UNIVERSITY TREATISE SERIES

CRIMINAL PROCEDURE

AN ANALYSIS OF CASES AND CONCEPTS

Seventh Edition

Charles H. Whitebread

Late George T. Pfleger Professor of Law
University of Southern California Law Center

Christopher Slobogin

Milton R. Underwood Chair in Law
Vanderbilt Law School

FOUNDATION
PRESS

© 1980, 1986, 1993, 2000 FOUNDATION PRESS
© 2008 by FOUNDATION PRESS
© 2015 LEG, Inc. d/b/a West Academic
© 2020 LEG, Inc. d/b/a West Academic
    444 Cedar Street, Suite 700
    St. Paul, MN 55101
    1-877-888-1330

West, West Academic Publishing, and West Academic are trademarks of West Publishing Corporation, used under license.

Printed in the United States of America

ISBN: 978-1-64242-262-7

For John T. Golden
After All These Years

For my parents
Peter M. and Becky P. Slobogin

Preface

This seventh edition of *Criminal Procedure* is a significant revision of the sixth edition (published in 2015). The content of each chapter is updated through the 2019 Term of the United States Supreme Court, and significant developments in the lower courts and Congress in the past five years have been added as well. The book devotes a chapter to every major area of criminal procedure, from the investigative phases through habeas corpus. The one exception is sentencing, but many aspects of that topic are covered where it intersects with the subject matter of the book's chapters.

As with previous editions, the principal goal of this effort is to provide an analytical framework for the subjects addressed. Thus, in addition to describing the law and how and why it developed, the book strives to provide a step-by-step methodology for evaluating the subject matter. The reader with a "problem" concerning search and seizure, interrogation, double jeopardy or effective assistance of counsel should be able to use this book to identify the crucial issues and discover the relevant caselaw and policy arguments. For those who need a quick rebriefing of the relevant law, both the numbered conclusion section at the end of each chapter and the relevant portion of the table of contents should serve as a reminder of the relevant principles.

Our belief is that this book is considerably richer than a canned "outline," because it describes the facts as well as the holdings of the cases, provides historical backdrop to the decisions, and samples the relevant scholarly literature. At the same time, the book does not drown the reader in detail concerning lower court decisions or minor nuances in the law. For those wishing to delve further into a given subject, an updated bibliography is provided at the end of each chapter. As with previous editions, this edition will be supplemented annually, after the completion of the Supreme Court's term.

This edition, like the last one, is dedicated to the late Charles Whitebread, whose unique pedagogical skills benefitted generations of law students and lawyers.

CHRISTOPHER SLOBOGIN

January 1, 2020

Summary of Contents

**PART B. THE FIFTH AMENDMENT'S PRIVILEGE
AGAINST SELF-INCRIMINATION**

PART H. THE RELATIONSHIP BETWEEN THE FEDERAL AND STATE COURTS

Table of Contents

PART B. THE FIFTH AMENDMENT'S PRIVILEGE AGAINST SELF-INCRIMINATION

CHAPTER 15. OVERVIEW OF THE PRIVILEGE AGAINST SELF-INCRIMINATION

PART C. IDENTIFICATION PROCEDURES

CHAPTER 17. GENERAL RESTRICTIONS ON IDENTIFICATION PROCEDURES

PART G. THE ROLE OF THE DEFENSE LAWYER

PART H. THE RELATIONSHIP BETWEEN
THE FEDERAL AND STATE COURTS

CRIMINAL PROCEDURE
AN ANALYSIS OF CASES AND CONCEPTS

Seventh Edition

Chapter 1

INTRODUCTION: THE STUDY OF CRIMINAL PROCEDURE

1.01 The Warren Court, Incorporation, and the Federalization of Criminal Procedure

As late as 1960, the study of criminal procedure was a fledgling discipline. Few law schools offered courses on the subject.[1] The relevant decisions of the United States Supreme Court focused on confessions and certain narrow problems connected with the conduct of trial. The task of monitoring the criminal process was in large part left up to the states, which varied widely in their approach.

The last several decades have witnessed an enormous increase in the amount of litigation concerning the procedural rights of the criminally accused. This upsurge has been the direct result of Supreme Court decisions in the early and mid-1960's that fashioned a wide variety of rules designed to provide those enmeshed in the criminal justice system with protection from overreaching by the state. In 1961, for example, the Court decided *Mapp v. Ohio*,[2] which held that any evidence seized in violation of the defendant's Fourth Amendment rights must be excluded from state as well as federal prosecutions. Two years later, the Court established a right to counsel for the indigent accused in all state felony prosecutions.[3] And in 1966, it enunciated the now well-known *Miranda* warnings as a constitutional prerequisite to the admissibility of any statement produced during custodial police interrogation.[4] Numerous other decisions reinforced Fourth, Fifth and Sixth Amendment guarantees having to do with searches, self-incrimination, double jeopardy, and the rights to counsel, confrontation, and speedy public jury trial.[5]

At least part of this judicial awakening was triggered by the Supreme Court's growing appreciation of the position occupied by the "underprivileged" of society—minority groups, the poor and the young. In decisions such as *Brown v. Board of Education*,[6] the Warren Court, so called after the appointment of Earl Warren as Chief Justice in 1953, attempted to break down some of the social barriers that operated to exclude these groups from mainstream society. It is no coincidence that the Court's rising interest in the procedural rights of the criminally accused—a group which is disproportionately composed of the minorities, the poor and the young—followed hard on its important civil rights decisions.

The Warren Court's activism focused primarily on the pretrial stages of the criminal process. Legal scholars had for some years been suggesting that the trial itself played a

---

[1]   See Abraham Goldstein, *Reflections on Two Models: Inquisitorial Themes in Criminal Procedure*, 26 Stan.L.Rev. 1009 (1974).

[2]   367 U.S. 643, 81 S.Ct. 1684 (1961).

[3]   *Gideon v. Wainwright*, 372 U.S. 335, 83 S.Ct. 792 (1963).

[4]   *Miranda v. Arizona*, 384 U.S. 436, 86 S.Ct. 1602 (1966).

[5]   See infra, this section.

[6]   347 U.S. 483, 74 S.Ct. 686 (1954).

1

relatively minor role in the criminal justice system.[7] The majority of cases never reach open court; they are settled through the plea bargaining process. Moreover, even if the accused pleads not guilty, the integrity of the resulting trial can still be tainted by police misconduct—an illegal search, a coerced confession or an inappropriately suggestive lineup. The Warren Court, sensitive to these concerns, shifted its attention to those stages of the criminal process where the exercise of police and prosecutorial discretion is most evident. *Mapp* and *Miranda* illustrate its attitude toward police investigation; the Court also sought to regulate other key elements of the pretrial process, from the preliminary hearing[8] and pretrial identification procedures[9] to plea taking itself.[10]

In order to ensure a uniform system of justice nationwide, the Warren Court made avid use of the "incorporation" concept. The Bill of Rights as ratified limited only the actions of the federal government. But the Fourteenth Amendment, ratified in 1868, provided that "no state" shall deprive citizens of life, liberty or property "without due process of law". This language was eventually interpreted to mean that provisions in the Bill of Rights that were a fundamental, intrinsic aspect of "due process" were "incorporated" into the Fourteenth Amendment and thus also applied to the states.[11] Pre-Warren Court decisions were reluctant to declare rights to be "fundamental," with nineteenth and early twentieth century cases refusing to find that due process encompassed the Fifth Amendment's provision for indictment by grand jury to the states,[12] the Eighth Amendment's cruel and unusual punishment prohibition,[13] the Fifth Amendment's privilege against self-incrimination,[14] and certain aspects of the double jeopardy clause.[15] But, during the Warren Court's tenure, the Court's focus shifted from an inquiry into whether a given right was "necessarily fundamental to fairness in every criminal system that might be imagined" to whether it was "fundamental in the context of the criminal processes maintained by the American states."[16] Guided by this principle, virtually every Bill of Rights guarantee pertaining to the criminal process other than the grand jury right was found to be inherent in due process of law and was thus imposed on the states through incorporation into the Fourteenth Amendment.[17] The following list

---

[7]   See, e.g., Abraham Goldstein, *The State and the Accused: Balance of Advantage in Criminal Procedure*, 69 Yale L.J. 1149 (1960).

[8]   *Coleman v. Alabama*, 399 U.S. 1, 90 S.Ct. 1999 (1970) (right to counsel at preliminary hearing).

[9]   *United States v. Wade*, 388 U.S. 218, 87 S.Ct. 1926 (1967) (right to counsel at lineups); *Stovall v. Denno*, 388 U.S. 293, 87 S.Ct. 1967 (1967) (prohibiting unnecessarily suggestive identification procedures).

[10]   *McCarthy v. United States*, 394 U.S. 459, 89 S.Ct. 1166 (1969); *Boykin v. Alabama*, 395 U.S. 238, 89 S.Ct. 1709 (1969) (requiring intelligent and voluntary pleas).

[11]   See generally, *Palko v. Connecticut*, 302 U.S. 319, 58 S.Ct. 149 (1937) (describing circumstances under which a Bill of Rights guarantee is "selectively incorporated" by the Fourteenth Amendment's prohibition on state laws that violate due process).

[12]   *Hurtado v. California*, 110 U.S. 516, 4 S.Ct. 111 (1884) (holding that an indictment by a grand jury is not necessary to due process of law under the Fourteenth Amendment).

[13]   *O'Neil v. Vermont*, 144 U.S. 323, 12 S.Ct. 693 (1892). See also, *Stack v. Boyle*, 342 U.S. 1, 72 S.Ct. 1 (1951) (explaining the meaning of the Eighth Amendment's bar against "excessive bail" without according it full constitutional status under the Fourteenth Amendment).

[14]   *Twining v. New Jersey*, 211 U.S. 78, 29 S.Ct. 14 (1908). See also, *Adamson v. California*, 332 U.S. 46, 67 S.Ct. 1672 (1947).

[15]   *Palko v. Connecticut*, 302 U.S. 319, 58 S.Ct. 149 (1937).

[16]   See *Duncan v. Louisiana*, 391 U.S. 145, 88 S.Ct. 1444 (1968).

[17]   Although *Schilb v. Kuebel*, 404 U.S. 357, 92 S.Ct. 479 (1971) intimated as much, the Eighth Amendment's excessive bail clause was not officially incorporated by the Court until *McDonald v. City of Chicago*, 561 U.S. 752, 130 S.Ct. 3020, 3034 n.12 (2010). Neither the Warren Court nor any subsequent Supreme Court decision has addressed the status of the Eighth Amendment excessive fines clause nor the Sixth Amendment guarantee that crimes be tried in the district where they occur, but these clauses are likely

outlines by amendment the relevant Warren Court decisions (and one much more recent decision) applying federal constitutional principles to the states:

(1) Fourth Amendment: the exclusionary remedy—*Mapp v. Ohio* (1961);[18] the full scope of the Fourth Amendment—*Ker v. California*[19] (1963);

(2) Fifth Amendment: the privilege against self-incrimination—*Malloy v. Hogan*[20] (1964); the ban against double jeopardy—*Benton v. Maryland*[21] (1969);

(3) Sixth Amendment: the right to speedy trial—*Klopfer v. North Carolina*[22] (1967); the right to jury trial—*Duncan v. Louisiana*[23] (1968); the right to appointed counsel—*Gideon v. Wainwright*[24] (1963); the right to confront and cross-examine witnesses—*Pointer v. Texas*[25] (1965); the right to compulsory process for obtaining witnesses—*Washington v. Texas*[26] (1967);

(4) Eighth Amendment: the ban against cruel and unusual punishment—*Robinson v. California*[27] (1962); the prohibition on excessive fines—*Timbs v. Indiana.*[28]

It is probable that many state courts resented this sudden upheaval in criminal procedure. In any event, the Warren Court felt that state court judges could not be counted upon to support enthusiastically its departures from tradition. Accordingly, in conjunction with its expansion of substantive constitutional causes of action, the Court opened wide the door to the federal court system through a series of cases redefining the scope of the writ of habeas corpus.[29] The increased availability of the writ, which under common law was designed to challenge the legality of detention by the government, handed to state prisoners a new method of attacking state judicial decisions on federal constitutional matters.

1.02   The Post-Warren Court: Four Themes

The Warren era, then, saw a dramatic expansion of the state defendant's federally protected constitutional rights and an equally dramatic widening of access to the federal courts as a means of vindicating those rights. With President Nixon's four appointments (Chief Justice Burger in 1969, Blackmun in 1970, Powell and Rehnquist in 1972), the Court's orientation in both of these areas began to shift noticeably, a shift which continued after Justice Rehnquist took over the Chief Justice position in 1987 and also appears to be a feature of the Court under Chief Justice Roberts, appointed in 2005. In

---

to be declared fundamental as well. Cf. *Browning-Ferris Industries v. Kelco Disposal*, 492 U.S. 257, 109 S.Ct. 2909 (1989) (O'Connor, J., concurring in part and dissenting in part).

[18] The Fourth Amendment was actually applied to the states in *Wolf v. Colorado*, 338 U.S. 25, 69 S.Ct. 1359 (1949), but *Mapp* was needed to give *Wolf* teeth. See § 2.02.

[19] 374 U.S. 23, 83 S.Ct. 1623 (1963).

[20] 378 U.S. 1, 84 S.Ct. 1489 (1964).

[21] 395 U.S. 784, 89 S.Ct. 2056 (1969).

[22] 386 U.S. 213, 87 S.Ct. 988 (1967).

[23] 391 U.S. 145, 88 S.Ct. 1444 (1968).

[24] 372 U.S. 335, 83 S.Ct. 792 (1963).

[25] 380 U.S. 400, 85 S.Ct. 1065 (1965).

[26] 388 U.S. 14, 87 S.Ct. 1920 (1967).

[27] 370 U.S. 660, 82 S.Ct. 1417 (1962).

[28] ___ U.S. ___, 139 S.Ct. 682 (2019).

[29] *Brown v. Allen*, 344 U.S. 443, 73 S.Ct. 397 (1953), discussed in § 33.02(a); *Fay v. Noia*, 372 U.S. 391, 83 S.Ct. 822 (1963), discussed in § 33.03(b).

analyzing the criminal procedure decisions of the post-Warren Court four themes seem to emerge as central.

The first theme is the "post-Warren Court's"[30] belief that the ultimate mission of the criminal justice system is to convict the guilty and let the innocent go free. The Warren Court tried to encourage respect for individual rights in the aggregate. In so doing, it often required the release of a factually guilty defendant in order to ensure an appropriate process. While some decisions of the post-Warren Court have produced the same result, it is clear that since the early 1970's the Court has been far more impressed than its predecessor with the importance of the defendant's guilt. Its decisions suggest that the rights enumerated in the Constitution are not all entitled to the same degree of judicial protection, but instead should be valued according to their impact on the adequacy of the guilt determining process.

In evolving this hierarchy among the provisions of the Bill of Rights, the Court has placed the Fourth Amendment's ban on unreasonable searches and seizures at the bottom. Suppose an individual is found in possession of a gram of cocaine. Whether the search that produced the cocaine is unlawful is irrelevant to the issue of the defendant's guilt. Yet if this evidence is excluded because the search *is* illegal then conviction for possession of the drug may be all but impossible. For this reason, application of the exclusionary rule to Fourth Amendment violations has received less than enthusiastic support from the post-Warren Court.

The most prominent illustrations of the lowly position the Amendment occupies in the hierarchy of rights are the Court's rulings that one who is not aware of his prerogatives under the Fourth Amendment can still "voluntarily" waive them[31] and that others can waive those prerogatives for him;[32] such is not the case with other rights.[33] The Court has also singled out Fourth Amendment claims by holding that they are not justiciable in federal habeas proceedings if they were fairly adjudicated by the state courts;[34] to date it has not extended this holding to other guarantees found in the Bill of Rights.

The right not to incriminate oneself, which derives from the Fifth Amendment, is more closely bound up with the truth-finding mission at trial. If a confession is extracted by methods that would make anyone say anything, the confession cannot be considered reliable. But while the post-Warren Court is not at all reticent about barring the courtroom use of statements produced in this manner,[35] it appears to be extremely hostile toward the *Miranda* rule, which can operate to exclude statements which are not directly "coerced." Thus, for example, the Court has permitted the use of a confession obtained in violation of *Miranda* for impeachment purposes, if the confession is shown

---

[30] The use of the terms "Warren Court" and "post-Warren Court" is not meant to imply that the same justices always voted as a bloc on the decisions discussed nor is it meant to suggest that those forming the majority of these decisions hold identical views. The terms are merely shorthand labels designed to symbolize the dichotomy between the Supreme Court's decisions in the past several decades.

[31] *Schneckloth v. Bustamonte*, 412 U.S. 218, 93 S.Ct. 2041 (1973).

[32] See *Illinois v. Rodriguez*, 497 U.S. 177, 110 S.Ct. 2793 (1990) (anyone with apparent authority of the defendant's property may consent to its search).

[33] See *Miranda v. Arizona*, 384 U.S. 436, 86 S.Ct. 1602 (1966) (Fifth Amendment waiver must be voluntary and intelligent); *Johnson v. Zerbst*, 304 U.S. 458, 58 S.Ct. 1019 (1938) (waiver of all fundamental rights must be knowing and intelligent).

[34] *Stone v. Powell*, 428 U.S. 465, 96 S.Ct. 3037 (1976).

[35] See, e.g., *Mincey v. Arizona*, 437 U.S. 385, 98 S.Ct. 2408 (1978).

to have been uncoerced.[36] It has also held that evidence obtained in violation of *Miranda* is still admissible in the prosecution's case-in-chief if the questioning was necessitated by an objective threat to the safety of the public or the arresting officer.[37] Even bad faith violations of *Miranda* do not require exclusion of fruits of the violation in many circumstances.[38] The Court also has had little problem finding that defendants cajoled into confessing nonetheless "voluntarily" waived their rights.[39]

A similar tension is evidenced in the Court's decisions regarding the Fifth Amendment's ban on trying an individual twice for the same offense—the double jeopardy clause. More recent Court decisions have shifted the emphasis away from the Warren Court's concern over the deleterious impact of two separate proceedings on the defendant's well-being toward whether the reason for aborting the first trial is bottomed on a decision that the defendant is not guilty.[40] If no acquittal occurs at the first proceeding, the post-Warren majority sees little sense in barring a second trial.

On the other hand, the current Court has been relatively zealous in scrutinizing such Sixth Amendment rights as the right to counsel at trial and the right to public jury trial, because these guarantees are viewed as essential to an accurate determination of guilt. The Court has staunchly supported the right to trial counsel as the key to ensuring a balance of power between the state and the accused, at least when confinement results,[41] and has bolstered the right to counsel on appeal.[42] Several decisions have also emphasized that the criminal trial is to be held in open court barring exceptional circumstances,[43] and interpreted the right to confront one's accusers expansively.[44] Less forcefully, the Court has maintained the jury's historic function as a buffer between the state and the criminal defendant.[45] It has also insisted that counsel be effective during the adjudication process,[46] and that prosecutors disclose exculpatory information prior to trial,[47] albeit in each case with the significant caveat, consistent with the factual guilt

---

[36] *Harris v. New York*, 401 U.S. 222, 91 S.Ct. 643 (1971).

[37] *New York v. Quarles*, 467 U.S. 649, 104 S.Ct. 2626 (1984).

[38] See *Missouri v. Seibert*, 542 U.S. 600, 124 S.Ct. 2601 (2004); *Wisconsin v. Knapp*, 542 U.S. 952, 124 S.Ct. 2932 (2004).

[39] See, e.g., *North Carolina v. Butler*, 441 U.S. 369, 99 S.Ct. 1755 (1979) (waiver despite confusion about admissibility of oral statements); *Davis v. United States*, 512 U.S. 452, 114 S.Ct. 2350 (1994) (waiver despite equivocal request for counsel); *Berghuis v. Thompkins*, 559 U.S. 98, 130 S.Ct. 1213 (2010) (waiver because no explicit statement asserting right to silent).

[40] *Burks v. United States*, 437 U.S. 1, 98 S.Ct. 2141 (1978)); *United States v. Scott*, 437 U.S. 82, 98 S.Ct. 2187 (1978).

[41] See *Argersinger v. Hamlin*, 407 U.S. 25, 92 S.Ct. 2006 (1972) (right to counsel in misdemeanor cases).

[42] *Evitts v. Lucey*, 469 U.S. 387, 105 S.Ct. 830 (1985) (failure to meet filing deadline for appeal is ineffective assistance).

[43] *Richmond Newspapers, Inc. v. Virginia*, 448 U.S. 555, 100 S.Ct. 2814 (1980); *Press-Enterprise Co. v. Superior Court*, 464 U.S. 501, 104 S.Ct. 819 (1984).

[44] *Crawford v. Washington*, 541 U.S. 36, 124 S.Ct. 1354 (2004).

[45] See generally Chapter 27. *Batson v. Kentucky*, 476 U.S. 79, 106 S.Ct. 1712 (1986) (peremptory challenges may not be used to exclude jurors solely on the basis of race); *Ballew v. Georgia*, 435 U.S. 223, 98 S.Ct. 1029 (1978) (five member jury unconstitutional); *Burch v. Louisiana*, 441 U.S. 130, 99 S.Ct. 1623 (1979) (nonunanimous vote by six member jury unconstitutional); *Taylor v. Louisiana*, 419 U.S. 522, 95 S.Ct. 692 (1975) (cross-representative jury pool required). But see, *Williams v. Florida*, 399 U.S. 78, 90 S.Ct. 1893 (1970) (six member jury constitutional); *Johnson v. Louisiana*, 406 U.S. 356, 92 S.Ct. 1620 (1972) (9–3 verdict constitutional).

[46] *Wiggins v. Smith*, 539 U.S. 510, 123 S.Ct. 2527 (2003) (capital sentencing); *Padilla v. Kentucky*, 559 U.S. 356, 130 S.Ct. 1473 (2010) (plea bargaining).

[47] *Kyles v. Whitley*, 514 U.S. 419, 115 S.Ct. 1555 (1995).

theme, that relief be granted only if the violation likely affected the outcome.[48] The focus on the trial as the central battleground between the accused and the government represents a substantial departure from the Warren Court's emphasis.

A second noticeable trait exhibited by the Court since 1970 is its devotion to "totality of the circumstances" analysis as distinct from a rule-oriented approach to criminal procedure. The Warren Court appeared to prefer the adoption of specific rules to guide law enforcement officers, as well as the courts which evaluate their behavior.[49] The post-Warren Court, on the other hand, has, with a few exceptions,[50] opted for a case-by-case approach which makes the precedential value of any one decision suspect.[51] Depending upon one's perspective, this tendency can be praised because it gives police and courts more flexibility in evaluating the propriety of particular acts and omissions, or criticized because it encourages standardless police conduct and judicial review. In practical terms, the end result of totality of the circumstances analysis has been a relaxation of constitutional restrictions on law enforcement.[52]

A third related theme running through the Court's decisions since the early 1970's is its greater faith in the integrity of the police and other officials who administer the criminal justice system. Whereas the Warren Court saw a need for strict judicial scrutiny of the law enforcement process, the post-Warren Court tends to give government officials wider latitude. Thus, it has frequently been willing to assume that police will act in good faith,[53] and has likewise assumed that magistrates,[54] prosecutors,[55] parole officers,[56] and

---

[48] *Strickland v. Washington*, 466 U.S. 668, 104 S.Ct. 2052 (1984) (Sixth Amendment violated only if attorney inadequacy deprived defendant of fair trial); *United States v. Bagley*, 473 U.S. 667, 105 S.Ct. 3375 (1985) (impeachment evidence must be likely to affect the outcome of trial to be "material").

[49] See e.g., *Miranda v. Arizona*, 384 U.S. 436, 86 S.Ct. 1602 (1966) (requiring specific warnings before custodial interrogation); *Chimel v. California*, 395 U.S. 752, 89 S.Ct. 2034 (1969) (adopting "armspan" rule for scope of search incident).

[50] See *United States v. Robinson*, 414 U.S. 218, 94 S.Ct. 467 (1973) (permitting search incident to arrest for all crimes); *Maryland v. Shatzer*, 559 U.S. 98, 130 S.Ct. 1213 (2010) (bar on re-initiation of interrogation lasts two weeks).

[51] See *Illinois v. Gates*, 462 U.S. 213, 103 S.Ct. 2317 (1983) (definition of probable cause); *United States v. Sharpe*, 470 U.S. 675, 105 S.Ct. 1568 (1985) (rejecting a time limitation on stops); *Rawlings v. Kentucky*, 448 U.S. 98, 100 S.Ct. 2556 (1980) (Fourth Amendment standing analysis); *Manson v. Brathwaite*, 432 U.S. 98, 97 S.Ct. 2243 (1977) (admissibility of lineup identifications); Chapter 13 (development of "special needs" balancing test); § 16.03 (emasculation of *Miranda* rule).

[52] See cases cited in previous note.

[53] See e.g., *Atwater v. City of Lago Vista*, 532 U.S. 318, 121 S.Ct. 1536 (2001) (police will not abuse authority to conduct custodial arrests for traffic offenses); *Nix v. Williams*, 467 U.S. 431, 104 S.Ct. 2501 (1984) (police will not knowingly violate Constitution merely because they think sought-after evidence will be discovered in any event); *Segura v. United States*, 468 U.S. 796, 104 S.Ct. 3380 (1984) (police will not illegally enter premises to secure evidence pending arrival of a warrant); *New York v. Quarles*, 467 U.S. 649, 104 S.Ct. 2626 (1984) (police will not take advantage of public safety exception to *Miranda* to obtain incriminating statements).

[54] *United States v. Leon*, 468 U.S. 897, 104 S.Ct. 3405 (1984) (magistrates will not rubber stamp warrant requests).

[55] *Connick v. Thompson*, 563 U.S. 51, 131 S.Ct. 1350 (2011) (multiple violations of duty to disclose exculpatory evidence do not demonstrate a predictable "pattern" of unconstitutional violations because prosecutors will generally abide by ethical obligations); *Wayte v. United States*, 470 U.S. 598, 105 S.Ct. 1524 (1985) (minimizing need for judicial supervision of charging process); *United States v. Ash*, 413 U.S. 300, 93 S.Ct. 2568 (1973) (prosecutor can be counted upon to treat defendant fairly at photo identification in absence of defendant's counsel); *United States v. Bagley*, 473 U.S. 667, 105 S.Ct. 3375 (1985) (prosecutor can be trusted to disclose to defense counsel information which might be exculpatory).

[56] *Pennsylvania v. Scott*, 524 U.S. 357, 118 S.Ct. 2014 (1998) (it's "unfair to assume that the parole officer bears hostility against the parolee that destroys his neutrality").

clerical personnel[57] can be trusted to protect the rights of criminal defendants. It has also granted state correctional officials broad authority in supervising those confined in jail or prison.[58]

The fourth theme underlying many modern Court decisions is a corollary of the third; the Court believes that state judges can be entrusted to enforce federal constitutional rights, with the caveat that when those rights impinge directly upon the question of guilt there should be no obstacle to seeking collateral relief in federal court.[59] Thus, it has prohibited federal habeas courts from announcing "new rules"—that is, rules that are not "dictated" by precedent—unless the habeas claim is one that questions the jurisdictional basis or the accuracy of the state court conviction.[60] And, as noted earlier, when the claim involves the Fourth Amendment, the Court has held that even well-accepted law cannot be applied by habeas courts when the petitioner has received a full and fair opportunity to raise the claim in state court.[61] The Court has also substantially narrowed the Warren Court's decisions governing the ability of those who fail to assert their constitutional claims in state court to assert them for the first time in federal court.[62] Finally, it has repeatedly emphasized and diligently applied the statutory requirement that state court determinations of legal and factual issues relating to federal constitutional claims be accorded a "presumption of correctness."[63] As a result of this "New Federalism," state court decisions are much less likely to be reviewed by the federal courts than in the Warren Court era.

As the substantive and procedural avenues of relief under the federal constitution have been narrowed by the post-Warren Court, two interesting counter-developments have occurred. First, some state courts have found Supreme Court precedent inapplicable in their jurisdictions by interpreting *state* constitutional provisions to provide more protection for criminal defendants.[64] At the same time, some federal courts, also apparently unsympathetic to the higher court's goals, resorted to their "supervisory" authority over the federal system as a means of redressing what they perceived as inappropriate, albeit "constitutional," actions in federal court. For instance, in *United States v. Payner*,[65] a federal district court suppressed evidence despite the defendant's inability to challenge its admission under the Court's standing cases, on the ground that the government had "affirmatively counsel[led] its agents that the Fourth Amendment standing limitation permits them to purposefully conduct an unconstitutional search and seizure of one individual in order to obtain evidence against third parties." In *United*

---

[57]   *Arizona v. Evans*, 514 U.S. 1, 115 S.Ct. 1185 (1995).

[58]   *Block v. Rutherford*, 468 U.S. 576, 104 S.Ct. 3227 (1984); *Hudson v. Palmer*, 468 U.S. 517, 104 S.Ct. 3194 (1984); *Bell v. Wolfish*, 441 U.S. 520, 99 S.Ct. 1861 (1979), discussed in § 20.04.

[59]   *Jackson v. Virginia*, 443 U.S. 307, 99 S.Ct. 2781 (1979); *Murray v. Carrier*, 477 U.S. 478, 106 S.Ct. 2639 (1986).

[60]   *Teague v. Lane*, 489 U.S. 288, 109 S.Ct. 1060 (1989).

[61]   Congress may have altered this rule, however. See § 33.02(b).

[62]   See generally, § 33.03(c) & (d).

[63]   *Williams v. Taylor*, 529 U.S. 362, 120 S.Ct. 1495 (2000) (an incorrect state court ruling is not unreasonable unless it is *clearly* opposite to a *holding* of the United States Supreme Court); *Wainwright v. Witt*, 469 U.S. 412, 105 S.Ct. 844 (1985) (applying presumption of correctness with respect to facts); *Marshall v. Lonberger*, 459 U.S. 422, 103 S.Ct. 843 (1983) (same).

[64]   For example, between 1970 and 1986, over 150 state court decisions repudiated Supreme Court criminal procedure rulings on independent state grounds. Ronald Collins & Peter Galie, *The Methodology of State Court Decisions*, Nat'l L.J., Sept. 29, 1986, at S-9. See generally, Chapter 34.

[65]   434 F.Supp. 113 (N.D.Ohio 1977).

States v. Hasting,[66] the Seventh Circuit admitted that a Fifth Amendment error committed by the prosecutor during closing argument was "harmless" under the Court's harmless error doctrine, but nonetheless reversed the conviction in an attempt to penalize the prosecutor's office for committing the error in case after case.

The Supreme Court has responded to both developments. In reaction to the rebellion at the state court level, it held, in *Michigan v. Long*,[67] that a state court decision relying on state constitutional provisions may nonetheless be subject to federal review unless the decision clearly indicates that it is based *solely* on state law. *Long* has meant that some ambiguously reasoned state court rulings have been considered and overturned by the Supreme Court. But it has not stifled state court activism; its "plain statement" requirement is easily met, thus permitting a competent state court to insulate from federal review any decisions that meet the federal minimum and are truly based on independent state grounds.[68] The Court has been more successful in curtailing the activism of lower federal courts. For example, in *Hasting*, it reinstated the conviction and held that local disciplinary action, not reversal, is the correct sanction for repeated prosecutorial error that is deemed harmless.[69] In *Payner*, it disapproved the district court's use of its supervisory power to accomplish something (i.e., suppression) the defendant had no constitutional authority to request.[70] Thus, the current Court appears committed not only to restricting defendants' rights, but also to ensuring, to the limits of its authority, that state and federal courts do not evade those restrictions.[71]

The foregoing is not meant to imply that the post-Warren Court's philosophy has in all respects been diametrically opposed to that of the Warren Court; many Supreme Court decisions since 1970 have reaffirmed the new law announced in the 1960's.[72] The point is that the post-Warren Court is more cautious in asserting the interests of the individual over those of the state in its monitoring of the criminal justice system.

1.03   The Crime Control and Due Process Models of Criminal Procedure

The difference in emphasis between the Warren and post-Warren Courts suggests the diverging approaches that can be taken toward the central problem encountered in the study of criminal procedure: how best to protect the rights and interests of the criminally accused without at the same time unduly inhibiting law enforcement. It is interesting to view the dichotomy between the two Courts against the backdrop of

---

[66]   660 F.2d 301 (7th Cir. 1981).

[67]   463 U.S. 1032, 103 S.Ct. 3469 (1983).

[68]   See § 34.02(c) for examples of state court decisions repudiating Supreme Court standards.

[69]   461 U.S. 499, 103 S.Ct. 1974 (1983).

[70]   447 U.S. 727, 100 S.Ct. 2439 (1980).

[71]   See also *Virginia v. Moore*, 553 U.S. 164, 128 S.Ct. 1598 (2008) (arrest invalid under state law does not necessarily invalidate ensuing search because state statutes do not define reasonableness under the Fourth Amendment); *Smith v. Phillips*, 455 U.S. 209, 102 S.Ct. 940 (1982) (federal courts hearing state habeas claims "may intervene only to correct wrongs of constitutional dimension," even when failing to intervene would permit prosecutorial misbehavior to "reign unchecked.").

[72]   See *Dickerson v. United States*, 530 U.S. 428, 120 S.Ct. 2326 (2000) (reaffirming *Miranda*). Compare *Hayes v. Florida*, 470 U.S. 811, 105 S.Ct. 1643 (1985) with *Davis v. Mississippi*, 394 U.S. 721, 89 S.Ct. 1394 (1969) (stationhouse detention for fingerprinting on less than probable cause unconstitutional); *Moore v. Illinois*, 434 U.S. 220, 98 S.Ct. 458 (1977) with *United States v. Wade*, 388 U.S. 218, 87 S.Ct. 1926 (1967) (right to counsel at lineups conducted after initial appearance or indictment).

Herbert Packer's study of the criminal process in his book *The Limits of the Criminal Sanction*.[73]

Packer posited two opposing trends in the administration of criminal justice, the Crime Control Model and the Due Process Model. He was careful to point out that neither model necessarily represents the "ideal." Rather each model offers advantages of its own and compromise between the two may often offer the best resolution, depending upon the issue at stake.

The Crime Control Model places a premium on efficiency and quick adjudication. The goal is to convey the guilty as rapidly as possible toward a conviction at trial or, better yet, a guilty plea, while ferreting out those who are unlikely to be offenders. Inherent in this model is what Packer called the "presumption of guilt"—that the person who enters the system is probably *factually* guilty. To ensure that these guilty parties are brought to justice, any limitations placed on law enforcement officials should be motivated solely out of a desire to promote the reliability of the outcome; purely "technical" controls on police behavior are unnecessary and inimical to this model of the criminal process.

The Due Process Model likewise stresses reliability in the accumulation and presentation of evidence but, given the "gross deprivation of liberty" resulting from conviction, mandates a higher degree of accuracy than the Crime Control Model. It assumes that, as Packer described it:

> People are notoriously poor observers of disturbing events . . . confessions and admissions by persons in police custody may be induced by physical or psychological coercion so that the police end up hearing what the suspect thinks they want to hear rather than the truth; witnesses may be animated by a bias or interest that no one would trouble to discover except one specially charged with protecting the interests of the accused (as the police are not).[74]

Thus, those administering the criminal process should be as certain as possible that the information used to convict an individual is accurate.

Beyond this heightened emphasis on reliability is a more global concern that the integrity of the criminal justice system, and therefore the integrity of society as a whole, be preserved. Thus, advocates of the Due Process Model are more willing to hinder the efficiency of the system through prophylactic rules designed to remind law enforcement officials of their duty toward the criminally accused. They are less concerned with letting off the factually guilty if, due to a failure on the part of the state to follow these rules, *legal* guilt has not been established.

Packer hypothesized that the means of implementing these two models are decidedly different:

> Because the Crime Control Model is basically an affirmative model, emphasizing at every turn the existence and exercise of official power, its validating authority is ultimately legislative. . . . Because the Due Process Model is basically a negative model, asserting limits on the nature of official

---

[73]   Herbert L. Packer, The Limits of the Criminal Sanction, ch. 8.

[74]   Id. at 163.

power and on the modes of its exercise, its validating authority is judicial and requires an appeal to supra-legislative law, the law of the Constitution.[75]

This hypothesis is especially interesting given the post-Warren Court's arguably greater deference to the legislative process.[76]

In any event, it should be evident that each of Packer's models has its appealing aspects. Choosing between the two, or arriving at some middle ground, is not an easy task, regardless of whether the judiciary or the legislature makes the ultimate decision.

Dispassionate discussion about the "rights" of criminal defendants is further hindered by the emotionally-charged nature of the subject. Opinions as to what to do with the "criminal element" can vary with the type of crime, the possible outcomes, and the experiences of the opinion-giver himself. One might prefer the full panoply of constitutional safeguards in cases involving minor crimes such as gambling or vagrancy, but tend to opt for the less technical "crime control" approach where a crime of violence is concerned.[77] Conversely, one could reasonably favor greater protections for those individuals most likely to receive the most significant sanctions and be willing to permit relaxed procedures when the consequences of mistake are not significant.[78] Regardless of the crime involved, the person who has been "busted" understandably may take a different view of the process than the student who has just been robbed of his prize record collection. There is no easy way to control for the impact of such personal biases, whether the debate takes place in the classroom, the legislature or the Supreme Court. But it is essential to be aware of the fact that they play a crucial role in the evolution of public policy.

The student of criminal procedure should also be aware of the relatively hidden world of discretion in the criminal process. The police, the prosecutor and the courts all have varying degrees of power to "push" a case or to drop it altogether, depending upon what stage the case has reached. Their decisions can have as much significance for the accused as any opinion delivered by the Supreme Court. A police officer may decide not to report a first offender, a prosecutor may refuse to accept a plea, a judge may divert a case out of the criminal system at a preliminary hearing. Existing statutory and case law may exert little or no influence over such decisions. Yet they are a part of the everyday workings of our criminal justice system.

1.04   The Stages of the Criminal Process

This book cannot hope to convey all of the nuances underlying the everyday operations of the criminal process, especially given the wide variations from state to

---

[75]   Id. at 173.

[76]   Compare *Miranda v. Arizona*, 384 U.S. 436, 86 S.Ct. 1602 (1966) (establishing detailed protections during interrogation) with *Missouri v. Hunter*, 459 U.S. 359, 103 S.Ct. 673 (1983) (legislative intent determinative as to whether two offenses are the "same offense" for purposes of deciding whether multiple punishment is permissible under double jeopardy clause) and Chief Justice Burger's dissent in *Bivens v. Six Unknown Named Agents*, 403 U.S. 388, 91 S.Ct. 1999 (1971) (arguing that legislative sanctions should replace the Fourth Amendment exclusionary rule).

[77]   See Malcolm Richard Wilkey, *The Exclusionary Rule: Why Suppress Valid Evidence?* 62 Judicature 214 (1978) (arguing that the rule should at least be eliminated with respect to serious crimes).

[78]   This apparently was the premise of the juvenile court movement in its early years, when procedural protections afforded juveniles were minimal given the belief that the consequences of a delinquency adjudication were principally "therapeutic." See Monrad Paulsen & Charles Whitebread, Juvenile Law and Procedure, ch. 1 (1974).

state. Nonetheless, the following outline of what could be called the "Ordinary Model" of the process may prove useful to the student as a preface to the rest of this book.

A typical case normally begins either with a complaint by a private citizen, or when police directly observe what looks like criminal activity. In the former instance, police usually have time to investigate the complaint through questioning of witnesses and examination of physical evidence. If they decide they have enough evidence to establish "probable cause"[79] that a particular individual committed the crime, they will often approach a magistrate and swear out an arrest warrant on the suspected culprit (as well as, perhaps, a search warrant authorizing search of his home). When police observe crime, on the other hand, there is normally no time to secure a warrant. In such cases, if the police have probable cause to believe the individual has committed or is committing a crime, they may arrest him without a warrant; if they do not have probable cause, they may still be able to question him and, if probable cause then develops, arrest him.

During arrest the police may conduct a search of the individual and begin to question him concerning the alleged offense. Soon after arrest, the arrestee is taken to the stationhouse for "booking," which usually involves being fingerprinted and photographed. At this point, when minor charges are involved, the police may release the arrestee on "stationhouse bail." For serious charges, the person usually remains in custody and a more formal interrogation may take place; additionally, the arrestee may be required to participate in a lineup or submit to scientific tests (such as blood tests) if they were not administered in the field, and further searches may also occur.

Fairly soon after arrest and booking (usually within 48 hours) comes the initial appearance in front of a judicial officer (sometimes called an "arraignment on the warrant"). Here the arrestee is informed of the charge (usually written up by the police or prosecutor in the form of a "complaint"), and of his rights to counsel and to remain silent. In many states, if the charges are minor, the magistrate may proceed to try the case at this time as well. In felony cases, if there is no arrest warrant, the magistrate must determine, either at the initial appearance or at a proceeding soon thereafter, whether there is probable cause to detain the individual.[80] If probable cause is found, or there is an arrest warrant, a decision is then made as to whether the arrestee can be released on personal recognizance, subjected to bail conditions, or detained preventively.[81]

In the meantime, the prosecutor formalizes the charges against the arrestee, now more appropriately called the defendant. In some states, the prosecutor need merely file an "information" describing the charges. In other states and the federal system, he must go to a grand jury to obtain an "indictment" stating the charges. In the former jurisdictions, he is usually required to make out a prima facie case on the charges in the information during a preliminary hearing in front of a magistrate. In the latter jurisdictions, he may have to go through the preliminary hearing before he can get to the grand jury.

The Constitution allows the defendant to *demand* counsel only at certain isolated "stages" of the pretrial process such as interrogation or a lineup identification.[82] But in

---

[79] This term, explicated in §§ 3.03 & 5.03, is found in the Fourth Amendment.

[80] The Supreme Court so held in *Gerstein v. Pugh*, 420 U.S. 103, 95 S.Ct. 854 (1975).

[81] See § 20.03.

[82] See § 31.03.

practice counsel is often appointed as early as the initial appearance. Once appointed, counsel can make several different types of pretrial motions, seeking dismissal of the case, change of venue, suppression of illegally obtained evidence, discovery of evidence, or the implementation of a statutory "speedy trial" right. Many of these motions cannot be made after trial or judgment. Defense counsel may also enter into negotiations with the prosecutor with a view to having his client plead guilty in exchange for a reduction in charges or a lenient sentence recommendation.

Sometime before trial, the defendant is brought before the court that will try him. With misdemeanants, as already noted, this is often the initial appearance. With more serious charges, a separate stage, called the "arraignment on the information" (or indictment) occurs, at which the court informs the defendant of his charges and asks him how he pleads. There are three basic pleas: not guilty, guilty and nolo contendere. If either of the latter two pleas are entered, the court conducts a hearing to ensure the plea is voluntarily and intelligently entered and to discover the terms of any plea agreement that has been reached between the defendant and the prosecution. Roughly 90 percent of all cases that are not dismissed previously by the police or the prosecutor are adjudicated via plea.

If the defendant pleads not guilty, the case is set for trial. In most cases, the defendant is entitled to a jury, which consists of twelve people in federal court and varies from six to twelve in state courts. In jury cases, voir dire of the jury panel is conducted, during which counsel for both sides, using peremptory and "for cause" challenges,[83] attempt to obtain a jury to their liking. Most states also require that notice of an alibi or insanity defense be made prior to or at this time.

At trial, the prosecution bears the burden of proving each element of the crime beyond a reasonable doubt.[84] After the presentation of evidence, with the defendant's case following the state's case, a verdict is reached and sentence imposed. In jury trials, the judge normally imposes sentence after a separate hearing, although some states permit sentencing by the trial jury.

An appeal may be automatic or discretionary, depending upon the level of the original trial court and the type of crime (misdemeanor or felony) involved. For instance, many states provide for automatic appeal from courts "not of record" to a higher court at which a record of the proceedings is kept (and at which the charges will usually be adjudicated *de novo*), but make further appeal to the state supreme court or intermediate appellate court discretionary with that court. An appeal must usually be taken within a specified time limit. If the defendant does appeal, the bail question may again arise. After sentence and appeal, the defendant may also "collaterally" attack the verdict through a writ of habeas corpus or coram nobis.

A major variation on the Ordinary Model described above occurs when the grand jury indictment *precedes* arrest. In these cases, typically involving political corruption or organized crime, the grand jury functions not as a check on charge selection but as an investigatory body. When arrest is predicated on an indictment, there is normally no need for a preliminary hearing other than an initial appearance to set bail, advise the

---

[83]   Each side receives a limited number of peremptory challenges permitting automatic removal of prospective jurors and an unlimited number of for cause challenges requiring the challenging party to prove potential prejudice toward it. See § 27.04(a).

[84]   *In re Winship*, 397 U.S. 358, 90 S.Ct. 1068 (1970).

defendant of his rights and appoint counsel, if necessary. No probable cause determination is necessary since the grand jury has already found it exists.

1.05 A Brief Outline of the Book

This book is devoted to examining the legal doctrines which govern the operation of the system described above. The first half of the book (Parts A through D) discusses the constraints the Constitution places on law enforcement officials in their effort to investigate crime. Specifically, it looks at the legal rules governing search and seizure (Part A), state compulsion of self-incriminating information (Part B), identification procedures (Part C), and police attempts to lure—or perhaps "entrap"—individuals into committing crime (Part D). The second half of the book (Parts E through H) examines the adversary system, including the formal stages of the pretrial process (Part E), trial and appeals (Part F), the role of defense counsel during these stages (Part G), and federal habeas review of state court decisions (Part H). In addition to the habeas issue, the last Part covers a second subject having to do with the relationship between the federal and state criminal justice systems—the tendency of state courts, discussed above, to ignore Supreme Court pronouncements and rely on their own constitutions to enforce stricter controls on law enforcement officials.

BIBLIOGRAPHY

Allen, Francis. The Judicial Quest for Penal Justice: The Warren Court and Criminal Cases. 1975 Ill.L.F. 518.

Amar, Akhil. The Constitution and Criminal Procedure: First Principles (1997).

Arenella, Peter. Rethinking the Functions of Criminal Procedure: The Warren and Burger Courts' Competing Ideologies. 72 Geo.L.J. 185 (1984).

Bradley, Craig. Criminal Procedure in the Rehnquist Court: Has the Rehnquisition Begun? 62 Ind.L.J. 273 (1987).

Chemerinsky, Erwin. The Roberts Court and Criminal Procedure at Age Five. 43 Texas Tech Law Review 13 (2010).

Clayton, Cornell W. and J. Mitchell Pickerell. The Politics of Criminal Justice: How the New Right Regime Shaped the Rehnquist Court's Criminal Jurisprudence. 94 Geo.L.J. 1385 (2006).

Damaska, Mirjan. Evidentiary Barriers to Conviction and Two Models of Criminal Procedure. 121 U. Pa.L.Rev. 506 (1972).

Feeley, Malcolm M. Two Models of the Criminal Justice System: An Organizational Perspective. 7 Law and Society Review 407 (1973).

Gizzi, Michael C. and R. Craig Curtis. The Fourth Amendment in Flux: The Roberts Court, Crime Control, and Digital Privacy (2016).

Israel, Jerold H. Criminal Procedure, the Burger Court and the Legacy of the Warren Court. 75 Mich.L.Rev. 1320 (1977).

Kamisar, Yale. The Warren Court (Was It Really So Defense-Minded?), The Burger Court (Is It Really So Prosecution-Oriented?) and Police Investigatory Practices. In: The Burger Court: The Counter-Revolution That Wasn't (V. Blasi ed. 1983).

Packer, Herbert. The Limits of the Criminal Sanction, Chap. 8. Stanford: Stanford University Press, 1968.

Saltzburg, Stephen A. Foreword: The Flow and Ebb of Constitutional Criminal Procedure in the Warren and Burger Courts, 69 Geo.L.J. 151 (1980).

Schulhofer, Stephen J. The Constitution and the Police: Individual Rights and Law Enforcement. 66 Wash. U.L.Q. 11 (1988).

Smith, Stephen F. The Rehnquist Court and Criminal Procedure. 73 Colorado L.Rev. 1337 (2002).

Stuntz, William J. The Uneasy Relationship Between Criminal Procedure and Criminal Justice. 107 Yale L.J. 1 (1997).

Symposium. The Fourteenth Amendment and the Bill of Rights. 18 J. Contemp. Legal Issues 469 (2009).

Whitebread, Charles. The Burger Court's Counter-Revolution in Criminal Procedure: The Recent Criminal Decisions of the United States Supreme Court. 24 Washburn L.J. 41 (1985).

Part A

THE FOURTH AMENDMENT: SEARCH AND SEIZURE LAW

The Fourth Amendment guarantees the "right of the people to be secure in their persons, houses, papers, and effects, against unreasonable searches and seizures. . . ." It also states that "no warrants shall issue, but upon probable cause, supported by oath or affirmation, and particularly describing the place to be searched, and the persons or things to be seized." The first part of the Amendment confers upon the citizenry protection against intrusion into their privacy. Under no circumstances will a governmental search or seizure of one's person or possessions be condoned if it is "unreasonable." The second section of the Amendment provides that warrants authorizing searches or seizures meet certain requirements before they can be regarded as valid. By implication, an invalid warrant will not support a search. The language of the Amendment does not require that every search be authorized by a warrant; indeed there has been considerable debate over whether the Amendment even expresses a *preference* for warrants.[1]

The following chapters describe how the Supreme Court and the lower courts have grappled with the language of the Fourth Amendment. Chapter 2 examines the exclusionary rule and other remedies available for violations of the Amendment's guarantees. Chapter 3 discusses the law of arrest and related seizures of the person. Chapters 4 through 14 cover the jurisprudence of searches. Chapter 4 explores the definition of "search" for purposes of the Fourth Amendment, Chapter 5 describes the components of a valid warrant and the probable cause concept, and the bulk of the remaining chapters deal with exceptions to the warrant and probable cause requirements. Chapter 14 discusses the special search context of technological surveillance.

---

[1]   See in particular § 4.05(a).

Chapter 2

THE EXCLUSIONARY RULE AND OTHER REMEDIES FOR FOURTH AMENDMENT VIOLATIONS

2.01 Introduction

In the criminal procedure setting, the phrase "exclusionary rule" has come to mean a prohibition against use of evidence obtained through methods violative of the Constitution. In the Fourth Amendment context, this rule has become the predominant means of sanctioning unconstitutional searches and seizures, despite the fact that exclusion, or "suppression", of evidence can often lead to dismissal of charges. The rationale for the rule has been variously described as an implementation of the ban against compelled testimony;[1] a means of returning property to its rightful owner;[2] an effort to restore the defendant and the state to the status quo existing at the time of the search;[3] a means of promoting judicial review of the Fourth Amendment;[4] and an expression of the sentiment that the judiciary should not be a partner to or otherwise sanction the lawlessness of a coordinate branch of government.[5] Today, however, the only purpose for the rule that is recognized by the Supreme Court is as a method of deterring the police from engaging in unconstitutional searches and seizures.

This chapter begins by tracing the history of the rule in the Fourth Amendment context. It then examines exceptions to the rule's application. It also describes the "fruit of the poisonous tree" doctrine, which has the effect of expanding the rule's application. Finally, it describes the civil and criminal alternatives to the exclusionary rule, with particular focus on the extent to which these alternatives might effectively replace or supplement the rule.

2.02 The Genesis of the Rule

Exclusion is a relatively new remedy for constitutional violations. The U.S. Supreme Court first endorsed the concept of exclusion in search and seizure cases in the 1886 case of *Boyd v. United States*.[6] There the Court held that a business invoice obtained through a subpoena should be excluded because "a compulsory production of the private books and papers of the owner of goods . . . is compelling him to be a witness against himself, within the meaning of the Fifth Amendment to the Constitution, and is the equivalent of a search and seizure—and an unreasonable search and seizure—within the meaning of the Fourth Amendment." As this passage indicates, the Court's conclusion that the evidence should be excluded rested as much on the Fifth Amendment, which states that

---

[1] *Boyd v. United States*, 116 U.S. 616, 6 S.Ct. 524 (1886).

[2] *Weeks v. United States*, 232 U.S. 383, 34 S.Ct. 341 (1914).

[3] *Nix v. Williams*, 467 U.S. 431, 104 S.Ct. 2501 (1984); Jerry E. Norton, *The Exclusionary Rule Reconsidered: Restoring the Status Quo Ante*, 33 Wake Forest L.Rev. 261 (1998).

[4] Thomas S. Schrock & Robert C. Welsh, *Up from Calandra: The Exclusionary Rule as a Constitutional Requirement*, 59 Minn. L.Rev. 251, 335–366 (1974).

[5] *Mapp v. Ohio*, 367 U.S. 643, 81 S.Ct. 1684 (1961).

[6] 116 U.S. 616, 6 S.Ct. 524 (1886).

"[n]o person . . . shall be compelled in any criminal case to be a witness against himself," as it does on the Fourth Amendment. Given the Fifth Amendment's reference to "witness", arguably only verbal and documentary evidence is subject to exclusion under this approach.

Perhaps for this reason, in its next major statement about the rule the Court relied solely on the Fourth Amendment. In *Weeks v. United States*,[7] the Supreme Court held that letters seized through an unlawful search and seizure of petitioner's home by federal officials should have been returned to him upon demand, and, further, that their use as evidence against the petitioner in a criminal trial constituted prejudicial error. The rationale for this ruling appeared to be that illegally seized property must be returned to its legitimate owner. Under a literal interpretation of this rationale, not only private papers of the type involved in *Weeks*, but any other legally possessed personal property unconstitutionally seized by the government had to be suppressed. In contrast, under this theory contraband and fruits of crime, which are not legitimately possessed by a criminal defendant, and perhaps instrumentalities of crime (such as a weapon), would not be excludable. But Justice Day, writing for a unanimous Court, also asserted that "[t]o sanction such proceedings [in which illegally seized evidence is used] would be to affirm by judicial decision a manifest neglect if not an open defiance of the prohibitions of the Constitution, intended for the protection of the people against such unauthorized action." Such strong language seemed to indicate the constitutional necessity of the exclusionary rule regardless of the type of evidence involved. Seven years later, in *Silverthorne Lumber Co. v. United States*,[8] Justice Holmes confirmed this view, stating that in the absence of the exclusionary rule, "the Fourth Amendment [is reduced] to a form of words." Later cases sanctioned exclusion of illegally seized evidence even when it was contraband.[9]

Weeks and *Silverthorne* involved federal prosecutions, however, and the Court applied the rule solely in federal cases for a number of years. When the Fourth Amendment ban was first applied to the states under the Fourteenth Amendment's Due Process clause in *Wolf v. Colorado*,[10] the Court refused to go so far as to say that the exclusionary rule was also constitutionally mandated to enforce that ban in state cases. The Court's reasoning in *Wolf* is epitomized by the following passage:

> Granting that in practice the exclusion of evidence may be an effective way of deterring unreasonable searches, it is not for this Court to condemn as falling below the minimal standards assured by the Due Process Clause a State's reliance upon other methods which, if consistently enforced, would be equally effective. . . . We cannot brush aside the experience of States which deem the incidence of such conduct by the police too slight to call for a deterrent remedy not by way of disciplinary measures but by overriding the relevant rules of evidence.

Thus, the Court left it for the states to decide how to safeguard the Fourth Amendment's guarantees.

---

[7] 232 U.S. 383, 34 S.Ct. 341 (1914).

[8] 251 U.S. 385, 40 S.Ct. 182 (1920).

[9] See, e.g., *Agnello v. United States*, 269 U.S. 20, 46 S.Ct. 4 (1925) (involving suppression of drugs).

[10] 338 U.S. 25, 69 S.Ct. 1359 (1949).

At the time *Wolf* was decided, eighteen states had adopted some form of the exclusionary rule. By 1960, eleven years later, eight more states had adopted the rule,[11] suggesting that, as far as a majority of states were concerned, there was no other effective remedy. Not surprisingly, the Court was called upon to overrule *Wolf* on more than one occasion. At first it was unwilling to consider the issue.[12] In *Rochin v. California*,[13] it did hold, three years after *Wolf*, that if a search or seizure conducted by state police "shocked the conscience," then exclusion is mandated as a matter of due process. In *Rochin*, the Court found that police use of an emetic to force the defendant to disgorge swallowed drugs was sufficiently repugnant to merit application of the exclusionary rule despite *Wolf*.[14] And, in *Elkins v. United States*,[15] it rejected the "silver platter" doctrine, which permitted *federal* use of evidence illegally obtained by state officials. It was not until 1961, however, in the case of *Mapp v. Ohio*,[16] that the Supreme Court finally agreed to undertake a full-fledged reconsideration of *Wolf*.

In *Mapp*, the Court decided, 5–4, to make the exclusionary rule binding on the states. The Court took a pragmatic approach to the question by recognizing that "the factual considerations supporting the failure of the *Wolf* Court to include the *Weeks* exclusionary rule . . . could not . . . now be deemed controlling." While the *Wolf* Court had felt that remedies other than exclusion might be applied to Fourth Amendment violations, the *Mapp* Court concluded that "other remedies have been worthless and futile," and viewed the exclusionary rule as necessary to the existence of the Fourth Amendment guarantee. "To hold otherwise," Justice Clark stated for the Court, "is to grant the right but in reality to withhold its privilege and enjoyment." Justice Clark recognized, using Justice Cardozo's famous words, that under the rule "[t]he criminal is to go free because the constable has blundered."[17] But he gave a second reason for the exclusionary rule—"the imperative of judicial integrity." Stated Clark:

> The criminal goes free, if he must, but it is the law that sets him free. Nothing can destroy a government more quickly than its failure to observe its own law, or worse, its disregard of the charter of its own existence.[18]

Thus, both deterrence of police misconduct and maintaining judicial "clean hands" justified applying the exclusionary rule to the states.

The final touch in terms of "constitutionalizing" the exclusionary rule came in *Ker v. California*.[19] While *Mapp* declared that state and federal officers were bound by "the same fundamental criteria," *Wolf* had spoken of applying only "the core of the Fourth Amendment" to the states, leaving some doubt as to whether all, or only some, Fourth Amendment rules applied to the states, and concomitantly leaving unclear whether exclusion was the appropriate remedy for all Fourth Amendment violations by state

---

[11]   See Appendix in *Elkins v. United States*, 364 U.S. 206, 80 S.Ct. 1437 (1960).

[12]   See, e.g., *Irvine v. California*, 347 U.S. 128, 74 S.Ct. 381 (1954); *Frank v. Maryland*, 359 U.S. 360, 79 S.Ct. 804 (1959).

[13]   342 U.S. 165, 72 S.Ct. 205 (1952).

[14]   However, it refused to apply the "due process exclusionary rule" to a month-long illegal wiretap, *Irvine v. California*, 347 U.S. 128, 74 S.Ct. 381 (1954), or extraction of blood from an unconscious person. *Breithaupt v. Abram*, 352 U.S. 432, 77 S.Ct. 408 (1957).

[15]   364 U.S. 206, 80 S.Ct. 1437 (1960).

[16]   367 U.S. 643, 81 S.Ct. 1684 (1961).

[17]   *People v. Defore*, 242 N.Y. 13, 150 N.E. 585 (1926), cert. denied 270 U.S. 657, 46 S.Ct. 353 (1926).

[18]   See also, *Elkins v. United States*, 364 U.S. 206, 80 S.Ct. 1437 (1960).

[19]   374 U.S. 23, 83 S.Ct. 1623 (1963).

government. In *Ker*, the Court emphasized that the Supreme Court had no "supervisory authority over state courts . . . , and, consequently, [*Mapp*] implied no *total* obliteration of state laws relating to arrests and searches in favor of federal law." However, the Court went on to hold that, while the states still had the general power to determine what constituted a reasonable search, seizure, or arrest, this finding of reasonableness could be "respected only insofar as consistent with federal constitutional guarantees." Thus, any time a claim of unconstitutional search and seizure or arrest is advanced as a defense to a criminal action in a state court, that court must apply federal standards to the lawfulness or reasonableness of the action in question, unless the state standard is *more* restrictive than the federal standard.[20] In light of this result, *Ker* is often said to be the culmination of the "federalization" of the exclusionary rule. It is important to recognize, however, that when the rule violated is not of constitutional dimension (but is imposed on the federal courts via the supervisory power or is a state rule), *Mapp* does not mandate exclusion.[21]

2.03   The Scope of the Rule

Mapp established that evidence obtained in violation of the Fourth Amendment must be excluded at trial in both federal and state prosecutions. But, beginning in the 1970's, the Court has made clear that the Fourth Amendment exclusionary rule does not operate in most settings outside of trial, and has slowly constricted its operation at trial as well. The premise of this retrenchment is the Court's conclusion that the rule is not a "personal constitutional right of the party aggrieved" but rather a "judicially-created remedy designed to safeguard Fourth Amendment rights generally through its deterrent effect."[22] In other words, as far as the Court is concerned, the only purpose of the exclusionary rule is to deter illegal police behavior; regardless of concerns about judicial integrity and the like, the rule should not apply when it is unlikely to deter, given the cost associated with its application (i.e., benefitting guilty persons and undermining the state's case).

(a)   Criminal Proceedings Other than Trial

After *Mapp* and *Ker*, courts were asked to apply the exclusionary rule in a variety of proceedings other than trial. The Supreme Court's first decision on this issue was *United States v. Calandra*,[23] which firmly established, using the language just quoted, the primacy of the deterrence objective, and demonstrated the Court's penchant for balancing the rule's deterrent effect against the costs of its application. In *Calandra*, the Court decided that a witness summoned to appear and testify before a grand jury could not refuse to answer questions merely because they were based on evidence obtained from an unlawful search and seizure. Justice Powell wrote for the Court that deciding whether the rule should apply in grand jury proceedings required weighing "the potential injury to the historical role and functions of the grand jury against the potential benefits of the rule as applied in this context." Application of this balancing test was relatively straightforward for the Court: while "extension of the exclusionary rule would

---

[20]   Several state courts have announced rules more restrictive than the federal standard based on their interpretation of state law. See § 34.02(c).

[21]   See, e.g., *Cady v. Dombrowski*, 413 U.S. 433, 93 S.Ct. 2523 (1973), where the Court strongly implied that rules governing the listing of items in a post-search inventory are a matter of state law.

[22]   *United States v. Calandra*, 414 U.S. 338, 94 S.Ct. 613 (1974).

[23]   Id.

seriously impede the grand jury" in its investigatory function, "[a]ny incremental deterrent effect which might be achieved by extending the rule to grand jury proceedings is uncertain at best," particularly since illegally seized evidence would still be barred at trial.

In *Stone v. Powell*,[24] the Court relied heavily on *Calandra's* balancing analysis in rejecting application of the exclusionary rule in habeas corpus proceedings. The Court held, 6–3, that where the state has provided an opportunity for the "full and fair litigation" of a Fourth Amendment claim,[25] a state prisoner may not be granted federal habeas relief on that claim regardless of its merit. Justice Powell, again writing the Court's decision, stated that the "deflection of truthfinding" inherent in the use of the exclusionary rule outweighed any deterrent force that use of the rule might have in a federal habeas corpus proceeding—a proceeding that takes place well after the initial criminal trial and therefore is unlikely to be of concern to police when deciding whether to make a search or arrest. The Court glossed over the possibility that the virtual elimination of federal review of state court decisions about the Fourth Amendment would reduce the rule's deterrent effect on state officers and state courts.

A third decision illustrating the Court's balancing approach is *Pennsylvania v. Scott*,[26] where the Court refused to apply the exclusionary rule to parole revocation proceedings. The five-member majority, in an opinion authored by Justice Thomas, stated that application of the exclusionary rule in this setting "would both hinder the function of state parole systems and alter the traditionally flexible administrative nature of parole revocation proceedings" (which are usually not conducted by judges). To the argument that the rule at least ought to apply to searches by parole officers looking for parole violations (because such officers will not be deterred by fear of exclusion at a criminal trial), the Court asserted that the relationship of the parole official with the parolee "is more supervisory than adversarial" and thus it is "unfair to assume that the parole officer bears hostility against the parolee that destroys his neutrality." Given the decision in *Scott*, it is highly likely the Court would hold that the rule does not apply in sentencing proceedings either, as several lower courts have already held.[27]

(b) Non-Criminal Proceedings

Four years after *Mapp*, the Warren Court was asked to decide, in *One 1958 Plymouth Sedan v. Pennsylvania*,[28] whether the exclusionary rule applies in a civil proceeding seeking the forfeiture of an automobile that had been used in the illegal transportation of liquor. The Court answered in the affirmative when, as here, there "is nothing even remotely criminal in possessing an automobile" and the nature of the proceeding would subject the person to significant penalties (here deprivation of a $1000 automobile). On the other hand, suggested the Court, when the individual subject to a forfeiture proceeding seeks to exclude contraband or other items which are illegal to

---

[24]   428 U.S. 465, 96 S.Ct. 3037 (1976).

[25]   See § 33.02(b) for a detailed discussion of the full and fair litigation issue.

[26]   524 U.S. 357, 118 S.Ct. 2014 (1998).

[27]   *United States v. Schipani*, 315 F.Supp. 253 (E.D.N.Y. 1970), aff'd 435 F.2d 26 (2d Cir. 1970), cert. denied 401 U.S. 983, 91 S.Ct. 1198 (1971). For a later decision, see *United States v. McCrory*, 930 F.2d 63 (D.C.Cir. 1991).

[28]   380 U.S. 693, 85 S.Ct. 1246 (1965).

possess, the result might be different.[29] In such cases, permitting exclusion would be tantamount to returning the items to the owner, which "would clearly . . . frustrate . . . the express public policy against the possession of such objects."

The continued viability of *Plymouth Sedan*, decided before *Calandra* and the post-Warren's Court's adoption of a deterrence approach to the rule, is tenuous. *United States v. Janis*,[30] a post-Warren Court decision, illustrates why. Janis successfully excluded cash and wagering records at his trial on illegal gambling charges and then moved to exclude them again in a subsequent civil action brought by the Internal Revenue Service. Despite evidence that the police officer involved in the illegal search routinely notified the IRS when he uncovered major gambling operations, the Court concluded that the gain in deterrence from suppression in an IRS proceeding would be negligible, since the civil proceeding "falls outside the offending officer's zone of primary interest." In other words, the Court assumed, because police officers are unlikely to conduct searches and seizures for the purpose of assisting the IRS in its regulatory endeavors, application of the rule in this context is unlikely to have much deterrent effect. This type of reasoning might also support foregoing application of the exclusionary rule in other civil proceedings that are subsidiary to criminal prosecutions investigated by the police, including the civil forfeiture actions at issue in *Plymouth Sedan*.[31]

At the same time, where the civil proceeding *is* the principal focus of the investigating agent, a different result seems proper. In these types of situations, many lower courts have applied the exclusionary rule. Thus, for instance, the rule has been applied in juvenile delinquency proceedings[32] and certain types of administrative proceedings[33] where the investigating agents work with the adjudicatory bodies in question.

Nonetheless, the Supreme Court has signaled that even the "zone of primary interest" test gives the rule too broad a scope. In *Immigration and Naturalization Service v. Lopez-Mendoza*,[34] the Court, relying on the more general balancing test adopted in *Calandra*, held that evidence illegally seized by INS officers need not be excluded in civil deportation hearings even though these proceedings are the principal "zone of interest" of INS officers. Looking first at the social benefits derived from applying the rule in such proceedings, the Court concluded that any deterrent value would be slight. Justice O'Connor's majority opinion pointed out, for instance, that since most illegal aliens agree to voluntary deportation without a formal hearing, INS officers know a Fourth Amendment challenge is rare and are therefore unlikely to be concerned about having evidence excluded. Moreover, the INS has its own comprehensive scheme for regulating detentions and searches and providing remedies for violations of the regulations. Among the social costs of imposing the rule, on the other hand, are the release of illegal aliens

---

[29] Cf. *United States v. Jeffers*, 342 U.S. 48, 72 S.Ct. 93 (1951) (government may refuse to return unlawfully seized narcotics); *Trupiano v. United States*, 334 U.S. 699, 68 S.Ct. 1229 (1948) (government may refuse to return unregistered still and mash).

[30] 428 U.S. 433, 96 S.Ct. 3021 (1976).

[31] E.g., addict commitment proceedings that take place after criminal conviction for drug use. Cf. *People v. Moore*, 69 Cal.2d 674, 72 Cal.Rptr. 800, 446 P.2d 800 (1968).

[32] *State in Interest of T.L.O.*, 94 N.J. 331, 463 A.2d 934 (1983), rev'd on other grounds *New Jersey v. T.L.O.*, 469 U.S. 325, 105 S.Ct. 733 (1985).

[33] *Donovan v. Sarasota Concrete Co.*, 693 F.2d 1061 (11th Cir. 1982) (OSHA proceedings, but adopting a good faith exception as well); *Midwest Growers Cooperative Corp. v. Kirkemo*, 533 F.2d 455 (9th Cir. 1976) (ICC); *Knoll Associates, Inc. v. FTC*, 397 F.2d 530 (7th Cir. 1968) (FTC).

[34] 468 U.S. 1032, 104 S.Ct. 3479 (1984).

in this country and a "severe" burden on the INS' "deliberately simple deportation hearing system, streamlined to permit the quick resolution of very large numbers of deportation actions." The Court concluded that the balancing test made exclusion of illegally obtained evidence unnecessary in such a system.

(c) The Reasonable "Good Faith" Exception

The Court's willingness to balance the social costs and benefits of the exclusionary rule has also been manifest in cases involving the rule's application at the criminal adjudication itself. Most important in this regard has been the Court's inexorable movement toward the position that the exclusionary rule should not apply when police are "reasonably" unaware they are violating Fourth Amendment principles; in this situation, the Court has reasoned, the exclusionary rule can have no deterrent effect and therefore, in light of the "enormous cost" associated with exclusion, should not operate to exclude evidence at trial. These decisions creating the "good faith" exception to the rule can be divided into search and seizures conducted in reliance on warrants, on statutes, on court records, and on the officer's own perceptions.

(1) Reliance on Warrants

Although a few decisions could be called forerunners on the issue,[35] the companion cases of *United States v. Leon*[36] and *Massachusetts v. Sheppard*[37] were the first significant decisions by the Court on the constitutionality of a good faith exception to the exclusionary rule. In *Leon*, the Court held, by a 6–3 margin, that evidence may be used in the prosecution's case-in-chief when obtained by police acting on authority of a warrant subsequently found to be unsupported by probable cause, provided that they had an objective good faith belief the warrant was valid and that the warrant was issued by a "neutral and detached" magistrate. In *Sheppard*, it concluded, again 6–3, that evidence obtained pursuant to a warrant for which there is probable cause but which is defective on its face is also admissible in the prosecution's case-in-chief, at least when the officer executing the warrant is the one who requested it. Both decisions mark a major change in the Court's stance on the exclusionary rule.

Justice White wrote the majority opinion for both decisions. He began by repeating *Calandra's* assertion that the exclusionary rule is not constitutionally required but rather is a judicially created remedy which may be modified when its social costs outweigh its benefits. In the specific context of searches conducted pursuant to a warrant, Justice White perceived few benefits to weigh against the cost of excluding relevant evidence of criminal activity. Imposing the exclusionary rule in such a situation could have virtually no deterrent effect on the police, he argued, because the judicial officer makes the decision to arrest or search. Nor, in White's opinion, would it act as a significant deterrent on judges and magistrates.

> [W]e cannot conclude that admitting evidence obtained pursuant to a warrant while at the same time declaring that the warrant was somehow defective will in any way reduce judicial officers' professional incentives to comply with the

---

[35] See in particular, *Michigan v. DeFillippo*, 443 U.S. 31, 99 S.Ct. 2627 (1979), discussed in § 2.03(c)(2); *United States v. Peltier*, 422 U.S. 531, 95 S.Ct. 2313 (1975) (declining to apply the rule retroactively to good faith police actions).

[36] 468 U.S. 897, 104 S.Ct. 3405 (1984).

[37] 468 U.S. 981, 104 S.Ct. 3424 (1984).

Fourth Amendment, encourage them to repeat their mistakes, or lead to the granting of all colorable warrant requests.

Thus, "when an officer acting with objective good faith has obtained a search warrant and acted within its scope" there is no point in imposing the exclusionary rule if the warrant happens to be invalid.

Justice White emphasized that the good faith test he announced is an objective one. From this, he derived several limitations. If the affidavit supporting the warrant is "so lacking in indicia of probable cause as to render official belief in its existence entirely unreasonable"[38] or if the warrant is "so facially deficient—i.e., in failing to particularize the place to be searched or things to be seized—that the executing officers cannot reasonably presume it to be valid,"[39] then the exception does not apply. Moreover, regardless of good faith, suppression will still occur when the magistrate is misled by information in the affidavit that the affiant knew was false,[40] or when the magistrate "wholly abandon[s] his judicial role" in issuing the warrant.[41]

Justice White's opinion relies heavily on several controversial assumptions about police and judicial behavior. For instance, commentators have long expressed fear that a good faith exception will encourage "shopping" for magistrates willing to act as "rubber-stamps" for police seeking judicial absolution for illicit actions. Although Justice White recognized the possibility of compliant or incompetent magistrates, he stated, despite evidence to the contrary,[42] that "we are not convinced that this is a problem of major proportions." He also may have been unduly sanguine about the willingness of even those magistrates who are competent to scrutinize warrant applications, now that a good faith exception exists. As Justice Brennan argued in dissent,

> [c]reation of this new exception for good faith reliance upon a warrant implicitly tells magistrates that they need not take much care in reviewing warrant applications, since their mistakes will from now on have virtually no consequence: If their decision to issue a warrant is correct, the evidence will be admitted; if their decision was incorrect but [not "entirely unreasonable" and] the police rely in good faith on the warrant, the evidence will also be admitted. Inevitably, the care and attention devoted to such an inconsequential chore will dwindle.

Similarly, Justice Brennan argued that police training programs will deemphasize Fourth Amendment jurisprudence as a result of *Leon* and *Sheppard*. Although the majority opinion asserted that the reasonableness standard would forestall such a

---

[38] See, e.g., *United States v. Hove*, 848 F.2d 137 (9th Cir. 1988) (obviously deficient affidavit cannot be cured by affiant's later testimony); *United States v. Huggins*, 733 F.Supp. 445 (D.D.C. 1990) (belief that probable cause existed unreasonable where no way for magistrate to determine whether information in affidavit stale).

[39] See, e.g., *United States v. Leary*, 846 F.2d 592 (10th Cir. 1988) (warrant so factually overbroad in description of items to be seized that agents could not reasonably rely on it).

[40] See, e.g., *United States v. Baxter*, 889 F.2d 731 (6th Cir. 1989) (exception does not apply where affidavit contained knowing misstatement as to nature of informant).

[41] *Lo-Ji v. State of New York*, 442 U.S. 319, 99 S.Ct. 2319 (1979), discussed in § 5.02.

[42] See Richard Van Duizend, L. Paul Sutton & Charlotte A. Carter, The Search Warrant Process: Preconceptions, Perceptions and Practices 32 (National Center for State Courts) (study of seven cities finding that "judge shopping" often occurs). See also Yale Kamisar, *Does (Did) (Should) the Exclusionary Rule Rest on a "Principled Basis" Rather than an "Empirical Proposition"?*, 16 Creighton L.Rev. 565, 569–71 (1983); William A. Schroeder, *Deterring Fourth Amendment Violations: Alternatives to the Exclusionary Rule*, 69 Geo.L.J. 1361, 1412 (1981).

development,[43] Brennan predicted that some officers will now merely be taught to recognize when, to use the majority's language, it is *"entirely* unreasonable" to believe probable cause exists. In all other cases, suggested Justice Brennan, police will be told simply to make sure the warrant has been signed, because "there will no longer be any incentive to err on the side of constitutional behavior."

Two additional concerns about the good faith exception that are given similarly short shrift by the majority opinion have to do with its effect on appellate review. First, as with other "totality of the circumstances" tests, the good faith exception might cause considerable judicial confusion. In response to this concern, Justice White simply stated that the exception, "turning as it does on objective reasonableness, should not be difficult to apply in practice." But the decision as to what is "entirely unreasonable" is sure to vary across jurisdictions depending upon a particular court's views on the costs of the exclusionary rule. Indeed, a survey of lower court cases between 1984 and 1990 found considerable conceptual confusion about the good faith exception and many examples of its "misapplication," in large part because the exception "introduces new uncertainty about when the [exclusionary] rule will apply, producing an excess of discretionary leeway."[44]

Secondly, the good faith exception might remove incentive to develop or clarify substantive Fourth Amendment law, since the courts can avoid such decisions, which are often difficult, simply by holding that the officer acted in reasonable good faith reliance on a warrant. This latter point is illustrated by both *Leon* and *Sheppard*. In *Leon*, the warrant application was based in part on information supplied by a confidential informant of unproven reliability who came to police over five months before the application was submitted. Although the police independently investigated this information, both the district court and the court of appeals concluded that the additional data failed to corroborate the details of the tip in the manner required under the Court's decisions in *Aguilar v. Texas*[45] and *Spinelli v. United States*.[46] However, as Justice Stevens pointed out in his dissent to *Leon*, the Court's subsequent decision in *Illinois v. Gates*[47] had modified the *Aguilar-Spinelli* test to the point where the tip might have been sufficient to issue the warrant.[48] Because the majority found that the officer in *Leon* acted in good faith, it neglected to decide whether the warrant was in fact valid under *Gates*, and thus failed to clarify this point.

Similarly, *Sheppard* conceivably could have been decided on substantive grounds rather than as a "good faith" case. In *Sheppard*, the Massachusetts Supreme Court had excluded certain evidence connecting the defendant to a murder because the search which produced it had been conducted pursuant to a warrant that, on its face, authorized only a search for controlled substances, thus violating the "particularity" requirement of

---

[43] The Court quoted Professor Israel to the effect that "the possibility that illegally obtained evidence may be admitted in borderline cases is unlikely to encourage police instructors to pay less attention to the Fourth Amendment" nor should it "encourage officers to pay less attention to what they are taught, as the requirement that the officer act in 'good faith' is inconsistent with closing one's mind to the possibility of illegality." Jerold Israel, *Criminal Procedure, the Burger Court and the Legacy of the Warren Court*, 75 Mich.L.Rev. 1319, 1412–13 (1977).

[44] David Clark Esseks, *Errors in Good Faith: The* Leon *Exception Six Years Later*, 89 Mich.L.Rev. 625 (1990).

[45] 378 U.S. 108, 84 S.Ct. 1509 (1964).

[46] 393 U.S. 410, 89 S.Ct. 584 (1969).

[47] 462 U.S. 213, 103 S.Ct. 2317 (1983).

[48] See § 5.03(b) for a discussion of the *Aguilar-Spinelli* rules and *Gates*' modification of them.

the Fourth Amendment.[49] The Supreme Court, relying on the newly created good faith exception, reversed this decision because the officer who conducted the search had drafted an affidavit which in fact set out sufficient facts to establish probable cause with respect to the seized items; the reason the warrant had not listed those items was because at the time the warrant was issued the issuing judge had only been able to find a warrant form for controlled substances and had neglected to replace the references to controlled substances with the appropriate evidentiary descriptions. As Justice Stevens pointed out, the same reasoning could have supported a holding that the particularity clause of the Fourth Amendment was not violated in the first place, since "the judge who issued the warrant, the police officers who executed it, and the reviewing courts all were able to ascertain the precise scope of the authorization provided by the court" by consulting the attached affidavit. Regardless of the validity of Justice Stevens' analysis, the point is that the majority failed even to consider it because the good faith analysis made such consideration unnecessary.

Subsequent cases have fleshed out when police reliance on a warrant might be "entirely unreasonable," and thus not eligible for the good faith exception. In *Groh v. Ramirez*,[50] the warrant, drafted by the police officer rather than the magistrate, neither listed the items to be seized nor cross-referenced the warrant application (which did list the items). The Supreme Court held that, on these facts, the plain language of the Fourth Amendment's Particularity Clause was violated and that, despite *Sheppard*, the good faith exception did not save the case.[51] Writing for five members of the Court, Justice Stevens quoted *Leon* in finding that the case provided an example of a warrant "so facially deficient . . . that the executing officers cannot reasonably presume it to be valid."[52]

In contrast, in *Messerschmidt v. Millender*,[53] the Court held the good faith exception applied. There, the police executed a warrant authorizing search of the Millenders' house for evidence against one Bowen, a foster child of theirs who was suspected of attempting to murder his girlfriend with a sawed-off shotgun. Pointing out that the warrant authorized seizure of "all" weapons found in their residence as well as "articles of evidence showing gang membership or affiliation," the Millenders argued that the police were "entirely unreasonable" in believing the warrant was sufficiently particularized and, thus, that *Leon*'s good faith standard was not met. The Court, in a 7–2 opinion, disagreed. Whereas the flaw in the warrant in *Groh* could have been discovered through a "cursory reading" or "just a simple glance," Chief Justice Roberts wrote for the Court, a reasonable officer seeing the *Millender* warrant could have believed that seizure of all firearms from the house in which Bowen was thought to reside was necessary to prevent further assaults on the girlfriend. Likewise, it was not entirely unreasonable to believe that seizure of gang-related evidence might be useful in proving motive, impeaching a trial claim that Bowen had no access to guns, or establishing a connection between Bowen and the articles found in the house. Justice Kagan, dissenting in part, disagreed with this last conclusion on the ground that "membership in even the worst gang does

---

[49] See § 5.04 for a discussion of the particularity requirement.

[50] 540 U.S. 551, 124 S.Ct. 1284 (2004).

[51] *Groh* was actually a civil suit brought against the executing officer, but the Court noted that the good faith defense in such actions is identical to *Leon*'s good faith exception. See *Malley v. Briggs*, 475 U.S. 335, 106 S.Ct. 1092 (1986), discussed in § 2.05(a)(3).

[52] *Groh* is discussed in more detail in § 5.04.

[53] 565 U.S. 535, 132 S.Ct. 1235 (2012).

not violate California law," while Justice Sotomayor's dissent argued that even the part of the warrant authorizing seizure of firearms was clearly overbroad, given the specific type of gun thought to be used in the offense.

(2) Reliance on Statutes

Michigan v. DeFillippo,[54] decided five years before *Leon* and *Sheppard*, in many ways presaged those cases.[55] DeFillippo was arrested by Detroit police for violating a city "Stop and Identify" ordinance. The ordinance provided that a police officer may stop and question an individual if the officer has reasonable cause to believe that the individual's behavior warrants further investigation for criminal activity. A 1976 amendment to the ordinance provided that it was unlawful for any person stopped under the section to refuse to identify himself and produce evidence of his identity. The Michigan courts held that the ordinance was unconstitutionally vague and that, because it was the basis for DeFillippo's arrest, both the arrest and subsequent search were invalid. The Supreme Court reversed, holding that "[a] prudent officer, in the course of determining whether respondent had committed an offense under all the circumstances shown by this record, should not have been required to anticipate that a court would later hold the ordinance unconstitutional." In terms echoing its *Calandra* balancing analysis,[56] the Court noted that excluding the evidence under such circumstances would be unlikely to deter police.

Like *DeFillippo*, *Illinois v. Krull*[57] involved police activity pursuant to a law subsequently found unconstitutional. However, *Krull* differed from *DeFillippo* in one respect. Whereas the ordinance in *DeFillippo* had unconstitutionally criminalized innocent behavior, the statute in *Krull* was found to authorize unconstitutional searches. The *DeFillippo* majority had carefully avoided applying its holding to the latter type of statute, noting that several previous Court decisions had excluded evidence seized pursuant to such laws after they were found unconstitutional.[58] The five-member majority in *Krull* saw no difference between the two types of enactments, however. Instead, it found that the situation in *Krull* was analogous to the situation in *Leon*, with the sole difference that the police were relying on a decision of the legislature rather than a magistrate. And just as the *Leon* Court had felt that the threat of exclusion was not necessary to ensure carefulness on the part of the magistrate, the Court in *Krull* asserted that a legislature was unlikely to pass unconstitutional statutes merely because the exclusionary remedy was unavailable to defendants searched under such laws. However, analogous to its holding in *Leon* permitting exclusion of evidence when the warrant issued by the magistrate is entirely unreasonable on its face, the Court stated

---

[54]   443 U.S. 31, 99 S.Ct. 2627 (1979).

[55]   See also, *United States v. Caceres*, 440 U.S. 741, 99 S.Ct. 1465 (1979). Respondent had challenged evidence obtained during an Internal Revenue Service monitoring, on the grounds that the I.R.S. had not complied with its own regulations governing such monitoring. The Court refused, 7–2, to adopt a rigid exclusionary rule in situations where the agency action demonstrates a reasonable, good faith attempt to comply with its regulations. Here the Court found there had been such a good faith effort. It should be noted, however, that *Caceres* did not involve a Fourth Amendment violation (the respondent had consented to the monitoring), but merely a violation of internal agency guidelines. While respondent (and Justice Marshall in dissent) argued that this oversight implicated a constitutional *due process* interest, the majority refused to so find.

[56]   See § 2.03(a).

[57]   480 U.S. 340, 107 S.Ct. 1160 (1987).

[58]   See, e.g., *Torres v. Puerto Rico*, 442 U.S. 465, 99 S.Ct. 2425 (1979); *Almeida-Sanchez v. United States*, 413 U.S. 266, 93 S.Ct. 2535 (1973); *Berger v. New York*, 388 U.S. 41, 87 S.Ct. 1873 (1967).

that in the statutory search context exclusion would be appropriate when the legislature "wholly abandon[s] its responsibility to enact constitutional laws."

In dissent, Justice O'Connor, joined by Justices Brennan, Marshall and Stevens, argued that the analogy to *Leon* was inapposite. Legislation affects many more individuals than a single warrant and is more likely to be the product of political pressure. Thus, O'Connor suggested, the need for deterrence is heightened. Yet without the exclusionary remedy, individual litigants are unlikely to challenge legislation (although, as the majority pointed out, injunctive and declaratory relief is still available). O'Connor also noted the difficulty of defining "good faith" in the statutory context. Whereas *Leon* merely requires proof of a facially valid warrant in order to trigger the good faith exception of that case, the rule in *Krull* requires courts "to determine at what point a reasonable officer should be held to know that a statute has, under evolving legal rules, become 'clearly' unconstitutional."[59]

(3) *Reliance on Records and Reports*

The Court once again relied on *Leon* in holding that an illegal search or seizure that results from good faith reliance on computer records should not trigger the exclusionary rule, at least when those records are generated by court personnel. In *Arizona v. Evans,*[60] the defendant was arrested by Phoenix police during a routine traffic stop after the patrol car's computer indicated he had an outstanding arrest warrant for a misdemeanor. In an ensuing search of the car, the police found marijuana. Evans moved to suppress the drugs based on the uncontested fact that the arrest warrant had been quashed 17 days prior to the arrest, an event that court clerks had failed to communicate to those who entered data into the computer. But Chief Justice Rehnquist concluded for the Court that, analogous to the assumption *Leon* made about magistrates, "there is no basis for believing that application of the exclusionary rule in these circumstances will have a significant effect on court employees responsible for informing the police that a warrant has been quashed."

The lone dissenter in *Evans*, Justice Stevens,[61] pointed out that neither the officer relying on a computer report nor the municipality which maintains the computer is likely to be civilly liable for an illegal arrest of the sort involved in *Evans*.[62] Thus he asserted, in a vein similar to Justice O'Connor's dissent in *Krull*, that deterrence of negligence like that involved in *Evans* can be achieved *only* through exclusion. Stevens registered particular concern over the effect *Evans* might have on innocent individuals erroneously stopped or searched based on faulty records. This concern is well-founded; an FBI study of the country's computerized criminal information systems in 1985 revealed that "[a]t least 12,000 invalid or inaccurate reports on suspects wanted for arrest are transmitted *each day* to Federal, state and local law-enforcement agencies."[63] Cognizant of these

---

[59]   As Justice O'Connor pointed out, the constitutionality of the statute at issue in *Krull* was still unclear six years after the search in that case.

[60]   514 U.S. 1, 115 S.Ct. 1185 (1995).

[61]   Justice Ginsburg dissented on procedural grounds, although her opinion suggested that she agreed with Stevens' views.

[62]   The officer would have a good faith defense and the municipality would be immune given the absence of a policy or custom sanctioning the practice. See § 2.05(a)(3) & (4).

[63]   David Burnham, *F.B.I. Says 12,000 Faulty Reports on Suspects are Issued Each Day*, N.Y. Times, Aug. 25, 1985, at 1 (emphasis added). See also, Jeffrey Rothfeder, Privacy for Sale 132 (1992) (recounting the discovery by a Midwest prosecutor that 73 percent of cases he examined that still had arrest warrants listed on the NCIC computer were no longer provable).

problems, three of the justices who joined the six member majority (O'Connor, Souter and Breyer) stated in a concurring opinion that while exclusion was not warranted on the facts of *Evans*, if a recordkeeping system "has no mechanism to ensure its accuracy over time and . . . routinely leads to false arrests," exclusion should be mandated.

An important issue left unresolved after *Evans* is the admissibility of evidence obtained in reliance on information generated by other *police*. In two earlier decisions, *Whiteley v. Warden*[64] and *United States v. Hensley*,[65] the Court strongly suggested that the admissibility of evidence obtained in reliance on a police bulletin hinges on whether the information in the bulletin withstands Fourth Amendment analysis, not on whether the arresting officer acted in good faith reliance on the bulletin. The *Evans* majority suggested that these cases are still good law by noting that its ruling would not necessarily apply if the persons maintaining the computer were "police personnel" rather than court employees. However, citing *Calandra* and other cases that stress that the exclusionary rule is not constitutionally required, the Court cleared the way for an eventual holding to the contrary by stating: "Although *Whiteley* clearly retains relevance in determining whether police officers have violated the Fourth Amendment, see *Hensley*, its precedential value regarding application of the exclusionary rule is dubious." If the Court decides to undo *Whiteley*, the police might be able to insulate an illegality simply by passing on the information so garnered to an officer who is not aware of the illegality (and thus would rely on it in good faith). That possibility, in turn, could diminish a wide range of Fourth Amendment protections, ranging from restrictions on use of informants[66] to fruit of the poisonous tree analysis.[67]

The Court inched closer to that type of regime in *Herring v. United States*,[68] where an arrest was made based on warrant that should have been withdrawn five months earlier. Although this error was attributable to the police department rather than, as occurred in *Evans*, the clerk's office, five members of the Court, in an opinion by Chief Justice Roberts, once again concluded that the "good faith" exception applied. According to the Court, suppression should occur only if the record-keeping error is "flagrant," "knowing" or "reckless", or, as suggested by the concurring justices in *Evans*, there is proof of systemic flaws in the database; in all other cases, the minimal deterrent effect of exclusion is outweighed by "the substantial costs of exclusion." This language suggests the Court is moving toward a rule of exclusion that is triggered only by non-negligent violations of the Fourth Amendment.

(4) Reliance on Previous Caselaw

The Court extended the good faith exception to cases in which police reasonably rely on appellate caselaw in *Davis v. United States*.[69] On his direct appeal, Davis conceded that the search of his car was legal under precedent existing at the time of search but argued that, since the Supreme Court's subsequent opinion in *Arizona v. Gant* had held

---

[64]   401 U.S. 560, 91 S.Ct. 1031 (1971), discussed in § 3.03(a)(3).

[65]   469 U.S. 221, 105 S.Ct. 675 (1985), discussed in § 11.03(c)(2).

[66]   For instance, information learned from a clearly unreliable informant could be passed on to another officer whose good faith reliance would prevent exclusion of evidence he finds as a result. Cf. § 5.03(b).

[67]   Overturning *Whiteley* would mean that exclusion would not result even though the second officer's search would be "fruit" of a defective police bulletin. See § 2.04.

[68]   555 U.S. 135, 129 S.Ct. 695 (2009).

[69]   564 U.S. 229, 131 S.Ct. 2419 (2011).

that such searches violated the Fourth Amendment,[70] the evidence found in his car should be excluded on retrial. Relying on *Leon, Krull, Evans* and, in particular, *Herring's* principle that exclusion is warranted only when a Fourth Amendment violation is flagrant or reckless, seven members of the Court, in an opinion by Justice Alito, rejected Davis' claim.

Justice Breyer's dissent, joined by Justice Ginsburg, made two arguments. First, Breyer claimed, the majority's holding violated retroactivity doctrine, which had long required that all litigants whose direct appeal is not final at the time of a new ruling, as was true of Davis when *Gant* was decided, should receive its benefit.[71] Justice Alito responded that this argument confused the retroactive application of a new substantive right, to which Davis was entitled, with the appropriate remedy when a right is retroactive. Since the exclusionary remedy is only apposite when deterrence would thereby be achieved, Alito reasoned, it was not the right remedy here. Justice Breyer also argued that, after *Davis*, litigants will not have any incentive to challenge Fourth Amendment precedent, because even a successful claim will not result in exclusion. The majority dismissed this concern as well, both on the ground that facilitating overruling of precedent is not "a relevant consideration in an exclusionary rule case" and on the ground that, even after *Davis*, litigants will still argue that their case is distinguishable from established precedent and thus provide courts with opportunities to change the law. However, the Court did state that, "if necessary" to prevent ossification of Fourth Amendment law, it might grant exclusion to the litigant who succeeds in convincing the Court its precedent should be overruled. Of course, such a resolution would result in the dissimilar treatment of similarly situated litigations that retroactivity doctrine is designed to avoid, but the majority apparently believed that its severance of the Fourth Amendment right from the exclusionary remedy handled this problem.

(5) Reliance on the Searching Officer's Observations

All of the decisions recognizing a good faith exception have involved the investigating officer's reliance on a source other than himself on the issue of whether his action violated the Fourth Amendment. The Court has yet to decide whether a reasonable good faith belief based on nothing other than the officer's own observations would provide a valid exception to the rule. The Court has dodged at least two opportunities to do so. In 1980 it denied *certiorari* on a decision that had adopted a full-blown good faith exception to the exclusionary rule.[72] In 1983, the Court asked the parties in *Illinois v. Gates*[73] to argue the validity of such an exception even though the state had not asserted good faith as a defense in the lower courts. Then, at least in part because the issue had not been argued below, the Court, "with apologies to all," decided *Gates* on other grounds.

Predicting the Court's eventual stance is difficult. Some relatively conservative justices, albeit justices who are no longer on the Court, have indicated a willingness to retract even the decisions already made if they result in widespread noncompliance.[74]

---

[70]   For a description of the Court's car search doctrine, see § 6.04(c).

[71]   For a discussion of the Court's retroactivity decisions involving cases on direct appeal, see § 29.06(b).

[72]   *United States v. Williams*, 622 F.2d 830 (5th Cir. 1980), cert. denied 449 U.S. 1127, 101 S.Ct. 946 (1981).

[73]   462 U.S. 213, 103 S.Ct. 2317 (1983).

[74]   In *Immigration & Naturalization Service v. Lopez-Mendoza*, 468 U.S. 1032, 104 S.Ct. 3479 (1984), discussed in § 2.03(b), Justices O'Connor, Blackmun, Powell and Rehnquist joined in that part of the opinion

However, given the direction of its decisions, there is a greater possibility that the Court will expand on the idea and apply it to any case, including those involving warrantless searches and seizures in which the officer reasonably believed he acted constitutionally. At least one federal court of appeals has adopted a broad good faith exception,[75] and several state legislatures have followed suit (although their police and courts still must apply the rule when violations of the Fourth Amendment occur).[76]

A good faith exception to exclusion of evidence illegally obtained via a warrantless search or seizure suffers from the same defects as the exception announced in *Leon*, *Krull*, and *Evans*: Fourth Amendment jurisprudence becomes secondary to what a "reasonable officer" would believe, thus encouraging police nonchalance toward the law and retarding its development. In addition, of course, the broader good faith exception does not offer whatever protection against abuse that review by a judicial officer, legislature or court personnel provides.

Nonetheless, exclusion under all circumstances seems silly. Sometimes the substantive law can be modified to take into account a minor divergence from the traditional rule (as demonstrated by how *Groh* dealt with the underlying situation involved in *Sheppard*). But, if not, something short of a full-blown good faith exception to the exclusionary rule may be appropriate, where there is a *de minimis* violation or clerical error.[77]

(d) Impeachment Evidence

Unless one of the good faith exceptions is met, evidence obtained through an illegal search and seizure is excludable from the prosecution's case-in-chief. However, if the prosecution seeks to use the evidence to impeach the defendant once he takes the stand, then exclusion is unlikely. Again, the Court has reasoned that such exclusion is unnecessary, because excluding the evidence from the prosecution's case-in-chief has sufficient deterrent effect. Rebuttal of testimony from persons other than the defendant, however, may not rely on evidence obtained through an illegal search and seizure.

(1) Against the Defendant

The Court first considered use of illegally seized evidence as an impeachment device in *Agnello v. United States*,[78] decided in 1925. There the Court held that such evidence may not be relied upon in federal cases for any purpose. Almost thirty years later, in *Walder v. United States*,[79] the Court permitted a limited exception to this rule, where the defendant in effect waives his Fourth Amendment protection by testifying on direct examination to matters going beyond the elements of the charge against him. In such cases, the Court held, the prosecution may rebut the tangential assertions with illegally

---

which, in the context of holding the exclusionary rule need not apply in civil deportation proceedings, stated: "Our conclusions concerning the exclusionary rule's value [in deportation proceedings] might change, if there developed good reason to believe that Fourth Amendment violations by INS officers were widespread."

[75] *United States v. Williams*, 622 F.2d 830 (5th Cir. 1980).

[76] Ariz.Rev.Stat. § 12–3925; Colo.Rev.Stat.1973, 16–3–308.

[77] See *United States v. Gordon*, 901 F.2d 48 (5th Cir. 1990) (good faith exception applies when warrant invalid because of incorrect street address, since executing officer was also the affiant and had recently viewed the location). An analogous exception has developed in determining the appropriate sanction under the federal electronic surveillance statute. See § 14.03(g)(2), (3).

[78] 269 U.S. 20, 46 S.Ct. 4 (1925).

[79] 347 U.S. 62, 74 S.Ct. 354 (1954).

obtained evidence. In *Walder*, involving a narcotics charge, the Court approved prosecution use of heroin illegally seized two years earlier to impeach statements the defendant made on direct to the effect that he had never purchased, sold or possessed narcotics. But the Court emphasized that the defendant must be "free to deny all the elements of the [current] case against him."

The next time the Court considered the impeachment issue, some twenty-five years later, it overruled *Agnello* (without mentioning the case) and ignored the limitations imposed in *Walder*. Building on its earlier decision permitting impeachment with evidence seized in violation of the Fifth Amendment,[80] the Court's decision in *United States v. Havens*[81] authorized use of illegally seized items to contradict direct testimony about the crime charged as well as testimony on collateral matters. In a 5–4 opinion, the Court, through Justice White, reasoned that exclusion in such cases would only minimally deter police misconduct, and at the same time encourage perjury by the defendant.

Concern about perjury also led the *Havens* Court to permit impeachment of statements first made on *cross*-examination. Because of "the importance of arriving at the truth in criminal trials, as well as the defendant's obligation to speak the truth in response to proper questions," there is "no difference of constitutional magnitude between the defendant's statements on direct examination and his answers to questions put to him on cross-examination that are plainly within the scope of the defendant's direct examination." The test of admissibility should be whether the questions on cross "would have been suggested to a reasonably competent cross-examiner" by direct testimony.

The Court found this test met in *Havens*. The defendant took the stand after one McLeroth testified that Havens had cut swatches out of his T-shirt and used them to sew pockets in McLeroth's undershirt for the purpose of carrying cocaine. On direct, Havens denied that he had engaged in any activity like that described by McLeroth, but made no mention of the T-shirt. On cross-examination, in response to questions, Havens more specifically denied having anything "to do with the sewing of the cotton swatches to make pockets on that T-shirt," and answered "Not to my knowledge" when asked if he had a T-shirt with missing patches in his luggage at the time he was arrested. In rebuttal, the government introduced a T-shirt, from which material had been cut, that had been found in Havens luggage after an illegal search. The Court found nothing improper in this action, noting that the trial judge instructed the jury to consider the impeachment evidence only on the issue of credibility.

Even if the Court is right that exclusion of such evidence is unlikely to deter illegal searches, *Havens* is sure to discourage some defendants from taking the stand, in derogation of their right to testify.[82] Defendants must now take into consideration that anything they say on direct examination, even if it merely involves denying the charge, might be impeached with illegally obtained evidence. And even if they avoid saying something rebuttable during direct, they may nonetheless be forced to do so during cross, since, as Justice Brennan pointed out in dissent, "even the moderately talented prosecutor [can] work in . . . evidence on cross-examination." *Walder's* waiver approach

---

[80]   *Harris v. New York*, 401 U.S. 222, 91 S.Ct. 643 (1971), discussed in detail in § 16.05(b)(1).

[81]   446 U.S. 620, 100 S.Ct. 1912 (1980).

[82]   The Court recognized this right in *Rock v. Arkansas*, 479 U.S. 1079, 107 S.Ct. 1276 (1987), discussed in § 28.06(a).

has been significantly undermined, if not rejected completely. *Havens'* ultimate impact on the accuracy of the fact-finding process is harder to gauge.

(2) *Against Other Witnesses*

While there are few restrictions on using illegally obtained evidence seized from the defendant to impeach the defendant, the state is prohibited from impeaching a witness other than the defendant with such evidence.[83] In *James v. Illinois*,[84] the Court decided, 5–4, that such a rule is necessary, despite its possible impact on truthfinding, for three reasons. First, while a perjury prosecution is unlikely to be a significant concern for a defendant already facing possible conviction and sentence, it is likely to deter outright falsification by other witnesses; accordingly, the additional incentive to tell the truth provided by impeachment with illegally obtained evidence is not as great. Second, a rule permitting such impeachment would chill the defendant's willingness to put on witnesses, thus detracting from, rather than enhancing, the truthseeking function of trial. Third, such a rule would give even more incentive to the police to violate the Fourth Amendment, since they would know that even though such a violation would mean exclusion from the prosecution's case-in-chief, it would permit impeachment not only of the defendant but of the defendant's witnesses.

The dissent, written by Justice Kennedy, labelled as speculative or unrealistic the assumptions made by the majority. Kennedy indicated he might be willing to distinguish between treatment of defendants and other witnesses to the extent of banning illegal evidence impeachment of cross-examination statements made by the latter (a rule *Havens* rejected as to statements by the defendant). But he characterized the majority's holding as "a wooden rule immunizing . . . defense testimony from rebuttal, without regard to knowledge that the testimony introduced at the behest of the defendant is false or perjured."

2.04   The "Fruit of the Poisonous Tree" Doctrine

(a) Rationale

Unlike the doctrines previously discussed, the "fruit of the poisonous tree" doctrine tends to expand the scope of the exclusionary rule. Suppose the police illegally arrest someone. The fruit of the poisonous tree doctrine would not only require exclusion of evidence obtained in a search incident to that arrest, but might also require exclusion of a confession obtained from the arrestee some hours later, even if the interrogation that produced the confession was conducted constitutionally. The doctrine thus may lead to exclusion of evidence procured through *lawful* means. The rationale for the doctrine is deterrence. Without it, police might knowingly violate the Fourth Amendment (e.g., by carrying out an illegal arrest) hoping to obtain evidence that would be admissible (e.g., a subsequent confession).

The doctrine is usually said to have originated in *Silverthorne Lumber Co. v. United States*.[85] In that case, the defendant company was convicted on contempt charges for failing to produce documents the existence of which the government discovered through

---

[83]   Note that if the evidence is illegally seized from the witness, the defendant would not have standing to exclude it. See § 4.04.

[84]   493 U.S. 307, 110 S.Ct. 648 (1990).

[85]   251 U.S. 385, 40 S.Ct. 182 (1920).

an illegal search. The Supreme Court, speaking through Justice Holmes, reversed the conviction, 7–2, holding that "[t]he essence of a provision forbidding the acquisition of evidence in a certain way is that not merely evidence so acquired shall not be used before the Court but that it shall not be used at all." To hold otherwise, reasoned Holmes, "reduces the Fourth Amendment to a form of words." The Court reaffirmed this notion in *Nardone v. United States*,[86] but recognized that merely establishing a logical connection between an illegality and the procurement of evidence should not automatically lead to exclusion. In doing so, the Court, through Justice Frankfurter, developed the colorful lexicon that today is associated with derivative evidence analysis. Frankfurter stated that it should be left to the discretion of "experienced trial judges" whether "a substantial portion of the case against [the accused] was a fruit of the poisonous tree." In some cases, "sophisticated argument may prove a causal link obtained through [illegality] and the Government's proof. As a matter of good sense, however, such a connection may have become so attenuated as to dissipate the taint."

In determining when "fruit" of police illegality is nonetheless admissible, three related doctrines have been developed by the courts: the attenuation doctrine (so-called as a result of Frankfurter's usage of that term in *Nardone*), the independent source doctrine, and the inevitable discovery doctrine. Here these doctrines will be examined primarily through cases in which the initial illegality was a violation of the Fourth Amendment. However, as subsequent discussion shows,[87] the triggering violation may be of other constitutional provisions as well. As one might expect in light of the Court's modern pronouncements concerning the exclusionary rule, all three doctrines are interpreted so as to exclude evidence only when the deterrence objective of the rule would be *significantly* furthered.

(b) The Attenuation Exception

Twenty-five years after *Nardone*, Justice Brennan, in the case of *Wong Sun v. United States*,[88] reframed Frankfurter's "attenuation" idea as an analysis of whether the derivative evidence "has been come at by exploitation of [the initial] illegality or instead by means sufficiently distinguishable to be purged of the primary taint."[89] Using this test, the Court excluded various admissions and confessions by one defendant because they were acquired immediately following his unlawful arrest, as well as narcotics obtained from another person because their whereabouts were discovered solely as a result of the defendant's declarations. However, the Court felt that the statement of a second defendant, voluntarily made when he returned to the stationhouse on his own initiative several days after he was released on his own recognizance, could not be said to have been obtained by exploitation of the illegally acquired information. Even though he too was located as a result of an unlawful arrest, the relation between the arrest and the defendant's voluntary statement "had 'become so attenuated as to dissipate the taint.'"

The attenuation doctrine has since been applied in a number of Supreme Court cases. Considered first are the cases, like *Wong Sun*, in which the "fruit" is a confession,

---

[86] 308 U.S. 338, 60 S.Ct. 266 (1939).

[87] See § 2.04(d). See also, § 16.05(c) (confession as poisonous tree) and § 17.05 (identification as poisonous tree).

[88] 371 U.S. 471, 83 S.Ct. 407 (1963).

[89] This phrase was taken from John MacArthur Maguire, Evidence of Guilt 221 (1959).

followed by discussion of cases in which other types of fruit are involved. Finally, cases in which the most important consideration appears to be the type of poisonous tree, rather than the nature of the fruit, are examined.

(1) Confessions as Fruit

Wong Sun made clear that the overriding issue in deciding whether the taint of an illegality has been dissipated is whether the resulting confession is "an act of free will." In *Brown v. Illinois*,[90] the Court catalogued several factors courts should consider in deciding whether a confession is an act of free will rather than tainted by previous illegality: (1) whether *Miranda* warnings[91] were given prior to any confession or admission; (2) the "temporal proximity" of the illegal police conduct and the verbal statements; (3) the presence of intervening circumstances or events; and (4) the "purpose and flagrancy of the official misconduct."

Several cases flesh out these factors. In *Dunaway v. New York*,[92] police brought the defendant to the stationhouse for an interrogation even though they did not have probable cause to arrest him. After being given *Miranda* warnings, Dunaway confessed to a robbery-murder. Justice Brennan, writing for the majority, first found that a detention merely for custodial interrogation "intrudes so severely on interests protected by the Fourth Amendment as necessarily to trigger the traditional safeguards against illegal arrest." He then stated that the confession deriving from this illegal detention should have been suppressed despite the police's compliance with *Miranda*. Citing *Brown*, he noted that the confession had followed so closely upon the detention and the police's conduct had so clearly violated Fourth Amendment policies that the confession could not be separated from the initial illegality. To hold otherwise would allow " 'law enforcement officers to violate the Fourth Amendment with impunity, safe in the knowledge that they could wash their hands in the "procedural safeguards" of the Fifth.' "

Similarly, in *Taylor v. Alabama*,[93] the Court held that even though: (1) the defendant had been given *Miranda* warnings three times between the illegal arrest and his confession; (2) six hours had elapsed between the arrest and the confession; and (3) the defendant was permitted to see two friends before the confession, there were insufficient intervening events to attenuate the taint of the arrest. In contrast, in *Rawlings v. Kentucky*,[94] even though the incriminating statements were made a mere 45 minutes after the illegal arrest, they were admissible because (1) the defendant received *Miranda* warnings just prior to making the statements; (2) the defendant was in a house, in a "congenial atmosphere" with several companions present, when he made the statements; (3) the statements were spontaneous rather than a response to direct questioning; (4) the police's violation of the Fourth Amendment was not flagrant but rather apparently was a good faith mistake; and (5) the defendant did not argue his admission was involuntary.

---

[90]   422 U.S. 590, 95 S.Ct. 2254 (1975).

[91]   See § 16.02(d) for a discussion of the warning requirement announced in *Miranda v. Arizona*, 384 U.S. 436, 86 S.Ct. 1602 (1966).

[92]   442 U.S. 200, 99 S.Ct. 2248 (1979).

[93]   457 U.S. 687, 102 S.Ct. 2664 (1982).

[94]   448 U.S. 98, 100 S.Ct. 2556 (1980).

These cases suggest that the most important factors of the four listed in *Brown* are the last two: intervening events (other than *Miranda* warnings) and the flagrancy of police conduct. As *Dunaway* recognized, if giving *Miranda* warnings were considered significant, police could too easily immunize their conduct. And as *Taylor* shows, a long lapse of time should not necessarily attenuate the taint; otherwise, police would be encouraged to hold those they have illegally arrested for long periods before questioning, which would only exacerbate the illegality. On the other hand, as *Rawlings* illustrates, the nature of the encounter, the overall spontaneity of the statement, and the good faith of the police can play an important role in determining whether the exclusionary rule applies. Recognizing these as factors to be considered in deciding whether exclusion should occur does not create as much of an incentive for police to abuse Fourth Amendment guarantees.

(2) Other Types of Fruit

As the preceding discussion suggests, most of the cases in which the attenuation doctrine has surfaced have involved analysis of when a confession obtained as a result of a Fourth Amendment violation is admissible. Occasionally, however, the fruit of an illegal seizure will be something else, such as identification of a person or another search. In such cases, the last three of *Brown's* factors are still relevant (*Miranda* warnings, of course, are relevant only to confessions). For instance, whether an identification during a properly conducted lineup should be admissible despite the fact it resulted from an illegal arrest depends upon intervening events (such as whether the defendant was taken before a magistrate), the voluntariness of the defendant's participation in the lineup, and the flagrancy of the arrest.[95] A similar analysis may also lead to admission of evidence found after an illegal stop if it is shown that the person stopped consented "voluntarily" to the search,[96] although here one must carefully analyze both the voluntariness and flagrancy issues.

In *United States v. Ceccolini*,[97] the Court used *Brown's* analysis in deciding whether a *witness* discovered as the result of an illegal search was inadmissible fruit. In *Ceccolini*, the Fourth Amendment violation occurred when a police officer stopped to talk to his friend Hennessey at work, in the defendant's shop. In the course of their conversation, the officer peeked into a package and saw money and gambling slips. He found out from Hennessey that the package belonged to her boss and reported the incident to local detectives. They alerted the FBI, which the year before had been conducting an investigation of gambling operations in the area, including surveillance of the defendant's shop. Four months after the illegal search of the package, the FBI conducted an interview with Hennessey, and a year and a half after the search her testimony in front of a grand jury and a later trial helped convict the defendant on perjury charges.

In upholding use of Hennessey's testimony, the Court, per Justice Rehnquist, noted the "length of the road" between the search and the testimony, the fact that the witness testified of her own free will, and the absence of evidence that the search's objective was obtaining a witness against Ceccolini. The latter finding may be the most important, assuming the ultimate goal is assuring that the deterrent effect of the exclusionary rule

---

[95] See, e.g., *Johnson v. Louisiana*, 406 U.S. 356, 92 S.Ct. 1620 (1972); see also, *United States v. Crews*, 445 U.S. 463, 100 S.Ct. 1244 (1980), discussed in § 17.05(b).

[96] See *State v. Fortier*, 113 Ariz. 332, 553 P.2d 1206 (1976).

[97] 435 U.S. 268, 98 S.Ct. 1054 (1978).

is not undermined. While it may be true, as the Court asserted in *Ceccolini*, that witnesses "can, and often do, come forward and offer evidence entirely of their own volition" (thus giving rise to an analogy to the Court's result in *Wong Sun*), a per se rule that witnesses should not ever be considered "fruit" (which Chief Justice Burger urged in a concurring opinion) would open the door to illegal searches designed to find them.[98]

More controversially, in *Utah v. Strieff*[99] the Court held that an outstanding arrest warrant can attenuate the taint of an illegal stop. In *Strieff*, the officer received an anonymous tip about drug activity at a particular residence, saw several people leave the house a few minutes after arriving, and then saw Strieff emerge. The officer demanded that Strieff tell him what he was doing in the house and asked for his identification, which matched with an outstanding warrant for a traffic violation; the ensuing arrest and search incident produced drugs. Assuming the stop was illegal, five members of the Court nonetheless concluded that the officer's violation of the Fourth Amendment was merely negligent, not flagrant, and that the search, while proximate to the illegal stop, was based on an intervening event, the warrant, that predated the stop and was unconnected to the arrest. In contrast, the three dissenters argued that, given the officer's admission that he was fishing for information, his conduct was flagrantly illegal and that this fact, combined with the proximity of the search to the stop, required exclusion.

Justice Sotomayor wrote a separate dissent contending that, given the huge number of outstanding arrest warrants (over 7.8 million nationally), many for minor offenses such as Strieff's, the majority's ruling would encourage police to stop people randomly with the hope of discovering admissible evidence, a scenario she thought would disproportionately affect minorities. Justice Thomas responded that completely suspicionless stops would call for exclusion on flagrancy grounds. Even if the Court adheres to that stance, *Strieff* gives police incentive to conduct stops based on hunches.

(3) Atypical Poisonous Trees

The typical poisonous tree—and the illegality in all of the cases discussed to this point—is an arrest, stop or search not founded on probable cause. When other types of Fourth Amendment illegalities are involved, the Court's attenuation analysis has often diverged from *Brown's* factors, or ignored them entirely. For instance, the Court refused to consider those factors in *New York v. Harris*.[100] There the police, acting without a warrant, arrested the defendant in his home several days after developing probable cause. They obtained incriminating statements from him both while he was still inside his home and after he had been taken to the stationhouse. The Supreme Court assumed with the lower courts that the arrest violated *Payton v. New York*,[101] which requires an arrest warrant for non-exigent home arrests. It further agreed with the lower courts that the statements made *in* the home should be excluded as fruit of the *Payton* violation. But while the lower appellate courts held that *Brown's* attenuation analysis also required

---

[98]   Another rationale for the result in *Ceccolini*, suggested by Justice Marshall in dissent, is that, in light of the ongoing FBI investigation, the government inevitably would have discovered Hennessey. See § 2.04(d).

[99]   ___ U.S. ___, 136 S.Ct. 2056 (2016).

[100]   495 U.S. 14, 110 S.Ct. 1640 (1990).

[101]   445 U.S. 573, 100 S.Ct. 1371 (1980), discussed in § 3.04(b).

exclusion of the stationhouse statement, the Supreme Court held, 5–4, that *Brown* was not even applicable.

Crucial to the Court's opinion, which was written by Justice White, was that a violation of *Payton* does not prevent the government from maintaining custody of an arrested defendant; the Fourth Amendment is implicated by a *Payton* violation because the police failed to get a warrant, not because they lacked probable cause to arrest. Thus, unlike in *Brown, Dunaway,* or *Taylor*—where the defendant's presence in the stationhouse was illegal because the police lacked probable cause—the stationhouse statement in *Harris* was not the product of an ongoing illegality. According to the majority, only statements made in the home are fruit of the illegality against which *Payton* was meant to protect.

As Justice Marshall, joined by Justices Brennan, Blackmun and Stevens, pointed out in dissent, this latter fact should be irrelevant to attenuation analysis. First, as contemplated by the attenuation cases, there was a clear connection between the *Payton* violation and out-of-home statements. The suspect who has been arrested in and removed from his home and family "is likely to be so frightened and rattled that he will say something incriminating. These effects, of course, extend far beyond the moment the physical occupation of the home ends." Second, Marshall argued, the majority's rule would encourage flagrant violations of *Payton* by officers who have probable cause to arrest but who want more information from the defendant and hope that a sudden warrantless home arrest will allow them to obtain it.

A similar type of attenuation analysis came into play in *Hudson v. Michigan*,[102] where the Court held that exclusion is not the appropriate remedy for a knock-and-announce violation. In *Hudson*, the government conceded that officers who searched Hudson's house and found drugs and weapons there violated the Fourth Amendment rule that police must knock and announce their presence unless they have reasonable suspicion to believe that evidence will be destroyed or a suspect will escape or harm others.[103] Nonetheless, the Supreme Court held that attenuation can occur not only when the causal connection is remote, but also when "the interest protected by the constitutional guarantee that has been violated would not be served by suppression of the evidence obtained." Thus, Justice Scalia wrote for five members of the Court, even if violation of the knock-and-announce rule could be said to be a proximate "cause" of the eventual seizure of evidence, exclusion is not the appropriate remedy because the knock-and-announce rule "has never protected . . . one's interest in preventing the government from seeing or taking evidence described in a warrant," which the Court asserted is the purpose of exclusion. Rather the knock-and-announce rule only protects against the violence that might be provoked by unannounced entry, the destruction of property that can be avoided if the occupants open the door, and the "privacy and dignity . . . destroyed by a sudden entrance" (for instance, entry when the occupant is in nightclothes).

A second reason the Court gave for its decision was based on *Calandra* cost-benefit analysis. The costs of exclusion in connection with knock-and-announce cases include the difficulty of resolving whether the rule applies and the danger posed to police and evidence when police knock unnecessarily. At the same time, Scalia asserted, "deterrence of knock-and-announce violations is not worth a lot" because the reasonable

---

[102] 547 U.S. 586, 126 S.Ct. 2159 (2006).

[103] For a discussion of the knock-and-announce rule, see § 5.05(c).

suspicion standard associated with the rule is so easily met police rarely have an incentive to commit them. Further, Scalia stated, damages actions and police professionalism sufficiently inhibit violations.

The dissent, written by Justice Breyer, contested the Court's cost-benefit analysis by noting that the Fourth Amendment has always exacted costs on law enforcement and asserting that the deterrent effect of damages actions is negligible; in fact he found no case in which more than nominal damages were awarded in a knock-and-announce case (although Scalia pointed out that many cases might have settled for larger amounts). Breyer also disputed Scalia's assertion that the knock-and-announce rule protects only against violence, property damage and surprise; the rule, he stated, is part of the "special protection for the privacy of the home." Finally, he argued that the purpose of the rule should not matter in any event; in no previous case, including *Harris*, had the Court permitted exclusion of evidence obtained as a direct result of an illegal entry.[104] The majority's "interest-based approach," Breyer suggested "could well complicate Fourth Amendment suppression law, threatening its workability."

Justice Kennedy was the necessary fifth vote for the majority. He appeared to be most persuaded not by the plurality's interest-based approach, but rather by the extent of attenuation in the traditional sense—that is, the lack of a close causal connection between the knock-and-announce violation and the later search. As he put it, "[w]hen . . . a violation results from want of a 20-second pause but an ensuing, lawful search lasting five hours discloses evidence of criminality, the failure to wait at the door cannot properly be described as having caused the discovery of evidence." His one caveat was that a pattern of such violations, especially if committed "against persons who lacked the means or voice to mount an effective protest," would be cause for "grave concern."

Hudson, like other cases decided by the post-Warren Court, sent strong signals that the court is willing to reconsider *Mapp*. At one point, for instance, the plurality opinion states "[w]e cannot assume that exclusion in this context is necessary deterrence simply because we found that it was necessary deterrence in different contexts and long ago," and went on to note the advent of damages actions and enhanced professionalism since *Mapp* was decided. The Court's expanded definition of attenuation, if followed, also suggests that violation of various other execution rules (entry during the daytime, avoidance of unreasonable force[105]) may not warrant exclusion either.

(c) The Independent Source Doctrine

Both *Silverthorne* and *Nardone* recognized that when the government can establish that evidence was obtained from a source independent of the illegal action, exclusion should not result. In such cases, there is no taint to attenuate. Thus, for instance, in *Segura v. United States*,[106] the Court held that evidence found in an apartment pursuant to a valid search warrant is admissible even if the police illegally entered the apartment prior to obtaining the warrant, so long as the warrant is based on information that is wholly unconnected with the initial entry and was known to the police before the entry. The illegal entry in *Segura* took place after Segura was arrested in the lobby of his

---

[104] Besides *Harris*, Scalia sought support in *Segura v. United States*, 468 U.S. 796, 104 S.Ct. 3380 (1984), discussed in the next section, and dictum in *United States v. Ramirez*, 523 U.S. 65, 118 S.Ct. 992 (1998), as precedent, but Breyer distinguished all three cases, and only four justices signed on to this part of his opinion.

[105] See generally § 5.05(c).

[106] 468 U.S. 796, 104 S.Ct. 3380 (1984).

apartment building. Upon taking him back into his apartment, the police found defendant Colon, arrested him as well, and took both into custody. Agents then secured the apartment for nineteen hours pending arrival of a warrant based on information developed before their entry.

The Court, in an opinion by Chief Justice Burger, assumed that the entry after Segura's arrest was illegal. But it emphasized the independent basis of the warrant, and thus concluded that evidence discovered pursuant to its execution was admissible. The defendant's argument that, "but for" the initial entry, Colon could have destroyed the evidence and thus prevented its discovery was dismissed by Burger as "pure speculation." "Even more important," stated Burger, "we decline to extend the exclusionary rule . . . to further 'protect' criminal activity." To the contention of the four dissenters that its holding would encourage illegal entries to "secure" the premises pending a warrant, the majority stated "[w]e are unwilling to believe that officers will routinely and purposely violate the law as a matter of course."

Segura left intact a disincentive to enter illegally because, under that decision, the police knew that anything they discovered during the illegal entry would be inadmissible, including items which they could have legally seized pursuant to a warrant. That is no longer the case, however, since *Murray v. United States*,[107] in which the Court held that evidence discovered during the initial illegal entry *is* admissible if it is also discovered during a later search pursuant to a warrant that is based on information obtained wholly independently of the initial entry. In *Murray*, the police suspected that the defendants were storing marijuana in a warehouse, but instead of seeking a warrant before searching the building, they went in without one, apparently believing that evidence would be destroyed or co-participants would escape if they did not do so. The search revealed numerous bales of marijuana, but no people. At this point the police successfully applied for a search warrant, based on an affidavit which did not mention the discovered bales nor the prior entry. On the basis of the warrant, they "rediscovered" the marijuana. The Supreme Court assumed without deciding that the initial entry was unlawful because, contrary to what the police allegedly thought, exigent circumstances had not existed. It went on to hold, however, that if the police could show they had probable cause sufficient for a warrant even had they not entered the warehouse, then the bales would be admissible because the second discovery would be based on an independent, untainted source.[108]

Unlike *Segura*, *Murray* encourages the police to enter illegally; once they think they have probable cause, they have nothing to lose if they enter without a warrant.[109] Justice Scalia, in his opinion for the Court, asserted that when the police who enter illegally subsequently attempt to get a warrant, they must meet the "onerous burden of convincing a trial court that no information gained from the illegal entry affected the law enforcement officers' decision to seek a warrant or the magistrate's decision to grant it." But, as Justice Marshall pointed out in dissent, police who are willing to manipulate the facts can easily meet this second burden. Moreover, regardless of the perjury problem, *Murray* is questionable because it clearly encourages warrantless searches of houses when the police believe they have probable cause. The decision to intrude should

---

[107]   487 U.S. 533, 108 S.Ct. 2529 (1988).

[108]   The case was remanded for a determination by the district court on this issue.

[109]   See William J. Stuntz, *Warrants and Fourth Amendment Remedies*, 77 Va.L.Rev. 881, 933–34 (1991).

not be left up to the police unless emergency circumstances dictate it.[110] Thus, the government should not be able to rely upon an "independent source" analysis to immunize from exclusion evidence found during an illegal entry.

An analogous practice engaged in by many lower courts—approving warrants based in part on tainted evidence so long as the untainted evidence supports a probable cause determination—is also suspect.[111] This approach encourages police to supplement borderline warrant applications with illegally obtained information. At the least, as some courts have held, this use of the independent source doctrine could be limited to those situations in which the tainted evidence constitutes an insignificant proportion of the basis for the warrant.[112]

(d) The Inevitable Discovery Exception

The inevitable discovery doctrine is closely related to the independent source idea (indeed some courts call it the "hypothetical independent source" rule). As described by most courts, if it can be proven that the derivative information *would have been* discovered by the police regardless of their unconstitutional acts, the evidence will be admissible. Since many courts have required a fairly high degree of proof in this regard, this exception is known as the "inevitable discovery" limitation. By the time the Supreme Court finally endorsed the inevitable discovery doctrine in *Nix v. Williams*,[113] every federal circuit had already adopted it.[114]

The illegality in *Williams* involved the Sixth Amendment right to counsel rather than the Fourth Amendment. The fruit in this case—the body of a young girl allegedly killed by the defendant—was found as a result of questioning the defendant about the body's location in the absence of counsel and in violation of an express promise not to do so.[115] However, the state was also able to show that, at the time the body was found, a volunteer search party organized by the police was two-and-one-half miles away from the culvert in which the body lay and would have searched the area within the next several hours. The Iowa Supreme Court affirmed use of the illegally obtained evidence because "(1) the police did not act in bad faith for the purpose of hastening discovery of the evidence in question, and (2) . . . the evidence in question would have been discovered by lawful means."[116]

In subsequent habeas proceedings, the Eighth Circuit accepted the Iowa court's two-prong test, which represented the typical formulation of the inevitable discovery doctrine at the time, but decided that the state produced insufficient evidence of good faith. The Supreme Court, in a 7–2 decision by Chief Justice Burger, reversed the Eighth Circuit and upheld the result of the Iowa court, on the ground that the motivation of the offending officer is irrelevant to inevitable discovery analysis. Burger reached this conclusion by analogizing to the independent source test.[117] As with the operation of that test, admitting evidence that would have been found in any event "ensures that the

---

[110] See generally, discussion of the warrant requirement in § 4.05(a).

[111] See, e.g., *James v. United States*, 418 F.2d 1150 (D.C.Cir. 1969).

[112] See, e.g., *United States v. Langley*, 466 F.2d 27 (6th Cir. 1972).

[113] 467 U.S. 431, 104 S.Ct. 2501 (1984).

[114] See cases cited at 467 U.S. 431 n. 2, 104 S.Ct. 2501 n. 2.

[115] See *Brewer v. Williams*, 430 U.S. 387, 97 S.Ct. 1232 (1977), discussed in § 16.04.

[116] *Iowa v. Williams*, 285 N.W.2d 248 (Iowa 1979).

[117] See § 2.04(c).

prosecution is not put in a worse position simply because of some earlier police error or misconduct." Requiring a good faith showing would violate this notion by placing "courts in the position of withholding from juries relevant and undoubted truth that would have been available to police absent any lawful activity."

It is true that, when discovery of the evidence was clearly inevitable, a good faith prerequisite would put police in a worse position than if there had been no police misconduct. But if deterrence is the basis of the exclusionary rule, this conclusion should not govern its scope. If it did, police would have no disincentive to engage in illegality when they believe that they already have a legal source for the evidence or that one will develop shortly. The result could be that, in cases like *Murray* (discussed in connection with the independent source doctrine), they will be able to justify an illegal warrantless search on the theory that they would have eventually obtained the evidence through a lawful warrant-based search. As one court put it, this type of inevitable discovery argument "would tend in actual practice to emasculate the search warrant requirement of the Fourth Amendment."[118] In response to this type of argument, Burger unrealistically asserted that police officers will "rarely, if ever, be in a position to calculate whether the evidence sought would inevitably be discovered," and that, even if they were, they "will try to avoid engaging in any questionable practice."

The Court's position in *Williams* might be more tenable if it had required the state to show that the discovery of the evidence through legal means was truly inevitable had the illegality not intervened. But the *Williams* Court held that proof of inevitability may be by a preponderance of the evidence, over the objection of the dissenters, Brennan and Marshall, who argued for a clear and convincing standard of proof. The elasticity of the majority's standard creates significant potential for speculative conclusions about what the police might have been able to accomplish, at the least increasing the possibility of hindsight justification and at worst encouraging police to take illegal shortcuts in the belief that legal investigatory methods can be imagined by the time of the suppression hearing. To avoid these problems, the inevitable discovery doctrine could be limited to those situations in which the government can show, as it did in *Williams*, that (1) a legal investigation (2) conducted by officers other than those who committed the illegality (3) was ongoing at the time of the illegality.[119]

2.05   Should the Rule Be Abolished?: Other Remedies for Constitutional Violations

Despite the Supreme Court's inroads, the exclusionary rule still operates to exclude most illegally obtained evidence from the guilt adjudication stage. Many critics have

---

[118] *United States v. Griffin*, 502 F.2d 959 (6th Cir. 1974). But see, *United States v. Hidalgo*, 747 F.Supp. 818 (D.Mass. 1990), where the Court refused to suppress evidence procured in violation of the warrant and knock-and-announce requirements because evidence would inevitably have been found pursuant to a valid search warrant which was being obtained at the time of the entry.

[119] See, e.g., *United States v. Rullo*, 748 F.Supp. 36 (D.Mass. 1990) (inevitable discovery doctrine does not permit admission of gun discovered by police as a result of involuntary statements made by defendant after his arrest, since the officers who directed the "inevitable" search for the gun were the same officers who were involved in beating the defendant and hearing him disclose location of weapon). But see, *United States v. Rodriguez*, 750 F.Supp. 1272 (W.D.N.C. 1990) (crack cocaine illegally found in defendant's pocket admissible because officer would inevitably have searched her person after discovering handgun in car and drugs in purse).

argued that this last vestige of *Mapp* should be eradicated as well.[120] The two principal arguments in favor of eliminating the rule entirely are that it does not deter police misconduct and that it allows a significant number of guilty persons to go free. Scholars have attempted to collect evidence on both these points, with mixed results.

Research on the deterrent effect of the rule is inconclusive. Professor Davies, after reviewing the methodological difficulties associated with testing the deterrence hypothesis, concluded:

> "When all factors are considered, there is virtually no likelihood that the Court is going to receive any 'relevant statistics' which objectively measure the 'practical efficacy' of the exclusionary rule. . . . Whichever side is required to prove the effect of the rule loses."[121]

In light of this empirical failure, commonsense must guide one's conclusions with respect to the deterrent effect of the rule. It is often pointed out that individual police officers are not directly affected by the exclusion of evidence they obtained illegally, because the exclusion takes place long after the search which produced the evidence.[122] Yet lessons are undoubtedly learned every time an officer testifies at a suppression hearing. More importantly, the exclusion of evidence does have a *systemic* effect. There is clear evidence that, since *Mapp*, prosecutors and police chiefs, fearful of losing cases on technicalities, have initiated programs designed to teach the individual officer relevant Fourth Amendment law.[123] Training classes and detailed search and seizure manuals are the surest legacy of the exclusionary rule. Given this fact, the rule presumably has had a positive impact on police behavior.[124]

As to the exclusionary rule's "costs," the word so often used by the Supreme Court in describing the convictions lost due to application of the rule, the available evidence suggests that only a small percentage of cases in which charges are brought are actually dismissed on Fourth Amendment grounds. For instance, Professor Nardulli examined the court records of 7,500 felony cases closed in 1979–80, and found that only 40 (or roughly one-half of one percent) ended in nonconvictions following a defendant's motion to suppress evidence seized illegally by police.[125] Similar figures are reported in most other studies.[126] Inserting this information into the equation favored by the current

---

[120] See Malcom Wilkey, *Why Suppress Valid Evidence*, 62 Judicature 214 (1978); Richard A. Posner, *Excessive Sanctions for Governmental Misconduct in Criminal Cases*, 57 Wash.L.Rev. 635 (1982).

[121] Thomas Y. Davies, *On the Limitations of Empirical Evaluations of the Exclusionary Rule: A Critique of the Spiotto Research and* United States v. Calandra, 69 Nw.L.Rev. 740, 763–64 (1974).

[122] See Wilkey, supra note 120, at 226–27; Chief Justice Burger's dissent in *Bivens v. Six Unknown Named Agents of Federal Bureau of Narcotics*, 403 U.S. 388, 416, 91 S.Ct. 1999, 2015 (1971).

[123] Bradley C. Canon, *Is the Exclusionary Rule in Failing Health: Some New Data and a Plea Against a Precipitous Conclusion*, 62 Ky.L.J. 681, 715 (1971); Yale Kamisar, *Does (Did) (Should) the Exclusionary Rule Rest on a 'Principled Basis' Rather Than an 'Empirical Proposition'?*, 16 Creighton 565, 590–1 (1983).

[124] Unfortunately, however, training does not appear to make a *significant* impression on the police. See L. Timothy Perrin et al., *If It's Broke, Fix It: Moving Beyond the Exclusionary Rule*, 83 Iowa L. Rev. 669, 727 (1999) (study finding a "widespread inability" of police to apply the law of search and seizure or interrogation); William C. Heffernan & Richard W. Lovely, *Evaluating the Fourth Amendment Exclusionary Rule: The Problem of Police Compliance with the Law*, 24 U. Mich. J. L. Ref. 311, 333 (1991) (officers tested on Fourth Amendment law did barely better than chance).

[125] Peter Nardulli, *The Societal Cost of the Exclusionary Rule: An Empirical Assessment*, 1983 Amer.Bar Found.J. 585 (1983).

[126] Less than .7% of 2,804 defendants handled during a two-month period in 1978 by U.S. Attorneys' offices won suppression motions and eluded conviction. Impact of the Exclusionary Rule on Federal Criminal Prosecutions (Report of the Comptroller General, April 19, 1979). Less than .8% of all felony complaints in

Court, the continued viability of the exclusionary rule is dependent upon how one balances the societal interest in increasing the proportion of those convicted by a figure somewhat under one percent against the value to society of ensuring that the police are informed of the privacy interests protected by the Fourth Amendment.

Of course, it can be argued that even if one values assuring Fourth Amendment protection over convicting a small group of defendants, the exclusionary rule is not the only or the best method of guaranteeing this protection. There are various other remedies for unconstitutional police conduct: civil suits seeking monetary and injunctive relief, criminal actions, and even non-judicial remedial measures. These alternatives will now be examined, with particular attention paid to each remedy's effectiveness as an alternative to the exclusionary rule.

(a) Damages

The elements of a damage action for a violation of the Constitution depend upon whether the civil defendant represents federal or state law enforcement and whether the defendant is an individual officer or a governmental entity. On the whole, the differences between state and federal causes of action are minimal, but there are enough variations to warrant separate treatment. The differences between suits aimed at individuals and those aimed at governments are significant, particularly in terms of defenses.

(1) Federal Officers: Bivens Actions

Until 1971, it was not clear that federal officers could be sued for failing to abide by the strictures of the Fourth Amendment. However, in *Bivens v. Six Unknown Named Agents*,[127] the Court created an implied private cause of action under the Fourth Amendment and permitted suit against federal officers who, without a warrant, had manacled, searched and arrested the plaintiff and ransacked his apartment. There are two essential elements in a *Bivens* action. First, the government official must have been acting "under color of authority." This is generally given a broad interpretation—an act is said to be within the scope of an official's authority if such act is "within the outer perimeter of [his] line of duty."[128] Second, the official must have deprived the individual of his constitutional rights under the Fourth Amendment or some other constitutional provision.[129]

After proving these two elements, a plaintiff has sustained his burden of persuasion. However, government officials may still have an immunity defense. Some government officials may be able to claim absolute immunity, while virtually all other officials, including the police, are entitled to qualified immunity, colloquially known as a "good

---

California during 1976–79 were rejected primarily for search and seizure problems. National Institute of Justice, The Effects of the Exclusionary Rule: A Study in California (1982). See also, Thomas Y. Davies, *A Hard Look at What We Know (and Still Need to Learn) About the 'Costs' of the Exclusionary Rule: The NIJ Study and Other Studies of 'Lost' Arrests*, 1983 Amer.Bar Found.J. 611 (1983).

[127] 403 U.S. 388, 91 S.Ct. 1999 (1971).

[128] *Barr v. Matteo*, 360 U.S. 564, 575, 79 S.Ct. 1335, 1341 (1959). However, private sector employees working for the government may not be sued under *Bivens*. See *Minneci v. Pollard*, 565 U.S. 118, 132 S.Ct. 617 (2012) (immunizing private prison employees).

[129] Since *Bivens*, other constitutional torts have been recognized. See, e.g., *Davis v. Passman*, 442 U.S. 228, 99 S.Ct. 2264 (1979) (Fifth Amendment remedy available for federal sex discrimination); *Carlson v. Green*, 446 U.S. 14, 100 S.Ct. 1468 (1980) (claim of incompetent care of federal prisoner recognized under Eighth Amendment); *Sonntag v. Dooley*, 650 F.2d 904 (7th Cir. 1981) (Bivens remedy under Fifth Amendment for coerced resignation from civil service position).

faith defense." In *Butz v. Economou*,[130] the Court identified several factors that should be considered in deciding whether a particular official should be afforded only qualified rather than absolute immunity: (1) the need to assure that the individual can perform his functions without harassment or intimidation; (2) the presence of safeguards that reduce the need for private damages actions as a means of controlling unconstitutional conduct; (3) insulation from political influence; (4) the importance of precedent set by the individual; (5) the adversary nature of the process used by the individual in making decisions; and (6) the correctability of error on appeal. In light of these factors, the Court has concluded that "qualified immunity represents the norm."[131] Thus, while federal judges[132] and prosecutors,[133] and officials who perform similar functions, enjoy absolute immunity, federal agency heads[134] presidential aides[135] and, most importantly for present purposes, the police,[136] have been extended only qualified immunity.

Even qualified immunity provides significant protection, however. According to the Court's decision in *Harlow v. Fitzgerald*,[137] an official protected by qualified immunity may not be held personally liable for an official action if the action meets the test of "objective legal reasonableness" in light of legal rules that were "clearly established" at the time the act occurred. If there is no clearly established rule governing the official's act, or if there is such a rule but the act, while in violation of the rule, was based on a reasonable interpretation of it, then no liability attaches. This formulation, stated the Court, should "permit the resolution of many insubstantial claims on summary judgment."[138]

In *Anderson v. Creighton*[139] the Court affirmed that *Harlow's* test applies to searches by police officers as well as actions by other government agents. In dissent, Justice Stevens argued that police should be more vulnerable to suit given the degree of discretion already afforded them by the "reasonableness" standard provided in the Fourth Amendment; he also noted the relatively minor interference litigation causes police who, unlike many other government officials, already spend considerable time testifying in court. But the majority refused to create different types of qualified immunity. Thus, the Court held, if the police activity as alleged by the plaintiff are actions that a reasonable police officer could have believed lawful, the suit may be dismissed on a motion for summary judgment prior to discovery. It also emphasized that the subjective beliefs of the officer are "irrelevant" to the immunity issue, thus making

---

[130]   438 U.S. 478, 98 S.Ct. 2894 (1978).

[131]   *Harlow v. Fitzgerald*, 457 U.S. 800, 102 S.Ct. 2727 (1982).

[132]   *Bradley v. Fisher*, 80 U.S. 335, 13 Wall. 335, 20 L.Ed. 646 (1871).

[133]   *Yaselli v. Goff*, 275 U.S. 503, 48 S.Ct. 155 (1927), affirming 12 F.2d 396 (2d Cir. 1926). But see infra notes 159–161, discussing prosecutorial liability under § 1983.

[134]   *Butz v. Economou*, 438 U.S. 478, 98 S.Ct. 2894 (1978).

[135]   *Harlow v. Fitzgerald*, 457 U.S. 800, 102 S.Ct. 2727 (1982).

[136]   *Bivens v. Six Unknown Named Agents of Federal Bureau of Narcotics*, 456 F.2d 1339 (2d Cir. 1972).

[137]   457 U.S. 800, 102 S.Ct. 2727 (1982).

[138]   The Court has also held, however, that this reasoning in *Harlow* does not necessarily justify placing other burdens on constitutional tort plaintiffs. For instance, in *Crawford-El v. Britton*, 523 U.S. 574, 118 S.Ct. 1584 (1998), it reversed a lower court ruling requiring plaintiffs to prove unconstitutional retaliatory motives by clear and convincing evidence, explaining that "[s]ocial costs that adequately justify the elimination of the subjective component of an affirmative defense do not necessarily justify serious limitations upon 'the only realistic' remedy for the violation of constitutional guarantees."

[139]   483 U.S. 635, 107 S.Ct. 3034 (1987).

clear that a police officer can escape liability for actions he knows are in violation of the Fourth Amendment so long as they were "objectively" legally reasonable.[140]

In *Saucier v. Katz*,[141] the Court held that a civil action may not be dismissed on immunity grounds without determining whether the facts as alleged by the plaintiff make out a constitutional violation, a rule primarily designed to promote the development of constitutional precedent. In *Pearson v. Callahan*,[142] however, a unanimous Court reversed *Saucier*, in an opinion by Justice Alito. Although admitting that moving directly to the issue of whether a rule is clearly established could mean that the relevant constitutional doctrine remains ambiguous, the Court noted that resolution of the doctrinal question in immunity cases, as required by *Saucier*, can expend significant judicial resources despite having no effect on the outcome of the case (if, for instance, the court can immediately determine that no established rule exists), may not have the precedential impact nor the benefit from adversarial briefing associated with a decision that is focused *solely* on establishing doctrine, and may not be appealable by the defendant if the defendant wins on the immunity issue.

The Court also noted, however, that lower courts are still free to decide the constitutional issue first if, in their view, these types of inefficiencies are minimal. In a subsequent decision, the Court held that it has the authority to grant certiorari in cases where the lower courts take this step and find in favor of the petitioner on the constitutional claim, but then grant the government official qualified immunity.[143] The Court explained that, to ensure that officials in this legal posture are able to contest the underlying constitutional issue at the Supreme Court level, it need not follow its usual practice of declining to hear appeals by prevailing parties.

(2) Federal Government: FTCA

Bivens explicitly left to Congress whether the federal government could be held liable for the "constitutional" torts of its officers, because "the federal purse was involved." At the time of *Bivens*, the Federal Tort Claims Act provided that a prima facie case against the government existed if the plaintiff could prove:

(1) damage to or loss of property, or death or bodily injury, which was

(2) caused by a negligent or wrongful act

(3) committed by a federal employee acting within the scope of employment

(4) in a state where the act committed would lead to legal liability for a private person.[144]

Although these elements would seem to encompass suits claiming police misconduct, the Act specifically barred recovery for a number of intentional torts that might normally form the basis for such suits, including false arrest, false imprisonment, abuse of process, assault, battery, and malicious prosecution. The Act also extended immunity to acts

---

[140] Compare this result to that reached under the good faith exception to the exclusionary rule, discussed in § 2.03(c).

[141] 533 U.S. 194, 121 S.Ct. 2151 (2001).

[142] 555 U.S. 223, 129 S.Ct. 808 (2009). *Callahan* was a § 1983 cases, see § 2.05(a)(3) & (4), but its ruling applies in this context as well.

[143] *Camreta v. Greene*, 563 U.S. 692, 131 S.Ct. 2020 (2011).

[144] 28 U.S.C.A. § 1346(b); see also, 28 U.S.C.A. §§ 1291, 1346(c), 1402(b), 1504, 2110, 2401(b), 2402, 2411(b), 2412(c), 2671–2680.

committed by a government employee in the exercise of his discretion, "whether or not the discretion involved be abused."

After *Bivens*, however, the Act was amended to make it applicable "to acts or omissions of investigative or law enforcement officers of the United States Government" on any claim arising out of such torts.[145] The term "law enforcement officers" was defined to include any officer "who is empowered by law to execute searches, to seize evidence, or to make arrests for violations of Federal law." The intent of the provision, according to the Senate report, is "to deprive the federal Government of the defense of sovereign immunity in cases . . . [involving] the same kind of conduct that is alleged to have occurred in *Bivens* and for which that case imposes liability upon the individual Government officials involved."[146] It is not clear whether this language means that the good faith defense recognized in *Bivens* is available to the government under the FTCA as well.[147]

Given the government's financial resources, an FTCA action is now clearly superior to a *Bivens* suit against the individual officer or officers, even if good faith is a defense in the former cause of action. The Supreme Court has held that the amendments to the FTCA were not meant to render *Bivens* obsolete, however; both causes of action may be brought simultaneously.[148] Thus the plaintiff whose constitutional rights have been violated by a federal police officer in bad faith can be assured of monetary compensation (under the FTCA) at the same time he can exact direct "revenge" against the official to the extent the official can afford it (under *Bivens*).

Some plaintiffs have tried to bring *Bivens* suits against the *government*, perhaps believing such actions to be more attractive than an FTCA claim that depends on state law rather than the Constitution and that might be barred by a good faith defense. But the Court has refused to recognize such suits. Reasoning that the purpose of a *Bivens* claim is to deter individual officers, and that allowing such suits against a governmental entity might even undermine that deterrent effect (given the likelihood that the agency would then almost always be the primary target), it held in *FDIC v. Meyer*[149] that *Bivens* actions may not be brought against federal agencies. In *Correctional Services Corporation v. Malesko*,[150] the Court extended that ruling to suits against private corporations performing federal functions (in this case, running a prison). Although the four-member dissent noted that *state* prisoners can sue such corporations under § 1983,[151] and that *Bivens* suits might be a particularly important mechanism for assuring accountability of private money-making enterprises, the Court repeated its statement in *Meyer* that *Bivens* suits are meant to deter individual federal officers, and

---

[145] 28 U.S.C.A. § 2680(h).

[146] Sen.Rep. No. 93–588, 93d Cong., 2d Sess., 1974 U.S.Code Cong. and Ad.News 2789, 2791 (1974).

[147] See *Norton v. United States*, 581 F.2d 390 (4th Cir. 1978), cert. denied 439 U.S. 1003, 99 S.Ct. 613 (1978) (defense available); *Bickley v. U.S. Dept. of Treasury*, 2000 WL 637345 (W.D.Va. 2007). But see *Owen v. City of Independence*, 445 U.S. 622, 100 S.Ct. 1398 (1980), which held that municipalities do not have a good faith defense in § 1983 actions.

[148] *Carlson v. Green*, 446 U.S. 14, 100 S.Ct. 1468 (1980). Furthermore, a *Bivens* suit against individual government officials may be maintained even if the FTCA suit is dismissed on the ground that the acts were "discretionary." *Simmons v. Himmelreich*, ___ U.S. ___, 136 S.Ct. 1843 (2016).

[149] 510 U.S. 471, 114 S.Ct. 996 (1994).

[150] 534 U.S. 61, 122 S.Ct. 515 (2001).

[151] See § 2.05(a)(4).

also noted the usual availability of alternative remedies under state tort law and the FTCA.

Another limitation on FTCA actions, found in the statute itself, is that sovereign immunity is not waived on claims "arising in a foreign country." In *Sosa v. Alvarez-Machain*,[152] a unanimous Supreme Court interpreted this language to bar claims against the United States that are based on injury suffered in another nation, even if other aspects of the tortious act or omission occurred in this country. Thus, even though the planning of the allegedly tortious kidnaping of the plaintiff occurred in California,[153] the fact that the kidnaping itself took place in Mexico barred an FTCA suit. The Court also held that the plaintiff's claim was barred under the Alien Tort Act (ATS), passed by the First Congress in 1789. The Court based this latter conclusion primarily on a reading of the Act's original intent (which was to permit claims such as those involving ambassadors, violations of safe conduct and piracy) and the finding that "binding customary international law" does not clearly recognize a claim for arbitrary arrest. A majority of the Court also stated, however, that "the door is still ajar" under the ATS for tort claims based on more definite and accepted "customary law," and mentioned "prolonged arbitrary detention" as one possible such claim.

(3) State Officers: § 1983

At one time, suits against state officers (or state governmental entities) were rare because of official (and governmental) immunity. Today most states have waived immunity either partially or wholly, thus making suits based on state tort law feasible. Even so, when the suit is against a municipality or county, or one of its officers (as opposed to a state-run institution or its employees), the most popular cause of action for damages arising out of non-federal conduct is provided by 42 U.S.C.A. § 1983, because it permits suit in federal court and significantly abrogates immunity protection for municipalities and similar governmental units regardless of state law on the subject, if filed in a timely fashion.[154]

Section 1983 provides that any "person" who "under color of" state law deprives another of "any rights, privileges, or immunities secured by the Constitution and laws shall be liable in an action at law, suit in equity, or other proper proceeding for redress." This provision, enacted as part of the Ku Klux Klan Act of 1871, was disinterred as a possible cause of action for police misconduct in *Monroe v. Pape*,[155] decided the same year as *Mapp*, and like that case, involving an illegal search and arrest.

The elements of a cause of action under § 1983, as laid out by the Supreme Court in *Pape* and summarized in *Parratt v. Taylor*,[156] are similar to those required for a *Bivens* suit. First, the conduct complained of must be committed by a person acting "under color of state law." Generally, as under *Bivens*, this term is construed broadly so as to include

---

[152] 542 U.S. 692, 124 S.Ct. 2739 (2004).

[153] In an earlier posture of the case, the Supreme had rejected the argument that the plaintiff's prosecution was unconstitutional because of the manner in which he was brought to the United States. See *United States v. Alvarez-Machain*, 504 U.S. 655, 112 S.Ct. 2188 (1992), discussed in § 3.01.

[154] *McDonough v. Smith*, ___ U.S. ___, 139 S.Ct. 2149 (2019) (holding that the three-year statute of limitations under § 1983 usually begins when the alleged violation occurred, but for a suit against a prosecutor for using fabricated evidence, akin to a malicious prosecution action, it begins at the time prosecution terminates in favor of the defendant).

[155] 365 U.S. 167, 81 S.Ct. 473 (1961).

[156] 451 U.S. 527, 101 S.Ct. 1908 (1981).

any actions of a law enforcement officer committed within the scope of his employment. Second, the conduct must have deprived the complainant of rights, privileges, or immunities secured by the Constitution or the laws of the United States.

Parratt suggested that the deprivation required for a § 1983 violation need not be intentional: "[S]imply because a wrong was negligently as opposed to intentionally committed [does] not foreclose the possibility that such action could be brought under § 1983." However, in *Daniels v. Williams*,[157] the Court explicitly overruled *Parratt* to the extent it held that negligent actions by state officials can lead to recovery under § 1983. The *Daniels* Court pointed out that no previous Court decision had permitted recovery under § 1983 for negligent conduct. It found this fact to be with good reason:

> [L]ack of due care suggests no more than a failure to measure up to the conduct of a reasonable man. To hold that injury caused by such conduct is a deprivation within the meaning of the Fourteenth Amendment would trivialize the centuries-old principle of due process of law.

Moreover, as with a *Bivens* suit, state and local police sued under § 1983 are entitled to qualified immunity protecting them from liability for actions that are reasonable in light of clearly established legal standards.[158] The Court has been particularly active in applying this limitation on liability in cases involving claims of excessive force by the police. Because every use of force case can differ factually, the Court has been prone to grant immunity on the ground that the officer's actions, even if extremely forceful, were not clearly unconstitutional.[159] Unfortunately, in many of these cases, the immunity finding begins and ends the Court's analysis, leaving unclear the Court's view on whether use of force under identical circumstances in the future would be unconstitutional.[160]

The Court has also held that, if the police action meets Fourth Amendment requirements, it will usually not run afoul of First Amendment requirements. In *Nieves v. Bartlett*,[161] the plaintiff argued he had been arrested in retaliation for his speech. Eight members of the Court concluded that if the plaintiff could produce "objective evidence" that he was "arrested when otherwise similarly situated individuals not engaged in the same sort of protected speech had not been," a First Amendment claim would lie. But otherwise, the Court held, such a claim should be rejected when the arrest is based on probable cause.

The Court has not always found immunity exists, however. Of particular relevance here is *Malley v. Briggs*,[162] which held that a warrant authorizing an officer's actions does *not* automatically make them reasonable. There, an officer being sued for wrongfully searching the plaintiff's home claimed that because he believed in good faith

---

[157] 474 U.S. 327, 106 S.Ct. 662 (1986).

[158] The qualified immunity defense in § 1983 actions was first recognized in *Pierson v. Ray*, 386 U.S. 547, 87 S.Ct. 1213 (1967). The holdings in both *Anderson v. Creighton* and *Pearson v. Callahan*, discussed in § 2.05(a)(1), are applicable here as well. But summary judgment on the issue should only be granted after considering the evidence in a light most favorable to the suspect. *Tolan v. Cotton*, 572 U.S. 650, 134 S.Ct. 1861 (2014).

[159] See, e.g., *City of Escondido v. Emmons*, ___ U.S. ___, 139 S.Ct. 500 (2019); *Kisela v. Hughes*, ___ U.S. ___, 138 S.Ct. 1148 (2018); *District of Columbia v. Wesby*, ___ U.S. ___, 138 S.Ct. 577 (2018); *City of San Francisco v. Sheehan*, 575 U.S. 600, 135 S.Ct. 1765 (2015).

[160] See § 3.03(b).

[161] ___ U.S. ___, 139 S.Ct. 1715 (2019).

[162] 475 U.S. 335, 106 S.Ct. 1092 (1986).

that information he provided a magistrate established probable cause and because the magistrate subsequently signed a warrant based on that information, he should be immune from suit under § 1983. But the Court held he would not have a defense if "a reasonably well-trained officer in petitioner's position would have known that his affidavit failed to establish probable cause and that he should not have applied for the warrant." The theoretical fact that no judge should issue a warrant when probable cause is absent did not persuade the Court that a judicially authorized warrant should immunize an officer, since "ours is not an ideal system, and it is possible that a magistrate, working under docket pressures, will fail to perform as a magistrate should." Thus, to minimize this possibility, officers should be exposed to liability for unreasonable warrant requests. The Court went on to hold that the reasonableness test in this context was the equivalent of the test established by the Court in *United States v. Leon*[163] for deciding whether a search based on a warrant is valid despite the absence of probable cause. In practice, this standard is likely to expose only the most incompetent or scurrilous officers to liability,[164] but it does mean that a warrant does not completely immunize the officer.[165]

The Court has also addressed the liability of other officials under § 1983. As at the federal level, while judges are immune from § 1983 damage suits,[166] most executive branch state and local officials—police chiefs, governors, and agency heads—can be sued individually under the statute.[167] They too have a good faith defense, however, the scope of which varies depending "upon the scope of discretion and responsibilities of the office and all the circumstances as they reasonably appeared at the time of the action on which liability is sought to be based."[168] Thus, for instance, while prosecutors are generally immune from liability under § 1983 for their discretionary actions,[169] one court has held a prosecutor liable for false statements made on the stand in response to a judicial inquiry as to whether there were any government informants among the witnesses called by the prosecutor.[170] Similarly, the Supreme Court has held that a prosecutor may be held liable under § 1983 for fabricating evidence (at least if the fabrication occurs prior

---

[163]   468 U.S. 897, 104 S.Ct. 3405 (1984), discussed in § 2.03(c)(1).

[164]   As Justice Powell noted in his concurring opinion in *Briggs*, "substantial weight should be accorded the judge's finding of probable cause in determining whether [police] will be personally liable."

[165]   For a comparison case, see *Messerschmidt v. Millender*, 565 U.S. 535, 132 S.Ct. 1235 (2012), discussed in § 2.03(c)(1).

[166]   In *Stump v. Sparkman*, 435 U.S. 349, 98 S.Ct. 1099 (1978), the Court upheld the absolute immunity of a state court judge even when he takes actions in excess of his authority, or acts maliciously or corruptly, so long as he has jurisdiction over the subject matter and the acts he takes in regard to it can be characterized as "judicial." However, when the § 1983 suit is for injunctive relief, judicial immunity is not absolute. See *Pulliam v. Allen*, 466 U.S. 522, 104 S.Ct. 1970 (1984).

[167]   *Scheuer v. Rhodes*, 416 U.S. 232, 94 S.Ct. 1683 (1974) (state governors); *Procunier v. Navarette*, 434 U.S. 555, 98 S.Ct. 855 (1978) (state prison officials); *Wood v. Strickland*, 420 U.S. 308, 95 S.Ct. 992 (1975) (school board members).

[168]   *Scheuer v. Rhodes*, 416 U.S. 232, 94 S.Ct. 1683 (1974). In *Gomez v. Toledo*, 446 U.S. 635, 100 S.Ct. 1920 (1980), the Court held that the defendant-official bears the burden of alleging and proving good faith.

[169]   *Imbler v. Pachtman*, 424 U.S. 409, 96 S.Ct. 984 (1976). Attorneys retained by a municipality to assist in investigation are also entitled to qualified immunity. *Filarsky v. Delia*, 566 U.S. 377, 132 S.Ct. 1657 (2012).

[170]   *Briggs v. Goodwin*, 569 F.2d 10 (D.C.Cir. 1977), cert. denied 437 U.S. 904, 98 S.Ct. 3089 (1978). But see *Taylor v. Kavanagh*, 640 F.2d 450 (2d Cir. 1981) (prosecutor not liable for making false statements during course of plea bargaining).

to charging),[171] for making false statements outside the courtroom,[172] and for giving unconstitutional advice to police officers.[173]

However, the entire Court held in *Van de Kamp v. Goldstein*[174] that prosecutorial failure to give the defense exculpatory impeachment evidence may not form the basis for suit because a decision about evidentiary disclosure is not an "investigative" task but rather is an action that is "intimately associated with the judicial phase of the criminal process." Nor, *Goldstein* further held, is a claim alleging supervisory failure to *train* prosecutors about when to disclose impeachment evidence actionable, because such training would also deal with "the prosecutor's basic trial advocacy duties." A further limitation on all of these suits is that a § 1983 suit seeking damages for a wrongful conviction does not lie unless and until the conviction has been overturned in state court or on federal habeas.[175]

(4) State Governmental Units: § 1983

In *Pape*, the Court held that the city of Chicago could not be held liable under § 1983 because Congress did not consider municipal corporations to be "persons" within the ambit of the section. But in *Monell v. Department of Social Services of New York*,[176] the Court overruled *Pape* insofar as it held that local governments are wholly immune from suit under § 1983. Rather, it permitted liability when the constitutional violation is sanctioned by official municipal policy or custom. This latter stipulation represented a compromise between making municipalities liable under a respondeat superior theory (which holds employers responsible for all acts of their employees within the scope of employment) and according them absolute immunity. It should be noted that suits against the federal government under the Federal Tort Claims Act need not allege or prove that official policy was being implemented at the time of the alleged official misconduct. This difference results entirely from the Court's reading of the legislative history associated with the two statutes at issue.

Monell included within its definition of "policy and custom" "custom [that] has not received formal approval through the body's official decisionmaking channels." This language suggests that unwritten, informal practice can form the basis for liability. The question then becomes how one establishes evidence of such a practice. In *Oklahoma City v. Tuttle*,[177] the Court found improper an instruction allowing the jury to infer a municipal policy of "inadequate training" from a single incident of "unusually excessive force" that resulted in serious injury. *Tuttle* seemed to suggest that an official act or failure to act not specifically authorized in writing by the appropriate body must cause more than an isolated occurrence in order to meet the policy or custom stipulation of *Monell*. Then, in *Pembaur v. Cincinnati*,[178] the Court held that an isolated incident *was* actionable under § 1983 when police, acting under instructions from the county prosecutor to "go and get" the petitioner, chopped down the petitioner's door after he had refused them entrance on the ground they had no warrant. Although no similar incident

---

[171] *Buckley v. Fitzsimmons*, 509 U.S. 259, 113 S.Ct. 2606 (1993).

[172] Id.

[173] *Burns v. Reed*, 500 U.S. 478, 111 S.Ct. 1934 (1991).

[174] 555 U.S. 335, 129 S.Ct. 855 (2009).

[175] *Heck v. Humphrey*, 512 U.S. 477, 114 S.Ct. 2364 (1994).

[176] 436 U.S. 658, 98 S.Ct. 2018 (1978).

[177] 471 U.S. 808, 105 S.Ct. 2427 (1985).

[178] 475 U.S. 469, 106 S.Ct. 1292 (1986).

by local police was proven, the Court's plurality opinion, written by Justice Brennan, distinguished *Tuttle* on the ground that the injury in the latter case was not committed "*pursuant*" to municipal policy. In *Pembaur*, on the other hand, the police acted under the orders of the prosecutor. Brennan concluded that so long as the official making the decision has authority to establish final policy on the action in question,[179] a single decision by that official, like a single legislative act by the municipality's legislative body, can form the basis for liability.

Two justices joined Justice Brennan's opinion and a fourth, Justice Stevens, concurred in the judgment on the ground that, under his interpretation of § 1983, municipalities should be liable on a *respondeat superior* theory. Two other justices, White and O'Connor, joined the result but wrote separate opinions to emphasize that, at the time the prosecutor gave his instruction, the type of act he authorized (a warrantless entrance in the absence of exigent circumstances to effect an arrest of an individual who did not own the premises) had not yet explicitly been held unconstitutional.[180] According to White and O'Connor, had a court decision or a statute made clear the action was impermissible, then a decision by the prosecutor in violation of the legal rule could not be said to be an execution of county policy. Thus, the stance of the current Court appears to be that a single unwritten decision by a municipal official who has authority to make such a decision can form the basis for municipal liability, but only if it does not run counter to established judicial or legislative rulings.

In many cases, the question is not whether an official custom or policy exists, but whether an official custom or policy can be said to have caused a deprivation of constitutional rights. In connection with suits over police conduct, the most common allegation in this vein, illustrated by *Tuttle*, is that the municipality's "policy" of failing to train its police to carry out particular types of duties has led to such a deprivation. In *City of Canton v. Harris*,[181] the Supreme Court explicitly held, 6–3, that a failure to train claim may be the basis for § 1983 liability, but only where such a claim "amounts to deliberate indifference to the rights of persons with whom the police come into contact." Moreover, held the Court, a training program is not to be found inadequate merely because "an otherwise sound program has occasionally been negligently administered" or because an injury could have been avoided had an officer received better training. Finally, "for liability to attach . . . the identified deficiency in a city's training program must be closely related to the ultimate injury." According to the Court, adopting lesser standards of fault and causation would open municipalities to "unprecedented liability" because "[i]n virtually every instance where a person has had his or her constitutional rights violated by a city employee, a § 1983 plaintiff will be able to point to something the city 'could have done' to prevent the unfortunate incident."

In a footnote, the Court provided illustrations of the rare situations where liability might be imposed under its "deliberate indifference" standard:

> For example, city policy makers know to a moral certainty that their police officers will be required to arrest fleeing felons. . . . Thus, the need to train officers in the constitutional limitations on the use of deadly force . . . can be said to be 'so obvious,' that failure to do so could properly be characterized as

---

[179] Under Ohio law, the prosecutor was specifically authorized to give instructions to police "in matters connected with their official duties." Ohio Rev. Code Ann. § 390.90 (1979).

[180] *Steagald v. United States*, 451 U.S. 204, 101 S.Ct. 1642 (1981) subsequently so held. See § 3.04(c).

[181] 489 U.S. 378, 109 S.Ct. 1197 (1989).

'deliberate indifference' to constitutional rights. It could also be that the police, in exercising their discretion, so often violate constitutional rights that the need for further training must have been plainly obvious to the city policy makers, who, nevertheless, are 'deliberately indifferent' to the need.

The standard adopted in *Harris* ensures that municipalities will not be liable under § 1983 for injuries stemming from most nonroutine violations of the constitution by their police, at least under a failure to train theory.[182]

The difficulty of prevailing on a failure-to-train theory became abundantly clear in *Connick v. Thompson*,[183] involving a claim that the prosecutor's office had failed to train its lawyers about *Brady v. Maryland's* requirement that prosecutors provide the defense with exculpatory evidence.[184] Over a two-decade period, involving several trials and hearings that resulted in Thompson's conviction for armed robbery and for a (separate) murder that preceded the robbery, prosecutors failed to hand over either a blood test that would have conclusively shown Thompson was not the perpetrator of the robbery or eyewitness testimony that strongly suggested he was not the perpetrator of the murder. Further, on the first day of the robbery trial the lead prosecutor removed the clothing swatch that contained the tested blood from the property room. That evidence was not discovered until a defense investigator came upon it a few weeks before Thompson's scheduled execution; it eventually led to reversal of both convictions. At Thompson's § 1983 trial claiming that the wrongful convictions resulted from a failure to train, testimony indicated that the head of the prosecutor's office and other supervisory officers were confused about the scope of *Brady*, that the office had one of the worst *Brady* violation records in the country, and that very little, if any, training about *Brady* occurred there. The jury upheld the failure-to-train claim, as did the lower courts, on the ground that the need for training was "obvious."

In a 5–4 opinion written by Justice Thomas, the Court reversed. While admitting that as many as four prosecutors involved in Thompson's case had not met their *Brady* obligations with respect to the blood test,[185] Justice Thomas concluded that Thompson failed to provide proof of a pattern of "similar" violations in other cases sufficient to give notice that training about *Brady* was needed, thus making "deliberate indifference" to the need for such training impossible. Justice Thomas distinguished *Canton's* police use of deadly force hypothetical, which had suggested that a pattern of violations was not necessary to win a failure-to-train claim, by contending that all prosecutors are "equipped" to interpret legal principles and ethically obligated to follow them in a way that police are not; thus, this case did not "present the same 'highly predictable' constitutional danger as *Canton's* untrained officer." Further, the prosecutors in Thompson's case clearly knew about the general *Brady* principle; the fact that *Brady* law has "gray areas" or is "difficult" to interpret does not mean that "prosecutors will so

---

[182] Similarly, the Supreme Court has stated that government hiring decisions will not be grounds for a § 1983 suit unless "adequate scrutiny of an applicant's background would lead a reasonable policymaker to conclude that the plainly obvious consequence of the decision to hire the officer would be the deprivation of a third party's federally protected right." *Board of County Commissioners of Bryan Cty., Okla. v. Brown*, 520 U.S. 397, 117 S.Ct. 1382 (1997).

[183] 563 U.S. 51, 131 S.Ct. 1350 (2011).

[184] See § 24.04 for a discussion of the *Brady* rule.

[185] In a concurring opinion, Justice Scalia, joined by Justice Alito, argued that failure to turn over the blood test was not a *Brady* violation because the government never conducted a blood test of Thompson and thus never found out that he was a different blood type than the perpetrator. See § 24.05 for a discussion of the constitutional duty to preserve evidence.

obviously make wrong decisions that failing to train them amounts to a 'decision by the city itself to violate the Constitution.' "

A Supreme Court decision which more clearly enhances the ability of the plaintiff to gain recovery from a municipality is *Owen v. City of Independence*,[186] which held that municipalities do not enjoy good faith immunity from liability. *Owen* found that the common law did not recognize immunity for municipalities and that the policies supporting good faith immunity for individuals—the injustice of subjecting an official acting in good faith to liability and the danger that the threat of such liability would inhibit the official's willingness to execute his office effectively—are "less compelling, if not wholly inapplicable, when the liability of the municipal entity is at issue." However, municipalities are not liable for punitive damages.[187]

Although municipalities may be sued under § 1983 with the limitations described above, states, and state officials acting in their official capacities,[188] may not be. In *Will v. Michigan Dept. of State Police*,[189] the Supreme Court held, 5–4, that a state is not a "person" under § 1983 and thus cannot be subject to a suit bringing such a claim. The Court pointed out that a "principal purpose" behind § 1983 was to provide a federal forum for civil rights claims, yet the Eleventh Amendment forbids suits in federal court against a *state* unless the state has waived immunity; thus, concluded the majority, "we cannot accept petitioner's argument that Congress intended nevertheless to create a cause of action against States to be brought in state courts, which are precisely the courts Congress sought to allow civil rights claimants to avoid through § 1983."[190] The Court held further that, because "a suit against a state official in his or her official capacity is not a suit against the official but rather is a suit against the official's office," filing against a state official rather than the state itself does not avoid the statutory bar. As Justice Brennan pointed out in dissent, the import of the Court's decision is to prohibit § 1983 suits against a state even if the state is willing to consent to such suits through abrogation of sovereign immunity.

(5) Summary

As the foregoing suggests, damages actions as currently structured should not be thought of as a substitute for the exclusionary rule. First, each remedy serves a purpose the other does not. A suit for damages does not as directly avoid the "tainting effect" that comes from using illegally obtained evidence in a court of law; the exclusionary rule cannot financially compensate victims for their injuries and provides no remedy at all for the innocent victim. Second, although both share the goal of deterring police misconduct, they diverge markedly in their impact on police behavior. A damages action, if successful, has the advantage of making the offending officer, rather than the prosecutor, "pay" for the violation. But because it is such a rare occurrence, it is much

---

[186] 445 U.S. 622, 100 S.Ct. 1398 (1980).

[187] *Newport v. Fact Concerts, Inc.*, 453 U.S. 247, 101 S.Ct. 2748 (1981).

[188] *McMillian v. Monroe County, Ala.*, 520 U.S. 781, 117 S.Ct. 1734 (1997), held, 5–4, that, depending upon a state's history, constitution and other laws, a sheriff can be a state official for § 1983 purposes.

[189] 491 U.S. 58, 109 S.Ct. 2304 (1989).

[190] The Eleventh Amendment literally forbids suit in federal court by the citizen of one state against another state. But the Court has held that the Amendment bars all nonconsensual suits against a state in federal court, *Edelman v. Jordan*, 415 U.S. 651, 94 S.Ct. 1347 (1974), and that *Monell* did not abrogate that immunity. *Quern v. Jordan*, 440 U.S. 332, 99 S.Ct. 1139 (1979). Of course, these decisions came well after passage of § 1983, which makes the majority's characterization of congressional intent somewhat disingenuous.

less likely than the exclusionary rule to actually shape police conduct. Under current law, a damages suit is not feasible when damages are negligible, as is the case with many Fourth Amendment (and other constitutional) violations,[191] and the victim poor, as are most persons investigated by the police. Even if damages are sizeable, a civil suit is unlikely to be attractive; since constitutional violations will often be the result of idiosyncratic misconduct rather than government policy, the (often judgment proof) officer will usually be the only legitimate defendant, at least in state litigation. Moreover, most individuals with possible damages claims will be charged with a criminal offense; because they will be incarcerated or feel estopped by some notion of "unclean hands" they will seldom bring a civil suit and, if not, juries might hold their association with criminal activity against them. Finally, even if suit is brought, the police know that good faith is a defense in any suit against an individual.

In contrast, the exclusionary rule operates in every case of illegality and is not dependent upon the status of the victim or the good faith of the police (except in those situations identified earlier).[192] Thus, as between the two remedies, the exclusionary rule is significantly more likely to be applied, a fact which both the police and their superiors surely know. Most importantly, whereas the exclusionary rule has clearly had an impact on police training, the threat of civil suit alone is unlikely to exert pressure on police departments to prevent any but the most egregious actions on the part of their employees. Indeed, because damages against a governmental entity under § 1983, if available at all, are possible only if a government policy or custom is violated, that statute provides some incentive for governmental units to *avoid* promulgating rules regulating police conduct and training. If substantive Fourth Amendment law is to be more than "a form of words," something more than the current damages regime is necessary.

(b) Injunctive Relief

For some time, injunctions against governmental officials were difficult to obtain because of sovereign immunity. As early as 1939, however, the Supreme Court recognized that unconstitutional acts by a state official could be enjoined under § 1983,[193] and ten years later it permitted injunctions against federal officials for such acts.[194] Traditionally, a court order enjoining particular conduct has only been available if there is no remedy at law, such as a damages action. In seeking to enjoin police actions, this requirement has usually meant that the plaintiff must prove that repeated violations have occurred and that further violations are imminent and cannot otherwise be stopped. Often, some showing of bad faith on the part of the police is also imposed.

---

[191] The Court has held that, to recover damages under § 1983, "actual injury" must be proven. *Carey v. Piphus*, 435 U.S. 247, 98 S.Ct. 1042 (1978). See also, *Memphis School Dist. v. Stachura*, 477 U.S. 299, 106 S.Ct. 2537 (1986) (damages based on abstract value of constitutional rights not awardable under § 1983). The FTCA stipulates that liability will lie only when a private individual could recover under state law (which often severely limits recovery for "mental distress" and will usually also limit compensation to "actual" damages). Additionally, of course, punitive damages cannot be obtained from the government under either § 1983 or the FTCA (*Newport v. Fact Concerts, Inc.*, supra note 188; 28 U.S.C.A. § 2674) and are not likely to be obtainable from individual officers.

[192] See § 2.03(c).

[193] *Hague v. C.I.O.*, 307 U.S. 496, 59 S.Ct. 954 (1939). In *Pulliam v. Allen*, 466 U.S. 522, 104 S.Ct. 1970 (1984), the Court, based on its reading of legislative history, held that judges are not immune from prospective relief sought under § 1983.

[194] *Larson v. Domestic & Foreign Commerce Corp.*, 337 U.S. 682, 69 S.Ct. 1457 (1949).

Lankford v. Gelston[195] illustrates these points. There, the police had, on 300 occasions over 19 days, conducted warrantless searches of the appellant's and other persons' homes, relying on uninvestigated and anonymous tips about the location of certain criminal suspects. The Fourth Circuit granted injunctive relief, focusing on the number of illegalities involved, the flagrancy of the misconduct, and the police officers' probable inability to satisfy any damage claim. The court also pointed out that since the proponents for relief were not being criminally prosecuted, the exclusionary rule would not deter the continued unconstitutional conduct of the police.

The Supreme Court has been cautious about granting such injunctive relief. In *Rizzo v. Goode*,[196] for instance, the Court emphasized that unless illegal action is (1) the product of deliberate action giving rise to a persistent pattern of police violation, or (2) the result of official policy, harm is not imminent and equitable relief should not be granted by the federal courts. In *Rizzo*, the district court found that while some Philadelphia police officers had engaged in misconduct against minority and other citizens, no policy on the part of the police department directed or encouraged such action. However, it also found that the city's procedures for handling citizen complaints discouraged the filing of complaints and minimized the consequences of police misconduct. The court thus ordered the city to develop a program for acting on citizen complaints. The Supreme Court refused to uphold the order, stating that a "*failure* to act in the face of a statistical pattern is distinguishable from . . . active conduct." It also emphasized that federal courts should be extremely reticent about interfering with the internal affairs of a state agency.

The Court made the same points in *Los Angeles v. Lyons*.[197] There the plaintiff alleged that he had been rendered unconscious and suffered damage to his larynx when police officers stopped him for a traffic violation and applied a "chokehold" to his neck. He also alleged that the Los Angeles police routinely apply such chokeholds in situations where they are not threatened by the use of deadly force. The Court held, in a 5–4 decision authored by Justice White, that these allegations "fall[ ] far short of the allegations that would be necessary to establish a case or controversy between these parties" for an injunction action. In order to meet this requirement, the Court explained, the defendant "would have had not only to allege that he would have another encounter with the police but also to make the 'incredible' assertion either, (1) that all police officers in Los Angeles *always* choke any citizen with whom they happen to have an encounter, whether for purposes of arrest, issuing a citation or for questioning, or, (2) that the city ordered or authorized police officers to act in such a manner." White also asserted that the plaintiff's proposed relief, which included a training program as well as an injunction against use of chokeholds in other than life-threatening situations, would entail "massive structural" changes that a federal court should generally be reluctant to order.

Clearly equitable relief is not a substitute for the exclusionary rule. Most obviously, an injunction is prospective in nature and thus cannot rectify past wrongs. Theoretically, injunctions could be a useful mechanism for bringing about systemic change. But, as *Rizzo* and *Lyons* demonstrate, to get an injunction, the plaintiff must usually show that an unconstitutional policy exists; further, even relatively flexible court orders that allow the state agency to devise and carry out its own programs will not be countenanced by

---

[195]   364 F.2d 197 (4th Cir. 1966).

[196]   423 U.S. 362, 96 S.Ct. 598 (1976).

[197]   461 U.S. 95, 103 S.Ct. 1660 (1983).

the Supreme Court. This "hands-off" attitude toward police departments, combined with the rigorous pleading requirements imposed by the Court's cases, mean that injunctive actions are unlikely to be effective in controlling the police.

(c) Criminal Remedies

At the *state* level, most jurisdictions provide criminal sanctions for illegal police conduct, including false arrest and trespass. Due to a large number of common law limitations on these actions, however, state prosecution for illegal police conduct is rare. In general, most states require criminal intent as an element of the crime, making subjective good faith *alone* (i.e., regardless of the reasonableness of the action) a complete defense to a criminal charge such as trespass or breach of the peace.[198]

As a supplement to state criminal remedies for police misconduct, 18 U.S.C.A. § 242 imposes a federal penalty on anyone who, under color of state law, willfully deprives a person of his constitutional rights.[199] As one might suppose from this language, this criminal action is similar to the civil action under § 1983. Indeed the elements for a cause of action under § 242 and § 1983 are essentially the same. However, because § 242 is a criminal statute, it is construed strictly. In *Screws v. United States*,[200] the Supreme Court, while upholding § 242 against an attack that it was void for vagueness, interpreted the statutory requirement of willful violation to mean that the defendant must have had or been motivated by a specific intent to deprive a person of his constitutional rights. The Court clarified in *United States v. Lanier*[201] that liability need not be based on a Supreme Court (as opposed to lower court) decision, nor need the facts in the defendant's case be "fundamentally similar" to the facts in the case allegedly violated; however, it also emphasized that the rule alleged to have been violated in a § 242 case, as with a § 1983 action, must have been "clearly established" in order to lead to liability.

This narrow construction of the statute, together with the natural reticence of prosecutors to bring actions against the police upon whom they rely to make their cases,[202] has rendered § 242 an ineffective deterrent to police misconduct. Although there have been a handful of cases brought under this provision and some convictions, this sanction has normally been applied only to the most outrageous kinds of police

---

[198] See *Henderson v. State,* 95 Ga.App. 830, 99 S.E.2d 270 (1957) (in criminal prosecution for false arrest defendant must have criminal intent); *White v. Mississippi Power & Light Co.,* 196 So.2d 343 (Miss. 1967) (criminal trespass to property must be accompanied by breach of peace). See also 75 Am.Jur.2d Trespass, § 86 (1974).

[199] The statute reads:

Whoever, under color of any law, statute, ordinance, regulation, or custom, willfully subjects any inhabitant of any State, Territory, or District to the deprivation of any rights, privileges, or immunities secured or protected by the Constitution or laws of the United States, or to different punishments, pains, or penalties, on account of such inhabitant being an alien, or by reason of his color, or race, than are prescribed for the punishment of citizens, shall be fined not more than $1,000 or imprisoned not more than one year, or both; and if death results shall be subject to imprisonment for any term of years or for life.

[200] 325 U.S. 91, 65 S.Ct. 1031 (1945).

[201] 520 U.S. 259, 117 S.Ct. 1219 (1997).

[202] This reticence is likely to increase with the Supreme Court's decision in *Garcetti v. Ceballos,* 547 U.S. 410, 126 S.Ct. 1951 (2006), holding that prosecutors who allege police perjury in connection with warrant applications do not enjoy First Amendment protection against supervisor retaliation when they make the allegations in the course of their official duties.

misconduct, usually involving brutality,[203] and thus is unlikely to apply in relatively nonviolent Fourth Amendment cases.

At the *federal* level, criminal sanctions for police misconduct are also relatively impotent. The criminal actions covered include unlawful search and seizure,[204] malicious procurement of a warrant, and exceeding the authority of a warrant.[205] Yet few cases have applied these provisions, graphically underscoring the fact that these federal criminal statutes serve as little deterrent to police misconduct.

Some mention should also be made of the long-standing suggestion that judges should use their contempt power to discipline offending officers. This remedy would be available at both the state and federal levels. The first formulation of this proposal came in the third edition of Wigmore's *Evidence*:[206]

> The natural way to do justice here would be to enforce the healthy principle of the Fourth Amendment directly, i.e., by sending for the high-handed, overzealous marshal who had searched without a warrant, imposing a thirty-day imprisonment for his contempt of the Constitution, and then proceeding to affirm the sentence of the convicted criminal.

More recent formulations of the suggestion also can be found.[207] However, the drawbacks of this sanction are obvious. Because judges are probably institutionally incapable of discovering on their own initiative instances of police misconduct, the contempt sanction would only be applied when the given facts in an adversary proceeding clearly indicate unlawful police action. Moreover, since the proposed "contempt of the Constitution" is an indirect criminal contempt, the accused police officer might have a right to a separate jury trial,[208] a burden the exclusionary rule does not require.

On the whole, though the exclusionary rule and criminal remedies are imposed for essentially the same reasons in the police misconduct area—i.e., to deter such conduct and to "purge" the legal system of its effect—the criminal remedy is shackled with substantive and procedural limitations that make it a poor mechanism for shaping police behavior. The exclusionary rule, on the other hand, does not require proof of criminal intent and operates automatically in the sense that it does not require a completely separate jury proceeding. In addition, unlike criminal remedies, its invocation is not controlled by the state but can occur at the behest of the aggrieved party.

(d) Non-Judicial Remedies

In addition to the traditional civil and criminal modes of relief, there are certain remedies for police misconduct that operate outside the judicial system. As such, they carry none of the stigma or force of law associated with the legal forms of redress. Rather,

---

[203] See, e.g., *Miller v. United States*, 404 F.2d 611 (5th Cir. 1968), cert. denied 394 U.S. 963, 89 S.Ct. 1314 (1969) (defendant bitten by dog acting at police direction); *Williams v. United States*, 341 U.S. 97, 71 S.Ct. 576 (1951) (defendant "beaten, threatened and unmercifully punished for several hours until he confessed"); *Lynch v. United States*, 189 F.2d 476 (5th Cir. 1951), cert. denied 342 U.S. 831, 72 S.Ct. 50 (1951) (police assault, battery and torture of black defendants).

[204] 18 U.S.C.A. § 2236.

[205] 18 U.S.C.A. §§ 2234, 2235.

[206] 8 John Wigmore, Evidence § 2184 (3d ed. 1940).

[207] Alfred W. Blumrosen, *Contempt of Court and Unlawful Police Action*, 11 Rutgers L.Rev. 526 (1957).

[208] See § 27.02(c).

their efficacy stems from the force of public and peer disapprobation which usually manifests itself in some form of political or economic pressure.

(1) Internal Review

One such non-judicial form of relief is a police department's internal review of its own misconduct. Every major police department has formal machinery for processing citizen complaints. There is much to be said for this form of police discipline, at least in the abstract. Internal review is potentially the most efficient method of regulating the conduct of peace officers because organizational superiors are in control of both the procedure and substance of the review. A punishment carried out by an insider for a violation of a regulation promulgated by an insider is likely to be accepted by both the miscreant officer and the department as a whole.[209]

Unfortunately, in practice, such machinery has proven ineffective. First, many complaints are never heard. For obvious reasons, the police do not encourage initiation of internal review procedures; indeed, there is evidence suggesting that potential allegations of police misconduct are withheld because of fear of retaliation.[210] Moreover, in some instances, complex procedural formalities operate as a disincentive to the filing of grievances.[211]

Second, internal review often produces inadequate discipline. For example, a review of 126 discipline cases—involving 234 officers—processed by Detroit's internal review board "led to the conclusion that even when serious misconduct was found, departmental sanctions were mild, often inconsistent, and that there appeared to be 'little likelihood the Department will impose *meaningful* discipline when a citizen complains genuinely.' "[212]

Third, even if all citizen complaints are properly processed and the misbehaving officers are appropriately disciplined, internal review is not likely to reach the more subtle privacy violations that the Fourth Amendment is meant to protect, either because citizens do not complain about them or because police departments do not see them as important and therefore do not regulate against them. Quite naturally, both citizens and police, lacking the perspective of the courts, may not put as great a premium on protection of societal privacy and autonomy.

(2) Civilian Review Boards

Dissatisfaction with both internal and judicial processing of police misconduct complaints has prompted a few cities to experiment with another remedy for such misconduct—civilian review boards.[213] These boards, sitting independently of the police

---

[209] See generally Anthony Amsterdam, *Perspectives on the Fourth Amendment*, 58 Minn.L.Rev. 349 (1974).

[210] Joanna Schwartz, *What Police Learn from Lawsuits*, 33 Cardozo L. Rev. 841, 862–67 (2012).

[211] Id. at 865–67.

[212] Edward J. Littlejohn, *The Civilian Police Commission: A Deterrent of Police Misconduct*, 59 Det.J.Urb.L.Rev. 5, 45 (1981) (emphasis in original). This article advocates a civilian review board (see below), but notes that there "remains a great reluctance among police officials to punish 'one of our own' when a citizen complains, [a phenomenon which] will not be changed through self-induced reforms or by the external review of complaints." See also Alison L. Patton, *The Endless Cycle of Abuse: Why 42 U.S.C. § 1983 Is Ineffective in Deterring Police Brutality*, 44 Hastings L.J. 753, 790–91 nn. 208–210 (1993) (citing multiple sources supporting the proposition that police discipline is ineffective).

[213] See generally, Samuel Walker & Morgan MacDonald, *An Alternative Model for Police Misconduct: A Model "State Pattern or Practice" Statute*, 19 Geo. Mason L. Rev. 479, 498–500 (2009).

structure, adjudicate the merits of citizen grievances, either dismissing them as groundless or recommending that departmental superiors discipline the miscreant officer. Such external review is designed to project an appearance of fairness unattainable by internal mechanisms. At the same time, the civilian review boards can pass judgment on discourteous or harassing police practices which do not constitute judicially remediable wrongs but that nevertheless annoy the complainant and intensify community hostility toward the police.

Yet civilian review boards have usually been a failure, in large part due to vigorous opposition by the police themselves. Officers express concern over civilian ignorance of police procedures, the adverse effect on morale, the intrusion into their work, and the informal nature of the review process.[214] In practice, the review boards have been relatively powerless in the face of police disenchantment, lack of political support, and weak authorizing legislation which leaves the ultimate authority to discipline officers up to the department itself; accordingly, many of them have been abolished.[215]

(3) Ombudsman

A third remedial system which, like the civilian review board, operates outside the judicial and internal police spheres, is the Scandinavian ombudsman system. The ombudsman is, most simply, an external critic of administration.[216] His goal is improvement of administration rather than punishment of administrators or redress of individual grievances. Thus, instead of conducting formal hearings associated with adjudicating individual complaints, he relies primarily on his own investigations to collect information. To facilitate his inquiries, he may request an explanation from appropriate officials, examine departmental files, or call witnesses and conduct a hearing. On the basis of his findings, he may recommend corrective measures to the department, although he cannot compel an official to do anything. In essence, unlike the exclusionary rule, the focus of an ombudsman's evaluation is not the guilt of a particular policeman, but the policies and procedures by which police superiors have assessed citizens' allegations of guilt. For this reason, any deterrent effect is extremely indirect.

(4) Quasi-Judicial Review

While these non-judicial forms of relief for police misconduct are potentially efficacious, those that have been tried have not provided an adequate alternative to the exclusionary rule. One reason for this is precisely the fact that these forms of relief are non-judicial and, as such, do not carry the force of law.

Two other proposals rely partially on judicial enforcement. A variation on the ombudsman approach would allow the ombudsman to authorize the appointment of private counsel at public expense to sue the offending official or officials, whenever he found probable cause to believe that a constitutional or other legal violation had occurred.[217] The proposal would also make recovery against the government possible, if a violation is found to have occurred but the offending official acted in good faith or is

---

[214] Id.

[215] For a description of the failed New York and Philadelphia boards, see Littlejohn, supra note 213, at 15–23. See also Samuel Walker, *Governing the American Police: Wrestling with the Problems of Democracy*, 2016 U. Chi. Legal F. 615, 636–37 (2016).

[216] The following description of the ombudsman's powers is taken from Sven Gwyn, *Transferring the Ombudsman*, in Ombudsmen for American Government? 37 (1968).

[217] Robert P. Davidson, *Criminal Procedure Ombudsman Revisited*, 73 J.Crim.L. & Criminol. 939 (1982).

unknown. This proposal corrects the basic deficiency of the Scandinavian approach by allowing individualized accountability. Because it provides for liquidated damages (calculated as a percentage of the typical officer's salary), it also ensures a meaningful sanction even when the police do not cause any concrete damage but "merely" infringe privacy, and could provide an incentive for departments to improve their training programs.

A variant of this approach came from Chief Justice Burger. He suggested, in *Bivens*, that a quasi-judicial body be established to allow recovery of damages against the government.[218] Under Burger's plan, if damages are awarded, the record of the condemned conduct would become part of the relevant officer's files. There would also be appellate judicial review of decisions made by the tribunal. To date, no jurisdiction has adopted such a system.

2.06   Conclusion

The exclusionary evidence rule operates to bar evidence that was unconstitutionally obtained. Originally created both to protect the integrity of the judicial process and to deter illegal police conduct, more recent Court decisions have made clear that deterrence is the dominant objective of the rule. The following can be said about its scope in the Fourth Amendment context.

(1)   Exclusion of illegally seized evidence is not required at grand jury, habeas corpus, sentencing, and parole revocation proceedings, nor at civil forfeiture proceedings (at least with respect to fruits of crime and contraband) or civil deportation or other civil proceedings, on the ground that holding otherwise would have little deterrent effect on government officials but would prevent access to probative information.

(2)   The rule has also been held inapplicable at *trial* when the illegally procured evidence (a) was obtained pursuant to an invalid warrant, so long as the warrant was issued by a neutral and detached magistrate and police reasonably believed it to be valid; (b) was obtained pursuant to statutory law subsequently found unconstitutional, so long as the law does not represent a total abandonment of the legislature's responsibility to enact constitutional laws; (c) was obtained in good faith reliance upon computer records; (d) was obtained in reliance on caselaw subsequently reversed; or (e) is used solely for the purpose of impeaching the defendant on issues raised during direct examination.

(3)   On the other hand, the "fruit of the poisonous tree" doctrine extends application of the rule to exclude even legally procured evidence, if a Fourth Amendment violation put the police in the position to obtain that evidence. This doctrine operates unless the government can show by a preponderance of the evidence (a) that the connection between the illegally obtained evidence and the evidence derived from it is so attenuated (by time or by an intervening event, such as discovery of a valid warrant) that the derivative evidence is not tainted with the illegality of the original evidence; (b) that in fact the proffered evidence was obtained from a source independent of the illegally obtained evidence; or (c) that the derivative evidence would eventually have been discovered legally.

(4)   The primary means of seeking damages for the misconduct of federal law enforcement officials are a *Bivens* action, which permits suit against the individual

---

[218] *Bivens v. Six Unknown Named Agents of Federal Bureau of Narcotics*, 403 U.S. 388, 422, 91 S.Ct. 1999, 2018 (1971) (Burger, C.J., dissenting).

official for actions depriving the plaintiff of constitutional rights, and a claim under the Federal Tort Claims Act, which permits suit against the federal government under similar circumstances. Individual federal officers may assert a reasonable good faith defense; it is not clear whether the federal government may do so. The primary method of seeking monetary compensation for the misconduct of local officials is a suit under 42 U.S.C.A. § 1983, which permits recovery against both the individual officer and the relevant government unit when the officer acts under color of state law to deprive the plaintiff of constitutional rights. However, only municipalities and other local government units and their officials may be sued under § 1983; states and state officials who are acting in their official capacity are immune from such suits. Moreover, as is true at the federal level, individual officers at the local level may assert a good faith defense. Local governments do not have such a defense, but they may be found liable only if the act of their employee is authorized by official policy or custom.

(5)   Other methods of controlling police misconduct include injunctive relief for repeated misconduct, criminal sanctions for willful trespass, breach of the peace or assault and battery, and non-judicial remedies such as internal review boards, civilian review boards, and ombudsmen.

Despite periodic criticism of the exclusionary evidence rule and despite the existence of several "alternative" remedies for unconstitutional police conduct, the rule remains one of the fundamental institutions of the American criminal law system. Only the exclusionary rule can serve the dual purpose of deterring police misconduct and maintaining the judiciary's "clean hands" when the government seeks to employ unconstitutionally obtained evidence to attach criminal stigma. Current civil, criminal, and non-judicial remedies can supplement the rule's deterrent impact but are either too cumbersome or too indirect in their effect to act as a complete substitute for it.

BIBLIOGRAPHY

Atkins, Raymond and Paul H. Rubin. Effects of Criminal Procedure on Crime Rates: Mapping Out the Consequences of the Exclusionary Rule. 46 J.L. & Economics 157 (2003).

Bradley, Craig C. *Murray v. United States*: The Bell Tolls for the Search Warrant Requirement. 64 Ind. L.J. 907 (1989).

Casper, Jonathan, Kennette Benedict, and Jo L. Perry. The Tort Remedy in Search and Seizure Cases: A Case Study in Jury Decisionmaking. 13 Law and Social Inquiry 279 (1988).

Davies, Thomas Y. A Hard Look at What We Know (and Still Need to Learn) About the "Costs" of the Exclusionary Rule: The NIJ Study and Other Studies of "Lost" Arrests. 1983 Am. B. Found. Res. J. 611.

Dripps, Donald. Living with *Leon*. 95 Yale L.J. 906 (1986).

Forbes, Jessica. The Inevitable Discovery Exception, Primary Evidence, and Emasculation of the Fourth Amendment. 55 Fordham L.Rev. 1221 (1987).

Heffernan, William C. On Justifying Fourth Amendment Exclusion. 1989 Wis. L. Rev. 1193.

Ingber, Stanley. Defending the Citadel: The Dangerous Attack of "Reasonable Good Faith." 36 Vand.L.Rev. 1511 (1983).

Kainen, James. The Impeachment Exception to the Exclusionary Rules: Policies, Principles and Politics. 44 Stan. L. Rev. 1301 (1992).

Kamisar, Yale. In Defense of the Search and Seizure Exclusionary Rule. 26 Harv. J.L. & Pub.Pol'y 119 (2003).

____. Does (Did) (Should) the Exclusionary Rule Rest on a "Principled Basis" Rather Than an "Empirical Proposition"? 16 Creighton L.Rev. 565, 590–1 (1983).

LaFave, Wayne. The Smell of *Herring*: A Critique of the Supreme Court's Latest Assault on the Exclusionary Rule. 9 J. Crim. L. & Criminology 757 (2009).

____. Controlling Discretion by Administrative Regulations: The Use, Misuse, and Nonuse of Police Rules and Policies in Fourth Amendment Adjudication. 89 Mich.L.Rev. 442 (1990).

Nardulli, Peter. The Societal Costs of the Exclusionary Rule Revisited. 1987 Ill.L.Rev. 223.

Orfield, Myron W. Deterrence, Perjury, and the Heater Factor: An Exclusionary Rule in the Chicago Criminal Courts. 63 Colo. L. Rev. 75 (1992).

Perrin, Timothy, H. Mitchell Caldwell, Carol A. Chase, Ronald W. Fagan. If It's Broken, Fix It: Moving Beyond the Exclusionary Rule. 83 Iowa L.Rev. 669 (1998).

Posner, Richard A. Rethinking the Fourth Amendment. 1981 Sup.Ct.Rev. 49.

Re, Richard. The Due Process Exclusionary Rule. 127 Harvard Law Review 1885 (2014).

Sack, Emily J. Illegal Stops and the Exclusionary Rule: The Consequences of *Utah v. Strieff*. 22 Roger Williams Law Review 263 (2017).

Schrock, Thomas S. and Robert C. Welsh, Up from *Calandra*: The Exclusionary Rule as a Constitutional Requirement. 59 Minn.L.Rev. 251 (1974).

Slobogin, Christopher. Why Liberals Should Chuck the Exclusionary Rule. 1999 Ill.L.Rev. 363.

Stuntz, William J. The Virtues and Vices of the Exclusionary Rule. 20 Harv. J.L. & Pub.Pol'y 443 (1997).

Symposium—Reasonable Remedies and (or) the Exclusionary Rule? 43 Texas Tech L. Rev. 373 et seq. (2010).

Symposium—The Exclusionary Rule: Is It on Its Way Out? Should It Be? Ohio State J. Crim. L. 341 et seq. (2012).

Wilkey, Malcolm Richard. A Call for Alternatives to the Exclusionary Rule: Let Congress and the Trial Courts Speak. 62 Judicature 351 (1979).

Chapter 3

THE LAW OF ARREST

3.01   Introduction

An unconstitutional or otherwise illegal arrest in itself has little significance in the prosecution of a given case. Of course, it is true, as Justice Powell has said, that "a search may cause only an annoyance and temporary inconvenience to the law-abiding citizen, assuming more serious dimensions only when it turns up evidence of criminality [, while an] arrest . . . is a serious personal intrusion regardless of whether the person seized is guilty or innocent."[1] Nevertheless, aside from the possibility of a civil action in particularly egregious cases, the remedy for an illegal arrest is simply the release from detention. Moreover, even in cases in which probable cause is lacking at the time of an arrest, the subsequent development of probable cause justifies a re-arrest. Most importantly, the Court has firmly established that an "illegal arrest does not void a subsequent prosecution."[2] That is, the defendant cannot escape prosecution or avoid being present in court simply because his initial arrest was illegal.[3] This is so even when the arrest consists of "kidnapping" the defendant from a foreign country over that country's protest.[4]

On the other hand, the legality of an arrest is often of crucial importance in determining the admissibility of evidence. As noted in the last chapter, it is well established that evidence seized pursuant to an unlawful arrest, as well as other evidence (e.g., confessions, identifications) that results from such an arrest, may constitute "fruit of the poisonous tree" and is generally subject to suppression under the exclusionary rule.[5] It is not surprising, therefore, that the bulk of arrest cases that have reached the Supreme Court arise from efforts by a convicted defendant to have his arrest declared unconstitutional in order to effect the suppression of damaging evidence. Like other aspects of Fourth Amendment jurisprudence, the development of the law of arrest is due in large measure to the development of the exclusionary rule and its application to the states in *Mapp v. Ohio*.[6]

With these points in mind, this chapter addresses the following components of the law of arrest: (1) the definition of arrest; (2) the level of suspicion (probable cause) necessary to justify an arrest; (3) the arrest warrant requirement; and (4) arrest procedure.

---

[1]   *United States v. Watson*, 423 U.S. 411, 428, 96 S.Ct. 820, 830 (1976) (Powell, J., concurring).

[2]   *Gerstein v. Pugh*, 420 U.S. 103, 95 S.Ct. 854 (1975).

[3]   *Frisbie v. Collins*, 342 U.S. 519, 72 S.Ct. 509 (1952).

[4]   *United States v. Alvarez-Machain*, 504 U.S. 655, 112 S.Ct. 2188 (1992); *Ker v. Illinois*, 119 U.S. 436, 7 S.Ct. 225 (1886). Note, that in cases where the arrest involves "outrageous" conduct by government officials, conviction may be barred. *Hampton v. United States*, 425 U.S. 484, 96 S.Ct. 1646 (1976) (Powell, J., concurring), discussed in § 19.02(d).

[5]   See § 2.04(a). Note, however, that exclusion is not required when an arrest is illegal for *non-*constitutional reasons. *Virginia v. Moore*, 553 U.S. 164, 128 S.Ct. 1598 (2008), discussed in § 6.02.

[6]   367 U.S. 643, 81 S.Ct. 1684 (1961), discussed in § 2.02.

3.02   The Definition of Arrest

Distinguishing between an arrest and lesser types of detentions is important, because only arrests require probable cause. Early decisions of the Court suggested that an arrest occurred any time police restricted a person's movement. For instance, in *Henry v. United States*,[7] the Court found that an arrest occurred when police stopped a car whose occupants were suspected of transferring stolen liquor. According to the Court, "[w]hen the officers interrupted the two men and restricted their liberty of movement, the arrest, for purposes of this case, was complete." Since the police did not have probable cause at that moment, their action was unconstitutional.

But nine years later, the Court made clear that something more than a restriction in movement is required for an arrest. In *Terry v. Ohio*,[8] an officer observed three men behaving in a manner that suggested they were planning a store robbery. He approached the men and asked what they were doing. When they failed to respond adequately, he grabbed each one of the suspects and patted down their outer clothing. In the process, he found two weapons. Clearly, the suspects' freedom was restricted at the moment the officer was frisking them. Had the Court considered this procedure an "arrest" it would have been unconstitutional, because the officer concededly lacked probable cause at that time. Instead, the Court distinguished between arrests—which "eventuate in a trip to the station house and prosecution for crime"—and lesser seizures, which can occur "whenever a police officer accosts an individual and restrains his freedom to walk away."[9] For the type of "stop-and-frisk" action involved in *Terry*, the officer needed only "reasonable suspicion" that criminal activity was afoot, a lower level of suspicion than probable cause.[10]

Since *Terry* the Court has had many occasions to distinguish between arrests, which require probable cause, and lesser detentions, which do not require as much justification. These cases can be categorized in terms of whether they deal with encounters in the stationhouse, in the field, at the border, in the home, and at the behest of a grand jury.

(a)   Detentions in the Stationhouse or Its Equivalent

In *Davis v. Mississippi*,[11] some 24 black youths, including Davis, were taken into custody for the purpose of fingerprinting during a rape investigation in which the only lead was the victim's broad description of her assailant as a black youth. Probable cause was clearly lacking for the detentions, yet Davis was twice held overnight and interrogated. On the basis of fingerprint evidence and damaging admissions made during the interrogations, he was convicted and sentenced to death. The Supreme Court reversed, finding that the length of the stationhouse detention, coupled with the interrogation, was too intrusive to be undertaken without probable cause.

Because the evidence available to police at the time Davis was detained had been so minimal, *Davis* left open the possibility that investigative stationhouse detentions of potential criminal defendants were permissible if police have reasonable suspicion of

---

[7]   361 U.S. 98, 80 S.Ct. 168 (1959).

[8]   392 U.S. 1, 88 S.Ct. 1868 (1968).

[9]   For further discussion of what constitutes a seizure, see § 11.02(a).

[10]   Although *Terry* focused on the constitutionality of the frisk rather than of the stop, later cases applied the reasonable suspicion concept to the latter as well as the former. For further discussion of the reasonable suspicion concept, see § 11.03(a).

[11]   394 U.S. 721, 89 S.Ct. 1394 (1969).

their involvement in crime. But in *Dunaway v. New York*,[12] the Court settled that stationhouse questioning of a suspect normally requires probable cause. In *Dunaway*, police officers took the defendant into custody in the course of investigating an attempted robbery and felony murder, gave him *Miranda* warnings, and subjected him to questioning, all without probable cause. In reversing Dunaway's conviction, the Supreme Court avoided the precise issue of whether the detention was an "arrest," but made clear that a detention for custodial interrogation requires probable cause. The majority found *Terry* inapplicable because the stop and frisk implicates only a "limited violation of individual privacy" while advancing substantial "interests in both crime prevention and detection and in the police officer's safety." The intrusive stationhouse encounter of the type involved in *Dunaway*, on the other hand, does little to prevent incipient criminal activity in the field.

The Court affirmed *Dunaway* in *Kaupp v. Texas*,[13] In that case, six police officers investigating a murder went to the home of a 17-year-old boy at 3:00 a.m., told him "we need to go and talk," and took him, barefoot and in his underwear, to the police station, where he made incriminating statements.[14] The police concededly did not have probable cause; in fact they had failed in their efforts to obtain an arrest warrant. Nonetheless, the Texas courts upheld the police action on the ground that no seizure occurred: the fact that Kaupp had said "O.K." after being told the police needed to talk to him made the trip to the station "voluntary." A unanimous Supreme Court, in a per curiam decision, rejected that conclusion, stating "[t]here is no reason to think Kaupp's answer was anything more than 'a mere submission to a claim of lawful authority.' "[15] To the argument that Kaupp was not seized because he had not resisted the police, the Court responded that the "failure to struggle with a cohort of deputy sheriffs is not a waiver of Fourth Amendment rights."

In *Florida v. Royer*,[16] the Court indicated that a nonconsensual investigative detention *outside* the stationhouse can also, under circumstances resembling a stationhouse encounter, require probable cause. In *Royer*, airport police stopped the defendant, suspected of carrying narcotics, and asked him to accompany them to a room in the airport approximately forty feet away. Royer followed them to what one of the detectives later described as "a large storage closet," containing a small desk and two chairs. The detectives then retrieved two pieces of Royer's luggage without his consent. Upon request, Royer produced a key and unlocked one of the suitcases, in which marijuana was found, and consented to the agents prying open the second piece of luggage, which also contained marijuana. He was then placed under arrest. The Court held that the detention in the "storage closet" prior to the opening of the luggage—an encounter that lasted fifteen minutes—constituted an "arrest" as well. As Justice White stated for the Court: "What had begun as a consensual inquiry in a public place had escalated into an investigatory procedure in a police interrogation room, where the police, unsatisfied with previous explanations, sought to confirm their suspicions." The

---

[12]   442 U.S. 200, 99 S.Ct. 2248 (1979).

[13]   538 U.S. 626, 123 S.Ct. 1843 (2003).

[14]   Kaupp indicated he was at the scene of the crime and had been handed the murder weapon by the perpetrator.

[15]   Compare this holding to the Court's analysis of voluntariness in consent to search cases, discussed in § 12.02(c).

[16]   460 U.S. 491, 103 S.Ct. 1319 (1983).

Court emphasized that the officers' conduct was "more intrusive than necessary to effectuate an investigative detention otherwise authorized by the *Terry* line of cases."[17]

Not all nonconsensual detentions at the stationhouse or its equivalent require probable cause, however. As discussed below, such detentions at the *border* are justifiable on reasonable suspicion. The Court has also intimated that detentions at the stationhouse for purposes other than holding a person on charges or for interrogation may not rise to the level of an arrest. In *Davis*, for instance, the Court called "arguable" the proposition "that, because of the unique nature of the fingerprinting process, [detentions for the sole purpose of obtaining fingerprints] might, under narrowly defined circumstances, be found to comply with the Fourth Amendment even though there is no probable cause in the traditional sense." Similarly, in *Hayes v. Florida*,[18] while the Court held impermissible a stationhouse fingerprinting because, as in *Davis*, the police had forcibly taken the suspect to the station without probable cause to arrest, the majority also recognized, with apparent approval, that several states had established procedures for *judicial authorization* of fingerprinting on less than probable cause.

Finally, of course, if the "detention" is consensual, then the police cannot be said to have arrested the person. Thus, the Supreme Court's *Miranda* decisions have consistently held that a person questioned at the police station is not in "custody" (and thus not under arrest) when *he* initiates a stationhouse encounter.[19]

(b) Detentions in the Field

While police questioning of a suspect in the stationhouse or its equivalent will normally require probable cause, such questioning pursuant to a stop conducted on the "street" will usually only require reasonable suspicion, as *Terry* held. However, *Terry* also held that the stop it authorized must be "brief," implying that a prolonged encounter would require probable cause. In *Royer* the Court explicitly stated that "an investigative detention [in the field] must be temporary and last no longer than is necessary to effectuate the purpose of the stop." Thus, at some point in time detentions in the field become arrests. The American Law Institute Code of Pre-Arraignment Procedure provides that a stop lasting over twenty minutes is not appropriate on less than probable cause.[20] In *United States v. Place*,[21] decided the same year as *Royer*, the Court seemed willing to consider this rule-oriented approach when it found that a 90-minute airport detention of luggage while awaiting a narcotics dog was "alone" sufficient to render the seizure impermissible under *Terry*.

But the Court ultimately refused to put a precise durational limit on stops. In *United States v. Sharpe*,[22] it stated:

> While it is clear that 'the brevity of the invasion of the individual's Fourth Amendment interests is an important factor in determining whether the seizure is so minimally intrusive as to be justifiable on reasonable suspicion' [citing *Place*], we have emphasized the need to consider the law enforcement

---

[17]   The Court went on to find that probable cause had not existed at the time of the detention and that the evidence found in the luggage was therefore inadmissible. See § 3.03(b)(3).

[18]   470 U.S. 811, 105 S.Ct. 1643 (1985).

[19]   See § 16.03(a)(3).

[20]   ALI, Model Code of Pre-Arraignment Procedure 110.2(1) (1975).

[21]   462 U.S. 696, 103 S.Ct. 2637 (1983).

[22]   470 U.S. 675, 105 S.Ct. 1568 (1985).

purposes to be served by the stop as well as the time reasonably needed to effectuate these purposes. . . . Much as a 'bright line' rule would be desirable in evaluating whether an investigative detention is unreasonable, common sense and ordinary human experience must govern over rigid criteria.

In *Sharpe* itself, the Court sanctioned a twenty minute detention of respondent Savage and his pickup truck on less than probable cause. For fifteen minutes of this period, Savage was held by State Trooper Thrasher pending arrival of Drug Enforcement Administration agent Cooke, who had become separated from Thrasher when he stopped Savage's accomplices and Thrasher had continued in pursuit of Savage. The final five minutes involved Cooke's investigation of Savage's documents and the truck itself, resulting in the discovery of what turned out to be marijuana and Savage's arrest.

The Supreme Court's majority opinion, authored by Chief Justice Burger, concluded that the seizure was merely a *Terry* stop. It was not an arrest because the police had not unnecessarily delayed Savage's detention; rather, they had conducted the investigation "in a diligent and reasonable manner." Cooke had attempted to raise Thrasher on the radio once the two had become separated and had arrived at the scene as soon as he could arrange for two other officers to detain the persons he had stopped. The state trooper's failure to conduct the search himself was justified because he had joined the pursuit late and thus "could not be certain that he was aware of all the facts that had aroused Cooke's suspicions," and because "as a highway patrolman, he lacked Cooke's training and experience in dealing with narcotics investigation." Burger contrasted the police behavior here with that in *Place*, where the Court had noted that the government agents had been remiss in not assuring the narcotic dog's presence at the time the luggage arrived in the airport.

Justice Marshall concurred in the result, concluding that the prolonged detention was Savage's fault: he should have pulled over when his accomplices were stopped by Cooke, but instead he continued to drive, necessitating Cooke's separation from the state trooper.[23] But both Justice Marshall and Justice Brennan, who dissented, rightfully pointed out that the due diligence of the police should be irrelevant to whether a field detention is an arrest. When the defendant does not contribute to the delay, they contended, no amount of effort by the police should convert an arrest into something less.

Marshall also argued that the due diligence test will "inevitably produce friction and resentment [among the police], for there are bound to be inconsistent and confusing decisions." Justice Brennan illustrated this last point by noting that the police in *Sharpe* could have been considerably more "diligent:" he suggested that a simultaneous stop of Savage and his accomplices should have been possible, that in any event Thrasher should have been able to conduct a competent investigation without Cooke, and that if he couldn't, *Cooke*, not Thrasher, should have followed Savage. He also pointed out that prior to the initial stop Cooke had had ample time to summon other DEA agents, who were "swarming throughout the immediate area," but that communications snafus had prevented his reaching them. Both Marshall and Brennan contended that the majority opinion would lessen pressure on the police to correct such problems and, more generally, to "structure their *Terry* encounters so as to confirm or dispel the officer's reasonable suspicion in a brief time."

---

[23] The majority indicated that its holding would be the same whether or not Savage had tried to elude the police.

Whether or not this latter observation is true, *Sharpe* does mean that determining whether prolonged detentions in the field are arrests will require careful case by case assessment of the extent to which the police attempt to minimize the duration of the detention.

(c) Detentions at the Border

The normal Fourth Amendment requirements are relaxed at the border, on the theory that the government's interest in protecting the integrity of the country's boundaries is paramount.[24] Relying heavily on this rationale, the Supreme Court, in *United States v. Montoya de Hernandez*,[25] granted the government broad authority to detain, on less than probable cause, individuals crossing the border. In *Montoya de Hernandez*, border officials had a reasonable suspicion that the defendant had ingested "balloons" containing drugs in an attempt to smuggle then into the country. After the defendant refused to undergo an x-ray examination, the police detained her incommunicado for 16 *hours* in an effort to produce the evidence via the "calls of nature." When this proved unsuccessful, due to what the court of appeals described as "heroic efforts" by the defendant, they obtained a warrant authorizing a search of her alimentary canal, which produced 88 balloons of cocaine.

Six members of the Court sanctioned the delay on the ground that the length and discomfort of the defendant's detention "resulted solely from the method by which she chose to smuggle illicit drugs into this country." To them, the only alternative to the officers' action was to allow the defendant to pass into the interior, which could not be countenanced in light of the officers' reasonable suspicion and the government's strong interest in protecting its borders. Justice Stevens agreed with the result, but on the ground—reminiscent of the holding in *Sharpe*—that the officers' attempt to minimize the delay by offering an x-ray examination had been rejected by the defendant.

Justice Brennan, joined by Justice Marshall, cogently argued that the detention in this case—"indefinite confinement in a squalid back room cut off from the outside world, the absence of basic amenities that would have been provided to even the vilest of hardened criminals, repeated strip-searches"—was tantamount to an arrest and should have been based on probable cause. Lacking probable cause the officers should either have allowed the defendant to enter the country *or* turned her away. Addressing Justice Stevens' rationale, Brennan pointed out that an x-ray examination can have damaging effects and involves bodily intrusion; thus, he argued, it should be undertaken nonconsensually only if judicially authorized.[26]

(d) Detentions in the Home

Nonconsensual confrontation in the home may or may not rise to the level of an arrest, depending upon its purpose. In *Beckwith v. United States*,[27] for instance, the Court found routine questioning by several IRS agents in the defendant's living room noncustodial. In contrast is *Rawlings v. Kentucky*.[28] There, police executing an arrest warrant in the home of the person named in the warrant failed to find the named person

---

[24] See § 13.05.

[25] 473 U.S. 531, 105 S.Ct. 3304 (1985).

[26] See § 13.05(b) for further discussion of this issue.

[27] 425 U.S. 341, 96 S.Ct. 1612 (1976), discussed in § 16.03(a)(2).

[28] 448 U.S. 98, 100 S.Ct. 2556 (1980).

but did discover evidence of drug possession as well as a number of occupants. Some of the officers detained the individuals in the house for 45 minutes while others went to obtain a search warrant for the house. The Supreme Court treated this detention as if it were an arrest and found it impermissible because probable cause with respect to the detained individuals was not shown to exist.

However, in *Michigan v. Summers*[29] the Court held that an individual may be detained during a search of his residence if the police arrive with a valid *search* warrant, even though probable cause to arrest him does not exist. A primary reason the Court gave for this result was that such a detention occurs on private property; detention in the home, the Court concluded, is neither as inconvenient nor as stigmatizing as detention elsewhere. A second rationale for the Court's decision was that a search warrant clearly indicates that there is probable cause to believe criminal activity has occurred or is occurring on the premises searched, thus implying that people on those premises may be involved in criminal activity. Thus, a warrantless search designed to prevent flight and protect the officers and evidence should be permitted. Given this reasoning, *Summers* is strictly limited to cases in which the detaining officers possess a valid search warrant based on probable cause to believe there is evidence of crime on the premises. When, as in *Rawlings*, they possess only an arrest warrant, they presumably may not detain individuals in the home who are not listed in the warrant unless probable cause to arrest develops as they legitimately execute the warrant.[30]

The Court applied *Summers* in *Muehler v. Mena*,[31] where police executing a search warrant for a home handcuffed the 5 foot, 2 inch Mena, held her in a room for two to three hours with three other occupants of the house, and questioned her about her immigration status. A bare majority of the Court, in an opinion by Chief Justice Rehnquist, concluded that this detention and questioning were reasonable under *Summers*. The handcuffing was justified initially because the search was for weapons in a house believed to belong to gang members, and its continuation was reasonable because it lasted no longer than the search. The questioning was permissible because it also took place during the lawful detention and because, as the Court has indicated in other cases,[32] questioning itself is not a seizure. The four dissenters would have remanded the case to determine whether excessive force was used, and Justice Kennedy, a member of the five-justice majority, cautioned that the decision did not permit routine handcuffing during house searches.

When, in contrast to the facts of *Summers* and *Mena*, occupants of the searched residence are detained outside the "immediate vicinity" of the house, the basis for detention cannot be the warrant authorizing search of the house. In *Bailey v. United States*,[33] police preparing to execute a warrant authorizing search of a home observed two men leave the house in a car. They stopped the car a mile from the house, frisked the men, and obtained incriminating evidence and statements. Justice Kennedy, writing for six members of the Court, concluded that none of the three law enforcement interests identified in *Summers*—protecting the officers conducting the house search, minimizing obstruction of the house search, or preventing flight of the house occupants—applied

---

[29] 452 U.S. 692, 101 S.Ct. 2587 (1981). See also § 5.05(e).

[30] See § 6.04(b).

[31] 544 U.S. 93, 125 S.Ct. 1465 (2005).

[32] See, e.g., *INS v. Delgado*, 466 U.S. 210, 104 S.Ct. 1758 (1984), discussed in § 11.02(a).

[33] 568 U.S. 186, 133 S.Ct. 1031 (2013).

"with the same or similar force to the detention of recent occupants beyond the immediate vicinity of the premises to be searched." The Court reached no conclusion as to whether the stop of the individuals could be justified on *Terry* grounds, however.

(e) Grand Jury Subpoenas

In the course of performing its investigative function, the grand jury may demand the appearance of witnesses and potential defendants through use of the subpoena *ad testificandum*.[34] The Supreme Court has indicated that such detentions may occur on less than probable cause and, indeed, on virtually no suspicion, for two reasons.[35] First, requiring a showing of probable cause would complicate the legitimate investigative objectives of the grand jury, which has traditionally possessed wide-ranging powers. More importantly, because a subpoena can be contested in court, is just as often served on concededly innocent persons as those suspected of crime, and does not require immediate compliance, this method of effecting an investigative detention is not considered as abrupt, demeaning, stigmatizing, or inconvenient as typical methods used by the police.[36]

(f) Summary

Determining whether a given detention is an arrest can often be a difficult endeavor. On the one hand, it seems apparent that seizures accompanied by handcuffing, drawn guns, or words to the effect that one is under arrest qualify as an "arrest" and thus require probable cause. On the other, brief questioning on the street will generally not rise to the level of an arrest. In analyzing the nature of those nonconsensual detentions lying in between, the key factors to consider are the purpose (e.g., questioning v. fingerprinting), manner (police detentions v. grand jury subpoenas), location (stationhouse confrontations v. seizures in the "field" or at the border), and duration of the detention. Also relevant are the degree of police diligence in minimizing the intrusion and the extent to which the defendant is responsible for prolonging the detention. None of these factors alone is determinative; the test is the familiar "totality of the circumstances" standard. Of course, regardless of what type of detention is involved, if the police have probable cause, the "arrest" issue is moot.

3.03   The Probable Cause Requirement for Arrests

In *Beck v. Ohio*,[37] the Supreme Court declared that police have probable cause to make an arrest when "the facts and circumstances within their knowledge and of which they [have] reasonably trustworthy information [are] sufficient to warrant a prudent man in believing that the [suspect] had committed or was committing an offense." As this language suggests, probable cause is an objective standard; a subjective test, as the *Beck* Court pointed out, would mean that arrests could take place "in the discretion of the police." The Supreme Court has also stated, not particularly helpfully, that the probable cause standard falls somewhere between a "mere suspicion" and the

---

[34]   See generally, § 23.05(a).

[35]   See, *United States v. Dionisio*, 410 U.S. 1, 93 S.Ct. 764 (1973) (grand jury subpoena for purpose of obtaining voice exemplar not a seizure or a violation of the Fifth Amendment); *United States v. Mara*, 410 U.S. 19, 93 S.Ct. 774 (1973) (grand jury subpoena of person's handwriting not a seizure or a violation of the Fifth Amendment).

[36]   Note that the grand jury cannot compel testimony from the subpoenaed witness. However, *non*-testimonial evidence, such as handwriting and voice exemplars, may be compelled. See § 23.05(a)(2).

[37]   379 U.S. 89, 85 S.Ct. 223 (1964).

reasonable-doubt showing imposed at trial.[38] As the name implies, probable cause may necessitate a more probable than not showing,[39] though many federal judges appear to think that the term refers to a level of certainty somewhat lower than that.[40] Defining such a fact-specific concept is obviously difficult. The discussion below will focus on the categories of information the courts have indicated can form the basis for probable cause to arrest.

(a) Secondhand Sources

Beck required that probable cause arise from "reasonably trustworthy information" that is "within [the officer's] knowledge." The Court has also established, however, that the arresting officer need not have personal, direct knowledge of the facts and circumstances which establish probable cause.[41] The three most common secondhand sources of information are "informants" who receive some specific benefit (e.g., reduced charges or money) for providing information to the police, victims and other eyewitnesses, and other police. Occasionally, police also obtain information from non-human sources; in particular, the use of dog sniffs has been the subject of much litigation.

(1) Informants

Police rely heavily on information from people who are acquainted with criminals or who may be criminals themselves. The usual issue in cases involving such informants is not whether their information, if believed, establishes probable cause, but the predicate issue of whether their information is accurate. Informants might give police distorted reports for a host of reasons, including a wish to curry favor with those who might charge them, a desire to exact revenge against a criminal colleague, or simply because they are liars. Some rules are necessary for assessing the credibility of their information, to reduce the chance that arrests will be conducted merely on the say-so of such an informer. A second reason for putting strictures on informant tips is to better enable magistrates and reviewing courts to determine when an "informant" has been concocted by police to cover the fact that their information has actually been acquired illegally.[42]

The Warren Court attempted to standardize analysis of informant credibility in *Aguilar v. Texas*,[43] where it held that an affidavit based on a tip from an informer must state: (1) sufficient underlying circumstances to demonstrate how the informant reached his conclusion, and (2) sufficient underlying circumstances establishing the reliability of the informant. The first, basis-of-knowledge prong attempts to discern whether the informant personally observed the reported criminal activity, or instead heard about it from other sources. If the latter, the information might be viewed more skeptically. The

---

[38] *Brinegar v. United States*, 338 U.S. 160, 69 S.Ct. 1302 (1949).

[39] See, e.g., *Mallory v. United States*, 354 U.S. 449, 77 S.Ct. 1356 (1957) (arrest of three black men with access to a basement where rape by a masked black man occurred was illegal, because police may not "arrest, as it were, at large . . . in order to determine whom they should charge before a committing magistrate on 'probable cause.' ").

[40] See C.M.A. McCauliff, *Burdens of Proof: Degrees of Belief, Quanta of Evidence, Or Constitutional Guarantees?*, 35 Vand.L.Rev. 1293, 1325 (1983) (when asked to quantify the degree of certainty represented by the phrase "probable cause," 166 federal judges gave, as an average response, 45.78%).

[41] *Jones v. United States*, 362 U.S. 257, 80 S.Ct. 725 (1960).

[42] For allegations that this occurs despite current rules, see Craig Bradley, Murray v. United States: *The Bell Tolls for the Search Warrant Requirement*, 64 Ind.L.J. 907 (1989).

[43] 378 U.S. 108, 84 S.Ct. 1509 (1964).

second, "veracity" prong directly attempts to evaluate whether the informant is lying or distorting the truth.

In *Spinelli v. United States*,[44] the Court elaborated on the first prong by concluding that insufficient information as to the informant's basis of knowledge can be overcome if "the tip describe[s] the accused's criminal activity in sufficient detail that the magistrate knows that he is relying on something more substantial than a casual rumor . . . or an accusation based merely on an individual's general reputation." And in *United States v. Harris*,[45] a plurality of the Court held that a failure to meet the second "veracity" prong was not fatal if the informant's statements were a declaration against penal interest.

The *Aguilar-Spinelli* test, as *Aguilar's* two-prong formulation came to be called, was modified even more substantially in *Illinois v. Gates*,[46] where the Court formally eschewed a requirement that both prongs be met. Rather, the credibility of an informant's information must be based on the "totality of the circumstances." Thus, while the basis-of-knowledge and veracity ideas are "highly relevant," "a deficiency in one may be compensated for . . . by a strong showing as to the other."

The above cases all involved searches and thus are discussed in more detail elsewhere in this book.[47] The focus here is their relevance to the probable cause determination in the arrest context. The leading case on this issue, *Draper v. United States*,[48] preceded *Aguilar* but is still informative. In *Draper*, an informant who had provided reliable information in the past advised police officers that the defendant was selling drugs, that he had gone to Chicago to secure a new supply and that he would be returning on a train carrying a tan bag that would contain the purchased drugs. Further, the informant described what Draper would be wearing and said that he would "walk real fast". The officers observed a man fitting the description emerge from the train carrying a tan zipper bag and walking very quickly. They arrested Draper without a warrant, searched him, and found drugs. In upholding Draper's conviction, the Supreme Court said the informant's tip, coupled with the corroboration of the information from the observation of the officers themselves, sufficed to establish probable cause to arrest.

Draper established that so long as the informant's tip "is reasonably corroborated by other matters within the officer's knowledge," the tip can be considered credible for consideration on the probable cause issue. Yet, as Justice Douglas, the lone dissenter, pointed out, a troubling aspect of *Draper* is the fact that the police observed nothing incriminating about Draper's actions before arresting him; the Court in effect held that because the informant had given an accurate description of Draper, the police were also justified in believing the informant's account of his criminal activity. Neither information as to how the informant knew about that activity (as required by *Aguilar*) or descriptive detail about the activity (as later permitted by *Spinelli*) was required.

Justice White, in a concurring opinion in *Gates*, explained how the Court in *Draper* should have analyzed the basis-of-knowledge prong to reach the result in that case: because the informant could predict two days in advance what Draper would be wearing, Draper must have "planned in advance to wear these specific clothes so that an

---

[44]   393 U.S. 410, 89 S.Ct. 584 (1969).

[45]   403 U.S. 573, 91 S.Ct. 2075 (1971).

[46]   462 U.S. 213, 103 S.Ct. 2317 (1983).

[47]   See § 5.03(b).

[48]   358 U.S. 307, 79 S.Ct. 329 (1959).

accomplice could identify him," giving rise to a "clear inference . . . that the informant was either involved in the criminal scheme himself or that he otherwise had access to reliable, inside information." Unfortunately, instead of adopting this interpretation of *Draper*, the majority in *Gates* reaffirmed the *Draper* majority's suggestion that the basis of knowledge about criminal activity need not be shown at all, and that informant veracity can be established through police corroboration of innocent information contained in the informant's tip, at least when the innocent information is detailed, as was the case in *Draper*. *Gates* also suggested that even the absence of corroboration would not be fatal, if the informant's reputation for veracity was well-known: if "a particular informant is known for the unusual reliability of his predictions of certain types of criminal activities in a locality, his failure, in a particular case, to thoroughly set forth the basis of his knowledge surely should not serve as an absolute bar to a finding of probable cause based on his tip."[49]

Based on the foregoing, factors to consider in determining whether an informant's information may form the basis for a probable cause determination include whether: (1) the informant gives a description of how he found out about the criminal activity; (2) the informant gives a detailed description of that activity; (3) there is evidence that the informant has been reliable in the past; (4) the informant predicts activity on the part of the suspect that is corroborated by the police; and (5) the informant implicates himself in the criminal activity. After *Gates*, no particular combination of these factors is required; a strong showing with respect to (1) or (3), for instance, might be sufficient.

An example of an arrest case in which this relatively relaxed test is *not* met is provided by *Beck*, decided well before *Gates* but reaffirmed by that case. There the informant merely stated that the suspect was engaged in gambling, with no detail as to time and place. This statement, even when combined with the officer's knowledge of Beck's prior gambling record, was insufficient; to hold otherwise, concluded the Court, would permit the state to arrest anyone with a prior record.

(2) Victims and Eyewitnesses

When the informant is a "respectable citizen" who has been a victim or otherwise an eyewitness to crime, the two prongs of *Aguilar-Spinelli*, while theoretically still relevant, are usually not applied with much rigor. In *Jaben v. United States*,[50] the Supreme Court held that "whereas some supporting information concerning the credibility of informants in narcotics cases or other common garden varieties of crime may be required, such information is not so necessary in the context of the case before us [where third parties provided information about the defendant's financial situation in a tax evasion case]." Similarly, in *Chambers v. Maroney*,[51] which did involve "garden-variety crime," the Court upheld an arrest for robbery of a service station for which probable cause was established through a report from two teenagers in the vicinity. *Chambers* recognizes that, with the typical eyewitness, the firsthand basis of the informant's knowledge is evident and there is usually no motive to fabricate information.

---

[49] An example of such a case might be *McCray v. Illinois*, 386 U.S. 300, 87 S.Ct. 1056 (1967), where the police informant had provided information on fifteen or sixteen previous occasions, which led to numerous arrests and convictions. Of course, there is much to be said, contrary to the rule in *Gates*, for the position that past accuracy should not be *dispositive* of the accuracy issue in a subsequent case. See § 5.03(b)(3).

[50] 381 U.S. 214, 85 S.Ct. 1365 (1965).

[51] 399 U.S. 42, 90 S.Ct. 1975 (1970).

Of course, as always, the information provided by such individuals, even if believed, must still establish probable cause to arrest. In *Chambers*, the teenagers told police investigating the robbery that a blue compact station wagon containing four men, one with a green sweater, had been circling in the vicinity of the gas station and later sped away from it. When the service station attendant verified that one of the two men who robbed the station had been wearing a green sweater, and that the other had been wearing a trench coat, "the police had ample cause to stop [within two miles of the station] a light blue compact station wagon carrying four men and to arrest the occupants, one of whom was wearing a green sweater and one of whom had a trench coat with him in the car."

(3) Other Police

When a police officer is the informant, the veracity inquiry is even further relaxed; indeed, in *United States v. Ventresca*,[52] the Supreme Court stated that "[o]bservations of fellow officers of the Government engaged in a common investigation are plainly a reliable basis for a warrant applied for by one of their number." Yet, again, those observations must amount to probable cause, or an arrest based on them will be invalid. Thus, in *Whiteley v. Warden*,[53] an arrest based on a radio bulletin from a sheriff in another jurisdiction advising that a warrant had been issued there for the suspect's arrest was held invalid, because the warrant affidavit failed to state any basis for the probable cause finding.

However, the *Whiteley* Court also stated that, had the warrant from the other jurisdiction been valid, the arrest would have been constitutional. *Whiteley* thus approves the common police practice of making arrests based on reports from other officers, whether or not information in the report was obtained firsthand, provided that it establishes probable cause. If the police bulletin is not based on probable cause, then an arrest founded on it is improper, regardless of how reasonable the arresting officer's belief in the report's validity may be. This rule deters the police from immunizing misconduct through reliance on other officers to conduct the actual arrest.[54]

(4) Dogs

Police often rely on trained dogs to detect drugs on the person of arrestees. In *Florida v. Harris*[55] an officer pulled Harris over on a routine traffic stop and asked for consent to search the car. When Harris refused consent, the officer deployed a drug-sniffing dog, which alerted to the presence of drugs. The ensuing search of the car turned up drugs, but not the type of drugs the dog was trained to detect. Harris was let out on bail, stopped again, and again the dog alerted to the presence of drugs in his vehicle, but none were found. The Florida Supreme Court suppressed the drug evidence found during the first search, primarily because, despite proof of the dog's training and certification, the state did not provide field performance records that could have exposed any tendency on the part of the handler to cue the dog to alert or that indicated the dog's inability to distinguish between "residual odors and actual drugs."

---

[52]   380 U.S. 102, 85 S.Ct. 741 (1965).

[53]   401 U.S. 560, 91 S.Ct. 1031 (1971).

[54]   But see *Arizona v. Evans*, 514 U.S. 1, 115 S.Ct. 1185, discussed in § 2.03(c)(3), which suggests that the exclusionary rule may not apply in such a situation.

[55]   568 U.S. 237, 133 S.Ct. 1050 (2013).

A unanimous Supreme Court concluded that the Florida Supreme Court's demand for field performance data was inconsistent with the totality of the circumstances definition of probable cause. The Court noted that, in the field, a dog may alert to substances that "were too well hidden or present in quantities too small for the officer to locate" or to the vestiges of drugs previously in the vehicle. Thus, Justice Kagan continued for the Court, the field performance tests demanded by the Florida Supreme Court are not necessarily the best measure of a dog's proficiency. If, as occurred in *Harris*, "a bona fide organization has certified a dog after testing his reliability in a controlled setting," or, as also occurred in *Harris*, "the dog has recently and successfully completed a training program that evaluated his proficiency in locating drugs," "a court can presume (subject to any conflicting evidence offered) that the dog's alert provides probable cause to search." Given the prevalence of drug residue on money and other items that are easily transferable, the Court's opinion glosses over the real possibility that dogs will routinely alert to people innocent of wrongdoing.[56]

(b) First-Hand Knowledge

When the arresting officer is also the "informant" then the key issue in most Supreme Court decisions has not been the accuracy or truthfulness of his observations but whether, based on what the officer knew, probable cause existed. A few recurring situations in which this issue has been raised are explored below.

(1) Post-Detention Information

A key tenet of arrest law is that probable cause must be established by evidence obtained independently of the arrest. In *Sibron v. New York*,[57] the Supreme Court stated: "It is axiomatic that an incident search may not precede an arrest and serve as part of its justification." This language should not be construed to prevent seizure of evidence before an arrest for which probable cause already exists becomes "official";[58] it is merely meant to deter police from illegally seizing and searching people solely for the purpose of establishing probable cause to arrest.

On the other hand, it is well-established that evidence noticed or seized during an encounter which has not yet reached the level of an "arrest" but which is nonetheless obtained legally may properly be used to establish probable cause. The clearest example of this rule is the situation where, upon "reasonable suspicion," a police officer stops a suspect, receives an inadequate explanation for his "suspicious" behavior, and discovers incriminating evidence during the course of a protective frisk. This was the situation in *Terry v. Ohio*,[59] the leading "stop and frisk" case, in which furtive conduct by three men alerted an experienced police officer that a robbery might be imminent. The officer approached the men and asked them what they were doing. They merely "mumbled something," whereupon the officer frisked them and discovered weapons. The defendant was then arrested, charged with carrying a concealed weapon, and convicted. The

---

[56] See Nakechi Taifa, *Civil Forfeiture vs. Civil Liberties*, 39 N.Y.L.S. L. Rev. 95, 106 (1995) (noting research indicated that an average of 96% of American money has been contaminated with drugs); see also *Roe v. Renfrow*, 631 F.2d 91, 95 (7th Cir. 1980) (involving strip search of 13 year-old after a dog alert, apparently triggered because the child had been playing with her dog, which was in heat, that morning).

[57] 392 U.S. 40, 88 S.Ct. 1889 (1968).

[58] See § 6.03.

[59] 392 U.S. 1, 88 S.Ct. 1868 (1968).

Supreme Court affirmed, holding that, if a protective frisk is justified and a weapon is discovered, probable cause to arrest may be established.[60]

Accordingly, if in the course of the temporary detention the suspect fails adequately to account for his suspicious actions, or if he affirmatively discloses incriminating evidence or makes incriminating statements, probable cause to arrest may be established.[61] Further, while the Supreme Court has suggested that the fact of flight alone does not create probable cause,[62] it noted in *Sibron* that flight to avoid a confrontation with police can also be an important factor in the probable cause determination (especially when the police already have reasonable suspicion). Lower courts have also held that an attempt to conceal from the view of the detaining police officer a highly suspicious object may give rise to probable cause.[63]

In *Hiibel v. Nevada Dist. Ct.*,[64] the Supreme Court held that failure to identify oneself may also be ground for an arrest, at least if the police already have reasonable suspicion that a crime has occurred. A police officer responding to a report of an assault involving a man and a woman in a vehicle found Hiibel, apparently intoxicated, standing next to a truck with a woman in it, and asked him for his name. Hiibel refused to give it, despite being asked to identify himself eleven times. He was arrested under a statute that criminalizes failure to identify oneself when there is reasonable suspicion the person has committed, is committing or will commit an offense. The Court had previously found less precise anti-loitering statutes unconstitutional under the due process clause,[65] but this statute clearly indicated that arrest is permitted only if reasonable suspicion exists and the detainee refuses to provide a name. In any event, the defendant contested the law's validity only on Fourth and Fifth Amendment grounds.

Hiibel's Fourth Amendment argument was that the Nevada statute permits circumvention of the probable cause requirement by authorizing arrest of someone who is merely suspicious. Justice Kennedy, writing for a five-member majority, rejected this claim on these facts, because the officer's question was a "commonsense inquiry, not an effort to obtain an arrest for failure to identify after a *Terry* stop yielded insufficient evidence." He noted that *Terry* and other stop-and-frisk cases had contemplated that an officer could question a legitimately stopped individual.[66] Requesting a name from such an individual, Kennedy reasoned, is a minor intrusion that is justified by the "purpose, rationale, and practical demands of a *Terry* stop."

The majority also rejected Hiibel's Fifth Amendment claim, holding that disclosure of identity "presented no reasonable danger of incrimination" in Hiibel's case, and would be likely to do so only in "unusual circumstances." That assertion is in obvious tension with the majority's explanation, in its Fourth Amendment analysis, of why the government interest in a detainee's identity outweighs the individual's interest in

---

[60] For further explication of this aspect of stop and frisk law, see § 11.03(c).

[61] See Joseph Cook, Constitutional Rights of the Accused: Pre-trial Rights 130–31 (1972).

[62] *Wong Sun v. United States*, 371 U.S. 471, 83 S.Ct. 407 (1963). But see *Illinois v. Wardlow*, 528 U.S. 119, 120 S.Ct. 673 (2000), discussed in § 11.03(a), which held that flight plus presence in a high crime area can constitute reasonable suspicion.

[63] *People v. Howell*, 394 Mich. 445, 231 N.W.2d 650 (1975).

[64] 542 U.S. 177, 124 S.Ct. 2451 (2004).

[65] See § 11.03(b)(4).

[66] See generally § 11.01. The majority dismissed as dictum language in other cases that had indicated detainees could refuse to answer an officer's questions. See, e.g., *Berkemer v. McCarty*, 468 U.S. 420, 104 S.Ct. 3138 (1984).

keeping it private. As Justice Stevens noted in dissent, presumably the officer wanted the name, and Nevada law authorizes him to obtain it, in order to facilitate investigation of criminal activity; a name can be valuable to the government even if it is not itself incriminating, especially given today's computerized criminal databases.[67]

(2) Proximity to Criminal Suspects

In *United States v. Di Re*,[68] government investigators justified their arrest of Di Re from the front passenger seat of a car on the ground that, at the time of his arrest, there were two other men in the car, both of whom were validly arrested for engaging in a transaction involving counterfeit ration coupons. The Court held that the police lacked probable cause to arrest Di Re, concluding that the circumstances were not such that a person in Di Re's position would necessarily know about or be involved in the illegal transaction. The Court noted that the transaction was not "secretive," but carried out in "broad daylight, in plain sight of passers-by, in a public street of a large city," and that "the alleged substantive crime [was] one which does not necessarily involve any act visibly criminal." If Di Re had seen the passing of coupons, "it would not follow that he knew they were ration coupons, and if he saw that they were ration coupons, it would not follow that he would know them to be counterfeit" (a fact apparently proven at trial by expert testimony). Thus, Di Re's proximity to criminal activity did not establish probable cause.

This principle has been reiterated by the Court on several occasions. In *Johnson v. United States*,[69] decided during the same term as *Di Re*, police were informed that some persons of unknown identity were smoking opium in a hotel room. From outside the room, the officers could smell burning opium. They entered the room, announced that all of its occupants were under arrest, and proceeded to search the premises.[70] Opium was discovered and introduced into evidence at trial. The Supreme Court reversed the convictions, holding that the officers had probable cause to believe that a crime had been committed but that they lacked sufficient information to determine which of the occupants had committed it. Consequently the arrests—and the search incident thereto—were illegal.

The *Johnson* analysis should be read in light of the Supreme Court's later holding in *Ker v. California*,[71] which indicated that under somewhat different circumstances probable cause might be more readily found. Armed with both their own visual observations and an informant's tip that George Ker had engaged in the purchase and sale of marijuana, police officers entered Ker's apartment. Inside were Ker and his wife. Upon spotting a brickshaped package of marijuana in the kitchen, they arrested both persons. The Supreme Court upheld both arrests, stating with respect to Mrs. Ker:

> Even assuming that her presence in a small room with the contraband in a prominent position on the kitchen sink would not alone establish a reasonable ground for the officers' belief that she was in joint possession with her husband,

---

[67] For further discussion of the meaning of "self-incrimination" under the Fifth Amendment, see § 15.03(c).

[68] 332 U.S. 581, 68 S.Ct. 222 (1948).

[69] 333 U.S. 10, 68 S.Ct. 367 (1948).

[70] The search in *Johnson* incident to the arrest was conducted long before the Court's opinion in *Chimel v. California*, 395 U.S. 752, 89 S.Ct. 2034 (1969), in which the permissible scope of searches incident was severely restricted to the area within the arrestee's reach. See § 6.04(a).

[71] 374 U.S. 23, 83 S.Ct. 1623 (1963).

that fact was accompanied by the officers' information that Ker had been using his apartment as a base of operations for his narcotics activities. Therefore, we cannot say that at the time of her arrest there were not sufficient grounds for a reasonable belief that Diane Ker . . . was committing the offense of possession of marijuana in the presence of the officers.

A subsequent Supreme Court case which helps define the extent to which police may infer probable cause from the defendant's presence at the scene of criminal activity is *Ybarra v. Illinois*.[72] In *Ybarra* police procured a valid search warrant authorizing both the search of a tavern believed to be a center of drug transactions and the search of the tavern's bartender. When executing the warrant, the police searched the dozen or so patrons of the tavern, including the petitioner, Ybarra. The Court held, 6–3 that the warrant did not give the officers authority "to invade the constitutional protections possessed individually by the tavern's customers." While the case thus dealt with the validity of a search, it contains language which is applicable to arrests:

> [A] person's mere propinquity to others independently suspected of criminal activity does not, without more, give rise to probable cause to search that person. Where the standard is probable cause, a search or *seizure of a person* must be supported by probable cause particularized with respect to that person. This requirement cannot be undercut or avoided by simply pointing to the fact that coincidentally there exists probable cause to search or seize another or to search the premises where the person may happen to be. [emphasis added]

Justice Stewart, writing for the majority, rejected the state's contention that when the police have a "reasonable belief" that individuals on "compact" premises "are connected with" drug trafficking and "may be concealing or carrying away the contraband," there is no bar to a search or seizure of those individuals. Citing *Di Re*, he emphasized that probable cause is necessary before such a search or seizure can take place, except when, as set out in *Terry*, there is a particularized fear that an individual is armed and dangerous. He noted that police could point to no specific fact that would have justified such a suspicion in Ybarra's case.

In contrast, in *Maryland v. Pringle*,[73] the Supreme Court noted that occupants of a car are much more likely to be engaged in a common enterprise than the patrons of a public tavern like the one searched in *Ybarra*. Thus, it unanimously upheld the arrest of all three persons in a car in which cocaine was found, after each had denied ownership of the drugs. *Di Re*, which had also involved arrest of car occupants, was distinguishable because there an informer had singled out someone other than Di Re as the guilty party. In *Pringle*, there was no such informant, so "a reasonable officer could conclude that there was probable cause to believe Pringle committed the crime of possession of cocaine, either solely or jointly."[74]

(3) Investigative Profiles

A relatively recent development in law enforcement has been the use of so-called "profiles," designed to take advantage of statistical or experiential information

---

[72]   444 U.S. 85, 100 S.Ct. 338 (1979).

[73]   540 U.S. 366, 124 S.Ct. 795 (2003).

[74]   All of these cases must be read against the backdrop of law that only requires a "nexus" between the defendant and illegal drugs for a conviction. See, e.g., *United States v. Hunte*, 196 F.3d 687 (7th Cir. 1999).

suggesting the common characteristics of certain types of criminal actors (e.g., hijackers, drug couriers). Several Supreme Court cases involve the use of such profiles.

In *Reid v. Georgia*,[75] for instance, the court of appeals held that a narcotics agent had reasonable grounds to stop two individuals because they met the following elements of an informal "drug courier profile:" (1) the petitioner had arrived from Fort Lauderdale, a principal place of origin for cocaine; (2) he arrived early in the morning, when law enforcement activity is diminished; (3) he and his companion appeared to be trying to conceal the fact that they were travelling together, and (4) they apparently had no luggage other than their shoulder bags. The Supreme Court concluded there were no grounds for a stop, much less an arrest, on these facts: only the third observation specifically related to the individuals concerned and this, in itself, was insufficient to give rise even to a reasonable suspicion, much less probable cause, that the individuals were carrying drugs.

In *Florida v. Royer*,[76] the police detained an individual in a small airport room because he fit the following elements of a drug courier profile: he was carrying American Tourister luggage which appeared to be heavy; was young and casually dressed; appeared nervous and evasive; paid for his ticket with cash; did not write his full name and address on his luggage identification tickets; and was departing from Miami, a major import center for illicit drugs and was destined for New York, a major drug distribution center. Further, the police determined that the name on the ticket was not Royer's. After finding that the detention constituted an arrest, the Court held that these factors did not constitute probable cause. "We cannot . . . agree that every nervous young man paying cash for a ticket to New York City under an assumed name and carrying two heavy American Tourister bags may be arrested and held to answer for a serious felony charge." However, the Court did hold that there were sufficient grounds in this case to stop the defendant.

The Court came to a similar conclusion in *United States v. Sokolow*,[77] again involving a seizure in an airport. There, at the time the defendant was stopped, his behavior "had all the classic aspects of a drug courier," according to an agent. More specifically, at the time of the stop, "the agents knew, *inter alia*, that (1) he paid $2,100 for two airplane tickets from a roll of $20 bills; (2) he traveled under a name that did not match the name under which his telephone number was listed; (3) his original destination was Miami, a source city for illicit drugs; (4) he stayed in Miami for only 48 hours, even though a round-trip flight from Honolulu to Miami takes 20 hours; (5) he appeared nervous during his trip; and (6) he checked none of his luggage." The Court found this information sufficient for a stop, but not an arrest.

The profiles at issue in these and other cases[78] barely deserve the name, given their transparently post hoc nature. As Justice Marshall pointed out in his dissent in *Sokolow*, the elements of drug courier profiles have been manipulated from case to case, apparently to justify seizures after the fact.[79] Probably wisely, therefore, the Court's

---

[75]   448 U.S. 438, 100 S.Ct. 2752 (1980).

[76]   460 U.S. 491, 103 S.Ct. 1319 (1983).

[77]   490 U.S. 1, 109 S.Ct. 1581 (1989).

[78]   See, e.g., *United States v. Mendenhall*, 446 U.S. 544, 100 S.Ct. 1870 (1980); *Florida v. Rodriguez*, 469 U.S. 1, 105 S.Ct. 308 (1984).

[79]   Marshall listed a number of seemingly contradictory factors that have been deemed important elements of various "profiles": person deplaned first, deplaned last, deplaned in the middle; one-way ticket,

penchant in "profile cases" seems to be to look at the underlying factual basis of the detention without squarely addressing the usefulness of the profiles, *qua* profiles, in determining reasonable suspicion or probable cause. Even in *Sokolow*, the case in which it came closest to explicitly authorizing their use, the Court was equivocal, merely stating that "the fact that these factors may be set forth in a 'profile' does not somehow detract from their evidentiary significance as seen by a trained agent."

On the other hand, a seizure based on a profile should not automatically be rejected, if two conditions are met: (1) the profile is empirically proven to produce a constitutionally adequate success rate (say, a 50% success rate to justify an arrest, or a 30% success rate to justify a *Terry* stop); and (2) it is filed with the court beforehand so as to prevent the post hoc manipulation of which Marshall complained. The mere fact that a profile allows police to base a detention on group data, rather than "particularized suspicion," should not defeat its use in the investigative context, where, as the Court has stated many times, probabilities are the issue.[80] The main reason profiles are unlikely to become the norm is the difficulty of arriving at a list of traits (at least with respect to drug couriers) that will lead to an empirically verifiable level of certainty sufficient to meet the dictates of probable cause or reasonable suspicion.

(c) Mistake

Once the objective facts known to the police establish probable cause, whether they come from informants or firsthand information, it is immaterial that some or all of those facts later turn out to be false,[81] so long as the officer reasonably believed them to be true at the time of arrest.[82] If, on the other hand, the arresting officer's mistake is unreasonable, the government may be liable under § 1983 for a violation of the Fourth Amendment. *Albright v. Oliver*[83] was a § 1983 action alleging that Oliver, a police officer, violated the Due Process Clause when he arrested Albright and subsequently testified at a preliminary hearing against him, on both occasions relying on uncorroborated information from an informant known to have provided unreliable information on 50 previous occasions; subsequent evidence showed that Albright was innocent. Although the Supreme Court held that due process was not the proper basis for such a claim and dismissed it,[84] at least four members of the Court indicated that Oliver's actions might be actionable under the Fourth Amendment, and another three justices definitively took this position. Among the latter group was Justice Ginsburg, who pointed out that, under the common law, an arrested person was considered "seized" for Fourth Amendment purposes even if released on bond, given the requirement that he appear in court on the

---

round trip ticket; non-stop flight, changed planes; no luggage, gym bag, new suitcases; traveling alone, traveling with companion; acted nervously, acted too calmly.

[80] For a more detailed investigation of the attack against profiles, see Christopher Slobogin, *The World Without a Fourth Amendment*, 39 U.C.L.A.L.Rev. 1, 380–85 (1991).

[81] *Henry v. United States*, 361 U.S. 98, 80 S.Ct. 168 (1959). See also, *United States v. Garofalo*, 496 F.2d 510 (8th Cir. 1974), cert. denied 419 U.S. 860, 95 S.Ct. 109 (1974).

[82] Id. See also, discussion of *Franks v. Delaware*, 438 U.S. 154, 98 S.Ct. 2674 (1978), in § 5.03(d).

[83] 510 U.S. 266, 114 S.Ct. 807 (1994).

[84] No single reason for doing so attracted a majority. A four-member plurality, in an opinion by Chief Justice Rehnquist, explained that "[w]here a particular amendment [i.e., the Fourth Amendment] 'provides an explicit textual source of constitutional protection' against a particular sort of government behavior, that Amendment, not the more generalized notion of 'substantive due process,' must be the guide for analyzing these claims." Justices Kennedy and Thomas concluded that state law provided an adequate ground for malicious prosecution, while Justice Souter concluded that, given the facts, the Fourth Amendment was the only possible basis for Albright's claim.

state's command. Further, "[i]f Oliver gave misleading testimony at the preliminary hearing, that testimony served to maintain and reinforce the unlawful haling of Albright into court, and so perpetuated the Fourth Amendment violation." Justices Blackmun and Stevens, in a separate opinion, agreed with these observations.

A variant of the mistaken probable cause situation is the mistaken offense scenario. In *Devenpeck v. Alford*,[85] Washington state police stopped Alford's car, initially on suspicion that he was impersonating an officer. But when they discovered he was taping their conversation during the stop, he was arrested for that conduct, in the belief that it violated state privacy law. It turned out that no such offense exists in Washington, and Alford sued the police for unlawful arrest. However, the jury denied Alford relief because it found there had been probable cause to arrest him for the offense of impersonating an officer. In refusing to reverse this verdict, the Supreme Court unanimously rejected Alford's claim and the Ninth Circuit's holding that, in order to avoid "sham" arrests, an arrest for an offense different from the one eventually pressed by the government is valid only if the former is closely related to and based on the same facts as the latter. Justice Scalia's opinion noted that previous caselaw had firmly established that the officer's motivation for arrest is immaterial as long as he knows of facts that are sufficient to establish probable cause for *some* crime.[86] Furthermore, Justice Scalia reasoned, the Ninth Circuit's rule would likely encourage officers either to cease providing reasons for arrest altogether, or to cite every class of offense for which probable cause might exist, consequences which he labeled "perverse."

A final type of mistake involves a mistake of law rather than fact. In *Heien v. North Carolina*,[87] a police officer stopped a car for having only a single back lamp, mistakenly believing that state law required two such lamps. Eight members of the Court held that this mistake did not make the ensuing stop and seizure of evidence unconstitutional. Heien argued that, whereas mistakes of fact can be reasonable when officers are confronted with volatile or fast-moving situations, the reasonable officer should always know the law. But the Court, pointing to the fact that the statute in this case was vaguely written, concluded that an officer can also "suddenly confront" a situation where application of the law is unclear. The Court also emphasized that the mistake must be reasonable, which two concurring justices suggested would only be the case when the relevant statue "is genuinely ambiguous, such that overturning the officer's judgment requires hard interpretive work."

3.04   The Arrest Warrant Requirement

The Fourth Amendment states that arrest warrants may only issue upon a showing of probable cause and must identify with particularity the person to be seized. The question addressed here is when such a warrant is required.[88] Under the common law rule, a warrantless arrest was permitted if the arresting officer had probable cause to believe that: (1) a person was committing or had committed a felony (although entry into

---

[85]   543 U.S. 146, 125 S.Ct. 588 (2004).

[86]   See, e.g., *Whren v. United States*, 517 U.S. 806, 116 S.Ct. 1769 (1996), discussed in § 10.04. Consistent with this ruling, the Court remanded the case for a determination as to whether probable cause existed as to the offense of impersonating an officer.

[87]   574 U.S. 54, 135 S.Ct. 530 (2015).

[88]   Other issues associated with the warrant process are dealt with in Chapter 5, dealing with search warrants, since they tend to be identical to those raised with respect to arrests.

a home to effect an arrest may have required a warrant[89]), or (2) a person was committing a misdemeanor involving a breach of the peace in the officer's presence, then an arrest warrant was not required. Thus, the only situation in which an arrest warrant was necessary was for arrest on a misdemeanor charge committed outside the officer's presence or not involving a breach of the peace.[90] The reasoning behind this rule was described by the Supreme Court in *Carroll v. United States*:[91]

> The reason for arrest for misdemeanors without warrant at common law was to promptly suppress breaches of the peace . . . while the reason for arrest without a warrant on a reliable report of a felony was because the public safety and the due apprehension of criminals charged with heinous offenses required that such arrests should be made at once without warrant.

As discussed below, since *Carroll* the Court has explicitly upheld the common law rule, except with respect to arrests in the suspect's home and the homes of third parties. Note, however, that even when an arrest need not be authorized by a warrant, the police must obtain a judicial determination of probable cause within a short time of the arrest.[92]

(a) Public Arrests

United States v. Watson[93] was the first case in which the Court squarely upheld, as a matter of constitutional law, the common law rule permitting warrantless arrest in public even when there is time to obtain a warrant. The Court expressed confidence in the ability of police officers to make determinations of probable cause and stated: "we decline to transform [a] judicial preference [for arrest warrants] into a constitutional rule when the judgment of the Nation and Congress has for so long been to authorize warrantless public arrests on probable cause." Since most public arrests are made under exigent circumstances, a different decision in *Watson* would have affected few cases.

The Court has also held that a warrant is not required to make an arrest on the "curtilage" of one's home. In *United States v. Santana*,[94] the police, with cause to arrest Santana, arrived at her house to find her standing in her front doorway. When she saw the officers approaching, she retreated into the vestibule and closed the door behind her. The officers followed her inside and there effected her arrest without a warrant. The Supreme Court affirmed the validity of the arrest procedure. When Santana stood in the doorway, the Court explained, "[s]he was not in an area where she had any expectation of privacy" and her arrest at that point would therefore have been permissible under a *Watson* public-arrest analysis. When she retreated into her house, she created exigent circumstances necessitating warrantless entry.[95]

---

[89]   See *Payton v. New York*, 445 U.S. 573, 590–98, 100 S.Ct. 1371, 1382–86 (1980).

[90]   Most jurisdictions have modified the misdemeanor arrest rule to permit warrantless arrests for *any* misdemeanor occurring in the officer's presence. The ALI's Model Code of Pre-Arraignment Procedure also permits, at § 120.1, a warrantless arrest for a misdemeanor "when the officer has reasonable cause to believe that the misdemeanant will not be apprehended or may cause injury to himself, to others, or to property, unless immediately arrested."

[91]   267 U.S. 132, 45 S.Ct. 280 (1925).

[92]   *Gerstein v. Pugh*, 420 U.S. 103, 95 S.Ct. 854 (1975), discussed in § 20.02.

[93]   423 U.S. 411, 96 S.Ct. 820 (1976).

[94]   427 U.S. 38, 96 S.Ct. 2406 (1976).

[95]   For further discussion of the exigency issue, see § 3.04(d).

(b) Arrests in the Home

For some time, the Court also seemed willing to permit warrantless arrests that *commence* inside the home. Most common law authorities held that a warrantless entry to effect a felony arrest in a private home constituted a reasonable exercise of the police power, regardless of the existence of exigent circumstances, and the validity of such a procedure was accepted *sub rosa* by the Supreme Court in a number of its early decisions.[96] It was not until *Payton v. New York*,[97] however, that the Court addressed directly the issue of warrantless home arrests. Despite the implications of its earlier decisions, the Court in *Payton* held, 6–3, that the Fourth Amendment prohibits a warrantless, nonconsensual entry into a suspect's home to make an arrest, unless exigent circumstances are present.[98]

The Supreme Court's majority opinion, written by Justice Stevens, emphasized that "physical entry of the home is the chief evil against which the wording of the Fourth Amendment is directed." He also noted that the Court had long established that a *search* of a home requires a warrant unless there are exigent circumstances.[99] To the dissenters' argument that a search is more intrusive than an arrest Stevens rightly responded that "any differences in the intrusiveness of entries to search and entries to arrest are merely ones of degree rather than kind," especially since a search may occur in the course of attempting to apprehend the subject of an arrest warrant.[100] Stevens also pointed out that, in comparison to the warrantless public arrest rule, the warrantless home arrest rule advanced by the dissent was not as widely supported. Although admitting that a large number of states followed the latter rule, he detected a trend toward the majority's position, noting that five of the seven federal circuit courts of appeal that had considered the question had found warrantless non-exigent home arrests unconstitutional.

The Court also concluded that the only probable cause showing that need be made to support an arrest warrant is that connecting the suspect with criminal activity. In contrast, Justice White's dissent, although arguing for warrantless arrests, contended that probable cause to believe the suspect was in his home should also be established before arrest can take place. The majority countered that "[i]f there is sufficient evidence of a citizen's participation in a felony to persuade a judicial officer that his arrest is justified, it is constitutionally responsible to require him to open his doors to the officers of the law."

(c) Arrests in Third Party Homes

When the police obtain an arrest warrant but seek to execute it in the home of someone other than the person named in the warrant, different considerations come into play. As Justice Marshall pointed out in the majority opinion in *Steagald v. United States*,[101] while an arrest warrant may protect the suspect "from an unreasonable

---

[96]   See, e.g., *Trupiano v. United States*, 334 U.S. 699, 68 S.Ct. 1229 (1948).

[97]   445 U.S. 573, 100 S.Ct. 1371 (1980).

[98]   In *Kirk v. Louisiana*, 536 U.S. 635, 122 S.Ct. 2458 (2002), the Court reversed, per curiam, a Louisiana Supreme Court decision that failed to inquire into whether exigent circumstances justified a warrantless home arrest, reaffirming that "police officers need either a warrant or probable cause plus exigent circumstances in order to make a lawful entry into a home."

[99]   See § 4.05(a).

[100]   See § 6.04(b).

[101]   451 U.S. 204, 101 S.Ct. 1642 (1981).

seizure, it [does] absolutely nothing to protect [a third party's] privacy interest in being free from an unreasonable invasion and search of his home." Thus, held the *Steagald* Court, in such situations the police must not only obtain an arrest warrant but also a search warrant, based upon a probable cause finding that the suspect is located in the third party's home.

The government in *Steagald* had contended that requiring a search warrant in such cases would unduly hamper law enforcement because the inherent mobility of the suspect might require several trips to the magistrate as the suspect moved from place to place. Marshall gave three reasons why the majority's rule would not "significantly impede effective law enforcement efforts." First, under *Payton*, an arrest warrant *is* sufficient authority to enter the suspect's *own* home. Secondly, under *Watson*, police can always arrest a suspect in public, and thus can wait to apprehend him as he leaves the dwelling. Finally, as with arrests in the defendant's own home, a warrant is not required to enter a house when exigent circumstances make obtaining one unfeasible.

As in *Payton*, Justices Rehnquist and White dissented, criticizing the Court's opinion primarily on practical grounds. They felt that, after the Court's ruling, police, magistrates and trial judges "will, in their various capacities, have to weigh the time during which a suspect for whom there is an outstanding arrest warrant has been in the building, whether the dwelling is the suspect's home, how long he has lived there, whether he is likely to leave immediately, and a number of related and equally imponderable questions." While the dissenters may be more realistic in their assessment of the impact of *Steagald* on law enforcement, the majority's concern that a contrary result would create significant potential for abuse is also well founded. As Justice Marshall pointed out, under such a ruling, the police, "[a]rmed solely with an arrest warrant for a single person, . . . could search all the homes of that individual's friends and acquaintances."

(d) Hot Pursuit: The Exception to the Warrant Requirement

Both *Payton* and *Steagald* indicated that "exigent circumstances" would justify warrantless entry to effect an arrest. The principal cases cited in support of this proposition were *Warden v. Hayden*[102] and *United States v. Santana*.[103] Both of these cases upheld warrantless home arrests relying on what has come to be known as the "hot pursuit" doctrine.

Under the hot pursuit doctrine, first announced in *Hayden*, if police have probable cause to believe a criminal suspect they are "hotly" pursuing has fled into a dwelling, they may make a warrantless entry of that dwelling for the purpose of arresting him. In *Hayden*, police were informed that the defendant had robbed a taxi company at gunpoint and had been followed to a particular house. Within five minutes of the defendant's entry into the house, the police had arrived at the home, gained entrance, and arrested the defendant. The Court upheld the arrest of the defendant because the "Fourth Amendment does not require police officers to delay in the course of an investigation if to do so would gravely endanger their lives or the lives of others."

A slightly different emergency rationale led to the Court's decision to uphold the warrantless home arrest in *Santana*. In *Santana*, it will be remembered, the police, with

---

[102]   387 U.S. 294, 87 S.Ct. 1642 (1967).

[103]   427 U.S. 38, 96 S.Ct. 2406 (1976).

probable cause to arrest the defendant, followed her inside her house after spotting her in her vestibule. To have required a warrant in this situation, the Court felt, would have permitted her almost certain escape. Thus, the Court has recognized both imminent danger to others and imminent escape of the suspect as exigencies permitting warrantless entry.

A third type of exigency which might justify such entries is when evidence would otherwise be destroyed. In *Minnesota v. Olson*,[104] the Court noted with approval the lower court's conclusion that "a warrantless intrusion may be justified by hot pursuit of a fleeing felon, or *imminent destruction of evidence* . . . or the need to prevent a suspect's escape, or the risk of danger to the police or to other persons inside or outside the dwelling."[105] This dictum is a sensible delineation of the exigency concept.[106] Thus, it seems likely that police may make a warrantless home arrest not only of suspects who are dangerous or escape risks, but also of those who might otherwise destroy evidence, at least when probable cause as to these exigencies exists.

In a case decided after *Payton* and *Steagald*, the Court has also held that a fourth factor—the gravity of the offense charged—is relevant in determining when exigent circumstances exist. In *Welsh v. Wisconsin*,[107] police had probable cause to believe the defendant was driving while intoxicated based on a witness' account that the defendant had been driving erratically, crashed his car, and acted bizarrely upon leaving his immobilized vehicle. Ascertaining the defendant's address from the registration left in the car, police proceeded to his home, arrested him and took a blood sample later used against him, all without a warrant. The Court, in a 7–2 decision, held the arrest invalid, because under Wisconsin law the defendant was guilty only of a civil traffic offense. Justice Brennan's majority opinion quoted Justice Jackson in *McDonald v. United States*[108] to justify its position: "When an officer undertakes to act as his own magistrate, he ought to be in a position to justify it by pointing to some real immediate and serious consequences if he postponed action to get a warrant." To the state's argument that exigency existed because evidence of the defendant's blood level needed to be preserved, the Court merely observed that when the offense is a noncriminal "minor" one, "a warrantless home arrest cannot be upheld simply because evidence of the petitioner's blood-alcohol level might have dissipated while the police obtained a warrant."

There are several potential problems with *Welsh*. First, there is the difficulty of determining when a crime is "minor." The crime involved in *Welsh*—driving while intoxicated—is considered quite serious in many states; presumably in these states warrantless home arrests would be permitted. Second, even if that problem is overcome (perhaps simply by declaring that all misdemeanors are "minor"), it is not clear why, if there is true exigency (for instance, where the misdemeanant is about to escape, harm someone, or destroy crucial evidence), the nature of the offense should prevent arrest when the suspect is at home. The real concern here appears to be the state's authority to criminalize relatively innocuous behavior, not the intrusion brought on by an arrest for a legitimately legislated crime.

---

[104]   495 U.S. 91, 110 S.Ct. 1684 (1990).

[105]   *State v. Olson*, 436 N.W.2d 92 (Minn. 1989) (emphasis added).

[106]   For further treatment of the exigency idea, in the context of warrantless entries to *search*, see §§ 6.04(b) & (c), 8.03, and 9.02(a).

[107]   466 U.S. 740, 104 S.Ct. 2091 (1984).

[108]   335 U.S. 451, 69 S.Ct. 191 (1948).

Most importantly, *Welsh* is suspect to the extent it suggests that warrants are *not* required for home arrests in *serious* cases. Unfortunately, many lower courts have so held, following the lead of the D.C. Circuit Court of Appeals in *Dorman v. United States*.[109] *Dorman* identified seven factors that might permit warrantless entry: (1) the offense under investigation is grave; (2) the suspect is reasonably believed to be armed; (3) the police have a high degree of probable cause for the arrest; (4) there is an especially strong reason to believe that the suspect is on the premises; (5) it is likely that the suspect will escape if not quickly apprehended; (6) the entry may be made peaceably; and (7) the entry is during the day. Factor (5) is a legitimate exigency that permits a warrantless entry, and factor (2) could be. The heightened probable cause findings required by factors (3) and (4) are perhaps justifiable given the absence of judicial intervention. But factor (1), either by itself or in combination, should not be relevant unless the nature of the offense somehow suggests imminent danger to others. Merely because the alleged offense is murder should not mean the warrant requirement may be dispensed with. Indeed, in such a situation judicial authorization is even more important, as the police naturally tend to become most zealous when serious offenses are involved.

The last two factors listed by the *Dorman* court, (6) and (7), are an admirable attempt to limit the intrusiveness of a warrantless entry. But if probable cause and true exigency are present, then the fact that a warrantless entry may have to be somewhat unruly or occur at night should not prevent it. Despite these observations, the lower courts continue to apply the *Dorman* factors, giving them different weights and applying them in different combinations depending upon the circumstances.[110]

3.05   Executing an Arrest

Several Fourth Amendment issues arise in connection with executing an arrest: (1) what time constraints does an arrest warrant place on the executing officer?; (2) when are the police required to knock and announce their presence when they make a home arrest?; (3) when may police use deadly force to effect an arrest?; (4) what are the consequences of mistakenly arresting the wrong person?; and (5) to what extent may the police search individuals whom they arrest, or search and detain third parties whom they discover in the course of making the arrest? The first topic is covered in this book's discussion of search warrants, since the issues are similar,[111] and the fifth topic is best dealt with in the context of the search incident to arrest exception.[112] The rest of these issues are discussed below. A final issue discussed here is the extent to which the *Due Process Clause* governs police attempts to apprehend suspects.

(a) The Method of Entry

In English law—a source to which the Supreme Court regularly refers in arrest entry cases—police were entitled to break into a house to effect an arrest after stating

---

[109]   435 F.2d 385 (D.C.Cir. 1970).

[110]   See, e.g., *United States v. Reed*, 572 F.2d 412 (2d Cir. 1978); *United States v. Anderson*, 2014 WL 1281062; *Gray v. Liriano*, 943 F.Supp.2d 1 (2013); *State v. Gregory*, 331 N.W.2d 140 (Iowa 1983), cert. denied 464 U.S. 833, 104 S.Ct. 115 (1983); *People v. Abney*, 81 Ill.2d 159, 41 Ill.Dec. 45, 407 N.E.2d 543 (1980). For an example of a warrantless entry case that does not rely on *Dorman*, see *United States v. Forker*, 928 F.2d 365 (11th Cir. 1991).

[111]   See § 5.05(a).

[112]   See § 6.04.

their authority and their purpose for demanding admission.[113] A similar rule was adopted early on in caselaw in this country.[114] Today the standards for arrest entries are usually set out in legislation. The federal statute, 18 U.S.C.A. § 3109, provides that an officer "may break open any outer or inner door or window of a house . . . to execute a search warrant, if, after notice of his authority and purpose, he is refused admittance." This statute has been held to govern arrests, as well as searches, both with and without a warrant.[115] The American Law Institute in its Model Code of Pre-Arraignment Procedure has promulgated a similar rule, which adds that an arrest entry without a prior demand is justified if the making of the demand would allow the arrestee to escape, subject the officer or another to harm, or permit the destruction of evidence or the damage or loss of property.[116]

The reasons for requiring notice in most cases are several: (1) needless property destruction will be avoided; (2) needless violence by surprised or fearful occupants will be prevented; and (3) the dignity and privacy of the occupants will be respected. At the same time, some sort of exigency exception is necessary to prevent against the same dangers (harm, escape or evidence destruction) that permit conducting an arrest without a warrant.[117]

Despite the longevity and widespread acceptance of such rules, the Supreme Court did not address their constitutional status until relatively recently. Although a plurality of the Court suggested in *Ker v. California*[118] that the common law also stated the constitutional standard, it was not until *Wilson v. Arkansas*,[119] decided in 1995, that the Court held that, given its historical pedigree, the knock and announce rule "is an element of the reasonableness inquiry under the Fourth Amendment." The Court also held, consistent with the common law and statute, that the police need not knock and announce their presence under exigent circumstances. In discussing what the latter circumstances might be, Justice Thomas' opinion for the Court made reference to the "threat of physical violence," the potential for escape, and the potential for evidence destruction. But the Court was reluctant to delineate these factors any further. In *Richards v. Wisconsin*,[120] it clarified its position by holding that police must knock and announce unless they have *reasonable suspicion* that such action "would be dangerous or futile, or that it would inhibit the effective investigation of the crime by, for example, allowing the destruction of evidence."[121]

The Supreme Court has also made clear that the *Richards* analysis does not change when police have to break down a door or otherwise damage premises in order to gain

---

[113] *Semayne's Case*, 50 Co.Rep. 91a, 11 E.R.C. 629, 77 Eng.Rptr. 194 (K.B. 1603), is the oft-cited authority for this proposition. "In all cases where the King is party," the Court declared, at 195, "the sheriff (if the doors be not open) may break the party's house, either to arrest him, or to do other execution of the K[ing]'s process, if otherwise he cannot enter. But before he breaks it, he ought to signify the cause of his coming, and to make request to open doors. . . ."

[114] *Read's Case*, 4 Conn. 166 (1822).

[115] See, e.g., *Miller v. United States*, 357 U.S. 301, 78 S.Ct. 1190 (1958).

[116] ALI, A Model Code of Pre-Arraignment Procedure § 120.6(1) and (2) (Official Draft 1975).

[117] See § 3.04(d).

[118] 374 U.S. 23, 83 S.Ct. 1623 (1963).

[119] 514 U.S. 927, 115 S.Ct. 1914 (1995).

[120] 520 U.S. 385, 117 S.Ct. 1416 (1997).

[121] For elaboration of these cases, see § 5.05(c).

entry. In *United States v. Ramirez*,[122] it held that reasonable suspicion of exigency justifies a no-knock entrance even when the entrance requires that the door be broken through. Five years later, in *United States v. Banks*,[123] the Court held that the same standard justifies breaking down the door after a knock and announcement fails to elicit a response. In *Banks*, police executing a warrant authorizing search for cocaine waited 15 to 20 seconds after they knocked and announced their presence, then used a battering ram on the door of Banks' two-bedroom apartment; inside they found drugs, as well as Banks, who had just gotten out of the shower and claimed to have not heard the police's knock. Although the lower courts had decided that a longer wait was necessary before police could damage property to gain entry, a unanimous Court held that damage necessary to effect an entry is always permissible if exigency exists. It concluded that such exigency existed here, because "15 to 20 seconds does not seem an unrealistic guess about the time someone would need to get in a position to rid his quarters of cocaine."

A few other Court cases have construed 18 U.S.C. § 3109, the federal statute dealing with arrest entries, doing so quite strictly. In *Miller v. United States*,[124] a D.C. police officer, accompanied by a federal narcotics agent, arrived at Miller's apartment at 3:45 a.m. without a warrant, for the purpose of arresting Miller for narcotics offenses. One of the officers knocked on the apartment door. Miller asked who it was, and the officers identified themselves simply as "police." Then Miller opened the door slightly—the door was secured by a chain—and inquired as to the officers' purpose. Without waiting for a response, Miller attempted to close the door. Before it could be shut, however, the officers reached inside, tore away the chain, entered the apartment and arrested Miller. While inside, the officers also seized several bills of incriminating marked currency.

The Supreme Court reversed Miller's conviction, holding that the method of entry failed to comport with § 3109. The officers, the Court concluded, never adequately announced their purpose prior to the forcible entry, and Miller's attempt to close the door on them was an ambiguous act that could not conclusively reflect an understanding that they had arrived to arrest him.

In *Sabbath v. United States*,[125] the Court focused on the meaning of "break open an outer or inner door or window" in § 3109. In *Sabbath* federal customs officers enlisted the aid of one Jones, whom they had caught trying to smuggle cocaine into the country, to apprehend "Johnny," the intended recipient of the drug. Jones agreed to deliver the cocaine while the police watched. Shortly after Jones entered "Johnny's" apartment, the officers knocked. Receiving no response, they entered through the unlocked door with guns drawn. Sabbath, the occupant of the apartment, was arrested, and a subsequent search resulted in the seizure of a quantity of cocaine. The Supreme Court reversed Sabbath's conviction, rejecting the court of appeal's judgment that the officers did not "break open" the door within the meaning of § 3109 and thereby trigger the identification and announcement requirements. Rather, it concluded: "An unannounced intrusion into a dwelling—what § 3109 basically proscribes—is no less an unannounced intrusion whether officers break down a door, force open a chain lock on a partially open door, open a locked door by use of a passkey, or, as here, open a closed but unlocked door." The Court was careful to note, however, that entries obtained by ruse or deception do not constitute

---

[122]   523 U.S. 65, 118 S.Ct. 992 (1998).

[123]   540 U.S. 31, 124 S.Ct. 521 (2003).

[124]   357 U.S. 301, 78 S.Ct. 1190 (1958).

[125]   391 U.S. 585, 88 S.Ct. 1755 (1968).

a "breaking" within the meaning of § 3109; otherwise, a good deal of undercover work by police would be in violation of federal law.

(b) The Use of Deadly Force

Virtually every state has a statute or, at the least, a police regulation specifying the circumstances in which violence or the threat of violence may be used to apprehend an arrestee. The statute promulgated by the American Law Institute in its Model Code of Pre-Arraignment Procedure is exemplary. Section 120.7 provides that an officer "may use such force as is reasonably necessary to effect the arrest, to enter premises to effect the arrest, or to prevent the escape from custody of an arrested person." *Deadly* force is authorized when the arrest is for a felony, the use of such force "creates no substantial risk to innocent persons," and the officer "reasonably believes" that the felony involved the use or threat of use of deadly force or there is "substantial risk" that the arrestee will cause other deaths or serious bodily harm if deadly force is not employed.[126]

In *Tennessee v. Garner*,[127] the Supreme Court held that the Model Code's approach to the use of deadly force, or one essentially like it, is required by the Fourth Amendment. *Garner* declared unconstitutional a Tennessee statute that permitted an officer who has given notice of an intent to arrest a criminal suspect to "use all the necessary means to effect the arrest" if the suspect flees or forcibly resists. Construing "all necessary means" to include deadly force, the Court held that, under the Fourth Amendment's reasonableness requirement, such means cannot be used to effect an arrest unless (1) it is necessary to prevent escape and (2) the officer has probable cause to believe the suspect poses a significant threat of death or serious physical injury to the officer or others. The Court also agreed with the court of appeals ruling that because the officer in *Garner* had been "reasonably sure" the suspect was unarmed, young and of slight build, he acted unreasonably in shooting (and killing) the suspect as he fled over a fence at night in the backyard of a house he was suspected of burglarizing. Justice O'Connor's dissent, joined by Chief Justice Burger and Justice Rehnquist, argued that statutes like the one struck down by the majority "assist the police in apprehending suspected perpetrators of serious crimes and provide notice that a lawful police order to stop and submit to arrest may not be ignored with impunity."

The Court later held, in *Graham v. Connor*,[128] that all claims of excessive force— whether deadly or not, and whether involving arrest or some other type of seizure—are governed by the Fourth Amendment reasonableness requirement. This inquiry, stated the Court, requires looking into a number of factors, including: (1) the severity of the crime; (2) whether the suspect poses an immediate threat; and (3) whether he is actively resisting arrest or attempting to evade arrest by flight. Moreover, it "must embody allowance for the fact that police officers are often forced to make split-second judgments—in circumstances that are tense, uncertain, and rapidly evolving—about the amount of force that is necessary in a particular situation." The Court applied the factors outlined in *Graham* in *Scott v. Harris*,[129] where Officer Scott engaged in a high-speed

---

[126] American Law Institute, A Model Code of Pre-Arraignment Procedure § 120.7 (Official Draft 1975).

[127] 471 U.S. 1, 105 S.Ct. 1694 (1985).

[128] 490 U.S. 386, 109 S.Ct. 1865 (1989).

[129] 550 U.S. 382, 127 S.Ct. 1769 (2007). See also *Plumhoff v. Rickard*, 572 U.S. 765, 134 S.Ct. 2012 (2014) (refusing to find excessive force was used by officers who shot and killed Rickard and a companion as they drove away from a police stop, almost hit an officer, and were chased at over 100 miles per hour while passing over a dozen motorists).

chase of Harris and eventually pushed Harris's rear bumper, which caused Harris to lose control, go down an embankment, and roll over. Rendered a quadriplegic because of the crash, Harris sued Scott, among others, under *Garner*. The Court assumed that Scott had seized Harris, using deadly force. But it also found that this use of force was reasonable, because Harris had endangered innocent lives for the entire 10-mile car chase, given his weaving in and out of car lanes on two-lane roads and at high speed (over 80 miles per hour). To Harris's contention that the police could have avoided this danger simply by aborting the chase, the Court pointed out that Harris would not necessarily have known the chase was over had they aborted and that such a rule would *encourage* reckless driving by suspects trying to elude the police, because they would know that such driving would lead to police calling off the chase.

Even if excessive force is used, an officer is liable under § 1983 only if prior law has clearly established that the particular way force was used is excessive. For example, in *Brosseau v. Haugen*,[130] while the Court declined to decide whether Officer Brosseau used excessive force when she shot a man in the back as he tried to drive away from her, it granted her immunity from suit, given the split in lower court case law as to when shooting a fleeing driver to prevent harm to pedestrians and other drivers is reasonable.[131] Similarly, in *San Francisco v. Sheehan*,[132] the Court held that there was no clearly established Fourth Amendment rule regarding when police may shoot a person with mental illness, in this case one who threatened them with a knife after they have confronted her in her apartment, left the apartment because of threats, and then re-entered. Further, as with all other Fourth Amendment inquiries, the excessive force inquiry is objective, "without regard to [the officers'] underlying intent or motivation." And if the use of deadly force is reasonable, it is irrelevant that the use of such force was triggered by an unconstitutional action, such as a failure to knock and announce.[133]

Because all of these cases involved damages claims, still unclear is whether, if excessive force is used, any evidence thereby obtained is inadmissible. Arguably, the deterrent effect of damages, unlike in other contexts,[134] is sufficient here to obviate the need for the exclusionary rule.

(c) Mistake as to Identity

Occasionally police have probable cause to arrest one person but arrest another. In such circumstances, the arrest is valid for purposes of determining the admissibility of any evidence thereby discovered if the mistake was reasonable. This scenario describes the facts of *Hill v. California*,[135] where the police, having probable cause to arrest Hill, went to his apartment and knocked; the person who answered the door, one Miller, fit Hill's description and was arrested. Although at this point Miller provided identification showing he was not Hill, the Court noted that "aliases and false identifications are not uncommon" and that Miller had denied knowledge of firearms in the apartment although a pistol and loaded ammunition clip were in plain view in the room. Thus, the police

---

[130] 543 U.S. 194, 125 S.Ct. 596 (2004).

[131] Note that, by deciding the case this way, the split is still unresolved, a result the Court has encouraged. See § 2.05(a)(1).

[132] 575 U.S. 600, 135 S.Ct. 1765 (2015); see also *White v. Pauly*, ___ U.S. ___, 137 S.Ct. 548 (2017).

[133] *Cty. of Los Angeles v. Mendez*, ___ U.S. ___, 137 S.Ct. 1539 (2017).

[134] See § 2.05(a)(5). Because of the threat of damage suits, police departments have been relatively active in regulating the use of deadly force. Samuel Walker, Taming the System 25–28 (1993).

[135] 401 U.S. 797, 91 S.Ct. 1106 (1971).

could reasonably have believed Miller was Hill and anything seized pursuant to a search incident to the arrest was admissible against Hill.[136] The Court emphasized that "sufficient probability, not certainty, is the touchstone of reasonableness under the Fourth Amendment and on the record before us the officers' mistake was understandable and the arrest a reasonable response to the situation facing them at the time."

(d) Due Process Limitations

While the manner of executing an arrest is governed principally by the Fourth Amendment, some *attempts* to arrest are not "seizures" under that amendment and thus are regulated only by the Due Process Clause, if at all. This was the unanimous holding in *Sacramento v. Lewis*,[137] which involved a civil suit against a police officer whose high speed chase of a motorcycle ended with him running over and killing the motorcycle's 16-year-old passenger. Following precedent,[138] the Court held that a police chase (as opposed to the physical bumping involved in *Harris*) is not a seizure within the meaning of the Fourth Amendment, and that the "stop" in this case was not a seizure either, because it did not involve "governmental termination of freedom of movement through means intentionally applied" (in contrast, to *Harris*, where the bump was intentional).[139] Although the officer had intended to stop the motorcycle, he presumably had not meant to do so by running over its riders, so the Fourth Amendment was not applicable.

However, the Court also held that, because it protects the individual against arbitrary government action, the Due Process Clause *would* be applicable in such a case if the police action "shocked the conscience", the Court's standard way of describing the scope of substantive due process protection.[140] In some settings, the shock-the-conscience standard merely requires the plaintiff to show deliberate or reckless indifference by the government.[141] Given the difficult and quick decisions that must be made in high speed chases, however, the Court defined the standard in that context to require a showing that the chasing officer intended to harm the suspects physically or "to worsen their legal plight."

In *Lewis*, the Court held that no such intent was shown. The officer began chasing the motorcycle when it forced its way between his car and another car and sped away despite being told to stop; he followed it at speeds up to 100 miles per hour, sometimes as closely as 100 yards away, through largely residential neighborhoods. According to the Court, "[w]hile prudence would have repressed the [officer's] reaction, the officer's instinct was to do his job as a law enforcement officer, not to induce [the driver of the motorcycle's] lawlessness, or to terrorize, cause harm, or kill."

---

[136] Note that one could also conclude that Hill lacked standing to challenge Miller's arrest. See § 4.04.

[137] 523 U.S. 833, 118 S.Ct. 1708 (1998).

[138] *California v. Hodari D.*, 499 U.S. 621, 111 S.Ct. 1547 (1991), discussed in § 11.02(a).

[139] Quoting *Brower v. County of Inyo*, 489 U.S. 593, 109 S.Ct. 1378 (1989).

[140] See *Rochin v. California*, 342 U.S. 165, 72 S.Ct. 205 (1952), discussed in § 2.02.

[141] See, e.g., *Estelle v. Gamble*, 429 U.S. 97, 97 S.Ct. 285 (1976) (finding a violation of the Eighth Amendment when prison officials were deliberately indifferent to the medical needs of someone jailed while awaiting trial).

3.06   Conclusion

The following comments summarize the law of arrest:

(1)   An illegal arrest or detention standing alone has little if any impact on the subsequent prosecution. The citizen's remedy for an illegal arrest is a separate civil suit for damages. However, tangible evidence sought to be introduced as incident to a lawful arrest and other types of evidence (confessions, lineup identifications) that are "fruit" of an unlawful arrest will often be suppressed.

(2)   An "arrest," at a minimum, is some type of restriction of an individual's liberty by the police. If the police detention is an arrest or its equivalent, it must be based on probable cause; for other seizures, police usually only need a reasonable suspicion of criminal intent, as contemplated under *Terry v. Ohio.* Any action by the police that makes it impossible for an individual to leave and which makes use of the formal trappings of police detention (e.g., handcuffs, full body searches, or forced movement to the stationhouse or other "private" area for interrogation) will usually constitute an arrest, although handcuffing the occupant of a home subject to lawful search may be permissible on less than probable cause. Whether seizures involving lesser restraints are "arrests" depends upon the purpose, manner, location and duration of the detention, and the extent to which the police or the defendant are responsible for any prolongation of the detention that occurs.

(3)   Probable cause to arrest is an objectively-defined standard, which focuses on whether there are reasonable grounds to believe the suspect has committed an offense. If the factual basis for the probable cause determination is hearsay, highly relevant is the two-prong test of *Aguilar*—that is, (a) whether sufficient facts are available to inform a magistrate of how the informant reached his conclusions, and (b) whether sufficient indicia of the informant's reliability exist. But a deficiency in one prong may be compensated for by a strong showing with respect to the other prong; the ultimate test is whether, under the totality of the circumstances, probable cause exists. When the arresting officer's own observations are the basis for arrest, only indicia of criminality noted prior to and independently of the arrest (but including evidence obtained as the result of a legitimate patdown based on reasonable suspicion) may be relied upon to develop probable cause. A failure to identify oneself, when combined with reasonable suspicion of crime, may justify arrest under a statute so providing, as can proximity to known criminal activity and the results of an alert from an adequately trained dog. A reasonable mistake as to the facts or law underlying the probable cause determination does not render the arrest invalid, nor does arrest for a non-existent crime as long as an actual crime has been committed.

(4)   An arrest warrant is not required to effect an arrest in public when the arresting officer has probable cause to believe that a felony has been or is being committed by the arrestee or that a misdemeanor is being committed by the arrestee in his presence. However, a warrant is required to make an arrest inside a private dwelling, unless exigent circumstances are present. Moreover, police must obtain a *search* warrant before they may enter the house of a third party to effect a non-exigent arrest.

(5)   The police must knock and announce their purpose before entering to make an arrest, though these requirements may be dispensed with if they have reasonable suspicion that by following them the suspect might escape, harm someone or destroy evidence. The use of deadly force is permitted in making an arrest only if there is

probable cause to believe it is necessary to prevent both escape and significant harm to the police or others (although police are immune from suit unless previous caselaw has clearly established that the force used is excessive). The Due Process Clause may prohibit actions short of arrest that "shock the conscience."

BIBLIOGRAPHY

Clancy, Thomas K. What Constitutes an "Arrest" Within the Meaning of the Fourth Amendment? 48 Vill.L.Rev. 129 (2003).

Cloud, Morgan. Search and Seizure by the Numbers: The Drug Courier Profile and Judicial Review of Investigative Formulas. 65 B.U.L.Rev. 843 (1985).

Edwards, Matthew A. Posner's Pragmatism and *Payton* Home Arrests. 77 Wash.L.Rev. 299 (2002).

Karsch, Mitchell. Excessive Force and the Fourth Amendment: When Does Seizure End? 58 Fordham L.Rev. 823 (1990).

LaFave, Wayne. Probable Cause from Informants: The Effects of Murphy's Law on Fourth Amendment Adjudication. 1977 U.Ill.L.F. 1 (1977).

Lee, Cynthia. Reforming the Law on Police Use of Deadly Force: De-escalation, Pre-Seizure Conduct and Imperfect Self-Defense. 2018 Illinois Law Review 629.

Logan, Wayne. Cutting Cops Too Much Slack. 104 Georgetown Online Journal 87 (2015).

Maclin, Tracey. The *Pringle* Case's New Notion of Probable Cause: An Assault on *Di Re* and the Fourth Amendment. 2004 Cato Sup. Ct. Rev. 395.

Richardson, L. Song. Arrest Efficiency and the Fourth Amendment. 95 Minn. L. Rev. 2035 (2011).

Schroeder, William. Factoring the Seriousness of the Offense into Fourth Amendment Equations—Warrantless Entries into Premises: The Legacy of *Welsh* v. Wisconsin. 38 U.Kan.L.Rev. 439 (1990).

Simeone, Joseph J. Duty, Power, and Limits on Police Use of Deadly Force in Missouri. 21 St.Louis U.Pub.L.Rev. 123 (2002).

Chapter 4

INTRODUCTION TO THE LAW OF SEARCHES: A FRAMEWORK FOR ANALYZING WHEN "SEARCHES" OCCUR AND WHEN THEY ARE REASONABLE

4.01   Introduction

This chapter attempts to make some sense out of search and seizure law apart from the law of arrest and other detentions. In other words, this chapter is concerned with searches, and with seizures of evidence. The bare words of the Fourth Amendment require only that such searches and seizures be reasonable and that, if and when a warrant is issued, it must be based on "probable cause," "supported by oath or affirmation," and particularly describe what is to be searched or seized. Over the years, the Supreme Court has added several layers of interpretation to this basic text. Without a framework for analyzing these decisions, one can quickly become lost in a maze of cases that seem neither consistent nor comprehensible.

This analysis can be divided into two stages. The first stage involves defining the types of activity that trigger the protections of the Fourth Amendment. On the assumption the Fourth Amendment is implicated, the second stage concerns the nature of the protection to be afforded. This chapter takes a comprehensive look at Stage I of the analysis. In addition, it provides a brief overview of Stage II, to assist in understanding the scope of the Fourth Amendment's protections. These protections—the warrant requirement and the specific situations in which it may be ignored—will then be discussed in greater detail in the chapters to follow.

In answering the question posed in Stage I—i.e., when is the Fourth Amendment implicated by the evidence-gathering activity in question?—three elements must be considered: whether the intrusion is the product of governmental action, whether it breaches society's "reasonable expectations of privacy," and whether it breaches the "legitimate expectations of privacy" of the individual intruded upon (the "standing" question). The Fourth Amendment is not implicated unless each of these elements is present.

4.02   The Definition of Governmental Conduct

The Fourth Amendment's proscription against illegal searches and seizures, like other Bill of Rights guarantees,[1] has been judicially construed to apply only to governmental conduct. Thus, when a *private* individual illegally acquires evidence that the government later seeks to use in a criminal prosecution, the Fourth Amendment is not violated.

The inapplicability of the Fourth Amendment to searches by private individuals was first recognized by the Supreme Court in *Burdeau v. McDowell.*[2] In that case, private

---

[1]   See generally, *Adamson v. California*, 332 U.S. 46, 67 S.Ct. 1672 (1947).

[2]   256 U.S. 465, 41 S.Ct. 574 (1921).

individuals, at the instigation of McDowell's former employer, illegally entered and searched McDowell's business office and seized certain papers. These papers were later turned over to Burdeau, a Special Assistant to the Attorney General of the United States, who intended to use them as evidence in a criminal prosecution against McDowell for fraudulent use of the mails. McDowell sought a court order for the return of the papers so that they could not be used against him. The district court granted his petition. The Supreme Court reversed, stating that the Fourth Amendment's "origin and history clearly show that it was intended as a restraint upon the activities of sovereign authority, and was not intended to be a limitation upon other than governmental agencies[.]"

The holding and rationale found in *Burdeau* have retained their validity through the years. In *Coolidge v. New Hampshire*,[3] the Supreme Court stated that if a private citizen "wholly on [his] own initiative" turns over certain articles to the police for use in a criminal investigation, "[t]here can be no doubt under existing law that the articles would later [be] admissible in evidence." And in *Walter v. United States*,[4] decided in 1980, the Court held that "a wrongful search and seizure conducted by a private party does not violate the Fourth Amendment and . . . does not deprive the government of the right to use evidence that it has acquired [from the third party] lawfully."[5]

In ascertaining whether governmental conduct has occurred for purposes of the Fourth Amendment, three questions commonly reoccur: (1) who is a government official?; (2) when is a private citizen, to use *Coolidge's* words, not acting "wholly on his own initiative," but rather at the behest of a government official?; and (3) once it is established that an action is purely private, what subsequent governmental action does the private search authorize? A fourth, related issue is when, if ever, actions by a *foreign* government implicate the Fourth Amendment.

(a) Government Officials

Clearly the actions of police officers employed by an American governmental entity are covered by the Fourth Amendment. However, the police represent only a small portion of those government officials whose primary or secondary task is enforcement of criminal and other laws. The Supreme Court has indicated that, even if their actions rarely or never result in criminal prosecution, the Fourth Amendment governs the actions of these other law enforcement officials as well, albeit often with less rigor than the police.[6] Thus, in *Camara v. Municipal Court*,[7] the Court held that searches by regulatory officials conducting safety and health inspections are subject to Fourth Amendment requirements. Since these searches can involve significant intrusions, it would be "anomalous to say that the individual and his private property are fully protected by the Fourth Amendment only when the individual is suspected of criminal behavior." The Court has explicitly extended this rationale to many other types of

---

3   403 U.S. 443, 91 S.Ct. 2022 (1971).

4   447 U.S. 649, 100 S.Ct. 2395 (1980).

5   See also, *State v. Oldaker*, 172 W.Va. 258, 304 S.E.2d 843 (1983) (search by landlord not subject to Fourth Amendment); *Commonwealth v. Goldhammer*, 322 Pa.Super. 242, 469 A.2d 601 (1983) (evidence procured by witness and attorney not subject to Fourth Amendment).

6   Thus, in virtually all the cases discussed below, the Court, after finding that the Fourth Amendment applied, relaxed the probable cause requirement, and in most it eliminated the warrant requirement as well. See generally, Chapter 13.

7   387 U.S. 523, 87 S.Ct. 1727 (1967).

government inspectors.[8] Similarly, the Court has held that government agencies pursuing internal, work-related investigations of their employees must abide by the Constitution.[9]

Public school teachers are also included within the rubric of government actors for purposes of the Fourth Amendment. Although some lower courts had held that teachers act *in loco parentis*, and thus that their searches of children should be no more restricted than those conducted by parents,[10] the Supreme Court, in *New Jersey v. T.L.O.*,[11] rejected this position, stating that "[t]oday's public school officials do not merely exercise authority voluntarily conferred on them by individual parents; rather, they act in furtherance of publicly mandated educational and disciplinary policies." Moreover, pointed out the Court, it had already found teachers answerable under both the Fifth Amendment[12] and the Due Process Clause.[13]

A more difficult question is whether the Fourth Amendment governs the actions of persons whom the government does not employ or influence in any other direct manner, but who conduct law enforcement-type searches and seizures on a routine basis as part of their job. Most courts have held that such individuals need not abide by constitutional strictures, whether they be store detectives,[14] security guards,[15] or insurance inspectors.[16] However, some have argued that, where the primary purpose of the privately paid personnel is to supplant the public police, then the Fourth Amendment should apply.[17]

(b) Government Agents

A purely private person may nonetheless become a "government official" for purposes of the Fourth Amendment if he acts at the behest of a bona fide official, as defined above. As *Coolidge* put it, "[t]he test . . . is whether [the private citizen] in light of all the circumstances of the case, must be regarded as having acted as an 'instrument' or agent of the state." Thus, where government officials actively join in the private search,[18] or instruct the private individual to conduct it,[19] there is sufficient state action.

---

[8]   See, e.g., *Michigan v. Tyler*, 436 U.S. 499, 98 S.Ct. 1942 (1978) (fire inspectors); *Marshall v. Barlow's, Inc.*, 436 U.S. 307, 98 S.Ct. 1816 (1978) (OSHA inspectors); *Donovan v. Dewey*, 452 U.S. 594, 101 S.Ct. 2534 (1981) (federal mine inspectors).

[9]   *O'Connor v. Ortega*, 480 U.S. 709, 107 S.Ct. 1492 (1987).

[10]   See, e.g., *R.C.M. v. State*, 660 S.W.2d 552 (Tex.App. 1983).

[11]   469 U.S. 325, 105 S.Ct. 733 (1985).

[12]   *Tinker v. Des Moines Independent Community School District*, 393 U.S. 503, 89 S.Ct. 733 (1969).

[13]   *Goss v. Lopez*, 419 U.S. 565, 95 S.Ct. 729 (1975).

[14]   *Gillett v. State*, 588 S.W.2d 361 (Tex.Crim.App. 1979); *People v. Horman*, 22 N.Y.2d 378, 292 N.Y.S.2d 874, 239 N.E.2d 625 (1968), cert. denied 393 U.S. 1057, 89 S.Ct. 698 (1969).

[15]   *Stanfield v. State*, 666 P.2d 1294 (Okl.Crim. 1983); *People v. Trimarco*, 41 Misc.2d 775, 245 N.Y.S.2d 795 (1963).

[16]   *Lester v. State*, 145 Ga.App. 847, 244 S.E.2d 880 (1978); *State v. Hughes*, 8 Ariz.App. 366, 446 P.2d 472 (1968), cert. denied 395 U.S. 940, 89 S.Ct. 2010 (1969).

[17]   See, e.g., *People v. Mangiefico*, 25 Cal.App.3d 1041, 102 Cal.Rptr. 449 (1972); John M. Burkoff, *Not So Private Searches and the Constitution*, 66 Cornell L. Rev. 627 (1981); Comment, 38 U.Chi.L.Rev. 555, 581–82 (1971) (arguing an analogy to *Marsh v. Alabama*, 326 U.S. 501, 66 S.Ct. 276 (1946), which held that the actions of a private company in running its own town are subject to the same constraints as the government of a public town).

[18]   See, e.g., *State v. Cox*, 100 N.M. 667, 674 P.2d 1127 (App. 1983); *Corngold v. United States*, 367 F.2d 1 (9th Cir. 1966).

[19]   See, e.g., *Machlan v. State*, 248 Ind. 218, 225 N.E.2d 762 (1967).

Analogously, the Supreme Court has indicated that when alcohol and drug tests carried out by a private employer are mandated or strongly encouraged by government regulations, the Fourth Amendment applies.[20]

On the other hand, where a government official does not "direct" the private action, but merely provides information that leads to it, courts often reach a different result. For instance, in *People v. Boettner*,[21] the court upheld a search by private university officials based on information supplied by the police, emphasizing that the private search had been conducted without the knowledge of the police, who had been proceeding with their own investigation. In *United States v. Lamar*,[22] a police officer notified an airline employee that he was interested in a certain unclaimed bag, believing it to belong to a person suspected of various narcotics violations. In the presence of the officer, the employee searched the bag for identification and found what he and the police officer suspected was heroin. Despite the officer's involvement in the search, the court found the Fourth Amendment not implicated because the officer had neither requested nor physically participated in the search, and the employee "was acting in the usual and ordinary course of his customary duties when he searched the bag for identification and address purposes."[23]

The result in the latter case is especially suspect because it encourages the police to use private parties as a means of evading Fourth Amendment requirements. Arguably, it runs counter to the Supreme Court's decision in *Elkins v. United States*,[24] which held, before *Mapp v. Ohio*[25] applied the exclusionary rule to the states, that the federal exclusionary rule should apply to evidence obtained in a search by state police when the federal and state police have a general understanding that the evidence would be used in federal prosecutions.

(c) What a Private Search Authorizes

A third area of concern occurs when the government, rather than directing or triggering the private search, later seeks to benefit from it. The Supreme Court's approach has been to look closely at whether the subsequent government action exceeds the scope of the private search. Thus, in *Walter v. United States*,[26] the Court invalidated a conviction which was based on the warrantless viewing of obscene films by the FBI, even though the packages containing the films had been opened by private parties and the markings on the canisters revealed that they contained obscene material. Since the private parties had not actually viewed the films, the FBI agents were constitutionally prohibited from viewing them without a warrant. However, the Court also accepted the notion that a government search which is not "a significant expansion of the search which had been previously conducted" is not violative of the Fourth Amendment.

---

[20]   *Skinner v. Railway Labor Executives' Ass'n*, 489 U.S. 602, 109 S.Ct. 1402 (1989). Although the Court noted that the regulations in *Skinner* left some testing to the discretion of the private railway, it pointed out that the law strongly encouraged and endorsed the tests and conferred upon the Federal Railway Administration the right to certain samples.

[21]   80 Misc.2d 3, 362 N.Y.S.2d 365 (1974).

[22]   545 F.2d 488 (5th Cir. 1977), cert. denied 430 U.S. 959, 97 S.Ct. 1609 (1977).

[23]   See also, *United States v. Morgan*, 744 F.2d 1215 (6th Cir. 1984) (same holding on similar facts).

[24]   364 U.S. 206, 80 S.Ct. 1437 (1960), discussed in § 2.02.

[25]   367 U.S. 643, 81 S.Ct. 1684 (1961).

[26]   447 U.S. 649, 100 S.Ct. 2395 (1980).

In *United States v. Jacobsen*,[27] a majority of the Court explicitly affirmed this latter rule. In *Jacobsen*, two Federal Express employees opened a package that had been damaged by a forklift and found five or six pieces of crumpled newspaper covering a tube about 10 inches long. They cut open the tube and discovered a series of four zip-lock plastic bags that contained white powder. After notifying the Drug Enforcement Administration of their find, they placed the bags back in the tube, and the tube and newspapers back in the box. Justice Stevens, writing for a six-member majority, sanctioned the subsequent warrantless search by a DEA official because his removal of the tube from the box and removal of the plastic bags from the tube "enabled the agent to learn nothing that had not previously been learned during the private search."

Carried to its logical extreme, this language would severely detract from the warrant requirement. Information about criminal evidence that the police do not directly acquire themselves always comes from private parties. Thus, under a loose interpretation of *Jacobsen*, police could conduct warrantless searches any time a private party has already done so and told the police about his discovery. In an attempt to avoid this result, the majority placed several limitations on its holding. It emphasized that the Federal Express employees had only recently examined the package, that they had invited the federal agent to view its contents, and that the agents had already learned a great deal about the contents of the package from the employees, "all of which was consistent with what they could see." Most importantly, the agent who searched the package had "a virtual certainty that nothing else of significance [other than the contraband] was in the package and that a manual inspection of the tube and its contents would not tell him anything more than he already had been told." Even with these restrictions, as Justice White pointed out in a separate opinion, it would be difficult to distinguish this case from "one in which the private party knew to a certainty that a container *concealed* contraband and nothing else as a result of conversations with its owner." Moreover, there is nothing in the majority opinion explicitly limiting its holding to searches of containers.[28] The better approach, as Justice White suggested, is to permit warrantless searches only of those items the police find in plain view as a result of the private party's search.[29]

(d) Searches in Foreign Countries

It is well-established that a search of an American citizen conducted in a foreign country by foreign police does not implicate the Fourth Amendment, even if the search is at the behest of, or based upon information provided by, American authorities.[30] This stance is generally justified on the ground that foreign police cannot be expected to know or abide by American law, nor will they be deterred by American sanctions. But if the United States government is *heavily* involved in the search, it would seem that, for reasons similar to those given above in connection with domestic searches by private agents of the police, the fact that it takes place outside American borders should not render the Constitution ineffective.

---

[27]   466 U.S. 109, 104 S.Ct. 1652 (1984).

[28]   Indeed, the majority pointed out that "warrantless searches of [letters and other sealed packages] are presumptively unreasonable," yet went on to conclude that they too could be searched under the circumstances present in *Jacobsen*.

[29]   Note that where a private party has legitimate access to the searched area, the issue in *Jacobsen* could be mooted by obtaining that person's consent. See § 12.04.

[30]   *United States v. Rose*, 570 F.2d 1358 (9th Cir. 1978).

If the target of the foreign search is an alien, even a search conducted solely by American officers is not likely to trigger Fourth Amendment protection, unless the foreign resident has a "substantial connection with our country." This was the holding of the Supreme Court, in *United States v. Verdugo-Urquidez*,[31] where DEA agents, assisted by Mexican authorities, conducted warrantless searches of two Mexican residences of a Mexican citizen who had been turned over to United States authorities two days earlier. Since, according to the Court, the defendant's sole connection with the United States was his detention, and this was not a "voluntary attachment," the defendant was not one of the "people" protected by the Fourth Amendment, a word that "refers to a class of persons who are part of a national community or who have otherwise developed sufficient connection with this community to be considered part of that community." The reach of *Verdugo-Urquidez* is unclear, however, since two members of the six-member majority emphasized that, even had the searchers wanted to comply with American law, there was no reasonable way they could have done so, given the absence of magistrates in the locality and the fact that American magistrates lacked jurisdiction. Under circumstances in which the functional equivalent of Fourth Amendment protections could be achieved, a different result might be reached by the Court. Many lower courts, however, have interpreted *Verdugo-Urquidez* broadly, denying Fourth Amendment rights even to aliens inside the country.[32]

4.03   The Definition of "Search" and "Seizure"

Not every attempt by government officials to obtain evidence is regulated by the language of the Fourth Amendment. Unless the investigative action involves a "search" or "seizure", as those terms are defined by the Court, the Fourth Amendment is not implicated. One might define the word "search" as a layperson would, to mean any action by government officials that involves looking for evidence of a violation of the law. By the same token, a "seizure" of something would mean an assertion of control over it for the purpose of using it in evidence. In defining the scope of the Fourth Amendment, however, the Supreme Court has chosen not to follow the semantic route. Instead, other considerations, primarily relating to expectations of privacy and a perceived need for fewer strictures on the police, have come into play.

Originally under the Court's cases, a "search" occurred solely when there was a physical intrusion into one of the "constitutionally protected areas" set out in the Fourth Amendment: persons, houses, papers and effects.[33] Thus, whereas police entry into a home (or the functional equivalent thereof)[34] was clearly a search, use of an electronic device to overhear conversations in the home was not, if it did not result in a trespass on private property.[35] Then, in *Katz v. United States*,[36] the Court, in an opinion by Justice Stewart, rejected the trespass approach to Fourth Amendment protection as both over- and under-inclusive:

---

[31]   494 U.S. 259, 110 S.Ct. 1056 (1990).

[32]   James Connell & René Valladares, *Search and Seizure Protections for Undocumented Aliens: The Territoriality and Voluntary Presence Principles in Fourth Amendment Law*, 34 Am. Crim. L. Rev. 1293 (1997).

[33]   *Silverman v. United States*, 365 U.S. 505, 81 S.Ct. 679 (1961).

[34]   See, e.g., *Stoner v. California*, 376 U.S. 483, 84 S.Ct. 889 (1964) (hotel room protected); *Amos v. United States*, 255 U.S. 313, 41 S.Ct. 266 (1921) (stores protected).

[35]   *Olmstead v. United States*, 277 U.S. 438, 48 S.Ct. 564 (1928) (tapping of telephone wires outside suspects' premises not a search).

[36]   389 U.S. 347, 88 S.Ct. 507 (1967).

[T]he Fourth Amendment protects people, not places. What a person knowingly exposes to the public, even in his own home or office, is not a subject of Fourth Amendment protections. . . . But what he seeks to preserve as private, even in an area accessible to the public, may be constitutionally protected.

Applying this "exposure-to-the-public" idea to the facts of *Katz*, the Court held that words spoken in a public telephone booth overheard on an electronic eavesdropping device were constitutionally protected even though the wording of the Fourth Amendment does not encompass phone booths and no trespass of private property had occurred. According to the Court, "a person who occupies [a phone booth], shuts the door behind him, and pays the toll that permits him to place a call is surely entitled to assume that the words he utters into the mouthpiece will not be broadcast to the world."

While the majority in *Katz* focused on the degree of exposure to the public, the Court's more recent cases have come to rely primarily on a slightly different formulation, first advanced in Justice Harlan's concurring opinion in *Katz*. While Harlan agreed with the majority that the Fourth Amendment protects "people," he also felt that it was hard to talk about the scope of that protection without referring to a place. Thus he suggested that the focus of the Amendment should be whether one's subjective and reasonable expectations of privacy in the place searched have been infringed by a police action. In a later decision, he wisely discarded the subjective component of his formulation, noting that if a person's beliefs about the privacy afforded him in a given place were relevant, the scope of the Fourth Amendment could be manipulated by the government, since it would depend upon what people are used to, not what they should be entitled to expect.[37] The expectation of privacy test, when relied upon by the Court, is now solely objective.

Despite *Katz*, the Court has not entirely abandoned property as the metric for defining searches under the Fourth Amendment. Many of its expectation-of-privacy cases are entirely consistent with a property-based approach to the Amendment. Moreover, in a few relatively recent cases, the Court has explicitly relied on property concepts in defining the Amendment's scope.[38] Property concepts also are the predominant method of defining "seizure" for Fourth Amendment purposes. Although the Court has occasionally referred to privacy interests in this setting,[39] usually it has focused on whether the government action deprives the individual of a "possessory interest" in the item.[40]

The following discussion fleshes out the Supreme Court's interpretation of these various definitions of the Fourth Amendment's scope in a number of contexts.

(a) Undercover and "Institutional" Agents

Under the old trespass doctrine, the Court decided several cases involving the use of undercover agents. In each, the issue was whether the defendant consented to the action taken by the agent. If so, then no trespass occurred and the Fourth Amendment was not implicated; if not, and the area searched was a constitutionally protected one,

---

[37] *United States v. White*, 401 U.S. 745, 91 S.Ct. 1122 (1971) (Harlan, J., dissenting).

[38] See § 4.03(f)(1) & (2).

[39] See § 4.03(b) (noting reliance on privacy language in addressing the seizure of voice and handwriting exemplars).

[40] See, e.g., *Hale v. Henkel*, 201 U.S. 43, 26 S.Ct. 370 (1906) (defining seizure as "a forcible dispossession of the owner.").

the Fourth Amendment applied. Thus, in *Gouled v. United States*,[41] the Court found a search occurred when an undercover agent looked through the defendant's desk; although the defendant had invited the agent into his office, he had not "consented" to him rummaging through his papers. In contrast, in *Lewis v. United States*,[42] the Court found the Fourth Amendment did not apply to an undercover agent's entry into a home for the purpose of completing a drug transaction, when the owner had invited him there over the phone.

The Court's analysis did not change when the police were after private conversations rather than a tangible object. The same term as *Lewis*, the Court held in *Hoffa v. United States*[43] that the Fourth Amendment does not prevent using acquaintances of the defendant to obtain information, so long as the defendant is aware the acquaintance is listening. Although the conversation "seized" in *Hoffa* took place in the defendant's private suite, a "constitutionally protected area," the agent—a union official who spent considerable time with Hoffa—"was not a surreptitious eavesdropper," but someone who "was in the suite by invitation, and every conversation which he heard was either directed to him or knowingly carried on in his presence."

A harder question under the trespass doctrine was whether the undercover agent could wear an electronic eavesdropping device. As Justice Burton pointed out in his dissent to *On Lee v. United States*[44] the addition of a concealed recorder "amount[s] to [the agent] surreptitiously bringing [the police] with him." Yet the five-member majority in *On Lee* held that because the defendant invited the agent who was "bugged" into his laundry and voluntarily conversed with him, no search occurred. The listening device merely improved the accuracy of the government's evidence. In a case involving substantially similar facts, *Lopez v. United States*,[45] the Court later affirmed *On Lee*, 6–3, again on the ground that no trespass occurred.

All of these cases were decided before *Katz* repudiated the trespass doctrine. Under either the "public exposure" or "reasonable expectation of privacy" analysis announced in that case, the argument for characterizing at least some types of undercover activity as searches becomes stronger. In particular, *Hoffa* (where the agent was the defendant's compatriot) and *On Lee* (where the agent was a former employee) are suspect. Private conversations are not "knowingly exposed to the public," nor is it unreasonable to expect that one's acquaintances are not government informers. The argument for applying the Fourth Amendment in *Lewis* is weaker, since the agent there was a stranger to the defendant and the intrusion was limited to that necessary to complete a drug sale, but even in that case the defendant was not knowingly exposing the privacy of his home to the public at large.

Nonetheless, on two occasions,[46] the post-*Katz* Court reaffirmed *On Lee*, the trespass case with the furthest reach, thus implicitly confirming the other cases as well. More understandably, it has also held, in *Maryland v. Macon*,[47] that an undercover

---

[41]   255 U.S. 298, 41 S.Ct. 261 (1921).

[42]   385 U.S. 206, 87 S.Ct. 424 (1966).

[43]   385 U.S. 293, 87 S.Ct. 408 (1966).

[44]   343 U.S. 747, 72 S.Ct. 967 (1952).

[45]   373 U.S. 427, 83 S.Ct. 1381 (1963).

[46]   *United States v. Caceres*, 440 U.S. 741, 99 S.Ct. 1465 (1979); *United States v. White*, 401 U.S. 745, 91 S.Ct. 1122 (1971) (plurality opinion).

[47]   472 U.S. 463, 105 S.Ct. 2778 (1985).

agent's entry of an adult bookstore during regular store hours and his examination of materials offered for sale there was not a "search," nor was his purchase of allegedly obscene publications a "seizure," given the public, consensual nature of the transactions involved. As a result of these decisions, most undercover activity is unregulated under the Fourth Amendment.

Even more questionable than its reaffirmance of the trespass cases are the Court's post-*Katz* cases permitting state use of everyday institutions as "undercover" agents, in what has come to be called the Court's "third party doctrine."[48] In *United States v. Miller*,[49] the Court held that a subpoena of records containing financial information voluntarily surrendered to a bank is not a search for Fourth Amendment purposes. The Court relied heavily on its undercover cases for the proposition that a "depositor takes the risk, in revealing his affairs to another, that the information will be conveyed by that person to the government . . . even if the information is revealed on the assumption that it will be used only for a limited purpose and the confidence placed in the third party will not be betrayed." Similarly, in *Smith v. Maryland*,[50] the Court held that a person does not have a reasonable expectation of privacy in the identity of phone numbers he calls, because he knows or should know that these numbers are recorded as a matter of routine by the phone company.

The voluntary "assumption of risk" rationale, however plausible it may be in the undercover agent cases, is wholly unrealistic in *Miller* and *Smith*, given the modern-day necessity of using the banking and telephone systems and most people's assumption that the information given to those systems will *not* be relayed to third parties without their explicit consent. Congress has passed legislation that requires the government to obtain a subpoena or court order before bank and phone records may be obtained,[51] and several state courts have rejected the reasoning of *Miller* and *Smith*, instead requiring a demonstration of reasonable suspicion or probable cause before such information must be handed over.[52] Nonetheless, in most jurisdictions documents in the possession of third parties are not protected by the Fourth Amendment.[53]

In a case purporting to apply solely to its facts, the Court more recently signaled a willingness to reconsider this view. In *Carpenter v. United States*,[54] five members of the Court held that a warrant is required to obtain cell site location information from the defendant's common carrier, at least when, as in *Carpenter*, multiple locations on multiple days are obtained. The government relied on *Miller* and *Smith* in arguing that the location data constituted a "business record" of the carrier that contained information knowingly surrendered by the defendant when he carried his cellphone. But Chief Justice Roberts' opinion for the Court distinguished those cases on two grounds.

---

[48] Orin Kerr, *The Case for the Third Party Doctrine*, 107 Mich. L. Rev. 561 (2009).

[49] 425 U.S. 435, 96 S.Ct. 1619 (1976).

[50] 442 U.S. 735, 99 S.Ct. 2577 (1979).

[51] Right to Financial Privacy Act, 12 U.S.C.A. § 3401 (permitting challenge of a subpoena for records unless notice would "seriously jeopardize the investigation"); Electronic Communications Privacy Act, 18 U.S.C.A. § 3121 (requiring a court order verifying that phone records are "relevant" to an ongoing investigation).

[52] See Stephen E. Henderson, *Learning from All Fifty States: How to Apply the Fourth Amendment and Its State Analogs to Protect Third Party Information from Unreasonable Search*, 55 Cath. U. L. Rev. 373 (2006).

[53] For more on the extent to which the Constitution protects papers, whether held by third parties or by the target, see §§ 15.06 and 23.05(a).

[54] ___ U.S. ___, 138 S.Ct. 2206 (2018).

First, "[t]here is a world of difference between the limited types of personal information addressed in *Smith* and *Miller* and the exhaustive chronicle of location information casually collected by wireless carriers today." Second, "[c]ell phone location information is not truly 'shared' as one normally understands the term [because] cell phones and the services they provide are . . . indispensable to participation in modern society" and because "there is no way to avoid leaving behind a trail of location data;" accordingly, Roberts stated, "in no meaningful sense does the user voluntarily 'assume[ ] the risk' of turning over a comprehensive dossier of his physical movements." While Roberts emphasized the holding in *Carpenter* does not necessarily apply to other surveillance techniques or business records, all of the dissents (filed separately by Kennedy, Alito, Thomas and Gorsuch) pointed out that much of what he says about cell phone location information could also apply to bank or phone records that *Miller* and *Smith* allow the government to obtain in virtually any quantity so long as they are relevant to an investigation.[55]

(b) Physical Characteristics

A second category of cases in which the Court has found that the Fourth Amendment is not implicated involves the "seizure" of a person's physical attributes. In *United States v. Dionisio*,[56] a grand jury subpoenaed about twenty persons, including Dionisio, to give voice exemplars for identification purposes. The Court, relying on *Katz's* public exposure doctrine, dismissed Dionisio's Fourth Amendment claim, stating:

> [t]he physical characteristics of a person's voice, its tone and manner, as opposed to the content of a specific conversation, are constantly exposed to the public. Like a man's facial characteristics, or handwriting, his voice is repeatedly produced for others to hear. No person can have a reasonable expectation that others will not know the sound of his voice, any more than he can reasonably expect that his face will be a mystery to the world.

Not surprisingly, given the above language, in *United States v. Mara*,[57] a companion case to *Dionisio*, the Court reached the same conclusion with respect to a person's handwriting. Presumably, any physical characteristic that is discernable by mere observation could be included among those things a person holds out to the public.[58]

It should be noted, however, that the seizure of the *person* necessary to obtain evidence of physical characteristics may have to meet certain Fourth Amendment requirements. *Dionisio* and *Mara* both held that the investigative traditions of the grand jury and the minimal intrusion associated with a grand jury subpoena allow relaxation of normal Fourth Amendment restrictions even in this respect.[59] But if the detention involves a forcible police seizure from the home, a warrant or at least a court order based

---

[55]   See § 23.04(a)(1) describing Fourth Amendment cases limiting the scope of the subpoena power.

[56]   410 U.S. 1, 93 S.Ct. 764 (1973).

[57]   410 U.S. 19, 93 S.Ct. 774 (1973).

[58]   Cf. *Davis v. Mississippi*, 394 U.S. 721, 89 S.Ct. 1394 (1969) (discussion of Fourth Amendment implications of fingerprinting). In *Cupp v. Murphy*, 412 U.S. 291, 93 S.Ct. 2000 (1973), respondent was held to have a Fourth Amendment right to privacy with respect to the scrapings from his fingernails, because "the search . . . went beyond mere 'physical characteristics . . . constantly exposed to the public.'" The characteristics of the scrapings could not have been obtained by mere observation.

[59]   See § 3.02(e).

on reasonable suspicion may be required, even if the sole purpose for the detention is to obtain evidence of physical characteristics.[60]

(c) Open Fields and Curtilage

While the home and private office are protected by the Fourth Amendment, areas adjacent to these localities may not be. In the pre-*Katz* case of *Hester v. United States*,[61] the Court upheld a warrantless search conducted by officers who were admittedly trespassing on the defendant's land, on the ground that the property searched was not "curtilage" immediately surrounding the defendant's home, but rather part of the "open fields." In *Oliver v. United States*,[62] decided after *Katz*, the Court reaffirmed the open fields doctrine in two cases involving entry onto private property which was fenced in and marked by "No Trespassing" signs. Justice Powell, writing for a 6–3 majority, held that landowners do not possess a legitimate expectation of privacy in fields that are far removed from the landowner's home and "curtilage," even if efforts have been made to maintain some degree of isolation. According to Powell:

> [O]pen fields do not provide the setting for those intimate activities that the Amendment is intended to shelter from government interference or surveillance. There is no societal interest in protecting the privacy of those activities, such as the cultivation of crops, that occur in open fields. Moreover, as a practical matter these lands usually are accessible to the public and the police in ways that a home, office or commercial structure would not be. It is not generally true that fences or no trespassing signs effectively bar the public from viewing open fields in rural areas.

Oliver involved land far removed from the defendant's home. The Court has also held that property immediately surrounding the defendant's premises (the "curtilage") is not protected by the Fourth Amendment, at least when it is viewed from the air. In *Dow Chemical Co. v. United States*,[63] the Environmental Protection Agency hired a commercial aerial photographer, using highly sophisticated equipment, to photograph the defendant's plant from the air. While recognizing that the area photographed did not fall squarely within the "open fields" doctrine, Chief Justice Burger, writing for the Court, found that it did not constitute curtilage either, apparently due to its size (the plant consisted of 2,000 acres). Yet, as Justice Powell, the author of *Oliver*, pointed out in dissent, the area was immediately adjacent to the plant, and well defined by fences and an elaborate security system designed to discourage competitors from discovering trade secrets. Perhaps realizing that a direct analogy to *Oliver* was not apposite, Burger also sought to justify the decision by pointing out that the aerial photography had not involved a physical intrusion, and that while it permitted better viewing of the premises than the naked eye, it did not reveal identifiable human faces, secret documents or any interior that implicated privacy interests. Finally, he pointed out that commercial enterprises had traditionally been accorded less privacy protection.[64]

---

[60]   See *Hayes v. Florida*, 470 U.S. 811, 105 S.Ct. 1643 (1985), discussed in § 3.02(d).

[61]   265 U.S. 57, 44 S.Ct. 445 (1924).

[62]   466 U.S. 170, 104 S.Ct. 1735 (1984).

[63]   476 U.S. 227, 106 S.Ct. 1819 (1986).

[64]   See § 4.03(g). See also, *Air Pollution Variance Bd. v. Western Alfalfa Corp.*, 416 U.S. 861, 94 S.Ct. 2114 (1974) (Fourth Amendment not implicated by outdoor pollution test conducted on "open fields" belonging to defendant company).

In *California v. Ciraolo*[65] the aerial photography occurred after police received an anonymous phone tip that the defendant had marijuana in his back yard and found they were unable to see it because of two high fences. The plane flew roughly 1,000 feet above the yard and a photograph was taken. This time, Chief Justice Burger conceded that the area under surveillance was "curtilage" and thus normally should be accorded Fourth Amendment protection. But, as he had in *Dow Chemical*, he found relevant the manner in which the surveillance was conducted. He pointed out that the police observation took place within public navigable airspace and that anyone casually flying over the property could have spotted the marijuana with the naked eye.

Similar in vein to *Ciraolo* and *Dow Chemical* is *Florida v. Riley*,[66] which involved police use of a helicopter hovering at 400 feet to discover marijuana in a backyard greenhouse. In an opinion by Justice White, four members of the Court held that this flight did not constitute a search, for three reasons. First, helicopter flights at this height do not violate Federal Aviation Administration regulations (which limit flights by fixed wing aircraft to 500 feet but permit helicopter flights at any altitude "if operation is conducted without hazard to persons or property on the surface.") Second, there was "nothing in the record or before us to suggest that helicopters flying at 400 feet are sufficiently rare in this country" to justify the defendant's claim of a reasonable expectation of privacy. Third, the helicopter did not interfere with the defendant's "normal use" of the greenhouse or reveal "intimate details connected with the use of the home or curtilage." Justice O'Connor joined the plurality because she believed that public use of airspace at 400 feet and above is "considerable". But she emphasized that public use of airspace below that altitude "may be sufficiently rare that police surveillance from such altitudes would violate reasonable expectations of privacy, despite compliance with FAA air safety regulations." Thus, a majority of the Court might be willing to limit warrantless overflights to the 400 foot region.

Although, after *Ciraolo* and *Riley*, aerial surveillance of the home's curtilage is largely ungoverned by the Fourth Amendment, *physical* intrusion into the curtilage remains a search. One year after *Ciraolo*, the Court established criteria for determining when an area is within the curtilage of the home, rather than in the open fields. In *United States v. Dunn*,[67] the Court held that curtilage questions "should be resolved with particular reference to four factors:"

> the proximity of the area claimed to be curtilage to the home, whether the area is included within an enclosure surrounding the home, the nature of the uses to which the area is put, and the steps taken by the resident to protect the area from observation by people passing by.

In *Dunn*, police entered the defendant's property without a warrant, climbed over several fences, and peered inside his barn, discovering evidence of drug production; they subsequently obtained a warrant to enter the barn and seized drug laboratory equipment and chemicals. The Court found that the initial viewing of the barn was valid because, under the four factor test set out above, the barn was not on the defendant's curtilage. The barn was 60 yards from the home, 50 yards outside the fence enclosing the home, used to produce drugs rather than to house "intimate activities of the home," and

---

[65]   476 U.S. 207, 106 S.Ct. 1809 (1986).

[66]   488 U.S. 445, 109 S.Ct. 693 (1989).

[67]   480 U.S. 294, 107 S.Ct. 1134 (1987).

surrounded only by low fences designed to corral livestock rather than prevent persons from viewing the barn. The majority emphasized that, even if the defendant did possess an expectation of privacy in the contents of the barn sufficient to require a warrant to enter it, the police could validly view the contents from the "open fields" outside the barn.

As Justice Brennan pointed out in dissent, the defendant had locked the entrance to his driveway off the main road, erected a wooden fence around the barn, and covered the barn's open end with a locked gate and fish netting that made it impossible to see inside the barn without standing immediately next to it. The consequence of the majority's decision is to require owners to take extraordinary measures to protect the privacy of the land around their buildings if they want to avoid unrestrained police surveillance.

The "flyover" cases (*Dow Chemical, Ciraolo, Riley*) and *Dunn* seriously erode Fourth Amendment protections. All of these decisions justify deliberate warrantless, suspicionless police searches by engaging in the fiction that the public could just as easily have viewed the searched areas through casual observance. In fact, it is unlikely, and the defendants in these cases undoubtedly thought it unlikely, that a member of the public would go to the trouble the police did to view the defendants' premises. These cases stretch to the breaking point the pronouncement in *Katz* that Fourth Amendment protection does not extend to what a person "knowingly exposes to the public".

(d) Containers and Other Effects

Very often evidence of criminal activity is not found in plain view, but rather within a container of some sort, which in Fourth Amendment terms is best thought of as an "effect." The Court has clearly established that if the object is "abandoned" then no Fourth Amendment right attaches. Under the old trespass doctrine, for instance, the Court indicated that property left by the owner in a hotel waste basket just before checking out could be seized and searched without implicating the Fourth Amendment.[68] In *California v. Greenwood*,[69] the Court reinvigorated this property-based holding by concluding that no legitimate expectation of privacy exists in garbage left in opaque bags outside the curtilage of the home. The Court reasoned that it is "common knowledge that plastic garbage bags left on or at the side of a public street are readily accessible to animals, children, scavengers, snoops, and other members of the public." Furthermore, one should know that once garbage is conveyed to a third party, it can easily be made accessible to the police.

Justice Brennan argued in dissent that trash contains information about one's intimate private thoughts and actions; the mere possibility that others might rifle through it should not authorize *police* to do so without probable cause or a warrant. Brennan also argued that the fact that the defendant left his garbage at curbside with the express purpose of conveying it to the city garbage collector should also be irrelevant to Fourth Amendment analysis; such an argument, he contended, would eliminate Fourth Amendment protection of mail surrendered to a mailman as well. While Brennan's arguments might still prevail in a case where the garbage is left *on* the curtilage, that result is unlikely, given the majority's reliance on the owner's "intent-to-

---

[68] *Abel v. United States*, 362 U.S. 217, 80 S.Ct. 683 (1960).
[69] 486 U.S. 35, 108 S.Ct. 1625 (1988).

convey," language which is reminiscent of *Miller's* reasoning allowing unregulated searches of bank records.

Where the abandonment notion cannot easily be applied to the effect, however, the post-*Katz* Court is much more likely to find a search and seizure has occurred. In *United States v. Chadwick*,[70] the Court held that a warrant is necessary to search a locked footlocker seized in public because a footlocker is likely to contain personal effects and is not subject to the type of public regulation a car is. In *Arkansas v. Sanders*,[71] the Court added that suitcases too are "inevitably associated with the expectation of privacy."[72] According to *Sanders*, the only non-abandoned containers that do not enjoy Fourth Amendment protection are those which somehow "reveal the nature of their contents," such as a transparent vial or a gun case.

This rule was confirmed in *Bond v. United States*,[73] in which a border patrol agent conducting an immigration check on a bus squeezed the defendant's opaque canvas bag and noticed that it contained a "brick-like" object. Seven members of the Court, in an opinion by Chief Justice Rehnquist, concluded that the methamphetamine subsequently discovered in the bag should be excluded because the officer's manipulation violated the Fourth Amendment. The Court reasoned that, although passengers on busses expect some handling of their luggage, they do not expect that it will be felt "in an exploratory manner." It also distinguished the squeezing in this case from the flyovers in *Ciraolo* and *Riley*, because the latter "involved only visual, as opposed to tactile, observation."

A more subtle case in this regard is *Lo-Ji Sales, Inc. v. New York*,[74] in which local government officials, entering after hours, seized books and films off the shelves of an "adult" book store without paying for them and examined them there despite the fact that they were packaged and not to be opened in the store. Although the Court would later hold that an undercover agent does not engage in a search or seizure when he buys material as a customer would,[75] here the police were not acting like the ordinary customer. Thus, a search and seizure occurred.

What the Court appears to be saying in *Chadwick*, *Sanders*, *Bond* and *Lo-Ji* is that only that portion of a container which the public would normally view or feel is denied Fourth Amendment protection. As Justice Stevens put it in *United States v. Ross*,[76] "just as the most frail cottage in the kingdom is absolutely entitled to the same guarantees of privacy as the most majestic mansion, so also may a traveler who carries a toothbrush and a few articles of clothing in a paper bag or a knotted scarf claim an equal right to conceal his possessions from official inspection as the sophisticated executive with the locked attaché case."

---

[70]   433 U.S. 1, 97 S.Ct. 2476 (1977).

[71]   442 U.S. 753, 99 S.Ct. 2586 (1979).

[72]   Although *Sanders'* holding that a warrant is required to search a suitcase seized from a car has been overruled, *California v. Acevedo*, 500 U.S. 565, 111 S.Ct. 1982 (1991), the aspect of *Sanders* discussed in the text remains intact. See generally, § 7.04.

[73]   529 U.S. 334, 120 S.Ct. 1462 (2000).

[74]   442 U.S. 319, 99 S.Ct. 2319 (1979).

[75]   See *Maryland v. Macon*, 472 U.S. 463, 105 S.Ct. 2778 (1985), discussed in § 4.03(a).

[76]   456 U.S. 798, 102 S.Ct. 2157 (1982).

(e) Controlled Delivery

There is one situation where a container that is neither abandoned nor revelatory of its contents may be opened without implicating the Fourth Amendment. In so-called "controlled delivery" cases, a container is lawfully intercepted and searched, found to contain contraband, repackaged, and then delivered to the addressee. The addressee is then eventually arrested for possession of the contraband. For instance, in *Illinois v. Andreas*,[77] during a routine inspection at an international airport,[78] customs agents opened a metal container that housed a wooden table, inside of which they found drugs. They resealed the container and delivered it to the defendant's apartment. Thirty to forty-five minutes later, the defendant came out of the apartment with the container, at which point the container was reopened and he was arrested.

The Supreme Court found that, on these facts, the Fourth Amendment was not implicated. According to the Court, "[n]o protected privacy interest remains in contraband in a container once government officers lawfully have opened that container and identified its contents as illegal." The fact that the container was resealed "does not operate to revive or restore the lawfully invaded rights." Thus, held the Court, so long as there is "a substantial likelihood that the contents of the container [remain the same] during the gap in surveillance," no search occurs when the container is reopened after the controlled delivery. In *Andreas*, the Court found that such a likelihood existed.

(f) Enhancement Devices

A particularly difficult area of Fourth Amendment jurisprudence involves the use of devices, ranging from flashlights to dog sniffs to satellite photography, designed to enhance the police's ability to discern criminal activity or evidence of crime. What should society's "reasonable expectations" be with respect to use of such devices? The courts have identified a number of factors that help answer this question, some of which may also be relevant in analyzing the search question even when use of technology is not at issue.

(1) The Nature of the Place Surveilled

Not surprisingly in light of *Katz'* public exposure language, the courts are reluctant to find a search has occurred when the place surveilled with an enhancement device is a public area. In *United States v. Knotts*,[79] federal agents obtained permission to place a beeper in a five gallon container of chloroform, which was subsequently picked up by one Petschen. Although the agents followed Petschen's car, they eventually lost sight of it and were able to track it to the defendant's cabin only with the aid of the beeper. The Supreme Court upheld this aspect of the police activity in *Knotts*, concluding that "[a] person travelling in an automobile on public thoroughfares has no reasonable expectation of privacy in his movements from one place to another," and that the fact that a beeper, rather than visual surveillance, was used in this case to track those movements "does not alter the situation." The Court stretched this notion a bit further in *United States v. Karo*,[80] where the beeper was used not only to track a container to a particular house, but also to track its departure from that house and its arrival at a

---

[77]   463 U.S. 765, 103 S.Ct. 3319 (1983).

[78]   As to inspections at airports considered the functional equivalent of borders, see § 13.05.

[79]   460 U.S. 276, 103 S.Ct. 1081 (1983).

[80]   468 U.S. 705, 104 S.Ct. 3296 (1984).

public warehouse. The Court found that no search occurred here either,[81] despite the fact that, in this case, the beeper was used to discover information that would have been difficult to obtain from a public vantage point, i.e., the removal of the container from the house and its re-location in the warehouse.

However, when a tracking device is used on a continuous basis, a different result might be required. In *United States v. Jones*,[82] the Court held that *placing* a Global Positioning device (GPS) on a car and using it to find something is a search, on the ground that planting the GPS is a trespass on an "effect" and thus constitutionally cognizable. This return to a property-based analysis did not address whether a search occurs when a GPS device is used to track a car or person in the absence of a trespass. However, Justice Sotomayor in the majority and four concurring justices seemed ready to declare that public tracking is a search, at least when, in contrast to *Knotts* and *Karo*, it is prolonged (in *Jones* the tracking lasted 28 days). Likewise in *Grady v. North Carolina*,[83] the Court held that the government conducts a search when, in the context of a sex offender monitoring program, it attaches a device to a person's body, without consent, for the purpose of tracking the individual's movements. The Court did not address whether "consent" by an offender who hopes wearing the tracking device will accelerate release from detention would be valid. As discussed in more detail elsewhere in this book,[84] these opinions may presage a more expansive view of the Fourth Amendment's scope.

As of now, however, *Knotts'* holding that non-trespassory observation of public activities using enhancement devices remains the law. Also not a search, according to the Court, is use of an illumination device to inspect the interior of a car through the window,[85] the interior of a barn located on open fields,[86] or the outside of a boat.[87] Nor, as recounted above, does use of telescopic equipment to surveil curtilage normally implicate the Fourth Amendment, at least when the curtilage is associated with a business.[88]

In contrast, a solid majority of the Court agreed, in both *Knotts* and *Karo*, that when a beeper is used to detect the movement of something once it is inside a house, then the Fourth Amendment is implicated.[89] The Court subsequently relied on this aspect of *Karo* and *Knotts* in holding that use of a thermal imaging device to detect activity inside a house is also a search for Fourth Amendment purposes. In *Kyllo v. United States*,[90] police used a device that registered relative degrees of heat as either white (hot), cool (black) or in-between (gray) to scan Kyllo's home, in an attempt to discover if the heat emanating

---

[81]   The Court also held that installation of the beeper in the defendant's container was not a "seizure"; to the dissent's argument that the installation was an assertion of control over the defendant's property, the Court responded that no possessory interest of the defendant's was compromised.

[82]   565 U.S. 400, 132 S.Ct. 945 (2012).

[83]   575 U.S. 306, 135 S.Ct. 1368 (2015).

[84]   The implications of *Jones* are discussed further in §§ 4.03(f)(7) and § 14.05(b).

[85]   *Texas v. Brown*, 460 U.S. 730, 103 S.Ct. 1535 (1983).

[86]   *United States v. Dunn*, 480 U.S. 294, 107 S.Ct. 1134 (1987).

[87]   *United States v. Lee*, 274 U.S. 559, 47 S.Ct. 746 (1927).

[88]   *Dow Chemical Co. v. United States*, 476 U.S. 227, 106 S.Ct. 1819 (1986), discussed in § 4.03(c).

[89]   These cases probably also impose Fourth Amendment strictures on use of beepers to locate an item within a particular apartment in an apartment complex, or within a particular locker in a bank of lockers. Clifford S. Fishman, *Electronic Tracking Devices and the Fourth Amendment:* Knotts, Karo, *and the Questions Still Unanswered*, 35 Cath. L.Rev. 277 (1979).

[90]   533 U.S. 27, 121 S.Ct. 2038 (2001).

from it was consistent with the high-intensity lamps typically used for indoor marijuana growth. Based in part on the results of this scan, they obtained a warrant to search his house and garage. Justice Scalia, writing for five members of the Court, concluded that "obtaining by sense-enhancing technology any information regarding the interior of the home that could not otherwise have been obtained without physical intrusion into a constitutionally protected area constitutes a search—at least where (as here) the technology in question is not in general public use."

The government and the dissent both argued that a thermal imaging device only detects heat after it has left the house, and analogized this situation to *Greenwood*, where the Court had held that looking at abandoned garbage is not a search.[91] But Scalia rejected "such a mechanical interpretation of the Fourth Amendment," pointing out that the listening device in *Katz*, where the Court found a search did occur, had only picked up sound that reached the exterior of the phone booth. To the contention that use of the device in *Kyllo* only detected non-intimate activities, the Court stated that "the Fourth Amendment's protection of the home has never been tied to measurement of the quality or quantity of information obtained," noting for instance that *Karo* involved detection of a can of ether. Scalia also pointed out the impracticality of basing the definition of search on such criteria, because police cannot know, before use of an enhancement device (or at least use of most enhancement devices[92]), precisely what types of items it will detect.

Kyllo provides homes significant protection from technologically-enhanced surveillance. However, its dictum that homes still do not receive Fourth Amendment protection from surveillance technology that is in "general public use" creates a major exception to that rule, given the growing ubiquity of many technological means of conducting investigations. That aspect of *Kyllo* is described further below.[93]

(2) The Nature of the Activity Surveilled

As the Court noted in *Kyllo*, in many cases the distinction between details that are "intimate" and those that are not will be very hard to make. Nonetheless, the nature of the activity observed by the police can sometimes be an important consideration. This is most evident in cases involving so-called "binary" searches, where the only information the government discovers through its use of technology is whether contraband or other evidence of crime exists. For instance, in *United States v. Jacobsen*,[94] the Court held that testing a substance strongly believed to be cocaine is not a search, and in *United States v. Place*,[95] it concluded that a dog sniff of luggage that alerts the police only to the presence of contraband does not implicate the Fourth Amendment. As Justice Stevens stated in *Jacobsen*, "Congress has decided . . . to treat the interest in 'privately' possessing cocaine as illegitimate; thus governmental conduct that can reveal whether a substance is cocaine, and no other arguably 'private' fact, compromises no legitimate privacy interest."

Of course, even if a "contraband-specific" device does not, by itself, infringe Fourth Amendment, the method of using it might. For example, *Place's* assumption that dog sniffs never intrude upon expectations of privacy is fanciful; especially if the sniff is of a

---

[91]   See § 4.03(d).

[92]   See § 4.03(f)(2).

[93]   See § 4.03(f)(5).

[94]   466 U.S. 109, 104 S.Ct. 1652 (1984).

[95]   462 U.S. 696, 103 S.Ct. 2637 (1983).

person, an insult to dignity is likely. Furthermore, even if an enhancement device detects only the presence of contraband and does so covertly (thus avoiding any insult to dignity), there may be Fourth Amendment limitations in certain contexts. For instance, Justice Brennan argued in his dissent in *Jacobsen* that the holding in that case should not be read to permit random use of contraband-specific devices to scan all passersby or all homes within a given area.[96] *Kyllo*, in particular its rejection of the idea that items inside the home should be differentiated based on their connection with intimate affairs, appears to provide support for that point of view.

In *Florida v. Jardines*,[97] the Court moved in this direction by holding that police use of a drug-sniffing dog to detect odors inside a home is a Fourth Amendment search, at least when effected by a physical intrusion on private property. In *Jardines*, officers acting on an unverified tip proceeded to the front door of the defendant's home with a drug-sniffing dog, using the driveway and a paved path to get there. The dog, on a six-foot leash, quickly signaled that it sensed the odor of drugs emanating from underneath the front door. Although conceding that normal use of the driveway and path would not be a trespass, Justice Scalia's opinion for the Court explained that the police behavior in this case went beyond the typical implicit license granted visitors: "To find a visitor knocking on the door is routine (even if sometimes unwelcome); to spot that same visitor exploring the front path with a metal detector, or marching his bloodhound into the garden before saying hello and asking permission, would inspire most of us to—well, call the police." While Scalia's opinion was predicated on the Court's newly rejuvenated trespass/property doctrine defining when a search occurs (introduced a year earlier in *Jones*), three members of the five-member majority stated in a concurring opinion that they would reach the same result under *Katz*' expectation of privacy test.

As Justice Kagan, who wrote the *Jardines* concurrence, stated, "[i]t is not surprising that in a case involving a search of a home, property concepts and privacy concepts should so align." Outside the home, however, the *Place* rationale continues to control. In *Illinois v. Caballes*,[98] Justice Stevens' opinion for the Court held that a dog sniff of a car is not a search so long as deployment of the dog does not require a seizure beyond that already authorized by a lawful stop. Reiterating *Place*, the Court stated that "[a] dog sniff conducted during a concededly lawful traffic stop that reveals no information other than the location of a substance that no individual has any right to possess does not violate the Fourth Amendment."

Given *Caballes*, a majority of the Court may resist finding that a Fourth Amendment search occurs when a dog is used to detect odors emanating from an apartment or from a home next to a public sidewalk. The four dissenters in *Jardines* made clear that they did not believe a person can have a reasonable expectation of privacy in odors that escape the abode, and Justices Scalia and Thomas, while in the majority in *Jardines*, did not sign on to Justice Kagan's concurrence, suggesting that they believe a trespass or at least a "physical intrusion" (to use the language of the majority opinion) is required in these situations. Even where a search outside the premises is not binary—that is, it discovers more than just evidence of crime—the nature of the sought-after activity probably still plays a role. For instance, in *Dow Chemical v.*

---

[96]   For further discussion of "detection devices" see § 14.06.
[97]   569 U.S. 1, 133 S.Ct. 1409 (2013).
[98]   543 U.S. 405, 125 S.Ct. 834 (2005).

United States,[99] the Court supported its decision finding no search by noting that the aerial photographs taken in that case revealed only physical details of Dow's plant, not "identifiable human faces, secret documents" or other "intimate details."

(3) The Care Taken to Ensure Privacy

In gauging the privacy associated with a place, whether a home or something else, the courts have also looked at the extent to which steps have been taken to enhance the privacy of that place. Thus, in holding a flashlight inspection of a barn to be outside the Fourth Amendment's purview in *United States v. Dunn*,[100] the Supreme Court noted that the upper portion of the "wall" through which police observed the interior consisted only of netting material. In *Ciraolo*, the fact that the defendant's fence was only 10-feet high and thus would not have kept observers on a truck or a double-decker bus from seeing his backyard helped justify the aerial surveillance in that case, even though it was of residential curtilage.

This inquiry into the defendant's efforts at privacy protection is problematic for two reasons. First, it may unfairly diminish constitutional guarantees for those who, for economic reasons, cannot take steps to protect their privacy through fences, thicker walls, or curtained windows. More importantly, placing too much reliance on the extent to which the target makes an effort to evade government surveillance would create the risk of encouraging a closed society, in which people routinely curtail contact with the outside world. With the advent of technologies that can see and hear through opaque surfaces over long distances, at night as well as during the day, greater and greater precautions will be necessary to render them ineffective.

(4) The Lawfulness of the Vantage Point

The lawfulness of the vantage point from which police make their observations is also relevant to the definition of "search," because surveillance undertaken from a vantage point outside a private area is more likely to be considered unintrusive. Thus, in *Ciraolo* and *Dow Chemical*, the Supreme Court implied that had the government physically intruded upon the curtilage rather than flown over it, a search would have occurred. Similarly, in *United States v. Place*, the Court stated in dictum that a dog sniff of luggage is not a search in part because it does not intrude into the luggage. In *Kyllo* also, the Court indicated that naked eye viewing of the home, or enhanced viewing of what such naked eye viewing could have discerned, is not a search if it takes place from a lawful vantage point.

As to what constitutes a "lawful vantage point," clearly the street, a sidewalk, an apartment hallway or public airspace would qualify. Private property can also be a "lawful" vantage point, despite the technical trespass involved. The Supreme Court has held that police can generally take up positions on any private property outside the curtilage without violating the Fourth Amendment.[101] And even curtilage might be a permissible vantage point if it is generally accessible to the public.[102] On the other hand,

---

[99]   476 U.S. 227, 106 S.Ct. 1819 (1986).

[100]   480 U.S. 294, 107 S.Ct. 1134 (1987).

[101]   *United States v. Dunn*, 480 U.S. 294, 107 S.Ct. 1134 (1987) (viewing the interior of a barn from private open fields is not a search).

[102]   See *Minnesota v. Carter*, 525 U.S. 83, 119 S.Ct. 469, 480–81 (1998) (Breyer, J., concurring) (concluding that viewing an apartment kitchen from a ground floor window while standing in an area used by other apartment dwellers was not a search).

visual surveillance of the home from bushes on the property or a fenced-in backyard is more than just a "technical" trespass.

(5) *The Availability and Sophistication of the Technology*

The overflight in *Dow Chemical* involved use of a mapmaking camera with a magnification capacity of 240. This fact did not give the Court pause, since the camera was purchasable on the "open market." However, the Court added, the same observation "using highly sophisticated surveillance equipment not generally available to the public, such as satellite technology, might be constitutionally prescribed absent a warrant." Further, use of "an electronic device to penetrate walls or windows so as to hear and record confidential discussions of chemical formulae or other trade secrets would raise very different and far more serious questions" than the camera-surveillance in *Dow Chemical*. *Kyllo* reiterated, albeit in dictum, that technology that is "in general public use" may be used to view the home interior without triggering the Fourth Amendment. Thus, the less available the particular surveillance equipment is and the greater its sophistication, the more reason there may be to deem its use invasive. In contrast, use of pervasive or primitive surveillance techniques, which can be more easily anticipated and protected against, might be viewed as relatively less likely to defeat expectations of privacy.

Here too caution must be exercised. The fact that the equipment is sometimes used by the public or has not been prohibited for public use does not necessarily mean that use of the same equipment by government officials is always an insignificant invasion. As suggested above, because many of the devices police use are already available to the public (e.g., binoculars, telescopes, and mapmaking cameras), placing too much weight on this factor would significantly reduce privacy in the home and elsewhere. The Supreme Court has recognized as much in *Florida v. Riley*,[103] where a majority indicated "that the reasonableness of Riley's expectation depends, in large measure, on the *frequency* of nonpolice helicopter flights at an altitude of 400 feet." In other words, in *Riley* it was not enough to defeat the defendant's claim that a private person could conceivably buy a helicopter and could fly at that level.

(6) *The Extent to Which Technology Enhances the Natural Senses*

A number of lower courts have distinguished between a device that "replaces" rather than simply "enhances" human senses. For example, a satellite or a device that can see through walls could be said to replace one's senses rather than enhance them because these devices can see things that the police would never be able to see with the eye. Conversely, as *Kyllo* suggested, when the enhancement device is used simply to "confirm" something already seen by the naked eye (e.g., use of binoculars to confirm an inadvertent sighting), its use is less likely to be viewed as a search, even if the surveillance is of the home.[104] The idea that minimal enhancement of naked eye observation is not a search also finds support in *Texas v. Brown*,[105] where the Supreme Court upheld the warrantless use of a flashlight to aid searching the interior of a car,

---

[103] 488 U.S. 445, 109 S.Ct. 693 (1989).

[104] See *United States v. Bassford*, 601 F.Supp. 1324, 1335 (D.Me. 1985) aff'd, 812 F.2d 16 (1st Cir. 1987) (holding that use of binoculars is not a search when they give a "view of a readily visible marijuana plot previously observed with the naked eye").

[105] 460 U.S. 730, 103 S.Ct. 1535 (1983).

stating that "the use of artificial means to illuminate a darkened area simply does not constitute a search, and thus triggers no Fourth Amendment protection."

A related assertion, more difficult to analyze, is that a search does not occur when the surveillance device merely allows police to see something that could have been viewed with the naked eye from a lawful vantage point but for fear that the observer would be discovered.[106] Despite its strong affirmance of Fourth Amendment protection for the home, *Kyllo* gave credence to this stance by permitting the use of sense-enhancing technology to collect any information about the home interior that could "otherwise have been obtained without physical intrusion into a constitutionally protected area." In other words, if activities viewed through binoculars or a nightscope could also have been seen with the naked eye from a public vantage point (but perhaps were not so viewed to avoid detection), the Fourth Amendment is apparently not implicated. Yet the fact that a naked eye observer could not have easily viewed the activity undiscovered may be precisely why the target expects privacy.

(7) Pervasiveness of the Surveillance

Numerous lower courts have expressed concern about dragnet, blanket or area-wide surveillance. Thus, while targeted aerial surveillance is not a search, courts have condemned random aerial patrols over wide-ranging areas.[107] Along the same lines, in his dissent in *Jacobsen* Justice Brennan cautioned against reading *Place* to permit police dogs to "roam the streets at random or to alert officers to people carrying cocaine," and also stated that the case should not be construed to allow drug scanning devices to "scan all passersby" or "to identify all homes in which [contraband] is present." Courts have also leveled criticism at prolonged observation or observation that is disruptive.[108]

In *Jones*, the Court inched further toward this position. Four members of the Court suggested in a concurring opinion that they would be willing to hold that "prolonged" technological surveillance, even in public, is a search, and a fifth justice, Justice Sotomayor, appeared ready to declare that the Fourth Amendment applies to surveillance of any length when carried out technologically. Sotomayor was concerned that GPS monitoring permits "a precise, comprehensive record of a person's public movements that reflects a wealth of detail about her familial, political, professional, religious, and sexual associations" and that can be stored and mined for information, all surreptitiously. The other concurring justices, led by Justice Alito, noted the 28-day GPS surveillance that took place in *Jones* "would have required a large team of agents, multiple vehicles, and perhaps aerial assistance" had the tracking device not been available and implicated the Fourth Amendment. At the same time, Alito suggested that the Fourth Amendment's protection ultimately depends upon the public's views on privacy, which might change over time. As he put it, "even if the public does not welcome the diminution of privacy that new technology entails, they may eventually reconcile themselves to this development as inevitable."

---

[106] Cf. *State v. Irwin*, 43 Wash.App. 553, 718 P.2d 826, 829–30 (1986) (holding that the use of an enhancement device from nearby woods in order to avoid detection is not a search).

[107] See, e.g., *People v. Agee*, 200 Cal.Rptr. 827, 836 (Cal. Ct. App. 1984).

[108] *Commonwealth v. Williams*, 431 A.2d 964, 966 (Pa. 1981) (involving officers who observed the interior of a home, including private sexual conduct, for nine days using binoculars and a nightscope); *Florida v. Riley*, 488 U.S. 445, 109 S.Ct. 693 (1989) (stating that a helicopter overflight that caused "hazard to person or property on the surface" or interferes with "normal use" of the home or curtilage might be a search).

A subsequent decision that, consistent with the concurring opinions in *Jones*, appeared to rest at least in part on the scope of the police action is *Carpenter v. United States*.[109] There the Court held that a search occurred when police obtained cell site location information for seven specific days over more than a 150-day period from the defendant's wireless carrier. In doing so, the Court noted that "historical cell-site records present even greater privacy concerns than the GPS monitoring of a vehicle we considered in *Jones* [because] a cell phone—almost a 'feature of human anatomy,'— tracks nearly exactly the movements of its owner . . . [and allows the government to] travel back in time to retrace a person's whereabouts, subject only to the retention polices of the wireless carriers, which currently maintain records for up to five years."

(g) Government Monitored Institutions

One final area in which the Court has utilized the public exposure doctrine involves intrusions that take place as part of a pervasive governmental regulatory scheme. In these cases, according to the Court, privacy interests are minimal because a person should know his personal effects will be exposed to government agents, if not the public at large. Thus, one has a limited expectation of privacy at the international border.[110] Similarly, while the Court has generally accorded businesses the same protection as residences because, as it stated in *See v. Seattle*,[111] "[t]he businessman, like the occupant of a residence, has a constitutional right to go about his business free from unreasonable official entries upon his private commercial property," it has recognized an exception for pervasively regulated industry. For example, in *United States v. Biswell*,[112] it permitted a federal agent's warrantless, "spot" inspection of a licensed gun dealer's storeroom, in part because "a dealer [who] chooses to engage in this pervasively regulated business and to accept a federal license, . . . does so with the knowledge that his business records, firearms and ammunition will be subject to effective inspection." In other words, a person selling firearms has no justifiable expectation his goods will be immune from exposure to government monitoring.[113]

Another decision along these lines is *Hudson v. Palmer*,[114] which held that a prisoner has no reasonable expectation of privacy in his prison cell and thus cannot claim a Fourth Amendment violation when his personal effects are confiscated or destroyed by prison authorities. Quoting from *Lanza v. New York*,[115] the Court concluded that, a prison "shares none of the attributes of privacy of a home, an automobile, an office or a hotel room," and that the need for institutional security outweighs this almost nonexistent expectation of privacy. Therefore, the prisoner's sole remedies against harassment or destruction of his property come from the Eighth Amendment's protection against "cruel and unusual punishment" and state tort and common-law provisions.

The Court resisted applying this analysis to schools, however. In *New Jersey v. T.L.O.*,[116] the state argued that because schoolchildren are subject to pervasive

---

[109] ___ U.S. ___, 138 S.Ct. 2206 (2018).

[110] See § 13.05.

[111] 387 U.S. 541, 87 S.Ct. 1737 (1967).

[112] 406 U.S. 311, 92 S.Ct. 1593 (1972).

[113] The Court has never explicitly held that such inspections are not searches. But it places very few restrictions on them. See § 13.03(a).

[114] 468 U.S. 517, 104 S.Ct. 3194 (1984).

[115] 370 U.S. 139, 82 S.Ct. 1218 (1962).

[116] 469 U.S. 325, 105 S.Ct. 733 (1985).

disciplinary supervision and because they have no need to bring personal property to school, they have no legitimate expectation of privacy on school grounds. In rejecting these arguments, the Court specifically distinguished *Hudson* from the situation before it: whereas security needs dictate the abrogation of privacy rights in prisons, discipline problems in the schools are "not so dire that students in the schools may claim no legitimate expectations of privacy." And students may, for perfectly sound reasons, bring highly personal items to school. However, the Court avoided the question whether a schoolchild has a legitimate expectation of privacy in school property, such as lockers and desks, in which he keeps personal items. Because this property is owned by the school, and may often be subject to periodic inspection, the Court may find a significantly reduced expectation of privacy in these areas.[117]

(h) An Alternative Definition

The question of when police have conducted a "search" for purposes of the Fourth Amendment is an important one since it determines whether the reasonableness and warrant requirements of that constitutional provision need be met. Ultimately, the issue involves defining the type of society in which we wish to live.[118] Under the Court's approach, if something is labelled a search it normally requires probable cause and a warrant (if there is time to get one), but if something is not a search, then no suspicion is required to justify it. An alternative to the Court's approach would be to construe the scope of the Fourth Amendment broadly—by, for instance, defining searches and seizures to encompass any action that meets the lay definition of those words—but to gauge the degree of Fourth Amendment protection by the level of intrusion involved in the action. Thus, both search of a home and search of open fields would require justification, but the former would require more justification (e.g., a warrant based on probable cause) than the latter (perhaps only a reasonable suspicion that evidence will be discovered). This "sliding scale" approach would subject to regulation a vastly greater number of police activities. But the cost to law enforcement, a factor which often seems to drive the Supreme Court's decisions in this area, would probably not be significantly greater; under this alternative approach, the results in many of the cases discussed above would have been the same, given the degree of suspicion possessed at the time of the search or seizure and the level of intrusion involved. The difference would be the absence of precedents telling the police that, for a wide variety of actions that most people would call a search or seizure, they need not worry about the Fourth Amendment at all.

4.04 Standing

Not every individual who is subjected to a "search," as defined above, has standing to contest the action. The Supreme Court has indicated that, as in other constitutional contexts,[119] the Fourth Amendment right cannot be asserted vicariously. That is, a right

---

[117] Compare *Zamora v. Pomeroy*, 639 F.2d 662 (10th Cir. 1981) ("Inasmuch as the school had assumed joint control of the locker it cannot be successfully maintained that the school did not have a right to inspect it.") with *State v. Engerud*, 94 N.J. 331, 463 A.2d 934 (1983) ("For the four years of high school, the school locker is a home away from home. In it the student stores the kind of personal 'effects' protected by the Fourth Amendment").

[118] See generally Anthony Amsterdam, *Perspectives on the Fourth Amendment*, 58 Minn.L.Rev. 349 (1974).

[119] See, e.g., *Warth v. Seldin*, 422 U.S. 490, 95 S.Ct. 2197 (1975) ("the [party] generally must assert his own legal rights and interests and cannot rest his claim to relief on the legal rights or interests of third

to exclude evidence that is illegally obtained does not automatically vest in the person against whom it is used, even when that person can prove that the purpose of the search was to gather evidence against him. Rather, under current law, that right may be asserted only by those individuals whose privacy is directly violated by the government action. Thus, in *United States v. Payner*,[120] the defendant was unable to contest admission of records concerning his financial affairs despite the fact that they were obtained when government agents burglarized a third party's hotel room. The Supreme Court upheld this result even though, according to the lower court, "the Government [had] affirmatively counsel[led] its agents that the Fourth Amendment standing limitation permits them to purposefully conduct an unconstitutional search and seizure of one individual in order to obtain evidence against third parties."

Although the Supreme Court did not arrive at this conceptualization of standing until 1978, its previous cases are illuminating and will be discussed prior to describing current standing rules.

(a) Property-Based Standing

Originally, as with the definition of "search," the courts did not use privacy language in grappling with the standing issue, but rather focused on property concepts. Only if one had a *possessory interest* in either the thing seized or the place searched was one able to assert a Fourth Amendment claim. Derived from the common law rules of trespass to real property, the requirement barred all but a very narrow class of persons from invoking the exclusionary rule. Among those who had standing under the old rubric were owners, lessees or licensees, persons with "dominion" over the property, occupants in a boarding house and guests in a hotel. House guests, business invitees, and employees, though legitimately on the premises, had no standing.[121]

(b) The *Jones* Criteria

In *Jones v. United States*,[122] the Supreme Court significantly reoriented standing law. Jones had been denied standing in the lower courts because he could claim no possessory interest in the place searched; the apartment in which both he and the drugs he was charged with possessing were found belonged to a friend, who had left for two weeks and given Jones a key and permission to stay there. In reversing the lower courts, the Court, through Justice Frankfurter, declared: "[I]t is unnecessary and ill-advised to import into the law surrounding the constitutional right to be free from unreasonable searches and seizures subtle distinctions, developed and refined by the common law in evolving the body of private property law." To replace the property-based rules, the Court developed two independent tests.

Frankfurter first addressed what he labeled a "dilemma" for the defendant charged with a possessory offense. For such a defendant, standing under the old approach would require the defendant to assert that which convicts him on the merits—namely, possession of the item seized. To avoid this dilemma, the Court held that defendants charged with possessory offenses have *automatic* standing. In addition to the avoidance

---

parties."); *Couch v. United States*, 409 U.S. 322, 93 S.Ct. 611 (1973) (privilege against self-incrimination a personal right).

[120] 447 U.S. 727, 100 S.Ct. 2439 (1980).

[121] See summary of case law in *Jones v. United States*, 362 U.S. 257, 80 S.Ct. 725 (1960).

[122] 362 U.S. 257, 80 S.Ct. 725 (1960).

of self-incrimination rationale, Frankfurter gave a second reason for an automatic standing rule:

> [T]o hold that petitioner's failure to acknowledge interest in the narcotics or the premises prevented his attack upon the search, would be to permit the Government to have the advantage of contradictory positions as a basis for conviction. Petitioner's conviction flows from his possession of the narcotics at the time of the search. Yet the fruits of that search, upon which the conviction depends, were admitted into evidence on the ground that petitioner did not have possession of the narcotics at that time. . . . It is not consonant with the amenities, to put it mildly, of the administration of criminal justice to sanction such squarely contradictory assertions of power by the Government.

The Court's second, independent basis for finding that Jones had standing to challenge the search in his case was more obviously a rejection of property-based standing. Reasoning that constitutional safeguards should not depend upon such "gossamer distinctions" as those between "lessee," "licensee," "invitee," "guest," and "owner," the Court held that "anyone legitimately on premises where a search occurs may challenge its legality by way of a motion to suppress, when its fruits are proposed to be used against him." Frankfurter made no effort to link this new test to any theoretical approach to the Fourth Amendment, however.

(c) Legitimate Expectations of Privacy Analysis

Seven years after *Jones*, the Court decided *Katz v. United States*,[123] the rationale of which eventually lead to elimination of both of *Jones'* standing criteria. Although *Katz*, as discussed earlier in this chapter,[124] focused on the definition of "search" rather than the standing question, the reasonable expectation of privacy language used by Justice Harlan in his concurring opinion soon found its way into the Court's standing decisions; indeed, in two cases decided within two years of *Katz*, the Court relied exclusively on expectation of privacy analysis and virtually ignored *Jones*.[125] Finally, in *Rakas v. Illinois*,[126] the Court explicitly recognized the connection between search and standing analysis. That is, the Court held that standing should depend on whether the police action sought to be challenged is a search (i.e., a violation of legitimate expectations of privacy) *with respect to the person challenging the intrusion.*

Rakas also used the expectation of privacy notion to justify rejection of *Jones'* legitimate presence test. Justice Rehnquist, who wrote the majority opinion in *Rakas*, concluded that, once privacy interests are seen as the focal point of standing analysis, the presence test creates "too broad a gauge for measurement of Fourth Amendment rights." Although the Court reaffirmed the result in *Jones*, it chose to read that case as standing for the "unremarkable proposition that a person can have a legally sufficient interest in a place other than his own home." Applying these ideas to the facts in *Rakas*, the Court held that the defendants there did not have standing to contest the search of

---

[123] 389 U.S. 347, 88 S.Ct. 507 (1967).

[124] See § 4.03.

[125] See, e.g., *Mancusi v. DeForte*, 392 U.S. 364, 88 S.Ct. 2120 (1968) (finding a union official had standing to contest documents taken from his office not because he was legitimately present but because a "reasonable expectation of freedom from governmental intrusion."); *Alderman v. United States*, 394 U.S. 165, 89 S.Ct. 961 (1969) (homeowner has standing to contest eavesdropping in house whether or not present during eavesdrop). Both of these cases are discussed further below.

[126] 439 U.S. 128, 99 S.Ct. 421 (1978).

a car merely because they were passengers in it at the time. Nor did the fact that the driver of the car was the ex-wife of one of the defendants impress the Court. Rehnquist noted that the defendants did not claim a possessory interest in the items seized—a sawed-off rifle and some shells—and could not assert "any legitimate expectation of privacy in the glove compartment or area under the seat of the car" where these items were found: "Like the trunk of an automobile, these are areas in which a passenger *qua* passenger simply would not normally have a legitimate expectation of privacy."

Rakas left unclear whether, had the defendants claimed a possessory interest in the items seized, they would have had standing to contest the search by virtue of that fact alone. Two years later, in *Rawlings v. Kentucky*,[127] the Court answered this question in the negative. The Court's version of the facts in *Rawlings* was as follows: just prior to police entering the dwelling in which Rawlings and Cox were guests, Rawlings dumped drugs into Cox's purse, despite Cox's protestations. When the police ordered Cox to empty her purse onto a table, Rawlings, with some hesitation, claimed they were his. The Court rejected Rawlings' claim that he should have standing to challenge the legality of this incident because of his possessory interest in the drugs, noting that he had no "right to exclude other persons" from the purse, and never had access to it prior to putting the drugs there. Further, the "precipitous nature" of his "bailment" to Cox "hardly supports a reasonable inference that petitioner took normal precautions to maintain his privacy." Finally, Rehnquist pointed out that, at the suppression hearing, Rawlings admitted to having no subjective expectation of privacy in the purse. Although thus suggesting a number of possible bases for standing under expectation of privacy analysis, *Rawlings* clearly established that possession of the seized item, by itself, is not one of them.

In *United States v. Salvucci*,[128] a companion case to *Rawlings*, the Court partially relied on this latter notion in abolishing the other doctrine announced in *Jones*, automatic standing. As Justice Rehnquist stated for the Court in *Salvucci*, "[w]e simply decline to use possession of a seized good as a substitute for a factual finding that the owner of the good had a legitimate expectation of privacy in the area searched." Given this conclusion, Rehnquist felt able to ignore the second of Frankfurter's rationales for automatic standing—the vice of prosecutorial contradiction: it is now possible, he concluded, for the prosecutor to assert, without contradiction, that the defendant does not have standing (i.e., a legitimate expectation of privacy in the place searched) and contend at trial that the defendant owns the property seized.[129] As to the self-incrimination rationale for automatic standing, as Rehnquist pointed out, by the time of *Salvucci* the dilemma to which Frankfurter referred in *Jones* had been eliminated by the Court's decision in *Simmons v. United States*,[130] which held that pretrial suppression hearing testimony is inadmissible on the issue of guilt.

(d) Current Standing Rules

With the endorsement in *Rakas* of the expectation of privacy approach to standing, the Court has moved toward a totality of the circumstances analysis. *Rakas* and

---

[127]   448 U.S. 98, 100 S.Ct. 2556 (1980).

[128]   448 U.S. 83, 100 S.Ct. 2547 (1980).

[129]   This latter reasoning is somewhat disingenuous, however, since at least some bases for standing may depend in part upon a property interest in the item seized. See § 4.04(d)(2) & (3).

[130]   390 U.S. 377, 88 S.Ct. 967 (1968), discussed in § 15.02(c).

Rawlings indicate that factors such as the individual's interest in the property searched, his interest in the property seized, and his presence in the area searched have been downgraded from dispositive rules to mere factors to be considered in the aggregate. Yet these factors remain relevant to standing analysis. From a reading of the Court's cases, there appear to be four situations in which a defendant may establish a legitimate expectation of privacy sufficient to permit challenge of a search or seizure.[131]

(1) The Right to Exclude Others

Most prominently, the defendant who can show he has the "right to exclude others" from the searched property will often have the capacity to contest the search. The Court used this language in both *Rakas* and *Rawlings* when describing its standing analysis. Clearly, as Justice Rehnquist recognized in *Rakas*, if one owns the area searched, one will generally possess a right to exclude others.[132] In *Alderman v. United States*,[133] a case decided before *Rakas* but affirmed by that decision, the Court held that a person not only has standing to contest the interception of his own conversations if they take place in his home but also the interception of any other conversations that occur there. The majority saw no difference between the latter situation and seizure of a third party's tangible property from a home; there too the homeowner would have standing "not because he had any interest in the seized items as 'effects' protected by the Fourth Amendment, but because they were the fruits of an unauthorized search of his house, which is itself expressly protected by the Fourth Amendment." This holding is consistent with the notion advanced in *Rakas* that expectations of privacy are not always associated with physical presence. Clearly, a homeowner should not have to be at home in order to enjoy a right to exclude unwanted eavesdroppers or intruders from the premises.

The right to exclude may also be asserted by non-owners. In *Rakas*, for instance, the Court stated that both the defendant in *Katz*, who "occupied a phone booth and closed the door," and the defendant in *Jones*, who had "complete dominion and control" over the searched premises by virtue of his possession of the absent owner's key, could "exclude all others" and thus had standing. Another pre-*Rakas* holding that was reaffirmed by that case was *Mancusi v. DeForte*,[134] in which the Court granted standing to a union official to contest the seizure of documents from a one-room office he shared with other officials. The reasoning underlying the result in that case, as described by Justice White, seems consistent with a right to exclude rationale:

> DeForte would have been entitled to expect that he would not be disturbed except by personal or business invitees, and that records would not be taken except with his permission or that of his union superiors. It seems to us that the situation was not fundamentally changed because DeForte shared an office with other union officers. DeForte still could reasonably have expected that

---

[131] Theoretically, one should distinguish between standing to contest searches and standing to contest seizures. In *Salvucci*, the Court noted that while a possessory interest in the item seized was insufficient for the former, it "may be sufficient in some circumstances to entitle a defendant to seek the return of the seized property if the seizure, as opposed to the search, was illegal." However, such standing will usually be superfluous and, if not, will rarely be useful because of the breadth of the plain view seizure doctrine, as described in Chapter 10. See Christopher Slobogin, *Capacity to Contest a Search and Seizure: The Passing of Old Rules and Some Suggestions for New Ones*, 18 Am.Crim.L.Rev. 387, 413–16 (1981).

[132] The one exception might be if ownership is in title only, such as in the case of a landlord's ownership of rented property.

[133] 394 U.S. 165, 89 S.Ct. 961 (1969).

[134] 392 U.S. 364, 88 S.Ct. 2120 (1968).

only those persons and their personal or business guests would enter the office, and that records would not be touched except with their permission or that of union higher-ups.

The Court has also held that the sole occupant of a rental car has standing on a right-to-exclude rationale, even when the occupant's name is not on the rental agreement and the agreement prohibits non-signees from driving the car. In *Byrd v. United States*,[135] a unanimous Court concluded that such a driver, if allowed to drive the car by the renter, is analogous to the defendant in *Jones*, because of the dominion and control over the car. However, the Court stressed that when such dominion is "wrongful," as in the case of a thief or a driver whose criminal record prevents him from renting the car under his own name, a different result would be required. In the course of analyzing the case, the opinion for the Court also clarified *Rakas* by stating that even passengers can have a legitimate expectation of privacy in a car if they can show some privacy interest beyond presence in it.

Although further elaboration of the right to exclude is needed, one way of thinking about its scope might be to analogize it to the capacity to consent to a search. As developed elsewhere in this book,[136] non-owners as well as owners may consent to search of property so long as they have sufficient control over that property. If an individual can be said to possess such control for purposes of consent, he should also have a right to exclude. These rights are but converse aspects of the same phenomenon—the effort to regulate one's privacy.

(2) Continuing Access Plus Possessory Interest

Another pre-*Rakas* case suggests a second basis upon which a non-owner can obtain standing. In *United States v. Jeffers*,[137] the Court granted standing to a defendant who not only did not own the searched apartment, but lacked the "complete dominion" and control possessed by Katz and Jones, and shared by DeForte. Although Jeffers did have a key to the apartment and could use it "at will," it was rented and occupied by his aunts and he did not live there. Thus, he did not have the right to exclude others from the apartment (nor a right to consent to its search). But he did have continuing access to the apartment; additionally, he claimed a possessory interest in the seized contraband. These two elements together are apparently sufficient to gain standing; according to the *Rakas* Court, "[s]tanding in *Jeffers* was based on Jeffers's possessory interest in both the premises searched and the property seized."[138] Note that this variety of standing, like the right to exclude, does not require that the defendant be present during the search; neither Jeffers nor his aunts were in the apartment when the contraband was found.

However, the mere fact that persons might have some control over the searched area does not automatically mean they have standing. This point was emphasized in *United States v. Padilla*,[139] where the Court rejected a standing rule developed by the Ninth Circuit providing that "a coconspirator's participation in an operation or arrangement that indicates joint control and supervision of the place searched establishes standing." In *Padilla*, the various defendants, all members of a drug

---

[135] ___ U.S. ___, 138 S.Ct. 1518 (2018).

[136] See § 12.04.

[137] 342 U.S. 48, 72 S.Ct. 93 (1951).

[138] Note also that *Rawlings* spoke of the degree of "previous access" to the searched area.

[139] 508 U.S. 77, 113 S.Ct. 1936 (1993).

smuggling ring, wanted to contest the stop of a drug-laden car driven by one of their "mules." Applying its test, the Ninth Circuit found that one defendant had standing to challenge the stop because he owned the car and had a "coordinating and supervisory role in the operation," that a second defendant had standing because she "provided a communication link" between various members of the conspiracy and "held a supervisory role tying everyone together and overseeing the entire operation," and that a third had standing because he "exhibited substantial control and oversight with respect to the purchase [and] the transportation through Arizona," where the car was stopped.

The Supreme Court, in a per curiam opinion, held that the Ninth Circuit's test conflicted with the well-established notion that Fourth Amendment standing exists only for persons whose own rights have been violated, and remanded the case for determination as to whether each defendant "had either a property interest protected by the Fourth Amendment that was interfered with by the stop of the automobile . . . , or a reasonable expectation of privacy that was invaded by the search thereof." While elimination of the Ninth Circuit's rule does conform to current standing doctrine, it also creates an incentive to violate the Fourth Amendment rights of suspected "mules" to get evidence against their bosses.

(3) Legitimate Presence Plus Possessory Interest

Even after *Rakas*, legitimate presence on the premises may remain a third way to establish standing, if it is combined with a possessory interest in the item seized. Although *Rakas* rejected as overbroad the legitimate presence test, Rehnquist noted that this conclusion "is not to say that [visitors in a house] could not contest the lawfulness of the seizure of evidence of the search if their own property were seized during the search."

The Court was later confronted with a version of this scenario in *Minnesota v. Olson*.[140] In contrast to Jones, Olson had slept in the apartment searched for only one night and was never left alone there. In contrast to Jeffers, he was never given a key. Despite these minimal contacts with the apartment, seven members of the Court held that the defendant had standing to contest the fact that the police did not have a warrant when they arrested him there.[141] Justice White, writing for the Court, rejected the state's argument that because the host had ultimate authority to admit and exclude visitors, a guest should lack standing. "If the untrammeled power to admit and exclude were essential to Fourth Amendment protection, an adult daughter temporarily living in the home of her parents would have no legitimate expectation of privacy because her right to admit or exclude would be subject to her parents' veto." While the "item" seized in *Olson* was the person of the defendant, the legitimate presence-possessory interest test probably also applies, as *Rakas* suggested, when the casual visitor's personal effects are seized: in *Olson*, the Court stated that an overnight guest "seeks shelter in another's home precisely because it provides him with privacy, a place where he and his *possessions* will not be disturbed by anyone but his host and those his host allows inside" (emphasis added).

On the other hand, parties who are in a residence for only a few hours and who have little or no previous relationship with the owner or occupants of the premises do not have

---

[140] 495 U.S. 91, 110 S.Ct. 1684 (1990).

[141] Note that a person always has standing to contest his arrest. Here the defendant was contesting the warrantless *entry* to make the arrest.

standing to contest a search of the premises. This was the holding in *Minnesota v. Carter*,[142] where six members of the Court concluded that two defendants who were observed bagging cocaine in a third defendant's apartment through a drawn window blind had no standing to contest the observation. Chief Justice Rehnquist's opinion for the Court reasoned that, because the defendants had never been in the apartment before (they in fact lived in another city) and had used it "simply [as] a place to do business" for two and a half hours, they possessed no legitimate expectation of privacy in the premises. Justice Ginsburg noted in dissent that the majority's result appeared to mean that "we have a more reasonable expectation of privacy when we place a business call to a person's home from a public telephone booth on the side of the street [the facts of *Katz*] than when we actually enter that person's premises to engage in a common endeavor."

Because no seizure of personal items was involved, *Carter* does not disturb the suggestion in *Rakas* that legitimate presence plus a possessory interest in any items seized will establish standing to contest the search and seizure of those items. But at best that suggestion is dictum. Furthermore, this dictum, if it becomes law, may not extend beyond searches of a residence. For instance, broadly construed, the legitimate presence-possessory interest rule would have conferred standing in *Rakas* had the defendants simply asserted ownership over the seized items. Yet the Court's conclusion that those defendants, as passengers, had no legitimate expectation of privacy in the glove compartment, under the seat or in the trunk suggests a more niggardly application of standing analysis. The Court's general derogation of privacy interests in the automobile, discussed elsewhere in this book,[143] is likely to end up justifying a distinction between homes and cars in the standing context as well.

Note, however, the difference between search of a car and its seizure in this regard. As six members of the Court pointed out in *Rakas*, because such a seizure clearly affects the passenger's freedom of movement, a passenger's ability to contest the legality of the stop (as opposed to the legality of a search) should not be diminished simply because he does not own it and is not driving it. Thus, for instance, if items belonging to a passenger are taken from the trunk after an illegal stop, the passenger should be able to exclude the evidence as fruit of the illegality.[144]

(4) Bailment

A fourth situation in which one may be able to claim standing is suggested by the facts in *Rawlings*. While the Court found that Rawlings' "bailment" of his drugs to Cox had been too "precipitous" to create an expectation of privacy, its focus on the bailment issue implies that, were one to make a valid bailment, a legitimate expectation of privacy might be established. To reason otherwise would be tantamount to saying that no one who shared his property with someone else can challenge a search of that property. On the other hand, the Court's holding in *United States v. Miller*,[145] that a person who voluntarily surrenders information to a bank lacks standing to contest a subpoena for records containing that information casts some doubt on this conclusion.

---

[142] 525 U.S. 83, 119 S.Ct. 469 (1998).

[143] See § 7.02.

[144] The one exception to this rule would be when the passenger is not "legitimately" present, as when the car is stolen. See, *State v. Bottelson*, 102 Idaho 90, 625 P.2d 1093 (1981).

[145] 425 U.S. 435, 96 S.Ct. 1619 (1976), discussed in § 4.03(a).

(5) *Subjective Expectations of Privacy*

A final factor which clearly should not play a role in the standing inquiry, but which unfortunately was given some credence by the Court in *Rawlings*, is the defendant's own perception of his privacy interests. As Professor Amsterdam pointed out in 1974:

> An actual, subjective expectation of privacy . . . can neither add to, nor can its absence detract from, an individual's claim to fourth amendment protection. If it could, the government could diminish each person's subjective expectation of privacy merely by announcing half-hourly on television that 1984 was being advanced by a decade and that we were all forthwith being placed under comprehensive electronic surveillance.[146]

4.05   Determining Whether a Search or Seizure Is Reasonable

If it is determined that a given search or seizure does not implicate the Fourth Amendment, either because no governmental conduct occurred, no "search" occurred, or the defendant's legitimate expectations of privacy were not infringed, then the evidence so procured is admissible in subsequent prosecution. If it is determined that a Fourth Amendment right does exist, the next step is to determine whether the government's conduct was reasonable. This stage requires determining whether a valid warrant has been issued, and, if not, whether one of the exceptions to the warrant requirement apply. These aspects of Fourth Amendment analysis are the subject of the next ten chapters. This section will briefly describe the structure of the Fourth Amendment, in particular its warrant and probable cause requirements, in the process explaining the organization of these chapters.

(a) The Warrant Requirement

Looking closely at the Fourth Amendment, one notices that the first clause bars unreasonable searches and seizures, while the second clause requires that warrants be based on probable cause and meet certain other requirements. The amendment is silent as to how the "Reasonableness Clause" and the "Warrant Clause" interact with one another, nor is it clear which clause should be considered the most important. As detailed in Chapter 3,[147] in the arrest context the manner in which the Supreme Court has interpreted the relationship between the two clauses is fairly straightforward. For other searches and seizures, the Court's jurisprudence has been somewhat more difficult to pin down.

Two competing approaches can be discerned in the Court's cases. The first assumes that the Warrant Clause is the predominate clause in the Fourth Amendment, thus establishing a presumption in favor of warrants for any given search. On this view, searches and seizures that are not based on a valid warrant are unreasonable unless the state can produce a very good justification (usually based on exigent circumstances) as to why obtaining such a warrant was not feasible. This perspective was most forcefully presented by Justice Stewart, who, in *Katz v. United States*,[148] stated that a warrant is required before every search or seizure, "subject only to a few specifically established

---

[146] Amsterdam, supra note 118, at 384.

[147] See § 3.04(b) (warrants only required for non-exigent home arrests).

[148] 389 U.S. 347, 88 S.Ct. 507 (1967).

and well-delineated exceptions." Since *Katz*, this phrase has been repeated in Court opinions many times.[149]

However, there is a competing perspective on the Fourth Amendment which, in practice if not in theory, seems to have gained the ascendancy. As summarized by the Court in *Terry v. Ohio*,[150] a case decided one year after *Katz*, "the central inquiry under the Fourth Amendment [is] the reasonableness in all the circumstances of the particular governmental invasion of a citizen's personal security." As construed by some members of the Court,[151] this approach treats the Reasonableness Clause as the most important command in the Fourth Amendment and the absence of a warrant as merely one factor among many to consider in evaluating the "reasonableness" of a search. On this view, the Warrant Clause was not included in the amendment to create a presumption in favor of warrants, but to describe the elements of a valid warrant (e.g., the probable cause, particularity, and oath requirements), should the state decide to seek one.

There is considerable historical support for this second version of the Fourth Amendment. Research indicates that, in drafting the amendment, the Framers' primary, if not *sole*, concern was avoiding a repetition of the British colonial practice of issuing so-called "general warrants," or warrants which were based on a "bare suspicion" and authorized fishing expeditions for evidence inside the home.[152] While such searches were clearly viewed with hostility by the colonists, warrantless searches, normally conducted in "hot pursuit" or incident to arrest and thus more restricted than general warrant searches, apparently were of little concern to the drafters of the Constitution. A second possible reason for preferring the "totality of the circumstances" analysis demanded by a "reasonableness" test is that it results in a more fine-tuned assessment of the competing values at stake.

On the other hand, if the goal is control of the police through relatively precise rules that eliminate much of their discretion, the *Katz* approach is more appealing.[153] Most searches for and seizures of evidence are conducted without a warrant. As Justice Jackson stated, the "forefathers were guilty of a serious oversight" if they assumed that by "controlling search warrants they had controlled searches."[154]

Both approaches have been adopted in Supreme Court opinions.[155] As noted, the Supreme Court continues to pay lipservice to the primacy of the Warrant Clause, and

---

[149] See, e.g., *United States v. Ross*, 456 U.S. 798, 102 S.Ct. 2157 (1982). More recently, the phraseology has sometimes varied. See, e.g., *Illinois v. Rodriguez*, 497 U.S. 177, 110 S.Ct. 2793 (1990) (speaking of the "ordinary requirement of a warrant").

[150] 392 U.S. 1, 88 S.Ct. 1868 (1968).

[151] See, e.g., Rehnquist's dissenting opinion in *Michigan v. Clifford*, 464 U.S. 287, 104 S.Ct. 641 (1984) ("In my view, the utility of requiring a magistrate to evaluate the grounds for a search following a fire is so limited that the incidental protection of an individual's privacy interests simply does not justify imposing a warrant requirement.").

[152] See Thomas Davies, *Recovering the Original Fourth Amendment*, 98 Mich. L. Rev. 547, 583 (1999) ("No one questions that the Framers despised and sought to ban general warrants."); Telford Taylor, Two Studies in Constitutional Interpretation 24–41 (1969).

[153] On the general desirability of rules versus case-by-case analysis when it comes to controlling the police, see Wayne LaFave, *The Fourth Amendment in an Imperfect World: On Drawing "Bright Lines" and "Good Faith*," 43 Pitt.L.Rev. 307 (1982).

[154] *Harris v. United States*, 331 U.S. 145, 196, 67 S.Ct. 1098 (1947) (Jackson, J., dissenting).

[155] For an early pair of cases in which these contrasting viewpoints were adopted, see *Johnson v. United States*, 333 U.S. 10, 68 S.Ct. 367 (1948) (apparently asserting the primacy of the Warrant Clause) and *United States v. Rabinowitz*, 339 U.S. 56, 70 S.Ct. 430 (1950) (adopting a totality of the circumstances analysis).

occasionally it strongly endorses that view. For instance, in *Mincey v. Arizona*,[156] it refused to adopt a "murder scene exception" to the warrant requirement under an Arizona statute that permitted "reasonable" searches of homes without a warrant. Quoting Justice Stewart's language from *Katz*, it unanimously held (in an opinion by Stewart) that the "seriousness of the offense" was not, by itself, a sufficient "exigency" to justify a warrantless search. Nonetheless, what may have been true at the time *Katz* was decided can no longer be seriously contended: the situations in which the Court has permitted warrantless searches are neither few in number nor "well-delineated." Rather, as Professor Bradley noted in 1985 (before many current exceptions came into being),[157] the various exceptions number well over twenty and become murkier as time goes on.

In order to facilitate analysis of Fourth Amendment cases, some reduction and categorization of the exceptions is important. Doing so in the broadest fashion possible, one might organize the caselaw described in the next ten chapters around four types of exceptions: (1) exceptions based on a perception that exigent circumstances make obtaining a warrant impossible or impractical (e.g., the "hot pursuit" exception);[158] (2) exceptions resting on a finding that the police action does not impinge upon a substantial privacy interest (e.g., the "heavily regulated industry" exception);[159] (3) situations involving "special needs" of law enforcement (a phrase coined by the Supreme Court) where warrants might frustrate legitimate purposes of the government other than crime control (e.g., the public school search exception);[160] and (4) situations where warrants are considered unnecessary because other devices already curb police discretion (e.g., the inventory search exception).[161] This book will break these conceptual categories down further into eight exceptions, based more directly on language from the Supreme Court's cases.

(b) The Probable Cause Requirement

The debate over the reach of the Warrant Clause concerns the procedural issue of when police should be forced to seek before-the-fact review. A separate issue is a substantive one: what level of certainty must the police have before they conduct a search, whether or not it is authorized by a warrant? The only level of certainty mentioned in the Fourth Amendment is probable cause, a standard which connotes something akin to a more-likely-than-not finding.[162] However, a number of Supreme Court decisions have recognized that some searches are "reasonable" even if carried out on less than probable cause. Thus, in attempting to develop a framework for analyzing Fourth Amendment cases, one must look not only at exceptions to the warrant requirement, but also exceptions to the probable cause requirement.

Of course, if a search requires a warrant, it must be based on probable cause, given the language of the Fourth Amendment. If a search does not require a warrant, then several factors have been considered by the Court in determining whether a level of suspicion lower than probable cause is permissible: (1) the intrusiveness of the search;

---

[156] 437 U.S. 385, 98 S.Ct. 2408 (1978). Reaffirmed in *Thompson v. Louisiana*, 469 U.S. 17, 105 S.Ct. 409 (1984).

[157] Craig M. Bradley, *Two Models of the Fourth Amendment*, 83 Mich.L.Rev. 1468, 1473, 1479 (1985).

[158] See Chapter 8.

[159] See § 13.03(a).

[160] See § 13.08.

[161] See § 13.07.

[162] See § 5.03(a).

(2) the nature of the harm being investigated; (3) the difficulty of detecting the harm if probable cause is required; and (4) the extent to which a probable cause requirement would disrupt smooth government functioning. For instance, in permitting suspicionless alcohol and drug testing of railway workers, the Court has asserted that such testing is less intrusive and less violative of expectations of privacy than many other types of searches, that the harm caused by drug- and alcohol-impaired railway workers is substantial, that such impairment would be difficult to detect if individualized suspicion were required, and that developing such suspicion would distract railway employers from their other, primary tasks.[163] The Court has relied on one or more of these four factors in every case in which it has permitted a search on less than probable cause.

(c) Adequacy of the Warrant

With these general points in mind, we can return to the roadmap for the next ten chapters' treatment of the Fourth Amendment, all of which assume that a government agent has engaged in a search and seizure that the defendant has standing to contest. Once it is established that the Fourth Amendment is implicated in this way, the next question is whether a valid warrant justified that action. As Chapter 5 spells out, to be valid, a warrant must meet several requirements. The most important of these are that the warrant:

(1)   be issued by a neutral and detached decisionmaker;

(2)   be based on probable cause that the items sought are in the place to be searched;

(3)   describe with particularity the place to be searched and the items to be seized; and

(4)   be executed within a reasonable period of time.

While Chapter 5's discussion of these and other aspects of the search warrant deal with the typical search, Chapter 14 discusses search warrants in the special context of technological surveillance using sophisticated eavesdropping and spying devices.

(d) Exceptions to the Warrant and Probable Cause Requirements

Most of the remaining chapters deal with warrantless searches. If a warrant is obtained, but is invalid, or if no warrant was ever obtained, evidence seized by government officials is still admissible if discovered:

(1)   "incident" to a lawful arrest (see Chapter 6);

(2)   in a movable vehicle in circumstances giving rise to the so-called "automobile exception;" (see Chapter 6);

(3)   while police are in "hot pursuit" of a suspected felon (see Chapter 8);

(4)   in an "evanescent" or "endangering" state (see Chapter 9);

(5)   in "plain view" from a lawful vantage point (see Chapter 10);

(6)   during a "frisk" after a valid stop (see Chapter 11);

---

[163]   See, *Skinner v. Railway Labor Executives' Association*, 489 U.S. 602, 109 S.Ct. 1402 (1989), discussed in § 13.09(b).

(7) in the course of a search authorized by a voluntary consent (see Chapter 12);

(8) in the course of inspections or searches conducted for certain "regulatory" purposes (see Chapter 13).

The first five doctrines listed above all require probable cause either to arrest or to search or seize, and thus can be viewed as exceptions to the warrant requirement alone. The sixth and seventh doctrines are exceptions to both the warrant and probable cause requirements. Finally, regulatory inspections (as opposed to searches and seizures conducted primarily to garner evidence of criminal activity) are placed in a special category because there are so many variations, although most also involve situations where neither a warrant nor probable cause is required.

The parameters of these exceptions are not always clear and occasionally overlap. But their organization in the manner described above should facilitate working through the large number of Supreme Court holdings concerning the Fourth Amendment. With respect to each exception, it is useful to ask three questions: (1) what is its rationale?; (2) when is it triggered?; and (3) what is the scope of the search and seizure it authorizes? Chapters Six through Thirteen provide the answers to these questions.

(e) Burdens and Standards of Proof

Whether a "search" occurred, the defendant has standing, a warrant was valid, or one of the exceptions applies is usually decided at a "suppression hearing" prior to trial. In practice, the burden and standard of proof at this proceeding are often not enunciated.

In the few cases in which it has addressed the issue, the Supreme Court has indicated that the burden varies between the defense and the prosecution, depending on the question involved. In *Bumper v. North Carolina*,[164] the Court appeared to hold that the prosecution bears the burden of proving the voluntariness of a consent. This holding might be said to follow from the Court's earlier decision that the government bears the burden of proving the voluntariness of a confession.[165] In *Florida v. Riley*,[166] on the other hand, five members of the Court asserted that the burden of proving a government action is a search should be on the defendant. Despite the contrast with *Bumper*, this decision makes some sense, since the defendant has the best access to information concerning expectations of privacy.

The Court has been silent with respect to the burden on other issues. Because the standing issue is similar to the search issue, the burden on the former point should probably be on the defendant.[167] In contrast, when the issue is whether probable cause existed, or a search was otherwise reasonable, the government is in the best position to prove the relevant facts, and should probably bear the burden. However, the lower courts' approach to this matter is not quite so simple.[168]

---

[164] 391 U.S. 543, 88 S.Ct. 1788 (1968).

[165] *Miranda v. Arizona*, 384 U.S. 436, 86 S.Ct. 1602 (1966).

[166] 488 U.S. 445, 109 S.Ct. 693 (1989).

[167] Cf. *Jones v. United States*, 362 U.S. 257, 80 S.Ct. 725 (1960) (holding it "entirely proper" to place the burden on the defendant on the standing issue).

[168] See, e.g., *United States v. Longmire*, 761 F.2d 411 (7th Cir. 1985) (burden on defendant if search with a warrant, on state if not, on ground that in the former case the state has already made out a prima facie case that search is reasonable). See also, *State v. Vrtiska*, 225 Neb. 454, 406 N.W.2d 114 (1987).

Whatever party bears the burden of proof, the constitutionally sufficient standard of proof is probably a preponderance of the evidence. This is the standard of proof the Court has imposed in the confessions context.[169] If the Court is willing to use the civil standard to resolve the admissibility of a confession, which can occasionally be unreliable, then it probably would be willing to apply the same standard in judging the admissibility of tangible evidence, which is virtually always reliable proof of guilt.

4.06   Conclusion

On the following page is a flow chart representing schematically the analysis of Fourth Amendment cases set forth in this chapter. The chart divides the analysis into two "Stages". Stage I asks whether the Fourth Amendment is implicated. Stage II asks whether, if the Amendment is implicated, the search or seizure was reasonable.

This chapter focused on Stage I, which deals with the scope of the Fourth Amendment right. An individual can claim Fourth Amendment protection only when "governmental conduct" infringes upon society's "reasonable expectations of privacy," and further infringes upon the individual's "legitimate expectations of privacy," concepts that can be summarized as follows:

---

[169] See discussion of *Lego v. Twomey*, 404 U.S. 477, 92 S.Ct. 619 (1972), discussed in § 16.06(b).

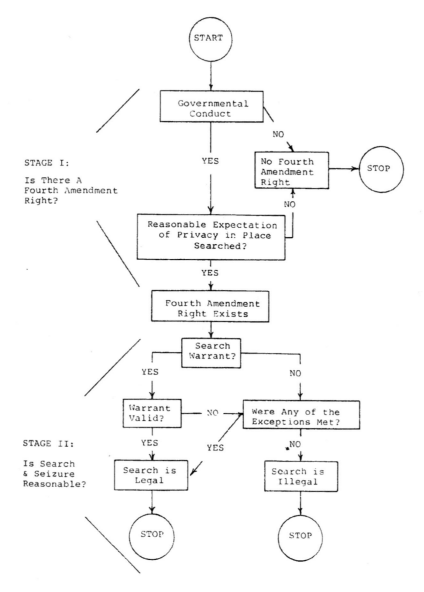

(1) Governmental conduct includes conduct by any public official, including law enforcement officials, fire, health and safety inspectors, and public school teachers. It also includes conduct by private persons acting as agents of these officials. Searches by private individuals who are not acting as agents of government officials do not implicate the Fourth Amendment; nor is the Amendment implicated by searches by governmental officials that essentially duplicate a previous independent search by a private individual, at least when the latter search reveals nothing of privacy significance other than contraband.

(2) Generally, one has a reasonable expectation of privacy in one's home, vehicles, personal effects, and person, meaning that the Fourth Amendment is implicated by governmental actions that physically intrude into these areas. The Fourth Amendment is also implicated by non-physical intrusions of the home using enhancement devices

that are not in general public use (at least if the activities viewed are not otherwise observable from a lawful vantage point), by prolonged tracking of a car effected through a trespass on the car, and by access to location data held by a third party communications carrier. However, generally a person does not have a reasonable expectation of privacy in what is exposed to the public, whether the exposure occurs in the home or elsewhere. In such situations, governmental intrusion is not a "search" for purposes of the Fourth Amendment. Relying on this rationale the Supreme Court has held that a search does not occur if government agents acquire information about an individual in any of the following ways: (a) from persons or institutions to whom the individual has "voluntarily" revealed information (other than location data held by common carriers); (b) from observation of the individual's physical characteristics and abilities; (c) from physical intrusion into the "open fields;" (d) from flying over either open fields or curtilage; (e) from containers that are "abandoned" (including garbage bags left at curbside), that reveal the nature of their contents to the casual observer, or that are searched after a controlled delivery under circumstances that make it unlikely the contents have changed; (f) from technological devices that are in general public use, that allow observation of activities that could also have been observed with the naked eye from a lawful vantage point, or that detect, in places other than the home, only incriminating evidence (e.g., field tests for drugs, dog sniffs of cars); (g) in the course of conducting a routine inspection of a jail cell.

(3) Even if a "search" has occurred, the person seeking the protection of the Fourth Amendment must show that *his* legitimate expectations of privacy were violated by the governmental conduct before he may contest the search. He can do this by showing: (a) the area searched was one from which he had the right to exclude others; or (b) continuing access to the place searched and a possessory interest in the item seized; and perhaps also by showing either (c) legitimate presence in the place searched and a possessory interest in the item seized; or (d) a valid bailment of the item seized to a person whose legitimate expectations of privacy were violated by the search for the item.

BIBLIOGRAPHY

Amsterdam, Anthony G. Perspectives on the Fourth Amendment. 58 Minn.L.Rev. 349 (1974).

Bentley, Eric Jr. Toward an International Fourth Amendment: Rethinking Searches and Seizures Abroad After *Verdugo-Urquidez*. 27 Vand. J. Trans. L. 329 (1991).

Bradley, Craig. Two Models of the Fourth Amendment. 83 Mich.L.Rev. 1468 (1985).

Burkoff, John M. Not So Private Searches and the Constitution. 66 Cornell L. Rev. 627 (1981).

Caminker, Evan. Location Tracking and Digital Data: Can *Carpenter* Build a Stable Privacy Doctrine? 2018 Supreme Court Review 411.

Colb, Sherry F. Standing Room Only: Why Fourth Amendment Exclusion and Standing Can No Longer Co-Exist. 28 Cardozo L. Rev. 1663 (2007).

Coombs, Mary I. Shared Privacy and the Fourth Amendment, or the Rights of Relationships. 75 Cal. L.Rev. 1593 (1987).

Joh, Elizabeth E. Conceptualizing the Private Police. 2005 Utah L. Rev. 573.

Kerr, Orin. The Case for the Third Party Doctrine. 107 Mich. L. Rev. 561 (2009).

Loewy, Arnold H. The Fourth Amendment as a Device for Protecting the Innocent. 81 Mich.L.Rev. 1229 (1983).

MacDonnell, Timothy C. *Florida v. Jardines*: The Wolf at the Castle Door. 7 N.Y.U. J. L. & Liberty 1 (2012).

Murphy, Erin. The Case Against the Case for the Third-Party Doctrine: A Response to Epstein and Kerr. 24 Berkeley Tech. L.J. 1239 (2009).

Re, Richard M. The Positive Law Floor. 129 Harvard Law Review Forum 313 (2016).

Sacharoff, Laurent. The Binary Search Doctrine. 42 Hofstra Law Review 1139 (2014).

Simmons, Ric. From *Katz* to *Kyllo*: A Blueprint for Adapting the Fourth Amendment to Twenty-First Century Technologies. 53 Hastings L. J. 1303 (2002).

Slobogin, Christopher. Making the Most of *United States v. Jones* in a Surveillance Society: A Statutory Implementation of Mosaic Theory. 8 Duke J. Constitutional L. & Pub. Pol'y 1 (2012).

_____. Peeping Techno-Toms and the Fourth Amendment: Seeing Through Kyllo's Rules Governing Technological Surveillance. 86 Minn. L. Rev. 1393 (2002).

Slobogin, Christopher and Joseph Schumacher. Reasonable Expectations of Privacy and Autonomy in Fourth Amendment Cases: An Empirical Look at "Understandings Recognized and Permitted by Society". 42 Duke L.J. 727 (1993).

Soree, Nadia B. Whose Fourth Amendment and Does It Matter?: A Due Process Approach to Fourth Amendment Standing. 46 Ind. L. Rev. 753 (2013).

Stuntz, William J. Privacy's Problem and the Law of Criminal Procedure. 93 Mich. L.Rev. 1016 (1995).

Sundby, Scott E. "Everyman's" Fourth Amendment: Privacy or Mutual Trust Between Government and Citizen? 94 Colum. L. Rev. 1751 (1994).

Wasserstrom, Silas. The Court's Turn Toward a General Reasonableness Interpretation of the Fourth Amendment. 27 Am.Crim.L.Rev. 119 (1989).

Yeager, Daniel. Search, Seizure and the Positive Law: Expectations of Privacy Outside the Fourth Amendment. 84 J. Crim. L. & Criminol. 249 (1993).

Chapter 5

THE SEARCH WARRANT

5.01   Introduction

Whether or not the Fourth Amendment states a preference for warrants,[1] the rationale for such a preference is clear. As Justice Jackson stated in *Johnson v. United States*:[2]

> The point of the Fourth Amendment . . . is not that it denies law enforcement the support of the usual inferences reasonable men draw from evidence. Its protection consists in requiring that those inferences be drawn by a neutral and detached magistrate instead of being judged by the officer engaged in the often competitive enterprise of ferreting out crime.

The assumption underlying this statement is that the interposition of a magistrate in the investigative decisionmaking process improves that process. While this premise can be questioned, it is probably sound. A study conducted by the National Center for State Courts found that magisterial review of warrant applications is often "perfunctory" (seldom lasting longer than five minutes), and rarely results in denial of an application.[3] At the same time, the study found that searches based on warrants are only occasionally subsequently found to be illegal,[4] and that the requirement that police obtain approval of their actions increases their "standard of care" because they, and the prosecutors advising them, know that a third party will be judging their decision to search.[5] According to the study, although the warrant requirement is perceived as "burdensome, time-consuming, intimidating, frustrating, and confusing" by the police, it seldom, if ever, results in the loss of "good cases."[6] Moreover, the advent of "telephonic warrants" and other time-saving devices can potentially improve the efficiency of the warrant process enormously.[7]

The language of the Fourth Amendment requires that a warrant be founded on "probable cause supported by oath or affirmation," and that it describe "with particularity the place to be searched and the things to be seized." As noted above, the Supreme Court has also held that the Fourth Amendment requires that the warrant be issued by a neutral and detached decisionmaker. Additional requirements, not clearly of constitutional stature, have been placed on the execution of warrants by statute or judicial decision. All of these issues are addressed in this chapter, beginning with the qualifications required of the decisionmaker.

---

[1]   See § 4.05(a).

[2]   333 U.S. 10, 68 S.Ct. 367 (1948).

[3]   See Richard Van Duizend, L. Paul Sutton & Charlotte A. Carter, The Search Warrant Process: Preconceptions, Perceptions, and Practices 31 (National Center for State Courts, undated).

[4]   The reversal rate appears to be less than 5%. Id. at 56.

[5]   Id. at 148–49.

[6]   Id. at 149, 96.

[7]   See Fed.R.Crim.P. 41(c)(2), permitting the police to call a magistrate and, based on recitation of the facts known to them, receive a judicial ruling over the phone, all of which is recorded and later transcribed.

5.02   The Neutral and Detached Decisionmaker

Because the primary purpose of the warrant requirement is to force the probable cause determination to be made by someone removed from the pressures of criminal investigation, the Supreme Court has taken pains to assure the decisionmaker is independent from law enforcement activities. Thus, in *Coolidge v. New Hampshire*,[8] search warrants issued by the state attorney general were declared invalid, even though he was authorized by state law to issue them. The Court concluded that the attorney general was not a "neutral and detached magistrate," especially since he was also the chief prosecutor in the case.

Although *Coolidge* left open the possibility that a prosecutor not involved in the case could constitutionally approve a warrant, the Court suggested otherwise in *United States v. United States District Court*.[9] At issue there was the President's power, acting through the Attorney General, to authorize electronic surveillance in internal security matters without prior judicial approval. The Court found the surveillances unlawful, again emphasizing the need for a neutral and detached magistrate. Justice Powell wrote:

> The Fourth Amendment does not contemplate the executive officers of Government as neutral and detached magistrates. Their duty and responsibility is to enforce the laws, to investigate and to prosecute. . . . [T]hose charged with this investigative and prosecutorial duty should not be the sole judges of when to utilize constitutionally sensitive means in pursuing their tasks. The historical judgment, which the Fourth Amendment accepts, is that unreviewed executive discretion may yield too readily to pressures to obtain incriminating evidence and overlook potential invasions of privacy and protected speech.

In some cases, even a magistrate may not be sufficiently neutral. In *Lo-Ji Sales, Inc. v. New York*,[10] the magistrate issued a search warrant for two specific "obscene" items, but also included in the warrant an authorization to seize any other items that he himself might find obscene upon examination at the searched premises. He then accompanied the police to the premises, decided which items beyond the two named in the warrant were to be seized, and added each to the initial warrant. The Supreme Court unanimously refused to accept the state's argument that the presence and participation of the magistrate in the search ensured that no items would be seized without probable cause. The Court found that the magistrate had failed to manifest the detached neutrality demanded of a judicial officer by the Fourth Amendment when he "conducted a generalized search under authority of an invalid warrant." In doing so, "he was not acting as a judicial officer but as an adjunct law-enforcement officer". The Court also found an infirmity in the fact that, upon finding a particular item obscene, the magistrate ordered the police to seize all "similar" items and allowed them to add the titles of the items they seized to the warrant. *Lo-Ji* demonstrates that a judicial officer, even if initially "independent" of the law enforcement process, can lose that independence through his own actions. It also stands for the proposition that the authority to decide probable cause cannot be delegated to police officers.

---

[8]   403 U.S. 443, 91 S.Ct. 2022 (1971).

[9]   407 U.S. 297, 92 S.Ct. 2125 (1972).

[10]   442 U.S. 319, 99 S.Ct. 2319 (1979).

The Supreme Court has also recognized that a magistrate's objectivity may be compromised by pressure from something other than a desire to "ferret out crime." In *Connally v. Georgia*,[11] the Court was confronted with a statute which provided that unsalaried justices of the peace were to receive five dollars for each warrant issued but nothing if they reviewed an application and denied it. Finding that this statute subjected suspects to "judicial action by an officer of a court who has 'a direct, personal, substantial, pecuniary interest' in his conclusion to issue or to deny the warrant," a unanimous Court found that it violated the Fourth Amendment.

If the necessary neutrality is present, warrants may be issued by judicial branch officials who are not judges, at least in some circumstances. In *Shadwick v. Tampa*,[12] the Court held that clerks of the Tampa municipal court were qualified as "neutral and detached" magistrates for the purpose of issuing arrest warrants for violations of city ordinances, because they were appointed from a classified civil service list, under the supervision of the municipal court judge, and removed from the prosecutor and police. The Court noted that nonlawyers not only have been acting as magistrates for years but have also been assumed to be competent to make decisions as members of grand juries and juries. The key inquiry is not the degree of legal training but whether the third party decisionmaker has sufficient objectivity to make a better decision than law enforcement officers on the "frontlines."

5.03   The Probable Cause Determination

Assuming the person making the probable cause determination is sufficiently divorced from law enforcement activity, the next question is whether the warrant issued was supported by probable cause. This section explores the meaning the Supreme Court has given this elusive term, the procedure for determining whether it exists, and ways of attacking that determination.

It is important to note that the probable cause concept is also extremely important in connection with many of the *exceptions* to the search warrant requirement, because they often require probable cause as a predicate, in addition to some type of exigent circumstances.[13] Thus, although the discussion below focuses on cases involving search warrants, it is relevant to several subsequent chapters in this book.[14]

(a) General Definition

The Supreme Court has explained that probable cause to search exists when the facts and circumstances in a given situation are sufficient to warrant a person of reasonable caution to believe that seizable objects are located at the place to be searched.[15] This language makes clear that probable cause is objectively defined, and not dependent upon the subjective views of the searching officer or authorizing magistrate. The degree of certainty required lies somewhere between "reasonable

---

[11]   429 U.S. 245, 97 S.Ct. 546 (1977).

[12]   407 U.S. 345, 92 S.Ct. 2119 (1972).

[13]   E.g., the "automobile exception" (Chapter 7) and the "plain view" exception (Chapter 10). Other exceptions require probable cause to arrest, e.g., the "search incident" exception (Chapter 6) and the "hot pursuit" exception (Chapter 8).

[14]   Where warrantless searches and seizures are involved, appellate review of probable cause (and reasonable suspicion) is *de novo*, although due weight is to be given inferences drawn by local judges and law enforcement officers. *Ornelas v. United States*, 517 U.S. 690, 116 S.Ct. 1657 (1996).

[15]   *Brinegar v. United States*, 338 U.S. 160, 69 S.Ct. 1302 (1949).

suspicion," the quantum of certainty required to justify a "stop and frisk,"[16] and "beyond a reasonable doubt," the standard of proof in a criminal trial. Literally interpreted, the term seems to require a more likely than not showing that the evidence sought will be found. Whether this is indeed the standard is open to question. The American Law Institute's formulation uses the term "reasonable cause" rather than probable cause, apparently to avoid the implication that a standard of "more probable than not" is required.[17]

Perhaps more importantly, the Supreme Court has made clear that probable cause is a flexibly defined concept. In *United States v. Ventresca*,[18] FBI agents observed repeated deliveries of loads of sugar in 60-pound bags, smelled the odor of fermenting mash, and heard sounds similar to that of a motor or a pump coming from the direction of Ventresca's house. In concluding that the agents' affidavit stating these facts amply established probable cause to support the issuance of the warrant, the Court held that affidavits should be tested in "a commonsense and realistic fashion," and reviewing courts should "not invalidate the warrant by interpreting the affidavit in a hypertechnical, rather than a commonsense, manner." The Court has vigorously reaffirmed *Ventresca* in more recent decisions to be discussed below.

The Court has also emphasized that the probable cause standard usually represents the same "level of certainty" regardless of the type of search contemplated. For example, in *New York v. P.J. Video*,[19] it held that searches for material that may be protected by the First Amendment need not be justified by any greater level of suspicion than searches seeking other types of evidence.[20] Occasionally, however, the Court has defined probable cause to mean a level of certainty below the more-likely-than not standard. In particular, some of its regulatory decisions, while requiring warrants based on "probable cause," actually permit inspections based on a very low probability that evidence of illegal activity will be found.[21]

Probable cause can refer to future as well as past facts or conditions. At issue in *United States v. Grubbs*[22] was the constitutionality of "anticipatory warrants"— warrants based on a finding that, at some future time, there will be probable cause to believe evidence will be located at a specified place. The warrant in *Grubbs* authorized search of Grubbs' residence upon a "controlled delivery" of a package containing a pornographic videotape that Grubbs had ordered.[23] Grubbs argued that the warrant was not based on probable cause, because at the time the warrant was issued the triggering condition had not yet occurred. A unanimous Court (Justice Alito not participating) dismissed this argument, emphasizing that probable cause exists *whenever* there is "a fair probability that contraband or evidence of a crime will be found in a particular place." As Justice Scalia stated for the Court, "all warrants are, in a sense, 'anticipatory' because they are based on a prediction that the evidence described will be in the

---

[16]   See § 11.03(a) for a discussion of the reasonable suspicion standard.

[17]   ALI, Model Code of Pre-Arraignment Procedure § 220.1(5) (1975).

[18]   380 U.S. 102, 85 S.Ct. 741 (1965).

[19]   475 U.S. 868, 106 S.Ct. 1610 (1986).

[20]   However, the Court has also indicated that when a seizure may act as a "prior restraint," an adversary proceeding must precede the seizure. *Marcus v. Search Warrants*, 367 U.S. 717, 81 S.Ct. 1708 (1961), discussed in § 5.06(b).

[21]   See, e.g., *Camara v. Municipal Court*, 387 U.S. 523, 87 S.Ct. 1727 (1967), discussed in § 13.02.

[22]   547 U.S. 90, 126 S.Ct. 1494 (2006).

[23]   See § 4.03(e) for a discussion of the controlled delivery technique.

identified house." Scalia also noted that electronic surveillance warrants had never been considered invalid even though they are always based on a prediction that the evidence—i.e., the conversations—will be seized at some time in the future. However, the Court also stated that, in an anticipatory warrant situation of the type involved in *Grubbs*, the issuing magistrate must be sure to find probable cause to believe the triggering condition will occur, as well as that evidence will be found once it does occur.

"Probable cause" is required to justify an arrest as well as a search and much of what is said in this book concerning probable cause in the former context is relevant here as well.[24] However, it should be clear that probable cause for a search does not automatically support an arrest, nor does a valid arrest warrant automatically support a search. Thus, for example, in order to obtain a search warrant, police need not allege that the place to be searched is controlled by a person connected with a crime (though this, of course, will frequently be the case). Conversely, the fact that a person believed to have committed a crime is in a certain location does not necessarily justify a search of every inch of that location. In short, a search is founded upon differing probabilities than an arrest.[25]

(b) Hearsay Information: Criteria for Use

Several Supreme Court cases have held that, as Federal Rule of Criminal Procedure 41(c) provides: "The finding of probable cause may be based upon hearsay evidence in whole or in part." Because the probable cause finding is based on probabilities, it may rely on evidence that would not be admissible at trial. However, as the Court stated in *Jones v. United States*,[26] there should be a "substantial basis for crediting the hearsay" before it forms the predicate for a probable cause determination. When the hearsay upon which the affiant-officer relies is from another police officer, or from a "respectable citizen" who has been the victim of a crime or witnessed it, the Court has been relatively relaxed about evaluating its basis.[27] But when the hearsay comes from "informants"—that is, people whose motivation to inform is money, or a reduction in charges or some other direct benefit from the police—the Court has been much more careful about gauging reliability.

The two leading cases in this regard during the Warren Court years were *Aguilar v. Texas*[28] and *Spinelli v. United States*.[29] In *Aguilar*, a search warrant had issued upon an affidavit from two police officers who swore only that they had "received reliable information from a credible person and do believe" that narcotics were being illegally stored on the described premises. The Court held the affidavit inadequate for two reasons: (1) The affidavit did not state sufficient underlying circumstances to permit a neutral and detached magistrate to understand how the informant reached his conclusion; and (2) the affidavit did not state sufficient underlying circumstances establishing the reliability or credibility of the informant. According to the Court, both the "basis-of-knowledge" prong and the "veracity" prong of this test had to be met to support a warrant's issuance.

---

[24]   See § 3.03.

[25]   See Edward Imwinkelreid, et al. Criminal Evidence 216, n. 14 (1976).

[26]   362 U.S. 257, 80 S.Ct. 725 (1960).

[27]   See §§ 3.03(a)(2) & (3), for a discussion of this issue, in the context of probable cause to arrest.

[28]   378 U.S. 108, 84 S.Ct. 1509 (1964).

[29]   393 U.S. 410, 89 S.Ct. 584 (1969).

In *Spinelli*, the Court reaffirmed *Aguilar's* two-prong test. There, a search warrant was issued on the basis of an FBI agent's affidavit alleging: (1) that an informant had told the agent that Spinelli was taking bets over two telephone numbers; (2) that FBI surveillance had independently resulted in knowledge that Spinelli had gone to the apartment where these two phones were located four times in a five-day period; and (3) that Spinelli was a known gambler and an associate of gamblers. The Court found this affidavit insufficient as well, because it failed to set forth the "underlying circumstances" describing how the informant obtained his information and did not contain reasons for the FBI agent's belief that the informant was reliable.[30] The information that Spinelli was a known gambler was viewed as irrelevant, by itself, on the issue of the informant's credibility.

The two-prong *Aguilar-Spinelli* test remained the law for over a decade. But in *Illinois v. Gates*,[31] a five-member majority explicitly "abandoned" the *Aguilar-Spinelli* rules and "reaffirm[ed] the totality of the circumstances analysis that traditionally has informed probable cause determinations." The search warrant issued in *Gates* was based on an anonymous handwritten letter sent to the Bloomingdale, Illinois police department. It charged that the defendants, Lance and Susan Gates, were involved in ferrying drugs from Florida to Illinois and that they had over $100,000 worth of drugs in their home. The letter also specified that the Gates were about to receive a new drug shipment. According to the letter, Sue Gates would drive to Florida to pick up the drugs on May 3rd, leave the car at West Palm Beach and fly back; Lance Gates would then fly down to drive the car back. The police verified that an L. Gates did in fact fly to Florida on May 5th; they also observed him rendezvous with a woman staying in a room registered to Susan Gates, and leave with her the next morning driving in the direction of Illinois. The warrant was issued on the basis of this information, and the subsequent search of the Gates' car and home after they arrived in Chicago uncovered several hundred pounds of marijuana, weapons and other contraband.

In invalidating the warrant and the search based on it, the Illinois Supreme Court evaluated the probable cause determination in light of each of the *Aguilar-Spinelli* prongs.[32] It concluded that the "veracity" prong of the test was not satisfied because, "[t]here was simply no basis" for concluding that the anonymous person who wrote the letter to the Bloomingdale police department was credible. In addition, according to the court, the letter gave no indication of the basis for the writer's knowledge of the defendants' activities. The United States Supreme Court, in an opinion by Justice Rehnquist, found the Illinois court's treatment of the warrant in *Gates* hypertechnical. While affirming that an informant's "veracity" and "basis of knowledge" are highly relevant to the probable cause determination, the Court did not view these elements as separate and independent requirements to be rigidly interpreted in every case. Rather, "they should be understood simply as closely intertwined issues that may usefully illuminate the commonsense, practical question whether there is 'probable cause.'" Thus, the Court concluded, "a deficiency in one may be compensated for, in determining the overall reliability of a tip, by a strong showing as to the other, or by some other indicia of reliability." Applying this "commonsense" approach to the *Gates* facts, the Court reversed the Illinois Supreme Court. It held that the letter alone would not have

---

[30]   Indeed, there was some indication the "informant" was an illegal wiretap of Spinelli's phone.

[31]   462 U.S. 213, 103 S.Ct. 2317 (1983).

[32]   *People v. Gates*, 85 Ill.2d 376, 53 Ill.Dec. 218, 423 N.E.2d 887 (1981).

furnished probable cause but that once most of its contents were corroborated by the police, a warrant could validly be issued.

The majority opinion in *Gates* reiterated at several points the need to avoid burdening the probable cause determination with "legal technicalities" or one "neat set of rules." But several lower court decisions after *Gates* suggested that while the decision had refocused the analysis of probable cause, it would have little impact on individual cases.[33] Perhaps aware of this tendency, the Supreme Court subsequently warned against dismissing *Gates* as a mere "refinement." In summarily reversing *Massachusetts v. Upton*,[34] a decision in which the Massachusetts Supreme Judicial Court stated that *Gates* did not mark a "significant change in the appropriate Fourth Amendment treatment of applications for search warrants,"[35] the Supreme Court insisted that *Gates* was not meant merely as a qualification of the two-pronged test, but rather sought to reject the test as "hypertechnical."

There follows an attempt to parse out the factors that are relevant to evaluating hearsay information after *Gates*. Because *Gates* and *Upton* have emphasized that "a deficiency in one [factor] may be compensated for . . . by a strong showing as to the other, or by some other indicia of reliability," any one of these factors, by itself, may be sufficient to establish that a tip is reliable enough to be used in evaluating whether probable cause exists.[36]

(1) Basis of Knowledge

As established in *Aguilar*, a good description of how the informant came to know about the alleged criminal activity is an important element in assessing credibility. If the informant persuasively shows that he was personally involved in the criminal transaction or otherwise observed it firsthand, his credibility will be viewed as relatively high. For instance, the affidavit which the Court upheld in *Jones v. United States*,[37] stated, among other things,[38] that the informant had "on many occasions . . . gone to [the suspects'] apartment and purchased narcotic drugs from the [suspects]," a statement which was bolstered by the affiant's own statement that he knew the informant to be a drug user and had seen needle marks on his arm. On the other hand, if the informant's allegations appear to be based on gossip, or do not have an identified basis, their credibility is questionable. As the Court's decisions indicate, the tips in *Aguilar* and *Spinelli*, and the anonymous letter in *Gates*, were completely lacking on this score.

(2) Detailed Description of Activity

In *Spinelli*, the Court announced an alternative method of conforming to the "basis-of-knowledge" prong. As Justice Harlan stated for the Court, "[i]n the absence of a statement detailing the manner in which the information was gathered, it is especially

---

[33]   See *Whisman v. Commonwealth*, 667 S.W.2d 394 (Ky.App. 1984); *State v. Ricci*, 472 A.2d 291 (R.I. 1984); *State v. Yananokwiak*, 65 N.C.App. 513, 309 S.E.2d 560 (1983). But see *United States v. Mendoza*, 722 F.2d 96 (5th Cir. 1983).

[34]   466 U.S. 727, 104 S.Ct. 2085 (1984).

[35]   *Commonwealth v. Upton*, 390 Mass. 562, 458 N.E.2d 717 (1983).

[36]   Note, however, that even if a tip is considered reliable, the information it provides may not establish probable cause. See, e.g., § 3.03(a)(2).

[37]   362 U.S. 257, 80 S.Ct. 725 (1960).

[38]   The affidavit also stated that the informant's information had been corroborated "by other sources of information" and that the informant had given reliable information in the past.

important that the tip describe the accused's criminal activity in sufficient detail that the magistrate may know that he is relying on something more substantial than a casual rumor . . . or an accusation based merely on an individual's general reputation." In *Spinelli*, this test was not met because the only facts supplied—that Spinelli was using two specified phones and that these phones were being used in gambling operations— "could easily have been obtained from an offhand remark heard at a neighborhood bar." A case in which suitable detail was provided, according to Harlan, was *Draper v. United States*,[39] in which the informant alleged that Draper would arrive on a particular train from Chicago on one of two specified mornings, wear particular clothes and be carrying a briefcase.

In a concurring opinion in *Gates*, Justice White suggested that the anonymous letter in that case provided detail on a par with the informant's information in *Draper*. According to White, given the amount of detail about the suspects' travel plans in the letter, "the magistrate could reasonably have inferred, as he apparently did, that the informant, . . . obtained his information in a reliable way." Of course, as Justice Stevens pointed out in his dissent in *Gates*, "each year dozens of perfectly innocent people fly to Florida, meet a waiting spouse, and drive off together in the family car." But the point of *Spinelli* is that when, as in both *Draper* and *Gates*, the informant states he knows or can predict *intimate* detail about the suspect, the probability that he has reliable "inside" information about the suspect's criminal activity is greater. A rich description of the suspect's home can be obtained from many sources and usually does not connote any knowledge about his crime; a point-by-point recitation of travel plans is likely to be available only to a few, and thus suggests the close relationship necessary to find out about criminal activity as well.

Spinelli also made clear, however, that no amount of detail is, by itself, enough; as noted above, it also required some showing of veracity on the part of the informant. Detailed information is not particularly helpful in this regard, since an informant can "fabricate in fine detail as easily as with rough brush strokes."[40] Yet the Court seemed to disregard this admonition in *Gates*. Justice Rehnquist stated that "even if we entertain some doubt as to an informant's motives, his explicit and detailed description of alleged wrongdoing, along with a statement that the event was observed firsthand, entitles his tip to greater weight than might otherwise be the case." If this statement is taken seriously, detailed allegations by informants would have to be treated with the same generosity as those made by police officers or "respectable" citizens.

(3) Past Reliability of Informant

The primary way of meeting the "veracity" prong of the *Aguilar-Spinelli* test was to establish that the informant had given reliable information in the past. Perhaps the strongest example of this sort from the Court's cases is *McCray v. Illinois*,[41] where the informant had provided information on fifteen or sixteen previous occasions, many of which resulted in arrests and convictions.[42] But the Court has also sanctioned boilerplate statements to the effect that the informant "has given reliable information in the past,"

---

[39]   358 U.S. 307, 79 S.Ct. 329 (1959), discussed in more detail in § 3.03(a)(1).

[40]   *Stanley v. State*, 19 Md.App. 507, 313 A.2d 847 (1974).

[41]   386 U.S. 300, 87 S.Ct. 1056 (1967).

[42]   Although information that results merely in arrest, as opposed to conviction, is not necessarily reliable, the recency of the arrest (and thus the likelihood the charge has not yet been adjudicated) should be taken into account.

albeit with the additional requirement that there should be some other indicia of reliability as well.[43]

In *Gates*, consistent with its totality of the circumstances ruling, the Court suggested that sufficient allegations of veracity may, by themselves, meet the standard announced in that case. As an example of how a deficiency in the basis-of-knowledge prong could be compensated for, Justice Rehnquist stated: if "a particular informant is known for the unusual reliability of his predictions of certain types of criminal activities in a locality, his failure, in a particular case, to thoroughly set forth the basis of his knowledge surely should not serve as an absolute bar to a finding of probable cause based on his tip." But this statement should be read narrowly. As Justice White stated in his concurrence, even *police officers* who are known to be honest should have to provide some basis for their belief that evidence is located in a particular area.

(4) Corroboration by Police

An informant's veracity can also be supported by police corroboration of his statements. In both *Draper* and *Gates*, for instance, the Court emphasized that the police observed events that fit the information given by the informant.[44] The fact that the corroboration in both cases was of "innocent detail" was not considered problematic because, as indicated above, the details were of the type only intimates were likely to know. Of course, to be useful to a magistrate making the probable cause determination, this corroboration should occur before a warrant is sought by the police. Thus, the fact that the police in *Gates* eventually found drugs in the suspects' basement, as predicted by the anonymous letter, was irrelevant, since the discovery came after the warrant was issued.

Apparently it is not fatal if, during their attempts to corroborate the informant's information, police find some of it to be in error. In his dissent in *Gates*, Justice Stevens pointed out that the anonymous letter had been incorrect with respect to what he termed a "material" fact (that Lance Gates would drive the car back to Illinois *alone*). Justice Rehnquist discarded this mistake as unimportant, on the ground that "[w]e have never required that informants used by the police be infallible, and can see no reason to impose such a requirement in this case."[45] It also appears, once again, that boilerplate language to the effect that corroboration has taken place may be sufficient if other factors are present as well.[46]

(5) Other Indicia of Reliability

In holding that "other indicia of reliability" besides the basis-of-knowledge and veracity prongs should be considered in evaluating the credibility of tips, *Gates* cited *United States v. Harris*.[47] That decision, handed down two years after *Spinelli*, advanced two additional ways of supporting an informant's allegations, in a melange of opinions which showed a Court already somewhat dissatisfied with the *Aguilar-Spinelli*

---

[43]   In *Jones v. United States*, 362 U.S. 257, 80 S.Ct. 725 (1960), the affidavit included the boilerplate about informant reliability but added that the informant's information had been corroborated by "other sources of information."

[44]   For further description of *Draper*, see § 3.03(a)(1).

[45]   While Rehnquist is correct that courts do not require informants to be infallible, the cases that stand for this proposition have involved discovery of the error *after* the search or seizure took place. See § 5.03(d).

[46]   See *Jones*, supra note 43.

[47]   403 U.S. 573, 91 S.Ct. 2075 (1971).

formulation. In *Harris*, the affidavit stated that the affiant had viewed the informant and judged him to be "prudent;" that the informant had purchased illegal whiskey from the suspect; and that the suspect had a reputation for trafficking in whiskey. A divided Court reversed the lower court's determination that the affidavit was insufficient under *Aguilar's* veracity prong. Four justices reached this result because they were willing to permit both police knowledge of the suspect's reputation and the informant's declaration against penal interest to bolster his credibility. In separate opinions, Justice Stewart was willing to subscribe only to the first rationale, while Justice White would only sign on to the second. The four dissenters criticized both methods of judging reliability.

Chief Justice Burger's opinion for the Court acknowledged that, in *Spinelli*, the Court had called the assertion that the suspect was known to the affiant as a gambler "bald and unilluminating" and had concluded that it was entitled to "no weight." But he disagreed with this pronouncement, stating that a suspect's reputation was a "practical consideration of everyday life" that should be considered in assessing reliability, and thus rejected *Spinelli's* indication to the contrary. With respect to declarations against interest, Burger asserted that "[p]eople do not lightly admit a crime and place critical evidence in the hands of the police in the form of their own admissions." Thus, such declarations "carry their own indicia of credibility—sufficient at least to support a finding of probable cause to search."

While the reputation of the suspect may bolster the informant's allegations to the extent they are consistent with that reputation, a conclusory statement in this regard is not particularly helpful to a magistrate because it does not tell him whether the reputation is deserved. At best, unless the reputation evidence is supported factually, it is useful only as support for an *officer's* probable cause determination in those situations where he is allowed to proceed without a warrant. And, as Justice Harlan pointed out in his dissenting opinion, declarations against interest in the informant context should be taken with a grain of salt, since the informant may be anonymous, or may have already received or be expecting to receive assurances that his indiscretions will not be prosecuted. Yet *Gates* apparently allows both conclusory statements about reputation and declarations against interest to be considered in the magistrate's totality of the circumstances analysis.

(c) Oath or Affirmation

Given the explicit language of the Fourth Amendment, all documents requesting a warrant (i.e., the application for a warrant and any accompanying documentation or affidavits) must be "affirmed" or sworn to by the officer making the application, usually in writing. If oral testimony is given, it too must be given under oath. For example, the federal rules provide that "[b]efore ruling on a request for a warrant the federal magistrate or state judge may require the affiant to appear personally and may examine under oath the affiant and any witness he may produce," provided the proceeding is recorded and made part of the affidavit.[48] Neither the oath nor the testimony need be made in the magistrate's presence, at least when pursuant to rules governing the issuance of telephonic warrants.[49]

---

[48] Fed.R.Crim.P. 41(c).

[49] See *United States v. Turner*, 558 F.2d 46 (2d Cir. 1977) (finding that magistrate's approval, over the phone, of warrant requested by officer in the field who swears to sufficient facts complies with oath or affirmation clause).

(d) Challenging the Probable Cause Determination; the Informant Privilege

A frequent issue in suppression hearings is whether the magistrate, or the police officer in cases where no warrant was necessary, had probable cause to act. In cases where there is a warrant, this challenge usually must be based entirely on information provided in the warrant application and supporting affidavits. As the Supreme Court stated in *Whiteley v. Warden*,[50] "an otherwise insufficient affidavit cannot be rehabilitated by testimony concerning information possessed by the affiant when he sought the warrant but not disclosed to the issuing magistrate." A contrary ruling, reasoned the Court, would "render the warrant requirement of the Fourth Amendment meaningless."

Occasionally, however, the defendant will want to challenge the accuracy of the statements made by the affiant or the affiant's informants. To do so requires going behind the warrant application and supporting documentation. Under the Supreme Court's cases, such challenges will rarely be successful. First, the Court seems to have held, and rightly so, that even if information underlying a probable cause determination turns out to be false, the warrant, or the warrantless search, is not defective if the information was such that a "prudent reasonable person" could rely on it and the officer honestly relied on it.[51] Second, even if the information was unreasonably relied upon, the defendant's ability to prove this fact at a hearing, and to have the tainted search declared invalid, has been severely circumscribed by the Court's decision in *Franks v. Delaware*.[52]

In *Franks*, the defendant sought a hearing to challenge a statement in the warrant affidavit to the effect that one of his co-workers had implicated him in criminal activity. In view of the defendant's proffer of testimony from the co-worker that such statements were never made, the Supreme Court was willing to grant a hearing. But in doing so, it required prospective challengers to meet three conditions before a hearing could take place, and also announced several government-oriented rules concerning the hearing itself, the combined effect of which is to ensure that most defendants will have great difficulty successfully mounting such challenges.

First, the allegation that the information was false must be more than conclusory and must be supported by more than a desire to cross-examine. Specifically, the defendant must: (1) allege that statements were made deliberately or with reckless disregard for the truth; (2) specifically point out the portion of the warrant that is claimed to be false; (3) accompany this proffer with a statement of supporting reasons; and (4) furnish affidavits of sworn or otherwise reliable statements of witnesses concerning the statements, or explain the absence of such witnesses. Allegations of negligent or innocent mistake are insufficient.

Secondly, the defendant is permitted to challenge only information supplied by affiants (i.e., police officers). With this limitation, the Court meant to implement the so-called "informant's privilege," which keeps the identity of police informants confidential

---

[50]   401 U.S. 560, 91 S.Ct. 1031 (1971).

[51]   *Henry v. United States*, 361 U.S. 98, 80 S.Ct. 168 (1959). The exception to this rule is when the information is provided by another police officer who knows or has reason to believe it is false. See infra note 56.

[52]   438 U.S. 154, 98 S.Ct. 2674 (1978).

in order to maintain their usefulness and prevent reprisals against them (and thus encourages others to inform as well).[53] In *McCray v. Illinois*,[54] the Court had already held that, despite the accused's right of confrontation under the Sixth Amendment, a defendant's motion to subpoena an informant for trial may be denied whenever the trial judge feels that the informant's testimony would not directly contradict other evidence before the court.[55] This wide-ranging discretion granted the trial judge in *McCray* was reinforced at the pretrial stage by the holding in *Franks*, which not only immunizes from pretrial attack the veracity of an informant, but also makes very difficult any challenge of a police officer's statement about what the informant said.[56]

As a third condition, the defendant must show that, assuming the challenged information is indeed false and thus must be deleted, the remainder of the information in the warrant application would not support a probable cause finding. Only if the rest of the evidence is insufficient for this purpose is the defendant entitled to a hearing under *Franks*. Finally, if the defendant is successful in making the showing required to earn a hearing, he must still establish at that hearing, by a preponderance of the evidence, that the false statement was made by the affiant deliberately, or with reckless disregard for the truth. If the defendant can make these showings, the search warrant is voided, and the fruits of the search are excluded in the same manner as if the defect appeared on the face of the warrant.

Franks can be criticized on a number of levels. First, its ban on challenging informant tips is an overly broad attempt to protect the informant privilege, particularly in light of the recognized tendency on the part of the police to invent informants.[57] As several lower courts have held, an informant can be interviewed *in camera* by the judge,[58] thus protecting against disclosure of his identity while at the same time permitting some assessment of a defendant's claims of falsehood. Second, *Franks'* requirement that the defendant allege and prove the affiant was reckless with respect to the truth disregards the Fourth Amendment's requirement that officers be "reasonable," a requirement which suggests that only negligence need be shown. Third, once the defendant shows a statement to be false, the burden of showing recklessness or negligence, as the case may be, should be on the officer, in line with the normal burden allocation in civil cases on the issue of a party's mental state (which only the party can truly know). Finally, *Franks'* "independent source" rule—that a warrant based on false statements will be allowed to stand if probable cause still exists upon removal of the tainted information—is suspect, to the extent it encourages officers to fabricate intentionally in cases where there is significant evidence against the defendant.[59]

---

[53] See 8 John Wigmore, Evidence § 2374 (1961).

[54] 386 U.S. 300, 87 S.Ct. 1056 (1967).

[55] The most likely situation in which the defense can overcome assertions of privilege is when the informant is the sole witness to the alleged criminal event (other than the defendant) and the defense is entrapment. See § 28.06(b).

[56] However, *Franks* suggested that, when the informant is another officer, police cannot "insulate one officer's deliberate misstatement merely by relaying it through an officer-affiant personally ignorant of its falsity." See § 3.03(c).

[57] See, e.g., Christopher Slobogin, *Testilying: Police Perjury and What To Do About It*, 67 Colo. L.Rev. 1037, 1043 (1996).

[58] See, e.g., *People v. Brown*, 207 Cal.App.3d 1541, 256 Cal.Rptr. 11 (4th Dist. 1989).

[59] See also, in this regard, § 2.04(c), discussing the independent source doctrine and the exclusionary rule.

5.04   The Particularity Requirement

The Fourth Amendment requires that warrants state with "particularity the place to searched and the things to be seized." The original purpose of this clause was to prevent the practice, common during colonial times, of relying on "general warrants" to search for "evidence of treason" and similarly broadly phrased objectives.[60] When a warrant specifies the place to be searched and things to be seized, it limits the scope of the search. Additionally, an application which is particular as to these two factors is more likely to be founded on a thorough investigation, and thus more likely to establish probable cause, which of course is required for any warrant to issue.

Thus, in *Groh v. Ramirez*,[61] the Court found unconstitutional a warrant that did not identify any of the items police wanted to seize, even though it did precisely indicate the residence to be searched and even though the underlying application set out in detail the items the police sought. Justice Stevens wrote for six members of the Court that, on these facts, "[t]he warrant was plainly invalid." Without a listing of the items sought on the face of the warrant, Stevens said, "there can be no written assurance that the Magistrate actually found probable cause to search for, and to seize, every item mentioned in the affidavit."[62] Here, for instance, a number of different weapons, as well as files and papers, were sought by police, yet the magistrate might have sanctioned seizure of only a portion of these items had he been forced to particularly describe what could be seized. Further, the Court stated, without a particularized warrant, "we ... cannot know whether the Magistrate was aware of the scope of the search he was authorizing," nor does the warrant inform the target of the search about the need for and limits on the search.

The Court has also indicated, however, that the Particularity Clause does not require the specification of anything *other* than the place to be searched and the items to be seized. In *Dalia v. United States*,[63] the Court held that a warrant authorizing electronic surveillance of particular conversations in a specified residence did not also need to authorize the covert entry necessary to install the eavesdropping device. And, as noted earlier, in *United States v. Grubbs*,[64] the Court held that an "anticipatory warrant" based on probable cause that evidence would be found in a particular residence after a "controlled delivery" need not specify the triggering condition of delivery. According to the Court, "[t]he Fourth Amendment ... does not set forth some general 'particularity requirement.' It specifies only two matters that must be 'particularly described[ed]' in the warrant: 'the place to be searched' and 'the persons or things to be seized.'"

(a) Place to Be Searched

The warrant need not state with precision the place to be searched. It "is enough if the description is such that the officer with a search warrant can, with reasonable effort, ascertain and identify the place intended."[65] Occasionally, the warrant description will

---

[60]   See Telford Taylor, Two Studies in Constitutional Interpretation 23–50 (1969).

[61]   540 U.S. 551, 124 S.Ct. 1284 (2004).

[62]   The Court did suggest, however, that a warrant that cross-referenced a detailed affidavit would suffice. See *United States v. McGrew*, 122 F.3d 847, 849–50 (9th Cir. 1997); *United States v. Williamson*, 1 F.3d 1134, 1136 n.1 (10th Cir. 1993).

[63]   441 U.S. 238, 99 S.Ct. 1682 (1979), discussed further in § 14.03(e)(1).

[64]   547 U.S. 90, 126 S.Ct. 1494 (2006), discussed in § 5.03(a).

[65]   *Steele v. United States*, 267 U.S. 498, 45 S.Ct. 414 (1925).

be mistaken. In *Maryland v. Garrison*,[66] the Supreme Court held that whether a mistake as to the place to be searched renders the warrant invalid depends upon the extent to which it was possible for an officer, acting reasonably, to discover a mistake at the time the warrant application was filed.

In *Garrison*, police officers sought and obtained a warrant to search the person of one Lawrence McWebb and "the premises known as 2036 Park Avenue third floor apartment," alleging that McWebb's apartment occupied the entire third floor of his apartment building. Actually, there were two apartments on the third floor, one belonging to Garrison, a fact the police claimed they did not discover until they had begun searching Garrison's apartment and found contraband. The Court, in a 6–3 opinion authored by Justice Stevens, found that the warrant did not violate the particularity requirement. Stevens noted that the informant who had provided police with information about McWebb had not mentioned a second apartment on McWebb's floor and that police inquiries at the local utility company had left the impression that the third floor had only one apartment. Finding that the officers had been sufficiently diligent in their attempts to ascertain who lived on the third floor prior to seeking the warrant, the Court held that the warrant was valid when issued.[67]

The Court emphasized, however, that the analysis of the particularity issue should not be influenced by events subsequent to the execution of the warrant.

> Just as the discovery of contraband cannot validate a warrant invalid when issued, so is it equally clear that the discovery of facts demonstrating that a valid warrant was unnecessarily broad does not retroactively invalidate the warrant. The validity of the warrant must be assessed on the basis of the information that the officers disclosed, or had a duty to discover and to disclose, to the magistrate.

(b) Things to Be Seized

The magistrate should ensure that the warrant is as specific as possible in identifying the items to be seized. A good example of a case where this admonition was not followed is *Lo-Ji Sales, Inc. v. New York*,[68] which concerned a warrant that authorized search of an adult book store not only to seize two specified films, but also to seize any items that the issuing magistrate might find "obscene" when he examined them at the store. A unanimous Court found that this warrant failed to "particularly describe . . . the things to be seized." In addition to surrendering his neutrality by going into the field, the magistrate had issued a warrant "reminiscent of the general warrants" meant to be prohibited by the Fourth Amendment.

In contrast, in *Andresen v. Maryland*,[69] the Court upheld a warrant that authorized seizure of a long list of specified documents, but ended with the phrase "together with other fruits, instrumentalities and evidence of crime at this [time] unknown." After construing this phrase to refer to the crime under investigation and noting that the crime was a complex one that "could be proved only by piecing together may bits of evidence," the Court upheld the warrant. The Court seemed impressed by the fact that the

---

[66]   480 U.S. 79, 107 S.Ct. 1013 (1987).

[67]   For discussion of *Garrison's* further holding with respect to execution of the warrant, see § 5.05(b).

[68]   442 U.S. 319, 99 S.Ct. 2319 (1979).

[69]   427 U.S. 463, 96 S.Ct. 2737 (1976).

investigating agents had included in the warrant application all the evidence then thought to be on the premises searched. Unfortunately, boilerplate language of the type involved in *Andresen* is often included (and upheld) in warrants under circumstances that are not as indicative of careful policework. For instance, in some jurisdictions warrants *routinely* authorize searches for and seizures of "rent receipts, personal correspondence and effects, keys, and other items that demonstrate dominion or control" of the premises.[70] As discussed below,[71] this type of language may improperly expand police authority to conduct searches.

5.05   Execution of the Warrant

Several issues arise with respect to executing a search warrant: (1) when may a warrant be executed?; (2) what is the effect of police mistake as to the premises to be searched? (3) must officers executing a warrant knock and announce their presence?; (4) are there any restrictions on the manner in which the search may be conducted? (5) what authority beyond that provided in the warrant do police have to search or seize persons or evidence found during its execution?; (6) when may the media accompany police?; and (7) what requirements are imposed on officers after they have seized the evidence? These issues are discussed here.

(a) Time Limitations

Service of the warrant should take place promptly so that the conditions underlying the probable cause determination do not dissipate. In some circumstances, delay may void the warrant. Two such situations would be if the language of the warrant itself commands that the search be conducted within a certain time, or if the underlying statute contains a time limit that will result in void service if it is exceeded. The federal rules, for instance, provide that the warrant must command the officer to search within a specified period of time not to exceed ten days.[72] Construing a predecessor to this rule in *Sgro v. United States*,[73] the Supreme Court found invalid a search of a hotel room for illegal intoxicants pursuant to a warrant affidavit that alleged a purchase of beer there three weeks earlier. *Sgro* also suggests that the Fourth Amendment itself prohibits undue delay in the absence of time constraints imposed by statute or warrant.

It is common to restrict service of warrants (both for arrests and searches) to the daytime unless nocturnal execution is specifically authorized. Federal Rule 41(e)(2) requires daytime execution unless the issuing authority, by provision in the warrant and for reasonable cause shown, authorizes execution at other times.[74] Some Supreme Court members have expressed the opinion that, given its intrusive nature, a nighttime search should only be permitted upon a showing of higher-than-normal probable cause.[75]

---

[70]   Van Duizend, Sutton & Carter, supra note 3, at 22.

[71]   See § 5.05(e).

[72]   Fed.R.Crim.P. 41(e)(2)(A)(i).

[73]   287 U.S. 206, 53 S.Ct. 138 (1932). See also, *State v. Burgos*, 7 Conn.App. 265, 508 A.2d 795 (1986) (search warrant executed within 10-day statutory limit may still violate constitutional reasonableness requirement).

[74]   The term "daytime" in this rule means the hours from 6:00 a.m. to 10:00 p.m. Fed.R.Crim.P. 41(a)(2)(B).

[75]   See opinion of Justice Marshall, joined by Justices Douglas and Brennan, in *Gooding v. United States*, 416 U.S. 430, 94 S.Ct. 1780 (1974). The majority found that the federal statute at issue in *Gooding* did not require such a showing.

However, it remains unclear whether the Fourth Amendment imposes any restrictions in terms of timing issues.[76]

(b) Mistake as to Premises to Be Searched

In *Maryland v. Garrison*,[77] the police searched Garrison's apartment even though the warrant only authorized search of McWebb's apartment. In seeking the warrant, the police has mistakenly asserted that there was only one apartment on McWebb's floor but, as discussed previously,[78] the Supreme Court found this mistake did not violate the Particularity Clause because it was reasonable in light of police efforts to ascertain the layout of the apartment building. The Court also held that the police acted reasonably during *execution* of the warrant. When they arrived on McWebb's floor, accompanied by McWebb, police found two open doors, with Garrison standing in his pajamas in front of one of them. The officers did not ask either McWebb or Garrison about the layout of the floor, but instead immediately conducted a sweep of both apartments, and then conducted a further search, during which they found marijuana in Garrison's room. The Court held that "[t]he objective facts available to the officers at the time suggested no distinction between McWebb's apartment and the third-floor premises." The dissent, authored by Justice Blackmun, found it "difficult to imagine that, in the initial security sweep, a reasonable officer would not have discerned that two apartments were on the third floor, realized his mistake, and then confined the ensuing search to McWebb's residence." While it is necessary to give police some leeway in their efforts to find premises to be searched given the occasional difficulty of the enterprise, *Garrison's* treatment of the facts is troubling. The actions of the police in that case at best constituted willful blindness of the "objective" facts.

(c) Announcement of Presence

At common law, officers executing a warrant were required to knock and announce their presence prior to executing a warrant, in order to avoid the unnecessary violence or property destruction that might result from a surprise entry. However, the Supreme Court has recognized a significant exception to this rule, suggesting in *Ker v. California*[79] and subsequently unanimously holding in *Wilson v. Arkansas*[80] that officers may dispense with the knock and announce requirement when they have reason to believe evidence may be destroyed, a suspect may escape, or harm may come to themselves or another. Furthermore, in *Richards v. Wisconsin*,[81] the Court unanimously held that police need only reasonable suspicion that such exigencies may be present. In *United States v. Ramirez*,[82] the full Court emphasized this holding by rejecting a Ninth Circuit rule requiring a heightened showing of "more specific inferences of exigency" before any no-knock entry that will cause destruction of the defendant's property.

---

[76]   Cf. *Conn & Najera v. Gabbert*, 526 U.S. 286, 119 S.Ct. 1292 (1999) (attorney who was searched pursuant to a warrant at the same time his client was testifying to a grand jury had standing "to complain of the allegedly unreasonable timing of the execution of the search warrant to prevent him from advising his client.").

[77]   480 U.S. 79, 107 S.Ct. 1013 (1987).

[78]   See § 5.04(a).

[79]   374 U.S. 23, 83 S.Ct. 1623 (1963).

[80]   514 U.S. 927, 115 S.Ct. 1914 (1995).

[81]   520 U.S. 385, 117 S.Ct. 1416 (1997).

[82]   523 U.S. 65, 118 S.Ct. 992 (1998).

At the same time, the Court has required that the suspicion of exigency be individualized. In *Richards* the Court invalidated a Wisconsin Supreme Court ruling that concluded that officers are never required to knock and announce their presence when executing a search warrant in a felony drug investigation.[83] The Court noted that not every drug investigation poses substantial risks (e.g., when the only individuals present in the residence are not involved with drug activity). Further, a blanket rule such as Wisconsin's could as easily be applied to searches of many other types of suspects (e.g., armed robbery suspects), which would effectively render the knock-and-announce requirement "meaningless." *Richards* calls into question state statutes that authorize magistrates to issue "no-knock" warrants,[84] given the fact that magistrates often have no individualized basis for deciding whether, at the time the police approach premises, evidence destruction or harm to others is imminent. It should also be noted, however, that the Court's decision in *Hudson v. Michigan*[85] rejecting exclusion as a remedy for knock-and-announce violations may, as a practical matter, significantly curtail any constraints that *Richards* and other decisions impose on the police.

Other issues associated with the knock and announce rule are also discussed in this book's treatment of arrest procedure.[86] The only such issue not replicated in arrest cases is whether surreptitious entry is permitted to install a listening device on a suspect's premises. In *Dalia v. United States*,[87] the Supreme Court held that such entry is not banned by the Fourth Amendment, so long as it is authorized by statute and is conducted in a reasonable manner (e.g., no property is destroyed). If these requirements are met, the entry does not even need to be authorized by a magistrate (although the magistrate must still issue a warrant based on probable cause to believe installation of the device is warranted).[88]

(d) Manner of Search

Federal law allows police to break open inner doors, containers, and so on if admittance is refused.[89] But such force must be reasonable, as several lower courts have held.[90] The Supreme Court itself has stated, in dictum, that "[e]xcessive or unnecessary destruction of property in the course of a search may violate the Fourth Amendment, even though the entry itself is lawful and the fruits of the search not subject to suppression."[91]

Likewise, excessive force directed at people occupying the place searched may violate the Fourth Amendment. In *Los Angeles Cty. v. Rettele*,[92] police with a valid warrant entered a house early in the morning expecting to find three African-Americans, one or more of them possibly armed. Instead they found two Caucasian individuals and ordered them out of bed at gunpoint, without permitting them to dress. It turned out that neither individual was wanted or armed. Nonetheless, the Court held that the police

---

[83] *State v. Richards*, 201 Wis.2d 845, 549 N.W.2d 218 (1996).

[84] For an example of such a "no-knock" statute, see McKinney's N.Y.Crim.Proc.Law § 690.35(3)(b).

[85] 547 U.S. 586, 126 S.Ct. 2159 (2006), discussed in § 2.04(b)(3).

[86] See § 3.05(a).

[87] 441 U.S. 238, 99 S.Ct. 1682 (1979).

[88] See § 14.03(e)(1).

[89] 18 U.S.C.A. § 3109.

[90] See *State v. Sierra*, 338 So.2d 609 (La. 1976).

[91] *United States v. Ramirez*, 523 U.S. 65, 118 S.Ct. 992 (1998).

[92] 550 U.S. 609, 127 S.Ct. 1989 (2007).

conduct was reasonable, in part because the police could have plausibly initially assumed that the individuals were in league with the suspects, and in part because once the deputies realized they had made a mistake, they apologized and left within five minutes of waking the individuals up. The Court reiterated, however, that "use of excessive force or restraints that cause unnecessary pain or are imposed for a prolonged and unnecessary period of time" in carrying out searches is a violation of the Fourth Amendment.[93]

(e) Seizures Not Authorized by the Warrant

Generally, any items found in plain view during a search of those areas indicated in a valid search warrant may be seized, even if they are not listed in the warrant, so long as there is probable cause to believe they are evidence of criminal activity. That has not always been the case. The rule as stated in *Marron v. United States*[94] was that only those items listed in the warrant could be seized; according to the Court, "[t]he requirement that warrants shall particularly describe the things to be seized makes general searches under them impossible and prevents the seizure of one thing under a warrant describing another." In *Marron*, for example, the Court found that a search warrant describing intoxicating liquors and articles for their manufacture did not authorize the seizure of a ledger and bills of account found in a search of the premises specified in the warrant.

In *Coolidge v. New Hampshire*,[95] however, the Court carved out a significant exception to the *Marron* rule: whenever police executing a valid warrant "inadvertently" find in "plain view" evidence of criminal activity that is "immediately apparent" as such, they may seize that evidence even if it is not listed in the warrant. Under such circumstances, stated the Court, "[a]s against the minor peril to Fourth Amendment protections, there is a major gain in effective law enforcement." Requiring the police to refrain from seizing such evidence and to seek another warrant based on what they have seen would not provide any appreciable protection of privacy, and might result in the loss of the evidence prior to execution of the second warrant.

As developed elsewhere in this book,[96] the "plain view" exception to the warrant requirement has been expanded substantially since *Coolidge*. Evidence need no longer be "immediately apparent" as such; rather the police need merely have probable cause to believe that what they see in plain view is evidence of crime.[97] Further, the "inadvertence" requirement has been eliminated, on the ground that even if police do not include in the warrant application all of the items that they suspect are on the premises to be searched, they have at least established probable cause to believe some evidence of criminal activity is there, and thus sufficient protection against arbitrary entries has been afforded.[98]

---

[93]   See also § 3.02(d), describing Fourth Amendment restrictions on execution of arrest warrants in the home.

[94]   275 U.S. 192, 48 S.Ct. 74 (1927).

[95]   403 U.S. 443, 91 S.Ct. 2022 (1971).

[96]   See Chapter 10.

[97]   *Texas v. Brown*, 460 U.S. 730, 103 S.Ct. 1535 (1983), discussed in § 10.03.

[98]   *Horton v. California*, 496 U.S. 128, 110 S.Ct. 2301 (1990), discussed and criticized in § 10.04.

Thus, a standard warrant clause of the type described earlier,[99] which authorizes searches for rent receipts and keys to establish dominion of the premises, would in effect authorize seizure of virtually any piece of evidence found in the house. In the absence of such boilerplate, however, the rule announced in *Marron* retains considerable force despite the plain view exception. First, the nature of the items listed in the warrant may prevent a plain view seizure in many instances. As stated by the Court in *Harris v. United States*,[100] "the same meticulous investigation which would be appropriate in a search for two small canceled checks could not be considered reasonable where agents are seeking a stolen automobile or an illegal still." When the warrant lists a 12-gauge shotgun as the item to be seized, the police may not look in a cookie jar or a desk drawer. Moreover, items that do not, by their appearance, provide probable cause may not be seized. An example of this situation is provided in *Stanley v. Georgia*,[101] in which agents executing a warrant authorizing a search for gambling paraphernalia found some film canisters, viewed the contents, and then seized them as pornographic. In *Coolidge*, the Court endorsed Justice Stewart's concurring opinion in *Stanley* arguing that, before viewing the films, the agents could not have known their contents "by mere inspection" and thus violated the Fourth Amendment by viewing and seizing them.[102]

A search warrant may also authorize seizure of *persons* as well as evidentiary items not listed. As discussed in Chapter 3,[103] in *Michigan v. Summers*,[104] the Supreme Court held that "a warrant to search for contraband founded on probable cause implicitly carries with it the limited authority to detain the occupants of the premises while a proper search is conducted." In *Illinois v. McArthur*,[105] the Court extended *Summers* to situations where no warrant exists. There it held that police may keep the occupant from *entering* the home while they *obtain* a warrant, as long as they have probable cause to believe the home contains evidence of crime that will be destroyed if the occupant is allowed free access inside, and the warrant is obtained in a timely fashion.

Both *Summers* and *McArthur* involved the detention of occupants who, as *Summers* indicated, are likely to be associated with the criminal activity that is the focus of the warrant and might in any event "elect to remain in order to observe the search of their possessions." Thus, it could be argued that the Fourth Amendment does not permit detention of people who neither live in the searched premises nor house their belongings there. However, in *Muehler v. Mena*,[106] the Court emphasized that when police are validly searching a house, they can seize, and even subject to brief questioning, any occupant of the premises.[107]

---

[99] See § 5.04(b).

[100] 331 U.S. 145, 67 S.Ct. 1098 (1947).

[101] 394 U.S. 557, 89 S.Ct. 1243 (1969).

[102] However, *if* probable cause exists, a "search" of an item in plain view is permitted to determine if the item is indeed evidence of crime. *Arizona v. Hicks*, 480 U.S. 321, 107 S.Ct. 1149 (1987), discussed in § 10.03.

[103] See § 3.02(d).

[104] 452 U.S. 692, 101 S.Ct. 2587 (1981).

[105] 531 U.S. 326, 121 S.Ct. 946 (2001).

[106] 544 U.S. 93, 125 S.Ct. 1465 (2005), discussed in § 3.02(d).

[107] This scenario is to be distinguished from when police are in a house on authority of an arrest warrant, in which case occupants not named in the warrant may have to be released. Cf. *Rawlings v. Kentucky*, 448 U.S. 98, 100 S.Ct. 2556 (1980), in which the Court assumed that detention of houseguests by police executing an arrest warrant for the owner was illegal. *Summers* may also be limited to searches for fruits and instrumentalities of crime, as opposed to searches for "mere evidence." See § 5.06(a).

Police may also conduct frisks of the occupants, but only when the conditions appropriate for a frisk are met. In *Ybarra v. Illinois*[108] police executing a search warrant authorizing a search of a tavern and its bartender also conducted a patdown of the tavern's patrons and a subsequent full search of Ybarra. The Court, in a 6–3 decision written by Justice Stewart, not only prohibited full searches in such a situation, but also rejected the state's argument that a more limited "frisk" should have been permitted under *Terry's* "stop-and-frisk" rule. Although the tavern was a "compact" area known to be a center for drug trafficking, the Court held that the state failed to provide any articulable suspicion that Ybarra, as a patron at the tavern, was a threat to the officers. Conversely, however, *Ybarra* suggests that if such suspicion does exist, then occupants of premises who cannot be detained under *Summers* may nonetheless be detained long enough to conduct a frisk.[109]

(f) Presence of the Media

In *Wilson v. Layne*[110] the Supreme Court unanimously held that police violate the Fourth Amendment when they allow the media to accompany them on searches, unless the media is somehow directly involved in helping to execute the warrant. Chief Justice Rehnquist's opinion for the Court emphasized that, "the Fourth Amendment . . . require[s] that police actions in execution of a warrant be related to the objectives of the authorized intrusion." According to Rehnquist, publicizing the government's efforts to combat crime and facilitating accurate reporting on law enforcement activities are not goals sufficiently related to the government's purpose in carrying out a particular search to outweigh the extra intrusion associated with media presence. The Court acknowledged the common law doctrine of allowing third parties to be present during searches for the specific purpose of identifying stolen property and also seemed willing to recognize that the presence of nonpolice could protect the police or suspects under some circumstances. But the press in this case was clearly not carrying out either purpose. The Court glossed over the First Amendment implications of its decision, simply stating that "the Fourth Amendment also protects a very important right, and in the present case it is in terms of that right that the media ride-alongs must be judged."

(g) Inventory of Seized Evidence

Statutes commonly require that an inventory be prepared of all property taken during the search, and that copies be given to someone on the searched premises and attached to the return of the warrant. Federal Rule 41(d) is a typical provision. It requires that the inventory be made in the presence of both the applicant for the warrant and the person from whose possession or premises the property was taken, or in the presence of at least one credible person if one of the first two individuals is not present. This type of provision is meant to protect against police theft and assure the person searched that his property is accounted for. However, in *Cady v. Dombrowski*,[111] the Supreme Court strongly suggested that failure to comply with a state requirement for submitting an inventory to the court raised only a question of state law. Thus, the Fourth Amendment probably does not require an inventory.

---

[108] 444 U.S. 85, 100 S.Ct. 338 (1979).

[109] *Ybarra* is discussed further in § 11.04 in the context of adequate grounds for a frisk.

[110] 526 U.S. 603, 119 S.Ct. 1692 (1999). See also *Hanlon v. Berger*, 526 U.S. 808, 119 S.Ct. 1706 (1999).

[111] 413 U.S. 433, 93 S.Ct. 2523 (1973).

5.06 When a Warrant Is Insufficient

Although a warrant is typically viewed as the preeminent protection afforded by the Fourth Amendment, in some situations it may be inadequate. This section explores those situations.

(a) The "Mere Evidence" Rule

At one time, warrants were insufficient to authorize searches for "mere evidence." In the 1921 decision of *Gouled v. United States*,[112] the Court held that only contraband, the fruits of crime, or the instrumentalities of crime could be seized under a warrant. Other types of evidence were viewed as so private that they were not seizable by any means, or were seizable only through a subpoena, which could be challenged through an adversary proceeding.[113] Thus, while a warrant could authorize searches for drugs, gambling proceeds, murder weapons, lottery tickets, and the like, a warrant was insufficient authority to gain entry into the home to search for most private documents and many types of circumstantial evidence.

In *Warden v. Hayden*,[114] the Court rejected *Gouled* to the extent it prevented seizure of "non-testimonial" evidence (as opposed to "testimonial," or documentary, evidence). There, the Court permitted the warrantless seizure of clothing subsequently shown to have been worn in a robbery that was not a fruit or instrumentality of the crime nor contraband; the Court clearly felt that the clothing could have been seized with a warrant as well. The majority noted that the Fourth Amendment's language did not make a distinction between different types of evidence and that "[privacy] is disturbed no more by a search directed to a purely evidentiary object than it is by a search directed to an instrumentality, fruit, or contraband." However, *Hayden* reserved the question of whether *documents* that are mere evidence could be seized with a warrant, out of concern not so much for Fourth Amendment values, but for reasons connected with the Fifth Amendment, which protects against compelled disclosure of "communicative" or "testimonial" evidence which is self-incriminating.[115]

Then, in *Andresen v. Maryland*,[116] the Court significantly reduced this last impediment to seizure of "mere evidence" by pointing out that, even though documents are communicative, their seizure pursuant to a warrant does not "compel" self-incrimination: such a seizure compels the possessor neither to create the document nor produce it.[117] While this reasoning, followed to its logical conclusion, removes Fourth Amendment protection from all documents, *Andresen* involved business papers, not personal papers. Other Court decisions suggest that some private papers, such as a diary, may be afforded special protection;[118] at least one justice has argued that the

---

[112] 255 U.S. 298, 41 S.Ct. 261 (1921).

[113] Note that, while a subpoena is less intrusive, in that the search for subpoenaed items is carried out by the owner rather than the police, and can be challenged in court, a subpoena issued by a grand jury need not be based on probable cause, but rather may be based on "tips" and "rumors." *United States v. Dionisio*, 410 U.S. 1, 93 S.Ct. 764 (1973), discussed in § 23.05(a).

[114] 387 U.S. 294, 87 S.Ct. 1642 (1967).

[115] See § 15.04.

[116] 427 U.S. 463, 96 S.Ct. 2737 (1976).

[117] On the other hand, when the document is seized via subpoena, there is compulsion to produce the document. For a discussion of the Fifth Amendment consequences of document production, see § 15.06.

[118] *Fisher v. United States*, 425 U.S. 391, 96 S.Ct. 1569 (1976).

Fourth Amendment prohibits the seizure of this type of documentary evidence even if police obtain a warrant.[119]

Theoretically, the mere evidence doctrine could focus not just on the types of documents being seized, but also on from whom they are being seized. In *Zurcher v. Stanford Daily*,[120] the police searched a newspaper office pursuant to a warrant, hoping to find photographs of a demonstration that had resulted in injury to several police officers. Justice Stevens, in his dissent in *Zurcher*, argued for the proposition that, when the premises of innocent third parties (such as the newspaper) are involved, warrants are inadequate authorization for searches for "mere evidence," unless it can be shown that the third party will destroy or remove the evidence if afforded a pre-search hearing. According to Stevens, "[m]ere possession of documentary evidence . . . is much less likely to demonstrate that the custodian is guilty of any wrongdoing or that he will not honor a subpoena or informal request to produce it." But the *Zurcher* majority rejected this view, primarily because it is often difficult, especially at the early stage of an investigation, to determine who is "innocent" and who is likely to destroy or remove evidence.

There is at least one instance in which a search for mere evidence is more circumscribed than other searches. In *Michigan v. Summers*,[121] the Court was unwilling to extend its holding—permitting detention of occupants of a home being searched pursuant to a search warrant—to searches solely for "mere evidence." Apparently, the Court felt that failing to recognize this exception would make much more likely the detention of persons who had no connection with criminal activity. This possibility is illustrated by the facts of *Zurcher: Summers* would presumably prohibit detention of the occupants of the newspaper office in *Zurcher*, in light of their tenuous connection with the criminal activity in question.

(b) First Amendment Material

A subtext in *Zurcher* was the fact that the search involved intrusion onto premises typically associated with the First Amendment's guarantees of free speech and press. In addition to rejecting the Fourth Amendment claim summarized above, the *Zurcher* majority refused to accept the contention that the First Amendment requires protections in this situation beyond those provided by a search warrant. But it did emphasize the need for courts to "apply the warrant requirement with particular exactitude when First Amendment interests would be endangered by the search." By this it meant not that a "higher standard" of probable cause should apply,[122] but that the government should avoid using warrants to effect a prior restraint on the material in question (by, for instance, preventing its dissemination). Moreover, Congress has directed that subpoenas should be the preferred method of seeking information from newspapers and others engaged in First Amendment activities.[123]

---

[119] *Couch v. United States*, 409 U.S. 322, 93 S.Ct. 611 (1973) (Marshall, J., dissenting).

[120] 436 U.S. 547, 98 S.Ct. 1970 (1978).

[121] 452 U.S. 692, 101 S.Ct. 2587 (1981), discussed in § 5.05(e).

[122] In *New York v. P.J. Video, Inc.*, 475 U.S. 868, 106 S.Ct. 1610 (1986), discussed in § 5.03(a), the Court overturned a lower court ruling that seizures of publications and films require a different showing of probable cause than in the normal case.

[123] Privacy Protection Act, 42 U.S.C.A. § 2000D. See also, 28 C.F.R. § 59.

In other contexts as well, the interests underlying the First Amendment have led to greater protections under the Fourth. Thus, in obscenity cases, when the government wants to seize large quantities of books or other materials, the Supreme Court has required a pre-search adversarial hearing in order to avoid the "danger of abridgement of the right of the public in a free society to unobstructed circulation of nonobscene books."[124] However, when a small number of copies, or a single item, are sought, the typical warrant procedure suffices, so long as a judicial proceeding takes place promptly after the seizure.[125]

(c) Bodily Intrusions

The Supreme Court has also indicated that certain types of investigative intrusions into the body are not permissible simply on the authority of a warrant. In *Rochin v. California*,[126] the Court held, under the Due Process Clause, that using an emetic to induce vomiting of drugs is never permissible. And while other, narrowly limited types of bodily intrusions have been permitted *without* a warrant when there is no time to obtain one,[127] in *Winston v. Lee*,[128] the Court suggested that, when there is no emergency, an adversarial hearing is required prior to such intrusions, at which a much heavier burden will be placed on the government than is usually the case.

In *Lee*, the government sought to have a bullet surgically removed from the defendant's collarbone. The Court not only required a warrant prior to such an intrusion, but also listed three other factors that should be considered before investigative surgery is authorized: (1) the extent to which the procedure threatens the safety or health of the individual; (2) the extent to which the intrusion impinges upon the individual's "dignitary interests in personal privacy and bodily integrity;" and (3) the extent to which prohibiting the intrusion would affect the "community's interest in fairly and accurately determining guilt or innocence." In applying these factors in *Lee*, Justice Brennan's opinion for the Court was very sensitive to the individual interests at stake. Confronted with a dispute as to how hazardous the procedure would be—with one witness indicating that considerable probing of muscle tissue might be necessary and could take as long as two and one-half hours, and another calling the surgery "minor"—Brennan upheld the court of appeals finding that the procedure might be medically risky. The Court also found that the defendant's dignitary interests would be harmed, primarily because the surgery would require use of anesthesia, which would render the defendant unconscious. Finally, the Court questioned the probative value of the bullet, given possible corrosion while in the shoulder, the difficulty with firearm identification generally, and the substantiality of the rest of the state's evidence. Although only six members of the Court joined Brennan's opinion, the Court was unanimous in finding the surgery proposed in *Lee* impermissible.

The Court did not specifically consider the procedural requirements for authorizing surgery, but did cite *United States v. Crowder*,[129] in which the D.C. Circuit Court of Appeals afforded the defendant an adversary hearing and immediate appellate review

---

[124] *Quantity of Copies of Books v. Kansas*, 378 U.S. 205, 84 S.Ct. 1723 (1964).

[125] *Heller v. New York*, 413 U.S. 483, 93 S.Ct. 2789 (1973).

[126] 342 U.S. 165, 72 S.Ct. 205 (1952).

[127] See, e.g., *Schmerber v. California*, 384 U.S. 757, 86 S.Ct. 1826 (1966) (warrantless blood test), discussed in § 9.02.

[128] 470 U.S. 753, 105 S.Ct. 1611 (1985).

[129] 543 F.2d 312 (D.C.Cir. 1976), cert. denied 429 U.S. 1062, 97 S.Ct. 788 (1977).

of a decision to permit surgery. At least one other court has overturned a conviction based on surgically seized evidence because the defendant had not been given such a hearing.[130]

(d) Forfeitures

A fourth situation in which a warrant based on probable cause may not be sufficient to authorize the government action, involving seizures rather than searches, is associated with real property confiscation pursuant to a forfeiture statute. As noted by the Supreme Court in *Calero-Toledo v. Pearson Yacht Leasing Co.*,[131] these statutes are designed to remove contraband and criminal instrumentalities from circulation, impose an economic penalty on owners of the seized property, compensate the government for its enforcement efforts and provide methods for obtaining security for subsequently imposed penalties and fines. Statutes providing for forfeiture allow government seizure of a wide array of items associated with criminal activity. For instance, the federal Comprehensive Drug Abuse and Control Act provides for civil forfeiture of illegal drugs, their containers, the conveyances that transported the drugs, money used in drug transactions, and real property purchased with drug money.[132]

The typical forfeiture statute provides that, after a seizure takes place, there must be a hearing to determine its validity. Under the federal statute, this proceeding can be either summary or judicial in nature. In a summary proceeding, which may occur if the property is worth less than $100,000, is contraband, or is a conveyance, the owner can either buy the property back from the government, or demand a judicial forfeiture proceeding. In a judicial proceeding, the government must prove that probable cause justified the forfeiture and that there is a "substantial connection" between the property and the underlying offense.[133] Upon such proof, the burden shifts to the claimant to prove his or her innocence. In *United States v. A Parcel of Land Known as 92 Buena Vista Avenue*,[134] the Court affirmed that, under the Forfeiture Act, a property owner who lacked knowledge of the fact that funds or property were proceeds traceable to illegal activity is entitled to assert an "innocent owner" defense to a forfeiture action.[135]

However, the federal statute does not require any type of *pre*seizure hearing.[136] Some courts have read an exigent circumstances requirement into the statute, thereby requiring *ex ante* review in all other situations.[137] In *Florida v. White*,[138] however, the

---

[130]　*State v. Overstreet*, 551 S.W.2d 621 (Mo. 1977).

[131]　416 U.S. 663, 94 S.Ct. 2080 (1974).

[132]　21 U.S.C.A. § 881(a)(1)–(7).

[133]　At least in civil forfeiture proceedings. See 18 U.S.C.A. § 983(c)(3).

[134]　507 U.S. 111, 113 S.Ct. 1126 (1993).

[135]　However, the Court has also held that such a defense is not constitutionally *required* by either the Due Process Clause or the Fifth Amendment Takings Clause, relying both on the history of forfeiture proceedings and the policy that such a defense might undermine the deterrent effect of forfeiture statutes. *Bennis v. Michigan*, 517 U.S. 1163, 116 S.Ct. 1560 (1996). Five justices hinted that such a defense might lie to the extent the confiscated *res* is unconnected to the underlying misconduct, but a majority was persuaded that, in *Bennis*, where the property confiscated was a car driven by a man soliciting prostitutes, such a connection existed; thus the wife's ownership interest in the car could be extinguished despite her ignorance of her husband's illegal activity.

[136]　A directive from the Justice Department does state that "[a] judicial determination of probable cause is required" prior to seizing real property, and "encouraged" in all other cases. Dir. No. 93–1, Justice Department Policy on Asset Forfeiture, 42 Crim.L.Rep. 2071 (Jan. 20, 1993).

[137]　See, e.g., *United States v. Spetz*, 721 F.2d 1457, 1465 (9th Cir. 1983).

[138]　526 U.S. 559, 119 S.Ct. 1555 (1999).

Supreme Court held that the police may seize personal property without a warrant and at their leisure, so long as they have probable cause to believe the property is forfeitable contraband and the seizure is made in public. In *White*, the Court upheld a warrantless seizure of a car known to have been used to carry drugs two months earlier. Similarly, in *Kaley v. United States*,[139] the Court held that a grand jury indictment, based on probable cause, is a sufficient finding of the crime predicate under a forfeiture statute, even when there is a colorable claim the resulting freezing of assets will deprive the defendant of the ability to pay the attorney of his choice.[140]

Thus, the Fourth Amendment apparently does not require any pre-seizure hearing for personal property. However, the Supreme Court has held that when the item confiscated under a forfeiture statute is real property, the *Due Process Clause* requires notice and an opportunity to be heard prior to the seizure, unless the government is able to demonstrate exigent circumstances (such as imminent destruction of buildings) that justify immediate seizure.[141] Furthermore, the Court has indicated that the breadth of forfeiture statutes is limited by the Eighth Amendment. In two companion decisions, *Alexander v. United States*[142] and *Austin v. United States*,[143] the Court held that seizures under a forfeiture statute may violate the "excessive fines" clause of that provision. In *Alexander*, the Court remanded the case to determine whether confiscation of the defendant's bookstore and nine million dollars earned through his illicit businesses was a disproportionate punishment for the offense of selling pornographic materials and engaging in widespread racketeering activities.[144] Similarly, in *Austin*, the government remanded for a determination as to whether the government's seizure of the defendant's mobile home and auto body shop for conviction of possession of cocaine (two ounces of which he transported from the home to the shop) was excessive under the Eighth Amendment.

United States v. Bajakajian,[145] another forfeiture case, was the first time the Court actually applied the Excessive Fines Clause to strike down a fine. Bajakajian had tried to take $357,144 out of the country and lied about doing so, thereby violating a federal statute prohibiting willful transportation of more than $10,000 across the border without reporting it. A separate federal statute provides that any person violating the reporting statute "shall . . . forfeit any property . . . involved in such an offense." Five members of the Supreme Court, in an opinion authored by Justice Thomas, found that construing the latter statute to require forfeiture of the full $357,144 would violate the Eighth Amendment.

The Court first emphasized its holding in *Austin* that any confiscation that is even "punitive in part" triggers the Excessive Fines Clause. Because the forfeiture in *Bajakajian* was explicitly authorized as part of the sentence for failure to report, cannot be imposed on an innocent owner, and resulted from an in personam proceeding against

---

[139]   571 U.S. 320, 134 S.Ct. 1090 (2014).

[140]   See § 31.05(b) for discussion of forfeiture laws and attorney's fees.

[141]   *United States v. James Daniel Good Real Property*, 510 U.S. 43, 114 S.Ct. 492 (1993).

[142]   509 U.S. 544, 113 S.Ct. 2766 (1993).

[143]   509 U.S. 602, 113 S.Ct. 2801 (1993).

[144]   The Court rejected a First Amendment prior restraint claim on the ground that the forfeiture was a punishment, which has never been subject to prior restraint analysis.

[145]   524 U.S. 321, 118 S.Ct. 2028 (1998).

the defendant,[146] it was sufficiently punitive in nature to be covered by the Clause. The Court then held that a confiscation that is determined to be a fine is excessive under the Clause only if it is "grossly disproportionate to the gravity of the defendant's offense." Because Bajakajian had not been found to have committed any crime other than failing to report (a crime for which the federal sentencing guidelines authorize a maximum fine of $5,000), and because failure to report, by itself "affected only one party, the Government, . . . in a relatively minor way", forfeiting the full $357,144 was excessive. Justice Kennedy argued in dissent that there is a direct correlation between the amount forfeited (i.e., the amount not reported) and the harm to the government that would have occurred had the currency not been detected. The majority disagreed, stating "[i]t is impossible to conclude, for example, that the harm respondent caused is anywhere near 30 times greater than that caused by a hypothetical drug dealer who willfully fails to report taking $12,000 out of the country in order to purchase drugs."

5.07   Conclusion

The warrant requirement is designed to implement the Fourth Amendment's prohibition against unreasonable searches and seizures by requiring that whenever feasible a neutral and detached magistrate determine whether a search is justified. The following elements are necessary for issuance of a valid warrant.

(1)   The person issuing the warrant must be "neutral and detached" in the sense that he is not involved in either the investigation or prosecution of crime. He should refrain from becoming involved in any search he authorizes and from delegating his authority to law enforcement officers. In cases involving minor crimes, non-judicial officers independent of the executive branch may be competent to issue warrants.

(2)   The official should issue a search warrant only if he finds, based on facts provided in an affidavit or oral testimony sworn by the complaining officer, probable cause to believe that there is or will be evidence of crime in the place to be searched. Relevant to this determination is whether there is evidence suggesting (a) that the informant—whether a police officer or a third party—is reliable (e.g., because of reliable information provided in the past, police corroboration of some details, or a declaration against interest), and (b) that the stated basis for the informant's belief is credible (e.g., there are sufficient facts or descriptive detail to believe the informant observed what is described rather than merely repeated rumor). In deciding whether probable cause exists, a deficiency in one of these two areas may be compensated for by a strong showing in the other, so that probable cause ultimately depends upon a flexible evaluation of the totality of the circumstances.

(3)   Subsequent evaluation of the probable cause determination usually focuses entirely on the warrant application and accompanying documents. However, if the

---

[146]   The Court also noted that the forfeiture could not be considered "remedial" because the only harm to the government that results from failure to report is loss of information and the forfeiture would not remedy that loss. In contrast, the Court stated, are civil in rem forfeiture proceedings (that proceed against the property rather than the person) that act like "liquidated damages" for failing to pay customs duties, and taxes associated with possessing narcotics (here, in contrast, no underlying "damage" was involved). See, cf., *One Lot Emerald Cut Stones v. United States*, 409 U.S. 232, 93 S.Ct. 489 (1972) (holding that a statute which required forfeiture of goods and a penalty equal to the value of the goods "provided a reasonable form of liquidated damages" and thus did not implicate the Double Jeopardy Clause); *Stockwell v. United States*, 80 U.S. 531, 13 Wall. 531, 20 L.Ed. 491 (1871) (finding nonpenal a statute which provided that persons who concealed goods liable to seizure for customs violations should "forfeit and pay a sum double the amount or value of the goods."). Compare the definition of punishment in double jeopardy cases, discussed in § 30.02(a)(1).

defendant can make a substantial preliminary showing that: (a) the affiant-officer (as opposed to an informant); (b) recklessly or intentionally; (c) made false statements; (d) that were necessary to the probable cause finding, he may obtain a hearing, which will result in invalidation of the warrant if he can show these elements by a preponderance of the evidence.

(4)   A warrant must state with particularity the place to be searched. However, a mistake as to the location of the place searched does not invalidate the warrant if it is based on information police obtain after a reasonably diligent investigation. A warrant must also state with particularity the items to be seized or at least reference a warrant application that does so, although some lack of specificity is permitted if other descriptions in the warrant provide reasonable guidance as to the general type of items that may be seized.

(5)   A warrant should be executed within the time prescribed by warrant, statute or rule, and, in any event, must be executed before probable cause dissipates. Reasonable mistakes as to the premises to be searched do not invalidate the subsequent search. Officers are generally required to knock and announce their presence, unless they have reasonable suspicion to believe a suspect will escape or evidence will be destroyed, and must conduct the search itself so as to avoid unnecessary force or destruction of property. Police may seize not only the evidence listed in the warrant but also items they have probable cause to believe are evidence that are spied in plain view in areas the warrant authorizes them to search. They may also detain occupants of the home while they execute the warrant and keep them from entering if they have probable cause for a warrant but do not yet have one, at least when the evidence named in the existing or soon-to-be-obtained warrant is contraband. They may also frisk those on the premises who are reasonably suspected to be dangerous. The media generally may not accompany police on a search. An inventory is usually mandated by statute, but is not a constitutional requirement.

(6)   When the government seeks large quantities of materials associated with First Amendment protection, evidence that necessitates a serious bodily intrusion, or forfeiture of real property, a pre-seizure adversarial hearing may be required in addition to or in lieu of a warrant.

BIBLIOGRAPHY

Blumenson, Eric and Eva Nilsen. Policing for Profit: The Drug War's Hidden Economic Agenda. 65 U. Chi. L. Rev. 35 (1998).

Borgmann, Caitlin E. The Constitutionality of Government-Imposed Bodily Intrusions. 2014 U. Ill. L. Rev. 1059 (2014).

Goldstein, Abraham. The Search Warrant, The Magistrate, and Judicial Review. 62 N.Y.U.L.Rev. 1173 (1987).

Grano, Joseph D. Probable Cause and Common Sense: A Reply to the Critics of *Illinois v. Gates*. 17 Mich.J.L.Ref. 465 (1984).

____. Rethinking the Warrant Requirement. 19 Amer.Crim.L.Rev. 603 (1982).

Hawthorne, Paul G. Tips, Returning to and Improving Upon *Aguilar-Spinelli*: A Departure from the *Gates* "Totality of the Circumstances". 46 How.L.Rev. 327 (2003).

Jia, Di, Kalle Spooner and Roland V. Del Carmen. An Analysis and Categorization of Supreme Court Cases Under the Exigent Circumstances Exception to the Warrant Requirement. 27 George Mason University Civil Rights Law Journal 37 (2016).

Kamisar, Yale. *Gates*, "Probable Cause," "Good Faith," and Beyond. 69 Iowa L.Rev. 551 (1984).

Kerr, Orin S. Search Warrants in an Era of Digital Evidence. 75 Miss.L.J. 85 (2005).

LaFave, Wayne R. Probable Cause from Informants: The Effects of Murphy's Law on Fourth Amendment Adjudication. 1977 U.Ill.L.F. 1 (1977).

Moylan, Charles E., Jr. *Illinois v. Gates*: What It Did and Did Not Do. 20 Crim.L.Bull. 93 (1984).

Project on Law Enforcement Policy and Rulemaking. Search Warrant Execution. Tempe, Arizona: The Project, 1974. (Model Rules for Law Enforcement Series).

Rash, Brandon C. *Groh v. Ramirez*: Strengthening the Fourth Amendment Particularity Requirement, Weakening Qualified Immunity. 39 Richmond L. Rev. 771 (2005).

Slobogin, Christopher. Cause to Believe What?—The Importance of Defining a Search's Object, or How the ABA Would Analyze the NSA Metadata Surveillance Program. 66 Oklahoma Law Review 725 (2014).

Stuntz, William J. Warrants and Fourth Amendment Remedies, 77 Va.L.Rev. 881 (1991).

Teeter, Dwight L., Jr. and Griffin S. Singer. Search Warrants in Newsrooms: Some Aspects of the Impact of *Zurcher v. The Stanford Daily*. 67 Kent.L.J. 847 (1978–79).

Van Duizend, Richard, L. Paul Sutton and Charlotte A. Carter. The Search Warrant Process: Preconceptions, Perceptions and Practices (1985).

Chapter 6

SEARCH INCIDENT TO A LAWFUL ARREST

6.01   Introduction

Suppose a person who has been arrested suddenly reaches into his coat pocket. Refraining from searching the suspect's pockets and seizing whatever they may contain until a search warrant is obtained could result in grave danger to the police or the destruction of crucial contraband. The search incident to a lawful arrest exception to the warrant requirement seeks to protect against these twin dangers. As the Court stated in *Chimel v. California*,[1] a search incident to arrest is permitted "to remove any weapons that the [arrestee] might seek to use in order to resist arrest or effect his escape" and to "seize any evidence on the arrestee's person in order to prevent its concealment or destruction."

Among all of the exceptions to the warrant requirement, the search incident doctrine is the oldest. In *Weeks v. United States*,[2] the Supreme Court noted that this exception has "always (been) recognized under English and American law." Three issues arise under search incident doctrine: (1) what types of arrests justify a search incident? (2) when must such searches be undertaken? and (3) what is the permissible scope of these searches?

6.02   Arrests Which Justify a Search

The most basic principle of search incident law is that the warrantless search is justified only if the arrest is lawful under the Constitution. When the arrest is not based on probable cause or is invalid for some other constitutional reason, the search is not valid.[3]

However, an arrest that is unlawful due solely to a violation of *non*-constitutional law does not invalidate a subsequent search as a Fourth Amendment matter. For instance, in *Virginia v. Moore*,[4] a unanimous Court held that even though, under Virginia law, the traffic arrest in that case should have resulted in a summons rather than an arrest, the fact that the police arrested the defendant did not invalidate the ensuing search, since the police had probable cause for the traffic offense. Justice Scalia, writing for the Court, found no historical evidence that the framers intended the Fourth Amendment reasonableness inquiry to be linked to state statutes. He also pointed to three practical reasons for the Court's decision. First, the Court has for some time adhered to the notion that a state's decision to provide more protection than the constitutional minimum, as the summons requirement did in this case, does not raise that minimum or render it unreasonable.[5] Second, a contrary decision would have resulted in the exclusion of the drugs found as a result of Moore's arrest, which would

---

[1]   395 U.S. 752, 89 S.Ct. 2034 (1969).

[2]   232 U.S. 383, 34 S.Ct. 341 (1914).

[3]   *Draper v. United States*, 358 U.S. 307, 79 S.Ct. 329 (1959). The various criteria for determining the legality of an arrest are discussed in Chapter 3.

[4]   553 U.S. 164, 128 S.Ct. 1598 (2008).

[5]   See § 34.01.

frustrate Virginia's policy, expressed in its statute, of remedying traffic violations through tort suits, not suppression of probative evidence. Finally, a contrary decision would also permit Fourth Amendment protections to vary from state to state and, where federal officers are involved, even within states.

A separate inquiry is whether the search incident doctrine permits searches when the underlying arrest, although valid, is for a crime that is unlikely to involve dangerous weapons or contraband. In other words, when the rationale for the exception (protection of police and prevention of evidence destruction) is unlikely to apply, does the exception still operate? In two controversial cases, the Supreme Court has answered this question in the affirmative. In *United States v. Robinson*,[6] an officer arrested the defendant for driving with a revoked license and then searched him; in the defendant's coat pocket he found a package, in which he discovered heroin. The court of appeals held the evidence inadmissible, on the ground that the crime of driving with a revoked license is not associated with any "fruits" or "instrumentalities;" thus, concluded the court, while a limited patdown of the arrestee's outer clothing for weapons was permissible under *Terry v. Ohio*,[7] a full search of the person arrested for such a crime was not necessary. The Supreme Court, in a 6–3 opinion written by Justice Rehnquist, reversed the lower court, holding that, under the Reasonableness Clause of the Fourth Amendment, *all* lawful custodial arrests justify a full search of the person without a warrant. Similarly, in a companion case to *Robinson, Gustafson v. Florida*,[8] the Court found no error when police searched the defendant—and opened a cigarette box found as a result—after his arrest for failure to have his driver's license in his possession.

The Court offered two reasons for these decisions. First, when police decide to take someone into custody, a mere patdown for weapons is insufficient protection. According to Rehnquist, "[i]t is scarcely open to doubt that the danger to an officer is far greater in the case of the extended exposure which follows the taking of a suspect into custody and transporting him to the police station than in the case of the relatively fleeting contact resulting from the typical *Terry*-stop." Second, the Court felt it important to adopt a "bright-line" rule that could be easily followed by police making arrests in the field. As Rehnquist stated the matter, "[a] police officer's determination as to how and where to search the person of a suspect whom he has arrested is necessarily a quick *ad hoc* judgment which the Fourth Amendment does not require to be broken down in each instance into an analysis of each step in the search." Thus, the legitimacy of a search incident should not depend upon "what a court may later decide was the probability in a particular arrest situation that weapons or evidence would in fact be found upon the person of the suspect."

Given the protection rationale, the one limitation on the *Robinson-Gustafson* holding is that the arrest result in the person being taken into custody. In *Knowles v. Iowa*,[9] the Court affirmed this point, by unanimously holding that a noncustodial arrest cannot form the basis for a search incident to arrest. In *Knowles* a police officer stopped the defendant for speeding and, rather than arresting him (which he had authority to do), issued a citation. The officer then conducted a warrantless search and found marijuana and a pot pipe. The Supreme Court noted that such a traffic stop rarely

---

[6]   414 U.S. 218, 94 S.Ct. 467 (1973).

[7]   392 U.S. 1, 88 S.Ct. 1868 (1968), discussed in § 11.01.

[8]   414 U.S. 260, 94 S.Ct. 488 (1973).

[9]   525 U.S. 113, 119 S.Ct. 484 (1998).

endangered the officer and never involved the need to procure evidence. Thus, it declined to extend *Robinson's* bright-line rule to such a situation.

After *Knowles*, there remained the question of whether any limitation existed on the type of offense that could trigger a custodial arrest and thus a search incident. In a concurring opinion in *Gustafson*, Justice Stewart had written that the defendant there might have prevailed had he asserted that his custodial arrest "for a minor traffic offense" violated his rights "under the Fourth and Fourteenth Amendments." Almost three decades later, however, that possibility was foreclosed by *Atwater v. City of Lago Vista*,[10] where the Court rejected the argument that the Fourth Amendment permits custodial arrest only for offenses that might carry jail time or when there is a compelling need for detention. As long as the police have probable cause, even arrest for "a very minor criminal offense" does not violate the Fourth Amendment, the Court held.

The five member majority, in an opinion by Justice Souter, rejected both historical and policy arguments against this ruling. Atwater, who was arrested, handcuffed and jailed for violating a seatbelt law, contended that at the time the Constitution was framed officers could not make a warrantless arrest for a misdemeanor unless it constituted a "breach of the peace." But Justice Souter pointed to evidence both in England and the colonies that constables were able to arrest for all sorts of minor offenses (evidence, it should be noted, that is quite slim when looked at closely[11]). He also refused to endorse Atwater's policy argument that arrest authority should be limited to jailable offenses to prevent police abuse. Such a rule was not desirable principally because, in light of the potential for civil liability, any attempt to draw lines "would come at the price of a systematic disincentive to arrest in situations where . . . arresting would serve an important societal interest," such as assuring that an out-of-state driver would pay a fine or that drugs discovered can be weighed to determine if jail time is warranted. To the concern about abuse, Souter pointed out that anyone arrested is entitled to judicial review of the detention within 48 hours,[12] that many jurisdictions limit police authority to make custodial arrests, that police are unlikely to engage in time-consuming arrests unless an important interest is at stake, and that the Fourth Amendment would still be violated by an arrest that is "unusually harmful to privacy or . . . physical interests."

Justice O'Connor's dissent focused primarily on the policy argument. Noting that in Texas, where Atwater was arrested, fine-only offenses include disobeying any sort of traffic warning sign, failing to pay a toll, driving with expired license plates, and littering, she argued that the Court's rule permitting a full arrest for such offenses "defies any sense of proportionality and is in serious tension with the Fourth Amendment proscription of unreasonable seizures." She pointed to the significant inconveniences associated with detention (including being housed with felons for up to 48 hours) and the fact that anyone arrested can, under authority of *Robinson*, be subjected to a search incident of his person and, if driving, his car (the latter a rule that has been somewhat modified since *Atwater*[13]). As an alternative to the Court's ruling, Justice O'Connor

---

[10]　532 U.S. 318, 121 S.Ct. 1536 (2001).

[11]　See Thomas Y. Davies, *The Fictional Character of Law and Order Originalism: A Case Study of Distortions and Evasions of Framing-Era Arrest Doctrine in* Atwater v. Lago Vista, 37 Wake Forest L. Rev. 239 (2002).

[12]　See § 20.02(c).

[13]　See § 6.04(c).

proposed the following rule: "when there is probable cause to believe that a fine-only offense has been committed, the police officer should issue a citation unless the officer is 'able to point to specific and articulable facts which, taken together with rational inferences form those facts, reasonably warrant [the additional] intrusion' of a full custodial arrest." She also noted that any concern about enhanced officer liability under such a standard was undercut by the existence of qualified immunity, which provides officers who act in reasonable good faith with a defense.[14]

As Justice Souter pointed out in *Atwater*, many states have reduced certain violations of their traffic codes to infraction (i.e., noncustodial) status,[15] thus preventing operation of the search incident doctrine in those situations. In other states, the highest state court has interpreted the state constitution to prohibit automatic searches incident in connection with minor crimes, specifically rejecting *Robinson*.[16] In states that have not taken such steps, *Robinson* and *Atwater* do relieve the police from engaging in an uncertain calculus each time they want to arrest or perform a search incident to arrest. But had the Court adopted Justice O'Connor's suggested approach in *Atwater*, or had it forbidden full searches of the person in the limited context of arrests for minor traffic violations in *Robinson*, it would have better implemented the rationale behind the search incident exception, reduced significantly police discretion to abuse the arrest power, and still produced a relatively precise rule. Nonetheless, the Court affirmed *Atwater* in *Moore*, where it asserted that any arrest, even one that is illegal under state law and is for a minor infraction, subjects police to the risks that justify a search incident of the person arrested.

6.03   The Timing of the Search

A fundamental tenet of search incident doctrine is that probable cause to make the arrest must *precede* the warrantless search.[17] The exception will not permit officers to conduct a "fishing expedition" in the hope that contraband or some other unlawful item is found that will support an arrest. The central idea is that the arrest justifies the warrantless search, not the reverse. However, as long as probable cause to arrest precedes the search, a formal "arrest" is not required to justify the search.[18]

Equally important to search incident doctrine is the requirement that the warrantless arrest take place *soon* after there is probable cause to arrest. As Justice Black, speaking for a unanimous Court, noted in *Preston v. United States*,[19] the "justifications [for the search incident] rule are absent where a search is remote in time or place from the arrest." Thus, in *Preston*, a warrantless search of a car towed to a garage after its occupants were arrested and taken to jail was not a valid search incident: neither destruction of evidence nor harm to the officers could have occurred at that time. The Court came to the same conclusion in *Chambers v. Maroney*,[20] involving similar facts. And in *United States v. Chadwick*,[21] a search of a footlocker more than an hour

---

[14]   See § 2.05(a)(3).

[15]   See, e.g., Ala. Code § 32–1–4 (1999); Md. Transp. Code Ann. § 26–202(a)(2).

[16]   See § 34.02(c).

[17]   *Sibron v. New York*, 392 U.S. 40, 88 S.Ct. 1889 (1968).

[18]   *Rawlings v. Kentucky*, 448 U.S. 98, 100 S.Ct. 2556 (1980).

[19]   376 U.S. 364, 84 S.Ct. 881 (1964).

[20]   399 U.S. 42, 90 S.Ct. 1975 (1970).

[21]   433 U.S. 1, 97 S.Ct. 2476 (1977).

after the defendant's arrest and after agents had gained exclusive control of it was also found invalid as a search incident.

One limited exception to the "contemporaneousness" element of search incident doctrine may have been announced in *United States v. Edwards*.[22] There the Court, in a 5–4 decision, approved the warrantless seizure and search of an arrestee's clothing ten hours after his arrest, while he was in jail. In the course of its opinion, the Court made the broad statement that "searches and seizures that could be made on the spot at the time of arrest may legally be conducted later when the accused arrives at the place of detention." But the Court also pointed out that taking Edwards' clothes at the time of arrest would have been impracticable, as it "was late at night[,] no substitute clothing was then available for Edwards to wear, and it would certainly have been unreasonable for the police to have stripped respondent of his clothing and left him exposed in his cell throughout the night." Noteworthy also is the fact that, while Edwards apparently was not aware of the clothing's evidentiary value, had he become so he could have easily destroyed it. *Edwards* should be narrowly construed to permit a later search incident only when an immediate search is virtually impossible and exigency still exists at the time of the later search.[23] A different rule would stretch search incident doctrine well beyond its twin rationales of protecting officers and evidence from harm.

It should also be noted, however, that other exceptions to the warrant and probable cause requirements might permit warrantless searches well after arrest. For instance, in *Chambers v. Maroney*, mentioned above, the Court found that, while not justified under search incident doctrine, the later warrantless search of the car was permissible under the "automobile exception" to the warrant requirement.[24] And, since *Edwards*, the Court has firmly held that routine "inventory" searches of cars, and of personal effects of arrestees detained in jail, are permissible in the absence of any suspicion.[25]

6.04 The Scope of a Search Incident

Originally, the scope of a search conducted contemporaneous with a lawful arrest was quite broad, permitting not just search of the arrestee but also of any nearby area that he "possessed," including areas not proximate to his person. The Supreme Court then adopted a rule that limited the search to the area within reach of the defendant. However, this so-called "armspan rule" has since been significantly modified in several situations.

(a) The Armspan Rule

In *United States v. Rabinowitz*,[26] the police, armed with a valid arrest warrant, arrested the defendant for forgery and then conducted a warrantless search of his one-room business, including the desk, safe, and file cabinets. Five members of the Court, evaluating the search under the totality of the circumstances, held that the search was

---

[22] 415 U.S. 800, 94 S.Ct. 1234 (1974).

[23] The Court also emphasized that the police had probable cause to believe the clothing had evidentiary value.

[24] The *Chambers* rationale requires that the police have probable cause to search the car, not just probable cause to arrest. See § 7.03(b).

[25] See *South Dakota v. Opperman*, 428 U.S. 364, 96 S.Ct. 3092 (1976) (cars); *Illinois v. Lafayette*, 462 U.S. 640, 103 S.Ct. 2605 (1983) (effects), discussed in § 13.07. However, these cases prohibit use of the inventory as a "pretext concealing investigatory motives," and thus would have been to no avail in *Edwards*.

[26] 339 U.S. 56, 70 S.Ct. 430 (1950).

reasonable. They gave a number of reasons, including the room's quasi-public nature and the fact that it "was small and under the immediate and complete control of respondent." But, as Justice Frankfurter pointed out in dissent, the agents had plenty of time to obtain a search warrant (they not only were able to obtain an arrest warrant, but also arranged to bring two forgery experts with them). Thus, the majority's disposition of the case encouraged unnecessary evasion of the particularity requirement and other guarantees afforded by a search warrant.

Almost twenty years later, in *Chimel v. California*,[27] the Court voted, 7–2, to overturn *Rabinowitz*. While the search in *Chimel* involved a three-bedroom home rather than a one-room business, the majority pointed out that *Rabinowitz* had come to stand for the broad proposition that "a warrantless search 'incident to a lawful arrest' may generally extend to the area that is considered to be in the 'possession' or under the 'control' of the person arrested." As *Rabinowitz* demonstrated, this vague standard gave police "the opportunity to engage in searches not justified by probable cause, by the simple expedient of arranging to arrest suspects at home rather than elsewhere." To replace the case-by-case "reasonableness" analysis endorsed in *Rabinowitz*, Justice Stewart, who wrote the Court's opinion, devised the "armspan" rule. As before, the arresting officer may search the arrestee's person to discover and remove weapons and to seize evidence. But beyond this, a search incident is limited to the area "within [the] immediate control" of the arrestee—that is, "the area from within which he might have obtained either a weapon or something that could have been used as evidence against him."

Although *Chimel* was an attempt to clarify the scope of a search incident, the armspan rule itself is subject to several interpretations. Does it, for instance, permit searches of opaque effects (e.g., wallets and purses) found on the arrested person, or closed containers (e.g., suitcases) near his person at the time of the arrest? Given the facts and results of *Robinson* and *Gustafson*, discussed earlier,[28] the Court appears to have held that the arresting officer may look into any containers found on the arrestee, even though, as the dissent in *Robinson* pointed out, it is impossible for the arrestee to obtain a weapon from the container once it is in the possession of the officer.

One significant exception to this rule is when the item found on the person is a cell phone. In *Riley v. California*,[29] the Court held unanimously that searches of cell phones may not be searched incident to arrest absent exigent circumstances indicating that failing to do so will endanger the police or evidence on the phone. Chief Justice Roberts' opinion dismissed as exaggerated concerns that the contents of the phone could be remotely "wiped" by the suspect's friends before a warrant could be obtained and noted that, in any event, remote wiping or encrypting is often preventable through removing the phone's battery, turning the phone off, or insulating it from radio waves. And the Court rejected the proposal that warrantless searches be permitted if limited to looking for evidence of the offense of arrest, the rule that applies to searches of cars under search incident doctrine.[30] In part this refusal was based on the concern that police would often be able to conjure up a reason to believe a phone contains evidence of some crime (e.g., GPS locational information in the pone could be said to be relevant to driving

---

[27]   395 U.S. 752, 89 S.Ct. 2034 (1969).

[28]   See § 6.02.

[29]   573 U.S. 373, 134 S.Ct. 2473 (2014).

[30]   See § 6.04(c).

infractions). But the principal reason for the Court's decision was the "quantitative and qualitative" difference between cell phones and other items an arrestee might have on his person. As Roberts put it, "Modern cell phones, as a category, implicate privacy concerns far beyond those implicated by the search of a cigarette pack, a wallet, or a purse."

A second exception to the general rule that searches incident to lawful arrest are unlimited in scope arises in connection with drunken driving. In *Birchfield v. North Dakota*,[31] five members of the Court held that nonconsensual blood tests after a DUI arrest may not take place without a warrant. At the same time, the Court held that breathalyzer tests may be conducted post-arrest without a warrant, on the ground that this procedure is less intrusive than a blood test and is necessary to prevent evidence dissipation. In dissent to this second holding, Justice Sotomayor, joined by Justice Kagan, disputed the need for an immediate test. Noting that most breathalyzer evidence used in court is produced by tests conducted at the stationhouse well after the arrest, she concluded search incident doctrine should not apply in this situation.

As for warrantless searches of effects not on the arrestee's person but proximate to him, the Court has not clearly spoken on the issue. In *United States v. Chadwick*,[32] it will be remembered, the Court prohibited a *later* warrantless search of a footlocker found in the arrestee's possession. But it was unclear as to whether a search incident at the time of arrest was permissible. One justice (Brennan) argued that an immediate search would not have been justified, since the footlocker was not within the "immediate control" of the arrestees, while two dissenting justices (Blackmun and Rehnquist) argued the opposite.

The armspan rule should be interpreted with the twin rationales of search incident doctrine in mind, as many lower courts appear to do. Thus, for instance, a search of an arrestee's backpack after she was arrested was found to violate search incident doctrine because agents were in possession of it when it was searched and were in no danger of harm.[33] Similarly, a search of a light fixture which turned up a cache of marijuana was held illegal because the fixture was outside the defendant's reach at the time of arrest.[34] In contrast, when the defendant, after his arrest, went to a locker to retrieve a bag, the police were authorized to conduct a warrantless search of it, because the defendant had extended the area of his immediate control by going to the locker.[35]

The Supreme Court has indicated that this "extension of control" rationale also allows *entries* into the home, if the arrestee chooses to go there after the arrest. In *Washington v. Chrisman*,[36] an officer stopped a student on suspicion of drinking underage, an action which the Court termed an "arrest." The officer asked the student for his identification and followed him to his room when he went to get it. While there, the officer saw in plain view marijuana and drug paraphernalia. In upholding the subsequent seizure of this evidence, the Court disagreed with the lower court's finding that no danger to either the officer or evidence was apparent on these facts; relying on

---

[31] ___ U.S. ___, 136 S.Ct. 2160 (2016).

[32] 433 U.S. 1, 97 S.Ct. 2476 (1977), discussed further in § 7.02.

[33] *United States v. Robertson*, 833 F.2d 777 (9th Cir. 1987).

[34] *State v. Rhodes*, 80 N.M. 729, 460 P.2d 259 (App. 1969).

[35] *Parker v. Swenson*, 332 F.Supp. 1225 (E.D.Mo. 1971), aff'd 459 F.2d 164 (8th Cir. 1972), cert. denied 409 U.S. 1126, 93 S.Ct. 943 (1973).

[36] 455 U.S. 1, 102 S.Ct. 812 (1982).

Robinson, the Court stated that "[e]very arrest must be presumed to present a risk of danger to the arresting officer. . . . Moreover, the possibility that an arrested person will attempt to escape if not properly supervised is obvious." Thus, the Court held, "it is not unreasonable, under the Fourth Amendment for an officer, as a matter of routine, to monitor the movements of an arrested person, as his judgment dictates, following the arrest."[37]

(b) Confederates and Destructible Evidence

All of the cases discussed above focus on the danger that the *arrestee* poses for the police. As Justice White pointed out in his dissent in *Chimel*, the arrestee is not the only legitimate focus of the police when making an arrest: "there must always be a strong possibility that confederates of the arrested man will in the meanwhile remove the items for which the police have probable cause to search." This concern about confederates, either as destroyers of evidence or as independent threats to the police, has led to significant modifications of the armspan rule, as the following discussion bears out.

(1) Searches for Confederates

In *Maryland v. Buie*,[38] the Court expanded the scope of a search incident in two ways. First, apparently for reasons similar to those used to justify the armspan rule, it held that the police may, incident to a home arrest, look in areas immediately adjoining the place of arrest for other persons who might attack the police, without having probable cause or even the lesser level of "reasonable suspicion."[39] Second, *Buie* held that if, at any moment up to the time the arrest is completed and the police depart, the police have reasonable suspicion that *other* areas of the premises harbor an individual who poses a danger to them, they may undertake a "protective sweep," limited to "a cursory visual inspection of those places in which a person might be hiding." In reaching the latter holding, the Court concluded that, in contrast to the type of search at issue in *Chimel*, such sweeps only minimally invade the arrestee's privacy. It analogized the protective sweep to the protective field patdown authorized in *Terry v. Ohio*,[40] and the limited "armspan" car search permitted by *Michigan v. Long*,[41] both of which are permissible based on a reasonable suspicion that the police or others are in danger. In dissent, Justice Brennan, joined by Justice Marshall, argued that, despite the majority's efforts at limiting its scope, the protective sweep authorized by *Buie* far exceeded in intrusiveness the police actions permitted by *Terry* and *Long*:

> A protective sweep would bring within police purview virtually all personal possessions within the house not hidden from view in a small enclosed space. Police officers searching for potential ambushers might enter every room including basements and attics; open up closets, lockers, chests, wardrobes, and cars; and peer under beds and behind furniture. The officers will view letters, documents and personal effects that are on tables or desks or are visible inside open drawers; books, records, tapes, and pictures on shelves; and

---

[37]   On remand, the Washington Supreme Court held that, under the state constitution, the evidence should be suppressed. *State v. Chrisman*, 100 Wn.2d 814, 676 P.2d 419 (1984).

[38]   494 U.S. 325, 110 S.Ct. 1093 (1990).

[39]   The reasonable suspicion standard is discussed in § 11.03(a).

[40]   392 U.S. 1, 88 S.Ct. 1868 (1968), discussed in § 11.01.

[41]   463 U.S. 1032, 103 S.Ct. 3469 (1983), discussed in § 11.05.

clothing, medicines, toiletries and other paraphernalia not carefully stored in dresser drawers or bathroom cupboards.

Thus, according to the dissent, protective sweeps should be permitted only if police have probable cause to believe they may otherwise be attacked; the majority's "articulable suspicion" standard was insufficient.

The flexibility of the latter standard is demonstrated by the Maryland Court of Appeals' decision in *Buie* on remand.[42] Although Buie was known to have an accomplice, the police had not seen the latter during three days of surveillance of Buie's house. More importantly the sweep took place *after* Buie had been arrested, handcuffed and taken outside. On these facts, the sweep (which turned up a red running suit in the basement) seems gratuitous.[43] Another lower court decision that reached a similarly questionable result is *United States v. Bennett*,[44] in which the court permitted a warrantless search of luggage despite the fact that the defendants were handcuffed and placed against the wall at the time, because the officers feared that an unspecified "someone else" would enter the room and obtain a weapon from the luggage in an effort to free the arrestees.[45]

(2) Searches for Evidence

Closely related to the fear that accomplices are on the premises is the concern, expressed by Justice White in *Chimel*, that these accomplices, or someone else sympathetic to the defendant, will destroy probative evidence once they know he has been discovered and arrested. To date, the Supreme Court has not clearly addressed this concern. A number of early Supreme Court decisions prohibited searches of a home, after an arrest made outside it, where there was no indication that evidence was being destroyed,[46] but only one decision explicitly deals with a government claim that a warrantless post-arrest search was needed to prevent evidence destruction, and that decision is difficult to interpret. In *Vale v. Louisiana*,[47] police had two warrants permitting arrest of the defendant for bond violations. While conducting surveillance of a house to see if the defendant lived there, they saw him come out and make what appeared to be a drug sale. They arrested him outside the house, but then searched the premises, apparently because two relatives of the defendant had arrived in the meantime and could have destroyed any narcotics inside.

The state claimed, and the Louisiana Supreme Court agreed, that the search was justified by exigent circumstances, but the Supreme Court reversed. In the course of its opinion, it stated: "We decline to hold that an arrest on the street can provide its own 'exigent circumstance' so as to justify a warrantless search of the arrestee's house." However, this broad conclusion, which would seem to prohibit post-arrest searches for

---

[42]   *Buie v. State*, 320 Md. 696, 580 A.2d 167 (1990).

[43]   Compare *United States v. Holzman*, 871 F.2d 1496 (9th Cir. 1989) (sweep not permissible upon officers' mere suspicion that accomplices may have been in hotel rooms or in general vicinity); *United States v. Baker*, 577 F.2d 1147 (4th Cir. 1978) (sweep permissible when police knew that a confederate of the arrestees had been seen with one of the arrestees the day before and was probably armed).

[44]   908 F.2d 189 (7th Cir. 1990).

[45]   Compare *United States v. Satterfield*, 743 F.2d 827 (11th Cir. 1984) (danger from unknown accomplices insufficient to justify search of house for shotgun after all occupants had been taken into custody).

[46]   See *Shipley v. California*, 395 U.S. 818, 89 S.Ct. 2053 (1969); *McDonald v. United States*, 335 U.S. 451, 69 S.Ct. 191 (1948) (warrant needed, as no "property in the process of destruction" or "likely to be destroyed.").

[47]   399 U.S. 30, 90 S.Ct. 1969 (1970).

evidence without judicial authorization, must be read in conjunction with the Court's further statement that there was "no reason, so far as anything before us appears, to suppose that it was impracticable for [the officers] to obtain a search warrant as well." Apparently the Court believed, as it had in *Chimel*, that the police were using the arrest warrants and surveillance as a pretext to gain warrantless entry into the home. The Court also seemed to think the relatives were not a threat to the evidence, as it stated "the goods ultimately seized were not in the process of destruction."

Whatever the reach of *Vale*, lower courts have routinely permitted warrantless searches of homes for evidence after an arrest, some requiring a probable cause belief, some only a reasonable suspicion, that the evidence is on the premises and would have disappeared by the time a warrant was obtained.[48] In this situation, in contrast to the protective sweep, probable cause should be required, since evidentiary searches are more intrusive than searches for confederates. Without this limitation, the possibility that police will use a warrantless arrest outside the home as a pretext to conduct a warrantless search within it is heightened considerably.[49]

(3) An Alternative: Securing the Premises

Another way of dealing with the "destructible evidence" problem is to secure the premises in which, or next to which, the arrestee is found, pending the procural of a search warrant. This practice would ensure that no evidence is destroyed, at least after a "sweep" of the premises ensures that no confederates are already there. Such a "seizure" of the home is arguably preferable to the search contemplated in *Vale*, since it is the less intrusive warrantless procedure. And it is often as feasible as a search, at least for smaller premises that can be secured with one or two officers.

In *Segura v. United States*,[50] the Court held, 5–4, "that where officers, having probable cause, enter premises . . . , arrest the occupants . . . and take them into custody and, for no more than the period here involved [i.e., 19 hours], secure the premises from within to preserve the status quo while others, in good faith, are in the process of obtaining a warrant, they do not violate the Fourth Amendment's proscription against unreasonable seizures." Whether one agrees with *Segura* may depend on a number of factors. In particular, if there are other occupants of the premises (besides those who have been arrested and taken into custody), a prolonged seizure may not be appropriate. But if, under the lower court cases described above, their presence authorizes an immediate warrantless search of the house, these other occupants might welcome the seizure option.

Following the logic of *Segura*, the Court held in *Illinois v. McArthur*[51] that when police have probable cause to believe evidence is in the home, they may not only secure the residence pending arrival of the warrant, but detain its occupants when they believe the occupants may otherwise destroy the evidence. As in *Segura*, the Court required that the warrant be obtained in a diligent manner. It also indicated that such a detention might not be permissible if the crime involved were extremely minor.[52]

---

[48] See, e.g., *United States v. Hoyos*, 892 F.2d 1387 (9th Cir. 1989) (reasonable suspicion); *United States v. Rubin*, 474 F.2d 262 (3d Cir. 1973), cert. denied 414 U.S. 833, 94 S.Ct. 173 (1973) (probable cause).

[49] See § 10.04 for a discussion of pretext doctrine.

[50] 468 U.S. 796, 104 S.Ct. 3380 (1984), discussed further in § 2.04(c).

[51] 531 U.S. 326, 121 S.Ct. 946 (2001).

[52] Cf. *Welsh v. Wisconsin*, 466 U.S. 740, 104 S.Ct. 2091 (1984), discussed in § 3.04(d).

(c) Search Incident Doctrine and Cars

There is at least one circumstance in which the police may rely on the search incident doctrine to justify searching an area beyond either the initial *or* "extended" control of the arrestee or his accomplices. In *New York v. Belton*,[53] the Supreme Court held, 6–3, that the search of a car and the contents of containers inside it is permissible even if the car's occupants have been removed from the car, so long as the occupants have been lawfully arrested and the search is contemporaneous with the arrest. The Court's decision seemed to be based entirely on the perception that the armspan rule had been difficult to apply in cases involving automobiles. Thus, stated Justice Stewart for the Court, the time had come to enunciate a "single, familiar standard" for the benefit of courts and police alike. With no further discussion, Stewart concluded:

> Our reading of the cases suggests the generalization that articles inside the relatively narrow compass of the passenger compartment of an automobile are in fact generally, even if not inevitably, within 'the area into which an arrestee might reach in order to gain a weapon or evidentiary item' . . . Accordingly, we hold that when a policeman has made a lawful custodial arrest of the occupant of an automobile, he may, as a contemporaneous incident of that arrest, search the passenger compartment of that automobile.

Belton thus permitted police who have lawfully arrested a car's occupants for a custodial crime to conduct a warrantless search of any part of the car's interior, as well as packages, clothing and other containers in it, so long as the search is contemporaneous with the arrest. Only the trunk and other relatively inaccessible areas (such as the area behind the dashboard) could not be searched during a search incident. Furthermore, this rule applied regardless of whether the occupants of the car outnumbered the police (as was true in *Belton*), and regardless of whether they were anywhere near the car at the time of the search. As the dissenters in *Belton* pointed out, the decision "adopts a fiction—that the interior of a car is always within the immediate control of an arrestee who has recently been in the car."

Twenty-eight years later the dissent's point of view won the day. In *Arizona v. Gant*,[54] the Court held, 5–4, that searches of cars incident to arrest may occur only when (1) the interior of the car is *actually* accessible to car occupants who might thereby obtain a weapon or destroy evidence, or (2) it is "reasonable to believe the vehicle contains evidence of the offense of arrest." In justifying the first holding, Justice Stevens' opinion for the Court analogized to the arm-span rule of *Chimel*, reasoning that "[i]f there is no possibility that an arrestee could reach into the area that law enforcement officers seek to search, both justifications for the search-incident-to arrest exception are absent." As Justice Scalia pointed out in his concurring opinion, because police almost always handcuff arrestees and put them in the squad car before contemplating a search of the car, this part of *Gant's* rule will seldom be met and represents a significant modification of *Belton's* broad search incident rule.[55]

The second holding in *Gant*, allowing searches incident when it is "reasonable to believe the vehicle contains evidence of the offense of arrest" will apply more often,

---

[53]   453 U.S. 454, 101 S.Ct. 2860 (1981).

[54]   556 U.S. 332, 129 S.Ct. 1710 (2009).

[55]   As Justice Alito pointed out in dissent, people arrested in the home are treated in the same fashion, which might significantly curtail searches incident to arrest under *Chimel* itself.

especially if, as the Court apparently intends, the "reasonable to believe" standard is somewhat easier to meet than "probable cause."[56] But if, as occurred in *Gant*, the arrest is for a traffic infraction, even this aspect of *Gant* will not apply. Thus, at the least, *Gant* eliminates the police practice, quite common since *Belton*,[57] of relying on arrests for minor traffic violations as authority for conducting a warrantless search of a car's interior.

6.05   Conclusion

Searches incident to arrest, traditionally conducted to prevent harm to the police and destruction of evidence, may be conducted without a warrant under the following circumstances:

(1)   The arrest must be lawful under the federal constitution (although it need not be lawful under the relevant state constitution), and must result in custodial detention rather than a summons, but may otherwise be for any offense, including a minor offense.

(2)   The search must take place soon after probable cause to arrest exists; it may not take place prior to that time.

(3)   The police may then, without a warrant: (a) search the person arrested and any containers thereby discovered, unless the search involves a blood draw or similar bodily intrusion or accessing a cellphone; (b) search the immediate area within the arrestee's actual control, meaning that area within the armspan of the defendant, including areas he may move to in the course of the arrest; (c) conduct a "protective sweep" of the premises adjoining the arrest; (d) conduct a sweep of any other area within the premises which they reasonably suspect might harbor persons who could endanger them; and (e) if the arrestee is an occupant of a car, search the interior when there is reason to believe evidence of the offense of arrest will be found. Additionally, some lower courts have allowed the police to (f) search any area within the arrestee's premises (when he is arrested on or near them) whenever they have a reasonable suspicion that evidence is in imminent danger of disappearing.

BIBLIOGRAPHY

Brennan-Marquez, Kiel and Stephen E. Henderson. Fourth Amendment Anxiety. 55 American Criminal Law Review 1 (2018) (discussing *Birchfield*).

Corn, Geoffrey S. *Arizona v. Gant*: The Good, the Bad, and the Meaning of "Reasonable Belief." 45 Conn. L. Rev. 177 (2012).

Dressler, Joshua. A Lesson in in Caution, Overwork and Fatigue: The Judicial Miscraftmanship of *Segura v. United States*. 26 Wm. & Mary L.Rev. 375 (1985).

Frase, Richard A. What Were They Thinking?: Fourth Amendment Unreasonableness in *Atwater v. City of Lago Vista*. 71 Fordham L.Rev. 329 (2002).

Kelder, Gary and Alan J. Statman. The Protective Sweep Doctrine: Recurring Questions Regarding the Propriety of Searches Conducted Contemporaneously With An Arrest On Or Near Private Premises. 30 Syracuse L.Rev. 973 (1979).

---

[56]   This rule had been suggested four years earlier by Justice Scalia in his concurring opinion in *Thornton v. United States*, 541 U.S. 615, 124 S.Ct. 2127 (2004).

[57]   See David A. Harris, "Driving While Black " and All Other Traffic Offenses: The Supreme Court and Pretextual Traffic Stops, 87 J.Crim. L. & Criminol. 544, 560–73 (1997).

LaFave, Wayne R. "Case-by-Case Adjudication" Versus "Standardized Procedures": The *Robinson* Dilemma. 1974 Sup.Ct.Rev. 172 (1974).

Logan, Wayne A. An Exception Swallows a Rule: Police Authority to Search Incident to Arrest. 19 Yale J. L. & Pol'y 381 (2001).

Ohm, Paul. The Life of *Riley (v. California)*. 48 Texas Tech L. Rev. 133 (2015).

Shoebotham, Leslie A. The Strife of *Riley*: The Search-Incident Consequences of Making an Easy Case Simple. 75 La. L. Rev. 29 (2014).

Tomkovicz, James J. Defining and Designing the Future of Search Incident to Arrest Doctrine: Avoiding Instability, Irrationality and Infidelity. 2007 Ill.Rev. 1417.

Chapter 7

THE "AUTOMOBILE EXCEPTION"

7.01   Introduction

In *Carroll v. United States*,[1] the Supreme Court laid down a set of principles governing searches of movable vehicles which has since been labelled the "automobile exception" to the warrant requirement. Specifically, *Carroll* held that a warrantless search of an automobile is permitted when: (1) there is probable cause to believe the vehicle contains evidence of crime; and (2) the police did not have time to obtain a search warrant prior to the search. Both of these elements were met in *Carroll*. There, agents stopped a person they knew had previously engaged in selling bootleg whiskey while he was driving what appeared to be a heavily-laden car, along a road known for its bootleg traffic. A search behind the car's upholstery produced 68 bottles of illicit liquor. The officers had not arrested the driver prior to the search (apparently because his crime was a misdemeanor that was not committed in their presence),[2] and thus search incident doctrine was irrelevant. But the Supreme Court sanctioned the search on the ground that the officers came upon the defendant unexpectedly, had full probable cause to believe his car contained evidence, and would have lost the evidence had they allowed the defendant to go on his way while they sought a warrant.

Unfortunately, lawyers and judges who have taken the words "automobile exception" literally have created considerable confusion about the parameters of the *Carroll* decision and its progeny. The exception is neither limited to automobile searches, nor does it cover all searches of automobiles. On the one hand, the exception may be applicable to searches of airplanes, boats, and other modes of transportation. In *United States v. Lee*,[3] for instance, the Court applied *Carroll* in upholding the warrantless search of a boat. Conversely, it should not be assumed that the automobile exception is relevant in every search and seizure case that involves an automobile or other movable vehicle. Many warrantless searches of movable vehicles are properly analyzed only in terms of other exceptions to the Fourth Amendment's warrant requirement. For instance, the Court has explicitly rejected use of the *Carroll* doctrine in analyzing searches of cars crossing the international border.[4] Likewise, a search of all or part of an automobile may be justified independently of the automobile exception if conducted incident to a lawful arrest,[5] in performing a stop and frisk of a car's occupants,[6] under the authority of the plain view doctrine,[7] while inventorying a car,[8] or upon the consent

---

[1]   267 U.S. 132, 45 S.Ct. 280 (1925).

[2]   Such arrests required a warrant under the common-law. See § 3.04.

[3]   274 U.S. 559, 47 S.Ct. 746 (1927).

[4]   See § 13.05(a).

[5]   See *Arizona v. Gant*, 556 U.S. 332, 129 S.Ct. 1710 (2009), discussed in § 6.04(c).

[6]   *Adams v. Williams*, 407 U.S. 143, 92 S.Ct. 1921 (1972), discussed in § 11.03(a).

[7]   *Harris v. United States*, 390 U.S. 234, 88 S.Ct. 992 (1968) (per curiam). See generally Chapter 10 for a discussion of plain view doctrine.

[8]   *South Dakota v. Opperman*, 428 U.S. 364, 96 S.Ct. 3092 (1976), discussed in § 13.07(a).

of a car's occupant.[9] Other constitutional searches of automobiles may not involve the Fourth Amendment at all.[10]

This chapter will focus on the automobile exception doctrine as set forth in *Carroll* and explicated in later cases. Other exceptions to the warrant requirement that may have an impact on searches of movable vehicles are discussed elsewhere.

7.02   The Rationale for the Exception

The automobile exception to the warrant requirement is based on two justifications. The first is the inherent mobility of cars and other conveyances. *Carroll's* most important contribution to analysis of Fourth Amendment cases is its differentiation between fixed and movable premises:

> The guaranty of freedom from unreasonable searches and seizures by the Fourth Amendment has been construed, practically since the beginning of the Government, as recognizing a necessary difference between a search of a store, dwelling house or other structure in respect of which a proper official warrant readily may be obtained, and a search of a ship, motor boat, wagon or automobile, for contraband goods, where it is not practicable to secure a warrant because the vehicle can be quickly moved out of the locality or jurisdiction in which the warrant must be sought.

The second rationale for the automobile exception is the public character of movable vehicles, in particular the automobile. The principal case supporting this point, ironically, did not involve a search of a vehicle. In *United States v. Chadwick*,[11] federal agents with probable cause to believe that the defendants' footlocker contained marijuana arrested the defendants and seized their footlocker at a train station. An hour and a half later they searched the footlocker without the defendants' consent or a warrant. The government attempted to justify this search primarily by relying on an analogy to the automobile exception: since the police had probable cause to search the footlocker and the footlocker was inherently mobile, the police should not have been required to seek a warrant before searching it. The Court admitted the police had probable cause. But it noted that once the police had seized the footlocker, exigent circumstances no longer existed. More significantly, the Court concluded that a search of a footlocker triggers stronger privacy considerations than does a search of a car.

The Court pointed out that cars are associated with a diminished privacy interest because: (1) automobiles function on the public thoroughfares; (2) they are subject to state registration and licensing requirements; (3) other aspects of automobile operation are strictly regulated; (4) periodic inspections are commonly mandated; and (5) automobiles may be impounded by police for public safety reasons. Footlockers, on the other hand, are not as heavily regulated or monitored by the state, and the expectation of privacy with respect to such repositories of personal belongings is greater than the privacy associated with a car. Therefore, concluded the Court, the automobile exception should not apply to searches of such items, despite their inherent mobility.[12]

---

    [9]   *Schneckloth v. Bustamonte*, 412 U.S. 218, 93 S.Ct. 2041 (1973), discussed in § 12.04.

    [10]   *New York v. Class*, 475 U.S. 106, 106 S.Ct. 960 (1986), discussed in § 7.03(b).

    [11]   433 U.S. 1, 97 S.Ct. 2476 (1977).

    [12]   The Court would later hold, however, that these items *lose* their heightened privacy protection when they are put in a car, *California v. Acevedo*, 500 U.S. 565, 111 S.Ct. 1982 (1991), discussed in § 7.04.

Chadwick made clear that the automobile exception is based on the twin premises that cars, and other vehicles such as boats and planes, are: (1) easily moved out of the jurisdiction and (2) associated with a lesser expectation of privacy than are other movable items. The first rationale makes some sense, although it can be questioned. Cars are *not* mobile once police have stopped them. If, as the Court has held, a house that is suspected of containing destructible evidence can be secured pending a warrant,[13] a car could be seized while police obtain judicial authorization to search it. But the Court, not without some reason, has been unwilling to require police to resort to this sometimes dangerous practice.[14]

The second rationale is much less supportable. The reasons the Court gave in *Chadwick* for distinguishing the privacy interest associated with cars from that associated with other effects do not explain why the areas in which evidence is usually found (e.g., glove compartments, trunks and so on) are less protected than other private areas which house personal property. More importantly, even if the car and its interior do have a diminished aura of privacy, it is not clear why this fact is relevant to whether a warrant is required. Assuming judicial decisionmaking is to be preferred over decisionmaking of officers in the field, only the presence of exigent circumstances should permit dispensing with a warrant.[15]

7.03   Elements of the Exception

Given the rationales for the automobile exception, three elements must be met before it applies. First, the area searched must be associated with a lessened expectation of privacy. Second, police must have probable cause to search the vehicle. Third, exigent circumstances must exist, although it appears that this last element of the exception, as now defined, adds virtually nothing beyond a showing that the vehicle is mobile. These elements are explored below.

(a) Vehicles Covered

As noted, searches of cars, boats and planes are covered by the exception, while searches of homes are not. In *California v. Carney*,[16] the Court was confronted with a hybrid situation: a warrantless search of a "mini" mobile home parked in a parking lot. While recognizing that the vehicle had "many of the attributes of a home," the six-member majority concluded that this type of mobile home is more like a car than a house. According to the Court, the test of whether a "vehicle" is one or the other should be whether the setting of the vehicle "objectively indicates that the vehicle is being used for transportation." Factors relevant to this determination are the vehicle's location, whether it is readily mobile or stationary (e.g., elevated on blocks), whether it is licensed, whether it is connected to utilities, and whether it has convenient access to the road. In dissent, Justice Stevens, making reference to *Chadwick*, argued that one has a *greater* expectation of privacy in vehicles such as the one at issue in *Carney* than in one's footlocker; he compared the mini-home to a hotel room or a hunting and fishing cabin.

---

[13]   See § 6.04(b)(3).

[14]   See *Chambers v. Maroney*, 399 U.S. 42, 90 S.Ct. 1975 (1970), discussed in § 7.03(c)(2).

[15]   For an argument to the contrary, see William J. Stuntz, *Warrants and Fourth Amendment Remedies*, 77 Va. L.Rev. 881 (1991) (arguing that, given the fact that justification is required ex ante, a warrant-based search requires more probable cause than a warrantless search and therefore it makes sense to reserve warrants for searches of more private areas such as houses).

[16]   471 U.S. 386, 105 S.Ct. 2066 (1985).

As he rightly pointed out, "searches of places that regularly accommodate a wide range of private human activity are fundamentally different from searches of automobiles which primarily serve a public transportation function."

As suggested above, the debate in *Carney* about whether the privacy associated with a mobile home makes it more like a car or a house should be beside the point; even if the majority had adopted Justice Stevens' position, it still could have upheld a warrantless search if exigent circumstances existed.[17] In other words, the focus in *Carney* should have been on whether the police had time to obtain a warrant before searching the vehicle, the same question that would arise in a search of a house. Unfortunately, the Court's attempt to distinguish cars from footlockers in *Chadwick* has led it to conclusions that lose sight of basic Fourth Amendment principles.

However, the Court has continued to maintain the distinction between cars on public streets and cars that are parked in private homes. A couple of twentieth century cases had implied that a warrant is required to search vehicles located on private property.[18] In *Collins v. Virginia*,[19] the Court explicitly so held. In a nearly unanimous opinion, the Court concluded that "the scope of the automobile exception extends no further than the automobile itself," thus invalidating the warrantless search of a motorcycle parked on the curtilage of the defendant's home.

(b) Probable Cause

Carroll warned that "where seizure is impossible except without warrant, the seizing officer acts unlawfully and at his peril unless he can show the court probable cause." Probable cause to search has been defined elsewhere.[20] The important point here is that, while probable cause to arrest and probable cause to search often co-exist, they are not congruent. Thus, in *Carroll*, the police could not arrest the defendant, but still had probable cause to search the car. In contrast the police may have sufficient grounds for arrest, but not for a search. In *Preston v. United States*,[21] the police arrested the occupants of a car for vagrancy. The Court held that this arrest did not, by itself, give police probable cause to search the car's glove compartment and trunk (in which guns and burglary tools were found).[22]

There is one situation where a warrantless, exigent search of an automobile does not require probable cause to believe evidence of crime is in the car. In *New York v. Class*,[23] the Court held, 5–4, that when the focus of the search is an automobile's Vehicle Identification Number (VIN), the car may be entered even when the police lack probable cause to believe the car is stolen and have no other reason for observing the VIN, so long as a valid stop for a traffic violation or some other offense has taken place. The Court based this holding both on the lessened expectation of privacy associated with the VIN

---

[17]   There was no analysis of this issue by the majority. The dissent stated that since curtains covered the windshield, there was "no indication of any imminent departure." On the other hand, the person who provided probable cause (a client of the defendant) might have alerted the occupant had police gone to get a warrant.

[18]   See *Coolidge v. New Hampshire* and *Florida v. White*, discussed in § 7.03(c)(1).

[19]   ___ U.S. ___, 138 S.Ct. 1663 (2018).

[20]   See § 5.03.

[21]   376 U.S. 364, 84 S.Ct. 881 (1964).

[22]   Note that the Court has solidified this type of reasoning in *Arizona v. Gant*, 556 U.S. 332, 129 S.Ct. 1710 (2009), discussed in § 6.04(c).

[23]   475 U.S. 106, 106 S.Ct. 960 (1986).

(which federal regulations require to be visible to someone outside the car) and the minimal intrusiveness of a search designed merely to obtain a VIN. This conclusion can be challenged. As the lower court in *Class* observed in explaining its decision to exclude a gun found by police during the VIN search, "[t]he fact that certain information must be kept, or that it may be of a public nature, does not automatically sanction police intrusion into private space in order to obtain it."

(c) Exigency

In discussing the nature of the exigency exception in automobile exception cases, it is useful to distinguish between exigency measured "backward" from the time the car is discovered or stopped and exigency measured "forward" from that time.[24] The first type of exigency has to do with whether a warrant could have been obtained between the development of probable cause and the discovery of the car. The second determines how long after the latter occurrence a warrantless search may occur.

(1) Measuring Exigency "Backward"

Carroll emphasized that exigency should be narrowly defined, stating that "[i]n cases where the securing of a warrant is reasonably practicable, it must be used." That holding appears to have been overruled in more recent cases, however. Instead, the emphasis is now merely whether the vehicle is "readily mobile," an inquiry that is virtually indistinguishable from the initial inquiry into whether the vehicle searched is associated with a lesser expectation of privacy.

Undoubtedly, many car searches are conducted in exigent situations. Often, as in *Carroll*, probable cause develops at the same time the car is sighted, thus leaving no time to obtain a warrant prior to its discovery. At other times, probable cause may exist some time before the car is encountered, but police justifiably act without a warrant because they reasonably believe the car may disappear if they don't. In *Husty v. United States*,[25] for instance, a police officer, acting on an informant's tip, found contraband whiskey in Husty's unattended car. To the contention that the officer had time to get a warrant, the Court responded: "[The officer] could not know when Husty would come to the car or how soon it would be removed." A slightly different variant of this scenario occurred in *Chambers v. Maroney*,[26] where a description of a car involved in a recently completed robbery went out over police radio, and the car was stopped soon thereafter.

In some cases, however, exigency measured "backward" does not exist. In *Coolidge v. New Hampshire*,[27] for instance, the Court found that the automobile exception did not justify the warrantless seizure and search of two cars located on the defendant's property because the police had had probable cause to search the cars for two-and-a-half weeks prior to the search. When the search warrant police had procured turned out to be invalid,[28] they could not, according to four members of the Court, fall back on the automobile exception, since exigency measured backward from the time the cars were "discovered" did not exist.

---

[24] See Charles E. Moylan, *The Automobile Exception: What It Is and What It Is Not—A Rationale in Search of a Clearer Label*, 27 Mercer L.Rev. 987 (1976).

[25] 282 U.S. 694, 51 S.Ct. 240 (1931).

[26] 399 U.S. 42, 90 S.Ct. 1975 (1970).

[27] 403 U.S. 443, 91 S.Ct. 2022 (1971).

[28] See § 5.02 for a discussion of this aspect of *Coolidge*.

Coolidge may be strictly limited to its facts, however. In *Cardwell v. Lewis*,[29] the police called the defendant to the station for questioning after developing probable cause to believe he had committed murder and that his car was used in the crime. They arrested him at the station, and then seized his car from a public parking lot and searched it, all without a warrant. While there was some indication that the defendant's wife could have driven the car away after his arrest, the police had time to obtain a warrant before the arrest. Yet four members of the Court upheld the search; they avoided the exigency issue almost entirely, instead resting the decision on the seemingly irrelevant ground that, unlike in *Coolidge*, the car had been located on public property.

In *Pennsylvania v. Labron*,[30] the Court more explicitly reduced the scope of the exigency prong of the automobile exception. Expressly rejecting two state court decisions that had required "exigency" prior to a warrantless car search, the Court's per curiam decision stated that the *Carroll* doctrine requires only probable cause and a "readily mobile vehicle." The latter requirement is not a measure of exigency as understood in the *Carroll* case, but rather is meant merely to ensure the vehicle searched is associated with a lessened expectation of privacy. This holding follows from the suggestion in *California v. Carney*[31] that the current rationale for the automobile exception is the lesser privacy interest in a car, not the likelihood it will leave the jurisdiction. Apparently, after *Labron*, the only time police with probable cause to search a vehicle need a warrant when they have time to get one is when the car is stationary, as defined in *Carney*, or it is located on private property, as in *Coolidge*.

The Court may have reinforced the latter (*Coolidge*) rule in *Florida v. White*.[32] There the Court upheld a warrantless seizure of White's car from his employer's parking lot (as well as its subsequent inventory) under a forfeiture statute, even though the seizure took place two months after police developed probable cause to believe it was contraband. But, in addition to citing the mobility of the car as a justification for this ruling, the Court explained: "our Fourth Amendment jurisprudence has consistently accorded law enforcement officials greater latitude in public places."

(2) Measuring Exigency "Forward"

In *Chambers v. Maroney*,[33] the Supreme Court held that if the elements of the automobile exception are met at the time the car is discovered—that is, if there is probable cause and the car is readily mobile—police may forego an immediate search and instead bring the car in from the field and conduct a warrantless search at the stationhouse. As later described by the Court,[34] "the actual search of the automobile in *Chambers* was made at the police station many hours after the car had been stopped on the highway, when the car was no longer movable, any 'exigent circumstances' had passed, and, for all the record shows, there was a magistrate easily available." Yet, noting only that the requirements of the automobile exception had been met in the field, the *Chambers* Court sanctioned the later search.

---

[29]   417 U.S. 583, 94 S.Ct. 2464 (1974).

[30]   518 U.S. 938, 116 S.Ct. 2485 (1996). See also, *Maryland v. Dyson*, 527 U.S. 465, 119 S.Ct. 2013 (1999).

[31]   471 U.S. 386, 105 S.Ct. 2066 (1985), discussed in § 7.03(a).

[32]   526 U.S. 559, 119 S.Ct. 1555 (1999), discussed further in § 5.06(d).

[33]   399 U.S. 42, 90 S.Ct. 1975 (1970).

[34]   *Coolidge v. New Hampshire*, 403 U.S. 443, 91 S.Ct. 2022 (1971).

As the Court itself admitted, considerations of exigency cannot explain this result. The Court could possibly have rationalized the holding by pointing to the fact that the arrest of the car's occupants in *Chambers* took place late at night under dangerous circumstances and that the police should not be prohibited from doing at the stationhouse what they could have done in the field but for the danger. But this gloss on *Chambers* was eliminated as a possibility in *Texas v. White*,[35] where the Court reaffirmed *Chambers* despite the absence of such dangerous circumstances. Thus, the only explanation for *Chambers* is the one offered in later cases: exigency is not a relevant consideration under the automobile exception; rather, because of its lessened privacy protection, any readily mobile vehicle on public property is subject to warrantless search whenever there is probable cause.[36]

There is one limitation on the police's ability to conduct a car search subsequent to its seizure. In *United States v. Johns*,[37] the Court held that a search under *Chambers* may not be postponed for so long that it "adversely affect[s] a privacy [or] possessory interest."[38] However, it appears that a long hiatus between the original stop and the later search will often be found reasonable; in *Johns* itself, the Court held that a three-day delay was permissible, in part because the owners, who had been arrested, had made no claim for the property in the interim. In any event, the *Johns* limitation makes little sense under the Court's new rationale for the automobile exception; the assumption of a lessened expectation of privacy that now justifies warrantless seizures and searches of cars does not change with time. Thus, if the Court is serious about putting some time limit on *Chambers* searches, *Johns* should be premised solely on property, rather than privacy, concerns, and should be read to mean that, if the delay in the search unreasonably deprives the owner of property, it may not be conducted even with a warrant.

7.04   Scope of the Search

Once the requirements of the automobile exception are met, police can obviously seize whatever they find in plain view. But what about items that are not immediately visible? Suppose, for instance, that the police have probable cause to believe that a car contains contraband and that they lawfully stop it. If they find a footlocker in the car, may they conduct a warrantless search of *it* as well, or does *United States v. Chadwick*, discussed above, forbid such a search? The Supreme Court has wrestled with this question in several cases, only many years later making clear that *Carroll* always "trumps" *Chadwick*: that is, once containers are placed in a car, they lose the relatively greater protection they usually possess and are treated like other areas within the car.

For some time, it appeared the Court would hold to the opposite result. In *Arkansas v. Sanders*,[39] the Court concluded that a warrantless search of a suitcase for which the police have probable cause was not permissible merely because police wait until it is put

---

[35]   423 U.S. 67, 96 S.Ct. 304 (1975).

[36]   It should be noted that even if *Chambers* had been decided differently (in line with the original exigency notion expressed in *Carroll*), the type of the search conducted there would today probably have been authorized under the Court's inventory cases. See § 13.07(a).

[37]   469 U.S. 478, 105 S.Ct. 881 (1985).

[38]   Additionally, the author of *Chambers*, Justice White, later stated in *Coolidge* that *Chambers* "contemplated some expedition in completing the [stationhouse] searches so that automobiles could be released and returned to their owners."

[39]   442 U.S. 753, 99 S.Ct. 2586 (1979).

in a car before they search it. Rather, as in *Chadwick*, the police must secure the luggage and obtain a warrant for its search. And in *Robbins v. California*,[40] the Court held, 6–3, that even containers that are discovered for the first time during a car search must be seized pending procural of a warrant, rather than subjected to a warrantless search at the time of discovery.

The majority in *Robbins* was tenuous, however; it was clear that the three dissenters were not alone in feeling uncomfortable with the result. In particular, Justice Powell—who wrote a tortured concurring opinion explaining why he would apply the majority's ruling to the type of package in *Robbins*, which had been "neatly wrapped," but not to other, less private receptacles, such as "a cigar box or a Dixie cup"—and Chief Justice Burger, who did not join in the majority opinion but merely entered a separate concurrence, seemed ambivalent about the decision. When the author of *Robbins*, Justice Stewart, was replaced by Justice O'Connor, the stage was set for a repudiation of *Robbins*.

One year later, the Court handed down *United States v. Ross*,[41] which overturned *Robbins* and which backed away from much of the reasoning in *Sanders*. *Ross* held that once the requirements of the automobile exception are met, the police have authority to conduct a warrantless search "that is as thorough as a magistrate could authorize in a warrant." The only limitations on the scope of the search are "defined by the object of the search and the places in which there is probable cause to believe that it may be found." Thus, the Court explained, police cannot conduct a warrantless search of a suitcase in a car when they are looking for illegal aliens. Conversely, however, if the police are looking for contraband, they may constitutionally search any area of the car in which the contraband might be contained, including luggage and other receptacles. In *Ross* itself, the Court upheld the warrantless search of a paper bag found in a car trunk after police, with probable cause to believe the trunk contained heroin, stopped the car, searched its interior, and then searched its trunk.

The Court's opinion, written by Justice Stevens, justified its about-face in *Ross* by carefully examining *Carroll* and its progeny. It noted, for instance, that the whiskey discovered in *Carroll* had not been in plain view, but rather had been found only after an officer opened the rumble seat and tore open its upholstery. Similarly, some of the whiskey used against the defendants in *Husty* was found in "whiskey bags" which could have contained other goods. After looking at other Court decisions, Stevens concluded:

> [T]he decision in *Carroll* was based on the Court's appraisal of practical considerations viewed in the perspective of history. It is therefore significant that the practical consequences of the *Carroll* decision would be largely nullified if the permissible scope of a warrantless search of an automobile did not include containers and packages found inside the vehicle. Contraband goods rarely are strewn across the trunk or floor of a car; since by their very nature such goods must be withheld from public view, they rarely can be placed in an automobile unless they are enclosed within some form of container.

---

[40] 453 U.S. 420, 101 S.Ct. 2841 (1981).

[41] 456 U.S. 798, 102 S.Ct. 2157 (1982).

Thus, containers found in a car are subject to no greater protection than the car itself.[42]

Ross explicitly refused to reconsider *Sanders*, thus leaving intact the rule that if probable cause to search a container exists *before* it is placed in a car, the police may not conduct a warrantless search of it. In *California v. Acevedo*,[43] the Court, by a 6–3 margin, took the last step toward removing warrant protection for searches of automobiles by overruling *Sanders*. Justice Blackmun, who wrote the Court's opinion, argued that *Sanders* provided only minimal protection of privacy in any event, quoting from his dissent in that case: "Since the police, by hypothesis, have probable cause to seize the property, we can assume that a warrant will be routinely forthcoming in the overwhelming majority of cases." He also noted that the warrantless search permitted in *Carroll* (which, it will be remembered, involved slashing the upholstery) was more intrusive than many container searches. Finally, Blackmun asserted that the "anomaly" created by the different treatment of containers in *Ross* and *Sanders* had confused and inconvenienced police and should be eliminated.

Police may now conduct a warrantless search of any container they have probable cause to search once it is placed in a car, at least one that is "readily mobile." The majority in *Acevedo* did emphasize that police may not search the *rest* of the car unless they have probable cause to search that area as well. That limitation is not likely to place much of a restriction on the police however. In *Wyoming v. Houghton*,[44] for instance, the Court permitted warrantless search of containers possessed by *passengers* in the car, even if the suspicion that such containers contain evidence is based solely on the car *driver's* involvement in crime. In reaching this conclusion, Justice Scalia's opinion for six members of the Court simply relied on the reduced privacy expectations associated with the car and the ease with which guilty drivers can secrete evidence in passenger's belongings. The majority did suggest, however, that a greater degree of suspicion would be required to search the *person* of the passenger.[45]

One final point about container searches must be emphasized. As Justice Stevens pointed out in dissent, an "anomaly" still exists after *Acevedo*: a container carried in the street is still protected by the warrant requirement (assuming search incident to arrest doctrine does not apply[46]), yet loses that protection as soon as it is put in a car. Recognizing this fact, Justice Scalia wrote a concurring opinion in *Acevedo* arguing that, in line with his perception of the common law, only searches of containers inside a private building should require a warrant. This rule is consistent with the Court's approach to cars; although it suggests, contrary to *Chadwick*, that containers have the same lessened expectation of privacy as cars, *Chadwick* has already been significantly undermined by *Ross* and *Acevedo*. The alternative approach—requiring seizure of containers pending issuance of a search warrant—is unlikely to be adopted by the Court.[47]

---

[42] The Court later made clear, in *United States v. Johns*, 469 U.S. 478, 105 S.Ct. 881 (1985), that any containers searchable under *Ross* are also searchable at a later point in time under the *Chambers* rule. See § 7.03(c)(3).

[43] 500 U.S. 565, 111 S.Ct. 1982 (1991).

[44] 526 U.S. 295, 119 S.Ct. 1297 (1999).

[45] Cf. *United States v. Di Re*, 332 U.S. 581, 68 S.Ct. 222 (1948) (search of a passenger after arrest of driver violated Fourth Amendment); *Ybarra v. Illinois*, 444 U.S. 85, 100 S.Ct. 338 (1979), discussed in § 5.05(e).

[46] See § 6.04(a).

[47] In *Chambers*, the Court concluded that immobilization of a car pending a warrant is just as intrusive as an immediate search; although this reasoning is curious, given the fact that seizing the car and searching

7.05   Conclusion

The basic tenets of the "automobile exception" can be summarized as follows:

(1)   The area searched must be a vehicle associated with a lessened expectation of privacy; that is, a vehicle that is not on private property and whose setting objectively indicates that it is being used for transportation.

(2)   There must be probable cause to believe the vehicle contains evidence of crime.

(3)   The vehicle must be readily mobile, although exigent circumstances that hinder or prevent obtaining a warrant need not be present unless the vehicle is on private property.

(4)   If these elements are met, any area of the car or any container therein for which probable cause exists may be searched immediately, or at some later time, provided any delay that occurs does not unreasonably interfere with privacy or possessory interests.

BIBLIOGRAPHY

Adams, James A. The Supreme Court's Improbable Justifications for Restrictions of Citizens' Fourth Amendment Privacy Expectations in Automobiles. 47 Drake L.Rev. 833 (1999).

Gardner, Martin R. Searches and Seizures of Automobiles and Their Contents: Fourth Amendment Considerations in a Post-*Ross* World. 62 Neb.L.Rev. 1 (1983).

Harris, David A. Car Wars: The Fourth Amendment's Death on the Highway. 66 Geo. Wash. L.Rev. 556 (1998).

Katz, Lewis R. *United States v. Ross*: Evolving Standards for Warrantless Searches. 74 J.Crim.L. & Criminol. 172 (1983).

Moylan, Charles E., Jr. The Automobile Exception: What It Is and What It Is Not—A Rationale in Search of a Clearer Label. 27 Mercer L.Rev. 987 (1976).

O'Connor, Martin L. Vehicle Searches—The Automobile Exception: The Constitutional Ride from *Carroll v. United States* to *Wyoming v. Houghton*. 16 Touro L. Rev. 393 (2000).

Tomkovicz, James J. *California v. Acevedo*: The Walls Close in on the Warrant Requirement. 29 Am. Crim. L.Rev. 1103 (1992).

---

it (pursuant to the warrant) seems more intrusive than an immediate warrantless search, it would also apply to containers.

Chapter 8

HOT PURSUIT

8.01   Introduction

As discussed in Chapter 3,[1] police are allowed to enter premises to make an arrest, without an arrest warrant, when they are in "hot pursuit" of a person they believe to have committed a crime. This chapter will look at the closely related issue of when police are permitted to enter premises to conduct a *search*, without a *search* warrant, while trying to find a suspect they are pursuing. The Supreme Court first explicitly recognized the hot pursuit exception to the search warrant requirement in *Warden v. Hayden*.[2] There, the police were summoned by taxi drivers who reported that their taxi company had been robbed and that they had followed the suspect to a particular house. The police were shown the house and were admitted by the wife of the defendant, who was upstairs feigning sleep. In the course of searching for the defendant they found clothing in a washing machine and under a mattress and a shotgun and a pistol in a bathroom. The clothing and weapons were later used in evidence against the defendant.

The Court, in an opinion by Justice Brennan, noted that this situation was not covered by search incident doctrine. That doctrine only permits a search *after* a person is seized pursuant to an arrest.[3] Here the evidence was found before and contemporaneously with the arrest, which occurred an entire floor away. Nevertheless, a unanimous Court found both the warrantless entry and the subsequent search "reasonable," because the "exigencies of the situation made that course imperative." As Brennan stated for the Court, the officers "acted reasonably when they entered the house," because "[t]he Fourth Amendment does not require police officers to delay in the course of an investigation if to do so would gravely endanger their lives or the lives of others." With respect to the search, "[s]peed here was essential, and only a thorough search of the house for persons and weapons could have insured that Hayden was the only man present and that the police had control of all weapons which could be used against them or to effect an escape."

The paradigmatic case of a hot pursuit search is clear. The police either witness or receive a "hot tip" on a felony and chase the alleged felon, who flees to shelter. They apprehend him there after a search that additionally happens to turn up evidence that is used at trial. The rapidity with which all of this occurs argues for dispensing with a warrant. But hot pursuit doctrine is more complicated than this typical scenario suggests. Several aspects require more development: (1) when hot pursuit justifies entry; (2) the definition of hot pursuit; and (3) the scope of a search while in pursuit.

---

[1]   See § 3.04(d).

[2]   387 U.S. 294, 87 S.Ct. 1642 (1967). Only Justice Fortas, in a concurring opinion, actually used the term "hot pursuit". The term was first used by the Court in *Johnson v. United States*, 333 U.S. 10, 68 S.Ct. 367 (1948).

[3]   See § 6.03.

8.02   When Hot Pursuit Justifies Entry

Not every hot pursuit of a suspect permits warrantless entry. The courts have imposed at least four limitations on hot pursuit doctrine which significantly circumscribe the extent to which a police chase can end up in the home.

(a) Probable Cause as to Crime and Location

Warrantless entry may not occur under the hot pursuit doctrine unless police have probable cause to believe that the person they are chasing has committed a crime and is on the premises entered. Although *Hayden* did not explicitly require a probable cause showing of these facts, probable cause was clearly present there, and other Supreme Court cases have established that an entry of the home must normally be preceded by a probable cause showing.[4] Of course, as *Hayden* demonstrates, neither the crime nor the suspect's entry into the home need be observed by the police. Rather, probable cause can come from third parties.[5]

(b) Cause as to Exigency

In addition to having probable cause to believe a suspect is on the premises, the police should also have reason to believe that the suspect will escape or that some further harm will occur unless the warrantless entry occurs immediately. As one court put it, "[a] hot pursuit, by itself, creates no necessity for dispensing with a warrant."[6] Hot pursuit may explain why police have not obtained a warrant up to the time they arrive at the suspect's house. But warrantless entry at that point should not be automatic. Rather, as summarized by the court in *United States v. George*,[7] a warrant should still be obtained unless the arresting officers reasonably believe (1) "that the suspects either know or will learn at any moment that they are in immediate danger of apprehension;" (2) that "evidence is being currently removed or destroyed and it is impractical to advert the situation without immediately arresting the suspects or seizing the evidence;" or (3) that "a suspect is currently endangering the lives of themselves or others."

Although, *Hayden* did not directly address this point, other Supreme Court cases have seemed to require proof of one of these emergency conditions before allowing police to proceed without a warrant,[8] and several lower courts besides *George* have explicitly come to this conclusion.[9] Whether the existence of such an exigency must be shown at the probable cause level, or whether a lesser showing is permitted, is not normally addressed by the courts. Since the issue is whether the home and similar premises may be entered, probable cause would seem to be the appropriate standard.

---

[4]   See *Payton v. New York*, 445 U.S. 573, 100 S.Ct. 1371 (1980); *Carroll v. United States*, 267 U.S. 132, 45 S.Ct. 280 (1925).

[5]   See § 5.03(b).

[6]   *State v. Wren*, 115 Idaho 618, 768 P.2d 1351 (1989).

[7]   883 F.2d 1407 (9th Cir. 1989).

[8]   See, e.g., *Johnson v. United States*, 333 U.S. 10, 68 S.Ct. 367 (1948) (no sufficient reason for dispensing with a warrant where there was no risk of imminent harm to any person, no evidence was being destroyed or likely to be destroyed, and the suspect was not likely to flee while the police obtained a warrant); *United States v. Jeffers*, 342 U.S. 48, 72 S.Ct. 93 (1951) (invalidating warrantless entry, noting that "[t]here was no question of violence, no moveable vehicle was involved, nor was there an arrest or imminent destruction, removal, or concealment of the property intended to be seized.").

[9]   See *Jeffcoat v. Hinson*, 851 F.2d 356 (4th Cir. 1988); *State v. Storvick*, 423 N.W.2d 398 (Minn.App. 1988), rev'd in part, 428 N.W.2d 55 (Minn. 1988).

(c) Lawful Starting Point

A third limitation on the hot pursuit doctrine is that the police start the pursuit from a legitimate place. In *Hayden*, this limitation was not an issue, since the police obviously began their pursuit of the suspect from a public area. But, as developed elsewhere in this book,[10] police may not initiate a search on *private* property unless they are already lawfully there. For instance, an officer who does not know about criminal activity until he has trespassed on private curtilage and looked in a window does not have legitimate grounds for invoking the hot pursuit exception to justify a subsequent entry. By the same token, if the police are legitimately on the premises when they begin their pursuit, then a warrant is not required (assuming the other elements of the hot pursuit doctrine are met). Thus, in *Mincey v. Arizona*,[11] the Court stated, in dictum, that police may make a "prompt warrantless search" of the scene of a homicide for the victim or the killer after they have lawfully entered the premises upon reports of a death.

In *United States v. Santana*,[12] the Court was confronted with a hybrid situation: the police started their pursuit on public property based on what they saw taking place on private property. In *Santana*, police had probable cause to believe Santana had marked money in her possession used to make a heroin buy. When they arrived at her house, she was standing in the doorway of the house with a brown paper bag in her hand. As the officers approached, Santana retreated into the vestibule, where she was arrested and the bag, containing narcotics, was searched. Justice Rehnquist, writing an opinion for four members of the Court,[13] held that Santana was in a "public" place for purposes of the Fourth Amendment since "[s]he was not in an area where she had any expectation of privacy," and thus the arrest and search were legitimate. Although the search in *Santana* was closer to a search incident than a hot pursuit search, the case apparently established that police may pursue from a public vantage point a suspect they first see on private property.

(d) Type of Crime

A final prerequisite of the hot pursuit doctrine is that the person chased be suspected of a law violation that is "serious." While this designation clearly includes felonies, and perhaps some misdemeanors as well, if the person pursued is suspected only of a minor infraction of the law, *Hayden* does not apply. In *Welsh v. Wisconsin*,[14] the police: (1) found a car abandoned in a ditch; (2) learned from a bystander that the driver had appeared to be drunk; (3) found the petitioner's address on the car's registration; and (4) entered the petitioner's home to make a warrantless arrest. Writing for six members of the Court, Justice Brennan found this action unconstitutional, despite the state's argument that an immediate entry was necessary to obtain evidence of the petitioner's blood-alcohol level. The Court held that warrantless entry, "the chief evil against which the wording of the Fourth Amendment is directed," is not permitted unless the state can point to "some real immediate and serious consequences if [the officer] postponed action to get a warrant." The "best indication" of how serious the state's

---

[10] See § 10.02.

[11] 437 U.S. 385, 98 S.Ct. 2408 (1978).

[12] 427 U.S. 38, 96 S.Ct. 2406 (1976).

[13] Justice White concurred on the ground that entry to make an arrest never requires a warrant, a position which was rejected four years later in *Payton v. New York*, 445 U.S. 573, 100 S.Ct. 1371 (1980).

[14] 466 U.S. 740, 104 S.Ct. 2091 (1984).

interest was in this case was the fact that Wisconsin classified the petitioner's offense as a noncriminal, civil forfeiture offense for which no imprisonment is possible. Given this minor penalty, concluded the Court, "a warrantless home arrest cannot be upheld simply because evidence of the petitioner's blood-alcohol level might have dissipated while the police obtained a warrant."

While, as a theoretical matter, it may make sense to prohibit warrantless entries when an offense is truly minor, the holding in *Welsh* does not follow. The civil scheme adopted by Wisconsin, requiring revocation of a drunk driver's license and civil fines, reflected a strong interest in deterring drunken driving. Nonetheless, under *Welsh*, until the state begins imprisoning such drivers, or at least begins prosecuting them as criminal, it may be prevented from obtaining probative evidence in cases where the driver reaches home before the officer does, an occurrence that is apparently fairly frequent.[15] Beyond this, there are good reasons for not basing the scope of the warrant requirement on the nature of the offense, discussed in detail elsewhere in this book.[16]

8.03   The Definition of "Hot Pursuit"

Suppose the police develop probable cause that a person is engaged in selling narcotics out of his home and, instead of seeking a warrant, stake out the house for several hours to see if the suspect is there. Suddenly the door opens, and the suspect comes out, sees one of the officers, and retreats into the living room. Would a warrantless entry be permitted out of fear that the suspect, now alerted to the officers' presence, will try to destroy the narcotics? The answer should be no.[17] Unless the police are in *hot* pursuit of a suspect *at the time they arrive at the home*, a warrantless entry should not be permitted, even when the police can show that an exigency—such as imminent destruction of evidence—existed. Otherwise, the police could engage in warrantless entries in situations where they had plenty of time to procure a warrant. Put another way, analogous to the analysis under the automobile exception,[18] exigency in hot pursuit cases should be shown to exist both forward (in terms of destruction of evidence, etc.) *and* backward (in terms of pursuit) from the time the police trace the suspect to the premises. While the Supreme Court, to date, has for the most part rigidly construed the pursuit notion, many lower courts have been less careful.

(a) Supreme Court Cases

The pursuit in *Hayden* was clearly "hot." The police answered the taxi driver's radio call "in less than five minutes" and proceeded directly to the house in which the suspect was located. In *Santana* too, there was exigency, although the exigency was arguably "created" by the police. There, the state sought to justify the lack of a warrant on the ground that they had just arrested an accomplice of Santana's a block and a half from her house and "word would have been back within a matter of seconds or minutes." No member of the Court disputed this contention. But, as Justice Brennan pointed out in dissent, "[t]he exigency that justified the entry and arrest was solely a product of police conduct." Had police made the arrest of the accomplice at some later point in time, which

---

[15]   See, e.g., *State v. Griffith*, 61 Wash.App. 35, 808 P.2d 1171 (1991); *Hamrick v. State*, 198 Ga.App. 124, 401 S.E.2d 25 (1990); *City of Wenatchee v. Durham*, 43 Wash.App. 547, 718 P.2d 819 (1986).

[16]   See § 3.04(d).

[17]   But cf. *United States v. Shye*, 492 F.2d 886 (6th Cir. 1974) (warrantless entry permitted when door opened after one-hour stakeout).

[18]   See § 7.03(c).

they easily could have done, no exigency would have arisen. Echoing the Court's search incident cases,[19] Brennan stated: "[w]hen an arrest is so timed that it is no more than an attempt to circumvent the warrant requirement, I would hold the subsequent arrest or search unlawful." Brennan's point was that if *Santana* were read to permit warrantless searches even when the exigency is police-created, it would seriously undermine the warrant requirement.

Nonetheless, in *Kentucky v. King*,[20] the Court held that so long as the pre-entry conduct of the police is lawful, it is irrelevant that the conduct precipitates an emergency that could have been avoided had the police not engaged in the conduct. In *King*, police smelled marijuana emanating from an apartment and knocked on the apartment's door, stating "This is the police" or "Police, police, police." When they heard noise inside the apartment consistent with attempts to destroy evidence, they announced they were going to enter and did so, all without a warrant. An eight-member majority, assuming that exigency existed at the time of entry, concluded that the warrantless action was permissible even if the police would have been able to obtain a warrant without losing the evidence. Justice Alito, writing for the Court, acknowledged that "[t]here is a strong argument" that a warrantless search is impermissible when police "threaten that they will enter without permission unless admitted." But the Court found that no such threat was made in this case, and that police do nothing illegal in simply knocking on a door and announcing their presence; to suggest otherwise, Alito noted, would prevent police from corroborating investigative information, obtaining consent, or carrying out any number of other legitimate actions. Thus, consistent with its decisions in other contexts,[21] police do not violate the Fourth Amendment if they use the knock-and-announce rule as a pretext in the hopes of creating an emergency that justifies warrantless entry.

In contrast to *Hayden*, *Santana* and *King* are decisions in which the Court found the trail too cold to justify a warrantless entry. In *Mincey v. Arizona*,[22] for instance, police first removed the defendant and the body of the victim from an apartment, and then returned to spend four days searching the premises. Two to three hundred items were inventoried, but no warrant was ever obtained. The state sought to justify the search on what it called a "murder scene" exception to the warrant requirement. Justice Stewart, writing for the majority, firmly rejected such an exception, stating that a warrantless search must be "strictly circumscribed by the exigencies which justify its initiation." He noted that by the time this search had begun, the police had already checked the apartment for other victims or suspects, thus eliminating any emergency.

Similarly, in *Thompson v. Louisiana*,[23] a unanimous Court refused to sanction a two-hour search of a murder scene by homicide squad members 35 minutes after the premises were secured by the police. The state pointed out that the duration of the search in this case was substantially shorter than that which occurred in *Mincey* and occurred on the same day as the murder. But the Court noted that "nothing in *Mincey* turned on the length of time taken in the search or the date on which it was conducted." Because the homicide squad had entered the premises "at a later time" to conduct a separate

---

[19]   See § 6.04(a).

[20]   563 U.S. 452, 131 S.Ct. 1849 (2011).

[21]   See § 10.04 for a discussion of pretext doctrine.

[22]   437 U.S. 385, 98 S.Ct. 2408 (1978).

[23]   469 U.S. 17, 105 S.Ct. 409 (1984).

search, a warrant was required. Although neither *Mincey* nor *Thompson* were explicitly hot pursuit cases, they both indicate that the Court believes the justification for a warrantless entry must be exigency. In neither case was there a "pursuit" which justified foregoing a warrant.

(b) Lower Court Cases

In seeking further clarification of the term "hot pursuit," one must turn to lower court decisions. Many have sanctioned warrantless entries after pursuits of somewhat longer duration than those involved in the Court's cases. Of course, if the pursuit is "immediate and continuous" (language the Court used in *Welsh* in defining hot pursuit), the fact that it is prolonged is not necessarily fatal. For instance, in *United States v. Holland*,[24] police began their pursuit of a suspected bank robber by following footprints made in the snow to a spot from which it appeared (based on analysis of impressions made in the snow) a car with two passengers had recently been driven. The pursuers obtained the name of the car's driver from the residents of a nearby house, located the driver, and obtained from him the name of his passenger (the eventual defendant). The officers then went to the home of the defendant, were admitted by one of the occupants and found the defendant hiding upstairs. Time in pursuit was approximately 30 minutes, but, as the court stated, "the fact that there were three houses involved in this chain of circumstances and, hence, a somewhat longer pursuit, neither breaks the chain nor alters the concept of hot pursuit."

In *United States v. Scott*,[25] four black males armed with a sawed-off shotgun and revolvers robbed a bank. A witness gave a general description of the getaway car along with part of the license number. When that vehicle was found abandoned, the police determined that the suspects had switched cars. They then followed a trail of tire marks produced by high acceleration to a parking lot of an apartment complex, where they found a car fitting the description of eye-witnesses who had observed the speeding car. By questioning the resident manager the police learned which apartments were occupied by black males. A search narrowed down the possible apartments to one; scuffling was heard inside, the police entered, made arrests, and seized evidence. Here entry and seizure took place 1 hour and 45 minutes after commission of the crime. The court nonetheless found sufficiently exigent circumstances, stating that "had the officers delayed their entry to apartment 7 to secure a search warrant for that apartment, the suspects might well have escaped or concealed evidence, and the risks of armed confrontation would have been increased."

More questionable are those cases which allow a warrantless pursuit that is neither immediate nor continuous. A notable example of this tendency is *Dorman v. United States*,[26] which in effect endorsed a "warm pursuit" doctrine. There, four men had held up a clothing store at gunpoint. In the ensuing investigation the police discovered Dorman's pants (discarded by Dorman after putting on a new suit), in which they found copies of his monthly probation report identifying him and his place of residence. Since it was late at night and a magistrate therefore difficult to find, the police made a warrantless entry into Dorman's residence, four hours after the commission of the crime. In upholding the entry, which did not produce Dorman but did result in the discovery of

---

[24]   511 F.2d 38 (6th Cir. 1975), cert. denied 421 U.S. 1001, 95 S.Ct. 2401 (1975).

[25]   520 F.2d 697 (9th Cir. 1975), cert. denied 423 U.S. 1056, 96 S.Ct. 788 (1976).

[26]   435 F.2d 385 (D.C.Cir. 1970) (en banc).

evidence behind a sofa, the District of Columbia Circuit Court of Appeals admitted that hot pursuit was not proven on these facts. Nonetheless, it found that the police had an "urgent need" to forego obtaining a warrant. It listed six conditions that might lead to a finding of "urgent need:" (1) the offense is a grave one, particularly one of violence; (2) the suspect is reasonably believed to be armed; (3) there is clear evidentiary support for a showing of probable cause; (4) there is strong reason to believe the suspect is on the premises entered; (5) there is a strong likelihood of escape if the suspect is not immediately apprehended; and (6) police entry is peaceable. The court focused on the facts that Dorman had been armed and abused his victims, the delay was not the fault of the police, and the entry was peaceable (Dorman's mother had let the police in). It also discussed magistrate availability and the preference for daytime entries as separate, somewhat offsetting, issues bearing on the reasonableness of the police's failure to obtain a warrant.

Dorman appears to expand the emergency concept considerably. Only the fifth factor listed above is directly related to exigency concerns and, as the court admitted, this factor did not weigh heavily in the court's analysis given the four-hour hiatus between the crime and the entry. Yet *Dorman's* factors have been widely cited.[27] One explanation for the popularity of *Dorman's* warm pursuit doctrine is that "pursuit" cases are concerned initially with the efficacy of obtaining an arrest warrant rather than a search warrant. Some courts might believe that a warrantless entry should be easier to justify when it is designed merely to apprehend a fleeing suspect, because the privacy intrusion is less. But, as the facts of *Dorman* illustrate, in relaxing the prerequisites for a warrantless arrest,[28] the courts are in effect expanding the scope of warrantless searches as well, and they should therefore proceed with greater caution.

8.04   Scope of the Search

The scope of a hot pursuit search is wide-ranging. As the *Hayden* Court stated: "The permissible scope of search must, at the least, be as broad as may reasonably be necessary to prevent the dangers that the suspect at large in the house may resist or escape." Thus, police may search any location that might hide the suspect or suspected accomplices, as well as any area that might contain weapons. Moreover, any evidence discovered in "plain view" while looking for the suspect or weapons is admissible as well.[29] In *Hayden* the Court held that clothing found in a washing machine was admissible because the officer who found it could have been looking for weapons.

There are two limitations on the hot pursuit search, however. First, the search, in the words of the *Hayden* Court, must be "prior to or immediately contemporaneous with" the arrest of the suspect; once the suspect is found, the scope of the search is determined by search incident to arrest doctrine, which adequately provides for police protection.[30] Of course, if more than one suspect is involved, police may look for all of them.[31] If no

---

[27]   See, e.g., *United States v. Kulcsar*, 586 F.2d 1283 (8th Cir. 1978); *United States v. Campbell*, 581 F.2d 22 (2d Cir. 1978).

[28]   See § 3.04(d) for criticism of this tendency.

[29]   See generally Chapter 10.

[30]   See § 6.04. However, *Hayden* indicated that for officers who are not aware of the arrest, hot pursuit doctrine applies.

[31]   See also *Simpson v. State*, 486 S.W.2d 807 (Tex.Crim.App. 1972) (police could search throughout house for wanted individual after occupants had scattered upon police's arrival).

suspect is found, however, the police must leave the premises; *Mincey* and *Thompson* hold that further scouring of the dwelling is not permissible.

The second limitation on the scope of a hot pursuit search is based on the protection rationale of the doctrine. Officers may search *only* where the suspect or weapons might reasonably be found. In *Dorman*, for instance, police did not exceed their authority by looking in the closet and behind the sofa but the court suggested that "rummaging through drawers" may have been inappropriate. Following this reasoning, if the suspect is not believed to be armed and there is no reason to believe weapons are in the house, then a hot pursuit search should be limited to those areas where a *person* could be located. Of course, after *Welsh*, the hot pursuit doctrine may not apply to nondangerous crimes in any event.

8.05   Conclusion

The hot pursuit doctrine permits warrantless entries of premises when suspects have fled there. The principal components of the doctrine are as follows:

(1)   Before entering the premises, the police must have probable cause to believe: (a) that the person they are pursuing has committed a serious crime (one that is not "minor"); and (b) that the person is on the premises they wish to enter. In addition, they should have reason to believe: (c) that the suspect will escape or harm someone or that evidence will be destroyed or lost unless a warrantless entry is made. The observations informing these beliefs must be lawfully acquired; that is, they must come from third parties or police observation from a lawful vantage point.

(2)   The pursuit must be immediate and continuous from the time of the crime or the time the suspect is spotted outside the premises, and should not be extremely prolonged; in other words, if the police have a reasonable amount of time to procure a warrant before they arrive at the premises, they should do so. The fact that their own conduct may have created the exigency that makes obtaining a warrant difficult is generally not relevant to the analysis, as long as the conduct does not itself violate the fourth amendment.

BIBLIOGRAPHY

Decker, John F. Emergency Circumstances, Police Responses, and Fourth Amendment Restrictions. 89 J. Crim. L. & Criminol. 433 (1999).

Donnino, William C., and Anthony J. Girese. Exigent Circumstances for a Warrantless Home Arrest. 45 Albany L.Rev. 90 (1980).

Evans, Jeffrey L. Constitutional Restraints on Residential Warrantless Arrest Entries: More Protection for Privacy Interests in the Home. 10 Amer.J.Crim.L. 1 (1982).

Williamson, Richard A. The Supreme Court, Warrantless Searches, and Exigent Circumstances. 31 Okla.L.Rev. 110 (1978).

Chapter 9

EVANESCENT EVIDENCE AND ENDANGERED PERSONS

9.01 Introduction

The previous three chapters—discussing the search incident, automobile and hot pursuit exceptions to the warrant requirement—cover most situations in which an emergency search is legitimately conducted by police investigating street crime.[1] But there remain some situations in which the criteria for these exceptions are not met, yet exigency justifies a full warrantless search by the police. In some cases an arrest has not occurred, or the search is not contemporaneous with or immediately prior to the arrest, so neither search incident nor hot pursuit doctrine applies. And while the primary objective in the automobile exception cases is evidence, the cases discussed here involving cars differ because the exigent circumstances come from the evidence itself, not from the fact it is in a movable vehicle.

Unlike the other exceptions described in this book, the Supreme Court has not attached a label to these types of cases; here the terms used will be the "evanescent evidence" and the "endangered persons" exceptions. The caselaw suggests that if the police have reason to believe either that something of evidentiary significance is about to disappear or that a person is in imminent danger of serious harm, they may engage in a search necessary to prevent the threat, even when apprehension of a suspect or search of a mobile vehicle is not involved. The various cases endorsing this notion will be discussed here within the framework provided by the language of the Fourth Amendment, beginning with searches of persons, the issue on which the Supreme Court has focused most of its attention in this context, and then continuing with searches of houses, papers and effects.

9.02 Persons

The classic example of "evanescent," or vanishing, evidence is alcohol in the blood. The first Supreme Court case upholding a warrantless intrusion into a person's body to obtain such evidence was *Breithaupt v. Abram*.[2] There, police took an injured and unconscious individual to a hospital where a routine blood test disclosed that he had been drinking. The defendant argued that this procedure violated *Rochin v. California*,[3] where the Court had found that forcible use of a stomach pump to obtain evidence violated the Due Process Clause because it "shocked the conscience." But the majority in *Breithaupt* distinguished *Rochin* by concluding that the blood test procedure used in the instant case "would not be considered offensive even by the most delicate," because it had "become routine in our everyday life." The three dissenters, Chief Justice Warren and Justices Black and Douglas, argued that neither the nature of the procedure, nor whether it was "forcibly" administered, should be relevant to due process analysis.

---

[1]   As to situations in which "frisks," as opposed to searches, are justified, see Chapter 11. As to emergency searches in the regulatory context, see Chapter 13.

[2]   352 U.S. 432, 77 S.Ct. 408 (1957).

[3]   342 U.S. 165, 72 S.Ct. 205 (1952).

Rather, "due process means at least that law-enforcement officers in their efforts to obtain evidence from persons suspected of crime must stop short of bruising the body, breaking skin, puncturing tissue or extracting body fluids, whether they contemplate doing it by force or by stealth."

The majority in *Breithaupt* was careful to note "that the indiscriminate taking of blood under different conditions or by those not competent to do so," might amount to "brutality" under the *Rochin* rule. Moreover, because it was decided under the Due Process Clause, *Breithaupt* did not directly address whether, or when, a warrant was required prior to a bodily intrusion. In *Schmerber v. California*,[4] the Supreme Court addressed both of these points in the course of upholding a warrantless blood test. The majority opinion, authored by Justice Brennan, first found that the Fourth Amendment was clearly meant to protect the dignity and privacy interests implicated by body searches. Second, it agreed with *Breithaupt* that such searches could be conducted without a warrant, provided that: (1) there is no time to obtain one; (2) there is a "clear indication" that the search will result in the desired evidence; and (3) the search is conducted in a "reasonable manner."

(a) The Exigency Requirement

Because a body search is particularly intrusive, the *Schmerber* Court authorized warrantless action only when "there [is] no time to seek out a magistrate and secure a warrant." The Court refused to resort to search incident doctrine, even though the defendant had been arrested at the time of the search. That doctrine requires only a valid arrest, not a showing that evidence is about to be destroyed, on the theory that protecting police or evidence from the arrestee is a paramount concern overriding the interest in ensuring that police are relatively certain their search will produce something.[5] According to the Court:

> Whatever the validity of these considerations in general, they have little applicability with respect to searches involving intrusions beyond the body's surface. The interests in human dignity and privacy which the Fourth Amendment protects forbid any such intrusions on the mere chance that desired evidence might be obtained. In the absence of a clear indication that in fact such evidence will be found, these fundamental human interests require law officers to suffer the risk that such evidence may disappear unless there is an immediate search.

Thus, an arrest by itself does not permit a warrantless bodily intrusion; there must be good reason to believe "an immediate search" will produce evidence.

A different type of body search confronted the Court in *Cupp v. Murphy*.[6] There, the defendant, after officially being informed of his wife's death by strangulation, volunteered to come to the police station for questioning. Soon after his arrival, the police noticed a spot on the defendant's finger and asked him if they could take a sample of scrapings from under his fingernails. He refused and began rubbing his hands behind his back and placing them in his pockets. At this point, the police forcibly, and without a warrant, removed some of the matter under his nails. As in *Schmerber*, the Court

---

4   384 U.S. 757, 86 S.Ct. 1826 (1966).

5   See § 6.01.

6   412 U.S. 291, 93 S.Ct. 2000 (1973).

reasoned that although the search incident doctrine might not apply (there being no arrest), the police had probable cause to believe that "highly evanescent evidence" was in the process of being destroyed and acted reasonably in preventing its destruction.

In *Missouri v. McNeely*,[7] however, the Court resisted an expansive definition of exigency, and specifically rejected the argument that the natural dissipation of alcohol in the blood constitutes a per se exigency. An officer stopped McNeely for speeding and driving over the centerline and, believing McNeely to be drunk, requested that McNeely undergo a breathalyzer test to determine his blood-alcohol concentration (BAC). When McNeely refused, the officer arrested him and took him to a hospital where, 25 minutes after the stop, McNeely's blood was drawn and tested. The state argued that exigent circumstances necessarily exist when an officer has probable cause to believe a person has been driving under the influence of alcohol, because BAC evidence is inherently evanescent. But eight members of the Court voted to remand the case to determine whether a warrant should have been obtained. Four justices, in an opinion by Justice Sotomayor, insisted that exigency must always be evaluated on a case-by-case basis. Noting the advent of telephonic warrants and other methods of expeditiously obtaining warrants, as well as the fact that alcohol in the blood dissipates "gradually and predictably," the plurality concluded that "the State's per se approach would improperly ignore the current and future technological developments in warrant procedures, and might well diminish the incentive for jurisdictions to pursue progressive approaches to warrant acquisition."

Justice Kennedy, who provided the fifth vote for the result, emphasized in a concurring opinion that at some point the Court might want to provide more rule-based guidance in such cases. Chief Justice Roberts, joined by two other justices, voted to remand the case in order to apply just such a rule, which he said should provide that exigency exists whenever the officer reasonably believes he cannot secure a warrant in the time it would take to obtain medical assistance. Only Justice Thomas agreed with the state's broader per se rule. He argued that officers can never know whether blood-alcohol levels will dissipate below the legal limit and that determining BAC at the time of the stop by reasoning backward from BAC at the time of a blood-draw—an analysis the plurality stated would minimize the evidentiary effects of any delay caused by seeking a warrant—will "devolve into a battle of the experts."

The concurring and dissenting justices in *McNeely* won the day in *Mitchell v. Wisconsin*.[8] There the defendant was stumbling and incoherent when police found him walking near a lake after a report that he had been driving while drunk, and he became unconscious by the time the police got him to a hospital. Without obtaining consent or a warrant, the hospital drew Mitchell's blood, which contained alcohol three times above the legal limit. The state had argued below that Wisconsin's "implied consent" statute (which, in line with laws in many other states, assumes that drivers "consent" to blood draws as a condition of obtaining a license) authorized such blood draws even of an unconscious person. But the four-member majority did not address that issue, instead holding that a warrant was not required because exigency existed. While acknowledging that *McNeely* had held that blood-alcohol dissipation was an insufficient exigency, the plurality asserted that a reasonable officer could believe exigency existed when, in addition, the defendant is unconscious, or when a car accident is involved, because of the

---

[7] 569 U.S. 141, 133 S.Ct. 1552 (2013).

[8] ___ U.S. ___, 139 S.Ct. 2525 (2019).

additional tasks (seeking medical attention, investigating the crime) such scenarios trigger. Justice Thomas added a fifth vote, for the reasons he gave in his *McNeely* dissent. Justice Sotomayor, the author of *McNeely*, wrote a dissent pointing out that the plurality's ruling would significantly undermine *McNeely*, because even conscious drunk drivers often require medical attention, and argued that these cases ought to be decided on their facts rather than handled through a per se rule. The plurality made a bow to the latter argument by stating that Mitchell could argue on remand that a reasonable officer would not believe obtaining a warrant in his case would "interfere with other pressing needs or duties," but also declared such cases should be "unusual."

(b) The Clear Indication Standard

As the passage quoted above indicates, *Schmerber* required that, in addition to exigency, there must be a "clear indication" that an immediate search will produce evidence before a warrantless body search may occur. This language could be construed to require more than probable cause, not only because of the word "clear" and not only because the Court suggested that probable cause to arrest did not necessarily authorize the blood test in *Schmerber*, but also because bodily intrusions can be seen as more intrusive than the ordinary search authorized on probable cause.[9] The *Schmerber* Court seemed to require at least probable cause for the blood test at issue in that case; the Court noted that the discovery of a near-empty whiskey bottle in the glove compartment of the defendant's car, his "glassy appearance," and the odor of liquor on his breath had given the police probable cause to believe there would be alcohol in his blood. *Murphy* as well noted that the police had probable cause to believe probative evidence being destroyed.

However, in *United States v. Montoya de Hernandez*,[10] the Court equated the clear indication phraseology with the lesser "reasonable suspicion" standard, at least when police want to determine whether an alien is smuggling drugs across the border in her alimentary canal.[11] The Court did not authorize any particular type of body search in that case, focusing instead on the constitutionality of a 16-hour detention designed to produce the drugs through the "call of nature."[12] It also declined to consider "what level of suspicion, if any, is required for nonroutine border searches such as strip, body cavity, or involuntary x-ray searches." But the Court emphasized that "not only is the expectation of privacy less at the border than in the interior, but the Fourth Amendment balance between the interests of the Government and the privacy right of the individual is struck much more favorably to the Government at the border."[13] Moreover, in a concurring opinion, Justice Stevens argued that the defendant's refusal to undergo an x-ray test legitimated the detention.

In short, the overall tone of the majority and concurring opinions in *Montoya de Hernandez* suggests that some forms of bodily intrusions will be allowed at the border

---

[9]   Cf. *Winston v. Lee*, 470 U.S. 753, 105 S.Ct. 1611 (1985), discussed in § 5.06(c) (requiring a warrant prior to shoulder surgery and stating that "a more substantial justification is required to make the search reasonable" where bodily intrusions are involved).

[10]   469 U.S. 1204, 105 S.Ct. 1164 (1985).

[11]   On the difference between probable cause and "reasonable suspicion," see § 11.03(a).

[12]   See § 3.02(c) for analysis of this aspect of the case.

[13]   See § 13.05 for further discussion of border searches.

on less than probable cause.[14] Indeed, the lower courts have permitted body searches at the border on less than probable cause for some time, relying on the rationale expressed in *Montoya de Hernandez*.[15] Some lower courts have also authorized a lesser showing for investigative body searches outside the border context, at least for the least intrusive procedures (such as blood and urine tests).[16]

(c) The Reasonable Manner Requirement

With respect to the conduct of the search, the Court looked at several factors in upholding the blood test in *Schmerber*. First, the test was an effective means of determining blood alcohol levels. Second, it involved "virtually no risk, trauma, or pain." And finally, it was conducted in a hospital environment, by a trained physician and in accordance with medical practices, thus minimizing any negative effects. These three requirements state the minimum limitations on performance of emergency bodily intrusions.[17]

In both *Schmerber* and *Murphy*, there are additional intimations that, to be reasonable, a warrantless search of the body must be the least intrusive method available to the police. In *Schmerber*, the Court noted that the defendant there was "not one of the few who on grounds of fear, concern for health, or religious scruple might prefer some other means of testing, such as the 'breathalyzer' test petitioner refused," although it went on to state that "[w]e need not decide whether such wishes would have to be respected." In *Murphy*, the Court stressed that the police action was not a full search of the person. But in *Montoya de Hernandez*, the Court, quoting from cases involving other types of searches and seizures, emphasized that "[t]he fact that the protection of the public might, in the abstract, have been accomplished by 'less intrusive' means does not, in itself, render the search unreasonable."[18] Further, "[a]uthorities must be allowed 'to graduate their response to the demands of any particular situation.' "[19] Whatever the validity of this point of view in the context of other types of searches, it is not appropriate where bodily intrusions are involved. In *Montoya de Hernandez*, for instance, when the defendant had not "produced" the suspected evidence after 16 hours of detention, the government resorted to an involuntary rectal examination, despite the availability of an x-ray. The Supreme Court did not consider the viability of either alternative, but had it done so, it should have required that the government use the less intrusive method of discovering the drugs given the dignity interests involved.

---

[14] The Supreme Court has also authorized *suspicionless* blood tests, urinalysis and breathalyzer tests designed to detect drug and alcohol use when the results will not be used for criminal prosecution. See § 13.09(b).

[15] See, e.g., *United States v. Couch*, 688 F.2d 599 (9th Cir. 1982).

[16] See, e.g., *Ewing v. State*, 160 Ind.App. 138, 310 N.E.2d 571 (1974) (warrantless taking of urine sample proper). See also, *United States ex rel. Guy v. McCauley*, 385 F.Supp. 193 (E.D.Wis. 1974) (search of vagina invalid, not because no probable cause, but because not conducted "by skilled medical technicians.").

[17] Procedures for conducting non-exigent searches of the body are discussed in § 5.06(c).

[18] See *United States v. Sharpe*, 470 U.S. 675, 105 S.Ct. 1568 (1985), discussed in § 3.02(b) (field detention of person).

[19] Quoting *United States v. Place*, 462 U.S. 696, 103 S.Ct. 2637 (1983), discussed in § 11.02(b) (detention of luggage).

9.03   Houses, Papers and Effects

Most warrantless searches for evidence in homes and other areas are governed by either the search incident, hot pursuit or automobile exceptions.[20] Occasionally, however, police may have reason to believe that evidence in a house or container will disappear, even though no suspect or vehicle is involved. In *United States v. Chadwick*,[21] for instance, the Supreme Court required a warrant prior to a non-exigent search of a footlocker, but noted that a warrant would not be required where officers believed "that it contained evidence which would lose its value unless the footlocker were opened at once." The *Chadwick* dissenters added that where an immediate search would "facilitate the apprehension of confederates or the termination of continuing criminal activity," a warrantless action might be permitted.

Chadwick also stated that a warrantless search would have been permissible in that case had the officers had "reason to believe that the footlocker contained explosives or other inherently dangerous items." As the reference to "dangerous items" suggests, protection of the public may also justify a warrantless search. Similarly, in *Mincey v. Arizona*,[22] the Supreme Court quoted favorably a lower court opinion which stated that "[t]he need to protect or preserve life or avoid serious injury is justification for what would be otherwise illegal absent an exigency or emergency."[23]

The Court explicitly recognized and explored the scope of this latter warrant exception in *Utah v. Stuart*,[24] where police made a warrantless entrance after responding to a loud party call and witnessing, through an open kitchen screen door, an altercation between four adults and a juvenile; they entered when they saw the juvenile punch one of the adults hard enough to make him spit blood into the sink. The Utah Supreme Court held that the conduct the police observed was not serious enough to justify the intrusion. But the Supreme Court, in a unanimous decision authored by Chief Justice Roberts, held that the Fourth Amendment does not require police "to wait until another blow rendered someone 'unconscious' or 'semi-conscious' or worse before entering." He went on to state that "[t]he role of a peace officer includes preventing violence and restoring order, not simply rendering first aid to casualties." Nor did the police violate the knock-and-announce rule when they entered without invitation, because their shout of "police" had gone unacknowledged during the tumult.[25]

The Utah Supreme Court had also found fault with the police action because the officers had entered "exclusively in their law enforcement capacity," rather than to aid any injured individuals. In a somewhat similar vein, other lower courts have held that a warrantless search is unconstitutional when "the officers consciously established the conditions which the government now points to as an exigent circumstance," such as when agents knock on a door of a house they think contains drugs and the ensuing attempt by the occupants to destroy the evidence creates the "exigency."[26] In *Stuart*, however, the Supreme Court suggested that limitations based on officer motivation are

---

[20]   See §§ 6.04; 8.04; 7.01.

[21]   433 U.S. 1, 97 S.Ct. 2476 (1977), discussed in § 7.02.

[22]   437 U.S. 385, 98 S.Ct. 2408 (1978).

[23]   *Wayne v. United States*, 318 F.2d 205 (D.C.Cir. 1963).

[24]   547 U.S. 398, 126 S.Ct. 1943 (2006).

[25]   For further discussion of the knock and announce doctrine, see § 3.05(a).

[26]   See, e.g., *United States v. Curran*, 498 F.2d 30 (9th Cir. 1974); *United States v. Allard*, 634 F.2d 1182 (9th Cir. 1980).

not required by the Fourth Amendment. Noting that it had repeatedly rejected contentions that the subjective motivations of the police are relevant to Fourth Amendment analysis,[27] the Court stated that "[i]t therefore does not matter here—even if their subjective motives could be so neatly unraveled—whether the officers entered the kitchen to arrest respondents and gather evidence against them or to assist the injured and prevent further violence."

A final question left unanswered by *Stuart* is whether the observations of the police must establish probable cause to believe exigency exists or whether instead some lesser level of suspicion is sufficient. The majority stated that police need an "objectively reasonable basis" to believe someone has been or will be injured. That language could be read to permit entry on reasonable suspicion.

The American Law Institute's Code of Pre-Arraignment Procedure provides a summary of the scenarios that might justify a warrantless entry to prevent harm or evidence destruction outside those situations covered by the search incident, hot pursuit and automobile exceptions. It allows warrantless entries upon "reasonable cause" to believe that the premises contain: "(1) individuals in imminent danger of death or serious bodily harm;[28] (2) things imminently likely to burn, explode, or otherwise cause death, serious bodily harm, or substantial destruction of property;[29] and (3) things subject to seizure . . . which will cause or be used to cause death or serious bodily harm if their seizure is delayed."[30]

Sometimes analyzed under the umbrella of what has been called the "community caretaker doctrine,"[31] the common thread joining all of these warrantless searches is that the nature of the evidence being sought, or the danger involved, creates a "compelling urgency" to act immediately. Thus, as is true of searches of the body, a warrantless entry to find evanescent evidence or avert harm should: (1) be based on probable cause to believe that an immediate entry is necessary to obtain the evidence or avert the harm; (2) offer an effective means of preventing the threat; (3) be limited in scope to the purpose of the search; and (4) be reasonably conducted.

9.04 Conclusion

In circumstances where the search incident, hot pursuit, and automobile exceptions do not apply, the "evanescent evidence" and "endangered person" exceptions to the warrant requirement permit warrantless searches of persons, houses, papers and effects when:

(1) There is an objectively reasonable basis (which may or may not equate with probable cause) to believe that an immediate search is necessary to prevent the imminent disappearance of evidence of criminal activity or bodily harm to a person. If this requirement is met, the fact that the police use the emergency to obtain evidence

---

[27] See *Whren v. United States*, 517 U.S. 806, 116 S.Ct. 1769 (1996), discussed in § 10.04. In a subsequent decision the Court affirmed this notion in the closely related hot pursuit context. *Kentucky v. King*, 563 U.S. 452, 131 S.Ct. 1849 (2011), discussed in § 8.03(a).

[28] See, e.g., *United States v. Brock*, 667 F.2d 1311 (9th Cir. 1982).

[29] See, e.g., *State v. McCleary*, 116 Ariz. 244, 568 P.2d 1142 (App. 1977).

[30] ALI, Model Code of Pre-Arraignment § 260.5. See also *People v. Mitchell*, 347 N.E.2d 608, 610–11 (N.Y. 1976).

[31] Mary E. Naumann, The Community Caretaker Doctrine: Still Another Fourth Amendment Exception, 26 Am. Crim. L. Rev. 325 (1999).

they otherwise couldn't obtain or created the exigency that results in the emergency does not render the entry and search unconstitutional.

(2) The search is otherwise reasonable. In the case of bodily intrusions, this requirement means, at the least: (a) that the procedure used is effective at obtaining the sought-after evidence; (b) that it does not involve a significant amount of pain or trauma; and (c) that the medical procedures followed are appropriate and necessary. Analogous requirements presumably apply to searches of houses, papers and effects. Assuming these requirements are met, it is doubtful that the search must be the least intrusive means of obtaining the evidence.

BIBLIOGRAPHY

Bacigal, Ronald J. Dodging a Bullet, But Opening Wounds in Fourth Amendment Jurisprudence. 16 Seton Hall L.Rev. 597 (1986).

Dix, George E. "Subjective Intent" as a Component of Fourth Amendment Reasonableness. 76 Miss. L. J. 373 (2006).

Mascolo, Edward. The Emergency Doctrine Exception to the Warrant Requirement Under the Fourth Amendment. 22 Buffalo L.Rev. 419 (1973).

Naumann, Mary E. The Community Caretaker Doctrine: Still Another Fourth Amendment Exception. 26 American Criminal Law Review 325 (1999).

Salken, Barbara. Balancing Exigency and Privacy in Warrantless Searches to Prevent Destruction of Evidence: The Need for a Rule. 39 Hastings L.J. 283 (1988).

Strossen, Nadine. The Fourth Amendment in the Balance: Accurately Setting the Scales Through the Least Intrusive Alternative Analysis. 63 N.Y.U.L.Rev. 1173 (1988).

Chapter 10

PLAIN VIEW

10.01 Introduction

The "plain view" exception to the warrant requirement was birthed in *Coolidge v. New Hampshire*.[1] The central issue in *Coolidge* was whether the police could seize and then search cars belonging to Coolidge without a warrant (the warrant the police possessed being invalid). The state argued that even though the warrant was deficient, evidence procured from one of the cars should still be admissible, because the car was in "plain view" from both the public street and from inside the house where Coolidge was arrested. A plurality of the Court, in an opinion by Justice Stewart, rejected this claim, noting that, "in the vast majority of cases, *any* evidence seized by police will be in plain view, at least at the moment of seizure." Thus, the mere fact that the police could see the car from the public street did not give them authority to search it. However, the Court went on to hold that, if the police are already lawfully *in* an area such as a house or car, evidence which is "immediately apparent as such" and which is discovered "inadvertently" may be *seized*. When a search is already underway, seizure of evidence in plain view works no additional intrusion. According to the Court, "[a]s against the minor peril to Fourth Amendment protections, there is a major gain in effective law enforcement."

From the foregoing, it should be clear that the plain view doctrine enunciated in *Coolidge* is designed to permit warrantless seizures, as opposed to searches. The doctrine can be more precisely stated as follows: police may seize items without a warrant authorizing such seizure if (1) their intrusion into the area in which the evidence is located is lawful; (2) the items are "immediately apparent" as evidence of criminal activity; and (3) the discovery of the evidence is "inadvertent." As the following discussion makes clear, the *Coolidge* plurality's holding on the first element seems to have withstood the test of time, while the second and third elements of the rule have been modified significantly.

10.02 Prior Valid Intrusion

In *Coolidge*, the Court stated:

[P]lain view *alone* is never enough to justify the warrantless seizure of evidence. This is simply a corollary of the familiar principle . . . that no amount of probable cause can justify a warrantless search or seizure absent "exigent circumstances." Incontrovertible testimony of the senses that an incriminating object is on premises belonging to a criminal suspect may establish the fullest possible measure of probable cause. But even where the object is contraband, this Court has repeatedly stated and enforced the basic rule that the police may not enter and make a warrantless seizure.

This passage from *Coolidge* distinguishes between plain view seizures from public places and plain view seizures from private premises. If a police officer sees marijuana on a

---

[1]   403 U.S. 443, 91 S.Ct. 2022 (1971).

public sidewalk, he may surely seize it without a warrant. In this situation, as discussed elsewhere in this book,[2] no search occurs. But suppose, instead, that the officer is walking on the public sidewalk and sees the marijuana inside one's home or car, through a window? In this situation, despite the existence of probable cause, the plain view doctrine would not permit intrusion into the house or vehicle to seize the evidence; such action would constitute a "search" that must be authorized in some other way.[3]

Of course, authorization to enter premises might derive from a number of sources, including search and arrest warrants, other exceptions to the warrant requirement, and legitimate non-investigative operations of government agencies. Once this authorization exists, the plain view doctrine is often unnecessary. Illustrative is *Colorado v. Bannister*,[4] in which a police officer approached a stopped vehicle in order to issue a traffic citation. Standing by the front door of the car, the officer happened to see, in "plain view," chrome lug nuts that matched a police radio description of some of those recently stolen in the vicinity, and observed also that the occupants of the car met the radio description of those suspected of the crime. The Supreme Court's per curiam decision upheld the officer's seizure of the lug nuts and other evidence, not on plain view grounds, but under the "automobile exception" announced in *Carroll v. United States*,[5] which permits warrantless searches of cars, and seizures and search of items therein, when there is probable cause to believe the car contains the items and some sort of exigency exists. The probable cause came from sighting the subjects matching the radio description, and the inherent mobility of the car provided the exigency. The Court rightly concluded that the automobile exception authorized both the intrusion *and* the seizure of the lug nuts; the plain view doctrine was not applicable.

In other situations, on the other hand, the plain view doctrine may come into play because the original authorization does not clearly permit seizure of the items in question. For instance, as discussed in connection with the particularity requirement,[6] when the police have a valid warrant to search a house, they may seize not only items in the warrant but also evidence that is not listed, if it is found in plain view in an area the warrant allows them to search. Similarly, evidence found by the police in hot pursuit of a suspect may be seized even though it is not a weapon that the suspect could use to escape or harm the officers.[7] And, as discussed in Chapter 12,[8] police may seize evidence found during a lawful consent search even if it is not the evidence the police or the consentor contemplated when the consent was given. Other plain view seizures have been upheld when executed by government officers who were: (1) accompanying an arrestee to his room;[9] (2) investigating a fire in a home;[10] (3) conducting an inventory

---

[2]   See § 4.03.

[3]   If, on the other hand, the marijuana were seen inside a *container* on the sidewalk, a seizure could take place, as the Fourth Amendment does not protect a container that somehow "reveals the nature of its contents." *Arkansas v. Sanders*, 442 U.S. 753, 99 S.Ct. 2586 (1979).

[4]   449 U.S. 1, 101 S.Ct. 42 (1980).

[5]   267 U.S. 132, 45 S.Ct. 280 (1925), discussed in § 7.01.

[6]   See § 5.04.

[7]   *Warden v. Hayden*, 387 U.S. 294, 87 S.Ct. 1642 (1967), discussed in § 8.04.

[8]   See § 12.03.

[9]   *Washington v. Chrisman*, 455 U.S. 1, 102 S.Ct. 812 (1982), discussed in § 6.04(a).

[10]   *Michigan v. Tyler*, 436 U.S. 499, 98 S.Ct. 1942 (1978), discussed in § 13.04.

search of a car;[11] (4) searching for a Vehicle Identification Number;[12] and (5) in a car rolling up a window to protect it against the rain.[13]

The scenarios in which the plain view doctrine could operate are as numerous as the situations in which police may validly intrude upon private premises. The important point to remember is that the doctrine does not justify the predicate intrusion.

10.03   Items That May Be Seized

The *Coolidge* plurality opinion sought to ensure that the plain view doctrine it announced would not encourage the type of behavior associated with the infamous "general warrants" of colonial times, which had authorized seizure of any object the executing officers thought relevant. Thus, the plurality required that items seized as evidence of criminal activity be "immediately apparent as such." As Justice Stewart explained, "the 'plain view' doctrine may not be used to extend a general exploratory search from one object to another until something incriminating at last emerges." Here he cited *Stanley v. Georgia*,[14] in which the three justices who reached the Fourth Amendment issue found that the warrantless seizure of film canisters, which later proved to contain obscene films, was not permissible even though the canisters had been in plain view, because their contents had not been.

However, in *Texas v. Brown*,[15] the Court made clear that the police need not be *certain* that the item seized is evidence of criminal activity. In *Brown*, a police officer stopped the defendant's car at a routine driver's license checkpoint late at night. As Brown reached across the passenger seat to open the glove compartment and look for his license, the officer observed him drop an opaque green party balloon, knotted at the opening, into the passenger's seat. Upon seeing the balloon, the officer shifted his position to obtain a view of the glove compartment. He noticed, with the help of a flashlight, that it contained several small plastic vials, quantities of loose white powder, and an open bag of party balloons. The officer eventually seized the green balloon, which later proved to contain heroin.

The Texas Court of Criminal Appeals, in reversing Brown's conviction, held that in order for the plain view doctrine to apply, the officer had to know that "incriminatory evidence was before him when he seized the balloon." A unanimous Supreme Court reversed, holding that *Coolidge* had not required such a high degree of certainty as to the nature of the seized item; to the extent the phrase "immediately apparent" connoted otherwise, it "was very likely an unhappy choice of words." Instead, concluded the Court, all that is required to meet this criterion of the plain view doctrine is probable cause.

Although the Court's equation of the "immediately apparent as such" language in *Coolidge* with probable cause is sensible, the fact that the Court reached this question on the facts in *Brown* is curious. All three of the opinions in *Brown* assumed that the plain view doctrine authorized the officer's intrusion into the car to obtain the balloon.

---

[11]   *South Dakota v. Opperman*, 428 U.S. 364, 96 S.Ct. 3092 (1976), discussed in § 13.07(a). See also, *Cady v. Dombrowski*, 413 U.S. 433 (1973) (police looking for an arrested officer's service revolver in officer's car found evidence of murder).

[12]   *New York v. Class*, 475 U.S. 106, 106 S.Ct. 960 (1986), discussed in § 7.03(b).

[13]   *Harris v. United States*, 390 U.S. 234, 88 S.Ct. 992 (1968) (per curiam).

[14]   394 U.S. 557, 89 S.Ct. 1243 (1969).

[15]   460 U.S. 730, 103 S.Ct. 1535 (1983).

But, as pointed out earlier in this chapter,[16] the plain view doctrine traditionally has not authorized intrusion, only seizure after the intrusion. It is highly likely that the officer's reach into the car and the ensuing search of the balloon in *Brown* was justified under the automobile exception to the warrant requirement,[17] given the Court's finding that probable cause existed. But recognition of this fact should have obviated the discussion of the plain view doctrine.

While *Brown* held that police need only probable cause in order to meet the second element of the plain view exception, *Arizona v. Hicks*[18] established that a *lesser* degree of suspicion is insufficient to meet this element. In *Hicks*, an officer validly in an apartment while investigating a shooting incident spotted two sets of expensive stereo components which he suspected were stolen. In order to check their serial numbers, he moved some of the components. The state conceded that at the time the officer moved the components he had only a reasonable suspicion that the equipment was stolen.

The Supreme Court held, 6–3, in an opinion by Justice Scalia, that the officer's moving of the components was a "search" of the equipment that required probable cause. The officer's act was a search because it involved an invasion of the defendant's privacy beyond that authorized by the initial intrusion to investigate the shooting. It required probable cause because to hold otherwise would "cut the 'plain view' doctrine loose from its theoretical and practical moorings." While efficiency concerns permit warrantless plain view seizures, "[n]o reason is apparent why an object should routinely be seizable on lesser grounds, during an unrelated search and seizure, than would have been needed to obtain a warrant for that same object if it had been known to be on the premises." To the dissent's argument that the officer's search in this case was merely "cursory" and therefore should be justified if based on reasonable suspicion, Scalia stated: "[w]e are unwilling to send police and judges into a new thicket of Fourth Amendment law, to seek a creature of uncertain description that is neither a plain-view inspection nor yet a 'full-blown search' ".

Note that *Hicks* allows warrantless "plain view searches" as well as warrantless seizures, so long as there is probable cause. That is, if police validly on premises develop probable cause to believe an item is evidence of criminal activity, they may not only seize that item without a warrant, but conduct a warrantless "search" of it as well. In most instances, such a preliminary inspection is preferable because it will help avoid unnecessary seizures. In others, however, it might tend to expand the scope of the plain view doctrine, which has traditionally authorized only seizures. Just as the Court has held that the "automobile exception" permits a warrantless search of all containers within the automobile that police have probable cause to believe contain evidence of crime,[19] *Hicks* may be construed to allow warrantless searches of all containers in a house that police have probable cause to believe contain such evidence.

Although the name of the plain view doctrine obviously focuses on what police discern visually, there is no reason, in theory,[20] to limit the doctrine's reach to such cases.

---

[16]   See § 10.02.

[17]   See Chapter 7.

[18]   480 U.S. 321, 107 S.Ct. 1149 (1987).

[19]   See § 7.04.

[20]   But see, Comment, *The Case Against a Plain Feel Exception to the Warrant Requirement*, 54 Chi.L.Rev. 683 (1987) (giving practical reasons for limiting the plain view doctrine to visible items).

As the Court has intimated, if police are validly on premises and smell an odor[21] or feel an object[22] that gives them probable cause to believe an item is evidence of criminal activity, they should be able to seize it, or at least the object in which it is contained, without a warrant. Similarly, whatever "items" police "plainly hear" from a lawful listening point is also admissible. This situation most commonly arises during properly authorized electronic surveillance, when police hear conversation about an offense or offenses that were not the original reason for the interception described in the surveillance warrant. Under Title III of the Omnibus Crime Control and Safe Streets Act of 1968, this information may be used in court if specific procedures are followed.[23]

10.04   Inadvertence and Pretextual Searches

A third requirement of the plain view doctrine announced by the *Coolidge* plurality, now eliminated, was that the discovery of the evidence must be inadvertent. This requirement was thought to flow from the general proposition that, when there is no exigency, a warrant must be obtained. As Justice Stewart stated in *Coolidge*:

> The rationale of the [plain view] exception to the warrant requirement . . . is that a plain view seizure not turn an initially valid (and therefore limited) search into a "general" one, wh[ere] the inconvenience of procuring a warrant to cover an inadvertent discovery is great. But where the discovery is anticipated, where the police know in advance the location of the evidence and intend to seize it, the situation is altogether different. The requirement of a warrant imposes no inconvenience in a legal system that regards warrantless searches as "*per se* unreasonable" in the absence of "exigent circumstances."

Thus, according to the *Coolidge* plurality, evidence that is "immediately apparent as such" and seized after a valid intrusion was still inadmissible if police anticipated its discovery and did not obtain a warrant authorizing a search for it.

The problem that arose as a result of the inadvertence requirement was determining precisely when a discovery was "inadvertent" for purposes of the plain view exception. Most courts allowed the exception to apply so long as the police did not have, prior to the search, probable cause to believe the evidence was on the premises; any lesser degree of suspicion that the evidence was there did not bar a finding of inadvertence.[24] This position reflects the reality that if the police do not have probable cause, they cannot obtain a warrant for the desired item even if they want to. On the other hand, such a stance might encourage an officer, acting on a mere "hunch" that evidence of criminal activity can be found on certain premises, to "create" a trivial purpose for entering the premises (e.g., a residential safety inspection or a traffic stop), hoping that in the ensuing search he will come across the evidence he really wants,

---

[21]   Cf. *United States v. Place*, 462 U.S. 696, 103 S.Ct. 2637 (1983), discussed in § 4.03(f)(2) (implying that a dog sniff of luggage that produces probable cause provides grounds for seizure of the luggage); *United States v. Villamonte-Marquez*, 462 U.S. 579, 103 S.Ct. 2573 (1983), discussed in § 13.06(d) (search based on smell of burning marijuana).

[22]   Cf. *Minnesota v. Dickerson*, 508 U.S. 366, 113 S.Ct. 2130 (1993), discussed in § 11.05 (implying that if police can develop probable cause by feeling an item through clothing, the item may be seized immediately).

[23]   18 U.S.C.A. § 2517(5), discussed in § 14.03(c)(3).

[24]   See, e.g., *United States v. Hare*, 589 F.2d 1291 (6th Cir. 1979); *United States v. Hillstrom*, 533 F.2d 209 (5th Cir. 1976), cert. denied 429 U.S. 1038, 97 S.Ct. 734 (1977); *United States v. Medows*, 540 F.Supp. 490 (S.D.N.Y. 1982).

without having to develop probable cause or seek a warrant.[25] In order to discourage such pretextual searches, one might advocate that *any* specific pre-search suspicion that evidence is on the premises should invalidate its seizure, unless the police obtain a warrant for that evidence or give a reasonable, non-pretextual explanation of why they did not obtain such a warrant.[26] A "non-pretextual explanation" would consist of proof that the officer's action was of a type *routinely* taken, as a matter of departmental policy, under the circumstances in question.[27]

In *Horton v. California*,[28] the Supreme Court mooted the debate over whether inadvertence should be equated with a lack of probable cause by eliminating the inadvertence requirement altogether. The majority opinion, by Justice Stevens, noted that this requirement only attracted a plurality of the Court in *Coolidge* and in any event was unnecessary to that decision. It then concluded that, contrary to Justice Stewart's statements in *Coolidge*, the inadvertence requirement was not needed to protect against general warrants. In doing so, the Court also seemed to dismiss the concern over pretextual searches described above:

> [E]venhanded law enforcement is best achieved by the application of objective standards of conduct, rather than standards that depend upon the subjective state of mind of the officer. The fact that an officer is interested in an item of evidence and fully expects to find it in the course of a search should not invalidate its seizure if the search is confined in area and duration by the terms of the warrant or a valid exception to the warrant requirement. . . . [I]f he or she has a valid warrant to search for one item and merely a suspicion concerning the second, whether or not it amounts to probable cause, we fail to see why that suspicion should immunize the second item from seizure if it is found during a lawful search for the first.

Stevens used the facts in *Horton* to illustrate the conclusion that the inadvertence requirement is unnecessary to protect against illegitimate intrusions. After investigating a robbery, an officer filed an application for a warrant that referred to police reports describing both the proceeds of the robbery and the weapons used. However, the warrant actually issued authorized a search only for the proceeds, including three specifically described rings. During the subsequent search, the officer did not find the rings but did find the weapons. He later admitted that when he entered the house he had been interested in finding not just the rings but other evidence connected with the robbery. According to the majority, despite the lack of inadvertence, no privacy interests would be vindicated by excluding the weapons. In conducting the search, the officer did not go beyond the boundaries prescribed by the warrant. "Indeed, if the three rings and other items named in the warrant had been found at the outset—

---

[25]   See, e.g., *United States v. Smith*, 799 F.2d 704 (11th Cir. 1986), in which a valid arrest for "weaving" from one lane to another was determined to be pretextual and the subsequent seizure of narcotics from the car illegal.

[26]   See Note, *The Pretext Problem Revisited: A Doctrinal Exploration of Bad Faith in Search and Seizure Cases*, 70 Boston Univ.L.Rev. 111 (1990).

[27]   Compare *United States v. Cardona-Rivera*, 904 F.2d 1149 (7th Cir. 1990) (officers' testimony that car later found to contain drugs was stopped for a traffic violation "not worthy of belief," since officers were not traffic police and did not have traffic books), with *State v. Bolton*, 111 N.M. 28, 801 P.2d 98 (1990) (stated purpose of police roadblock to detect license violations not a pretext to enforce immigration or drug laws even though Border Patrol officers were also present and police asked to search all vehicles referred to secondary checkpoint).

[28]   496 U.S. 128, 110 S.Ct. 2301 (1990).

or if petitioner had them in his possession and had responded to the warrant by producing them immediately—no search for weapons could have taken place."

Justice Brennan's dissent, joined by Justice Marshall, claimed that since the facts of *Horton* did not involve an obviously pretextual search its holding did not authorize such searches. However, in *Whren v. United States*,[29] the Court specifically held that pretextual stops and searches do not violate the Fourth Amendment, at least so long as the police have probable cause to believe a violation of *some* law has occurred. In *Whren*, plainclothes officers driving an unmarked car in a "high drug area" saw the driver of a truck look down into the lap of his passenger as they passed. The truck then remained stopped at an intersection for more than 20 seconds. When the officers made a U-turn to head back toward the truck, it suddenly turned right, without signalling, and sped off at an "unreasonable" speed. The officers stopped the car and subsequently observed drugs in Whren's hands. The defendants admitted that they had violated traffic laws, but claimed that the officers stopped them based on an inarticulable hunch that they possessed drugs and thus violated the Fourth Amendment.

In a unanimous opinion written by Justice Scalia, the Supreme Court rejected this argument. As it had intimated in several other cases,[30] including *Horton*, the Court concluded that the Fourth Amendment's emphasis on reasonableness means that "subjective intentions play no role in ordinary, probable cause Fourth Amendment analysis." The defendants had argued that, at the least, a determination should be made as to whether the police actions in the case deviated from normal police practices (here, for instance, D.C. police regulations permit plainclothes officers in unmarked vehicles to enforce traffic laws only in emergency situations). But the Court held that the objective approach means that even an inquiry into what a "reasonable police officer" would have done under the circumstances is not required, because ultimately this inquiry too is an attempt to ascertain the subjective motivations of the officer. Scalia also noted the difficulty a contrary result would create for the courts: either they would have to ascertain the subjective intentions of the officer or determine the reaction of a hypothetical officer which, in the absence of regulations, would often be pure speculation.

The Court expressed three exceptions to its ruling rejecting a pretext doctrine. First, proof that a search or seizure was the product of intentional racial discrimination might provide a basis for relief under the Fourteenth Amendment. Second, where the basis for the search or seizure is not probable cause, as for instance is the case with inventory searches and many types of regulatory inspections,[31] the Fourth Amendment might still prohibit pretextual actions. Third, there might be some situations where the search and seizure works such a significant harm on the individual that pretextual actions would be barred even when there is probable cause for the police action.[32] However, the Court concluded, such harm would never arise from a minor traffic violation.

---

[29] 517 U.S. 806, 116 S.Ct. 1769 (1996).

[30] See, e.g., *United States v. Villamonte-Marquez*, 462 U.S. 579, 103 S.Ct. 2573 (1983), discussed in § 13.06(d); *Scott v. United States*, 436 U.S. 128, 98 S.Ct. 1717 (1978), discussed in § 14.03(e)(2).

[31] See Chapter 13, in particular §§ 13.02 & 13.10. However, the Court has since intimated that any level of "individualized suspicion," even if short of probable cause, can provide an objective basis for ignoring pretext claims. See *Ashcroft v. al-Kidd*, 563 U.S. 731, 131 S.Ct. 2074 (2011), discussed in § 20.03(c)(5).

[32] The Court gave as examples the use of deadly force, see *Tennessee v. Garner*, discussed in § 3.05(b); unannounced entry into a home, *Wilson v. Arkansas*, discussed in § 5.05(c); entry in to a home without a warrant, see *Welsh v. Wisconsin*, discussed in § 3.04(d); and physical penetration of the body, see *Winston v. Lee*, discussed in § 5.06(c).

Relevant to this latter point, the defendants had argued that, given the wide discretion the ubiquity of traffic violations gives the police, the *collective* harm, in terms of confusion and alarm, that is produced by allowing plainclothes officers to stop cars for such violations outweighs the government interest in traffic safety. To this the Court responded:

> We are aware of no principle that would allow us to decide at what point a code of law becomes so expansive and so commonly violated that infraction itself can no longer be the ordinary measure of the lawfulness of enforcement. And even if we could identify such exorbitant codes, we do not know by what standard (or what right) we would decide, as petitioners would have us do, which particular provisions are sufficiently important to merit enforcement.

10.05   Conclusion

The principles relevant to plain view analysis can be summarized as follows:

(1)   A prior valid intrusion is required, based on a warrant, an exception to the warrant requirement, or some other circumstance (such as a lawful inspection).

(2)   Items not contemplated by the initial authorization may nonetheless be seized (or searched) without a warrant, so long as—by look, feel, smell or sound—they give police probable cause to believe they are evidence of criminal activity.

(3)   Proof that the justification given for the intrusion was pretextual does not establish a constitutional violation so long as the pretextual justification meets objective Fourth Amendment standards, unless the pretextual justification does not require individualized suspicion, involves significant harm to the individual, or is a cover for intentional racial bias.

BIBLIOGRAPHY

Burkoff, John M. Rejoinder: Truth, Justice, and the American Way—or Professor Haddad's "Hard Choices." 18 U.Mich.L.Ref. 695 (1985).

Butterfoss, Edwin. A Suspicionless Search and Seizure Quagmire: The Supreme Court Revives the Pretext Doctrine and Creates Another Fine Fourth Amendment Mess. 40 Creighton L. Rev. 419 (2007).

Cloutier, Denise Marie. *Arizona v. Hicks*: The Failure to Recognize Limited Inspections as Reasonable in Fourth Amendment Jurisprudence. 24 Colum. J.L. & Soc. Probls. 351 (1991).

Harris, David A. "Driving While Black" and All Other Traffic Offenses: The Supreme Court and Pretextual Traffic Stops. 87 J.Crim.L. & Criminol. 544 (1997).

Moylan, Charles E., Jr. Plain View Doctrine: Unexpected Child of the Great "Search Incident" Geography Battle. 26 Mercer L.Rev. 1047 (1975).

O'Neill, Timothy P. Beyond Privacy, Beyond Probable Cause, Beyond the Fourth Amendment: New Strategies for Fighting Pretext Arrests. 69 U.Colo. L.Rev. 693 (1998).

Poulin, Anne Bowen. The Plain Feel Doctrine and the Evolution of the Fourth Amendment. 42 Vill. L.Rev. 741 (1997).

Salken, Barbara. The General Warrant of the Twentieth Century? A Fourth Amendment Solution to Unchecked Discretion to Arrest for Traffic Offenses. 62 Temple L.Rev. 221 (1989).

Stinsman, James T. Computer Seizures and Searches: Rethinking the Applicability of the Plain View Doctrine. 83 Temple L. Rev. 1097 (2011).

Wallin, Howard. Plain View Revisited. 22 Pace L. Rev. 307 (2002).

Yankah, Ekow N. Pretext and Justification: Republicanism, Policing and Race. 40 Cardozo Law Review 1543 (2019).

Yeager, Daniel B. The Stubbornness of Pretexts. 40 San Diego L. Rev. 611 (2003).

Chapter 11

STOP AND FRISK

11.01   Introduction

In *Terry v. Ohio*,[1] the Supreme Court recognized for the first time that a search or seizure might be constitutional on less than probable cause. Specifically, *Terry* held that a frisk, or patdown of outer clothing, is authorized when the police have "reasonable suspicion," a lesser level of certainty than probable cause. It also strongly suggested that the predicate "stop," or temporary detention, is also permissible on reasonable suspicion. The "stop and frisk" doctrine thus announced represents an exception to both the warrant and probable cause requirements.

Long before *Terry*, legislatures had authorized stops and frisks on less than probable cause. For instance, as early as 1942, several states had adopted the Uniform Arrest Act,[2] which empowered an officer to stop a person in public based upon "reasonable ground to suspect" that the person "is committing, has committed, or is about to commit a crime," and then search him "for a dangerous weapon" if the officer has "reasonable ground to believe that he is in danger."[3] By 1967, the stop and frisk concept had been endorsed by both the American Law Institute,[4] the President's Commission on Law Enforcement and Administration of Justice,[5] and several lower courts.[6]

Thus, when the Supreme Court decided *Terry* in 1968, it was not working on a blank slate. In *Terry*, a detective of 30 years' experience noticed Terry and a companion hovering about a street corner for an extended length of time. He observed them pace alternately along an identical route, pause to stare in the same store window some 24 times and confer on the corner immediately thereafter. A third man appeared to join in one of these conferences, left swiftly, and was followed and rejoined a few minutes later by the other two. Suspecting that the men were contemplating a daylight robbery, the detective approached the men, identified himself as a policeman, and asked their names. When they mumbled a response, the officer, fearing they were armed, spun Terry around and patted down his outer clothing. He felt and subsequently removed a revolver from Terry's overcoat pocket, and charged him with carrying a concealed weapon.

In upholding this action, Chief Justice Warren, who wrote the opinion for the Court, stated:

> We merely hold that where a police officer observes unusual conduct which
> leads him reasonably to conclude in light of his experience that criminal

---

[1]   392 U.S. 1, 88 S.Ct. 1868 (1968).

[2]   Interstate Commission on Crime, The Handbook on Interstate Crime Control 86–89 (1942).

[3]   See, e.g., Del.Code tit. 11, §§ 1901–12 (1953); N.H.Rev.Stat.Ann. 594:1–25 (1955).

[4]   ALI, Model Code of Pre-Arraignment Procedure § 2.02 (Tent.Draft No. 1, 1966). The ALI eventually adopted a modified version of this draft, reprinted in § 11.07.

[5]   President's Commission on Law Enforcement and Administration of Justice, The Challenge of Crime in a Free Society 95 (1967).

[6]   *State v. Williams*, 97 N.J.Super. 573, 235 A.2d 684 (1967), cert. denied 397 U.S. 1069, 90 S.Ct. 1510 (1970); *People v. Rivera*, 14 N.Y.2d 441, 252 N.Y.S.2d 458, 201 N.E.2d 32 (1964), cert. denied 379 U.S. 978, 85 S.Ct. 679 (1965).

activity may be afoot and that the persons with whom he is dealing may be armed and presently dangerous, where in the course of investigating this behavior he identifies himself as a policeman and makes reasonable inquiries, and where nothing in the initial stages of the encounter serves to dispel his reasonable fear for his own or others' safety, he is entitled for the protection of himself and others in the area to conduct a carefully limited search of the outer clothing of such persons in an attempt to discover weapons which might be used to assault him. Such a search is a reasonable search under the Fourth Amendment, and any weapons seized may properly be introduced in evidence against the person from whom they were taken.

While the Court explicitly purported to "decide nothing today concerning the constitutional propriety of an investigative 'seizure' upon less than probable cause for purposes of 'detention' and/or interrogation," it shortly followed this disavowal with the declaration that "a police officer may in appropriate circumstances and in an appropriate manner approach a person for purposes of investigating possibly criminal behavior even though there is no probable cause to make an arrest."

The Court's rationale for approving stops and frisks on reasonable suspicion rather than probable cause came from the Reasonableness Clause of the Fourth Amendment. According to the *Terry* Court, this clause requires an analysis of whether a given police action "was justified at its inception" and "was reasonably related in scope to the circumstances which justified the interference in the first place." The Court felt that the strong state interest in preventing criminal activity, combined with the relatively minor intrusion associated with a stop (as opposed to an arrest) and a frisk (as opposed to a full search), justified such actions on a lesser showing of suspicion than probable cause.

The *Terry* Court could have analyzed the constitutionality of stops and frisks in at least two other ways. It could have ruled that an investigative stop is not a "seizure" and that a frisk is not a "search," thus eliminating any Fourth Amendment regulation of these actions. But this approach would have immunized a vast segment of police conduct from constitutional challenge. Alternatively, after holding, as it did, that a seizure and search were involved, it could have adhered to the traditional "probable cause" language, but held that this standard varies depending upon the circumstances. This was the approach the Court adopted for administrative searches in *Camara v. Municipal Court*,[7] decided a year earlier. There, the Court held that residential health and safety inspections require "probable cause", but also made clear that, given the "valid public interest" and "limited invasion" involved, the term in this context did not require *any* level of suspicion with respect to a particular house, but only a showing that the area as a whole required inspection. This "sliding scale" definition of probable cause has been criticized as well, as likely to convert the Fourth Amendment "into one immense Rorschach blot."[8] As subsequent discussion will show, however, *Terry's* holding is very similar to this approach.[9] Indeed, the Court's application of *Terry* in later cases suggests that, without admitting to doing so, the Court has endorsed a sliding scale perspective on the Fourth Amendment when less intrusive seizures and searches are involved.

---

[7]   387 U.S. 523, 87 S.Ct. 1727 (1967), discussed in § 13.02(a).

[8]   Anthony Amsterdam, *Perspectives on the Fourth Amendment*, 58 Minn.L.Rev. 349 (1974).

[9]   See also Christopher Slobogin, *Let's Not Bury* Terry: *A Call for Rejuvenation of the Proportionality Principle*, 72 St. John's L.Rev. 1053, 1071–77 (1998).

Terry raises four distinct issues: (1) the definition of "stop," which also requires defining the word "seizure" for Fourth Amendment purposes; (2) the justification for a stop and lesser seizures; (3) the justification for a frisk; and (4) the scope of the frisk. This chapter examines how the Supreme Court has addressed these issues and then provides a sampling of how the lower courts have handled them.

11.02　The Definition of "Seizure"

(a)　Of the Person

Until *Terry*, the Supreme Court's cases suggested that the only seizure of the person governed by the Fourth Amendment was an arrest. *Terry's* recognition that seizures short of an arrest are permissible under the Reasonableness Clause raises two issues concerning the nature of police-citizen confrontations. First, because arrests must be based on probable cause, while stops and other seizures may be based on a lower level of certainty, it is important to determine the dividing line between arrests and other seizures. Second, it is important to determine whether some police-citizen confrontations are not seizures at all and, if so, when.

As discussed in detail in this book's treatment of arrests,[10] distinguishing between an arrest and an investigative stop depends upon a number of factors, including the purpose of the detention (e.g., fingerprinting versus interrogation), its location (e.g., the field versus the stationhouse), and, probably most importantly, its duration (e.g., a temporary confrontation versus a custodial detention). The Supreme Court has been unwilling to set a precise time limit on stops, but has indicated that a twenty-minute detention is a *Terry* stop, not an arrest, so long as the police exercise "diligence" in expediting the detention, and are not unreasonable in failing to recognize or to pursue less intrusive alternatives.[11]

The focus here will be on the other end of the spectrum: when has a "seizure" of the person occurred so as to implicate the Fourth Amendment and the *Terry* balancing analysis? In *Terry*, the Court stated that "whenever a police officer accosts an individual and restrains his freedom to walk away, he has 'seized' that person." It also stated, however, that "not all personal intercourse between policemen and citizens involves 'seizures' of persons. Only when the officer, by means of force or show of authority, has in some way restrained the liberty of a citizen may we conclude that a seizure has occurred." The Supreme Court has since narrowed the definition of "seizure" even further, holding, in *California v. Hodari D.*,[12] that while restraint is a necessary condition for a seizure, it is not necessarily sufficient. Rather the question is a more complex one that is very fact specific. Thus, a close look at the cases is necessary.

In *United States v. Mendenhall*,[13] a twenty-two-year-old black woman was confronted in the Detroit airport by two plain-clothes DEA officials who identified themselves and asked her for her ticket and identification. After returning her ticket and license, the agents asked her why her ticket was not in her name and, when she became incoherent, asked her to accompany them to a private room in the airport. Two members of the Court, Justices Stewart and Rehnquist, felt that this confrontation was

---

[10]　See § 3.02.

[11]　*United States v. Sharpe*, 470 U.S. 675, 105 S.Ct. 1568 (1985), discussed in § 3.02(b).

[12]　499 U.S. 621, 111 S.Ct. 1547 (1991).

[13]　446 U.S. 544, 100 S.Ct. 1870 (1980).

not a seizure and that therefore the agents did not need to meet the reasonable suspicion standard set forth in *Terry*. They stated that the test for determining when someone was "seized" under the Fourth Amendment should be when "a reasonable person would have believed that he was not free to leave," and suggested several factors that might be considered in determining whether this test was met: "[T]he threatening presence of several officers, the display of a weapon by an officer, some physical touching of the person of the citizen, or the use of language or tone of voice indicating that compliance with the officers' request might be compelled." None of the other members of the Court directly addressed the seizure issue, however, in large part because it was not addressed by the lower courts. Thus, *Mendenhall* did not provide a clear message as to what constitutes a seizure.

In *Florida v. Royer*,[14] the Court was more explicit on the issue. *Royer* involved facts virtually identical to *Mendenhall* with one exception: the officers did not return Royer's ticket or driver's license. The Court held, 5–4, that under these circumstances, and when the officers did not indicate in any way that Royer was "free to depart," a Fourth Amendment seizure had taken place. Similarly, in *Brendlin v. California*[15] the Court unanimously rejected the claim that a passenger in a car is not seized during a car stop. Even when the car stop is clearly for a driving violation attributable only to the driver, "any reasonable passenger would [understand] the police officers to be exercising control to the point that no one in the car was free to depart without police permission." Thus, in *Brendlin*, where the police concededly lacked reasonable suspicion when they stopped the car in which Brendlin was a passenger, Brendlin's subsequent arrest for a parole violation was deemed fruit of an illegal stop.

The Court has indicated that no seizure takes place, however, when police merely question an individual for a few moments, at least if the questioning occurs at his place of work. In *Immigration & Naturalization Service v. Delgado*,[16] the INS obtained two warrants authorizing a "survey" of the work force at a factory in southern California to determine whether any illegal aliens were present. The warrants were based on a probable cause showing that numerous illegal aliens were employed at the factory, but did not name any specific individuals. In executing the survey, several agents positioned themselves near the buildings' exits, while other agents dispersed throughout the factory questioning most, but not all, of the employees at their work stations. The agents displayed badges, carried walkie-talkies, and were armed, although no weapons were drawn. Employees were asked from one to three questions relating to their citizenship; if they gave credible answers, the questioning ended. Respondent Delgado and the three other respondents were all questioned in this manner and, after answering apparently satisfactorily, were left alone.

Justice Rehnquist, writing for a six-member majority, noted that in *Royer* the Court had implicitly permitted both questioning relating to one's identity and a request for identification; neither, by itself, constituted a Fourth Amendment seizure. Rehnquist also rejected the respondents' argument that the stationing of agents at the doors of the factory constituted a seizure. He pointed out that the employees' freedom was already somewhat restricted by the demands of their workplace and that the surveys did not prevent the employees from pursuing their ordinary business. He went on to conclude

---

[14]   460 U.S. 491, 103 S.Ct. 1319 (1983).

[15]   551 U.S. 249, 127 S.Ct. 2400 (2007).

[16]   466 U.S. 210, 104 S.Ct. 1758 (1984).

that had the questioning taken place at the exits, it would have been no more a seizure than what occurred inside the factory. "[T]he mere possibility that [the employees] would be questioned if they sought to leave the buildings should not have resulted in any reasonable apprehension by any of them that they would be seized or detained in any meaningful way."

The Court reaffirmed *Delgado* and favorably cited Stewart's opinion in *Mendenhall* in another airport stop case, *Florida v. Rodriguez*.[17] There the Court held that a seizure did not occur when a plain-clothes officer approached the defendant in a public airport, showed his badge, obtained agreement from the defendant to talk, and requested him to move approximately 15 feet to where his companions were standing with another police officer. The Court termed these events "clearly the sort of consensual encounter that implicates no Fourth Amendment interest."

A unanimous Court also found no seizure in *Michigan v. Chesternut*,[18] where the defendant started running upon spying a police patrol car and the officers in the car accelerated to catch up with him "to see where he was going." The Court noted that the police did not activate a siren or flashers, command the defendant to halt, display any weapons, or operate the car so as to block the defendant's course. While admitting that operating a police car parallel to a running pedestrian could be "somewhat intimidating" it found that this action was not so intimidating that, under *Mendenhall's* test, the defendant could reasonably have believed that he was not free to disregard the police presence. The Court noted that a different situation might be presented if the officers had been on foot and visibly chased the defendant.

Yet, three terms later, the Court decided that even this latter situation does not result in a seizure for purposes of the Fourth Amendment. In *California v. Hodari D.*,[19] police in an unmarked vehicle came upon four or five youths huddled around a red car. When the youths saw the officers' vehicle they took flight, and the red car left at high speed. An officer gave chase to one of the youths, who tossed away crack cocaine just before being tackled. The defendant argued that at the time of the chase he had been "seized," and that the cocaine was inadmissible because the officers lacked reasonable suspicion at that point. In a 7–2 decision authored by Justice Scalia, the Court held that a mere show of authority, absent physical contact or submission to that authority, is not a seizure as that word is commonly understood, and is therefore not a seizure under the Fourth Amendment. Scalia also contended that this ruling would not encourage improper police behavior, "[s]ince policemen do not command 'Stop!' expecting to be ignored, or give chase hoping to be outrun . . . ." The dissent, by Justice Stevens, argued that the attempted detention in this case presented a situation in which "a reasonable person would not feel free to leave." But the majority, as noted earlier, countered that this language, from *Mendenhall*, merely stated a necessary, rather than a sufficient, condition for a seizure.

The Court continued its movement away from *Mendenhall's* definition of seizure in a pair of cases involving police boarding of busses, *Florida v. Bostick*[20] and *United States v. Drayton*.[21] In *Bostick*, two police officers, one of them armed, boarded a bus as part of

---

17 469 U.S. 1, 105 S.Ct. 308 (1984).
18 486 U.S. 567, 108 S.Ct. 1975 (1988).
19 499 U.S. 621, 111 S.Ct. 1547 (1991).
20 501 U.S. 429, 111 S.Ct. 2382 (1991).
21 536 U.S. 194, 122 S.Ct. 2105 (2002).

a routine drug interdiction effort. They asked selected passengers for their ticket and identification, checked those items and handed them back, and then asked if they could search the passengers' luggage. The Court rejected the Florida Supreme Court's holding that the passengers were seized at the point of the request to search, reasoning, *inter alia*, that even had the police not been there the passengers would have wanted to stay on the bus, given the imminence of its departure. Justice O'Connor stated for the Court that the proper test for determining whether a seizure takes place is whether "a reasonable person . . . was not at liberty to ignore the police presence and go about his business." It remanded the case for a redetermination under that test,[22] and without resolving whether police must tell individuals confronted in such a manner that they are free to not cooperate.

In *Drayton*, the Court made clear that no such "warning" need be given. There, two plainclothes police positioned themselves at the front and back of the bus, with a third moving from passenger to passenger. None of the officers were visibly armed, and the officer conducting the questioning stood to the side of each passenger while he stated that the officers were conducting a "drug and weapons interdiction." He then said "we would like for your cooperation" and asked to search the passenger's bags. At the suppression hearing, this officer testified that he sometimes told people they did not have to cooperate, but that he did not do so on this occasion. He also admitted that everyone on this bus "cooperated," and that in his experience with bus interdiction efforts only a few people had refused to cooperate. The Court held, in a 6–3 opinion, that no seizure occurred. Justice Kennedy pointed out that bus passengers often left the bus for snacks or cigarettes during the interdiction process. "And of more importance," he stated, "bus passengers answer officers' questions and otherwise cooperate not because of coercion but because the passengers know that their participation enhances their own safety and the safety of those around them."

The dissent, authored by Justice Souter, argued that, on these facts, "[t]he reasonable inference was that the 'interdiction' is not a consensual exercise, but one the police would carry out whatever the circumstances; that they would prefer 'cooperation' but would not let the lack of it stand in their way." Referring to *Bostick's* definition of seizure, he also noted "[t]he bus was going nowhere, and with one officer in the driver's seat, it was reasonable to suppose no passenger would tend to his own business until the officers were ready to let him." Although the Court has held that police need not inform people of their right to refuse consent a request to *search*,[23] at least in that context they must ask to carry out their action, which suggests the absence of an entitlement on the part of the police. The statement made in *Drayton* ("we would like for your cooperation") suggests a different balance of power.

While the Court's definition of seizure is acceptable, its application of that definition tortures the spirit of the Fourth Amendment, which is designed to regulate coercive government intrusions into privacy and autonomy. People who are questioned by armed police at their place of work (as in *Delgado*), asked to accompany a police officer elsewhere (as in *Mendenhall* and *Rodriguez*), chased by the police (as in *Chesternut* and *Hodari*), or confronted by armed officers in the cramped confines of a bus (as in *Bostick* and *Drayton*) are unlikely to feel they are free to go about their business, especially if they are not told they may do so. At the same time, assuming that all of these cases

---

[22]   On remand the Florida Supreme Court found that no seizure had occurred. 593 So.2d 494 (Fla. 1992).

[23]   See § 12.02(a).

involved seizures, applying *Terry's* balancing approach might produce the same result in at least some of them. For instance, in *Delgado*, the "warrant" obtained by the police was based on probable cause to believe there was a significant percentage of illegal aliens employed in the surveyed factory.[24] In *Rodriguez*, the seizure did not occur until after the defendant and his two companions acted furtively upon sighting plain-clothes officers, one told the other to "Get out of here," and the defendant made a half-hearted running effort. And in *Hodari*, the flight from the police, although something an innocent person might do in neighborhoods where police harassment is routine, nonetheless gave police ample reason to believe some sort of investigation was called for.[25] In contrast, the complete lack of suspicion in *Bostick*[26] should prevent any intrusion that would be unwanted by a reasonable person.

(b) Of Effects

While *Terry* and its progeny have focused on seizures of the person, a few cases have also addressed the validity of seizures of effects on less than probable cause. As with seizures of the person, both ends of the spectrum must be examined. On the one hand, probable cause is required for any seizure of personal property which, because of its owner's proximity to it or desire to retain it, amounts to an arrest of the owner. Thus, in *United States v. Place*,[27] a 90-minute detention of the defendant's luggage at the airport to arrange for a dog sniff was held unconstitutional because of its duration, and "the failure of the agents to accurately inform respondent of the place to which they were transporting his luggage, of the length of time he might be dispossessed, and of what arrangements would be made for return of the luggage if the investigation dispelled the suspicion." This language suggests, conversely, that if luggage can be detained without interrupting a person's travel plans or other liberty interests, a seizure of luggage on less than probable cause would be permissible. Indeed, *Place* also stated that, under the *Terry* balancing test, "some brief detentions of personal effects may be so minimally intrusive of Fourth Amendment interests that strong countervailing governmental interests will justify a seizure based only on specific articulable facts that the property contains contraband or evidence of a crime."

Furthermore, consistent with the Court's cases concerning detentions of persons, at the far end of the spectrum there are some situations in which restraints on effects do not even amount to a seizure. For instance, in *United States v. Van Leeuwen*,[28] the police, contacted by a suspicious postal clerk, asked postal officials to hold two packages of coins for 29 hours while they investigated the situation and obtained a search warrant. Although a unanimous Court noted that the suspicious circumstances "certainly justified detention, without a warrant, while an investigation was made," it went on to hold that no suspicion was even necessary, since "[n]o interest protected by the Fourth Amendment was invaded by forwarding the packages the following day rather than the day when they were deposited." The warrantless police action did not invade either the defendant's privacy interest in the content of the packages or any possessory interest.

---

[24] For additional discussion of this "generalized" type of suspicion, see § 11.03(c)(3).

[25] See discussion of *Illinois v. Wardlow*, 528 U.S. 119, 120 S.Ct. 673 (2000), in § 11.03(a).

[26] One court noted that in a sweep of 100 buses (potentially involving four to five thousand people), only seven arrests resulted. *United States v. Flowers*, 912 F.2d 707 (4th Cir. 1990), cert. denied 501 U.S. 1253, 111 S.Ct. 2895 (1991).

[27] 462 U.S. 696, 103 S.Ct. 2637 (1983).

[28] 397 U.S. 249, 90 S.Ct. 1029 (1970).

11.03 Permissible Grounds for Stops and Other Seizures

Generally, as *Terry* provided, a seizure is not permitted unless police possess at least a reasonable suspicion that criminal activity is afoot. But since *Terry*, the Court has sanctioned some types of seizures on less than reasonable suspicion, and has made it clear that *Terry's* standard is not to be rigidly applied.[29] In the discussion that follows, the Court's decisions applying the reasonable suspicion standard will be treated chronologically, in order to gain an historical perspective on the Court's evolving (and occasionally vacillating) approach. A separate discussion will focus on the sources of information upon which police may rely in deciding whether reasonable suspicion exists and the types of crimes which justify a stop.

(a) *Terry* Stops and the Reasonable Suspicion Standard

In *Terry*, the Court defined reasonable suspicion as "specific and articulable facts" that lead the officer to believe "criminal activity is afoot." Such suspicion may not be based upon an "inchoate or unparticularized suspicion or 'hunch,' " but must be grounded on facts which, in light of the officer's experience, support "specific reasonable inferences" that justify the intrusion. The level of suspicion contemplated by this language is clearly something less than probable cause, although how much less has not been spelled out by the Court.[30] The Court's cases suggest that the level will vary, depending upon the level of intrusion on the one hand and the importance of the state's interest on the other.

Thus, in *Sibron v. New York*,[31] a companion case to *Terry*, the Court held that the "mere act of talking to a number of known addicts" and reaching into a pocket does not produce a reasonable inference that criminal activity is afoot sufficient to justify an officer's search of the pocket. In contrast, in *Peters v. New York*,[32] another companion case to *Terry*, the Court found that an off-duty officer had sufficient grounds for a stop and a patdown of two individuals when he saw them tiptoe down a hallway and run when they saw him. According to the Court, "deliberate furtive actions and flight at the approach of strangers or law officers are strong indicia of *mens rea*."

The first major post-*Terry* decision to deal comprehensively with the reasonable suspicion standard was *United States v. Brignoni-Ponce*.[33] Like many other cases concerning the definition of reasonable suspicion, *Brignoni-Ponce* involved enforcement of the immigration laws, in this case by roving car patrols operating on roads near the border. Although the federal statute was unclear on their authority, in practice these patrols made random stops of cars in an effort to detect the entry of illegal aliens. One of these patrols stopped Brignoni-Ponce's car; after questioning revealed that his two passengers had entered the country illegally, he was arrested and later convicted for transporting illegal aliens.

---

[29] The Court has also held that reasonable mistakes of fact and law about whether there is reasonable suspicion that criminal activity is afoot are not violations of the Fourth Amendment. *Heien v. North Carolina*, 574 U.S. 54, 135 S.Ct. 530 (2015), discussed in § 4.03(f)(1).

[30] A survey of federal judges indicated that, on average, they would attribute a 31% level of certainty to a finding of reasonable suspicion (compared to 46% for probable cause). C.M.A. McCauliff, *Burdens of Proof: Degrees of Belief, Quanta of Evidence, or Constitutional Guarantee?* 35 Vand.L.Rev. 1293, 1325 (1982).

[31] 392 U.S. 40, 88 S.Ct. 1912 (1968).

[32] 392 U.S. 40, 88 S.Ct. 1889 (1968).

[33] 422 U.S. 873, 95 S.Ct. 2574 (1975).

The government contended that, given the proportions of the immigration problem, it should be able to stop any persons near the border for "limited" questioning about their immigration status. The Supreme Court disagreed in a unanimous opinion, holding that, except at the border or its functional equivalents,[34] border patrol officers are prohibited from stopping vehicles unless they know of specific articulable facts, together with rational inferences from those facts, that a particular vehicle contains illegal aliens. Noting that the sole justification border patrol officers gave for the stop of Brignoni-Ponce was that he and his companions had appeared to be of Mexican ancestry, the Court reversed his conviction. The Court listed a number of factors the patrol could consider in deciding whether reasonable suspicion existed: the characteristics of the area where the vehicle is found and its proximity to the border, information about recent illegal border crossings in the area, the driver's behavior, aspects of the vehicle itself, *and* the appearance of the automobile's occupants. But it emphasized that the latter factor by itself could not justify a stop: "[t]he likelihood that any given person of Mexican ancestry is an alien is high enough to make Mexican appearance a relevant factor, but standing alone it does not justify stopping all Mexican-Americans to ask if they are aliens."

In *Delaware v. Prouse*,[35] the Court held inadmissible marijuana found by a police officer on the floor of a car he had stopped for the purpose of checking the driver's license and car registration. The stop was not prompted by either the officer's observance of a traffic or equipment violation or by any suspicious behavior by any of the car's occupants. In finding this seizure violative of the Fourth Amendment, the Court stated that such "discretionary spot checks" were no less offensive than the roving border patrol stops it had earlier found impermissible in *Brignoni-Ponce*. Thus, other than at a designated checkpoint,[36] an officer may stop an automobile to undertake a license check only when he holds an "articulable and reasonable suspicion that a motorist is unlicensed or that an automobile is not registered, or that either the vehicle or an occupant is otherwise subject to seizure for violation of law."

The same term it decided *Prouse*, the Court invalidated the seizure in *Brown v. Texas*.[37] In *Brown*, two police officers were cruising in a patrol car when they observed Brown and another man walking away from one another in an alley. Officer Venegas later testified that both officers had believed their arrival either broke up or prevented a meeting between the two. Venegas got out of the patrol car and asked Brown to identify himself and explain his presence there; the other individual was not detained. Brown refused to identify himself and asserted that the officers had no right to stop him. Venegas replied that Brown was in a "high drug problem area;" the other officer then frisked Brown, but found nothing. Brown was arrested and later convicted under a Texas statute that makes it a criminal act for a person to refuse to give his name and address to an officer "who has lawfully stopped him and requested the information."

The Supreme Court concluded that reasonable suspicion did not exist on these facts. The sole justification the officers gave for the stop was that the situation "looked suspicious and we had never seen that subject in that area before." Although the area in which Brown was stopped did have a high incidence of drug traffic, the officers did not

---

[34] At these locations, the Court has held a citizen has no reasonable expectation of privacy and is not entitled to the usual Fourth Amendment protection. See § 13.05(a).

[35] 440 U.S. 648, 99 S.Ct. 1391 (1979).

[36] See § 13.06(c).

[37] 443 U.S. 47, 99 S.Ct. 2637 (1979).

claim any specific misconduct on the part of Brown, nor did they believe he was armed. Reminiscent of its holding in *Sibron*, the Court stated:

> There is no indication in the record that it was unusual for people to be in the alley. The fact that the appellant was in a neighborhood frequented by drug users, standing alone, is not a basis for concluding that the appellant himself was engaged in criminal conduct. In short, the appellant's activity was no different from the activity of other pedestrians in that neighborhood.

Although the Court did not invalidate the statute under which Brown was arrested and convicted, it did hold that stops pursuant to it must be based on reasonable suspicion that the person stopped "was engaged or had engaged in criminal conduct."[38]

But the Court seemed to retreat from this strong statement in *United States v. Mendenhall*.[39] In that case, it will be remembered, narcotics agents stopped the defendant as she got off an airplane in Detroit. The officers decided to stop the defendant because she fit a "drug courier profile," an informal compilation of characteristics considered typical of individuals carrying illicit drugs.[40] Specifically, the agents relied upon the facts that the defendant arrived from Los Angeles (regarded as frequent source of drugs), that she was the last person to leave the plane, that she appeared to be very nervous, that she "scanned" the area as she left the plane, that she did not claim any luggage, and that she went to the desk of another airline than the one on which she arrived, apparently for the purpose of leaving Detroit. At least three members of the Court[41] felt the stop was reasonable, emphasizing that the difficulty in detecting the transportation of drugs had prompted the training of special drug enforcement agents who are "able to perceive and articulate meaning in given conduct which would be wholly innocent to the untrained observer." The four dissenters, on the other hand, felt that none of the defendant's actions noticed by the police were unusual, but were "rather the kind of behavior that could reasonably be expected of anyone changing planes in an airport terminal." They labeled the officers' suspicion a "hunch" rather than one based on "specific reasonable inferences."

In sharp contrast to *Mendenhall* is *Reid v. Georgia*,[42] another airport stop case decided the same term. In *Reid*, the entire Court indicated that reasonable suspicion of criminal activity does *not* exist when a person (1) gets off a plane from Ft. Lauderdale (a supposed drug source) at a time in the morning when law enforcement activity is minimal; (2) has no luggage other than a shoulder bag; (3) apparently makes efforts to conceal he is travelling with someone else; and (4) occasionally looks back at that person. The per curiam opinion stated that with the exception of the last factor, these "circumstances describe a very large category of presumably innocent travellers, who would be subject to virtually random seizures were the Court to conclude that as little foundation as there was in this case could justify a seizure."

---

[38] If, on the other hand, the police *do* have reasonable suspicion, they may arrest for failure to identify, at least as long as the request for identity is warranted by the facts, rather than a pretext to secure an arrest, and a reasonable person would not believe the identity is incriminating. See *Hiibel v. Nevada*, 542 U.S. 177, 124 S.Ct. 2451 (2004), discussed in § 3.03(b)(1).

[39] 446 U.S. 544, 100 S.Ct. 1870 (1980).

[40] See §§ 3.03(b)(3) & 11.03(c)(3) for a discussion of investigative profiles.

[41] As noted in § 11.02(a), two members of the Court concluded that no seizure occurred, and thus did not reach the reasonable suspicion issue.

[42] 448 U.S. 438, 100 S.Ct. 2752 (1980).

Certainly, much, if not all, of Mendenhall's behavior was "innocent" as well; at least some members of the Court seemed to be sending mixed signals. A third airport stop case, *Florida v. Royer*,[43] did not provide much further clarification. The principal focus of the decision was on other issues, including, as previously described, when a Fourth Amendment seizure occurs. Moreover, there were four separate opinions in *Royer*. But it appears that eight members of the *Royer* Court sanctioned the initial encounter in that case between the defendant and two drug enforcement agents, based on the following factors: (1) the defendant's American Tourister luggage, which appeared to be heavy; (2) his youth and casual dress; (3) his pale and nervous appearance; (4) his use of cash to pay for his ticket; (5) his failure to give full identifying information on his luggage tags, and (6) his arrival from a known drug import center (Miami) and expected departure from a known distribution center (New York). Justice Brennan was the only member who explicitly dissented on this point, stating that the agents' observations, "considered individually or collectively, . . . are perfectly consistent with innocent behavior and cannot possibly give rise to any inference supporting a reasonable suspicion of activity." Perhaps somewhat less "innocent" were the factors used to justify the stop in *United States v. Sokolow*,[44] where the Court found reasonable suspicion exists when a person buys two roundtrip tickets from Honolulu to Miami, with a return time 48 hours after arrival in Miami, pays for the tickets with $2,100 in cash from a roll of what appeared to be $4,000, and gives the ticket agent a false phone number.

The Court has also held that unprovoked flight after noticing the presence of the police may give rise to reasonable suspicion. In *Illinois v. Wardlow*,[45] eight officers in a four car caravan were converging on an area known for heavy drug trafficking when the defendant, who was standing on a corner, looked in their direction and began running away from them. Five members of the Court, in an opinion by Chief Justice Rehnquist, concluded that these facts provided reasonable suspicion. Although an individual's presence in a high crime area "standing alone" is insufficient to meet this standard, "officers are not required to ignore the relevant characteristics of a location." And although flight from officers "is not necessarily indicative of wrongdoing, . . . it is certainly suggestive of such." Together, these facts provided enough to justify a stop. The Court distinguished this situation from cases holding that citizens may refuse to cooperate with the police with impunity,[46] on the ground that flight is an act of evasion, not merely a failure to cooperate. The four dissenters, while agreeing that flight from the police in a high crime area could furnish reasonable suspicion, pointed to ambiguity in the record as to whether the police cars were marked as such and whether the defendant was in the drug trafficking area to which the police were going. They also emphasized that people might flee from the police for any number of innocent reasons, including unwillingness to be a witness, fear of criminal activity, and fear of the police themselves.

The majority stance toward *Terry* analysis appears to be premised on a healthy respect for the deductive processes of trained officers, once they have diligently accumulated as much information about the suspect's behavior as they can. The language of Chief Justice Burger in *United States v. Cortez*,[47] handed down a year after

---

[43]   460 U.S. 491, 103 S.Ct. 1319 (1983).

[44]   490 U.S. 1, 109 S.Ct. 1581 (1989).

[45]   528 U.S. 119, 120 S.Ct. 673 (2000).

[46]   See, e.g., *Brown v. Texas*, 443 U.S. 47, 99 S.Ct. 2637 (1979); *Florida v. Royer*, 460 U.S. 491, 103 S.Ct. 1319 (1983); *Florida v. Bostick*, 501 U.S. 429, 111 S.Ct. 2382 (1991), all discussed in § 11.02(a).

[47]   449 U.S. 411, 101 S.Ct. 690 (1981).

Mendenhall and *Reid*, captures the approach. The assessment of a police action under *Terry*, stated Burger, should be based on "the whole picture." It should take into account "all of the circumstances," including observations, information from police reports, and "consideration of the modes or patterns of operation of certain kinds of lawbreakers." And, most importantly, this information should be viewed from the perspective "of those versed in the field of law enforcement," not "in terms of library analysis by scholars." Finally, as have several Court opinions, *Cortez* reminds courts that the trained officer may often be able to deduce more from given facts than the untrained layperson.

Indeed, in *United States v. Arvizu*,[48] a *unanimous* Court upheld a vehicle stop based on seemingly innocuous factors, emphasizing both the need to defer to officer expertise and the appropriateness of totality of the circumstances analysis. In this case, a border patrol officer, carrying out a routine patrol in a remote part of Arizona, grew suspicious when the defendant slowed at the sight of the agent but failed to acknowledge him, and the children in the back seat of defendant's car waved oddly at the officer and had their knees in a raised position as if resting on something. Although the Court conceded that, in an urban area, this behavior might be considered normal, in this region of Arizona a different conclusion could have been warranted, and the officer "was entitled to make an assessment of the situation in light of his specialized training and familiarity with the customs of the area's inhabitants." Additionally, the defendant was driving on a dirt road often traveled by smugglers, in a minivan (a type of vehicle said to be often used by smugglers) that was registered to a residence in an area "notorious for alien and narcotics smuggling," at a time proximate to the border patrols' shift change (when fewer patrols would be watching for illegal activity), along a route that made little sense for normal traffic. Although "each of these factors alone is susceptible to innocent explanation . . . [t]aken together . . . they sufficed to form a particularized and objective basis" for the stop, the Court stated.

(b) Other Types of Seizures

The prototypical seizure short of arrest is the *Terry* stop. But the Court has confronted a number of other situations that involve a seizure not amounting to an arrest. As described in detail in Chapter 13, which deals with regulatory and programmatic searches and seizures, the Court has approved "dragnet" seizures at various types of checkpoints and in connection with drug testing programs, despite the absence of *any* individualized suspicion, reasonable or otherwise. Two other situations, involving seizures that are more closely analogous to one-on-one *Terry* stops aimed at investigating crime, are discussed here: seizures of car occupants and seizures pursuant to loitering statutes.

(1) Seizures of Car Occupants

In *Pennsylvania v. Mimms*,[49] two officers stopped a car for driving with expired license plates. One of the officers asked the driver to step out of the car. The Pennsylvania Supreme Court held that this act was a "seizure" and that it was unlawful because the officer could not point to objective facts supporting a suspicion of criminal activity or danger. The Supreme Court agreed that a seizure occurred and that no suspicion existed, but found the seizure reasonable, in a per curiam opinion.

---

[48]   534 U.S. 266, 122 S.Ct. 744 (2002).

[49]   434 U.S. 106, 98 S.Ct. 330 (1977).

The Court pointed out that, once a car has been stopped, the added intrusion associated with requesting the driver to alight is *de minimis*. The driver "is being asked to expose very little more of his person than is already exposed," and the restriction of the driver's liberty will occur whether he stays inside or comes outside the car. At the same time, according to the Court, a police officer takes an "inordinate risk" when he approaches a person seated in an automobile, even when the only offense suspected is a traffic violation and the driver has done nothing to make the officer feel uneasy.[50] Thus, such seizures are legitimate, provided they occur after a lawful stop for some violation of the law.

Maryland v. Wilson[51] extended *Mimms* by holding that the police can order passengers out of the car as well. The seven-member majority, in an opinion by Chief Justice Rehnquist, conceded that in the typical traffic case there is no basis for stopping or detaining passengers, as opposed to the driver. But since the passengers are already detained because of the stop of the car, the order to exit the car merely changes their location. Balanced against this "minimal" intrusion is the possibility that passengers inside the car have greater access to weapons. In separate dissents, both Justice Stevens and Justice Kennedy decried the majority's willingness to permit police to force innocent passengers to stand in full view of the public and in the elements for long periods of time merely because their driver has committed a minor traffic violation.[52]

The Court has also held that the detention associated with a traffic stop may continue even once the warning or citation has been issued and the defendant's license returned, at least long enough to ask questions designed to obtain a consent to search. In *Ohio v. Robinette*,[53] after the defendant was stopped for speeding, given a verbal warning and handed back his license, the officer stated: "One question before you get gone: are you carrying any illegal contraband in your car? Any weapons of any kind, drugs, anything like that?" The defendant responded, "No," at which point the officer asked if he could search the car and the defendant consented. The defendant subsequently argued that the consent was invalid because, once the traffic stop was complete, the officer had no grounds for detaining him (other than an unsupportable hunch he was carrying drugs), and yet did so with his questions. The Supreme Court assumed, with the defendant, that a "continued detention" had occurred, and focused solely on whether the pretextual nature of the continued detention invalidated the consent. On that issue, following its precedent,[54] the majority stated that so long as there is probable cause authorizing a citation (here for speeding) the officer's subjective reasons for detaining an individual are irrelevant. This disposition of the case suggests that a traffic violation authorizes some seizure beyond that necessary to deal with the violation.

In *Arizona v. Johnson*,[55] the Court appeared to affirm that car passengers as well as drivers may be held beyond the duration of the initial stop, so long as the additional

---

[50]   To this claim, the three dissenters responded that the available data, as well as some police manuals, suggest that harm is more likely when a car occupant gets out of the car than when he stays inside.

[51]   519 U.S. 408, 117 S.Ct. 882 (1997).

[52]   Recall, however, that the Court has also held that passengers *are* seized in this situation, see *Brendlin v. California*, discussed in § 11.02(a), and thus could conceivably sue or exclude evidence if the stop of the car is illegitimate because not based on reasonable suspicion.

[53]   519 U.S. 33, 117 S.Ct. 417 (1996).

[54]   *Whren v. United States*, 517 U.S. 806, 116 S.Ct. 1769 (1996), discussed in § 10.04.

[55]   555 U.S. 323, 129 S.Ct. 781 (2009).

seizure is minimal. Johnson was a passenger in the back seat of a car pulled over by three officers in Arizona's gang task force on the ground that the vehicle's registration had been suspended for insurance-related reasons. While two officers dealt with the driver and the passenger in the front seat, Officer Trevizo questioned Johnson. Trevizo noticed that Johnson was wearing clothing that she considered consistent with gang membership and that Johnson had a scanner in his jacket pocket, which she believed normally meant involvement in criminal activity. In response to Trevizo's questions, Johnson said that he had no identification, that he came from Eloy, Arizona, which Trevizo knew was home to a Crips gang, and that he had served time in prison for burglary. Suspecting that Johnson might have a weapon, Trevizo asked Johnson to get out of the car and frisked him, which led to discovery of a gun.

The lower court held that, while Johnson was initially lawfully seized because he was a passenger in a car legitimately stopped for a traffic violation, the prolonged encounter with Trevizo required a separate showing of reasonable suspicion of criminal activity, which the court concluded did not exist on these facts. The Supreme Court, in an opinion written by Justice Ginsburg, rejected this reasoning, stating that Trevizo "surely was not constitutionally required to give Johnson an opportunity to depart the scene after he exited the vehicle without first ensuring that, in so doing, she was not permitting a dangerous person to get behind her." While that conclusion may be necessary to protect the police, the opinion leaves unclear how long and for what purpose a passenger who has been ordered or asked to exit the vehicle (as authorized in *Wilson*) may be detained during a traffic stop. Of most concern is Justice Ginsburg's statement that "[a]n officer's inquiries into matters unrelated to the justification for the traffic stop . . . do not convert the encounter into something other than a lawful seizure, so long as those inquiries do not measurably extend the duration of the stop." This language solidifies a rule that was insinuated in *Robinette*, and in effect allows police to use routine traffic violations as a means of carrying out criminal investigations on mere hunches.[56]

However, in *Rodriguez v. United States*,[57] the Court emphasized that post-citation seizures may not be prolonged. In that case, six members of the Court, in an opinion by Justice Ginsburg, found invalid a canine-sniff of the defendant's car some seven or eight minutes after the officer had issued a citation and taken "care of all the business" associated with a traffic stop for driving on a road shoulder. The government had argued that the delay occurred solely because the arresting officer called for backup and that, in any event, it was *de minimis*. But Justice Ginsburg wrote that, unless highway or officer safety is involved (as in *Mimms* and *Johnson*), police may not seize a person stopped for a traffic violation to "detect evidence of ordinary criminal wrongdoing," but only for the purpose of carrying out duties "incident of a traffic stop." The Court included within "traffic stop duties" not only checking license and registration information but also "determining whether there are outstanding warrants against the driver." To the dissenting justices, this latter task could not be distinguished from other efforts to detect evidence of ordinary crime. The dissent, written by Justice Thomas, also pointed out that the Court's rule will be contingent on how efficient or aggressive the arresting officer is, since those who are less efficient or who make a custodial arrest will in effect have more time to summon other officers or a canine. Conversely, Thomas noted, officers might now

---

[56] Undercutting somewhat this interpretation of *Johnson*, however, is the Court's decision in *Arizona v. United States*, 567 U.S. 387, 132 S.Ct. 2492 (2012), which stated that "[d]etaining individuals solely to verify their immigration status would raise constitutional concerns."

[57] 575 U.S. 348, 135 S.Ct. 1609 (2015).

feel compelled to carry out further investigation without backup, to their detriment. If the pretextual use of traffic stops is to be regulated at all, however, the Court's rule is necessary.

(2) Stops for Loitering

Governments have long resorted to loitering and vagrancy statutes as a method of preventing criminal behavior. These statutes authorize the police to stop or arrest suspicious-looking individuals or persons considered disreputable on grounds short of an articulable suspicion that criminal activity is afoot. Precisely because of the discretion they give police, many loitering and vagrancy statutes have been declared unconstitutional, usually on the ground that they are impermissibly vague.

In *Papachristou v. City of Jacksonville*,[58] the Supreme Court struck down a municipal ordinance that authorized arrest of "vagrants," a group defined to include "rogues and vagabonds, or dissolute persons who go about begging . . . common drunkards, lewd, wanton and lascivious persons, . . . persons wandering or strolling around from place to place without any lawful purpose or object, habitual loafers, [and] disorderly persons." The Court concluded that the ordinance provided "no standards governing the exercise of . . . discretion", and thus "permit[ted] and encourage[d] an arbitrary and discriminatory enforcement of law" and resulted "in a regime in which the poor and the unpopular are permitted to 'stand on the sidewalk . . . only at the whim of any police officer.' "

Similarly, in *Kolender v. Lawson*,[59] the Court struck down on vagueness grounds a statute that made a misdemeanant of anyone "[w]ho loiters or wanders upon the streets or from place to place without apparent reason or business and who refuses to identify himself and to account for his presence when requested by any peace officer to do so, if the surrounding circumstances are such as to indicate to a reasonable man that the public safety demands such identification." A state court had construed the statute to require that "credible and reliable" identification be given to any police officer who had "reasonable suspicion" of criminal activity, and specified "credible and reliable" to mean "carrying reasonable assurance that the identification is authentic and providing means for later getting in touch with the person who has identified himself." Despite these limitations, the Supreme Court found the law deficient, concluding that it "vests virtually complete discretion in the hands of the police to determine whether the suspect has satisfied the statute and must be permitted to go on his way in the absence of probable cause to arrest."

After *Kolender*, a number of jurisdictions tried to devise statutes that were even more specific.[60] The City of Chicago passed an ordinance that provided that "whenever a police officer observes a person whom he reasonably believes to be a criminal street gang member loitering in any public place with one or more other persons, he shall order all such persons to disperse and remove themselves from the area." The ordinance defined "loiter" to mean "to remain in any one place with no apparent purpose" and allowed arrest upon a failure to disperse after a legitimate police order. The Chicago police department construed the statute to require "probable cause" that a person was a

---

[58]   405 U.S. 156, 92 S.Ct. 839 (1972).

[59]   461 U.S. 352, 103 S.Ct. 1855 (1983).

[60]   See generally, Debra Livingston, *Police Discretion and the Quality of Life in Public Places: Courts, Communities, and the New Policing*, 97 Colum. L. Rev. 551, 622–24 (1997).

gang member before arrest could take place and limited its operation to areas known to be experiencing significant problems due to gang activity. The primary purpose of the ordinance was to enable police to arrest gang members who engaged in drug dealing, vandalism, and more serious crimes, but who seldom engaged in these acts in the presence of the police and who threatened citizens who reported such acts.

In *Chicago v. Morales*,[61] the Supreme Court struck down this law as well. Although a three-member plurality of the Court advanced a number of reasons for the holding, the majority rationale, endorsed by six members, was that the ordinance was void on vagueness grounds. The city had argued that the ordinance limited police discretion in three ways: (1) it only permitted dispersal orders directed toward those who were not moving and had no apparent purpose; (2) it did not permit arrest of those who obeyed a dispersal order; and (3) an order of dispersal was only permitted if the officer reasonably believed a gang member was among the loiterers. The justices in the majority found these limitations insufficient. They reasoned that the ordinance still gave police too much discretion to decide who, among those who were not moving, had "no apparent purpose" in doing so. The plurality did indicate it might have reached a different result had the ordinance limited arrests *solely* to gang members or to those who were loitering with "an apparently harmful purpose or effect." But because the statute applied "to everyone in the city who may remain in one place with one suspected gang member as long as their purpose is not apparent to an officer observing them," it was constitutionally deficient.[62]

Justice O'Connor, joined by Justice Breyer in concurrence, elaborated on the type of statute that might be permissible. She asserted that had the term "loiter" been construed to mean "to remain in any one place with no apparent purpose other than to establish control over identifiable areas, to intimidate others from entering those areas, or to conceal illegal activities," the ordinance may have been valid. Justice Scalia's dissent countered that this type of ordinance would not deal with the perceived law enforcement problem, because "the intimidation and lawlessness do not occur when the police are in sight." Justice Thomas's dissent, joined by Scalia and Chief Justice Rehnquist, concluded that "remaining in one place with no apparent purpose" was not so vague that the statute should be struck down as invalid on its face (as opposed to as applied), and noted that limiting the law's application to gang members, as the plurality suggested, would not solve the supposed vagueness of that language. He also echoed Scalia's view that, by undermining Chicago's efforts at addressing the pervasive intimidation of gangs, the Court's action did little to protect people's "right" to stand in one place but did much to deny vulnerable innocent citizens "freedom of movement."

(c) Permissible Sources of Information

Most of the time, as in *Terry* itself, reasonable suspicion develops as a result of direct police observation of ongoing events. But, as with probable cause, reasonable suspicion may be based on information provided by third parties. Where probable cause is

---

[61]   527 U.S. 41, 119 S.Ct. 1849 (1999).

[62]   The plurality also dismissed the relevance of the police department's self-imposed limitations with respect to the statute, stating "[t]hat the police have adopted internal rules limiting their enforcement to certain designated areas in the city would not provide a defense to a loiterer who might be arrested elsewhere[, n]or could a person who knowingly loitered with a well-known gang member anywhere in the city safely assume that they would not be ordered to disperse no matter how innocent and harmless their loitering might be."

concerned, the police must have fairly substantial grounds for crediting the hearsay information, particularly when it is from an informant.[63] When reasonable suspicion is the standard, however, the *"Aguilar-Spinelli"* requirements that the informant's basis-of-knowledge and reliability be established, already modified for probable cause determinations by modern Court decisions,[64] have been relaxed even further.

(1) Informants

In *Adams v. Williams*,[65] a police officer confronted and then frisked a person on the basis of a tip from an informant. The Court held that because the informant was known to the officer and had provided information in the past, had come forward "personally to give information that was immediately verifiable at the scene," and was "subject to immediate arrest for making a false complaint" had the tip proven incorrect, there was "enough indicia of reliability to justify [the] stop." These facts provide no information as to how the informant came by his information, and very little information about his reliability, particularly since it is unlikely people are aware they can be arrested for making a false complaint. But at least the presence of the informant at the scene of the stop provided some incentive to be truthful.

In contrast, in *Alabama v. White*,[66] the police acted on an anonymous tip that a certain female person would leave a certain room in a particular apartment complex, get into a brown Plymouth station wagon with a broken right taillight, and drive toward Dobey's Hotel while in possession of an ounce of cocaine inside a brown attache case. Police proceeded to the designated apartment complex, spotted the Plymouth as described, and shortly thereafter observed the defendant, without a briefcase, leave the indicated apartment and get in the car. They then followed her as she took the most direct route to Dobey's Hotel. They stopped her just short of the hotel, obtained consent to search her vehicle, and found cocaine in a brown briefcase. The Court found, 6–3, that although the information possessed by the police prior to the stop did not rise to the level of probable cause, it was sufficient to give them reasonable suspicion. Justice White, writing for the Court, was particularly impressed with the fact that the caller accurately *predicted* what the defendant would do, because this demonstrated inside information rather than information that could easily be obtained by any casual observer. Although calling it a "close case," White felt that this fact, plus the other corroboration by the police, was sufficient to justify a stop.

As Justice Stevens, joined by Justices Brennan and Marshall, noted in dissent:

> Anybody with enough knowledge about a given person to make her the target of a prank, or to harbor a grudge against her, will certainly be able to formulate a tip about her like the one predicting Vanessa White's excursion. In addition, under the Court's holding, every citizen is subject to being seized and questioned by any officer who is prepared to testify that the warrantless stop was based on an anonymous tip predicting whatever conduct the officer just observed.

---

[63] See § 5.03(b).

[64] See *Illinois v. Gates*, 462 U.S. 213, 103 S.Ct. 2317 (1983), discussed in § 5.03(b) (*Aguilar-Spinelli* two-prong test rejected in favor a totality of the circumstances approach).

[65] 407 U.S. 143, 92 S.Ct. 1921 (1972).

[66] 496 U.S. 325, 110 S.Ct. 2412 (1990).

The better approach in such cases, the dissenters implied, is to require informant information to meet the same credibility test that is required for probable cause findings. While the police need only reasonable suspicion in stop cases, that suspicion should be based on facts as credible as the facts relied upon in making probable cause determinations.

Florida v. J.L.[67] also involved an anonymous tip, and this time a unanimous Court found for the defendant. Police received an anonymous phone call that a young black male standing at a particular bus stop and wearing a plaid shirt was carrying a gun. Police went to the bus stop and saw three black males, one of whom was wearing a plaid shirt, but observed nothing else suspicious. They frisked the youth and found a gun. The Court, in an opinion by Justice Ginsburg, distinguished this case from *White* by noting that in the latter case the informant had accurately predicted the suspect's movements, which suggested that the tipster had inside knowledge about the suspect and therefore may have been right about the cocaine possession. Here "[a]ll the police had to go on . . . was the bare report of an unknown, unaccountable informant who neither explained how he knew about the gun nor supplied any basis for believing he had inside information about J.L." The Court also refused to adopt the government's proposed "firearm exception" to *Terry*, meant to allow frisks on less than reasonable suspicion when illegal gun possession is suspected, because it would permit harassment and embarrassment through the simple ruse of an anonymous phone call stating that a given person had a gun. However, the Court indicated that a different result might be merited in connection with reports of concealed bombs, or of guns being carried near schools and other areas associated with a lesser expectation of privacy.

Fitting somewhere in-between *White* and *J.L.* are the facts of *Navarette v. California*,[68] where the police stopped a truck matching the description given by an anonymous 911 caller who reported the vehicle had run her off the road. The police discovered the truck moving in the direction and at the approximate location given by the caller. Five members of the Court concluded that, unlike in *J.L.*, the anonymous caller claimed to have witnessed dangerous behavior by the target and also had little time to fabricate the report, given the short time between the alleged incident and the call. Furthermore, the fact that anonymous calls in this jurisdiction were recorded and could be linked to particular geographic areas could lead a "reasonable officer [to] conclude that a false tipster would think twice before using such a system." On the basis of this information, the majority continued, police had reasonable suspicion to believe the driver was drunk.

The dissent, written by Justice Scalia, pointed out that, unlike in *White*, the caller provided virtually no detail other than the truck description, and did not predict any behavior other than the truck's likely route. Scalia also disputed the spontaneity of the call, as well as the relevance of the 911's recording and location capacities, since the caller's anonymity made it impossible to ascertain whether she knew of them. He also challenged the conclusion that officers had reasonable suspicion of drunken driving, especially given the fact that they witnessed no erratic driving for the five minutes they followed the car. He concluded, "The Court's opinion serves up a freedom-destroying cocktail consisting of two parts patent falsity: (1) that anonymous 911 reports of traffic violations are reliable so long as they correctly identify a car and its location, and (2)

---

[67]   529 U.S. 266, 120 S.Ct. 1375 (2000).

[68]   572 U.S. 393, 134 S.Ct. 1683 (2014).

that a single instance of careless or reckless driving necessarily supports a reasonable suspicion of drunkenness."

(2) Police Flyers

The Court's stop cases have analogized to probable cause analysis where the "informant" is another police officer or department. In *United States v. Hensley*,[69] the Court unanimously held that police are entitled to rely on notices and "wanted flyers" from other jurisdictions in stopping individuals, so long as the jurisdiction that issued the flyer had specific and articulable facts to suspect the individual of past or present criminal activity at the time the flyer was issued and the stop is not significantly more intrusive than would have been permitted the issuing department. This holding follows the rule established in *Whiteley v. Warden*,[70] which permitted arrests based on radio bulletins so long as the source of the bulletin had probable cause to arrest.

(3) Profiles and Plans

In a number of the Court's cases, the police have relied on so-called "drug-courier profiles" in determining whom to stop.[71] As discussed in more detail in connection with arrests,[72] the Court has been cautious about authorizing use of such profiles, instead requiring an independent assessment of the facts to determine whether probable cause or reasonable suspicion exists. A second type of "generalized," as opposed to "individualized," method of showing adequate suspicion is through an investigative "plan." This type of plan was relied upon by border officials in *I.N.S. v. Delgado*,[73] in which a warrant was obtained based on a showing that numerous illegal aliens were employed at a particular factory, without naming any specific individuals. Although the Court did not directly address its validity, such a "general" warrant might permit some types of seizures, if a statistical correlation between the factors in the plan and the alleged activity (e.g., employment of illegal immigrants) exist.

(d) Types of Crimes

In *Sibron v. New York*,[74] the Court suggested that a stop merely to obtain evidence of narcotics possession was never permissible. Such a rule arguably makes sense under the *Terry* balancing test, since where there is no imminent danger to the officer or the public, the intrusion associated with a stop may not be justifiable without greater suspicion. In contrast, in *Adams v. Williams*,[75] a stop and frisk to obtain narcotics and a *gun* was permitted, even though the officer acted on a tip that was relatively unreliable and there was no indication the gun was unlicensed. The nature of the criminal situation being investigated may have made the difference in *Adams*.

---

[69] 469 U.S. 221, 105 S.Ct. 675 (1985).

[70] 401 U.S. 560, 91 S.Ct. 1031 (1971), discussed in § 3.03(a)(3).

[71] See, e.g., *Florida v. Royer*, 460 U.S. 491, 103 S.Ct. 1319 (1983); *United States v. Sokolow*, 490 U.S. 1, 109 S.Ct. 1581 (1989).

[72] See § 3.03(b)(3).

[73] 466 U.S. 210, 104 S.Ct. 1758 (1984).

[74] 392 U.S. 40, 88 S.Ct. 1889 (1968).

[75] 407 U.S. 143, 92 S.Ct. 1921 (1972).

Since these cases, the Court has permitted stops for a number of lesser crimes.[76] However, these decisions all involved stops for imminent or ongoing crimes. In contrast, in *United States v. Hensley*,[77] the police stopped the defendant on the basis of a flyer issued by another department indicating that he was suspected of committed an aggravated robbery twelve days earlier. While, as described above, the Court found that requiring probable cause in such situations "would not only hinder the investigation, but might also enable the suspect to flee in the interim and to remain at large," it left open the possibility that stops on a reasonable suspicion of past criminal activity might be impermissible if the crime is minor.

11.04   Permissible Grounds for a Frisk

A valid stop does not automatically justify a frisk. *Terry* permitted a frisk only when the officer has, in addition to the suspicion necessary to justify a stop, a reasonable suspicion that the person stopped is "armed and dangerous." This rule follows from the *Terry* balancing test: each intrusion by the government must be justified by a legitimate objective.

Terry's holding also suggested that, before a frisk takes place, the officer must "identif[y] himself as a policeman and make[ ] reasonable inquiries." One type of reasonable inquiry, the Court held in *Hiibel v. Nevada Dist. Ct.*,[78] is a request for the person's name. The majority reasoned that the request for identity has "an immediate relation to the purpose, rationale, and practical demands of a *Terry* stop." While Justice Stevens' dissent pointed to the myriad ways in which a name can provide the police with incriminating information beyond that needed to effect a preventive stop (especially in light of today's nationalized computer databases), the majority insisted that a demand for a name is a "commonsense inquiry" rather than an attempt to circumvent the Fourth and Fifth Amendments, at least when the demand is not pretextual and there is no reason to believe at the time it is made that the name in itself will be incriminating. If the individual does not respond to a request for identity under these conditions, *Hiibel* held that not only may the officer carry out a frisk, but he may effect an arrest, if state law so provides.

Presumably, in addition to an identity request, the officer may ask the lawfully stopped individual what he is up to. As the Court later recognized in *Adams v. Williams*,[79] however, the exigencies of the situation often do not permit such niceties. As described earlier, in *Adams*, the officer, acting on a tip that a person seated in a nearby car was carrying narcotics and a gun at his waist, approached the person and asked him to open the door. When the defendant rolled down the window instead, the officer reached into the car and removed a revolver from his waistband. Although the officer's question was the only exchange between the officer and the defendant, the Court found the officer's seizure of the weapon reasonable in light of the defendant's apparent unwillingness to cooperate.

A few other Court cases flesh out the types of situations in which a frisk may be justified. In *Terry* itself, the officer's observations of the defendants' actions, plus their

---

[76]   See, e.g., *United States v. Brignoni-Ponce*, 422 U.S. 873, 95 S.Ct. 2574 (1975) (stops for violations of immigration laws).

[77]   469 U.S. 221, 105 S.Ct. 675 (1985).

[78]   542 U.S. 177, 124 S.Ct. 2451 (2004), discussed further in § 3.03(a).

[79]   407 U.S. 143, 92 S.Ct. 1921 (1972).

furtive, "mumbling" behavior once he had accosted them, permitted a frisk. Similarly, in *Pennsylvania v. Mimms*,[80] the Court approved a frisk when the officer observed a large bulge under the sports jacket of a driver who had just been asked to get out of his car. On the other hand, in *Ybarra v. Illinois*,[81] the Court held that the police did not have sufficient grounds for a frisk. There, police executing a warrant for search of a tavern and its bartender frisked each of the twelve patrons after announcing they were going to conduct "a cursory search for weapons." One officer felt what he described as a "cigarette pack with objects in it" on Ybarra, and later returned to remove it from his person. The Court refused to uphold this action, despite the state's and the dissent's contention that the tavern was a "compact, dimly lit" area that needed to be "frozen" to prepare for the search. As Justice Stewart stated for the Court, "[t]he 'narrow scope' of the *Terry* exception does not permit a frisk for weapons on less than reasonable belief or suspicion directed at the person to be frisked, even though that person happens to be on premises where an authorized narcotics search is taking place."

Ybarra also emphasized that the frisk must be directed at discovering weapons, not evidence. The government had argued that its interest in controlling the sale of hard drugs and the ease with which such drugs can be concealed also justified the frisk in that case. But the Court concluded that the *Terry* doctrine should not be expanded from a device for protecting the police to an "aid [to] the evidence-gathering function of the search warrant."

However, in *Minnesota v. Dickerson*,[82] the Court seemed to forget this admonition. There, two officers saw Dickerson leave a "crack house," initially walk toward them, and then walk away toward an alley, where they stopped him. Without any inquiries, they immediately frisked him. Arguably, this frisk was conducted in the absence of an articulable suspicion of danger. Yet the Court did not even address this issue, apparently assuming that such suspicion existed.[83] This assumption flies in the face of *Ybarra's* language cautioning that a *Terry* frisk is not meant to assist police in gathering evidence.

11.05   The Scope of a Frisk

Once a frisk is justified, *Terry* allows the officer to undertake "a carefully limited search of the outer clothing . . . in an attempt to discover weapons which might be used to assault him." In *Sibron v. New York*,[84] one of *Terry's* companion cases, the Court suggested that reaching into a person's pocket is impermissible when the officer makes "no attempt at an initial limited exploration for arms." But in *Adams*, the Court upheld the officer's reaching into the defendant's waistband when he had information that a gun was there and the defendant was uncooperative, again illustrating the proposition that the danger defines the scope of the intrusion. Of course, if the officer feels a weapon-like object, he may seize the item to protect himself.[85]

Furthermore, even if the officer feels only *contraband* he may remove it from the suspect's pocket, so long as, at the time he initially feels it, he has probable cause to

---

[80]   434 U.S. 106, 98 S.Ct. 330 (1977).

[81]   444 U.S. 85, 100 S.Ct. 338 (1979).

[82]   508 U.S. 366, 113 S.Ct. 2130 (1993).

[83]   The Court did decide, however, that the police exceeded the bounds of a valid frisk. See § 11.05.

[84]   392 U.S. 40, 88 S.Ct. 1889 (1968).

[85]   *Pennsylvania v. Mimms*, 434 U.S. 106, 98 S.Ct. 330 (1977) (permitting a seizure of a gun felt through sports jacket).

believe it is contraband. The Court adopted this "plain feel" doctrine in *Minnesota v. Dickerson*,[86] where officers, after stopping a person who had come out of a "crack house," immediately frisked him. Although the frisking officer found no weapons, he did feel a lump which, after some manipulation, he judged was crack cocaine in cellophane. The Court concluded that an officer conducting a valid frisk may seize *any* evidence he "feels" during the frisk. It reasoned that this rule flowed from the plain view doctrine, which permits seizure of evidence in plain view from a place the officer has validly intruded upon.[87] However, the Court went on to hold that its new rule did not justify the seizure in this case, since the officer's manipulation of the package went beyond the scope of a valid weapons frisk. The Court analogized this situation to *Arizona v. Hicks*,[88] where it held that movement of a stereo to see its serial numbers, on less than probable cause, violated the plain view doctrine.

Even thus limited, *Dickerson's* plain feel rule is questionable. Although it does bear a conceptual relationship to the plain view idea, as a practical matter it significantly increases police discretion. An officer's sense of touch is unlikely to be as reliable as his vision. More importantly, whereas a court can independently gauge whether an item was in plain view at the time it was seized, it will likely have to rely on the officer's word in gauging the accuracy of his tactile skills. Finally, it allows seizures of items other than weapons, an arguable expansion of *Terry's* holding.

The scope of a frisk has been expanded in other ways as well. Analogous to the armspan rule in the search incident context,[89] the police may search any area from which the person stopped might be able to obtain a weapon. This was the holding of *Michigan v. Long*,[90] where two officers on evening patrol stopped to investigate a car that they had observed driving erratically and that had ended up in a ditch. They met the defendant, the only occupant of the car, at the rear of the vehicle and noted that he appeared to be intoxicated. When asked for his license and registration, the defendant returned to the car and the officers followed; while doing so they saw a hunting knife on the floorboard of the car. After patting down the defendant and finding no weapons, one of the officers shined his flashlight into the car and saw something protruding from the armrest under the frontseat. Lifting the armrest revealed an open leather pouch which the officer "determined" to contain marijuana.

Although the defendant had not been arrested for any crime at the time of the search, the Court disagreed with the Michigan Supreme Court's holding that the search of the passenger compartment was invalid. Instead, the Court emphasized that *Terry* did not restrict the "frisk" for weapons to the person but rather permitted a protective search of any area which might contain a weapon posing danger to the police. Here, the Court concluded, the observance of the hunting knife, the intoxicated state of the defendant, and the fact that the encounter took place at night in an isolated rural area gave the police specific and articulable facts which, taken together with the rational inferences from those facts, reasonably warranted the search. The Court noted that the search had been limited to "those areas to which Long would generally have immediate control, and that could contain a weapon."

---

86   508 U.S. 366, 113 S.Ct. 2130 (1993).

87   See generally, Chapter 10.

88   480 U.S. 321, 107 S.Ct. 1149 (1987), discussed in § 10.03.

89   See § 6.04(a).

90   463 U.S. 1032, 103 S.Ct. 3469 (1983).

While the *Long* Court's extension of *Terry* is an appropriate means of protecting the police, its application of this concept to the facts of *Long* is questionable, given the location of the pouch and the fact that Long was in the control of the officers at the time of the search.[91] To the suggestion that the officers could have moved the defendant further from the car if they were worried about his use of a weapon in the car, the Court stated that police are not required to "adopt alternate means to insure their safety in order to avoid the intrusion involved in a *Terry* encounter," a statement that does not explain why the police are allowed to go *beyond* the intrusion associated with a *Terry* encounter when it is not necessary. *Long* should be read in light of the long list of Supreme Court decisions minimizing Fourth Amendment protection of automobiles.[92]

Terry itself spoke only of admitting weapons discovered in the course of a lawful frisk. Following that rule would deter the police from engaging in fishing expeditions in situations where they know they are not in danger but the objective facts provide "reasonable suspicion" that a person is armed and dangerous. However, *Dickerson* and *Long* clearly permit the seizure and admission into evidence of contraband found during a frisk. These decisions are of a piece with other Court decisions holding that a clearly guilty person should not go free when his objectively-defined rights have not been violated.[93]

11.06   Stop and Frisk in the Lower Courts

A look at lower court decisions helps flesh out the standards set by *Terry* and later decisions. The discussion of these cases is organized under the same four headings used in the last section.

(a) The Definition of Seizures and Stops

Consistent with the Supreme Court's decisions, most lower courts hold that no seizure occurs when an officer merely confronts a citizen and asks questions.[94] In *State v. Tsukiyama*,[95] the Hawaii Supreme Court found that no seizure occurred when a policeman asked Tsukiyama a number of questions, including his name, after Tsukiyama had requested a flashlight from the officer to use in fixing his automobile. The defendant here initiated the conversation, and the court specifically found no element of command, force or coercion, and no physical restraint.

Even when the officer initiates contact, courts are willing to find no seizure occurs in some circumstances. In *Login v. State*,[96] a detective approached the defendant as he was walking in the Miami airport and displayed his badge and identification. He stated: "I am a narcotics officer with the sheriff's office and I would like to talk to you; do you have a minute?" The defendant replied, "Yes." At that moment, the officer noticed cocaine

---

[91]   In interesting contrast to this reasoning is the reasoning in *Arizona v. Gant*, 556 U.S. 332, 129 S.Ct. 1710 (2009), discussed in § 6.04(c), where the Court held that a search incident to arrest of a car occupant only authorizes a protective search of areas over which the occupant has "actual" control.

[92]   See, e.g., *New York v. Belton*, 453 U.S. 454, 101 S.Ct. 2860 (1981), discussed in § 6.04(d); *California v. Acevedo*, 500 U.S. 565, 111 S.Ct. 1982 (1991), discussed in § 7.04; *South Dakota v. Opperman*, 428 U.S. 364, 96 S.Ct. 3092 (1976), discussed in § 13.07(a).

[93]   Cf. § 11.04 (discussing the Court's resistance to pretextual search arguments).

[94]   See, e.g., *State v. Davis*, 543 So.2d 375 (Fla. 3d D.C.A. 1989) (no seizure when uniformed officer inquires if he might speak with bicyclist and bicyclist stops); *People v. King*, 72 Cal.App.3d 346, 139 Cal.Rptr. 926 (1977) (no seizure when officer overtakes a pedestrian and asks him to halt).

[95]   56 Hawaii 8, 525 P.2d 1099 (1974).

[96]   394 So.2d 183 (Fla. 3d D.C.A. 1981).

residue around the defendant's nostrils, which observation eventually led to the defendant's arrest. The Florida District Court of Appeal held that no Fourth Amendment seizure had taken place at the time the cocaine was observed. The court recognized the practical advantage of a rule holding that a stop occurs as soon as police initially approach the individual, identify themselves and begin to question him. But it rejected a per se rule, based on the following reasoning:

> [A]pplication of such a rule would cover a multitude of police-citizen street encounters which in no way approach a police seizure of the person, such as police questioning of a probable witness to a crime or police inquiries directed to a stranded motorist in need of assistance. To label all police encounters with the public as seizures when accompanied by questioning, no matter how cordial, would tremendously impede the police in the effective performance of both their criminal investigation and community assistance functions. . . .

The court did note, however, that it would not hesitate to find a seizure when police use language which "in tone and content bespeak an order to stop, particularly when employed during a fast moving criminal investigation on the street." Other courts have been even more willing to hold that a seizure occurs, but at the same time have required much less than reasonable suspicion to justify it. Illustrative is *People v. De Bour*,[97] which held that police must have "some objective credible reason" for the "minimal intrusion of approaching [an individual] to request information."

Toward the other end of the seizure spectrum, the courts have had to interpret the Supreme Court's ruling that the permissible duration of a stop is dependent upon the reasonableness of the officer's attempts to reduce delay.[98] In *Courson v. McMillian*,[99] for example, the court held in the context of a damages action that a deputy did not violate clearly established law when he stopped the occupants of a car on a suspicion that they were involved in growing marijuana, and then held them at gunpoint for 30 minutes, most of which was spent awaiting assistance. The Court pointed out that, even though the officer lacked probable cause for an arrest, the deputy was alone late at night at a vacant construction site, the occupants of the car appeared uncooperative and one of them was abusive; thus, the court granted summary judgment against the plaintiffs.

(b) Permissible Grounds for Seizures and Stops

Many lower courts require rather specific facts linking the individual to criminal activity before they are willing to find an investigatory stop valid. For example, the Michigan Supreme Court, in *People v. Parisi*,[100] found the police unjustified in stopping an automobile based upon: (1) the officer's concern that the occupants were "sleeping or ill;" (2) the fact that the car was traveling more slowly than the posted speed; and (3) the youthful appearance of the occupants, noting that there was no minimum speed and the local juvenile curfew did not apply to cars. The court in *United States v. Bell*[101] found inadequate cause for an investigatory stop of a van on suspicion of criminal drug-related activity where: (1) the van, which had out-of-state license plates, was traveling eastward (away from California) on an interstate highway; and (2) the van was driven by a

---

[97] 40 N.Y.2d 210, 386 N.Y.S.2d 375, 352 N.E.2d 562, 571–72 (1976).

[98] *United States v. Sharpe*, 470 U.S. 675, 105 S.Ct. 1568 (1985), discussed in § 3.02(b).

[99] 939 F.2d 1479 (11th Cir. 1991).

[100] 393 Mich. 31, 222 N.W.2d 757 (1974).

[101] 383 F.Supp. 1298 (D.Neb. 1974).

youthful driver. In interesting contrast to the Supreme Court's decision in *Dickerson*, the court in *State v. Saia*[102] found a stop unreasonable where officers observed a woman leave a known drug outlet and saw her reach twice inside her waistband while apparently aware of police surveillance. Similarly, *State v. Kupihea*[103] held that police acted unreasonably when they stopped two individuals in an automobile who had looked back at the police and then crouched down. In short, as the court in *State v. Key*[104] stated: where the "conduct of the defendant [is] just as consistent with innocent as with illicit behavior," reasonable suspicion does not exist.

Other cases have found adequate cause for an investigative stop when the defendant's conduct is less than innocent. For instance, in *State v. Purnell*,[105] the police were justified in stopping a defendant who was seen looking into every business at 2:00 a.m. when all the stores were closed, and who walked away hurriedly when the police car approached. Also found permissible was a stop of four large tractor-trailers on a highway in a coastal area where drug smuggling often took place, after the trucks had left a deep-water docking facility at a time of night when no commercial activity occurred there and the weather was such that no boats were available for transporting goods.[106] Much more questionable is the decision, by a divided Supreme Court of Indiana, upholding a police stop of a car driven by a single black male based upon knowledge: (1) that two black men, one armed with a sawed-off shotgun, had robbed a motel several miles away; (2) that they were believed to be traveling in the general direction of the police officers; and (3) that they might reasonably be passing the officer's position about that time.[107]

Some cases have also considered the usefulness of informants in making the reasonable suspicion determination. For instance, in *Commonwealth v. Anderson*,[108] the police received an anonymous tip scrawled upon a newspaper that had been thrown into a toll booth from a passing bus. The tip stated that police would find an armed and dangerous drug courier on a particular bus, and included a description of the supposed drug courier. Presaging the Supreme Court's decisions in *White* and *Navarette*, the court held that the tip had the requisite indicia of reliability to support a stop of an individual who matched the description and who got off the indicated bus, walked quickly through the bus terminal while glancing back at the police several times, and made a gesture to get rid of a bag in his possession when he came face to face with two other officers.

As these descriptions indicate, there is no bright-line test for reasonable suspicion. However, there appear to be at least three factors that routinely influence both the police and the courts which find such suspicion to be present: (1) evasiveness (e.g., running or walking quickly away from police; attempts to hide something or avoid eye contact); (2) incongruity (e.g., looking out of place, ethnically or otherwise); and (3) the nature of the defendant's location (e.g., high crime area). With the possible exception of running at the sight of the police, these factors are at least as likely to be consistent with innocence as

---

[102] 302 So.2d 869 (La. 1974), cert. denied 420 U.S. 1008, 95 S.Ct. 1454 (1975).

[103] 59 Hawaii 386, 581 P.2d 765 (1978).

[104] 375 So.2d 1354 (La. 1979).

[105] 621 S.W.2d 277 (Mo. 1981).

[106] *United States v. Ogden*, 703 F.2d 629 (1st Cir. 1983).

[107] *Williams v. State*, 261 Ind. 547, 307 N.E.2d 457 (1974).

[108] 366 Mass. 394, 318 N.E.2d 834 (1974).

with guilt. Most court decisions recognize this fact. But if two or more of these types of factors are present, most courts easily find reasonable suspicion.[109]

(c) Permissible Grounds for a Frisk

Many lower courts have conscientiously applied the requirement that police have articulable grounds for believing a stopped individual is armed and dangerous before they undertake a frisk. In *United States v. Johnson*,[110] for instance, the Tenth Circuit found the police justified in stopping a car for having a noisy muffler, but held illegal a frisk of a passenger in the car when both the driver and his wife were very cooperative but the passenger could not produce identification. Similarly, in *People v. Superior Court of Los Angeles County*,[111] police stopped an automobile that was being driven at night without lights. The driver could produce no identification, license or registration and was therefore arrested pursuant to state law. The driver was then frisked, although the officer conducting the search admitted having no fear for his safety. In holding the search unlawful, the California Supreme Court concluded that a patdown search in the context of a detention for a traffic violation must be supported by specific facts or circumstances that could give rise to a reasonable belief that a weapon is concealed on the motorist. The minor infractions involved in this case, by themselves, were not sufficient, to support such a belief. Although the U.S. Supreme Court has since held that a *full* search is permitted incident to a custodial arrest,[112] a few lower courts continue to invalidate frisks incident to non-custodial traffic arrests unless there is articulable suspicion.[113]

Unfortunately, unlike the *Johnson* and *Superior Court* decisions, some lower court opinions have handled the power to frisk and the authority to stop as aspects of a single question. One result of this analytical impurity is that the case law reflects a substantial correlation between the adequacy of the grounds for an investigative stop and the likelihood that a frisk will be found permissible; the more convincing the justification for investigation, the more willing the courts have been to find that a protective search is warranted. It is possible, however, to parse from the decisions a number of discrete factors that have consistently been found relevant to a judgment by police that an individual may be armed and presently dangerous and thus worthy of a frisk after the initial stop.

The specific criminal activity which the police suspect may be afoot is always a relevant and often a dispositive consideration in the determination of the reasonableness of a frisk. If a crime of violence or serious property theft is suspected, it is rare that a court will fail to find reasonable grounds to conclude that the suspect may be armed and presently dangerous.[114] If, on the other hand, the suspected criminal activity merely

---

[109] See David Harris, *Particularized Suspicion, Categorical Judgements: Supreme Court Rhetoric versus Lower Court Reality Under* Terry v. Ohio, 72 St. John's L.Rev. 975, 988–1001 (1998); Margaret Raymond, *Down on the Corner, Out in the Street: Considering the Character of the Neighborhood in Evaluating Reasonable Suspicion*, 60 Ohio St. L.J. 99, 115–124 (1999).

[110] 463 F.2d 70 (10th Cir. 1972).

[111] 7 Cal.3d 186, 101 Cal.Rptr. 837, 496 P.2d 1205 (1972).

[112] *United States v. Robinson*, 414 U.S. 218, 94 S.Ct. 467 (1973), discussed in § 6.02. The California Supreme Court, however, has rejected this stance, based on an interpretation of the state constitution. *People v. Brisendine*, 13 Cal.3d 528, 119 Cal.Rptr. 315, 531 P.2d 1099 (1975).

[113] *United States v. Wanless*, 882 F.2d 1459 (9th Cir. 1989).

[114] *United States v. Walker*, 924 F.2d 1, 4 (1st Cir. 1991) (frisk of burglar permissible because "burglars often carry weapons or other dangerous objects"); *Wright v. State*, 88 Nev. 460, 499 P.2d 1216 (1972) (frisk

United States v. Del Toro,[140] the Second Circuit found as a matter of law that a ten dollar bill, folded 2″ by ¾″ and containing cocaine, could not reasonably be considered a weapon when felt in a suit pocket, and therefore was illegally seized. However, the "weapon-like object" limitation to the permissible scope of a frisk has been substantially diluted by other courts through imaginative definition of what reasonably might be considered a weapon. Courts have condoned the seizure of: a marijuana cigarette which the searching officer pulled from a pocket at the same time as a lipstick container that the officer believed to be a 12-gauge shotgun shell;[141] a cigarette lighter containing hashish because it could be used in a doubled up fist, or thrown, or used to burn the officer;[142] a large envelope containing lottery slips on the theory that it could have hidden a thin knife or blade;[143] and a bag of marijuana cigarettes which came out of a pocket along with a long-stemmed smoking pipe that the officer believed to be a knife.[144]

Once an object that may pose a threat to the officer is discovered and in his possession, it would seem that the protective function of a search during an investigative stop has been accomplished and further investigation of the object is not necessary. In *Jackson v. Alaska*,[145] the court prohibited searches of small containers, such as wallets, absent articulable reasons for believing it may contain an "atypical weapon." But in *Taylor v. Superior Court*,[146] the court found the further examination of a cigarette lighter in police possession to be reasonable because it might have concealed dangerous razor blades. In *Nash v. State*,[147] the opening of a box already seized was held to be reasonable. Such cases, though not uncommon, appear to be deviations from, rather than elaborations of, the underlying rationale of the *Terry* decision.

11.07   Conclusion

Based on the Supreme Court's decisions and the lower courts' interpretation of those decisions, the following general principles about the stop and frisk doctrine can be stated:

(1)   A police-citizen encounter is not governed by the Fourth Amendment unless it is considered a "seizure." Factors to consider in deciding whether a "seizure" has taken place include: (a) the duration of the detention; (b) whether police actions were threatening; (c) whether the person detained was physically touched by the police; (d) whether the detention took place in an enclosed area as opposed to an area open to public view; and, most importantly, (e) whether the police action would have communicated to a reasonable, innocent person that the person was not free to decline police requests or otherwise terminate the encounter. The Supreme Court has held that confrontations of bus passengers, chases of fleeing individuals, and brief questioning are not seizures, unless accompanied by clearly coercive gestures or tones.

(2)   Generally, a person may be seized on less than probable cause to arrest only if the seizing officer (a) observes the person engage in conduct leading to a reasonable suspicion that criminal activity has recently occurred, is occurring or is about to occur

---

[140]   464 F.2d 520 (2d Cir. 1972).

[141]   *People v. Atmore*, 13 Cal.App.3d 244, 91 Cal.Rptr. 311 (2d Dist. 1970).

[142]   *Taylor v. Superior Court*, 275 Cal.App.2d 146, 79 Cal.Rptr. 677 (4th Dist. 1969).

[143]   *State v. Campbell*, 53 N.J. 230, 250 A.2d 1 (1969).

[144]   *People v. Watson*, 12 Cal.App.3d 130, 90 Cal.Rptr. 483 (3d Dist. 1970).

[145]   791 P.2d 1023 (Alaska App. 1990).

[146]   275 Cal.App.2d 146, 79 Cal.Rptr. 677 (4th Dist. 1969).

[147]   295 A.2d 715 (Del. 1972).

and can point to specific and articulable facts warranting the suspicion (such as repeatedly walking by a store after consulting with colleagues, exhibiting characteristics consistent with a bona fide drug courier profile, or running from the police in a high crime area); (b) receives information from an informant having some indicia of reliability (but not necessarily that required for probable cause) from which such a suspicion can be drawn; or (c) possesses information from the police department that the person is a suspect in a felony, which belief is based on specific and articulable facts. However, even reasonable suspicion is not required to justify requests to disembark from a car following a legal stop or orders to disperse pursuant to valid anti-loitering statutes (although the Court has yet to uphold such a statute).

(3)   If a stop is authorized by reasonable suspicion or a lesser level of suspicion, reasonable inquiries designed to test the suspicion may be made, including a request for identity; however, a separate finding of reasonable suspicion is required if the seizure becomes prolonged (e.g., extends beyond the time necessary to carry out duties incident to a traffic stop). If the officer reasonably believes after these inquiries or for other reasons that the person may be armed and presently dangerous, he may also frisk the person. Factors determining the reasonableness of the frisk include the type of criminal activity that is thought to be afoot, the person's reputation for dangerousness, visual clues as to the presence of a weapon, and suggestive movements by the suspect. Mere proximity to wanted persons is an insufficient ground for a frisk.

(4)   If a frisk is authorized, it may include not only a patdown of the person's outer clothing but also a search of the area immediately surrounding the person when there is a reasonable fear that it might contain an instrument of assault. Weapon-like objects may be removed. It is likely that containers so removed may be searched without a warrant. However, objects that do not initially feel like weapons may not be manipulated to determine their nature.

BIBLIOGRAPHY

American Law Institute. A Model Code of Pre-Arraignment Procedure. Philadelphia: American Law Institute, 1975. 110.2 commentary, pp. 262–303.

Bellin, Jeffrey. The Inverse Relationship Between the Constitutionality and Effectiveness of New York City's "Stop and Frisk." 94 B.U. L.Rev. 1495 (2014).

Butterfoss, Edwin. Bright Line Seizures: The Need for Clarity in Determining When Fourth Amendment Activity Begins. 79 J.Crim.L. & C. 437 (1988).

Clancy, Thomas K. Protective Searches, Pat-Downs, or Frisks?: The Scope of the Permissible Intrusion to Ascertain if a Detained Person is Armed. 82 Marq.L.Rev. 491 (1999).

Cloud, Morgan. Search and Seizure by the Numbers: The Drug Courier Profile and Judicial Review of Investigative Formulas. 65 B.U.L.Rev. 843 (1985).

Cooper, Frank Rudy. The Un-Balanced Fourth Amendment: A Cultural Study of the Drug War, Racial Profiling, and *Arvizu*. 47 Vill. L. Rev. 851 (2002).

Grunwald, Ben and Jeffrey Fagan. The End of Intuition-Based High Crime Areas. 107 California L. Rev. 345 (2019).

Harris, David A. Particularized Suspicion, Categorical Judgements: Supreme Court Rhetoric versus Lower Court Reality Under *Terry v. Ohio*. 72 St. John's L.Rev. 975, 988–1001 (1998).

____. Frisking Every Suspect: The Withering of *Terry*. 28 U.C. Davis L.Rev. 1 (1994).

Johnson, Sheri Lynn. Race and the Decision to Detain a Suspect. 93 Yale L.J. 214 (1983).

LaFave, Wayne R. Seizures Typology: Classifying Detentions of the Person to Resolve Warrant, Grounds, and Search Issues. 17 Univ.Mich.J.L.Ref. 417 (1984).

____. "Street Encounters" and the Constitution: *Terry, Sibron, Peters*, and Beyond. 67 Mich.L.Rev. 40 (1968).

Lerner, Craig S. Reasonable Suspicion and Mere Hunches. 59 Vand. L.Rev. 407 (2006).

Maclin, Tracey. "Black and Blue Encounters"—Some Preliminary Thoughts About Fourth Amendment Seizures: Should Race Matter? 26 Val.U.L.Rev. 243 (1991).

____. The Decline of the Right of Locomotion: The Fourth Amendment on the Streets. 75 Cornell L.Rev. 1258 (1990).

Miller, Eric J. Role-Based Policing: Restraining Police Conduct "Outside the Legitimate Investigative Sphere." 94 Calif.L.Rev. 617 (2006).

Raymond, Margaret. Down on the Corner: Out in the Street: Considering the Character of the Neighborhood in Evaluating Reasonable Suspicion. 60 Ohio St.L.J. 99, 115–124 (1999).

Richardson, L. Song. Police Efficiency and the Fourth Amendment. 87 Ind.L.J. 1143 (2012).

Rudstein, David S. White on *White*: Anonymous Tips, Reasonable Suspicion, and the Constitution. 79 Ky.L.J. 661 (1990–91).

Saltzburg, Stephen. *Terry v. Ohio*: A Practically Perfect Doctrine. 72 St. John's L.Rev. 911 (1998).

Slobogin, Christopher. Let's Not Bury *Terry*: A Call for Rejuvenation of the Proportionality Principle. 72 St. John's L. Rev. (1998).

Stulin, Jamie. Does *Hiibel* Redefine *Terry*?: The Latest Expansion of the *Terry* Doctrine and the Silent Impact of Terrorism on the Supreme Court's Decision to Compel Identification. 54 Am.U.L.Rev. 1449 (2005).

Symposium. Terry v. Ohio at Fifty: The Past, Present and Future of Stop and Frisk. 54 Idaho Law Review 279 (2018).

Chapter 12

CONSENT SEARCHES

12.01   Introduction

As early as 1921, the Supreme Court recognized that a valid consent waives the protections afforded by the Fourth Amendment.[1] The theory is that giving police permission to enter an area surrenders one's expectation of privacy in that area. Thus, a valid consent eliminates both the warrant and suspicion requirements.

This chapter discusses the elements of a valid *overt* consent. In a number of cases, the Supreme Court has sometimes used the language of consent in analyzing encounters with undercover agents, typically holding that the Fourth Amendment does not regulate such activity when its target voluntarily deals with the agent.[2] These cases are distinguishable from those discussed here for two reasons. First, despite the Court's characterization of undercover encounters as consensual, these cases have nothing to do with consent as that concept is normally understood, since the nature of what is being agreed upon is never made clear to the "consentor." Second, the central issue in the undercover cases is whether or not the Fourth Amendment should apply at all; thus, they are treated in the portion of this book dealing with that question.[3] Consent given to an identified officer, on the other hand, only obviates the need for a warrant or probable cause *if* other Fourth Amendment requirements are met. In particular, determining whether a consent is valid under the Fourth Amendment requires close attention to: (1) whether the consent is voluntary; (2) whether the search conforms to the consent given; and (3) whether the consentor had authority to give consent to the area searched.

12.02   The Voluntariness Requirement

If the police search an area over the owner's objection, then the owner has not surrendered her expectation of privacy. In *Schneckloth v. Bustamonte*,[4] the Supreme Court held that "the Fourth and Fourteenth Amendments require that a consent not be coerced, by explicit or implicit means, by implied threat or covert force." *Schneckloth* went on to define voluntariness in terms of the same "totality of the circumstances" analysis that the Court had already adopted in confession cases.[5] According to the Court, by looking at the "surrounding circumstances" of the consent, including the impact of "subtly coercive police questions" and the "possibly vulnerable subjective state of the person who consents," invalid searches can "be filtered out without undermining the continuing validity of consent searches." The following discussion looks at various circumstances that might affect this analysis.

---

[1]   *Amos v. United States*, 255 U.S. 313, 41 S.Ct. 266 (1921).

[2]   See e.g., *On Lee v. United States*, 343 U.S. 747, 72 S.Ct. 967 (1952) (no search, since agent entered defendant's laundry with defendant's "consent"); *Gouled v. United States*, 255 U.S. 298, 41 S.Ct. 261 (1921) (search, because defendant only "consented" to agent entering home, not rummaging through drawers).

[3]   See § 4.03(a).

[4]   412 U.S. 218, 93 S.Ct. 2041 (1973).

[5]   See § 16.02(a).

(a) Knowledge of the Right

In *Johnson v. Zerbst*,[6] the Supreme Court held that, at least when constitutional rights are involved, a waiver "is ordinarily an intentional relinquishment or abandonment of a known right or privilege." Thus, for instance, the Court has held that a person in custody must be told he has a right to remain silent and a right to have an attorney present during questioning, or any statement he makes will be the product of an invalid waiver.[7] This warning is meant to inform the person of his rights under the Fifth and Sixth Amendments. One of the more controversial issues in the consent search area is whether the prosecution must show that the defendant knew of his right to refuse consent. Must a consent to search be "knowing," or is "voluntariness" the sole standard? Even if voluntariness is the standard, does it make any sense to say that a consent is voluntary when the person giving that consent was unaware of the right to refuse?

Early decisions of the Court suggested it might adopt a voluntary and knowing standard. In *Johnson v. United States*,[8] for instance, the Court held a consent invalid because it "was granted in submission to authority rather than as an understanding and intentional waiver of a constitutional right." But in *Schneckloth* the Court held that knowledge of the right to refuse consent is only one of the circumstances to be considered in the totality of the circumstances analysis. The Court gave three reasons for holding that "the prosecution is not required to demonstrate such knowledge as a prerequisite to establishing a voluntary consent." First, the need to show the consenting party was aware of his rights would "create serious doubt whether consent searches could continue to be conducted" in light of the difficulty of proving such awareness. Second, trying to eradicate this difficulty by imposing a requirement on the police to warn prospective targets of their right, as the Court had done in the confession context with its warnings requirement in *Miranda v. Arizona*,[9] "would be thoroughly impractical." Consent searches:

> normally occur on the highway, or in a person's home or office, and under informal and unstructured conditions. The circumstances that prompt the initial request to search may develop quickly or be a logical extension of investigative police questioning. The police may seek to investigate further suspicious circumstances or to follow up leads developed in questioning persons at the scene of a crime. These situations are a far cry from the structured atmosphere of a trial where, assisted by counsel if he chooses, a defendant is informed of his trial rights ... And, while surely a closer question, these situations are still immeasurably far removed from "custodial interrogation" where, in *Miranda v. Arizona*, we found that the Constitution required certain now familiar warnings as a prerequisite to police interrogation.

As a third reason for not requiring knowledge of the right to refuse consent, the Court stated that the *Zerbst* standard for waiver applies only "to those rights guaranteed to a criminal defendant to insure ... a fair criminal trial," and thus does not extend to the protections of the Fourth Amendment, which "are of a wholly different order, and have

---

[6]   304 U.S. 458, 58 S.Ct. 1019 (1938).

[7]   *Miranda v. Arizona*, 384 U.S. 436, 86 S.Ct. 1602 (1966). See also, *United States v. Wade*, 388 U.S. 218, 87 S.Ct. 1926 (1967) (counsel at pretrial lineups); *Patton v. United States*, 281 U.S. 276, 50 S.Ct. 253 (1930) (jury trial).

[8]   333 U.S. 10, 68 S.Ct. 367 (1948).

[9]   384 U.S. 436, 86 S.Ct. 1602 (1966), discussed in § 16.02(d).

nothing whatever to do with promoting the fair ascertainment of truth at a criminal trial."

Schneckloth's distinction between Fourth Amendment protections and other rights accorded defendants is questionable. A simple warning can easily be given to those the police wish to search, as the experience of the F.B.I. and the Bureau of Narcotics and Dangerous Drugs bears out.[10] More importantly, the Court's willingness to treat the privacy interests protected by the Fourth Amendment as inferior to the interests protected by the Fifth and Sixth Amendments is suspect as a matter of constitutional interpretation, since neither the language nor the history of the Bill of Rights suggests any such hierarchy.[11]

Nonetheless, the Court expanded *Schneckloth's* holding in *Ohio v. Robinette*.[12] There, after giving a person stopped for speeding a verbal warning and handing him back his license, the officer stated: "One question before you get gone: are you carrying any illegal contraband in your car? Any weapons of any kind, drugs, anything like that?" The Ohio Supreme Court held that the defendant's subsequent consent to search the car was invalid because he had not been told he was free to go once his license was handed back.[13] Eight members of the Court held, however, that "just as it 'would be thoroughly impractical to impose on the normal consent search the detailed requirements of an effective warning' [citing *Schneckloth*], so too would it be unrealistic to require police officers to always inform detainees that they are free to go before a consent to search may be deemed involuntary." Instead, as *Schneckloth* held, the voluntariness of a consent is to be evaluated in the totality of the circumstances, with the dialogue between officer and detainee being one such circumstance.

It should be re-emphasized that, even after *Schneckloth*, the subject's knowledge of his right to refuse consent remains a crucial factor to be considered in determining the validity of a consent. Thus, in *United States v. Mendenhall*,[14] the Supreme Court judged "highly relevant" the fact that the defendant had twice been told of her right to refuse consent, and found the defendant's acquiescence to the search of her handbag and person voluntary. Conversely, in *Rosenthall v. Henderson*,[15] a lower court case decided before *Schneckloth*, the failure to give such a warning was found relevant to a finding of involuntariness.

(b) Custody

Schneckloth suggested, in dictum, that an arrested person may be under more duress than one who is not, and thus more likely to feel coerced into consenting. This observation, combined with the admission in *Schneckloth* that, however "impractical" they are otherwise, warnings are possible in the "structured" setting following a custodial arrest, suggested that the Court might find that an unwarned person who has been arrested cannot give a valid consent. But three years later, in *United States v. Watson*,[16] the Court found valid the consent of a person who was arrested on a public

---

[10]   See commentary to ALI Model Code of Pre-Arraignment § 240.2(2), at 532–37.

[11]   See Lloyd L. Weinreb, *Generalities of the Fourth Amendment*, 42 U.Chi.L.Rev. 47 (1974).

[12]   519 U.S. 33, 117 S.Ct. 417 (1996).

[13]   *State v. Robinette*, 73 Ohio St.3d 650, 653 N.E.2d 695 (1995).

[14]   446 U.S. 544, 100 S.Ct. 1870 (1980).

[15]   389 F.2d 514 (6th Cir. 1968).

[16]   423 U.S. 411, 96 S.Ct. 820 (1976).

street and then asked if his car could be searched. The police did tell the individual that anything they found could be used against him, but did not state that he had a right to refuse consent. And in a pre-*Schneckloth* case, *Davis v. United States*,[17] the Court found that the agreement of a filling station owner, after an initial objection, to unlock a room and allow police to search for rationing coupons was a valid consent, even though he was under arrest at the time and not warned.

These cases present an interesting contrast to *Miranda* and its progeny, which rely on the assumption that arrest is "inherently coercive" and require warnings about the right to remain silent to counteract this coercive atmosphere.[18] While these two lines of cases seem inconsistent, they might be reconciled on the ground that, while police do not have to ask if they can interrogate a suspect, they do have to ask if they can search, signaling that refusal is possible. Furthermore, of course, *Schneckloth* made clear that the Fourth Amendment is at the bottom of the rights hierarchy.

(c) Force, Show of Force and Threats

As noted above, *Schneckloth* concluded that a consent is not valid if "coerced, by explicit or implicit means, by implied threat or covert force." *Schneckloth* itself did not provide an indication of how the Court would construe this language, since there the consent was clearly voluntary. In that case, a police officer lawfully stopped a car with six occupants. To his request to search the car, the brother of the absent owner of the car responded "Sure, go ahead" and even assisted the police in opening the glove compartment and trunk. The consentor apparently had nothing to hide, since the car was not his and the evidence subsequently found was used against another occupant of the car.

Of course, use of direct threats of physical violence ("Consent or else . . . ") will render consent involuntary. The same appears to be true of a threat of criminal punishment. In *Birchfield v. North Dakota*,[19] the Court held that consent to a blood test by a motorist arrested for drunken driving is invalid if given after being told that a refusal to take the test would result in a criminal penalty. However, the Court has also held that telling a driver that a refusal will result in losing one's driver's license or be used at trial to prove a DUI offense does not vitiate a subsequent consent.[20]

In earlier cases, the Court seemed willing to construe "coercion" quite broadly beyond physical coercion or threats of criminal punishment. In *Amos v. United States*,[21] for instance, two government agents showed up at the defendant's home, identified themselves to his wife, and told her they had come to search the premises "for violations of the revenue laws." Recounting nothing but these facts, the Court found her consent to their subsequent search involuntary, stating simply that "under the implied coercion here presented, no such waiver was intended or effected."

Similarly, in *Johnson v. United States*,[22] the Court held that coercion exists when the police, lacking the requisite warrant or suspicion, announce they are going to search.

---

[17]   328 U.S. 582, 66 S.Ct. 1256 (1946).

[18]   See § 16.02(d)(1).

[19]   ___ U.S. ___, 136 S.Ct. 2160 (2016).

[20]   *South Dakota v. Neville*, 459 U.S. 553, 103 S.Ct. 916 (1983).

[21]   255 U.S. 313, 41 S.Ct. 266 (1921).

[22]   333 U.S. 10, 68 S.Ct. 367 (1948).

A somewhat more subtle situation was presented in *Bumper v. North Carolina*,[23] where the Supreme Court found invalid the consent of the defendant's grandmother, a 66-year-old African-American widow, to a search of her house after four white police officers appeared at her door and announced they had a search warrant. The primary ground for the Court's conclusion was that the officers' "show of authority" coerced the consent. As Justice Stewart stated for the Court, "[w]hen a law enforcement officer claims authority to search a home under a warrant, he announces in effect that the occupant has no right to resist the search. The situation is instinct with coercion." On the other hand, in *Coolidge v. New Hampshire*,[24] where the police came to the defendant's house merely to ask his wife questions and she volunteered to procure items that they wanted, no coercion was found.

United States v. Mendenhall[25] is a more recent example of how the Court has applied the totality of the circumstances analysis to situations where no direct force or threat is involved. In *Mendenhall*, officers of the Drug Enforcement Administration posted at the Detroit airport to check for signs of narcotics trafficking observed several aspects of the defendant's conduct that suggested to them she might be carrying narcotics. They approached her, identified themselves, and asked her to produce identification and her plane ticket. After examining both, the agents questioned her as to why the ticket was in another name, to which she responded that she "just felt like using that name." Their suspicions were further aroused when she told them that she had been in California only two days, and they were strengthened again when she began shaking and became somewhat incoherent after one agent told her that he was a federal narcotics agent. Asked to accompany the agents for further questioning to the DEA office located elsewhere in the airport, Mendenhall walked with them to the office. There she was asked if she would allow them to search her person and handbag. Although she was told that she could decline, she agreed. A search of the handbag yielded another ticket in a third name. A female police officer, assigned to search Mendenhall further, again asked if she consented. Although Mendenhall stated she had a plane to catch, she agreed to the search. After partially disrobing, she handed over two packages of heroin.

The Court examined both the consent to accompany the officers to the DEA office and the consent to the searches conducted there. As to the voluntariness of the first consent, the Court noted that Mendenhall was not *told* that she had to go to the office but rather was simply *asked* if she would accompany the officers. "There were neither threats nor any show of force." The Court also pointed out that the initial questioning by the narcotics agents had been brief. The Court dismissed Mendenhall's argument that, as a 22 year-old black female who had not graduated from high school, she felt unusually threatened by the officers, who were white males. "While these factors were not irrelevant . . . neither were they decisive, and the totality of the evidence in this case was plainly adequate to support the District Court's finding that the respondent voluntarily consented to accompany the officers to the DEA office." Turning to an analysis of the consent to have her handbag and her person searched, the Court was most impressed with the fact that the agents twice told Mendenhall she was free to decline to consent to those searches. As noted earlier, the Court termed this fact "highly relevant" to its conclusion that the consents were voluntary. It also refused to view Mendenhall's

---

[23]　391 U.S. 543, 88 S.Ct. 1788 (1968).

[24]　403 U.S. 443, 91 S.Ct. 2022 (1971).

[25]　446 U.S. 544, 100 S.Ct. 1870 (1980).

statement that she had a plane to catch as evidence of resistance to the body search, but rather agreed with the District Court that this statement could be seen simply as an expression that the search be conducted quickly.

Mendenhall suggests that, in determining whether a consent is voluntary, the Court is reluctant to consider subtly coercive factors that may play on the individual who is confronted by government officials or to attribute importance to *non*verbal responses, such as "shaking" or incoherence, that may indicate some degree of intimidation. As the four dissenters in *Mendenhall* pointed out: "On the record before us, the Court's conclusion can only be based on the notion that consent can be assumed from the absence of proof that a suspect resisted police authority."

The lower courts have dealt with a number of situations involving subtle and not so subtle forms of coercion. Representative is *United States v. Whitlock*,[26] in which the defendant was approached at gun point, handcuffed and escorted to his apartment where he was surrounded by five drug enforcement agents. The federal District Court found that, given these circumstances of "surprise, confusion and fright," the consent was involuntary.[27] However, on substantially similar facts, the Virginia Supreme Court found consent voluntary.[28] The crucial distinction appeared to be that in this case the defendant had been told he had the right to refuse.

The lower courts have also invalidated consents that are the product of verbal threats. In *Jones v. Unknown Agents of the Federal Election Commission*,[29] the defendant's consent was found involuntary because an FEC official had threatened him with 10 years in jail, a $10,000 fine, and the possibility of losing his house if he did not turn over incriminating evidence. In *Lightford v. State*,[30] the suggestion by one of several officers detaining the defendant that they kick in the defendant's door if he did not produce the key to it was found unconstitutionally coercive.

(d) Personal Characteristics

Schneckloth noted that, in determining the validity of a consent, the "traditional definition of voluntariness we accept today has always taken into account evidence of minimal schooling [and] low intelligence." The Court also mentioned age as a consideration in totality of the circumstances analysis. Lower courts have also considered these factors important,[31] and have indicated that illiteracy,[32] substance abuse,[33] emotional state,[34] and difficulty with the English language[35] are pertinent as well. Presumably, the same variables found relevant in confessions cases will be relevant here.[36] *Mendenhall* seems to indicate that, as far as the Court is concerned, these factors

---

[26]   418 F.Supp. 138 (E.D.Mich. 1976), aff'd 556 F.2d 583 (6th Cir. 1977).

[27]   See also, *Rodriquez v. State*, 262 Ark. 659, 559 S.W.2d 925 (1978) (consent invalid when defendant surrounded by police officers).

[28]   *Lowe v. Commonwealth*, 218 Va. 670, 239 S.E.2d 112 (1977), cert. denied 435 U.S. 930, 98 S.Ct. 1502 (1978).

[29]   613 F.2d 864 (D.C.Cir. 1979), cert. denied 444 U.S. 1074, 100 S.Ct. 1019 (1980).

[30]   90 Nev. 136, 520 P.2d 955 (1974).

[31]   See, e.g., *United States v. Mayes*, 552 F.2d 729 (6th Cir. 1977) (age and immaturity).

[32]   *Suggars v. State*, 520 S.W.2d 364 (Tenn.Crim.App. 1974).

[33]   *United States v. Leland*, 376 F.Supp. 1193 (D.Del. 1974).

[34]   *People v. Gonzalez*, 39 N.Y.2d 122, 383 N.Y.S.2d 215, 347 N.E.2d 575 (1976).

[35]   *United States v. Wai Lau*, 215 F.Supp. 684 (S.D.N.Y. 1963).

[36]   See § 16.02(a)(2).

must have a significant effect on the defendant's ability to consent voluntarily before they will result in a finding that waiver was invalid.

A separate issue is whether a waiver that is subsequently established to be involuntary due to some dysfunction is nonetheless valid if the police could not have recognized the problem under the circumstances. One might conclude that if a personal trait renders consent truly involuntary, then the fact that the police could not reasonably have discerned its effect should be irrelevant.[37] In such an instance, the person has not actually surrendered any expectation of privacy. But, as discussed below, the Supreme Court has found third party consents valid even when the third party does not have actual authority to consent, so long as it reasonably *appears* the third party has authority.[38] And, in the confession context, the Court has held that the confession of a mentally ill individual is "voluntary" so long as police do not recognize and exploit the illness in their attempts to obtain information.[39] These decisions flow from the premise that the Constitution is meant to impose constraints on the police, not protect individual rights in situations where the police could not have been deterred by a constitutional ruling.

12.03   The Scope of a Consent Search

The scope of a search conducted pursuant to a consent is governed by the nature of the consent. If a person consents to a search of area X but specifically denies access to area Y, the police may not search area Y on authority of the consent. On the other hand, *any* articles within area X may be examined, if it is "objectively reasonable" for the officer to believe that the scope of the person's consent permits him to do so. This was the holding of *Florida v. Jimeno*,[40] which involved a search of a folded, brown paper bag on the floorboard of a car after the driver had told police they could search the car. Although the driver later contended that he had meant to consent only to a search of the visible interior of the vehicle and not closed containers within it, the Supreme Court pointed out that the consent came after the officer had informed the defendant that he believed the defendant was carrying narcotics. Under these circumstances, the Court concluded, 7–2, that the officer was reasonable in assuming that the consent authorized search of any items within the car that might contain drugs. The Court distinguished this situation from one in which the defendant consents to search of a trunk, where the police find a locked briefcase and pry it open. In the latter instance, the Court stated, "[i]t is very likely unreasonable" to believe the person consented to search of the briefcase (apparently even if the person knew the police were looking for drugs).[41]

If the officer in *Jimeno* had obtained consent based on a representation that he wanted to look for weapons instead found drugs in an area where weapons would not normally be placed, a different result might be reached. In *State v. Gonzales*,[42] for

---

[37]   See, e.g., *United States v. Elrod*, 441 F.2d 353 (5th Cir. 1971).

[38]   See *Illinois v. Rodriguez*, 497 U.S. 177, 110 S.Ct. 2793 (1990), discussed in § 12.04.

[39]   *Colorado v. Connelly*, 479 U.S. 157, 107 S.Ct. 515 (1986).

[40]   500 U.S. 248, 111 S.Ct. 1801 (1991).

[41]   Compare *United States v. Pena*, 920 F.2d 1509 (10th Cir. 1990) (consent to search for drugs in car authorized tapping of external fender and probing of rear door panel after officer observed loose, crooked and missing screws); *United States v. Lechuga*, 925 F.2d 1035 (7th Cir. 1991) (consent to search for drugs in apartment authorized search of suitcase in closet).

[42]   46 Wash.App. 388, 731 P.2d 1101 (1986). See also, *Graves v. Beto*, 424 F.2d 524 (5th Cir. 1970) (consent to take blood sample for purpose of determining alcohol content not admissible to establish identity in a rape case).

instance, a Washington appellate court held that a person's consent to search his residence for stolen jewelry, radios, and equipment did not contemplate a search which turned up marijuana in a paper bag. On the other hand, if a consent search is limited to intrusion into those areas that a reasonable person would assume is covered by the consent, then the mere fact that the police find in plain view items other than those contemplated by the police or the consentor usually should not render the search illegal. More questionably, the Supreme Court is likely to subscribe to this position even if the police act pretextually—that is, even if they ask for consent to search for item X when in fact they wish to obtain item Y and then discover Y.[43]

A second issue regarding the scope of a consent search is whether it can be modified after consent is given. The American Law Institute's Model Code of Pre-Arraignment Procedure would permit the withdrawal or limitation of consent at any time prior to the completion of the search.[44] Although noting that caselaw on the issue is scanty and divided, the Reporters for the Code felt that the reasoning behind the decisions permitting withdrawal of a waiver to police questioning[45] supported a similar rule in the consent search context. The analogy to confessions seems appropriate in light of *Schneckloth's* use of the voluntariness standard employed in confession cases.

Some courts have also recognized what could be called "constructive withdrawal." For instance, in *State v. Brochu*,[46] the Maine Supreme Court held that a defendant's consent to search of his house for evidence concerning his wife's murder did not survive his subsequent arrest for that crime; the court noted that when he consented the defendant was still in the role of a husband assisting the police in investigating his wife's death, not a suspect. Accordingly, a second search the day following his arrest was not authorized by the consent.

In *Thompson v. Louisiana*[47] the Supreme Court appeared to endorse the idea of constructive withdrawal. Mrs. Thompson called her daughter to tell her that Mr. Thompson was dead and that she had swallowed some pills but no longer wanted to commit suicide. The daughter summoned police to the defendant's home, let them in, and showed them the location of Mrs. Thompson and her husband. Some 35 minutes after deputies had transported the defendant to the hospital, two members of the homicide squad arrived to conduct a follow-up investigation, which they termed a "general exploratory search for evidence of crime." During this second entry, the police found evidence that helped prove Mrs. Thompson had killed her husband. While the Court sanctioned the initial entry on a combination emergency/consent ground, it invalidated the subsequent search, which had not been authorized by a warrant. The Court stated that the defendant's "call for help can hardly be seen as an invitation to the general public that would have converted her home into the sort of public place for which no warrant to search would be necessary."

12.04   Third Party Consent

In most of the consent search cases that have reached the Supreme Court, the consent to search was not given by the person against whom the evidence was used. In

---

[43]   See discussion of pretextual searches in § 10.04.

[44]   ALI Model Code of Pre-Arraignment Procedure § 240.3(3) (1975).

[45]   See cases discussed in § 16.03(e)(1) & (2).

[46]   237 A.2d 418 (Me. 1967).

[47]   469 U.S. 17, 105 S.Ct. 409 (1984).

Schneckloth, the car search that produced evidence against the defendant was authorized by another passenger, whose absent brother owned the car. In *Coolidge v. New Hampshire*,[48] consent was given by the wife of the defendant. And, although the consent in *Bumper v. North Carolina*[49] was ultimately found invalid on involuntariness grounds, the Court never questioned the authority of the defendant's grandmother to consent to a search of her house.

These decisions flow from the Court's view of the scope of the Fourth Amendment. Originally, that scope was defined by property concepts. Thus, if a person owned or had a significant possessory interest in the area in question, he could consent to its search. Although the majority opinion in *Katz v. United States*[50] later rejected a property-based understanding of the Fourth Amendment, stating that the Amendment "protects people, not places," Justice Harlan's concurring opinion in that case averring that discussion about Fourth Amendment protection usually requires reference to a place has dominated subsequent Court decisionmaking.[51] The Court's post-*Katz* focus on "reasonable expectations of privacy" in the area searched has meant that when a place is shared by more than one person, more than one person may consent to its search. Thus, once again, the Fourth Amendment is treated differently than the right to remain silent or the right to counsel, neither of which can be waived by a third party.[52]

The property-based rationale for this view is reflected in several cases pre-dating *Katz*. For instance, in *Chapman v. United States*,[53] the Court held invalid a consent by a landlord of a tenant's home, despite the state's claim that a landlord has authority to view premises that are being "wasted and used for criminal purposes." The Court was unable to find any state or common law "holding that a landlord, in the absence of an express covenant so permitting, has a right forcibly to enter the demised premises without the consent of the tenant 'to view waste.' " And in *Stoner v. California*,[54] consent by a hotel clerk of a room in the hotel was found insufficient because a guest can surrender his Fourth Amendment right only "directly or through an agent" and there was nothing in the record to indicate that "the night clerk had been authorized by the petitioner to permit the police to search the petitioner's room."

After *Katz*, the Court's cases began analyzing third party consent cases in terms of reasonable expectations concerning the searched area. For example, in *Frazier v. Cupp*,[55] the Court upheld a consent by the defendant's cousin to search a duffel bag that both of them used and that had been left in the cousin's house, because the defendant had "assumed the risk that [the cousin] would allow someone else to look inside." And in *United States v. Matlock*[56] the Court firmly discarded a property-based view of third party consents in favor of an analysis asking whether the third party possesses "common authority or other sufficient relationship to the premises or property or effects sought to be inspected." In a footnote the Court explained:

---

[48]   403 U.S. 443, 91 S.Ct. 2022 (1971).

[49]   391 U.S. 543, 88 S.Ct. 1788 (1968).

[50]   389 U.S. 347, 88 S.Ct. 507 (1967).

[51]   See § 4.03 for further discussion of this development.

[52]   See § 15.05 (right to remain silent); § 31.04(b) (right to counsel).

[53]   365 U.S. 610, 81 S.Ct. 776 (1961).

[54]   376 U.S. 483, 84 S.Ct. 889 (1964).

[55]   394 U.S. 731, 89 S.Ct. 1420 (1969).

[56]   415 U.S. 164, 94 S.Ct. 988 (1974).

Common authority, is of course, not to be implied from the mere property interest a third party has in the property. The authority which justifies the third-party consent does not rest upon the law of property, with its attendant historical and legal refinements, but rests rather on mutual use of the property by persons generally having joint access or control for most purposes, so that it is reasonable to recognize that any of the coinhabitants has the right to permit the inspection in his own right and that the others have assumed the risk that one of their number might permit the common area to be searched.

The Court's application of this language to the facts of *Matlock* is instructive. There, the defendant was arrested in the front yard of a house in which he lived with several others. Instead of asking the defendant if they could search his room, the police proceeded to the house, where they were admitted by a Mrs. Graff, one of the other tenants. Although she later denied that she acted voluntarily, Mrs. Graff consented to a search of the house, including the bedroom which she said she shared with the defendant. There, in a closet on the floor, the police found incriminating evidence in a diaper bag. The Court assumed Mrs. Graff's consent was voluntary and found it sufficient authorization for the search, because she had "common authority" over the searched area. The Court did not consider whether she had common authority over the diaper bag, presumably because, as it had stated in response to the defendant's argument in *Frazier* that his cousin had access to only part of the duffel bag, "[w]e will not . . . engage in such metaphysical subtleties." Based on the Court's treatment of the facts in *Matlock*, it appears that if the state can establish that the third party shares an area with another more or less equally,[57] that party's consent authorizes a search of the entire area.[58] Thus, the common authority test, to the extent it differs from the property-agency theory earlier endorsed by the Court, probably broadens the scope of third party consent.

The Court's finding in *Matlock* that Mrs. Graff possessed actual authority over the bedroom meant that the Court did not reach the government's further contention in that case that a third party consent should be deemed valid whenever the searching officers reasonably believe that the party has such authority, whether or not it actually exists. When given the opportunity to consider this so-called "apparent authority" doctrine, in *Illinois v. Rodriguez*,[59] six members of the Court voted to adopt it. In *Rodriguez*, police obtained evidence used to convict the defendant after his ex-girlfriend let them into his apartment with her key. Prior to the search she referred to the premises as "our" apartment and said she had clothes and furniture there. In fact, however, she had moved out of the apartment almost a month earlier, taking with her most of her belongings; since that time she had visited Rodriguez infrequently, never invited her friends there, and never went there herself when he was not at home. On these facts, both the lower courts and the Supreme Court held that she had no actual authority to consent to a

---

[57]   Note that when the third party's authority over a place is clearly inferior, as in *Chapman* and *Stoner*, then the consent is not valid. The same should hold true of an area within premises that is clearly within the exclusive control of the defendant. See, e.g., *United States v. Heisman*, 503 F.2d 1284 (8th Cir. 1974) (consent by one tenant not valid as to another tenant's room).

[58]   Some courts appear to stretch even this broad rule a bit far. See, e.g., *United States v. Clutter*, 914 F.2d 775 (6th Cir. 1990) (children 12 and 14 years of age could consent to search of bedroom occupied by their mother and her male companion since they "were routinely left in exclusive control of the house.").

[59]   497 U.S. 177, 110 S.Ct. 2793 (1990).

search of the apartment. But the Court then held that this conclusion did not necessarily invalidate the search.

According to Justice Scalia, who wrote the Court's opinion, the question to be addressed in such cases is whether the facts available to the officer warranted "a man of reasonable caution in the belief that the consenting party had authority over the premises." This rule is justified, he asserted, because the Fourth Amendment does not require that factual determinations made by magistrates or police be correct, but only that they be reasonable. However, Scalia also cautioned that "[e]ven when the invitation is accompanied by an explicit assertion that the person lives there, the surrounding circumstances could conceivably be such that a reasonable person would doubt its truth and not act upon it without further inquiry." The case was remanded for consideration in light of these points.[60]

One justification for the third party consent doctrine is that the autonomy of the third party would be undermined if his consent is ignored.[61] However, when the third party lacks *actual* authority, as might have been the case in *Rodriguez*, the third party's autonomy interest is not implicated. Furthermore, as Justice Marshall pointed out in dissent, third party consent searches are usually not conducted under exigent circumstances. Thus, when the police fail to get a warrant, instead relying on the consent of a third party who may not have authority to consent, arguably the police, rather than the defendant, should "accept the risk of error."

The one situation where police may not act on a consent from a third party with actual authority is when the defendant (or another occupant of the area) is present and refuses consent. In *Georgia v. Randolph*,[62] police came to Randolph's house after his estranged wife called from there to complain that he had taken their son and left the house. Randolph soon returned and told police where his son was; once police had secured the boy and returned with him, the wife volunteered that there were "items of drug evidence" in the house. When police asked Randolph if they could search the premises, he refused; his wife, however, was willing to consent. Justice Souter, in an opinion for five members of the Court, held that Randolph's refusal trumped his wife's consent. Stressing the significance of "widely shared social expectations" to Fourth Amendment analysis, he asserted that "[w]ithout some very good reason, no sensible person would go inside under those conditions." Souter also relied on property law, pointing to the "want of any recognized superior authority among disagreeing tenants."

Justice Roberts, joined by Justices Scalia and Thomas, disputed the majority's reliance on social expectations, noting that "slight variations in the fact pattern" (e.g., two consentors, one refuser; an invitation from a friend countered by a refusal from an unknown roommate) "yield vastly different expectations about whether the invitee might be expected to enter or to go away." He also emphasized, as had *Matlock*, that once one shares space with another individual, privacy has been surrendered: "What the majority's rule protects is not so much privacy as the good luck of a co-owner who just happens to be present at the door when the police arrive." He noted that both *Matlock*,

---

    60   Compare *State v. Penn*, 61 Ohio St.3d 720, 576 N.E.2d 790 (1991) (police would not reasonably believe pharmacist had authority to consent to search of pharmacy when they were "on notice" that he had terminated his employment there four days earlier).

    61   See Mary Irene Coombs, *Shared Privacy and the Fourth Amendment, or the Rights of Relationships*, 75 Cal. L.Rev. 1593, 1642–44 (1987).

    62   547 U.S. 103, 126 S.Ct. 1515 (2006).

where the defendant was in a police car on the street, and *Rodriguez*, where the defendant was asleep in the apartment that police entered, were still good law. Finally, Roberts pointed out that, under the Court's rule, the objecting co-owner was likely to destroy evidence and inflict retribution on the consenting individual once the police leave. While Souter had suggested that the police would not need unopposed consent to intervene where there are "exigent circumstances," Roberts argued that cognizable exigency may not always exist in potential domestic abuse situations and other common scenarios.

Fernandez v. California[63] involved just such a domestic altercation. Police chasing a robbery suspect tracked him to an apartment building and heard screams coming from one of the apartments. The woman who answered the apartment door appeared to be battered and bleeding, but when police indicated they wanted to conduct a protective sweep the defendant came to the door and objected. Police identified him as the robbery suspect, arrested him and took him to the police station. When they returned to the apartment, the woman consented to a search. The Supreme Court held, 6–3, that the consent was valid. While repeating *Randolph's* admonition that consent by one occupant might not be valid if police have removed a potentially objecting occupant, Justice Alito's opinion concluded that this dictum did not apply when the objecting occupant is legitimately arrested. Applying *Randolph's* "widely shared social expectations" formulation, Alito asserted that the woman's relatives and others would not have felt obligated to abide by the absent defendant's objection, and the police should not have to do so either.

In dissent, Justice Ginsburg argued that, even if third parties would feel free to enter the premises under such circumstances, they would not rummage through the house looking for evidence as the police did. She emphasized that the proper conduct by the police in this case would have been to obtain a warrant based on the same probable cause that led to the arrest. As Justice Alito noted, however, probable cause to arrest may not equate with probable cause to search and, in any event, the point of consent doctrine is to obviate the warrant requirement. Furthermore, if, as suggested above, the third party doctrine is meant to honor the third party's autonomy, that person's decision about whether a place over which the person has actual control can be searched should be just as valid as the defendant's, where or not he is present.

12.05   Conclusion

The principal tenets of the consent search exception to the warrant requirement can be described as follows:

(1) In order for a consent to be valid it must be voluntary under the totality of the circumstances test developed in confessions cases. In determining whether a consent is voluntary, one of the factors that may be considered is whether the consentor knew of his right to refuse the search, but failure of the police to apprize the consentor of this right is not an automatic ground for exclusion of the evidence. Other factors that might impinge upon the voluntariness decision are (a) whether the consentor was in custody at the time of consent; (b) the extent to which police used force, shows of force or threats, including threats of a criminal penalty upon refusal, to obtain the consent; (c) whether police claimed to have authority to conduct a search; and (d) the extent to which the

---

[63]   571 U.S. 292, 134 S.Ct. 1126 (2014).

consentor, due to personal characteristics, found it particularly difficult to resist police suggestions.

(2)   The scope of a consent search can be limited by the consentor to specific areas or types of items. Theoretically, at least, the consent search may be terminated at any time by the consentor. In either case, however, the nature of the consent is governed by what an "objectively reasonable" police officer would believe under the circumstances, not by the subjective beliefs of the consentor or the officer.

(3)   In general, the voluntary consent of a person who shares authority over an area more or less equally with another party will authorize a search of that area and seizure of property within it, unless the other party is present and refuses consent. Also valid is a voluntary consent by anyone whom the police reasonably believe possess such actual authority.

BIBLIOGRAPHY

Bookspan, Phyllis. Reworking the Warrant Requirement: Resuscitating the Fourth Amendment. 44 Vand. L.Rev. 473 (1991).

Coombs, Mary. Shared Privacy and the Fourth Amendment, or the Rights of Relationships. 75 Calif.L.Rev. 1593 (1987).

Donahoe, Diana R. Not So Great Expectations: Implicit Racial Bias in the Supreme Court's Consent to Search Doctrine. 55 Am. Crim. L. Rev. 619 (2018).

Gardner, Martin. Consent as a Bar to Fourth Amendment Scope: A Critique of a Common Theory. 71 J.Crim.L. and Criminol. 443 (1980).

Lassiter, Christo. Consent to Search by Ignorant People. 39 Tex. Tech.L.Rev. 1171 (2007).

Maclin, Tracey. The Good News and the Bad News About Consent Searches in the Supreme Court. 39 McGeorge L. Rev. 27 (2008).

Nadler, Janice. No Need to Shout: Bus Sweeps and the Psychology of Coercion. 2002 Sup.Ct. Rev. 153.

Rausch-Chabot, Meagan. The Home as Their Castle: An Analysis of *Randolph v. Georgia*'s Implications for Domestic Disputes. 30 Harv. J. L. & Gender 37 (2007).

Simmons, Ric. Not "Voluntary" But Still Reasonable: A New Paradigm for Understanding the Consent Searches Doctrine. 80 Ind. L.J. 773 (2005).

Sommers, Roseanna and Vanessa K. Bohms. The Voluntariness of Voluntary Consent: Consent Searches and the Psychology of Compliance. 128 Yale L.J. 1962 (2019).

Stuntz, William J. Waiving Rights in Criminal Procedure. 75 Va.L.Rev. 761 (1989).

Ward, Robert V. Consenting to a Search and Seizure in Poor and Minority Neighborhoods: No Place for a "Reasonable Person". 36 How. L.J. 239 (1993).

Williams, Daniel R. Misplaced Angst: Another Look at Consent-Search Jurisprudence. 82 Ind. L.J. 69 (2007).

Chapter 13

REGULATORY INSPECTIONS AND SEARCHES

13.01   Introduction

Federal and state governments have established a vast array of regulatory schemes designed to monitor the activities of their constituents, ranging from highway license checks and safety inspections of residential and commercial buildings to border patrols and school disciplinary rules. Although differentiating precisely between regulatory searches and other searches is difficult, all of these actions share two features: (1) their predominant objective is to procure evidence for "administrative" purposes rather than aid prosecution for serious crime (although sometimes evidence of serious crime is discovered in plain view during such searches); and (2) they are usually conducted either by officials other than the police or by police who are carrying out some function other than investigation of a particular crime.

The Supreme Court has recognized that many of these regulatory efforts can result in significant intrusions on personal privacy or autonomy, and thus has usually held that they implicate the Fourth Amendment. At the same time, the Court has been willing to relax the typical warrant and probable cause requirements in virtually all of the regulatory situations it has confronted. In doing so, the Court has relied on a balancing analysis first developed in *Camara v. Municipal Court*.[1] In that case, dealing with residential health and safety inspections, the Court concluded that "there can be no ready test for determining reasonableness other than by balancing the need to search against the invasion which the search entails."

In applying the *Camara* invasion-versus-need balancing test to regulatory inspections, the Court has looked at several factors. On the individual side of the balance, the Court has emphasized the lesser intrusion involved when the government's motivation is regulatory rather than investigative. On the government side, it has pointed to one or more of the following factors: (1) the difficulty of detecting the harm caused by regulatory violations if a warrant and probable cause are required; (2) the likelihood that regulatory officials will experience difficulty mastering the warrant procedure and the "niceties" of probable cause; and (3) the disruption a warrant and probable cause requirement will cause to the smooth operation of the government. Application of these factors has always led to a modification of the probable cause standard, and often resulted in the elimination of a warrant requirement. Indeed, beginning in the 1980's, the Court has been referring to situations in which one or more of these criteria are met as "exceptional circumstances in which special needs, beyond the normal needs for law enforcement, make the warrant and probable cause requirement impracticable."[2] This chapter looks at a wide array of "special needs" situations, including residential, business and fire inspections, border searches, airport and traffic screenings, inventory searches, school and workplace searches, drug testing programs, searches of probationer's homes, and DNA testing.

---

[1]   387 U.S. 523, 87 S.Ct. 1727 (1967).

[2]   As Justice Blackmun first put it in his concurring opinion in *New Jersey v. T.L.O.*, 469 U.S. 325, 105 S.Ct. 733 (1985), discussed in § 13.08.

13.02   Inspections of Homes

(a)   Health and Safety Inspections

One of the first types of administrative searches addressed by the Supreme Court concerned health and safety inspections of residential buildings. For some time, the Court refused to apply Fourth Amendment strictures to such inspections. In *Frank v. Maryland*,[3] for instance, it upheld the constitutionality of a statute punishing property holders for refusing to cooperate with a warrantless inspection. Because a safety inspection does not ask the property owner to open his doors to a search for "evidence of criminal action," the Court stated, it "touch[es] at most upon the periphery of the important interests safeguarded by the Fourteenth Amendment's protection against official intrusion."

In 1967, however, the Court overruled *Frank* in *Camara v. Municipal Court*.[4] Noting that most regulatory violations *can* result in criminal penalties, and that a warrantless search gives the occupant inadequate proof of the inspector's authority to conduct the search, the Court, in an opinion by Justice White, held that nonconsensual administrative searches of private residences constitute a "significant intrusion upon the interests protected by the Fourth Amendment" and thus are unreasonable without a warrant.

At the same time, the majority significantly modified the basis for obtaining a warrant in the administrative search context. Rather than requiring that the magistrate find probable cause with respect to each building inspected, the Court found sufficient a "probable cause" finding that the area, "as a whole," needed inspection, based on such factors as the age of the buildings, the passage of time, and other conditions. This type of probable cause is not "individualized," nor does it resemble the more-likely-than-not finding to which traditional probable cause has often been analogized.[5] But Justice White gave three reasons for adopting it when the search is a residential health or safety inspection:

> First, such programs have a long history of judicial and public acceptance. Second, the public interest demands that all dangerous conditions be prevented or abated, yet it is doubtful that any other canvassing technique would achieve acceptable results. . . . Finally, because the inspections are neither personal in nature nor aimed at the discovery of evidence of crime, they involve a relatively limited invasion of the urban citizen's privacy.

These reasons all make sense. While, in contrast to White's language, the dissent in *Frank* had spoken of "acquiescence" to, rather than acceptance of, these inspection programs, it is not farfetched to conclude that, on the whole, the public welcomes government efforts to make their homes safer, and that this attitude lessens the sense of intrusion associated with such searches. The Court is also correct in asserting that the types of problems these inspections are designed to correct—faulty wiring, ventilation, plumbing and other unsafe or unhealthy conditions—would be very difficult to detect (or would lead to an unacceptable increase in undercover activity and similar efforts) if probable cause were required. And an inspection is a relatively limited

---

[3]   359 U.S. 360, 79 S.Ct. 804 (1959).

[4]   387 U.S. 523, 87 S.Ct. 1727 (1967).

[5]   See § 5.03(a).

invasion, in the sense that it does not involve rummaging through personal belongings or the stigmatization associated with a criminal investigation. Taken together, these reasons support the idea that such inspections may be authorized based on the type of low-level, "generalized" suspicion described by the majority.

The three-member dissent did not disagree with these findings. Rather, it inveighed against *Camara's* warrant requirement, arguing that it would result in the advent of "boxcar warrants . . . identical as to every dwelling in the area, save the street number itself . . . printed up in pads of a thousand or more . . . and issued by magistrates in broadcast fashion as a matter of course." But because most residents consent to such inspections,[6] warrants will seldom be necessary. If a refusal does occur, a resident is unlikely to be able to hide any unsafe conditions by the time a warrant is obtained; further, if the condition is corrected, the government's objective will have been achieved in any event. A more telling criticism of *Camara* is that it did not require the inspecting agency, when conducting the initial warrantless inquiry, to give the resident notice regarding its intention and the right to refuse consent. Without such notice, the resident is more likely to succumb to the implicit "claim of authority" that any inspector carries with him.[7]

It should also be noted that there are some situations when even the watered-down warrant requirement of *Camara* is inapplicable, because the inspection must take place immediately. Usually, residential inspections do not involve an emergency, because, as noted above, if the violation is corrected before the inspectors arrive, the government's objective is achieved. However, occasionally exigency does exist. The Supreme Court has permitted warrantless entries in cases involving unwholesome food,[8] compulsory small pox vaccination,[9] and health quarantines.[10] Elimination of a warrant requirement does not, of course, eliminate the need to show some level of suspicion that the entry is necessary to avert the perceived harm.

(b) Welfare Inspections

In *Wyman v. James*,[11] the Supreme Court upheld a New York law that permitted caseworkers to make warrantless visits to the homes of welfare beneficiaries, the consequence of which could be the termination of benefits. Compared to health and safety inspections, such visits are arguably less "accepted," more "invasive," and not as indispensable to the government's aim of detecting welfare fraud. Yet the Supreme Court did not rely on the *Camara* factors in analyzing the statute. Rather it declared that welfare visitations are not searches under the Fourth Amendment, primarily because they cannot result in criminal sanctions.

---

[6]   In his dissenting opinion in *Camara*, Justice Clark noted that in one voluntary inspection program initiated in Oregon the consent rate was 5 out of 6, a fact which he used to support his argument that warrants would have to be obtained in an inordinate number of cases, but which can also support the conclusion that most people welcome such inspections.

[7]   The Court has held that warning a person of his right to refuse consent is not required. *Schneckloth v. Bustamonte*, 412 U.S. 218, 93 S.Ct. 2041 (1973), discussed in § 12.02(a). But the primary reason for that holding was the often unstructured setting of a field search. In the regulatory context, this rationale does not apply.

[8]   *North American Cold Storage Co. v. Chicago*, 211 U.S. 306, 29 S.Ct. 101 (1908).

[9]   *Jacobson v. Commonwealth of Massachusetts*, 197 U.S. 11, 25 S.Ct. 358 (1905).

[10]   *Compagnie Francaise De Navigation a Vapeur v. Louisiana State Board of Health*, 186 U.S. 380, 22 S.Ct. 811 (1902).

[11]   400 U.S. 309, 91 S.Ct. 381 (1971).

This reasoning, which was also the basis of *Frank*, had been squarely rejected in *Camara*. At the least, such visitations should require administrative warrants in all non-exigent situations, based on neutral factors that correlate with violation of welfare rules. Given the intrusion involved, one could even make a case for requiring normal warrants, based on the usual individualized probable cause. A countervailing factor in this regard is that, if invasiveness is judged from the perspective of the children who are often protected by welfare legislation,[12] such visits might be welcomed as readily as the health and safety inspections at issue in *Camara*.

13.03   Inspections of Businesses

See v. Seattle,[13] a companion case to *Camara*, involved a city-wide inspection of businesses for violations of the fire code. The Court, again through Justice White, concluded that "[t]he businessman, like the occupant of a residence, has a constitutional right to go about his business free from unreasonable official entries upon his private commercial property." Thus, *Camara*-type warrant and probable cause requirements were held to apply to the type of inspections at issue in *See*. The Court seemed determined to ensure that "the decision to enter and inspect will not be the product of the unreviewed discretion of the enforcement officer in the field." Within five years of *See*, however, the Court had created an exception to this rule that has since come to be called the "closely regulated business" exception to the warrant requirement. The scope of this exception has become so broad that it appears to apply to all but a few types of business inspections, without regard to their invasiveness or the difficulty of otherwise detecting statutory violations, the types of factors considered important in *Camara*. To be distinguished from the programmatic, area-wide or industry-side inspections involved in cases like *See* are those searches that target a particular business. In these types of cases, a warrant or subpoena is required, as discussed in the second subsection below.

(a)   The Closely Regulated Business Doctrine

The first decision tempering *See* was *Colonnade Catering Corp. v. United States*.[14] In a brief opinion, the Court approved a federal statute criminalizing refusal to allow warrantless entry of liquor stores by government inspectors, who in this case were attempting to discover if liquor bottles had been refilled illegally. Two years later came *United States v. Biswell*,[15] which upheld a warrantless entrance of a gun store to inspect documents and check whether any unlicensed guns were on the premises. Justice White, who wrote for eight members of the Court, distinguished his opinion in *See* by noting that the conditions sought to be discovered in the latter case were relatively difficult to conceal or to correct in a short time; requiring a warrant after refusal would thus not frustrate the regulatory purpose. Effective implementation of the Gun Control Act, on the other hand, required "unannounced, even frequent inspections." Of course, a *Camara*-type warrant issued *ex parte* would permit such surprise inspections. Moreover, the Court's approach in *Colonnade* and *Biswell* ignored *See's* conclusions about the importance of protecting business privacy from the unmonitored discretion of field officers. On the first point, the *Biswell* Court apparently felt that requiring a warrant in

---

[12]   See Robert A. Burt, *Forcing Protection on Children and Their Parents: The Impact of* Wyman v. James, 69 Mich.L.Rev. 1259 (1971).

[13]   387 U.S. 541, 87 S.Ct. 1737 (1967).

[14]   397 U.S. 72, 90 S.Ct. 774 (1970).

[15]   406 U.S. 311, 92 S.Ct. 1593 (1972).

each instance would be inefficient, perhaps having in mind the *Camara* dissent's lamentation about "boxcar warrants." As to the second objection, the *Biswell* majority concluded: "When a dealer chooses to engage in this pervasively regulated business and to accept a federal license, he does so with the knowledge that his business records, firearms and ammunition will be subject to effective inspection." The Court did state, however, that "unauthorized force" cannot be used to gain entrance, apparently meaning to prohibit unnecessarily rough entry.

Biswell's "pervasively" or "closely" regulated business exception to the warrant requirement appeared to consist of two elements: (1) the violations sought to be discovered must be of the type that are easily hidden—as opposed to easily correctable—thus allowing the business owner to frustrate government policy if the usual process of seeking consent and obtaining a warrant or subpoena upon refusal were followed; (2) the industry in question must be pervasively regulated so that an owner is put on notice as to the types of surprise inspections to which he will be subjected. In *Marshall v. Barlow's, Inc.*,[16] however, the Court indicated that merely satisfying these two requirements might not be enough. There, the Secretary of Labor argued that inspections under the Occupational Health and Safety Act met both conditions; the safety violations targeted under the Act could be subject to "speedy alteration and disguise" and the regulations under the Act specified in detail the types of things that would be inspected. But the Court held otherwise, in an opinion remarkable for its opaqueness.

Justice White, again writing for the (six-member) majority, glossed over the government's "speedy alteration" argument, merely asserting that most business owners would consent to OSHA inspections. Apparently the Court had in mind, as it had in *Camara* and *See*, that in most instances the government objective of achieving a safe workplace would be achieved even if the officials had to seek a warrant after being refused entry, either because the deficiencies would be corrected before their return or violations subjected to "alterations" or "disguise" could be discerned by the inspectors. As to the government's argument that the Act provided precise inspection guidelines, White simply stated that *Barlow's* did not involve a "closely regulated industry," since OSHA applied to a wide range of businesses, not all of which were associated with the long tradition of extensive regulation experienced by the liquor and gun industries at issue in *Colonnade* and *Biswell*. Apparently the reasoning here was that the "implied consent" rationale of *Biswell* would be meaningless if it applied to virtually any type of business. In any event, the Court went on to hold that, to make a nonconsensual entry under OSHA, the government must obtain a *Camara*-type warrant based on a showing that the inspection is part of a general enforcement plan based on neutral criteria such as number of employees and accident experience.

In its next business inspection case, *Donovan v. Dewey*,[17] the Court, this time in an opinion by Justice Marshall, further modified the "closely regulated industry" exception, in the course of concluding that warrantless inspections of coal mines under the Federal Mine Safety and Health Act were permissible. First, its holding made clear that, contrary to the Court's implication in *Barlow's* (as well as in *Colonnade* and *Biswell*), an industry need not have experienced a long tradition of regulation to be "closely regulated;" as Justice Stewart pointed out in dissent, the coal mining industry had been extensively monitored for less than two decades when *Dewey* came to the Court. The

---

[16]   436 U.S. 307, 98 S.Ct. 1816 (1978).

[17]   452 U.S. 594, 101 S.Ct. 2534 (1981).

duration of regulation is only one factor to consider, concluded the majority; the key threshold issue is the comprehensiveness of regulatory scheme. However, the Court also held that a finding that an industry is pervasively regulated is not enough to justify warrantless business inspections. Three criteria additional must be met: (1) the government must have a "substantial" interest in the activity being regulated; (2) warrantless searches must be necessary to the effective enforcement of the law, as in *Biswell*; and (3) the inspection program must provide "a constitutionally adequate substitute for a warrant." The Court found that all three criteria were met in *Dewey*. With respect to the all-important third criterion, the Court noted that the Act required inspection of "*all* mines," defined the frequency of inspection, provided precise standards "with which a mine operator is required to comply," and established "a specific mechanism for accommodating any special privacy concerns that a specific mine operator might have" by allowing the owner to refuse entry and force the government to seek an injunction in federal court.

The OSHA inspection at issue in *Barlow's* had provided the same sort of protections (including, in practice, the refusal-and-injunction process). But the majority in *Dewey* explained that the Federal Mine Safety Act applied to a specific industry "with a notorious history of serious accidents and unhealthful conditions," whereas the statute in *Barlow's* would have permitted indiscriminate inspections of many businesses with no history of safety violations. In any event, it would appear that the injunction process mandated by the Federal Mine Safety Act provides as much protection as does a warrant (at least to refusing owners). Indeed, given this latter aspect of *Dewey*, the decision called into doubt the broad scope of *Biswell's* ruling allowing "unannounced" nonconsensual, warrantless inspections of any closely regulated industry.

But the Court's next business inspection decision, *New York v. Burger*,[18] reinvigorated that ruling. The junkyard industry at issue in that case did not have a "notorious history" of violations, nor did the statute regulating it provide any type of judicial procedure. But the inspection process was upheld nonetheless by a vote of 6–3. The statute involved in *Burger* allowed warrantless, surprise inspections of junkyards and "vehicle dismantlers" for the purpose of checking whether they are licensed as required by the statute and, if so, whether their records are in order and any vehicles or parts on the premises were stolen. Unlike the Federal Mine Safety Act at issue in *Dewey*, the statute did not purport to regulate the condition of the premises, the method of operation, or the equipment utilized. But the Court, finding the registration and record-keeping aspects of the statute "extensive" (and relying as well on the "history of regulation of *related* industries"), held that the New York junkyard industry is "closely regulated." The Court went on to reiterate that, even if an industry is closely regulated, the statute regulating the industry must meet the three criteria established in *Dewey* in order to satisfy the Fourth Amendment. But Justice Blackmun, writing for the Court, quickly found that the New York law met all three criteria. First, the state had a "substantial interest" in regulating the vehicle dismantling industry because this industry is closely associated with motor vehicle theft, a significant problem in New York. Second, the statute serves this interest effectively; its surprise inspection provision was "crucial" if stolen vehicles and parts are to be detected. Third, the statute provided a constitutionally "adequate substitute for a warrant" by informing operators of junkyards that inspections would be made on a regular basis and by limiting the

---

[18]   482 U.S. 691, 107 S.Ct. 2636 (1987).

inspection to regular business hours and to vehicles and parts subject to its record-keeping requirements.

As Justice Brennan argued in dissent, "if New York City's administrative scheme renders the vehicle-dismantling business closely regulated, few businesses will escape such a finding." And even if the junkyard industry is heavily regulated, the New York statute did not meet *Dewey's* criteria. In particular, it provided no standard to guide inspectors and no injunction process: government officials are allowed to search any junkyard without any justification any time they are open. Brennan also cautioned that the administrative scheme was merely a pretext for allowing police to uncover evidence of crime without obtaining a warrant. He noted that the statute specifically authorized police to conduct such inspections.

Brennan's warning in *Burger* that the "implications of the Court's decision, if realized, will virtually eliminate Fourth Amendment protection of commercial entities in the context of administrative searches," is not far off the mark. As long as the statutory scheme is aimed at a discreet industry (rather than at all businesses, as in *Barlow's*), and provides a minimal amount of guidance (as in *Burger*), then an immediate, warrantless entry is apparently permitted, assuming "unauthorized force" is not used. Of particular concern is the possibility, noted by Brennan, that warrantless business inspections will hide pretextual searches. The Court itself has recognized that the regulatory inspection process can be abused unless it is monitored, and schemes like those at issue in *Burger*, where the police are often involved, are likely to encourage such abuse if not subjected to some outside scrutiny.[19]

The potential for pretextual use of business inspections was the primary rationale for the Court's decision in *City of Los Angeles v. Patel.*[20] That case involved police inspections of hotel registries that a Los Angeles ordnance required hotel owners to keep in an effort to deter and detect use of hotels for prostitution, drug dealing and other crimes. Justice Scalia's dissent argued that, based on the licensure, tax, sanitation and like requirements to which they are subject, hotels are a closely regulated business and that *Dewey's* other criteria for the closely regulated business exception to the warrant requirement were met as well. But Justice Sotomayor, joined by four other justices, concluded that "[i]f such general regulations were sufficient to invoke the closely regulated industry exception, it would be hard to imagine a type of business that would not qualify." Instead, as in *See* and *Camara*, the majority held that government officials must seek "precompliance review" before searching a non-consenting owner's property. According to the majority, "[a]bsent an opportunity for precompliance review, the ordinance creates an intolerable risk that searches authorized by it will exceed statutory limits, or be used as a pretext to harass hotel operators and their guests." To Justice Scalia's complaint that such review would significantly undermine the purpose of the inspection scheme by creating cumbersome procedural requirements and alerting hotel owners that police are aware of their complicity in criminal activity, Justice Sotomayor

---

[19]　Long ago, the Court also noted the possibility that inspectors may serve as a "front" for the police. *Abel v. United States*, 362 U.S. 217, 80 S.Ct. 683 (1960). See, e.g., *Turner v. Dammon*, 848 F.2d 440 (4th Cir. 1988) (civil suit alleging police made a disproportionate number of "bar checks"); *People v. Tillery*, 211 Cal.App.3d 1569, 260 Cal.Rptr. 320 (1989) (finding inadmissible marijuana plants discovered by police officers executing an administrative building-inspection warrant over the occupant's resistance). Although the Court has held that, where there is probable cause for a search the fact that the searchers may have had a hidden agenda is irrelevant, when there is no individualized suspicion, as in the cases described here, proof of pretextuality might result in a finding that the Fourth Amendment was violated. See § 10.04.

[20]　___ U.S. ___, 135 S.Ct. 2443 (2015).

replied that a "simple" administrative subpoena would suffice; further, in the event an officer "reasonably suspects that a hotel operator may tamper with the registry while the motion to quash is pending, he or she can guard the registry until the required hearing can occur, which ought not take long."

Patel reinforces *Barlow's* holding that the mere fact that businesses are regulated does not make them so "closely" regulated that they lose the protection of ex ante review. At the same time, the decision clarifies that even those business searches that do not fall within the closely regulated exception are "special needs" or "administrative" searches that do not require a warrant.

(b) Non-Programmatic Searches of Businesses

When a search of a business is focused on investigating a particular company rather than conducted pursuant to an inspection scheme, then the usual Fourth Amendment protections apply. Occasionally, those protections will require a warrant. For instance, in *G.M. Leasing Corp. v. United States*,[21] the government searched the petitioner's business offices for papers relating to a tax assessment. The government argued, inter alia, that *Biswell*, or at least *Camara* and *See*, were applicable. But the Court held that the search of G.M. Leasing's office was not pursuant to a regulatory plan. Nor was the intrusion into the company's office "based on the nature of its business, its license, or any regulation of its activities." Thus, the "usual" quantum of probable cause was required before agents from the Internal Revenue Service could enter to seize assets to satisfy tax assessments.[22]

More typically, investigation of a company does focus on its business and its activities, and the government relies not on physical entry into the company's offices but on the issuance of subpoenas calling on the business to surrender documents that are "relevant," a standard that is much looser and less particular than probable cause. In *Hale v. Henkel*,[23] the Court rejected the argument that a warrant was required in this situation, because such a requirement would make it " 'utterly impossible to carry on the administration of justice'." The only limitation the Court imposed on such subpoenas is that they not be so "sweeping" that responding to them would "completely put a stop to the business of that company." Forty years later, in *Oklahoma Press v. Walling*,[24] the Court emphasized that, when seeking business records, the Fourth Amendment "at the most guards against abuse only by way of too much indefiniteness or breadth in the things required to be 'particularly described,' if also the inquiry is one the demanding agency is authorized by law to make and the materials specified are relevant."[25] The Court has held that this standard applies even when the records sought are to further prosecution of a customer or client whose information the company possesses rather than of the company itself.[26]

---

[21]   429 U.S. 338, 97 S.Ct. 619 (1977).

[22]   See also, *Go-Bart Importing Co. v. United States*, 282 U.S. 344, 51 S.Ct. 153. (1931) (warrant required to search company offices for evidence of bootlegging violations).

[23]   201 U.S. 43, 26 S.Ct. 370 (1906).

[24]   327 U.S. 186, 66 S.Ct. 494 (1946).

[25]   See also *United States v. Morton Salt Co.*, 338 U.S. 632, 70 S.Ct. 357 (1950); *United States v. Powell*, 379 U.S. 48, 85 S.Ct. 248 (1964).

[26]   *Ryan v. United States*, 402 U.S. 530, 91 S.Ct. 1580 (1971). See generally § 4.03(a), discussing the absence of Fourth Amendment protection for third party records.

As discussed in more detail elsewhere in this book,[27] there are at least two justifications for this very relaxed standard. First is *Hale's* statement that a more stringent standard would make regulation impossible. Without easy access to business records, the information necessary to ensure businesses are following the myriad laws that govern their operation would, at the least, be very difficult. The second rationale for the relaxed subpoena standard is more closely tied to typical Fourth Amendment analysis. *Oklahoma Press* suggested that a subpoena does not involve an "actual search," because no physical entry is involved and the target can challenge the subpoena prior to handing over the requested documents.[28]

Note that, in theory, the Fifth Amendment could impose some limitations on subpoenas, because they "compel" incriminating information from the business. However, the Court has made clear that these limitations only apply in rare circumstances.[29]

13.04   Fire Inspections

In *Michigan v. Tyler*,[30] the Court approved a warrantless search and seizure of burned premises the night of the fire and another seizure the next morning while the cause of the fire was still undetermined. However, it held unconstitutional a warrantless search weeks later that produced further evidence on which to ground prosecution of the defendant property owner for arson. It concluded that once the exigency produced by the fire (including the need to determine its cause after it is extinguished) is ended, the police and fire marshal must secure an administrative warrant to conduct further searches. Moreover, *Tyler* required a more particularized inquiry than that demanded by *Camara/See*, on the ground that a fire scene search is necessarily responsive to an individualized event, rather than to a random inspection pattern. The Court listed several factors to consider in making this individualized determination, including: (1) the number of prior entries, (2) the scope of the search, (3) the time of day when it is proposed to be made, (4) the time lapse since the fire, (5) the continued use of the building, and (6) the owner's efforts to secure the building against intruders.

In *Michigan v. Clifford*,[31] the Court partially reaffirmed *Tyler* but also appeared to reject at least some of its reasoning. *Clifford* involved an inspection of burned premises five hours after the extinction of the blaze, during which evidence of arson was discovered, as well as a second search for further evidence of arson. The entire Court agreed that the second phase of the search required a conventional warrant, since the government admitted it was part of a criminal investigation. But only four members of the Court agreed that the first search required a *Camara*-type search warrant of the type outlined in *Tyler*. Four other justices concluded that no warrant was needed to support this search, on the ground that it was a continuation of the original entry to extinguish the blaze. Justice Stevens, the swing vote, reasoned that a *Camara* warrant would provide no real protection in such cases. He concluded that instead "the home

---

[27] See § 23.05(a).

[28] See also *Donovan v. Lone Steer, Inc.*, 464 U.S. 408, 104 S.Ct. 769 (1984) (approving a subpoena *duces tecum* against a company employee because (a) it does not contemplate nonconsensual entry and (b) no penalty may be imposed for failure to comply with the subpoena until the employer has the opportunity to question, in open court, its reasonableness).

[29] See § 15.06.

[30] 436 U.S. 499, 98 S.Ct. 1942 (1978).

[31] 464 U.S. 287, 104 S.Ct. 641 (1984).

owner is entitled to reasonable advance notice that officers are going to enter his premises for the purposes of ascertaining the cause of the fire." After *Clifford* then, it appears any inspection conducted within a reasonable time after the fire must be preceded by notice but need not be authorized by a warrant of any type. After such time, the modified administrative warrant described in *Tyler* is required, unless suspicion develops as to a criminal motive, in which case a traditional warrant must be sought.

These rules seem needlessly complicated. An immediate warrantless post-fire search is justified by the indisputable facts that a fire has occurred and that determining its origins is an important task which requires quick entry. If further entries are necessary to determine the fire's origins, a requirement that a magistrate make a probable cause finding to that effect would prevent arbitrary decisions by fire officials and not be unduly burdensome. Trying to distinguish between routine post-fire inspections and situations where inspectors develop a "suspicion" that arson has occurred is likely to create considerable confusion as to when an ongoing investigation must stop to obtain a conventional warrant.

13.05   Border Inspections

Unfortunately, the heavy volume of litigation on the subject leaves the impression that "border searches" constitute a separate exception to the warrant requirement. It is true, as developed below, that at the border itself the authority of the United States to exclude illegal aliens and contraband from the country can be exercised through the mechanism of warrantless inspections and searches. But searches and seizures conducted *near* the border are treated no differently than searches and seizures conducted elsewhere in the country. The Supreme Court's border search decisions rely on traditional analysis, in particular the automobile exception to the warrant requirement, "stop and frisk" doctrine and vehicle roadblock jurisprudence applicable nationwide. Thus, for instance, in *Almeida-Sanchez v. United States*[32] and *United States v. Ortiz,*[33] the Court reaffirmed that the elements of the automobile exception, including probable cause, must be met before a car found on the highway may be searched, even when the search takes place near the border.[34] In *United States v. Brignoni-Ponce,*[35] it made clear that the fact that a car is stopped near the border does not eliminate the reasonable suspicion requirement for brief investigative detentions.[36] And the analysis in *United States v. Martinez-Fuerte*[37] used to justify warrantless and suspicionless illegal immigrant checkpoints has since been applied to other types of checkpoints having nothing to do with illegal immigration and border searches and seizures.[38]

These cases are thus more relevant to other search and seizure issues. Here the focus will be on the government's authority *at* the border to conduct searches and seizures as a way of regulating who and what enters the country. The rules discussed here also apply at "functional equivalents" of the border, including "an established

---

[32]   413 U.S. 266, 93 S.Ct. 2535 (1973).

[33]   422 U.S. 891, 95 S.Ct. 2585 (1975).

[34]   For a description of the automobile exception, see Chapter 7.

[35]   422 U.S. 873, 95 S.Ct. 2574 (1975).

[36]   For discussion of stop jurisprudence, see § 11.03(a).

[37]   428 U.S. 543, 96 S.Ct. 3074 (1976).

[38]   See *Michigan Dept. of State Police v. Sitz*, 496 U.S. 444, 110 S.Ct. 2481 (1990), discussed in § 13.06(b).

station near the border, at a point marking the confluence of two or more roads that extend from the border,"[39] and international airports.[40]

(a) Routine Searches

In *Carroll v. United States*,[41] the Supreme Court stated that "national self-protection" permits the government to require "one entering the country to identify himself as entitled to come in, and his belongings as effects which may be lawfully brought in." Sixty years later, in *United States v. Montoya de Hernandez*,[42] the Court put the matter more explicitly: "Routine searches of the persons and effects of entrants [at the border] are not subject to any requirement of reasonable suspicion, probable cause, or warrant." The Court gave two justifications for this stance. First, "one's expectation of privacy [is] less at the border" than in the interior, and second, the Fourth Amendment balance between the interests of the government and the individual is struck much more favorably to the Government at the border. These rationales reflect the *Camara* balancing analysis: the invasiveness of routine searches at the border is said to be minimal because people expect and understand the need for such searches, and the significant government interest in monitoring what enters the country could not be effectively protected unless such routine searches are permitted. Thus, neither a warrant nor any individualized suspicion need be shown before a frisk of one's person or a search of one's effects by border authorities.

(b) Nonroutine Searches

Whatever the validity of this reasoning when a "routine" search is conducted at the border, it is considerably harder to swallow when the government engages in more intrusive searches and prolonged seizures. Yet the courts are willing to relax Fourth Amendment protections in these situations as well. In *Montoya de Hernandez*, the Supreme Court permitted a 16-hour detention at the border based on reasonable suspicion,[43] despite conceding that the seizure "undoubtedly exceeds any other detention we have approved under reasonable suspicion." There, at least, the defendant was in part at fault for the length of the detention, since she refused an x-ray examination to determine whether she was carrying "drug balloons" in her alimentary canal. Lower courts, however, have permitted rectal examinations and other body cavity searches on less than probable cause, regardless of the defendant's expressed wishes.[44] Strip searches have also been permitted on reasonable suspicion.[45]

When a nonroutine search is of a vehicle rather than a person, even reasonable suspicion is not required. In *United States v. Flores-Montano*,[46] the Supreme Court unanimously held that border officials may detain a person and his car for at least one to two hours in order to remove and inspect the gas tank of the car (which officials in

---

[39]   *Almeida-Sanchez v. United States*, 413 U.S. 266, 93 S.Ct. 2535 (1973).

[40]   See also *Illinois v. Andreas*, 463 U.S. 765, 103 S.Ct. 3319 (1983), discussed in § 4.03(e).

[41]   267 U.S. 132, 45 S.Ct. 280 (1925).

[42]   473 U.S. 531, 105 S.Ct. 3304 (1985).

[43]   The reasonable suspicion stemmed from the following facts: (1) the defendant had made eight recent trips from South America to either Miami or Los Angeles; (2) this trip was from Bogota, Columbia, a "source city" for drugs; and (3) the defendant had no appointments with vendors, no order forms, and no hotel reservations, despite claiming that she was in Los Angeles to buy goods for her husband's store.

[44]   See, e.g., *United States v. Carpenter*, 496 F.2d 855 (9th Cir. 1974).

[45]   *United States v. Guadalupe-Garza*, 421 F.2d 876 (9th Cir. 1970).

[46]   541 U.S. 149, 124 S.Ct. 1582 (2004).

this case thought might contain drugs). Chief Justice Rehnquist reiterated that, at the border, the government's interest is "at its zenith," while privacy interests are minimal. This is especially so, he stated, with respect to vehicle gas tanks, which can thus be subjected to suspicionless seizures and inspections. The price of this relaxation of Fourth Amendment requirements was made evident by government statistics, noted in the majority opinion, showing that 348 gas tank searches conducted along the southern border in 2003 produced *no* evidence of crime.

(c) International Mail

Federal law authorizes inspection of international mail whenever there is "reasonable cause to suspect" that the mail contains illegally imported merchandise.[47] Neither a warrant nor probable cause is required. However, the implementing regulations do prohibit reading correspondence without a warrant.

In *United States v. Ramsey*,[48] customs officials opened incoming international mail because they knew that the envelopes were from Thailand, often a source of illegal drugs, and because they had observed the envelopes were bulky and heavier than normal airmail letters. The Supreme Court held that these facts gave the inspectors reasonable cause to suspect, within the statutory framework. It also held that the Fourth Amendment did not prohibit the actions taken by the inspectors, despite the absence of a warrant and probable cause, because the search was the equivalent of one conducted at the border, where the sovereign's right to control what enters the country prevails. Justice Rehnquist, writing for the majority, reasoned that because INS agents may search the citizen's person without a warrant as he crosses the border and seize and inspect the contents of any envelope he may have in his possession, there is no persuasive reason to require more in order to inspect a letter arriving through the mail. The Court left open, however, whether a warrant is required before an official may read written material in letters. Given current regulations, and First as well as Fourth Amendment concerns, such a result seems likely.

13.06   Checkpoints

Checkpoints are useful as a means of investigating a large number of people in an efficient manner; typically, only a small portion of those stopped are likely to be in violation of the law. The border searches just discussed are one example. Inside the country, checkpoints are also common. The Supreme Court has held that stops at domestic checkpoints established solely or primarily to implement a "general interest in crime control" or for "ordinary" law enforcement purposes (such as narcotics interdiction) are impermissible unless police have individualized suspicion.[49] But the Court has upheld the constitutionality of checkpoints used on the highways to detect illegal immigration, drunk driving, and violation of licensing laws, and on the waterways to check for proper documentation. These cases are discussed here, along with lower court decisions on checkpoints situated at airports to discover weapons.

---

[47]   19 U.S.C.A. § 482.

[48]   431 U.S. 606, 97 S.Ct. 1972 (1977).

[49]   *Indianapolis v. Edmond*, 531 U.S. 32, 121 S.Ct. 447 (2000), discussed in § 13.06(f).

contention that license and inspection checkpoints are necessary to achieve the government's objectives is more realistic.

Assuming such roadblocks are constitutional, a separate issue that has arisen in the lower courts is whether a motorist's attempt to evade the roadblock authorizes chase. In *Martinez-Fuerte*, the Court had suggested that one reason a fixed checkpoint is constitutional is that it does not take motorists "by surprise" and can be avoided. But some courts have nonetheless held that turning around prior to a license check roadblock provides reasonable suspicion of involvement in some sort of illegality.[55] Others have held to the contrary, emphasizing that the mere act of avoiding contact with the police should not create an articulable suspicion of criminal activity.[56]

(d) Boat Inspections

Boats on inland waterways could be analogized to cars using public thoroughfares. But the Supreme Court has concluded that a better analogy is with border searches, at least when the waterways have ready access to the sea. In *United States v. Villamonte-Marquez*,[57] customs officials (as well as an ordinary police officer) boarded the defendants' boat to inspect their papers pursuant to 19 U.S.C.A. § 1581(a), which authorizes officers to board any vessel at any time and at any place in the United States to examine the vessel's manifest and other documents. While examining a document, the officer smelled what he thought to be burning marijuana and, looking through an open hatch, saw burlap-wrapped bales that proved to be marijuana. The Supreme Court distinguished this case from *Prouse* by noting that such boardings are essential to ensure enforcement of the complex documentation requirements for boats, "particularly in waters where the need to deter or apprehend drug smugglers is great". According to the Court, "fixed checkpoints" are an impractical means of achieving the document-inspection objective on waterways that have access to the sea.

Thus, so long as the detention is "brief" and limited to inspecting documents, a suspicionless boarding of a boat by customs officials is constitutional and any evidence in plain view is admissible. However, precisely because such a boarding is suspicionless, a Fourth Amendment violation may occur if it is pretextual.[58] Given the presence of the police officer, atypical in customs work, and allegations that customs agents had received a tip that drugs were on board, such an argument was possible in *Villamonte-Marquez*, but the Court did not address it.

(e) Airport Screenings

The first case to consider the constitutionality of airport screening procedures was *United States v. Lopez*.[59] The procedure considered there consisted of four stages: (1) identification of a person as one who fit a "behavioral profile" of a plane hijacker; (2) who would then be required to pass through a magnetometer; (3) which, if triggered, would be followed by an interview; and, (4) if suspicion were not thereby eliminated, a frisk of the person and a search of his luggage. The *Lopez* Court purported to apply the *Terry*

---

[55]   *Coffman v. Arkansas*, 26 Ark.App. 45, 759 S.W.2d 573 (1988).

[56]   *Utah v. Talbot*, 792 P.2d 489 (Utah App. 1990).

[57]   462 U.S. 579, 103 S.Ct. 2573 (1983).

[58]   See § 10.04.

[59]   328 F.Supp. 1077 (E.D.N.Y. 1971).

criteria,[60] finding that if a person progressed through the first three stages, there was reasonable suspicion to frisk the individual and search the luggage.[61]

Most other courts permit frisks on little or no suspicion, given "the enormous consequences" that can flow from a hijacking and the fact that persons can choose not to fly if they wish to avoid the intrusion.[62] The most balanced approach, currently followed in most airports, is to subject all passengers to the relatively uninvasive magnetometer procedure and all luggage to an x-ray. Those who are thereby suspected of carrying something dangerous might then be subject to a frisk of their person and a search of their luggage.

(f) Checkpoints Aimed at Ordinary Crime Control

Prouse, *Martinez-Fuerte*, *Sitz* and the Court's other checkpoint cases notwithstanding, checkpoints established primarily "to uncover evidence of ordinary criminal wrongdoing" are not permissible under the Fourth Amendment. This was the holding of *Indianapolis v. Edmond*,[63] which involved a checkpoint specifically set up to allow drug-sniffing dogs access to cars in an effort to detect narcotics. Although approximately five percent of those stopped at the checkpoint were arrested for drug-related crimes, a proportion well above the success rate in *Sitz*, the Court emphasized that the roadblock in the latter case was permitted because it was designed to eliminate an "immediate, vehicle-bound threat to life and limb." Similarly, the Court noted, *Prouse's* approval of license checkpoints was based specifically on concerns about roadway safety. The Court was somewhat less convincing in distinguishing *Martinez-Fuerte*, noting simply that "the border context [in that case] was crucial." But all three of the latter cases, the Court insisted, involved something other than a "general interest in crime control," and thus did not authorize the roadblock in *Edmond*, which was announced by signs indicating it was a "Narcotics Checkpoint."

Justice O'Connor's opinion for the six-member majority also discounted the argument that *Whren v. United States*[64] prevented the Court from inquiring into the roadblock's "primary purpose." She noted that *Whren's* holding that the subjective intent behind police search and seizures is irrelevant applies only when the police clearly have an objectively legitimate reason for stopping in the first instance, which did not exist here.[65] Nonetheless, *Edmond* left open whether a roadblock set up "primarily" for legitimate purposes (e.g., a license checkpoint) may constitutionally have as a secondary purpose the detection of narcotics. In *Illinois v. Caballes*,[66] the Court signaled the answer to this question is yes. There the police stopped the defendant for speeding and, while issuing a citation, arranged for a drug-sniffing dog to examine his car. In a 6–2 opinion (Chief Justice Rehnquist not participating), the Court held that the drugs discovered by

---

[60]   See § 11.03(a).

[61]   The data showed that a person who went through the first three stages was found to be carrying a weapon six percent of the time.

[62]   *Corbett v. Transportation Security Administration*, 767 F.3d 1171 (11th Cir. 2014); *United States v. Lindsey*, 451 F.2d 701 (3d Cir. 1971), cert. denied 405 U.S. 995, 92 S.Ct. 1270 (1972); *United States v. Skipwith*, 482 F.2d 1272 (5th Cir. 1973).

[63]   531 U.S. 32, 121 S.Ct. 447 (2000).

[64]   517 U.S. 806, 116 S.Ct. 1769 (1996), discussed in § 10.04.

[65]   *Whren* also specifically declined to apply its holding to situations where the legitimating police action is based on less than probable cause, as was the case in *Edmond*.

[66]   543 U.S. 405, 125 S.Ct. 834 (2005).

the dog were admissible, because the dog sniff did not extend the stop beyond the time necessary to issue the ticket and to conduct associated inquiries and because a dog sniff, by itself, is not a search.[67] Although *Caballes* did not involve a roadblock, a dog sniff at a license checkpoint that does not extend the duration of the license check might similarly be permissible, as several lower courts have held.[68]

The Court also distinguished *Edmond* in upholding the roadblock in *Illinois v. Lidster*,[69] which was set up at the location of a hit-and-run accident, one week after the accident occurred and at approximately the same time of night, in an effort to identify possible witnesses to the accident. Although no witnesses were discovered, police operating the checkpoint did notice Lidster's drunken actions and arrested him for driving under the influence. Justice Breyer noted for a unanimous Court that, unlike the roadblock in *Edmond*, the checkpoint here was designed to "apprehend, not the vehicle's occupants, but other individuals," that such a stop was "less likely to provoke anxiety or to prove intrusive," and that the questioning at the checkpoint was analogous to soliciting information from pedestrians, which the Court has always permitted.[70] Although Justice Stevens agreed with this reasoning, he, along with Justices Souter and Ginsburg, dissented in part because he believed the case should have been remanded to allow the lower courts to consider more carefully whether the roadblock was necessary in light of the alarm an unpublicized nighttime stop might occasion. He noted that a more effective, less intrusive method of finding witnesses might have been simply to put flyers on the cars of workers at nearby businesses whose shifts ended at about the time of the accident.

13.07   Inventories

(a)   Of Vehicles

Car inventories occur after a car has been impounded for a traffic or parking violation, or because its occupants have been arrested or abandoned it. Assuming probable cause to search does not exist at the time of impoundment, warrantless inventories of cars cannot be justified under the automobile exception. Nor would that exception apply if probable cause subsequently developed because, say, police see evidence of criminal activity through the car window; once impounded the car will not leave the impoundment lot until the owner collects it, and thus no exigency exists.[71] In *South Dakota v. Opperman*,[72] however, the Supreme Court held that warrantless inventories are permissible on *regulatory* grounds. In *Opperman*, the police impounded the defendant's locked, unoccupied automobile after issuing two parking tickets warning that the car was parked illegally in a restricted zone. At the impound lot, an officer observed through the car's windows a watch and other items of personal property. At his direction, the car was unlocked and the contents of the car inventoried. In the glove compartment police found a bag of marijuana. The Court upheld the search, concluding

---

[67]   See § 4.03(f)(2).

[68]   See Brooks Holland, *The Road 'Round* Edmond: *Steering Through Primary Purpose and Crime Control Agendas*, 111 Penn St. L. Rev. 293, 298 (2006) ("The weight of authority so far indicates that a secondary purpose of crime control will not upset a checkpoint with a lawful primary purpose.").

[69]   540 U.S. 419, 124 S.Ct. 885 (2004).

[70]   See § 11.02(a).

[71]   See § 7.03(c)(2) for discussion of this aspect of the automobile exception.

[72]   428 U.S. 364, 96 S.Ct. 3092 (1976).

that inventory searches are permissible, provided they are: (1) pursuant to a lawful impoundment; (2) of a routine nature "essentially like that followed throughout the country;" and (3) not a mere "pretext concealing an investigatory police motive."

The Court offered three justifications for an inventory: avoiding harm to the police, avoiding false claims of theft, and preventing vandalism of property. All of these justifications can be challenged. If an explosive or some other harmful device is in the car and for some reason hasn't already been triggered, opening the car doors and compartments would often *increase* the risk to the police. If a person is willing to make a claim of theft by the police, then he will probably also be willing to claim (just as persuasively) that police falsified any inventory tending to disprove that claim. And vandalism can be prevented by putting the car in a secure impound lot or, if one is not available, contacting the owner and asking if he wants the contents of his car secured (in *Opperman*, the Court merely noted that the owner "was not present to make other arrangements for the safekeeping of his belongings"). At bottom, the problem with inventory searches is the ease with which they can be used to evade the warrant and probable cause requirements any time a car may be lawfully impounded. Only if the inventory search is strictly limited can the pretextual actions prohibited by the Court actually be avoided.

Instead, the Court has not only affirmed *Opperman* but significantly expanded its scope. In *Colorado v. Bertine*,[73] for instance, the Court opted for a crime control resolution of several issues not explicitly addressed in *Opperman*. First, it made clear that containers found in the course of an inventory search may be searched, so long as such a search is authorized by departmental inventory regulations.[74] It rejected the Colorado Supreme Court's finding that such searches violated the Court's "container cases" requiring a warrant prior to the search of an opaque container,[75] on the ground that these cases involved investigations of criminal conduct whereas inventory searches do not. Second, it refused to alter the inventory search rule when a secure impound facility is available. As Chief Justice Rehnquist stated for the Court, "the security of the storage facility does not completely eliminate the need for inventorying; the police may still wish to protect themselves or the owners of the lot against false claims of theft or dangerous instrumentalities." The fact that the inventory in *Bertine* was sloppily carried out, suggesting that the goal of the inventory was to find evidence, not protect against false claims, was ignored by the Court. Finally, the Court was unwilling to adopt as a constitutional ruling a requirement that police allow owners of cars about to be impounded an opportunity to make alternate arrangements, stating that "[t]he reasonableness of any particular governmental activity does not necessarily or invariably turn on the existence of alternative 'less intrusive' means."

Although *Opperman* and *Bertine* at least suggest that an inventory search is limited to those areas where valuables might normally be kept, the Court has also indicated that under certain circumstances police may search other areas of the car as well. In

---

[73]   479 U.S. 367, 107 S.Ct. 738 (1987).

[74]   In *Florida v. Wells*, 495 U.S. 1, 110 S.Ct. 1632 (1990), the Court held unconstitutional an inventory search of a container when no such regulations existed. However, the Court indicated that virtually any regulations that *are* promulgated would pass constitutional muster. In dictum, it stated that such regulations would be adequate if they mandated that all containers be opened, that no containers be opened, or that the police officer in his discretion determine which containers should be opened based on "the nature of the search and characteristics of the container itself."

[75]   See § 7.04.

Michigan v. Thomas,[76] the car in which Thomas was a passenger was stopped for a traffic violation committed by its 14-year-old driver. The driver was issued a citation for driving without a license; Thomas was arrested for possession of open intoxicants in a motor vehicle. The car was then impounded and, pursuant to departmental policy, was inventoried prior to towing. The arresting officer found two bags of marijuana in the unlocked glove compartment. A second officer then searched the car more thoroughly, including under the front seat, inside the locked trunk, and under the dashboard. In the air vents located under the dashboard, he found a loaded .38 revolver.

The Michigan state appellate court reversed Thomas' subsequent conviction for possession of a concealed weapon on the ground that an inventory inspection, while permissible under *Opperman*, should not include searches of air ducts, which are neither customary places for the storage of valuables nor in plain view. Although discovery of the marijuana gave rise to probable cause, the police should then have sought a warrant, since the car was securely immobilized. The Supreme Court's per curiam opinion reversed, concluding that once discovery of the marijuana gave the police probable cause to believe further contraband was in the car, exigent circumstances were not required to authorize a warrantless search. By analogy to *Chambers v. Maroney*,[77] which authorized stationhouse searches of cars that could have been searched in the field under the "automobile exception," the police were permitted to conduct a thorough warrantless search of the car any time after the marijuana was discovered.

In *Florida v. Meyers*,[78] the Court relied on the *Chambers* analogy again in the course of extending the scope of the inventory search even further. In *Meyers*, police arrested the defendant and conducted a search of his car that the lower state court characterized "as an incident thereto and for inventory purposes." A second search some eight hours later after the car was in the impound lot was also lawful, according to the Court, because, as in *Thomas*, the *Chambers* rationale applied. In effect, then, an inventory search for valuables may take place well after the original impoundment, despite the seeming inconsistency between this rule and the supposed purpose of inventories, to wit, protecting against theft of valuables or danger to police.

After the Court's car inventory decisions, police departments have every incentive to promulgate car impoundment policies that are as broad as possible. Once a car is lawfully impounded (which, again, can occur for something as insignificant as unpaid parking tickets), police may inventory any "accessible" items in it without a warrant, so long as the scope of the inventory is authorized by departmental procedures. If police discover evidence giving rise to probable cause, they may conduct an even more intrusive search, again without a warrant. Furthermore, the inventory may take place well after impoundment, so long as it was authorized at the time of the impoundment. The only limitations on the initial inventory, aside from those police departments gratuitously place on themselves, are that the police may not intrude into areas where valuables are not normally kept and that, as required in *Opperman*, the inventory not be a pretext for an investigative search. Given Court decisions in other areas,[79] this second limitation may also be moot, so long as the requirements of the inventory search exception are met.

---

[76]   458 U.S. 259, 102 S.Ct. 3079 (1982).

[77]   399 U.S. 42, 90 S.Ct. 1975 (1970), discussed § 7.03(c)(2).

[78]   466 U.S. 380, 104 S.Ct. 1852 (1984).

[79]   See § 10.04.

(b) Of Persons

The effects of a person who has been lawfully arrested and taken into custody are subject to an inventory search as well. In *Illinois v. Lafayette*,[80] the defendant was arrested for disturbing the peace and taken to the police station where, in the process of booking him, police removed the contents of a shoulder bag and found amphetamine pills. The Illinois appellate court affirmed the trial court's suppression of the pills on the grounds that no warrant had been obtained and that the search could not be justified as an inventory search or a search incident to a lawful arrest. The Supreme Court unanimously reversed, citing *Opperman* in holding that "[t]he justification for such searches does not rest on probable cause and hence the absence of a warrant is immaterial to the reasonableness of the search."

According to the Court, protection of a suspect's property, deterrence of false claims of theft against the police, concern over security, and identification of the suspect all provide valid reasons for permitting examination of an arrested suspect and his personal effects, so long as it is part of a routine police procedure. As it had in *Opperman*, the Court refused to require police to set aside for safekeeping items that did not appear to be evidence of criminal activity or usable as weapons. "Even if less intrusive means existed of protecting some particular type of property, it would be unreasonable to expect police officers in the everyday course of business to make fine and subtle distinctions in deciding which containers or items may be searched and which must be sealed as a unit."

13.08   School and Workplace Searches

In *New Jersey v. T.L.O.*,[81] a school teacher discovered the 14 year-old respondent smoking cigarettes in a school lavatory in violation of school rules. When questioned about the smoking incident by the Vice Principal, the respondent denied she had been smoking or had ever smoked. The Vice Principal looked through her purse, found a pack of cigarettes and noticed a package of rolling papers. He then searched the purse more carefully and found several incriminating items, including some marijuana and two letters implicating the respondent in marijuana dealing. Upon appeal from a delinquency conviction in juvenile court, the New Jersey Supreme Court ordered the suppression of the evidence.

The Supreme Court reversed in a decision written by Justice White. It first held, unanimously, that public school officials are government agents for purposes of the Fourth Amendment[82] and that schoolchildren are entitled to some protection under the Amendment because they have a legitimate expectation that school officials will not intrude unreasonably upon their privacy.[83] However, six members of the Court refused to apply the warrant or probable cause requirements to the school search situation involved in *T.L.O.* A warrant requirement "would unduly interfere with the maintenance of the swift and informal disciplinary procedures needed in the schools." And a high suspicion requirement would be unduly burdensome in light of "the substantial need of teachers and administrators for freedom to maintain order in the schools."

---

[80]   462 U.S. 640, 103 S.Ct. 2605 (1983).

[81]   469 U.S. 325, 105 S.Ct. 733 (1985).

[82]   See § 4.02(a) for further discussion of this issue.

[83]   See § 4.03(g) for further discussion of this issue.

Justice Blackmun's concurring opinion is also important, because it introduced the "special needs" label that would become popular in future Court cases. As he put it, "[o]nly in those exceptional circumstances in which special needs, beyond the normal need for law enforcement, make the warrant and probable-cause requirement impracticable, is a court entitled to substitute its balancing of interests for that of the Framers." Blackmun found that such an "exceptional circumstance" existed here, because of the government's "heightened obligation to safeguard students whom it compels to attend school" and the inefficiency of meeting that obligation if the investigation necessary to meet the probable cause standard were required.

In place of the warrant and probable cause requirements, the Court substituted the "reasonableness" analysis, first developed in *Camara* and *Terry*. That analysis, according to the majority, "involves a twofold inquiry: first, one must consider 'whether the . . . action was justified at its inception; second, one must determine whether the search as actually conducted' was reasonably related in scope to the circumstances which justified the interference in the first place.'" The Court felt that an added advantage of this test was that it would relieve school officials from "schooling themselves in the niceties of probable cause."

Applying this test to the facts, Justice White found that the report from the teacher about the smoking in the lavatory gave the Vice Principal sufficient suspicion that the purse contained cigarettes, and that the discovery of rolling papers gave him reason to suspect that marijuana was in the purse. This in turn allowed a search of all the purse's contents. When the Vice Principal found an index card containing a list of "people who owe me money" as well as drug paraphernalia, the inference that respondent was dealing in drugs was strong enough to permit reading the letters he had discovered.

The principal thrust of Justice Brennan's dissent was that, for the first time outside the programmatic context, the Court had authorized a full search in the absence of probable cause despite the conclusion that reasonable expectations of privacy existed. Although the Vice Principal probably had probable cause to search the purse for cigarettes—a reliable informant had told him he had just seen the respondent smoking— he did not, according to Brennan, have probable cause to continue the search of the purse after finding the rolling papers: "Just as a police officer could not obtain a warrant to search a home based solely on his claim that he had seen a package of cigarette papers in that home, Mr. Choplick was not entitled to search possibly the most private possession of T.L.O. based on the mere presence of a package of cigarette papers."

As Justice Brennan pointed out, *Terry* and *Camara* do not support the majority's position in *T.L.O.*, at least in any direct sense. *Terry's* holding recognizing the lesser "reasonable suspicion" standard involved a frisk. And *Camara* and its progeny also involved relatively unintrusive searches, together with a showing that a significant government objective would be difficult to achieve if a full quantum of probable cause were required. *T.L.O.*, on the other hand, involved a full search of personal effects on less than probable cause in a situation where a probable cause requirement would not render the government's objective impossible.

One might justify *T.L.O.* on the ground that it, like *Camara*, applies only to "administrative" searches. The initial search in *T.L.O.* was for evidence of a disciplinary infraction, not a crime, and the majority indicated that its holding did not necessarily apply to searches by the police or by school officials acting at the behest of the police. But even if the Court adheres to this limitation, its ruling is questionable. A search of a purse is equally intrusive whether the wrong being investigated is administratively or criminally defined. And the assertion that lay investigators would be burdened by the police model is suspect as well. As Justice Brennan noted, if the police can fathom probable cause, so can school administrators, especially now that the Court has rejected a rule-bound approach to the issue.[84] Further, if resorting to a judicial warrant procedure for disciplinary infractions is overly cumbersome, some sort of in-house pre-search review could replace it for all non-exigent searches.[85] Similar points can be made in connection with the Court's other "special needs" cases, discussed in subsequent sections. Among these cases is the Court's decision in *Vernonia School District 47J v. Acton*,[86] which upheld random drug testing of school athletes; this decision in discussed below in connection with the Court's other drug testing cases.

Similar in tone to *T.L.O.* is *O'Connor v. Ortega*,[87] which held that neither a warrant nor probable cause is required to justify a search of a government employee's office, at least when the search is not a criminal investigation but rather "a noninvestigatory work-related intrusion or an investigatory search for evidence of suspected work-related employee misfeasance."[88] As in *T.L.O.*, the validity of such searches is to be measured by the general standard of "reasonableness." Again, a majority[89] of the Court was willing to discard the warrant requirement because of the perceived hardship it would impose on those conducting the search (in this case, employers). And, as in *T.L.O.*, the Court saw no reason to impose a probable cause standard on work-related investigations when the primary purpose is not criminal investigation but the smooth functioning of the institution. According to Justice O'Connor, "[t]he delay in correcting the employee misconduct caused by the need for probable cause rather than reasonable suspicion will be translated into tangible and often irreparable damage to the agency's work, and ultimately to the public interest." Moreover, analogous to its reasoning in *T.L.O.*, the Court felt that employers should not be expected to school themselves in the "niceties" of probable cause determinations. Balanced against these government interests was what Justice O'Connor termed the "relatively limited invasion" of the work-related search: the employee "may avoid exposing personal belongings at work by simply leaving them at home."

Justice Blackmun, who had concurred in *T.L.O.*, dissented in *Ortega*, joined by three other justices. While he had been willing to recognize a "special need" for relaxed Fourth Amendment requirements in the school context, he found no such special need in *Ortega*. The search in the case was of the entire contents of a doctor's office desk and files. The search took place while the doctor was on administrative leave and not permitted to enter the hospital. Thus, Dr. Ortega's employers could have obtained a warrant based on probable cause "[w]ithout sacrificing their ultimate goal of maintaining an effective institution. . . ." Furthermore, seeking a warrant would have forced the employers "to

---

[84]   See *Illinois v. Gates*, 462 U.S. 213, 103 S.Ct. 2317 (1983), discussed in § 5.03(b).

[85]   See Christopher Slobogin, *A World Without the Fourth Amendment*, 39 U.C.L.A. 1, 34–36 (1991).

[86]   515 U.S. 646, 115 S.Ct. 2386 (1995), discussed in § 13.09(b).

[87]   480 U.S. 709, 107 S.Ct. 1492 (1987).

[88]   The Court stated: "we do not address the appropriate standard when an employee is being investigated for criminal misconduct or breaches of other nonwork-related statutory or regulatory standards."

[89]   Justice Scalia refused to join language in the Court's four-member plurality opinion stating that expectations of privacy in the office should be determined on a case-by-case basis rather than assumed. But he agreed with the plurality that, in his words, "government searches to retrieve work-related materials or to investigate violations of workplace rules—searches of the sort that are regarded as reasonable and normal in the private-employer context—do not violate the Fourth Amendment."

articulate their exact reasons for the search and to specify the items in Dr. Ortega's office they sought, which would have prevented the general rummaging through the doctor's office, desk, and file cabinets" that occurred in the case. Although the dissent could envisage routine situations in which a warrant should not be required prior to a work-related investigation, it found the Court's formulation too sweeping.

Without saying so, the Court also applied special needs analysis in upholding an audit of text messages on a police officer's department-issued pager, an audit that resulted in disciplinary (but not criminal) action against the officer because so many of the messages were personal in nature. In *City of Ontario v. Quon*,[90] the Court assumed without deciding that employees can have a reasonable expectation of privacy in messages sent over a government-owned pager, at least when the relevant privacy policy is ambiguous about its coverage.[91] But echoing its formulation in *Ortega*, the Court also found, unanimously, that the police department's audit of Quon's messaging was motivated by a "noninvestigatory work-related purpose," and thus did not trigger the warrant or probable cause requirements. The search was reasonable because Quon (as well as other officers) had routinely exceeded the monthly character limit for the pager, and the department needed to ascertain whether the limit needed to be extended for work purposes or instead should be reduced because the pagers were being used for personal communications. Further, Justice Kennedy concluded for the Court, the search was not excessive in scope because it accessed only two months' worth of messages and, given the fact that the pager was a workplace device, "was not nearly as intrusive" from an expectation of privacy perspective as a search of "personal" e-mail or a wiretap of the officer's own phone.

In *Safford Unified School District v. Redding*,[92] the Court made clear that, although special needs analysis governs school and workplace searches, its reasonableness test requires more than reasonable suspicion for particularly intrusive searches. In this case, a school official developed reasonable suspicion to believe Redding was distributing contraband pills to other students. After searching her backpack and outer clothing (a search the Court held was reasonable given information the official obtained from other students), the official told Redding to disrobe down to her underwear and pull it away from her body, which exposed her breasts and pelvic region "to some degree." Justice Souter, writing for eight members of the Court, found that this "strip search" violated the Fourth Amendment given the absence of "any indication of danger to the students from the power of the drugs or their quantity and any reason to suppose that [Redding] was carrying pills in her underwear."

13.09   Testing for Drug and Alcohol Use

The Court has been willing to relax Fourth Amendment strictures even further when the school or employer "search" consists of a test to determine whether the employee is using drugs or alcohol. In *Skinner v. Railway Labor Executives' Association*[93] and *National Treasury Employees Union v. Von Raab*[94] the Court upheld regulations

---

[90]   560 U.S. 746, 130 S.Ct. 2619 (2010).

[91]   The department's written policy, which stated that employees had no expectation of privacy in electronic communications, did not explicitly apply to text messaging, but a lieutenant had stated at a staff meeting that it did apply to such messaging.

[92]   557 U.S. 364, 129 S.Ct. 2633 (2009).

[93]   489 U.S. 602, 109 S.Ct. 1402 (1989).

[94]   489 U.S. 656, 109 S.Ct. 1384 (1989).

that permit such tests, not only without a warrant or probable cause, but also in the absence of any individualized suspicion. In *Skinner*, the Court considered regulations promulgated by the Federal Railroad Administration (FRA) which require drug and alcohol testing of any employee who is involved in an accident or who is suspected of having violated certain rules (such as failing to heed a signal). *Von Raab* concerned an employee drug test program administered by the Customs Service which permits testing of anyone who applies for or seeks promotion to a customs job connected with one of three functions—interdicting drugs, use of arms, or access to classified material. Under either program, if an employee tests positive, dismissal may result.[95]

Justice Kennedy, who wrote the majority opinion in both cases, began each by analyzing whether the types of tests used were "searches" under the Fourth Amendment. Because the FRA regulations focus on investigations of accidents and rules violations, they rely primarily on blood and breath tests (which are best at discerning very recent drug and alcohol use), and reserve urinalysis as a backup procedure. In contrast, because the Customs Service regulations aim at screening job and promotion applicants who will be notified of the test, they authorize only urinalysis, which can detect substances in the blood stream that were ingested 60 days or more before the test. The Court found that all three types of tests are searches when administered by the government or a government agent.[96] Blood and breath tests violate "bodily integrity", and urinalysis may reveal private facts about persons other than their drug or alcohol usage, in addition to requiring a significant invasion of privacy if implemented properly.[97] However, the majority was unwilling to hold that the nature of these intrusions justified imposing the warrant or probable cause requirements, or even a requirement of reasonable suspicion.[98] Once again, it relied on *T.L.O.'s* "special need" rubric in deciding to forego these traditional Fourth Amendment protections.

As to the warrant requirement, analogous to its decisions in *T.L.O.* and *Ortega* the Court found that mandating a warrant before testing would frustrate the smooth operation of the testing programs. Additionally, Kennedy concluded that the specificity of the regulations obviated the need for a magistrate. In *Skinner*, for instance, he stated that "in light of the standardized nature of the tests and the minimal discretion vested in those charged with administering the program, there are virtually no facts for a neutral magistrate to evaluate." Similarly, in *Von Raab*, Kennedy concluded that because the testing is automatic for anyone who applies for a job, the Service does not exercise any discretion in deciding who to test; "there are simply 'no special facts for a neutral magistrate to evaluate.' "

In holding that individualized suspicion was also unnecessary under the regulations at issue, the Court found that the employees' interest in avoiding suspicionless invasions of privacy was outweighed by the government's interest in blanket testing. On the

---

[95] While approving both these programs the Court, as it had in *Ortega*, reserved the question as to whether they would be allowed if the test results were routinely used for law enforcement rather than the avowed regulatory purposes.

[96] Under FRA regulations, the railroads administer the tests and private hospitals analyze the results. But the Court found sufficient government involvement to implicate the Fourth Amendment. See § 4.02(b).

[97] Under the Customs Service regulations, monitors are to accompany the subject to the bathroom and listen for the "usual sounds of urination."

[98] See also *Consolidated Rail Corp. v. Railway Labor Executives' Ass'n*, 491 U.S. 299, 109 S.Ct. 2477 (1989), decided the same term as *Skinner* and *Von Raab*. There, the Court held that private railroad and airline companies may unilaterally require random drug and alcohol tests under existing labor contracts because such a requirement is only a "minor change" in the existing relationship between employers and employees.

employee's side of the balance, both *Skinner* and *Von Raab* emphasized *Ortega's* conclusion that an individual's privacy right is often significantly diminished by the demands of the workplace. In *Von Raab*, for instance, Kennedy stated that the " 'operational realities of the workplace' may render entirely reasonable certain work-related intrusions by supervisors and co-workers that might be viewed as unreasonable in other contexts." Customs employees who are involved in drug interdiction or carry firearms should expect that information about their fitness will be elicited.[99] Similarly, in *Skinner*, the Court stated that railway workers cannot expect as much privacy at work as they enjoy at home because they are aware that their employer may subject them to various examinations to determine their ability to operate the railways safely.

Ranged against this diminished privacy interest, stated Kennedy, are "compelling" governmental interests. One such interest, which the Court found to be present in both cases, is preventing impairment of employees with important responsibilities. Without suspicionless testing, Kennedy asserted, employees will know that use of psychoactive substances might go undetected and thus may be more likely to engage in such use, with possibly serious consequences. In the railway industry lives might be lost; with customs agents the "national interest in self protection could be irreparably damaged if those charged with safeguarding it were, because of their own drug use, unsympathetic to their mission of interdicting narcotics" or impaired while using their weapons. In *Skinner*, the Court identified a second reason, in addition to the deterrence rationale, for supporting suspicionless testing: the railways' interest in obtaining information about the causes of major accidents and taking appropriate steps to counteract them.

It was this second rationale that prompted Justice Stevens to join the majority in *Skinner*. In a concurring opinion, he cogently explained why the deterrence rationale was unsatisfactory:

> Most people—and I would think most railroad employees as well—do not go to work with the expectation that they may be involved in a major accident, particularly one causing such catastrophic results as loss of life or the release of hazardous material requiring an evacuation. Moreover, even if they are conscious of the possibilities that such an accident might be a contributing factor, if the risk of serious personal injury does not deter their use of these substances, it seems highly unlikely that the additional threat of loss of employment would have any effect on their behavior.

Only Justices Marshall and Brennan dissented in *Skinner*. In *Von Raab*, they were joined by Justices Scalia and Stevens. Scalia's dissent provides persuasive reasons for distinguishing the two cases:

> I joined the Court's opinion [in *Skinner*] because the demonstrated frequency of drug and alcohol use by the targeted class of employees, and the demonstrated connection between such use and grave harm, rendered the search a reasonable means of protecting society. I decline to join the Court's opinion in the present case because neither frequency of use nor connection to harm is demonstrated or even likely. In my view the Customs Service rules are

---

[99]   With respect to the third group covered by the Services' testing program—those who sought jobs permitting access to classified materials—the Court remanded for a determination as to whether the specific job categories that the regulations included within this group—among them, for instance, baggage clerk, animal caretaker, and electric equipment repairer—in fact had such access. It suggested however, that, in theory, this group of people could be subjected to suspicionless testing as well.

a kind of immolation of privacy and human dignity in symbolic opposition to drug use.

Scalia pointed to statistics that showed the rarity of drug use among customs agents compared to high usage of drugs and alcohol among railway workers. He also found it implausible that customs officers in charge of drug interdiction will be less "sympathetic" to this mission if they use drugs, "any more than police officers who exceed the speed limit in their private cars are appreciably less sympathetic to their mission of enforcing the traffic laws." Similarly, he did not believe that a drug testing program would be more effective at reducing such usage among those officers who carry firearms than the fear of being impaired when confronted by danger.

Today, drug testing by the government is widespread. Lower court cases have considered the legality of programs that permit warrantless, suspicionless testing of teachers, police, utility workers, horse jockeys and several other groups.[100] After *Skinner* and *Von Raab*, the constitutionality of such programs will depend in large part on three factors: (1) the extent to which the type of employee to be tested is subject to privacy intrusions as a routine aspect of the job; (2) the extent to which the job involves potential harm to the public or is otherwise deemed "sensitive"; and (3) the extent to which drug or alcohol use can be deterred by a testing program.

Applying these three factors in *Vernonia School District 47J v. Acton*,[101] the Court upheld a random drug testing program directed at students who want to participate in school athletic programs. The Court found that such students have minimal privacy expectations for a number of reasons. First and foremost, wrote Justice Scalia for a six-member majority, they are "(1) children, who (2) have been committed to the temporary custody of the State as schoolmaster." Additionally, athletes expect less privacy given the semi-public nature of locker rooms and the fact that going out for a team is generally accompanied by significant intrusions (e.g., physical exams). The Court also found that the tests, which involved collecting urine samples from fully clothed students while they were monitored from behind, involved "negligible" privacy intrusion,[102] especially since positive results would at most lead to suspension from the athletic program.

As to the harm sought to be prevented by the testing, Scalia characterized the government interest in deterring drug use among physiologically vulnerable children "compelling." He also pointed to the school district's evidence that drug and disciplinary infractions had increased in recent years, that students were in a "state of rebellion . . . fueled by alcohol and drug abuse, as well as by the student's misperceptions about the drug culture," and that student athletes were the leaders in this rebellion.

Finally, the program was necessary because an individualized suspicion requirement would be "impracticable." Parents willing to accept random drug testing might not be willing to accept "accusatory drug testing for all students," because such a program "transforms the process into a badge of shame." Further, a suspicion-based

---

[100] See, e.g., *Policemen's Benevolent Ass'n. of New Jersey v. Washington Township*, 850 F.2d 133 (3d Cir. 1988), cert. denied 490 U.S. 1004, 109 S.Ct. 1637 (1989) (police). See generally, Phyllis Bookspan, *Jar Wars: Employee Drug Testing, The Constitution, and the American Drug Problem*, 26 Am.Crim.L.Rev. 359 (1988).

[101] 515 U.S. 646, 115 S.Ct. 2386 (1995).

[102] The Court did express reservation about the program to the extent it requires students to reveal prescription medication they are taking and then permits that information to be relayed to school authorities and coaches, but since the record was unclear on this point, it did not directly address the Fourth Amendment implications of such a procedure.

program would be more likely to lead to discriminatory action by teachers, increase litigation, and divert teachers from their normal functions.

Justice O'Connor, joined by Justices Stevens and Souter, wrote a dissent that primarily attacked this last facet of the majority opinion. In her view, a suspicion requirement *would* work, as evidenced by the number of disciplinary infractions discovered and acted upon by school authorities. Further, she argued, the "blanket" nature of the drug testing program in *Vernonia* (which, applied nationwide, could involve millions of students) was unprecedented. She distinguished Vernonia's program from those in *Skinner* and *Von Raab* on two grounds: (1) the suspicionless testing in the latter two cases was the only way to achieve the government's purpose;[103] and (2) both "involved situations in which even one undetected instance of wrongdoing could have injurious consequences for a great number of people."

Justice Ginsburg wrote a concurring opinion emphasizing that the Court's decision would not necessarily authorize schoolwide testing, beyond those who participate in athletics. However, given the majority's reasoning, it seems unlikely that a school district which can muster evidence similar to that introduced by Vernonia would have difficulty convincing a five-member majority of the current Court to support such a program.

Pottawatomie County School District v. Earls[104] was a major step in that direction. There a five-member majority of the Court upheld a drug testing program aimed at students involved in *any* extracurricular activity, ranging from band and choir to the National Honor Society. To participate in such activities, students had to submit to a drug test (using the urinalysis procedure at issue in *Von Raab*), and also had to agree to further random tests once involved in the activities; positive results could result in suspension from the activity but were not given to law enforcement. Unlike the athletes targeted in *Vernonia*, students in nonathletic extracurricular activities are not as likely to be involved in "communal undress" and similar surrenders of privacy. Nor, at least in this case, were they shown to be engaging in significant drug use, in contrast to the proof of increased drug abuse in *Vernonia*. Finally, to the extent drug use does occur during such activities, it is not as likely to endanger the students or others as is drug use during sports.

Nonetheless, the majority, in an opinion by Justice Thomas, discounted all three distinctions. The lesser privacy of athletes "was not essential to our decision in *Vernonia*, which depended primarily upon the school's custodial responsibility and authority." Likewise, proof of substantial drug use is not necessary to justify a drug testing program. The majority refused to adopt the Tenth Circuit's requirement that the school demonstrate "some identifiable drug abuse problem among a sufficient number of those subject to the testing, such that testing that group of students will actually redress its drug problem." That type of test would be too difficult to administer, Thomas stated; in any event, "it would make little sense to require a school district to wait for a substantial portion of its students to begin using drugs before it was allowed to institute a drug testing program destined to deter drug use." Finally, "the safety interest furthered by drug testing is undoubtedly substantial for all children, athletes and nonathletes alike." This reasoning would easily support a school-wide drug testing program, although

---

[103] She also noted that, in *Skinner* at least, the fact that the testing took place after accidents and safety violations ensured some degree of individualized suspicion, in contrast to the program at issue in *Vernonia*.

[104] 536 U.S. 822, 122 S.Ct. 2559 (2002).

Justice Breyer, the fifth vote for the majority, expressed discomfort at such a rule, just as Justice Ginsburg had in *Vernonia*.

Not every government attempt to discover drug use through testing is constitutional, however. *Chandler v. Miller*[105] struck down on Fourth Amendment grounds a Georgia statute that required every person seeking nomination or election to a state office to undergo a test for illegal drugs. Georgia argued that the statute deterred illegal drug use that could call into question an official's judgement and integrity, jeopardize discharge of public functions (including antidrug law enforcement efforts), and undermine public confidence and trust in elected officials. The eight-member majority dismissed these interests as "hypothetical." Under special needs analysis, Justice Ginsburg wrote for the Court, there must be "concrete danger"; here the state admitted there was no evidence of drug abuse by public officials in Georgia. Ginsburg distinguished this case from *Von Raab*, where evidence of drug use had also been minimal, by noting that drug interdiction was the primary purpose of the customs agency and that customs law enforcement agents, in contrast to political candidates, are not subject to the day-to-day scrutiny that could reveal evidence of drug abuse.[106] In conclusion, the Court stated, "[t]he need revealed [by the Georgia statute] is symbolic, not 'special,' as that term draws meaning from our case law."

The majority did note that its previous decisions had given states wide leeway in establishing conditions of candidacy for state office that were not violative of constitutional protections.[107] Perhaps this is why it chose not to address the constitutionality of medical examinations "designed to provide certification of a candidate's general health." In dissent, Chief Justice Rehnquist made much of this demurral: "The only possible basis for distinction is to say that the State has a far greater interest in the candidate's 'general health' than it does with respect to his propensity to use illegal drugs . . . the sort of policy judgment that surely must be left to legislatures, rather than being announced from on high by the Federal Judiciary."

Ferguson v. City of Charleston[108] involved a somewhat different type of drug testing program than those considered in the Court's previous cases. In consultation with the police, staff at the Medical University of South Carolina developed a policy that authorized drug testing of pregnant patients suspected of drug use and also permitted turning over positive results to the police, who then might initiate prosecution, albeit usually with the intent of encouraging the woman to obtain treatment. Assuming (contrary to the jury finding in the case) that these tests were nonconsensual, the Court, in an opinion by Justice Stevens, found them to be unreasonable under the Fourth Amendment. These tests differed from those in *Skinner, Vernonia* and the other drug testing cases, Stevens reasoned, because in those cases "there was no misunderstanding about the purpose of the test or the potential use of the test results," whereas the patients in *Ferguson* apparently believed the tests were primarily diagnostic, the results of which reasonable patients would assume were confidential. More important to the five-member

---

[105] 520 U.S. 305, 117 S.Ct. 1295 (1997).

[106] As Rehnquist pointed out in dissent, however, the *Von Raab* Court had also permitted drug testing of customs officials who deal with classified documents (although it did remand to determine who such officials were). See supra note 99. These officials do not deal with drug interdiction and may be subject to daily scrutiny.

[107] *Compare Gregory v. Ashcroft*, 501 U.S. 452, 111 S.Ct. 2395 (1991) (state may set mandatory retirement age for judges) *with Bond v. Floyd*, 385 U.S. 116, 87 S.Ct. 339 (1966) (cannot exclude elected representative on ground that his antiwar statements cast doubt on his ability to take an oath).

[108] 532 U.S. 67, 121 S.Ct. 1281 (2001).

majority, and the key justification for Justice Kennedy in concurrence, was that, in contrast to most of the Court's previous special needs cases, law enforcement officials were involved in developing and implementing the Charleston policy from its inception. Thus, this case was more analogous to the narcotics checkpoint in *City of Indianapolis v. Edmond*,[109] where the Court held that individualized suspicion was required given the focus on "ordinary law enforcement."

Justice Scalia in dissent argued that turning the test results over to the police did not violate the Fourth Amendment because, even if the patients were unclear about the tests' purpose, they voluntarily submitted to them and thus, under authority of the Court's undercover agent cases,[110] assumed the risk the results would be used for criminal evidence purposes. Scalia also could find no distinction between this case and *Griffin v. Wisconsin*,[111] which also upheld a law enforcement search, specifically a search by a probationer officer that was triggered by information received from a police detective. Perhaps the best response to Scalia's observations about the Court's precedents is that information exchanged between doctor and patient, like that which passes between client and lawyer, should be entitled to greater privacy protection than evidence and communications voluntarily surrendered in other contexts.

13.10 Probation and Parole Supervision

The same term that *Ortega* was decided, the Court recognized still another special need situation in which the warrant and probable cause requirements may be relaxed. In *Griffin v. Wisconsin*,[112] the Court upheld a warrantless search of a probationer's home under a Wisconsin statute authorizing such searches whenever a probation officer has "reasonable grounds" to believe the home contains items unauthorized by the probation order. The 5–4 decision, written by Justice Scalia, found that, in light of the rehabilitative and preventive goals of probation, probation supervision "is a 'special need' of the State permitting a degree of impingement upon privacy that would not be constitutional if applied to the public at large."

According to Scalia, a warrant requirement would interfere with the probation officer's ability to respond quickly to evidence of misconduct and thus reduce the rehabilitative and deterrent effects of supervision. Moreover, the need for the independent review of a magistrate is reduced when a probation officer—who is "supposed to have in mind the welfare of the probationer"—rather than a police officer is making the decision to search. The probable cause requirement would also make searches more difficult and thus again "reduce the deterrent effect of the supervisory arrangement". Additionally, the greater degree of reliability required by the probable cause standard might prevent intervention at the first sign of trouble, before a probationer does damage to himself or society.

Griffin did not make clear what standard should govern searches of probationers' homes. The dissenters all agreed that the basis of the search in *Griffin*—a tip from an unidentified police officer that Griffin "had or might have guns"—did not amount to reasonable suspicion, and yet the majority found it sufficient. Later cases indicated that

---

[109] 531 U.S. 32, 121 S.Ct. 447 (2000), discussed in § 13.06(f).

[110] See § 4.03(a).

[111] 483 U.S. 868, 107 S.Ct. 3164 (1987), discussed in § 13.10.

[112] 483 U.S. 868, 107 S.Ct. 3164 (1987).

even this level of suspicion is usually not required when the search is of a probationer's or parolee's residence.

The search of the probationer's apartment in *United States v. Knights*[113] was by a sheriff's deputy involved in a routine criminal investigation, who developed suspicion that Knights was engaged in making pipe bombs and planning arson. Knights argued that, because this search was not a probationary status check, it fell outside the "special needs" exception, and thus required probable cause. But a unanimous Supreme Court held that, regardless of the searcher's purpose, a probationer is generally entitled to less Fourth Amendment protection. The probationer's status allows the imposition of "reasonable conditions that deprive the offender of some freedoms enjoyed by law-abiding citizens," including the type of condition imposed on Knights as part of his probation (allowing a search by any "probation officer or law enforcement officer"). By virtue of this condition, Knights had a "diminished" reasonable expectation of privacy.[114] And the government's interest is heightened in this setting because probationers are less likely to be law-abiding. The "balance of these considerations," stated the Court, "requires no more than reasonable suspicion to conduct a search of this probationer's house" (and presumably the homes of most other probationers, who are usually subject to the same type of condition).

While *Knight* required "no more than reasonable suspicion," in *Samson v. California*,[115] the Court made clear that this language and *Knight's* balancing analysis does not *require* that level of justification. Reiterating the points in *Knights* that probationers and parolees have "severely diminished privacy expectations" (especially in California where parolees must sign an order accepting as a condition of release that they can be searched at "any time"[116]) and that these individuals also require "intense supervision" given their high recidivism rates, Justice Thomas wrote for six members of the Court that the Fourth Amendment permits *random* searches of parolees, by *police officers* as well as parole officers. In dissent, Justice Stevens asserted that "the Court for the first time upholds an entirely suspicionless search unsupported by any special need." The latter category might have applied, Stevens said, were the searches conducted solely by parole officers for the purpose of "guid[ing] the parolee's transition back into society" or pursuant to "programmatic safeguards to ensure evenhandedness;" outside of those situations, however, individualized suspicion should be required. Thomas did allude favorably to California law's injunction against "arbitrary, capricious or harassing" searches of parolees. Perhaps to this extent, at least, the Fourth Amendment imposes limits on law enforcement discretion in this context.

13.11   DNA Testing

Every state permits the collection of DNA samples from convicted felons, and over half the states permit DNA collection from people arrested for serious offenses.[117] The buccal swab necessary to obtain DNA consists of a light touch inside the cheek. The

---

[113]   534 U.S. 112, 122 S.Ct. 587 (2001).

[114]   The Court avoided deciding whether a probationer's acceptance of such a condition constituted consent, however.

[115]   547 U.S. 843, 126 S.Ct. 2193 (2006).

[116]   Despite this provision, the Court again refused, as it had in *Knights*, to address whether the suspicionless searches could also be justified via consent doctrine.

[117]   See *Maryland v. King*, 569 U.S. 435, 133 S.Ct. 1958 (2013).

sample can help determine whether a person is who he says he is, but more commonly is used as a way of linking the individual to unsolved or future crimes.

In *Maryland v. King*,[118] a closely divided Supreme Court held that swabs to obtain DNA are Fourth Amendment searches, but that they may be conducted on all people validly arrested for a "serious offense," without demonstration of any suspicion the swab will produce evidence of crime. Instead of relying on special needs analysis to reach this conclusion, the Court used the balancing test adopted in *Samson*, which it said was more apposite in cases involving people who are arrested. Justice Kennedy's opinion for five members of the Court stated that the government's interests in comparing DNA to existing records—e.g., identifying arrestees and determining whether they have committed other crimes, are dangerous or are a flight risk—outweighed the slight intrusion associated with a buccal swab, at least when the DNA is used only for identification purposes, does not reveal genetic traits and is destroyed if the arrestee is acquitted. Justice Kennedy likened the DNA matching process to fingerprinting, which has long been seen by the lower courts as "a natural part of the administrative steps incident to arrest."

In dissent, Justice Scalia argued that DNA is more likely than fingerprinting to be used to match an arrestee to another crime, and that the matching process is the type of "general search" barred by the Fourth Amendment. He also noted that the arrestees most directly affected by the majority's decision would be those who are eventually acquitted, because those who are convicted would have their DNA sampled in any event. Finally, he did not see how the Court's balancing analysis distinguished between swabs of those arrested for serious offenses and those arrested for traffic offenses and predicted that DNA sampling would soon spread to every arrestee.

The majority is right that the search in this case was minimal, particularly in light of other intrusions that can permissibly take place upon arrest.[119] Further, the potential for DNA databanks to solve crime and deter it is significant. What is not as clear is why arrestees can be singled out for DNA sampling while others are not. Arrestees may be no more likely to have committed other crimes than those who have not been arrested. Furthermore, if, as Justice Scalia predicts, *King* is not limited to serious crimes, the case provides an incentive to use minor offenses as a pretext for gathering DNA evidence.

13.12   Conclusion

The Supreme Court has addressed the Fourth Amendment implications of a number of so-called "administrative" or "regulatory" search situations. Its pronouncements are summarized below.

(1)   Nonconsensual health and safety inspections of residences and of businesses not governed by (2) below are permissible only if authorized by a *"Camara* warrant" or some other type of pre-compliance review, such as an administrative subpoena. The court order need not be based on probable cause to believe that the particular residence or business is in violation of health and safety laws, but may instead be issued if it is carried out pursuant to a general inspection plan. The schedule of inspections should be based on "neutral" criteria (e.g., geographic area to be inspected in the case of residence

---

[118]   Id.

[119]   See *Florence v. Burlington*, 566 U.S. 318, 132 S.Ct. 1510 (2012), discussed in § 20.03 (permitting body cavity searches in jail).

inspections, number of employees in the case of business inspections) that inhibit arbitrary or pretextual intrusions.

(2) Inspections of "closely regulated" businesses do not require a warrant nor, apparently, even *Camara*-type suspicion, if: (a) the government has a substantial interest in regulating the business; (b) surprise inspections are required to implement the interest effectively; and (c) the statute provides an adequate substitute for a warrant. Where violations of the regulations are easily hidden, this latter requirement may be met if the time, place and scope limitations of the inspection are spelled out in the statute. In other cases, the government may, in addition, have to seek an injunction to enter if the owner refuses. In any case, "unauthorized force" may not be used to gain entry. Entry into a business to obtain evidence of criminal activity not associated with the operation of the business requires a traditional warrant. Documents and other items sought without physical entry may also be obtained pursuant to a subpoena based on a finding that the items are relevant to a legitimate investigation.

(3) Searches of a building conducted during and immediately after a fire may be made without a warrant. Once exigent circumstances are no longer present, however, the owner is entitled either to notice of the government's intention to inspect the scene or a "*Camara* warrant." If the inspection evolves into a search for evidence of crime, a warrant meeting the requirements of a typical criminal search warrant must authorize it.

(4) Routine stops and searches at the border do not implicate the Fourth Amendment, as persons crossing the border have no reasonable expectation that their possessions will be immune from government scrutiny. International mail may be searched without a warrant or probable cause (although *reading* mail may require a warrant). Prolonged detention or nonroutine searches of people (as opposed to cars) at the border require at least reasonable suspicion but does not require probable cause, at least when necessitated by the detained person's refusal to contemplate less intrusive alternatives.

(5) The Supreme Court has approved checkpoints to detect illegal immigration, drunken driving, automobile licenses and registration violations, violations of boating rules on waterways connected to the sea, and witnesses to a crime. Lower courts have approved airport checkpoints to detect hijackers and other dangerous individuals. No individualized suspicion is required at any of these specialized checkpoints, so long as the intrusion is minimal and there is some attempt to minimize discretion (by having higher authorities establish the checkpoint, or by checking those who pass through according to a pre-specified pattern). However, checkpoints established to carry out "ordinary" law enforcement are impermissible without individualized suspicion.

(6) An inventory of a car that has been lawfully impounded or of the personal effects of an individual who has been lawfully arrested does not require a warrant so long as conducted pursuant to police department regulations. A car inventory must be limited to a search of places in which valuables might reasonably be kept (which includes glove compartments and trunks). If the inventory reveals items giving rise to probable cause to believe that contraband or other illegal items are somewhere in the car, a warrantless search of other parts of the car may be conducted at that time or at a later time.

(7) Searches of public schoolchildren's personal effects for evidence of disciplinary infractions are governed by the Fourth Amendment. However, neither a warrant nor probable cause are required to conduct such searches; rather, the validity of the search depends upon the reasonableness of the initial intrusion and the reasonableness of the search's scope in light of the surrounding circumstances. Suspicionless drug testing of students, at least those involved in extracurricular activities, is also constitutional.

(8) Searches of government employees' offices are governed by the Fourth Amendment, but neither a warrant nor probable cause is required to conduct such searches if they are work-related rather than criminal investigations; as with public school searches, the governing test is "reasonableness." A warrantless test of government employees or other groups for drug or alcohol use is reasonable, even if not based on individualized suspicion, if the government's interest in detecting such use is "compelling" enough to outweigh the individuals' privacy interest. Under this balancing test, suspicionless drug testing is permissible when aimed at railway workers involved in accidents or safety violations and customs agents, but not if it targets pregnant women in the hospital (at least when the testing program is initiated by the police) or individuals seeking political office.

(9) Searches of probationers' or parolees' homes do not require either a warrant or any particular level of suspicion.

(10) DNA testing using a buccal swap of persons arrested for serious offenses requires neither a warrant nor any level of suspicion.

The Court's regulatory search cases have created a "second class" Fourth Amendment right, applicable when the government can justify its desire to intrude on some ground other than a need for evidence of criminal law violations (and *Burger*, *Samson* and *King* in effect do away with even the latter limitation). This second class recognizes neither a warrant requirement nor a probable cause requirement. Government officials need only act "reasonably," which will often be the case if they can articulate statute- or regulation-based justification for the search. Depending upon the government's willingness to create "administrative" rationales for its searches, this second class right could supercede in significance the original Fourth Amendment right. Given the deference to police these cases evidence, one must be particularly alert to the possibility that these special needs doctrines are being used pretextually.

BIBLIOGRAPHY

Arcila, Fabio. Special Needs and Special Deference: Suspicionless Civil Searches in the Modern Regulatory State. 56 Admin.L.Rev. 1223 (2004).

Bookspan, Phyllis. Jar Wars: Employee Drug Testing, The Constitution, and the American Drug Problem. 26 Am.Crim.L.Rev. 359 (1988).

Brensike-Primus, Eve. Disentangling Administrative Searches. 111 Colum. L. Rev. 254 (2011).

Christenson, Steven. *Colorado v. Bertine* Opens the Inventory Search to Containers. 73 Iowa L.Rev. 771 (1988).

Friedman, Barry and Maria Ponomarenko. Democratic Policing. 90 N.Y.U. Law Review 1827 (2015).

Holland, Brooks. The Road 'Round *Edmond*: Steering Through Primary Purpose and Crime Control Agendas. 111 Penn St. L. Rev. 293 (2006).

Mandell, Leonard B. and Richardson, L. Anita. Lengthy Detentions and Invasive Searches at the Border: In Search of a Magistrate. 28 Ariz.L.Rev. 331 (1986).

Murphy, Erin. License, Registration, Cheek Swab: DNA Testing and the Supreme Court. 127 Harv. L. Rev. 161 (2013).

Rosenweig, Paul. Functional Equivalents of the Border, Sovereignty, and the Fourth Amendment. 52 Univ. Chicago L.Rev. 1119 (1985).

Rothstein, Mark A. OSHA Inspections after *Marshall v. Barlow's, Inc.* 1979 Duke L.J. 63 (1979).

Slobogin, Christopher. Policing as Administration. 165 University of Pennsylvania Law Review 191 (2016).

Stack, Rebecca. Airport Drug Searches: Giving Content to the Concept of Free and Voluntary Consent. 77 Va.L.Rev. 183 (1991).

Steinberg, David E. High School Drug Testing and the Original Understanding of the Fourth Amendment. 30 Hastings Const.L.Q. 263 (2003).

Strossen, Nadine. *Michigan Department of State Police v. Sitz*: A Roadblock to Meaningful Judicial Enforcement of Constitutional Rights. 42 Hastings L.J. 285 (1991).

____. The Fourth Amendment in the Balance: Accurately Setting the Scales Through the Least Intrusive Alternative Analysis. 63 N.Y.U. L.Rev. 1173 (1988).

Stuntz, William J. Implicit Bargains, Government Power, and the Fourth Amendment. 44 Stan. L.Rev. 553 (1992).

Sundby, Scott E. Protecting the Citizen "Whilst He Is Quiet": Suspicionless Searches, "Special Needs," and General Warrants. 74 Miss.L.J. 501 (2004).

Worf, Richard C. The Case for Rational Basis Review of General Suspicionless Searches and Seizures. 23 Touro L.Rev. 93 (2007).

Chapter 14

TECHNOLOGICAL SURVEILLANCE

14.01   Introduction

The term technological surveillance, as used in this chapter, is meant to encompass a wide variety of techniques that enhance the ability to eavesdrop or spy on the activities of others. These techniques include wiretapping (involving the interception of telephone calls by physical penetration of the wire circuitry), "bugging" (listening to conversations over a transmitting device installed either on premises or on individuals), hacking (the interception of computer transmissions and the accessing of stored transmissions), electronic tracking of movements, video surveillance, and x-ray-type devices that can "see" through opaque surfaces. Sophisticated techniques in each of these categories are being developed at a rapid pace. For instance, conversations can now be discerned from the vibrations they make on window panes; cathode ray technology can be used to access electronic mail from locations hundreds of yards from the relevant computer; vehicles can be tracked using beepers, Global Positioning Systems, signals from a cell phone, or satellite imagery; cameras can be equipped with wide-angle, pinhole lenses allowing their placement virtually anywhere, and can also be equipped with magnification and infrared, darkness piercing capacity; the outlines of objects underneath clothing can be discerned not only by x-ray machines but by hand-held thermal-imaging devices.[1] All of this technology permits surveillance, without detection if so desired, of private conversations and actions.

When used by the government, technological surveillance creates a particularly dramatic threat to the privacy of individual citizens. Yet the legal system has been slow to respond to this unique type of "search and seizure." While law enforcement agencies began using some wiretapping and bugging techniques as early as the 1920's,[2] the first comprehensive effort toward regulating their use did not occur until the late 1960's. And recent developments suggest that scientific advancement and law enforcement ingenuity will continue to outpace judicial and legislative monitoring.

This chapter first explores regulation of "communications surveillance" (i.e., wiretapping, bugging, and interception of electronic mail), concentrating on Title III of the Omnibus Crime Control and Safe Streets Act,[3] which was passed by Congress in 1968, has been amended significantly once since then, and presently governs both federal and state practice with respect to electronic eavesdropping. It also looks at efforts to regulate tracking devices, video surveillance, and detection devices that can penetrate walls and clothing.

---

[1]   See generally, Christopher Slobogin, *Technologically-Assisted Physical Surveillance: The American Bar Association's Tentative Draft Standards*, 10 Harv. J. Law & Technology 383 (1997); Lewis Katz, *In Search of a Fourth Amendment for the Twenty-First Century*, 65 Ind.L.Rev. 549 (1990).

[2]   See *Olmstead v. United States*, 277 U.S. 438, 48 S.Ct. 564 (1928).

[3]   18 U.S.C.A. §§ 2510–2520.

14.02   Regulation of Communications Surveillance Prior to Title III

(a) The Trespass Doctrine

The first case involving communications surveillance to reach the Supreme Court was *Olmstead v. United States*.[4] There, federal agents had set up a tap of the telephone wires outside the defendants' premises, without a warrant. Over strong dissents by Justice Brandeis and Justice Holmes, the Court held that since the tap was not a "trespass" on the defendants' property and did not seize tangible "things" protected by the language of the Fourth Amendment, no search or seizure occurred. Although it eventually discarded the notion that conversations were not "things" for Fourth Amendment purposes, for the next forty years the Court continued to analyze electronic surveillance cases in terms of whether the surveillance worked a trespass. Thus, in *Goldman v. United States*,[5] the Court held that the use of a detectaphone placed against an office wall in order to hear private conversations in the office next door did not violate the Fourth Amendment because there was no physical trespass in connection with the relevant interception. Conversely, in *Silverman v. United States*,[6] eavesdrop evidence was excluded because it was obtained through use of a "spike mike" inserted under the baseboard of a wall until it made contact with a heating duct running throughout Silverman's house.

Even when the surveillance involved a physical invasion of property by a government agent, the Court refused to apply the Fourth Amendment if there was "consent." Thus, in *On Lee v. United States*,[7] the Court upheld, 5–4, use of a "body bug" concealed on an ex-employee of the defendant who entered the defendant's laundry without objection and engaged him in conversation. Neither the argument that the government's actions were fraudulent nor the contention that the body bug allowed another agent, outside the laundry, to listen to the defendant swayed the Court; these facts did not convert the action into a trespass. Similarly, in *Lopez v. United States*,[8] the Court sanctioned use of a recording device on a government agent, because "the device was used only to obtain the most reliable evidence possible of a conversation in which the Government's own agent was a participant" and "was not planted by means of an unlawful physical invasion of petitioner's premises."

(b) The Federal Communications Act

While the Court was reluctant to regulate communications surveillance, Congress, six years after *Olmstead*, did undertake that task in cases involving federal agents. In § 605 of the Federal Communications Act of 1934, Congress provided that "no person not being authorized by the sender shall intercept any communication and divulge or publish the existence, contents, purport, effect or meaning of such intercepted communications to any person." As with the trespass doctrine, if a party to the conversation allowed the eavesdropping, the Act was not triggered.[9] But nonconsensual wiretapping was curtailed

---

[4]   277 U.S. 438, 48 S.Ct. 564 (1928).

[5]   316 U.S. 129, 62 S.Ct. 993 (1942).

[6]   365 U.S. 505, 81 S.Ct. 679 (1961).

[7]   343 U.S. 747, 72 S.Ct. 967 (1952).

[8]   373 U.S. 427, 83 S.Ct. 1381 (1963).

[9]   *Rathbun v. United States*, 355 U.S. 107, 78 S.Ct. 161 (1957).

significantly under § 605. In *Nardone v. United States*,[10] the Supreme Court held that, in federal cases, § 605 required exclusion of all evidence obtained from a surreptitious interstate wiretap; to hold otherwise, explained the Court, would be to allow an unauthorized person to "divulge" the contents of the message.[11] The Court later held that this rule applied to *intra*state taps as well,[12] and also to evidence procured by state officers that was later used in federal court.[13]

However, these cases, all of which preceded *Mapp v. Ohio*,[14] made clear that the Act did not mandate exclusion in state cases.[15] It was not until 1968, seven years after *Mapp*, that violations of the Act were found to require exclusion in state prosecutions.[16] Moreover, § 605 applied only to tapping of phone, telegraph or radiotelegraph lines. It did not cover use of more sophisticated devices that did not involve tapping. Finally, the Act did nothing to prevent private eavesdropping. Developments in Fourth Amendment jurisprudence and, eventually, the passage of Title III, would make the Federal Communications Act of tangential relevance to regulation of eavesdropping law.[17]

(c) *Katz* and Expectation of Privacy Analysis

In 1967, the Supreme Court decided the seminal case of *Katz v. United States*.[18] There, government agents attached an electronic listening and recording device to the outside of a booth known to be used by the defendant for phone conversations. Although no physical trespass of the booth occurred (and in any event the booth was not the defendant's property), the Court excluded the conversations thereby obtained, in the process overturning *Olmstead* and rejecting the trespass doctrine. Because the government action "violated the privacy upon which Katz justifiably relied while using the telephone booth," the Fourth Amendment was implicated and the agents should have obtained a warrant. Justice Harlan's concurring language referring to the defendant's "reasonable expectations of privacy" soon became the theoretical basis of Fourth Amendment protection.[19]

However, the post-*Katz* Court has refused to back away from the holdings in *On Lee* and *Lopez* involving "consensual" eavesdropping. In *United States v. White*,[20] a plurality of the Court upheld the result in those cases despite *Katz'* rejection of the trespass rationale. Noting that one assumes the risk that one's acquaintances will be government agents, the majority stated "it is only speculation to assert that the defendant's utterances would be substantially different or his sense of security any less if he also thought it possible that the suspected colleague is wired for sound." In dissent, Justice

---

[10]   302 U.S. 379, 58 S.Ct. 275 (1937).

[11]   Two years later, the Court held in the same case that "fruit" of the wiretap could not be used in federal court. *Nardone v. United States*, 308 U.S. 338, 60 S.Ct. 266 (1939), discussed in § 2.04(a).

[12]   *Weiss v. United States*, 308 U.S. 321, 60 S.Ct. 269 (1939).

[13]   *Benanti v. United States*, 355 U.S. 96, 78 S.Ct. 155 (1957).

[14]   367 U.S. 643, 81 S.Ct. 1684 (1961).

[15]   The Court explicitly so held in *Schwartz v. Texas*, 344 U.S. 199, 73 S.Ct. 232 (1952).

[16]   *Lee v. Florida*, 392 U.S. 378, 88 S.Ct. 2096 (1968).

[17]   With the enactment of Title III, Congress amended § 605 to limit its coverage solely to interception of radio communications, which Title III does not cover. Act of June 19, 1968, Pub.L. No. 90–351, § 803, 82 Stat. 212.

[18]   389 U.S. 347, 88 S.Ct. 507 (1967).

[19]   See § 4.03 for further discussion of *Katz*.

[20]   401 U.S. 745, 91 S.Ct. 1122 (1971). *White* was affirmed by a majority of the Court in *United States v. Caceres*, 440 U.S. 741, 99 S.Ct. 1465 (1979).

Harlan argued otherwise: "Were third-party bugging a prevalent practice, it might well smother that spontaneity—reflected in frivolous, impetuous, sacrilegious, and defiant discourse—that liberates daily life." Thus, the Fourth Amendment should protect "the expectation of the ordinary citizen, who has never engaged in illegal conduct in his life, that he may carry on his private discourse freely, openly, and spontaneously without measuring his every word against the connotations it might carry when instantaneously heard by others unknown to him and unfamiliar with his situation or analyzed in a cold, formal record played days, months, or years after the conversation." As developed elsewhere in this book,[21] the deeper problem with *White* lies in the failure of either the majority or the dissent to recognize that even undercover activity that is not electronically assisted violates normal expectations of privacy.

(d) The Fourth Amendment Warrant Requirement

If a particular type of eavesdropping does implicate the Fourth Amendment, one must determine the kind of protection thereby afforded. The same term as *Katz*, the Supreme Court decided *Berger v. New York*,[22] which, for the first time, addressed the precise application of the Fourth Amendment to communications surveillance cases.

At issue in *Berger* was a New York eavesdropping statute which permitted an eavesdrop order to be issued by a magistrate if a specified state law enforcement officer stated that there was reasonable ground to believe that evidence of a crime could thus be obtained. Since this was the only requirement for an order to issue, the Supreme Court determined that the statute was deficient on its face in six specific areas: (1) it failed to require a showing of probable cause that a particular offense had been or was being committed; (2) it did not require a particularized description of the communications, conversations or discussions that were to be seized; (3) it provided for the grant of a two-month period eavesdrop that could and often did lead to a series of intrusions, searches and seizures pursuant to a single showing of cause whereby all conversations were seized, not just incriminating ones; (4) the statute failed to provide for a termination date on the eavesdrop once the conversation sought was seized; (5) it provided no requirement for notice, as do conventional warrants, but rather permitted uncontested "entry" for the purpose of setting up wiretaps without any showing of exigency; and (6) it failed to require return on the warrant, thus making judicial supervision of the eavesdropping difficult.

In short, *Berger* notified the states that statutes authorizing eavesdropping under court order would, at the least, have to comply with traditional Fourth Amendment search warrant requirements.[23] The precise reach of *Berger* is discussed in more detail in the discussion of Title III, which was enacted one year after *Berger*.

14.03   Federal Eavesdropping Law: Title III

In apparent response to the legal uncertainties regarding communications surveillance, and spurred on by the *Berger* and *Katz* decisions, Congress passed Title III of the Omnibus Crime Control and Safe Streets Act of 1968.[24] The law is particularly

---

[21] See § 4.03(a).

[22] 388 U.S. 41, 87 S.Ct. 1873 (1967).

[23] See Chapter 5 for a description of these requirements.

[24] 18 U.S.C.A. §§ 2510–20 (originally enacted as Act of June 19, 1968, Pub.L. No. 90–351, § 802, 82 Stat. 212). The textual references throughout the rest of this chapter refer to Title III.

important because it preempts state law pertaining to electronic eavesdropping.[25] Pursuant to § 2516(2) of Title III, a state court judge may grant an eavesdropping order only if the entire application process is in conformity with Title III as well as with the applicable state statute.[26] If a state statute does not conform to Title III with regard to the procedures for obtaining a valid wiretap order, the order will be unlawful even though authorized by state law. At the same time, Congress clearly intended that the states could enact more restrictive communications surveillance statutes or construe existing statutes narrowly to protect privacy more fully than Title III.[27]

In 1986, Congress enacted the Electronic Communications Privacy Act,[28] which significantly amended Title III in several ways. A summary of Title III, as amended, and the decisions by the Supreme Court relevant to it follow.

(a) The Scope of Title III

Title III prohibits the "interception" of "wire, oral or electronic communications," unless such interception is authorized by the statute. As originally enacted, Title III protected only wire communications and oral communications. In 1986, responding to the explosion of telecommunication and computer technologies, Congress passed the Electronic Communications Privacy Act (ECPA), which added "electronic communications" as a protected category.[29] The 1986 amendments also make clear that Title III protects *private* wire and electronic communications;[30] the previous version had referred exclusively to wire communications "operated by any person engaged as a common carrier."

Finally, the amendments extend protection to electronic storage and processing of information.[31] To the extent such storage or processing is under the auspices of a third party computer operator, the amendments thus provide protection the Fourth Amendment may not, since the Fourth Amendment is not implicated when information is sought from a party to whom it has voluntarily been surrendered.[32] However, the 1986 amendments do not require a "Title III" warrant, but only a regular warrant for access to information that is in storage less than 180 days, and only a subpoena for access to information in storage over 180 days.[33] Furthermore, the USA Patriot Act of 2001 amended this portion of Title III by providing that an *ex parte* subpoena (one which does not require notice to the target) is sufficient to obtain basic subscriber information, defined as name, address, session times and durations, length and type of service, means and source of payment (including credit card numbers), and the identity of Internet users who use a pseudonym. Even if the government seeks additional transactional information—such as account logs and e-mail addresses of other individuals with whom the accountholder has corresponded—it still need not alert the subscriber, but it must

---

[25]   18 U.S.C.A. § 2516(2), cf. *United States v. Tortorello*, 480 F.2d 764 (2d Cir. 1973), cert. denied 414 U.S. 866, 94 S.Ct. 63 (1973).

[26]   18 U.S.C.A. § 2516(2).

[27]   Sen.Rep. No. 1097, 90th Cong., 2d Sess. (1968), U.S.Code Cong.Adm.News 2177, 2187.

[28]   Pub.L. No. 99–508 (1986).

[29]   18 U.S.C.A. § 2511(2)(a)(ii).

[30]   See 5 U.S.Code Congressional and Administrative News 3559 (99th Cong.2d Sess.1986) [hereafter referred to as 5 U.S.Code News].

[31]   18 U.S.C.A. § 2701 et seq.

[32]   Cf. *United States v. Miller*, 425 U.S. 435, 96 S.Ct. 1619 (1976), discussed in § 4.03(a).

[33]   18 U.S.C.A. § 2703.

allege "specific and articulable facts showing that there are reasonable grounds to believe that . . . the records or other information sought are relevant and material to an ongoing criminal investigation."[34] Although this language sounds like reasonable suspicion is required, note that it only demands that the information be "relevant and material" to an investigation.

The discussion that follows focuses solely on interception of communications in real time, rather than on accessing stored records or transactional information. With that limitation,[35] it describes Title III's scope, its warrant and execution requirements, and the suppression and civil and criminal remedies it provides.

(1) Types of Communications Protected

The three types of communications covered by Title III are precisely defined. Wire communication is defined as:

> "any aural transfer made in whole or in part through the use of facilities for the transmission of communications by the aid of wire, cable, or other like connection . . . [that affects interstate commerce] . . . [S]uch term includes any electronic storage of such communication."[36]

In 1986, the Act was amended to exclude "the radio portion of a cordless telephone communication that is transmitted between the cordless telephone handset and the base unit" on the dubious ground that communications "on some cordless telephones can be intercepted easily with readily available technologies, such as an AM radio."[37] In 1994 Congress reversed itself, extending full Title III protection to conversations over such phones.[38]

Oral communication is defined as "any oral communication uttered by a person exhibiting an expectation that such communication is not subject to interception under circumstances justifying such expectation, but such term does not include any electronic communication."[39] The 1968 legislative history suggests that this language would not cover conversations in certain quasi-public areas, such as a jail cell or "open fields."[40] Admittedly, the Supreme Court has found the Fourth Amendment inapplicable to searches for *effects* in these areas.[41] But the reasoning in these cases does not necessarily apply to "searches" for conversations which the parties expect to be private.

Electronic communication means

> any transfer of signs, signals, writing, images, sounds, data, or intelligence of any nature transmitted in whole or in part by wire, radio, electromagnetic, photoelectronic, or photooptical systems that affects interstate or foreign commerce but does not include (A) [the radio portion of cordless phones]; (B)

---

[34]   18 U.S.C.A. § 2703(c).

[35]   See § 23.05(a)(1) for discussion of subpoenas for records of communications under ECPA and the Patriot Act.

[36]   Id. § 2510(1).

[37]   5 U.S.Code News, supra note 30, at 3566. See also *State v. Howard*, 235 Kan. 236, 679 P.2d 197 (1984) (same); *Dorsey v. State*, 402 So.2d 1178 (Fla. 1981) (same).

[38]   Pub. L. No. 103–414, § 202 (1994).

[39]   18 U.S.C.A. § 2510(2).

[40]   Sen.Rep. No. 1097, 90th Cong.2d Sess. 89–90 (1968).

[41]   *Oliver v. United States*, 466 U.S. 170, 104 S.Ct. 1735 (1984) (open fields); discussed in § 4.03(c); *Hudson v. Palmer*, 468 U.S. 517, 104 S.Ct. 3194 (1984), discussed in § 4.03(g).

any wire or oral communication; (C) any communication made through a tone-only paging device; (D) any communication from a tracking device. . . .[42]

In general, according to the legislative history of ECPA, "a communication is an electronic communication protected by the federal wiretap law if it is not carried by sound waves and cannot fairly be characterized as containing the human voice."[43] The term is meant to cover electronic mail, computer-to-computer communications, microwave transmissions, and cellular telephones, among other modern communication techniques. Tone-only paging devices were excluded by analogy to "pen registers" which, for reasons discussed below,[44] are exempted from coverage. Tracking devices are handled under separate provisions.[45] The distinction between electronic communications and other types of communications is important in several respects; most significantly, as discussed below, violation of the rules relating to the former type of communication does not require suppression of illegally obtained evidence.

(2) The Definition of "Interception"

Interception is defined as "the aural or other acquisition of the contents of any wire, electronic, or oral communication through the use of any electronic, mechanical, or other device."[46] Telephone and telegraph equipment used in the ordinary course of business and hearing aids are not considered a "device" under the statute.[47] Moreover, using a device that does not intercept the "contents" of a communication, as defined by the Act, does not violate Title III. Contents for purposes of the Act "includes any information concerning the identity of the parties to such communication or the existence, substance, purport, or meaning of that communication."[48]

In *United States v. New York Telephone Co.*,[49] the Supreme Court held that a "pen register," which merely records numbers dialed on a telephone without overhearing verbal communications, does not fall within this definition. Thus after *New York Telephone*, the government could obtain pen register information simply by seeking a typical warrant rather than the more protective warrant required by Title III.

Two years later, in *Smith v. Maryland*,[50] the Court eliminated even this requirement by finding that use of pen registers does not constitute a "search" under the Fourth Amendment. The Court reasoned that there is no reasonable expectation of privacy in numbers dialed because (1) individuals assume the risk of disclosure when they voluntarily convey such information to the phone company; and (2) the phone company, in its daily operations, regularly records numbers dialed. In 1986, Congress mitigated this holding somewhat by requiring in the ECPA that police obtain a court order finding the pen register data "relevant" to an ongoing criminal investigation.[51]

---

[42]   Id. § 2510(12).

[43]   5 U.S.Code News, supra note 30, at 3568, 3562–64.

[44]   See § 14.03(a)(2).

[45]   See § 14.04.

[46]   18 U.S.C.A. § 2510(4).

[47]   Id. § 2510(5).

[48]   Id. § 2510(8).

[49]   434 U.S. 159, 98 S.Ct. 364 (1977).

[50]   442 U.S. 735, 99 S.Ct. 2577 (1979).

[51]   18 U.S.C.A. § 3121 et seq. The court need not make an independent investigation of the facts, however; its function is to certify the completeness of the application. Id. § 3123(a).

(b) Authorized Interceptions

As should be clear from the above, Title III is meant to regulate interception of almost all varieties of communication. However, there are several exceptions to its ban on interception of wire, oral or electronic transmissions. First, analogous to Fourth Amendment jurisprudence, a party to a communication or a person authorized by one of the parties to the communication may intercept the communication.[52] Second, for obvious reasons, the Act permits interception of electronic communication made through an "electronic communication system that is configured so that such electronic communication is readily accessible to the general public" and of radio communications meant to be heard by the public.[53] Third, quality control checks by common carriers and government agencies are allowed for that specific purpose.[54] A fourth exception arises in certain emergency situations involving "immediate danger of death or serious physical injury to any person," and "conspiratorial activities . . . characteristic of organized crime."[55] Application for a court order approving the emergency interception must be made within 48 hours, however.

Still another, increasingly important exception to the Title III ban on interception of communications concerns national security surveillance.[56] Here the key distinction is between threats from domestic organizations and foreign entities, with the latter subject to lesser regulation. In *United States v. United States District Court*,[57] the Court held (1) that the national security exception in Title III did not purport to eliminate the necessity of a court order for federal investigations of "internal security matters" that are not linked to foreign powers and (2) that, in any event, the Fourth Amendment would not allow this practice. The Court also held, however, that it might be permissible to relax some of Title III's requirements when domestic activities directly implicate national security.

Even when surveillance is aimed at gathering foreign intelligence, the government must abide by certain rules. The Foreign Intelligence Surveillance Act (FISA) of 1978 created a secret court to monitor such surveillance.[58] The initial version of the Act required a warrant for non-emergency national security surveillance, based on a probable cause finding that a foreign power or agent of a foreign power would be the target of the surveillance and that national security intelligence was the "primary purpose" of the surveillance. The USA Patriot Act of 2001 amended that provision to permit a FISA warrant to be issued whenever intelligence-gathering is a "significant purpose" of the surveillance, a change upheld by the FISA appellate court.[59] The Protect America Act, enacted in 2007, went even further, eliminating judicial review entirely when the Director of National Intelligence and the Attorney General certify that intelligence-gathering is a significant purpose of the surveillance and that there is

---

[52]   Id. § 2511(2)(c), (d). "Retroactive" consent is not permitted, however. Sen.Rep., supra note 39, at 94.

[53]   Id. § 2511(2)(g).

[54]   Id. § 2511(2)(a)(i), (b). This exception permits interceptions to procure evidence of wire fraud, even if they last several weeks, in an effort to identify all the perpetrators. *United States v. Harvey*, 540 F.2d 1345 (8th Cir. 1976).

[55]   18 U.S.C.A. § 2518(7).

[56]   Id. § 2511(2)(e), (f).

[57]   407 U.S. 297, 92 S.Ct. 2125 (1972). This decision is sometimes referred to as the *Keith* decision, after the district court judge who tried the case.

[58]   50 U.S.C.A. § 1801 et seq.

[59]   *In re Sealed Case*, 310 F.3d 717, 744 (2002).

"reasonable belief" that it is targeted at a person outside the United States.[60] However, one year later this provision was amended to require a FISA warrant for national security surveillance aimed at a U.S. person outside the country or a non-U.S. person "reasonably believed" to be in the U.S. Even under the amendments, the government need not demonstrate probable cause to believe the target is a foreign power or agent of the foreign power, nor need it specify where the surveillance will occur.[61]

Finally, of course, domestic interceptions aimed at ordinary criminals may be made if authorized by a proper court order.[62] As detailed below, Title III sets out specific rules governing the application for the eavesdrop order, its content, and procedures for performing an interception pursuant to the order. It also provides specific remedies, including suppression of illegally seized evidence and civil and criminal penalties if its provisions are violated.

(c) Application for an Order

The application for a Title III warrant must meet several requirements,[63] many of which go beyond that required for the typical warrant application. The application must provide: (1) the identity of the investigative officer making the application and of the officer authorizing the application; (2) "a full and complete statement of the facts and circumstances relied upon by the applicant to justify his belief that an order should be issued," including "details as to the particular offense;" (3) "a particular description of the nature and location of the facilities from which or the place where the communication is to be intercepted," "a particular description of the type of communications sought to be intercepted;" and "the identity of the person, if known, committing the offense and whose communications are to be intercepted;" (4) a "full and complete statement as to whether or not other investigative procedures have been tried and failed or why they reasonably appear to be unlikely to succeed if tried or to be too dangerous;" (5) "a statement of the period of time for which the interception is required to be maintained," including, if necessary, "a particular description of facts establishing probable cause to believe that additional communications of the same type will occur" after "the described type of communication has been first obtained;" (6) "a full and complete statement of the facts concerning all previous applications . . . involving any of the same persons, facilities or places specified in the application, and the action taken by the judge on each such application;" and (7) where an extension of an order is at issue, "a statement setting forth the results thus far obtained from the interception, or a reasonable explanation of the failure to obtain such results." These seven elements are discussed below, with the focus on their relationship to Fourth Amendment law.

(1) Identity of the Applicant

The original Act required that an application for an order be authorized by the Attorney General, or any Assistant Attorney General specifically designated by the Attorney General. The 1986 amendments allow any acting Assistant Attorney General

---

[60]   50 U.S.C.A. § 1804. This law, which was being amended at the time this book went to press, also requires that annual reports be submitted to Congress about the number of such certifications (but no details about their purpose or execution) and that the FISA court review the "procedures" designed to ensure that targets of surveillance are in fact overseas, under a "clearly erroneous" standard.

[61]   50 U.S.C.A. § 1881a.

[62]   18 U.S.C.A. § 2511(a)(ii).

[63]   These are set out in 18 U.S.C.A. § 2518(1).

and any Deputy Assistant Attorney General (Criminal Division) to sign applications to intercept wire and oral communications[64] and "any attorney for the Government" to authorize applications for interception of electronic communications.[65] Further, only the attorneys authorizing wire and oral communications need be specially designated by the Attorney General. Thus, the number of federal officials who can authorize surveillance applications has been expanded by the 1986 amendments and the number of attorneys who can authorize surveillance applications for electronic communications is vastly greater than the number who can authorize applications for wire and oral communications.[66] (On the state level, officials holding positions analogous to those federal officials described above may authorize applications.[67])

(2) Details of the Offense

As originally enacted, Title III specified that communications surveillance may be used only to investigate certain types of crimes. Under the 1986 amendments, however, the list of federal crimes that can trigger interception of wire and oral communications was expanded to include virtually any felony;[68] when electronic communications are to be intercepted, the amendments specifically allow application concerning "any Federal felony."[69] State statutes may authorize court orders to obtain evidence regarding "murder, kidnapping, gambling, robbery, bribery, extortion, or dealing in [drugs], or other crime dangerous to life, limb, or property, and punishable by imprisonment for more than one year . . . or any conspiracy to commit any of the foregoing offenses."[70] So long as one of these crimes is alleged in the application, this component of Title III is met.

(3) Particularity Requirements

The provisions of Title III that mandate descriptions of what is to be "seized" and from where and whom it is to be seized may be constitutionally required by *Berger v. New York*,[71] which held that merely naming the person whose communications are to be overheard or recorded violates the particularity requirement of the Fourth Amendment.[72] The *Berger* Court reasoned that "the need for particularity . . . is especially great in the case of eavesdropping [because it] involves an intrusion on privacy that is broad in scope." But while lower courts generally require an indication in the application of the identity of the target and the facility to be tapped,[73] most have not

[64]   Id. § 2516(1).

[65]   Id. § 2516(3).

[66]   For this reason, decisions strictly limiting the authorizing authority under Title III are now moot. See *United States v. Giordano*, 416 U.S. 505, 94 S.Ct. 1820 (1974) and *United States v. Chavez*, 416 U.S. 562, 94 S.Ct. 1849 (1974).

[67]   See, e.g., *State v. Farha*, 218 Kan. 394, 544 P.2d 341 (1975), cert. denied 426 U.S. 949, 96 S.Ct. 3170 (1976).

[68]   18 U.S.C.A. § 2516(1).

[69]   Id. § 2516(3).

[70]   Id. § 2516(2).

[71]   388 U.S. 41, 87 S.Ct. 1873 (1967), discussed in § 14.02(d).

[72]   For a discussion of this requirement, see § 5.04.

[73]   Where "roving taps" are necessary because it is not known where the subject will make the designated communication or the subject is shown to be deliberately changing locations to avoid tapping, the 1986 amendments allow specification of a limited geographic area, the number of phones to be intercepted and the time in which the interception is to be accomplished. Id. § 2518(11). See also, 5 U.S.Code News, supra note 30, at 3586.

required, beyond a description of the offense being investigated, a precise delineation of the "type of communications sought to be intercepted," on the ground that such a requirement would be very difficult to meet.[74]

Whether the lower courts' approach conforms with *Berger* has not yet been ruled on by the Court. But the Supreme Court has held that investigating agents need not list the identity of *everyone* they believe might be overheard, thus suggesting that they need not predict all types of conversations they will uncover. In *United States v. Kahn*,[75] the government intercepted conversations between the defendant and his wife, as well as between his wife and other gamblers, pursuant to a warrant that named the defendant but not his wife. The court of appeals suppressed all of these conversations, including the defendant's, reasoning that the government should have discovered the wife's involvement in the defendant's gambling operations prior to the search and included her name on the application. But the Supreme Court reversed, holding that "Title III requires the naming of a person in the application or interception order only when the law enforcement authorities have probable cause to believe that that individual is 'committing the offense' for which the wiretap is sought." Pre-application investigation of all possible suspects is not required.

This holding is analogous to the Court's later ruling in *Horton v. California*,[76] which eliminated the inadvertence requirement in plain view cases on the ground that, if probable cause exists to obtain a warrant, other evidence discovered in plain view in the course of executing the warrant is admissible even if police suspected it might be discovered. The difference where eavesdropping is concerned is that considerable additional private material will almost always be "discovered" when an unnamed third party is involved. The Court concluded, however, that the "minimization" requirement, discussed below,[77] would reduce unnecessary privacy invasions.[78]

(4) The Last Resort Requirement

In *Giordano*, the Supreme Court stated that the provision in Title III requiring a showing that other investigative procedures have failed is designed to ensure that electronic eavesdropping is not "routinely employed as the initial step in criminal investigation." Language in *Kahn* also endorses this notion. But the lower courts have not construed the provision literally, instead permitting communications surveillance when other methods might be considered dangerous or more difficult.[79] The Supreme Court itself has generally looked with disfavor on least drastic means analysis in the investigative context,[80] although it has yet to speak directly on the issue when electronic surveillance is concerned.

---

[74]   See, e.g., *United States v. Fino*, 478 F.2d 35 (2d Cir. 1973).

[75]   415 U.S. 143, 94 S.Ct. 977 (1974).

[76]   496 U.S. 128, 110 S.Ct. 2301 (1990), discussed in § 10.04.

[77]   See § 14.03(e)(2).

[78]   The Court has also held that, if the police fail to list a person for whom they *do* have probable cause, this error is harmless, because the listing requirement does not play a "substantive role" in the regulatory scheme. *United States v. Donovan*, 429 U.S. 413, 97 S.Ct. 658 (1977), discussed further in § 14.03(g)(1).

[79]   See James Carr, The Law of Electronic Surveillance 179 (1977).

[80]   See, e.g., discussion of checkpoints in § 13.06 and inventories in § 13.07.

(5) Durational Elements

Discussed here are the last three elements of the application process, all of which relate to the duration of an interception. Not only must investigators indicate the amount of time they need to complete the interception (which in any event may not exceed 30 days per order),[81] but they must also explain why the interception should not be "automatically terminated when the described type of communication has been first obtained." Of course, the significance of this latter requirement is diminished by the lower courts' previously discussed disinclination to require any specificity with respect to type of communication sought to be intercepted. The investigators must also describe any previous applications for the same persons or places, again a provision designed to sensitize the judge to any overly intrusive or prolonged surveillance. As this provision only requires disclosure of past interceptions of previously *named* targets, the holding in *Kahn* (which does not require listing all possible targets in an application) assumes greater significance.[82] Finally, any attempt to continue interception beyond the statutory 30-day period requires a second application, including an explanation of why the first interception failed.

Relevant to interpretation of all of these provisions is the Supreme Court's opinion in *Berger*. There the Court seemed particularly concerned about the duration of the typical eavesdrop. In finding the New York statute unconstitutional, it stressed that the law permitted an extension of an order "without a showing of present probable cause for the continuance of the eavesdrop," and placed "no termination date on the eavesdrop once the conversation sought is seized." Title III, at least on its face, seems to avoid both of these problems. But the Court also emphasized that the 60-day surveillance in *Berger* was "the equivalent of a series of intrusions, searches, and seizures pursuant to a single showing of probable cause." *Berger* would seem to require that orders be sought on a more frequent basis than the 30 day duration authorized by Title III, at least when the number of participants or types of conversations expand.

The lower courts have not adopted this interpretation of *Berger*, however. Instead, they have permitted, based on a single application, wiretaps that last several weeks and involve many different conversations.[83] As Justice Harlan argued in his *Berger* dissent, a prolonged electronic eavesdrop can be seen as a single search, during which particularly described categories of conversations may be seized. If one is to adopt this stance, however, it becomes important to be as specific as possible with respect to the types of conversations sought to be seized, a requirement which, as noted above, the lower courts have been reluctant to impose. As an additional protection, serious effort must be made to minimize interception of conversations that are irrelevant to the investigation; unfortunately, as discussed below, this requirement too is often ignored.[84] At the least, courts can monitor prolonged surveillance by requiring periodic reports, as authorized under Title III.[85]

---

[81] 18 U.S.C.A. § 2518(5).

[82] As does the holding in *Donovan*, described supra note 78, which does not penalize the government for failure to list even those targets for whom the government has probable cause.

[83] See, e.g., *Hanger v. United States*, 398 F.2d 91 (8th Cir. 1968). According to the Administrative Office of the United States Courts, federal wiretaps average over 60 days (thus requiring two judicial extensions), and intercept the conversations of over 100 people during that period.

[84] See § 14.03(e)(2).

[85] See 18 U.S.C.A. § 2518(5).

(d) The Wiretap Order

The judge must make several findings before a Title III warrant may be issued,[86] and include within the order certain provisions.[87] The required findings are four in number: (1) a probable cause belief that an enumerated offense has been, is being, or will be committed; (2) a probable cause belief that particular communications concerning that offense will be obtained through the proposed interception; (3) a belief that "normal investigative procedures have been tried and failed or reasonably appear to be unlikely to succeed if tried or to be too dangerous;" and (4) a probable cause belief that the facilities to be subject to surveillance are connected with the offense or the person named. In *Berger*, the majority suggested that the probable cause required for electronic surveillance is higher than normal. As stated by Justice Stewart, "[o]nly the most precise and rigorous standard of probable cause should justify an intrusion of this sort." But the lower courts have not so held in interpreting Title III.[88]

If the judge decides the order should issue, the order must: (1) identify "the person, if known, whose communications are to be intercepted;" (2) identify "the nature and location of the communications facilities as to which, or the place where, authority to intercept is granted;" (3) describe "the type of communications sought to be intercepted, and a statement of the particular offense to which it relates;" (4) identify the person authorizing the application and the agency performing the interception; (5) provide "that the authorization to intercept shall be executed as soon as practicable;" (6) specify "the period of time during which such interception is authorized," and "whether or not the interception shall automatically terminate when the described communication has been first obtained;" (7) provide that the interception "be conducted in such a way as to minimize the interception of communications not otherwise subject to interception;" and (8) at the discretion of the court, "require reports to be made to the judge who issued the order showing what progress has been made toward achievement of the authorized objective and the need for continued interception." The order must also, in cases where so requested by the applicant, order relevant common carriers, landlords, and similar agencies or individuals to cooperate with the investigation.

As the provisions of the order track very closely the elements of the application, the comments made earlier with respect to the application process are equally applicable here. In particular, it should be noted that since the government is not required to list in the application those individuals for whom it does not have probable cause, the order need not list these individuals either. To hold otherwise, reasoned the Court in *Kahn*, would require the judge to conduct his own investigation of nonlisted parties.

(e) Executing the Order

Execution of a Title III warrant is governed by several rules. First, Title III provides that all interceptions "shall, if possible, be recorded on tape or wire or other comparable device . . . in such way as will protect the recording from editing or other alterations."[89] This provision helps ensure accuracy by making the evidence procured through electronic surveillance as "tangible" as the evidence obtained in a more typical search.

---

[86]   These are described in 18 U.S.C.A. § 2518(3).

[87]   Id. § 2518(4) and (5).

[88]   *United States v. Falcone*, 505 F.2d 478 (3d Cir. 1974).

[89]   18 U.S.C.A. § 2518(8)(a).

Second, as noted above, the Title III order places several limitations on the manner in which the interception is carried out. Most important are the commands concerning durational limits, periodic reports, and the minimization requirement.

This latter issue requires elaboration. In addition, two other execution issues—the amendment process which is required when evidence of other crimes is obtained and the propriety of covert entry to plant an eavesdropping device—will be explored in some detail, in the order in which they are likely to occur during an interception.

(1) Covert Entry

Occasionally, agents must enter private property to install or remove the eavesdropping device. Title III is silent as to the circumstances under which this type of action may take place. In *Dalia v. United States*,[90] the Supreme Court held that such entries are reasonable under the Fourth Amendment and permitted under Title III as well, so long as no property is damaged and the entry is otherwise conducted reasonably. More questionably, five members of the Court held that the covert entry need not be authorized by the court but can be carried out at the discretion of the officers. The majority, via Justice Powell, found nothing in the language of the Fourth Amendment regulating the method by which a search is carried out and called the imposition of such a requirement in the electronic surveillance context "an empty formalism," given the obvious necessity of covert entry in some cases. As two of the dissenters pointed out, however, a court can meaningfully regulate such entries by requiring proof that they are necessary and limiting the extent of intrusion they entail.

(2) The Minimization Requirement

In *Berger*, the Supreme Court stressed that one unconstitutional aspect of the statute under consideration there was that it allowed seizure of "the conversations of any and all persons coming into the area covered by the device . . . indiscriminately and without regard to their connection to the crime under investigation." Title III seeks to avoid this problem by providing that the interception "be conducted in such a way as to minimize the interception of communications not otherwise subject to interception."

Scott v. United States[91] illustrates the difficulty of implementing this provision. In *Scott*, the officers admitted to having made no efforts to minimize the intrusion into defendant's privacy. For a month, with only one short exception, virtually every call made on the phone was intercepted, although only 40% were pertinent (narcotics related) calls. However, apparently no patterns developed that indicated to listening agents that nonpertinent matters were being intercepted and that the remainder of the conversation would be nonpertinent as well. The Supreme Court, speaking through Justice Rehnquist, held that, in analyzing whether minimization has occurred, courts should take into account: (1) the percentage of nonpertinent calls, (2) the length of the calls, (3) the ambiguity of the language used, (4) the type of use to which the telephone is normally put, (5) the scope of the investigation, (6) whether the calls involve one or more of the co-conspirators and (7) at what point during the authorized period the interception was made (with less minimization required at the outset as officers establish the pattern of calls). In *Scott* itself, despite the officers' admitted bad faith, no violation of the minimization rule was found, because the 60% of the calls which were not pertinent were

---

[90]   441 U.S. 238, 99 S.Ct. 1682 (1979).
[91]   436 U.S. 128, 98 S.Ct. 1717 (1978).

either "very short," "ambiguous in nature," or "one-time conversations" that did not fit any known pattern.

The majority also held that the investigators' subjective attitude toward minimization was irrelevant to the analysis. This holding, which replicates the Court's objective approach in other Fourth Amendment situations,[92] tells officers to err on the side of interception, since plausible explanations for a failure to minimize can often be made. It also undercuts the Court's ruling in *Kahn* (which, it will be remembered, had relied on the minimization requirement in permitting a failure to list in the application all possible parties whose conversations would be intercepted), and undermines as well the rationale for allowing thirty-day surveillance based on one showing of probable cause.

(3) Amendments

If officers overhear conversations about offenses not named in the warrant, they may, in circumstances analogous to those found in plain view cases,[93] "seize" these conversations as well. However, Title III requires that, to be admissible in criminal proceedings, these communications must be forwarded to the court "as soon as practicable" and the court must find that "the contents were otherwise intercepted in accordance with the provisions of this chapter."[94] This would appear to mean, for instance, that if the communications were overheard during a period when the minimization requirement should have applied, they may not be used in court.[95] *Scott* made clear, however, that bad faith failure to follow minimization requirements does not require exclusion under either the statute or the Fourth Amendment unless the court also finds that, as an objective matter, those requirements were violated.

(f) Post-Interception Procedures

Once an interception has been completed, two important steps must be taken. First, sealing provisions protect against the editing or alteration of recorded interceptions and the destruction, editing, or alteration of eavesdrop orders or applications.[96] If these provisions are not followed, and a "satisfactory explanation" is not provided, exclusion of the evidence must result.[97] Second, within 90 days of the termination of the order, the issuing judge must have an inventory served on the persons named in the order or application.[98] The inventory must give notice of the entry of the order or application, the disposition of the application, and information as to whether there was an interception. Here too exclusion is mandated if the inventory does not reach the relevant parties within 10 days of trial or other proceeding.[99] This inventory provision also allows the judge to give discretionary notice to other parties to the intercepted communications if the judge concludes that such notice would be in the "interests of justice."[100]

---

[92] See § 10.04 for a description of the cases.

[93] See § 10.04.

[94] 18 U.S.C.A. § 2517(5).

[95] See Sen.Rep., supra note 40, at 100.

[96] Id. § 2518(8)(a)–(b).

[97] Id.

[98] Id. § 2518(8)(d).

[99] Id. § 2518(9).

[100] Id. § 2518(8)(d).

In *United States v. Donovan*,[101] the Court held that, as an aid to the inventory process, the government has a duty to classify all persons whose conversations have been intercepted and to transmit this information to the judge. If instead, as in *Donovan*, the government merely supplies the judge with a list of all *identifiable* persons whose conversations were intercepted that list must at least be complete. Although the inadvertent failure to include the names of two "non-target" persons on the list was held to be "harmless" in *Donovan*, when names are deliberately withheld or prejudice to the defendant results from the exclusion, the Court suggested a different result might be reached.

An individual who suspects that the government will use or is using information obtained or derived from an illegal wiretap, but who does not receive notice under the statute, may force the prosecution to affirm or deny the existence of the surveillance.[102] This provision is designed to assist the defendant who otherwise would have a difficult time proving surveillance took place. However, courts have held that the allegation of surveillance must be supported by specific facts.[103]

(g) The Suppression Remedy

Of course, any communications seized in violation of the Fourth Amendment must be suppressed unless an exception to the Fourth Amendment exclusionary principle, such as the good faith rule announced in *United States v. Leon*,[104] applies. Thus, in light of *Berger*, for example, evidence obtained pursuant to a Title III warrant that fails to provide any description of what is being seized, or that does not indicate the duration of the order, should be excluded, barring the unlikely finding that police were reasonable in believing the warrant to be valid.

Title III also contains its own exclusionary rules, which have independent effect. Already noted are the provisions requiring exclusion when: (1) communications not related to the offense being investigated are intercepted and are not disclosed to the judge "as soon as practicable;" (2) intercepted communications are not sealed and no satisfactory explanation is given for the oversight; and (3) the inventory is not provided to parties named in the order or application at least 10 days before trial or other proceeding. Title III also has a general exclusion provision that requires suppression when: (4) "the communication was unlawfully intercepted;" (5) "the order of authorization or approval under which it was intercepted is insufficient on its face;" or (6) "the interception was not made in conformity with the order of authorization or approval."[105]

(1) General Scope

Title III's rules provide protection beyond that afforded by the Fourth Amendment in at least two ways: they apply to private, as well as government, interceptions,[106] and require exclusion at all hearings, not just trial.[107] At the same time, unlike the Fourth

---

[101] 429 U.S. 413, 97 S.Ct. 658 (1977).

[102] Id. § 3504(a).

[103] *Matter of Grand Jury*, 529 F.2d 543 (3d Cir. 1976), cert. denied 425 U.S. 992, 96 S.Ct. 2203 (1976).

[104] 468 U.S. 897, 104 S.Ct. 3405 (1984), discussed in § 2.03(c)(1).

[105] 18 U.S.C.A. § 2518(10)(a).

[106] 5 U.S.Code News, supra note 30, at 3559. Compare § 4.02.

[107] 18 U.S.C.A. § 2518(10)(a). Compare § 2.03(a) and (b). But see, *Gelbard v. United States*, 408 U.S. 41, 92 S.Ct. 2357 (1972) (where Justice White joined the plurality ruling that Title III required suppression of

Amendment rule, these exclusionary provisions apply only to interceptions of wire and oral communications, not to interceptions of electronic communications. The legislative history to the ECPA offers no rationale for this difference in treatment, merely stating that the position was adopted "as a result of discussions with the Justice Department."[108] Thus, outside any protection afforded by the Fourth Amendment, the civil and criminal remedies described in the next section are the sole remedies afforded those whose electronic communications have been illegally intercepted.

Even when wire and oral communications are intercepted in violation of Title III, exclusion is not always required under the statute (or under the Fourth Amendment). The effect of Title III's rules is limited by the "central rule" test, a good faith exception, and standing requirements.

(2) The "Central Role" Test

Because Title III's substantive rules are so complex, the Supreme Court has been cautious about giving full sway to its general exclusionary remedies. Instead, as the Court stated in *United States v. Giordano*,[109] suppression is required only when the statutory provision that was violated "was intended to play a central role in the statutory scheme."

The central role test idea has been applied in several cases. In *Giordano*, the Court held that the pre-1986 requirement that all applications be authorized by the Attorney General or his designee did play a central role in the statutory scheme, because it was "reasonable to believe that such a precondition would inevitably foreclose resort to wiretapping in various situations where investigative personnel would otherwise seek intercept authority from the court and the court would very likely authorize its use." In *United States v. Chavez*,[110] on the other hand, the provision requiring accurate identification of the authorizing official was viewed as not "substantive" enough to require suppression upon violation (although the dissent pointed out that this provision played the important role of holding the authorizing official accountable for his actions). In *United States v. Donovan*,[111] the Court came to a similar conclusion regarding the provision requiring identification in the application and order of all parties for whom the government has probable cause. So long as at least one such party is identified in the order, it is "sufficient on its face," according to the Court, and thus suppression is not required even if other parties are left out. This conclusion is debatable; as noted above, the listing provision arguably does play a "central role" in the statutory scheme, since both the provision requiring notification of previous applications and the requirement for inventory notice only operate with respect to parties *named* in the application.

Donovan also held that suppression is not required by a failure to send a post-surveillance inventory to persons whose communications have been intercepted but who were not named in the application or order. This holding is probably correct as a matter of statutory interpretation, since none of the general exclusionary rules (numbers four through six above) deals with post-interception matters, and the specific rule dealing

---

illegally obtained evidence at a grand jury proceeding only because no warrant had been obtained; where there is a warrant "the deterrent value of excluding the evidence will be marginal at best.").

[108] 5 U.S.Code News, supra note 30, at 3577.

[109] 416 U.S. 505, 94 S.Ct. 1820 (1974).

[110] 416 U.S. 562, 94 S.Ct. 1849 (1974).

[111] 429 U.S. 413, 97 S.Ct. 658 (1977).

with inventories (number three) only requires exclusion when the inventory is denied to a person named in the order or application. Whether failure to provide a discretionary inventory should result in exclusion as a *Fourth Amendment* matter is not as clear; *Donovan* left open the possibility that a deliberate, prejudicial action might require suppression.

The Court has not applied the central role test to most other aspects of Title III,[112] but some predictions about likely outcomes can be made, based on analogous Fourth Amendment provisions. Presumably, the probable cause requirements with respect to the offense, the communications sought, and the parties to be intercepted play a central role in Title III's statutory scheme, given their congruence with Fourth Amendment principles. Similarly, violation of the 30-day limitation on a single warrant is likely to require exclusion, given the Court's concern in *Berger* over the length of the interception in that case.

With less confidence, one can predict that the minimization requirement will be viewed as central, because it provides the only concrete means of avoiding a "general" search during the time period authorized by the order. Although *Scott v. United States*[113] suggested as much, it also stated, in dictum, that had the minimization requirement been violated in that case, only the improperly intercepted conversations would have to be suppressed. The Court is likely to confirm this stance when given an opportunity to do so. While exclusion of all intercepted communications would maximize deterrence, it would prevent use of evidence that is not fruit of a violation.

The "centrality" of Title III's provision mandating a finding that other investigative methods have been tried is even more difficult to predict. On the one hand, Title III's intent is to reserve electronic surveillance as a back-up investigative tool. On the other, as indicated in the discussion of the last resort requirement, the lower courts have not adhered rigidly to this requirement and the Supreme Court has rejected less intrusive means analysis in other search contexts. As it has with the minimization requirement, the Court will probably give lipservice to the provision, but make clear that the government's burden in meeting it is not particularly heavy.

(3) The Good Faith Exception

Even if exclusion is mandated under Title III, the government may be able to take advantage of a good faith exception analogous to that which exists in Fourth Amendment cases. *United States v. Ojeda Rios*[114] involved Title III's requirement that the government seal tapes immediately after the expiration of the surveillance order or provide a "satisfactory explanation" for failing to do so, under one of the provisions that requires exclusion for violation of its terms. Relying on this provision, the district court in *Ojeda Rios* excluded evidence obtained from two wiretaps because of long delays (82 and 118 days, respectively) between the termination of the orders for each tap and sealing of the tapes, a decision that the Second Circuit affirmed.

The Supreme Court agreed with the lower courts that the government must provide a satisfactory explanation not only for a failure to seal the tapes but also for any delay

---

[112] In *Dahda v. United States*, ___ U.S. ___, 138 S.Ct. 1491 (2018), the Court held that a warrant that invalidly permitted eavesdropping outside the authorizing court's jurisdiction did not violate the *Giordano* test when no conversations intercepted outside that jurisdiction were introduced into evidence.

[113] 436 U.S. 128, 98 S.Ct. 1717 (1978).

[114] 495 U.S. 257, 110 S.Ct. 1845 (1990).

in sealing. It also rejected the government's argument that a "satisfactory explanation" includes a showing that the tapes had not been altered during the delay, for "even if we were confident that tampering could always be easily detected, . . . it is obvious that Congress had another view when it imposed the sealing safeguard." But six members of the Court nonetheless voted to remand the case for a determination as to whether the prosecutor reasonably believed that when a tap is one of many in the same investigation, as was true of both wiretaps at issue in *Ojeda Rios*, the tapes for the wiretap do not need to be sealed until the entire investigation is terminated. The relevant caselaw appeared to permit a delay in sealing the tapes in such cases only when subsequent court orders are continuous extensions of the first order; in *Ojeda Rios*, there was a gap between the surveillance periods authorized by the first orders and the orders authorizing the taps in question. But, according to the Court, "[t]he government is not required to prove that a particular understanding of the law is correct but rather only that its interpretation was objectively reasonable at the time." The result in *Ojeda Rios* permits a type of good faith defense akin to that recognized in *United States v. Leon*.[115]

(4) Standing

Under the Fourth Amendment, only those persons who can show that a search infringed their "legitimate expectations of privacy" may challenge the search.[116] In *Alderman v. United States*,[117] the Supreme Court held that this test gives Fourth Amendment standing to the parties to an intercepted conversation, as well as to the owners of premises on which an intercepted conversation took place, whether or not they were present at the time. However, *Alderman* does not grant standing to bring a Fourth Amendment claim to other persons who may be incriminated by the interception. Under Title III, in contrast, any "aggrieved person" may move to suppress oral or wire communications, a term which is defined as one "who was a party to any intercepted . . . communication or a person against whom the interception was directed."[118] This definition confers standing on any target of an interception, even if that person's "legitimate expectations of privacy" are not infringed by the interception.

The contradictions between Fourth Amendment and Title III standing are apparently resolved in the legislative history to Title III, which indicates that the phrase "aggrieved person" is to be construed "in accordance with existent standing rules."[119] *Alderman* itself noted this language, and concluded that Title III was intended "to reflect existing law," not "extend" the exclusionary rule to all targets of an interception.

Alderman also held that a defendant should receive *all* surveillance records as to which he has standing, not just those considered relevant by the judge exercising *in camera* review. The Court reasoned that a judge might not be able to ascertain the relevance of every communication: "An apparently innocent phrase, a chance remark, a reference to what appears to be a neutral person or event, the identity of a caller or the individual on the other end of a telephone, or even the manner of speaking or using words may have special significance to one who knows the more intimate facts of an accused's life." The Court also held, however, that the court could order the defendant and his

---

[115] 468 U.S. 897, 104 S.Ct. 3405 (1984), discussed in § 2.03(c)(1).

[116] See § 4.04(c).

[117] 394 U.S. 165, 89 S.Ct. 961 (1969).

[118] 18 U.S.C.A. § 2518(11).

[119] Sen.Rep., supra note 40, at 106.

counsel to avoid unwarranted disclosures that might harm innocent third parties. Additionally, in *Taglianetti v. United States*,[120] it concluded that the defendant is not entitled to examine surveillance records for which he does not have standing, and that the judge can be trusted to identify the defendant's voice to determine whether such standing exists.

Litigation brought against covert surveillance schemes by persons who are not subject to prosecution face particularly difficult standing challenges. In *Clapper v. Amnesty International, USA*,[121] the plaintiffs wanted to challenge the constitutionality of the 2007 amendments to the FISA, which permit issuance of a FISA warrant authorizing interception of communications originating in the United States made to any non-citizen believed to be outside the United States if the government can show simply that "a significant purpose of the acquisition is to obtain foreign intelligence information."[122] To establish standing, the plaintiffs, many of whom were lawyers or human rights activists, contended that, although they could not prove their conversations had been intercepted, the likelihood of such interception was high, given the nature of their clients and associations and the government's strong interest in detecting terrorists. But the Court held, 5–4, that the threat of interception was "speculative" and not, as required by previous standing precedents, "certainly impending."[123]

To the argument that, given the covert nature of the surveillance, the 2007 amendments might otherwise be immune from challenge, Justice Alito responded for the majority that defendants who are prosecuted using intercepted information have standing to challenge the statute, as do electronic service providers directed to assist the government in carrying out the surveillance. Both alternatives are problematic. The first basis for standing depends upon the government's willingness to abide by its statutory duty to provide notice of an intent to use the results of such surveillance, notice that has not always been forthcoming.[124] And third party service providers do not necessarily share the same concerns that those subject to prosecution have.[125]

(h)　Criminal and Civil Remedies

In addition to the exclusionary remedy, the Act provides for criminal and civil remedies similar to those available for typical Fourth Amendment violations.[126] "Intentional" violations of the Act are punishable as criminal offenses and carry penalties of a fine of not more than $10,000, or imprisonment for not more than five years, or both.[127] Additionally, any person whose wire, oral or electronic communications

---

[120]　394 U.S. 316, 89 S.Ct. 1099 (1969).

[121]　568 U.S. 398, 133 S.Ct. 1138 (2013).

[122]　See § 14.03(b).

[123]　See, e.g., *Whitmore v. Arkansas*, 495 U.S. 149, 110 S.Ct. 1717 (1990).

[124]　Adam Liptak, *A Secret Surveillance Program Proves Challengeable in Theory Only*, N.Y. Times, July 15, 2013 (noting cases in which federal prosecutors refused to disclose the source of their evidence, despite the high likelihood it came from NSA surveillance).

[125]　Stephen Wm. Smith, *Gagged, Sealed and Delivered: Reforming ECPA's Secret Docket*, 6 Harv. L. & Pol'y Rev. 313, 328 (2012) (noting that "[t]he provider's own privacy interests are not at stake, and it is compensated for most expenses of complying with the order" and that, "[a]lthough there may well be instances in which a provider might 'push back" against law enforcement in response to particular orders, providers rarely appeal to a higher court.").

[126]　See § 2.05.

[127]　18 U.S.C.A. § 2511.

are intercepted, disclosed, or used in violation of Title III has a civil cause of action for damages under Title III against the transgressor.[128] Recovery may include actual damages, punitive damages, and reasonable attorney's fees and litigation expenses. The actual damages provision establishes minimum liquidated damages of $100 for each day of violation or $1,000, whichever is higher.[129] In both criminal and civil cases, good faith is a defense.[130]

Under limited circumstances, the First Amendment may also provide a defense to criminal and civil penalties under the Act. In *Bartnicki v. Vopper*,[131] the Supreme Court held that persons who disclose unlawfully intercepted communications may be able to escape liability under Title III even when they know or have reason to know the information was obtained illegally, if they themselves acquired the intercepted information lawfully and the information is of "public concern." The respondents in *Vopper* were all media outlets which played or printed a transcript of tape of a cell phone conversation between two union officials. Although the conversation was intercepted by an unidentified person (and therefore was obtained in violation of the statute), the media entities themselves, including Vopper, a radio talk show host, came by the tape legally (it was given to them by an anti-union partisan who found the tape in his mailbox). Justice Stevens, writing for six members of the Court, rejected the argument that punishment of people like Vopper, whom he assumed knew that the tape was illegally intercepted, was needed to deter unlawful interception. According to Stevens, "there is no evidence that Congress viewed the prohibition [against disclosure of illegal interceptions] as a response to the difficulty of identifying persons making improper use of scanners and other surveillance devices, and accordingly deterring such conduct, and there is no empirical evidence to support the assumption that the prohibition against disclosure reduces the number of illegal interceptions." Although the Court did recognize a strong privacy interest in conversations that take place over phones, it concluded that, for matters of public concern like those involved in this case, that interest is outweighed by the interest in freedom of speech.

However, the Court reserved the question whether media disclosure of illegally intercepted conversations about "trade secrets, domestic gossip, and other information of purely private concern" would be immunized by the First Amendment. More importantly, two members of the six-member majority, Justices Breyer and O'Connor, emphasized they were joining the opinion only because the intercepted conversation included threats of potential physical harm to others[132] by people who were at least "limited public figures." Whether other types of illegally intercepted conversations could be legally disclosed by those who know or should know of the illegality therefore remains in serious doubt.

14.04   Tracking Devices

Tracking devices come in many forms. One of the simplest is the beeper, which emits a signal that can be traced electronically and can be placed in virtually any vehicle or

---

[128] Id. § 2520.

[129] Id. § 2520(a).

[130] Id. § 2511(4)(a).

[131] 532 U.S. 514, 121 S.Ct. 1753 (2001).

[132] The tape recorded comments to the effect that if the school district didn't change its position someone might have to "blow off their front porches" and "do some work on those guys."

item. Other tracking devices under development or already in use include radar that can monitor vehicles over the horizon; bistatic sensor devices that passively pick up various types of emissions (e.g., from a cellular phone or a GPS device) or rely instead on an active sonar-like capacity; and tagging systems that use a projectile launcher to attach a beeper to a fleeing vehicle. Also of relevance are efforts to construct "intelligent transportation systems," which involve fitting every vehicle in a given transportation network with radio units that transmit to a base station. While being studied principally as a way of controlling traffic patterns, these systems would also provide a way of tracking individual vehicles, or of discovering where they were located at a previous point in time.[133]

Use of these devices is minimally regulated by Title III.[134] But the Supreme Court has imposed significant restrictions on their use, not only to detect movements inside premises but also movements in public.

The Court's first tracking device case, decided in 1983, pointed in the opposite direction. In *United States v. Knotts*,[135] federal agents placed a beeper in a container of chloroform housed in a store, with the consent of the storeowner. The container was subsequently picked up by Petschen, who put it in his car. The police lost visual track of Petschen sometime after he left the store but, relying on the beeper, they were able to trace his car to Knotts' cabin. Based on visual surveillance of the cabin, they obtained a search warrant and discovered a drug laboratory on the premises. Knotts argued that the police should also have obtained a warrant before placing the beeper in the chloroform can. But the Supreme Court held that, because Petschen's car travelled public thoroughfares, no expectation of privacy was violated when police relied on the beeper rather than eyesight to track the car.

The decision in *Knotts* can be viewed as a variant of the "untrustworthy ear" doctrine discussed earlier.[136] Like defendants who "voluntarily" talk to government agents wearing concealed body bugs, Petschen knowingly exposed his car to the public when he used public roads. The beeper merely assisted police in keeping track of him while he was on those public roads.

However, thirty years later, in *United States v. Jones*,[137] the Court called this reasoning into question. There, the Court held that using a tracking device to follow a car does implicate the Fourth Amendment, at least when the device is attached to the car in a way that amounts to a trespass. Justice Scalia's opinion for the majority concluded that placing a GPS on a car is a physical intrusion on an "effect" (the car) and, when used to obtain information, "would have been considered a search within the meaning of the Amendment at the time it was adopted." *Knotts* was distinguished on the ground that the suspect did not own the receptacle at the time the beeper was placed in it. Thus, irrespective of whether a government action infringes *Katz'* reasonable-expectation-of-privacy test, Scalia concluded, when "the Government obtains information by physically intruding on a constitutionally protected area" a search occurs.

---

[133]   See Slobogin, supra note 1, at 406.

[134]   18 U.S.C.A. § 3117(a) simply provides: "[I]f a court is empowered to issue a warrant or other order for the installation of a mobile tracking device, such order may authorize the use of that device within the jurisdiction of the court, and outside the jurisdiction if the device is installed in that jurisdiction."

[135]   460 U.S. 276, 103 S.Ct. 1081 (1983).

[136]   See § 14.02(a).

[137]   565 U.S. 400, 132 S.Ct. 945 (2012).

Justice Sotomayor was the fifth vote for this view, but also strongly suggested that a search occurs under *Katz'* test even when police rely on a non-trespassory act (e.g., tracking using signals from a phone's GPS or from a transponder installed in the car by the manufacturer). She pointed out that tracking can covertly generate and record a "wealth of detail" about a person's life in a way that "chills association and expressive freedoms." The net result, she concluded, is that "GPS monitoring—by making available at a relatively low cost such a substantial quantum of intimate information about any person whom the Government, in its unfettered discretion chooses to track—may alter the relationship between citizen and government in a way that is inimical to democratic society."

Justice Alito's concurrence, joined by three other justices, agreed that a search occurred in *Jones*, but did not agree with the majority's trespass rationale for that result. He complained that the majority's approach was a throwback to the property-based analysis of *Olmstead*, which *Katz* had discredited. Further, Justice Alito contended, even on a common-law trespass theory the majority's approach failed: the minimal trespass that occurred in *Jones* probably would not have been actionable under the common law and the majority's colonial analogue to a GPS search (a constable hiding in a coach trunk) was fanciful. Instead, Alito argued, *Katz'* test should be the sole test for determining when a search occurs. For reasons similar to those advanced by Justice Sotomayor, Justice Alito suggested that under that test the Fourth Amendment would apply to "prolonged tracking" unless "extraordinary offenses" were under investigation. Since the tracking in *Jones* lasted 28 days and focused on obtaining information about drug dealing, he concluded it met this test.

Thus, five justices seem ready to overturn *Knotts* or at least limit it to short-term tracking, even when no trespass is involved. If so, the Court will have to sort out at what point public tracking becomes a search, and perhaps also will need to define Justice Alito's "extraordinary offenses." Additionally, *Jones* left unclear the consequence of labeling tracking a search. Is a warrant based on probable cause always required for such tracking or might a lesser justification suffice? (For instance, in *United States v. Karo*, discussed below, the Court suggested that even tracking *inside* a house might only require a court order based on reasonable suspicion.) Alternatively, the Court might decide that even short-term tracking makes creation of "personality mosaics" so cheap and easy that a traditional warrant is always required.[138]

More fundamentally, *Jones* calls into question a number of the cases that have narrowly construed *Katz*. Justice Sotomayor wondered in *Jones* whether, given the large amount of information that the digital age allows other individuals or institutions to acquire about us, it is now "necessary to reconsider the premise that an individual has no reasonable expectation of privacy in information voluntarily disclosed to third parties." That reconsideration might result not only in a rethinking of *Knotts*, but of other Court cases that have refused to apply the Fourth Amendment on an "assumption of risk" rationale.[139]

When a tracking device is used to locate a person or item within a dwelling, the Fourth Amendment is clearly implicated, whether or not a trespass is involved. In

---

[138] Cf. *United States v. Maynard*, 615 F.3d 544, 562 (D.C. Cir. 2010) (discussing the mosaic theory of the Fourth Amendment).

[139] See § 4.03(a).

United States v. Karo[140] agents placed a beeper in a can containing ether, with the owner's consent. They saw Karo pick up the can from the owner and, using visual and beeper surveillance, followed the can to his house. Up until this point, the case paralleled *Knotts*. But then, undetected by police visually, the can was moved to other locations on four occasions. Had it not been for the beeper, police would not have discovered any of these transfers, except the last one, when they used visual as well as beeper surveillance to follow a truck containing the ether from a warehouse to a residence in Taos.

Seven members of the Court held that the police should have obtained a warrant before placing the beeper in the can because the beeper allowed the covert monitoring of the can inside the Taos residence. As the Court stated: "Had a DEA agent thought it useful to enter the Taos residence to verify that the ether was actually in the house and had he done so surreptitiously and without a warrant, there is little doubt that he would have engaged in an unreasonable search within the meaning of the Fourth Amendment."

The Court was willing, however, to tailor the warrant requirement to meet the specific needs of tracking. The government had contended that requiring judicial authorization of beeper installations would render them useless: the particularity requirement of the warrant clause mandates a description of the location of any evidence to be seized,[141] but the whole point of the beeper is to ascertain that location. The Court took the government's observations into account in holding that to obtain a warrant for purposes of beeper installation the government need merely show: (1) the object into which the beeper is to be placed; (2) the circumstances that led the police to want to install the beeper; and (3) the length of time for which beeper surveillance is requested. It also expressly left open the question of whether mere reasonable suspicion of criminal activity would be sufficient to issue a warrant.[142] Since police often cannot know when public tracking will end up also tracking the inside of premises, *Karo's* warrant requirement, however framed, will often need to be met in cases where the tracking begins on public thoroughfares.

A different form of tracking relies not on real-time surveillance of the type that occurred in *Knotts*, *Jones* and *Karo*, but on access to records from a subject's cellphone carrier detailing the person's location over time. As discussed in § 4.03(a), in *Carpenter v. United States*,[143] the Supreme Court held that under some circumstances this type of access is a search, rejecting the contention that a person voluntarily surrenders location information simply by using the phone. As with *Jones*, still an open question is whether a warrant is always required to obtain such information, although in *Carpenter* itself, where the police accessed over 150 days of location information, and focused on seven days in particular to determine the defendant's whereabouts, the Court held that the police should have obtained a warrant.

---

[140] 468 U.S. 705, 104 S.Ct. 3296 (1984).

[141] See § 5.04.

[142] Note that even if the Court eventually holds that only reasonable suspicion is required to use a beeper for *monitoring*, a warrant based on probable cause may be required if *installation* of a beeper requires entry into a private dwelling. Although the Court has not required a particularized showing that entry is necessary in the communications surveillance context, see § 14.03(e)(1), in that context the court has already found probable cause to believe surveillance is necessary.

[143] ___ U.S. ___, 138 S.Ct. 2206 (2018), discussed further in § 4.03(a).

14.05   Video Surveillance

Probably the most invasive type of technological surveillance in use today is video surveillance, especially of private spaces. Cameras not only allow police to hear what is said but also, of course, permit observation of what occupants of the premises are doing, all of which can be recorded. Nothing more dramatically conjures up the image of an "Orwellian society" than a surreptitiously planted government "eye" in one's living room. This discussion looks first at video surveillance of private areas and then examines video surveillance of public spaces.

(a) Private Areas

Legislation purporting to regulate video surveillance of private dwellings was introduced during the 1984 session of Congress (and several subsequent sessions).[144] The 1984 proposal, intended as an amendment to Title III, would have treated video surveillance no differently from communications surveillance, with two exceptions. First, it would have added a provision making bad faith failure to minimize irrelevant interceptions automatic grounds for exclusion. Second, it sought to limit surveillance to ten days per warrant, as opposed to the thirty-day term permitted for electronic eavesdropping. To date, however, no federal legislation regulating this type of surveillance has been passed.

Several courts have held that Title III applies to video surveillance by analogy.[145] The leading case in this regard is *United States v. Torres*.[146] There, the FBI obtained judicial authorization to install cameras in "safehouses" used by four members of FALN, a Puerto Rico separatist group, thought to be making explosives for terrorist purposes. The district court held the videotapes thus obtained inadmissible in the absence of any statutory basis for the authorizing order. The Seventh Circuit reversed, holding that although Title III did not cover video surveillance, its provisions could be applied by analogy. In its opinion, the FBI's warrant met the particularity, least restrictive means and minimization requirements in that statute. Two features of the case particularly impressed the Seventh Circuit. First, it felt that no other investigative alternatives to video surveillance existed. The terrorists were allegedly aware that the "safehouses" in which they assembled bombs might be bugged and thus played the radio loudly and spoke in code; furthermore, as the FBI pointed out, the act of making bombs is largely a silent affair. Second, the "safehouses" in which the bombs were assembled were more like businesses than homes and thus were associated with a lesser expectation of privacy.[147]

Some courts have rejected *Torres'* analogy approach, holding that only those aspects of Title III that are required by the Fourth Amendment apply to video surveillance. This means, for instance, that the provisions of Title III that require applications to be signed by certain types of prosecutors and that limit surveillance to certain crimes would not apply to video surveillance.[148]

---

[144] H.R. 6343, 98th Cong., 2d Sess. (1984).

[145] See *United States v. Falls*, 34 F.3d 674 (8th Cir. 1994); *United States v. Koyomejian*, 970 F.2d 536 (9th Cir. 1992).

[146] 751 F.2d 875 (7th Cir. 1984).

[147] See § 13.03(a).

[148] See, e.g., *United States v. Cuevas-Sanchez*, 821 F.2d 248 (5th Cir. 1987); *United States v. Biasucci*, 786 F.2d 504 (2d Cir. 1986).

Torres states the better rule. Indeed, given its heightened level of intrusiveness, video surveillance of the interior of private residences arguably ought to be subject to greater restrictions than even that case establishes. In particular, three such restrictions are worth considering. First, because minimization is particularly difficult to enforce where cameras are involved, a stringent prohibition (like that in the proposed federal statute) against bad faith viewing of activities that are innocent or that do not involve the suspects is appropriate. Given the invasion of privacy involved, perhaps even negligent failures to minimize should result in exclusion. One appropriate minimization method, approved by the district court in *Application of Order Authorizing Interception*,[149] is prohibition of video surveillance until audio surveillance indicates criminal activity is taking place.

Second, a warrant for video surveillance should not be issued unless no other method can accomplish the investigative objective. Sometimes eavesdropping will provide sufficient information. In other cases, more traditional techniques can suffice. In *Torres*, for instance, there may have been probable cause sufficient to obtain a search warrant authorizing entry of the safehouses while the bombs were being made. This alternative may not have produced as much evidence as video surveillance but may still have been preferable to it. In *People v. Teicher*,[150] on the other hand, there probably was no alternative to installing a camera focused on the dental chair of a dentist suspected of sexually abusing his patients. Before applying for the warrant granted in that case, police had questioned the defendant about one of the complaints of sexual abuse, had equipped two of the female complainants with hidden recorders and transmitters in an attempt to elicit admissions from the defendant, and had tapped the telephone of a complainant who had received repeated calls from the defendant, all to no avail. Furthermore, stated the court, "the use of a police decoy without the protection of visual surveillance would not have produced the needed evidence in this case, since the decoy, of necessity, would have been heavily sedated and might not have been able to relate what transpired."

A third worthwhile extension of Title III is the federal proposal's provision shortening the duration of video surveillance under each warrant. Given the intrusiveness of video surveillance, if evidence of criminal activity sufficient to make a case is not obtained within a very short time, police should have to justify further surveillance.

Finally, there is the issue of consent. If one follows the analogy to aural surveillance, video surveillance should not require a warrant if one of the parties observed consents to it. However, a few courts have held that, given its heightened intrusiveness, warrantless video surveillance should be prohibited even when one of those surveilled consents.[151] This rule makes sense in many cases, since what a video camera "observes" may be quite different from what a government agent sees, especially if the consentor leaves the room. On the other hand, if the consentor owns the area subjected to camera surveillance, his absence should perhaps not be dispositive, by analogy to *Alderman v.*

---

[149] 513 F.Supp. 421 (D.Mass. 1980).

[150] 52 N.Y.2d 638, 439 N.Y.S.2d 846, 422 N.E.2d 506 (1981).

[151] *People v. Henderson*, 220 Cal.App.3d 1632, 270 Cal.Rptr. 248 (1990); *United States v. Shabazz*, 883 F.Supp. 422 (D.Minn. 1995).

United States,[152] which gives an absent owner standing to contest interception of conversations in his home.

(b) Public Spaces

The presence of video cameras, steadily panning the city streets, directly compromises the desire and ability to remain anonymous in one's comings and goings. The feeling of unease that conspicuously-positioned video cameras might create is likely to be particularly acute when the cameras are permanent and designed to monitor everyone in the area, at all times of the day. Yet such cameras can also identify culprits and gather information about suspicious activity or groups of people. Further, cameras facilitate law enforcement by providing accurate documentation of crimes when there are no witnesses and facilitating interviewing when there are. These capacities are augmented further when a "zoom" capacity, in real-time or subsequent to the event, is available to magnify what is monitored. Given their perceived success at deterring and detecting crime, a number of cities have installed such cameras.

The Court's tracking cases, discussed in the previous section, are relevant here. Given *United States v. Knotts*, the case which upheld use of beepers to track vehicles in public spaces, such public video surveillance might not be subject to either warrant or suspicion requirements. However, the five justices in *Jones v. United States* who signaled that public tracking for "prolonged" periods implicates the Fourth Amendment might also be willing to impose some limitations on camera systems, especially if these systems allow law enforcement to monitor a particular person's activities for the entire period he is in public.

Assuming, however, that a traditional warrant or some modicum of individualized suspicion is not required in such cases, several other limitations might be imposed under the Fourth Amendment's Reasonableness Clause or as a legislative mandate. First, because this type of surveillance allows government monitoring of large numbers of people 24 hours a day, the law might require a finding by an elected body or a politically accountable police official that surveillance of the locations at issue will deter a specified criminal activity, and, if the surveillance is approved, a periodic review of that finding. Second, the public to be affected by the surveillance could be afforded an opportunity to give input on the proposed surveillance. Third, if cameras are installed, the public should be notified of their existence,[153] both to ensure that people who frequent the area will know their actions will be monitored and to promote the deterrent effect of the surveillance. Fourth, use of audio and zoom capacity might be limited to those situations in which individualized suspicion of crime exists, and certainly use of the cameras to surveil private areas should require probable cause. Finally, limitations on the maintenance and use of any recordings should be imposed.[154]

---

[152] 394 U.S. 165, 89 S.Ct. 961 (1969), discussed in § 14.03(g)(4).

[153] Cf. *United States v. Martinez-Fuerte*, 428 U.S. 543, 96 S.Ct. 3074 (1976) (upholding illegal immigrant checkpoints in part on ground that sufficient notice was given to prevent motorists from being taken by surprise).

[154] For instance, Baltimore requires destruction of videotapes within 96 hours unless probative evidence of criminal activity needs to be maintained. For a coherent approach to this surveillance technique, see ABA Standards for Criminal Justice: Technologically-Assisted Physical Surveillance, Standard 2–9.3(b) (1999).

14.06   Detection Devices

Several different types of detection devices—devices that can "see" through opaque, inanimate surfaces—exist or are on the verge of production. One such device registers the degree of radiation emitted from the body and objects concealed on it. Because these waves readily pass through clothing, and because the body is a good "emitter" while metal and other dense, inanimate objects tend to be bad "emitters," the latter objects show up on the device as outlines against the body. Another device aims a low intensity electromagnetic pulse at the subject and measures the time decay of each object radiated, a period which differs depending upon the object. The device then compares the time-decay of the object with known "signatures" of items like guns; no image is produced. A third device measures the fluctuations in the earth's magnetic field produced by ferromagnetic material (like the metal in a gun) which moves through it.[155] There are also a number of thermal imaging devices that measure the heat emitted from behind opaque barriers.[156]

One of the most heavily litigated detection techniques has been the use of thermal imagers to ascertain the presence of heat sources associated with drug manufacturing. Prior to 2001, a majority of courts had held that use of such a device to discern activity inside a home is not a search,[157] on one of two grounds: (1) it detects only "abandoned heat waste" and thus is immune from Fourth Amendment regulation by analogy to *California v. Greenwood*[158] (which held that going through garbage found at curbside is not a search) or (2) it detects only evidence of criminal activity and thus is authorized by *United States v. Place*[159] (which held that a dog sniff for drugs is not a search). However, in *Kyllo v. United States*,[160] the Supreme Court held that use of a thermal imaging device to learn about activities inside the home is a Fourth Amendment search. It rejected the abandonment argument as "mechanical," and noted that even the listening device at issue in *Katz* had only picked up "abandoned" sound waves. To the *Place* argument it responded that "the Fourth Amendment's protection of the home has never been tied to measurement of the quality or quantity of information obtained," pointing out, for instance, that *Karo* involved detection of a can of ether in a home.

Outside the home, however, the Court is more willing to countenance the second argument—that devices that detect only contraband (i.e., are "contraband-specific") do not require justification under the Fourth Amendment. In *Illinois v. Caballes*,[161] for instance, the Court held that a dog sniff of a lawfully stopped car that detects the presence of drugs is not a Fourth Amendment event, as long as the sniff does not prolong

---

[155] For a description of these devices, see David A. Harris, *Superman's X-Ray Vision and the Fourth Amendment: The New Gun Detection Technology*, 29 Temple L. Rev. 7–8 n. 38 (1996).

[156] One such device looks like a 35 millimeter camera, has a range of up to 400 meters, and can detect temperature differences as small as one-half a degree. Matthew L. Zabel, *Thermal Imagery vs. the Fourth Amendment*, 90 Nw. U. L.Rev. 267, 269 (1995).

[157] See, e.g., *United States v. Penny-Feeney*, 773 F.Supp. 220 (D.Haw. 1991); *United States v. Pinson*, 24 F.3d 1056, 1058 (8th Cir. 1994).

[158] 486 U.S. 35, 108 S.Ct. 1625 (1988), discussed in § 4.03(d).

[159] 462 U.S. 696, 103 S.Ct. 2637 (1983), also discussed in § 4.03(f)(2).

[160] 533 U.S. 27, 121 S.Ct. 2038 (2001).

[161] 543 U.S. 405, 125 S.Ct. 834 (2005).

the stop. Use of a mechanical device that detects only illegal drugs or weapons might be justified under similar circumstances.[162]

Even aiming a detection device at a home does not implicate the Fourth Amendment under two circumstances recognized in *Kyllo* (albeit both in dictum). First, if the device is in "general public use," *Kyllo* stated, the government may use it to surveil activities inside the home without worrying about the Fourth Amendment, apparently on the ground that people cannot reasonably expect privacy vis-à-vis commonly used technology. The Court did not specify the types of devices that fit within this exception, but certainly flashlights and binoculars are eligible; indeed, in discussing the general public use exception the Court cited *Dow Chemical v. United States*,[163] which involved use of a $22,000 mapmaking camera. The second exception recognized in *Kyllo* permits suspicionless surveillance of homes even with devices that are not in general public use when what is observed could also have been seen by the naked eye from a lawful vantage point. This exception is likely to generate considerable litigation about what the police could or could not have seen unaided by technology, and leaves unclear whether it applies when the reason police used a detection device instead of the naked eye is fear of detection.[164]

14.07　Conclusion

This chapter has examined the most prominent forms of technological surveillance. There follow some general points that can be made about this problematic type of search and seizure.

(1)　Government's use of technology to enhance what the normal senses could see or hear from a lawful vantage point normally does not infringe upon the interests protected by the Fourth Amendment. Thus, the Supreme Court has held that electronic eavesdropping on a conversation does not implicate the Fourth Amendment when one party to the conversation consents to the eavesdropping (the "untrustworthy ear" exception). Nor can one reasonably expect protection from technologically-enhanced visual surveillance if the observer is situated at a lawful vantage point and observes only what the naked eye could see. Even technology that detects more than the normal senses may escape Fourth Amendment regulation if it detects only the presence of contraband or other illicit items or is in general public use. However, as described in (5) below, technological surveillance that requires a trespass on the target's property or that is prolonged or permits aggregation of significant amounts of public data may, in some circumstances, implicate the Fourth Amendment.

(2)　A defendant only has Fourth Amendment standing to contest government surveillance when one's privacy interests are infringed. Thus, in the eavesdropping context, a person may contest an electronic search on constitutional grounds only if it intercepted his own conversation or the conversation took place on his property. By analogy, one may only be able to contest electronic tracking, video surveillance, or use of detection devices when the surveillance is of oneself or intrudes into one's property.

---

[162] Note, however, that a device that detects only *weapons*, as is true with many devices under development, may not be contraband-specific, because in a majority of states today carrying a concealed weapon is legal (at least outside of airports and similar areas).

[163]　476 U.S. 227, 106 S.Ct. 1819 (1986), discussed in § 4.03(f)(2).

[164]　See Christopher Slobogin, *Peeping Techno-Toms and the Fourth Amendment: Seeing Through* Kyllo's *Rules Governing Technological Surveillance*, 86 Minn. L. Rev. 1393, 1411–15 (2002).

Furthermore, until a person is prosecuted, he does not have standing to challenge the constitutionality of a covert surveillance regime because any injury thereby suffered is too speculative.

(3) Statutory regulation of communications surveillance (e.g., wiretapping, bugging, accessing of electronic mail) at both the federal and state level is governed by Title III of the Omnibus Crime Control and Safe Streets Act of 1968, as amended by the Electronic Communications Privacy Act of 1986, or by state statutes substantially similar to it. Consistent with Fourth Amendment requirements set out by the Supreme Court, the Act requires that all nonconsensual surveillance for the purpose of investigating domestic crime must take place pursuant to a warrant and establishes a detailed regulatory scheme for implementing this objective. Of particular note is that surveillance warrants may only be issued by specified judges, in cases involving probable cause to believe those named in the warrant engaged or are engaging in specified crimes, and after a finding that no other investigative techniques are likely to obtain evidence the government needs.

(4) Title III provides for both civil and criminal penalties against those who violate its provisions, as well as a suppression remedy that supplements the Fourth Amendment's exclusionary remedy. However, the criminal and civil penalties do not apply to people who broadcast illegally intercepted communications, even if they know the communications were intercepted illegally, as long as they did not participate in the illegality and the communications are of "public interest" (defined to encompass, at the least, communications that prevent serious harm to others). And the Act's suppression remedy applies only in the case of illegally intercepted "wire" and "oral" communications, not in the case of illegally intercepted "electronic" communications, and even then probably does not apply if the agents act in good faith.

Moreover, the Supreme Court has held that only violation of provisions that play a "central role" in the regulatory scheme will lead to suppression of evidence discovered as a result of the violation. The provisions most likely to be considered "central" include those described in (3), plus the provision that mandates that the initial surveillance period to be limited to 30 days. Title III's requirement that agents "minimize" interception of non-relevant communications might also require exclusion under some circumstances. However, if, as an objective matter, minimization was not required, bad faith on the part of the agents does not require exclusion. Further, exclusion of evidence about crimes not named in the warrant is not required if it was obtained while carrying out a legitimate surveillance (the "plain hear" rule).

(5) The Fourth Amendment is implicated when the police use a tracking device to monitor public travel, at least when use of the device involves a trespass on the defendant's property. Even when no trespass is involved, accessing location records from a common carrier is a search, and long-term real-time tracking of public travel is likely to be. Use of a tracking device to locate evidence or a person in a private dwelling requires a warrant, which may issue if police adequately describe (a) the object into which the device is to be placed; (b) the circumstances that suggest the device will provide evidence of crime; and (c) the length of time for which the device is requested. The Court has not settled whether such a warrant requires probable cause or instead can be based on reasonable suspicion.

(6) Most courts have held that video surveillance of private areas is governed by rules analogous to those in Title III regulating communications surveillance. The Fourth

Amendment may not impose any restrictions on video surveillance of public spaces, but authorization by high level officials, public input, periodic review, and rules governing maintenance and use of recordings are components of a reasonable surveillance program.

(7) Use of detection devices such as thermal imagers to detect activities or conditions inside a private dwelling requires a warrant unless, as noted in (1), it merely replicates what the naked eye could view from a public vantage point or is in general public use. Technology that is "contraband-specific" (i.e., detects only contraband) may implicate the Fourth Amendment when aimed at the home, but not when aimed at luggage or cars.

BIBLIOGRAPHY

Arcila, Fabio. GPS Tracking Out of Fourth Amendment Dead Ends: *United States v. Jones* and the *Katz* Conundrum. 91 N. Car. L. Rev. 1 (2012).

Bloom, Robert J. and William J. Dunn. The Constitutional Infirmity of the Warrantless NSA Surveillance: The Abuse of Presidential Power and the Injury to the Fourth Amendment. 15 Wm. & Mary Bill Rts.Rev. 147 (2006).

Butler, Alan. Standing Up to *Clapper*: How to Increase Transparency and Oversight of FISA Surveillance. 48 New England L. Rev. 55 (2013).

Clancy, Thomas K. Coping with Technological Change: *Kyllo* and the Proper Analytical Structure to Measure Fourth Amendment Rights. 72 Miss.L.J. 525 (2002).

Fishman, Clifford S. The "Minimization" Requirement in Electronic Surveillance: Title III, the Fourth Amendment and the Dread *Scott* Decision. 28 Am.U.L.Rev. 315 (1979).

Harris, David A. Superman's X-Ray Vision and the Fourth Amendment: The New Gun Detection Technology. 29 Temple L. Rev. 7–8 n. 38 (1996).

Kastenmeier, Robert, Deborah Leavy and David Beier. Communications Privacy: A Legislative Perspective. 1989 Wisc.L.Rev. 715 (1989).

Kerr, Orin S. The Next Generation Communications Privacy Act. 162 University of Pennsylvania Law Review 373 (2014).

Maclin, Tracey. *Katz*, *Kyllo*, and Technology: Virtual Fourth Amendment Protection in the Twenty-First Century. 72 Miss.L.J. 51 (2002).

Pulaski, Charles. Authorizing Wiretap Applications Under Title III: Another Dissent to *Giordano* and *Chavez*. 123 U.Pa.L.Rev. 750 (1977).

Simmons, Ric. From *Katz* to *Kyllo*: A Blueprint for Adapting the Fourth Amendment to Twenty-First Century Technologies. 53 Hastings L.J. 1303 (2002).

Slobogin, Christopher. Making the Most Out of *Jones v. United States* in a Surveillance Society: A Statutory Implementation of Mosaic Theory. 8 Duke J. Const'all L. & Pub. Pol'y 1 (2012).

____. Public Privacy: Camera Surveillance of Public Places and the Right to Anonymity. 72 Miss. L.J. 213 (2002).

Symposium: The Future of Internet Surveillance Law. 72 Geo. Wash. L. Rev. 1139 (2004).

Terrell, Timothy P. and Anne R. Jacobs. Privacy, Technology and Terrorism: *Bartnicki*, *Kyllo* and the Normative Struggle Behind Competing Claims of Solitude and Security. 51 Emory L.J. 1469 (2002).

Part B

THE FIFTH AMENDMENT'S PRIVILEGE AGAINST SELF-INCRIMINATION

The portion of the Fifth Amendment that governs the content of the next two chapters guarantees that "no person shall be compelled in any criminal case to be a witness against himself. . . ." This language, applied to the states in *Malloy v. Hogan*,[1] has not been interpreted literally. Rather the Supreme Court has sought to balance the values underlying the privilege against the needs of an efficient system of criminal justice. According to *Malloy*, the objectives sought to be implemented by the privilege are manifold: the prevention of abuse of citizens by government officials; the protection of privacy; the fear that coerced statements will be unreliable; "our unwillingness to subject those suspected of crime to the cruel trilemma of self-accusation, perjury or contempt;" the "preference for an accusatorial rather than an inquisitorial system of criminal justice;" and "our sense of fair play which dictates 'a fair state-individual balance . . . by requiring the government in its contest with the individual to shoulder the entire load. . . .' " Particularly important is the idea that ours is an accusatorial system, in which the government is required to obtain evidence of guilt by its own labors, rather than from the accused through inquisitional practices. Thus, when the government confronts a person with the "cruel trilemma of self-accusation, perjury or contempt" of which *Malloy* speaks, the protections of the Fifth Amendment are usually implicated. However, occasionally a fair state-individual balance will permit the government to force an individual to make such a choice.

Chapter 15 explores the complex elements constituting the constitutional right which has become known as the "privilege against self-incrimination." Chapter 16 then applies these principles to one of the most heavily litigated, and after the Supreme Court's decision in *Miranda v. Arizona*,[2] also one of the best-known areas of constitutional criminal procedure—the law of confessions.

---

[1]   378 U.S. 1, 84 S.Ct. 1489 (1964).
[2]   384 U.S. 436, 86 S.Ct. 1602 (1966).

Chapter 15

OVERVIEW OF THE PRIVILEGE
AGAINST SELF-INCRIMINATION

15.01   Introduction

The privilege against self-incrimination can be broken down into four components. Literally, it states that no person (1) shall be compelled; (2) in any criminal case; (3) to be a witness; (4) against himself. First, the privilege is not triggered unless there is *compulsion* to talk; of course, as with all of the other criminal process rights, this compulsion must come from the state. Second, the compulsion must lead to the revelation of *incriminating* material, material that will help lead to criminal punishment. Third, state compulsion of incriminating material may nonetheless be permissible if it does not require the person to be a "witness"—that is, a person who provides *testimonial*, as opposed to "non-communicative," evidence. And only the person who is compelled may assert the privilege; to implicate the Fifth Amendment, the compelled evidence must be *self*-incriminating. The first four sections of this chapter look at these components of the privilege against self-incrimination. The final section applies them to a particularly complex area of Fifth Amendment jurisprudence: use of the subpoena *duces tecum*.

15.02   Compulsion

As Chief Justice Burger wrote in *United States v. Washington*,[1] "absent some officially coerced self-accusation, the Fifth Amendment privilege is not violated by even the most damning admissions." Another way the Court has characterized this issue, as Justice Powell recognized in *Garner v. United States*,[2] is in terms of "waiver." That is, the Court has attempted to determine whether the failure to assert the privilege against self-incrimination is "voluntary, knowing and intelligent."

For some time, it appeared that the only type of compulsion or involuntary waiver that would implicate the Fifth Amendment was that resulting from "legal" process imposed as a result of a failure to talk, such as a contempt citation, a criminal penalty or some other type of sanction imposed by statute or a court. But the Court eventually recognized that unconstitutional compulsion can result from other types of pressure, in particular pressure exerted by the police. As the Court stated, in the landmark case of *Miranda v. Arizona*,[3] unless the Fifth Amendment applied during interrogation, "all the careful safeguards erected around the giving of testimony, whether by an accused or a witness, would become empty formalities in a procedure where the most compelling possible evidence of guilt, a confession, would have already been obtained at the unsupervised pleasure of the police." Thus, compulsion implicating the Fifth Amendment can occur in both formal and informal settings. Here the discussion will be

---

[1]   431 U.S. 181, 97 S.Ct. 1814 (1977).

[2]   424 U.S. 648, 96 S.Ct. 1178 (1976).

[3]   384 U.S. 436, 86 S.Ct. 1602 (1966). In the much earlier case of *Bram v. United States*, 168 U.S. 532, 18 S.Ct. 183 (1897), the Court also seemed to hold that police interrogation implicated the Fifth Amendment, but *Bram* was ignored until *Miranda*. See § 16.02(d).

organized under three broad categories: compulsion during questioning, statutory compulsion, and compulsion by threat of noncriminal sanctions.

(a) During Questioning

Governmental questioning comes in many forms. For the purpose of defining compulsion under the Fifth Amendment, the Court has distinguished between custodial interrogation, cross-examination during trial, questioning of grand jury witnesses, and non-custodial questioning outside the courtroom.

(1) Defendants in Custody

In *Miranda*, the Supreme Court held that "custodial interrogation" is "inherently coercive." Thus, unless special precautions are taken, statements made during such interrogation are unconstitutionally compelled. The Court held that the coercive nature of an interrogation setting can be ameliorated only if two steps take place: (1) the suspect is told he has a right to remain silent, that anything he says may be used against him, and that he has a right to an attorney during interrogation, at state expense if necessary; and (2) the suspect "voluntarily and intelligently" waives his right to remain silent and his right to an attorney before interrogation proceeds. *Miranda* and police interrogation are discussed in detail in the next chapter;[4] the brief description here is useful for comparison purposes.

(2) Trial Witnesses

In contrast to its holding in *Miranda*, the Supreme Court has repeatedly held that a witness at trial is not entitled to warnings, nor to an assessment of whether any subsequent testimony is a voluntary and intelligent waiver of his right to remain silent; rather, the mere act of speaking is seen as a valid waiver. As Justice Frankfurter stated in *United States v. Monia*,[5] "if [a witness] desires the protection of the privilege, he must claim it or he will not be considered to have been 'compelled' within the meaning of the Amendment."[6]

A witness in the trial setting does not necessarily *feel* less "compelled" to talk than the suspect subjected to interrogation. But there are good reasons for the Court's different treatment of the compulsion/waiver concept in these two situations. First, the physical setting of the government-citizen encounter is different. It seems fair to assume that questioning conducted at a public proceeding with a judge is less coercive than interrogation at the stationhouse. At the same time, the trial witness, having had time to prepare for trial, is much more likely to know about and understand his right to remain silent than is the suspect who has just been arrested. Of course, if the witness is the defendant, he will also have counsel to make sure his statements are not coerced and are the product of an intelligent waiver. Second, when the witness is *not* a defendant or putative defendant, the government's attitude is not aggressively adversarial or prosecutorial, but rather inquisitive. This attitude is not only likely to diminish coercion, but also means that putting the onus on the government to assure that any waiver is "intelligent" makes less sense. Because "only the witness knows whether the apparently

---

4   See, in particular, §§ 16.03(c)(d) & (e).

5   317 U.S. 424, 63 S.Ct. 409 (1943) (Frankfurter, J., dissenting).

6   See also, *United States v. Kordel*, 397 U.S. 1, 90 S.Ct. 763 (1970); *United States ex rel. Vajtauer v. Commissioner of Immigration*, 273 U.S. 103, 47 S.Ct. 302 (1927).

innocent disclosure sought may incriminate him,"[7] the witness should bear the burden of asserting the privilege.

(3) Grand Jury Witnesses

A grand jury proceeding falls in between custodial interrogation and trial questioning. On the one hand, its objective is primarily investigative and some of the witnesses questioned may be suspects or putative defendants; moreover, the proceedings are secret,[8] and counsel is usually not permitted in the grand jury room.[9] On the other, the proceeding is conducted in front of members of the public, usually numbering over ten,[10] is monitored by the court (although a judge is not present),[11] and does not take the questioned individual by "surprise" in the same way custodial interrogation after arrest does. Responding to this hybrid situation in three separate cases, the Supreme Court has declined to hold that grand jury witnesses are entitled to Miranda warnings prior to their testimony, but has also held that any subsequent use of grand jury testimony requires the state to show that the statements represented a voluntary and intelligent waiver of the Fifth Amendment.

In *United States v. Mandujano*,[12] the respondent was charged with perjury for admittedly false statements he made while testifying before a grand jury. He successfully moved in the lower court to suppress the false statements because he was a putative defendant and had not received the *Miranda* warnings prior to testifying. The Supreme Court reversed, holding that failure of the state to provide *Miranda* warnings at a grand jury hearing is no basis for the suppression of false statements in a subsequent perjury proceeding. Similarly, in *United States v. Wong*,[13] the Court rejected petitioner's claim that the absence of *Miranda* warnings meant that his grand jury statements could not be used in a perjury prosecution. It stated that whether or not the average witness might be entitled to the warnings, no witness was permitted to lie; therefore, the absence of the warnings could not bar the perjury charge. Because *Mandujano* and *Wong* considered perjury hearings, however, they were not entirely determinative of what warnings would be required as a prerequisite to the admissibility of a putative defendant's statements in the more typical case.

United States v. Washington[14] involved such a case. The respondent was a putative defendant who, before testifying in front of a grand jury, had been warned of his right to remain silent and of the admissibility of his statements in future criminal proceedings; he had not, however, been told his testimony could lead to indictment. The Supreme Court held that the warnings given to the respondent before his testimony were sufficient to remove any possibility of compulsion. Chief Justice Burger wrote for the majority: "[I]t seems self-evident that one who is told he is free to refuse to answer questions is in a curious posture to later complain that his answers were compelled." Thus, warning a grand jury witness that he is a "target" of the investigation is not necessary under the Fifth Amendment. The Court also stopped short of holding that the

---

[7]   *Garner v. United States*, 424 U.S. 648, 96 S.Ct. 1178 (1976).

[8]   See § 23.03.

[9]   See § 23.04(c).

[10]   See § 23.02(b).

[11]   See § 23.05(d).

[12]   425 U.S. 564, 96 S.Ct. 1768 (1976).

[13]   431 U.S. 174, 97 S.Ct. 1823 (1977).

[14]   431 U.S. 181, 97 S.Ct. 1814 (1977).

grand jury setting is inherently coercive, suggesting that even the abbreviated warning given in *Washington* may not be required.[15] However, the Court did at least consider whether a voluntary and intelligent waiver occurred, which is more than has been required in the trial context. Moreover, because they are so easily given, most jurisdictions provide the *Miranda* warnings prior to grand jury testimony of putative defendants and many also give the "target warning" to putative defendants.[16]

(4) The Fair Examination Rule

If a witness at either a trial or a grand jury proceeding testifies and provides incriminating information, the government is permitted to compel answers to questions asking for explication of that information, apparently on a waiver theory. This rule is most broadly interpreted when the witness is a defendant at trial. In *Brown v. United States*,[17] the petitioner testified at a denaturalization proceeding that she had not engaged in communist activities for the ten years prior to her application for citizenship. On cross-examination, she claimed the Fifth Amendment privilege when asked whether she was presently a member of the Communist Party. The Supreme Court affirmed her contempt conviction for refusing to answer. Justice Frankfurter, writing for the Court, stated that holding otherwise would be "a positive invitation to mutilate the truth." According to the Court, testifying defendants may be cross-examined, provided that the questions are directed to the purpose of impeaching their credibility or to the substance of their testimony on direct examination.

Some courts have construed *Brown* broadly to stand for the proposition that when the accused testifies concerning the offense for which he is on trial, he forfeits the privilege as to all facts relevant to that offense, even if they were not mentioned on direct.[18] Others apparently permit cross-examination to the extent permitted by the normal rules relating to the scope of cross-examination,[19] which in some jurisdictions allow questioning on any subject about which the subject has knowledge.[20] Although a fair state-individual balance would seem to support the general holding in *Brown*, the cross-examination allowed should be limited to whatever is necessary to test the truth of the statements made on direct. Allowing cross-examination beyond this point unfairly tips the state-individual balance or, if one prefers waiver language, works an involuntary "waiver" of the Fifth Amendment.

When the person testifying is not the accused, the same general rule applies, but courts have been more careful about limiting cross-examination. In *Rogers v. United States*,[21] the petitioner appeared before a grand jury and testified concerning her relationship with the Communist Party. She admitted, without asserting a Fifth

---

[15]   Note also that in *Minnesota v. Murphy*, 465 U.S. 420, 104 S.Ct. 1136 (1984), the Court held that a probationer questioned by his probation officer is not entitled to *Miranda* warnings, in part because this setting was "less intimidating" than the grand jury setting, where the Court had "never held that [the warnings] must be given."

[16]   See, e.g., *State v. Cook*, 11 Ohio App.3d 237, 464 N.E.2d 577 (1983); Idaho Code § 19–1121; South Dakota Laws § 23–A–5–12.

[17]   356 U.S. 148, 78 S.Ct. 622 (1958).

[18]   McCormick, Evidence § 132, at 323–24 (3d ed. 1984). See also *Johnson v. United States*, 318 U.S. 189, 63 S.Ct. 549 (1943).

[19]   See *People v. Perez*, 65 Cal.2d 615, 55 Cal.Rptr. 909, 422 P.2d 597 (1967), writ dism'd 395 U.S. 208, 89 S.Ct. 1767 (1969).

[20]   McCormick, Evidence § 21, at 51 (3d ed. 1984).

[21]   340 U.S. 367, 71 S.Ct. 438 (1951).

Amendment objection, that she had at one time possessed Party documents. She then refused to divulge to whom she had given the documents, relying on her Fifth Amendment privilege. The Supreme Court, affirming her contempt conviction for refusing to answer, held that a witness' admission of an incriminating fact constitutes a waiver of Fifth Amendment protection with respect to the details surrounding that admission. Justice Vinson, writing for the majority, reasoned that extending Fifth Amendment protection to the details associated with an admission that had already been made would allow the witness to pick and choose those details she would admit, resulting in distortion of the testimony. The Court viewed the witness' incriminating admission as a waiver because, by making the admission, she had voluntarily subjected herself to the criminal sanction resulting from the admission. The increased possibility that criminal sanctions would be imposed due to the forced admission of details was not considered important, in light of the need for reliable testimony. The Court did recognize the abuses this exception might permit, however, and held that details may not be compelled if they present a " 'real danger' of further incrimination."

Early applications of the *Rogers* holding in federal courts had rather harsh effects on witnesses. *Rogers* was interpreted to prevent only compelled admissions of new crimes not divulged in prior testimony.[22] More recent cases have demonstrated greater sensitivity to the possibility of incrimination by compelled admission of details; thus, while questions about other parties (such as those in *Rogers* itself) must be answered,[23] most courts now will not allow the compulsion of any self-incriminating details that "might provide a link not already provided."[24]

A variation on the fair examination rule occurs when the state wants to introduce an expert to rebut a mental state issue raised by the defendant. Just as the prosecution's ability to cross-examine the defendant depends on whether and to what extent the defendant testifies on direct, the admissibility of the prosecution psychiatric expert's findings are directly related to the defendant's decisions at trial about whether to introduce evidence on mental state issues. In *Estelle v. Smith*,[25] the Court held that the prosecution may not compel an evaluation on issues regarding mental defenses or introduce a psychiatrist who conducted such an evaluation unless the defendant has put at issue his mental state at the time of the offense. But in *Buchanan v. Kentucky*,[26] the Court held that, if the defendant has raised such an issue at trial, the state may introduce the results of an examination initiated *jointly* by the defense and the prosecution. And in *Kansas v. Cheever*,[27] the Court, analogizing to the principle that the Fifth Amendment does not allow a defendant to refuse to answer cross-examination questions relating to his testimony on direct, unanimously concluded that even the results of an evaluation ordered solely at the request of the prosecution may be described by the expert in rebuttal of a defense claim. *Cheever* also held that the triggering claim can relate to any mental state defense, not just insanity. In *Cheever* itself, the Court upheld prosecution use of an expert to rebut a defense of voluntary intoxication.

---

[22]   National Lawyers Guild, Representation of Witnesses before Federal Grand Juries § 13.7(b) (1976).

[23]   Id.

[24]   *Shendal v. United States*, 312 F.2d 564 (9th Cir. 1963); see Note, 92 Harv.L.Rev. 1752, 1754–60 (1979).

[25]   452 U.S. 454, 101 S.Ct. 1866 (1981).

[26]   483 U.S. 402, 107 S.Ct. 2906 (1987).

[27]   571 U.S. 87, 134 S.Ct. 596 (2013).

(5) The Continuing Waiver Theory

Normally, if a witness does waive the Fifth Amendment by testifying, that waiver is applicable only throughout that proceeding. However, some courts have held that, under certain circumstances, a waiver at a grand jury proceeding also operates at trial. For instance, in *Ellis v. United States*,[28] the court ruled that a grand jury witness who voluntarily makes incriminating statements may not invoke the privilege for the same statements at a criminal trial (at least when the witness is not the defendant), primarily because the government already has access to the grand jury testimony and thus the compelled trial testimony poses little or no danger of eliciting additional incriminating material. Other courts have adopted this "continuing waiver" theory, but, as in *Ellis*, do not apply it to criminal defendants, out of fear that a contrary rule would "chill" their right to testify.[29] Another useful limitation of the continuing waiver rule would be to prohibit its operation unless the grand jury witness is given warnings apprizing him of the consequences of a decision to testify.

(6) Non-Custodial Questioning; the "Exculpatory" No Doctrine

Non-custodial questioning outside the courtroom is generally treated like questioning in the courtroom. *Miranda* warnings are not required,[30] and unless the interviewee asserts the right to remain silent and that assertion is overridden, no Fifth Amendment violation occurs, barring some evidence of coercion on the questioners' part. For a time, some federal courts were willing to assume such coercion existed in connection with a specific type of noncustodial questioning. Under 18 U.S.C. § 1001 a person who makes a false statement to a federal investigator may be penalized with a fine of up to $10,000, a prison sentence of up to five years in prison, or both. A number of federal courts construed the statute narrowly, holding that § 1001 prosecutions should be dismissed when based simply on the fact that the defendant falsely stated "no" in answer to a question about whether he had committed a particular crime or an element thereof.[31] The Fifth Amendment rationale for this "exculpatory no" doctrine is that operation of the false statement statute creates the "cruel trilemma" banned by the Fifth Amendment: because of the statute, a guilty person asked an incriminating question either has to admit guilt, violate § 1001 by falsely denying guilt, or refuse to answer, a refusal that the subject might believe can be used against him (since *Miranda* warnings need not be given).

In *Brogan v. United States*[32] the Supreme Court rejected this argument. Justice Scalia, writing for seven members of the Court, concluded that the trilemma did not exist in this situation. He dismissed as "implausible" the assertion that people are not aware of their right to remain silent "in the modern age of frequently dramatized '*Miranda*' warnings;" in any event, he added, fear that silence will be used "does not exert a form of pressure that exonerates an otherwise unlawful lie." Even if the "trilemma" did exist, however, Scalia asserted it did not violate the Constitution.

---

[28]   416 F.2d 791 (D.C.Cir. 1969).

[29]   *Salim v. United States*, 480 A.2d 710 (D.C.App. 1984); see also *United States v. Miller*, 904 F.2d 65 (D.C.Cir. 1990). On chilling exercise of the right, see § 15.02(c).

[30]   See § 16.03(a).

[31]   See, e.g., *United States v. Lopez-Iraeta*, 136 F.3d 143 (11th Cir. 1998); *United States v. Equihua-Juarez*, 851 F.2d 1222, 1224 (9th Cir. 1988).

[32]   522 U.S. 398, 118 S.Ct. 805 (1998).

(b) Statutory Compulsion

Many federal and state statutes require citizens to create documents, or answer questions posed on a document, that may prove self-incriminating. As with compulsion of witnesses, the Supreme Court's analysis of this type of compulsion has focused on the setting in which the information is given and the purpose behind the government's request for information. As a general rule, the Court has held that, like the trial witness, the person subject to statutory compulsion loses the privilege if he does not assert it by refusing to answer. However, the Court has also identified situations in which the statutory compulsion is more "adversarial," and the privilege accordingly provides more comprehensive protection. Finally, a third series of cases hold that where the statute requires disclosure of "public" information for legitimate, non-criminal purposes, the Fifth Amendment provides no protection at all.

(1) Innocently-Posed Questions

In *United States v. Sullivan*,[33] the Court upheld the defendant's conviction for failure to file an income tax return. The defendant argued that submission of the return would have been self-incriminating, but the Court concluded that the privilege entitled the taxpayer, at most, to refrain from answering specific questions that might tend to incriminate him. As to what information the taxpayer could have withheld, the Court's only statement, in dictum, was that "[i]t would be an extreme if not an extravagant application of the Fifth Amendment to say that it authorized a man to refuse to state the amount of his income because it had been made in crime."

Fifty years later, the Court explicated this holding in *Garner v. United States*,[34] where the defendant was convicted of conspiring to fix sporting events, based in part upon admissions contained in his tax form. As in *Sullivan*, the defendant argued that not submitting the form would have led to a conviction, but added that returning an incomplete form would result in punishment under a federal statute criminalizing the filing of incomplete returns. Noting that prosecution for a good faith assertion of the privilege is not permitted under the latter statute, a unanimous Court refused to find that use of the tax statements violated the Fifth Amendment. As with the trial witness, a person who answers an innocently posed question on the tax form cannot be said to have been "compelled" by the state to answer. Indeed, "a taxpayer, who can complete his return at leisure and with legal assistance, is even less subject to . . . psychological pressures . . . than a witness who has been called to testify in judicial proceedings." On the other hand, the Court confirmed that a taxpayer may assert the privilege with impunity with respect to specific incriminating items on the form at the time it is prepared.[35]

The *Sullivan-Garner* approach to statutory compulsion would seem to apply to many situations in which the government asks citizens for information via registration

---

[33] 274 U.S. 259, 47 S.Ct. 607 (1927).

[34] 424 U.S. 648, 96 S.Ct. 1178 (1976).

[35] The majority opinion, joined by seven members of the Court, concluded by stating that the Fifth Amendment claim must be *valid*, not just in good faith. But, as the two concurring members pointed out, 26 U.S.C.A. § 7203 provides that the failure to provide information on the return must be "willful," and the government conceded that a defendant cannot properly be convicted for an erroneous claim of privilege asserted in good faith.

forms, welfare applications, professional license applications and the like.[36] Unless the privilege is asserted at the time the forms are filled out, the privilege is lost, since the questions posed are not adversarial, and thus not instinct with coercion.

(2) The Suspect Class Exception

When, in contrast to the situation in *Sullivan* and *Garner*, the statutory request is not "innocently posed" but rather prosecutorial in nature, the privilege not only permits a refusal to answer specific questions but also a refusal to file the forms in the first instance. The leading case in this regard is *Albertson v. Subversive Activities Control Board*,[37] which involved a statute requiring communists to register with the government. The petitioners, who were communists, claimed this provision violated their right against self-incrimination, given the fact that mere association with the Communist Party could lead to criminal charges. In agreeing with this argument and reversing their convictions for failing to register, the Court rejected the government's contention that, in light of *Sullivan*, the petitioners were only permitted by the Fifth Amendment to refrain from answering specific questions on the Communist registration form. Justice Brennan, writing for the majority, observed:

> In *Sullivan* the questions in the income tax return were neutral on their face and directed at the public at large, but here they are directed at a highly selective group inherently suspect of criminal activities. Petitioners' claims are not asserted in an essentially noncriminal and regulatory area of inquiry, but against an inquiry in an area permeated with criminal statutes, where response to any of the form's questions in context might involve the petitioners in the admission of a crucial element of a crime.

Cases applying *Albertson* have focused on the extent to which the statutory purpose requires revelation of obviously incriminating information from "a highly selective group inherently suspect of criminal activities." In *Marchetti v. United States*,[38] the Court held that registration and occupational tax laws that applied only to gamblers violated the Fifth Amendment rights of those who were required to register. These statutes had the "direct and unmistakable consequence of incriminating" the respondents because wagering is "permeated with criminal statutes" and gamblers are "inherently suspect of criminal activities." Thus Marchetti's conviction for a failure to file the required forms was reversed. The Court applied a similar analysis to two companion cases, *Haynes v. United States*,[39] which involved a statute requiring registration of firearms possessed by those who had violated other provisions of the National Firearms Act, and *Grosso v. United States*,[40] dealing with a statute providing for registration of those who paid excise taxes on wagering. In *Leary v. United States*,[41] decided a year later, the Court voided the self-reporting provisions of the Marijuana Tax Act, which required informing authorities of drug possession for tax purposes, relying heavily on the fact that such reporting necessarily involved an admission of conduct that was a crime under state law.

---

[36] But see *Selective Service System v. Minnesota Public Interest Research Group*, 468 U.S. 841, 104 S.Ct. 3348 (1984), discussed in § 15.02(b)(2).

[37] 382 U.S. 70, 86 S.Ct. 194 (1965).

[38] 390 U.S. 39, 88 S.Ct. 697 (1968).

[39] 390 U.S. 85, 88 S.Ct. 722 (1968).

[40] 390 U.S. 62, 88 S.Ct. 709 (1968).

[41] 395 U.S. 6, 89 S.Ct. 1532 (1969).

In all of these cases, the Court recognized that by filing an incomplete form, or explicitly invoking their Fifth Amendment privilege on the form itself (as required in *Sullivan* and *Garner*), the petitioners would incriminate themselves by informing the government that they were involved in illegal activities. As the Court stated in *Grosso*, a "statutory system . . . utilized to pierce the anonymity of citizens engaged in criminal activity, is invalid." Even a grant of immunity as to prosecutorial use of the identification was seen as insufficient protection by the Court. In *Albertson*, for instance, the Court expressed its concern that, once possessed of the individual's identity, the government could use it to acquire other incriminating information that would be hard to trace back to the registration form, and thus evade the immunity grant.[42]

At times, it can be difficult to determine when *Albertson* rather than *Garner* should apply. *Selective Service System v. Minnesota Public Interest Research Group*,[43] involved a federal statutory scheme that required male college students to show they had registered for the draft before they could receive federal financial assistance. Under this statute, those students who wanted assistance but who had not registered by the statutory deadline (within 30 days of their 18th birthday) would have to register late, conduct that was a criminal offense. Nonetheless, a majority of the Court upheld the statute and permitted the use of any incriminating responses discovered on the late registration forms that were necessary to document eligibility for student aid. At the same time, citing *Garner*, the Court strongly implied that students could exercise their Fifth Amendment right when registering and applying for aid and that the government could not compel their answers at that point without immunization. The problem with this holding, as Justice Marshall pointed out in dissent, is that, unlike the tax laws at issue in *Garner* but like the statute in *Albertson*, the late registration provision in this case was aimed at discovering the identity of an inherently suspect group, "the 674,000 existing nonregistrants." Thus, allowing assertion of the privilege would provide insufficient protection to these people; the government could still discover the identity of individuals who had not registered on time and, armed with that information, make its case against them.

Another analytically difficult situation arises in connection with stop-and-identify statutes that permit arrest of persons who fail to identify themselves once police have legitimately stopped them based on reasonable suspicion. Arguably, this group of people is, by definition, "inherently suspect of criminal activities." But in *Hiibel v. Nevada*[44] a majority of the Supreme Court ignored this assertion in Justice Stevens' dissent and upheld a stop-and-identify law against a Fifth Amendment challenge. The Court did state, however, that a Fifth Amendment violation might occur "where there is a substantial allegation that furnishing identity at the time of a stop would have given the police a link in the chain of evidence needed to convict the individual of a separate offense."

---

[42]　Of course, total (or "transactional") immunity from prosecution would solve this problem, but the Court has been unwilling to read an immunity provision into legislation, see *Marchetti v. United States*, 390 U.S. 39, 88 S.Ct. 697 (1968), and in other settings has held that the Fifth Amendment requires only use and derivative use immunity. *Kastigar v. United States*, 406 U.S. 441, 92 S.Ct. 1653 (1972), discussed in § 15.03(c)(1).

[43]　468 U.S. 841, 104 S.Ct. 3348 (1984).

[44]　542 U.S. 177, 124 S.Ct. 2451 (2004).

(3) The "Regulatory Purpose" Doctrine

A final series of cases which further complicates the analysis of statutory compulsion stands for the proposition that when a statutory reporting requirement is essential to a public, regulatory scheme, rather than designed to obtain private information (as in *Garner*) or evidence of criminal activity (as in *Albertson*), it does not implicate the Fifth Amendment at all, even when it happens to compel incriminating disclosures. The Court's first case in this regard was *Shapiro v. United States*,[45] which upheld the conviction of a business owner based in part on information found in records he was required to keep and produce for the government under the Emergency Price Control Act. In *Grosso*, the Court later described the rationale for *Shapiro* as follows:

> [F]irst the purposes of the United States' inquiry must be essentially regulatory; second, information is to be obtained by requiring the preservation of records of a kind which the regulated party has customarily kept; and third, the records themselves must have assumed "public aspects" which render them at least analogous to public documents.

The first requirement distinguished *Shapiro* from the *Albertson* line of cases, which were aimed at discovering evidence of criminal activity rather than regulating a non-criminal enterprise. The latter two requirements differentiated *Shapiro* from cases like *Sullivan* and *Garner*, since tax forms are not routinely kept records nor are they public in nature.

However, in *California v. Byers*,[46] a plurality of the Court significantly modified this characterization of the regulatory purpose doctrine, shedding any requirement that the incriminating information be found in routinely kept records. The defendant in *Byers* left the scene of a traffic accident without reporting his name and was charged with unsafe passing and failure to stop and identify himself. He demurred to the second charge, claiming that California's reporting requirement under its hit-and-run statute violated his privilege against self-incrimination. Chief Justice Burger's opinion reasoned that where there is a "strong polic[y] in favor of disclosure," such as here, the defendant must demonstrate "substantial hazards of self-incrimination." Applying the *Albertson* criteria, he found that the disclosure requirement under the hit-and-run statute did "not entail the kind of substantial risk of self-incrimination involved in *Marchetti, Grosso,* and *Haynes.*" The vehicle code's requirements were directed at the public at large rather than an inherently suspect group, and the reporting provision was motivated by a non-criminal purpose, "to promote the satisfaction of civil liabilities arising from automobile accidents."

As the four dissenters pointed out, contrary to Burger's assertion, the vehicle code provision at issue in *Byers* was not directed at the public at large, but rather was aimed at a more select group, namely drivers involved in accidents causing property damage, and clearly requires them to surrender their "anonymity," a concern in *Albertson*. At the same time, the statute in *Byers* does seem different from the statutes involved in the *Albertson* line of cases in that, as in *Shapiro*, the group it focused on was not "inherently suspect" of criminal activity; many drivers involved in accidents are not chargeable criminally. Justice Harlan's concurring opinion offers a better rationale for the decision. He concluded, contrary to the plurality, that the risk of incrimination in *Byers* was "real." But, he argued that, balancing the state's interest against the individual's, the

---

[45]   335 U.S. 1, 68 S.Ct. 1375 (1948).
[46]   402 U.S. 424, 91 S.Ct. 1535 (1971).

"assertedly non-criminal governmental purpose in securing information, the necessity for self-reporting as a means of securing the information, and the nature of the disclosures required" meant Byers could not assert the privilege in this situation. As Harlan pointed out:

> Byers having once focused attention on himself as an accident-participant, the State must still bear the burden of making the main evidentiary case [under the vehicle code]. To characterize this burden as a merely ritualistic confirmation of the "conviction" secured through compliance with the reporting requirement in issue would be a gross distortion of reality; on the other hand, that characterization of the evidentiary burden remaining on the [government] after compliance with the regulatory scheme involved in *Marchetti* and *Grosso* seems proper.

Harlan's rationale seems to be the one preferred by the Court in later cases. In *Garner*, in distinguishing the hit-and-run statute in *Byers* from the income tax laws involved in that case, the Court emphasized that *Byers* only involved questions about name and address and that the various opinions in that case had "suggested that the privilege might be claimed appropriately against other questions." *Byers*, continued the *Garner* Court, thus holds "only that requiring certain basic disclosures fundamental to a neutral reporting scheme does not violate the privilege."[47] Similarly, in *Baltimore City Department of Social Services v. Bouknight*,[48] while the Court held that the privilege does not prevent the government from compelling a woman to produce her child in custody proceedings given the regulatory purpose of those proceedings, it cautioned that if the state subsequently sought to use the act of production (or lack thereof) against the mother in a criminal prosecution, the Fifth Amendment might be implicated.[49]

Most lower court decisions seem to apply *Byers* consistently with this approach. For instance, in *United States v. San Juan*,[50] the court upheld against a Fifth Amendment challenge the provisions of the Bank Secrecy Act that require disclosure of amounts in excess of $5,000 transported across United States borders. The court found that the government had a clear and continuing interest in controlling international transactions, that the provisions were neutral on their face, in that they apply to all international travelers, and that they do not require admissions of criminal activity (although disclosure may lead to inquiry). In contrast, in *Bionic Auto Parts & Sales, Inc. v. Fahner*,[51] the court struck down statutory requirements that auto parts dealers record and report altered serial numbers, given "the degree to which the information request in and of itself is incriminatory and the degree to which those required to keep the records are suspected of criminal activity." The statute at issue imposed absolute criminal liability for possession or sale of parts with altered serial numbers.

One might analyze the cases adopting the public records exception to the privilege in terms of waiver; that is, one could say that organizations or persons who choose to

---

[47]   Indeed, the disclosures in *Byers* could be seen as nontestimonial. See § 15.04.

[48]   493 U.S. 549, 110 S.Ct. 900 (1990).

[49]   The Court also sought to explain *Bouknight* by analogy to its collective entity cases, which hold that a subpoena may compel information that is held in a "representative" capacity. See § 15.06(d). Here, the Court asserted, the child was held in such a capacity by the mother, who had reacquired custody, after an initial determination of unfitness, on condition that she meet several requirements, including cooperating with the social services department.

[50]   405 F.Supp. 686 (D.Vt. 1975), rev'd on other grounds 545 F.2d 314 (2d Cir. 1976).

[51]   721 F.2d 1072 (7th Cir. 1983).

operate in certain highly regulated activities automatically forego Fifth Amendment protection of certain information. But it makes more sense to say that these cases rest on a conclusion that, in light of the strong public interest involved, a "fair state-individual balance" means there is no right to waive. The key question addressed in these cases appears to be "whether a particular reporting requirement is designed to facilitate the government's legitimate needs for regulatory information rather than undercut the adversary system by covertly aiding the investigation and prosecution of crime."[52]

(c) Compulsion Through Non-Criminal Sanctions

In the cases discussed above, state compulsion was implemented through the threat of criminal contempt citation or some other criminal punishment. A final group of cases dealing with compulsion focuses on the extent to which exercise of the Fifth Amendment right is "chilled" by state actions that do not involve direct use of criminal sanctions. The first case explicitly examining this problem was *Griffin v. California*,[53] in which the Court held that a prosecutor's reference to the defendant's failure to testify, designed to convince the jury to draw an adverse inference therefrom, was reversible error. The Court held that "the imposition of any sanction which makes assertion of the Fifth Amendment 'costly' is constitutionally impermissible compulsion." Here, the types of comments made by the prosecutor could inhibit exercise of the defendant's Fifth Amendment right to refrain from testifying, a corollary of the right to remain silent.

While the reach of *Griffin* has since been limited significantly,[54] its basic premise—that the state should not be able to inhibit free exercise of the right to remain silent in any way—is reflected in several other cases. In *Garrity v. New Jersey*,[55] for instance, police officers summoned during an investigation of police corruption were informed that they would be discharged if they refused to answer questions. The Court held that such compulsion violated their rights and required reversal of convictions based on their testimony. In *Simmons v. United States*,[56] the Court held that the defendant's pretrial testimony at a hearing to determine the validity of a search and seizure could not be used against him at trial on the question of guilt, concluding that forcing a choice between one's Fourth and Fifth Amendment rights was "intolerable." In *Lefkowitz v. Turley*,[57] the Court invalidated a New York statute requiring public contractors either to waive immunity or to suffer forfeiture of existing and future state contracts for the next five years. And in *Lefkowitz v. Cunningham*,[58] it held unconstitutional a statute which provided that an officer of a political party must either answer questions posed by the grand jury or be immediately disqualified from holding any other party or public office for a period of five years.

In contrast, conditioning a prisoner's entry into a sexual abuse treatment program on disclosure of all prior sexual offenses, including those not yet charged and for which no immunity is granted, is not a violation of the Fifth Amendment. This is so, the Court

---

    52   Robert Mosteller, *Simplifying Subpoena Law: Taking the Fifth Amendment Seriously*, 73 Va.L.Rev. 1, 67 (1987).

    53   380 U.S. 609, 85 S.Ct. 1229 (1965).

    54   See § 28.03(c) for further discussion of *Griffin* and its progeny.

    55   385 U.S. 493, 87 S.Ct. 616 (1967).

    56   390 U.S. 377, 88 S.Ct. 967 (1968).

    57   414 U.S. 70, 94 S.Ct. 316 (1973).

    58   431 U.S. 801, 97 S.Ct. 2132 (1977).

held in *McKune v. Lile*,[59] even if the refusal also results in curtailment of visitation rights, earnings, work opportunities, the ability to send money to family, canteen expenditures, access to personal television, and the potential for transfer to a maximum security unit. Justice Kennedy, writing for a four-member plurality, concluded that these "minimal incentives" to participate in Kansas' sexual abuse treatment program did not amount to Fifth Amendment compulsion. The plurality also sought to characterize these consequences of remaining silent as simply a loss of benefits rather than a penalty of the type involved in *Garrity* and *Lefkowitz*.

The fifth vote for the majority came from Justice O'Connor. She did not agree with the plurality's assertion that the consequences of remaining silent constituted loss of a benefit rather than a penalty. Rather, she straightforwardly concluded that the reduction in incentives and the transfer from medium to maximum security were "minor" compared to the penalties involved in *Lefkowitz* and the other penalty cases. O'Connor noted that the prisoner who refuses to participate in the treatment would still be able to see his attorney, family and clergy, and does not require wages given the prison's provision of his basic needs. Further, she asserted, Lile would not be threatened unduly by transfer to maximum security, where "we may be assume that the prison is capable of controlling its inmates so that respondent's personal safety is not jeopardized."

Justice Stevens, writing for a four-member dissent, agreed with O'Connor that the plurality's description of the consequences of silence as a non-penalty was specious. He also disputed the plurality's and O'Connor's characterization of those consequences as minimal, pointing out that they were the same sanctions that follow a disciplinary conviction for an offense such as theft, sodomy, riot, arson, or assault. He noted that the state could simply provide immunity if it needed information about past sex offenses, or could make the program entirely voluntary, as it is in the federal prisons, so that no loss of privileges occurs if there is a refusal to participate. The plurality had concluded that the state should not have to grant immunity to get the information it wanted, because inhibiting prosecution on past crimes would minimize the seriousness of sex offenses and thus undermine rehabilitation and deterrence. But Stevens pointed out that most sex offenders were, like Lile, serving very long sentences for their sex offense and had thus already learned the serious consequences of their behavior.[60]

Lile purportedly does not change the principle that the Fifth Amendment is violated if a sentence is extended as a result of silence, because this would be a criminal sanction imposed for exercise of the right. Apparently, however, it is permissible to give an offender a reduction in sentence for cooperating with law enforcement,[61] and it is clearly constitutional to condition a reduction in charge or sentence on a plea of guilty.[62] Although the difference between these latter two situations and a sentence enhancement due to silence may seem clear in the abstract, functionally they amount to the same thing. *Lile* brings the Court one step closer to confronting that conundrum. For now, however, as Justice O'Connor recognized, a majority of the Court has failed "to set forth a comprehensive theory of the Fifth Amendment privilege against self-incrimination" with respect to compulsion.

---

[59]   536 U.S. 24, 122 S.Ct. 2017 (2002).

[60]   Of course, prisoners could still misrepresent their prior history, and in fact no prisoner involved in the program had yet been prosecuted based on disclosures made to obtain entry into it.

[61]   United States Sentencing Commission, Guidelines Manual § 3E1.1 (Nov. 2000).

[62]   See *Bordenkircher v. Hayes*, 434 U.S. 357, 98 S.Ct. 663 (1978), discussed in § 26.02(c)(2).

It should also be noted that, in some situations, the "Hobson's choice" confronting the defendant may not involve the Fifth Amendment, despite first appearances. This was the case in *South Dakota v. Neville*,[63] involving a statute that required a driver stopped for drunken driving either to take a blood-alcohol test or suffer revocation of his driver's license. The Supreme Court upheld the admission of the defendant's refusal to take the test, in part because "the state did not directly compel respondent to refuse the test, for it gave him the choice of submitting to the test or refusing." More importantly, this choice did not include sacrificing the privilege against self-incrimination as one option because, concluded the Court, the results of a blood-alcohol test are "nontestimonial."[64]

15.03   Incrimination

The Fifth Amendment prohibits the state from compelling information only if it might be used in a "criminal proceeding." Indeed, if the government does not use a person's statement in a criminal proceeding, the Fifth Amendment is not violated even when the statement is clearly compelled. That basic tenet was made evident in *Chavez v. Martinez*.[65] There the Court held the Fifth Amendment was not violated by an officer's hospital questioning of a severely injured suspect who was screaming in pain, thought he was dying, and stated he did not want to talk until he was treated, because the suspect's subsequent incriminating statements were never used against him in a criminal prosecution. Justice Thomas, in an opinion joined by Chief Justice Rehnquist and Justices O'Connor and Scalia, reasoned that Martinez "was never made to be a 'witness' against himself in violation of the Fifth Amendment's Self-Incrimination Clause." Justice Souter, joined by Justice Breyer, similarly concluded that Martinez' claim was "well outside the core of Fifth Amendment protection."[66]

At the same time, as Justice Souter explained in his *Martinez* opinion, "extensions of the bare guarantee may be warranted if clearly shown to be desirable means to protect the basic right against invasive pressures of contemporary society." Thus, the Court has consistently held that the Fifth Amendment protects the individual who *refuses* to answer questions when the answers may be used in a criminal proceeding. As the Court stated in *Lefkowitz v. Turley*,[67] the privilege not only permits an individual to remain silent at grand jury and trial proceedings in which he is a criminal defendant, but also to refuse "to answer official questions put to him in any . . . proceeding, civil or criminal, formal or informal, where the answers might incriminate him in future criminal proceedings."[68]

It follows, however, that if an individual subject to questioning can be assured that the information will not be used in a "criminal" proceeding, he has no right to remain silent. Such assurance may derive from: (1) the nature of the information requested (e.g., its irrelevance to any criminal matter); (2) a grant of immunity protecting against its

---

[63]   459 U.S. 553, 103 S.Ct. 916 (1983).

[64]   See § 15.04 for further discussion of the testimonial/nontestimonial distinction.

[65]   538 U.S. 760, 123 S.Ct. 1994 (2003).

[66]   However, these two Justices, plus three others, also concluded that Martinez might have a valid due process claim.

[67]   414 U.S. 70, 94 S.Ct. 316 (1973).

[68]   This "right" is sometimes called the "witness privilege," to be distinguished from the "defendant's privilege," which permits the defendant in criminal proceedings to exclude compelled statements already made.

future use; or (3) some other guarantee that the information cannot be used to prosecute for a given crime (e.g., expiration of the relevant statute of limitations). The definition of "criminal proceeding," and these three related aspects of the incrimination concept are taken up here.

(a) The Definition of Criminal Proceeding

In deciding whether a proceeding is "criminal" for purposes of the privilege, courts look principally at whether "punitive" sanctions could be imposed at the proceeding in question, not at the label—i.e., "civil" or "criminal"—traditionally affixed to the proceeding. In other words the *purpose* of the sanction, not whether it results in loss of liberty, is the important variable. Thus, proceedings that require the convicted defendant to pay fines or forfeit property as "punishment" rather than for compensatory reasons may be characterized as "criminal,"[69] whereas, as developed below, proceedings that can result in prolonged confinement meant to be rehabilitative rather than punitive may be termed "civil" for Fifth Amendment purposes.

For some time, it appeared that loss of liberty was more than a secondary factor in Fifth Amendment analysis. In *In re Gault*,[70] the Court justified its holding that the privilege may be raised at all stages of a juvenile delinquency proceeding with the following words: "our Constitution guarantees that no person shall be 'compelled' to be a witness against himself when he is threatened with deprivation of his liberty." The Court found that the state's designation of delinquency proceedings as "civil" in nature was irrelevant; what was important in determining the availability of the privilege is "the nature of the statement or admission and the exposure which it invites." Justice Fortas, who wrote the majority opinion, concentrated on the fact that in over half the states children adjudicated delinquent could be housed with adults and that in every state children over a certain age could be transferred to adult court jurisdiction for trial, thereby creating exposure to imprisonment.

However, in *Minnesota v. Murphy*,[71] the Court stated in a footnote that if questions put to a probationer were relevant only to his probationary status (e.g., questions about residence) and "posed no realistic threat of incrimination in a separate criminal proceeding", then the probationer could not refuse to answer them. The Court further stated that the probationer could even be forced to answer questions about *crimes* he may have committed (and that the answers could be used at a revocation proceeding), so long as the state is prevented from using these disclosures in separate criminal proceedings. Since a probation revocation proceeding can obviously result in a loss at liberty, *Gault's* language was called into question.

In *Allen v. Illinois*[72] the Court settled that *Gault's* deprivation of liberty criterion "is plainly not good law" and that the extent to which a given proceeding is punitive in nature is the sole factor to be considered in determining the applicability of the privilege. *Allen* involved application of the Fifth Amendment to psychiatric evaluations and adjudicatory proceedings under the Illinois Sexually Dangerous Persons Act. The Act permits the prosecutor to initiate "civil" proceedings designed to commit an individual

---

[69] See, e.g., *United States v. United States Coin & Currency*, 401 U.S. 715, 91 S.Ct. 1041 (1971); *Boyd v. United States*, 116 U.S. 616, 6 S.Ct. 524 (1886).

[70] 387 U.S. 1, 87 S.Ct. 1428 (1967).

[71] 465 U.S. 420, 104 S.Ct. 1136 (1984).

[72] 478 U.S. 364, 106 S.Ct. 2988 (1986).

who has been found beyond a reasonable doubt to have committed at least one criminal sexual offense and to be "sexually dangerous." Justice Rehnquist, writing the 5–4 opinion, focused entirely on the purpose of the Act, as construed by the Illinois Supreme Court. He noted that the Act created a statutory obligation to provide care and treatment for those adjudicated sexually dangerous and that release was required if the "patient was found to be no longer dangerous." Thus, the Court concluded, the "Act does not appear to promote either of 'the traditional aims of punishment—retribution or deterrence.'" The fact that the Act provided the individual subjected to commitment proceedings with procedural rights akin to those accorded the criminal defendant was deemed irrelevant. Nor was the fact that the petitioner had been confined in a psychiatric unit located at the state's maximum security prison material. The Court did note, however, that had the petitioner shown that the confinement of sexually dangerous individuals "imposes on them a regimen which is essentially identical to that imposed upon felons with no need for psychiatric care, this might well be a different case."

The Court's decision in *Allen* is insensitive to the reality of the commitment system. As Justice Stevens noted in dissent, the maximum penalty for the petitioner's crime was less than a year's imprisonment and a $500 fine, yet under authority of the Illinois act he had been committed for five years at the time of the Court's decision. While loss of liberty should perhaps not be the dispositive factor in determining the applicability of the Fifth Amendment, a statute that permits indeterminate confinement in the equivalent of prison, should not, regardless of its purpose, be designated "civil" in nature. Even analyzing the statute in the Court's terms, the result in *Allen* seems misguided. The principal goal of the Illinois statute, as indicated by its release provisions, is not treatment but incapacitation, a primary goal of punishment, and one which is closely related to retribution where individuals thought to be "sexually dangerous" are concerned. Yet *Allen* now permits the states to compel individuals charged with sexual offenses to submit to psychiatric evaluations and answer questions, upon penalty of contempt, that will assist the state in committing them indefinitely under such statutes, so long as any disclosures made are not used to convict the individual in separate criminal proceedings.

Presumably, after *Allen*, there is no Fifth Amendment privilege in civil commitment proceedings either.[73] While *Gault's* holding that the privilege applies to juvenile delinquency proceedings is still good law, its application to other juvenile court matters (such as Children in Need of Supervision cases) is doubtful, given the rehabilitative goals of these proceedings. The Court has also indicated that child custody proceedings, in which the goal of the state is to remove a child from the mother's custody, are not "criminal" for purposes of the Fifth Amendment.[74] Nor are civil deportation proceedings of illegal aliens.[75]

Even proceedings that are directly associated with the criminal process are not necessarily "criminal" proceedings for purposes of the Fifth Amendment. As noted earlier, in *Murphy* the Court explicitly stated that a probation revocation hearing is not a "criminal proceeding" and that "a State may validly insist on answers to even

---

[73] The court has already indicated as much by summarily affirming *French v. Blackburn*, 428 F.Supp. 1351 (M.D.N.C. 1977), which held that the Fifth Amendment does not apply in civil commitment proceedings.

[74] *Baltimore City Department of Social Services v. Bouknight*, 493 U.S. 549, 110 S.Ct. 900 (1990) (state may compel mother to produce her child at custody hearings in juvenile court, although state use of act of production in subsequent criminal proceedings might be prohibited).

[75] See *INS v. Lopez-Mendoza*, 468 U.S. 1032, 104 S.Ct. 3479 (1984), discussed in § 2.03(b).

incriminating questions and hence sensibly administer its probation system, so long as it recognizes that the required answers may not be used in a criminal proceeding and thus eliminates the threat of incrimination." In the same vein, in *Estelle v. Smith*,[76] the Supreme Court held that the state may compel answers from the defendant during a pretrial psychiatric evaluation to determine his competency to stand trial, so long as the information obtained is used for its "avowed purpose"—as evidence at a proceeding to determine competency. Under such circumstances, the pretrial competency proceeding is not "criminal" for purposes of the Fifth Amendment.

Smith also held, however, that a capital sentencing proceeding *is* a "criminal proceeding;" thus, on the facts of that case, the privilege was violated when competency results were used at capital sentencing without obtaining a valid waiver. According to the seven member majority, "[g]iven the gravity of the decision to be made at the penalty phase" of a capital sentencing proceeding, there is "no basis to distinguish between the guilt and penalty phases . . . so far as the protection of the Fifth Amendment privilege is concerned." The Court concluded that when the defendant "neither initiates a psychiatric evaluation nor attempts to introduce any psychiatric evidence, [he] may not be compelled to respond to a psychiatrist if his statements can be used against him at a capital sentencing proceeding." However, as indicated earlier in this chapter,[77] if the defendant does initiate the evaluation, or the evaluation is requested by the prosecution in a case where the defense has indicated it will introduce psychiatric testimony at sentencing, then the defendant cannot assert the Fifth Amendment with impunity. In these two situations, the Court appears willing to hold that the defendant has "waived" the privilege.

The majority in *Smith* left open the question of whether the Fifth Amendment may be asserted at noncapital sentencing proceedings. Of course, if the information sought at sentencing can be used in a future prosecution against the defendant, he need not provide it.[78] And in *Mitchell v. United States*,[79] the Court appeared to hold that a defendant may assert the right to remain silent at sentencing even with respect to the offense for which he is being sentenced. In *Mitchell*, the government argued that, analogous to the rule that a defendant who takes the stand at trial cannot avoid cross-examination,[80] the defendant who makes statements at the plea hearing may not later refuse to answer questions at sentencing. However, a unanimous Court rejected that argument, reasoning that the inability to question statements made at a plea hearing does not threaten the integrity of the factfinding process the way an uncross-examined trial witness would, because "the defendant who pleads guilty puts nothing in dispute regarding the essentials of the offense." Instead, noted Justice Kennedy for the Court, "the defendant takes those matters out of dispute, often by making a joint statement with the prosecution or confirming the prosecution's version of the facts."

Presumably a defendant who is convicted at trial has the same right to remain silent at sentencing, since in that situation he either has been cross-examined or has not made any type of statement at adjudication. Indeed, the Court stated that "to maintain that sentencing proceedings are not part of 'any criminal case' [the language of the Fifth

---

[76] 451 U.S. 454, 101 S.Ct. 1866 (1981).

[77] See § 5.02(a)(4).

[78] Id.

[79] 526 U.S. 314, 119 S.Ct. 1307 (1999).

[80] See § 15.02(a)(4).

Amendment] is contrary to law and common sense", because "[w]here the sentence has not yet been imposed a defendant may have a legitimate fear of adverse consequences from further testimony."

More importantly, five members of the Court also held, in line with *Griffin v. California*,[81] that the sentencing court may not use a defendant's silence against him. Thus, a convicted defendant may be able to avoid speaking about his crime not only at the sentencing hearing but also at any pre-sentence interviews, such as those conducted by probation officers, without fear of sanction from the court.[82]

(b) Foreign Prosecutions

In *United States v. Balsys*[83] the Court for the first time squarely confronted the issue of whether a foreign prosecution is a "criminal case" under the Fifth Amendment, such that a person could invoke the Amendment to avoid statements in this country that might be used in another. Balsys, who immigrated to the U.S. in 1961, was subpoenaed by the Justice Department in 1996 in an effort to discover whether he had been involved in Nazi-sponsored persecutions during World War II, contrary to statements in his immigration application that he had been in hiding in Lithuania during the war. Answers to the Justice Department's questions could not be used to prosecute him in this country because the statute of limitations had run on the crime of perjury regarding his wartime activities, the only crime with which he could be charged in the U.S. However, Balsys alleged, and the government conceded, that if he were to admit such involvement in the Justice Department's proceedings his statements could well form the basis for prosecution in various other countries such as Lithuania and Germany.

The majority opinion in *Balsys*, authored by Justice Souter, concluded that such concern about foreign prosecution does not implicate the Fifth Amendment. Balsys argued that because the Fifth Amendment's privilege against self-incrimination speaks of "any criminal case", whereas the Sixth Amendment's provisions regarding jury, counsel, and confrontation rights clearly refer to domestic "criminal prosecutions", the former phrase should be read expansively to include foreign prosecutions. However, Souter noted that not even the other clauses of the *Fifth* Amendment (i.e., the grand jury, double jeopardy, due process and takings clauses) reached so broadly; they all clearly apply only to American cases. He also suggested that the expansive "any criminal case" language of the privilege against self-incrimination more probably was included to distinguish the privilege's scope from the Fifth Amendment's Grand Jury Clause, which applies only in "capital, or otherwise infamous crime."[84] The Supreme Court case that most strongly supports the contrary position, *Murphy v. Waterfront Comm'n of N.Y. Harbor*,[85] speaks of "the inviolability of human personality and . . . the right of each individual to a private enclave where he may lead a private life."[86] But to the extent this

---

[81]   380 U.S. 609, 85 S.Ct. 1229 (1965), see § 15.02(c).

[82]   However, the Court reserved the question of whether the sentencing court could use silence as evidence of lack of remorse or unwillingness to accept responsibility, both of which may affect the sentence under the federal sentencing guidelines. In *White v. Woodall*, 572 U.S. 415, 134 S.Ct. 1697 (2014), discussed in § 28.03(b)(1), it also intimated that, when a jury is involved in sentencing, the judge need not instruct it to avoid drawing an adverse inference from the defendant's silence.

[83]   524 U.S. 666, 118 S.Ct. 2218 (1998).

[84]   See § 23.01.

[85]   378 U.S. 52, 84 S.Ct. 1594 (1964).

[86]   See Introduction to Part B.

language suggested that *any* potential subsequent prosecution should be a concern recognized by the Fifth Amendment, the majority rejected it as overbroad, finding that this language was more probably focused on emphasizing that the states and the federal government were one "sovereign" for purposes of the Fifth Amendment.

The majority did state that if international cooperation were to develop to the point that its decision in *Balsys* were abused, a different result would be indicated. As Souter put it, "[i]f it could be said that the United States and its allies had enacted substantially similar criminal codes aimed at prosecuting offenses of international character, and if it could be shown that the United States was granting immunity from domestic prosecution for the purpose of obtaining evidence to be delivered to other nations as prosecutors of a crime common to both countries, then an argument could be made that the Fifth Amendment should apply based on fear of foreign prosecution simply because that prosecution is not fairly characterized as distinctly 'foreign.' " In such cases, the two countries could be said to be operating as one sovereign and the Fifth Amendment might be implicated.

(c) The Link-in-the-Chain Rule

Only if information is usable in a "criminal proceeding," as defined above, may it be withheld under the Fifth Amendment. A witness cannot invoke the privilege merely to avoid a non-criminal sanction or revelation of information that tends to "disgrace him or bring him into disrepute."[87] On the other hand, any information that might be used at a criminal proceeding need not be disclosed. In *Hoffman v. United States*,[88] the Supreme Court held that a witness may refuse to answer any question the response to which might "furnish a link in the chain of evidence needed to prosecute."

The *Hoffman* language has been given broad construction. In *Hoffman* itself, the Court overruled the lower court's holding that there was "no real danger of incrimination" from questions about a grand jury witness' current occupation and contacts with a person who was a fugitive witness. Since the grand jury investigation was about racketeering, the Court noted, answers to the first question might have revealed information relating to violations of various gambling laws, and answers to the second question might have disclosed information about the witness' attempt to hide the fugitive. Similarly, in *Simpson v. United States*,[89] the Court summarily reversed, with no explanation, a lower court decision upholding a contempt of Congress conviction of a witness who had refused to divulge to the House Un-American Activities Committee his address, present occupation, where he had attended school, and whether he had ever been in the armed services. In contrast, in *Hiibel v. Nevada Dist. Ct.*[90] the Court held that forcing an individual stopped on the street to reveal his name, by itself, will normally not implicate the Fifth Amendment, even if the name will allow the police to link him to crime databases or to locate and arrest him at some subsequent time; to the

---

[87] *Brown v. Walker*, 161 U.S. 591, 16 S.Ct. 644 (1896). See also *Ullmann v. United States*, 350 U.S. 422, 76 S.Ct. 497 (1956) (holding that a person may not refuse to acknowledge membership in the Communist party to avoid subsidiary repercussions such as "loss of job, expulsion from labor unions, state registration and investigation statutes, passport eligibility, and general public opprobrium.").

[88] 341 U.S. 479, 71 S.Ct. 814 (1951).

[89] 355 U.S. 7, 78 S.Ct. 14 (1957) (per curiam), rev'g *Wollam v. United States*, 244 F.2d 212 (9th Cir. 1957).

[90] 542 U.S. 177, 124 S.Ct. 2451 (2004), discussed further in § 3.03(a).

Court, these possibilities did not present a "reasonable danger of incrimination," at least on the facts of *Hiibel*.

Hoffman also set out the procedure for asserting the privilege and determining the validity of the assertion. A witness intending to refuse to answer a question because of possible self-incrimination must inform the court that his refusal is based on his Fifth Amendment privilege. Unexplained silence may result in a valid contempt citation. However, the court may not require the witness to assert that the response is actually incriminating or to prove the possibility of incrimination; *Hoffman* held that either burden would force the witness to surrender the very protection the Fifth Amendment provides. If the prosecutor does not believe that a witness's assertion of the Fifth Amendment is justified, he may object. The prosecutor then bears the burden of proving to the court that the witness's claim is unfounded. To sustain an assertion of the Fifth Amendment privilege, *Hoffman* stated, "it need only be evident from the implications of the question, in the setting in which it is asked, that a responsive answer . . . might be dangerous because injurious disclosure could result." In adjudicating the validity of the claim, the judge "must be governed as much by his personal perception of the peculiarities of the case as by the facts actually in evidence." To overrule a witness's Fifth Amendment claim, the judge must be *"perfectly clear . . . that the witness is mistaken, and that the answer(s) cannot possibly have such tendency to incriminate."* Further, the witness has a right to present evidence demonstrating the validity of his Fifth Amendment claim.

Overall, in any "criminal proceeding," or when one is in the offing, the evidentiary burden established in *Hoffman* to protect a witness's Fifth Amendment claim is virtually insurmountable. Generally, prosecutors who object to an individual's assertion of the right to silence cannot meet this burden, and instead confer immunity or attempt to establish the point with other evidence.

(d) Immunity

Persons may not claim a Fifth Amendment right to be free from compelled self-incrimination if their testimony has been rendered nonincriminating by a governmental grant of immunity. Immunity statutes developed out of the state's need to compel from witnesses testimony that facilitates prosecution of other individuals considered more important. They have been attacked on the ground that, while preventing prosecution of the witness based on his immunized statements, they do not protect against the opprobrium, civil liability and danger from third parties that may result from the disclosure of criminal acts. Yet the courts have uniformly rejected such challenges on the ground that a grant of immunity need merely provide protection congruent with the privilege, which only prevents compelled *incrimination*.[91]

(1) Types of Immunity

Immunity exists in two forms, "use and derivative use" immunity, and "transactional" immunity. The former forbids the admission of any testimony that is specifically immunized, and any evidence derived therefrom. In contrast, transactional immunity protects the individual from prosecution for any activity mentioned in the immunized testimony. Thus, witnesses given transactional immunity may testify about

---

[91]   See, e.g., *Ullmann v. United States*, 350 U.S. 422, 76 S.Ct. 497 (1956); *Patrick v. United States*, 524 F.2d 1109 (7th Cir. 1975).

matters far beyond the subject of the questions asked in order to "bathe" themselves in immunity. To limit such unjustified benefits most jurisdictions now utilize use and derivative use immunity. New York, which has transactional immunity, immunizes only answers that are responsive to the questions asked.[92]

The Supreme Court first approved the concept of statutory immunity in *Counselman v. Hitchcock*.[93] In subsequent cases, *Counselman* was initially interpreted to require transactional immunity because, at the end of that opinion, the Court stated that a valid immunity grant "must afford absolute immunity against future prosecution for the offense to which the question relates."[94] But in *Murphy v. Waterfront Commission*,[95] the Court seemed willing to recognize use and derivative use immunity as constitutionally adequate. In that case, the Court held that, in order to ensure the full protection guaranteed by the Fifth Amendment, testimony obtained pursuant to a grant of immunity by a state must also be excluded from federal prosecutions, and vice versa.[96] In doing so, it spoke only of use and derivative use immunity, not immunity from prosecution for the crime in question. Finally, in *Kastigar v. United States*,[97] the Court explicitly approved use and derivative use immunity. Reasoning that the Fifth Amendment does not protect against prosecution, which is the effect of transactional immunity, but only against incrimination resulting from compelled disclosure, the Court concluded that use and derivative use immunity is "coextensive with the scope of the privilege against self-incrimination."

The dissent's major objection to this ruling was its perception that prosecutors would be able to disguise when evidence in a subsequent prosecution is derived from leads developed from the immunized testimony. The majority responded by referring to the heavy burden the government must bear in showing the subsequent prosecution is based on an independent source. This burden "imposes on the prosecution the affirmative duty to prove that the evidence it proposes to use is derived from a legitimate source wholly independent of the compelled testimony." Since it can often be difficult to meet this burden, it is common for prosecutors to deliver sealed files to the court containing the evidence they have secured against the immunized witness before the witness testifies.

(2) Use of Immunized Testimony to Impeach

In *New Jersey v. Portash*,[98] the Court relied on its reasoning in *Kastigar* in prohibiting the use of immunized testimony even for impeachment purposes. In *Portash*, the respondent, who had testified before a grand jury pursuant to an immunity grant, was indicted for official misconduct and extortion. At Portash's trial, the judge ruled that the immunized grand jury testimony would be admissible for the purpose of exposing inconsistencies in the respondent's trial testimony. As a consequence of the judge's ruling, Portash did not testify at his trial. Affirming the reversal of the respondent's conviction, the Supreme Court held that immunized testimony "is the essence of coerced

---

[92] N.Y.—McKinney's Crim.Proc.Law § 190.40(2)(b) (1984–85).

[93] 142 U.S. 547, 12 S.Ct. 195 (1892).

[94] Edward Imwinkelreid, et al., Criminal Evidence (1979), at 304.

[95] 378 U.S. 52, 84 S.Ct. 1594 (1964).

[96] *Murphy* also supports the proposition that immunity extends to other state prosecutions as well.

[97] 406 U.S. 441, 92 S.Ct. 1653 (1972).

[98] 440 U.S. 450, 99 S.Ct. 1292 (1979).

testimony." Thus, the admission of immunized testimony in a criminal proceeding to impeach the defendant's testimony at trial is a violation of his Fifth Amendment right.

The majority opinion in *Portash* reserved a possible exception to its decision in the case of perjury trials. In *United States v. Apfelbaum*,[99] the Court explicitly held that not only alleged false statements, but also any other statements made during immunized testimony that are relevant to whether the alleged false statements are in fact perjured, are admissible at a subsequent perjury trial in the prosecution's case-in-chief. Writing for a unanimous Court, Justice Rehnquist pointed out that while the Fifth Amendment guarantees protection against self-incrimination, it has never been held by the Court to protect "false swearing." Because the immunity statute in question likewise provided protection against self-incrimination with regard to immunized true statements, but not from prosecution for making false statements, its protection was co-extensive with the Fifth Amendment. In short, any immunized statements, whether true or untrue, can be used in a trial for making false statements.

(3) The Effect on Testimony in Later Proceedings

A separate immunity issue the Court has confronted is the extent to which an immunity grant permits the individual who has been immunized to refuse to testify in later proceedings. In *Pillsbury Co. v. Conboy*,[100] Conboy had been granted use immunity on testimony before a federal grand jury. In a subsequent civil antitrust suit, the plaintiff sought Conboy's deposition. At the deposition, Conboy was asked the same questions he had been asked at the grand jury proceeding and then was read the answers he gave at that proceeding in an effort to determine whether he had "so testified." He refused to answer, asserting his privilege against self-incrimination. The trial court held Conboy in contempt, apparently in the belief that the grant of immunity protected against prosecution use of any disclosures Conboy made during the antitrust suit. But Conboy argued that even if no new information came from his being asked to adopt his answers to the grand jury, he was at risk because other parties in the suit had the right to cross-examine him. Thus, they might demand information that would not be seen as derivative of the immunized testimony. The Supreme Court agreed, holding that unless the government expressly grants a new assurance of immunity at the civil trial, no contempt citation may be issued for refusal to repeat answers previously immunized in the criminal setting.

(4) The Procedure for Granting Immunity

In *Conboy*, the Court stated that the authority for granting immunity rests with the executive branch.[101] Generally, to the extent courts are involved at all in immunity procedure,[102] they merely ensure that the relevant statutory procedures are followed. Under the federal statute,[103] the court must issue an order if the request for immunity is approved by the Attorney General, the Deputy Attorney General or a designated

---

[99]   445 U.S. 115, 100 S.Ct. 948 (1980).

[100]   459 U.S. 248, 103 S.Ct. 608 (1983).

[101]   On the authority of defense counsel to grant immunity, see § 28.06(c)(3).

[102]   Although many jurisdictions require a court order, in virtually all jurisdictions prosecutors can avoid even this minimal limitation through an informal promise of non-prosecution, a practice which accomplishes the same objective as immunization, but can be seen as an exercise of the prosecutorial prerogative. See § 21.02.

[103]   18 U.S.C.A. § 6003.

Assistant Attorney General, and the attorney making the request states that the "testimony or other information [sought from the witness] may be necessary to the public interest" and is not likely to be disclosed by the witness voluntarily. As indicated earlier,[104] if a properly immunized witness refuses to testify under such an order, he may be held in contempt, even if he fears retaliation for his testimony or some other non-criminal liability.

(e) Other Means of Avoiding Incrimination

The privilege may not be invoked with respect to the facts of an offense for which the statute of limitations has run, the person has been finally sentenced, or the person has been pardoned. In none of these cases can compulsion of admissions result in a criminal penalty. The government bears the burden of demonstrating that the relevant event has occurred.[105] Until the government makes this showing, the witness may validly refuse to answer questions under the Fifth Amendment.

15.04　　The "Testimonial Evidence" Requirement

Unless the compulsion of incriminating information requires a person to be a "witness" against himself, the Fifth Amendment is not implicated. The Supreme Court has relied on this language in concluding that only "testimony" or "communication" is protected by the Fifth Amendment. As Justice Holmes stated in *Holt v. United States*,[106] "the prohibition of compelling a man in a criminal court to be witness against himself is a prohibition of the use of physical or moral compulsion to extort communications from him, not an exclusion of his body as evidence when it may be material." To hold otherwise, Holmes asserted, "would forbid a jury to look at a prisoner and compare his features with a photograph in proof." The modern formulation of this idea was stated by Justice Brennan in *Schmerber v. California*:[107] "We hold that the privilege protects an accused only from being compelled to testify against himself, or otherwise provide the State with evidence of a testimonial or communicative nature."

Relying on this testimonial/nontestimonial distinction, the Court has permitted the government to force the accused to don clothing in order to facilitate identification (in *Holt*), submit to the extraction of blood (in *Schmerber*), participate in a line-up,[108] produce a writing exemplar,[109] and produce a voice exemplar.[110] It has also stated in dictum that the Fifth Amendment "offers no protection against compulsion to submit to fingerprinting, photography, or measurements, . . . to appear in court, to stand, to assume a stance, to walk, or to make a particular gesture."[111]

However, the Court has also noted that not all "physical" or "real" evidence obtained from a person is necessarily noncommunicative. In *Schmerber*, the forcible extraction of blood in that case was permissible not only because it did not involve "the cruel, simple expedient of compelling [evidence] from [the accused's] own mouth," but also because

---

[104] See § 15.03(d).

[105] McCormick, Evidence § 139 (3d ed. 1984).

[106] 218 U.S. 245, 31 S.Ct. 2 (1910).

[107] 384 U.S. 757, 86 S.Ct. 1826 (1966).

[108] *United States v. Wade*, 388 U.S. 218, 87 S.Ct. 1926 (1967).

[109] *Gilbert v. California*, 388 U.S. 263, 87 S.Ct. 1951 (1967); *United States v. Mara*, 410 U.S. 19, 93 S.Ct. 774 (1973).

[110] *United States v. Dionisio*, 410 U.S. 1, 93 S.Ct. 764 (1973).

[111] *United States v. Wade*, 388 U.S. 218, 87 S.Ct. 1926 (1967).

"his participation, except as a donor, was irrelevant to the results of the test, which depend on chemical analysis and on that alone." On the other hand, suggested the Court, physical evidence from a lie detector test might be testimonial: "To compel a person to submit to testing in which an effort will be made to determine his guilt or innocence on the basis of physiological responses, whether willed or not, is to evoke the spirit and history of the Fifth Amendment."

A few other Court cases shed further light on the testimonial evidence requirement. In *California v. Byers*[112] a plurality of the Court held that statutory provisions requiring accident-involved drivers to stop and leave their names "does not provide the State with 'evidence of a testimonial or communicative nature.' " Chief Justice Burger reasoned that stopping is no more testimonial than standing in a lineup and that giving one's name "is an essentially neutral act." This analysis has been criticized by several commentators, who believe that the statute compels drivers to admit participation in criminal acts[113] and to surrender the anonymity[114] that protects them from criminal prosecution. In this regard, the statute in *Byers* is like the statutes at issue in the line of cases beginning with *Albertson v. Subversive Activities Control Board*,[115] which also sought identifying information in connection with a specific crime. In any event, in *Hiibel v. Nevada Dist. Ct.*[116] the Court was willing to assume that "stating one's identity" or producing an identification document is testimonial in nature.

The Court looked more closely at the circumstances under which verbal responses may be nontestimonial in *Pennsylvania v. Muniz*.[117] There the state introduced the defendant's somewhat slurred and unresponsive answers to a series of booking questions about his height, weight and so on in an effort to prove him guilty of drunken driving. The Court held unanimously that, under *Schmerber* and *Holt*, the "physical inability to articulate words in a clear manner" was not testimonial evidence and could be used against the defendant. However, the Court split on the admissibility of the defendant's answers to one of the questions asked, specifically, "Do you know what the date was of your sixth birthday?" The defendant's first response to this question was inaudible; when asked again he replied, "I don't know." Five members of the Court agreed that asking the sixth birthday question, at least when no *Miranda* warnings have been given, subjected the defendant to the cruel trilemma of choosing between truth, falsity or silence. As Justice Brennan put it for the majority:

> By hypothesis, the inherently coercive environment created by the custodial interrogation precluded the option of remaining silent. Muniz was left with the choice of incriminating himself by admitting that he did not then know the date of his sixth birthday, or answering untruthfully by reporting a date that he did not then believe to be accurate (an incorrect guess would be incriminating as well as untruthful).

---

[112] 402 U.S. 424, 91 S.Ct. 1535 (1971).

[113] Note, 26 Ark.L.Rev. 81, 84–85 (1972).

[114] *The Supreme Court, 1970 Term*, 85 Harv.L.Rev. 3, 269 (1971).

[115] 382 U.S. 70, 86 S.Ct. 194 (1965), discussed in § 15.02(b)(2).

[116] 542 U.S. 177, 124 S.Ct. 2451 (2004).

[117] 496 U.S. 582, 110 S.Ct. 2638 (1990).

Since the *content* as well as the delivery of the answer to the birthday question was incriminating and went beyond mere identification, it was testimonial.[118] In dissenting to this part of the Court's opinion, Chief Justice Rehnquist, joined by three others, contended that "[i]f the police may require Muniz to use his body in order to demonstrate the level of his physical coordination, there is no reason why they should not be able to require him to speak or write in order to determine his mental coordination."

15.05　The Personal Basis of the Right

The Fifth Amendment's prescription that "no person" shall be compelled to be a witness "against himself" has been construed literally by the Court. Thus, the only person who can prevent revelation of incriminating, testimonial information is the person being compelled. As the Supreme Court stated in *Couch v. United States*:[119] "The Constitution explicitly prohibits compelling an accused to bear witness 'against himself': it necessarily does not proscribe incriminating statements elicited from another. Compulsion upon the person asserting it is an important element of the privilege."

In *Couch* itself the Court found that a sole proprietor could not rely on the Fifth Amendment to prevent production of papers possessed by her tax accountant. The accountant, not the defendant, was "the only one compelled to do anything." And because the accountant made no claim that the records would incriminate him, the Fifth Amendment was not implicated. Although recognizing that the defendant was the owner of the papers, the Court stated that "possession [not ownership] bears the closest relationship to the personal compulsion forbidden by the Fifth Amendment." In *Fisher v. United States*[120] the Court explained further that "[w]e cannot cut the Fifth Amendment completely loose from the moorings of its language and make it serve as a general protector of privacy—a word not mentioned in its text and a concept directly addressed in the Fourth Amendment."

However, the Court has recognized two exceptions to the general rule that only the person against whom the compulsion is directed may assert the privilege. In *Couch*, the Court noted that "situations may well arise where constructive possession is so clear or the relinquishment of possession is so temporary and insignificant as to leave the personal compulsions upon the accused substantially intact," a statement reiterated in *Fisher*. The lower courts have construed this idea very restrictively,[121] as indeed they should if the locus of compulsion is the key issue. The second exception to the personalized compulsion idea comes from *Fisher*. When documents are transferred to an attorney "for the purpose of obtaining legal advice," then the attorney may assert the Fifth Amendment claim for the client's protection. This exception is not based on the Fifth Amendment, however. Rather, it is founded on a desire to implement the purpose underlying the attorney-client privilege—that of encouraging the uninhibited exchange of information between attorneys and their clients.

---

[118] The Court avoided deciding whether two other questions—asking the defendant to count while performing a "walk-the-line" test and during a "one leg stand" test—were testimonial. But the four dissenters indicated they were willing to hold that neither these "statements" nor the "*Byers*-type" responses to the booking questions were testimonial.

[119] 409 U.S. 322, 93 S.Ct. 611 (1973).

[120] 425 U.S. 391, 96 S.Ct. 1569 (1976).

[121] See *Matter of Grand Jury Empanelled February 14, 1978*, 597 F.2d 851 (3d Cir. 1979).

It should be noted that the personalized compulsion concept applies in the interrogation context as well. Of course, a person cannot prevent another from voluntarily waiving his Fifth Amendment right merely because the waiver will provide the state with evidence against him. More dramatically, the *Couch* rationale means that even an *involuntary*, coerced statement may be used against someone else without violating the Fifth Amendment.[122]

15.06   The Fifth Amendment and Subpoenas

This section examines the complicated set of rules dealing with the extent to which the privilege against self-incrimination may be used to prevent the government from obtaining evidence via a subpoena *duces tecum* or similar compulsory process. The previous section noted that only the person against whom the subpoena is directed, usually the "custodian" of the records, may assert the privilege (and thus, a "third-party subpoena," compelling a third-party recordholder to disclose the documents, does not violate the *target's* Fifth Amendment right). As it turns out, in most cases even the custodian is afforded very little protection by the Amendment.

(a) *Boyd* and the "Zone of Privacy"

For a time, beginning in 1886, it appeared that the Fifth Amendment would provide very wide-ranging protection against document subpoenas. In that year, the Supreme Court decided *Boyd v. United States*,[123] which relied on both the Fourth and Fifth Amendments in holding unconstitutional a court order requiring an importing firm to produce an invoice concerning items it allegedly had imported illegally. The Court pointed to the common law prohibition against forcing documentary evidence "out of the owner's custody by process,"[124] and averred that compulsory production of books and papers, even when sought to obtain evidence of a serious crime, is "contrary to the principles of free government." With respect to the Fifth Amendment in particular, the Court concluded that just as the Fifth Amendment prohibited "compulsory discovery by extorting the party's oath," so it prohibited discovery by "compelling the production of his private books and papers" that are not fruits or instrumentalities of crime. *Boyd* thus appeared to hold that government could never use a subpoena to force an individual to turn over these types of papers, whether private or business, given their association with the individual's personal sphere of privacy.[125]

(b) The Collective Entity Doctrine

In 1906, the Court significantly eroded the "zone of privacy" created by *Boyd* by removing Fifth Amendment protection of most business papers. In *Hale v. Henkel*,[126] the Court upheld a subpoena of corporate records against a Fifth Amendment challenge on the ground that a corporation is a fictional entity (and thus not a "person" to which the Fifth Amendment refers), and because, as a "creature of the state," it is entitled to less protection from the government than is the individual. In *United States v. White*,[127] the

---

[122] See § 16.05(a).

[123] 116 U.S. 616, 6 S.Ct. 524 (1886).

[124] The Court relied primarily on *Entick v. Carrington*, 19 Howell, St.Tr. 1029 (1765).

[125] Although *Boyd* did permit subpoena of papers that are a fruit or instrumentality of crime, this issue rarely arises, since a search warrant is the preferred method of obtaining readily destructible evidence.

[126] 201 U.S. 43, 26 S.Ct. 370 (1906).

[127] 322 U.S. 694, 64 S.Ct. 1248 (1944).

Court extended this exception to unincorporated organizations, in this case a labor union. As in *Henkel*, the Court held that whenever an organization takes on an impersonal quality rather than embodying "the purely private or personal interests of its constituents," Fifth Amendment protection is not available to the organization. It also emphasized "the inherent and necessary power of the federal and state governments to enforce their laws" against business organizations, which would be stymied if a Fifth Amendment challenge were sustained. This same reasoning led the Court to hold, in *Bellis v. United States*,[128] that a partnership with an "established institutional identity" is not protected by the privilege.

Bellis suggested that the only organizations that might assert the privilege are "small family partnerships" and sole proprietorships (of any size). Why these business organizations should be exempted from the collective entity exception to the privilege is not entirely clear. Except in a technical legal sense, their business records are no more "personal" than the records of corporations, and the organizations themselves are just as subject to the state's regulatory interests as other business entities.[129]

(c) The Rejection of a Privacy Basis for the Amendment

The next major change in Fifth Amendment jurisprudence relating to subpoenas occurred in *Fisher v. United States*.[130] There, the Court upheld a subpoena of documents prepared by the defendant's accountant that were in the possession of the defendant's attorney. Although the papers at issue were business records, the collective entity doctrine did not apply, since the defendant was a sole proprietor. And, as noted earlier,[131] *Fisher* was willing to recognize an exception to the personalized compulsion rule when a client seeks to prevent surrender of documents he gives to his attorney for the purpose of seeking legal advice; thus, the client had standing to assert the privilege despite the fact the documents were not in his possession. But the Court went on to hold that, in this case, the client had no privilege to assert. In doing so, it modified even further the scope of *Boyd* by rejecting its conceptual basis and indicating that "private," as well as business, papers are entitled to considerably less protection than the latter decision had indicated.

Boyd had focused on the privacy interest in papers afforded by the Fourth and Fifth Amendments. *Fisher* separated the Fourth and Fifth Amendment issues and held that, while the Fourth Amendment does protect privacy, the Fifth Amendment does not. Rather it protects only against compulsion of incriminating, testimonial information. On this assumption, concluded Justice White for the Court, the Fifth Amendment generally does not prevent use of subpoenas as a means of obtaining documents, because subpoenas usually compel nothing of incriminating value.

In reaching this latter conclusion, White first noted that a subpoena clearly does not compel *creation* of the documents; thus, the privilege cannot be asserted with respect to their contents. In his concurring opinion, Justice Brennan argued that if the Fifth Amendment prohibits "compelling one to disclose the contents of one's mind," it must

---

[128] 417 U.S. 85, 94 S.Ct. 2179 (1974).

[129] See also § 15.06(d). Note that under the Court's "regulatory purpose" cases, see § 15.02(b)(3), even "personal" organizations can be compelled to produce records that are regularly kept as part of a neutral reporting scheme. However, in the context at issue here, the government has usually already focused on the business as a defendant, and the contention that the compulsion has a "non-criminal" purpose will be weak.

[130] 425 U.S. 391, 96 S.Ct. 1569 (1976).

[131] See § 15.05.

also prohibit "compelling the disclosure of the contents of that scrap of paper [on which] persons would, at their peril, record their thoughts and the events of their lives." But the fact remains that, unlike compulsion of verbal testimony, a document has already been created at the time of the compulsion. As Justice O'Connor latter stated in *United States v. Doe*[132] (which permitted a subpoena of the *defendant's* business records from the *defendant's* possession) this fact suggests that "the Fifth Amendment provides absolutely no protection for the contents of private papers of any kind."[133] Although this may prove to be an exaggeration,[134] the reasoning in *Fisher* and *Doe* supports her conclusion.

As *Fisher* noted, however, a subpoena does compel the act of *producing* the documents, an act that will occasionally have incriminating aspects. Specifically, White pointed out, incriminating evidence will be compelled by a subpoena if the government needs to use the act of producing the records to prove, in a prosecution against the custodian: (1) that they existed; (2) that the custodian possessed or controlled the documents; or (3) that they are authentic. In the normal case, proof of existence, possession, or authentication are not important. For instance, in *Fisher*, the Court held that it was a "foregone conclusion" both that the tax documents existed and that either the defendant or an agent possessed them; these "admissions" inherent in the act of producing the documents added "little or nothing to the sum total of the Government's information." Likewise, because the documents were authored by the accountant, the act of production by itself did not, and could not, authenticate their source or accuracy.

In some cases, however, such admissions are not "foregone conclusions." For instance, if the mere existence of a particular item proves the crime being investigated,[135] or if the document cannot be authenticated on its face or by testimony of a non-custodian, the fact that a particular person produced it can be very useful to the prosecution's case against that person. In such situations, suggested *Fisher*, the prosecution must either forego use of a subpoena or grant use and derivative use immunity as to the act of production. To obtain such immunity, the prosecution should have to show that it can prove existence, possession or authentication in some other way (otherwise, there is no need for the documents, since they would not be admissible). In some cases, such as, for instance, a subpoena for contraband, records of illegal activities, or private records accessed by only one person, such proof may be impossible.[136]

United States v. Hubbell[137] demonstrated another, more powerful way the foregone conclusion test might bar a subpoena. There the Independent Counsel investigating violations of federal law relating to the Whitewater Development Corporation served Hubbell with a subpoena requesting the production of 11 categories of documents, in response to which Hubbell produced 13,120 pages. Relying on information in these documents, the Independent Counsel subsequently indicted Hubbell for various tax-

---

[132] 465 U.S. 605, 104 S.Ct. 1237 (1984).

[133] However, the *Fourth* Amendment requires a showing of relevance. See 23.05(a)(1). Moreover, a subpoena for a very private document such as a diary might require a showing of probable cause. See § 5.06(a).

[134] The majority in *Fisher* noted that the case did not raise the "special problems of privacy which might be presented by subpoena of a personal diary" or direct compulsion of other "private papers."

[135] See *United States v. (Under Seal)*, 745 F.2d 834 (4th Cir. 1984) (subpoena for records of purchases and sales of controlled substances).

[136] See generally, Robert Mosteller, *Simplifying Subpoena Law: Taking the Fifth Amendment Seriously*, 73 Va.L.Rev. 1, 40–49 (1987). Note that, in some of these situations, use of a search warrant to obtain records which the prosecution has probable cause to believe exist in a certain location may be possible. *Andresen v. Maryland*, 427 U.S. 463, 96 S.Ct. 2737 (1976). A search warrant does not "compel" an act of production.

[137] 530 U.S. 27, 120 S.Ct. 2037 (2000).

related crimes and mail and wire fraud, all unrelated to the Whitewater investigation. Eight members of the Court, in an opinion by Justice Stevens, concluded that the prosecution's use of the documents to obtain the indictment against Hubbell violated the Fifth Amendment.[138] The Court found that *Fisher's* foregone conclusion test was not met, because the Independent Counsel had not shown it had "any prior knowledge of either the existence or the whereabouts" of the documents;[139] further, a showing that a business person such as Hubbell will always possess general business and tax records "cannot cure this deficiency."

The degree to which *Hubbell* requires prosecutors to be precise about the documents sought remains unclear. The subpoena in *Hubbell* was abnormally exploratory (indeed, Hubbell was not tried for the crimes it contemplated); at the same time *Hubbell* reaffirmed *Fisher*, which involved a subpoena broadly asking for "working papers prepared by the taxpayer's accountants that the IRS knew were in their possession of the taxpayer's attorneys." Noting these facts and responding to the practicalities of investigation, lower courts have held that the government is not required "to have actual knowledge of each and every responsive document."[140] But *Hubbell* has nonetheless provided authority for quashing subpoenas in a number of cases.[141]

Hubbell also dismissed *Fisher's* intimation that the act of production might not be "testimonial." To the government's contention that Hubbell's production of the documents was only a "physical act," the Court responded that "[i]t was unquestionably necessary for [Hubbell] to make extensive use of 'the contents of his own mind' in identifying the hundreds of documents responsive to the requests in the subpoena." It continued: "The assembly of those documents was like telling an inquisitor the combination to a wall safe, not like being forced to surrender the key to a strongbox."

As this last statement suggests, to be distinguished from the act of production is the act of facilitating production by another party, which may often not be testimonial. In *Doe v. United States*[142] (not to be confused with *United States v. Doe*, discussed above), the Court held that forcing the defendant to sign a blanket consent form authorizing disclosure of records related to his bank accounts, but not requiring him to indicate the location or number of any account, did not "explicitly or implicitly, relate a factual assertion or disclose information." At most it required the *banks* to declare that certain records of the defendant were in their possession. Thus, the government was not forcing the defendant to be a "witness" against himself.

(d) Custodians of Impersonal Records

Prior to *Fisher*, the Court had repeatedly held that the custodian of records owned by collective entities could not resist a subpoena even if the records would clearly

---

[138] The Court rejected the Government's contention that, because none of the documents would actually be used against Hubbell at trial, the Fifth Amendment was not violated. The fact that the information in the documents played a "substantial role" in obtaining the indictment was a sufficient derivative use for the Court.

[139] Indeed, the Independent Counsel had conceded that it could not demonstrate with "reasonable particularity" that it had known, prior to the subpoena, that the documents requested existed and were in Hubbell's possession.

[140] See *In re Grand Jury Subpoena, dated April 18, 2003*, 383 F.3d 905 (9th Cir. 2004).

[141] See id. (requiring "reasonable particularity"); *In re Grand Jury Subpoena Duces Tecum Dated March 25, 2011*, 670 F.3d 1335 (11th Cir. 2012); *Bear Sterns & Co. v. Wyler*, 182 F.Supp.2d 679 (N.D.Ill. 2002).

[142] 487 U.S. 201, 108 S.Ct. 2341 (1988).

incriminate him as well.[143] These decisions made sense given the prevailing theory that the Fifth Amendment protected personal records, not impersonal ones. But after *Fisher's* replacement of the privacy theory with one focusing on compulsion, the stage seemed to be set for holding that custodians of records held by collective entities could resist a subpoena if the act of production thereby compelled would tend to incriminate them and immunity were not granted.

However, in *Braswell v. United States*,[144] the Court decided to adhere to its earlier collective entity cases in situations where a custodian asserts the privilege on personal grounds. Although recognizing that *Fisher* and *Doe* had "embarked upon a new course of Fifth Amendment analysis," Chief Justice Rehnquist, who wrote the Court's 5–4 opinion, reasoned that the collective entity cases were not obsolete because "the custodian of corporate or entity records holds those documents in a representative rather than a personal capacity," and agents who accept custody of such documents accept the same responsibility to permit inspection as the entity is required by law to assume. As the Court had in *Henkel*, he also stressed that recognizing a privilege in this setting would hinder the government's efforts to prosecute white collar crime. The defendant had offered two solutions to this latter problem: allowing the corporation to choose an alternative custodian who would not be incriminated by the act of production or granting immunity for that act. But Rehnquist rejected both proposals. The alternative custodian solution does not work if, as is often the case, the subpoenaed custodian is the only person who knows the location of the records: unless he is willing to give the alternate self-incriminating information, the custodian cannot tell the alternate where the records are, thus inhibiting the production of the records. And an immunity grant would make any derivative use of the act of production impossible, which could have "serious consequences," given the heavy burden the government must meet in showing the independent source of its evidence.[145]

Rehnquist did state that the government "may make no evidentiary use of the 'individual act' against the individual." Thus, "in a criminal prosecution against the custodian, the Government may not introduce into evidence before the jury the fact that the subpoena was served upon and the corporation's documents were delivered by one particular individual, the custodian." Instead, the government should be limited to showing that the entity had produced the records and were authentic, and let the jury draw its own conclusions about what the custodian knew. Rehnquist also left open the question of "whether the agency rationale supports compelling a custodian to produce corporate records when the custodian is able to establish, by showing for example that he is the sole employee and officer of the corporation, that the jury would inevitably conclude that he produced the records." The importance of this last caveat was diminished by the failure of the Court to make such a finding in *Braswell*, despite the fact that the custodian there was the only shareholder in one of the two corporations involved, and the only person with any authority over either corporations' business affairs.

Left intact by *Braswell* was the Court's earlier decision in *Curcio v. United States*.[146] That case held that, in a prosecution against the collective entity, a custodian could be

---

[143]   *Wilson v. United States*, 221 U.S. 361, 31 S.Ct. 538 (1911). See also § 15.06(b).

[144]   487 U.S. 99, 108 S.Ct. 2284 (1988).

[145]   See § 15.03(d)(1).

[146]   354 U.S. 118, 77 S.Ct. 1145 (1957).

forced to produce records, and to testify as to their authenticity (something implicit in the act of production in any event), but could not be compelled to give further oral testimony incriminating himself. Further, of course, if the subpoenaed records truly are personal, rather than organizational, the privilege may be asserted even by an employee of a collective entity. Thus, for instance, whereas desk calendars—provided by the corporation, used for scheduling corporate business, and accessible to secretaries and other employees—are probably not privileged, pocket calendars owned by the witness, containing personal as well as corporate entries and not accessible to others, may be privileged.[147] Again, however, all that is protected is the act of production to the extent it is incriminating, not the contents of the record.

15.07   Conclusion

The Fifth Amendment privilege against self-incrimination precludes state compulsion of incriminating, testimonial statements from the person whom the state seeks to compel. The four components of this rule are summarized below, with a separate synopsis of the privilege's application to disclosures pursuant to subpoena.

(1) *Compulsion.* The extent to which failure to assert the right to remain silent will be viewed as the product of compulsion rather than a valid waiver depends primarily upon: (a) the setting of the state's attempt to get information, and (b) the extent to which the government's purpose is to elicit self-incriminating information. Thus, in the custodial interrogation setting, the suspect must be told of his right to remain silent and the government must show that any subsequent statements were voluntarily and intelligently made. In the trial setting, neither the warnings nor proof of waiver is necessary, and cross-examination of a defendant who testifies on direct, as well as evaluations of the defendant necessary to rebut expert witnesses presented by the defendant, are permitted as long as the prosecution's proffers stay within the scope of the defendant's. In the grand jury setting, witnesses are entitled, at most, to the first two *Miranda* warnings, and in other non-custodial settings only proof of a valid waiver (i.e., proof that no overt coercion occurred) is required.

A statute that has as its primary purpose the disclosure of incriminating information from an inherently suspect group violates the Fifth Amendment, while a statute that has as its primary purpose the implementation of a non-criminal, regulatory reporting scheme does not. A statute, such as the Internal Revenue Act, which falls somewhere in between is valid, but sanctions may not be imposed on a person who refuses, in good faith, to report specific information thought to be incriminating. Exercise of the right to remain silent might be unconstitutionally inhibited not only by imposition of criminal or contempt sanctions for not talking, but also by noncriminal sanctions such as, for instance, conditioning continuance in a job on disclosure of incriminating statements. However, given the lesser constitutional protection afforded prisoners, conditioning privileges, special treatment programs and custody in a medium rather than maximum security prison on revelation of prior crimes, including those not charged or immunized, does not violate the Fifth Amendment.

(2) *Incrimination.* The privilege may only be asserted to prevent compulsion of information that is relevant to and sought to be used in a criminal proceeding. A criminal proceeding is one that may result in criminal punishment, which, in addition to criminal

---

[147] See *Grand Jury Subpoena Duces Tecum Dated April 23, 1981*, 657 F.2d 5 (2d Cir. 1981).

trials, includes juvenile delinquency proceedings, grand jury proceedings, and capital sentencing hearings, but does not include commitment proceedings, child custody proceedings, civil deportation proceedings, other proceedings the purpose of which is primarily rehabilitative or regulatory, and foreign prosecutions. Disclosures may also be compelled at a criminal proceeding if the statute of limitations for the crime in question has expired or if immunity is granted. To be valid, a grant of immunity must guarantee, at the least, that the government will not use the disclosures or evidence derived therefrom in subsequent proceedings, unless those proceedings are aimed at proving the immunized person committed perjury during the earlier proceeding.

(3) *Testimonial evidence.* The privilege applies only to information that is testimonial in nature, which means that it communicates something beyond the physical characteristics of a person, the identity of a person, or his appearance in certain clothing.

(4) *Personalized compulsion.* A person's Fifth Amendment privilege is not violated by compulsion against another unless the compulsion seeks documents from the person's attorney, given to that attorney for the purpose of obtaining legal advice, or unless the person has only temporarily surrendered the items compelled and still constructively possesses them.

(5) *Subpoenas.* A subpoena for documents compels only the production of the documents, not their creation, and thus is not subject to quashing through assertion of the privilege unless the act of production by the target provides evidence of existence, possession or authentication that is not a foregone conclusion (which is most likely to be the case when the prosecutor has no prior knowledge of the existence or location of the documents beyond knowledge that such documents are usually kept). When the subpoena is for documents owned by a collective entity, such as a corporation or sizeable partnership, then the privilege may not be asserted even when the act of production might incriminate the custodian. However, at any subsequent trial of the custodian, the act of production may not be directly linked with him.

BIBLIOGRAPHY

Alito, Samuel. Documents and the Privilege Against Self-Incrimination. 48 U.Pitt.L.Rev. 27 (1986).

Allen, Ronald J. and M. Kristin Mace. The Self-incrimination Clause Explained and Its Future Predicted. 94 J. Crim. L. & Criminol. 243 (2004).

Amar, Akhil Reed and Renne Lettow. Fifth Amendment First Principles: The Self-Incrimination Clause. 98 Mich. L.Rev. 857 (1995).

Ayer, Donald B. The Fifth Amendment and the Inference From Silence: *Griffin v. California* After Fifteen Years. 78 Mich.L.Rev. 841 (1980).

Cole, Lance. The Fifth Amendment and Compelled Production of Personal Documents After *United States v. Hubbell*: New Protection for Private Papers? 29 Am.Crim.L.Rev. 123 (2002).

Davies, Thomas. Farther and Farther from the Original Fifth Amendment: The Recharacterization of the Right Against Self-Incrimination as a "Trial Right" in *Chavez v. Martinez.* 70 Tenn. L. Rev. 987 (2003).

Dolinko, David. Is There a Rationale for the Privilege Against Self-Incrimination? 33 U.C.L.A. L.Rev. 1063 (1986).

Dripps, Donald A. Self-Incrimination and Self-Preservation: A Skeptical View. 1991 U. Ill. L.Rev. 329.

Frantz, Carolyn J. *Chavez v. Martinez*'s Constitutional Division of Labor. 55 Sup.Ct.Rev. 269 (2004).

Garrett, Brandon. Corporate Confessions. 30 Cardozo L. Rev. 917 (2008).

Henning, Peter. Finding What Was Lost: Sorting Out the Custodian's Privilege Against Self-Incrimination from the Compelled Production of Records. 77 Neb. L.Rev. 34 (1998).

Langbein, John H. The Historical Origins of the Privilege Against Self-Incrimination at Common Law. 92 Mich. L.Rev. 1047 (1994).

Levy, Leonard. The Origins of the Fifth Amendment (1968).

Menza, Alexander J. Witness Immunity: Unconstitutional, Unfair, Unconscionable. 9 Seton Hall Const. L.J. 505 (1999).

Mosteller, Robert. Simplifying Subpoena Law: Taking the Fifth Amendment Seriously. 73 Va.L.Rev. 1 (1987).

Saltzburg, Stephen. The Required Records Doctrine: Its Lessons for the Privilege Against Self-Incrimination. 53 U.Chi.L.Rev. 6 (1986).

Schulhofer, Stephen. Some Kind Words for the Privilege Against Self-Incrimination. 26 Val. U. L.Rev. 311 (1991).

Seidmann, Daniel J. and Alex Stein. The Right to Silence Helps the Innocent: A Game-Theoretic Analysis of the Fifth Amendment. 114 Harv. L. Rev. 430 (2000).

Slobogin, Christopher. Subpoenas and Privacy. 54 De Paul L.Rev. 804 (2005).

____. *Estelle v. Smith*: The Constitutional Contours of the Forensic Evaluation. 31 Emory L.J. 71 (1982).

Stuntz, William. Self-Incrimination and Excuse. 88 Colum L.Rev. 1227 (1988).

Uviller, Richard H. *Fisher* Goes on the Quintessential Fishing Expedition and *Hubbell* is Off the Hook. 91 J.Crim.L. & Criminol. 311 (2001).

Westen, Peter. Answer Self-Incriminating Questions or Be Fired. 37 Am. Crim. L. Rev. 97 (2010).

Chapter 16

CONFESSIONS

16.01   Introduction

Confessions have long been recognized as an essential and accepted part of law enforcement. A confession not only provides direct evidence against the accused, but also furnishes leads to additional evidence against him or his colleagues in crime, at the same time it clears the name of other individuals suspected of the offense. The principal question with respect to attempts at obtaining confessions is not whether they should be allowed but how they should be regulated.

Today, as a result of *Miranda v. Arizona,*[1] most litigation about confessions centers on the applicability of the Fifth Amendment. But until 1966, when *Miranda* was decided, the courts relied on other principles in determining the validity of confessions. Under the common law, the courts' principal focus was simply an evidentiary inquiry into whether the confession was reliable, a finding that was most likely when the statement was perceived to be "voluntary" rather than the product of promises or torture.[2] In 1936, the Supreme Court gave the "voluntariness" test constitutional stature under the Due Process Clause,[3] and for the next twenty-eight years the due process standard held sway. Then, for a short time beginning in 1964, it appeared the Court might treat the admissibility of confessions primarily in terms of whether questioning in the absence of an attorney violates the accused's Sixth Amendment right to counsel.[4] But, two years later, the Court decided *Miranda,* which made the Fifth Amendment "the pervasive perspective for evaluating statements of the accused."[5] Since *Miranda,* the requirement that persons subjected to custodial interrogation be told of their right to remain silent has been the predominant focus of the Court. The due process and right to counsel approaches remain important in various settings, however; indeed, both have been rejuvenated in more recent years.

This chapter begins with an overview of the Supreme Court's confessions jurisprudence, from the due process test through *Miranda.* The initial section also looks at competing approaches to regulating interrogation that have developed since *Miranda.* The chapter then closely examines the various elements of *Miranda,* as well as the Sixth Amendment rules governing interrogation. It ends with a discussion of the exclusionary rule as it applies to confessions, and of the procedure for determining the admissibility and credibility of confessions.

---

[1]   384 U.S. 436, 86 S.Ct. 1602 (1966).

[2]   *The King v. Warickshall,* 168 Eng.Rep. 234, L. Leach Cr. Cases 263 (K.B. 1783); *Hopt v. Utah,* 110 U.S. 574, 4 S.Ct. 202 (1884).

[3]   *Brown v. Mississippi,* 297 U.S. 278, 56 S.Ct. 461 (1936). In one early case, *Bram v. United States,* 168 U.S. 532, 18 S.Ct. 183 (1897), the Court excluded a confession on Fifth Amendment grounds, but this case remained dormant until *Miranda.*

[4]   *Massiah v. United States,* 377 U.S. 201, 84 S.Ct. 1199 (1964).

[5]   Joseph Cook, Constitutional Rights of the Accused: Pretrial Rights 305 (1974).

16.02   Approaches to Regulating the Interrogation Process

The Supreme Court's confessions cases reflect both a desire to protect against police misconduct that might lead to an unwilling confession and a belief that reliable confessions should be admitted into evidence whenever possible. While these objectives are not necessarily contradictory, a broad definition of misconduct could exclude many confessions that are clearly reliable; at the same time, permitting use of all reliable confessions might sanction a wide range of unpleasant, degrading or painful police practices that pressure or trick persons into giving confessions they do not "want" to give. Each of the approaches described below reflects this tension.

(a)   The Due Process "Voluntariness" Test

At the time of *Brown v. Mississippi,*[6] the first Supreme Court case involving a state confession, neither the Fifth nor Sixth Amendment had been applied to the states. The Court thus analyzed the case under the Due Process Clause. The facts in *Brown* presented an extreme situation which the Court could not ignore. Police officers investigating a murder resorted to severe whippings and other brutal methods as a means of obtaining the signatures of three black defendants to confessions that had been dictated by the police. Convictions were obtained on the basis of these confessions alone. The Court found the convictions invalid because the interrogation methods were so offensive.

After *Brown,* the Court decided roughly 35 confessions cases relying solely on the due process approach.[7] In *Fikes v. Alabama,*[8] the Court reviewed a number of its decisions since *Brown* and summarized the standard applied in these cases in terms of whether the "totality of the circumstances that preceded the confessions" deprived the defendant of his "power of resistance." Applying this standard requires a fact specific case-by-case analysis. But the factors that the courts have identified in assessing the voluntariness of a confession can be broken down into two broad categories: the police conduct involved and the characteristics of the accused.

(1)   Police Conduct

The most obviously unacceptable type of police conduct is the use of physical brutality to coerce a confession, such as occurred in *Brown.* As stated by Justice Douglas in *Williams v. United States,*[9] confessions obtained through the use of physical brutality and torture "cannot be admissible under any concept of due process." In the years immediately following *Brown,* physical mistreatment of suspects and the threat of violence were the predominant concerns of the Court.[10]

As time went on, however, the Court began to confront cases involving more subtle police conduct. In *Rogers v. Richmond,*[11] the defendant confessed after the police told him they were going to take his wife into custody. In *Lynumn v. Illinois,*[12] the defendant

---

[6]   297 U.S. 278, 56 S.Ct. 461 (1936).

[7]   B. James George, Constitutional Limitations on Evidence in Criminal Cases 260–61 (1973).

[8]   352 U.S. 191, 77 S.Ct. 281 (1957).

[9]   341 U.S. 97, 71 S.Ct. 576 (1951).

[10]   See, e.g., *Chambers v. Florida,* 309 U.S. 227, 60 S.Ct. 472 (1940); *Ward v. Texas,* 316 U.S. 547, 62 S.Ct. 1139 (1942).

[11]   365 U.S. 534, 81 S.Ct. 735 (1961).

[12]   372 U.S. 528, 83 S.Ct. 917 (1963).

made incriminating statements after being told that cooperation would lead to leniency, but that failure to cooperate could result in loss of welfare payments and the custody of her children. Both confessions were found to be coerced.

A modern case involving subtler coercion is *Arizona v. Fulminante*.[13] Fulminante was suspected of molesting and killing his 11-year-old stepdaughter. Incarcerated in prison for another crime, he was approached by one Sarivola, a fellow inmate who was a paid informant for the FBI but who posed as an organized crime figure. Sarivola raised the subject of the stepdaughter's death with Fulminante on several occasions, but the defendant at first denied any participation. The FBI instructed Sarivola to find out more. Eventually, Sarivola told Fulminante that he knew other inmates were giving Fulminante "tough treatment" because of the rumor that he was a child-murderer and that he, Sarivola, could protect him, but only if Fulminante disclosed what he knew. Calling it a "close question," Justice White, joined by four other members of the Court, concluded that Fulminante's subsequent statement to Sarivola was coerced by a "credible threat." According to the majority, "it was fear of physical violence, absent protection from his friend (and Government agent) Sarivola, which motivated Fulminante to confess."[14]

Fulminante can also be seen as an example of the "false friend" technique confronted in earlier cases. A classic example of this type of case came in *Spano v. New York*,[15] in which detectives brought in a young police officer, a close friend of the accused, to question him. The officer falsely stated that if he did not get a statement from the accused his job was in jeopardy, and that the loss of job would be disastrous to his wife and children. The Court considered the sympathy thus aroused one of the factors in the totality of the circumstances, and concluded that the will of the accused had been overborne. Similarly, in *Leyra v. Denno*,[16] a state-employed psychiatrist was introduced to the accused as a "doctor" brought to give him medical relief from a painful sinus. By subtle and suggestive questioning the psychiatrist induced the accused to admit his guilt. The Court found the suspect's ability to resist interrogation had been broken by the "arts" of the psychiatrist, and held the use of confessions extracted in this manner inconsistent with due process.

While the "false friend" technique, carried to an extreme, will often be unconstitutional, mere misrepresentation does not necessarily violate due process. In *Frazier v. Cupp*,[17] for instance, the police falsely told the defendant that his co-defendant had already confessed. The Court found this fabrication "relevant," but "insufficient in our view to make this otherwise voluntary confession inadmissible." Similarly, in *Bobby v. Dixon*,[18] a per curiam decision, the Court stated that "no holding of this Court suggests, much less clearly establishes, that police may not urge a suspect to confess before another suspect does so." Numerous lower court decisions echo the view that many

---

[13]   499 U.S. 279, 111 S.Ct. 1246 (1991).

[14]   The Court also noted that Fulminante was of slight build and had not adapted well to the stress of prison life on previous occasions.

[15]   360 U.S. 315, 79 S.Ct. 1202 (1959).

[16]   347 U.S. 556, 74 S.Ct. 716 (1954).

[17]   394 U.S. 731, 89 S.Ct. 1420 (1969).

[18]   565 U.S. 23, 132 S.Ct. 26 (2011).

types of deception, including pretending to be a "friend" and fabrications about evidence, are not coercive.[19]

The extent to which the accused is isolated from family, friends, or counsel is also frequently cited as a factor bearing upon the voluntariness determination.[20] In *Fikes v. Alabama*,[21] for example, the fact that the accused had been questioned far from his home, and had seen no one other than his accusers for over a week before confessing, was weighed heavily by the Court in holding his confession inadmissible. A similar crucial inquiry is whether an accused is provided with items such as food or cigarettes during an extended interrogation. Many of the interrogations found to be improper by the Court in its due process days involved a denial of these amenities.[22] In *Crooker v. California*,[23] however, the accused was questioned only intermittently, was given milk and a sandwich shortly after his arrest, and was provided with coffee and permitted to smoke whenever he wished, factors that led the Supreme Court to find that his confession was voluntary.

Still another factor the Court has looked at in deciding voluntariness is the length of the interrogation.[24] In *Ashcraft v. Tennessee*[25] relays of police questioned the suspect continuously for thirty-six hours without allowing him rest or sleep. The confession ultimately obtained was ruled inadmissible. A similar ruling came in *Chambers v. Florida*,[26] where the suspects had steadfastly refused to confess through five days of interrogation, only to break down after an all-night examination on the fifth day. The timing of the interrogation is also important. In *Spano*, for instance, the Court noted that the questioning occurred after indictment, which the Court felt showed "the undeviating intent of the officers to extract a confession." According to the Court, "when such intent is shown, this Court has held this confession obtained must be examined with the most careful scrutiny."

Finally, even prior to *Miranda*, police failure to apprise the accused of his right to remain silent or his rights respecting counsel was a significant factor in judging the voluntariness of his statements. In *Davis v. North Carolina*,[27] for instance, the Court noted that "the fact that Davis was never effectively advised of his rights gives added weight to the other circumstances described [in the opinion] which made his confessions involuntary." Several due process decisions overturning confessions also relied in part on the fact that the accused was prevented from consulting with his attorney after asking

---

[19]   See, e.g., *Miller v. Fenton*, 796 F.2d 598 (3d Cir. 1986) (confession admissible despite repeated statements by officer that he was suspect's friend and would help him, as well as false statements by officer about the strength of the evidence against the suspect). See generally, Paul Marcus, *It's Not Just About Miranda: Determining the Voluntariness of Confessions in Criminal Prosecutions*, 40 Val. U.L. Rev. 601, 612–13, 623 (2006) (noting that courts have permitted lies about "witnesses against the defendant, earlier statements by a now-deceased victim, an accomplice's willingness to testify, whether the victim had survived an assault, 'scientific' evidence available, including DNA and fingerprint evidence, and the degree to which the investigating officer identified and sympathized with the defendant," as well as lies about providing treatment if a confession is forthcoming).

[20]   See *Darwin v. Connecticut*, 391 U.S. 346, 88 S.Ct. 1488 (1968), for a discussion of cases.

[21]   352 U.S. 191, 77 S.Ct. 281 (1957).

[22]   See, e.g., *Payne v. Arkansas*, 356 U.S. 560, 78 S.Ct. 844 (1958) (two sandwiches in 40 hours).

[23]   357 U.S. 433, 78 S.Ct. 1287 (1958).

[24]   See *Davis v. North Carolina*, 384 U.S. 737, 86 S.Ct. 1761 (1966) for citations to cases.

[25]   322 U.S. 143, 64 S.Ct. 921 (1944).

[26]   309 U.S. 227, 60 S.Ct. 472 (1940).

[27]   384 U.S. 737, 86 S.Ct. 1761 (1966). See, also *Haynes v. Washington*, 373 U.S. 503, 83 S.Ct. 1336 (1963); *Culombe v. Connecticut*, 367 U.S. 568, 81 S.Ct. 1860 (1961); *Turner v. Pennsylvania*, 338 U.S. 62, 69 S.Ct. 1352 (1949).

to see him.[28] However, in *Moran v. Burbine*,[29] decided after *Miranda*, the Court held that deliberately lying to the defendant's attorney in order to keep him from being present during interrogation does not violate due process when the defendant has been told of his right to counsel and does *not* ask to see him. In this type of situation, no compulsion occurs.

(2) Characteristics of the Accused

The second category of factors to be weighed in the "totality of the circumstances" relates to the special characteristics of the accused. If the case is close, obvious disabilities tip the balance in favor of the defendant. Thus, for instance, in *Haley v. Ohio*,[30] the Court reversed the conviction of a fifteen-year-old boy who had confessed after a night-long interrogation. Justice Douglas wrote: "Mature men possibly might stand the ordeal from midnight to 5 a.m. But we cannot believe that a lad of tender years is a match for the police in such a contest." The Court has also considered the level of intelligence and education of the accused in determining the voluntariness of a confession. In *Davis v. North Carolina*,[31] the confession of a borderline intellectually disabled individual with a third or fourth grade education was found invalid; in contrast, in finding the statements in *Crooker v. California*[32] voluntary, the Court considered extremely important the fact that the accused was 31 years-old and a college graduate who had attended law school for one year and studied criminal law. Similarly, any evidence of mental illness will weigh heavily in the totality of the circumstances analysis. In *Blackburn v. Alabama*,[33] the Court found involuntary a confession by an accused with a lengthy history of mental problems who might have been "insane" at the time of the interrogation.

Physical fatigue or pain that could impair the accused mentally have also been considered important. In *Ashcraft v. Tennessee*,[34] the fatigue brought on by 36 hours of continuous questioning was the major reason for excluding the confession in that case. In *Beecher v. Alabama*,[35] a confession was found to be the product of "gross coercion" when it was made to a hospital doctor one hour after arrest, while the accused was in extreme pain from a gunshot wound and was under the influence of morphine. A post-*Miranda* case arriving at a similar result was *Mincey v. Arizona*,[36] which involved questioning of an accused who was in the hospital for treatment of a gunshot wound, had received some drugs (albeit none that impaired his ability to remain alert), and was in "unbearable" pain. In finding the accused's incriminating admissions involuntary, the Court noted that the questioning had taken place over a four-hour period (punctuated by treatment and occasional losses of consciousness), and had continued despite Mincey's physical helplessness, his often incoherent answers, and his entreaties that the questioning be postponed until the next day or until his attorney could be present.

---

[28] See, George, supra note 7, at 260–61.

[29] 475 U.S. 412, 106 S.Ct. 1135 (1986), discussed further in § 16.03(d)(2).

[30] 332 U.S. 596, 68 S.Ct. 302 (1948).

[31] 384 U.S. 737, 86 S.Ct. 1761 (1966).

[32] 357 U.S. 433, 78 S.Ct. 1287 (1958).

[33] 361 U.S. 199, 80 S.Ct. 274 (1960).

[34] 322 U.S. 143, 64 S.Ct. 921 (1944).

[35] 408 U.S. 234, 92 S.Ct. 2282 (1972).

[36] 437 U.S. 385, 98 S.Ct. 2408 (1978).

In none of these cases were the characteristics of the accused alone enough to support a finding of involuntariness. Some evidence of abusive police conduct was also necessary. In *Colorado v. Connelly,*[37] the Court made explicit that, unless the state somehow takes advantage of the disabilities of an accused, no constitutional violation has taken place. In *Connelly,* the defendant approached an officer in the street and stated that he wanted to talk about a murder he had committed. He was given the *Miranda* warnings, but continued to talk about the murder and showed police the supposed location of the crime. It later developed that the defendant was mentally ill at the time of his incriminating statements and actions; at a preliminary hearing, a psychiatrist testified that Connelly had approached the police because he thought he had been commanded to do so by the "voice of God." The Supreme Court held that, even assuming this testimony to be correct, neither the Due Process Clause nor the Fifth Amendment was violated, since no action by the police "coerced" the defendant into waiving his rights. While the fact of his mental illness might have affected the *reliability* of Connelly's statements and thus their admissibility under local evidence rules, the Constitution did not require exclusion on involuntariness grounds.

While the Court's conclusion that some sort of state action is required in order to find that a confession is "coerced" is consistent with the usual treatment of criminal process rights,[38] it is not obvious that Connelly's post-warning confession should have been admissible. Subsequent discussion will make clear that determining when police have exploited weaknesses of the accused is extremely difficult.[39] As Justice Stevens stated in a separate opinion, once a defendant like Connelly is in a "custodial relationship" with the police, questioning takes on a "presumptively coercive character." Moreover, as Justice Brennan's dissent noted, even if confessions which are not "caused" by the police are never involuntary under the Constitution, their reliability, a matter traditionally subsumed in the voluntariness inquiry, should still be a matter of constitutional concern because the state is relying on them in its courts of law. *Connelly* appears to hold, however, that the Constitution does not address the reliability issue independently of the voluntariness issue.

(3) Analysis of the "Voluntariness" Test

The major problem with the voluntariness test is a practical one: it gives neither the police nor the courts much guidance. As the preceding discussion illustrates, a host of factors can be relevant in the "totality of the circumstances;" rarely does one factor predominate. The difficulty of applying the test is exacerbated by the murkiness of its rationale. Although the common law voluntariness test was bottomed on a concern about reliability, the due process voluntariness test, as applied by the Court, slowly changed the focus to police behavior. Indeed, by 1961, Justice Frankfurter's opinion in *Rogers v. Richmond,*[40] went so far as to say that involuntary confessions are excluded "not because such confessions are unlikely to be true but because the methods used to extract them offend an underlying principle in the enforcement of our criminal law: that ours is an accusatorial and not an inquisitorial system—a system in which the State must establish guilt by evidence independently and freely secured and may not by coercion prove its

---

[37]   479 U.S. 157, 107 S.Ct. 515 (1986).

[38]   See, e.g., § 4.02, discussing the scope of Fourth Amendment.

[39]   See, e.g., §§ 16.03(b) & (d).

[40]   365 U.S. 534, 81 S.Ct. 735 (1961).

charge against an accused out of his own mouth."[41] While determining the reliability of a confession is no easy task, evaluating whether it is "coerced" is even more difficult, given the unlimited ways in which police conduct and individual characteristics might interact, and the metaphysical nature of the inquiry into whether that interaction results in the accused's "will" being "overborne" or merely exercised.

The practical and conceptual difficulties with the voluntariness test helped smooth the way for more prophylactic approaches—that is, approaches which set out straightforward, if somewhat rigid, rules for the police to follow when they want to interrogate a suspect. As discussed below, the Supreme Court has, since *Brown* and the initial due process cases, endorsed three different prophylactic approaches, ending with *Miranda*. But the advent of these more rule-oriented tests has not spelled the end of due process analysis, as indicated by the number of post-*Miranda* decisions described above in which the Court resorted to this analysis (e.g., *Fulminante, Burbine, Mincey* and *Connelly*).

Due process precedents remain important for a number of reasons. First, there are points in the criminal process at which *Miranda* and the other prophylactic approaches may not apply (e.g., grand jury proceedings,[42] or pre-custodial questioning) and thus the voluntariness test may come into play. For instance, *Fulminante* represents a case in which the *Miranda* and Sixth Amendment approaches did not apply (because the defendant was not in "custody" as defined by *Miranda* jurisprudence and had not been indicted for the charge in question[43]), but a colorable claim of involuntariness remained. Second, the post-*Miranda* Court has indicated that, for purposes of determining whether a confession may be used for impeachment purposes or whether it taints any "fruits" it helps police obtain, the appropriate standard is whether the confession was "coerced" in the due process sense, not whether it was obtained in violation of *Miranda*.[44] In *Mincey*, for example, due process analysis was important because the prosecution, which implicitly conceded that the statements at issue in that case were obtained in violation of *Miranda*, sought to use them for impeachment purposes rather than in its case-in-chief. Third, and perhaps most importantly, under all the prophylactic approaches waiver is still possible under certain circumstances, making a determination of whether the statements were "voluntarily" made the primary issue.[45] In both *Burbine* and *Connelly*, for example, the defendants received warnings as required by *Miranda;* the question was whether their subsequent statements were voluntary. In short, the analysis of confessions that was refined during the "due process period" remains a significant facet of confessions jurisprudence.

(b) The *McNabb-Mallory* Rule

At the same time the Court was developing the voluntariness test as a limitation on confessions used in state courts, it experimented with a second approach to interrogation regulation under its supervisory power over the federal courts. In 1944, it decided

---

[41] Ironically, the Court's move away from reliability as the touchstone of due process analysis also made possible its decision in *Connelly*, which in essence holds that the Constitution does not have anything to say about *un*reliable confessions that are not coerced by the police.

[42] See § 15.02(a)(3).

[43] See §§ 16.03(a)(5) & 16.04(a).

[44] See § 16.05(b) & (c).

[45] See §§ 16.03(d) and 16.04(c).

McNabb v. United States,[46] which involved the admissibility of confessions of several individuals suspected of murdering a federal revenue agent. The Court avoided addressing the constitutionality of the police conduct, relying instead on its supervisory authority over the administration of criminal justice in the federal courts. Pointing to a number of federal statutes calling for prompt arraignment of arrested persons, the Court held that confessions obtained during an unnecessary delay between the time of arrest and arraignment (at which time a lawyer is usually appointed) should be excluded. Although the statutes did not specifically call for exclusion of confessions made during this period, "to permit such evidence to be made the basis of conviction in the federal courts would stultify the policy which Congress has enacted into law."

Because the Court's opinion in *McNabb* also spent considerable effort analyzing the voluntariness of the confessions in that case, it was not clear how important the decision was. But five years later the Court restated that "a confession is inadmissible if made during illegal detention due to failure promptly to carry a prisoner before a committing magistrate."[47] And in 1957, in *Mallory v. United States,*[48] a unanimous Court held that Federal Rule of Criminal Procedure 5(a), enacted in 1946 to replace the prompt arraignment statutes at issue in *McNabb,* prohibits delay that would "give opportunity for the extraction of a confession."

In 1968, as part of an unsuccessful attempt to "repeal" *Miranda,* Congress also addressed the situation covered by the *McNabb-Mallory* rule. Section (c) of 18 U.S.C. § 3501 provides that no confession shall be excluded "solely because of delay" if it was obtained within six hours of arrest, and permits extension of the six-hour period when the location of the magistrate makes it necessary.[49] That language still implies, consistent with *McNabb-Mallory,* that a confession obtained *after* the six-hour period or a reasonable extension thereof must be excluded, even if it is voluntary. But other sections of the statute state that all voluntary confessions are admissible,[50] and that delay in bringing a suspect before a judge is merely one of the factors to be considered in deciding whether the confession is voluntary.[51]

In *Corley v. United States,*[52] the Supreme Court held, 5–4, that section (c) trumps the other provisions, primarily because a contrary interpretation would render it "nonsensical and superfluous;" if Congress had meant to provide that all voluntary confessions are admissible and that delay alone can never lead to exclusion, Justice Souter wrote for the majority, then it would not have needed to include a separate provision stating that delay alone is not ground for exclusion when the confession is obtained within six hours of arrest. Although *McNabb-Mallory* thus remains viable, it applies only in federal cases. Indeed, the Court has emphasized that § 3501(c) does not operate to exclude confessions in state cases even when the questioning is by federal officers who later charge the defendant with a federal crime.[53] Furthermore, a voluntary

---

[46]   318 U.S. 332, 63 S.Ct. 608 (1943).

[47]   *Upshaw v. United States,* 335 U.S. 410, 69 S.Ct. 170 (1948).

[48]   354 U.S. 449, 77 S.Ct. 1356 (1957).

[49]   18 U.S.C.A. § 3501(c).

[50]   Id. § 3501(a).

[51]   Id. § 3501(b).

[52]   556 U.S. 303, 129 S.Ct. 1558 (2009).

[53]   *United States v. Alvarez-Sanchez,* 511 U.S. 350, 114 S.Ct. 1599 (1994). Cf. *Powell v. Nevada,* 511 U.S. 79, 114 S.Ct. 1280 (1994), discussed in § 20.02(c) (noting but not addressing the issue of suppressing

confession obtained after the six-hour period is admissible even in federal court if the delay is not the fault of the police.[54]

(c) *Massiah* and *Escobedo*: The Sixth Amendment Approach

The first constitutionally-based deviation from the due process approach was predictable. In its due process cases, two factors that the Court often mentioned as tending to make a confession "involuntary" were the formal charging of the suspect and police efforts to prevent access to an attorney. For instance, as noted earlier, in *Spano v. New York*,[55] the Court considered significant the fact that Spano had been indicted, because that event meant the police had clearly focused their attention on him; the majority also noted that Spano had asked for his attorney. Four members of the Court who concurred in finding Spano's confession invalid argued that it was inadmissible solely on the ground that, just as an accused is accorded trial counsel, an indicted individual should be afforded counsel during post-charge interrogation.

In *Massiah v. United States*,[56] a six-member majority finally held that the Sixth Amendment guarantee of "the assistance of counsel" in all "criminal prosecutions" is violated when government agents "deliberately elicit" statements from an indicted person in the absence of counsel. In *Massiah,* the accused, who had been indicted for violating federal narcotics laws, was released on bail. A friend of his allowed the government to install a radio transmitter in his car, and then invited Massiah to enter the car and discuss the pending case. Massiah made incriminating statements that were overheard by the police. The dissent noted that no coercion was present on these facts and that Massiah's access to counsel was not infringed in any way, nor was counsel's ability to prepare for trial impaired by the police action. But Justice Stewart wrote for the majority that if the right to counsel is "to have any efficacy it must apply to indirect and surreptitious interrogations as well as those conducted in the jailhouse." According to Stewart, "Massiah was more seriously imposed upon . . . because he did not even know that he was under interrogation by a government agent."

Massiah was a significant step away from the case-by-case voluntariness analysis; it provided a relatively precise rule by which the admissibility of confessions could be determined.[57] Yet, as one commentator writes: "The lower courts . . . generally construed *Massiah* as narrowly as possible."[58] When the "interrogation" in *Massiah* took place, the defendant had already been indicted and had retained an attorney. Thus, *Massiah*, read literally, does not apply at any time before indictment or the retention or appointment of counsel. Moreover, given the facts of that case, application could be limited to confrontations initiated by the police that involved trickery. In any event, *Massiah* lay dormant at the Supreme Court level for another thirteen years, perhaps because *Miranda* and the Fifth Amendment occupied the Court's attention. Later developments

---

statements obtained in violation of the rule that a first appearance take place within 48 hours of a warrantless arrest).

[54]   *Williams v. United States*, 273 F.2d 781 (9th Cir. 1959); *Proctor v. United States*, 338 F.2d 533 (D.C.Cir. 1964).

[55]   360 U.S. 315, 79 S.Ct. 1202 (1959).

[56]   377 U.S. 201, 84 S.Ct. 1199 (1964).

[57]   *Massiah* was applied to the states in *McLeod v. Ohio,* 381 U.S. 356, 85 S.Ct. 1556 (1965) (per curiam).

[58]   Cook, supra note 5, at 299.

in Sixth Amendment jurisprudence will be discussed after looking at *Miranda* and its progeny.[59]

Escobedo v. Illinois,[60] an offshoot of *Massiah* handed down five weeks later, is important primarily as the most significant precursor to *Miranda.* Escobedo was arrested for murder, questioned, and then released the same day, after his lawyer obtained a writ of *habeas corpus.* Ten days later an alleged accomplice implicated Escobedo and he was rearrested. On route to the station he was advised of his accomplice's accusation. His request to consult with his attorney was denied, as were several requests by counsel to consult with Escobedo. The two were kept apart until Escobedo, after four hours of questioning, made a damaging statement. He was convicted of murder, based in part on the statement, and the Supreme Court of Illinois affirmed.

Justice Goldberg stated the Supreme Court's holding as follows:

> We hold . . . that where, as here, the investigation is no longer a general inquiry into an unsolved crime but has begun to focus on a particular suspect, the suspect has been taken into police custody, the police carry out a process of interrogations that lends itself to eliciting incriminating statements, the suspect has requested and been denied an opportunity to consult with his lawyer, and the police have not effectively warned him of his absolute constitutional right to remain silent, the accused has been denied "the Assistance of Counsel" in violation of the Sixth Amendment . . . and that no statement elicited by the police during the interrogation may be used against him at a criminal trial.

To the five-member majority, the fact that the interrogation was conducted before the accused was formally indicted, as was the case in *Massiah,* made no difference. The investigation had begun to focus on the accused, so the purpose of the interrogation was to induce him to confess. The opinion reviewed various decisions in which the "guiding hand of counsel" was thought to be essential, and concluded that Escobedo's need for a lawyer's help at this stage was no less critical. Justice Goldberg wrote that "no system of criminal justice can, or should, survive if it comes to depend for its continued effectiveness on the citizens' abdication through unawareness of their constitutional rights."

Escobedo muddied the waters that *Massiah* had tried to clear up. *Escobedo* held that once an individual is the focus of investigation by the police, he may not be denied access to his attorney—if he has one *and* if he asks for him. But it did not define precisely when a suspect becomes "the accused." More importantly, the decision did not state what rights accrue to a person who does not have, and cannot afford, an attorney, or to a person who has an attorney but does not ask to see him. In *Miranda,* the Court took a significant step toward resolving those questions, effectively limiting the *Escobedo* holding to its facts.[61]

---

[59] See § 16.04.

[60] 378 U.S. 478, 84 S.Ct. 1758 (1964).

[61] See *Kirby v. Illinois,* 406 U.S. 682, 92 S.Ct. 1877 (1972).

(d) *Miranda* and Fifth Amendment Analysis

The same year it decided *Massiah* and *Escobedo*, the Supreme Court handed down *Malloy v. Hogan*,[62] which held that the Fifth Amendment applied to the states. In doing so, it announced that "today the admissibility of a confession in a state criminal prosecution is tested by the same standard applied in federal prosecution since 1897." In that year, the Court decided *Bram v. United States*,[63] which had relied on the privilege against self-incrimination in evaluating the admissibility of a confession in federal court. But no other case since then had done so; rather, the voluntariness standard had dominated analysis of confessions. Even *Massiah* and *Escobedo*, decided after *Malloy*, did not pick up on its message.

Two terms later, however, the Court firmly shoved aside both due process analysis and the *Massiah* approach. In *Miranda v. Arizona*,[64] Chief Justice Warren, for a five-member majority, announced the following rule: "[T]he prosecution may not use statements, whether exculpatory or inculpatory, stemming from custodial interrogation of the defendant unless it demonstrates the use of procedural safeguards effective to secure the privilege against self-incrimination." With these words, *Miranda* established the Fifth Amendment as the basis for ruling on the admissibility of a confession.

(1) The Holding

The *Miranda* holding[65] has two important components. First, a person subjected to custodial interrogation must be warned that he has a right to remain silent, that any statement he does make may be used in evidence against him, and that he has the right to the presence of an attorney, either retained or appointed, before and during questioning. Second, a defendant may waive these rights, but only if the waiver is made voluntarily, knowingly, and intelligently will it render subsequent confessions admissible.

The procedural safeguards announced in *Miranda* are required "unless other fully effective means are devised to inform accused persons of their right of silence and to assure a continuous opportunity to exercise it." The Court recognized that Congress and state legislatures might be able to devise effective alternatives that would protect the rights of the individual and promote effective law enforcement. In the absence of a fully effective legislative or judicial equivalent, however, the proper warnings must be given and a valid waiver must be found before any statement may be admitted.

The opinion explains further that if, at any stage of the interrogation, an accused indicates that he wishes to speak with a lawyer, there can be no more questioning. Similarly, if the accused indicates in any other way that he does not wish to be interrogated, the police may not question him. Even if he has answered some questions or volunteered some statements, he may refuse to answer further questions until he sees an attorney and thereafter consents to be questioned. The decision is unclear about the limits of interrogation when counsel is present, although the Court suggests in a footnote

---

[62] 378 U.S. 1, 84 S.Ct. 1489 (1964).

[63] 168 U.S. 532, 18 S.Ct. 183 (1897).

[64] 384 U.S. 436, 86 S.Ct. 1602 (1966).

[65] *Miranda* actually combined consideration of four cases: *State v. Miranda*, 98 Ariz. 18, 401 P.2d 721 (1965); *People v. Vignera*, 15 N.Y.2d 970, 259 N.Y.S.2d 857, 207 N.E.2d 527 (1965); *Westover v. United States*, 342 F.2d 684 (9th Cir. 1965); *People v. Stewart*, 62 Cal.2d 571, 43 Cal.Rptr. 201, 400 P.2d 97 (1965).

that when an individual indicates a desire to remain silent, there may be circumstances in which further questioning will be permitted if counsel is there.

The Court believed this sweeping set of rules was necessary to counter what it called the "inherently coercive" nature of interrogation that occurs in the stationhouse. As support for this view of the interrogation process, it described a number of practices found in "police manuals and texts", which it stated were "observed and noted around the country."[66] It emphasized, first, that police are taught to isolate the suspect to deprive him of outside support and to engage in lengthy interrogation sessions if necessary. When these tactics fail, the Court stated, various deceptive tactics are often employed to confuse or threaten the suspect, including intimations that the police have more evidence than they really have and the "Mutt and Jeff" routine, in which one officer poses as the "relentless investigator who knows the subject is guilty" while the other acts as a "kindhearted man" who can only hold Mutt off for so long. To counteract use of these types of practices, the Court held, warnings and the right to presence of counsel are necessary.

(2) *Research on* Miranda

Several empirical studies have attempted to assess the impact of *Miranda* and to check the validity of the Court's assumptions regarding the reality of police interrogation. One of the best known studies, conducted in New Haven,[67] found the interrogation process to be somewhat different from that pictured by the majority. First, the study found that only rarely were any directly coercive methods used to secure a confession. And it suggested that if custody and confrontation with police exert a more subtle pressure to confess, the warnings do not appear to alleviate that pressure in most cases because few warned suspects refrained from talking or asked for counsel. Tempering the findings of the New Haven study, however, was the fact that, largely because *Miranda* had just been decided, the police seldom gave the full warnings in the interrogations studied. Other studies, apparently conducted in jurisdictions experiencing better compliance with *Miranda*, found a significant (10 to 20%) drop in confessions after *Miranda* went into effect.[68] These findings suggest the warnings did have some impact.

The results of the New Haven study and similar studies were also at variance with some of the views expressed by the dissenters in *Miranda*. The dissenters were concerned that, given the reduction in confessions likely to occur after *Miranda*, a substantial number of crimes would go unsolved or unpunished. The New Haven study suggested otherwise. Relying on their own evaluation as well as that of the police officers, the study's authors concluded that interrogation was necessary to solve a crime in less than ten percent of the felony cases where arrests were made. And confessions were needed to convict in an even smaller percentage of the cases. These findings have been

---

[66]　E.g., Fred E. Inbau & John Reid, Criminal Interrogation and Confessions (1962). The Court also quoted extensively from the Wickersham Report of 1931, IV National Comm'n on Law Observance and Enforcement, Report on Lawlessness in Law Enforcement, and from the 1961 U.S. Commission on Civil Rights Report.

[67]　Michael Wald, et al., *Interrogations in New Haven: The Impact of* Miranda, 76 Yale L.J. 1519 (1967). One of the authors participated in this study while a student at Yale Law School.

[68]　See Richard H. Seeburger & R. Stanton Wettick, Miranda *in Pittsburgh: A Statistical Study*, 29 U.Pitt.L.Rev. 1, 23–6 (1967) for a description of *Miranda's* impact in three cities.

replicated in other studies conducted around the same time.[69] Thus, assuming *Miranda has* reduced the proportion of confessions obtained by 10 to 20%, these studies suggested that the warnings prevent conviction in far less than 2% of all felony cases. A related argument, made by Justice Harlan in dissent, was that *Miranda* would bring more lawyers to the stationhouse and that those lawyers would urge their clients to remain silent. In fact, the New Haven study found that when suspects did ask for a lawyer and a lawyer came, he most often advised the suspect to cooperate with the police.

More recent research continues to fuel the debate about the extent to which *Miranda* reduces confession and conviction rates. One study conducted in 1994 in Salt Lake City found that incriminating statements occurred in only 33% of all cases presented by police for prosecution, compared to the 60+% confession rate found in the *Miranda* era studies.[70] However, another study conducted in 1993 in three other jurisdictions obtained a 64% confession rate post-*Miranda*.[71] After carefully looking at all the research, one commentator concluded that *Miranda* has had "no net effect" on confession rates.[72]

(3) *The Conceptual Importance of* Miranda

While the nature of *Miranda's* impact on the conduct and efficacy of interrogations is still open to some debate, it is clear the decision represented a significant modification of the law of confessions in at least three ways. First, it completed the gradual shift of focus from concern over the reliability of confessions to concern over whether the police practices used to obtain them are coercive. *Miranda* is designed to counteract the "inherently coercive" nature of custodial interrogation; any improvement in the reliability of confessions it might produce was clearly of secondary importance to the majority. Second, *Miranda* represented a repudiation of the due process case-by-case analysis; as had *Massiah,* it relied on a rule-oriented mode of decisionmaking. Indeed, the decision appeared to have announced the most straightforward rule possible: proper warnings and a valid waiver—meaning an express statement that one wants to talk and does not want an attorney beforehand—are required before any "custodial interrogation;" otherwise any statements made are not admissible for any purpose. Although subsequent cases, described later in this chapter,[73] significantly undercut its prophylactic nature, *Miranda* remains an example of a relatively "bright-line" rule.

The third important conceptual aspect of *Miranda* is that it redefined "coercion" in the interrogation context. Whereas under the due process "voluntariness" test unconstitutional coercion was said to exist only if, in the totality of the circumstances, the suspect's will was overborne, *Miranda* created what later cases would call an "irrebuttable presumption" of coercion when police fail to give warnings prior to custodial interrogation.[74] Justice White argued in his dissent in *Miranda* that this definition of

---

[69]   Seeburger & Wettick, supra note 66, at 26; Richard J. Medalie, et al., *Custodial Police Interrogation in Our Nation's Capital: The Attempt to Implement* Miranda, 66 Mich.L.Rev. 1347 (1968).

[70]   Paul G. Cassell & Bret S. Hayman, *Police Interrogation in the 1990s' An Empirical Study of the Effects of* Miranda, 42 UCLA L.Rev. 839 (1996).

[71]   Richard A. Leo, *Inside the Interrogation Room*, 86 J. Criminal L. & Criminol. 266 (1996).

[72]   George C. Thomas, III, *Plain Talk About the* Miranda *Empirical Debate: A 'Steady-State' Theory of Confessions*, 43 UCLA L. Rev. 933 (1996).

[73]   See § 16.03.

[74]   *Oregon v. Elstad*, 470 U.S. 298, 105 S.Ct. 1285 (1985). On the other hand, if warnings are given, the presumption is rebuttable.

coercion cannot possibly be countenanced by the Fifth Amendment, which prohibits only "compelled" testimony. He contended, for instance, that simply asking a single question after arrest would not normally be coercive in any sense, even if no warnings are given. And if such a question *were* said to be coercive simply because of the setting in which it is asked, then *Miranda* is internally inconsistent: the waiver prescribed by *Miranda* could never be voluntary, because it too would be the product of the inherent coercion of the interrogation room.

Although the majority did not provide it, there is a counter to these arguments. *Miranda* can be seen as indulging in the reasonable assumption that the typical person subjected to custodial interrogation either is not aware of his right to remain silent or will be led to believe he does not have one, despite what he "knows." Absent such certainty that he can remain silent, the unwarned individual *thinks* he is faced with the very "trilemma" the Fifth Amendment is meant to prevent: a choice between self-accusation, fabrication, or some type of sanction for silence (i.e., use of his silence against him, or a contempt citation or some other extrajudicial punishment).[75] The warnings tell him that this trilemma does not exist. If this analysis is correct, the warnings requirement in *Miranda* should have constitutional stature and statutory attempts to nullify it are themselves a nullity.

Nonetheless, several Court decisions subsequent to *Miranda*, while affirming that failure to give the warnings requires exclusion in the prosecution's case-in-chief, have stated or implied that this exclusionary rule "sweeps more broadly than the Fifth Amendment itself."[76] If so, some have argued, *Miranda* may not be imposed on the states, which only have to abide by constitutional guarantees.[77] Although, as discussed in the next section, the Court clearly does not agree with this stance,[78] it has relied on the notion that *Miranda's* definition of coercion extends beyond the Constitution's to bolster several of the decisions that limit *Miranda's* scope.[79]

The Court has also held that a *Miranda* violation does not infringe the Constitution for purposes of a damages action under § 1983,[80] unless and until the statement obtained through that violation is introduced in court. The Fifth Amendment, the Court noted in *Chavez v. Martinez*,[81] expressly states that a violation occurs only when a person has been "compelled to be a witness against himself in a criminal case." Thus, although Martinez was not warned before being questioned, the fact that he was never prosecuted for the incident that triggered the questioning meant that his Fifth Amendment right was not violated.[82]

---

[75] See William J. Stuntz, *Self-Incrimination and Excuse*, 88 Colum.L.Rev. 1227 (1988). The "trilemma," described in *Malloy v. Hogan*, 378 U.S. 1, 84 S.Ct. 1489 (1964), is discussed in the Introduction to Part B.

[76] In *Michigan v. Tucker,* 417 U.S. 433, 94 S.Ct. 2357 (1974), the Court stated that *Miranda* "recognized that [its] procedural safeguards were not themselves rights protected by the Constitution but were instead measures to insure that the right against compulsory self-incrimination was protected." Eleven years later the Court reaffirmed the notion that *Miranda* is merely a "procedural" safeguard. *Oregon v. Elstad*, 470 U.S. 298, 105 S.Ct. 1285 (1985).

[77] See, e.g., Joseph Grano, Miranda v. Arizona *and the Legal Mind: Formalism's Triumph Over Substance and Reason*, 24 Am. Crim. L. Rev. 243 (1987).

[78] *Dickerson v. United States*, 530 U.S. 428, 120 S.Ct. 2326 (2000), discussed in § 16.02(e)(1).

[79] See *Harris v. New York* and *Oregon v. Elstad*, discussed in §§ 16.05(b) & (c).

[80] For discussion of § 1983 claims against individual officers, see § 2.05(a)(3).

[81] 538 U.S. 760, 123 S.Ct. 1994 (2003).

[82] However, five members of the Court also concluded that the manner of questioning—which occurred at a hospital over a 45-minute period while Martinez was in severe pain, partially blinded and in fear of death

(e) Other Approaches

As noted above, *Miranda* stated that its warnings requirement could be replaced by "other fully effective means" of informing "accused persons of their right of silence." After *Miranda,* several alternatives were proposed or implemented, some of which provide less protection than *Miranda* and some of which provide more.

(1) *The Congressional Voluntariness Test*

18 U.S.C. § 3501, the same congressional provision that curtailed the *McNabb-Mallory* rule, attempted to repeal *Miranda* and *Massiah* as well, at least in the federal courts. The statute provides that a confession "shall be admissible in evidence if it is voluntarily given,"[83] thus essentially endorsing the due process voluntariness test. Whether police gave warnings, counsel was present, or counsel was requested are all factors to be considered in deciding voluntariness but, the statute provides, these factors "need not be conclusive on the issue."[84]

In *Dickerson v. United States,*[85] the Supreme Court invalidated § 3501 on the ground that it was inconsistent with the "constitutional rule" announced in *Miranda.* Noting that the statute did not require warnings about the right to remain silent or the right to counsel, Chief Justice Rehnquist, who wrote for seven justices, reasoned that it was not "an adequate substitute" for *Miranda.* In dissent, Justice Scalia asserted that the voluntariness inquiry mandated by § 3501 is all that the Fifth Amendment requires. He bolstered this conclusion by pointing to numerous Court decisions, alluded to above,[86] that were based on the premise that *Miranda* swept more broadly than the Fifth Amendment. Accordingly, Scalia charged, the majority's invalidation of § 3501 "flagrantly offends fundamental principles of separation of powers, and arrogates to itself prerogatives reserved to the representatives of the people."

But the majority insisted that *Miranda* was based on the Constitution, and therefore that overturning the statute was within the Court's prerogatives. Rehnquist conceded that some of the Court's decisions supported the contrary view, but stated that these decisions "illustrate the principle—not that *Miranda* is not a constitutional rule—but that no constitutional rule is immutable." He pointed to language in both the majority and dissenting opinions of *Miranda* indicating that the justices believed they were debating a constitutional proposition, as well as the fact that, in *Miranda* and in later decisions, *Miranda* and its progeny were applied to the states, which would be impermissible if *Miranda* were not a constitutional rule. The majority also noted that, if it were to uphold the statute, it would be reinstating the totality of the circumstances test that *Miranda* found difficult for courts and police to apply. Finally, it stated that stare decisis "weighs heavily" against overruling a decision that has become "part of our national culture." Although the Court's reasoning is somewhat strained, its holding is supported by the fact that prophylactic rules imposing restrictions beyond that

---

from gunshot wounds, and despite his statement that he did not want to talk until treated—might provide a basis for a § 1983 claim framed as a due process violation. Accordingly, the Court remanded the case for consideration of that ground.

[83]   18 U.S.C.A. § 3401(a).

[84]   Id. § 3501(b).

[85]   530 U.S. 428, 120 S.Ct. 2326 (2000).

[86]   See supra notes 76–79 and accompanying text.

mandated by the Constitution are a natural, if not necessary, aspect of effective constitutional decisionmaking.[87]

(2) The Waiver-with-Counsel Approach

In New York as a matter of state law, police may not question a suspect once a complaint or indictment against the defendant issues, unless there is an affirmative waiver in the presence of counsel.[88] This rule clearly provides more protection than either the Fifth or Sixth Amendment rights, both of which can be waived in the absence of counsel.[89] New York also has a special rule governing questioning *prior* to formal charging: an uncounseled waiver is invalid if, at the time of the waiver, defense counsel has become involved in the case.[90] This rule provides more protection than *Miranda* for those uncharged suspects who have alert attorneys (like the one in *Escobedo*) or who have been able to contact an attorney, but not for those who do not have and do not ask for one. Some commentators have gone further, arguing that "[a]ll suspects in custody should have a nonwaivable right to consult with a lawyer before being interrogated by the police."[91]

(3) Judicial Questioning

In the early years of the republic, most questioning of suspects was conducted by justices of the peace. But this practice fell into disuse as judicial officers took on other roles and police investigatory powers grew.[92] In 1932, Professor Kauper made a proposal to reinstate the practice with some modifications.[93] As he described it, "[t]he remedy proposed consists of two essentials: (1) That the accused be promptly produced before a magistrate for interrogation; and, (2) That the interrogation be supported by the threat that refusal to answer questions of the magistrate will be used against the accused at trial."

Subsequent developments in Fifth Amendment jurisprudence might invalidate the latter method of compelling answers from suspects.[94] But even without this device, it has been argued there may still be some validity to Professor Kauper's claim that "inauguration of a scheme of magisterial interrogation will greatly weaken the police motive for private interrogation" and ensure that questioning is carried out by "officers who are better qualified to exercise the power of interrogation fairly and effectively."[95] While the number of confessions produced under such a system, particularly in combination with *Miranda* type warnings, would probably fall, its proximity to the time

---

[87] David A. Strauss, *The Ubiquity of Prophylactic Rules*, 55 U.Chi.L.Rev. 190 (1988).

[88] *People v. Samuels*, 49 N.Y.2d 218, 424 N.Y.S.2d 892, 400 N.E.2d 1344 (1980).

[89] *Miranda* stated so explicitly with respect to the Fifth Amendment. With respect to Sixth Amendment waiver, see *Brewer v. Williams*, 430 U.S. 387, 97 S.Ct. 1232 (1977), discussed in § 16.04(c).

[90] *People v. Rogers*, 48 N.Y.2d 167, 422 N.Y.S.2d 18, 397 N.E.2d 709 (1979).

[91] Charles J. Ogletree, *Are Confessions Really Good for the Soul? A Proposal to Mirandize* Miranda, 100 Harv. L. Rev. 1826, 1842 (1987).

[92] See generally, Eben Moglen, *Taking the Fifth: Reconsidering the Origins of the Constitutional Privilege Against Self-Incrimination*, 92 Mich. L.Rev. 1086 (1994).

[93] Paul G. Kauper, *Judicial Examination of the Accused—A Remedy for the Third Degree*, 30 Mich.L.Rev. 1224 (1932).

[94] See *Griffin v. California*, 380 U.S. 609, 85 S.Ct. 1229 (1965), discussed in § 15.02(c). *Griffin*, however, only prevented comments on silence *at trial*, because of the negative effect on the fairness and accuracy of the trial. See § 28.03(c)(1).

[95] Henry Friendly, *The Fifth Amendment Tomorrow: The Case for Constitutional Change*, 37 U. Cin. L. Rev. 671, 713–16 (1968).

of arrest would mean that those who do talk would not have time to work out a coherent fabricated alibi. Several others have proposed variants on Kauper's proposal.[96]

(4) Videotaping of Interrogations

As either a substitute or a supplement to *Miranda*, many commentators, from all points on the political spectrum, have suggested that interrogations be videotaped.[97] Arguably, taping will help the government as much, if not more, than defendants. Taping can provide proof against false accusations aimed at the police, professionalize the interrogation process, and preserve the details of statements that might come in handy later, all of which has been shown to increase guilty pleas.[98] At the same time, taping can deter the worst interrogation abuses and apprise judges of the tactics police use during interrogation, and thus increase the chances that confessions are truly voluntary. A number of courts and police departments have adopted taping requirements either for all interrogations or a subset of them.[99]

The grounds for judicially imposing a taping requirement are numerous. Some courts have resorted to their supervisory power,[100] others to constitutional doctrines. In mandating a "full recording" of any interrogation in a place of detention, or proof as to why such recording was not feasible, the Alaska Supreme Court reasoned that because interrogation continues to take place largely incommunicado, the testimony of police and defendants often conflict, and human memory is fallible, the absence of an accurate record can infringe the suspect's constitutional rights to silence, to an attorney, and to a fair trial.[101] For similar reasons, a few courts have held that failure to tape interrogations creates, in effect, a presumption of involuntariness.[102]

16.03   The Elements of *Miranda*

Of the many different approaches to the regulation of interrogation, *Miranda's* holding has assumed the most importance. The primary issues raised by that decision are: (1) the definition of custody; (2) the definition of interrogation; (3) the content and necessity of the warnings; and (4) the circumstances under which a waiver of the rights to silence and counsel is valid. These issues are addressed here. It is fair to say that every one of *Miranda's* pronouncements on these issues has been undercut to at least some extent by subsequent decisions.

---

[96] Akhil Reed Amar & Renee B. Lettow, *Fifth Amendment First Principles: The Self-Incrimination Clause*, 93 Mich. L. Rev. 857, 908–09 (1995); Donald A. Dripps, *Foreword: Against Police Interrogation—and the Privilege Against Self-Incrimination*, 78 J. Crim. L. & Criminol. 699, 730 (1988).

[97] Compare Paul G. Cassell, *Miranda's Social Costs: An Empirical Reassessment*, 90 Nw.U.L.Rev. 387, 489–92 (1996) to Welsh S. White, *False Confessions and the Constitution: Safeguards Against Untrustworthy Confessions*, 32 Harv. C.R.-C.L. L.Rev. 105, 153–55 (1997).

[98] William A. Geller, *Videotaping and Confessions*, in The *Miranda* Debate: Law, Justice and Policing 303, 307–09 (Richard A. Leo & George C. Thomas III eds., 1998).

[99] Thomas P. Sullivan, *Electronic Recording of Custodial Interrogations: Everybody Wins*, 95 J. Crim. L. & Criminol. 1127 (2005).

[100] *State v. Scales*, 518 N.W.2d 587 (Minn. 1994).

[101] *Stephan v. State*, 711 P.2d 1156 (Alaska 1985).

[102] *Commonwealth v. DiGiambattista*, 442 Mass. 423, 813 N.E.2d 516 (2004) (holding, under court's supervisory power, that if a confession was not videotaped, the jury could be instructed that the statement was to be evaluated with "particular caution."); *State v. Jerrell*, 283 Wis.2d 145, 699 N.W.2d 110 (2005) (same, in juvenile cases).

(a) Custody

The *Miranda* Court limited its holding to situations in which "a person has been taken into custody or otherwise deprived of his freedom of action in any significant way." It further explained that this point in the criminal process is what was meant in *Escobedo* when it spoke of an investigation that has focused on the accused. Subsequent developments have made clear that the definition of custody is narrower than suggested by either statement in *Miranda*. In short, the Court's more recent cases indicate that a person is in custody only if the circumstances would indicate to a reasonable suspect that he was under arrest or its functional equivalent. If such circumstances exist, then any interrogation, even if it is about a different crime than the one which led to the arrest, triggers *Miranda*.[103] On the other hand, interrogation during a detention short of arrest or its equivalent is not enough to require warnings, even when the police have clearly "focused" on the person detained.

As with analysis of when an arrest has occurred for Fourth Amendment purposes,[104] determination of whether a person is in custody depends in large part on the location of the confrontation and its duration and purpose. In other words, this determination is based on objective factors; neither the beliefs of the officer or the suspect are pertinent in deciding whether a person is in custody. As the Court has stated, "the only relevant inquiry [in analyzing the custody issue] is how a reasonable man in the suspect's position would have understood his situation."[105]

(1) Field Stops

The first decision to put forth explicitly the twin propositions that arrest and "custody" are congruent and that only objective factors are to govern the custody determination was *Berkemer v. McCarty*.[106] There the Court held that warnings need be given only before interrogation of a person whose freedom of action has been curtailed to a "degree associated with formal arrest," as judged by a reasonable person in the person's situation. In *Berkemer*, an officer stopped the defendant for weaving in and out of a highway lane. When he noticed the defendant was having difficulty standing, he decided the defendant would have to be charged with a traffic offense and that he would not be allowed to leave the scene, but did not so inform the defendant. When the defendant could not perform a field sobriety test without falling, the officer asked him if he had been using intoxicants, to which the defendant replied that he had consumed two beers and had smoked marijuana a short time before. The officer then formally arrested the defendant.

The Court's opinion, written by Justice Marshall, admitted that a traffic stop does curtail the motorist's freedom of action and that the Court had on several occasions labeled such a stop a "seizure" for Fourth Amendment purposes. However, because the detention resulting from such a stop is "presumptively temporary and brief" and because the typical traffic stop is public, the motorist should not feel unduly coerced. Here, only a short period of time elapsed between the stop and the arrest and at no time was the

---

[103] *Mathis v. United States*, 391 U.S. 1, 88 S.Ct. 1503 (1968).

[104] See § 3.02.

[105] *Berkemer v. McCarty*, 468 U.S. 420, 104 S.Ct. 3138 (1984). See also, *Stansbury v. California*, 511 U.S. 318, 114 S.Ct. 1526 (1994) (officer's uncommunicated belief that suspect was not in custody irrelevant to custody issue).

[106] 468 U.S. 420, 104 S.Ct. 3138 (1984).

defendant informed his detention would be more than temporary. The officer's unexpressed intention to detain the defendant was irrelevant: "From all that appears in the stipulation of facts, a single police officer asked [the defendant] a modest number of questions and requested him to perform a simple balancing test at a location visible to passing motorists."

On the more general question of whether *Miranda* warnings are required after an investigative stop of the type authorized by *Terry v. Ohio,*[107] *Miranda* itself declared that "[g]eneral on-the-scene questioning as to facts surrounding a crime or other general questioning of citizens in the factfinding process is not affected by our holding." Consistent with this statement, the *Berkemer* Court stated that "[t]he comparatively nonthreatening character of [investigative] detentions explains the absence of any suggestion in our opinions that *Terry* stops are subject to the dictates of *Miranda.*" However, if the stop becomes prolonged, or in any other way takes on aspects of an arrest (such as handcuffing or persistent questioning in an isolated setting), then a finding of custody is more likely.[108] The same can be said for questioning at the border: routine questions do not implicate *Miranda,* but once a person is taken to a private room, or questioned for a prolonged period, a different result might be required.[109]

(2) Questioning in the Home

In *Orozco v. Texas,*[110] the Court found that *Miranda* was implicated when four police officers woke up the accused in his bedroom at 4 a.m. and began questioning him about a murder. The Court focused on the testimony of one of the officers that, as far as the police were concerned, the accused was not free to leave, a subjective factor which has since been discounted in *Berkemer*; however, the holding could also be supported by the objectively coercive nature of the confrontation.

In contrast, in *Beckwith v. United States,*[111] a daytime interview by a number of IRS agents in a private home was found to be noncustodial. The defendant claimed that the questioning should have been preceded by the full warnings (rather than the modified warning he received) because he was the "focus" of a criminal investigation and was placed under " 'psychological restraints' which are the functional, and therefore, the legal equivalent of custody." Chief Justice Burger, writing for the majority, dismissed this argument, noting that "*Miranda* specifically defined 'focus,' for its purposes, as 'questioning initiated by law enforcement officers *after* a person has been taken into custody or otherwise deprived of his freedom of action in any significant way.' " After *Beckwith,* investigative questioning in the home is unlikely to implicate *Miranda* unless

---

[107] 392 U.S. 1, 88 S.Ct. 1868 (1968), discussed in § 11.01.

[108] See, e.g., *State v. Myers,* 118 Idaho 608, 798 P.2d 453 (1990) (normal traffic stop turned into custody when four police cars participated in stop and officer asked the defendant if he was carrying any drugs or syringes); *United States v. Beraun-Panez,* 812 F.2d 578 (9th Cir. 1987) (custody where stop took place away from public view where no passersby would likely be present and defendant repeatedly accused of lying).

[109] *United States v. Salinas,* 439 F.2d 376 (5th Cir. 1971).

[110] 394 U.S. 324, 89 S.Ct. 1095 (1969).

[111] 425 U.S. 341, 96 S.Ct. 1612 (1976).

it becomes prolonged or is particularly intrusive, as in *Orozco*.[112] Of course, if there is a formal arrest in the home, then failure to give the warnings violates *Miranda*.[113]

(3) Questioning at the Stationhouse or Its Equivalent

Miranda strongly suggested that stationhouse questioning is always "inherently coercive." However, the post-*Miranda* Court has adhered to the arrest analogy in looking at the custody question in the stationhouse setting. In *Oregon v. Mathiason*,[114] the police initiated contact with Mathiason, a parolee, when an officer left a note at his apartment saying "I'd like to discuss something with you." When Mathiason called in response to this note and expressed no preference as to a meeting place, the officer chose the state patrol office about two blocks from the defendant's apartment. Ninety minutes later, the two met in the hallway adjacent to the office, where the officer assured the defendant he was not under arrest. Once in the office with the door closed, the officer told the defendant he wanted to talk to him about a burglary and that his truthfulness would possibly be considered by the district attorney or judge. He further advised Mathiason that the police believed he was involved in the burglary and then stated, falsely, that the defendant's fingerprints were found at the scene. A few minutes after these statements, and a total of five minutes after he had come into the room, the defendant admitted to taking the property. He then received *Miranda* warnings, made a full confession, and was allowed to leave.

In overturning the Oregon Supreme Court's finding that Mathiason's incriminating statement was made in a "coercive environment," the Court stated:

> Any interview of one suspected of a crime by a police officer will have coercive aspects to it, simply by virtue of the fact that the police officer is part of a law enforcement system which may ultimately cause the suspect to be charged with a crime. But police officers are not required to administer *Miranda* warnings to everyone whom they question. Nor is the requirement of warnings to be imposed simply because the questioning takes place in the station house, or because the questioned person is one whom the police suspect.

Consistent with its focus on coercion, the Court also held that the officer's false statement about the fingerprints was irrelevant to the custody question under *Miranda*.

In a later case, *California v. Beheler*,[115] the Court stated that *Mathiason* stands for the proposition that *Miranda* is not implicated "if the suspect is not placed under arrest, voluntarily comes to the police station, and is allowed to leave unhindered by the police after a brief interview." In *Beheler* itself, the Court relied on this proposition in finding that warnings were not required where the defendant voluntarily confessed over the phone, confessed again at the stationhouse after agreeing to come there, and then was allowed to leave.

---

[112] See, e.g., *United States v. Griffin*, 922 F.2d 1343 (8th Cir. 1990) (robbery suspect in custody when agents sent family members to another part of the house and followed suspect into another room when he went there to get cigarettes).

[113] See also, *Rawlings v. Kentucky*, 448 U.S. 98, 100 S.Ct. 2556 (1980) (three house occupants in custody when police detained them for 45 minutes while warrant sought).

[114] 429 U.S. 492, 97 S.Ct. 711 (1977).

[115] 463 U.S. 1121, 103 S.Ct. 3517 (1983).

Even when the defendant is under considerable pressure to meet with police, the fact of custody is not necessarily established. In *Minnesota v. Murphy*,[116] a probationer was ordered to meet with his probation officer, as part of the probation supervision process; during their interview he confessed to a rape and a murder. The Court held that *Miranda* did not apply because, as in *Berkemer,* Murphy's "freedom of movement [was] not restricted to the degree associated with formal arrest." While "[c]ustodial arrest is said to convey to the suspect a message that he has no choice but to submit to the officers' will and to confess ... [i]t is unlikely that a probation interview, arranged by appointment at a mutually convenient time, would give rise to a similar impression." The Court continued:

> Many of the psychological ploys discussed in *Miranda* capitalize on the suspect's unfamiliarity with the officers and the environment. Murphy's regular meetings with his probation officer should have served to familiarize him with her and her office and to insulate him from psychological intimidation that might overbear his desire to claim the privilege. Finally, the coercion inherent in custodial interrogation derives in large measure from an interrogator's insinuation that the interrogation will continue until a confession is obtained. ... Since Murphy was not physically restrained and could have left the office, any compulsion he might have felt from the possibility that terminating the meeting would have led to revocation of probation was not comparable to the pressure on a suspect who is painfully aware that he literally cannot escape a persistent custodial interrogator.

Although the fact that the suspect was allowed to leave (as in *Mathiason* and *Beheler*), or could have left (as in *Murphy*), has only a tenuous connection to what a reasonable suspect would have felt *during* the interrogation, these cases indicate that Court places great emphasis on such factors.

The Court has also indicated, however, that at least one characteristic that is not an objective indicator of the degree of restraint—the suspect's degree of immaturity—may be considered in determining whether a person is in custody. In its first opinion on this issue, *Yarborough v. Alvarado*,[117] a plurality of the Court suggested that a suspect's age and degree of experience with the criminal justice system are *not* relevant to the custody question because that inquiry "states an objective rule designed to give clear guidance to the police," who should not have to determine a suspect's degree of immaturity or criminal history. However, Justice O'Connor, the fifth vote for the result in *Alvarado*, wrote a concurring opinion stating that a suspect's youth might sometimes be relevant to the custody inquiry. In *J.D.B. v. North Carolina*,[118] involving a 13 year-old questioned for 30 to 45 minutes at his school by two officers and two administrators, five members of the Court affirmed this stance. Justice Sotomayor stated for the majority that the Court's precedents, state laws recognizing differences between children and adults, and "commonsense" all made clear that juveniles are not "miniature adults" and that "a reasonable child subjected to police questioning will sometimes feel pressured to submit when a reasonable adult would feel free to go." Thus, when an officer knows or

---

[116] 465 U.S. 420, 104 S.Ct. 1136 (1984).
[117] 541 U.S. 652, 124 S.Ct. 2140 (2004).
[118] 564 U.S. 261, 131 S.Ct. 2394 (2011).

should know a suspect's age, that factor should be taken into account in determining the custody issue.

The four dissenters, in an opinion by Justice Alito, pointed out that various other factors, such as IQ, immigration status or educational background might also be known to the police at the time of interrogation and thus, under the majority's reasoning, should be relevant to the custody determination. Even if limited to age, Alito continued, the majority's opinion undermined *Miranda's* goal of establishing bright-line rules, particularly since the opinion provided no guidance as to how age affects the extent to which a person feels free to leave. Finally, the dissent contended that the majority's rule was unnecessary, because the Due Process Clause already permits courts to investigate the effects of immaturity on a person's ability to resist police pressure.

In cases involving more typical juvenile suspects—those in their older teens—age is not likely to be a major consideration in making the custody determination, at least if the result in *Alvarado* is any indication. At the request of the police Alvarado, a 17 year-old, was brought to the station by his parents, who were told to wait in the lobby while Alvarado was questioned by a female officer for approximately two hours. Before the interview began, an officer called Alvarado a "suspect," and during the interview he was not told he could leave until after he had confessed. However, five members of the Court, in an opinion by Justice Kennedy, concluded that the state court was "reasonable" in finding that Alvarado was not in custody at the time of the interview. Kennedy emphasized that Alvarado was not put under arrest or threatened during the interview; that Alvarado's parents, not the police, had brought him to the station; that the parents had remained at the station (thus "suggesting the interview would be brief"); and that the officer had twice asked Alvarado if he wanted to take a break. Justice Breyer argued in dissent that most of these factors would have suggested to a reasonable person he was *not* free to leave: Alvarado did not come to the station of his own accord (in contrast to the suspect in *Beheler*); his parents were kept out of the interview room; the interview, contrary to the initial impression created by the police, was not brief (four times longer than the interview in *Mathiason*); and the invitation to take a "break" suggested that Alvarado was there until the officer believed the interview was over. Although *Alvarado* was a habeas case decided under a more relaxed standard of review seven years before *J.D.B.*,[119] its holding signals that a majority of the present Court is not likely to treat older adolescents much differently than adults.

Once a suspect is put in custody, questioning should usually be preceded by warnings. In *Mathis v. United States*,[120] the Court held that an accused interrogated by I.R.S. officers while in jail serving a sentence on a state charge was in custody for *Miranda* purposes. Because the accused was clearly detained against his will, the fact that the questioning concerned a crime different from the one for which he was serving time was irrelevant. Similarly, in *Estelle v. Smith*,[121] the Court held that a post-arrest, court-ordered psychiatric evaluation requested by the state must be preceded by *Miranda* warnings when its results are used for adjudication of guilt or capital sentencing; otherwise, a psychiatrist who later testifies based on such an examination is "essentially like . . . an agent of the State recounting unwarned statements made in a

---

[119] Because *Alvarado* came to the Court as a habeas case, the issue before the Court was not whether *Miranda* was violated, but whether the state court was reasonable in holding it wasn't. See § 33.03(b) & (c).

[120] 391 U.S. 1, 88 S.Ct. 1503 (1968).

[121] 451 U.S. 454, 101 S.Ct. 1866 (1981).

post-arrest custodial setting."[122] However, the Court has intimated that under some circumstances a person who is in prison is no longer in custody for *Miranda* purposes. Thus, in *Howes v. Field*,[123] the Court held that a state court was not unreasonable in holding that a prisoner is not in custody when he is removed from the general population and questioned in a separate room about events outside the prison, at least when he is told he can go back to his cell whenever he wanted.[124]

(4) Minor Crimes

Consistent with the arrest analogy, sufficient coercion to trigger the warnings requirement exists *whenever* a person is in custody, regardless of the crime. This was a second aspect of *Berkemer*, which, it will be remembered, involved a traffic stop. Although the Court found that custody did not occur there, it also unanimously rejected a "misdemeanor exception" to *Miranda* for persons who are in custody. To the state's argument that police would have no reason to subject those arrested for a traffic offense to strenuous interrogation, the Court noted that police sometimes have difficulty obtaining evidence relating to certain types of misdemeanors such as driving under the influence of narcotic drugs, and that "[u]nder such circumstances, the incentive for police to try to induce the defendant to incriminate himself may well be substantial."

In addition to deciding that there was no necessary distinction between serious and minor crimes in terms of the coercive impact of custody, the *Berkemer* Court pointed to several practical reasons for its conclusion. There are many situations, noted Justice Marshall, in which an officer taking a driver into custody for causing a collision would be unable to tell whether the driver will eventually be charged with a felony or a misdemeanor. Moreover, the nature of the offense may depend upon circumstances unknowable to the police, such as whether the suspect has previously committed a similar offense or has a criminal record, or whether the victim will die. Finally, because officers are accustomed to giving *Miranda* warnings to persons in custody, an across-the-board rule would work no undue hardship while it would maintain the prophylactic advantage of *Miranda*.

(5) Questioning by Non-Police

When the interrogator is a government official who is not a police officer, the custody issue can sometimes become murky. Public "civilian" investigators, such as health inspectors and school officials, may not be as intimidating as the police. Moreover, given the nature of their jobs, the questions they ask may not be aimed at obtaining "incriminating" answers.[125] But if a government action amounts to the equivalent of an arrest for a criminal offense, then *Miranda* should apply. At least three Supreme Court decisions support this conclusion. In *Mathis*, the Court found that *Miranda* was

---

[122] See § 15.03(a) for further discussion of *Smith*. The Court also seems to have accepted the idea that a police confrontation with a hospitalized person, at least one who is non-ambulatory and in some pain, is in custody for purposes of *Miranda*. *Mincey v. Arizona*, 437 U.S. 385, 98 S.Ct. 2408 (1978).

[123] 565 U.S. 499, 132 S.Ct. 1181 (2012).

[124] The Court has also held that when an offender is returned to the prison population after an interrogation, a hiatus of two weeks or more before the next interrogation creates a "break in custody". However, in this situation, warnings are required before the second interrogation. See *Maryland v. Shatzer*, 559 U.S. 98, 130 S.Ct. 1213 (2010), discussed in 16.03(e)(4).

[125] Note that, even when a person is in custody, if his answers will not be used in a "criminal proceeding," either because they are not relevant to any criminal offense or because immunity has been granted, then *Miranda* does not apply; in such cases, there is no right to remain silent. See § 15.03.

implicated even though the questioning was conducted by I.R.S. agents. Similarly, in *Smith*, the Court stated: "That respondent was questioned by a psychiatrist designated by the trial court to conduct a neutral competency examination, rather than by a police officer, government informant, or prosecuting attorney is immaterial." And the Court strongly implied that, had the probationer in *Murphy* been in custody, the warnings should have been given by the probation officer who conducted the questioning.

As with other criminal process rights, *Miranda* requires "state action." Thus, as a general rule, questioning by a private individual (e.g., an employer or a journalist) does not trigger *Miranda*.[126] When a private individual conducts a "custodial interrogation" as an agent of the police, however, the Fifth Amendment is implicated,[127] at least when the suspect knows that the questioner is acting for the police.[128] Even when the interrogator is not a direct agent of the police, a good case for applying *Miranda* exists if he is acting with the primary purpose of enforcing the law and significantly restrains a person's liberty; consistent with the above discussion, if the private action amounts to an "arrest" for a crime, then *Miranda* should apply. But most courts, defining state action narrowly, have held that questioning by security guards and the like does not implicate *Miranda*, regardless of its custodial aspects.[129]

(b) Interrogation

The mere fact of custody does not trigger the warnings requirement. The person must be subjected to "interrogation" as well. *Miranda* defined interrogation as "questioning initiated by law enforcement officers." But *Miranda* was also concerned with "techniques of persuasion" that produce a "compulsion to speak," apparently aiming to regulate any police action that suggest a response is called for. While later decisions paid lipservice to this view, they have tended to undermine it in practice.

(1) The Innis Formulation

Rhode Island v. Innis[130] was the Court's first attempt to flesh out the definition of interrogation. The Court began by stating that interrogation "must reflect a measure of compulsion above and beyond that inherent in custody itself." It then went on to define interrogation to mean not only "express questioning" but also its "functional equivalent," including "any words or actions on the part of the police (other than those normally attendant to arrest and custody) that the police should know are reasonably likely to elicit an incriminating response from the suspect." Using examples from *Miranda*, the Court listed as "functional equivalents" of interrogation situations where the police coach witnesses to identify the defendant in a line-up, suggest to the suspect that he was guilty, or minimize the seriousness of the offense or the perpetrator's role in it.

The apparent breadth of the Court's definition of interrogation was called into question, however, by its application in *Innis*. In that case police officers, while driving Innis to the police station after arresting him for armed robbery, engaged in a conversation about the danger the missing robbery weapon would present to

---

[126]　George, supra note 7, at 437–38.

[127]　See *Wilson v. O'Leary*, 895 F.2d 378 (7th Cir. 1990).

[128]　When, instead, the questioner is "undercover," the coercion associated with custody does not exist. See *Illinois v. Perkins*, 496 U.S. 292, 110 S.Ct. 2394 (1990), discussed in § 16.03(b)(2).

[129]　*City of Grand Rapids v. Impens*, 414 Mich. 667, 327 N.W.2d 278 (1982); George, supra note 7, at 438.

[130]　446 U.S. 291, 100 S.Ct. 1682 (1980).

handicapped children; apparently in response to this conversation, Innis directed them to the hiding place of a shotgun later used as evidence to convict him. The Court's opinion, written by Justice Stewart (a *Miranda* dissenter), found that this exchange did not constitute interrogation. The Court characterized it as "nothing more than a dialogue between the two officers to which no response from the respondent was invited."

In dissent, Justice Stevens argued that evidence in the record suggested the officers' actions were not entirely "innocent." He pointed out that the officer whose statement triggered Innis' response was not regularly assigned to the transport vehicle, that he may have been—the record was unclear—sitting in the back seat next to Innis, and that the triggering statement was particularly emotionally charged ("God forbid" that a "little girl" might find the weapon). He also disputed the majority's implicit assumption that a criminal suspect will not respond to "indirect appeals to his humanitarian impulses." He pointed out that such an assumption "is directly contrary to the teachings of police interrogation manuals, which recommend appealing to a suspect's sense of morality as a standard and often successful interrogation technique."

Post-*Innis*, the Court continued to define interrogation narrowly. In *Arizona v. Mauro*,[131] after Mauro indicated his desire to remain silent, the police allowed his wife, upon her request, to talk to him. An officer was present during the conversation and tape-recorded it. The conversation was later used to rebut Mauro's insanity defense. The Supreme Court, in a 5–4 opinion authored by Justice Powell, held that no interrogation had taken place on these facts because Mauro "was not subjected to compelling influences, psychological ploys, or direct questioning." The Arizona Supreme Court had unanimously concluded that interrogation *did* occur, largely on the ground that the detectives had admitted that they knew incriminating statements were likely to be made if the conversation took place.[132] But Powell concluded that police "do not interrogate a suspect simply by hoping that he will incriminate himself." The dissent, again authored by Justice Stevens, admitted that there had been no explicit police subterfuge in the case. But because the police "exploited the custodial situation and the understandable desire of Mrs. Mauro to speak with [her husband]" by arranging for and listening to their conversation, he concluded that "interrogation" had taken place.

The definition of interrogation in *Innis* clearly focused on what the *officers* knew or should have known. This approach might be justified on the ground that police should not be penalized through exclusion of statements which they could not have known would be coerced by their actions. However, if the issue is the degree of coercion on the suspect, then coercion must ultimately be measured from the suspect's perspective. Indeed, that is the perspective adopted by the Court in defining "custody," appropriately narrowed by a "reasonableness" requirement.[133] Both *Innis* and *Mauro* are less than sensitive to the fact that a reasonable suspect, who otherwise would remain silent, can be induced to talk through police action short of questioning.

(2) *When Custodial Questioning Is Not Interrogation*

Even direct questioning of a person in custody does not always implicate *Miranda*. According to *Innis*, interrogation must add to the compulsion inherent in custody. Thus, when a person in custody does not know his questioner is a government agent, no

---

[131]　481 U.S. 520, 107 S.Ct. 1931 (1987).

[132]　*State v. Mauro*, 149 Ariz. 24, 716 P.2d 393 (1986).

[133]　See *Berkemer v. McCarty*, 468 U.S. 420, 104 S.Ct. 3138 (1984), discussed in § 16.03(a)(1).

interrogation takes place. In *Illinois v. Perkins*,[134] the police placed an undercover agent in the cell of the defendant, who was in custody on a charge of aggravated battery. In response to questions by the agent, the defendant made incriminating statements about a murder unrelated to the battery charge. The Court held, 8–1, that admission of these statements did not violate *Miranda* because they were not made in the type of "police-dominated atmosphere" that concerned the *Miranda* majority.[135]

The Court has also held that, even when the suspect is subjected to custodial questioning by someone he knows to be an agent, "interrogation" has not occurred if the questions asked are part of a legitimate police procedure, such as booking or field tests, that is "not intended to elicit information for investigatory purposes." In *Pennsylvania v. Muniz*,[136] the defendant, arrested for drunk driving and taken to the stationhouse, was asked seven questions regarding his name, address, height, weight, eye color, date of birth and current age. In addition, he was given instructions on how to perform various sobriety tests and how to take a breathalyzer test and then asked whether he understood these instructions. A plurality of four members of the Court joined Justice Brennan's opinion holding that the seven identifying questions came within a "routine booking question" exception to *Miranda,* thus permitting, despite the absence of warnings, use of the defendant's responses (some of which indicated he was confused and incoherent).[137] Eight members of the Court also agreed that statements made by the defendant during the sobriety and breathalyzer tests were not prompted by "interrogation;" the police statements prior to and during these tests either were "not likely to be perceived as calling for any verbal responses" or were "focused inquiries . . . necessarily 'attendant to' the [legitimate] police procedure. . . ."

In dissent, Justice Marshall argued that, without warnings, both the booking questions and the test communications violated *Innis;* given their belief that the defendant was intoxicated, the police should have known that incriminating responses were likely to be elicited. Although technically correct, Marshall's interpretation of *Innis* neglects the spirit of that case, which attempted to define when interrogation adds to the coercion already present in any custodial situation.

(c) The Warnings

When the accused is in custody and the police wish to "interrogate" him, *Miranda* requires that the warnings be given. The thrust of the opinion is that the warnings should *always* be given, regardless of context. Thus, *Miranda* specifically held that *all* suspects are to be informed of their rights, with no presumption of any prior awareness of those rights. And, in a footnote, the Court recognized that while the warning concerning the right to appointed counsel is technically unnecessary when the person is known to have an attorney or ample funds to retain one, "giving a warning is too simple and the rights involved too important to engage in *ex post facto* inquiries into financial ability when there is any doubt at all on that score." In short, the Court in *Miranda* seemed determined to fashion an easily applied rule that would cover all custodial

---

[134]   496 U.S. 292, 110 S.Ct. 2394 (1990).

[135]   Nor was the Sixth Amendment violated, since the defendant had not yet been charged. See § 16.04(a). However, in a concurring opinion, Justice Brennan argued that such deception violated Due Process.

[136]   496 U.S. 582, 110 S.Ct. 2638 (1990).

[137]   Four other members of the Court contended that the defendant's answers to the questions were not testimonial in any event, see § 15.04, thus giving clear support to the rule that warnings do not have to precede routine booking questions.

interrogation situations and provide suspects with the necessary information to make voluntary and intelligent decisions about their rights.

However, since *Miranda*, the Court has not adhered to this preference. It has permitted "de minimis" variations in the warnings even when they might create ambiguity, refused to require clarifying warnings, and created a "public safety" exception to *Miranda*.

(1) De Minimis *Variations*

In *California v. Prysock*,[138] the Supreme Court emphasized that "*Miranda* itself indicates that no talismanic incantation was required to satisfy its strictures." In *Prysock*, this notion was interpreted to mean that failure to inform an indigent defendant that he has a right to an appointed lawyer prior to interrogation is not violative of *Miranda*. In *Prysock* the defendant, a juvenile, was told the following: "You have the right to talk to a lawyer before you are questioned, have him present with you while you are being questioned, and all during the questioning." Shortly thereafter, the defendant was also told he had the right to a *court-appointed* lawyer if he could not afford one, but was not told when such an attorney could be appointed. As Justice Stevens noted in his dissent, the California Court of Appeals found that this warning was constitutionally inadequate because "the minor was not given the crucial information that the services of the free attorney were available *prior* to the impending questioning." The Supreme Court's per curiam decision concluded, however, that the warnings given in *Prysock* were a "fully effective equivalent" to the *Miranda* litany. It intimated that had police improperly associated the right to an appointed attorney solely with some future time in court, the result would have been different.

However, in *Duckworth v. Eagan*,[139] where it was confronted with such a case, the Court found that this variation in the warnings was also *de minimis*. In *Eagan*, the following warnings were given to the defendant shortly after his arrest:

> Before we ask you any questions, you must understand your rights. You have the right to remain silent. Anything you say can be used against you in court. You have a right to talk to a lawyer for advice before we ask you any questions, and to have him with you during questioning. You have this right to the advice and presence of a lawyer even if you cannot afford to hire one. We have no way of giving you a lawyer, but one will be appointed for you, if you wish, if and when you go to court. If you wish to answer questions now without a lawyer present, you have the right to stop answering questions at any time. You also have the right to stop answering at any time until you've talked to a lawyer.

Although this language suggests that a person who cannot afford an attorney is entitled to one only "if and when [the person] goes to court," the Court held, 5–4, that it "touched all the bases required by *Miranda*." Chief Justice Rehnquist, writing for the Court, noted that, under Indiana procedure, a person who asserts his right to an attorney cannot be questioned until one is appointed for him at the initial appearance in front of a judicial officer. Thus, the "if and when" language was accurate and the warnings, "in their totality", satisfied *Miranda*.

---

[138] 453 U.S. 355, 101 S.Ct. 2806 (1981).

[139] 492 U.S. 195, 109 S.Ct. 2875 (1989).

In dissent, Justice Marshall faulted the majority for its assumption that "frightened suspects unlettered in the law" will understand the warnings given in *Eagan* to mean that if they cannot afford an attorney they may ask for one and avoid questioning until one is appointed at the initial appearance. Moreover, as Marshall pointed out, even if a defendant does correctly understand the warnings he is not told when the court appearance will take place. "The threat of an indefinite deferral of interrogation, in a system like Indiana's, thus constitutes an effective means by which the police can pressure a suspect to speak without the presence of counsel." Finally, Marshall emphasized that the confusion produced by the warnings could easily be eradicated merely by eliminating the sentence with the "if and when" language in it.

This latter point is perhaps the strongest. Any possibly misleading statement ought to be excised from the warnings, because it is so easy to do so. Thus, for instance, lower court holdings permitting the second warning to read that anything said might be used "for or against you" reach the wrong result.[140] This statement's distorting implication that the police want to help the suspect, combined with the ease with which the implication can be removed, should lead to the opposite finding.

The Court has continued to approve ambiguous *Miranda* language, however. In *Florida v. Powell*,[141] the warning included the usual first two warnings as well as statements that the suspect had a right to counsel "before" questioning and a right to state-paid counsel "before" questioning. It then ended with the statement "You have the right to use any of these rights at any time you want during this interview." The Florida Supreme Court concluded that these warnings only associated the right to counsel with the pre-interrogation period, because, despite the last sentence, "a right that has never been expressed cannot be reiterated." But the Supreme Court, in an opinion written by Justice Ginsburg for a seven-member majority, held that the last warning "confirmed" that the right to counsel could be exercised during interrogation. The Court admitted that the warnings "were not the *clearest possible* formulation of *Miranda*." But it discounted the possibility that its ruling provided an incentive for police across the country to formulate similarly unclear warnings, citing the assertion of the Solicitor General that "it is 'in law enforcement's own interest' to state warnings with maximum clarity." The outcome in *Powell* belies that assertion.

(2) Collateral Information

A second issue associated with the warnings requirement is whether any information other than that contained in the original *Miranda* litany must be communicated to the defendant in order to ensure a valid waiver. For instance, it has been argued that defendants should be told that their silence cannot be used against them at trial; otherwise, they are less likely to see any benefit to remaining silent.[142] Similarly, defendants have contended that they are entitled to be told the crime that has triggered the investigation and to be informed that they may cut off questioning at any time (the latter a right specifically granted by *Miranda*).[143]

---

[140]   *State v. Melvin,* 65 N.J. 1, 319 A.2d 450 (1974).

[141]   559 U.S. 50, 130 S.Ct. 1195 (2010).

[142]   Sheldon H. Elsen & Arthur Rossett, *Protections for the Suspect Under* Miranda v. Arizona, 67 Colum.L.Rev. 645, 654 (1967).

[143]   Id. See also, *People v. Prude,* 66 Ill.2d 470, 6 Ill.Dec. 689, 363 N.E.2d 371 (1977), cert. denied 434 U.S. 930, 98 S.Ct. 418 (1977).

In *Colorado v. Spring*,[144] however, the Supreme Court seemed to adopt the position that the Fifth Amendment does not require that any collateral information be communicated to the defendant. In *Spring,* the defendant was arrested and questioned on charges of transporting stolen firearms, and then was questioned about a homicide as well. Although admitting that he had been given and understood the *Miranda* warnings, he argued that statements made in response to the homicide-related questions were inadmissible because he was not informed he would be interrogated about the murder. Justice Marshall's dissent in *Spring* supported this stance, contending that "[a]dditional questioning about entirely separate and more serious suspicions of criminal activity can take unfair advantage of the suspect's psychological state, as the unexpected questions cause the compulsive pressures [that the warnings are supposed to dissipate] suddenly to reappear"; moreover, he stated, had Spring known the homicide was to be the subject of the interrogation, he might have insisted on consulting with an attorney at the outset.

But the majority found that "a suspect's awareness of all the possible subjects of questioning in advance of interrogation is not relevant to determining whether the suspect voluntarily, knowingly, and intelligently waived his Fifth Amendment privilege." As long as the defendant understands "the basic privilege guaranteed by the Fifth Amendment" and "the consequences of speaking freely to law enforcement officials," as was true in this case, *Miranda* is not violated. While the Court did not explicitly state that the *Miranda* rights are the *only* subjects about which a defendant must be informed prior to interrogation, this language indicates it will be hostile to suggestions that other types of collateral information be included in the pre-interrogation litany.

When the suspect is a foreign national, another type of warning that might be added to the *Miranda* litany would describe the right of such individuals to consult with consular officials upon arrest. This right is recognized in Article 36(1)(b) of the Vienna Convention on Consular Rights, to which the U.S. is a signatory. In *Medellin v. Texas*,[145] however, the Supreme Court held that until this treaty is made self-executing by Congress, it cannot be the basis for a claim in domestic courts.

(3) The "Public Safety" Exception

By far the most significant exception to the general rule that *Miranda* warnings must precede custodial interrogations was announced in *New York v. Quarles*.[146] There the Court held that the warnings need not be given at all if the prosecution can show that warning a suspect could have endangered the public. The "public safety exception" to *Miranda* not only substantially erodes the prophylactic nature of the *Miranda* doctrine but for the first time authorizes the use of clearly coerced statements in the prosecution's case-in-chief.

Quarles aptly illustrates both points. Based on information that a man with a gun had just entered a supermarket, Officer Kraft, assisted by three other officers, entered the store, spotted the defendant, and with gun drawn ordered him to stop and put his hands over his head. After frisking the defendant and discovering an empty shoulder holster, Kraft handcuffed the defendant and asked him where the gun was. The

---

[144] 479 U.S. 564, 107 S.Ct. 851 (1987).

[145] 552 U.S. 491, 128 S.Ct. 1346 (2008).

[146] 467 U.S. 649, 104 S.Ct. 2626 (1984).

defendant responded "the gun is over there" while nodding in the direction of some empty cartons, from which Kraft retrieved a loaded revolver. At that point, Kraft formally placed the defendant under arrest and read him his *Miranda* rights. In response to further questioning, the defendant admitted to owning the gun. The trial court and the lower appellate courts excluded the gun on the ground it was obtained in violation of *Miranda* and excluded all of the defendant's statements about the gun on the ground that they were "fruit" of the illegal interrogation.

Justice Rehnquist, in an opinion joined by four other Justices, admitted that the defendant had been in custody at the time Officer Kraft asked him about the location of the gun. But he held that the fear of coerced admissions which led to *Miranda* no longer justified reliance on a rigid rule; rather this concern must be balanced against the needs of the public. He then concluded:

> [T]he need for answers to questions in a situation posing a threat to the public safety outweighs the need for the prophylactic rule protecting the Fifth Amendment's privilege against self-incrimination. We decline to place officers such as Officer Kraft in the untenable position of having to consider, often in a matter of seconds, whether it best serves society for them to ask the necessary questions without the Miranda warnings and render whatever probative evidence they uncover inadmissible, or for them to give the warnings in order to preserve the admissibility of evidence they might uncover but possibly damage or destroy their ability to obtain that evidence and neutralize the volatile situation confronting them.

Justice Rehnquist also made clear that the public safety exception is a purely objective standard. Given the "kaleidoscopic situation" confronting officers when public safety is threatened, "where spontaneity rather than adherence to a police manual is necessarily the order of the day, the application of the [public safety] exception . . . should not be made to depend on *post hoc* findings at a suppression hearing concerning the subjective motivation of the arresting officer." To the majority, the events in the supermarket clearly presented such an objectively threatening situation. As long as the whereabouts of the gun remained unknown, "it obviously posed more than one danger to the public safety: an accomplice might make use of it, a customer or employee might later come upon it." The existence of these dangers outweighed, in the majority's eyes, the fact that the defendant had been handcuffed and confronted by four armed officers when he was asked, without being told he could remain silent, about the gun.

Quarles is a questionable decision at best, both as to the rule it announced and as to the manner in which it applied the rule. With respect to the latter issue, Justice Marshall pointed out, in dissent, that since the defendant's apprehension took place after the store was closed and there was no known accomplice the threat to the public in *Quarles* was minuscule. In fact, the New York Court of Appeals had specifically found "no evidence in the record before us that there were exigent circumstances posing a risk to public safety. . . ." Thus, even assuming the validity of a public safety exception to *Miranda, Quarles* seems an inappropriate case in which to apply it.

The divergence between the New York court's conclusion concerning the facts and the majority's characterization of them also illustrates the danger of departing from the prophylactic rule in the first place. Police and courts will no longer have the relative clarity offered by *Miranda* but will disagree, as they did in *Quarles,* over when the public is threatened. The majority recognized this possibility but argued that, at least with respect to police, the public safety exception "will not be difficult . . . to apply" because "officers can and will distinguish almost instinctively between questions to secure their own safety or the safety of the public and questions designed solely to elicit testimonial evidence from a suspect." Justice O'Connor—who agreed with the majority that the gun should be admissible,[147] but dissented with respect to the adoption of the public safety exception—was more realistic about the consequences of *Quarles:* "The end result will be a finespun new doctrine on public safety exigencies incident to custodial interrogation, complete with the hair-splitting distinctions that currently plague our Fourth Amendment jurisprudence."[148] As an illustration of Justice O'Connor's point, imagine that the police in *Innis* had *directly* interrogated the accused about the location of the robbery weapon without giving a warning. Presumably, prior to *Quarles,* the evidence thus obtained would have been excluded because no warning preceded the questioning. But now courts must decide: given the apparent danger the gun represented to neighborhood children, does the public safety exception to the warnings requirement apply?[149]

More importantly, as this example illustrates, *Quarles* disregards the underlying premise of *Miranda.* Justice O'Connor once again put the matter succinctly when she stated:

> *Miranda* has never been read to prohibit the police from asking questions to secure the public safety. Rather, the critical question *Miranda* addresses is who shall bear the cost of securing the public safety when such questions are asked and answered: the defendant or the State. *Miranda,* for better or worse, found the resolution of that question implicit in the prohibition against compulsory self-incrimination and placed the burden on the State.

Quarles, on the other hand, ignores the issue of coercion in favor of ensuring that evidence obtained under exigent circumstances is not excluded but rather used to convict the guilty. The balancing analysis it employs could also end up undermining *Miranda* in a host of other situations where the state's interests are perceived to be particularly weighty.[150]

(d) Waiver: Generally

Miranda stated that if a person talks after the warnings, "a heavy burden rests on the government to demonstrate that the defendant knowingly and intelligently waived his privilege against self-incrimination and his right to retained or appointed counsel." Moreover, "a valid waiver will not be presumed simply from the silence of the accused

---

[147] O'Connor argued that the gun should have been admitted because it was "nontestimonial" in nature and thus, under *Schmerber v. California,* 384 U.S. 757, 86 S.Ct. 1826 (1966), discussed in § 15.04, not covered by the Fifth Amendment.

[148] See generally, Note, *The Public Safety Exception to* Miranda: *Careening Through the Lower Courts,* 40 Fla.L.Rev. 989 (1988).

[149] The Court did provide *some* guidance on this issue, by indicating that its decision in *Orozco v. Texas,* 394 U.S. 324, 89 S.Ct. 1095 (1969), involving questioning at home about a gun used in a murder several hours earlier, was not affected by its holding.

[150] The booking exception recognized in *Pennsylvania v. Muniz,* 496 U.S. 582, 110 S.Ct. 2638 (1990), discussed in § 16.02(b)(2), could be seen as an example of this analysis. Conceivably, special needs analogous to those recognized in Fourth Amendment cases could also affect *Miranda* analysis in cases where the interrogators are not police and are seeking information designed to combat "serious" regulatory problems such as drug use in schools. Cf. § 13.09.

after warnings are given or simply from the fact that a confession was in fact eventually obtained:"

> Whatever the testimony of the authorities as to waiver of rights by an accused, the fact of lengthy interrogation or incommunicado incarceration before a statement is made is strong evidence that the accused did not validly waive his rights. In these circumstances the fact that the individual eventually made a statement is consistent with the conclusion that the compelling influence of the interrogation finally forced him to do so. It is inconsistent with any notion of a voluntary relinquishment of the privilege. Moreover, any evidence that the accused was threatened, tricked, or cajoled into a waiver will, of course, show that the defendant did not voluntarily waive his privilege.

Since *Miranda,* this language has been interpreted narrowly. Although the Court has been careful to insist that the government bears the burden on the waiver issue,[151] it has also held, in *Colorado v. Connelly,*[152] that the government need only prove the validity of a waiver by a "preponderance of the evidence."[153] This is obviously not a particularly "heavy" burden. Further, the Court's cases suggest that waiver analysis after the warnings have been given will be very similar to the voluntariness analysis found in the Court's due process cases.[154] Indeed, in *Fare v. Michael C.,*[155] the Court explicitly held that the "totality of the circumstances approach is adequate to determine whether there has been a waiver" under *Miranda*. This development has resulted in substantial modification of *Miranda's* wide-ranging dictum.

(1) Express v. Implied Waiver

Most significant in this regard is the post-*Miranda* Court's rejection of a requirement that the government prove that the defendant expressly waived his rights; rather, circumstantial proof of waiver is sufficient. *Miranda's* statement that "a valid waiver will not be presumed" from the fact that a confession was eventually obtained, together with the holding in *Westover v. United States* (one of the cases joined in *Miranda*) that an "articulated waiver" is required before a confession will be considered admissible, suggested that the *Miranda* majority strongly favored an express written or oral waiver. But in *North Carolina v. Butler,*[156] the Court held otherwise. Justice Stewart, a dissenter in *Miranda*, reasoned for the Court that "[t]he question is not one of form, but rather whether the defendant in fact knowingly and voluntarily waived his rights delineated in the *Miranda* case." A "course of conduct *indicating* waiver" (emphasis added) is sufficient grounds for such a finding. As the three dissenters noted, this decision undermines the prophylactic effect of *Miranda* and runs counter to its premise that, in the "inherently coercive" atmosphere of custodial interrogation, ambiguity should be resolved in favor of the defendant.

The *Butler* majority did not resolve whether the waiver in that case was valid, but merely overruled the state court's decision that an express waiver was required. Butler

---

[151] *Tague v. Louisiana,* 444 U.S. 469, 100 S.Ct. 652 (1980) (overturning state court decision placing burden on defendant to show lack of capacity).

[152] 479 U.S. 157, 107 S.Ct. 515 (1986).

[153] See § 16.06(b).

[154] See generally, § 16.02(a).

[155] 442 U.S. 707, 99 S.Ct. 2560 (1979).

[156] 441 U.S. 369, 99 S.Ct. 1755 (1979).

had been read his rights and had also read an "Advice of Rights" form, which he said he understood. However, he also refused to sign the form and made no statement about whether he wanted to waive the right to remain silent or the right to counsel. He then indicated he was willing to talk. The difficulty of determining, after the event, whether this conduct "indicates" a voluntary and intelligent waiver, or is instead a misunderstanding on the part of the defendant as to the importance of his signature, illustrates the usefulness of an express waiver requirement. If such a requirement existed, the burden would be on the government to ascertain what the defendant's ambiguous actions meant and to provide proof of a clear decision from Butler with respect to his rights. Under the Court's test, on the other hand, the government's burden is to prove the more amorphous proposition that there was a voluntary waiver in light of "the particular facts and circumstances surrounding [the] case, including the background, experience, and conduct of the accused."

The practical impact of this test was illustrated in *Berghuis v. Thompkins*,[157] where the Court held *Miranda* was not violated despite the fact that the suspect's incriminating statement came at the end of a three-hour interrogation (during which the police did virtually all of the talking) and consisted simply of a "Yes" in response to a question about whether he had prayed for forgiveness for the crime. Citing *Butler*, Justice Kennedy wrote for five members of the Court that "where the prosecution shows that a *Miranda* warning was given and that it was understood by the accused, an accused's uncoerced statement establishes an implied waiver of the right to remain silent." Justice Sotomayor's dissent stressed that, while *Butler* permitted implicit waivers, it also reiterated *Miranda's* statement that waiver may not be presumed "simply from the fact that a confession was in fact eventually obtained." She also pointed out that, while Butler had said he would talk to the police and made incriminating statements fairly quickly, Thompkins never indicated a desire to talk, was mute or non-responsive during most of the interview, and did not say anything incriminating until two hours and forty-five minutes into the interrogation.

One twist to the facts in *Thompkins* is that the police added a fifth warning to the usual four, telling Thompkins that he could "use" the right remain silent "any time before or during questioning." The majority pointed to this fact in concluding that Thompkins understood that the right to silence could be asserted at any time. Left unresolved is whether the Court would have found a valid waiver had such a warning not been proffered. Even with such a warning, some suspects could believe that the way to exercise the right to silence is to remain silent; if police nonetheless continue to ask questions, these suspects might conclude that in reality they have no such right, thereby undercutting the voluntariness of subsequent statements.

(2) *The Knowing and Intelligent Requirement*

While *Miranda* insisted that all waivers be "knowing and intelligent," the Court has since indicated that full understanding of the warnings is not necessary for a waiver to be valid. In *Connecticut v. Barrett*,[158] the defendant explicitly refused to give police any written statements before he talked to counsel but just as unequivocally stated that he had "no problem" *talking* with them. The most reasonable interpretation of Barrett's post-warning behavior was that he erroneously believed that only written statements

---

[157] 560 U.S. 370, 130 S.Ct. 2250 (2010).
[158] 479 U.S. 523, 107 S.Ct. 828 (1987).

could be used against him.[159] The Court itself admitted Barrett's actions might have been "illogical." But, emphasizing that Barrett had said he understood the warnings, it held that his oral statements were admissible. The result in *Barrett* suggests that, had it reached the issue, the Court would have found in the government's favor in *Butler* (where the defendant also said he understood the warnings), despite the apparent confusion of the defendant in that case.[160]

Sometimes the defendant alleges confusion about the duration of a waiver. In *Wyrick v. Fields,*[161] the defendant, who had retained counsel, agreed in his counsel's absence to take a polygraph examination. Before doing so he signed a consent form, including a waiver of his right to counsel, and was read a statement informing him of his right to refuse to answer questions at any time. After taking the examination, the defendant answered questions from the examiner about his reactions toward the examination, which eventually led to damaging disclosures. To Fields' contention that neither he nor his attorney believed the procedure would involve post-test questioning, the Court responded, "it would have been unreasonable for Fields and his attorney to assume that Fields would not be informed of the polygraph readings and asked to explain any unfavorable result." The Court also concluded that "the questions put to Fields after the examination would not have caused him to forget the rights of which he had been advised and which he had understood moments before." Thus, despite the absence of proof of actual awareness that the waiver applied to post-test questioning, the Court found the waiver valid.

The related issue of whether, under *Miranda,* the police may use "trickery" to procure a statement has also arisen. In *Colorado v. Spring,*[162] the Court declined to apply this term to a police failure to inform the defendant that he would be questioned about a crime other than the one for which he was arrested. It further suggested that trickery does not occur unless police engage in "affirmative representation," and even as to this situation it was coy about how the matter should be decided.[163] This position is reminiscent of that taken in the due process cases, where trickery, by itself, does not lead to a finding that a confession was involuntary.[164] It is in marked contrast to the language in *Miranda* quoted above, in which the Court stated that "any evidence that the accused was ... tricked ... into a waiver will, of course, show that the defendant did not voluntarily waive his privilege."

"Trickery" was also at issue in *Moran v. Burbine,*[165] where the police assured the defendant's attorney that the defendant would not be questioned until the next day, but then proceeded to question the defendant about a murder, without telling him the attorney had called. The Court held, 6–3, that the fact that the police kept the defendant ignorant of his attorney's effort to reach him was irrelevant to whether the confessions

---

[159] According to one study, 45 percent of defendants given the warnings mistakenly believed that oral statements could not be used against them. Lawrence S. Leiken, *Police Interrogation in Colorado: The Implementation of* Miranda, 47 Denver L.J. 1, 15–16, 33 (1970).

[160] Compare *McDonald v. Lucas,* 677 F.2d 518 (5th Cir. 1982) (merely talking to police after refusing to sign a waiver is not, by itself, evidence of a course of conduct implying waiver).

[161] 459 U.S. 42, 103 S.Ct. 394 (1982).

[162] 479 U.S. 564, 107 S.Ct. 851 (1987).

[163] The Court stated that it need "not reach the question whether a waiver of *Miranda* rights would be valid in such a circumstance."

[164] See *Frazier v. Cupp,* 394 U.S. 731, 89 S.Ct. 1420 (1969), discussed in § 16.02(a)(1).

[165] 475 U.S. 412, 106 S.Ct. 1135 (1986).

were coerced. As Justice O'Connor pointed out for the Court, "the same defendant, armed with the same information and confronted with precisely the same police conduct, would have knowingly waived his *Miranda* rights had a lawyer not telephoned the police station to inquire about his status."[166] The purpose of *Miranda,* O'Connor emphasized, was to dissipate compulsion directed toward the defendant, not monitor how police treat the defendant's attorney.[167] The same term as *Burbine,* the Court vacated the judgments of two state courts excluding confessions made after counsel present at the stationhouse had been refused permission to see their clients.[168]

To help in understanding, if not justifying, the Court's decisions in this area, it may be useful to make a distinction between trickery as to the contents of the warnings and trickery as to other aspects of the case. If the police lead a guilty defendant to believe he has no right to remain silent or right to counsel, despite the warnings, then he is faced with the "trilemma" against which the Fifth Amendment is meant to protect; as far as the suspect is aware, he must either confess, lie, or face some penalty for remaining silent. On the other hand, if instead of leading the defendant to believe there is no point in remaining silent, the police fail to correct a misimpression about how to assert the right (as in *Butler* or *Barrett*), do not make clear how they plan to proceed (as in *Fields* or *Spring*), or fail to inform him of all possible facts relevant to his decision (as in *Burbine*), the trilemma is not resurrected. Any confession that occurs in the latter situations could be said to be "voluntary," even if not completely "knowing."[169]

(3) *The Voluntariness Requirement*

As the above discussion makes clear, separating the voluntariness component of waiver analysis from the knowing and intelligent component is somewhat artificial. The only point to be made here is that, just as physical force, threats, promises and prolonged, incommunicado questioning are prohibited under due process analysis, they are impermissible under *Miranda* after the warnings are given.[170] By the same token, as with due process analysis, if the police do not "cause" the confession through some sort of conduct, proof that it was not the product of "free and deliberate choice" because of the defendant's mental condition will be insufficient to show an "involuntary" waiver.[171]

An example of the Court's post-*Miranda* treatment of the voluntariness idea is found in *Fare v. Michael C.,*[172] where the Court held, 5–4, that a post-warning confession by a 16½-year-old was not involuntary. Justice Powell, in dissent, emphasized the Court's long tradition of solicitude toward juveniles,[173] and noted that the juvenile here "was immature, emotional, and uneducated, and therefore was likely to be vulnerable to the skillful, two-on-one, repetitive style of interrogation to which he was subjected." The

---

[166] The Court also found no violation of the Sixth Amendment right to counsel, since the interrogation took place before arraignment. See § 16.04(a).

[167] As to a possible due process claim against the police action, the Court held this too would fail, because the conduct of the police did not "shock the conscience."

[168] *Maryland v. Lodowski,* 475 U.S. 1078, 106 S.Ct. 1452 (1986); *Florida v. Haliburton,* 475 U.S. 1078, 106 S.Ct. 1452 (1986). Although these cases are similar in some respects to *Escobedo v. Illinois,* 378 U.S. 478, 84 S.Ct. 1758 (1964), discussed in § 16.02(c), Escobedo knew his attorney was trying to reach him and asked to see his attorney.

[169] William J. Stuntz, *Self-Incrimination and Excuse,* 88 Colum.L.Rev. 1227 (1988).

[170] See § 16.02(a) for a discussion of due process analysis.

[171] *Colorado v. Connelly,* 479 U.S. 157, 107 S.Ct. 515 (1986), discussed in § 16.02(a)(2).

[172] 442 U.S. 707, 99 S.Ct. 2560 (1979).

[173] See *Haley v. Ohio,* 332 U.S. 596, 68 S.Ct. 302 (1948), discussed in § 16.02(a)(2).

record also showed that the defendant had cried during the interrogation and had indicated on several occasions that he could not or would not answer the police's questions. But the majority concluded that the defendant understood his rights, especially in light of his extensive previous involvement with the criminal justice system, and that the officers did not prolong the questioning nor "intimidate or threaten respondent in any way."

(e) Waiver: After Assertion of Rights

When the defendant's reaction to the warnings is not an express or implied waiver of his rights but rather an assertion of them, the Supreme Court has developed special waiver rules, albeit different from those apparently intended by the *Miranda* Court. According to *Miranda:*

> If the individual indicates in any manner, at any time prior to or during questioning, that he wishes to remain silent, the interrogation must cease. . . . Without the right to cut off questioning, the setting of in-custody interrogation operates on the individual to overcome free choice in producing a statement after the privilege has been once invoked. If the individual states that he wants an attorney, the interrogation must cease until an attorney is present. . . . If the individual cannot obtain an attorney and he indicates that he wants one before speaking to police, they must respect his decision to remain silent. . . . If authorities conclude that they will not provide counsel during a reasonable period of time in which investigation in the field is carried out, they may refrain from doing so without violating the person's Fifth Amendment privilege so long as they do not question him during that time.

This passage strongly suggests that if a suspect states either that he wishes to remain silent or that he wants an attorney, questioning must cease and may not resume. While the post-*Miranda* Court has been unwilling to give this language its fullest reach, it has indicated that, as discussed further below, a suspect who invokes his right to counsel is entitled to special solicitude. When the suspect merely states he wishes to remain silent the appropriate waiver analysis is not as clear, but is also likely to make police efforts to resume questioning more difficult.

(1) Assertion of the Right to Remain Silent

The leading case on the latter issue is *Michigan v. Mosley,*[174] in which the Court permitted questioning after an assertion of the right to remain silent, but only under special circumstances. There, two hours after the defendant stated he did not want to talk, a different officer confronted him in a different room about another crime and gave him a second set of warnings, after which he gave incriminating statements. The Court held, 7–2, that, on these facts, the "right to cut off questioning" referred to in the above passage from *Miranda* had been "scrupulously honored." The majority was impressed with the facts that "the police here immediately ceased the interrogation, resumed questioning only after the passage of a significant period of time and the provision of a fresh set of warnings, and restricted the second interrogation to a crime that had not been a subject of the earlier interrogation."

---

[174] 423 U.S. 96, 96 S.Ct. 321 (1975).

The key issue after *Mosley* was whether later questioning on the *same* crime is permissible after an assertion of the right to remain silent.[175] Justice White, concurring in the decision, concluded that, at the least, new information further implicating the defendant for that crime could be communicated to him. But this type of recurring confrontation might tend to "wear down" the defendant in the manner feared by the *Miranda* majority, which expressly noted that references to the strength of the evidence against the defendant should be seen as "interrogation."[176] On this view, the police should, at a minimum, refrain from such confrontation unless the defendant initiates the contact with the police.

Of course, the analysis in *Mosley* is not triggered if the suspect does not invoke the right to silence. In *Berghuis v. Thompkins*,[177] the Court held, consistent with its doctrine in connection with assertions of the right to counsel,[178] that the suspect must "unambiguously" assert the right. This requirement, the Court stated, provides a clear rule and avoids forcing police "to make difficult decisions about an accused's unclear intent," the same reasons it had given in support of its rule about asserting the right to counsel. But Justice Sotomayor's dissent contended that invocations of the right to silence are different from invocations of the right to counsel. While *Mosley* permits re-initiation of interrogation after assertion of the right to silence, the Court's right to counsel cases *prohibit* re-initiation after assertion of that right, unless the suspect indicates a desire to do so.[179] Thus, requiring police to clarify whether the suspect wants to talk in the face of an ambiguous assertion of the right to silence would not hinder police to the same extent as a clarification requirement in connection with the right to counsel, and would more adequately adhere to *Mosley's* stipulation that the right to silence be "scrupulously honored." Furthermore, Justice Sotomayor noted, *Miranda's* right to counsel warning specifically states that counsel will be provided the suspect "if he so desires," whereas *Miranda's* right to silence warning does not make clear how the right is to be asserted. Some suspects might believe that the right to silence is best exercised by remaining silent rather than saying anything.

(2) Assertion of the Right to Counsel

Assertions of the right to counsel are treated differently than assertions of the right to remain silent. The key difference is that, when the former right is asserted, police must not only stop questioning but may not reinitiate it unless the suspect indicates a desire to resume contact with the police. In *Edwards v. Arizona*,[180] the Court held that an accused, "having expressed his desire to deal with the police only through counsel, is not subject to further interrogation by the authorities until counsel has been made available to him, unless the accused himself initiates further communication, exchanges or conversation with the police." The defendant in *Edwards* told the officer who initially interrogated him that he wanted to see an attorney "before making a deal." The next day, two detectives arrived at Edwards' cell to question him further. When the detention

---

[175] In *Moran v. Burbine*, 475 U.S. 412, 106 S.Ct. 1135 (1986), the suspect invoked his right to remain silent and then was questioned again less than five hours later, apparently about the same crime the police had wanted to question him about during the first interrogation. Although the Court held the ensuing statements were admissible, it did not directly address the *Mosley* issue.

[176] See § 16.03(b)(1).

[177] 560 U.S. 370, 130 S.Ct. 2250 (2010).

[178] See § 16.03(e)(3).

[179] See § 16.03(e)(2).

[180] 451 U.S. 477, 101 S.Ct. 1880 (1981).

officer told Edwards about the detectives, he refused to talk to them. The officer told Edwards he "had" to talk to them, and took him to meet the detectives. After receiving *Miranda* warnings from the detectives, Edwards implicated himself on robbery and murder charges. The Court held that, on these facts, Edwards had not validly waived his Fifth Amendment right to counsel; the police interrogation had not taken place "at his suggestion or request."

Edwards raises three issues: (1) when has the defendant asserted his right to counsel, thus triggering *Edwards?;* (2) what protection does *Edwards* afford after such an assertion and prior to any initiation of contact by the defendant?; and (3) what is initiation and how does it affect subsequent waiver analysis?

(3) How Rights Must Be Asserted

The Court has established that *Edwards* is not triggered unless: (a) the *suspect*; (b) requests *counsel*; (c) during *interrogation*; (d) in an *unequivocal* fashion. Relevant to the first point is *Moran v. Burbine*.[181] There, the police assured the suspect's attorney they would not question her client until the next morning. They then proceeded to question the suspect without telling him about his attorney's call. The Court held that *Edwards* was not implicated because the suspect had been given the warnings and voluntarily signed a form indicating he did not want to talk to an attorney. The fact that a third party had, unbeknownst to Burbine, invoked his right to counsel was irrelevant.

A request for someone other than counsel is also unlikely to trigger *Edwards'* protection. In *Fare v. Michael C.*,[182] the suspect, a juvenile, asked for assistance from his probation officer. The Court found, 5–4, that this request was not an invocation of the right to counsel. The majority stated that *Miranda's* right to counsel is "based on the unique role the lawyer plays in the adversary system of criminal justice in this country." A probation officer is not legally trained nor trained in advocacy, nor is he obligated to keep confidences as is an attorney; moreover, he is an employee of the state who, at the least, would be subject to conflicting pressure at a police-conducted interrogation. The majority rejected the dissenters' contention that a request for a probation officer "constitutes both an attempt to obtain advice and a general invocation of the right to silence." Although *Fare* preceded *Edwards,* it is obviously relevant to the application of that case. Whether the Court would reach the same result when a parent or minister is requested remains open.

In *McNeil v. Wisconsin,*[183] the Court further constricted the *Edwards* rule by holding that it is not triggered unless the defendant requests an attorney during *interrogation.* In *McNeil,* the defendant appeared with an attorney at a bail hearing on robbery charges. Later the police approached him regarding a murder. After receiving *Miranda* warnings, the defendant agreed to talk about the murder and made statements linking him to it. He subsequently sought to exclude these statements on the ground that his request for an attorney at the hearing triggered the *Edwards* rule, thus barring the police's unsolicited interrogation about the murder. But the Supreme Court held, 6–3, that *Edwards* "requires, at a minimum, some statement that can reasonably be construed to be expression of a desire for the assistance of an attorney *in dealing with custodial interrogation by the police* (emphasis in original)," and that requesting the

---

[181]   475 U.S. 412, 106 S.Ct. 1135 (1986).
[182]   442 U.S. 707, 99 S.Ct. 2560 (1979).
[183]   501 U.S. 171, 111 S.Ct. 2204 (1991).

assistance of an attorney at a bail hearing did not constitute such an expression. According to the Court, *Edwards* was designed to prevent badgering of defendants who have expressed an unwillingness to talk to police in the absence of counsel, a situation not present on the facts of *McNeil*.

A final issue with respect to invoking the right to counsel is how clear the invocation must be. In *Smith v. Illinois,*[184] the Court divided 6–3 over whether *Edwards* had been invoked. After the defendant in *Smith* was given the first two *Miranda* warnings and had indicated that he understood them, the following colloquy took place:

Q.   You have a right to consult with a lawyer and to have a lawyer present with you when you're being questioned. Do you understand that?

A.   Uh, yeah. I'd like to do that.

Q.   Okay. . . . If you want a lawyer and you're unable to pay for one a lawyer will be appointed to represent you free of cost, do you understand that?

A.   Okay.

Q.   Do you wish to talk to me at this time without a lawyer being present?

A.   Yeah and no, uh, I don't know what's what, really.

Q.   Well. You either have to talk to me this time without a lawyer being present and if you do agree to talk with me without a lawyer being present you can stop at any time you want to.

A.   All right. I'll talk to you.

The defendant subsequently made incriminating statements which were used to convict him.

The Illinois Supreme Court held that Smith's statements after his statement, "I'd like to do that" were ambiguous with respect to his desire for an attorney and that therefore *Edwards* was not invoked and the defendant's confession could be admitted. The United States Supreme Court reversed, finding that "post-request responses to further interrogation may not be used to cast retrospective doubt on the clarity of the initial request itself."

However, in *Davis v. United States,*[185] the Court significantly undercut *Smith*. *Davis* held that, to trigger *Edwards*, a defendant "must articulate his desire to have counsel present sufficiently clearly that a reasonable police officer in the circumstances would understand the statement to be a request for an attorney." More importantly, it concluded that police need not ask clarifying questions when a request is equivocal, but may instead continue questioning until an unequivocal request is forthcoming. The five-member majority rejected Davis' argument that even an ambiguous request should immediately end questioning, "because it would needlessly prevent the police from questioning a suspect in the absence of counsel even if the suspect did not wish to have a lawyer present." Justice O'Connor's opinion went on to uphold the lower courts' conclusion that the statement Davis made during his interrogation, "Maybe I should talk to a lawyer," was not a cognizable request for a lawyer.

---

[184]   469 U.S. 91, 105 S.Ct. 490 (1984).

[185]   512 U.S. 452, 114 S.Ct. 2350 (1994).

Four justices concurred with the result because Davis had subsequently indicated he did not want a lawyer, but disagreed with the majority's resolution of the ambiguous request issue. In an opinion by Justice Souter, they argued that a better rule would be to bar government agents from further questioning "until they determine whether a suspect's ambiguous statement was meant as a request for counsel." Justice Souter noted that "individuals who feel intimidated or powerless are more likely to speak in equivocal or nonstandard terms when no ambiguity or equivocation is meant." Further, Souter pointed out, "[w]hen a suspect understands his (expressed) wishes to have been ignored . . . in contravention of the 'rights' just read to him by his interrogator, he may well see *further* objection as futile and confession (true or not) as the only way to end his interrogation." At the same time, the concurring justices agreed with the majority's rejection of Davis' position. Although recognizing that police might continue to badger a suspect even under his rule, Souter noted that ceasing questioning upon any statement about an attorney, as Davis advocated, would lead to a loss of voluntary confessions; in addition, Souter concluded, "the strong bias in favor of individual choice may . . . be disserved by stopping questioning when a suspect wants it to continue."

(4) Protection Afforded by Assertion of Right to Counsel

If the suspect does unequivocally request an attorney during interrogation, *Edwards* directs the police to refrain from questioning the suspect until an attorney arrives or the defendant initiates contact. Contrary to the rule when the right to remain silent is asserted, this prohibition applies even if the questioning concerns a different offense than the one for which the defendant is originally detained. In *Arizona v. Roberson*,[186] the defendant was arrested for burglary and given the warnings, at which point he stated that he wanted a lawyer "before answering any questions." Three days later, while still in custody and as yet without counsel, he was questioned by another officer about another burglary. Although he was given warnings before this second interrogation, the Court held that *Edwards* barred admission of the inculpatory statements he made at this point.

The state argued that *Roberson*'s request for counsel had been limited to provision of an attorney for the first burglary. To this the Court responded by noting that Roberson had refused to answer "any" questions; more generally, it held that "the presumption raised by a suspect's request for counsel—that he considers himself unable to deal with the pressures of custodial interrogation without legal assistance—does not disappear simply because the police have approached the suspect, still in custody, still without counsel, about a separate investigation." Thus, this case was different from *Mosley,* where the Court found that the defendant's assertion of the right to remain silent did not prohibit police from a second interrogation on a separate crime, because there the defendant had asserted *only* his right to remain silent, not signaled an inability to proceed without a lawyer's advice. The state also argued that when the police are pursuing truly independent investigations, the chance that the defendant will feel coerced by the second interrogation is more remote than on the *Edwards* facts. But the Court did not agree, "especially in a case such as this, in which a period of three days elapsed between the unsatisfied request for counsel and the interrogation about a second offense."

---

[186]   486 U.S. 675, 108 S.Ct. 2093 (1988).

The Court has also made clear that, once an attorney is requested (and assuming no reinitiation of contact by the defendant), mere consultation with the attorney prior to questioning is insufficient under *Edwards;* according to *Minnick v. Mississippi,*[187] the attorney must be present during the questioning. In *Minnick,* the defendant, after answering some questions during interrogation, stopped the interview by stating, "Come back Monday when I have a lawyer." Counsel was then appointed and consulted with the defendant on three separate occasions. On Monday, the police returned and, without the attorney, the defendant made statements later used at trial. The Supreme Court, in an opinion by Justice Kennedy, held that the statements should have been excluded because interrogation took place in the absence of counsel. According to the Court, "[a] single consultation with an attorney does not remove the suspect from persistent attempts by officials to persuade him to waive his rights, or from the coercive pressures that accompany custody and that may increase as custody is prolonged." The Court was unwilling to endorse a rule that would make the protection afforded by *Edwards* dependent upon the defendant resignalling his desire for an attorney after every consultation with one, especially since defining "consultation" might prove difficult.

However, if there is a "break in custody" that lasts at least two weeks after the invocation of the right to counsel, police may unilaterally re-initiate contact, assuming the contact is prefaced by warnings. This was the rule announced in *Maryland v. Shatzer,*[188] where the Court reasoned that if a suspect has "returned to his normal life" for that period of time, his willingness to talk to police (after warnings are re-given) is not likely to be coerced. Rather, Justice Scalia wrote for the majority, after two weeks "[h]is change of heart is . . . likely attributable to the fact that further deliberation in familiar surroundings has caused him to believe (rightly or wrongly) that cooperating with the investigation is in his interest." Admitting that setting such a precise time limitation was somewhat unusual, Scalia pointed out that the Court had adopted time limitations in other situations,[189] and that *Edwards* was itself a court-made prophylactic rule. The Court also held that a break in custody can occur even in prison (in *Shatzer,* the suspect had been in prison for two and a half years after the invocation), so long as the suspect is housed with the general prison population. In this situation, suspects "are not isolated with their accusers" and the "interrogator has no power to increase the duration of incarceration."

(5) *Initiation and Waiver*

Roberson and *Minnick* combined indicate that once an attorney's presence at interrogation is requested, no unsolicited questioning may take place in the absence of counsel, even about separate offenses and even if a new set of warnings are given. But *Shatzer* limited this protection to two weeks if there is a break in custody. And even during this two week period, *Edwards* permits questioning to resume if the defendant initiates contact with the police after his request for an attorney.

A plurality of the Court has indicated that it takes very little to "initiate" contact for purposes of *Edwards.* In *Oregon v. Bradshaw,*[190] the defendant was given the *Miranda* warnings while being questioned in a homicide case and again after being

---

[187] 498 U.S. 146, 111 S.Ct. 486 (1990).

[188] 559 U.S. 98, 130 S.Ct. 1213 (2010).

[189] See *County of Riverside v. McLaughlin,* 500 U.S. 44, 111 S.Ct. 1661 (1991), discussed in § 20.02(c).

[190] 462 U.S. 1039, 103 S.Ct. 2830 (1983).

arrested on a related charge. After denying guilt on both charges, he asked for his attorney. While being transferred to jail, and in the absence of his attorney, he asked an officer, "[w]ell, what is going to happen to me now?" The officer advised him that they did not have to talk; the defendant said he understood. The officer then described the charge against the defendant. He also suggested that the defendant take a polygraph test, which the defendant did, after again being given his *Miranda* rights. When the polygraph examiner told the defendant he did not believe the defendant's story, the defendant admitted his guilt. Justice Rehnquist, writing for the plurality of four justices, admitted the ambiguity of the defendant's initial question, but concluded that it "evinced a willingness and a desire for a generalized discussion about the investigation; it was not merely a necessary inquiry arising out of the incidents of the custodial relationship." He gave as examples of the latter type of communication requests for water or access to a telephone. Here, on the other hand, the question "could reasonably have been interpreted by the officer as relating generally to the investigation." The four dissenters seem much closer to the mark with their conclusion "that respondent's only 'desire' was to find out where the police were going to take him."

Both the plurality and the dissent in *Bradshaw* agreed that a finding that initiation has occurred does not end the analysis under *Edwards*.[191] It must still be decided whether, in the totality of the circumstances, including the fact of initiation, the suspect voluntarily and intelligently waived his rights. This question feeds back into the general waiver analysis discussed earlier. On this issue, the plurality and the four dissenters once again disagreed. But Justice Powell joined the plurality in holding that Bradshaw's post-initiation actions constituted a valid waiver.

16.04   The Resurgence of the Sixth Amendment Approach

The holding in *Massiah v. United States*[192]—that police may not deliberately elicit information from an indicted defendant in the absence of counsel—lay dormant for over a decade. During that period, the Supreme Court and the lower courts virtually ignored the Sixth Amendment perspective endorsed in that case, focusing instead on the application of *Miranda*. But then, in *Brewer v. Williams*[193] and subsequent cases, the Supreme Court reaffirmed the continuing significance of *Massiah* and even seemed to expand its scope.

In *Williams*, the defendant was suspected of killing a 10 year-old girl. Before the defendant was to be taken by police officers to another city, the defendant's lawyers advised him not to make any statements during the trip and extracted a promise from the police that they would not question the defendant during the journey. Nonetheless, during the trip, a detective who knew that Williams was a former mental patient and deeply religious suggested that the girl deserved a "Christian burial." Addressing the defendant as "Reverend," the detective mentioned the possibility that an upcoming snow storm would make it difficult to locate the girl's body unless the defendant assisted police in finding it soon. He then said: "I do not want you to answer me. I don't want to discuss it further. Just think about it as we're riding down the road." Later during the ride the defendant made incriminating statements and directed police to the body.

---

[191]   Justice Powell, in concurrence, felt that separating the initiation and waiver issues would confuse the lower courts; as noted below, he voted with the plurality on the ground that a valid waiver occurred.

[192]   377 U.S. 201, 84 S.Ct. 1199 (1964), discussed in § 16.02(c).

[193]   430 U.S. 387, 97 S.Ct. 1232 (1977).

The Court, in a 5–4 decision by Justice Stewart, reversed the defendant's subsequent conviction. The detective had "deliberately and designedly set out to elicit information from Williams just as surely as—and perhaps more effectively than—if he had formally interrogated him," yet had not told Williams of his right to have counsel present and "made no effort at all to ascertain whether Williams wished to relinquish that right." Thus, Williams had been denied his right to counsel and the state had failed to sustain its burden of showing that he had waived his constitutional protection.

In dissent, Justice White, joined by Justices Blackmun and Rehnquist, argued that Williams' revelations had been spontaneous and that, even if they had not been, there was no evidence of coercion by the police. The "Christian burial speech" had been "accompanied by a request that respondent not respond to it; and it was delivered hours before respondent decided to make any statement. Respondent's waiver was thus knowing and intentional."

The most important aspect of *Williams* is the analytical basis of the decision. Although the same result could have been reached under *Miranda* (at least had the Court been willing to announce the *Edwards* rule four years ahead of time), neither the majority nor the dissent discussed the applicability of that case. Instead, the focus in *Williams* was entirely on the Sixth Amendment. While there were obvious differences among members of the Court as to whether "deliberate elicitation" had taken place and a valid waiver had occurred, only Chief Justice Burger, who wrote a separate dissenting opinion, appeared to question the necessity of the original *Massiah* ruling. Several issues must be resolved under the rejuvenated *Massiah* doctrine: (1) at what point in the criminal process is the Sixth Amendment right to counsel triggered?; (2) when has the government engaged in "deliberate elicitation;"? and (3) when is such elicitation permissible because the defendant has waived his Sixth Amendment right?

(a) The Initiation of Criminal Prosecution

Massiah is based on the Sixth Amendment's guarantee of counsel in "all criminal prosecutions." Because the case involved an indicted defendant, lower court decisions interpreting *Massiah* initially defined prosecution as beginning with an indictment.[194] However, eight years after *Massiah,* in *Kirby v. Illinois,*[195] the Supreme Court established that the Sixth Amendment is implicated whenever the "adverse positions of the government and defendant have solidified" so that "a defendant finds himself faced with the prosecutorial forces of organized society, and immersed in the intricacies of substantive and procedural criminal law." Quoting from *Kirby,* the Court in *Williams* held that the *Massiah* right is triggered by any event which indicates that the government has committed itself to prosecute, "whether by way of formal charge, preliminary hearing, indictment, information, or arraignment." In *Rothgery v. Gillespie Cty., Texas,*[196] the Court stated even more explicitly that a finding of probable cause made at an initial appearance in front of a judicial officer can also trigger the right to counsel, even if formal charges have not yet been brought by the prosecutor.[197] In *Williams* itself, no indictment had been issued but the defendant had been arraigned on an arrest warrant; this was enough for the Court.

---

[194] See *United States ex rel. Forella v. Follette,* 405 F.2d 680 (2d Cir. 1969).

[195] 406 U.S. 682, 92 S.Ct. 1877 (1972).

[196] 554 U.S. 191, 128 S.Ct. 2578 (2008), discussed further in § 31.03(a)(3).

[197] See § 20.02 for a discussion of the initial appearance.

Before charging, however, *Massiah* is not applicable. Thus, the mere fact that the defendant has an attorney is not dispositive. In *Moran v. Burbine,*[198] the Court discounted "the fortuity of whether the suspect or his family happens to have retained counsel." Rather, the important question is whether "the government's role [has] shift[ed] from investigation to accusation." In *Burbine,* police interference with the attorney's attempts to see her client did not violate the Sixth Amendment because no charges had yet been brought. A similar result was reached in *Maine v. Moulton,*[199] where a surreptitious investigation of the defendant (obviously undertaken in the absence of counsel), revealed evidence of two crimes, only one of which had been formally charged at the time. The Court excluded evidence pertaining to the crime for which the defendant had been indicted, but admitted evidence concerning the crime for which no formal proceedings had begun. According to the majority, "to exclude evidence pertaining to charges as to which the Sixth Amendment right to counsel had not attached at the time the evidence was obtained, simply because other charges were pending at that time, would unnecessarily frustrate the public's interest in the investigation of criminal activities."[200]

It may seem somewhat artificial to use formal charging as the demarcation for the Sixth Amendment right. But that stage in the process serves as the best proxy for determining when a suspect needs an attorney's "assistance" in a "criminal prosecution." Before that point, an attorney is useful primarily to combat police compulsion, a need that *Miranda* is designed to meet. It is after that point that the special qualifications of counsel are most likely to be called upon in confrontations with the government.

This point seemed to be ignored by the Court in *Texas v. Cobb,*[201] where the defendant was indicted for burglary. Over a year after counsel was appointed to defend him on that charge, he confessed, under questioning preceded by *Miranda* warnings, to murdering the woman and child who had lived in the burglarized home and had disappeared at the time the burglary occurred. Cobb argued that this confession should be excluded because it was factually related to the burglary charge, about which interrogation was clearly barred because of his request for counsel at arraignment for that crime. Five members of the Court disagreed. Chief Justice Rehnquist reasoned for the majority that whether offenses are the same for Sixth Amendment purposes should be governed by the *Blockburger* test used to determine when offenses are the same for double jeopardy purposes.[202] Under that test, offenses are not the same if they each include an element the other does not. Because burglary requires proof of theft and murder requires proof of death, the two offenses involved in *Cobb* were clearly not the same under this test and the indictment on the burglary charge did not trigger Sixth Amendment protection for the murder charge.

In dissent, Justice Breyer pointed out that the majority's rule allows police to ignore the Sixth Amendment right to counsel when questioning about a given crime "through the simple device of asking questions about any other related crime not actually charged

---

[198]   475 U.S. 412, 106 S.Ct. 1135 (1986).

[199]   474 U.S. 159, 106 S.Ct. 477 (1985).

[200]   See also, *Hoffa v. United States,* 385 U.S. 293, 87 S.Ct. 408 (1966) (Sixth Amendment not violated where undercover work concerned charges unrelated to those on which defendant was tried); *McNeil v. Wisconsin,* 501 U.S. 171, 111 S.Ct. 2204 (1991), discussed in § 16.03(e)(3).

[201]   532 U.S. 162, 121 S.Ct. 1335 (2001).

[202]   See § 30.04(a)(2) for a discussion of the *Blockburger* test, announced in *Blockburger v. United States,* 284 U.S. 299, 52 S.Ct. 180 (1932).

in the indictment." He noted that both *Moulton* (which involved questioning on a burglary charge and theft charges, at a time when Moulton had only been charged with theft) and *Williams* (which involved questioning that led to murder charges, at a time when Williams had only been charged with child abduction) would have come out differently under the majority's test. He also pointed out that the factual relation test proposed by Cobb and used by many lower courts prior to *Cobb* relies on commonsense to a much greater extent than the *Blockburger* test, and thus was more likely to be effectively applied by police. In response to these points the majority emphasized that suspects in Cobb's position still must receive *Miranda* warnings prior to questioning and that the dissent's approach would negate "society's interest in the ability of police to talk to witnesses and suspects, even those who have been charged with other offenses." Neither of these comments address the dissent's concerns. Nor do they deal with the underlying purpose of the Sixth Amendment in ensuring representation of those subject to prosecution. Suspects should be entitled to expect that a request for counsel during interrogation extends Sixth Amendment protection to *all* offenses against which that counsel is likely to be defending.[203]

(b) Deliberate Elicitation

The phrase "deliberate elicitation," found in both *Massiah* and *Williams,* suggests that the Sixth Amendment is implicated by any government attempt, after formal charging, to get information from the defendant in the absence of counsel. In *United States v. Henry,*[204] the Court reinforced this notion by referring to whether officers "intentionally create[ed] a situation likely to induce Henry to make incriminating statements without the assistance of counsel." There, the incriminating evidence was obtained by one Nichols, an inmate at the jail in which Henry was confined. Government agents working on a robbery case had approached Nichols shortly after Henry was incarcerated and told him to be alert to any statements Henry might make about the robbery. However, they also cautioned Nichols not to initiate any conversation with Henry regarding the crime. Despite this last caveat, the Court found that the officers had "created a situation likely to induce" incriminating statements. It noted that Nichols had been a paid government informant for over a year, that the government agent who contacted Nichols had known he would be able to engage Henry in conversation, and that Nichols had incentive to encourage conversation because he knew he would be paid only if he produced useful information.

However, when the government merely "plants" an informant in the same cell as the defendant, deliberate elicitation does not occur, the Court concluded in *Kuhlmann v. Wilson.*[205] Whereas in *Henry* the informant had "stimulated" conversations with the defendant, in *Kuhlmann* the informant asked no questions concerning the pending charges and, in the words of the state court, "only listened" to the defendant's "spontaneous" and "unsolicited" statements, which had been triggered by a meeting with his brother. The dissent argued that "elicitation" had occurred, as the informant had tried to develop a relationship with the defendant, responded to his initial denial of guilt by saying his story "didn't sound too good," and, as in *Henry,* was paid for his efforts. In any event, *Kuhlmann* explicitly allows "passive" means of obtaining information from

---

[203] Cf. § 21.04(b), discussing joinder of charges.

[204] 447 U.S. 264, 100 S.Ct. 2183 (1980).

[205] 477 U.S. 436, 106 S.Ct. 2616 (1986).

uncounseled defendants. After that decision, electronic bugs positioned in a jail cell clearly would not violate the Sixth Amendment.

The "deliberate elicitation" concept introduced in *Massiah,* as refined in later cases, appears to differ in two ways from the "custodial interrogation" which triggers Fifth Amendment analysis. First, as *Henry* and *Kuhlmann* indicate, it does not require custody; questioning by undercover agents who exert no "compulsion," as that term is used in Fifth Amendment cases, may still implicate the Sixth Amendment. Second, even when a person is in custody, police conduct that would not be interrogation may nonetheless constitute deliberate elicitation. A comparison of the facts and results of *Williams* and *Rhode Island v. Innis,*[206] makes the point: the "Christian burial speech" in the former case was enough to implicate the Sixth Amendment, but *Innis* refused to find that the police comments made there—about the danger posed by a hidden weapon, in the presence of a similarly suggestible defendant—amounted to interrogation. The distinction between Fifth and Sixth Amendment analysis is also illustrated by *Fellers v. United States,*[207] where police conversed with an indicted defendant in his home for about 15 minutes, politely but without giving him warnings. Although the defendant was probably not in custody on these facts, a unanimous Court excluded his statements, reiterating the point it had made in *Innis* and other cases that the deliberate elicitation standard is to be "distinguished" from the "Fifth Amendment custodial-interrogation standard."[208]

These differences are explicable if one considers the differing purposes of the Fifth and Sixth Amendments. The privilege against self-incrimination is meant to protect against state compulsion, while the Sixth Amendment, *inter alia,* is meant to prevent state interference with the attorney-client relationship.[209] Thus, at the least, government attempts to induce statements after the right to counsel attaches should implicate the latter Amendment, even if the "inherent coercion" of custodial interrogation is not present. Indeed, an argument can be made that *any* "elicitation" requirement unduly narrows Sixth Amendment protection because, as *Kuhlmann* illustrates, police attempts to avoid having to deal with a counseled defendant can involve "passive" as well as "active" techniques.

(c) Waiver

Williams recognized that the Sixth Amendment right to counsel may be waived in the absence of counsel but, as in *Miranda,* required that the waiver be knowing, intelligent and voluntary. Of course, in "undercover cases" like *Henry* and *Kuhlmann,* a "knowing" waiver is impossible; the focus in these cases is entirely on whether there has been deliberate elicitation. But in cases like *Williams,* where the suspect is aware he is dealing with the police, a knowing waiver can occur. Some language in *Williams* suggested that waiver would be harder to show in this setting than under *Miranda.* In particular, the *Williams* Court at one point stated that the "strict standard" associated

---

[206] 446 U.S. 291, 100 S.Ct. 1682 (1980), discussed in § 16.03(b)(1).

[207] 540 U.S. 519, 124 S.Ct. 1019 (2004).

[208] The Court remanded the case for an admissibility determination concerning a second set of incriminating statements made by the defendant, at the stationhouse after he had received *Miranda* warnings. The lower courts had held that these latter statements were admissible under *Oregon v. Elstad,* see § 16.05(c), but the Supreme Court intimated that *Elstad,* a Fifth Amendment case, might not apply in the Sixth Amendment context.

[209] See § 32.04(a)(3).

with waiver of trial counsel should also apply to a waiver during questioning that takes place after the Sixth Amendment attaches.[210] But a complete differentiation between the Fifth and Sixth Amendment rights to counsel has not come to pass.

Thus, in *Patterson v. Illinois*,[211] the Court held that, when a suspect does not yet have counsel, the analysis for determining whether a Sixth Amendment waiver has occurred mimics Fifth Amendment analysis. According to *Patterson,* the stringent waiver of counsel standard adopted at trial is not apposite during pretrial questioning by the police "because the full 'dangers and disadvantages of self-representation' during questioning are less substantial and more obvious to an accused than they are at trial." Further, "[b]ecause the role of counsel at questioning is relatively simple and limited, we see no problem in having a waiver procedure at that stage which is likewise simple and limited." Accordingly, when the defendant does not yet have an attorney, administration of the *Miranda* warnings and a waiver satisfactory for purposes of *Miranda* are also sufficient for Sixth Amendment purposes.

Fifth and Sixth Amendment waiver analysis also merge when a suspect requests counsel. In *Michigan v. Jackson*,[212] the Court held that the *Edwards* rule—providing that under the Fifth Amendment police must stop questioning a defendant who asserts his right to counsel but may renew questioning if the defendant initiates contact with the police—also applies in the Sixth Amendment context. *Jackson* did recognize one difference between the two contexts: In a Sixth Amendment case, the request for counsel triggering *Edwards'* protection may occur at arraignment as well as during. But in *Montejo v. Louisiana*,[213] a majority of five reversed this aspect of *Jackson.* Justice Scalia's opinion rejected the dissent's assertion (quoting from *Patterson*) that "once an accused has a lawyer, a distinct set of constitutional safeguards aimed at preserving the sanctity of the attorney-client relationship take effect." Rather, Scalia retorted, the interest to be protected is the same in both contexts: prevention of police badgering of defendants who state they need counsel's assistance *during interrogation*.

Despite the outcome and rationale of *Montejo*, there may still be a few differences between Fifth and Sixth Amendment waiver analysis (other than the obvious one that the Sixth Amendment applies to post-charge undercover cases like *Massiah* while the Fifth Amendment does not). In *Patterson*, the Court noted that, whereas police efforts to prevent attorney access to a client do not violate the Fifth Amendment,[214] they would violate the Sixth Amendment once it has attached. *Patterson* may also mean that, in contrast to waiver of the Fifth Amendment right to counsel, waiver of Sixth Amendment counsel, once he has been appointed, must be explicit.[215]

Arguably, *Patterson* did not go far enough. As suggested above, the further a case moves in the criminal process, the more complicated it becomes. Immediately after arrest, the police are usually interested only in getting information about the alleged crime. After arraignment the government is more likely to want to engage in quasi-plea bargaining and other legally technical matters. Under such circumstances, it is more

---

[210] For a discussion of the waiver of trial counsel standard, see § 31.04(b).

[211] 487 U.S. 285, 108 S.Ct. 2389 (1988).

[212] 475 U.S. 625, 106 S.Ct. 1404 (1986).

[213] 556 U.S. 778, 129 S.Ct. 2079 (2009).

[214] See *Moran v. Burbine*, 475 U.S. 412, 106 S.Ct. 1135 (1986), discussed in § 16.03(d)(2).

[215] *People v. Kidd,* 129 Ill.2d 432, 136 Ill.Dec. 18, 544 N.E.2d 704 (1989). Compare to cases discussed in § 16.03(d)(1).

difficult for the defendant to understand what he is giving up by talking. A rule that prohibited waiver after the defendant is formally charged, whether or not he has counsel, would make some sense from this perspective.[216]

16.05   Confessions and the Exclusionary Rule

As in the Fourth Amendment context, the fact that police conduct was unconstitutional under *Miranda, Massiah* or due process analysis does not automatically lead to exclusion of evidence obtained by that conduct.[217] The three most significant issues relating to the exclusionary rule as applied to confessions are the scope of the standing requirement, use of illegally obtained evidence for impeachment purposes, and the scope of the derivative evidence, or fruit of the poisonous tree, rule.

(a)   Standing

As a general proposition, a person may not exclude evidence obtained in violation of another person's rights.[218] Moreover, the Supreme Court has specifically held that the Fifth Amendment privilege against self-incrimination, upon which *Miranda* is based, is a personal right.[219] Thus, courts have held that one person cannot exclude, on Fifth Amendment grounds, the confession of another or evidence derived from it, even if that confession was obtained in flagrant violation of *Miranda*.[220] There is little reason to think the same analysis would not hold true if a confession were obtained in violation of the Sixth Amendment or the Due Process Clause; when a third party's rights are at issue, the defendant has no standing to claim they were violated.[221]

Two very narrow constitutional limitations on the use of such third party evidence may remain. First, the Confrontation Clause prohibits use of a person's statements against a defendant who does not have the opportunity to cross-examine the declarant before or during trial (a scenario which most commonly occurs when the declarant is a co-defendant who has "taken the Fifth" at trial).[222] Thus, a third party's confession may occasionally be inadmissible against the defendant on Sixth Amendment confrontation grounds. Second, a confession which is the product of coercion so intense that it is likely to be "untrustworthy" may be inadmissible in anyone's trial.[223] But this rule only bars use of the confession itself; fruit of the confession is likely to have independent indicia of reliability.

---

[216] See discussion of New York's approach in § 16.02(e)(2).

[217] This is true even though the Fifth Amendment, by prohibiting compulsion of testimony, arguably contains its own exclusionary rule, whereas the Fourth Amendment and Due Process Clause do not. See generally, Arnold Loewy, *Police-Obtained Evidence and the Constitution: Distinguishing Unconstitutionally Obtained Evidence from Unconstitutionally Used Evidence*, 87 Mich.L.Rev. 907 (1989).

[218] *Tileston v. Ullman,* 318 U.S. 44, 63 S.Ct. 493 (1943).

[219] *Couch v. United States,* 409 U.S. 322, 93 S.Ct. 611 (1973), discussed in § 15.05.

[220] *People v. Varnum,* 66 Cal.2d 808, 59 Cal.Rptr. 108, 427 P.2d 772 (1967), appeal dism'd 390 U.S. 529, 88 S.Ct. 1208 (1968).

[221] However, Loewy, supra note 217, has argued that, because the due process clause is a "substantive right" mean to deter illegalities against all people (whereas the Fifth and Sixth Amendments are procedural rights personal to the defendant) third party standing should exist in due process cases.

[222] See *Bruton v. United States,* 391 U.S. 123, 88 S.Ct. 1620 (1968), discussed in § 28.04(d).

[223] Cf. *Harris v. New York,* 401 U.S. 222, 91 S.Ct. 643 (1971), discussed in § 16.05(b)(1).

(b) The Impeachment Exception

Miranda's only reference to use of illegally obtained statements on cross-examination occurred in its discussion of "exculpatory statements." The Court noted that because such statements are often used to "impeach" trial testimony, they "may not be used without the full warnings and effective waiver required for any other statement." *Miranda* thus appeared to hold that a confession obtained in violation of its rules should be rendered inadmissible for any purpose. But in subsequent decisions the Court has rejected this interpretation in favor of one that permits use of confessions which are "voluntary," in the due process sense, to challenge statements made by the defendant at trial, even if obtained in contravention of *Miranda*.

(1) Use of Statements

Harris v. New York[224] was the first case to carve an exception out of *Miranda's* total exclusion policy. In *Harris*, the defendant denied in court that he had made a sale of heroin to an undercover agent. On cross examination he was asked if he had made certain statements following his arrest that were inconsistent with this testimony. Although the prosecution conceded that the proffered statements were obtained in violation of *Miranda*, the trial judge instructed the jury that they could be considered in passing on the defendant's credibility. The Supreme Court agreed that confessions obtained in violation of *Miranda's* warnings requirements, but otherwise voluntary, may be used to impeach the testimony of a defendant who takes the stand. It rejected as dicta any language in *Miranda* suggesting otherwise. The primary rationale for the decision was the belief that the privilege against self-incrimination should not "be construed to include the right to commit perjury." Further, the Court noted that the police were unlikely to violate *Miranda* in reliance on its decision: "sufficient deterrence flows when the evidence in question is made unavailable to the prosecution in its case in chief."

The same could not be said in support of the Court's decision in *Oregon v. Hass*,[225] in which the police violated *Miranda* by continuing to question the defendant after he had requested his attorney. As the dissent pointed out, unless statements made in response to such questioning are excluded for any purpose, police have every incentive to continue questioning a person who has asked for counsel; although any statements thereby obtained cannot be used in the case-in-chief, they may still be used to impeach.[226] However, the seven member majority was more worried, as it had been in *Harris*, that barring this evidence for all purposes would pervert the shield provided by *Miranda* "to a license to testify inconsistently, or even perjuriously, free from the risk of confrontation with prior inconsistent utterances." The Court stressed the importance of "the search for truth in a criminal case," and found that since there was no evidence of coercion in this case, the statements should be admitted to further the truth-finding function of criminal adjudication.

However, it is also important to emphasize that the decisions allowing confessions to be used for impeachment purposes apply only when the confession is voluntary under the totality of the circumstances. The state may not use a confession that is "involuntary"

---

[224] 401 U.S. 222, 91 S.Ct. 643 (1971).

[225] 420 U.S. 714, 95 S.Ct. 1215 (1975).

[226] The dissent's criticism is diminished, though only minimally, by the fact that, after *Hass* the Court decided *Edwards v. Arizona*, 451 U.S. 477, 101 S.Ct. 1880 (1981), discussed in § 16.03(e)(2), which held that police may resume questioning of a defendant who invokes the right to counsel *if* he initiates contact.

in the due process sense for any purpose, even if it may be reliable and expose perjury. The Supreme Court has made this clear on at least two occasions. In *New Jersey v. Portash*,[227] the state argued that *Harris* permits the use of immunized testimony to impeach a witness. The Court disagreed, noting that statements given in response to a grant of legislative immunity are "the essence of coerced testimony." The witness is told simply to testify or face a conviction for contempt. Since this situation invokes "the constitutional privilege against compulsory self-incrimination in its most pristine form," any balancing of the need to deter unsavory police practices and the need to prevent perjury is "impermissible." The Court came to a similar conclusion in *Mincey v. Arizona*.[228] In *Mincey,* the defendant was hospitalized and barely able to speak when the police questioned him, on several different occasions and despite his requests for an attorney. The state's use of inculpatory statements he made during this questioning were found inadmissible for any purpose, despite his receipt of *Miranda* warnings.

The same rule—allowing use of illegally obtained statements for impeachment unless they are the result of physical coercion—applies when the statements sought are obtained in violation of the Sixth Amendment. In *Michigan v. Harvey*,[229] two police officers violated *Michigan v. Jackson's* prohibition on questioning after a request for counsel by reinitiating contact with the defendant in his jail cell.[230] The Court held, 5–4, that the statements could be used for impeachment purposes, although it left open the possibility that post-charge statements that are not the product of a knowing waiver (such as those obtained by an informant or jailhouse snitch rather than officers who identify themselves to the defendant) would be inadmissible for impeachment purposes.

Nineteen years later, in *Kansas v. Ventris*,[231] the latter possibility was foreclosed. Justice Scalia, writing for seven members of the Court, conceded that the "core" of the Sixth, like the core of the Fifth Amendment, is a "trial right." He also conceded that *Massiah*, which involved statements made to an informant, had indicated that the Sixth Amendment right is violated when an improperly obtained pretrial statement is "used" at trial, which strongly suggested that such statements should not be admissible even for impeachment purposes. But Justice Scalia countered that it is "illogical to say that the right is not violated until trial counsel's task of opposing conviction has been undermined by the statement's admission into evidence;" the defendant still enjoys the assistance of counsel at trial. Instead, Scalia asserted, the real violation occurs when police badger defendants during interrogation. To prevent that type of illegality, exclusion is only necessary when its benefits outweigh its costs. Relying on the same reasoning it had in *Havens* and *Harris*, the Court concluded that statements obtained in violation of *Jackson* may, if voluntarily made, be used to impeach defendants who have taken the stand even when they are deceived about the identity of their questioners.

Justice Stevens' dissent in *Ventris* argued that failing to prevent impeachment use of such statements "compound[s]" the infringement on the right to pretrial counsel because trial counsel "may be unable to effectively counter the potentially devastating, and potentially false, evidence subsequently introduced." He also asserted that the Court's opinion would promote "shabby tactics" by police; presumably here he had in

---

[227] 440 U.S. 450, 99 S.Ct. 1292 (1979).

[228] 437 U.S. 385, 98 S.Ct. 2408 (1978), discussed in § 16.02(a)(2).

[229] 494 U.S. 344, 110 S.Ct. 1176 (1990).

[230] 475 U.S. 625, 106 S.Ct. 1404 (1986), discussed in § 16.04(c).

[231] 556 U.S. 586, 129 S.Ct. 1841 (2009).

mind the possibility that police may now conclude that, once the right to counsel is asserted during interrogation, they have nothing to lose by getting their informants to continue asking questions in the hopes of at least obtaining impeachment evidence. But the majority in *Ventris* emphasized that *Massiah's* rule is only "prophylactic," meaning that it provides protection beyond what is required by the Sixth Amendment. This holding thus equates *Massiah* with *Miranda*, which the Court has also held is a prophylactic rule that provides protection beyond the core of the Fifth Amendment.[232] Because, according to the current Court, prophylactic rules are not dictated by the Constitution, they can be subject to cost-benefit analysis, and the Court rarely finds that the benefit of excluding probative evidence exceeds its cost.

(2) Use of Silence

A different line of cases concerns use of the defendant's silence for impeachment purposes. In *Doyle v. Ohio*,[233] the defendants, who were given *Miranda* warnings after their arrest, took the stand and told an exculpatory story that they had not previously told the police or the prosecutor. Over their counsel's objection, they were asked on cross-examination why they had not given the arresting officer their explanations. The defendant's post-arrest "silence" on this issue would seem to be "voluntary," and therefore admissible for impeachment purposes under *Harris* and *Hass*. But, relying on a due process fairness notion rather than the Fifth Amendment, the Court held that a suspect's post-arrest silence is "insolubly ambiguous" once he has been assured by the *Miranda* warnings that silence will carry no penalty, and thus it is not admissible for the purpose of impugning the suspect's credibility. Similarly, in *Wainwright v. Greenfield*,[234] the Court found unconstitutional a prosecutor's closing argument that the defendant's repeated post-warning refusals to answer questions without first consulting an attorney demonstrated a degree of comprehension inconsistent with the defendant's insanity plea at trial. Efforts to prove the defendant's mental state at the time of arrest must be made without reference to the invocation of rights he has been expressly told he has.[235]

On the other hand, if the defendant *talks* after the warnings, the prosecutor may ask the defendant why he didn't tell his current, trial story to the police instead of the one he did tell them after his arrest. According to the Court in *Anderson v. Charles*,[236] such questioning at trial "makes no unfair use of silence because a defendant who voluntarily speaks after receiving *Miranda* warnings has not been induced to remain silent." Further, if the suspect is silent *before* receiving his *Miranda* warnings, that silence may be used against him. In *Jenkins v. Anderson*,[237] the Court so held, on the ground that such a defendant has not yet been told that he has a right to remain silent and thus his silence is less ambiguous than after such a warning has been given. Whether such silence is sufficiently probative on the issue of the defendant's credibility during his trial testimony is solely a matter of state law. In *Jenkins*, for instance, the

---

[232] See § 16.05(c).

[233] 426 U.S. 610, 96 S.Ct. 2240 (1976).

[234] 474 U.S. 284, 106 S.Ct. 634 (1986).

[235] However, if a prosecutor's question about post-warning silence is followed by a sustained objection and an instruction to disregard the question, no *Doyle* violation occurs. *Greer v. Miller*, 483 U.S. 756, 107 S.Ct. 3102 (1987).

[236] 447 U.S. 404, 100 S.Ct. 2180 (1980).

[237] 447 U.S. 231, 100 S.Ct. 2124 (1980).

Court held that the fact that the defendant waited two weeks to report his commission of a homicide could be used to impeach his self-defense testimony if, under state evidentiary law, such pre-arrest "silence" is considered relevant. It stressed that, since Jenkins had not been in contact with police prior to the time he confessed, his silence was not in response to any warning received from the police.[238]

The Court carried the analysis in *Jenkins* one step further in *Salinas v. Texas*.[239] Salinas voluntarily agreed to be interviewed at the police station about a murder; it was stipulated he was not in custody at the time. During the hour-long interview, Salinas answered most of the police's questions, but when asked about whether his shotgun would match the shells found at the crime scene he looked down at the floor and remained silent for a few moments. At Salinas' trial, Salinas did not take the stand, but the prosecutor nonetheless used this reaction in his *case-in-chief*. Three members of the Court, in an opinion by Justice Alito, held that because Salinas did not formally invoke the Fifth Amendment privilege, his silence could be used against him. The Court distinguished this situation from a number of cases in which no invocation is required, either because the invocation would serve no purpose (as in *Griffin v. California*,[240] which held that the defendant has an absolute right to avoid testifying at trial, regardless of his reasons for refusing) or where assertion of the right would be costly (as in cases where assertion of the right triggers civil or criminal penalties[241]). Salinas argued that silence itself is an invocation, especially when police have reason to suspect an answer to their question might be incriminating. But the plurality reasoned that something more is required, because courts need to know the reason for the silence (e.g., incrimination, embarrassment, protection of a third party) in order to determine whether the Fifth Amendment applies. The opinion analogized to a number of cases consistent with this holding, including *Berghuis v. Thompkins*,[242] which requires an unequivocal assertion of the right to silence in order to trigger its protections after warnings are given.[243] Finally, the plurality rejected the argument that unschooled interviewees will, in the absence of an attorney, be unlikely to know how to assert the privilege or think that they do not need to do so, and left open whether variations on "I want to assert the Fifth Amendment" will suffice.

Justice Thomas, in an opinion joined by Justice Scalia, agreed that Salinas' silence could be used in the prosecution's case-in-chief, but solely on the ground that *Griffin v. California* was wrongly decided. His view was that, as a matter of Fifth Amendment law, silence can always be used against a defendant, whether it occurs prior to custody, during custodial interrogation, or during trial, because fear of such use does not amount to the compulsion barred by that Amendment.

As a result of this lineup of the Court's members, the rule appears to be that pre-custody silence that is not preceded by an invocation may be used at trial for any purpose, at least as far as the Constitution is concerned. However, as noted earlier, evidentiary rules may bar use of such silence when its ambiguity reduces its probative value. For the

---

[238] See also, *Fletcher v. Weir*, 455 U.S. 603, 102 S.Ct. 1309 (1982).

[239] 570 U.S. 178, 133 S.Ct. 2174 (2013).

[240] 380 U.S. 609, 85 S.Ct. 1229 (1965), discussed in § 15.02(c).

[241] See §§ 15.02(b) & (c).

[242] 560 U.S. 370, 130 S.Ct. 2250 (2010), discussed in § 16.03(e)(1).

[243] See also *Roberts v. United States*, 445 U.S. 552, 100 S.Ct. 1358 (1980) (requiring invocation of the right to avoid use of incriminating information at sentencing); *Hoffman v. United States*, 341 U.S. 479, 71 S.Ct. 814 (1951), discussed in § 15.03(c).

same reason, *Salinas* does not disturb *Doyle's* holding that, as a matter of due process, silence that occurs *after Miranda* warnings may not be used either in the case-in-chief or to impeach.

Finally, implicit in the opinion of the three-member plurality is the assumption that the Fifth Amendment applies to pre-custody situations, a view with which the four-member dissent clearly agrees. Thus, while an individual in Salinas' situation must invoke the right to avoid use of silence, that invocation presumably cannot be used against him. According to Justice Breyer's dissent, a better approach would be to prohibit use of pre-custodial silence if one can "fairly infer from an individual's silence and surrounding circumstances an exercise of the Fifth Amendment's privilege." But Justice Thomas' approach seems preferable to either of these rules in this context. While his rejection of *Griffin's* prohibition on the use of silence at trial may go too far, he is closer to the mark in his assertion that, when an individual is not in custody, fear that silence will be used at a later trial is not compulsion for Fifth Amendment purposes.

Doyle was also at issue in *South Dakota v. Neville,*[244] where the defendant was stopped for drunk driving. He was told that he could refuse a blood alcohol test but that, if he did so, he would lose his license. The Court first held that the defendant had no right to refuse to take the test under the Fourth or Fifth Amendments because it was "safe, painless and commonplace," and did not compel testimonial evidence.[245] It then rejected his next argument: that the Due Process Clause, as construed in *Doyle,* prevented use of his refusal to take the test at trial because, just as *Miranda* warnings indicate that silence may not be used, he had, in effect, been told it would not be used (by virtue of the fact that the police had only mentioned loss of license as an adverse consequence). The Court found it "unrealistic" that the defendant believed his refusal was otherwise harmless: "[i]mportantly, the warning that he could lose his driver's license made it clear that refusing the test was not a 'safe harbor,' free of adverse consequences."

(c) Derivative Evidence

The admissibility of evidence obtained as a result of an arrest made in violation of the Fourth Amendment is judged under so-called "fruit of the poisonous tree" analysis.[246] But when the illegality is an improperly obtained confession, the Supreme Court has been reluctant to apply its "fruits" doctrine. Instead, similar to its treatment of the impeachment issue, it has held that a violation of *Miranda,* not rising to a due process-type violation, will generally not lead to exclusion of subsequently obtained evidence, even if that evidence was clearly derived from the violation. Only evidence that results from "due process level" coercion will be excluded under the Fifth Amendment. Whether the same restrictive rule will apply to violations of the Sixth Amendment remains unclear.

The Court's first explicit indication that it would treat "poisonous" confessions differently from "poisonous" searches came in 1947, in *United States v. Bayer.*[247] There

---

[244]   459 U.S. 553, 103 S.Ct. 916 (1983).

[245]   See § 15.04 for further discussion of the testimonial evidence requirement.

[246]   See § 2.04 for a discussion of the doctrine in the Fourth Amendment setting.

[247]   331 U.S. 532, 67 S.Ct. 1394 (1947). A still earlier decision, *Lyons v. Oklahoma,* 322 U.S. 596, 64 S.Ct. 1208 (1944), presaged *Bayer* in holding that the admissibility of a subsequent confession depended on whether it was "voluntary." Fruits doctrine was not mentioned.

the Court stated that its Fourth Amendment fruit of the poisonous tree cases "did not control" the admissibility of evidence derived from an illegally obtained confession because the latter involves a "quite different category" of evidence. In *Michigan v. Tucker,*[248] the Court intimated that its intervening decision in *Miranda* had not changed this position. *Miranda* had stated that "no evidence obtained as a result of interrogation [conducted in violation of *Miranda*] can be used against [the defendant]." But *Tucker* treated this language as dictum. In *Tucker,* a suspect was arrested for rape and questioned without being told of his right to counsel. During the interrogation he stated that he had been with a friend during the time of the crime. The police later obtained incriminating information from the friend. Although this information was clearly derived from the illegally conducted interrogation, the Court stated that "[t]he police conduct at issue here did not abridge respondent's constitutional privilege against compulsory self-incrimination, but departed only from the prophylactic standards later laid down by this Court in *Miranda* to safeguard this privilege." The Court thus saw no reason to exclude the friend's statement.

Tucker was of limited force, however, because the interrogation in that case took place before *Miranda* was decided; accordingly, the decision could be seen as an effort to avoid penalizing good faith actions by the police who were following practice considered acceptable at that time. But in *Oregon v. Elstad,*[249] the Court made clear that it would continue to treat *Miranda* as a "prophylactic rule," at least for most types of derivative evidence. According to *Elstad, Miranda* created a "presumption of compulsion" which is irrebuttable when the state seeks to introduce unwarned statements in its case-in-chief, but which may be rebutted when the state's objective is to introduce evidence derived from the statements.[250] Such a rebuttal is accomplished if the prosecution can show that the police conduct leading to discovery of the evidence was not "coercive," which the majority defined as action constituting "physical violence or other deliberate means calculated to break the suspect's will."

Evidence derived from a violation of *Massiah, Jackson* and other cases implementing the Sixth Amendment are likely also admissible under *Elstad*-type reasoning. In *Kansas v. Ventris,*[251] the Court made clear that the rules established in these cases, like the rules developed in *Miranda* and its progeny, are "prophylactic" and thus only require exclusion when exclusion's deterrent effect outweighs its costs. Accordingly, while evidence directly obtained from violation of one of these rules will be excluded, evidence that has a more tenuous connection to the illegality will often be admissible. The discussion below examines the admissibility of three different types of evidence—other statements, witness identities, and physical evidence—when they are indirectly derived from *Miranda, Massiah*, or due process violations.

(1) Other Confessions

In *Elstad*, the police interrogated the defendant and obtained an incriminating statement from him after they had arrested him in his home. The defendant received no warnings, however, until he arrived at the stationhouse. After he was warned, he signed

---

[248]   417 U.S. 433, 94 S.Ct. 2357 (1974).

[249]   470 U.S. 298, 105 S.Ct. 1285 (1985).

[250]   The Court noted that the same analysis also explained its impeachment decisions, discussed in § 16.05(b).

[251]   556 U.S. 586, 129 S.Ct. 1841 (2009).

a written confession. The Oregon Court of Appeals concluded that because of the brief period separating the defendant's initial, unwarned statement and his subsequent confession, the "cat was sufficiently out of the bag to exert a coercive impact" on the defendant and render his second confession inadmissible. In other words, the court felt that the defendant's second confession may well have resulted from his inaccurate conclusion that his first confession could be used against him and that thus no further harm could come from making further incriminating statements. In a 6–3 decision written by Justice O'Connor, the Court reversed the Oregon court, finding it "an unwarranted extension of *Miranda* to hold that a simple failure to administer the warnings, unaccompanied by any actual coercion or other circumstances calculated to undermine the suspect's ability to exercise his free will so taints the investigatory process that a subsequent voluntary and informed waiver is ineffective for some indeterminate period." Here, the psychological pressure exerted by the previous confession on the decision to make the second confession was "speculative and attenuated at best."

As Justice Brennan pointed out in dissent, there is little to distinguish what occurred in *Elstad* from the typical Fourth Amendment "fruit" case in which only a short period of time and *Miranda* warnings separate an illegal *arrest* and a signed confession.[252] If anything, an arrest would seem to exert less of an impact on subsequent behavior by the defendant than would a confession. Yet, he noted, the Court has refused to presume that a post-warning confession obtained after arrest is "sufficiently an act of free will to purge the primary taint of the unlawful invasion."[253] Brennan argued that derivative evidence analysis in Fifth Amendment cases should be governed by considerations similar to those applied in the Fourth Amendment area. In successive confession cases such as *Elstad,* the relevant criteria should be the second confession's proximity in time and place to the first confession, intervening factors such as consultation with friends or a lawyer, and the purpose and flagrancy of the police misconduct resulting in the first confession.

Another factor Brennan thought should be considered in deciding whether a subsequent confession should be admissible is whether the suspect was told his earlier statements might not be admissible. The majority had held that it would be too burdensome to require such a warning, given the "murky and difficult" state of Fifth Amendment jurisprudence. But Brennan disagreed, because "the vast majority of confrontations implicating this question involve obvious *Miranda* violations." To Justice Brennan's point can be added the observation that *Miranda* warnings must be given at some point if *any* statements are to be admissible; surely it is not that difficult to tell the suspect, after these warnings are read to him, that if similar warnings were not given him prior to his last statements, those statements may not be admissible. If police are not required to do so, there is little to inhibit them from pursuing improper questioning prior to every "formal" interrogation in an effort to create "momentum" toward a usable confession.

Nonetheless, the *Elstad* majority insisted that the admissibility of statements by the defendant after an improper interrogation has taken place should depend solely upon whether they are considered "voluntary" in light of "the surrounding circumstances and the entire course of police conduct with respect to the suspect." "Highly probative" to this

---

[252] See § 2.04(b)(1).

[253] *Wong Sun v. United States,* 371 U.S. 471, 83 S.Ct. 407 (1963).

analysis is whether such statements were preceded by warnings. Given the Court's pronouncement that the "cat's out of the bag" rationale is "speculative and attenuated," the police can thus insulate most confessions from the poison of previous *Miranda* violations simply by giving the *Miranda* warnings. The *Elstad* majority did make favorable reference to *Westover v. United States*,[254] one of the cases decided with *Miranda*. *Westover* had held inadmissible a confession made after warnings were given because prior to the warnings the accused had been subjected to intermittent interrogations over a fourteen hour period, none of which was preceded by warnings. But the more typical case today will involve a much shorter pre-warning interrogation period which is unlikely to render "coerced", in the due process sense, any statements made after the warnings.

In *Missouri v. Seibert*,[255] the Court carved an exception out of *Elstad*, the precise scope of which is not entirely clear given the lineup of the Justices. In *Seibert*, an officer intentionally refrained from warning a suspect before questioning her about whether she had burned down her house knowing someone was inside. Once she confessed to the crime he gave her a short break, administered *Miranda* warnings, and then got her to repeat her confession, using her previous statements to prod her when she hesitated to admit she knew the house had been occupied at the time of the arson. The officer later testified he deliberately followed this procedure in the belief, endorsed by his department and many police training programs around the country,[256] that the second statement would be admissible under *Elstad*. Nonetheless, a four-member plurality of the Court, in an opinion by Justice Souter, concluded that the second statement was inadmissible. The officer's procedure, Souter stated, was designed "to render *Miranda* warnings ineffective by waiting for a particularly opportune time to give them, after the suspect has already confessed." The plurality distinguished this situation, where the second interrogation immediately followed the first and occurred in the same location, from *Elstad*, where "a reasonable person in the suspect's shoes could have seen the station house questioning as a new and distinct experience, [and] the *Miranda* warnings could have made sense as presenting a genuine choice whether to follow up on the earlier admission."

The four dissenting justices, in an opinion written by *Elstad's* author, Justice O'Connor, saw no distinction between the two cases because *Elstad* had declared the cat-out-of-the bag phenomenon at work in *Seibert* constitutionally irrelevant.[257] Because of the 4–4 split between the plurality and the dissent, Justice Kennedy's concurrence appears to provide the governing opinion.[258] Kennedy agreed with the plurality that the officer had used the two-step interrogation technique "in a calculated way to undermine the *Miranda* warning," and thus concluded that the second confession had to be suppressed. But he also stated that when the two-step procedure is not "deliberate," or if "curative measures" are taken (such as taking a "substantial break in time and circumstances" between the two interrogations or providing a warning that the pre-warning statement is inadmissible), the second statement should be admissible. The

---

[254] For the lower court opinion, see 342 F.2d 684 (9th Cir. 1965).

[255] 542 U.S. 600, 124 S.Ct. 2601 (2004).

[256] See generally, Charles Weisselberg, *Saving* Miranda, 84 Cornell L. Rev. 109, 110, 132–39 (1998).

[257] Consistent with this point of view, in *Bobby v. Dixon*, 565 U.S. 23, 132 S.Ct. 26 (2011), the Court suggested that when the suspect does not confess during the first interrogation and nothing said during the first interrogation is used to obtain an admission in the second interrogation, *Seibert's* rule does not apply.

[258] See *Marks v. United States*, 430 U.S. 188, 97 S.Ct. 990 (1977).

problem with accepting this rule as the Court's holding is that an inquiry into whether the procedure was deliberate calls for a subjective inquiry into the questioner's state of mind, which both the plurality and dissent rejected on pragmatic grounds.

(2) Witnesses

In speaking of *Tucker*, *Elstad* stressed the conclusion in that decision that the officer's conduct—which led to discovery of a witness against the defendant—involved no "actual compulsion." Thus, this type of derivative evidence will usually be admissible as well, so long as the interrogation that results in the discovery of a witness is not designed to "break the suspect's will." Even in the latter situation, exclusion may not be mandated if Fourth Amendment cases are any guide. When the witness' identity is discovered through an illegal search, the Court has been reluctant to hold that witnesses are "tainted" by police conduct, given the fact that witnesses, unlike tangible evidence, can make themselves known to police, thus making it more likely they would have been discovered in any event.[259]

When the testimony "discovered" is from the defendant himself, an earlier case may have created a limited exception to the *Tucker-Elstad* rule. In *Harrison v. United States*,[260] the government introduced three confessions, improperly obtained under the now defunct *McNabb-Mallory* rule,[261] at the defendant's first trial. The defendant then took the stand and made an admission of guilt. After reversal of the conviction based on the unlawfulness of the admitted confessions, a new trial took place at which the prosecutor read into evidence the admission made during the first trial. The Supreme Court noted that, had the three confessions not been admitted, the defendant might not have testified at all at the first trial, and in any event probably would not have admitted guilt. Thus, stated the Court, the admission was "fruit of the poisonous tree."

Despite this language, *Harrison* may not diverge from *Elstad's* reasoning. Although confessions obtained in violation of the *McNabb-Mallory* rule are not necessarily the result of efforts to break the suspect's will, the *Harrison* Court emphasized that the "fruit" of those confessions—the defendant's testimony—was itself "impelled" by the tactical situation in which the defendant found himself. Thus, consistent with *Elstad*, *Harrison* could be read to hold that a defendant's testimony is not inadmissible "fruit" of an improperly obtained confession unless its use somehow "coerces" him to testify.

(3) Physical Evidence

When the "fruit" of the illegally obtained confession is tangible evidence rather than another confession or testimony from a witness, exclusion is even less likely. In *United States v. Patane*,[262] the Supreme Court held that a gun obtained as a result of questioning an unwarned suspect was admissible. Five members of the Court rejected the argument that Fourth Amendment fruits analysis should apply when tangible evidence is discovered through a *Miranda* violation. Rather the majority reiterated *Elstad's* holding that *Miranda* merely creates a presumption of coercion, and thus its effect on criminal prosecutions should be kept as narrow as possible. The majority added

---

[259] *United States v. Ceccolini*, 435 U.S. 268, 98 S.Ct. 1054 (1978), discussed in § 2.04(b)(2).

[260] 392 U.S. 219, 88 S.Ct. 2008 (1968).

[261] See § 16.02(b) for a discussion of this rule.

[262] 542 U.S. 630, 124 S.Ct. 2620 (2004).

that *Dickerson v. United States*,[263] which had reaffirmed *Miranda's* constitutional status after *Elstad*, did not require a rethinking of this proposition; rather by describing the "core" of *Miranda* as a rule that unwarned statements are inadmissible, that case had emphasized that "the closest possible fit be maintained between the Self-Incrimination Clause and any rule designed to protect it."

Three members of the Court, in an opinion by Justice Thomas, went further, stating that the Fifth Amendment is only violated when unwarned statements are introduced at trial, not when police fail to give warnings.[264] Thus, they argued, fruit of the poisonous tree analysis, designed to deter constitutional violations, is inapposite; "there is, with respect to mere failures to warn, nothing [unconstitutional] to deter," and thus exclusion of anything other than the statements is not mandated. In a concurrence, Justices O'Connor and Kennedy, found this "trial-right" characterization of *Miranda* to be unnecessary to reach the Court's result. O'Connor's opinion did contend, however, that the case for admissibility here was even stronger than in *Elstad* and *Tucker*, because tangible evidence is "nontestimonial" and thus not governed by the Fifth Amendment's prohibition of compelled testimony.[265]

The four dissenters pointed out that, in contrast to exclusion that would have the effect of preventing a defendant's impeachment,[266] exclusion in a case like *Patane* would not "handicap the traditional truth-testing devices of the adversary process." The dissent was even more concerned that *Patane* would provide an inducement for police to ignore *Miranda* in the hopes of obtaining physical evidence. Yet in the subsequent case of *Wisconsin v. Knapp*,[267] the Court cited *Patane* in vacating a judgment excluding such evidence, despite a substantial showing that *Miranda* was purposely violated to facilitate its discovery, a ruling indicating that the Court is unconcerned about deterrence of *Miranda* violations in this context. Following *Elstad*, *Patane* and *Knapp* then, the only situation in which physical evidence derived from a confession might be inadmissible is when the confession is obtained through "actual coercion or other circumstances calculated to undermine the suspect's ability to exercise his free will." Even then, if Justice Thomas' or Justice O'Connor's rationale wins the day, that exclusion will have to occur on due process grounds, given the Fifth Amendment's focus on preventing trial use of testimonial evidence.

The Court has also indicated that the inevitable discovery exception to the fruit of the poisonous tree doctrine, which is routinely applied in Fourth Amendment cases, applies as well when the poisonous fruit is an illegally obtained statement. Indeed, the Court first endorsed the inevitable discovery exception in a case involving a pretrial Sixth Amendment violation. In *Nix v. Williams*,[268] the Court held that the body of a murder victim was admissible even though it was found as a result of statements obtained in violation of *Massiah* because, at the time the statements were made, a search party was nearing the area in which the body was located. The exception applies when the government can show by a preponderance of the evidence that physical evidence

---

[263] 530 U.S. 428, 120 S.Ct. 2326 (2000), discussed in § 16.02(e).

[264] For further discussion of this theory of the Fifth Amendment, see § 16.02(d)(3).

[265] See § 15.04 for a discussion of the definition of "testimonial" evidence under the Fifth Amendment.

[266] See § 16.05(b).

[267] 542 U.S. 952, 124 S.Ct. 2932 (2004).

[268] 467 U.S. 431, 104 S.Ct. 2501 (1984).

obtained as a result of illegally obtained statements would have been discovered through legitimate means independent of the illegality.[269]

16.06   Assessing the Admissibility and Credibility of a Confession

From the foregoing, it should be obvious that despite the *Miranda* Court's efforts to construct an easily applied rule that does not require case-by-case analysis, judging the admissibility of a confession will often be a difficult endeavor. This section discusses the procedures for determining the admissibility issue. It also addresses the evidentiary rules governing assessment of a confession's credibility once it has been found admissible.

(a) The Decisionmaker

Before *Miranda*, when the validity of confessions was analyzed under the Due Process Clause, at least three different procedures were devised for determining whether a confession was voluntarily made. Two of these procedures are still in use today. In states following the so-called orthodox rule, the trial judge alone determines the issue of voluntariness. Under the Massachusetts rule, the trial judge makes an independent judgment regarding voluntariness, but if he concludes that the confession was voluntary, the jury may reconsider the issue and conclude otherwise. Before 1964, many states, including New York, followed a third procedure under which the question of voluntariness of the confession was put to the jury unless the trial judge in a preliminary determination found that under no circumstances could the confession be deemed voluntary.

In *Jackson v. Denno*,[270] decided in that year, the Supreme Court found this latter procedure unconstitutional. The trial court in *Jackson* had submitted the issue of voluntariness to the jury in accordance with state practice. The jury members were instructed to disregard the confession if they found it was involuntary, but if they found it voluntary they were to determine its truth or reliability and weigh it accordingly. In rejecting this procedure, the Supreme Court held that the admissibility of a confession must be decided prior to its submission to the jury. Under the New York procedure, the Court observed, prejudice could result in two ways. First, the jury could impermissibly base its decision regarding the voluntariness of the confession on its assessment of its truthfulness. Second, even if the jury found the confession involuntary, it might be unable to disregard it in determining guilt.

In a footnote, the Court indicated that the trial judge, another judge, or another jury may make the voluntariness decision; only the jury that decides guilt or innocence may not do so. Although not required in most states, the Court's reasoning in *Jackson* suggests that the same practice should govern admissibility determinations in bench trials. At least when he finds a confession involuntary, a judge should refrain from trying the case; knowing the defendant has confessed is likely to affect his deliberations no matter how involuntary the confession.

The orthodox rule and the Massachusetts rule survived the Court's holding in *Jackson*. However, now that *Miranda* and *Massiah* have for the most part replaced the totality of the circumstances test with technical legal rules, a good argument can be made

---

[269]   For further discussion of the inevitable discovery exception, see § 2.04(d).

[270]   378 U.S. 368, 84 S.Ct. 1774 (1964).

that the Massachusetts approach, which allows the legally unsophisticated jury to make the "admissibility" decision a second time after the judge's determination, is not appropriate. Given the complexity of modern confessions law, the best procedure is the judge-based orthodox rule, which is followed in the federal courts.[271]

Even under the orthodox rule, the jury is prohibited only from *making* the ultimate admissibility decision, not from *hearing* the evidence which is relevant to that decision. In *Pinto v. Pierce*,[272] for instance, the trial judge permitted the jury to be present during a voluntariness hearing and then ruled the confession admissible. The Supreme Court held that because the defendant didn't object to this procedure and because the confession was ruled admissible in any event, the jury's verdict should stand. So limited, *Pinto* may be unobjectionable. But had the confession been ruled inadmissible, the same type of prejudice concerns which led to the Court's holding in *Jackson* should have required reversal. In many jurisdictions, juries are forbidden to hear evidence presented in a voluntariness hearing for this reason.[273]

(b) Burden and Standard of Proof

It seems clear that, whether a claim about a confession is based on the Due Process Clause, *Miranda* or the Sixth Amendment, the burden is on the government to show that no violation occurred. In *Miranda*, for instance, the Court spoke of the "heavy burden" on the prosecution of demonstrating the validity of any waiver of *Miranda* rights. If the burden is on the state in these cases, then it is presumably on the government when the defendant makes a due process or Sixth Amendment claim—claims the current Court takes even more seriously.

The more controversial issue has been the standard of proof imposed on the government. *Miranda's* statement that the burden is a "heavy" one suggested that the government should have to show a confession was invalid beyond a reasonable doubt. But in *Lego v. Twomey*,[274] the Court held that the prosecution need only prove voluntariness under the Due Process Clause by a preponderance of the evidence. And in *Colorado v. Connelly*,[275] the Court found that the same standard applies to *Miranda* claims as well, on the ground that if "the voluntariness of a confession need be established only by a preponderance of the evidence, than a waiver of the auxiliary protections established in *Miranda* should require no higher burden of proof."

Lego in particular is questionable, since an involuntary confession may also be unreliable, yet, if given to the jury (under the Massachusetts procedure), still prove highly persuasive. In response to this argument, the *Lego* Court simply stated that, while the reasonable doubt standard "is necessary . . . to ensure against unjust convictions by giving substance to the presumption of innocence[, a] guilty verdict is not rendered any less reliable . . . simply because the admissibility of a confession is determined by a less stringent standard." Given this reasoning, the government's burden on a Sixth Amendment claim is probably also a preponderance of the evidence.

---

[271] 18 U.S.C.A. § 3501(a).

[272] 389 U.S. 31, 88 S.Ct. 192 (1967).

[273] See, e.g., Fed.R.Evid. 104(c).

[274] 404 U.S. 477, 92 S.Ct. 619 (1972).

[275] 479 U.S. 157, 107 S.Ct. 515 (1986).

Relevant to the government's burden with respect to proving the admissibility of confessions is the common law rule that an uncorroborated confession, even if voluntary, is not sufficient to support a conviction. In most jurisdictions, unless the government produces independent proof of the *corpus delicti* (i.e., proof that the criminal act occurred), the confession is not admissible.[276] As *Miranda* noted, the judge must be careful not to let this independent evidence influence the ultimate determination of the confession's admissibility.

(c) Challenging the Confession at Trial

Assuming a confession is found to be admissible, the defendant may still attack its *reliability* at trial. In both *Jackson* and *Lego* the Court made clear that its decision in *Jackson* was not meant to undercut the defendant's prerogative to challenge the confession's credibility once found admissible. In *Crane v. Kentucky*,[277] the Court conferred constitutional status on the rule that testimony calling into question a confession's reliability is not limited to the initial voluntariness determination but may also be presented at trial if the confession is found voluntary. Left unresolved by *Crane*, however, is what type of testimony is permitted. Some jurisdictions will allow the defendant to attack a confession's reliability by presenting to the trial jury all of the evidence adduced at the voluntariness hearing, so that the jury can make an independent judgment of the weight to be accorded to the confession;[278] other jurisdictions only permit the jury to hear "controverted testimony" (that is, evidence that was challenged during the hearing).[279]

Of course, the defendant can also decide to take the stand and try to convince the jury that his confession was involuntary. Doing so might entail the risk of questioning about other issues. But most jurisdictions, in an effort to prevent undue inhibition of defendants seeking to impeach their confession, either directly forbid prosecution questions on matters collateral to the voluntariness issue,[280] or enforce the so-called "American" (or federal) rule pertaining to the scope of cross-examination, which generally restricts cross-examination to subjects covered on direct examination and to matters affecting credibility.[281] Thus, if the defendant's testimony on direct addresses only the circumstances surrounding his confession, the prosecution may not question him about the alleged offense itself.

16.07 Conclusion

The original *Miranda* doctrine has been substantially eroded by decisions limiting the situations to which it applies and the extent to which it need be enforced by an exclusionary policy. But despite these inroads, or perhaps because of them, the

---

[276] McCormick on Evidence § 145 (4th ed. 1992).

[277] 476 U.S. 683, 106 S.Ct. 2142 (1986).

[278] See, e.g., *People v. Carroll,* 4 Cal.App.3d 52, 84 Cal.Rptr. 60 (Ct.App. 1970); *Karl v. Commonwealth,* 288 S.W.2d 628 (Ky. 1956). Note that this procedure does not permit the jury to address the admissibility question, as does the Massachusetts rule, see § 16.06(a), but only the reliability issue.

[279] See, e.g., *Malone v. State,* 452 So.2d 1386 (Ala.Crim.App. 1984); *Taylor v. State,* 337 So.2d 1368 (Ala.App. 1976).

[280] *Calloway v. Wainwright,* 409 F.2d 59 (5th Cir. 1968) (applying Florida law), cert. denied 395 U.S. 909, 89 S.Ct. 1752 (1969); *State v. Lovett,* 345 So.2d 1139 (La. 1977); *Washington v. Commonwealth,* 214 Va. 737, 204 S.E.2d 266 (1974).

[281] Fed.R.Evid. 611(b); cf. *Tucker v. United States,* 5 F.2d 818 (8th Cir. 1925) (breach of American rule held to violate privilege against self-incrimination). See generally McCormick on Evidence § 21 (4th ed. 1992).

prophylactic core of *Miranda* is firmly ensconced, as the Court's reaffirmation of *Miranda* in *Dickerson v. United States* indicates. While more recent Court decisions have harkened back to the case-by-case approach associated with the Due Process Clause, a full retreat to the law of voluntariness is unlikely.

As the jurisprudence of confessions stands today:

(1)   Disclosures made to the police before an individual is in "custody" or that are not the product of "interrogation" are admissible for any purpose, at least under the Fifth Amendment. Custody occurs when an individual is placed under arrest or in any similar way is significantly restrained by law enforcement officials and is more likely when the suspect is a juvenile. But *Miranda's* requirements are not triggered by a *Terry* stop or simply because the suspect is in the stationhouse (at least when the suspect agrees to come there). Interrogation includes not only express questioning but also any words or actions on the part of the police other than those normally attendant to arrest and custody that the police should know are reasonably likely to elicit an incriminating response from the suspect. Under this definition, interrogation does not include questions asked as part of a legitimate police procedure, such as booking or a field test, that are not intended to elicit information for investigatory purposes. Moreover, interrogation must involve coercion beyond that inherent in custody itself. Thus, the Court has held that questioning by an undercover agent, even if it occurs in prison, is not interrogation, nor are comments to other officers about the possible harms undiscovered weapons might cause.

(2)   Disclosures made in response to custodial interrogation are not admissible in the prosecution's case-in-chief for any criminal offense unless (a) they are preceded by warnings, or the fully effective equivalent of warnings, telling the suspect he has the right to remain silent, that anything he says may be used against him, that he has the right to an attorney before and during police questioning, and that an attorney will be appointed for him if he cannot afford one; or unless (b) they result from questioning triggered by exigent circumstances suggesting an objective threat to police or public safety. *De minimis* variations from the warnings are permitted, even if they obfuscate when state-paid counsel will be provided. Warnings about the subject matter of the interrogation, the right to cut off questioning, or the fact that post-warning silence may not be used against the defendant need not be given.

(3)   Disclosures made after receipt of the warnings are admissible in the prosecution's case-in-chief if they are the product of a valid waiver of the right to remain silent and the right to have an attorney present during questioning. Any statement or course of conduct indicating an understanding of one's rights and a willingness to talk to police will suffice as a valid waiver if it is voluntary given the totality of the circumstances. Relevant circumstances are the conduct of the police, including their use of physical or psychological pressure, and the age, education and intelligence of the suspect. Disclosures procured through use of physical violence and other deliberate means calculated to break the suspect's will are not the product of a valid waiver. On the other hand, statements that result from mere deception about police motivation or evidence in their possession are admissible, as are statements that are not "caused" by the police, even if they are "compelled" by the defendant's mental condition.

(4)   Custodial interrogation may not begin or, if begun, must end if the suspect *unequivocally* asserts the right to remain silent or requests an attorney during interrogation. However, police may reinitiate interrogation after an assertion of the right

to remain silent so long as they scrupulously honor the decision to stop the questioning, which probably requires no more than waiting a significant period of time before attempting any new interrogation and rewarning the person before this interrogation. Police may reinitiate interrogation after assertion of the right to an attorney when the suspect initiates further communication with the police by evincing a willingness and desire for a discussion about the investigation or confesses during an interrogation preceded by warnings that takes place more than two weeks after his assertion. In either case, the waiver must be voluntary as assessed in the totality of the circumstances.

(5)   Assuming the police do not use physical violence or other means calculated to break the suspect's will, the prosecution may introduce in its case-in-chief: (a) disclosures by the defendant prior to being taken into custody; (b) post-warning disclosures that the defendant makes as a result of previous disclosures obtained in violation of *Miranda*, unless the police acted in bad faith in obtaining the post-warning disclosures; (c) tangible evidence and witnesses discovered as a result of disclosures obtained in violation of *Miranda*, even if the police acted in bad faith. The prosecution may also use as impeachment evidence: (d) disclosures made after a request for an attorney and before the suspect's initiation of any further communication with the police, if they are otherwise voluntary; and (e) "silence" that is not the result of being informed of the right to remain silent, when silence is relevant under local evidentiary rules.

(6)   In a jury trial, the admissibility of a confession must initially be determined by a decisionmaker other than the jury itself. The government bears the burden of proving a confession is admissible by a preponderance of the evidence. The defendant has a due process right to challenge at trial the credibility of a confession found to be admissible.

(7)   Disclosures that are admissible under the above rules may nonetheless be inadmissible under the Sixth Amendment, if they: (a) occur in the absence of counsel; (b) are obtained after the initiation of adversary proceedings (e.g., arraignment, indictment or preliminary hearing); (c) concern the charge that triggers Sixth Amendment's protection or the "same offense," as defined under double jeopardy doctrine; (d) are deliberately elicited by police either directly or by intentionally creating a situation likely to induce incriminating statements; and (e) are not the product of a valid waiver. Waiver and exclusion rules under the Sixth Amendment are identical to those described in (3), (4) and (5)(d), except that a "knowing" waiver cannot be made if police do not tell a suspect of his attorney's attempts to contact him.

BIBLIOGRAPHY

Amar, Akhil Reed and Renee B. Lettow. Fifth Amendment First Principles: The Self-Incrimination Clause. 93 Mich. L.Rev. 857 (1995).

Brensike-Primus, Eve. The Future of Confession Law: Toward Rules for the Vountariness Test. 114 Michigan L.Rev. 1 (2015).

Caplan, Gerald. Questioning *Miranda*. 38 Vand.L.Rev. 1417 (1985).

Cassell, Paul G. Protecting the Innocent from False Confessions and Lost Confessions—and from *Miranda*. 88 J. Crim. L. & Criminol. 497 (1998).

Covey, Russell D. Interrogation Warrants. 26 Cardozo L.Rev. 1867 (2005).

Dery, George M. The Supposed Strength of Hopelessness: The Supreme Court Further Undermines *Miranda* in *Howes v. Florida*. 40 Am. J. Crim. L. 69 (2012).

Dripps, Donald. Constitutional Theory for Criminal Procedure: *Dickerson*, *Miranda*, and the Continuing Quest for Broad-But-Shallow. 43 Wm. & Mary L.Rev. 1 (2001).

Godsey, Mark A. Reformulating the Miranda Warnings in Light of Contemporary Law and Understandings. 90 Minn. L. Rev. 781 (2006).

Grano, Joseph. *Miranda v. Arizona* and the Legal Mind: Formalism's Triumph Over Substance and Reason. 24 Am. Crim. L.Rev. 243 (1986).

____. Voluntariness, Free Will and the Law of Confessions. 65 Va.L.Rev. 859 (1979).

____. *Rhode Island v. Innis*: A Need to Reconsider the Constitutional Premises Underlying the Law of Confessions. 17 Am.Crim.L.Rev. 1 (1979).

Grossman, Steven P. Separate But Equal: *Miranda*'s Rights to Silence and Counsel. 96 Marq. L. Rev. 151 (2012).

Gugenheim, Martin and Randy Hertz. *J.D.B.* and the Maturing of Juvenile Confession Suppression Law, 38 Wash. U. J. L. & Pol'y 109 (2012).

Holland, Brooks. A Relational Sixth Amendment During Interrogation. 99 J. Crim. L. & Criminology 381 (2009).

Howe, Michael J. Tomorrow's *Massiah*: Towards a "Prosecution Specific" Understanding of the Sixth Amendment Right to Counsel. 104 Colum.L.Rev. 134 (2004).

Inbau, Fred E. Overreaction—The Mischief of *Miranda v. Arizona*. 73 J.Crim.L. & Criminol. 797 (1982).

Interrogations in New Haven: The Impact of *Miranda* [Note]. 76 Yale L.J. 1521 (1967).

Kamisar, Yale. The Rise, Decline and Fall(?) of *Miranda*. 87 Wash. L. Rev. 965 (2012).

____. *Brewer v. Williams*, *Massiah* and *Miranda*: What Is "Interrogation?" When Does It Matter? 67 Georgetown L.J. 1 (1978).

____. A Dissent from the *Miranda* Dissents: Some Comments on the "New" Fifth Amendment and the Old "Voluntariness" Test. 65 Mich. L.Rev. 59 (1966).

Kassin, Saul. Inside Interrogation: Why Innocent People Confess. 32 Am. J. Trial Advoc. 525 (2009).

Kinports, Kit. The Supreme Court's Love-Hate Relationship with *Miranda*. 101 J. Crim. L. & Criminology 375 (2011).

Klein, Susan R. *Miranda's* Exceptions in a Post-*Dickerson* World. 91 J.Crim.L & Criminol. 567 (2001).

Leo, Richard A. Questioning the Relevance of *Miranda* in the Twenty-First Century. 99 Mich.L.Rev. 1000 (2001).

____. Inside the Interrogation Room. 86 J.Crim.L. & Criminol. 266 (1996).

Loewy, Arnold H. Police-Obtained Evidence and the Constitution: Distinguishing Unconstitutionally Obtained Evidence from Unconstitutionally Used Evidence. 87 Mich. L.Rev. 907 (1989).

Marcus, Paul. It's Not Just About *Miranda*: Determining the Voluntariness of Confessions in Criminal Prosecutions. 40 Val. U.L.Rev. 601 (2006).

Moreno, Joëlle Anne. Faith-Based *Miranda*?: Why the New *Missouri v. Seibert* Police "Bad Faith" Test is a Terrible Idea. 47 Ariz.L.Rev.395 (2005).

Parry, John T. Constitutional Interpretation, Coercive Interrogation, and Civil Rights Litigation after *Chavez v. Martinez*. 39 Ga.L.Rev. 73 (2005).

Posner, Eric. A. Should Coercive Interrogation Be Legal? 104 Mich.L.Rev. 671 (2006).

Rogers, Richard et al., The Comprehensibility and Content of Juvenile *Miranda* Warnings. 14 Psychol. Pub. Pol'y & L. 63 (2008).

Rosenberg, Irene and Yale Rosenberg. A Modest Proposal for the Abolition of Custodial Confessions. 68 N.Car.L.Rev. 69 (1989).

Schulhofer, Stephen. Reconsidering *Miranda*. 54 U.Chi.L.Rev. 435 (1987).

Slobogin, Christopher. Manipulation of Suspects and Unrecorded Questioning: After Fifty Years of *Miranda* Jurisprudence, Still Two (or Maybe Three) Burning Issues. 97 B.U. L. Rev. 1157 (2017).

Stuntz, William J. Lawyers, Deception and Evidence-Gathering. 79 Va. L.Rev. 1903 (1993).

____. Waiving Rights in Criminal Procedure. 75 Va. L. Rev. 761 (1989).

Sullivan, Thomas. Recording Federal Custodial Interviews. 45 Am. Crim. L. Rev. 1297 (2008).

Symposium. *Miranda* at 40. 10 Chapman L. Rev. 532 (2007).

Thomas, George C. III. Plain Talk About the *Miranda* Empirical Debate: A "Steady-State" Theory of Confessions. 43 UCLA L.Rev. 933 (1996).

Thomas, George C. III and Richard A. Leo. Confessions of Guilt: From Torture to *Miranda* and Beyond (2012).

Tomkovicz, James. An Adversary System Defense of the Right to Counsel Against Informants: Truth, Fair Play, and the Massiah Doctrine. 22 U.C. Davis L.Rev. 1 (1988).

Uviller, H. Richard. Evidence from the Mind of the Criminal Suspect: A Reconsideration of the Current Rules of Access and Restraint. 87 Colum.L.Rev. 1137 (1987).

Weisselberg, Charles D. Mourning *Miranda*. 96 California L.Rev. 1519 (2008).

White, Welsh S. *Miranda's* Waning Protections: Police Interrogation Practices After *Dickerson* (2001).

Part C

IDENTIFICATION PROCEDURES

Procedures for identifying the perpetrator of a crime can take many forms: lineups, photo arrays, one-on-one confrontations, fingerprinting, blood tests, voice exemplars, and handwriting exemplars are among the most common. The primary focus in this Part will be on the first three procedures, which make use of eyewitness identifications. An eyewitness identification is a particularly powerful piece of evidence in a criminal prosecution. Few scenarios in a criminal trial are more convincing than when a witness points to the defendant and says "He's the one." Yet, for reasons described below, such identifications can easily be wrong, whether they are made soon after the crime or in court. The potentially devastating impact of such identifications, combined with their suspect reliability, has made them a special concern of the courts.

Chapter 17 provides an overview of the constitutional constraints on the admissibility of both pretrial and in-court identifications. Chapter 18 then examines in detail the proper methods for conducting pretrial identification procedures.

Chapter 17

GENERAL RESTRICTIONS ON IDENTIFICATION PROCEDURES

17.01   Introduction

Judges and jurors naturally assume that an eyewitness to a crime can accurately discern and remember the physical characteristics of the person who committed the crime.[1] Yet extensive research indicates that both our ability to observe what someone looks like under the type of circumstances likely to be present during a crime and our capacity to recall what we observe is surprisingly deficient.[2] Many factors can cause faulty perception.[3] Aside from the obvious problems associated with lighting conditions and distance, for instance, there are proven difficulties connected with cross-racial identifications, which are notoriously inaccurate, and identifications in crimes involving weapons, which often draw the witness' attention away from the assailant. Even assuming optimum observation conditions, our inability to process more than a few stimuli at any given moment, *especially* when under stress, leads to difficulty in observing multiple details. Recall of an event is also often faulty.[4] Memory of what we perceive decays very rapidly—beginning within minutes of the event.

If people readily recognized and admitted to these failures of perception and memory, then reliance on eyewitness evidence might not be problematic: not only would there be less eyewitness testimony, but any such testimony that is presented would be discounted appropriately. Unfortunately, eyewitnesses are often not aware of how inaccurate their perceptions and memory are. Worse, they often unknowingly fill in their perceptual and recall gaps with possibly unreliable information obtained from other sources (e.g., preconceptions about criminals, newspaper accounts, what other witnesses say, or leading questions by the police). The ironic result, according to research, is that sincere confidence in one's identification, especially if it grows over time, may be negatively correlated with accuracy.[5]

These and other problems with eyewitness identification cannot be fully rectified by the legal system. In particular, the law cannot have much of an effect on witness' perceptual and recall capabilities. But it can try to control any conscious or unconscious conduct by the police or the prosecution that supplies what perception and memory

---

[1]   See Patrick Wall, Eyewitness Identification in Criminal Cases 19–13 (1965) (detailing numerous cases in which jurors disregarded convincing alibi evidence in convicting defendant on the basis of less impressive eyewitness identification testimony).

[2]   One of the best known examples of inaccurate identification is the "New York City television" study conducted by Dr. Robert Buckhout. In this study, viewers of the nightly news on a New York City TV station were shown a videotape of a mugging incident, and then a lineup of six men. They were then asked to phone in their opinion as to who committed the mugging. Less than 15% of the more than 2,000 respondents, or a percentage equal to random selection, correctly identified the culprit. Robert Buckhout, *Nearly 2,000 Witnesses Can Be Wrong*, Soc.Act. & L. at 7 (May, 1975).

[3]   A summary of the studies on perception is found in Ralph Norman Haber & Lyn Haber, *Experiencing, Remembering and Reporting Events*, 6 Psychol. Pub. Pol'y & L. 1057 (2000).

[4]   Studies are summarized in Haber & Haber, supra note 3.

[5]   Note, *Did Your Eyes Deceive You?: Expert Psychological Testimony on the Unreliability of Eyewitness Testimony*, 29 Stanford L.Rev. 969, 985 (1977).

cannot. Such conduct might include "sore thumb" lineups or photo array procedures that point to a favored suspect, failure to separate eyewitnesses during the identification process to ensure they do not influence one another, and subtle suggestions by the officers administering the procedure that try to influence an eyewitness' identification. The Supreme Court has indicated that both the Sixth Amendment right to counsel and the Due Process Clause place some constraints on the use of these types of techniques.[6] This chapter discusses these constraints, as well as the applicability of the Fourth Amendment and the privilege against self-incrimination to identification procedures. It also examines how the courts have analyzed the admissibility of identifications that are the "fruit" of a constitutional violation and the procedures for determining the admissibility of identification evidence.

17.02   The Right to Counsel

In *United States v. Wade*,[7] the defendant participated in a lineup conducted without notice to and in the absence of his counsel after he had been indicted. The Supreme Court held that the Sixth Amendment invalidated his subsequent conviction because the post-indictment lineup was a "critical stage,"[8] at which "the presence of counsel is necessary to preserve the defendant's basic right to a fair trial." The Court pointed to two factors that made the lineup in *Wade* deserving of Sixth Amendment protection. First, "substantial prejudice to defendant's rights" could result from the confrontation because "the trial which might determine the accused's fate may well be not that in the courtroom but at the pretrial confrontation." Second, counsel could help avoid that prejudice by observing the lineup and using what he observed at trial to contest its results. The Court was not comfortable forcing the attorney to rely on other sources of information about the lineup. In particular, it noted that the defendant is unlikely to know what to look for even if he is calm enough to do so, and will in any event often be an unwilling or relatively unconvincing witness at trial (at least compared to the police). The eyewitness too will probably be impervious to the effect of subtle suggestions, and thus also an inadequate source of information. To the Court's observations can be added the likely fact that neither the eyewitness nor the police who conduct the lineup will be highly motivated to cooperate with the defense.

The Court's apparent concern that counsel have sufficient information to mount an effective subsequent challenge of a lineup procedure suggested that *Wade* was based as much on the Sixth Amendment right to effective cross-examination and confrontation of one's accusers[9] as it was on a Sixth Amendment right to assistance of counsel at the identification. So construed, *Wade* would stand in contrast to cases like *Miranda v. Arizona*[10] and *Massiah v. United States*,[11] which required counsel during police questioning primarily to assist the defendant in dealing with police conduct at the time it occurs, rather than in exposing its impropriety in future proceedings. But *Wade* also

---

[6]   Other techniques for combatting the vagaries of eyewitness testimony, not derived from the Constitution, include cautionary instructions to the jury, see *United States v. Telfaire*, 469 F.2d 552 (D.C.Cir. 1972), and expert psychological testimony pointing out the various problems with eyewitness evidence. See, e.g., *State v. Chapple*, 135 Ariz. 281, 660 P.2d 1208 (1983).

[7]   388 U.S. 218, 87 S.Ct. 1926 (1967).

[8]   See § 31.03(a)(1) for a detailed discussion of critical stage analysis.

[9]   See § 28.05(b) for a discussion of the right to cross-examine witnesses.

[10]   384 U.S. 436, 86 S.Ct. 1602 (1966), discussed in § 16.02(d).

[11]   377 U.S. 201, 84 S.Ct. 1199 (1964), discussed in § 16.02(c).

talks about counsel's ability to "avert prejudice" at the lineup. As subsequent discussion develops, the scope of the right to counsel could differ significantly, depending upon which conceptual basis for *Wade* is chosen. In any event, both *Wade* and subsequent cases have indicated that its holding is a narrow one, heavily dependent upon the type of procedure at issue and the stage of the criminal process at which it takes place.

(a) Type of Procedure

Certain types of identification procedures do not, by their nature, trigger the Sixth Amendment right to counsel. *Wade* itself distinguished the lineup from "various other preparatory steps, such as systematized or scientific analyzing of the accused's fingerprints, blood sample, clothing, hair and the like." In such cases, counsel is not required because

> [k]nowledge of the techniques of science and technology is sufficiently available, and the variables in techniques few enough, that the accused has the opportunity for a meaningful confrontation of the Government's case at trial through the ordinary processes of cross-examination of the Government's expert witnesses and the presentation of the evidence of his own experts.

Thus, in *Gilbert v. California*,[12] a companion case to *Wade*, the Court held that the taking of handwriting exemplars is not a "critical stage" of the criminal proceeding requiring counsel because such exemplars can easily be duplicated and analyzed at trial. As the Court's reasoning suggests, *Gilbert* and the other cases of "systematized" identification procedures mentioned in *Wade* are more easily explained on right to effective cross-examination grounds than assistance-of-counsel grounds: while one might require counsel if the objective were to ensure that no police misconduct occurs during the taking of the sample or its analysis, the opposite result is supportable because the accuracy of the procedure can be adequately tested even if counsel does not observe it while it occurs.

The Court less successfully relied on this type of reasoning in finding, in *United States v. Ash*,[13] no right to counsel at photo arrays. As one reason for this result, the *Ash* Court made the dubious assertion that the ability to preserve the photo array makes such a procedure easier to reconstruct than a lineup. As *Wade* indicated, to enable effective challenge at subsequent proceedings counsel is required at a lineup not just to observe its composition (which, it should be noted, can easily be "preserved", via photograph) but to witness police and eyewitness conduct during the procedure and observe any conscious or unconscious manipulation of the procedure (e.g., a statement like "Look at photo number two again."). With a photo array, an attorney is arguably even more necessary since, in contrast to a lineup, the defendant is not present and cannot provide any information about what happened.

Perhaps realizing this, the *Ash* majority relied more heavily on another justification: the conclusion that, because photo arrays do not involve situations in which the defendant must deal with the "intricacies of the law and the advocacy of the public prosecutor," they do not call for counsel's presence. This so-called "trial-like confrontation" analysis is a version of the assistance-of-counsel approach, but in effect marked a significant departure from previous right to counsel jurisprudence, which had

---

[12]   388 U.S. 263, 87 S.Ct. 1951 (1967).
[13]   413 U.S. 300, 93 S.Ct. 2568 (1973).

recognized that counsel can provide the defendant non-technical as well as legal aid.[14] More importantly for present purposes, it failed to distinguish the result in *Ash* from *Wade*. *Wade* required counsel at lineups, yet a defendant's participation in a lineup does not involve an "adversarial" confrontation with the prosecutor, nor require an understanding of the legal process. While the defendant in a lineup has an interest in ensuring that the procedure is properly conducted, an interest which counsel can help protect, this is also true of a photo procedure, and is not related to the defendant's presence.[15]

Ash left unresolved whether the right to counsel applied to the third type of eyewitness identification procedure, the one-on-one confrontation or showup. Given the fact that such an event is both difficult to reconstruct *and* requires the defendant's presence, the Court later held, in *Moore v. Illinois*,[16] that a defendant is entitled to an attorney in such situations. Under current law, then, lineups and showups are the only identification procedures that implicate the right to counsel.

(b) Timing of the Procedure

Not every lineup or showup implicates the right to counsel, however. Consistent with the Court's movement away from an effective cross-examination analysis and toward its "trial-like confrontation" assistance-of-counsel approach, the Court in *Kirby v. Illinois*[17] held that a defendant has no right to an attorney during identification procedures that take place before "prosecution has commenced." This holding derives both from the language of the Sixth Amendment, which speaks of the assistance of counsel in all "criminal prosecutions," and the perception, later echoed in *Ash*, that only after the initiation of "adversary judicial criminal proceedings" is a defendant "faced with the prosecutorial forces of organized society, and immersed in the intricacies of substantive and procedural criminal law." Thus, until such proceedings are initiated, "by way of formal charge, preliminary hearing, indictment, information, or arraignment," a person is not entitled to counsel at lineups or showups. In *Moore*, the Court reaffirmed *Kirby*, making clear, however, that the right to counsel can be triggered *during* arraignment on the warrant, as well as after.

Kirby can be subjected to the same type of criticism as *Ash*: a post-charge identification is no more (or less) likely than a pre-charge identification to involve the defendant in the "intricacies of substantive or procedural law;" at the same time, the substantial degree of prejudice that can result from a pretrial identification procedure exists *whenever* it takes place. The *Kirby* Court may have had in mind the practical reality that obtaining counsel for persons subjected to identifications at an early stage of the criminal process can be very difficult. Police often use showups, and to a lesser extent lineups, to eliminate as well as identify, suspects soon after a crime is committed; appointing counsel for every person so displayed would be impractical. If this was the Court's concern, however, a better rule might have been to create an "exigency" exception

---

[14]   See, e.g., *Miranda v. Arizona*, 384 U.S. 436, 86 S.Ct. 1602 (1966), discussed in § 16.02(d).

[15]   Perhaps the best explanation for *Ash* is found in the Court's insinuation that, had it found otherwise, it would have also been required to find a right to counsel during routine government interviews with witnesses, despite the defendant's absence and despite the concomitant interference with the prosecution's development of its case. For discussion of this point in the context of the Court's other cases dealing with the right to counsel, see § 31.03(a)(2).

[16]   434 U.S. 220, 98 S.Ct. 458 (1977).

[17]   406 U.S. 682, 92 S.Ct. 1877 (1972).

for emergency identifications,[18] rather than artificially limiting counsel to identifications conducted at or after arraignment proceedings.

Along these lines, *Wade* indicated that, even after formal charging, "substitute counsel" might be sufficient "where notification and presence of the suspect's own counsel would result in prejudicial delay." While the majority in *Wade* apparently had in mind a "human" substitute, in some cases, particularly lineups or showups conducted at the stationhouse, a videotape of the identification might prove adequate in emergency circumstances. Indeed, as suggested in the next chapter,[19] videotaping the identification might meet Sixth Amendment requirements even when there is no emergency.

(c) Waiver and Alternatives to Counsel

A confrontation theory of the right to counsel would suggest that the right can never be waived. Because the defendant's direct involvement in the procedure makes him less observant and because he may not witness all phases of the identification process, it could be argued that counsel, or some "substitute" for counsel, must be present to ensure an opportunity for adequate reconstruction at trial. But, under the ascendant "assistance" approach, waiver would seem permissible, since a defendant might reasonably feel that he can confront the "intricacies" of the adversary system on his own. *Wade* itself, perhaps somewhat contradictorily given its primary emphasis on the right to effective cross-examination, indicated that a defendant subjected to a lineup could waive counsel, if the waiver is "intelligent." Presumably, this language requires, at the least, that a person be told he has a right to counsel and that an explicit waiver be obtained.[20]

Wade also stated that "legislation or other regulations, such as those of local police departments, which eliminate the risks of abuse and unintentional suggestion at lineup proceedings and the impediments to meaningful confrontation at trial may . . . remove the basis for regarding the stage as 'critical.' " Here, the Court seemed to be saying that the right to counsel would be eliminated if standardized procedures: (1) minimize the suggestiveness of the procedure; and (2) make adequate reconstruction of the identification possible without the attorney being present. The methods of accomplishing these goals derive in large part from due process analysis, to which we now turn.

17.03   Due Process

In *Stovall v. Denno*,[21] a companion case of *Wade* and *Gilbert*, the Supreme Court made clear that, in addition to the safeguards provided by the Sixth Amendment, the accused is entitled to protection under the Fifth Amendment against an identification procedure "so unnecessarily suggestive and conducive to irreparable mistaken identification" as to amount to denial of due process of law. Unlike the Sixth Amendment right to counsel, this due process standard applies to identification procedures without regard to whether adversary judicial criminal proceedings have begun.[22]

---

[18]   See § 18.03(b) for examples of emergencies where counsel might not be required.

[19]   See § 18.02(d).

[20]   *People v. Coleman*, 43 N.Y.2d 222, 401 N.Y.S.2d 57, 371 N.E.2d 819 (1977); cf. *Patterson v. Illinois*, 487 U.S. 285, 108 S.Ct. 2389 (1988) (discussing waiver of Sixth Amendment right to counsel during questioning), discussed in § 16.04(c).

[21]   388 U.S. 293, 87 S.Ct. 1967 (1967).

[22]   *Kirby v. Illinois*, 406 U.S. 682, 92 S.Ct. 1877 (1972).

However, as with other due process guarantees,[23] the suggestiveness of the identification procedure and the potential for unreliable identifications must be caused by government misconduct, rather than happenstance. Thus, in *Perry v. New Hampshire*,[24] the Court held, 8–1, that an eyewitness' identification of the defendant from her kitchen window as he was standing next to a police car, while perhaps made in a suggestive situation, was merely a response to a routine police question about who broke into her car and thus not excludable on due process grounds.

Stovall established that the totality of circumstances must be examined to determine whether the accused was deprived of the due process of law. In *Stovall*, for instance, the Court held that the identification challenged (a one-on-one emergency confrontation between the accused and an injured witness in a hospital room who was on the verge of dying) did not violate the Fifth Amendment because it was not *unnecessarily* suggestive, and there was not a substantial likelihood of misidentification. To elucidate the *Stovall* rule, the three elements of suggestiveness, necessity and likelihood of misidentification must be examined.

(a) Suggestiveness

An identification procedure is suggestive if it, in effect, dictates to the witness, "this is the man." For example, a lineup is suggestive if the accused is the only one who faintly resembles the person who committed the offense or if the police point out the accused to the suspect. A one-on-one confrontation in which the police present a suspect to a witness is, of course, highly suggestive.[25] The use of suggestive identification procedures is disapproved because it is feared that the suggestion, and not the remembrance, will trigger an identification.

Illustrative is *Moore v. Illinois*,[26] where the Court relied not only on the Sixth Amendment right to counsel but also seemed to base its reversal on due process grounds. The majority opinion's description of the facts suggests the dual basis for holding Moore's identification unconstitutional:

> It is difficult to imagine a more suggestive manner in which to present a suspect to a witness for their critical first confrontation than was employed in this case. The victim, who had seen her assailant for only 10 to 15 seconds, was asked to make her identification after she was told that she was going to view a suspect, after she was told his name and heard it called as he was led before the bench, and after she heard the prosecutor recite the evidence believed to implicate petitioner. Had petitioner been represented by counsel, some or all of this suggestiveness could have been avoided.

Suggestiveness alone will not automatically render a particular identification procedure unconstitutional, however. The Court has indicated that if a suggestive procedure was "necessary" and did not create a substantial likelihood of misidentification, it will withstand a due process challenge. More recently, it has

---

[23]   *Colorado v. Connelly*, 479 U.S. 157, 107 S.Ct. 515 (1986), discussed in § 16.02(a)(2) (holding that a confession "coerced" by suspect's mental illness does not implicate the due process clause).

[24]   *Perry v. New Hampshire*, 565 U.S. 228, 132 S.Ct. 716 (2012).

[25]   See *United States v. Wade*, 388 U.S. 218, 87 S.Ct. 1926 (1967) (delineating other types of suggestive lineups). See also, *United States ex rel. Kirby v. Sturges*, 510 F.2d 397 (7th Cir. 1975), cert. denied 421 U.S. 1016, 95 S.Ct. 2424 (1975).

[26]   434 U.S. 220, 98 S.Ct. 458 (1977).

indicated that even an unnecessarily suggestive procedure is permissible if the resulting identification has indicia of reliability.

(b) Necessity

The Supreme Court has on several occasions sanctioned the use of a suggestive procedure on the grounds of exigent circumstances. As noted earlier, *Stovall* found a one-man confrontation at a hospital constitutionally permissible because the witness was in danger of dying. In *Simmons v. United States*,[27] a bank robbery had been committed and the felons were still at large. The police showed six snapshots to witnesses of the robbery, from which the defendants were identified. Although the Supreme Court found that the photo display of the snapshots fell "short of the ideal," "[i]t was essential for the FBI agents swiftly to determine whether they were on the right track, so that they could properly deploy their forces in Chicago and, if necessary, alert officials in other cities." This justification, and the Court's finding that there had been little danger of misidentification, led to a conclusion that the procedure did not deny the accused due process of law. Thus, the Warren Court indicated that a suggestive procedure may be upheld if its use was unavoidable, especially if there is no indication that the resulting identification was unreliable.

(c) Reliability

More recent cases indicate that the most critical factor in the totality of the circumstances is the reliability of the identification. *Stovall* had seemed to suggest that the results of an unnecessarily suggestive procedure should be inadmissible, regardless of its reliability. But in *Neil v. Biggers*,[28] decided five years later, the Court intimated that reliability and not suggestiveness should govern admissibility analysis. In *Biggers*, the accused was identified at a station-house showup conducted seven months after the crime. Although the Court conceded that the procedure had been unnecessarily suggestive, it held that the accused had not been denied due process of law. It is "the likelihood of misidentification which violates a defendant's right to due process." The Court offered a list of factors to be considered in evaluating the likelihood of misidentification, including:

> The opportunity of the witness to view the criminal at the time of the crime, the witness' degree of attention, the accuracy of the witness' prior description of the criminal, the level of certainty demonstrated by the witness at the confrontation, and the length of time between the crime and the confrontation.

The Supreme Court reaffirmed the precept that reliability is the "linchpin" in the analysis of pretrial identification procedures in *Manson v. Brathwaite*.[29] In *Manson*, an undercover police officer purchased heroin from a seller while standing near him in a well-lit hallway for two to three minutes. A few minutes after the sale was consummated, the officer described the seller to another officer, who suspected the defendant and gave the undercover officer a picture of him. Two days after receiving the picture, the undercover officer identified it as a picture of the person from whom he had bought heroin. The Supreme Court, in an opinion by Justice Blackmun, held that the single-photograph display, while suggestive (unnecessarily so, given the possibility of a photo

---

[27]   390 U.S. 377, 88 S.Ct. 967 (1968).
[28]   409 U.S. 188, 93 S.Ct. 375 (1972).
[29]   432 U.S. 98, 97 S.Ct. 2243 (1977).

array), did not create a substantial likelihood of irreparable misidentification in the "totality of the circumstances". The witness was a trained police officer, had a sufficient opportunity to view the suspect, accurately described him, positively identified his photograph, and made the photographic identification only two days after the crime. These factors counterbalanced the suggestiveness of the identification procedure used and the fact that less suggestive alternatives were readily available.

If the reliability of identifications could be adequately gauged there would be little problem with the *Biggers-Manson* rule that unnecessarily suggestive identification procedures are permissible. But as the discussion in the introduction to this chapter suggests, difficult-to-discern perceptual and memory deficiencies often affect the accuracy of identifications. And even if such deficiencies are "recognized," their magnitude may not be apparent to courts assessing the admissibility of identification evidence. Thus, when a suggestive procedure is *unnecessary*, it is difficult to justify.[30]

17.04   Other Constitutional Considerations

Identification procedures could arguably implicate both the Fourth Amendment and the privilege against self-incrimination as well as the Sixth Amendment and the Due Process Clause. Taking a handwriting sample, for instance, could be viewed both as a "seizure" and as coercive production of incriminating information. But the Supreme Court has indicated challenges on Fourth or Fifth Amendment grounds will rarely succeed.

(a) Fourth Amendment

With respect to the Fourth Amendment, the Court has held that one has no "reasonable expectation of privacy" in characteristics that are exposed to the public such as one's visage, one's handwriting and the sound of one's voice.[31] Thus, only the seizure of the person necessary to obtain such identifying information need meet the reasonableness requirement of that Amendment; subsequently viewing a face or taking a handwriting sample is not a "seizure" and need not be justified by probable cause or even reasonable suspicion that it will produce evidence.

Fourth Amendment restrictions on the seizure of the person necessary to obtain identifying information depend upon the entity doing the seizing. When the grand jury is the investigating body, the Supreme Court has held that, so long as the requirements for a subpoena are met, a person can be required to appear for purposes of providing voice and handwriting exemplars.[32] Presumably, the same rule would apply to grand jury efforts to obtain other types of identifying information. As discussed elsewhere in this book,[33] generally a subpoena cannot be quashed unless it requests information clearly irrelevant to the investigation or is overbroad.

When the *police* want to seize a person for the purpose of obtaining identifying information, the Fourth Amendment imposes more onerous requirements, although

---

[30]   The necessity principle is discussed further in §§ 18.02(e) and 18.03(a).

[31]   See, e.g., *United States v. Dionisio*, 410 U.S. 1, 93 S.Ct. 764 (1973), discussed in § 4.03(b). Note that when the identifying "information" is not exposed to the public, as is true with blood, then a seizure requires probable cause. *Schmerber v. California*, 384 U.S. 757, 86 S.Ct. 1826 (1966), discussed in § 9.02.

[32]   *United States v. Dionisio*, 410 U.S. 1, 93 S.Ct. 764 (1973); *United States v. Mara*, 410 U.S. 19, 93 S.Ct. 774 (1973).

[33]   See § 23.05(a)(1).

probably not at the level required for seizures motivated by other objectives. Typically, probable cause is required for an arrest or any other prolonged detention.[34] But in *Hayes v. Florida,*[35] the Court stated in dictum: "There is . . . support in our cases for the view that the Fourth Amendment would permit seizures for the purpose of fingerprinting, if there is reasonable suspicion that the suspect has committed a criminal act, if there is a reasonable basis for believing that fingerprinting will establish or negate the suspect's connection with that crime, and if the procedure is carried out with dispatch."[36] The majority also stated that, while such a seizure would require judicial authorization if it involved entry into the home or removal to the police station, the police could act on their own for an "identification-only" seizure on the street. The apparent rationale for both these conclusions was the temporary, relatively unintrusive nature of the fingerprinting process. In his concurring opinion in *Hayes*, Justice Brennan argued in favor of the traditional probable cause standard. With respect to on-site fingerprinting in particular, Brennan noted that it might take place "in full view of any passerby" and thus "would involve a singular intrusion on the suspect's privacy, an intrusion that would not be justifiable . . . as necessary for the officer's protection."

The reasoning of the dictum in *Hayes* would also justify seizures from the home for the purpose of a line-up or showup based on a judicial finding of reasonable suspicion. Further, again assuming reasonable suspicion, *Hayes* would allow police to act on their own in arranging on-the-scene lineups or showups. On the other hand, suspicionless or random seizures of a person for such identification procedures would be impermissible.

(b) Fifth Amendment

In *Wade*, the Court made clear that the privilege against self-incrimination does not limit the use of identification procedures. Although incriminating evidence can result from these procedures, such evidence is "real" or "physical," not "testimonial"; therefore it is not protected by the Fifth Amendment.[37] Thus, *Wade* found no violation of the privilege when the state requires the accused to exhibit himself for observation in a lineup. Nor, according to *Wade*, is there a Fifth Amendment violation when a lineup participant is required to utter words purportedly uttered by the perpetrator of the crime, because "his voice [is used] as an identifying physical characteristic, not to speak his guilt." On the same rationale, *Gilbert* held that the taking of handwriting exemplars does not violate the privilege. Compelled fingerprinting and other identification procedures could be justified similarly.

17.05 Identifications as Fruit

(a) Of Previous Illegal Identifications

A trial identification is made under extremely suggestive circumstances. Not only is it a one-on-one confrontation, but the eyewitness knows that the prosecution has identified the defendant as the suspect. Nonetheless, most courts routinely permit such identifications,[38] perhaps in part to avoid hearsay concerns associated with introduction

---

[34]   See § 3.02 for a discussion of the types of detentions which require probable cause.

[35]   470 U.S. 811, 105 S.Ct. 1643 (1985).

[36]   See also, *Davis v. Mississippi*, 394 U.S. 721, 89 S.Ct. 1394 (1969).

[37]   See § 15.04 on the "testimonial evidence" requirement.

[38]   See *State v. White*, 160 Ariz. 24, 770 P.2d 328 (1989); *State v. Hannah*, 312 N.C. 286, 322 S.E.2d 148 (1984).

of pretrial identifications,[39] but primarily because there has almost always been a previous, properly conducted identification of the defendant that the in-court identification merely corroborates.[40] If this previous identification is invalid on Sixth Amendment, due process, or Fourth Amendment grounds, should the in-court identification be prohibited as well? The answer to this question depends upon whether the latter identification is "tainted" by the previous illegality. In such cases, analogous to analysis under the Fourth Amendment, one must decide whether the in-court identification is "fruit of the poisonous tree."[41]

In *Wade*, the Supreme Court explicitly recognized the analogy to its Fourth Amendment cases and held that an illegally conducted lineup does not invalidate subsequent identifications if the subsequent identification derives from an "independent source." The majority mentioned several factors, many of them picked up later in *Biggers'* reliability test, which a court should consider in determining whether an in-court identification derives from an independent source. These include:

> the prior opportunity to observe the alleged criminal act, the existence of any discrepancy between any pre-lineup description and the defendant's actual description, any identification prior to lineup of another person, the identification by picture of the defendant prior to the lineup, failure to identify the defendant on a prior occasion, and the lapse of time between the alleged act and the lineup identification.

Courts have also considered other factors in making the independent source determination. For example, the fact that a witness did not experience extreme anxiety or extraordinary pressure during the event he allegedly witnessed has been found to create a lesser likelihood of distorted observation and to increase the probability that an in-court identification was based on the original observation and not a tainted pretrial identification.[42]

While conceptually the independent source test makes sense, in practice it is often impossible to implement. As pointed out in the introduction to this chapter, a person's "memory" of an event is composed not just of perceptions registered at the time the event occurs but also of subsequent "data" which helps fill in gaps as the recall of the event inevitably decays. Asking a judge to discern the extent to which a new identification is the product of the original perceptions instead of the new "filler" data created by the illegal procedure is usually a futile task, especially since the witness is likely to be unaware of this substitution process himself.

Nonetheless, the lower courts have had little trouble applying the independent source doctrine to validate subsequent identifications, often reciting nothing more than a conclusion that the witness had a "good" opportunity to view the incident in question.[43]

---

[39]   Traditionally, evidence of pretrial identification was viewed as inadmissible hearsay. However, most courts today allow such evidence to corroborate an in-court identification or under a hearsay exception. See Thomas A. Mauet, *Prior Identifications in Criminal Cases: Hearsay and Confrontation Issues*, 24 Ariz.L.Rev. 29 (1982).

[40]   If the in-court identification is the first identification, it is more likely to be found invalid. See § 18.03(a)(6).

[41]   See § 2.04 for a general discussion of this doctrine.

[42]   *United States v. Johnson*, 412 F.2d 753 (1st Cir. 1969), cert. denied 397 U.S. 944, 90 S.Ct. 959 (1970).

[43]   See Note, *Pretrial Identification Procedures—Wade to Gilbert to Stovall: Lower Courts Bobble the Ball*, 55 Minn.L.Rev. 779 (1971) (courts have "easily found an 'independent source' for an in-court

Given the vagaries of memory, the better rule might well be to bar from evidence all identifications made subsequent to an identification that is found to be unreliable. An alternative to such a rule is the practice, discussed below,[44] of permitting the reliability of an identification to be challenged in front of the jury even after it is found admissible on independent source grounds. Some lower courts have developed elaborate instructions, based on the type of research referenced at the beginning of this chapter, designed to inform the jury about the vagaries of eyewitness identifications.[45] In the absence of steps like these, violation of the right to counsel and due process guarantees during the pretrial process seldom prejudice the prosecution, since an in-court identification is usually found to be "independent" of the previous identification.

(b) Of Other Illegalities

Suppose that the defendant is illegally arrested and then placed in a lineup. Or suppose that he is subjected to an unconstitutionally coercive interrogation during which he names a person who later identifies him as the perpetrator. If the identification procedure in these cases is conducted properly—that is, if the defendant is provided with counsel and unnecessary suggestivity is avoided—then the identification will very likely be reliable. Should such an identification nonetheless be excluded from evidence, on the ground that it is fruit of the poisonous arrest or confession, actions which should be deterred through application of the exclusionary rule?

In *Davis v. Mississippi*[46] the Court answered this question in the affirmative. There it suppressed the fingerprints of a person who had been illegally detained as part of a dragnet roundup of scores of individuals during a rape investigation. Fingerprints are even more trustworthy than a properly obtained eyewitness identification, yet the Court held that the egregious police action in *Davis* required that they be suppressed.

However, when the fruit of an illegal detention is an eyewitness identification a different result will often be called for. In *United States v. Crews*,[47] the police originally detained the defendant based on the general descriptions of three separate robbery victims, and a tentative face-to-face identification by a fourth person who had seen the defendant on the day of the first robbery "hanging around" the area in which all three crimes were committed. While at police headquarters, Crews was briefly questioned, photographed, and then released. On the following day, the police showed the victim of the first robbery an array of eight photographs, including one of the defendant. Although she had previously viewed over one hundred pictures without identifying the assailant, she immediately selected Crews' photograph on this occasion. Three days later, one of the other victims made a similar identification. Crews was again taken into custody and positively identified by the two women who had made the photographic identifications.

The trial judge found that Crews' initial detention had been an arrest without probable cause and that the products of that arrest—the photographic and lineup identifications—could not be introduced at trial. But he also concluded that the victims would still be able to identify the defendant in court based upon recollection untainted

---

identification"). See also, *United States v. Dring*, 930 F.2d 687 (9th Cir. 1991); *United States v. Lewin*, 900 F.2d 145 (8th Cir. 1990); *United States ex rel. Kosik v. Napoli*, 814 F.2d 1151 (7th Cir. 1987).

[44] See § 17.06.

[45] The best example of this approach is *State v. Henderson*, 208 N.J. 208, 27 A.3d 872 (2011).

[46] 394 U.S. 721, 89 S.Ct. 1394 (1969).

[47] 445 U.S. 463, 100 S.Ct. 1244 (1980).

by these identifications. At trial, all three victims identified Crews as their assailant. Crews was convicted of the first armed robbery, but found not guilty of the other two robberies. The lower federal courts reversed the conviction, finding that, under the "fruit of the poisonous tree" doctrine, the in-court identification which led to the conviction was at least indirectly the product of official misconduct (the illegal arrest).

The Supreme Court, while agreeing the arrest was illegal, unanimously upheld the conviction, although the reasons for doing so varied. Justice Brennan, writing for three members of the Court, noted that "[i]n the typical fruit of the poisonous tree case . . . the challenged evidence was acquired by the police *after* some initial Fourth Amendment violation." Here no new evidence was acquired through the illegal arrest; the "fruit" had already been obtained by the time the illegal detention took place. Brennan reached this conclusion by dividing a victim's in-court identification into three components: (1) the victim's presence in the courtroom; (2) the victim's ability to give an accurate identification based on observations made at the time of the crime; and (3) the physical presence of the defendant in the courtroom. He concluded that, in *Crews*, none of these elements " 'ha[d] been come at by exploitation' of the violation of the defendant's Fourth Amendment rights." The victim's identity had been known to the police before the defendant's illegal arrest. The trial court "expressly found that the witness's courtroom identification rested on an independent recollection of her initial encounter with the assailant." Finally, given the fact that the police had already known Crews' identity and had some basis for suspecting his involvement before the illegal arrest, Brennan argued that the Court did not need to decide whether the defendant's visage was "fruit" of the police misconduct.

Five members of the Court, in two separate opinions, diverged from the last part of this analysis, relying on *Frisbie v. Collins*,[48] which held that an illegal arrest does not alone bar prosecution or conviction. As one of the two opinions put it, this ruling "forecloses the claim that [a defendant's] face can be suppressible as a fruit of the unlawful arrest." On this view, even if the police had *not* known of Crews prior to the illegal detention, the results of the properly conducted identifications could have been admitted. In practice, this holding means that a properly obtained courtroom identification by an eyewitness (i.e., one which the judge finds is based on an "independent" source) is virtually never suppressible as fruit of an illegal arrest (or an illegal interrogation), even if the defendant's "visage" is in court solely because of the illegal action.[49]

17.06 Procedure for Determining Admissibility

Wade and *Stovall* make clear that evidence of an identification found to violate the defendant's rights to counsel or due process, and any subsequent "tainted" identification, must be suppressed. Generally, the state bears the burden of establishing the presence of counsel or an intelligent waiver by the accused,[50] while the defendant must prove a

---

[48]   342 U.S. 519, 72 S.Ct. 509 (1952), discussed in § 3.01.

[49]   The one caveat to this conclusion might be if the illegal arrest (or interrogation) of the defendant also produced the name of the eyewitness who eventually identified him (Brennan's first component of an identification). But see, *United States v. Ceccolini*, 435 U.S. 268, 98 S.Ct. 1054 (1978), discussed in § 2.04(b)(2), which suggests that when the fruit of an illegality is a witness, exclusion will usually not occur, in part because the witness might well have been discovered independently.

[50]   *United States v. Garner*, 439 F.2d 525 (D.C.Cir. 1970). See also, Nathan A. Sobel, Eyewitness Identification § 85 (New York 1972).

violation of due process.[51] The prosecution also bears the burden of showing in-court identification testimony derives from an origin independent of tainted pretrial identification.[52]

Normally the suppression hearing is held prior to trial or, if during trial, in the absence of the jury. However, in *Watkins v. Sowders*,[53] the Supreme Court held that these procedures are not constitutionally mandated. The Court recognized that hearings to determine the admissibility of *confessions* should generally be held with the jury excused, given the effect a confession found to be inadmissible can have on the jury's deliberations even when they are instructed to disregard it.[54] But Justice Stewart, writing for the Court, argued that even if this procedure were constitutionally required when confessions are involved, identification hearings are distinguishable. He pointed out that the admissibility of a confession depends upon more than its reliability; the police conduct involved may require its exclusion regardless of how accurate it is. Where identifications are concerned, on the other hand, reliability is the principal determinant of admissibility. Thus, judging the admissibility of an identification involves "the very task our system must assume juries can perform," and need not require the jury's dismissal. This reasoning ignores the fact that an identification is as powerful as a confession in its effect on jurors; as with a confession, once an identification is found inadmissible, every effort should be made to keep them from knowing about it. Since the identifications in *Watkins* were admissible, the Court did not have to confront this problem in that case. But it conceded that a judicial determination with the jury excused "may often be advisable,"[55] and acknowledged that "[i]n some circumstances such a determination may be constitutionally necessary."

As *Watkins* recognized, if identification evidence is found admissible, then its credibility is for the jury to decide. A determination by the judge that an identification is reliable does not foreclose the issue. Thus, for instance, even though a suggestive procedure may have been justified by exigent circumstances, its unreliability may be argued to the jury. It should also be noted that equivocation or indefiniteness on the part of the identifying party affects the weight of the evidence and not its admissibility.[56] For example, in *United States v. Hines*,[57] a witness inspecting a police book of photographs stated that one of the pictures looked like, but was not, the assailant. The court held that evidence of the "looks like" description was relevant to the issue of identification. The probative value of the evidence was a matter for the jury.

17.07 Conclusion

The vagaries of eyewitness identifications have led the courts to place several restrictions on the means used to obtain them. These restrictions are summarized at the

---

[51] *Stovall v. Denno*, 388 U.S. 293, 87 S.Ct. 1967 (1967); *Allen v. Rhay*, 431 F.2d 1160 (9th Cir. 1970), cert. denied 404 U.S. 834, 92 S.Ct. 116 (1971).

[52] *United States v. Wade*, 388 U.S. 218, 87 S.Ct. 1926 (1967).

[53] 449 U.S. 341, 101 S.Ct. 654 (1981).

[54] See § 16.06(a).

[55] The Court suggested that if the defendant could show specific instances when the presence of the jury inhibited his attorney's cross-examination, a due process claim might lie.

[56] See, e.g., *United States v. Peterson*, 435 F.2d 192 (7th Cir. 1970), cert. denied 403 U.S. 907, 91 S.Ct. 2212 (1971); *Russell v. United States*, 408 F.2d 1280 (D.C.Cir. 1969), cert. denied 395 U.S. 928, 89 S.Ct. 1786 (1969).

[57] 460 F.2d 949 (D.C.Cir. 1972).

conclusion of the next chapter, after a closer look at the various identification techniques. The bibliography also appears at the end of the next chapter.

Chapter 18

EYEWITNESS IDENTIFICATION TECHNIQUES

18.01   Introduction

The discussion in the previous chapter treated the various pretrial identification techniques together in an effort to provide an overview of the Supreme Court's approach to identification issues. This chapter will examine separately those identification techniques that rely on eyewitnesses—specifically, lineups, showups and confrontations, and photographic identifications—so as to better focus on the special problems associated with each. To some extent, this will necessitate repeating the holdings discussed in the last chapter.

18.02   Lineups

Of the three identification techniques discussed in this chapter, properly conducted lineups are the least likely to result in misidentification. As such, they can help police apprehend suspects, relieve the innocent and provide valuable trial evidence. But, improperly conducted, they can also be unnecessarily suggestive and produce unreliable results. The rules governing the conduct of lineups that are described below are aimed at preventing misidentifications while at the same time permitting full prosecutorial exploitation of lineups.

(a)   Compelling Participation

In *United States v. Wade,*[1] the Supreme Court held that the privilege against self-incrimination is not violated by forcing a person to participate in a lineup, because the procedure requires only the exhibition of physical characteristics and thus is not testimonial in nature. For the same reason, a person in a lineup can be "required to use his voice as an identifying characteristic." Because the privilege is not implicated, a refusal to participate in a court ordered lineup can subject a person to contempt sanctions.[2] Further, a defendant who refuses to participate may be asked about his refusal or, if he does not take the stand, he may be subject to prosecutorial comment about his failure to participate.[3]

Under some circumstances, the Fourth Amendment may prohibit indiscriminate use of a person as a lineup subject. When the person is not already in custody, the Supreme Court has suggested that, unless there is a reasonable suspicion that the person has committed the crime being investigated, "seizing" that person for the purpose of placing him in a lineup is unconstitutional.[4] On the other hand, several lower courts have held that, if a person is already in custody, he may be made to stand in a lineup for

---

[1]   388 U.S. 218, 87 S.Ct. 1926 (1967), this aspect of which is discussed in § 17.04(b).

[2]   *Doss v. United States*, 431 F.2d 601 (9th Cir. 1970).

[3]   *United States v. Parhms*, 424 F.2d 152 (9th Cir. 1970), cert. denied 400 U.S. 846, 91 S.Ct. 92 (1970); *United States v. Franks*, 511 F.2d 25 (6th Cir. 1975), cert. denied 422 U.S. 1042, 95 S.Ct. 2656 (1975) (refusal to comply with court order to give voice exemplar admissible to show guilt).

[4]   *Hayes v. Florida*, 470 U.S. 811, 105 S.Ct. 1643 (1985), discussed in § 17.04(a). See also, *United States v. Allen*, 408 F.2d 1287 (D.C.Cir. 1969) (forced participation in lineup for crime other than that for which defendant arrested permissible given that the similarity in modus operandi created a reasonable suspicion that he was responsible).

any crime as "filler material" (sometimes called a "distractor") without judicial authorization or any showing of suspicion.[5]

(b) Defense Request for a Lineup

The defendant may ask for a lineup prior to trial in an attempt to counteract the results of a previous, more suggestively conducted identification procedure, or merely to prove that the eyewitness cannot identify him. At least one lower court has held that due process requires granting a defense motion for a lineup where "eyewitness identification is shown to be a material issue and there exists a reasonable likelihood of a mistaken identification which a lineup would tend to resolve."[6] Most lower courts have held, however, that the matter is solely within the discretion of the trial court. In *United States v. Ravich*,[7] for instance, the court rejected the defendant's contention that he was constitutionally entitled to a lineup when the prosecution had chosen not to conduct one. Rather, it directed the trial court to consider carefully the defense request, taking into account a number of factors, including:

> the length of time between the crime or arrest and the request, the possibility that the defendant may have altered his appearance . . . , the extent of inconvenience to prosecution witnesses, the possibility that revealing the identity of the prosecution witnesses will subject them to intimidation, the propriety of other identification procedures used by the prosecution, and the degree of doubt concerning the identification.

The court found that the trial court had not abused its discretion in denying the defendant's request, in particular because prior photo identifications of the defendant had been conducted properly.

A defense request for a lineup *at* trial (as an alternative to an in-court identification while the defendant is seated at the defense table) is arguably on stronger ground. An in-court identification is often inherently suggestive, mainly because the defendant is seated conspicuously at the defense table. Indeed, in *Moore v. Illinois*,[8] the Supreme Court suggested that, at least when the in-court identification is the first confrontation between the witness and the defendant, counsel could postpone the proceeding until a lineup is arranged. But, again, many lower courts have left a ruling on such a request up to the trial court.[9] Thus, wide variation in practice exists. In *United States v. Moss*,[10] the court granted a continuance so that the defense attorney could bring in other members of the defendant's race to sit with him.[11] But in *Dent v. State*,[12] the appellate court found that an in-court, one-on-one identification was not improper simply because the defendant was the only member of his race in the courtroom.

---

[5]   *United States v. Anderson*, 490 F.2d 785 (D.C.Cir. 1974).

[6]   *Evans v. Superior Court*, 11 Cal.3d 617, 114 Cal.Rptr. 121, 522 P.2d 681 (1974).

[7]   421 F.2d 1196 (2d Cir. 1970), cert. denied 400 U.S. 834, 91 S.Ct. 69 (1970).

[8]   434 U.S. 220, 98 S.Ct. 458 (1977).

[9]   *Commonwealth v. Small*, 10 Mass.App.Ct. 606, 411 N.E.2d 179 (1980); *United States v. Williams*, 436 F.2d 1166 (9th Cir. 1970), cert. denied 402 U.S. 912, 91 S.Ct. 1392 (1971).

[10]   410 F.2d 386 (3d Cir. 1969), cert. denied 396 U.S. 993, 90 S.Ct. 488 (1969).

[11]   See also *State v. Talbot*, 408 So.2d 861 (La. 1981) (discussing trial court decision to allow defendant to sit with spectators in courtroom during witness identification).

[12]   423 So.2d 327 (Ala.Cr.App. 1982).

A slightly different argument was raised, and rejected, in *United States v. Hamilton*.[13] There, the defendant contended that the admissibility of an in-court identification derived from an initial photo identification should be conditioned upon an additional confirmatory procedure, such as a lineup. Although emphasizing the greater relative reliability of lineups and acknowledging the merit of the defendant's proposal, the court concluded that "confirmation of a photographic identification is not an imperative of due process." The court also declined to exercise its supervisory process to require such a confirmation. *Hamilton* would seem to follow from the Supreme Court's reliance on reliability as the "linchpin" of due process analysis, without regard to the suggestiveness or necessity of the identification procedure used.

(c) The Role of Counsel

The holding in *United States v. Wade* with respect to the right to counsel was based on the premise that "the presence of . . . counsel [at a post-indictment lineup] is necessary to preserve the defendant's basic right to a fair trial as affected by his right meaningfully to cross-examine the witnesses against him and to have effective assistance of counsel at the trial itself." This language suggests that counsel for the defendant should serve primarily as an observer of the identification procedure. As such, he will be able to reconstruct the circumstances of the pretrial lineup or confrontation at a suppression hearing, where he might be able to argue due process was violated, or at trial, where he can cast doubt on the credibility of the pretrial identification or an in-court identification.[14]

Other language in *Wade*, however, suggests a more active role. For instance, the opinion speaks of counsel's ability to "avert prejudice" and assist the police "by preventing the infiltration of taint in the prosecution's identification evidence." This conflicting language raises the issue, discussed in the previous chapter,[15] of whether the right to counsel should be based on a cross-examination/confrontation theory, or an assistance of counsel theory. Under the latter theory, counsel would not only observe, but might also be under an obligation to object to improper police procedures and, in an effort to avoid tainting eyewitness memory, attempt to prevent them from occurring.

The lower courts appear to take a middle tack. They have permitted counsel to make suggestions about the composition of the lineup, but do not require the police to follow them.[16] This stance has the practical advantage of minimizing attorney interference with police work, at the same time avoiding a subsequent claim by the prosecution that the defense attorney waived any due process claim by not raising it at the time of the lineup. Ideally, of course, the very presence of counsel will "avert prejudice" without the need for strenuous objections. The downside of this practice is that, once a suggestive lineup results in an identification, it will likely heavily influence any future identification.

The assistance of counsel theory also apparently limits counsel to situations in which the defendant is present.[17] Because the actual identification at a lineup (as

---

[13]   420 F.2d 1292 (D.C.Cir. 1969).

[14]   The attorney might also testify as to what he saw, but this action raises difficult ethical issues. See ABA Code of Professional Responsibility, DR 5–102 (lawyer who is to testify in client's case should withdraw, unless doing so "would work a substantial hardship," given possible conflicts of interest).

[15]   See § 17.02(a).

[16]   *People v. Borrego*, 668 P.2d 21 (Colo.App. 1983); *United States v. Eley*, 286 A.2d 239 (D.C.App. 1972); *United States v. Allen*, 408 F.2d 1287 (D.C.Cir. 1969).

[17]   See discussion of *United States v. Ash*, 413 U.S. 300, 93 S.Ct. 2568 (1973), in § 17.02(a).

opposed to the process of viewing it) can take place in the absence of the defendant, it may not be unconstitutional to bar counsel at this point. Under a right to confrontation interpretation of *Wade*, on the other hand, the opposite result would be required, since government manipulation, conscious or not, may have its most significant impact at the time the witness communicates a decision. Again, the lower courts have usually taken a middle ground, allowing counsel to be present during the viewing and the actual identification,[18] but not during questioning of the identifying witnesses after the identification.[19]

(d) Substitute Counsel

Wade held that use of substitute counsel is permissible if waiting for the suspect's counsel would result in "prejudicial delay." Given the time it takes to construct a good lineup, there will usually be enough time to contact the client's counsel if he is available. If substitute counsel is used, however, then appointed or retained counsel is under a duty to discover what he observed.[20] One court has suggested that the burden is on the government to provide trial counsel with a report of the substitute counsel's observations, and that failure to meet that burden should result in suppression of the identification.[21]

(e) Unnecessary Suggestiveness and Lineups

The "totality of circumstances" due process analysis discussed in the preceding chapter provides the touchstone for the determination of whether a lineup is unnecessarily suggestive.[22] The Court in *Wade* noted that lineup procedures have been suggestive when, for example,

> all in the lineup but the suspect were known to the identifying witness, . . . the other participants in a lineup were grossly dissimilar in appearance to the suspect, . . . only the suspect was required to wear distinctive clothing which the culprit allegedly wore, . . . the suspect is pointed out before or during a lineup, and . . . the participants in the lineup are asked to try on an article of clothing which fits only the suspect.

Another example of a suggestive lineup procedure is provided by *Foster v. California*.[23] There, the manager of a robbed Western Union office viewed a three-person lineup in which the defendant was the only one wearing a leather jacket similar to that worn by the robber and was a half-foot taller than the other two persons. Even so, the manager's identification was only tentative. The police then arranged a one-on-one confrontation with the defendant; again the identification was tentative. Finally, ten days later, the police arranged a second lineup in which the defendant was the only person who appeared in the first lineup. At this point, the manager became "convinced" that the defendant was the perpetrator. The Supreme Court reversed the conviction, noting that "[i]n effect, the police repeatedly said to the witness, '*This* is the man.'"

---

[18] *People v. Williams*, 3 Cal.3d 853, 92 Cal.Rptr. 6, 478 P.2d 942 (1971).

[19] Id.; see also, *United States v. Bierey*, 588 F.2d 620 (8th Cir. 1978); *United States v. Cunningham*, 423 F.2d 1269 (4th Cir. 1970).

[20] *United States v. Estes*, 485 F.2d 1078 (D.C.Cir. 1973), cert. denied 415 U.S. 923, 94 S.Ct. 1426 (1974).

[21] *Marshall v. United States*, 436 F.2d 155 (D.C.Cir. 1970).

[22] See § 17.03.

[23] 394 U.S. 440, 89 S.Ct. 1127 (1969).

To minimize the risk of suggestiveness, the Model Rules for Law Enforcement[24] propose the following procedures:

a.   All lineups should consist of at least 4 persons in addition to the suspect.

b.   Persons in the lineup should have approximately similar physical characteristics.

c.   The suspect should be permitted to select his own place in the line.

d.   All persons should be required to take whatever special action is required such as making gestures, speaking, showing profile or donning distinctive clothing.

e.   Persons present at the lineup should be warned to conduct themselves so as not to single out the suspect.

f.   Each lineup should be photographed or videotaped.[25]

Other protocols recommend that multiple witnesses not be present at the same time, that witnesses be given the option of identifying no one, and that the officer conducting the lineup not know who the suspect is.[26] Some have also suggested a "blank lineup" procedure, which includes only "innocent" people, to be followed by a lineup in which the suspect appears. If the witness picks someone out of the first lineup his accuracy is open to serious question, whereas if he selects no one out of the first lineup and the suspect out of the second, the identification is more trustworthy.[27] A modern version of this procedure is the sequential lineup, which presents one individual or picture at a time.[28] This procedure has been shown to be better than a simultaneous lineup at avoiding false identifications, but it is also less likely to result in identification of the true perpetrator.[29]

The utilization of such procedures might, as a practical matter, eliminate a due process challenge. Additionally, *Wade* suggested that this type of standardization would obviate the Sixth Amendment right to counsel at the lineup. In particular, the videotaping provision of the Model Rules would ensure that counsel receives a depiction of how the procedure was conducted. However, the actual identification, as well as the lineup session, should be videotaped if the tape is to provide a substitute for counsel.

18.03   Showups

On-the-scene "showups" and other types of witness-suspect "confrontations" differ from lineups in that the victim or witness is exposed to only one person for identification. The constitutional requirements imposed by due process and the right to counsel should apply with even more force to these more suggestive types of pretrial identification.

---

[24]   Arizona State University and Police Foundation, Model Rules for Law Enforcement, Eyewitness Identification 52 (1974) [hereinafter cited as Model Rules].

[25]   See, also *United States v. Smallwood*, 473 F.2d 98 (D.C.Cir. 1972).

[26]   *How Fair Is Your Lineup?*, 2 Social Action in Law 9–10 (1975).

[27]   Gerald D. Lefcourt, *The Blank Lineup: An Aid to the Defense*, 14 Crim. L. Bull. 428 (1978).

[28]   See Roy Malpass, *A Policy Evaluation of Simultaneous and Sequential Lineups*, 12 Psychol., Pub. Pol'y, & L. 1057 (2001).

[29]   Nancy K. Steblay, Jennifer E. Dysart & Gary L. Wells, *Seventy-Two Tests of the Sequential Lineup Superiority Effect: A Meta-Analysis and Policy Discussion*, 17 Psychol., Pub. Pol'y & L. 99 (2011).

(a) When Permissible

As a general rule, police should use lineups when feasible because confrontations are inherently suggestive.[30] However, the "totality of circumstances" still determines whether due process is violated in any individual case, and the courts have made clear that there are several circumstances in which one-on-one encounters are not only permissible but to be encouraged.

(1) Immobility or Loss of Witness

In *Stovall v. Denno*,[31] the Supreme Court approved a showup at the hospital where the victim of an assault was being treated for serious wounds. "Faced with the responsibility for identifying the attacker, with the need for immediate action and with the knowledge that [the victim] could not visit the jail, the police followed the only feasible procedure and took [the accused] to the hospital room." When the victim is on the verge of dying or in some other way will soon be unable to identify the perpetrator, a showup is clearly permissible. When there is no danger of losing the witness, but he is confined to the hospital, a showup may also be permissible.[32] But if a lineup or photo array can be arranged in the hospital, a showup may not be necessary; if so, it should be avoided, given its suggestive nature.

(2) Inaccessibility of Suspect

Suspects may also be incapable of participating in a lineup procedure. For instance, the suspect may be hospitalized, in which case a lineup is usually impossible.[33] A harder question arises when the police do not have the reasonable suspicion necessary to seize a person for an appearance in a lineup.[34] In such cases, it might be argued that the police are justified in taking the witness to the person's place of work,[35] or to any other place the suspect can be found. While this practice is suggestive, it does not involve a seizure and may be the only way in which the police can obtain a positive or negative identification. The possibility of a photo array should be considered, however.

(3) On-the-Scene Identifications

Courts have also been reluctant to overturn convictions based upon "on the scene" showups, despite their inherent suggestivity, for two reasons. Prompt identification is generally viewed as reasonable police procedure aimed at the quick solution of crime. In addition, the short lapse of time between the crime and the showup supports the reliability of the identification. Thus, the D.C. Circuit Court of Appeals, in *United States v. Perry*,[36] commented that a police regulation restricting on-the-scene confrontations to those instances where the suspect is arrested near the scene and within sixty minutes of the alleged offense represented a commendable effort "to balance the freshness of such a confrontation against its inherent suggestiveness, and to balance both factors against the need to pick up the trail while fresh if the suspect is not the offender." Another

---

[30]   *Foster v. California*, 394 U.S. 440, 89 S.Ct. 1127 (1969).

[31]   388 U.S. 293, 87 S.Ct. 1967 (1967).

[32]   *People v. Taylor*, 52 Ill.2d 293, 287 N.E.2d 673 (1972).

[33]   *Jackson v. United States*, 412 F.2d 149 (D.C.Cir. 1969).

[34]   See § 18.02(a).

[35]   Cf. *People v. Bradley*, 12 Ill.App.3d 783, 299 N.E.2d 99 (1973).

[36]   449 F.2d 1026 (D.C.Cir. 1971).

proposal would allow the suspect to be shown to the witness at any appropriate place if the apprehension occurs within two hours of the crime.[37]

It is debatable whether a short lapse of time between the crime and the identification automatically justifies a one-on-one confrontation. The suggestion that "this is the perpetrator" may well inaccurately fill in the perceptual and memory gaps that can plague any observer. But, properly conducted, a show-up within a short period after the offense may be permissible. For instance, in *United States v. McCoy*,[38] suspects were taken to the scene of a robbery within forty-eight minutes of its commission. A witness identification made at the on-the-scene showup was held admissible because a number of factors supported the reliability of the identification: the witness had had a good opportunity to observe the robber; the time lapse was short; the police refused to reply to inquiries by the witness as to whether the suspects were the robbers and whether the stolen property had been recovered; the witness identification was firmly positive; and the witness had previously refused to identify another man as the robber. In *United States v. Hines*,[39] the court held that an on-the-scene showup of a suspect in handcuffs did not automatically violate due process when four of five witnesses simultaneously identified him only ten minutes after the crime.

(4) Non-Emergency Showups

Even when no emergency exists, a one-on-one encounter may be permissible if the identification it produces is considered reliable in the totality of the circumstances. In *Neil v. Biggers*,[40] the Supreme Court sanctioned an arranged stationhouse encounter, involving Biggers, the victim and five officers, that was not necessitated by exigency; the victim was not in *extremis* and the encounter took place seven months after the crime had occurred. Although the justification for the confrontation was somewhat weak—police claimed to be unable to find other individuals with the defendant's "unique" characteristics and thus did not hold a lineup—the Court found the identification reliable.

While the Court may well have been right, a close look at the facts of *Biggers* illustrates why suggestive procedures should be avoided.[41] According to the Court, the victim had viewed her assailant for almost one-half hour, under adequate lighting conditions. The Court ignored or discounted the facts that the rape occurred in an unlit kitchen (although light filtered through from another room), and that during much of the incident the victim was either being threatened with a knife—which might have triggered weapons focus—or had her back to the assailant as he forced her to walk ahead of him after the rape occurred). The Court also stated that the victim had given police, prior to the showup, a description of her assailant that fit the defendant; however, that description—depicting the assailant as flabby, smooth skinned, and bushy-haired, with a youthful voice—was extremely vague. The court also emphasized that the victim had refused to identify anyone as her assailant during several previous identification procedures, while on this occasion she had had "no doubt" the defendant was the person

---

[37] *Model Rules*, supra note 24, Rule 202. See also, *Johnson v. Dugger*, 817 F.2d 726 (11th Cir. 1987) ("immediate confrontations allow identification before the suspect has altered his appearance and while the witness' memory is fresh, and permit the quick release of innocent persons.").

[38] 475 F.2d 344 (D.C.Cir. 1973).

[39] 455 F.2d 1317 (D.C.Cir. 1971), cert. denied 406 U.S. 975, 92 S.Ct. 2427 (1972).

[40] 409 U.S. 188, 93 S.Ct. 375 (1972).

[41] Some of these facts are found only in the lower court opinion, 448 F.2d 91 (6th Cir. 1971).

who had attacked her. At the same time, after eight months of searching for the perpetrator, frustration (on the part of both the victim and the police) and the vicissitudes of memory may have played a significant role in the identification.

(5) Accidental Confrontations

When a confrontation occurs accidentally, the possibility of improper police action is removed, and courts are understandably even more reluctant to find a violation of due process in an ensuing identification. In *United States v. Pollack*,[42] the witness had been unable to identify the defendant in photographs but unexpectedly encountered and recognized the defendant in a courthouse corridor. A subsequent in-court identification was held admissible. In *United States v. Evans*,[43] a chance street encounter between the witness and the defendant led to the identification of the defendant. A police officer assisted the witness in re-identifying the defendant a few minutes after the initial confrontation. The court, finding the police conduct to be reasonable and in good faith, approved the identification.[44]

(6) In-Court Identifications

Probably the most suggestive type of showup is the in-court identification. The defendant is clearly labelled as such, and the witness is under considerable public pressure not to contradict the state's decision to prosecute. Where there has been a previous, properly conducted identification of the same person, this course of action might be justifiable.[45] However, when the in-court identification is the first identification, courts should be more cautious.[46] As noted earlier, the Supreme Court itself has stated, in *Moore v. Illinois*,[47] that it "is difficult to imagine a more suggestive manner in which to present a suspect to a witness for their critical first confrontation." *Moore* suggested that, in this situation, the court should consider a lineup or seating the defendant in the courtroom with the audience. Yet other courts have indicated that, at trial at least (*Moore* involved a preliminary hearing), a first-time in-court identification need not be avoided, since the "defendant's protection against the obvious suggestiveness in any courtroom identification confrontation is his right to cross-examine."[48]

(b) The Right to Counsel

After *Kirby v. Illinois*,[49] it was clear that a showup that occurs once prosecution has commenced, "by way of formal charge, preliminary hearing, indictment, information, or arraignment," requires counsel. Because most showups occur prior to this point in the process, the right to counsel is usually inapplicable to this procedure. Even for post-charge showups, the same exigencies that justify a showup, described above, may justify foregoing notification of counsel.[50] If there is no time to arrange a lineup, then there may

---

[42]   427 F.2d 1168 (5th Cir. 1970), cert. denied 400 U.S. 831, 91 S.Ct. 63 (1970).

[43]   438 F.2d 162 (D.C.Cir. 1971), cert. denied 402 U.S. 1010, 91 S.Ct. 2196 (1971).

[44]   Note that an identification resulting from an accidental confrontation may still be excluded as unreliable.

[45]   As to the proper result when the previous identification was not properly conducted, see § 17.05(a).

[46]   Cf. *United States ex rel. Haywood v. O'Leary*, 827 F.2d 52 (7th Cir. 1987).

[47]   434 U.S. 220, 98 S.Ct. 458 (1977).

[48]   *State v. Smith*, 200 Conn. 465, 512 A.2d 189 (1986).

[49]   406 U.S. 682, 92 S.Ct. 1877 (1972).

[50]   Cf. the lower court decision in *United States ex rel. Stovall v. Denno*, 355 F.2d 731 (2d Cir. 1966).

be no time to contact counsel, if the suspect has one, or to appoint counsel, if the suspect does not. On the other hand, when the showup is due solely to the immobility of the witness or the suspect, counsel or a substitute should be present.

The role of counsel at showups is similar to his role at lineups. The conduct of the police and the witness should be observed with an eye to challenging the credibility of the identification at a later stage. Counsel might also be able to persuade the police to conduct a less suggestive identification procedure. When the showup occurs in court, *Moore* suggests that counsel may be even more active and argue for alternative procedures, including a lineup.

18.04 Photograph Identification

Law enforcement officers often use photographic displays to identify suspects prior to arrest. Usually, analogous to a lineup, the police use a photo array, in which pictures of several individuals are displayed. Occasionally, however, they rely on the photo version of a showup—a showing of one photograph. The Supreme Court has approved both techniques, despite the likelihood that they are less reliable than their in-person counterparts.[51] In *Simmons v. United States*,[52] the Court noted that identification by photographs "has been used widely and effectively in criminal law" and approved use of an array in that case. In *Manson v. Brathwaite*,[53] it refused to find invalid an in-court identification based on an earlier identification from a single photograph, since the totality of the circumstances indicated the earlier determination was reliable. Further, the Court has held that, in contrast to lineups and showups, there is no right to counsel at a photo identification procedure.[54]

(a) When Permissible

Given its lesser reliability, a photo array should not be used when a lineup is possible. For instance, the Model Rules for Law Enforcement suggest that photo displays only be relied upon when the suspect has not been apprehended, the suspect threatens to be disruptive, or there is a lack of suitable persons for a lineup.[55] The Supreme Court lent some credence to this view in *Simmons*, when it emphasized, in approving the photo array in that case, that a swift identification was necessary to apprehend the suspect, who was still at large. However, most courts do not make the admissibility of a photo identification dependent upon whether a lineup was feasible; instead, they focus on the danger of mistaken identification in light of the way in which the photo identification was conducted.[56]

(b) Due Process Requirements

As a general rule, suggestiveness varies inversely with the number of pictures displayed. Most obviously, if the police show the witness a single picture of the suspect, the potential for suggestiveness is quite high. The Model Rules for Law Enforcement

---

[51] P. Wall, Eyewitness Identification in Criminal Cases 83 (1965).

[52] 390 U.S. 377, 88 S.Ct. 967 (1968).

[53] 432 U.S. 98, 97 S.Ct. 2243 (1977).

[54] *United States v. Ash*, 413 U.S. 300, 93 S.Ct. 2568 (1973), discussed in § 17.02(a).

[55] Model Rules, supra note 24, Rule 305.

[56] *State v. Emerson*, 149 Vt. 171, 541 A.2d 466 (1987).

recommend that photographs of at least seven individuals of substantially similar appearance be displayed to avoid suggestiveness.[57]

As *Manson* demonstrates, however, the display of a single photograph is not prohibited even when the procedure is unnecessary. Several cases have approved this practice under questionable circumstances. For instance, in *Chaney v. State*,[58] the court held that police investigating a rape case were justified in showing the victim a single photograph of the defendant, who was a suspect in another rape case, because the rapist had mentioned to the victim that he had previously been jailed on a rape charge. In *Virgin Islands v. Petersen*[59] a photo identification array was held admissible even though it consisted of only two photographs, both of the defendant. Although both decisions emphasized that the witnesses had a good opportunity to view the perpetrator, in both the suggestive use of photos was also unnecessary. In contrast, in *United States v. Cox*,[60] the flight of the criminal presented urgent circumstances dictating that no time be spent on arranging a display.

Assuming a full display is used, it should not be arranged so that a particular individual's picture is in some way emphasized. In *People v. Citrino*,[61] for instance, the court rejected an identification based on a photo array shown to the witness shortly before trial in which the defendant was pictured three times in a five-picture display. In another case, an alteration of only the suspect's photograph to show a "fu manchu" was disapproved.[62]

The danger of the misidentification may be exacerbated by other factors as well. Multiple witnesses should be separated during the viewing of a display. The police should not indicate to the witness that a particular individual pictured in a display has been implicated in the crime by other evidence.[63] Showing a number of photograph arrays in which the suspect is the only repeater may also single out the suspect to the witness.[64] As with the single photo display cases, however, the courts generally indicate that none of these practices automatically invalidates an identification; instead, the "linchpin" of the analysis is whether the identification is reliable.[65]

18.05 Conclusion

The rules governing the conduct of identification procedures and use of their results that have been discussed in this and the preceding chapter can be summarized as follows:

---

[57] Model Rules, supra note 24, Rule 306.

[58] 267 So.2d 65 (Fla. 1972).

[59] 553 F.2d 324 (3d Cir. 1977).

[60] 428 F.2d 683 (7th Cir. 1970), cert. denied 400 U.S. 881, 91 S.Ct. 127 (1970).

[61] 90 Cal.Rptr. 80, 11 Cal.App.3d 778 (1970).

[62] *State v. Alexander*, 108 Ariz. 556, 503 P.2d 777 (1972). Compare *Rudd v. State*, 477 F.2d 805 (5th Cir. 1973) (each photo was altered).

[63] See *People v. Brown*, 52 Ill.2d 94, 285 N.E.2d 1 (1972), for an arguably appropriate method of proceeding in such situations.

[64] See *King v. State*, 18 Md.App. 266, 306 A.2d 258 (1973).

[65] See, e.g., *Nicholson v. State*, 523 So.2d 68 (Miss. 1988) (fact that defendant was the only person in display to have tattoo was suggestive in light of earlier description, but no risk of misidentification); *State v. Pigott*, 320 N.C. 96, 357 S.E.2d 631 (1987) (only one of 9 other pictures similar to defendant's, but no risk of misidentification).

(1)   The accused has a right to counsel at any pretrial lineup or showup that occurs at or after the initial appearance before a judicial officer, unless waiting for counsel would cause "prejudicial delay," in which case substitute counsel is required. There is no right to counsel at accidental or spontaneous confrontations, photographic displays, or "scientific" identification procedures that do not rely on eyewitnesses, such as fingerprinting or the taking of handwriting exemplars. Further, regulations governing the conduct of identification procedures along the lines provided in (3) below could eliminate the need for, and thus the right to, counsel in those situations where it attaches.

(2)   In addition to meeting any Sixth Amendment requirement, an identification procedure must meet the demands of due process. Reliability is the linchpin of due process analysis. Thus, a lineup, showup, or photo display that suggests a particular result, even if unnecessarily so, is not unconstitutional if the identification it produces is considered reliable after evaluating the totality of the circumstances. Factors to be considered in evaluating reliability include (a) the opportunity of the witness to view the criminal at the time of the crime; (b) the witness' degree of attention; (c) the accuracy of the witness' prior description of the criminal; (d) the level of certainty demonstrated by the witness at the confrontation; (e) the length of time between the crime and the confrontation; and (f) any discrepancies in identifications, if there is more than one.

(3)   Although suggestivity is not dispositive of the due process issue, every effort should be made to avoid suggestive procedures. Lineups and photo displays should include a number of alternatives to the suspect, of approximately similar physical characteristics, and should avoid singling out the suspect in any way. Show-ups and one-photo displays should be avoided unless emergency circumstances dictate their use. There is no right to demand the least suggestive procedure available, however.

(4)   If evidence of an identification is found inadmissible under the above rules, then not only that identification but also any later identification by the same person must be excluded, unless the prosecution can show that evidence of the subsequent identification is derived from a source independent of the tainted identification. Factors to be considered in gauging the degree of taint in a subsequent identification are virtually identical to those considered in evaluating reliability, including: (a) the witness' prior opportunity to observe the alleged criminal act; (b) any discrepancy between the witness' pre-identification descriptions and the defendant's actual description; (c) any pre-identification naming of another person by the witness; (d) any failure to identify the defendant on a prior occasion, and (e) the lapse of time between the alleged act and the identification alleged to be tainted.

(5)   The admissibility of a pretrial or in court identification is determined by the judge, although the jury may be present during the hearing, at least when its presence does not significantly inhibit the defendant's cross-examination and when the identification is ultimately found admissible.

BIBLIOGRAPHY

Cicchini, Michael D. and Joseph G. Easton. Reforming the Law of Show-Up Identifications. 100 J. Crim. L. and Criminology 381 (2010).

Clark, Steve E., Ryan T. Howell and Sherrie L. Davey. Regularities in Eyewitness Identification. 32 Law & Hum. Beh. 198 (2008).

Davis, Deborah and Elizabeth Loftus. The Dangers of Eyewitnesses for the Innocent: Learning from the Past and Projecting into the Age of Social Media. 46 New Eng. L. Rev. 769 (2012).

Garrett, Brandon. Eyewitnesses and Exclusion. 65 Vand. L. Rev. 951 (2012).

Grano, Joseph. *Kirby*, *Biggers*, and *Ash*: Do Any Constitutional Safeguards Remain Against the Danger of Convicting the Innocent? 72 Mich.L.Rev. 717 (1974).

Gross, Samuel. Loss of Innocence: Eyewitness Identification and Proof of Guilt. 16 J.Leg.Studies 395 (1987).

Haber, Ralph Norman and Lyn Haber. Experiencing, Remembering and Reporting Events. 6 Psychol. Pub. Pol'y & L. 1057 (2000).

Levine, Felice J. and June L. Tapp. The Psychology of Criminal Identification: The Gap from *Wade* to *Kirby*. 121 U.Pa.L.Rev. 1079 (1973).

Loftus, Elizabeth. Eyewitness Testimony (1979).

Malpass, Roy. A Policy Evaluation of Simultaneous and Sequential Lineups. 12 Psychol., Pub. Pol'y & L. 394 (2006).

O'Toole, Timothy and Giovanna Shay. *Manson v. Braithwaite* Revisited: Towards a New Rule of Decision for Due Process Challenges to Eyewitness Identification Procedures. 49 Val. U. L. Rev. 109 (2006).

Sonenshein, David A. and Robin Nilon. Eyewitness Errors and Wrongful Convictions: Let's Give Science a Chance. 89 Or. L. Rev. 362 (2010).

Steblay, Nancy. Scientific Advances in Eyewitness Identification Evidence. 41 Wm. Mitchell L. Rev. 1090 (2015).

Thompson, Sandra Guerra. Eyewitness Identifications and State Courts as Guardians Against Wrongful Convictions. 7 Ohio St. J. Crim. L. 603 (2010).

Trenary, Amy. *State v. Henderson*: A Model for Admitting Eyewitness Identification Testimony. 84 Colo. L. Rev. 1247 (2013).

Uviller, Richard H. The Role of the Defense Lawyer at a Lineup in Light of the *Wade*, *Gilbert* and *Stovall* Decisions. 4 Crim.L.Bull. 273 (1968).

Wells, Gary L. Eyewitness Identification: Systemic Reforms. 2006 Wisc. L. Rev. 615.

Part D

ENTRAPMENT

The defense of entrapment arises when a defendant, who has admittedly committed a crime, can prove that the actions of law enforcement authorities caused him to commit it. As presently interpreted by the Supreme Court, the defense is "substantive" rather than procedural in nature, in the sense that it focuses on the defendant's mental state at the time of the offense rather than on the nature of the police conduct prior to and during commission of the crime. It is included in this book because the minority view of the defense holds that it should be construed as a constraint on police practices. As such, the entrapment defense operates like the exclusionary rule to deter police engaging in particularly egregious behavior.

Chapter 19

THE ENTRAPMENT DEFENSE

19.01 Introduction

The defense of entrapment is grounded in the belief that the government should not be able to convict a person for a crime which the government itself instigated. But this simple idea can be framed in many ways. In deciding whether the government has been an "instigator," some courts consider only whether the defendant was predisposed to commit the crime at the time of the instigation (the "predisposition" or "subjective" test). If he was, then regardless of how coercive or egregious the government conduct, he is not entitled to a defense.[1] Other courts have considered the predisposition of the defendant relatively insignificant, and focused instead on the conduct of the government (the "conduct of the authorities" or "objective" test).[2] As described in the American Law Institute's Model Penal Code, under this test if the government "employ[ed] methods of persuasion or inducement which create a substantial risk that such an offense will be committed by persons other than those who are ready to commit it," then a defense will lie regardless of the particular defendant's willingness to commit the offense.[3] This test has also been called the "hypothetical person" test, because it looks at whether the reasonable innocent person would give in to the government's blandishments. Still other courts combine the two approaches, looking first at whether the conduct of the authorities was improper and, if not, then looking at whether the defendant was predisposed to commit the crime (the "hybrid" test).[4]

Finally, several courts have held that, regardless of the test used in the typical case, if the government conduct is so "outrageous" as to shock the conscience, then acquittal should result as a matter of constitutional due process (the due process test).[5] Although this last test is similar to the conduct of authorities standard, it is both broader and narrower. It is broader because it covers any government conduct that is outrageous, whether or not it might encourage crime; it is narrower because, to the extent it does cover government instigation, it applies only to the most egregious official conduct. Under this test and the conduct of authorities test, the burden of proof is usually on the defendant, whereas the government must prove predisposition beyond a reasonable doubt.[6]

As the first section of this chapter indicates, the Supreme Court has consistently applied the predisposition test, although some members of the Court have argued strongly for the conduct of authorities approach, and a few have contended that a very limited due process defense should also be recognized. As the second section

---

[1] *Hampton v. United States*, 425 U.S. 484, 96 S.Ct. 1646 (1976) (plurality opinion); *United States v. Rey*, 811 F.2d 1453 (11th Cir. 1987) (defendant who was predisposed to commit crime cannot be entrapped, regardless of how outrageous or overreaching government's conduct may be).

[2] *People v. Barraza*, 23 Cal.3d 675, 153 Cal.Rptr. 459, 591 P.2d 947 (1979).

[3] ALI Model Penal Code § 2.13 (1962).

[4] *Moore v. State*, 534 So.2d 557 (Miss. 1988).

[5] *United States v. Twigg*, 588 F.2d 373 (3d Cir. 1978), discussed in § 19.03(a).

[6] *Jacobson v. United States*, 503 U.S. 540, 112 S.Ct. 1535 (1992). Note also that, in federal court, a defendant may plead both guilty and "guilty but entrapped." *Mathews v. United States*, 485 U.S. 58, 108 S.Ct. 883 (1988).

demonstrates, because the Supreme Court has refused to constitutionalize the defense, the lower courts have been much more diverse in their approach.

19.02 Supreme Court Cases

(a) The Statutory Basis of the Defense

A consistent majority of the Court has held that the availability of the entrapment defense is purely a matter of statutory interpretation and does not derive from the Constitution. The Court's first explicit entrapment opinion, the 1932 decision of *Sorrells v. United States*,[7] laid down what remains today the Court's approach to entrapment. Chief Justice Hughes stated: "We are unable to conclude that it was the intention of Congress in enacting [the National Prohibition Act] that its processes of detection or enforcement should be abused by the instigation by government officials of an act on the part of persons otherwise innocent in order to lure them to its commission and punish them." The idea that the defense is derived purely from legislative intent was repeated over twenty-five years later by Chief Justice Warren in *Sherman v. United States*,[8] and restated by Justice Rehnquist in *United States v. Russell*,[9] where he noted that the defense is rooted "in the notion that Congress could not have intended criminal punishment for a defendant who has committed all the elements of a proscribed offense, but was induced to commit them by the Government."

In *Sorrells*, Chief Justice Hughes noted that one consequence of this interpretation of the defense was that certain defendants may not be able to claim it. In particular, he cautioned that a defendant who has committed "heinous" or "revolting" crimes may not assert the defense. Apparently, this limitation is based on the idea that, whatever legislative intent is with respect to other offenses, the legislature would not permit acquittal of someone who could be persuaded to commit a violent crime, regardless of the strength of the persuasion or the original innocence of the perpetrator. Furthermore, as the language in both *Sorrells* and *Russell* indicates, the entrapment defense has been limited to situations in which the instigator was a government official or agent. Although a person could just as easily be induced to commit crime by a private individual (indeed, as far as the offender is concerned, there is no difference between a private and governmental instigator), the Court has again justified this limitation as a matter of legislative intent.

Justice Frankfurter, in his concurring opinion in *Sherman*, argued that the legislative intent rationale for the entrapment defense is "sheer fiction." In his opinion, "the Courts refuse to convict an entrapped defendant, not because his conduct falls outside the proscription of the statute, but because, even if his guilt be admitted, the methods employed on behalf of the Government to bring about conviction cannot be countenanced." But Frankfurter too avoided a constitutional view of entrapment. Rather, he felt that the defense derived from the federal courts' "supervisory jurisdiction over the administration of criminal justice." This latter position has been the usual stance of those members of the Court who prefer the conduct of the authorities test. No member of the Court has viewed the entrapment defense as constitutionally based

---

7   287 U.S. 435, 53 S.Ct. 210 (1932).
8   356 U.S. 369, 78 S.Ct. 819 (1958).
9   411 U.S. 423, 93 S.Ct. 1637 (1973).

although, as discussed below,[10] some have recognized the narrow due process defense, which they view as separate and apart from the entrapment test.

(b) Predisposition v. Conduct of Authorities

The Court's few decisions on entrapment demonstrate a deep split among its members. In each case, the majority focused primarily, if not entirely, on the predisposition of the defendant to commit the act alleged, while the minority view opted for the conduct of the authorities approach.

In *Sorrells*, the defendant was charged with selling whiskey to a prohibition agent in violation of the National Prohibition Act. The agent was introduced to the defendant at the latter's house. After two unsuccessful attempts, the agent finally convinced the defendant to sell him whiskey by "taking advantage of the sentiment aroused by reminiscences of their experiences as companions in arms in the World War." The lower courts ruled as a matter of law that there was no entrapment.

Chief Justice Hughes concluded in the majority opinion that the issue of entrapment should have been submitted to the jury. He described the case as one in which "the criminal design originates with the officials of the Government and they implant in the mind of an innocent person the disposition to commit the alleged offense and induce its commission in order that they may prosecute." But, in discussing the conduct of the prohibition agent, he was careful to point out that in several cases decided by the Court "artifice and stratagem" were found to be permissible methods of catching those engaged in criminal enterprise. Most importantly, he noted that, in addition to evidence tending to show reprehensible conduct by the authorities, testimony relevant to the defendant's inclination to commit the alleged act is admissible in such cases: "[I]f the defendant seeks acquittal by reason of entrapment, he cannot complain of an appropriate and searching inquiry into his own conduct and predisposition as bearing upon that issue."

In a concurring opinion, Justice Roberts, joined by Justice Brandeis and Justice Stone, clearly set out for the first time the "conduct of authorities" test.[11] The basis for this approach to entrapment is "the public policy which protects the purity of government and its processes." On this view, the government should not use its machinery to consummate a wrong. Nor should it be allowed to introduce evidence showing "that the defendant had a bad reputation or had previously transgressed. . . ." Allowing the authorities' conduct to be "rendered innocuous" by such evidence "in effect, pivots convictions in such cases, not on the commission of the crime charged, but on the prior reputation or some former act or acts of the defendant not mentioned in the indictment." Thus, according to the minority view, where entrapment is raised, only the conduct of the authorities should be examined. Furthermore, Roberts concluded, it is the province of the court, not the jury, to determine whether there was entrapment. This role falls to the court because it is a necessary step in the "preservation of the purity" of the judicial process, a duty obviously belonging to the court. While the court may seek the jury's help in resolving the facts, the judge must make the ultimate determination.

---

[10]   See § 19.02(d).

[11]   The *Roberts* opinion restated and refined a dissent by Justice Brandeis in *Casey v. United States*, 276 U.S. 413, 48 S.Ct. 373 (1928), which stated in part: "This prosecution should be stopped, not because some right of [the defendant's] has been denied, but in order to protect the Government. To protect it from illegal conduct of its officers. To preserve the purity of its courts."

The Supreme Court next addressed the entrapment defense in *Sherman*, where a government informant met the defendant at a doctor's office where both were being treated to cure narcotics addiction. Thereafter, the two met accidentally several times at the office or at a pharmacy. After progressing in conversation from mere greetings to discussions of mutual experiences and problems, the informant first asked the defendant if he knew a supplier of drugs and then whether the defendant himself could supply the narcotics. The defendant attempted to avoid the issue, but after repeated requests, apparently predicated on the informant's suffering and his failure to respond to institutionalized treatment, the defendant agreed. Thereafter, the defendant procured drugs and shared them with the informant several times, at a cost approximately equal to the defendant's expenses incurred when obtaining the drug. The defendant was arrested after government agents observed many of these transactions. The defendant was convicted by a jury over his claim of entrapment and the circuit court of appeals affirmed.

The Supreme Court reversed, finding entrapment was "patently clear" as a matter of law. But Chief Justice Warren's majority opinion adhered to the predisposition test. According to Warren, in determining whether entrapment has occurred, "a line must be drawn between the trap for the unwary innocent and the trap for the unwary criminal." As for the propriety of adopting Justice Roberts' conduct of the authorities standard, he noted that the issue had not been argued. But he ventured that such a test was too broad; if the government could not reply to a claim of improper inducement with a showing that the conduct was due to the defendant's "own readiness," the prosecution would suffer a "handicap [that] is obvious." He then quoted Judge Learned Hand from the court below, to the effect that, under the official conduct test, "it would be impossible ever to secure convictions of any offences which consist of transactions that are carried on in secret." Although this point is certainly exaggerated, it is true that judging the conduct of undercover agents can be difficult without knowing how predisposed the defendant was. Conduct that may seem impermissible with respect to an "unwary innocent" might be justifiable in connection with a "wary criminal," who is familiar with and leery of sting operations and the like. The Court also refused to address Roberts' contention that entrapment issues should be decided by the court, but noted that all of the circuit courts of appeals had held otherwise.

Undaunted, Justice Frankfurter, in a concurring opinion, argued that the official conduct test would best serve the "transcending value at stake," which he defined as "public confidence in the fair and honorable administration of justice, upon which ultimately depends the rule of law." He noted that if the predisposition test, which is focused on the individual rather than the police, is the correct standard, then encouragement by private individuals, as well as entrapment by government officials, would also have to be a defense for the "unwary innocent." To Frankfurter, the inquiry should instead be "whether the police conduct revealed in the particular case falls below standards, to which common feelings respond, for the proper use of governmental power." Echoing Roberts, he contended that this test would avoid the "grave prejudice that a defendant suffers if hearsay and other reputation evidence is admitted to show predisposition."[12] Further, he stated that the subjective test would produce inconsistent results: "surely if two suspects have been solicited at the same time in the same manner,

---

[12]   Note that reputation evidence need not be admissible in entrapment cases. Rather, the government could be forced to rely on the defendant's behavior between the time of government contact and the commission of the offense. Roger Park, *The Entrapment Controversy*, 60 Minn.L.Rev. 163, 272 (1976). But see § 19.02(c).

one should not go to jail simply because he has been convicted before and is said to have a criminal disposition." He also expressed concern that the predisposition test might encourage police abuse of those defendants who are predisposed; he noted "the possibility that no matter what his past crimes and general disposition the defendant might not have committed the particular crime unless confronted with inordinate inducements."

But the minority view was definitively discarded by the Court in its next entrapment case, *Russell*. There, a government narcotics agent posed as a narcotics manufacturer and distributor who was interested in controlling the manufacture and distribution of methamphetamine. He offered to supply the defendants with one of the difficult-to-obtain ingredients for manufacture of the drug in return for half of the drug produced. This offer was accepted. There was also testimony that the defendants had obtained from another source the scarce ingredient both before and after they obtained it from the narcotics agent. The court of appeals overturned the conviction, saying that there had been "an intolerable degree of governmental participation in the criminal enterprise," on either of two alternative theories: (1) that there is entrapment as a matter of law whenever the government supplies contraband to defendants,[13] or (2) that there is entrapment whenever the government is so enmeshed in the criminal activity that the prosecution is repugnant to the American criminal justice system.[14]

Justice Rehnquist's majority opinion dismissed both theories, finding that there was sufficient predisposition on the part of the defendants to invalidate an entrapment defense. Though acknowledging that "we may some day be presented with a situation in which the conduct of law enforcement agents is so outrageous that due process principles would absolutely bar the government from invoking judicial processes to obtain a conviction," he concluded that the present case was "distinctly not of that breed" because the government had merely supplied a legal and harmless substance to a person who had previously been "an active participant in an illegal drug manufacturing enterprise." Two dissents, by Justices Stewart and Douglas, argued that the majority applied the wrong standard. Stewart contended that the courts *must* look at official conduct in order to ensure that the conduct does not drop to a level "not to be tolerated by an advanced society." At the least, he suggested, the predisposition test should not be applicable when the substance provided the defendants is "wholly unobtainable from . . . sources" other than the government.

In a fourth Supreme Court entrapment case, *Hampton v. United States*,[15] the defendant was convicted of distributing heroin that was supplied to the defendant by a government informant and then sold by the defendant to two government agents. Justice Rehnquist's plurality opinion again reaffirmed the *Sorrells-Sherman* predisposition approach and rejected the governmental conduct approach. In its strongest statement to date against the latter test, the Court averred that its previous decisions had ruled out the "possibility that the defense of entrapment could ever be based upon governmental misconduct . . . where the predisposition of the defendant to commit the crime was established." In response to petitioner's argument that the government's provision of contraband should be ruled a *per se* denial of due process, Rehnquist admitted that "[t]he Government obviously played a more significant role in enabling petitioner to sell contraband in this case than it did in *Russell*." But "[i]f the police engage in illegal

---

[13]   Citing *United States v. Bueno*, 447 F.2d 903 (5th Cir. 1971).

[14]   Citing *Greene v. United States*, 454 F.2d 783 (9th Cir. 1971).

[15]   425 U.S. 484, 96 S.Ct. 1646 (1976).

activity in concert with a defendant beyond the scope of their duties the remedy lies, not in freeing the equally culpable defendant, but in prosecuting the police under the applicable provisions of state or federal law."

The dissent, authored this time by Justice Brennan and joined by two others, expressed the by now firmly entrenched minority approach and called for reversal of the conviction because "[t]he Government is doing nothing less than buying contraband from itself through an intermediary and jailing the intermediary." The dissent felt that this type of governmental activity could not be tolerated and that, at a minimum, the Court should adopt the principle that there is entrapment "as a matter of law where the subject of the criminal charge is the sale of contraband provided to the defendant by a government agent."

(c) The Definition of Predisposition

By the time of the *Hampton* decision, the Court had clearly settled on the subjective, predisposition test for entrapment. But it had yet to offer guidance on the contours of this test. In the three cases in which it came to a definite decision on the entrapment issue—*Sherman, Russell,* and *Hampton*—the existence of predisposition, or the absence thereof, was obvious. In *Sherman,* where the Court found entrapment as a matter of law, the defendant had apparently never engaged in selling drugs prior to his contact with the government agent, only reluctantly became involved after repeated government inducements, and even then did so only as a favor and not in an effort to gain money. In the latter two cases, on the other hand, the defendants were known to have previously been involved in illegal drug activity.

In *Jacobson v. United States,*[16] the Court confronted a more difficult case, and thus had to be more explicit about its views on the predisposition issue. In the process, the Court appeared to adopt a relatively expansive view of the entrapment defense. First, it held that predisposition to commit the crime must pre-exist the government's initial contact with the defendant. Second, it suggested that proof of predisposition requires more than showing a mere "inclination" to engage in the illegal activity.

In *Jacobson,* the defendant was convicted of knowingly receiving child pornography through the mails. Over a two and one-half year period prior to his arrest the government had sent him various mailings, from five fictitious organizations, asking about his sexual attitudes toward boys, extolling the value of free sexual expression, and suggesting that government laws banning pornography were unconstitutional. The defendant responded to many of these mailings, disclosing an interest both in seeing pictures of pre-teen sex and in supporting a (fictitious) group lobbying to change pornography laws. However, on only two occasions, at the end of the two and one-half year period, did he order child pornography materials; the first order was never filled, the second resulted in his arrest. Furthermore, there was no evidence that the defendant ordered any similar material from any other organization during this time. Prior to this period, on the other hand, he had ordered two child pornography magazines from a private organization (apparently thinking they would only contain pictures of boys 18 and older), at a time when possession of child pornography was not a crime under either federal or state law.

A five-member majority held that the defendant was entrapped as a matter of law. Justice White, who wrote the majority opinion, stated that "although [the defendant]

---

[16]   503 U.S. 540, 112 S.Ct. 1535 (1992).

had become predisposed to break the law [by the time of the arrest], it is our view that the Government did not prove that this predisposition was independent and not the product of the attention that the Government had directed at petitioner [over the two and-one-half years preceding the arrest]." Rejecting the argument that the defendant's pre-contact purchase of magazines met the government's burden, he stated that "[e]vidence of predisposition to do what once was lawful is not, by itself, sufficient to show predisposition to do what is now illegal, for there is a common understanding that most people obey the law even when they disapprove of it." Quoting from *Sorrells*, he concluded that "[l]aw enforcement officials go too far when they 'implant in the mind of an innocent person the *disposition* to commit the alleged offense and induce its commission in order that they may prosecute.'"

Justice O'Connor, in dissent, argued that the majority's definition of predisposition might lead lower courts to require the government to show that it had a "reasonable suspicion of criminal activity before it begins an investigation," which would run counter to the Court's cases holding that the Fourth Amendment does not apply to undercover activity.[17] While the majority explicitly denied it was imposing such a requirement, O'Connor is right that showing the existence of predisposition prior to the initial contact will be difficult in connection with some types of government sting operations, such as advertising campaigns aimed at culling from the general population those who are interested in pornography and similar types of illegal activity. Yet such random inducement operations probably *should* be inhibited, if only because they are likely to cause crime that otherwise would never have occurred.[18] The FBI itself provides that inducement to commit a crime should not be offered unless "(a) there is a reasonable indication, based on information developed through informants or other means, that the subject is engaging, has engaged, or is likely to engage in illegal activity of a similar type; or (b) the opportunity for illegal activity has been structured so that there is reason for believing that persons drawn to the opportunity, or brought to it, are predisposed to engage in the contemplated illegal activity."[19]

A second aspect of *Jacobson* may ultimately have greater impact on entrapment law. To bolster the conclusion that the defendant lacked predisposition independent of the government's blandishments, White not only discounted his original magazine purchases but also refused to characterize the defendant's conduct during the two and one-half year inducement period as evidence of a desire to commit crime; as he put it, "[p]etitioner's responses to the many communications prior to the ultimate criminal act were at most indicative of certain personal inclinations, including a predisposition to view photographs of preteen sex and a willingness to promote a given agenda by supporting lobbying organizations." Justice O'Connor did not see any difference between an "inclination to view photographs of preteen sex" and a predisposition to commit the crime of possessing child pornography. In fact, there is a difference: for instance, a desire to use illegal drugs is not the same as a desire to commit the crime of buying illegal

---

[17] See § 4.03(a).

[18] Cf. *United States v. Valdovinos-Valdovinos*, 588 F.Supp. 551 (N.D.Cal. 1984), rev'd 743 F.2d 1436 (9th Cir. 1984) (finding a due process violation where the Immigration and Naturalization Service set up an undercover telephone, disseminated the number in Mexico, and advised Mexican nationals to violate U.S. law).

[19] Attorney General's Guidelines on FBI Undercover Operations (Dec. 31, 1908), reprinted in Sen.Rep. No. 97–682, p. 551 (1982). To date, however, no federal court has adopted a reasonable suspicion requirement. In *United States v. Luttrell*, 889 F.2d 806 (9th Cir. 1989), a panel of the Ninth Circuit adopted such a requirement, but the full court later rejected it. 923 F.2d 764 (9th Cir. 1991).

drugs. Yet in many cases the difference between an "inclination" to do something that is criminal and a "predisposition" to commit the crime will undoubtedly be subtle.

Jacobson may make the government's burden more difficult in entrapment cases. At the same time, given the relatively harmless nature of the offense involved in that case,[20] and the prolonged, intense nature of the government's inducement, which the Court appeared to view as excessive, it may be readily distinguished from more typical entrapment cases.

(d) A Due Process Test?

Although the minority view of entrapment is clearly disfavored, it is important to note that many members of the modern Court have not accepted the position that the government's conduct is irrelevant if the government can prove predisposition on the part of the defendant. For instance, in his concurring opinion in *Hampton*, Justice Powell, joined by Justice Blackmun, argued that under *Rochin v. California*,[21] a case in which police used brutal physical means to obtain evidence, behavior that shocks the conscience should permit a finding for the defendant on due process grounds, regardless of predisposition. In a footnote, Powell quoted Judge Friendly in *United States v. Archer*:[22]

> [T]here is certainly a [constitutional] limit to allowing governmental involvement in crime. It would be unthinkable, for example, to permit government agents to instigate robberies and beatings merely to gather evidence to convict other members of a gang of hoodlums. Governmental "investigation" involving participation in activities that result in injury to the rights of its citizens is a course that courts should be extremely reluctant to sanction.

Powell also noted that the Court's earlier cases had not required the Court "to consider whether overinvolvement of Government agents in contraband offenses could ever reach such proportions as to bar conviction of a predisposed defendant as a matter of due process."

However, Justice Powell emphasized that "[p]olice overinvolvement in crime would have to reach a demonstrable level of outrageousness before it could bar conviction." He also preferred treating due process "outrageousness" claims separately from "entrapment" cases, reserving the latter term for those situations where a non-predisposed defendant was lured into committing crime. This distinction might explain, although it does not necessarily justify, the apparent contradiction between Powell's willingness, under the Due Process Clause, to consider the defense when the government instigates violence, and *Sorrell's* admonition that the entrapment defense should not be available for "heinous" crimes. It also makes clear that, in the federal courts, the conduct of the authorities is relevant only to the extent it coincides with due process concerns. To this limited extent, then, the minority view of an "encouragement" defense may remain viable at the Supreme Court level.

---

[20] Cf. *United States v. Bogart*, 783 F.2d 1428 (9th Cir. 1986) ("where the police control and manufacture a victimless crime, it is difficult to see how anyone is actually harmed, and thus punishment ceases to be a response, but becomes an end in itself—to secure the conviction of a private criminal. . . . [U]nder such circumstances, the criminal justice system infringes upon personal liberty and violates due process.").

[21] 342 U.S. 165, 72 S.Ct. 205 (1952), discussed in § 9.02.

[22] 486 F.2d 670 (2d Cir. 1973).

19.03   Entrapment in the Lower Courts

(a)   The Conduct of Authorities and Due Process Tests

As noted above, the official conduct and due process standards both focus on the government's actions. Although the latter test, as characterized by Justice Powell in *Hampton*, is harder to meet, the two tests raise sufficiently similar issues that they will be treated together here. A growing number of state courts, persuaded by Justice Frankfurter's arguments in *Sherman*, have adopted the official conduct, or "objective" test.[23] And many federal courts, although apparently prohibited from adopting that test by *Hampton*, have nonetheless recognized a due process defense.[24] But very few courts, regardless of the test used, have found the defense to exist in a particular case.

United States v. Twigg[25] is one of the few federal court decisions that has found entrapment as a matter of law on governmental misconduct/due process grounds. There, the entrapment process began when Drug Enforcement Administration agents sought out a convicted felon, Kubica, and offered to reduce the severity of his sentence if he agreed to cooperate with them. At the request of DEA officials, Kubica contacted an acquaintance, Neville, and suggested setting up a laboratory to manufacture speed. Neville expressed an interest and later introduced Kubica to Twigg, who became involved in the operation to repay a debt to Neville. The government supplied Kubica with glassware and a difficult to find ingredient indispensable to the manufacture of speed. The DEA also made arrangements with chemical supply houses to facilitate the purchase of the rest of the necessary materials. In addition, the government provided an isolated farmhouse in which to set up the laboratory. During the production process, Kubica, the government agent, was completely in charge and furnished all the technical laboratory expertise.

The court found that the only evidence that Neville was predisposed to commit the crime was his receptivity to Kubica's proposal and Kubica's testimony that he had worked with Neville in a similar laboratory several years earlier. The court also considered the fact that the plan did not originate with the defendants. When Kubica, at the insistence of the DEA, had first reestablished contact with Neville, the latter was not engaged in any illegal activity. In fact, found the court, Kubica had implanted the criminal plan in Neville's mind. In addition, the court found that neither Neville nor Twigg had the technical expertise as chemists to have accomplished the criminal enterprise without Kubica.

While the court thus suggested a lack of predisposition on the defendants' part, it did not explicitly reject the jury's finding that there had been predisposition. Instead, its principal focus was the conduct of the authorities. It concluded that the government's involvement in the crime reached a "demonstrable level of outrageousness," substantial enough to bar prosecution of the defendants as a matter of due process. The court thus seemed not only to reject Justice Rehnquist's approach and endorse Justice Powell's, but to broaden Powell's exception beyond its original scope. Powell's concurrence in *Hampton* had specifically noted that the level of outrageousness he had in mind "would be

---

[23]   See cases listed in *State v. Wilkins*, 144 Vt. 22, 473 A.2d 295 (1983).

[24]   See, e.g., *United States v. Bogart*, 783 F.2d 1428 (9th Cir. 1986); *United States v. Twigg*, 588 F.2d 373 (3d Cir. 1978); *United States v. Pardue*, 765 F.Supp. 513 (W.D.Ark. 1991).

[25]   588 F.2d 373 (3d Cir. 1978).

especially difficult to show with respect to contraband offenses, which are so difficult to detect in the absence of undercover Government involvement."

Yet the facts in *Twigg* do suggest egregious conduct by the police. *Russell* and *Hampton*, both of which involved contraband offenses, are distinguishable. The laboratory in *Russell* was already in existence at the time the government approached the defendants, whereas the government was totally responsible for the establishment of the drug facility in *Twigg*. And although the government instigated the crime in *Hampton*, its involvement was not nearly as pervasive in that case as it was in *Twigg*; the crime in the latter case would have been inconceivable without the substantial government participation that occurred. If due process is to provide a defense in narcotics cases, *Twigg* is a good case for its application.

Only a few other decisions have held government conduct has, as a matter of law, exceeded reasonable bounds. Some courts, for instance, have held that acquittal should result when a person is induced to commit crime by an informant who is offered a contingent fee to implicate him.[26] But this holding is generally limited to situations in which payment is made upon a *conviction*, an arrangement which can encourage perjury by the informant. If the contingency agreement, like other deals with an informant, merely encourages action designed to lead to arrest, the matter is said to be one for the jury.[27] The Florida Supreme Court has also found objectionable a decoy operation in a high-crime area using an officer posing as a "drunk" with money sticking out of his pocket. According to *Cruz v. State*,[28] this conduct "carries with it the 'substantial risk' that . . . an offense will be committed by persons other than those who are ready to commit it." Finally, a few courts have considered adopting, as a matter of due process, a reasonable suspicion requirement like the dissent accused the majority of adopting in *Jacobson*.[29]

(b) The Predisposition Test

A few lower courts have found entrapment as a matter of law under the predisposition test. In *United States v. Lard*,[30] two undercover agents and one government informant told defendant Rigsby that they needed guns and asked him if he knew anyone who would sell them guns. Rigsby subsequently took the undercover agents to defendant Lard's home. Once inside, the agents asked Lard if his shotgun was for sale; Lard answered no. An agent then asked Lard if he had any other firearms for sale and Lard replied that he only had a small detonator. The agent, however, implored Lard that to accomplish his purpose he needed a pipe bomb. Lard persisted in trying to sell merely the detonator and some shotgun shells. The agent argued these items were not worth the price. Lard then said he could make a pipe bomb and that it would be ready in three hours. The agents later returned and completed the sale.

---

[26] *United States v. Yater*, 756 F.2d 1058 (5th Cir. 1985), cert. denied 474 U.S. 901, 106 S.Ct. 225 (1985). See also, *People v. Isaacson*, 44 N.Y.2d 511, 406 N.Y.S.2d 714, 378 N.E.2d 78 (1978) (informant tricked into believing he would receive a stiff prison sentence entrapped defendant with no prior criminal record).

[27] *United States v. Valona*, 834 F.2d 1334 (7th Cir. 1987); *United States v. Gentry*, 839 F.2d 1065 (5th Cir. 1988).

[28] 465 So.2d 516 (Fla. 1985), over'd *Munoz v. State*, 629 So.2d 90 (Fla. 1993).

[29] See supra note 19. Arguably, *Twigg* adopted such a requirement as well, given its emphasis on the fact that, in that case, the defendant was "lawfully and peacefully minding his own affairs" when the government made contact.

[30] 734 F.2d 1290 (8th Cir. 1984).

The Eighth Circuit found that no reasonable juror could have found beyond a reasonable doubt that Lard was predisposed to commit the crime and that the agents simply gave him the opportunity to do so. The court emphasized the fact that Lard had no prior criminal record and no record of making or dealing in firearms. It also noted that Lard's possession of and attempt to sell the detonator and shotgun shells were not unlawful acts. The pipe bomb idea was raised only after the agent repeatedly insisted he needed something more powerful than these items. The court concluded: "Law enforcement officials may not arbitrarily select an otherwise law abiding person, gain his confidence, and then lure him into committing a crime."

In one of the few other lower court cases in which an entrapment claim was viewed favorably, *United States v. Borum*,[31] the Circuit Court of Appeals for the District of Columbia held that the defendant was entitled to an instruction on entrapment given the evidence of government inducement and lack of predisposition. The case arose out of an undercover fencing operation in which policemen bought stolen goods and contraband from individuals and recorded the transactions on video tape. The primary aim of the fencing operation was to get unregistered and stolen guns off the street. Borum visited the fencing operation twenty-seven times; on twenty of those occasions the agents asked him for guns. Borum repeatedly told them he refused to handle guns, because, given a previous felony conviction, he faced a stiff penalty if caught with firearms. Even after explaining why he was unwilling to deal in guns, the police rejected his offers of other contraband, insisting on firearms. Borum, in need of money to support his drug habit, then brought the fence operators a stolen pistol.

The court of appeals concluded that there was sufficient evidence for a jury to find inducement by government agents and lack of predisposition on Borum's part. While recognizing that entrapment is not a defense when the defendant merely shows that an agent made an offer and the defendant acquiesced, here the government initiated and repeated solicitations for guns, and the evidence suggested both Borum's unwillingness to deal in guns and his avoidance of firearms in the past.

In contrast to *Twigg, Lard* and *Borum*, most lower court decisions have rejected entrapment claims, taking their cue from the Supreme Court. Probably the best known such cases are the series of holdings which arose from the "ABSCAM sting."[32] ABSCAM was an extensive undercover operation aimed at exposing political corruption. FBI agents posed as representatives of wealthy Arab sheiks who wanted to emigrate to the United States and invest in American real estate and businesses. Their aim was to attract public officials into accepting generous bribes in exchange for furthering the "sheiks'" objectives. Through Melvin Weinberg, a reputed "con" man who received probation and a salary for his cooperation with the government, word of "big money" was spread in various circles, including the United States Congress. The FBI planned to take appropriate action if any criminal proposals resulted from this "offer."

When the FBI finally terminated the operation, one U.S. Senator, at least seven U.S. representatives, and several lesser officials had been indicted. Although the facts in each indictment varied, each defendant was recorded and filmed accepting money in return for some political favor concerning investments, immigration matters, or both.

---

[31]　584 F.2d 424 (D.C.Cir. 1978).

[32]　For an extensive factual description of ABSCAM (Short for ABdul SCAM), see *United States v. Myers*, 527 F.Supp. 1206 (E.D.N.Y. 1981).

While many of the public officials readily accepted payments, FBI agents had more difficulty with Senator Williams of New Jersey and Congressman Kelly of Florida. Over a period of one year, the "sheiks" met with Senator Williams seven times.[33] Williams initially repeatedly refused to exploit his position as a public official. He also rejected plans to conceal profits from the Internal Revenue Service. At a final meeting, however, he consented to a deal and accepted a bribe. Although Williams raised an entrapment defense at trial, the court refused to find entrapment as a matter of law and the jury convicted him of bribery. His conviction was confirmed at the appellate level.[34]

Congressman Kelly also, at first, rejected the idea of payments.[35] At the initial meeting, he expressed interest only in the legitimate aspects of the Arab ventures. He rejected the bribes a second and third time as well, insisting he was only interested in legitimate projects that would benefit his district. But the agents persisted; more pressure and the display of $25,000 spread on a table in stacks of one hundred dollar bills finally persuaded Kelly to take the bribe.

Although Kelly was also convicted by the jury, the trial judge overturned the jury's verdict. He stated that the government may not tempt an individual beyond that which he "is likely to encounter in the ordinary course." The agents should have stopped when Kelly rejected the first bribe since it was unrealistic for a Congressman to receive further bribe offers once the first one had been refused. The D.C. Circuit Court of Appeals reversed and remanded, however, with instructions to reinstate the jury verdict.[36] Considering the genuine need to detect corrupt public officials and the difficulties inherent in doing so, the court concluded that the government's conduct did not reach an intolerable degree of outrageousness nor did Kelly show a suitable lack of predisposition. Notably, this was the same court that decided *Borum*.

These cases show that, inevitably, the courts consider both government conduct and defendant predisposition in assessing entrapment claims. Unless the government conduct is clearly outrageous, however, any predisposition on the part of the defendant will usually mean entrapment will not be found as a matter of law.

19.04   Conclusion

The law of entrapment can be summarized as follows:

(1) The two major competing interpretations of the entrapment defense are the predisposition, or subjective, test and the conduct of the authorities, or objective, test. Under the former, entrapment exists only if the defendant was not predisposed to commit the crime. Under the latter, entrapment exists only if the government conduct was such that a reasonable person would have been induced to commit the crime.

(2) The Supreme Court and the federal courts have adopted the predisposition test. Under the Court's interpretation of this test, the prosecution must show beyond a reasonable doubt that the defendant was predisposed to commit the offense prior to its

---

[33] *United States v. Williams*, 529 F.Supp. 1085 (E.D.N.Y. 1981) describes the facts of the case.

[34] *United States v. Williams*, 705 F.2d 603 (2d Cir. 1983), cert. denied 464 U.S. 1007, 104 S.Ct. 524 (1983).

[35] *United States v. Kelly*, 539 F.Supp. 363 (D.D.C. 1982).

[36] *United States v. Kelly*, 707 F.2d 1460 (D.C.Cir. 1983), cert. denied 464 U.S. 908, 104 S.Ct. 264 (1983), appeal after remand 748 F.2d 691 (D.C.Cir. 1984).

initial contact with him. The conduct of the government is irrelevant. Furthermore, the defense may not exist for "heinous" or violent crimes.

(3) Some federal courts also recognize a due process defense, which leads to acquittal if the government conduct was outrageous. Although rare, some situations which might give rise to such a due process defense are: (a) when police use physical violence to create and gather evidence of criminal activity; (b) when the government supplies contraband wholly unobtainable from other sources; or (c) when, in a "criminal enterprise" situation, the government initiates, finances and exercises control over the operations of the enterprise.

It should also be remembered that even if undercover work does not give rise to an entrapment claim it may implicate the right to counsel[37] and, rarely, the Fourth Amendment's protection against unreasonable searches and seizures.[38]

BIBLIOGRAPHY

Allen, Ronald, Melissa Luttrell and Anne Kreeger. Clarifying Entrapment. 89 J.Crim.L. & Criminol. 407 (1999).

Camp, Damon D. Out of the Quagmire After *Jacobson v. United States*: Towards a More Balanced Entrapment Standard. 83 Crim L. & Criminol. 1055 (1993).

Carlson, Jonathan. The Act Requirement and the Foundations of the Entrapment Defense. 73 Va.L.Rev. 1011 (1987).

Carter, Derrick Augustus. To Catch the Lion, Tether the Goat: Entrapment, Conspiracy and Sentencing Manipulation. 42 Akron L. Rev. 135 (2009).

Colquitt, Joseph A. Rethinking Entrapment. 41 Am.Crim.L.Rev. 1389 (2004).

Daniels, Richard. "Outrageousness!" What Does It Really Mean—An Examination of the Outrageous Conduct Defense. 18 Southwestern U.L.Rev. 105 (1988).

Gershman, Bennett L. Abscam, the Judiciary, and the Ethics of Entrapment, 91 Yale L.J. 1565 (1982).

Joh, Elizabeth. Breaking the Law to Enforce It: Undercover Police Participation in Crime. 62 Stanford L.Rev. 155 (2009).

Marcus, Paul. Presenting, Back From the [Almost] Dead, the Entrapment Defense. 47 Fla. L Rev. 105 (1996).

McAdams, Richard H. Reforming Entrapment Doctrine in *United States v. Hollingsworth*. 74 U. Chi. L. Rev. 1795 (2007).

Roth, Jessica A. The Anomaly of Entrapment. 91 Wash. L. Rev. 979 (2014).

Seidman, L. Michael. The Supreme Court, Entrapment, and Our Criminal Justice Dilemma. 1981 Sup.Ct.Rev. 111.

Stevenson, Dru. Entrapment and the Problem of Deterring Police Misconduct. 37 Conn.L.Rev. 67 (2004).

---

[37] See § 16.04(b).

[38] See § 4.02(a).

Whelan, Maura F.J. Lead Us Not Into (Unwarranted) Temptation: A Proposal to Replace the Entrapment Defense with a Reasonable Suspicion Requirement. 133 U.Pa.L.Rev. 1193 (1985).

Part E

THE PRETRIAL PROCESS

Up to this point, the primary focus of this book has been on the types of constraints the Constitution places on the conduct of law enforcement authorities as they pursue their investigatory duties. Part E of the book examines the formal process used to move the criminally accused from arrest to adjudication of the charges against him. Each state has erected a multi-stage procedure designed to afford the accused some type of hearing regarding issues such as the legality of his arrest, the advisability of bail, and whether there is probable cause to prosecute. The following chapters examine these various stages, as well as other aspects of the pretrial process, with particular emphasis on how the constitutional mandates of the Fourth, Fifth and Sixth Amendments apply at each stage.

It would be impossible to describe accurately the "typical" pretrial process, since the states vary so widely in their practices and because certain types of cases are handled differently from others.[1] For example, although the Federal Rules of Criminal Procedure provide for a "preliminary examination" to investigate whether there is probable cause to prosecute the accused,[2] several states do not provide for such a proceeding. As a second example, some cases, such as those involving governmental corruption, are usually pursued initially through grand jury indictment, while in the typical criminal case, where apprehension occurs soon after commission of the crime, indictment *follows* arrest, if it occurs at all. Indeed, most states do not normally proceed by indictment in the typical case, but rather make use of the prosecutor's "information," a document subscribed by the prosecutor that recites the charge. These and other differences are discussed here, but no attempt has been made to describe all existing variations.

The following chapters are arranged to reflect the most likely chronological order in the usual pretrial process. Chapter 20 discusses the initial custodial decisions—most prominently the so-called "bail" determination—which are made immediately following the arrest of a suspect. Chapter 21 addresses the rules governing the prosecutor's charging decision, including joinder and venue rules; while some sort of charge must of course be brought to initiate the criminal process, the types of decisions discussed in this chapter are normally not formalized until the evidence can be sifted, which usually occurs after the bail determination. The preliminary hearing—the procedure many jurisdictions have established to check this formal charging decision—is the subject of Chapter 22. There follows, in Chapter 23, an examination of the grand jury, which as noted above, performs not only a prearrest investigative function but also, in many jurisdictions, a post-arrest function similar to the preliminary hearing, in that it formalizes the charges against the accused. Chapter 24 discusses the discovery process, which usually begins, at least informally, soon after arrest and continues through to adjudication of the charges. Finally, placing a time limit on these proceedings is the right to speedy trial, discussed in Chapter 25. Other pretrial issues are examined elsewhere in this book, including suppression hearings for the purpose of assessing the

---

[1]   For a brief description of the "Ordinary Model" of the criminal process, see § 1.04.

[2]   Fed.R.Crim.P. 5.

admissibility of evidence gathered by the police[3] and hearings to evaluate competency to stand trial.[4]

---

[3] See, e.g., §§ 4.05(e), 16.06, 17.06.

[4] See § 28.03(b).

Chapter 20

INITIAL CUSTODIAL DECISIONS: PRETRIAL DETENTION AND RELEASE

20.01 Introduction

In most jurisdictions, once an individual is arrested, he is taken before a judicial officer (usually a magistrate or lower court judge) for his "initial appearance" or "first appearance" in court. In misdemeanor cases, trial of the accused may occur at this point.[1] In serious cases, the judicial officer will tell the accused his charges, warn him of his right to refrain from self-incrimination, and appoint counsel. The official may also set preliminary bail, although normally a separate hearing is reserved for the formal determination of this issue.

At the bail hearing, for those crimes which are "bailable," the judicial officer decides what conditions to impose on the accused to assure his appearance at trial and at any preliminary proceedings. These conditions may range from merely extracting a promise to reappear to a hefty cash deposit with the court. In some cases, the defendant is unable to meet the imposed conditions, with the result that he is detained pending adjudication of his charges. And in some jurisdictions, if the prosecution can prove the accused is unlikely to remain in the community or is likely to commit a crime if released, the accused may be explicitly subject to "preventive detention."

Logically precedent to both the initial appearance and the pretrial release decision, of course, is a determination that the state has the right to detain the accused in the first place. In cases where arrest was authorized by a warrant or grand jury indictment, an official determination of probable cause has already been made, and the initial proceedings may take place without further findings. But when, as is common, an arrest is made "in the street," the only pre-arrest determination of probable cause is the police officer's. As described below, the Supreme Court has held that a judicial check of the officer's decision is required in this situation. In cases where it is necessary, many states combine this probable cause assessment with the initial appearance described above.

The first section of this chapter discusses further the rationale for and nature of the probable cause to detain determination. The second section examines the bail system and preventive detention. Finally, the chapter discusses the legal privileges of those who are detained pending trial.

20.02 The Probable Cause Hearing

(a) When a Hearing Is Required

Gerstein v. Pugh[2] involved a challenge of the preliminary hearing system used in Florida at the time. Under that system, prosecutors could charge all crimes, other than capital offenses, by information, without a prior preliminary examination and without obtaining leave of court. A suspect could obtain a judicial determination of probable

---

[1] Usually, a "complaint" filed by the prosecutor is sufficient basis for such a proceeding. Only felony prosecutions normally require an information or an indictment.

[2] 420 U.S. 103, 95 S.Ct. 854 (1975).

cause only through a preliminary hearing, not required until 30 days after arrest, or during arraignment, which also often took place a month or more after arrest.

The Supreme Court held this scheme unconstitutional, concluding that the Fourth Amendment requires as a condition for any significant pretrial restraint on liberty a judicial determination of probable cause made either before or promptly after arrest. While the Court recognized the practical necessity of allowing warrantless arrests so long as they are supported by probable cause, the Court pointed out that exigent circumstances no longer exist once a suspect is taken into custody. At that time, a suspect's rights to be free from unlawful detention becomes paramount:

> [W]hile the State's reasons for taking summary action subside, the suspect's need for a neutral determination of probable cause increases significantly. The consequences of prolonged detention may be more serious than the interference occasioned by arrest. Pretrial confinement may imperil the suspect's job, interrupt his source of income, and impair his family's relationship. . . . Even pretrial release may be accompanied by burdensome conditions that effect a significant restraint of liberty. . . . When the stakes are this high, the detached judgment of a neutral magistrate is essential if the Fourth Amendment is to furnish meaningful protection from unfounded interference with liberty.

Gerstein rejected the contention that the prosecutor's decision to file an information is itself a sufficient determination of probable cause to detain a defendant pending trial. But it also made clear that a probable cause hearing is not necessary after every arrest. When an arrest is based on a grand jury indictment or an arrest warrant, a preliminary hearing is not constitutionally required. *Gerstein* stands only for the proposition that before a suspect may be detained some official entity other than an executive branch official must make a determination of probable cause.

Moreover, this probable cause determination is required only when a "significant pretrial restraint on liberty" is to be imposed by the state. *Gerstein* explained that the restraint must be something other than the mere condition that the suspect appear for trial, but offered nothing else by way of defining when a restraint might be "significant." It would seem that any imposition of bail would constitute enough restraint to justify a *Gerstein* hearing; even release on personal recognizance can result in a significant infringement on liberty if any conditions are attached to release. Given these facts, the simpler approach would be to hold a *Gerstein* hearing in the absence of a warrant or indictment.

A final limitation on *Gerstein,* noted in the decision, is that, like other constitutional rights, the right to a *Gerstein* hearing may be waived by the accused.

(b) Procedural Protections

The lower courts in *Gerstein* held that the determination of probable cause must be accompanied by the full scheme of adversary safeguards—counsel, confrontation, cross-examination, and compulsory process for witnesses. The Supreme Court reversed the lower courts on this issue, finding that the probable cause determination was not a "critical stage" that would require appointed counsel, because the consequences of the proceeding—although possibly a significant restraint on liberty—do not approximate the possible consequences of trial, sentencing and other stages of the criminal process where counsel has been found necessary.[3] The Court conceded that confrontation and cross-examination might enhance the reliability of probable cause determinations in some cases. But it concluded that the value of such actions would be too slight to justify a constitutional mandate that these formalities be employed in making the Fourth Amendment determination of probable cause; this determination, the Court pointed out, is always made without benefit of counsel on those occasions when the police approach a magistrate for an arrest warrant *prior* to arrest.

For the same reasons, the Court also approved informal modes of proof at the hearing, including hearsay and written testimony. The standard of proof is simply whether there is probable cause to believe the suspect has committed a crime. As such, there need be only a reasonable belief in guilt, not proof beyond a reasonable doubt or by a preponderance of the evidence.

The Court had administrative concerns in mind as well. A footnote explained:

> Criminal justice is already overburdened by the volume of cases and the complexities of our system. The processing of misdemeanors, in particular, and the early stages of prosecution generally are marked by delays that can seriously affect the quality of justice. A constitutional doctrine requiring adversary hearings for all persons detained pending trial could exacerbate the problem of pretrial delay.

Given the Court's eschewal of the full panoply of procedural protections during a *Gerstein* hearing, such a hearing may and often does consist merely of a brief appearance in front of a magistrate after arrest. The proceeding will often be *ex parte* and, in effect, rarely be a "hearing" in anything but name. Since it serves the same purpose as a hearing to secure an arrest warrant, the *Gerstein* hearing will resemble such proceedings.

(c) Timing of the Hearing

Gerstein required that the hearing it mandated take place "promptly after arrest." But *Gerstein* did not attempt to define this phrase further. In *Riverside County v. McLaughlin,*[4] the Supreme Court held, 5–4, that a hearing that takes place within 48 hours of arrest will be presumptively reasonable. Although such a hearing might still violate *Gerstein* if it is delayed "unreasonably,"[5] "unavoidable delays in transporting arrested persons from one facility to another, handling late-night bookings where no magistrate is readily available, obtaining the presence of an arresting officer who may be busy processing other suspects or securing the premises of an arrest, and other practical realities" are valid excuses for postponement within the two-day period. Moreover, Justice O'Connor, who wrote the Court's opinion, indicated that administrative efficiency is another legitimate reason for delay; relying on *Gerstein's* statement that flexibility during the pretrial stages of the criminal process is important as a means of promoting state experimentation, she referred favorably to a scheme that routinely defers the *Gerstein* hearing for up to 48 hours in order to combine it with other types of proceedings, such as bail determinations.

---

[3]   See § 31.03(a)(1) for a discussion of critical stage analysis.

[4]   500 U.S. 44, 111 S.Ct. 1661 (1991).

[5]   E.g., "delays for the purpose of gathering additional evidence to justify the arrest, a delay motivated by ill will against the arrested individual, or delay for delay's sake."

Justice Scalia in dissent argued that *Gerstein's* language about experimentation focused on the *procedures* for conducting the hearing, not its timing, and that the need to avoid incarceration of an innocent individual far outweighs the state's interest in efficient processing. He also contended that the majority's approach violated the common law notion that judicial review of an arrest must take place as soon after arrest as possible.[6] He concluded that, at most, the Fourth Amendment allows a 24-hour delay between arrest and the *Gerstein* hearing. Justice Marshall, joined by Justices Blackmun and Stevens, wrote a separate dissent that did not mention Scalia's 24-hour rule, but agreed that "a probable cause hearing is sufficiently 'prompt' under *Gerstein* only when provided immediately upon completion of the 'administrative steps incident to arrest.' "

Assuming a violation of *McLaughlin's* rule, what is the remedy? In *Powell v. Nevada,*[7] the Court avoided definitively answering this question, but stated that finding such a violation does not necessarily mean a defendant must be released from custody or that any statements he makes after the 48-hour period expires must be suppressed. On the custody issue, other decisions by the Court strongly suggest that a defendant is not entitled to release simply because of a procedural error.[8] Whether statements obtained after a *McLaughlin* violation should be suppressed is not as clear. Justice Thomas wrote an opinion in *Powell,* joined by Chief Justice Rehnquist, arguing that exclusion of such statements should result only if a timely hearing would have found no probable cause for the arrest. This reasoning ignores the Court's traditional attenuation analysis, which bases the fruit of the poisonous tree inquiry on whether police might perpetrate the illegality (here delay of the first appearance) in order to secure the evidence.[9] But it might be supportable under more recent decisions which tend to de-emphasize attenuation analysis.[10] At the same time, it is clear that when the defendant can show that the police did not have *probable cause,* damages for any resulting detention may be obtained on Fourth Amendment grounds.[11]

20.03 Bail and Other Pretrial Release Conditions

In large jurisdictions, approximately 60% of felony defendants are released prior to the final disposition of their case.[12] This section describes the various approaches to pretrial release that have developed over the centuries and analyzes their current constitutional status. It also describes the procedures required for a pretrial release hearing, the right to post-conviction release, and the procedures for appealing the bail decision.

(a) The History of Pretrial Release

Once a person has been arrested pursuant to a warrant or indictment, or has been found detainable at a *Gerstein* hearing, the question becomes whether he should be

---

[6]   See, e.g., *Wright v. Court,* 107 Eng.Rep. 1181 (K.B. 1825) ("[I]t is the duty of a person arresting any one on suspicion of felony to take him before a justice as soon as he reasonably can.").

[7]   511 U.S. 79, 114 S.Ct. 1280 (1994).

[8]   See § 3.01.

[9]   See § 2.04(b). See also § 16.02(b), discussing the *McNabb-Mallory* rule, which excludes statements that result from delayed arraignment under certain circumstances.

[10]   See in particular, *New York v. Harris,* 495 U.S. 14, 110 S.Ct. 1640 (1990), discussed in § 2.04(b)(1).

[11]   *Manuel v. City of Joliet, Ill.,* ___ U.S. ___, 137 S.Ct. 911 (2017).

[12]   Gerard Rainville & Brian A. Reeves, Felony Defendants in Large Urban Counties, 2000 (Bureau of Justice Statistics, Dec. 2003).

released pending the next judicial proceeding. Pretrial release, traditionally known as release on "bail," facilitates preparation of a defense and prevents incarceration of a possibly innocent person. At the same time, it may allow the defendant to flee the jurisdiction, tamper with evidence, or harm others. As the history of pretrial release shows, several different approaches to pretrial release are possible.

(1) English Antecedents

In England, the practice of bail developed as an alternative to holding accused persons for prolonged periods of time in diseased-ridden jails. Bail literally meant the bailment or delivery of an accused from the jail to third parties of his own choosing. If the third party could not produce the accused for trial, he had to surrender himself to custody, or in later times, surrender property or money. Given the size of the community, the releasing sheriff or justice of the peace knew most bailed offenders, as well as their sureties.[13]

(2) The Money Bail and Bondsman System

The practice of pretrial release was carried over to the United States. In 1789, the federal government provided, by statute, that "upon all arrests in criminal cases, bail shall be admitted, except where the punishment may be death."[14] Most states followed suit in their own constitutions or statutes.[15] For instance, California's constitution, in language which is widely copied, provides that "all persons shall be bailable by sufficient sureties, unless for capital offenses when the proof is evident or the presumption great."[16]

As the United States grew, its system for ensuring appearance of a person diverged significantly from English practice, which functioned in a much smaller community. First, the principal hold on the accused came to be a money deposit, as opposed to the surety himself or his property. Second, as a "supplement" to the private surety known to the sheriff or judge, a professional "bondsman" took on the job of surety.[17] The premise of this money bail system was and continues to be that risk of a sufficiently high financial loss will provide a deterrent to flight and assure the accused's presence at trial.

There are several practical difficulties connected with the money bail system. The first of these weaknesses results from the method by which the magistrate sets the amount of bail. Instead of being an informed, individualized decision based on a calculation of the proper financial deterrent, the process is often mechanical—the amount of bail is set according to the offense charged.[18] Because this process makes no allowance for the accused's ability to pay, the great majority of indigent defendants must submit to detention.[19]

---

[13]   Daniel J. Freed & Patricia M. Wald, Bail in the United States 1–3 (1964).

[14]   18 U.S.C.A. § 3142 (originally in Judiciary Act of 1789).

[15]   Freed & Wald, supra note 13, at 2. See, e.g., N.J. Const.Art. I, par. 11.

[16]   Cal. Const.Art. I, § 6.

[17]   Freed & Wald, supra note 13, at 4.

[18]   Monrad Paulsen, *Pre-Trial Release in the United States*, 66 Colum.L.Rev. 109, 113 (1966); Charles Ares, Anne Rankin & Herbert Sturz, *The Manhattan Bail Project: An Interim Report on the Use of Pre-Trial Parole*, 38 N.Y.U.L.Rev. 67, 71 (1963).

[19]   Ares et al., supra note 18, at 71.

Another problem with the money bail system is the role of the bondsman. In most jurisdictions, the bondsman puts up the financial security required by the magistrate for a percentage fee paid by the accused. If the accused fails to appear at trial, the bondsman's security is forfeited, providing incentive for the bondsman to locate the defendant. But if the defendant appears for trial, no portion of the fee paid to the bondsman is refunded to the defendant (otherwise, the bond profession would be singularly unremunerative). This widespread practice removes any deterrent effect from money bail. Whether he appears at trial or not, the defendant loses the same amount of money, i.e., the fee he paid to the bondsman. Thus, the financial premise on which the system is grounded is seriously undermined. More importantly, this system places the bondsman, rather than the judge, in the position of jailkeeper.[20] Those able to meet the bondsman's fee buy their freedom while those who cannot, or those whom the bondsman deems "bad risks" (for he is ostensibly risking forfeiture), remain in jail. The courts are relegated to the rather ministerial role of fixing the amount of bail and holding deposits that are made.[21]

A final practical problem with the money bail system is the fact that so many people are detained under it. Not only does this overload the jails; it also causes significant hardship for many people. Families are left without financial support and jobs are lost. Moreover, for a number of reasons, including their inability to contact witnesses, make amends with victims, and continue their connections in the community, pretrial detainees are more likely than others to be convicted and to receive a severe sentence upon conviction.[22]

(3) The First Reform Movement: Personal Recognizance

Dissatisfaction with the money bail system led to nationwide recognition of the need for reform in bail procedures. The primary aim of the reform movement was to abolish, or at least reduce reliance on, the money bail system through approaches that minimized detention and maximized release on recognizance.

The pilot bail reform project was conducted by the Vera Institute in New York City. The Manhattan Bail Project, as it was called, focused on indigent defendants who, according to a carefully selected and weighted set of criteria, presented a low risk of flight if release were granted. Among the factors considered important in recommending release on recognizance were previous convictions, roots in the community, employment history, and the gravity of the charge. The Project achieved a high degree of success. Over the first three years of its operation, from 1961–1964, only 1.6 percent of those defendants recommended for release willfully failed to appear at trial. During the same period, three percent of those released under the traditional system of bail failed to appear, nearly twice as many as had been released without bail.[23]

---

[20]   If a person *is* released on bail and does not return for trial, other problems arise. Bondsmen often employ professional bounty hunters in such situations. Because most courts hold that bounty hunters are not state actors for constitutional purposes and many states refuse to impose licensing or training requirements on them, returning defendants can result in "unnecessary violence, destruction of property, and arrests of innocent victims." Jonathan Drimmer, *When Man Hunts Man: The Rights and Duties of Bounty Hunters in the American Criminal Justice System*, 33 Hou. L.Rev. 731, 736–37 (1996).

[21]   *Pannell v. United States*, 320 F.2d 698 (D.C.Cir. 1963).

[22]   Anne Rankin, *The Effect of Pretrial Detention*, 39 N.Y.U.L.Rev. 641 (1964).

[23]   Vera Institute of Justice, Programs in Criminal Justice Reform, Ten Year Report, 1961–1971, 35 (1972).

These results spurred reform efforts in other cities,[24] with the culmination of the movement coming in 1966. In that year, Congress passed the Federal Bail Reform Act,[25] which furnished a model for several state statutes.[26] The Act provided that any person charged with a non-capital offense "be ordered released pending trial on his personal recognizance or upon the execution of an unsecured appearance bond in an amount specified by the judicial officer, unless the officer determines . . . that such a release will not reasonably assure the appearance of the person as required." If the latter determination was made, the officer could impose, in addition to the above conditions, any other conditions that would assure the appearance of the accused, including placing the person in another's custody, restrictions on travel or association, the execution of a secured appearance bond with a percentage deposited with the court, or other condition the officer might consider necessary.[27] Note that under this statute and its state counterparts money bail is only one of the conditions to be considered; further, when money *is* used as assurance, it is deposited directly with the court, not through a bondsman.

More importantly, in deciding which conditions to impose, the Act provided that "the judge shall . . . take into account the available information concerning: the nature and the circumstances of the offense charged, the weight of evidence against the accused, the accused's family ties, employment, financial resources, character and mental condition, the length of his residence in the community, his record of convictions, and his record of appearances at court proceedings or of flight to avoid prosecution or failure to appear at court proceedings."[28] This list of considerations requires much greater individualization than the mechanical reference to schedules under the money bail system, which sets the amount of bail according to the offense charged.

The Act had a significant impact on the release rate of federal defendants, which increased by as much as 40%.[29] State jurisdictions that reduced their reliance on financial incentives also reduced substantially the number of state defendants detained from arrest to disposition.[30] At the same time, the nonappearance rate in jurisdictions with these new laws was low, and may often have been related more to the time between arrest and disposition than to the seriousness of the penalty involved.[31]

(4) The Second Reform Movement: Preventive Detention

Under the 1966 Act, the pretrial release decision focused on whether the defendant would return for trial. But public concern over crimes committed by released defendants eventually led to modification of the original reforms.[32] In 1970, the District of Columbia passed the first explicit "preventive detention" statute, authorizing denial of bail to

---

[24] Over 100 Vera-type projects exist nationwide. Wayne H. Thomas, Pretrial Release Programs (1977).

[25] 18 U.S.C.A. §§ 3146–3152.

[26] See, e.g., Mass.Gen.Laws Annot., 276, §§ 58, 82A.

[27] 18 U.S.C.A. § 3146(a). These provisions are now found in 18 U.S.C.A. § 3142(a) & (c).

[28] Id. § 3146(b). Similar provisions are now found in 18 U.S.C.A. § 3142(g).

[29] See Wayne H. Thomas, Bail Reform in America 27 (1976).

[30] Id. at 37–39 (over a 10-year period, the percentage of felony defendants detained from arrest to disposition dropped from 52% to 33%, the percentage of misdemeanants detained from 40% to 28%).

[31] Id. at 103 (percentage of defendants who failed to appear was roughly five percent across all offenses).

[32] Estimates of crimes committed by arrestees on release vary from 10 to 15% of all crimes, Mark H. Moore, et al. Dangerous Offenders: The Elusive Target of Justice 126 (1984), to a finding that only 5% of all those released were rearrested within 60 days. Note, *Preventive Detention: An Empirical Analysis*, 6 Harv.Civ.Rts-Civ.Lib.L.Rev. 291 (1971).

"dangerous" persons charged with certain offenses for a period of up to 60 days.[33] The Act was infrequently used,[34] and no state followed the District's lead for some time. But fourteen years later, the U.S. Congress passed the Federal Bail Reform Act of 1984.[35] This Act continued to express a preference for individualized pretrial release and specifically stated that the "judicial officer may not impose a financial condition that results in pretrial detention of the person."[36] But it also authorized preventive detention of dangerous individuals, and amended the 1966 Act in several other ways as well.

First, the 1984 Act permits the judge making the pretrial release decision to impose conditions on the accused that are only tangentially related to assuring reappearance and are obviously designed to inhibit the commission of crime. Under the new Act, for instance, release may be revoked (if the judge so indicates when permitting pretrial release) for possession of a firearm or other destructive device; failure to maintain or commence employment, an educational program, or a treatment program; failure to report to a local agency; failure to comply with a specified curfew; and failure to return to custody for employment, schooling or other limited purposes.[37] Second, the Act permits detention for not more than ten days of any person: (1) who is, and was at the time the alleged offense was committed, on release pending trial for a felony, pending sentencing or appeal, or pursuant to a grant of probation or parole; or (2) who "may flee or pose a danger to any other person or the community."[38]

Third, and most controversially, the Act permits continued detention after the ten-day period if, after a hearing, it appears that no condition "will reasonably assure the appearance of the person as required and the safety of any other person and the community."[39] This hearing must be held upon motion of the government in any case involving a crime of violence, an offense punishable by life imprisonment or death, a drug-related offense for which the penalty is greater than ten years, or a felony committed by a person who has already been convicted of two of the above-described offenses. A hearing is also to be held if, on motion of the government or the judge's own motion, the case "involves a serious risk that the person will flee; [or] a serious risk that the person will obstruct or attempt to obstruct justice, or threaten, injure, or intimidate, or attempt to threaten, injure, or intimidate, a prospective witness or jury."[40] If the judge finds, apparently by a preponderance of the evidence, that "no condition or combination of conditions will reasonably assure the appearance of the person," or by clear and convincing evidence that "no condition or combination of conditions will reasonably assure the safety of any other person and the community," detention until trial is appropriate. The accused is entitled to counsel during the hearing, but "[t]he rules concerning admissibility of evidence in criminal trials do not apply to the presentation

---

[33]   D.C.Code 1970, § 23–1322.

[34]   Out of the first 600 felony defendants to enter the criminal justice system in the year following the Act's passage, only ten persons were preventively detained, five of whom had their detention orders reversed. Paul Wice, Freedom for Sale: A National Study of Pre-Trial Release 1–3, 164 (1974).

[35]   18 U.S.C.A. §§ 3141–3150 (1984).

[36]   Id. § 3142(c)(2).

[37]   Id. at § 3142(c)(1).

[38]   Id. at § 3142(d).

[39]   Id. at § 3142(e).

[40]   Id. at § 3142(f).

and consideration of information at the hearing."[41] Several states have enacted similar statutes.[42]

The Act increased the number of federal prisoners by 32 percent in 1985.[43] The provision allowing preventive detention of "dangerous" offenders was successfully invoked over 1600 times per month over a one year period.[44] Thus, the Act has clearly put a strain on correctional and judicial resources. The evidence concerning its effect on the crime rate is equivocal.[45] Research investigating pretrial detention practices in the states, most of which have statutes that mimic the federal statute, concluded that "if the goal is to prevent crime, judges are often releasing and detaining the wrong groups."[46]

(b) The "Right" to Pretrial Release

The Eighth Amendment states that "[e]xcessive bail shall not be required," a clause that has long been assumed to be applicable to the states[47] (although it was only officially incorporated in 2012[48]). One might argue that a denial of pretrial freedom subjects an accused to "excessive" constraints in violation of the Eighth Amendment because it entails incarceration without conviction and hampers preparation of his defense. But this argument has never succeeded; as noted above, for instance, from the beginning bail has always been denied in capital cases when the "proof is evident or the presumption great." As the Supreme Court stated in *Carlson v. Landon*:[49]

> [i]n England, [the Bail] clause has never been thought to accord a right to bail in all cases, but merely to provide that bail shall not be excessive in those cases where it is proper to grant bail. When this clause was carried over into our Bill of Rights, nothing was said that indicated any different concept.

Another, similar argument for an absolute right to pretrial release could derive from the presumption of innocence. As argued by Professor Tribe, one could contend that a denial of pretrial release infringes the presumption because it takes away the freedom to which an innocent person is entitled.[50] But in *Bell v. Wolfish*,[51] the Court held that the presumption of innocence is merely "a doctrine that allocates the burden of proof in criminal trials," telling the factfinder to judge the defendant on the evidence rather than on the fact that he has been charged; thus, according to the Court, it has no effect outside of the trial context.

---

[41]   Id.

[42]   See, e.g., West's Fla.Stat.Ann. § 907.041.

[43]   Howard Kurtz, *Detention Law, Further Crowds Prisons*, The Washington Post, January 9, 1986, at A4. As of early 1986, the federal prison system was 42% over capacity. Id.

[44]   Id.

[45]   Marc Miller & Martin Guggenheim, *Pretrial Detention and Punishment*, 75 Minn. L.Rev. 335, 383–388 (1990).

[46]   Shima Baradharan & Frank L McIntyre, *Predicting Violence*, 90 Tex. L. Rev. 497, 558 (2012).

[47]   *Schilb v. Kuebel*, 404 U.S. 357, 92 S.Ct. 479 (1971).

[48]   *McDonald v. City of Chicago*, 561 U.S. 752, 130 S.Ct. 3020, 3034 n.12 (2010).

[49]   342 U.S. 524, 72 S.Ct. 525 (1952).

[50]   Laurence Tribe, *An Ounce of Prevention: Preventive Justice in the World of John Mitchell*, 56 Va.L.Rev. 371, 404 (1970).

[51]   441 U.S. 520, 99 S.Ct. 1861 (1979).

(c) Constitutional Criteria for Pretrial Release

Since there is no constitutional right to bail, the question becomes: under what circumstances may bail be denied? As the historical discussion illustrates, statutory pretrial release criteria are wide-ranging. Addressed here are the three most prominent reasons for denying release: likelihood of flight, dangerousness to others, and lack of financial resources. Also discussed are special pretrial detention situations, involving non-citizens and "material witnesses." The Supreme Court's early cases indicated that assuring appearance for trial was the only constitutionally acceptable criterion for evaluating pretrial release. However, the Court has more recently held that other "regulatory" goals are permissible as well, including prevention of harm to the public. In analyzing the constitutionality of the various criteria, the courts have looked not only at the Eighth Amendment's language but also considered the implications of substantive due process and the Equal Protection Clause.

(1) Likelihood of Flight

In *Stack v. Boyle*,[52] the Supreme Court stressed that the purpose of bail is to permit pretrial release of an accused with the assurance that he will return for trial:

> Like the ancient practice of securing the oaths of responsible persons to stand as sureties for the accused, the modern practice of requiring a bail bond or the deposit of a sum of money subject to forfeiture serves as additional assurance of the presence of an accused. . . . Since the function of bail is limited, the fixing of bail for any individual defendant must be based upon standards relevant to the purpose of assuring the presence of that defendant.

Construing this language, lower courts concluded that, in setting bail or other pretrial release conditions, the sole consideration was preventing flight from the jurisdiction.[53] Clearly, the Bail Reform Act of 1966 reflected this view.

Further, *Stack* indicated that the language of the Eighth Amendment meant that bail should rarely be set so high as to prevent release under this criterion:

> Admission to bail always involves a risk that the accused will take flight. That is a calculated risk which the law takes as the price of our system of justice. . . . In allowance of bail, the duty of the judge is to reduce the risk by fixing an amount reasonably calculated to hold the accused available for trial and its consequence. But the judge is not free to make the sky the limit, because the Eighth Amendment to the Constitution says: "Excessive bail shall not be required."

In *Stack,* the Court held that a uniform bond of $50,000 for each of several unregistered Communist Party members needed to be reconsidered by the trial court. On remand, each defendant's bail was to be set in light of "the nature and circumstances of the offense charged, the weight of the evidence against him, the financial ability of the defendant to give bail and the character of the defendant." This language presaged the federal Act of 1966 and parallel state legislation that put emphasis on an individualized assessment of the accused's likelihood of returning for trial.

---

[52] 342 U.S. 1, 72 S.Ct. 1 (1951).

[53] See Freed & Wald, supra note 13, at 6–7.

(2) Dangerousness

For at least three decades after *Stack*, prevention of flight was the only *avowed* aim of the bail system. However, the money bail system was often used, *sub rosa*, to detain "dangerous" individuals.[54] And, of course, once preventive detention statutes like the 1984 Bail Reform Act were passed, courts could openly consider such factors as danger to the community or witnesses. Both of these practices appeared to be in violation of *Stack*. But in *United States v. Salerno*,[55] the Supreme Court rejected a facial challenge of the Bail Reform Act of 1984, finding that *Stack* provided "far too slender a reed on which to rest" the argument that detention for the purpose of preventing crime by arrestees was unconstitutional:

> Nothing in the text of the Bail Clause limits permissible government considerations solely to questions of flight. The only arguable substantive limitation of the Bail Clause is that the Government's proposed conditions of release or detention not be "excessive" in light of the perceived evil. . . . [W]hen the government has admitted that its only interest is in preventing flight, bail must be set by a court at a sum designed to ensure that goal, and no more. . . .
>
> We believe that when Congress has mandated detention on the basis of a compelling interest other than prevention of flight, as it has here, the Eighth Amendment does not require release on bail.

The defendants in *Salerno* also challenged the preventive detention portion of the statute on substantive due process grounds, claiming that such detention amounted to punishment without trial. A similar argument had been made and rejected in the earlier case of *Schall v. Martin*,[56] where the Court upheld a state statute authorizing detention of juveniles who were charged with a delinquent act and posed a "serious risk" of committing a crime before their adjudicatory hearing. The Court in *Schall* reasoned that whether a government action is "punishment" depends upon whether the government's intent is to punish or, if it is not, whether the action "appears excessive in relation to [a legitimate] alternative purpose."[57] Using these criteria, the Court found that children confined under the statute were not punished: the duration of detention could be no longer than 17 days and even those children kept in "secure detention" wore street clothes, participated in education and recreational programs, and were disciplined for misbehavior solely by confinement in their rooms. This type of confinement did not indicate an intent to punish and was not excessive in relation to the important government interest of protecting the public from such juveniles.

Similarly, in *Salerno,* the Court found the government's interests to be "regulatory" rather than punishment oriented.[58] Confinement under the Act is not meant to be

---

[54]   See John Mitchell, *Bail Reform and the Constitutionality of Preventive Detention*, 55 Va.L.Rev. 1223, 1235 (1969).

[55]   481 U.S. 739, 107 S.Ct. 2095 (1987).

[56]   467 U.S. 253, 104 S.Ct. 2403 (1984).

[57]   Relying on *Bell v. Wolfish*, 441 U.S. 520, 99 S.Ct. 1861 (1979), discussed in § 20.04.

[58]   The Court noted several other instances where pretrial detention was permitted for "regulatory" purposes, among them *Jackson v. Indiana*, 406 U.S. 715, 92 S.Ct. 1845 (1972) (pretrial detention of incompetent defendants), discussed in § 28.03(b)(4); *Gerstein v. Pugh*, 420 U.S. 103, 95 S.Ct. 854 (1975) (temporary detention pending probable cause hearing), discussed in § 20.02(a).

punishment, because it is limited by the Speedy Trial Act,[59] and must occur in a facility separate, "to the extent practicable," from those who have been convicted. As to the justification for this regulatory confinement, the Court pointed to the strong government interest in preventing crime by arrestees. It also noted that the Act focuses on those charged with serious offenses, and requires clear and convincing proof "that no conditions of release can reasonably assure the safety of the community or any person." By implication, a preventive detention statute that does not impose these two limitations may not pass constitutional muster.[60]

Perhaps the weakest aspect of the Court's due process analysis in *Schall* and *Salerno* is its assumption that the government's interests can be reasonably implemented. In both opinions it stated that, "from a legal point of view[,] there is nothing inherently unattainable about a prediction of future criminal conduct," given the traditional reliance on such predictions in many other contexts, such as sentencing, parole and probation. But research indicates that a prediction that someone will recidivate is often wrong.[61] If this is so, preventive detention will not effectuate the government's purpose of detaining those most likely to commit crime.[62] At the same time, it is likely to detain a number of people who are not dangerous. Further, it provides the government with a means of manipulating defendants. As Justice Marshall pointed out in his *Salerno* dissent, one of the defendants in that case who had been preventively detained because he was "dangerous" was released when he agreed to be a covert government agent, suggesting that the Act might be used for purposes other than protecting the community. Aware of these difficulties, many lower courts have required fairly stringent proof of dangerousness.[63]

(3) Lack of Financial Resources

As noted in this chapter's historical account,[64] pretrial release was, and still is in some states, often denied simply because a person is poor and cannot produce any money (or enough money to meet the bondsman's requirements). The lower courts have, on the whole, found nothing wrong with this result. As one court put it, bail "is not excessive merely because the defendant is unable to pay it."[65] This position makes sense only in those situations where one can predict that no amount of money will assure the defendant's presence (a scenario which may often be true with drug kingpins, for instance),[66] or that the defendant is dangerous. When such predictions cannot be made,

---

[59]   The Act usually limits the time between arrest and trial to 100 days, but there are several exceptions. See § 25.05(c) and (d). The Court did indicate that if confinement became prolonged, it might be deemed "punitive." See *United States v. Hare,* 873 F.2d 796 (5th Cir. 1989).

[60]   Reinforcing that view is *Zadvydas v. INS,* 533 U.S. 678, 121 S.Ct. 2491 (2001), which held that aliens subject to deportation but who cannot be immediately deported may be preventively confined for only six months, at which time the government must either release the alien or show good reason to believe he will be removed to another country in the "reasonably foreseeable future."

[61]   See Baradharan & McIntyre, supra note 46.

[62]   The prevention of flight criterion also calls for a speculative prediction. But as noted in § 20.03(a)(3), these predictions tend to be wrong in only a very small percentage of the cases (under 5%).

[63]   See, e.g., *United States v. Townsend,* 897 F.2d 989 (9th Cir. 1990) (doubts regarding propriety of release to be resolved in favor of defendant); *United States v. Jackson,* 845 F.2d 1262 (5th Cir. 1988) (mere fact that defendant in a drug ring was member of a notorious motorcycle gang not enough); *United States v. Ploof,* 851 F.2d 7 (1st Cir. 1988) (generalized danger to the community insufficient).

[64]   See § 20.03(a)(2) & (3).

[65]   *Hodgdon v. United States,* 365 F.2d 679 (8th Cir. 1966).

[66]   See *United States v. Jessup,* 757 F.2d 378 (1st Cir. 1985).

even a modest bail may be "excessive" for many indigent defendants, in the sense that a smaller, affordable amount, as low as it might be, will still assure appearance for trial. The federal Reform Act of 1984 seems to recognize this fact by prohibiting imposition of "a financial condition that results in pretrial detention of the person."

The few lower courts that have found unconstitutional a failure to take into account financial circumstances when setting bail have generally done so on equal protection rather than Eighth Amendment grounds. For instance, in *Ackies v. Purdy*,[67] the court held that setting bail solely according to the nature of the offense would lead to an irrational distinction between the rich and the poor, as "a poor man with strong ties in the community may be more likely to appear than a man with some cash and no community involvement." With the advent of alternatives to money bail, a different type of equal protection might also be made. The federal court in *Pugh v. Rainwater*[68] concluded that equal protection requires that nonfinancial means of assuring appearance should be considered before money bail. As the court put it, "[r]equiring a presumption in favor of non-money bail accommodates the State's interest in assuring the defendant's appearance at trial as well as the defendant's right to be free pending trial, regardless of his financial status."

But the Supreme Court has not viewed the equal protection argument favorably in another context. In *Schilb v. Kuebel*,[69] it upheld a state statute which provided that a defendant who was not released on his own recognizance could be required either to deposit cash equal to 10% of the bond set by the court, 10% of which would be forfeited as "bail bond costs" even if the defendant reappeared, or to deposit the full amount of bail, all of which would be refunded if the defendant returned. The defendant argued, in effect, that this statute unfairly taxed the indigent accused, who was forced to pick the first alternative and thus lose money. But the Court found the statute did not necessarily discriminate against the poor, since "[i]t should be obvious that the poor man's real hope and avenue for relief is the personal recognizance provision" and since, given "these days of high interest rates," "it is by no means clear that [the second route] is more attractive to the affluent defendant." Neither of these conclusions addressed the defendant's claim contending that indigents have *no* choice; the dissent argued that, at the least, the state should have to impose a similar retention fee on those who paid the full deposit.

(4) Non-Citizenship

A series of Supreme Court decisions deal with the authority of the government to detain aliens prior to or after their deportation hearings. In 1896, the Court stated that deportation proceedings "would be vain if those accused could not be held in custody pending the inquiry into their true character."[70] The Court has since made clear that the Constitution places very few restrictions on detentions of aliens prior to such proceedings. As it stated in *Demore v. Kim*,[71] "this Court has firmly and repeatedly endorsed the proposition that Congress may make rules as to aliens that would be unacceptable if applied to citizens."

---

[67]   322 F.Supp. 38 (S.D.Fla. 1970).

[68]   557 F.2d 1189 (5th Cir. 1977).

[69]   404 U.S. 357, 92 S.Ct. 479 (1971).

[70]   *Wong Wing v. United States*, 163 U.S. 228, 16 S.Ct. 977 (1896).

[71]   538 U.S. 510, 123 S.Ct. 1708 (2003).

Two cases decided in the 1950's are illustrative. In *Carlson v. Landon*,[72] the government detained several aliens, whom the government alleged were dangerous members of the Communist party, prior to their deportation hearing. Relying on *Stack v. Boyle*,[73] in which the Court a mere year earlier had suggested that risk of non-appearance was the sole ground on which bail could be denied,[74] the petitioners challenged their detention on the ground that no finding of flight risk had been made. But the Court held, 5–4, that bail in cases involving aliens could be denied upon proof of danger to society as well as proof of flight risk. The majority also found that the government had produced adequate evidence of the petitioners' dangerousness, over dissents by Justices Frankfurter and Black charging that the evidence for at least some of the detainees was "insufficient," based on "rank hearsay," or stale. The next year, the Court held, again 5–4, that an alien who had lived lawfully in the United States for twenty-five years but who was returning from nineteen months behind the "Iron Curtain" could be denied re-entry and indefinitely detained at Ellis Island, without a judicial hearing to determine his dangerousness. The Court concluded that, in such cases of "exclusion" (as opposed to deportation), the Attorney General has discretion to make such a determination on his own.[75]

Forty years later, in *Reno v. Flores*,[76] the Court remained deferential to legislative schemes and the executive branch's exercise of discretion regarding detention of aliens. There the regulation in question gave the Attorney General discretion to detain alien juveniles prior to their deportation proceedings if no parent, close relative or legal guardian was available to assume custody. The Court held that this regulation did not violate substantive due process, because its presumption against granting custody to other individuals besides those listed was "rationally related" to preserving the welfare of juveniles and was not punitive in purpose.

Two other cases involving detention of aliens appear at first glance to be different in tone from this precedent, but in fact do not veer dramatically from it. In *Zadvydas v. Davis*,[77] the Court held, 5–4, that an alien who has been found deportable but who encounters difficulty finding residence in another country is entitled to a hearing within six months to determine whether he should be released back into the United States. At the hearing, Justice Breyer stated for the Court, "once the alien provides good reason to believe that there is no significant likelihood of removal in the reasonably foreseeable future, the Government must respond with evidence sufficient to rebut that showing." In *Clark v. Martinez*,[78] the Court held that, because the statutory provision at issue in *Zadvydas* also governs detention of aliens who have been denied admission to the U.S. in the first instance, the same six-month presumption applies to that group as well. However, in both *Zadvydas* and *Martinez* the Court also made clear that if Congress passed an amendment to the statute that granted the Attorney General the power to

---

[72]   342 U.S. 524, 72 S.Ct. 525 (1952).

[73]   342 U.S. 1, 72 S.Ct. 1 (1951).

[74]   See § 20.03(c)(1). *Stack* had stated: "The right to release before trial is conditioned upon the accused's giving adequate assurance that he will stand trial and submit to sentence if found guilty."

[75]   *Shaughnessy v. United States ex rel. Mezei*, 345 U.S. 206, 73 S.Ct. 625 (1953).

[76]   507 U.S. 292, 113 S.Ct. 1439 (1993).

[77]   533 U.S. 678, 121 S.Ct. 2491 (2001).

[78]   543 U.S. 371, 125 S.Ct. 716 (2005).

detain an alien indefinitely, "the Court would be required to give it effect," as Justice Breyer put it in *Zadvydas*.

This deferential attitude was also on display in *Demore v. Kim*, noted above. That case involved a federal immigration statute which clearly stated that an alien who commits one of a specific set of crimes must be detained pending the removal hearing to determine whether the deportation criteria are met.[79] Kim, who had been detained under this statute after being convicted of burglary and petty theft, brought a habeas corpus action alleging that it violated substantive due process because it *mandated* detention without a showing that he was *either* a flight risk or dangerous.[80] Five members of the Court, in an opinion by Chief Justice Rehnquist, rejected this contention. Rehnquist noted that the Court had not required individualized judicial assessments in previous cases involving detention of aliens and, relying on congressional findings that up to 20% of aliens failed to appear for their deportation proceedings, concluded that "when the Government deals with deportable aliens, the Due Process Clause does not require it to employ the least burdensome means to accomplish its goal." He also pointed out that, in contrast to *Zadvydas*, which involved a potentially indefinite detention, detentions prior to deportation proceedings are of limited duration (usually under 60 days).[81]

The Court's cases in this area establish that aliens may be detained at the discretion of the government, without recourse to judicial review of the basis for their detention, in at least three situations: when they attempt to enter or re-enter the country, when they have been found deportable but are unable to find a country in which to reside or, most relevant to this chapter, pending deportation proceedings. The only procedural limitations on the executive branch imposed by the Due Process Clause in these three situations are those Congress recognizes.

(5) Material Witnesses

A final type of pre-proceeding detention involves individuals who are thought to have knowledge of crime rather than be guilty of one. A brief discussion of this situation is included here because statutes authorizing such detentions can be used as a pretext for detaining suspects. Under federal law and the law in many states, a person may be "arrested" as a "material witness" if "it appears from an affidavit filed by a party that the testimony of a person is material in a criminal proceeding, and if it is shown that it may become impracticable to secure the presence of the person by subpoena."[82] Under the federal law, the detention is limited to a "reasonable period of time" necessary to take a deposition, although detention may continue if the person refuses to be deposed or if "necessary to prevent a failure of justice." The statute has been upheld against Fourth Amendment challenge, even though it does not require a probable cause showing

---

[79] 8 U.S.C.A. § 1226(c).

[80] The statute also provided that the Attorney General's judgment to detain such individuals "shall not be subject to review." 8 U.S.C.A. § 1226(e). The Court held, over a four-member dissent authored by Justice O'Connor, that this language only prevents challenge of individual determinations, not challenges to the constitutionality of the legislation.

[81] Dissenting to this portion of the opinion, Justice Souter, joined by two others, noted that Kim was a permanent resident alien (a status that allows permanent residence and employment in the United States) and that such aliens are both much less likely to flee the jurisdiction and, if detained, more likely to be detained for longer than average, given the greater likelihood they will challenge the detention (in proceedings that can take several months).

[82] 18 U.S.C.A. § 3144.

with respect to a crime, the materiality of the testimony, or the necessity of the detention.[83]

In *Ashcroft v. al-Kidd*[84] the Court held that pretextual use of the material witness statute does not violate the Fourth Amendment. Al-Kidd argued that the federal government detained him (for over a week) under the material witness statute not because he possessed information relevant to another person's prosecution but because of unsupported suspicions that he was consorting with terrorists. The government's material warrant application had claimed that his detention was necessary because his testimony was crucial to a criminal prosecution and he was on the verge of leaving for Saudi Arabia on a one-way ticket; in fact, al-Kidd asserted, his ticket was round-trip, his parents, wife and children were all citizens and residents of the U.S., and he had already cooperated with the FBI on several occasions, all of which suggested the real reason for the material witness warrant was to detain him despite a lack of probable cause to arrest. Five members of the Court, in an opinion by Justice Scalia, held that the Fourth Amendment was not violated even if al-Kidd's allegations were true. The Court interpreted *Whren v. United States*[85] to stand for the proposition that seizures or searches based on "individualized suspicion" are permissible even if the police have an ulterior motive.

In an opinion concurring only in the judgment granting qualified immunity to Attorney General Ashcroft, Justice Sotomayor, joined by Justices Ginsburg and Breyer (Justice Kagan did not participate) argued that *Whren* had only prohibited pretext arguments when the government has probable cause to believe a crime has been committed, which was clearly not shown in this case. Similarly, Justice Ginsburg's separate opinion noted that cases applying *Whren* typically have required individualized suspicion of "wrongdoing," also not established here. But the majority stated that "[e]fficient and evenhanded application of the law demands that we look to whether the arrest is objectively justified, rather than to the motive of the arresting officer." Because al-Kidd only advanced the pretext argument and did not challenge the material witness warrant itself, the Court left unresolved whether a material witness detention is permissible on the facts of *al-Kidd*, or indeed whether material witness warrants are even governed by the Fourth Amendment.[86]

(d) The Pretrial Release Hearing

Stack indicated that the Eighth Amendment would be violated if a court set bail according to some predetermined schedule, without considering "the nature and circumstances of the offense charged, the weight of the evidence against [the defendant], the financial ability of the defendant to give bail and the character of the defendant." In upholding preventive detention, *Schall* and *Salerno* also seemed to find important that the statutes in question provided for "case-by-case" determinations of dangerousness at a pretrial hearing presided over by a judge. These cases suggest that, at least where American citizens are involved, each defendant should be afforded, as a matter of

---

[83]   *United States v. Awadallah*, 349 F.3d 42 (2d Cir. 2003); *Bacon v. United States*, 449 F.2d 933, 943–45 (9th Cir. 1971).

[84]   563 U.S. 731, 131 S.Ct. 2074 (2011).

[85]   517 U.S. 806, 116 S.Ct. 1769 (1996), discussed in § 10.04.

[86]   Because of this legal ambiguity, the relevant law was not "clearly established" at the time of al-Kidd's detention, and thus all members of the Court dismissed al-Kidd's petition on qualified immunity grounds. See § 2.05(a)(1).

procedural due process, some sort of hearing before the long-term pretrial release decision, at which an individualized assessment is made. Thus, they also suggest that the non-individualized bail schedules frequently used under the money bail system are unconstitutional.[87]

These conclusions are bolstered by the type of reasoning found in *Hunt v. Roth,*[88] where the Eighth Circuit struck down a Nebraska constitutional amendment that denied bail in cases of "sexual offenses involving penetration by force or against the will of the victim . . . where the proof is evident or the presumption great." The court concluded:

> The fatal flaw in the . . . amendment is that the state has created an irrebuttable presumption that every individual charged with this particular offense is incapable of assuring his appearance by conditioning it upon reasonable bail or is too dangerous to be granted release. . . . The state may be free to consider the nature of the charge and the degree of proof in granting or denying bail but it cannot give these factors conclusive force.

Note that *Hunt's* reasoning applies with equal force to the most time-honored exception to bail practices, capital cases "where the proof is evident or the presumption great."[89] While, on the whole, a person charged with a capital offense may be more likely to flee the jurisdiction than other defendants, *Hunt* suggests that the state should not be able to assume that is the case even where capital charges are involved.

If a hearing is held, there are good reasons to require far more formality than the nonadversarial probable cause hearing approved in *Gerstein v. Pugh,*[90] despite the fact that it may take place at approximately the same point in the criminal process. Research indicates that counsel can have a significant effect on whether release occurs and on what terms.[91] Further, the Supreme Court's cases require counsel at any stage after "prosecution commences" and the defendant is "immersed in the intricacies of substantive and procedural criminal law."[92] A post-arrest bail hearing appears to meet both of these requirements. Additionally, because the information relevant to this proceeding can come from many sources, the defendant should have the right to present evidence and cross-examine the government's witnesses.

However, a large number of lower courts have refused to apply the right to counsel and related rights to bail hearings.[93] In support of this position, it can be pointed out that, in *Salerno,* the Supreme Court found the federal preventive detention statute's provision for counsel, evidence presentation, and cross-examination rights acceptable because it "far exceed[ed] what we found necessary" in *Gerstein.* This language clearly

---

[87]   Preliminary bail, applicable only for a few days, can probably be set according to a schedule, however. *Ackies v. Purdy,* 322 F.Supp. 38 (S.D.Fla. 1970).

[88]   648 F.2d 1148 (8th Cir. 1981), vac'd for mootness 455 U.S. 478, 102 S.Ct. 1181 (1982).

[89]   In those states which had to revise their capital punishment statutes because of constitutional developments, some eliminated this exception, see e.g., *Martinez v. State,* 26 Ariz.App. 386, 548 P.2d 1198 (1976), while others continue to apply it those offenses which once were designated capital. *Jones v. Sheriff, Washoe County,* 89 Nev. 175, 509 P.2d 824 (1973).

[90]   420 U.S. 103, 95 S.Ct. 854 (1975), discussed in § 20.02(b).

[91]   See Douglas L. Colbert et al. *Do Attorneys Really Matter?: The Empirical and Legal Case for the Right to Counsel at Bail,* 23 Cardozo L.Rev. 1719 (2002); Paul B. Wice, Freedom for Sale 49 (1974).

[92]   *Kirby v. Illinois,* 406 U.S. 682, 92 S.Ct. 1877 (1972), discussed in § 31.03(a)(3).

[93]   See, e.g., *Fenner v. State,* 381 Md. 1, 846 A.2d 1020 (2004). As of 2006, 42 two states did not provide counsel either statewide or within certain jurisdictions. See Douglas L. Colbert, *Coming to a Court Near You: Convicting the Unrepresented at the Bail Stage,* 36 Seton Hall L. Rev. 656 n.21 (2006).

does not *require* that these various rights be accorded a defendant subject to preventive detention. Also noteworthy in this regard is a later holding of the Court that, despite the federal statute's "prompt hearing" provision, a delayed hearing is harmless error where the person is subsequently found eligible for detention.[94] Finally, it remains uncertain, despite the emphasis the Court placed on it in *Salerno,* whether the statute's requirement that proof of dangerousness be by "clear and convincing evidence" is constitutionally mandated.[95]

A number of states, in their constitutions, by statute or both, as well as the federal government through the Crime Victims' Rights Act of 2004,[96] recognize that victims have a right to be heard on the matter of pretrial release.[97] Victims might have information relevant to the strength of the case against the defendant, the seriousness of the offense, and the danger presented by the defendant.[98] Not yet clear under all of these provisions is whether the victim is permitted to submit oral testimony or can be limited to written submissions.

(e) Trial and Post-Conviction Bail

The focus to this point has been on the scope of pretrial release. Similar release questions can arise during trial or after conviction pending appeal. In *Bitter v. United States,*[99] the Supreme Court held that, if granted prior to trial, bail may be revoked during trial "only when and to the extent justified by danger which the defendant's conduct presents or by danger of significant interference with the progress or order of the trial." Bail revocation at trial may not be based, as was the case in *Bitter,* on "a single, brief incident of tardiness." Thus, pretrial release establishes a strong preference for continued release during trial.

With respect to bail after conviction and pending appeal, many states merely leave the issue to the discretion of the trial judge. But the federal Bail Reform Act of 1966, which at the pretrial stage focused purely on assuring appearance for trial, at the post-conviction stage also allowed detention if the person would pose a danger to the community.[100] Under the Bail Reform Act of 1984, post-conviction release is even harder to obtain, as the judge must find by clear and convincing evidence that the offender will *not* pose a danger or flee before release may occur.[101]

(f) Appeal of the Pretrial Release Decision

Most jurisdictions have statutes authorizing an interlocutory appeal from a decision denying pretrial release.[102] If there is no such statute, habeas corpus is considered the proper remedy for review.[103] Furthermore, a state defendant who is unable to make bail

---

[94] *United States v. Montalvo-Murillo,* 495 U.S. 711, 110 S.Ct. 2072 (1990).

[95] See *United States v. Salerno,* 829 F.2d 345 (2d Cir. 1987).

[96] 18 U.S.C.A. § 3771(a) (recognizing, inter alia, the right of the victim "to be reasonably heard at any public proceeding in the district court involving release, plea, sentencing, or any parole proceeding").

[97] See generally, Paul G. Cassell, *Recognizing Victims in the Federal Rules of Criminal Procedure: Proposed Amendments in Light of the Crime Victims' Rights Act,* 2005 B.Y.U.L.Rev. 835.

[98] See *United States v. Marcello,* 370 F.Supp.2d 745 (N.D.Ill. 2005).

[99] 389 U.S. 15, 88 S.Ct. 6 (1967).

[100] 18 U.S.C.A. § 3148.

[101] 18 U.S.C.A. § 3143(b).

[102] See § 29.03(a) for a discussion of interlocutory appeals generally.

[103] *Ex parte Brumback*, 46 Cal.2d 810, 299 P.2d 217 (1956).

before trial may seek habeas review in federal court when the state appellate court docket is so backlogged that effective relief would otherwise be denied.[104] However, it is unlikely that any appellate court, federal or state, will overrule a lower court pretrial release decision, unless a gross abuse of discretion can be proved. Moreover, the Supreme Court has held that, unless the defendant brings a class action in favor of all pretrial detainees similarly situated, an appeal of a pretrial bail decision is moot once the defendant is convicted.[105]

20.04   Disposition of Pretrial Detainees

Relevant to the debate over the scope of pretrial detention are the conditions in which the detention occurs. The Supreme Court has been confronted with several cases claiming that particular government practices at detention facilities are unconstitutional. To date, it has rejected all of these claims.

The leading case is *Bell v. Wolfish,*[106] where the Court analyzed a number of rules promulgated by New York City's Metropolitan Correctional Center (MCC), a federally-operated short-term facility used primarily to house pretrial detainees. The majority opinion, by Justice Rehnquist, decided that the issue was whether these rules constituted "punishment" of unconvicted individuals, in which case due process was violated, or were instead "reasonably related to [another] legitimate governmental objective." Using this expansive test, the Court sanctioned: a "publisher-only" rule prohibiting detainees from receiving books or magazines from anyone other than the publisher, book clubs, or bookstores;[107] a prohibition against packages from outside (except a package of food at Christmas); unannounced searches of living areas at irregular intervals; and visual body cavity searches after contact visits. All of these practices were viewed as legitimate means of ensuring the security of the prison and preventing smuggling of weapons and contraband. In *Block v. Rutherford,*[108] the Court relied on the same reasoning in upholding a pretrial detention center's blanket prohibition of contact visits.

Although arising out of the post-conviction prison setting, the Court's decision in *Hudson v. Palmer*[109] is also of relevance here. In that case, Palmer sought damages under § 1983 for an arbitrary "shakedown" of his cell by a prison guard who intentionally destroyed some of his property, including legal materials and letters. Accepting these factual allegations as true, the majority found that the guard's actions violated neither the Due Process Clause nor the Fourth Amendment. The Due Process Clause was not implicated because intentional misconduct of this sort could not be prevented by the state and the state provided adequate postconduct remedies.[110] The Fourth Amendment's prohibition of unreasonable searches and seizures was not implicated because prisoners have no reasonable expectation of privacy in their cells. Balancing society's interest in prison security against the prisoner's interest in privacy, Chief Justice Burger concluded for the majority that "society would insist that the prisoner's

[104] *Boyer v. City of Orlando,* 402 F.2d 966 (5th Cir. 1968); see 28 U.S.C.A. § 2254(b).

[105] *Murphy v. Hunt,* 455 U.S. 478, 102 S.Ct. 1181 (1982).

[106] 441 U.S. 520, 99 S.Ct. 1861 (1979).

[107] The Court also found that this rule did not violate the First Amendment, especially since it was usually limited to a maximum sixty day detention period.

[108] 468 U.S. 576, 104 S.Ct. 3227 (1984).

[109] 468 U.S. 517, 104 S.Ct. 3194 (1984).

[110] See *Parratt v. Taylor,* 451 U.S. 527, 101 S.Ct. 1908 (1981), discussed in § 2.05(a)(3).

expectation of privacy always yield to what must be considered the paramount interest in institutional security." Therefore, "unfettered access" to prison cells is permissible and prison officials may seize "any articles which, in their view, disserve legitimate institutional interests," including, apparently, Palmer's letters and legal materials. To Palmer's argument that without the reasonableness guarantee incorporated in the Fourth Amendment prisoners would be subject to harassment by prison officials, Chief Justice Burger pointed out that the Eighth Amendment protected against cruel and unusual punishments and that state tort and common-law remedies were available.

Justice Stevens, joined by Justices Brennan, Marshall and Blackmun, agreed that random searches of a prisoner's cell are reasonable in order to ensure that it contains no contraband or dangerous weapons. But the dissenters saw "no need for seizure and destruction of noncontraband items found during such searches." As the dissent pointed out, *Palmer* reinforces the impression that the Court has adopted a "hands-off" attitude toward prison and jail administration.

That impression was furthered by the Court's decision thirty years later in *Florence v. County of Burlington*,[111] which upheld a strip search procedure that applied to all arrestees. Florence was arrested for failing to appear at a hearing to enforce a fine and, once in jail, was required to disrobe, open his mouth, lift his tongue, lift his genitals, and cough while squatting. He argued that this procedure was unnecessary for someone who was not suspected of concealing drugs or weapons. But the Supreme Court, in an opinion by Justice Kennedy, held that this procedure was a reasonable seizure under the Fourth and Fourteenth Amendments because of concerns about infectious diseases, gang violence, and drug-connected transactions in jail. Kennedy reasoned that the seriousness of the offense of arrest "is a poor predictor of who has contraband," that minor offenders can be coerced into sneaking weapons into prison, and that jail personnel do not have access to criminal history.

The four dissenters, in an opinion by Justice Breyer, argued that frisking, metal detectors, searches of clothing, and showers and delousing could adequately meet the government's safety objectives where minor offenders are concerned. Breyer referred to one study in New York involving 23,000 arrestees taken to jail, only five of whom had drugs in their anal cavity or underwear; further, only one of these five had not already been suspected of having contraband on their person. He also noted that several professional correctional associations forbid suspicionless strip searches, even for those arrested for felonies, as do at least 10 states. Finally, he pointed out that people presumably do not hide contraband on their person with the intent of smuggling it into jail if they happen to be arrested that day. The dissent concluded by arguing that, at the least, the Constitution required that minor offenders be segregated until the first appearance in front of a judicial officer, at which time many charges are dismissed or otherwise disposed of. One of the justices in the majority, Justice Alito, agreed with this stance, and both he and Chief Justice Roberts, also in the majority, adverted to a possible exception to the Court's holding if the jurisdiction had the capacity to house arrestees for minor offenses separately from the general jail population.

---

[111] 566 U.S. 318, 132 S.Ct. 1510 (2012).

20.05 Conclusion

The initial custodial decisions made after arrest are relatively unregulated by the Constitution. Set out below is a summary of the relevant Supreme Court pronouncements and some of the more common statutory rules that govern these decisions.

(1) If arrest is not authorized by either an arrest warrant or a grand jury indictment, the Fourth Amendment requires a prompt post-arrest judicial assessment of whether probable cause to detain exists. The assessment may be *ex parte,* in the absence of counsel, and informal in nature—in short, similar to the pre-arrest determination of probable cause when a warrant is sought. If such a hearing takes place within 48 hours of arrest, it is presumptively reasonable.

(2) After arrest, the typical procedure is to determine whether the individual is eligible for bail or other type of pretrial release. While the money bail system is still in force in many states, the trend is to require an individualized assessment of the likelihood an accused will appear for trial and to encourage release of defendants on their own recognizance or on other non-financial conditions. A second, contrary trend is the enactment of laws that permit the government to detain "preventively" suspects who are likely to commit crimes while on pretrial release.

(3) Neither the Eighth Amendment's prohibition of excessive bail nor the Due Process Clause prohibits a denial of pretrial release, so long as the denial is related to a legitimate government objective, is not disproportionate to the perceived danger, and is not intended as punishment. Thus, the federal Bail Reform Act of 1984, which permits pretrial detention when no reasonable pretrial release condition can assure reappearance at trial, prevent harm to witnesses, or prevent the commission of a crime, is constitutional. However, the Equal Protection Clause may prohibit denial of pretrial release solely on the grounds of indigency or at least require serious consideration of other means of deterring flight, even if the Eighth Amendment or the Due Process Clause do not.

(4) Prior to a pretrial release determination that can have long-term consequences, procedural due process probably requires a judicial hearing, with counsel and the right to call and cross-examine witnesses. Non-citizens subject to deportation hearings may be denied pre-hearing release at the discretion of the executive branch, if such power is authorized by statute. Clear constitutional limitations on material witness statutes have yet to be established.

(5) The government has wide-ranging authority to administer pretrial detention facilities, which can include body cavity searches of individuals arrested for minor offenses, so long as its practices are related to legitimate security rationale.

BIBLIOGRAPHY

Alschuler, Albert W. Preventive Pretrial Detention and the Failure of Interest-Balancing Approaches to Due Process. 85 Mich. L.Rev. 510 (1986).

Appelman, Laura. Justice in the Shadowlands: Pretrial Detention, Punishment, and the Sixth Amendment. 69 Wash. & Lee L. Rev. 1297 (2012).

Baradharan, Shima. The Bail Book: A Comprehensive Look at Bail in America's Criminal Justice System (2018).

Baradharan, Shima and Frank L McIntyre. Predicting Violence. 90 Tex. L. Rev. 497 (2012).

Bargava, Shalini. Detaining Due Process: The Need for Procedural Reform in "*Joseph* Hearings" after *Demore v. Kim*. 31 N.Y.U. J. L. Soc.Change 51 (2006).

Bascuas, Ricardo J. The Unconstitutionality of "Hold Until Cleared": Reexamining Material Witness Detentions in the Wake of the September 11th Dragnet. 58 Vand.L.Rev. 677 (2005).

Cohen, Richard A. Wealth, Bail and Equal Protection of the Laws. 23 Vill.L.Rev. 977 (1978).

Colbert, Douglas L. Prosecution Without Representation. 59 Buff. L. Rev. 333 (2011).

Colbert, Douglas L. et al. Do Attorneys Really Matter?: The Empirical and Legal Case for the Right to Counsel at Bail. 23 Cardozo L.Rev. 1719. (2002).

Damon, Hallie T. A Reasonable Detention?: Rethinking the Material Witness Probable Cause Standard After *Al-Kidd*. 44 Colum. Human Rights L. Rev. 537 (2013).

Dery, George M. Florence and the Machine: The Supreme Court Upholds Suspicionless Strip Searches Resulting from Computer Error. 40 Am. J. Crim. L. 173 (2013).

Foote, Caleb, ed. Studies on Bail. University of Pennsylvania Law School, 1966.

Goldkamp, John S. Danger and Detention: A Second Generation of Bail Reform. 76 J.Crim.L. & Criminol. 1 (1985).

Kalhous, Clara and John Meringolo. Bail Pending Trial: Changing Interpretations of the Bail Reform Act and the Importance of Bail from Defense Attorneys' Perspectives. 32 Pace L. Rev. 800 (2012).

Klein, Douglas J. The Pretrial Detention "Crisis": The Causes and the Cure. 52 Wash U. J. Urb. & Contemp. L. 281 (1997).

Martin, David A. Graduated Application of Constitutional Protection for Aliens: The Real Meaning of *Zadvydas* v. Davis. 2001 Sup.Ct.Rev. 47.

Miller, Marc and Martin Guggenheim. Pretrial Detention and Punishment. 75 Minn.L.Rev. 335 (1990).

Richards, Edward P. The Jurisprudence of Prevention: The Right of Societal Self-Defense Against Dangerous Individuals. 16 Hastings Const. L.Q. 329 (1989).

Scott, Thomas E. Pretrial Detention Under the Bail Reform Act of 1984: An Empirical Analysis. 27 Am.Crim.L.Rev. 1 (1989).

Tribe, Laurence H. An Ounce of Detention: Preventive Justice in the World of John Mitchell. 56 Va.L.Rev. 371 (1970).

Wiseman, Samuel R. Pretrial Detention and the Right to be Monitored. 123 Yale L.J. 1344 (2014).

Chapter 21

CONSTRAINTS ON PROSECUTORIAL DISCRETION: CHARGING, JOINDER AND VENUE RULES

21.01   Introduction

Article II, Section 3 of the United States Constitution provides that the executive branch of the federal government "shall take Care that the Laws be faithfully executed." Similar provisions are found in most state constitutions. Where the criminal law is concerned, the obligation to "execute the law," at both the federal and state levels, falls primarily on the prosecutor.[1] Its principal manifestation is the charging decision, the determination whether a particular individual should formally be accused of crime and, if so, on precisely what charge or charges.

Traditionally, the prosecutor has been vested with wide-ranging authority in making this decision. As the Supreme Court stated in *Bordenkircher v. Hayes,*[2] "so long as the prosecutor has probable cause to believe that the accused committed an offense defined by statute, the decision whether or not to prosecute, and what charge to file or bring before a grand jury, generally rests entirely in his discretion."

Prosecutorial discretion in this area is not unfettered, however. Some constraints derive from the Constitution, some come from statutory regulation, and many are self-imposed by the executive branch itself. The first two sections of this chapter examine the constitutional limitations, as well as some exemplary legislative and administrative restrictions, on the prosecutor's authority to decide who to prosecute and on what charges. The third section discusses the rules regulating joinder of charges and joinder of parties; these rules also tend to restrict the prosecutor's control over the charging process. The final section discusses the constitutional and statutory rules regarding venue, which require that prosecution take place in a geographic area associated with the crime. The intent of this chapter is to give an overview of the complex nature of the charging decision and the law's attempts to regulate it.

The procedural devices that review the validity of a charge once it has been chosen by the prosecutor—the preliminary hearing and the grand jury review process—are discussed in the following chapters.

21.02   The Decision to Forego Prosecution

The prosecutor has the authority to dismiss charges even over the complainant-victim's objection. Additionally, through the plea bargaining process,[3] he has the ability to accept a guilty plea on a lesser charge than that originally brought. Both of these

---

[1]   Of course, the police exercise considerable discretion in the field when making the initial arrest decision. See generally, Kenneth C. Davis, Police Discretion (1975).

[2]   434 U.S. 357, 98 S.Ct. 663 (1978).

[3]   The procedures normally followed during plea bargaining, and the constitutional restrictions placed on the prosecutor once a bargain has been reached, are discussed in Chapter 26. Here plea bargaining will be discussed only from the standpoint of the prosecutor's authority to reduce charges.

privileges are exercised frequently. In the federal courts, approximately 75% of all criminal cases brought to the attention of the prosecutor result in dismissal;[4] the proportion of nonprosecutions in state jurisdictions is probably closer to fifty percent,[5] but is obviously still sizeable. Of those cases that are prosecuted, perhaps 95% in both federal and state jurisdictions result in a conviction by guilty plea, often on a charge lower than that originally brought.[6]

(a) Reasons for Non-Prosecution

The most obvious, and most justifiable, reason for not prosecuting an individual on a particular charge is insufficient evidence. A dismissal on lack of evidence grounds could involve an assessment that the individual is in fact innocent of the charge, or it could mean that, while the prosecutor believes the defendant is guilty, he also believes certain crucial evidence is inadmissible because of police misconduct or evidentiary rules. Another evidentiary reason for not proceeding is an inability to secure the cooperation of a key witness, who might not want to undergo the inconvenience or possible harassment associated with testimony in court. Even when the prosecutor has access to sufficient admissible evidence to convict, however, he may decide to forego prosecution or to agree to a plea bargain on a lesser charge than the evidence would support. The reasons for such a decision are legion;[7] only a few will be mentioned here.

The prosecutor may reach the conclusion that, despite the ability to make out a prima facie case, he will have a particularly difficult time obtaining a conviction, given the strength of the defense's evidence or the likely reaction of a jury to the defendant's plight, and thus that his time is better spent focusing on other cases. He may feel that particular charges, although legitimate under prevailing law, are not appropriately brought because of the minor nature of the crime, alternative methods of redressing the harm (e.g., restitution), or societal condonation of the behavior involved (as in adultery cases).[8] Or he may believe that application of the law at issue would impose a draconian penalty under the circumstances (e.g., a statute allowing imposition of a mandatory life sentence on a person with three felonies regardless of degree). The characteristics of the potential defendant—that is, age, prior record, or family situation—may also influence the prosecutor toward leniency,[9] either through outright dismissal, charge reduction, or referral to a so-called "pretrial diversion program" designed to help the defendant deal with the problems that allegedly precipitated the criminal activity.[10]

---

[4]   Richard S. Frase, *The Decision to File Federal Criminal Charges: A Quantitative Study of Prosecutorial Discretion*, 47 U.Chi.L.Rev. 246 (1980).

[5]   See Adam M. Gershowitz, *Prosecutorial Screening Before Arrest*, 2019 Ill. L.Rev. 293; Peter Greenwood, et al., Prosecution of Adult Felony Defendants in Los Angeles County: A Policy Perspective (1976) (prosecution rate varies from 46% to 55%).

[6]   See § 26.01.

[7]   See Wayne LaFave, *The Prosecutor's Discretion in the United States*, 18 Am. J.Comp.L. 532, 533–35 (1970) for a detailed discussion of the reasons a prosecutor might decide not to prosecute.

[8]   In the Frase study, supra note 4, federal attorneys cited the minor nature of the crime as the principal reason for declining prosecution in 44% of the cases, while insufficiency of the evidence was responsible for nonprosecution in only 22% of the cases.

[9]   See Richard H. Kuh, *Plea Bargaining: Guidelines for the Manhattan District Attorney's Office*, 11 Crim.L.Bull 48 (1975) (listing as "mitigating factors" the defendant's prior record, age, military and work record and the "genuineness of the defendant's contrition"). In the Frase study, supra note 4, federal attorneys cited characteristics of the defendant as the principal reason for declining prosecution in 21% of the cases.

[10]   See Franklin E. Zimring, *Measuring the Impact of Pretrial Diversion from the Criminal Justice System*, 41 U.Chi.L.Rev. 224 (1974).

More practical concerns may dictate prosecutorial decisions as well. Charge reduction or dismissal may meet a perceived need to develop informants or to reward the defendant for helping to apprehend others. If prosecution requires a complicated extradition process, it may be dropped. Federal prosecutors may dismiss charges that can also be tried in state court, on the ground that the federal interest in prosecuting the case is minimal.[11]

An underlying consideration in all of these instances is economic. While the conscientious prosecutor may want to convict every individual who has committed crime on the charge that best describes the illegal conduct, lack of attorney time and investigative and other resources may force him to consider lenient treatment of defendants. In particular, the institution of plea bargaining has received powerful impetus because of the belief that, if not offered concessions, defendants will seldom choose a guilty plea over trial, thus severely overburdening the criminal justice system.

Although there is a sense in which all of the reasons for nonprosecution and charge reduction given above are "legitimate," one can argue that, to the extent prosecutors are dismissing or downgrading charges for reasons unrelated to the available evidence, they are failing to "execute" the laws of the state. At the least, it must be admitted that the decision to dismiss or reduce charges for other than evidentiary reasons will often be a complex one. As a result, prosecutorial leniency may frustrate legislative and public will and is susceptible of abuse.

(b) Limitations on Non-Prosecution

Judicial and legislative response to the possible abuses of non-prosecution has not been energetic. A failure to pursue charges may occasionally be overridden by a court on a writ of mandamus[12] or by the prosecutor's superior,[13] and in extremely rare instances, a private party may be able to bring prosecution (often called a *qui tam* action)[14] or the prosecutor may be removed.[15] But none of these devices provides an institutional approach to the everyday problem of arbitrary nonprosecution.

In some jurisdictions, more comprehensive schemes for avoiding arbitrary exercise of discretion to dismiss or reduce charges have been developed. Many prosecutorial offices have taken it upon themselves to develop guidelines for prosecutors to follow. One district attorney's office, for example, established criteria that tell prosecutors when to seek the lesser of two possible sentences authorized by the legislature.[16] Unlike

---

[11]   In the Frase study, supra note 4, the availability of state prosecution was cited as a reason for declining federal prosecution in 26% of the cases.

[12]   See *NAACP v. Levi,* 418 F.Supp. 1109 (D.D.C. 1976), dismissed as moot, *NAACP v. Bell,* 76 F.R.D. 134 (D.D.C. 1977). But see, *Inmates of Attica Correctional Facility v. Rockefeller,* 477 F.2d 375 (2d Cir. 1973).

[13]   "Many states by statute confer upon the attorney general the power to initiate prosecution in cases where the local prosecutor has failed to act. In practice, however, attorneys general have seldom exercised much control over local prosecuting attorneys." Yale Kamisar, Wayne LaFave, Jerold Israel, Nancy I. King, Modern Criminal Procedure 997 (11th ed. 1999).

[14]   Annot., 66 A.L.R.3d 732 (1975). But see *Tonkin v. Michael,* 349 F.Supp. 78 (D.Vi. 1972) (holding that notwithstanding a court rule permitting private prosecution, it should not be allowed over the prosecutor's objection). A number of states have victim's rights provisions that require prosecutors to consult with victims, but usually only after charges are filed. Cf. *Ex parte Littlefield,* 343 S.C. 212, 540 S.E.2d 81 (2000) (Victims' Bill of Rights Act does not detract from prosecutors' broad discretion to decide what charges to bring); *Town of Castle Rock v. Gonzales,* 545 U.S. 748, 125 S.Ct. 2796 (2005) (refusing to recognize a § 1983 claim against police for failure to enforce a restraining order despite a mandatory arrest policy).

[15]   Kamisar, et al., supra note 13, at 998.

[16]   Greenwood, et al., supra note 5, at 60.

prosecutorial rules dictating when charges should be dismissed outright (e.g., "cases involving less than a gram of cocaine will not be prosecuted," "defendants with no prior record and a job shall normally have misdemeanor charges dismissed"), such criteria do not ignore legislative intent, since the applicable statute explicitly authorizes the lesser sentence. There remains a question as to the impact these and other types of guidelines have on actual practice; unless they are made known to the public, they may be inconsistently applied by the prosecutor. On the other hand, their publication would tend to lessen the deterrent effect of the law and encourage time-consuming litigation over whether they are rational and equitably applied.

Another approach to the practice of charge dismissal or reduction when sufficient evidence to convict exists is to forbid it. In West Germany, for instance, if a file is closed it must include a written statement of reasons for the dismissal which, in important cases, must be approved by the prosecutor's superior.[17] Apparently, only reasons having to do with evidentiary insufficiency are acceptable in most instances. It has been suggested that West German prosecutors may dismiss cases for the same reasons American prosecutors do, but conceal this fact with claims of incomplete evidence.[18] Even if this is true, the written justification requirement presumably facilitates review of the prosecutor's decision and discourages dismissals based on improper considerations.

A similar approach has been adopted, at least technically, by those American jurisdictions that provide for judicial approval of a *nolle prosequi,* the formal prosecutorial declaration that no prosecution will be sought on a particular charge.[19] In order to protect against excessive use of this device, these jurisdictions require the prosecutor to explain to the court in writing his reasons for failing to prosecute when the failure occurs after an indictment has been issued or an information filed. If routinely and conscientiously applied, such a requirement would act as a significant check on prosecutorial charging and plea bargaining decisions.

The requirement does not seem to be routinely applied, however.[20] Indeed, the "principal object" of this judicial review is not to protect the public's interest but "is apparently to protect a defendant against prosecutorial harassment, e.g., charging, dismissing and recharging, when the Government moves to dismiss an indictment over the defendant's objection."[21] Moreover, the Supreme Court itself has expressed misgivings about judicial supervision of the charging process. In *Wayte v. United States*[22] it gave two reasons for avoiding such supervision. First, "[s]uch factors as the strength of the case, the prosecution's general deterrence value, the Government's enforcement priorities, and the case's relationship to the Government's overall enforcement plan are not readily susceptible to the kind of analysis the courts are competent to make." Second, law enforcement might be "chilled" if the prosecutor's motives and actions are subjected to outside scrutiny and the government's enforcement policies revealed publicly.

Despite these concerns, the benefits of judicial monitoring of the charging process may well outweigh the costs, especially if the court's evaluation is not a rigid one. The

---

[17]   See Kenneth C. Davis, Discretionary Justice: A Preliminary Inquiry 188–196 (1969).

[18]   Abraham S. Goldstein & Martin Marcus, *The Myth of Judicial Supervision in Three 'Inquisitorial' Systems: France, Italy, and Germany,* 87 Yale L.J. 240, 275–6 (1977).

[19]   See Note, 103 U.Pa.L.Rev. 1057, 1064–67 (1955).

[20]   Note, 65 Yale L.J. 209, 214 (1955).

[21]   *Rinaldi v. United States,* 434 U.S. 22, 98 S.Ct. 81 (1977).

[22]   470 U.S. 598, 105 S.Ct. 1524 (1985).

focus should be on whether there is sufficient evidence to bring charges and if so, whether the government's failure to bring them is due to factors that are part of a rational law enforcement policy.[23] The prosecution is already subject to some judicial oversight when disposition is by guilty plea;[24] theoretically, even under the present system it should be ready to justify any reduction in charge resulting from the plea bargaining process. When the prosecutorial action being evaluated is dismissal rather than charge reduction, the judicial assessment need not be public, which should reduce the state's reluctance to reveal its policies to the court.

(c) Agreements Not to Prosecute

On occasion, a prosecutor will agree to dismiss criminal charges if the defendant waives any civil claims that might arise from government conduct during the arrest or prosecution. In *Town of Newton v. Rumery*,[25] the Supreme Court sanctioned such an agreement, so long as the defendant is not coerced into it. Here, the defendant's agreement to forego a civil suit in exchange for dismissal of witness tampering charges against him was found to be voluntary, because he had been released from custody and consulted his attorney beforehand. The Court pointed out that the agreement not only protected the state against suit, but also saved the witness who had allegedly been intimidated from having to testify in criminal and civil court, something she had indicated she did not want to do. The four dissenters argued that such agreements should usually be declared invalid, even if voluntary, because they placed the prosecutor in a conflict of interest between his public duty to prosecute criminal offenses and his desire to protect the police and municipality from civil suit.

21.03   Constraints on Bringing Charges

If the prosecutor does decide to prosecute an individual for a particular act, she possesses wide-ranging authority with respect to the precise charge or charges to be brought. For instance, if the evidence indicates that X, intending to kill Y, fires at Y and hits her in the leg, in many jurisdictions X could be charged with attempted murder, malicious wounding, or unlawful wounding, each carrying a significantly different penalty. In addition to being able to choose the severity of the charge, the prosecutor is often able to charge a number of crimes based on the same incident if the appropriate statutory authority exists. For instance, a robbery of six men at a poker game can result in six separate robbery charges.[26] Theft using a gun can result in an armed robbery charge and a charge involving use of a gun to commit a crime.[27]

Generally, the choice the prosecutor makes with respect to these options is unchallengeable. In rare cases, as discussed above, an especially lenient charge might be called into question by the courts, government entities or the public. Equally rarely, the *defendant* may be able to challenge a prosecution, even though based on a valid

---

[23] The National Advisory Commission on Criminal Justice Standards, in its 1973 Report on Courts, recommended that a decision not to prosecute (as opposed to a decision to prosecute) be subject to review at the instance of the police or the complainant, under a standard for review which contemplates whether the decision "was so unreasonable as to constitute an abuse of discretion."

[24] See § 26.04(c).

[25] 480 U.S. 386, 107 S.Ct. 1187 (1987).

[26] See *Ashe v. Swenson*, 397 U.S. 436, 90 S.Ct. 1189 (1970), discussed in § 30.04(a)(3).

[27] Such dual charging does not violate the Double Jeopardy Clause if the legislature intended the two offenses to be separate crimes. See § 30.04(a)(2).

statute and even though the defendant appears to come within its terms. There are essentially three grounds for a challenge by the defendant: selective prosecution, vindictive prosecution, or a prosecution in disregard of legislative will. This section discusses the legal restrictions that have developed in response to these three possibilities.[28]

(a) Discriminatory Prosecution

The Supreme Court has recognized that, in limited circumstances, a prosecutor's decision to prosecute can violate the Equal Protection Clause. As early as 1886, in *Yick Wo v. Hopkins,*[29] the Court stated:

> Though the law itself be fair on its face and impartial in appearance, yet, if it is applied and administered by public authority with an evil eye and an unequal hand, so as practically to make unjust and illegal discriminations between persons in similar circumstances, material to their rights, the denial of equal justice is still within the prohibition of the Constitution.

Yick Wo was convicted under a city ordinance making it unlawful for any person to maintain a laundry in the city of San Francisco without first obtaining the permission of the board of supervisors, unless the laundry was located in a building constructed of brick or stone. The Court admitted that the statute was, on its face, a reasonable exercise of the police power. But the evidence indicated that those refused permission to continue using wooden facilities were principally Chinese. On this evidence, the Court held that criminal enforcement of the law was illegal. Since *Yick Wo*, the courts have refined the equal protection analysis considerably.

(1) The Three-Prong Test

In *Oyler v. Boles,*[30] the Supreme Court emphasized that selective prosecution has to be both intentional and the result of an arbitrary classification before an equal protection claim will succeed. In *Oyler*, the defendant presented statistics showing that, of the six men sentenced in the Taylor County Circuit Court who should have been sentenced to life imprisonment under West Virginia's habitual offender statute, only he was so sentenced. The Court rejected his equal protection claim, finding that these statistics did not show whether the failure to sentence the other five individuals as habitual offenders was due to ignorance concerning their prior offenses or "the result of a deliberate policy of proceeding only in a certain class of cases or against specific persons." Only in the latter instance would there be proof of an equal protection violation. "Moreover," the Court stated:

> the conscious exercise of some selectivity in enforcement is not in itself a federal constitutional violation. Even though the statistics in this case might imply a policy of selective enforcement, it was not stated that the selection was deliberately based upon an unjustifiable standard such as race, religion, or other arbitrary classification.

---

[28] A fourth ground, malicious prosecution, might be recognized under state tort law, but is apparently not actionable as a constitutional matter except to the extent it constitutes an unreasonable seizure under the Fourth Amendment. Cf. *Albright v. Oliver,* 510 U.S. 266, 114 S.Ct. 807 (1994), discussed in § 3.03(c). Federal criminal defendants may also seek damages for bad faith criminal prosecutions under 28 U.S.C.A. § 2412.

[29] 118 U.S. 356, 6 S.Ct. 1064 (1886).

[30] 368 U.S. 448, 82 S.Ct. 501 (1962).

Courts since *Oyler* have devised a three-prong test for determining whether a given prosecution has been discriminatory. The defendant must show: (1) a failure to prosecute those who are similarly situated (2) that is intentionally based on (3) an arbitrary rather than a rational classification.[31] As *Oyler* indicates, a showing that no one else in the defendant's position has been prosecuted under the same statute is not enough. The defendant must also show that this state of affairs is by design, not due to ignorance or inadvertence. And even if the discrimination is intentional, it is not a violation of equal protection unless the reason for the discrimination is race, religion or some other impermissible or irrational classification. Even so limited, the discriminatory prosecution claim can arise in many different contexts. This section will look at a few of the recurring issues.

(2) *Prosecution of Conspicuous Lawbreakers*

Several courts have held that "[s]elective enforcement may . . . be justified when a striking example or a few examples are sought in order to deter other violators."[32] Since such prosecutions intentionally select from among many who are similarly situated, the justification for this type of decision is that the classification is not arbitrary; the courts find the deterrence rationale a rational basis for selective prosecution. Even when the "example" is selected because the violation is meant as a protest of the law, thus implicating the First Amendment, courts generally find no constitutional problem. For instance, in *United States v. Catlett*,[33] a prosecution under an IRS policy targeting cases "involving . . . individuals who have achieved notoriety as tax protesters" was upheld by the Eighth Circuit.

Catlett and similar protester-prosecution cases can be justified on the ground that the mere fact of protest should not immunize lawbreakers from prosecution and that, so long as other people who break the same law are prosecuted, no invidious discrimination has occurred.[34] The Supreme Court appeared to adopt this type of reasoning in *Wayte v. United States*.[35] The defendant there was one of 674,000 men who refused to register for the draft: some had actively protested against the Selective Service laws; some, like the defendant, had submitted letters to the government declaring their refusal to register and giving reasons; some indicated their refusal in less dramatic ways; some had been reported by others; some had neither reported themselves nor been reported by anyone else. The defendant was among a handful of these individuals prosecuted under a "passive" enforcement policy that targeted the nonregistrants who were easiest to identify—those who somehow publicly disclosed their unwillingness to register. In rejecting the defendant's equal protection claim, the Court, in an opinion by Justice Powell, concluded that the defendant had "not shown that the enforcement policy selected nonregistrants for prosecution on the basis of their speech." He noted that the government did not prosecute those protesters who eventually registered; at the same

---

[31] See, e.g., *Commonwealth v. Franklin,* 376 Mass. 885, 385 N.E.2d 227 (1978). See also, Steven Alan Reiss, *Prosecutorial Intent in Constitutional Criminal Procedure*, 135 U.Pa.L.Rev. 1365 (1987).

[32] *People v. Utica Daw's Drug Co.,* 16 A.D.2d 12, 225 N.Y.S.2d 128 (1962). See also, *Falls v. Town of Dyer, Indiana,* 875 F.2d 146 (7th Cir. 1989) ("A government legitimately could enforce its law against a few persons (even just one) to establish a precedent, ultimately leading to widespread compliance.").

[33] 584 F.2d 864 (8th Cir. 1978).

[34] See also, *United States v. Bassford,* 812 F.2d 16 (1st Cir. 1987) (prosecution for violating marijuana laws not impermissibly selective even though defendant may have been chosen for prosecution in part because he was vocally against drug laws).

[35] 470 U.S. 598, 105 S.Ct. 1524 (1985).

time, Powell asserted, of those who never registered, the government prosecuted not only "vocal" nonregistrants, such as the defendant, but also "people who reported themselves or were reported by others but who did not publicly protest."[36]

The Court went on to say that even if vocal nonregistrants were discriminated against, there was no evidence of discriminatory purpose. Quoting from equal protection cases in other contexts,[37] it defined such purpose as "more than . . . awareness of consequences." Intentional discrimination "implies that the decisionmaker . . . selected or reaffirmed a particular course of action at least in part 'because of,' not merely 'in spite of,' its adverse effects upon an identifiable group." Here there was no showing that the government prosecuted Wayte *"because"* of his protest activities; rather he was prosecuted because his speech made him more easily identifiable.

The Court also concluded that the defendant's prosecution did not violate the First Amendment, because the "speech" affected (i.e., protesting the draft) was combined with "nonspeech" (i.e., the failure to register) in the same course of conduct, and the government interest in regulating the latter was sufficiently important to justify incidental infringement of the former. Applying the test of *United States v. O'Brien,*[38] Powell concluded that prosecuting nonregistrants was a strong governmental interest in light of government's constitutional duty to secure the nation's defense, and that the government's "passive" enforcement policy was a cost effective way of implementing this interest, given the difficulty of identifying all draft evaders and the danger that "failing to proceed against publicly known offenders would encourage others to violate the law." Further the policy was merely an "interim enforcement system," pending development of a method of identifying all nonregistrants.

When it can be shown, contrary to the Court's finding in *Wayte,* that the defendant was selected solely "on the basis of speech," a different result may be called for. In *Federov v. United States,*[39] the defendants, demonstrators being prosecuted for unlawful entry, offered to prove that all other first time offenders charged with unlawful entry had been found eligible for pretrial diversion rather than prosecuted. The trial court ruled that this proffer was insufficient to warrant discovery and an evidentiary hearing on the selective prosecution claim, because the correct comparative group was not all others charged with trespass but other *demonstrators* charged with trespass; the court noted, for instance, that demonstrators might be more disruptive than other trespassers and thus merit greater sanction. But the appellate court reversed this ruling, noting that *Wayte* had "treated all those who refused to register [i.e. vocal and nonvocal nonregistrants] as members of a single class and considered whether those selected from the class for prosecution were selected on an impermissible basis."

Thus, in this case, the defendants' claim that the courts should focus on the larger group of all first-time trespassers was correct. Since, based on the record, it appeared that the only difference between the latter group and the defendants' was that the first-

---

[36]   Contrary to the Court's assertion, the district court appeared to have found that all of those being prosecuted were "vocal" nonregistrants (meaning those who declared their intent not to register via letter or public pronouncement). *United States v. Wayte,* 549 F.Supp. 1376 (D.C.Cal. 1982).

[37]   See *Personnel Administrator of Massachusetts v. Feeney,* 442 U.S. 256, 99 S.Ct. 2282 (1979).

[38]   391 U.S. 367, 88 S.Ct. 1673 (1968). *O'Brien* permits government regulation of speech "if it is within the constitutional power of the Government; if it furthers an important or substantial governmental interest; if the government interest is unrelated to the suppression of free expression; and if the incidental restriction of alleged First Amendment freedoms is no greater than is essential to the furtherance of that interest."

[39]   580 A.2d 600 (D.C.App. 1990), aff'd 600 A.2d 370 (D.C.App. 1991).

time trespassers' "alleged conduct was not associated with the expression of views protected by the First Amendment," a colorable claim of selective prosecution was made out. "To conclude otherwise is to maintain that persons whose trespass had First Amendment ramifications have, as a result of that fact alone, committed a crime of greater 'magnitude' than persons whose trespass was not politically motivated." *Federov* illustrates how the result in a selective prosecution case can be determined by the choice of the group to which the defendant must be similarly situated.

(3)　*Prosecution of "Significant" Offenders*

To be distinguished from "conspicuous lawbreaker" prosecution just discussed is a governmental policy that results in prosecution of one offender but not his colleague in crime, on the ground that the former poses the more significant threat to the community. For example, one court has upheld a policy that enforces gambling laws against bookmakers but not against those placing bets with them.[40] A variant of this policy is one that focuses on the most egregious offenders. Thus, a policy of enforcing a law prohibiting sale of securities without a license only against those who sell more than ten securities was upheld.[41] Although these policies all intentionally select certain offenders from among a pool of "similarly situated" offenders, they can be said to do so on a rational rather than arbitrary ground, and thus do not violate the Equal Protection Clause. As one court put it, "the prosecutor may conserve resources for more important cases."[42]

However, as with the conspicuous offender cases, when a suspect classification is connected with a "significant offender" enforcement policy, courts are less reluctant to recognize a selective prosecution claim, even when the government can proffer "rational" reasons for the policy. For instance, in *State v. McCollum,*[43] the court dismissed prostitution charges against female nude dancers who, during a private party at a club, received money for sexual conduct with male patrons. The court pointed out that the males involved were not arrested despite the fact that Wisconsin law criminalized the behavior of both the payor and payee in a prostitution arrangement. It rejected the government's arguments that it was harder to develop evidence against the males and that prosecution of the females would result in "maximum deterrence."[44]

Even when no suspect classification is involved, if there is *no* rational basis for selective prosecution, the courts will dismiss the prosecution. Thus, in *United States v. Robinson,*[45] the court refused to uphold a policy of prosecuting only private detectives, and not government officials, for illegal wiretapping. The court noted that the degree of intrusion occasioned by a wiretap and the divulgence of what is discovered does not depend on who conducts it. In effect, the court concluded that the significance of the crime was the same in both instances and thus differentiation based on the type of perpetrator was unconstitutional.

---

[40]　*People v. Garner,* 72 Cal.App.3d 214, 139 Cal.Rptr. 838 (1977).

[41]　*State v. Steurer,* 37 Ohio App.2d 51, 66 O.O.2d 89, 306 N.E.2d 425 (1973), cert. denied 416 U.S. 940, 94 S.Ct. 1943 (1974).

[42]　*Falls v. Town of Dyer, Indiana,* 875 F.2d 146 (7th Cir. 1989).

[43]　159 Wis.2d 184, 464 N.W.2d 44 (App. 1990).

[44]　See also, *Commonwealth v. King,* 374 Mass. 5, 372 N.E.2d 196 (1977).

[45]　311 F.Supp. 1063 (W.D.Mo. 1969).

(4) Pretextual Prosecution

Occasionally, a defendant will contend that prosecution for one crime occurred solely because the prosecutor has been unable to obtain sufficient evidence on another, more serious offense. For instance, in *United States v. Sacco*,[46] the court assumed that the government targeted the defendant for investigation under the alien registration laws "based on his suspected role in organized crime." Nonetheless, the court went on to conclude that "[i]t cannot be said that [such a] standard for selection is not rationally related to the purposes of the various criminal laws [under which the defendant] was being investigated, including the alien registration laws." However, in *United States v. Cammisano*,[47] a case involving prosecution under the Federal Meat Inspection Act of a person allegedly associated with "organized crime," the district court stated that "not all classifications used by the government may be found rationally related to the purpose of the particular criminal law being invoked," and held that a colorable claim of selective prosecution had been made out sufficient to grant discovery against the prosecution.

Perhaps the difference between these two cases is that in *Sacco* there was strong evidence of organized crime activity by the defendant, whereas in *Cammisano* there was a suggestion that the defendant was selected purely because of his Italian ancestry, which "would obviously be an impermissible and arbitrary classification." Some have argued that a pretextual prosecution might be impermissible even when there is some evidence of involvement in other criminal activity on the part of the defendant. Professor Freedman, for instance, notes that "few of us . . . have led such unblemished lives as to prevent a determined prosecutor from finding some basis for an indictment or an information." From this, he argues that "to say that the prosecutor's motive is immaterial, is to justify making virtually every citizen the potential victim of arbitrary discretion."[48]

(5) Discovery

As the discussion above illustrates, a number of the reported cases focus not on the ultimate issue of whether selective prosecution has occurred, but rather on whether the defendant has made out a good enough case to merit discovery and an evidentiary hearing on the claim. In *Wayte*, the two dissenters took the majority to task for proceeding directly to the merits without considering whether the trial court's discovery order should have been upheld. As the dissenters pointed out, a selective prosecution claim is difficult to make out without such discovery, since "most of the relevant proof in [such] cases will normally be in the Government's hands."

In *United States v. Armstrong*,[49] the Supreme Court directly addressed the threshold for discovery in selective prosecution cases and opted for a stringent showing. The defendants there, African-Americans charged with possession of and conspiracy to possess crack cocaine, sought government disclosure of the race of defendants in cocaine prosecutions for the past three years, as well as information regarding the levels of law enforcement involved in investigating those cases and the criteria for prosecuting them. The Supreme Court overturned the lower court decisions granting this request. It first

---

[46]   428 F.2d 264 (9th Cir. 1970).

[47]   413 F.Supp. 886 (W.D.Mo. 1976), mod'd 546 F.2d 238 (8th Cir. 1976).

[48]   Monroe Freedman, *The Professional Responsibility of the Prosecuting Attorney*, 55 Geo.L.J. 1030, 1034 (1967). But see, Richard L. Braun, *Ethics in Criminal Cases: A Response*, 55 Geo.L.J. 1048 (1967).

[49]   517 U.S. 456, 116 S.Ct. 1480 (1996).

held that such discovery was not authorized under the federal rule governing discovery (Rule 16) because that rule speaks solely of material in the possession of the government that is "material to the defendant's defense." Eight members of the Court concluded that this language encompasses only information that acts as a "shield" against the prosecution's case, not any and all information which might be useful in attacking the government's conduct of the prosecution.[50] Although the majority went on to hold that there may be a non-statutory basis for discovering information relevant to a selective prosecution claim, it stressed that the standard for discovery in such cases must be "rigorous" given its potential for diverting prosecutorial resources and divulging prosecutorial strategy.

The precise language chosen by the Court to describe this threshold came from *United States v. Berrios*,[51] a Second Circuit decision that required "some evidence tending to show the existence of the essential elements of the defense" (i.e., discriminatory effect and discriminatory intent). Although this language does not seem particularly restrictive on its face, the Court's application of it in *Armstrong* evidenced considerable resistance to discovery requests in such cases. The defendants had produced a study showing that every one of the 24 cases closed by the Federal Public Defender in 1991 for the crimes of possession or conspiracy to possess crack cocaine had involved black defendants. To counteract a prosecution claim that most crack users and dealers are black, they also produced affidavits from two defense attorneys, one of whom alleged that an intake coordinator at a drug treatment center had told her that there were "an equal number of Caucasian users and dealers to minority users and dealers," and another of whom stated that, in his experience, state courts often prosecuted nonblacks for crack offenses. The Court of Appeals had given credence to this information and been willing to presume that "people of all races commit all types of crimes" in sustaining the District Court order granting discovery.

However, the Supreme Court found that the defense's showing in *Armstrong* was insufficient under the *Berrios* test, even as a demonstration of discriminatory effect, much less of discriminatory intent. It noted that the lower court's assumption about perpetrators of crack crimes was "contradicted" by United States Sentencing Commission statistics showing that 90% of persons sentenced in 1994 for crack cocaine trafficking were black (although this statistic is of course meaningless if the selective prosecution claim is correct). The Court also dismissed the affidavits of the two defense attorneys as based on hearsay and anecdotal evidence. Finally, it ignored the fact that the prosecution was unable to name a single white defendant who had been prosecuted for possession of crack cocaine in the past three years.

Along the same lines is *United States v. Bass*,[52] where the defendant asked for discovery of information about the Department of Justice's charging practices in capital cases. His *Armstrong* showing consisted of nationwide statistics demonstrating that blacks were charged with federal death-eligible offenses more than twice as often as whites, and that the United States entered into plea bargains more frequently with whites than it does with blacks. Although the Sixth Circuit granted the discovery request, the Supreme Court held, per curiam, that the defendant had failed to make a sufficient showing of discriminatory effect, much less discriminatory intent. These data

---

[50] See § 24.03(b) for further discussion of this case.
[51] 501 F.2d 1207, 1211 (2d Cir. 1974).
[52] 536 U.S. 862, 122 S.Ct. 2389 (2002).

did not represent a "credible showing" that defendants "*similarly situated*" to the defendant (i.e., those with similar aggravating and mitigating factors) had been discriminated against. Further the fact that the defendant had been offered a plea bargain made the statistics about plea bargaining "even less relevant."

In interesting contrast to *Armstrong* and *Bass* is *State v. Kennedy*, a lower court decision.[53] There the public defenders' office produced a survey which disclosed that, over a three-year period, it had represented 43 persons for traffic violations on the road on which the defendants, both non-Caucasians, were stopped for speeding. Of these individuals, 70% were African-Americans, 7% were Hispanics and 23% were Caucasians. In contrast, the office's caseload for all crimes committed in the county comprised 76% Caucasians and 17% African-Americans. The New Jersey state court recognized that this study was deficient because it did not provide information as to the racial composition of all those who travelled this particular road, and did not state the race of those who were arrested, as opposed to formally charged, with crimes. But, stressing that only a "colorable basis," not a prima facie showing, was necessary, it held the survey "raises disturbing questions concerning whether . . . members of minority groups are being targeted or singled out for prosecution of traffic infractions," sufficient to warrant discovery of State Police logs, reports, training materials, and names of instructors. It ordered that these materials be submitted to the court for in camera inspection to determine "their relevance and the State's need for confidentiality," and noted that the state could apply for a protective order as it deemed necessary.

(b) Vindictive Prosecution

The Due Process Clause imposes a limited prohibition on prosecutorial use of the charging prerogative to the extent that prerogative is used to penalize the exercise of legal rights. This principle was first announced in *Blackledge v. Perry*.[54] There the defendant was convicted in misdemeanor court on the misdemeanor charge of assault with a deadly weapon, and sentenced to six months. After the defendant filed notice of appeal to a county superior court for a trial *de novo*, which under North Carolina law annuls the previous conviction and requires a new trial, the prosecutor obtained an indictment covering the same conduct at issue in the misdemeanor trial but charging Perry with the *felony* of assault with intent to kill. Perry pleaded guilty in the superior court and was sentenced to a term of five to seven years.

In overturning the new sentence, the Supreme Court relied on *North Carolina v. Pearce*,[55] which held that "vindictiveness against a defendant for having successfully attacked his first conviction must play no part in the sentence he receives after a new trial." Although *Pearce* had involved judicial imposition of a harsher sentence after a successful appeal, the Court found the rationale of that decision relevant to prosecutorial charging decisions after the defendant indicates a desire to appeal a conviction. It emphasized the prosecution's possible motivation to "up the ante" in such situations and the consequent chilling effect on the right to pursue the statutory appellate remedy. Given the "realistic likelihood of vindictiveness" when a felony charge is brought against a convicted misdemeanant who is appealing the conviction, the Court held that any new punishment must be overturned unless, analogous to what it had held in *Pearce,* the

---

[53]   247 N.J.Super. 21, 588 A.2d 834 (App.Div. 1991).

[54]   417 U.S. 21, 94 S.Ct. 2098 (1974).

[55]   395 U.S. 711, 89 S.Ct. 2072 (1969) discussed in § 29.02(d).

prosecutor can identify specific reasons explaining the increased charge. In other words, it established a "presumption of vindictiveness" in such situations.[56]

The courts have provided limited guidance as to the types of reasons that can overcome this presumption. In *Blackledge,* the Court noted that one such reason would be where "it was impossible to proceed on the more serious charge at the outset," because, for instance, the victim of an assault did not die until after charges were filed. Beyond this, the lower courts are split on whether proffer of any non-vindictive explanation will suffice or whether, instead, new conduct by the defendant justifying the new charge is required.[57] To be of practical use to a defendant, the presumption should be hard to overcome, given the difficulty of evaluating the validity of any proffered prosecutorial reason.

The situations in which the *Blackledge* presumption arises are very limited. First, it applies only when the change in charge occurs after exercise of a legal right, such as the right to appeal, which would otherwise be "chilled." Second, it generally does not apply if the prosecutor "ups the ante" during the pretrial process. This is because, as explained by the Supreme Court in *United States v. Goodwin,*[58] during this process, "the prosecutor's assessment of the proper extent of prosecution may not have crystallized." New evidence, or a different interpretation of already existing evidence, might lead to an honest reappraisal of the original charge. Thus, in *Goodwin,* a pretrial adjustment of the defendant's charge from a misdemeanor to a felony after the defendant chose to be tried by a jury rather than a judge did not implicate the *Blackledge* presumption.

The *Goodwin* Court noted that, while the *presumption* of vindictiveness would not apply in the pretrial setting, there was still "the possibility that a defendant in an appropriate case might prove objectively that the prosecutor's [pretrial] charging decision was motivated by a desire to punish him for doing something that the law plainly allowed him to do." But it found no such proof where the defendant's decision to seek a jury trial meant the case was transferred from the magistrate to a district court and the prosecutor who charged the felony was different from the one who charged the misdemeanor.[59] Moreover, it approved the state's observation that, while the "defendant is free to tender evidence to the court to support a claim that enhanced charges are a direct and unjustifiable penalty for the exercise of a procedural right . . . only in a rare case [will] a defendant be able to overcome the presumptive validity of the prosecutor's actions through such a demonstration." In short, when the change in charge takes place prior to trial, the presumption shifts from vindictiveness to non-vindictiveness.

Furthermore, when the change in charge is part of the plea negotiation process, the defendant will apparently never be able to make out a vindictiveness claim. In *Bordenkircher v. Hayes,*[60] the prosecutor offered Hayes a five-year term on a forged check

---

[56] *Thigpen v. Roberts,* 468 U.S. 27, 104 S.Ct. 2916 (1984) involved substantially the same factual situation as *Blackledge* except that the prosecuting agent responsible for the stiffer charge at the defendant's *de novo* trial was not involved in the initial prosecution. In vacating the defendant's sentence, the Court noted that a district attorney faced with the retrial of an already-convicted defendant might be vindictive even if he did not bring the initial prosecution.

[57] *United States v. Andrews,* 633 F.2d 449 (6th Cir. 1980). In the sentencing context, the Supreme Court has held that *any* "new information," not just new conduct by the defendant, overcomes the presumption. *Texas v. McCullough,* 475 U.S. 134, 106 S.Ct. 976 (1986), discussed in § 29.02(d)(2).

[58] 457 U.S. 368, 102 S.Ct. 2485 (1982).

[59] Compare to *Thigpen,* supra note 56.

[60] 434 U.S. 357, 98 S.Ct. 663 (1978).

charge; he also made clear that if Hayes (who had two prior forgery convictions) did not accept the offer, he would be prosecuted as an habitual offender, a charge which carried a mandatory life sentence. Although the Court suggested that there are some limits on the prosecutor's broad discretion to plea bargain, it held that due process is not violated when, as here, the "conduct engaged in by the prosecutor . . . no more than openly presented the defendant with the unpleasant alternatives of foregoing trial or facing charges on which he was plainly subject to prosecution."

Prohibiting a due process claim in such cases seems extreme. As Justice Blackmun, with two others, stated in dissent, "[p]rosecutorial vindictiveness in any context is still prosecutorial vindictiveness." Justice Powell, in a separate dissent, focused on a slightly different proposition:

> Only in the most exceptional case should a court conclude that the scales of the bargaining are so unevenly balanced as to arouse suspicion. In this case, the prosecutor's actions denied respondent due process because their admitted purpose was to discourage and then to penalize with unique severity his exercise of constitutional rights. Implementation of a strategy calculated solely to deter the exercise of constitutional rights is not a constitutionally permissible exercise of discretion.

(c) Duplicative Statutes

The legislature will occasionally provide two maximum sentences, under two different statutes, for the same conduct.[61] Whether this duplication is intended or due to carelessness is not always clear. Whatever the reason for the duplication, it appears that the federal constitution does not dictate which statute the prosecutor must choose.

In *United States v. Batchelder*,[62] the defendant received a sentence of five years under a statute that prohibited various persons, including those previously convicted of a crime "punishable by imprisonment for a term exceeding one year," from receiving firearms that have travelled in interstate commerce. In reversing his conviction, the court of appeals pointed out that another federal statute imposed a maximum of two years on those who have been convicted of a "felony" who receive, possess or transport any firearm in interstate commerce. It concluded that Congressional intent had been to limit the punishment for the defendant's conduct to the latter term.

The Supreme Court could find no evidence of such intent. Nor did it think that duplicative statutes gave the prosecutor "unfettered discretion." It could find "no appreciable difference between the discretion a prosecutor exercises when deciding whether to charge under one of two statutes with different elements and the discretion he exercises when choosing one of two statutes with identical elements." Although in the latter situation the prosecutor may be influenced by the penalties available, the defendant has neither a due process nor equal protection right to choose the penalty scheme. Finally, the Court did not agree with the court of appeals' suggestion that duplicative statutes might impermissibly delegate to the executive branch the legislative function, since the statutes plainly demarcated the range of penalties available.

---

[61] This situation is thus distinguishable from that involved in *Hayes*, which involved a prosecutorial choice between a forgery statute and an habitual offender statute providing enhanced penalties for various crimes, including forgery, *if* the offender had two other convictions.

[62] 442 U.S. 114, 99 S.Ct. 2198 (1979).

After *Batchelder,* a federal constitutional challenge of a prosecutor's charging decision when duplicative statutes are involved is unlikely to be successful. But a state court could still find a violation of equal protection as a matter of state constitutional law. In *People v. Marcy,*[63] the Colorado Supreme Court concluded that

> equal protection of the laws requires that statutory classification of crimes be based on differences that are real in fact and reasonably related to the general purposes of criminal legislation. [Such protection is lacking] if different statutes proscribe the same criminal conduct with disparate criminal sanctions.

The implication of this reasoning for prosecutors confronted with two statutes covering precisely the same conduct may be that, barring a clear showing of contrary legislative intent, they should only prosecute under the most recent statute.

21.04 Joinder

Every jurisdiction has rules that dictate when a defendant may be tried on more than one charge at the same trial, and when more than one defendant may be tried at the same trial. These rules are discussed here because they may affect the types of charges the prosecutor brings against a particular defendant or defendants.

(a) Joinder Analysis

Joinder analysis under the typical statute proceeds in two stages. The first stage asks whether joinder—of charges or of defendants—is permissible. If so, the second stage asks whether the joinder would nonetheless prejudice one or both of the parties, in which case severance is granted. It appears that the party seeking joinder, usually the prosecution, bears the burden of showing joinder is proper, while the party seeking severance, usually the defendant, bears the burden of showing prejudice.[64]

This simple framework is complicated by the fact that a misjoinder finding often comes after trial. When this occurs, some courts have held that new, separate trials must be held automatically; to require a showing of prejudice at this point, they reason, would mean the trial court would have little incentive to consider carefully the first stage of the analysis, because whether or not joinder rules were followed, the ultimate question on appeal would be whether the parties were prejudiced.[65] Most courts, however, hold that misjoinder is subject to harmless error analysis. In *United States v. Lane,*[66] for instance, the Supreme Court held that, on appeal in federal court, the question is whether the misjoinder "had a substantial and injurious effect or influence in determining the jury's verdict," language taken from its cases discussing harmless error analysis.[67]

It is probable that this post-trial, harmless error test is equivalent to the prejudice test applied prior to trial. In any event, the discussion below on joinder of charges and joinder of defendants does not distinguish between the two tests.

---

[63]   628 P.2d 69 (Colo. 1981).

[64]   *Johnson v. United States,* 356 F.2d 680 (8th Cir. 1966).

[65]   *United States v. Graci,* 504 F.2d 411 (3d Cir. 1974).

[66]   474 U.S. 438, 106 S.Ct. 725 (1986).

[67]   See *Kotteakos v. United States,* 328 U.S. 750, 66 S.Ct. 1239 (1946), discussed in § 29.05(b).

(b) Joinder of Charges

Under the federal rules, charges against the same defendant may be joined as separate counts in the same indictment or information under a number of circumstances: (1) when the charges arise out of the same transaction (e.g., burglary of a house, theft in the same house, and assault while escaping); (2) when they arise out of two different transactions that are "connected together" or are part of a "common scheme or plan" (e.g., burglarizing a gun store to obtain a gun later used in a bank robbery); and (3) when they arise out of two or more different acts that are "the same or similar in character" (e.g., two robberies committed in a similar way).[68] Virtually all states have rules akin to the first two, and about a third of the states have rules similar to the last rule.

The primary justification for these rules is efficiency. Joinder clearly avoids duplication of effort on the part of the prosecution and the witnesses. The defendant too may want a joint trial, to "eliminate the harassment, trauma, expense, and prolonged publicity of multiple trials . . . increase the possibility of concurrent sentences in the event of conviction, and . . . prevent the application of enhanced sentencing statutes."[69] At the same time, as noted above, every jurisdiction also permits severance of properly joined charges if prejudice would otherwise result. For example, under the federal rules, "[i]f it appears that a defendant or the government is prejudiced by a joinder of offenses . . . the court may order an election or separate trials of counts . . . or provide whatever other relief justice requires."[70]

Most severance motions are by defendants, who usually claim that joinder will cause one of three types of prejudice: (1) the factfinder will simply infer criminal disposition from the number and types of crimes charged, rather than consider the specific evidence against the accused; (2) the factfinder will "cumulate" the evidence, rather than compartmentalize it according to each charge; or (3) the defendant will be inhibited in presenting separate defenses.[71] These various objections are considered below.

(1) Inferring Criminal Disposition

This potential source of prejudice arises most often with the third type of joinder: joinder of similar offenses. The fear is that the factfinder will decide the defendant is guilty of one crime and then, because the crimes are similar, blithely decide he is also guilty of the others without considering specific evidence. A worse scenario is that the factfinder decides that a person charged with so many offenses must be guilty of something and convict accordingly.

Drew v. United States[72] provides a good illustration of how a court might resolve this dilemma. There, the defendant was tried jointly for a robbery and an attempted robbery. The evidence underlying the first charge indicated that a black male wearing sun glasses had announced to a lone sales clerk in a neighborhood convenience store that he was robbing the store. When the clerk hesitated, the man pulled a gun from his pocket. She gave him money and he left. In a lineup seventeen days later, she identified Drew as the offender. Prior to the arrest and identification of Drew, another store in the

---

[68] Fed.R.Crim.P. 8(a).

[69] 2 ABA Standards for Criminal Justice § 13–2.1, Commentary (2d ed. 1980).

[70] Fed.R.Crim.P. 14.

[71] *Drew v. United States,* 331 F.2d 85 (D.C.Cir. 1964).

[72] 331 F.2d 85 (D.C.Cir. 1964).

same convenience chain was unsuccessfully robbed. The sales clerk testified that a black man wearing sun glasses asked to buy some peanuts, then demanded the store's money. The sales clerk refused the demand and the robber left. The police apprehended Drew in the store's vicinity shortly thereafter and returned him to the store, where the clerk identified him as the person who attempted to rob her.

The court agreed with Drew that the trial judge had erred in not granting Drew's motion for severance of these two charges. As a guideline for determining when two similar crimes can be joined, the court found applicable the rules governing the admissibility of evidence about other crimes. Such evidence is generally admissible when relevant to motive, intent, absence of mistake, the existence of a common plan, a particular *modus operandi*, or the identification of the accused.[73] Yet even if relevant, such evidence may not be admitted if its probative value is substantially outweighed by the risk that its admission will result in unfair prejudice to the defendant.[74] In *Drew,* the evidence concerning the attempted robbery was at most only barely suggestive of a *modus operandi* similar to that involved in the robbery, yet could easily have prejudiced the defendant by suggesting criminal disposition and inhibiting individualized consideration of the charges. Indeed, the record showed repeated confusion as to which of the two crimes involved was being referred to during trial. Thus, the court held, the probative value of the additional crime was outweighed by the possibility that it prejudiced the defendant and joinder was inapposite.

This kind of analysis suggests that same or similar crimes should rarely be joined. It is reinforced by clear research evidence that, even when limiting instructions are given, conviction rates are higher when a jury has knowledge of multiple offenses, especially when they are the same or similar in nature.[75] In contrast to the federal rules, many states prohibit joinder of such offenses, allowing simultaneous trial only when the crimes arise from the same episode or transaction or series of transactions.[76] The American Bar Association's Criminal Justice Standards accomplish essentially the same result by providing for unlimited joinder, but permitting severance as of right for either party as to those offenses which are not "based upon the same conduct, upon a single episode, or upon a common plan."[77] If joinder of same or similar crimes is allowed, as suggested in *Drew*, prejudice should be minimized by joining only those crimes that meet an exception to the general rule barring evidence of other crimes (e.g., similarity in *modus operandi*).

(2) Cumulation of Evidence

The prejudice associated with cumulation of evidence—that is, the danger that the jury will decide that sufficient evidence on one charge means there is probably sufficient evidence on another joined charge—is closely related to the type of prejudice just discussed. But it usually arises when the joined charges reflect crimes stemming from the same episode or transaction; in this situation, the jury might see evidence of one crime as dispositive of liability on the other.

---

[73]　Federal Rule of Evidence 404(b).

[74]　See Charles A. Wright & Kenneth W. Graham, Federal Practice and Procedure, § 5235 (1978).

[75]　See Roselle L. Wisler & Michael J. Saks, *On the Inefficacy of Limiting Instructions: When Jurors Use Prior Conviction Evidence to Decide on Guilt*, 9 Law & Human Behavior 37 (1985).

[76]　See e.g., Fla.R.Crim.Pro. 3.150(a)(1984).

[77]　See 2 ABA Standards for Criminal Justice §§ 13–2.1, 13–3.1, 13–1.2.

Courts rarely consider the possibility of cumulation ground for reversal however. In *United States v. Adams*,[78] the defendant allegedly bought heroin and sold it to an undercover policeman. Nine months later, when he was arrested for the sale, he was found in possession of heroin. The defendant was tried and convicted of selling heroin and of possession of heroin. On appeal, the defendant argued that joinder was inappropriate under Rule 8(a) and that, even if it were proper, the jury's deliberations on the first charge could easily have been unduly influenced by the fact of possession. The Second Circuit disagreed on both points. Despite the fact that the sale and the possession were separated by nine months, the court approved the trial judge's recognition "as matter of common knowledge that the pattern here was typical of conduct in the narcotics traffic," and thus could be joined as parts of "a common scheme or plan." It then went on to hold that the defendant was not prejudiced by the joinder. The court emphasized that the trial judge had instructed the jury to delineate carefully the factors essential to each charge and to find the defendant guilty only if the specific charge had been proven. The court also noted that the evidence supporting each charge was substantial and "simple."

The Second Circuit's conclusion that joinder of the two counts was permissible is questionable, but not unusual.[79] The court's prejudice analysis is more difficult to assess. The deficiencies of instructions in correcting for jury confusion has been noted. It may be, however, that joinder situations involving offenses arising out of the same episode or transaction are not as inherently prejudicial as those involving same or similar offenses. The research on the effect of limiting instructions is most critical of multiple crime evidence when the crimes are similar in nature; in "same transaction" joinder, on the other hand, the crimes involved are often quite different (e.g., possession as contrasted with sale). Jurors may be more likely to assume a criminal disposition toward robbery when confronted with evidence of several robberies than they are likely to assume guilt for a greater crime (i.e., drug sale) from a finding of guilt on a lesser crime (i.e., mere possession).

(3) Inhibition of Defense

The situation most likely to give rise to this third problem is when the defendant wishes to testify concerning one charge but not another. In *Cross v. United States*,[80] for instance, the defendant was charged with robbery of a church rectory in one count and robbery of a tourist home in a second count. He obtained an acquittal on the second robbery charge as a result of his alibi testimony, but "to avoid the damaging implication of testifying on only one of the two joined counts," he offered "dubious testimony" about the first robbery, which included admissions about prior convictions and other "unsavory activities." He was ultimately convicted on that charge. The court held that joinder had "embarrassed and confounded Cross in making his defense," and thus was prejudicial under Rule 14.[81]

---

[78]   434 F.2d 756 (2d Cir. 1970).

[79]   *Kindred v. State*, 524 N.E.2d 279 (Ind. 1988) (perjury properly joined with forgery a month later because necessary to obtain false identification used in forgery).

[80]   335 F.2d 987 (D.C.Cir. 1964).

[81]   As an aside, it is not clear that the two charges should have been joined in the first place, given the interpretation of the "similar act" joinder provision by *Drew,* discussed in § 21.04(b)(3), decided the same term by the same court.

If, in an attempt to avoid the type of "dubious testimony" given in *Cross,* the defendant decides not to testify about one of the counts, may the prosecutor comment on his silence? Generally, adverse reference to a defendant's failure to take the stand is a violation of the Fifth Amendment, since a defendant's knowledge that such a reference will occur might "compel" self-incriminating testimony.[82] But some courts have held that the government may force a defendant to "elect to testify as to both charges or to none at all."[83] A more discriminating approach was taken in *People v. Perez,*[84] where the California Supreme Court permitted prosecutorial comment about the defendant's failure to testify about two of the four counts joined against him because the crimes charged in those counts exhibited similar *modus operandi* to the first two charges; under California's rules of evidence, these charges could have been referred to during cross-examination even had they not been joined. Had the crimes not carried a similar "signature," on the other hand, the prosecutorial comment may have violated the Fifth Amendment. Thus, as with prejudice that might result from inferring criminal disposition, this type of prejudice might be defined by the rules of evidence.

(4) Double Jeopardy Concerns

The Double Jeopardy Clause, found in the Fifth Amendment, protects a person from being "twice put in jeopardy" for the "same offense." As developed in detail elsewhere in this book,[85] despite its apparent meaning, the term "same offense" may include more than one statutory crime on a given set of facts. When two or more crimes are the "same offense" for double jeopardy purposes, the prosecutor must join them, or forfeit the ability to try whichever charges are not joined. Any attempt to try these charges separately would mean the defendant would be "twice put in jeopardy." However, an exception to this rule occurs when the second trial on the same offense results from a severance motion by the defendant.[86] As common sense would seem to dictate, if the defendant successfully argues that severance is necessary because prejudice would result from the simultaneous trial of two charges, the Double Jeopardy Clause does not prevent the government from prosecuting on the second charge.

(c) Joinder of Defendants

Generally, a prosecutor may join two or more defendants in the same indictment or information, and thus try them jointly, if they are alleged to have participated in an offense or offenses arising out of the same course of conduct. Federal Rule of Criminal Procedure 8(b) is illustrative:

> Two or more defendants may be charged in the same indictment or information if they are alleged to have participated in the same act or transaction or in the same series of acts or transactions constituting an offense or offenses.

Joinder of defendants is most likely to occur with alleged co-conspirators or co-defendants.

---

[82] *Griffin v. California,* 380 U.S. 609, 85 S.Ct. 1229 (1965), discussed in § 15.02(c).

[83] *Holmes v. Gray,* 526 F.2d 622 (7th Cir. 1975), cert. denied 434 U.S. 907, 98 S.Ct. 308 (1977).

[84] 65 Cal.2d 615, 55 Cal.Rptr. 909, 422 P.2d 597 (1967), cert. granted 390 U.S. 942, 88 S.Ct. 1055 (1968).

[85] See § 30.04.

[86] See *Jeffers v. United States,* 432 U.S. 137, 97 S.Ct. 2207 (1977), discussed in § 30.04(b)(2).

The principal reason for allowing such joinder is prosecutorial efficiency.[87] Unlike joinder of charges, joinder of defendants seldom provides any benefit to the defendant.[88] Furthermore, such joinder can often be extremely prejudicial, in a number of ways. For example: (1) a co-defendant's confession which implicates the defendant as well as the co-defendant might be introduced despite the defendant's inability to challenge it effectively, because the co-defendant refuses to take the stand under the Fifth Amendment;[89] (2) also for Fifth Amendment reasons, a co-defendant's account tending to *exculpate* the defendant (while inculpating the co-defendant) may *not* be introduced;[90] (3) the factfinder may convict merely out of the confusion or disgust created by conflicting defense strategies (e.g., the defendants accuse one another of the crime);[91] or (4) the factfinder may convict merely because the defendant is associated with other clearly guilty defendants.[92]

As discussed elsewhere in this book, the first situation may run afoul of the Sixth Amendment's Confrontation Clause and often results in severance.[93] When confronted by the other three situations, the courts sometimes grant severance motions. But they are usually reluctant to do so.[94] In part, this may be due to a valid concern that severance will allow defendants to prevent accurate factfinding. For instance, granting severance in an attempt to avoid the second type of prejudice (exclusion of exculpatory information) might occasionally present an opportunity for defendants to "swap alibis" (e.g., X falsely exculpating Y at Y's trial, and then Y—now acquitted and protected against retrial by the Double Jeopardy Clause—returning the favor at X's trial).

Similarly, severance to avoid the third type of prejudice (contradictory defenses) runs counter to the notion that differing stories are most effectively tested when all of the players put on their best defense in the same room. As one court put it, "conflicting versions of what took place, or the extent to which [the defendants] participated in it," is "a reason for rather than against a joint trial" because "it is easier for the truth to be determined if all are required to be tried together."[95] In *Zafiro v. United States*,[96] a unanimous Supreme Court agreed that, under the federal rules, severance is not automatically required when codefendants disclaim knowledge of the crime and try to blame each other. Rather, it should be granted only when the trial court finds "a serious risk that a joint trial would compromise a specific trial right of one of the defendants [such as the previously mentioned right to confront accusers], or prevent the jury from making a reliable judgment about guilt or innocence." The Court noted that even if the defendants were granted severance, the state could present the testimony of the other

---

[87]   Even this assumption can be questioned, since evidence suggests that, if the defendants are tried separately, the second defendant will plead guilty after conviction of the first. Peter Langrock, *Joint Trials: A Short Lesson From Little Vermont*, 9 Crim.L.Bull. 612 (1973).

[88]   See Robert O. Dawson, *Joint Trials of Defendants in Criminal Cases: An Analysis of Efficiencies and Prejudices*, 77 Mich.L.Rev. 1379, 1381–97 (1979).

[89]   See *Bruton v. United States*, 391 U.S. 123, 88 S.Ct. 1620 (1968).

[90]   *United States v. Ford*, 870 F.2d 729 (D.C.Cir. 1989).

[91]   *People v. Boyde*, 46 Cal.3d 212, 250 Cal.Rptr. 83, 758 P.2d 25 (1988).

[92]   *Krulewitch v. United States*, 336 U.S. 440, 69 S.Ct. 716 (1949) ("It is difficult for the individual to make his own case stand on its own merits in the minds of jurors who are ready to believe that birds of a feather are flocked together.").

[93]   See § 28.04(d).

[94]   See generally, Dawson, supra note 88.

[95]   *Ware v. Commonwealth,* 537 S.W.2d 174 (Ky. 1976).

[96]   506 U.S. 534, 113 S.Ct. 933 (1993).

suspects at the independent trials. Thus, the Court could see "no reason why relevant and competent testimony would be prejudicial merely because the witness is also a codefendant [in the same proceeding]."

These possibilities make evaluation of the prejudicial impact of joinder very difficult. The Supreme Court's decision in *Schaffer v. United States*[97] provides a typical illustration of how prejudice of the fourth, "guilt-by-association" type is evaluated by the courts. *Schaffer* involved a trial with seven defendants. Four of these defendants, the two Schaffer brothers and Marco and Karp, appealed the joinder of their cases with the case against the other three, the Stracuzzas. The latter three had been the "brains" of a group that had transported stolen clothing across state lines. According to the state, they and the Schaffers had transported goods to Pennsylvania. They and Marco had transported goods to West Virginia. And they had joined with Karp in transporting goods to Massachusetts.

Justice Clark, writing for the majority, found that even though the conspiracy charge linking these defendants together was dismissed after presentation of the state's case, there was insufficient prejudice to warrant severance. He noted that proof of the common scheme was competent as to all the petitioners and that during trial proof of each shipment was related to a specific petitioner and proven by different witnesses with respect to each shipment. Thus, the evidence against each petitioner "was carefully compartmentalized." Furthermore, the judge's instructions "meticulously set out separately the evidence as to each of the petitioners and admonished the jury that they were 'not to take into consideration any proof against one defendant and apply it by inference or otherwise to any other defendant.' " The Court also refused to fashion a hard and fast rule that when a conspiracy count fails, joinder is error as a matter of law.

In addition to challenging this last holding, the four-member dissent, written by Justice Douglas, questioned the usefulness of instructions as a means of separating the defendants:

> [W]here, as here, there is no nexus between the several crimes, the mounting proof of the guilt of one is likely to affect another. There is no sure way to protect against it except by separate trials, especially where, as here, the several defendants, though unconnected, commit the crimes charged by dealing with one person, one house, one establishment. By a joint trial of such separate offenses, a subtle bond is likely to be created between the several defendants though they have never met nor acted in unison[.]

Schaffer illustrates that, in analyzing joinder of defendants, concrete concerns about judicial economy may often override speculative concerns about prejudice.

21.05   Venue

Another constraint on the prosecutor's charging decision stems from Article III, section 2 of the Constitution, which states that the trials of all crimes are "to be held in the State where said crimes shall have been committed."[98] Further, every jurisdiction

---

[97]   362 U.S. 511, 80 S.Ct. 945 (1960).

[98]   The Sixth Amendment, which states that juries shall be selected from "the State and district wherein the crime shall have been committed," could also be relevant here, but this provision, which focuses on "vicinage" (or the neighborhood) from which the jury is drawn, has generally been held inapplicable to the states. See, e.g., *Price v. Superior Ct.*, 25 Cal.4th 1046, 108 Cal.Rptr.2d 409, 25 P.3d 618 (2001); *Davis v. Warden*, 867 F.2d 1003 (7th Cir. 1989).

has rules governing where, within its confines, criminal adjudications may take place, usually based on where the crime was committed. For instance, the federal rules provide that, "[u]nless a statute or these rules permit otherwise, the government must prosecute an offense in a district where the offense was committed."[99] In federal court and many states, venue is an element of the crime and must be alleged in the charging instrument.[100]

Although the location of most crimes is obvious, various aspects of some crimes—such as kidnaping, Internet offenses, or conspiracy—may take place across several jurisdictions. In such cases, the Supreme Court has held, the *locus delicti* [of the charged offense] must be determined from the nature of the crime alleged and the location of the act or acts constituting it."[101] This analysis often involves a close reading of the relevant statute.

For instance, in *United States v. Lombardo*,[102] the Court held that the owner of a prostitution house in Seattle, charged with failing to "file" a report with the Commissioner General of Immigration about harboring an alien, could only be tried in Washington D.C., where the Commissioner was located, because filing "is not complete until the document is delivered and received." Similarly, in *Travis v. United States*,[103] venue for the crime of making false statements "in a matter within the jurisdiction of any department or agency of the United States" was in Washington D.C. because, under the statute, jurisdiction was not triggered until the filing of the allegedly false document, and "when a place is explicitly designated where a paper must be filed, a prosecution for failure to file lies only at that place." In contrast, in *United States v. Johnson*,[104] the Court held that venue for trying the crime of "using" the mails for the purpose of "sending" dentures into another state lay in the state from which the dentures were sent. But in *Johnston v. United States*,[105] failure to obey the order of a local draft board to report to a hospital for civilian work could only be tried where the failures to report occurred (the hospitals), not where the draft boards were established. Although these decisions sometimes referenced their effects on the defendants, witnesses, and judicial resources, in none of them did resource and efficiency considerations trump the statutory analysis.[106]

Congress has resolved many of the issues raised by these early cases by providing that continuing offenses can be tried "in any district in which such offense was begun, continued, or completed."[107] Nonetheless, in more recent cases the Court has still paid

---

[99] Fed.R.Crim. P. 18.

[100] See *United States v. Miller*, 111 F.3d 747 (10th Cir. 1997).

[101] *United States v. Anderson*, 328 U.S. 699, 66 S.Ct. 1213 (1946).

[102] 241 U.S. 73, 36 S.Ct. 508 (1916).

[103] 364 U.S. 631, 81 S.Ct. 358 (1961).

[104] 323 U.S. 273, 65 S.Ct. 249 (1944).

[105] 351 U.S. 215, 76 S.Ct. 739 (1956).

[106] When more than once district is appropriate for venue purposes, these considerations do become paramount. See *Platt v. Minn. Mining & Manu. Co.*, 376 U.S. 240, 84 S.Ct. 769 (1964).

[107] 18 U.S.C.A. § 3237(a). In a provision that is of suspect constitutionality, the statute also provides that "[a]ny offense involving the use of the mails, or transportation in interstate or foreign commerce, is a continuing offense and . . . may be inquired of and prosecuted in any district from, *through*, or into which such commerce or mail matter moves." [emphasis added] However, the expansive effect of this statute is mitigated by the defendant's ability to move for a change of venue, Fed.R.Crim.P. 21(b), and the court's obligation to "set the place of trial within the district with due regard for the convenience of the defendant and the witnesses, and the prompt administration of justice." Fed.R.Crim.P. 18.

close attention to the language of the criminal statutes in deciding venue questions. In *United States v. Cabrales*,[108] it held that a prosecution for money laundering could only take place where the money was laundered, in Florida, not where the laundered funds were generated, in Missouri, despite government arguments that the underlying offense (drug dealing) was an essential element of and facilitated by the laundering charge and that the major harm from that offense occurred in Missouri. And in *United States v. Rodriguez-Moreno*,[109] the Court held that the crime of "using or carrying" a firearm "during and in relation to any crime of violence"—in this case kidnapping—could be tried in New Jersey, even though the kidnapping occurred in Texas and the kidnappers only stayed in New Jersey a short while before moving to Maryland, where the defendants used a gun on the kidnaping victim for the first time. While it is well established that venue for kidnapping lies in every jurisdiction in which the victim is taken,[110] the defendants argued that venue for the firearm charge was appropriate only in Maryland, since that was the only place a gun was "used" or "carried." However, the Court, in an opinion by Justice Thomas, concluded that the gun was used "during and in relation to" the kidnapping, which occurred in a number of states.

21.06   Conclusion

The various rules discussed in this chapter that govern the prosecutor's charging decision can be summarized as follows:

(1) A prosecutor's decision not to prosecute on a particular charge is rarely challenged. A few jurisdictions require the prosecutor who dismisses a case to justify his action in writing if the dismissal occurs after the information or indictment has been filed. The only other realistic controls on a prosecutor's decision to dismiss or drop charges are those imposed by the prosecutor's office on itself. This state of affairs conforms with the Supreme Court's expressed preference against judicial review of most prosecutorial decisions.

(2) A prosecutor's decision to prosecute is subject to two types of constitutional constraints, both narrowly construed. Equal protection is violated if a defendant is (a) intentionally selected for prosecution (b) from among similarly situated offenders (c) for an arbitrary reason or based on a suspect classification connected with race, gender, expression or the like. Due process is violated if the prosecutor's charging decision is a vindictive response to exercise of a legal right (such as the right to appeal) which challenges a previous decision by the prosecutor, a protection that has the following contours:: (a) there is a "presumption" of vindictiveness if the prosecutor raises the initial charge after the defendant has exercised the right during or after trial; (b) imposition of a higher, legitimate charge during plea bargaining, in response to the defendant's rejection of the prosecutor's offer, cannot be challenged on vindictiveness grounds; (c) in other situations in which a charging decision appears to have been made in response to exercise of a legal right, there is, in effect, a presumption against vindictiveness.

(3) Joinder of charges and parties is governed by statute or rule. In the federal courts, the prosecutor may join charges (a) of the same or similar character; or those based on (b) the same act or transaction; or on (c) two or more acts or transactions

---

[108]   524 U.S. 1, 118 S.Ct. 1772 (1998).

[109]   526 U.S. 275, 119 S.Ct. 1239 (1999).

[110]   Cf. *United States v. Lombardo*, 241 U.S. 73, 36 S.Ct. 508 (1916) ("where a crime consists of distinct parts which have different localities the whole may be tried where any part can be proved to have been done").

connected together or constituting parts of a common scheme or plan. Many states permit joinder only in the latter two situations. Joinder of defendants is permitted in virtually all jurisdictions if they participated in the same act or transaction or in the same series of acts or transactions constituting an offense or offenses. Once joinder is found to be proper, the defendant(s) bears the burden of proving that joinder would prejudice their interests by making it difficult for the factfinder to give each charge or defendant individualized consideration. On appeal, misjoinder is usually subject to harmless error analysis, although some jurisdictions may require automatic reversal.

(4) Charges may be adjudicated only in venues where the crime was committed. Determining the location of a crime requires close attention to its statutory definition.

BIBLIOGRAPHY

Amsterdam, Anthony. The One-Sided Sword: Selective Prosecution in Federal Courts. 6 Rutgers-Camden L.J. (1974).

Bales, Richard A. A Constitutional Defense of Qui Tam. 2001 Wis.L.Rev. 381.

Bibas, Stephanos. Prosecutorial Regulations Versus Prosecutorial Accountability. 157 U. Pa. L. Rev. 959 (2009).

Bowers, Josh. Legal Guilt, Normative Innocence, and the Equitable Decision Not to Prosecute. 110 Colum. L. Rev. 1655 (2010).

Davis, Angela. The American Prosecutor: Independence, Power and the Threat of Tyranny. 86 Iowa L.Rev. 393 (2001).

____. Prosecution and Race: The Power and Privilege of Discretion. 67 Fordham L. Rev. 13 (1998).

Dawson, Robert O. Joint Trials of Defendants in Criminal Cases: An Analysis of Efficiencies and Prejudices. 77 Mich.L.Rev. 1379 (1979).

Engel, Steven A. The Public's Vicinage Right: A Constitutional Argument. 75 N.Y.U.L.Rev. 1658 (2000).

Erlinder, C. Peter and David C. Thomas. Prohibiting Prosecutorial Vindictiveness While Protecting Prosecutorial Discretion: Toward a Principled Resolution of a Due Process Dilemma. 76 J. Crim. L. & Criminol. 341 (1985).

Frase, Richard S. The Decision to File Federal Criminal Charges: A Quantitative Study of Prosecutorial Discretion. 47 U.Chi.L.Rev. 246 (1980).

Freedman, Monroe H. The Professional Responsibility of the Prosecuting Attorney. 55 Geo. L.J. 1030 (1967).

Gershman, Bennett L. Prosecutorial Decisionmaking and Discretion in the Charging Function. 62 Hastings L.J. 1259 (2011).

Gershowitz, Adam M. and Laura R. Killinger. That State (Never) Rests: How Excessive Prosecutorial Caseloads Harm Criminal Defendants. 105 Nw. U. L. Rev. 261 (2011).

Gifford, Donald. Equal Protection and the Prosecutor's Charging Decision: Enforcing an Ideal. 49 Geo.Wash.L.Rev. 659 (1981).

Gold, Russell M. Promoting Democracy in Prosecution. 86 Wash. L. Rev. 69 (2011).

Green, Bruce A. and Fred C. Zacharias. "The U.S. Attorneys Scandal" and the Allocation of Prosecutional Power. 69 Ohio St. L.J. 187 (2008).

____. Prosecutorial Neutrality. 2004 Wisc.L.Rev. 837.

Hanna, Cheryl. No Right to Choose: Mandated Victim Participation in Domestic Violence Prosecutions. 109 Harv. L.Rev. 1849 (1996).

LaFave, Wayne. The Prosecutor's Discretion in the United States. 18 Am.J.Comp.L. 532 (1970).

Leipold, Andrew D. The Impact of Joinder and Severance on Federal Criminal Cases: An Empirical Study. 59 Vand.L.Rev. 349 (2006).

Miller, Marc and Ronald Wright. The Black Box. 94 Iowa L. Rev. 125 (2008).

Ramsey, Carolyn B. The Discretionary Power of "Public" Prosecutors in Historical Perspective. 39 Am.Crim.L.Rev. 1309 (2002).

Seigel, Michael L. and Christopher Slobogin. Prosecuting Martha: Federal Prosecutorial Power and the Need for a Law of Counts. 109 Penn St.L.Rev. 1107 (2005).

Simons, Michael A. Prosecutorial Discretion and Prosecution Guidelines: A Case Study in Controlling Federalization. 75 N.Y.U.L.Rev. 893 (2000).

Stuntz, William J. and Daniel C. Richman. Al Capone's Revenge: An Essay on the Political Economy of Pretextual Prosecution. 105 Colum.L.Rev. 583 (2005).

Viera, Norman. Registration, Protest, and the Rationale of *Wayte v. United States*. 40 Ark.L.Rev. 841 (1987).

Vorenberg, James. Decent Restraint of Prosecutorial Power. 94 Harv.L.Rev. 1521 (1981).

Chapter 22

THE PRELIMINARY HEARING

22.01   Introduction

The preliminary hearing or examination is to be distinguished from the initial appearance,[1] the *Gerstein* determination,[2] and the bail hearing.[3] The preliminary hearing normally takes place after all of these proceedings, is adversarial in nature, and is designed primarily to assess the propriety of the prosecutor's charging decision. In particular, it is meant to prevent "hasty, malicious, improvident, and oppressive prosecutions" and to assure "there are substantial grounds upon which a prosecution may be based."[4] The hearing may also provide an opportunity for discovery, obtaining statements for impeachment purposes, perpetuating testimony and facilitating pretrial release.[5]

This chapter addresses three issues concerning the preliminary hearing: (1) when it is required; (2) the appropriate standard for determining whether the prosecution has a case; and (3) the procedural rights accorded at the hearing, including the extent to which the hearing should be used for discovery purposes.

22.02   When the Hearing Is Required

(a)   Under the Federal Constitution

Despite the important functions associated with the preliminary hearing, the Supreme Court has held, in *Lem Woon v. Oregon,*[6] that it is not required by the Constitution. In *Lem Woon*, the Court noted that it had already refused to apply to the states the Fifth Amendment's requirement that serious crimes be tried only on grand jury indictment,[7] and found no relevant distinction between the functions served by the preliminary hearing and the grand jury indictment process. *Lem Woon* was reaffirmed in *Gerstein v. Pugh,*[8] which required a nonadversarial hearing to determine probable cause to detain when no warrant or indictment has authorized arrest. The Court in *Gerstein* specifically recognized that this prompt post-arrest determination is required by the Fourth Amendment and is thus distinguishable from judicial oversight of the decision to prosecute, which is not constitutionally mandated.

(b)   Under Federal and State Statutes

Although the preliminary hearing is not constitutionally required, most jurisdictions make some provision for it by statute or court rule. Assuming the hearing

---

[1]   See § 20.01.

[2]   See § 20.02.

[3]   See generally § 20.03.

[4]   *Thies v. State,* 178 Wis. 98, 189 N.W. 539 (1922).

[5]   See *Coleman v. Alabama,* 399 U.S. 1, 90 S.Ct. 1999 (1970).

[6]   229 U.S. 586, 33 S.Ct. 783 (1913).

[7]   *Hurtado v. California,* 110 U.S. 516, 4 S.Ct. 111 (1884), discussed in § 23.01.

[8]   420 U.S. 103, 95 S.Ct. 854 (1975), discussed in § 20.02.

is not waived,[9] the availability of the preliminary hearing in virtually all of these jurisdictions is contingent upon the prosecutor's ability and desire to proceed by grand jury indictment. In "indictment jurisdictions"—jurisdictions that *require* prosecution by indictment (including the federal courts, which must abide by the Fifth Amendment)—the defendant is entitled to a preliminary hearing to determine whether to bind his case over to the grand jury, *unless* the prosecutor first secures, normally within a certain time period, an indictment. For example under the federal rules,[10] a "preliminary examination" must be held not later than 10 days after the initial appearance if the defendant is in custody and no later than 20 days if he is not in custody, unless the defendant is indicted before that time. In those jurisdictions that allow prosecution by either information or indictment ("information jurisdictions"), if the prosecutor proceeds by information the defendant is usually entitled to a preliminary hearing before the information is filed. As in indictment jurisdictions, however, in most of these information jurisdictions the prosecutor may also proceed by indictment, in which case no hearing is necessary.

This ability to "moot" the hearing by obtaining an indictment has meant that, in some jurisdictions, a preliminary examination is a rare event. In response, some courts have specifically disapproved the practice of granting a prosecutor's request to postpone the preliminary hearing so that he can obtain an indictment.[11] The California Supreme Court even held the "mooting" practice illegal under the state constitution's equal protection clause, on the ground that the disparity between the rights accorded a defendant during a grand jury proceeding and a preliminary hearing is "considerable."[12] As developed below, the defendant has a right to counsel and an opportunity to challenge the prosecution's case at the preliminary hearing and may be able to use it for discovery purposes as well; in contrast, as described in the next chapter,[13] the defendant does not even have a right to be present during a grand jury proceeding.

In federal court, if the defendant is entitled to a hearing but it does not take place, the defendant is released from custody.[14] Although the defendant may also be able to have his charges dismissed, the prosecution is not prevented from refiling the charges, assuming the statute of limitations has not expired. Moreover, if the prosecution successfully obtains an indictment in the meantime, neither release nor dismissal is usually required.

22.03   The "Probable Cause" Standard

(a) Definition

The prosecution bears the burden of showing that a case should be "bound over" to the grand jury or for trial. The standard of proof required, usually referred to as "probable cause," is not easily defined. Clearly, the prosecution should not have to show

---

[9]   One study found that waiver can occur in as many as 50% of the cases in some jurisdictions. Leo Katz, Lawrence Letwin & Richard Bamberger, Justice is the Crime 46–47 (1972).

[10]   Fed.R.Crim.P. 5.1(a)(2).

[11]   See e.g., *United States ex rel. Wheeler v. Flood,* 269 F.Supp. 194 (E.D.N.Y. 1967); *United States v. Pollard,* 335 F.Supp. 868 (D.D.C. 1971).

[12]   *Hawkins v. Superior Court,* 22 Cal.3d 584, 150 Cal.Rptr. 435, 586 P.2d 916 (1978). *Hawkins,* however, was overruled by an amendment to article I, section 7 of the California Constitution in 1990.

[13]   Compare § 22.04 with § 23.04.

[14]   See, e.g., 18 U.S.C.A. § 3060(d).

guilt beyond a reasonable doubt at this preliminary stage of the proceedings. On the other hand, merely requiring the probable cause determination necessary to issue an arrest warrant, as many courts do,[15] seems to serve no useful purpose, since this determination has presumably already been made at least by the time of the initial appearance in front of a judicial officer. Moreover, as one court put it, "probable cause to arrest does not automatically mean that the Commonwealth has sufficient competent legal evidence to justify the costs both to the defendant and to the Commonwealth of a full trial."[16]

Thus, a number of courts require the state to make out a "prima facie" case at the preliminary hearing stage.[17] This standard means the prosecutor must present enough evidence to convince the magistrate that a directed verdict for the defendant would not be necessary after the state rests at trial. But even this standard does not necessarily require the prosecution to present the case it would at trial; for instance, hearsay inadmissible at trial might nonetheless be allowed at the preliminary hearing if there is a showing that the out-of-court declarant will be available for trial.[18]

A question that has troubled the courts is the extent to which the implausibility of the prosecution's witnesses, or the strength of various defenses, such as entrapment or self-defense, should influence the magistrate. If the standard is probable cause to arrest, the magistrate can justifiably disregard such matters completely. Even if the issue is whether the prosecution has a prima facie case, one might conclude that assessment of both credibility and the validity of defenses should be left to the jury. As discussed below,[19] based on this assumption, some courts have limited the defense's ability to cross-examine and present witnesses. However, whether so limited or not, if the defense is able to show that the prosecution's witnesses are entirely implausible, or that a defense would make the state's case completely untenable, many courts seem willing to permit dismissal of the case.[20]

(b) Consequences of Probable Cause Finding

If probable cause is not found and the charges are dismissed, the defendant is released. But in many states, dismissal after a preliminary hearing does not prohibit the prosecutor from filing a second information and seeking a second preliminary hearing on the same charge or different charges.[21] Other states require a showing of new evidence before refiling of an information is permitted.[22] In any event, the prosecutor whose case has been dismissed at the preliminary hearing can usually secure an indictment and proceed against the defendant on that basis.[23] One study found that, in

---

[15] *State v. Clark*, 20 P.3d 300 (Utah 2001); *State v. Morrissey*, 295 N.W.2d 307 (N.D. 1980).

[16] *Myers v. Commonwealth*, 363 Mass. 843, 298 N.E.2d 819 (1973).

[17] Id.; *Commonwealth v. Beatty*, 281 Pa.Super. 85, 421 A.2d 1159 (1980); *People v. Veal*, 101 Mich.App. 772, 300 N.W.2d 516 (1980).

[18] See § 22.04(b).

[19] See § 22.04(c).

[20] On witness credibility, see decisions discussed in *Hunter v. District Court*, 190 Colo. 48, 543 P.2d 1265 (1975). On defenses, see *Jennings v. Superior Court*, 66 Cal.2d 867, 59 Cal.Rptr. 440, 428 P.2d 304 (1967).

[21] See, e.g., *State v. Bloomer*, 197 Kan. 668, 421 P.2d 58 (1966), cert. denied 387 U.S. 911, 87 S.Ct. 1697 (1967); *Commonwealth v. Hetherington*, 460 Pa. 17, 331 A.2d 205 (1975).

[22] *Jones v. State*, 481 P.2d 169 (Okl.Crim. 1971).

[23] *People v. Uhlemann*, 9 Cal.3d 662, 108 Cal.Rptr. 657, 511 P.2d 609 (1973).

such cases, grand juries virtually always indict, but only 50% of the indicted cases end in conviction.[24]

If probable cause is found, the defendant is bound over to the grand jury in indictment jurisdictions and tried on the information in information jurisdictions. If interlocutory appeal of the decision is permitted, it is rarely successful. Even if it is successful, however, the prosecutor presumably has the same options described above with respect to seeking an indictment or refiling. If the bindover decision is not challenged until *after* trial, a conviction usually moots the issue, although some courts have held that the absence of probable cause means the trial court was without jurisdiction and that a new trial is required.[25]

22.04 Procedural Rights

(a) Right to Counsel

In *Coleman v. Alabama,*[26] the Supreme Court held that when the state does provide the defendant with a preliminary hearing, it must also provide him with counsel if he is indigent. The Alabama Court of Appeals had sanctioned the denial of counsel, reasoning that the accused is not foreclosed from advancing defenses at trial which were not raised at the preliminary hearing and that, given the Supreme Court's decision in *Pointer v. Texas,*[27] testimony at the hearing which is not subject to cross-examination could not be used at trial in any event. The Supreme Court nonetheless found the hearing a "critical stage"[28] of the criminal process: "Plainly the guiding hand of counsel at the preliminary hearing is essential to protect the indigent accused against an erroneous or improper prosecution."

The Court's opinion listed four ways in which the presence of counsel at the preliminary hearing may protect the accused. First, a lawyer's skill in examining and cross-examining witnesses may turn up weaknesses in the case that could lead the magistrate to refuse to bind the accused over for trial. Second, even if the case goes to trial, the lawyer may use witnesses' answers to impeach their testimony at trial or to preserve favorable testimony. Third, discovery of the state's case may take place, enabling the lawyer to prepare a more effective defense at trial. Finally, the lawyer might make effective arguments for the accused with respect to fixing bail[29] or determining the necessity for a psychiatric examination.[30]

If the state does not provide counsel at the preliminary hearing, however, reversal of conviction is not automatic. The Court in *Coleman* remanded the case to determine whether the denial of counsel prejudiced preparation of the defendant's defense or instead was harmless error. The usual inquiry in such situations, suggested by Justice White in *Coleman*, is whether "important testimony of witnesses unavailable at the trial

---

[24] Janet Gilboy, *Prosecutors' Discretionary Use of the Grand Jury to Initiate or to Reinitiate Prosecution*, 1984 Am.B.Found.Res.Journ. 1.

[25] *State v. Mitchell*, 200 Conn. 323, 512 A.2d 140 (1986); *People v. Martinovich,* 18 Mich.App. 253, 170 N.W.2d 899 (1969).

[26] 399 U.S. 1, 90 S.Ct. 1999 (1970).

[27] 380 U.S. 400, 85 S.Ct. 1065 (1965). See § 28.05(b).

[28] See § 31.03(a)(1) for a discussion of critical stage analysis.

[29] Usually, however, the bail decision takes place at an earlier stage of the proceedings. See § 20.01.

[30] See § 28.03(b)(2).

could have been preserved had counsel been present to cross-examine opposing witnesses or to examine witnesses for the defense."

(b) Rules of Evidence

The federal rules clearly contemplate use of hearsay at preliminary hearings.[31] Moreover, although the rules do not explicitly state whether the probable cause determination may be based on illegally obtained evidence, they do state that the defendant "may not object to evidence on the ground that it was unlawfully acquired."[32] In contrast, several state jurisdictions bar use of both hearsay and illegally-obtained evidence,[33] presumably on the ground that the preliminary hearing should test the prosecution's case as it will be presented at trial.

As suggested above, even in those jurisdictions in which the prosecution must make out a prima facie case at the preliminary hearing, it does not follow that all of the evidence he presents there must be admissible at trial, so long as that evidence convinces the magistrate there will be sufficient admissible evidence to make out such a case when trial occurs. Thus, admitting the out-of-court declarations of an absent witness who will be available at trial is not necessarily inconsistent with the prima facie standard. Two other reasons can be advanced in favor of the use of hearsay at such proceedings. First, as recognized by a 1990 California constitutional amendment that specifically provides that hearsay is admissible at preliminary hearings,[34] such a rule might help "protect victims and witnesses in criminal cases" because they will not be required to appear. Second, it is firmly established that the grand jury may consider hearsay.[35] Thus, given the prosecutor's ability to obtain an indictment regardless of the outcome of the preliminary hearing, it may make little sense to bar use of hearsay. Some courts adopt an intermediate position, holding that the probable cause determination is much more suspect if founded *solely* on hearsay testimony.[36]

Basing a bindover decision in whole or in large part on illegally obtained evidence can be supported on the latter ground as well; the exclusionary rule does not apply at grand jury proceedings.[37] There are two additional reasons for permitting use of such evidence. First, as the Supreme Court has reasoned in the grand jury context, excluding evidence at the preliminary hearing will not add to the deterrent effect on police that is already provided by excluding evidence at trial.[38] Second, the suppression decision may have yet to be made by the time of the hearing, and the magistrate may not want to delay the hearing to make such a determination. As noted above, the federal rule provides that the magistrate need not consider a suppression motion at this stage.

---

[31] Fed.R.Crim.P. 5.1 used to state that the probable cause determination could be "based upon hearsay in whole or in part." That language was deleted in 2002, but the Advisory Committee notes make clear that the deletion is not meant to change the practice of allowing hearsay, given "administrative necessity" and the fact that hearsay is admissible in grand jury proceedings.

[32] Fed.R.Crim.P. 5.1(e).

[33] See, e.g., *People v. Walker*, 385 Mich. 565, 189 N.W.2d 234 (1971); *Myers v. Commonwealth*, 363 Mass. 843, 298 N.E.2d 819 (1973); *State v. Marshall*, 92 Wis.2d 101, 284 N.W.2d 592 (1979).

[34] Cal. Const. Art. I., § 30(b).

[35] See § 23.06(a)(1).

[36] See, e.g., *Commonwealth ex rel. Buchanan v. Verbonitz*, 525 Pa. 413, 581 A.2d 172 (1990), cert. denied 499 U.S. 907, 111 S.Ct. 1108 (1991) (commonwealth failed to make prima facie showing where only evidence presented was hearsay testimony of investigating police officer).

[37] See § 23.06(a)(2).

[38] *United States v. Calandra*, 414 U.S. 338, 94 S.Ct. 613 (1974).

(c) Right to Cross-Examine and Subpoena Witnesses

Under the Sixth Amendment, the defendant subject to a trial has the right to confront and cross-examine material prosecution witnesses who are available, and to use compulsory process to subpoena his own witnesses.[39] The usual rule at the preliminary hearing is not as broad. While every jurisdiction allows, by rule or statute, some cross-examination of the witnesses the prosecution proffers, the Supreme Court has held there is no federal constitutional right to cross-examination at the preliminary hearing.[40] Thus, cross-examination may be limited by the magistrate if it goes beyond challenging the prima facie case. For example, questioning designed to prove affirmative defenses may be prohibited.[41] For the same reason, the defense's ability to call its own witnesses and question them may be limited.[42] Furthermore, the defense may be prohibited from calling *prosecution* witnesses that the prosecution did not call.[43] Of course, the magistrate has discretion to relax these rules; they are most strictly enforced when defense tactics will be time-consuming.[44]

Occasionally, a court has suggested that the defense is entitled to greater latitude at the preliminary hearing. One such decision is *Myers v. Commonwealth.*[45] There, the court relied heavily on *Coleman,* which had indicated that counsel's role at the hearing was not only to expose weaknesses in the prosecution's case, but also to preserve testimony for use as an impeachment device and to discover other elements of the prosecution's case. According to *Myers,* while preliminary hearing cross-examination should be limited, as at trial, to relevant issues in dispute, the defendant should have "reasonable latitude" in questioning prosecution witnesses "in order to effectuate the ancillary discovery and impeachment functions of the hearing noted in *Coleman.*" Further, the magistrate should not be able to decide when to limit defendants' ability to "present testimony in their own behalf," not only because *Coleman* suggested that presentation of evidence was a right, but also because allowing such an exercise of discretion "would create a situation where some defendants would be afforded a full adversary hearing upon demand while others received summary hearings," in possible violation of equal protection principles. The court went on to admonish the hearing judge for preventing defense counsel's attempts to ask the sole prosecution witness in a rape case about her beliefs in witchcraft and to present the results of a psychiatric evaluation showing the witness had a hysterical neurosis that might lead her to make up stories about people. The appellate court held that both cross-examination and the introduction of the additional evidence should have been allowed because "the examining magistrate could not have possibly made an informed judgment on the question of whether there was sufficient credible evidence of the defendant's guilt to support a bind-over until he had considered all of this evidence."

---

[39] See §§ 28.05; 28.06.

[40] *Goldsby v. United States,* 160 U.S. 70, 16 S.Ct. 216 (1895).

[41] *State v. Altman,* 107 Ariz. 93, 482 P.2d 460 (1971).

[42] Id. The federal rules permit cross-examination of "adverse witnesses" but do not authorize any further defense presentation of evidence. Fed.R.Crim.P. 5.1(e).

[43] See *Schiermeister v. Riskedahl,* 449 N.W.2d 566 (N.D. 1989) (accused not entitled to cross-examine complaining witness at preliminary hearing where complaining witness did not testify).

[44] Kenneth Graham & Leon Letwin, *The Preliminary Hearing in Los Angeles: Some Field Findings and Legal-Policy Observations,* 18 U.C.L.A. L.Rev. 916, 922 (1971).

[45] 363 Mass. 843, 298 N.E.2d 819 (1973). See also Comm. ex rel. *Buchanan v. Verbonitz,* 525 Pa. 413, 581 A.2d 172 (1990).

Weighed against the valid reasons for permitting trial-like confrontation and compulsory process at the preliminary hearing are two concerns. First, as the prosecution argued in *Myers,* permitting these rights at the preliminary hearing might transform the hearing "into a full-blown trial." To this argument the *Myers* court responded: "past experience indicates that trial strategy usually prevents such a result as both the prosecution and the defense wish to withhold as much of their case as possible." Defense attorneys prefer to save attacks on credibility for trial, "rather than tip their hand at this early stage." Further, "defense tactics usually mitigate against putting the defendant on the stand or presenting exculpatory testimony at the preliminary hearing unless defense counsel believes this evidence is compelling enough to overcome the prosecution's case."

The second concern with a more open approach to the preliminary hearing is the fear that the defense attorney will use confrontation and compulsory process mechanisms to convert the hearing into a discovery device. Several courts have forcefully stated that the sole purpose of the preliminary hearing is to make the screening determination.[46] As one court put it, "the accused may lay claim to the benefit of only so much discovery as may become incidental to a properly conducted inquiry into probable cause."[47] This attitude seems sensible to the extent formal discovery devices provide the defense with a good picture of the prosecution's case.[48] But in those jurisdictions where discovery procedures are lacking, as Judge Weinstein observed in *United States ex rel. Wheeler v. Flood,*[49] the preliminary hearing "may provide the defendant with the most valuable discovery technique available to him."

California's approach, adopted in 1990, tries to address the tension between the defendant's right to a meaningful screening and the state's desire to conserve resources. The state's statutes provide that the defendant may call any witness, including the declarant of a hearsay statement offered by the prosecutor, provided that, if the prosecutor so requests, the defendant makes an offer of proof to the satisfaction of the magistrate "that the testimony of that witness, if believed, would be reasonably likely to establish an affirmative defense, negate an element of a crime charged, or impeach the testimony of a prosecution witness or the statement of a declarant testified to by a prosecution witness."[50] This approach prevents the defense from engaging in a fishing expedition, at the same time it appears to give counsel in cases like *Myers* the power to force the prosecution to prove it has a solid case.

22.05   Conclusion

The preliminary hearing is designed to act as a check on the prosecutor's charging decision. Its essential elements can be summarized as follows:

---

[46]   See, e.g., *United States ex rel. Haywood v. O'Leary,* 827 F.2d 52 (7th Cir. 1987); *Hennigan v. State,* 746 P.2d 360 (Wyo. 1987). But see, *Avery v. State,* 555 So.2d 1039 (Miss. 1990) (purposes of a preliminary hearing include discovery and the confrontation of witnesses, as well as determining probable cause and setting bond.).

[47]   *Coleman v. Burnett,* 477 F.2d 1187 (D.C.Cir. 1973).

[48]   But see § 24.03(b).

[49]   269 F.Supp. 194 (E.D.N.Y. 1967).

[50]   West's Ann.Cal.Evid.Code § 1203.1; West's Ann.Cal.Penal Code § 872.

(1) Although not constitutionally required, the preliminary hearing is available by statute or court rule in almost every state, unless waived by the defendant or unless the prosecutor procures an indictment within the statutory time limit.

(2) To obtain a bindover decision in some jurisdictions, the prosecutor need merely show probable cause sufficient to arrest and his evidence need not be admissible at trial. In a number of states, however, the prosecutor must make out a prima facie case.

(3) The defendant has a right to counsel at the hearing under the Sixth Amendment. But the extent to which the defendant may prevent use of hearsay and illegally obtained evidence, cross-examine prosecution witnesses, and subpoena witnesses at the preliminary hearing depends upon the jurisdiction's standard of proof and its attitude toward use of the preliminary hearing as a discovery device. On the latter score, the usual position appears to be that discovery incidental to challenging the prosecution's case is permissible, but that otherwise discovery should be conducted through other means.

BIBLIOGRAPHY

Arenella, Peter. Reforming the Federal Grand Jury and the State Preliminary Hearing to Prevent Conviction Without Adjudication. 78 Mich.L.Rev. 463 (1980).

Berend, Laura. Less Reliable Preliminary Hearings and Plea Bargains in Criminal Cases in California: Discovery Before and After Proposition 115. 48 Am.U.L.Rev. 465 (1998).

Cassell, Paul G. and Thomas E. Goodwin. Protecting Taxpayers and Crime Victims: The Case for Restricting Utah's Preliminary Hearings to Felony Cases. 2011 Utah L. Rev. 1377.

Gilboy, Janet. Prosecutors' Discretionary Use of the Grand Jury to Initiate and Reinitiate Prosecution. 1984 Am.B.Found.Res. J. 2.

Graham, Kenneth and Leon Letwin. The Preliminary Hearing in Los Angeles: Some Field Findings and Legal-Policy Observations. 18 U.C.L.A. L.Rev. 635 and 916 (1971).

Hammer, William J. Preliminary Hearings in Virginia. 20 Wm. & Mary L.Rev. 625 (1979).

McIntyre, Donald M. A Study of Judicial Dominance of the Charging Process. 59 J.Crim.L. & Criminol. & P.S. 463 (1968).

Miller, Frank W. and Robert O. Dawson. Non-Use of the Preliminary Examination: A Study of Current Practices. 1964 Wisc.L.Rev. 252 (1964).

Stoegbauer, Jay. Proposition 115 After *Crawford v. Washington*: It is Time to Revisit the Constitutionality of Police Officer Hearsay in Preliminary Hearings. 34 West. St. U. L. Rev. 143 (2007).

Von Dam, John. Preliminary Hearings in a Truckload. 8 Crim. Just. J. 195 (1986).

Chapter 23

THE GRAND JURY

23.01   Introduction

The Fifth Amendment states in part: "No person shall be held to answer for a capital, or otherwise infamous crime, unless on a presentment or indictment of a grand jury." The eighteenth century English grand jury, usually consisting of 23 persons and acting in secret, was able to charge both on its own (an accusation called a "presentment") and based on a prosecutor's recommendation (an accusation called an "indictment").[1] The framers of the American Constitution included the grand jury provision in the Bill of Rights because the grand jury was perceived to be a "bulwark against oppression," in terms of both its ability to investigate the government and its authority to deny the government an indictment. For example, during the Revolution the grand jury often charged British soldiers and other royal officers with crimes against the citizenry; at the same time it refused to indict colonists for perceived "political" crimes and frequently issued reports critical of England's colonial policies.[2]

Today, the grand jury is much more dependent upon the prosecutor than it was two centuries ago. But it still performs both an investigative and a screening function. As an investigating body, it has wide-ranging powers—including subpoena, immunity and contempt authority—that can be used not only to develop evidence against individual offenders but also to conduct broad-based examinations of organized crime, or "watchdog" inquiries into government operations. As a screening body, it has the authority, although seldom exercised,[3] to refuse to return an indictment (or to find "no bill"). Because it has so much power, and at the same time, is often perceived as merely a tool of the prosecutor, it has become the focus of considerable controversy.[4]

Perhaps wisely, then, the Supreme Court, in the 1884 decision of *Hurtado v. California*,[5] held that indictment by grand jury is not guaranteed by the Fourteenth Amendment, making the Indictment Clause one of the few Bill of Rights' provisions that is not applicable to the states. After emphasizing the need to encourage experimentation among the states and noting that historically the preliminary hearing had often served as a check on the charging decision, the Court stated "we are unable to say that the substitution for a presentment or indictment by a grand jury of [a] proceeding by information after examination and commitment by a magistrate, certifying to the probable guilt of the defendant, with the right on his part to the aid of counsel, and to the cross-examination of the witnesses produced for the prosecution, is not due process of law." Thus, at least in those states that have the type of preliminary hearing described

---

[1]   Great Britain has since abolished the grand jury.

[2]   See generally, Richard Younger, The People's Panel (1963).

[3]   In 1976, .1% of indictments sought from federal grand juries were refused, while approximately 10% of indictments sought from New York grand juries were refused. Hearings before the Subcommittee on Immigration, Citizenship, and International Law of the House Committee on Judiciary in H.R. 94, 95th Cong., 1st Sess. (1977), at 738, 525. Other reports indicate returned "no-bills" in less than 1% of federal cases and from 2 to 20% in state cases. Wayne LaFave, Jerold Israel, Nancy King, Criminal Procedure § 15.03(a) (1999).

[4]   See in particular, § 23.07.

[5]   110 U.S. 516, 4 S.Ct. 111 (1884).

in the previous chapter, the Constitution does not require a grand jury indictment to prosecute.

However, several state constitutions provide that, with certain limited exceptions, felonies are to be prosecuted solely by indictment.[6] Many other states follow the same practice pursuant to statute.[7] The rest, perhaps thirty in all, allow prosecution either by indictment or information.[8] In these latter states, the prosecutor usually performs his own investigation (aided by the police) and proceeds by information, the validity of which is tested at a preliminary hearing presided over by a judicial officer.[9] Apparently, prosecutors view the grand jury process to be cumbersome and time-consuming. However, occasionally indictments from a grand jury are sought in these "information" jurisdictions as well.[10] Most commonly, an indictment is sought when: (1) the case is of great public interest and the prosecutor, for political reasons, wants to share the charging responsibility with a group of citizens; (2) the investigative powers of the grand jury are useful, as in antitrust, fraud, organized crime and political corruption cases; (3) the grand jury process would be speedier than a preliminary hearing, as in cases involving multiple defendants; (4) a scared or reluctant witness can be coaxed to testify because of the secrecy shrouding grand jury proceedings or, more coercively, because of the immunity-granting and contempt powers the grand jury possesses.[11]

This chapter addresses the following issues: (1) the structure and selection of the grand jury; (2) the extent to which grand jury deliberations should be kept secret; (3) the rights of a grand jury witness; (4) the grand jury's investigative powers; (5) the grand jury's screening power, including the common grounds for challenging an indictment; and (6) the value of the grand jury as presently utilized.

23.02   Structure and Composition

(a)   Creation and Duration

In most states, the court is the entity charged with deciding whether a grand jury is necessary for investigative or screening purposes and with summoning the grand jury. However, the court is usually prodded in this regard by the prosecutor and, in an increasing number of jurisdictions, the prosecutor may directly impanel a grand jury.[12] Some states also allow a specified number of the electorate to force creation of a grand jury for particular types of investigations.[13] In large jurisdictions, several grand juries may be impanelled, with some designated as "regular" grand juries that handle everyday

---

[6]   The states are Alaska, Delaware, Hawaii, Illinois, Kentucky, Maine, Mississippi, New Jersey, New York, North Carolina, Ohio, Oregon, Pennsylvania, South Carolina, Tennessee, and Texas. The Connecticut, Florida, and Louisiana constitutions require indictment for capital offenses.

[7]   See, e.g., Va.Code § 19.2–217; W.Va.Code, 62–2–1; Mass.Gen.Laws Ann. 263, § 4.

[8]   Some states allow use of the judicial-inquest or "one-man grand jury." See, e.g., Kan.Stat.Ann. 22–3101. Florida requires neither a grand jury nor a preliminary hearing in noncapital cases, so long as an information is filed within 21 days of arrest. West's Fla.S.A.R.Crim.Proc. 3.133(b).

[9]   See Chapter 22.

[10]   In California at one time, for instance, indictments were sought in roughly 5% of the cases. Bureau of Criminal Statistics, Crime and Delinquency in California 90 (1968) (indictment procedure employed in 4.3% of the cases in 1968).

[11]   Comment, *The California Grand Jury—Two Current Problems*, 52 Calif.L.Rev. 116 (1964).

[12]   See, e.g., West's Ann.Cal.Penal Code § 913.

[13]   See, e.g., Neb.Rev.Stat. § 29–1401(3).

investigation and screening, while others are designated "special" grand juries, whose job is to focus on particular cases.[14]

Once summoned, a grand jury sits for a specified term, although this term may be cut short if the court believes further deliberation is unnecessary. A term can last from a month to as long as three years for special grand juries.[15] Under the federal rules, a "regular" grand jury may serve no longer than 18 months, unless the court extends the service of the grand jury for a period of six months "upon a determination that such extension is in the public interest."[16] During its term, the grand jury usually meets several days each month.

(b)　Size and Voting Requirements

The large size of the English grand jury (24 or 23) allowed a majority vote larger than the unanimous verdict by twelve individuals that was required of the petit jury at trial. Most American jurisdictions have reduced the size and changed the voting requirement for the grand jury. At the federal level, a grand jury is usually composed of twenty-three jurors but can be as small as sixteen (a range that allows up to seven jurors to be excused during the long grand jury term), with twelve votes necessary for an indictment.[17] One state (Tennessee) has a thirteen-member grand jury, twelve of whom must concur for an indictment,[18] while another (Virginia) sits grand juries of from five to nine members, with four votes needed for a true bill.[19] There are many other variations.[20]

As with petit juries, each grand jury has a foreman, whose duties vary. Under federal practice, the court appoints both a foreman (as well as a "deputy" foreman), who is to administer oaths and sign all indictments, as well as keep a record of all votes by the grand jury.[21]

(c)　Selection

Parallel to the selection process for petit juries,[22] the selection of a grand jury proceeds in two stages. The first involves choosing the jury pool or venire, the second selecting a grand jury from that pool. Various constitutional and statutory rules govern both stages of the process. Under most circumstances, an indictment issued by an unconstitutionally selected grand jury may be quashed, and a conviction based on it overturned.[23]

(1)　The Venire

Prospective grand jurors are normally selected from the same pool as petit jurors. Most jurisdictions draw this pool randomly from voting lists, tax returns or telephone

---

[14]　Cf. 18 U.S.C.A. § 3332(b).

[15]　See 18 U.S.C.A. § 3333(e) (permitting extension beyond 36 months if necessary).

[16]　Fed.R.Crim.P. 6(g).

[17]　Fed.R.Crim.P. 6(a)(1).

[18]　Tenn.Code.Ann. §§ 40–12–206; 40–13–105.

[19]　Va.Code §§ 19.2–194; 19.2–202.

[20]　See John A. Van Dyke, *The Grand Jury: Representative or Elite?* 28 Hastings L.J. 37 (1976).

[21]　Fed.R.Crim.P. 6(c).

[22]　See § 27.03.

[23]　See § 23.06(c).

directories, although a few still use the "key-man" system, which relies on designated individuals to nominate prospective jurors. Either of these selection methods, but in particular the latter, is subject to two different types of constitutional challenges.

The first is grounded on the Equal Protection Clause and requires a showing that the defendant's racial group was purposefully excluded from the grand jury venire. In *Castaneda v. Partida*,[24] the Supreme Court held that, to make out such a claim, actual discriminatory intent need not be proven, but rather may be presumed if there is a significant disparity between the group's representation in the community and its representation in the grand jury pool, particularly when the selection procedure used provides an opportunity for abuse. In *Castaneda*, the Court found that a 40% disparity between the proportion of Mexican-Americans in the community and the proportion summoned for grand jury service, combined with an easily abused "key-man" procedure, established a prima facie case of discrimination. The Court also held that the presumption of discrimination, once established, may be overcome by evidence showing the selection procedure was not abused. In *Castaneda*, however, no rebuttal evidence was offered.

The second constitutional basis for challenging the grand jury selection process derives by analogy from the "fair cross-section" requirement for petit juries announced in *Taylor v. Louisiana*.[25] In that case, the Court held that "systematic exclusion" of a "large, distinct group" from the pool or venire from which the petit jury is chosen violates the Sixth Amendment, because it infringes upon the defendant's right to have a representative jury and the community's interest in participating in the criminal justice system. This fair cross-section claim has two possible advantages over an equal protection claim. Most significantly, it does not require a showing of purposeful exclusion but only that it be "systematic" (e.g., via statute), and can be based on exclusion of groups defined by other than racial or gender characteristics (e.g., youth).[26]

Three members of the Court, in a dissenting opinion in *Castaneda*, indicated that they would find *Taylor's* cross-section requirement inapplicable to grand jury venires because the Sixth Amendment speaks only of petit juries and the Fifth Amendment's grand jury clause does not apply to the states. But in *Hobby v. United States*[27] it appeared that a majority of the Court was willing to apply the cross-section requirement to the grand jury as a matter of due process, as several lower courts had done.[28] Although *Hobby* focused on the constitutionality of a judge's selection of the grand jury foreman, the Court's opinion also stated that the selection of the grand jury panel must meet the requirement that "no 'large and identifiable segment of the community [be] excluded from jury service.'"

(2) The Jury

Once a jury pool is selected, the grand jury is selected through a process of exclusion. Those who do not meet residency, citizenship, or other statutory requirements are

---

[24]   430 U.S. 482, 97 S.Ct. 1272 (1977), discussed in detail in § 27.03(b).

[25]   419 U.S. 522, 95 S.Ct. 692 (1975), discussed in § 27.03(c).

[26]   See *Sweet v. U.S.*, 449 A.2d 315, 324 n.20 (D.C.App. 1982); *Cerrone v. People*, 900 P.2d 45 (Colo. 1995).

[27]   468 U.S. 339, 104 S.Ct. 3093 (1984).

[28]   See, e.g., *State v. Jenison*, 122 R.I. 142, 405 A.2d 3 (1979). But see, *Commonwealth v. Bastarache*, 382 Mass. 86, 414 N.E.2d 984 (1980).

excused. Further, a large number of people are excluded on hardship grounds, given the long duration of the grand jury term.[29] If a person who was not legally qualified to be on the grand jury somehow slips through, any subsequent indictment still stands if there were a sufficient number of legally qualified grand jurors voting for the indictment.[30]

Under the Court's petit jury jurisprudence, a defendant can challenge the makeup of the jury that sits on his case on equal protection grounds, or on the ground that the jury was not impartial; both of these claims can be aimed at the grand jury as well.[31] In *Rose v. Mitchell*,[32] the Court held that a defendant has "a right to equal protection of the laws [which is] denied when he is indicted by a grand jury from which members of a racial group purposefully have been excluded." In *Campbell v. Louisiana*,[33] the Court also held, consistent with its petit jury holdings,[34] that a white defendant has standing to challenge racial discrimination against African-Americans in the selection of a grand jury. Such standing is necessary because of the harm such discrimination can cause to the integrity of the grand jury, the white defendant's "close relationship" to the excluded jurors given their common interest in eradicating discrimination, and the fact that an excluded grand juror has little economic incentive to vindicate his own rights.[35]

The ability to challenge a grand jury on lack of impartiality grounds is not as firmly grounded. Lower courts have pointed out that, unlike the right to jury clause in the Sixth Amendment, the Grand Jury Clause does not include the word "impartial," and that in any event the latter clause does not apply to the states.[36] However, in *Beck v. Washington*,[37] the Court stated that "[i]t may be that the Due Process Clause of the Fourteenth Amendment requires the State, having once resorted to a grand jury procedure, to furnish an unbiased grand jury." The Court went on to hold that, if so, the trial judge in *Beck* had discharged his obligations under the Clause when he asked prospective jurors if they were conscious of any prejudice due to pretrial publicity and excused three jurors on the ground of possible bias. The problem here is that, in contrast to the petit jury selection process, no state allows the defense to conduct a pre-indictment *voir dire* of the grand jury. At most, as in *Beck*, the defendant may request that the judge question grand jurors and remind them of their oath not to base their decisions merely on antipathy toward the defendant. Further, a post-indictment *voir dire* is unlikely to be granted, especially since such an inquiry might reveal the grand juror's vote, supposedly cast in secrecy. Finally, most courts hold that, without proof of actual bias on the part of

---

[29]   Van Dyke, supra note 20, at 58–62.

[30]   See, e.g., Fed.R.Crim.P. 6(b)(2).

[31]   § 27.04(c) & (d). See, e.g., Fed.R.Crim.P. 6(b)(2). A lack of representativeness claim might also be possible, although the Supreme Court has yet to settle whether this type of claim may be raised even against a petit jury (as opposed to the jury pool), when the jury is otherwise impartial. See *Lockhart v. McCree,* 476 U.S. 162, 106 S.Ct. 1758 (1986), discussed in § 27.04(c).

[32]   443 U.S. 545, 99 S.Ct. 2993 (1979).

[33]   523 U.S. 392, 118 S.Ct. 1419 (1998).

[34]   See *Powers v. Ohio*, 499 U.S. 400, 111 S.Ct. 1364 (1991), discussed in § 27.04(d)(1).

[35]   Such a challenge is permissible even with respect to the grand jury foreperson, unless he has mostly clerical duties or was picked from an already-sitting grand jury. See *Hobby v. United States*, 468 U.S. 339, 104 S.Ct. 3093 (1984).

[36]   *United States v. Knowles*, 147 F.Supp. 19 (D.D.C. 1957).

[37]   369 U.S. 541, 82 S.Ct. 955 (1962).

one or more grand jurors whose vote was necessary for the indictment, a conviction by an impartial petit jury moots the grand jury impartiality issue.[38]

23.03 Secrecy

(a) Rationale

Although the original reason for maintaining the secrecy of grand jury proceedings is in some dispute,[39] the modern justifications for confidentiality are fairly widely agreed upon. These were spelled out by the Supreme Court in *Pittsburgh Plate Glass Co. v. United States*:[40]

> (1) to prevent the escape of those whose indictment may be contemplated; (2) to insure the utmost freedom to the grand jury in its deliberations, and to prevent persons subject to indictment or their friends from importuning the grand jurors; (3) to prevent subornation of perjury or tampering with the witnesses who may testify before the grand jury and later appear at the trial of those indicted by it; (4) to encourage free and untrammeled disclosures by persons who have information with respect to the commission of crimes; (5) to protect the innocent accused who is exonerated from disclosure of the fact that he has been under investigation, and from the expense of standing trial where there was no probability of guilt.

An additional, practical reason for secrecy, at least until modern times, was that most grand jury proceedings were not transcribed.

Prior to the 1960's, reasons like these were invoked to deny the defendant and third parties access to evidence produced for the grand jury. Since that time, however, most jurisdictions have provided for recording grand jury testimony and have developed some exceptions to the general rule that this record may not be divulged outside the grand jury room.

(b) Disclosure by Witnesses

Probably the most widely adopted exception to grand jury secrecy is that witnesses at the proceeding may disclose their own testimony.[41] By making such a public disclosure, the witness could bring about all the dangers which secrecy is designed to avert, including alerting the suspect to the fact that he is being investigated, wrongfully stigmatizing that person, endangering other witnesses mentioned in the testimony, or creating a situation that might lead to intimidation of the grand jury. But most jurisdictions apparently believe that preventing witnesses from talking is too difficult, and might also prevent monitoring how the grand jury is treating its witnesses.[42]

---

[38] *United States v. Brien,* 617 F.2d 299 (1st Cir. 1980), cert. denied 446 U.S. 919, 100 S.Ct. 1854 (1980). See also, *United States v. Mechanik,* 475 U.S. 66, 106 S.Ct. 938 (1986), discussed in § 23.06(b) & (c).

[39] Compare G. Edwards, The Grand Jury 21 (1906) with Richard M. Calkins, *Grand Jury Secrecy,* 63 Mich.L.Rev. 455, 458 (1965).

[40] 360 U.S. 395, 79 S.Ct. 1237 (1959).

[41] See, e.g., Fed.R.Crim.P. 6(e)(2) (prohibiting disclosure only by grand jurors, prosecutors, those who record the proceedings and those who receive legitimately disclosed information).

[42] William Soroky, *Grand Jury Secrecy: Should Witnesses Have Access to Their Grand Jury Testimony as a Matter of Right?,* 20 U.C.L.A.L.Rev. 804, 819 (1973).

In *Butterworth v. Smith,*[43] the Supreme Court indicated that the First Amendment may provide another reason for this exception to the secrecy requirement. *Smith* held that a Florida statute that barred a grand jury witness from recounting his own testimony, or its "content, gist, or import," violated freedom of speech to the extent it operated after the grand jury's term has ended. Chief Justice Rehnquist, writing for a unanimous Court, pointed out that by the end of the grand jury term the target of the investigation will usually either have been arrested or exonerated; thus, secrecy is not needed to prevent the target from fleeing or to avoid manipulation of grand jury deliberations. And while removing a secrecy requirement might allow a defendant to learn a witness' identity, modern discovery rules often permit discovery of witness identity in any event. Finally, while such a requirement might help avoid unfair stigmatization of an exonerated defendant, "reputational interests alone cannot justify the proscription of truthful speech." Balanced against these interests, Rehnquist pointed out, was the fact that the statute's broad proscription against revealing the content, gist or import of the testimony could keep vital information from the public forever, especially if there is no trial. In *Smith,* it had the effect of enjoining a newspaper reporter from writing about discoveries made while investigating alleged misconduct of government officials.

Smith does not prevent muzzling a witness while the grand jury is still in session. Nor, as Justice Scalia pointed out in a concurring opinion, does it prevent a state from prohibiting a witness from disclosing the testimony of other witnesses at the grand jury session. Finally, Scalia asserted, a state might still be able to prevent a witness from revealing what he *said* at the grand jury proceeding, as opposed to what he *knows* about the events in question.

(c) Disclosure to the Defendant

Most jurisdictions permit disclosure of grand jury proceedings to the defendant when, to use the words of the federal rule, the defendant makes "a showing that a ground may exist to dismiss the indictment because of a matter that occurred before the grand jury."[44] Having mostly to do with prosecutorial misconduct, these grounds are very limited, as discussed further later in this chapter.[45] Thus disclosure for this purpose rarely occurs.

Much more frequent is disclosure to the defendant for discovery purposes, although the extent and timing of the disclosure varies considerably. With the exception of the defendant's own testimony,[46] in many states and the federal courts only testimony by witnesses who will testify at trial is provided the defendant.[47] Moreover, apparently out of fear that witnesses might otherwise be intimidated, this testimony is usually not disclosed until after, or just before, the witness testifies at trial.[48] Other states are even more restrictive, requiring a special showing of need before any grand jury testimony is

---

[43]   494 U.S. 624, 110 S.Ct. 1376 (1990).

[44]   See, e.g., Fed.R.Crim.P. 6(e)(3)(E)(ii).

[45]   See § 23.06(b).

[46]   See, e.g., Fed.R.Crim.P. 16(a)(3) (defendant to be provided with transcript of his own testimony).

[47]   See 18 U.S.C.A. § 3500(e); *State v. CPS Chemical Co., Inc.,* 198 N.J.Super. 236, 486 A.2d 944 (1985).

[48]   18 U.S.C.A. § 3500(e). The federal provision has been strictly construed to authorize pretrial disclosure only at the option of the prosecutor. See § 24.03(b). See, e.g., *United States v. Algie,* 667 F.2d 569 (6th Cir. 1982).

divulged.[49] Only about ten states automatically give the defendant the entire transcript.[50] If one agrees with *Smith* that, after indictment, many of the dangers associated with disclosure are mitigated, then the more restrictive approaches seem inappropriate. As the Supreme Court stated in *Dennis v. United States,*[51] in the course of reversing a decision denying a request at trial for the grand jury testimony of four key prosecution witnesses, "[i]n our adversary system for determining guilt or innocence, it is rarely justifiable for the prosecution to have exclusive access to a storehouse of relevant fact. Exceptions to this are justifiable only by the clearest and most compelling considerations."

(d) Disclosure to Third Parties

Any number of parties other than the prosecutor and the defendant in a given case might seek access to parts or all of the grand jury proceeding. The general rule as to disclosure in this situation, at least at the federal level, comes from *Douglas Oil Co. of California v. Petrol Stops Northwest.*[52] There, the Supreme Court stated that the parties requesting disclosure "must show that the material they seek is needed to avoid a possible injustice to another judicial proceeding, that the need for disclosure is greater than the need for continued secrecy, and that their request is structured to cover only material so needed." *Douglas Oil* also noted, presaging *Smith,* that another factor militating in favor of disclosure exists when the grand jury has finished its deliberations, although it cautioned that courts must still be careful to consider the impact of disclosure on the behavior of witnesses at *future* grand jury proceedings.

A much earlier case, *United States v. Procter & Gamble Co.,*[53] demonstrates how the *Douglas Oil* calculus might be applied. There, the defendants in an antitrust suit sought disclosure of transcripts from grand jury proceedings of which they had been the target (but which had not resulted in an indictment). The Supreme Court upheld the district court's denial of the request, finding that there had been no showing of "particularized need." The Court noted that the request was not specifically aimed at information designed "to impeach a witness, to refresh his recollection, to test his credibility and the like," and thus impermissibly asked for "*wholesale* discovery." Further, some of the witnesses at the grand jury proceedings were employees and customers of the defendant companies, who might face some sort of retaliation if their identities became known (an event which would certainly intimidate witnesses in future cases). The Court also noted that alternatives to discovery were available and that the savings in time and expense that would come from disclosure of grand jury transcripts did not by itself establish the requisite need.

When the party requesting the information is the government, the Supreme Court has taken a more generous stance toward disclosure. First, it seems clear that the prosecutor should be able to disclose information to those who are assisting in the prosecution of the case being considered by the grand jury. Indeed, the federal rules

---

[49]   *Valles v. State,* 90 N.M. 347, 563 P.2d 610 (1977); *Silbert v. State,* 12 Md.App. 516, 280 A.2d 55 (1971).

[50]   See, e.g., West's Ann.Cal.Penal Code § 938.1; Nev.Rev.Stat. § 172.225.

[51]   384 U.S. 855, 86 S.Ct. 1840 (1966).

[52]   441 U.S. 211, 99 S.Ct. 1667 (1979).

[53]   356 U.S. 677, 78 S.Ct. 983 (1958).

require no showing of "particularized need" in such cases.[54] When disclosure is sought by government attorneys who are not assisting in "prosecutorial duties" connected with the federal criminal law, the Supreme Court has held, in *United States v. Sells Engineering, Inc.,*[55] that a showing of need does have to be made, despite language in the federal rules suggesting otherwise.[56] But *Sells* also characterized as having "some validity" the statement that "disclosure of grand jury materials to government attorneys typically implicates few, if any, of the concerns that underlie the policy of grand jury secrecy." More specifically, *Sells* stated that such disclosure might pose "less risk of further leakage or improper use than would disclosure to private parties or the general public."

Also supporting a less stringent approach to disclosure when the supplicant is the government is the Court's decision in *United States v. John Doe, Inc. I.*[57] In interesting contrast to its reasoning in *Proctor & Gamble* (which had counted as one consideration in "particularized need" analysis the availability of other sources of information when private litigants make a request), the Court there pointed out that disclosure to government officials (here lawyers in the Justice Department's antitrust division) could "sav[e] the Government, the potential defendants, and witnesses, the pains of costly and time consuming depositions and interrogatories which might later have turned out to be wasted if the Government decided not to file a civil action after all." The Court also noted that such disclosure might prevent the government from abusing other investigative techniques. On the other hand, it indicated some concern over whether, when their civil counterparts are making the request, federal grand jury prosecutors might be tempted to "manipulate the grand jury's powerful investigative tools to root out additional evidence useful in the civil suit." Of importance to the Court's holding in *Doe*—granting the antitrust division's request for a portion of a grand jury transcript from a case brought by the Justice Department's criminal division—was the fact that the grand jury attorneys had submitted an affidavit attesting to their good faith in conducting the investigation (despite the fact that it had ended without an indictment).

Another limitation under the federal rules, applicable when grand jury information is sought for a non-criminal, investigation, is that the requested information be relevant to pending *judicial proceedings.*[58] This provision has been strictly construed by the Supreme Court.[59] However, the USA Patriot Act of 2001 amended the rules to authorize prosecutors to provide intelligence and immigration agencies national security

---

[54] Fed.R.Crim.P. 6(e)(3)(A)(ii) (automatic disclosure to "government personnel . . . that an attorney for the government considers necessary to assist in performing that . . . in the performance of such attorney's duty to enforce federal criminal law.").

[55] 463 U.S. 418, 103 S.Ct. 3133 (1983).

[56] Fed.R.CrimP. 6(e)(3)(A)(i) (authorizing disclosure to "an attorney for the government for use in performing that attorney's duty"). In a companion case to *Sells,* the Court decided that need must also be shown by state attorneys seeking federal grand jury transcripts. *Illinois v. Abbott & Associates, Inc.,* 460 U.S. 557, 103 S.Ct. 1356 (1983). *Abbott* triggered a congressional amendment to Rule 6(e), which now allows disclosure to state attorneys if a federal attorney shows that "such matters may disclose a violation of state, Indian tribal, or foreign criminal law." Fed.R.Crim.P. 6(e)(3)(E)(iv).

[57] 481 U.S. 102, 107 S.Ct. 1656 (1987).

[58] Fed.R.Crim.P. 6(e)(3)(E)(I).

[59] *United States v. Baggot,* 463 U.S. 476, 103 S.Ct. 3164 (1983) (IRS not entitled to disclosure for purpose of assessing tax liability when no litigation pending).

information obtained through the grand jury even though no judicial proceedings may be in the offing.[60]

23.04   Rights of Grand Jury Witnesses

Whether conducting its own investigation or screening the prosecutor's decision to prosecute, the grand jury relies heavily on witnesses. The scope of the constitutional rights accorded a grand jury witness regarding testifying, remaining silent and consulting counsel differs significantly from those granted a trial witness, a defendant at a preliminary hearing, or a suspect during custodial interrogation.

(a) Right to Testify

At trial, the defendant has a constitutional right to testify.[61] The same is probably true of the defendant at a preliminary hearing.[62] But few states grant the target of a grand jury investigation the right to appear before the grand jury.[63] Apparently, this practice is justified on two grounds: (1) the need for secrecy during such an investigation; and (2) the fact that the target may not become known until the conclusion of the proceeding.[64] Of course, in those jurisdictions where a preliminary proceeding precedes the grand jury, neither of these reasons make sense. Where the grand jury is the sole charging mechanism, a failure to inform the target may, in some cases, be justified to prevent his escape. But, at least where a person who is clearly a target of the investigation requests an appearance, a strong argument can be made that he should be given the same right that he would have during a preliminary hearing.[65]

(b) Warnings

When a person does appear in front of the grand jury (either voluntarily or under subpoena), he has a right to refuse to answer any question put to him by the grand jury if the answer would be self-incriminating. A frequently litigated question is whether the grand jury witness must be told he may remain silent (and that anything he says may be used against him), by analogy to the Court's decision in *Miranda v. Arizona*[66] requiring that such warnings be given to persons subjected to custodial interrogation. Analysis of this issue boils down to whether questioning by the grand jury is more like interrogation by the police or cross-examination at trial. At trial and the preliminary hearing, a witness who decides to testify is not warned that he has the right to remain silent, on the sensible ground that, because he has counsel, he already knows about and can effectively assert the right; further, such a witness is undoubtedly aware the

---

[60]   Pub.L.No. § 203(a), incorporated in Fed.R.Crim.P. 6(e)(3)(D).

[61]   *Rock v. Arkansas,* 479 U.S. 1079, 107 S.Ct. 1276 (1987) (basing the right on the Due Process Clause, the Sixth Amendment right to call witnesses in the defendant's favor, and the Fifth Amendment's protection of silence unless the defendant "chooses to speak"), discussed in § 28.06(a).

[62]   See § 22.04(c).

[63]   Most jurisdictions allow the grand jury to grant a request at its discretion. A few require that a requesting accused be heard, Okla.Stat.Ann. tit. 22, § 335, and others require that certain individuals be given the opportunity to appear. Ga.Code Ann. §§ 45–15–11, 44–11–4 (public officials accused of misconduct).

[64]   See, e.g., *State v. Salazar,* 81 N.M. 512, 469 P.2d 157 (1970) (giving a third reason: that the right to appear only attaches during "criminal prosecution," which has not yet commenced).

[65]   But see, *People v. Newton,* 8 Cal.App.3d 359, 87 Cal.Rptr. 394 (1970) (rejecting an equal protection claim on this ground).

[66]   384 U.S. 436, 86 S.Ct. 1602 (1966), discussed in § 16.02(d).

prosecution is after incriminating information.[67] In contrast, as discussed below,[68] a grand jury witness may not have counsel in the grand jury room with him, if he has one at all, and is less likely to know when he is the target of an investigation. Moreover, the secrecy of the grand jury process makes it more akin to a stationhouse interrogation than a publicly conducted trial or preliminary hearing.

Perhaps for these reasons, many states have mandated warnings by statute, either just for targets,[69] or for all witnesses.[70] But, as a matter of constitutional law, most courts have held that prosecutorial questioning of a grand jury witness does not implicate *Miranda* because the grand jury atmosphere is not as "inherently coercive" as custodial interrogation.[71] A few have adopted the position that once the grand jury's investigation focuses on a witness, the Fifth Amendment requires that he be told of his right to remain silent.[72] The Supreme Court has yet to rule on the issue, although it has indicated its reluctance to require such a warning as a constitutional matter.[73]

The Supreme Court *has* clearly held that a putative defendant need not be told that he is being investigated by the grand jury. In *United States v. Washington,*[74] the defendant was informed of his right to remain silent and that anything he said could be used against him. But he was not told that his testimony could lead to his indictment by the grand jury. The Supreme Court held that the defendant's status as a target did not affect his constitutional protections. Because he "knew better than anyone else" whether his answers would be incriminating, and was not compelled to answer, the Fifth Amendment was not violated, despite the absence of a "target warning."

(c) Right to Counsel

Whatever the necessity of informing a grand jury witness of his right to remain silent, it seems clear that the second half of the *Miranda* warnings concerning the right to counsel need not be given, for the simple reason that there is no such right, at least at the typical grand jury proceeding. In *In re Groban's Petition,*[75] the Supreme Court stated, in dictum, that a grand jury "witness cannot insist, as a matter of constitutional right, on being represented by counsel." This dictum was repeated in the Court's opinion in *United States v. Mandujano,*[76] where four members of the Court concluded that a grand jury proceeding takes place before the initiation of adversary criminal proceedings, and thus is not part of the "criminal prosecution" which the Sixth Amendment indicates is the threshold for application of the right to counsel. Based on the reasoning of the plurality in *Mandujano,* a person who has already been formally charged (through a

---

[67]   See generally § 15.02(a)(2).

[68]   See § 23.04(c).

[69]   See, e.g., New Mex.Stat.Ann., § 31–6–12.

[70]   Idaho Code § 19–1121.

[71]   See, e.g., *Gollaher v. United States,* 419 F.2d 520 (9th Cir. 1969), cert. denied 396 U.S. 960, 90 S.Ct. 434 (1969); *United States v. Corallo,* 413 F.2d 1306 (2d Cir. 1969), cert. denied 396 U.S. 958, 90 S.Ct. 431 (1969).

[72]   *United States v. Reed,* 631 F.2d 87 (6th Cir. 1980); *State v. Falcone,* 195 N.W.2d 572 (Minn. 1972).

[73]   See § 15.02(a)(3). See also, *United States v. Mandujano,* 425 U.S. 564, 96 S.Ct. 1768 (1976) (distinguishing the grand jury setting from the "inherently coercive" atmosphere of custodial interrogation).

[74]   431 U.S. 181, 97 S.Ct. 1814 (1977).

[75]   352 U.S. 330, 77 S.Ct. 510 (1957).

[76]   425 U.S. 564, 96 S.Ct. 1768 (1976).

warrant or an information) might have a right to counsel in the grand jury room,[77] but such persons are usually not the targets of grand jury investigations.

Although the Sixth Amendment probably does not require counsel in the grand jury room, one could still argue, as Justice Brennan did in his dissent in *Mandujano,* that the *Fifth* Amendment mandates that result. Analogous to the reasoning in *Miranda* concluding that counsel must be provided the person subjected to custodial interrogation, Brennan contended that the counselless grand jury witness cannot effectively exercise the right to remain silent. A number of courts have, in effect, accepted this analysis, but concluded, contrary to Brennan, that it merely entitles a grand jury witness to consult with counsel *outside* the grand jury room.[78]

The rationale for limiting the right to counsel to periodic consultation in the grand jury anteroom are several. If counsel is present during the actual questioning, he might: (1) obstruct the investigation by consulting with the witness after each question and, in effect, putting words in the witness' mouth (something even trial counsel cannot do once his client is on the stand); (2) disrupt the proceeding through objections or arguments; and (3) breach grand jury secrecy. On the other hand, when counsel is relegated to the anteroom, a witness may feel reluctant to leave the room more than occasionally, and thus make unwise decisions concerning assertion of the right to remain silent or other privileges or rights.[79] And even if consultation occurs, the witness may not be able to report accurately to the lawyer what has transpired in the grand jury room. Some legislatures have allowed counsel to accompany target witnesses into the grand jury room, but limit them to giving advice; no questions or objections may be raised.[80]

23.05   Investigative Powers

As the Supreme Court stated in *Branzburg v. Hayes,*[81] the grand jury has "a right to every man's evidence," meaning it may compel testimony and documents subject only to "constitutional, common law or statutory privilege." This "right" exists, the Court later explained in *United States v. Dionisio,*[82] because the "obligation of every person to appear and give testimony [to the grand jury is] indispensable to the administration of justice." In the absence of such an obligation, the grand jury process would become a series of "mini-trials," replete with constitutional and evidentiary objections that would impede the investigative process. Thus, as the Court stated in *United States v. Calandra,*[83] a grand jury "may compel the production of evidence or the testimony of witnesses as it considers appropriate, and its operation generally is unrestrained by the technical procedural and evidentiary rules governing the conduct of criminal trials."

In concrete terms, the courts' insistence on the grand jury's right to "every man's evidence" has provided it with three related investigative tools: (1) the power to subpoena

---

[77]   See *Kirby v. Illinois,* 406 U.S. 682, 92 S.Ct. 1877 (1972), holding that the Sixth Amendment attaches "by way of formal charge, preliminary hearing, indictment, information, or arraignment." See § 31.03(a)(3).

[78]   See, e.g., *United States v. Corallo,* 413 F.2d 1306 (2d Cir. 1969), cert. denied 396 U.S. 958, 90 S.Ct. 431 (1969); *People v. Ianniello,* 21 N.Y.2d 418, 288 N.Y.S.2d 462, 235 N.E.2d 439 (1968).

[79]   Walter Steele, Jr., *Right to Counsel at the Grand Jury Stage of Criminal Proceedings*, 36 Mo.L.Rev. 193, 203 (1971).

[80]   See, e.g., Mich.Comp.Laws.Ann. § 767.3; *Commonwealth v. Griffin,* 404 Mass. 372, 535 N.E.2d 594 (1989).

[81]   408 U.S. 665, 92 S.Ct. 2646 (1972).

[82]   410 U.S. 1, 93 S.Ct. 764 (1973).

[83]   414 U.S. 338, 94 S.Ct. 613 (1974).

testimony and tangible evidence deemed useful to its investigation; (2) the power to grant immunity from prosecution; and (3) the power to hold in contempt a person who refuses to comply with a subpoena or to testify after being immunized. In modern times the utilization of these powers is largely controlled by the prosecutor and, to a much smaller extent, the court. This section describes the grand jury's investigative authority, and the roles of the prosecutor and the court in implementing it.

(a) The Subpoena Power

There are two types of subpoenas available to the grand jury—the subpoena *ad testificandum,* which compels witness attendance, and the subpoena *duces tecum,* which compels production of tangible evidence. There are very few limitations, constitutional or otherwise, on the use of either of these devices, although some courts have begun imposing more strenuous requirements for issuance of a subpoena *duces tecum.* The following discussion illustrates this point not only in connection with grand jury subpoenas but also through discussion of subpoenas issued by other entities.

(1) Fourth Amendment Limitations

In the companion cases of *United States v. Dionisio* and *United States v. Mara,*[84] the Court held that a summons to appear before a grand jury and provide evidence was not a "seizure" under the Fourth Amendment because it did not involve the degree of compulsion, stigma, or abruptness of an arrest or an investigative stop. The Court admitted that such an appearance might be "inconvenient" or "burdensome," but this was incidental to the "historically grounded obligation of every person to appear and give his evidence before the grand jury." Further, the imposition of Fourth Amendment strictures on the grand jury "would assuredly impede its investigation and frustrate the public's interest in the fair and expeditious administration of the laws." Thus, the grand jury "could exercise its 'broad investigative powers' on the basis of 'tips, rumors, evidence offered by the prosecutor, or [the jurors'] own personal knowledge' " without making any preliminary showing.

Although *Dionisio* and *Mara* settled that a subpoena *ad testificandum* is not a Fourth Amendment seizure, and need not be based on any showing of suspicion,[85] they did not specifically address the Fourth Amendment's application to subpoenas *duces tecum* for documents or other tangible evidence found in the home or office. In its 1886 decision of *Boyd v. United States,*[86] the Court appeared to hold that the government could not use such a subpoena to seize "mere evidence," as opposed to contraband or instrumentalities or fruits of crime. This conclusion, based in part on privacy concerns underlying the Fourth Amendment, and in part on Fifth Amendment concerns about the compulsion of testimony, would have placed a significant limitation on the subpoena *duces tecum.* Largely for this reason, the Supreme Court soon retreated from this position. In *Hale v. Henkel,*[87] the Court held that the Fourth Amendment's requirement that a search and seizure be reasonable did not bar subpoenas of documents, at least those possessed by corporations.

---

[84] 410 U.S. 1, 93 S.Ct. 764 (1973) (*Dionisio*); 410 U.S. 19, 93 S.Ct. 774 (1973) (*Mara*).

[85] *Dionisio* did caution that subpoenas may not be "too sweeping." But it went on to find that the subpoena of approximately 20 persons for voice exemplars, which the lower court had characterized as a "dragnet procedure," did not violate this prohibition.

[86] 116 U.S. 616, 6 S.Ct. 524 (1886).

[87] 201 U.S. 43, 26 S.Ct. 370 (1906).

However, *Hale* also held that these subpoenas may not be "too sweeping." Like a search warrant, a subpoena must state with "particularity" the items to be produced. The Court found that this requirement was not met in *Hale,* where the subpoena required production of numerous different records, delivery of which might have prevented the defendant corporation from carrying on its business (there being no capacity for photocopying).

Despite their general antipathy toward Fourth Amendment limitations on subpoenas, *Dionisio* and *Mara* too could be read as suggesting that subpoenas *duces tecum* should be treated differently than subpoenas *ad testificandum*, at least outside the corporate context. The witnesses summoned in *Dionisio* were required to provide voice exemplars and the witness summoned in *Mara* was directed to provide a handwriting exemplar. The Court found that these identification procedures were not "seizures" because they merely obtained physical characteristics "constantly exposed to the public," and thus invaded no privacy interest.[88] The Court also indicated, however, that a different result might be called for if the grand jury sought a blood sample, given its greater intrusiveness. Although a subpoena *duces tecum* is not as intrusive or as "abrupt" as a search conducted by police, it does require the production of documents or other items that are not "exposed to the public" and may be very private. Thus, such a subpoena could be characterized as a "search." Yet, until relatively recently, most courts rejected Fourth Amendment challenges to such subpoenas, on the ground that they seek records held by third parties, and thus are governed by the doctrine of *United States v. Miller*[89] and *Smith v. Maryland,*[90] which held that Fourth Amendment protection dissipates once information is voluntarily surrendered to a third party institution.

However, some courts have required a greater showing to obtain medical documents and other records that might contain particularly personal information.[91] And forty years after *Miller* and *Smith* the Supreme Court appeared to undermine those cases by holding that a warrant is required to access cell-site location data from the defendant's phone company. In *Carpenter v. United States,*[92] it stated "[t]here is a world of difference between the limited types of personal information addressed in *Smith* and *Miller* and the exhaustive chronicle of location information casually collected by wireless carriers today." Although the majority claimed that its decision was limited to the type and amount of information involved in *Carpenter*—which was sought by the government, not via a grand jury—the dissenters asserted, with some cause, that there is no clear distinction between location records and the bank and phone records of the type at issue in *Miller* and *Smith.*

In those situations in which a warrant or its equivalent is not required, some showing of need might still be constitutionally mandated for subpoenas. Many lower courts follow the rule announced in *United States v. Gurule,*[93] which identifies three components of "reasonableness" that must be met by a subpoena *duces tecum:*

---

[88]   See § 4.03(b) for further discussion of this point.

[89]   425 U.S. 435, 96 S.Ct. 1619 (1976), discussed in § 4.03(a).

[90]   442 U.S. 735, 99 S.Ct. 2577 (1970).

[91]   See e.g., *United States v. Warshak,* 631 F.3d 266 (6th Cir. 2010) (content of emails); *State v. Skinner,* 10 So.3d 1212 (La. 2009) (medical and prescription records); *Doe v. Broderick,* 225 F.3d 440 (4th Cir. 2000) (medical); *King v. State,* 272 Ga. 788, 535 S.E.2d 492 (2000) (medical).

[92]   ___ U.S. ___, 138 S.Ct. 2206 (2018), discussed in § 4.03(a).

[93]   437 F.2d 239 (10th Cir. 1970).

(1)   the subpoena may command only the production of things relevant to the investigation being pursued;

(2)   specification of things to be produced must be made with reasonable particularity; and

(3)   production of records covering only a reasonable period of time may be required.

Some courts read into the second component a requirement that the subpoena not result in the party being "harassed or oppressed to the point that he experiences an unreasonable business detriment,"[94] which would seem to follow from the Court's holding in *Hale*.[95]

Although it did not address the constitutional issue, the Supreme Court's decision in *United States v. R. Enterprises, Inc.*[96] is not inconsistent with this approach. There, the Court construed Rule 17(c) of the Federal Rules of Criminal Procedure, which permits quashing of a subpoena on motion "if compliance would be unreasonable or oppressive." Emphasizing the special investigative role of the grand jury, the Court rejected the Court of Appeals' holding that a subpoena would be "unreasonable" under this provision unless it could be shown the evidence it requested was "relevant" to its investigation in the sense required at trial.[97] Rather, it concluded that, to quash a subpoena under Rule 17(c), the subpoenaed party must show "that there is no reasonable possibility that the category of materials the Government seeks will produce information relevant to the general subject of the grand jury's investigation." While this standard sets an extremely low threshold, it does recognize that there must be some connection between the evidence sought and the subject of the grand jury investigation.[98] Further, the Court suggested that there might be a duty on the part of the government to apprise the court, *in camera,* of the subject of the investigation, "so that the court may determine whether the motion to quash has a reasonable prospect for success before it discloses the subject matter to the challenging party." *R. Enterprises* also acknowledged, as does the *Gurule* formulation, that a subpoena can be challenged on two other grounds as well: that it is "too indefinite" or that it would be "overly burdensome."

Other types of subpoenas or subpoena mutations, issued by entities other than grand juries, are similarly lightly regulated, although *Carpenter* may change things. For instance, administrative subpoenas, issued by agencies such as the IRS or the Federal Communications Commission, are valid if they seek information "relevant" to a "legitimate investigation" authorized by statute,[99] a standard that the Supreme Court has held is met even if the subpoena is the result of "official curiosity,"[100] and one that lower courts have indicated is more deferential than the "arbitrary and capricious"

---

[94]   *In re Grand Jury Subpoena Duces Tecum (Corrado Brothers)*, 367 F.Supp. 1126 (D.Del. 1973).

[95]   See also *Donovan v. Lone Steer, Inc.*, 464 U.S. 408, 104 S.Ct. 769 (1984) (stating that the Fourth Amendment protects against "an unreasonably burdensome . . . subpoena requiring the production of documents)."

[96]   498 U.S. 292, 111 S.Ct. 722 (1991).

[97]   The relevant case on trial subpoenas is *United States v. Nixon*, 418 U.S. 683, 94 S.Ct. 3090 (1974), which the Court in *R. Enterprises* held was inapplicable to grand jury subpoenas.

[98]   The Court refused to express a view on the respondents' further contention that the records sought related to First Amendment activities and thus could be subpoenaed only if the government demonstrated that they were "particularly relevant to its investigation."

[99]   *United States v. Powell*, 379 U.S. 48, 85 S.Ct. 248 (1964).

[100]   *United States v. Morton Salt*, 338 U.S. 632, 70 S.Ct. 357 (1950).

test.[101] Also requiring only a relevance showing are subpoenas for medical records under the Health Insurance Portability and Accountability Act, financial records under the Fair Credit Reporting Act,[102] bank records under the Right to Financial Privacy Act,[103] and phone and email logs under the Electronic Communications Act.[104] Other than subpoenas for medical and bank records, most subpoenas may also be *ex parte*, meaning that the target need not receive notice they have been served.[105]

A subpoena variant know as a National Security Letter *must* be ex parte,[106] and is valid if an FBI agent certifies that financial information relevant to a national security investigation is sought.[107] Lower courts have held that these Letters, which are used quite frequently,[108] are subject to judicial review to ensure that the necessary certification has been made and that they do not impinge unduly on "First Amendment activities," but as one court noted, "the stand of review for administrative subpoenas similar to NSLs is so minimal that most such NSLs would likely be upheld in court."[109] In any event, as of now the *Miller* doctrine probably applies here as well, meaning the Fourth Amendment is inapplicable. For the same reason, the vast accumulation of records that occurs in connection with government "data mining" programs, which have proliferated since September 11, 2001, are subject to little or no regulation, at least under the Fourth Amendment.[110]

(2) Fifth Amendment Limitations

Clearly, both types of subpoenas (*ad testificandum* and *duces tecum*) compel the subpoenaed party to produce evidence. Occasionally, that evidence may be self-incriminating. Nonetheless, a Fifth Amendment claim will rarely lead to the quashing of a subpoena.

As discussed previously, a grand jury witness, like a trial witness, may refuse to answer questions on Fifth Amendment grounds.[111] But most courts agree that, unlike a defendant at trial (who can avoid the prejudicial effect of continually claiming the privilege by avoiding taking the stand), a person subpoenaed *ad testificandum* by a grand jury may not refuse to appear as a witness, even if it is clear he is the object of the

---

[101] *United States v. Hunton & Williams*, 952 F.Supp. 843 (D.D.C. 1997).

[102] 15 U.S.C.A. § 1681(b)(1).

[103] 12 U.S.C.A. § 3409.

[104] 18 U.S.C.A. § 2703(c).

[105] Ellen S. Podgor & Jerold H. Israel, White Collar Crime in a Nutshell 296 (2004). See *SEC v. Jerry T. O'Brien, Inc.*, 467 U.S. 735, 104 S.Ct. 2720 (1984) (holding that the Fourth Amendment does not require notice to targets of subpoenas).

[106] 12 U.S.C.A. § 3414(a)(5)(D); 18 U.S.C.A. § 2709(c) (third party recordholders prohibited from telling the target about the NSL for at least one year).

[107] 18 U.S.C.A. §§ 2709(f); 3511(a) & (b).

[108] Eric Lichtblau, *Congress Nears Deal to Renew Antiterror Law*, N.Y. Times, Nov. 17, 2004, at A1, A21 (30,000 to 50,000 NSLs issue every year since 2001).

[109] *Doe v. Ashcroft*, 334 F.Supp.2d 471 (S.D.N.Y. 2004); *Doe v. Gonzales*, 386 F.Supp.2d 66, 67 (D.Conn. 2005). Both decisions were vacated in light of new legislation which incorporated their requirements. See *Doe v. Gonzales*, 449 F.3d 415 (2d Cir. 2006).

[110] See Christopher Slobogin, *Datamining by the Government and the Fourth Amendment*, 75 Chicago L.Rev. 317 (2008).

[111] See § 23.04(a). Note, however, that some types of self-incriminating evidence can be compelled from a grand jury witness because it is considered "non-testimonial." Thus, in *Dionisio* and *Mara* the Court found the Fifth Amendment was not implicated by compelled disclosure of voice and handwriting because this was "noncommunicative" evidence. See § 15.04.

grand jury inquiry and will claim the privilege in its presence.[112] This conclusion follows from the premise that the grand jury must be given broad scope in its efforts to ferret out crime. To fulfill this obligation, the grand jury needs a crack at "every man" who might have evidence, including a target who, even if he refuses to provide *self-incriminating* information, may provide exculpatory information or information inculpating others. Further, prospective witnesses cannot know precisely what questions the grand jury will ask and thus cannot make an intelligent assertion of the right before they have made an appearance.[113]

A subpoena *duces tecum* is more likely to implicate the Fifth Amendment, but only in very narrow circumstances. As discussed in detail in this book's treatment of the Fifth Amendment,[114] the Supreme Court has held, in *Fisher v. United States,*[115] that the contents of documents are not protected by the privilege against self-incrimination, because they are voluntarily created. A subpoena compels only the act of producing the documents, which is usually not incriminating unless it is used to prove authenticity or ownership or the description of the nature or location of the documents sought is so vague (because the prosecutor is guessing about either or both) that the defendant is in essence finding the information for the prosecution.[116] Even if the fact of production does somehow incriminate the custodian of the records (because, for instance, it proves the source of those records, which is an element of the prosecution's case), *Fisher* held that, if the prosecution grants immunity with respect to use of this fact, the records may be compelled via subpoena. Of course, if the records are compelled from a third party, which is often the case, the target has no standing to bring a Fifth Amendment challenge.[117]

(3) Miscellaneous Limitations

Although seldom successful, a number of other grounds for resisting a subpoena have been recognized. For instance, some courts have indicated that if a party can show that the grand jury is investigating matters entirely unrelated to criminal activity, an objection may be sustained.[118] But these challenges are usually denied on the authority of the Supreme Court's decision in *Blair v. United States,*[119] which concluded that, given the broad investigative powers of the grand jury, a witness should not be allowed "to set limits to the investigation that the grand jury may conduct." Another sometimes successful challenge to a subpoena is to show that the grand jury is being manipulated by the prosecutor. For instance, if the subpoena power is being used for the purpose of obtaining discovery for civil litigation,[120] in order to obtain evidence of crime that should

---

[112] See *United States v. Friedman,* 445 F.2d 1076 (9th Cir. 1971), cert. denied 404 U.S. 958, 92 S.Ct. 326 (1971); *United States v. Capaldo,* 402 F.2d 821 (2d Cir. 1968), cert. denied 394 U.S. 989, 89 S.Ct. 1476 (1969).

[113] Nonetheless, the American Bar Association has recommended that the court should prohibit the prosecution from compelling a target to take the stand if he states he intends to assert the privilege in response to its questions, on the ground that otherwise he will be "prejudice[d] . . . in the eyes of the grand jury." ABA Standards Relating to the Prosecution Function 90 (1971).

[114] See § 15.06(c).

[115] 425 U.S. 391, 96 S.Ct. 1569 (1976).

[116] See *United States v. Hubbell,* 530 U.S. 27, 120 S.Ct. 2037 (2000), discussed in § 15.06(c).

[117] *Johnson v. United States,* 228 U.S. 457, 33 S.Ct. 572 (1913).

[118] See, e.g., *Franzi v. Superior Court,* 139 Ariz. 556, 679 P.2d 1043 (1984).

[119] 250 U.S. 273, 39 S.Ct. 468 (1919).

[120] *United States v. Procter & Gamble Co.,* 356 U.S. 677, 78 S.Ct. 983 (1958) (use for civil discovery would be "flouting the policy of the law").

normally be obtained in other ways,[121] or, most commonly, for the purpose of getting more information on an already-indicted defendant,[122] a subpoena may be quashed. Finally, courts recognize that subpoenas used purely for harassment purposes must be quashed.[123]

(b) The Immunity Power

As noted above, a grand jury witness who validly exercises his right to remain silent cannot be sanctioned. But the grand jury is not necessarily stymied in this situation. It retains the power to grant immunity to any person asserting the privilege, in an effort to force him to testify. As explained in detail in Chapter 15,[124] immunity is of two types. The broadest form, "transactional" immunity, bars the witness' future prosecution as to any transaction to which he has testified. "Use and derivative use" immunity bars the use, or derivative use, of his own testimony in a prosecution against him. Thus, under the latter type of immunity, later prosecution is possible if independent evidence of the witness' crime is found. In *Kastigar v. United States,*[125] the Supreme Court upheld the constitutionality of use immunity, despite its lesser protection.

However, *Kastigar* also held that, in a subsequent prosecution of a witness granted use immunity, the burden of proof would be on the government to show that the evidence had been derived from "a legitimate source wholly independent of the compelled testimony." Generally, therefore, in those states that provide for use immunity (i.e., a substantial majority of the states), those who are immunized are either "minor players" who are given immunity in exchange for information about other suspects, or individuals concerning whom the prosecution has already developed considerable evidence, which can be sealed and delivered to the court as proof of its "independence" from any admissions made during immunized testimony.

(c) The Contempt Power

The grand jury's ability to issue subpoenas and grant immunity is backed up by the authority to impose civil and criminal contempt citations for those who refuse to respond. If held in civil contempt, which is the usual sanction, the individual may be fined or jailed until he "purges" himself of contempt by producing the evidence or testifying.[126] He is released at the end of the grand jury's term if he has not purged himself by then, although a subsequent grand jury may once again subpoena or immunize him.[127] If civil contempt fails, the grand jury may resort to criminal contempt, which results in a fixed sentence or fine.

---

[121] *In re Grand Jury Subpoena (Kiefaber),* 774 F.2d 969 (9th Cir. 1985) (subpoenas quashed because prosecutor used them to obtain evidence for police, in circumvention of Rule 6(e)), vac'd 823 F.2d 383 (9th Cir. 1987).

[122] *United States v. Star,* 470 F.2d 1214 (9th Cir. 1972); *United States v. Dardi,* 330 F.2d 316 (2d Cir. 1964), cert. denied 379 U.S. 845, 85 S.Ct. 50 (1964).

[123] *Branzburg v. Hayes,* 408 U.S. 665, 92 S.Ct. 2646 (1972).

[124] See § 15.03(d)(1).

[125] 406 U.S. 441, 92 S.Ct. 1653 (1972).

[126] *Shillitani v. United States,* 384 U.S. 364, 86 S.Ct. 1531 (1966).

[127] The Ninth Circuit has rejected claims that successive jailings for civil contempt constitute double jeopardy, a denial of due process, or cruel and unusual punishment. *United States v. Duncan,* 456 F.2d 1401 (9th Cir. 1972), vac'd on other grounds 409 U.S. 814, 93 S.Ct. 161 (1972).

The contempt device is not unlimited. In *Wood v. Georgia*,[128] the Supreme Court held unconstitutional, under the First Amendment, a contempt order against a sheriff who had publicly criticized as racist a recently initiated grand jury investigation of bloc voting by blacks; according to the Court, the sheriff's statements had not presented a "clear and present danger" to the grand jury's deliberations. Although the contempt order in *Wood* was not initiated by the grand jury itself, but by the judges who convened it, presumably a contempt order requested by the grand jury attempting to suppress criticism of its actions would be analyzed similarly.

(d) The Role of the Prosecutor and the Court

In medieval England, the grand jury initiated investigations either on its own or, most commonly, at the behest of the local justice of the peace. A refusal to indict, at least in the latter instance, had to be explained to the court. Later, in both England and colonial America, the grand jury was occasionally able to distance itself further from both the government and the court.[129] But, in the United States today, the grand jury's independence, especially vis-a-vis the prosecutor, is minimal.

Almost every state makes the prosecutor the primary "legal adviser" of the grand jury, and requires or allows him to be present during all grand jury sessions.[130] Theoretically, the grand jury can choose who or what it wants to investigate, issue its own subpoenas, and decide who to immunize. But, in most cases these decisions are actually made by the prosecutor, who in any event is usually granted independent authority to exercise these functions to assist the grand jury in its deliberations.[131] Even the grand jurors' right to ask questions of witnesses, recognized in every jurisdiction, is diminished by the prosecutor's role of primary inquisitor.

As the prosecutor's dominance over the grand jury has increased, the court's has diminished. Although the grand jury has traditionally been seen as an arm of the court, it is usually impanelled either directly or at the request of the prosecutor. After impanelment, the judge's role is primarily ministerial. He "charges" the grand jury, usually speaking of the nature and tradition of grand jury investigation, and the grand jury's independence from the prosecutor. He may also provide legal advice. Most importantly, he enforces the grand jury's subpoena, immunity, and contempt powers. But because he is not present during the grand jury's deliberations,[132] the judge exerts very little practical control over them. Even when possible abuses are brought to his attention, a judge usually does not intercede. Many courts endorse the view that "there should be no curtailment of the inquisitorial power of the grand jury except in the clearest case of abuse, and mere inconvenience not amounting to harassment does not justify judicial interference with the functions of the grand jury."[133]

---

[128] 370 U.S. 375, 82 S.Ct. 1364 (1962).

[129] Younger, supra note 2, at 84.

[130] See, e.g., West's Fla.Stat.Ann. § 905.19. But see North Carolina Gen.Stat. § 15A–622(f) et seq. (providing for judicial supervision of grand jury).

[131] See, e.g., Fed.R.Crim.P. 17(a).

[132] See Fed.R.Crim.P. 6(d), Va.Code § 19.2–199.

[133] *United States v. Johns-Manville Corp.*, 213 F.Supp. 65 (E.D.Pa. 1962). See also, *United States v. Williams*, 504 U.S. 36, 112 S.Ct. 1735 (1992) (court has no authority to sanction prosecutorial conduct not expressly prohibited by Constitution, statute, or rule), discussed in § 23.06(b).

23.06   Grand Jury Screening: Challenges to the Indictment

While the grand jury remains an important investigative body in some types of cases, its major function in most states is to decide, based on the evidence before it, whether an indictment should be issued, or whether instead it should find "no bill." In the federal system and a little over a third of the states, an indictment by grand jury is required, whereas in the remainder of the states the prosecutor has the option of proceeding via information and the preliminary hearing. Below are discussed the major grounds upon which an indictment may be quashed: (1) evidentiary insufficiency; (2) prosecutorial misconduct; (3) discriminatory practices in the selection of the grand jury; and (4) variance from the indictment. With the exception of the third claim, these claims seldom result in an overturned indictment. Indeed, decisions by the Supreme Court narrowing the grounds upon which an indictment may be challenged seem to emasculate many of the rules governing the grand jury process, at least at the federal level.

(a) Sufficiency and Admissibility of Evidence

As with the preliminary hearing,[134] jurisdictions diverge on the proper standard for indictment. In some states, the statutory test is whether there is "probable cause" to believe the accused committed a crime.[135] Others use a prima facie standard.[136] This latter standard is phrased in various ways. For instance, in Arkansas, the grand jury is to return an indictment "when all the evidence before [it], taken together, would in [its] judgement, if unexplained, warrant a conviction by the trial jury."[137] In Utah, "[a]n indictment may not be found unless the grand jurors who vote in favor of the indictment find there is clear and convincing evidence to believe the crime to be charged was committed and the person to be charged committed it."[138]

Ultimately, the standard applied matters very little as far as indictment challenges are concerned. In *Costello v. United States,*[139] the Supreme Court inveighed against evidentiary challenges of grand jury indictments, primarily on efficiency grounds. According to the majority, "[i]f indictments were to be held open to challenge on the ground that there was inadequate or incompetent evidence before the grand jury, the resulting delay would be great indeed." Although an indictment might be challengeable when it is based on "no substantial or rationally persuasive evidence,"[140] the lower courts generally follow *Costello's* lead on this issue.

(1) Application of Evidentiary Rules

Closely related to the standard of proof question is whether an indictment may be quashed if it is based on evidence that would be inadmissible at trial. Similar to the typical preliminary hearing,[141] grand juries in most states usually ignore the rules of

---

[134] See § 22.03(a).

[135] Wash.Code Ann. § 10.27.150.

[136] See, e.g., West's Ann.Cal.Penal Code § 939.8.

[137] Ark.Stat. § 16–85–513(a).

[138] Utah Code Ann. § 77–10a–14.

[139] 350 U.S. 359, 76 S.Ct. 406 (1956).

[140] See id. (Burton, J., concurring). Even this basis for challenge is unlikely to succeed in the federal courts, given the Court's decision in *United States v. Mechanik,* 475 U.S. 66, 106 S.Ct. 938 (1986), discussed in § 23.06(b).

[141] See § 22.04(b).

evidence, whether based on common law, statute, or the Constitution. Again, *Costello* is the leading case upholding this practice. The Court's explicit ruling in *Costello* was that admitting hearsay evidence at grand jury proceedings does not violate the Fifth Amendment's Indictment Clause. But the Court used broad language suggesting that other types of evidence inadmissible at trial could be considered by the grand jury as well, at one point stating, "an indictment returned by a legally constituted and unbiased grand jury, . . . if valid on its face, is enough to call for a trial of the charge on the merits."

The Court reached this conclusion based on several factors: (1) inadmissible evidence does not necessarily lack probative value; (2) many of the rules of evidence, such as the hearsay rule, are rooted in and dependent upon an adversary proceeding and cross-examination, which is antithetical to the grand jury process; (3) any infringement of the accused's right may be remedied by operation of the evidentiary rules at trial; and (4) a contrary result would require grand jurors to apply the evidentiary rules and subject their judgment to the court's review, thereby delaying the grand jury proceeding and sacrificing their independence to the court. Some state legislatures and courts apparently disagree with this reasoning, requiring the grand jury to consider only admissible evidence under the rules of evidence,[142] while at least one federal court has held that hearsay evidence may not serve as a basis for an indictment when better evidence is readily available.[143]

(2) *Application of Exclusionary Rules*

The Supreme Court has also held that evidence which is inadmissible for constitutional reasons may be considered by the grand jury. In *Lawn v. United States*,[144] the Court, repeating *Costello's* statement that an indictment valid on its face is a sufficient basis for trial, held that the grand jury could consider statements obtained in violation of the privilege against self-incrimination.[145] And in *United States v. Calandra*,[146] again relying heavily on *Costello*, the Court concluded that an indictment cannot be quashed simply because it is based on evidence seized in violation of the Fourth Amendment. To the argument that this situation differed from *Costello* because the Fourth Amendment exclusionary rule was designed to punish and deter unconstitutional conduct, the Court responded that application of the rule at trial would sufficiently advance its deterrent purpose.

Calandra also held that the Fourth Amendment does not provide protection against questions *based* on illegally seized evidence; thus, answers to such questions may form the basis for an indictment. A narrow exception to this rule was announced in *Gelbard v. United States,*[147] which held that, under Title III, the federal wiretapping statute, a grand jury witness is a "party aggrieved" and thus may refuse to answer questions based on conversations obtained through an illegal wiretap, even if immunized. *Calandra* made clear that *Gelbard* was not the product of constitutional doctrine but rather

---

[142] Nev.Rev.Stat. § 172.135; N.Y.—McKinney's Crim.Pro.Law § 190.30; *Adams v. State*, 598 P.2d 503 (Alaska 1979) (requiring reversal of conviction if inadmissible evidence is the basis for the indictment).

[143] *United States v. Arcuri*, 282 F.Supp. 347 (E.D.N.Y. 1968), aff'd 405 F.2d 691 (2d Cir. 1968), cert. denied 395 U.S. 913, 89 S.Ct. 1760 (1969).

[144] 355 U.S. 339, 78 S.Ct. 311 (1958).

[145] See also, *United States v. Blue*, 384 U.S. 251, 86 S.Ct. 1416 (1966).

[146] 414 U.S. 338, 94 S.Ct. 613 (1974), also discussed in § 2.03(a).

[147] 408 U.S. 41, 92 S.Ct. 2357 (1972).

stemmed from an interpretation of Title III, which explicitly bars the use of evidence obtained or derived from an illegal wiretap at trial *or* at a grand jury proceeding.[148]

(b) Prosecutorial Misconduct

Many courts have recognized that egregious prosecutorial conduct—such as, for instance, knowing use of perjured testimony,[149] or failure to provide the grand jury with clearly exculpatory evidence[150]—can lead to a successful challenge of the resulting indictment. These rulings can be squared with *Costello,* despite its presumption in favor of facially valid indictments, if one construes the premise of that decision to be an "unbiased" grand jury; prosecutorial malfeasance can create a "biased" indictment that must be quashed despite its facial validity.

However, in *United States v. Williams,*[151] the Supreme Court held that, in federal jurisdictions at least,[152] a court cannot dismiss an indictment for prosecutorial misconduct unless the misconduct violates a pre-existing constitutional, legislative, or procedural rule. In *Williams,* the prosecutor withheld from the grand jury exculpatory information that might have led to a "no bill" finding. While the prosecutor clearly has an obligation, grounded in the Due Process Clause, to provide exculpatory information to the defendant prior to trial,[153] there is no constitutional obligation to give the grand jury such information; as the *Williams* majority stated, "requiring the prosecutor to present exculpatory as well as inculpatory evidence would alter the grand jury's historical role, transforming it from an accusatory to an adjudicatory body." Nor does federal legislation or the Federal Rules of Criminal Procedure require such disclosure. Thus, according to Justice Scalia, who wrote the opinion for a five-member majority, a trial court has no authority to sanction this type of misconduct. "Because the grand jury is an institution separate from the courts, over whose functioning the courts do not preside, we think it clear that, as a general matter at least, no such 'supervisory' judicial authority exists."

Even when the prosecutorial misconduct violates a clearly established rule, indictment challenges will rarely succeed, especially if made after conviction.[154] In *United States v. Mechanik,*[155] the Supreme Court appeared to hold that virtually all such post-conviction challenges will be denied on harmless error grounds, because conviction nullifies the error. Although *Mechanik* involved only a violation of federal rule 6(d), which limits the types of individuals who may attend a grand jury hearing, the Court's rationale for holding that violation harmless was broadly applicable:

> Both [of the lower courts] observed that Rule 6(d) was designed, in part, "to ensure that grand jurors, sitting without the direct supervision of a judge, are

---

[148] 18 U.S.C.A. § 2515. For further discussion of this point, see § 14.03(g).

[149] *United States v. Basurto,* 497 F.2d 781 (9th Cir. 1974).

[150] *Ostman v. Eighth Judicial Dist. Court,* 107 Nev. 563, 816 P.2d 458 (1991); *Johnson v. Superior Court,* 15 Cal.3d 248, 124 Cal.Rptr. 32, 539 P.2d 792 (1975).

[151] 504 U.S. 36, 112 S.Ct. 1735 (1992).

[152] For a state court ruling contra to *Williams,* see *State v. Gaughran,* 260 N.J.Super. 283, 615 A.2d 1293 (Law Div. 1992).

[153] See § 24.04.

[154] Even if the misconduct is discovered and objected to prior to trial, the harmless error standard of *Nova Scotia,* discussed below, must be met, and interlocutory appeal of an adverse decision is not allowed, at least in federal court. *Midland Asphalt Corp. v. United States,* 489 U.S. 794, 109 S.Ct. 1494 (1989).

[155] 475 U.S. 66, 106 S.Ct. 938 (1986).

not subject to undue influence that may come with the presence of an unauthorized person." The Rule protects against the danger that a defendant will be required to defend against a charge for which there is no probable cause to believe him guilty. . . . But the petit jury's subsequent guilty verdict not only means that there was probable cause to believe that the defendants were guilty as charged, but that they are in fact guilty as charged beyond a reasonable doubt. Measured by the petit jury's verdict, then, any error in the grand jury proceeding connected with the charging decision was harmless beyond a reasonable doubt. . . .

[Further], there is no simple way after the verdict to restore the defendant to the position in which he would have been had the indictment been dismissed before trial. He will already have suffered whatever inconvenience, expense, and opprobrium that a proper indictment may have spared him.

Many courts have followed this reasoning in rejecting indictment challenges based on other types of prosecutorial misconduct.[156]

In the subsequent case of *Bank of Nova Scotia v. United States*,[157] the Court appeared to back off somewhat from *Mechanik's* harmless error analysis, by making clear that conviction does not moot all challenges to prosecutorial misconduct. But the Court continued to emphasize the heavy burden faced by the defendant bringing such challenges, holding that dismissal of the indictment in this situation "is appropriate only 'if it is established that the violation substantially influenced the grand jury's decision to indict,' or if there is 'grave doubt' that the decision to indict was free from the substantial influence of such violations." Applying this standard in *Bank of Nova Scotia,* the Court found that the following illegal actions by the prosecutor were not grounds for quashing the indictment, since they did not prejudice the grand jury's decision: (1) use of the grand jury to gather evidence for use in civil matters; (2) public identification of the targets; (3) imposition of secrecy oaths on witnesses; (4) permitting misleading summaries of the evidence by government agents; (5) granting immunity to witnesses with the implicit threat that they would be charged if they testified for the defendant; (6) making abusive comments to an expert witness that were overheard by grand jury members; and (7) failure to prevent two witnesses from appearing in front of the grand jury simultaneously. In dismissing the fourth complaint above, the Court also suggested that the defense must show not only prejudice but that the prosecution knew, rather than just suspected, that evidence presented to the grand jury was misleading.

Mechanik and *Bank of Nova Scotia* send prosecutors the message that most of the rules governing the conduct of grand jury proceedings are precatory only. The opinion in *Bank of Nova Scotia* did indicate, however, that if the prosecutorial misconduct "overreached or deceived in some significant way" or spanned several cases and was "so systematic and pervasive as to raise a substantial question about the fundamental fairness of the process which resulted in the indictment," then prejudice might be found, language which has led some lower courts to reverse convictions based on indictments affected by particularly egregious and pervasive prosecutorial misconduct.[158] It should

---

[156] See, e.g., *United States v. Fenton*, 1998 WL 356891 (W.D.Pa. 1998) (violation of ABA ethical standards not ground for invalidating indictment); *United States v. Fountain,* 840 F.2d 509 (7th Cir. 1988). But see, *United States v. Taylor,* 798 F.2d 1337 (10th Cir. 1986).

[157] 487 U.S. 250, 108 S.Ct. 2369 (1988).

[158] See, e.g., *United States v. Sigma International, Inc.,* 244 F.3d 841 (11th Cir. 2001).

also be noted that the Court borrowed its prejudice standard in *Bank of Nova Scotia* from *Kotteakos v. United States,*[159] a petit jury harmless error case, which eschewed looking at whether there was sufficient evidence to convict after deleting the error, but rather focused on whether the error influenced the jury's decision, a standard that is arguably easier to meet.

(c) Discrimination in the Selection Process

As discussed earlier in this chapter,[160] both the Equal Protection Clause and the Due Process Clause may provide a basis for challenging the grand jury's indictment. In contrast to cases involving evidentiary insufficiency and prosecutorial misconduct, the Supreme Court has indicated that these types of claims, if proven, will lead to quashing of the indictment whether raised before or after conviction. Because it "strikes at the fundamental values of our judicial system and our society as a whole," the Court has held, in two different decisions,[161] that discrimination in the selection of a grand jury can never be harmless, even when the person has been convicted by a fairly selected and impartial petit jury.[162]

This notion was reiterated in *Mechanik,* which distinguished these cases on the ground that "racial discrimination in the selection of grand jurors is so pernicious and other remedies so impractical, that the remedy of automatic reversal was necessary as a prophylactic means of deterring grand jury discrimination in the future." Similarly, with respect to a pre-trial challenge on due process representativeness grounds, *Bank of Nova Scotia* explained that a proven violation should result in automatic reversal because the "nature of the violation allow[s] a presumption that the defendant was prejudiced, and any inquiry into harmless error would . . . require[ ] ungrounded speculation."

(d) The Essential Elements Requirement and Variance

The Supreme Court's cases have established that an indictment must meet at least three constitutional requirements: (1) as a matter of due process, it must "fairly inform" a defendant of the charge against which he must defend; (2) it must enable him "to plead an acquittal or conviction in bar of future prosecutions for the same offense," as provided under the Double Jeopardy Clause; and (3) under the Fifth Amendment's Indictment Clause, it must "contain the elements of the offense charged," and thus reflect that the grand jury found probable cause with respect to all of the "essential elements" of the alleged crime.[163] Normally, all of these concerns are taken care of if the indictment tracks the language of the relevant statute, "accompanied by such a statement of facts and circumstances as will inform the accused of the specific offense."[164] If the first two concerns remain, they are usually mooted through other mechanisms. If the defendant

---

[159] 328 U.S. 750, 66 S.Ct. 1239 (1946), discussed in § 29.05(b).

[160] See § 23.02(c).

[161] *Rose v. Mitchell,* 443 U.S. 545, 99 S.Ct. 2993 (1979); *Vasquez v. Hillery,* 474 U.S. 254, 106 S.Ct. 617 (1986).

[162] As a result, a resulting conviction must apparently be reversed and a new trial held, although another alternative would be to reinstate the conviction if a duly constituted grand jury reindicts the defendant. See Tom Stacy and Kim Dayton, *Rethinking Harmless Constitutional Error,* 88 Colum.L.Rev. 79 (1988).

[163] See *Hamling v. United States,* 418 U.S. 87, 94 S.Ct. 2887 (1974); *United States v. Debrow,* 346 U.S. 374, 74 S.Ct. 113 (1953).

[164] *United States v. Hess,* 124 U.S. 483, 8 S.Ct. 571 (1888).

is still unsure of the charge, he can ask for a bill of particulars,[165] and the transcript of the grand jury proceeding or arraignment (or of trial itself) will provide adequate basis for making double jeopardy determinations.

The third requirement—that the indictment indicate the grand jury has found probable cause for all essential elements of the crime charged—is more likely to result in a concrete constitutional violation. As the Supreme Court noted in *Russell v. United States*,[166] if a defendant is "convicted on the basis of facts not found by, and perhaps not even presented to, the grand jury which indicted him," he is deprived "of a basic protection which the guaranty of the intervention of the grand jury was designed to secure." This type of claim was raised in *United States v. Resendiz-Ponce*,[167] where the defendant's indictment alleged that he "knowingly and intentionally attempted to enter the United States of America at or near San Luis in the District of Arizona." The defendant argued, both pretrial and on appeal, that this indictment failed to allege an essential element of attempt, namely a specific overt act such as entering an inspection station or presenting a misleading identification card. But the Supreme Court held that use of the word "attempt" both provided sufficient notice and assured that conviction "would arise out of the theory of guilt presented to the grand jury," as required by *Russell*. The lone dissenter, Justice Scalia, countered that "[a] reasonable grand jury, relying on nothing but that term [i.e., attempt] might well believe that it connotes intent plus any minor action toward the commission of the crime, rather than the 'substantial step' that the Court acknowledges is required."

The Ninth Circuit decision in *Resendiz-Ponce* had held that the omission of the overt act in the indictment was a "fatal flaw" not subject to harmless error analysis. Given its resolution of the case, the Supreme Court did not address this aspect of the Ninth Circuit's holding, but Justice Scalia agreed that such an error is "structural" and requires automatic reversal. In an earlier case, however, the Court indicated that, at least when the Fifth Amendment claim is not raised until after trial, it is subject to plain error analysis. The indictment in *United States v. Cotton*[168] alleged, parallel to the relevant statute, that the defendants possessed "a detectable quantity of cocaine or cocaine base," a crime that brings a maximum penalty of 20 years. After conviction, the trial judge found that all of the defendants had possessed at least 500 grams of cocaine and decided to sentence two of the defendants to 30 years and the other defendants to life, under authority of a separate statute that permitted sentences of up to life in prison for possession of more than 50 grams of the drug.

The Court first concluded that the amount of drugs possessed by the defendants was an essential element of the crime under *Apprendi v. New Jersey*,[169] which held that facts that enhance a sentence beyond the statutory maximum must be found by a jury. But despite the failure to include this element in the indictment, the Court refused to reverse the conviction because the error did not "seriously affect the fairness, integrity or public reputation of judicial proceedings" given the overwhelming nature of the evidence against the defendants and the Court's assumption that the grand jury, having

---

[165] See Fed.R.Crim.P. 7(f).

[166] 369 U.S. 749, 82 S.Ct. 1038 (1962). See also, *Stirone v. United States,* 361 U.S. 212, 80 S.Ct. 270 (1960).

[167] 549 U.S. 102, 127 S.Ct. 782 (2007).

[168] 535 U.S. 625, 122 S.Ct. 1781 (2002).

[169] 530 U.S. 466, 120 S.Ct. 2348 (2000), discussed in § 27.02(a)(2).

found that the conspiracy existed, "surely . . . would have also found that the conspiracy involved at least 50 grams of cocaine base." This reasoning appears to reject Scalia's later assertion in *Resendiz-Ponce* that this type of error is structural,[170] and also suggests that even had the *Apprendi* claim been raised prior to trial and thus been subject to the harmless error standard,[171] reversal might not have occurred, given the Court's willingness to assume the outcome of the grand jury process would have been the same.

A closely related issue arises when the proof offered by the prosecution at trial is at "variance" with the allegations in the grand jury's indictment. If the variance between the indictment and the proof at trial is minimal, modern courts typically take no notice of the fact. But, as *Russell* indicated, a substantial variance can result in the quashing of an indictment and the reversal of a conviction based on it, on the ground that it violates the Indictment Clause of the Fifth Amendment.[172]

As an extension of this reasoning, federal courts sometimes overturn convictions based on some but not all of the material allegations in the indictment, concluding that if the grand jury had heard only the evidence related to the proven allegations, it might have failed to indict. In *United States v. Miller,*[173] however, the Supreme Court held that when the indictment facts that the prosecution fails to prove at trial are "in no way essential to the offense on which the jury convicted," they can be regarded as "surplusage."[174] This was the case in *Miller,* where the indictment had specified that the defendant had fraudulently used the mails to obtain insurance proceeds by (1) consenting to a "burglary" that resulted in the "loss" of his property and (2) misrepresenting the value of the loss to his insurance company. The government was unable to have the first allegation stricken from the indictment and was unable to prove it at trial. But the second allegation was a sufficient basis for, and led to, a conviction. Thus, concluded the Court, the indictment should be upheld.

23.07   An Assessment of the Grand Jury

Should the grand jury continue as an investigative and screening body? Looking first at the grand jury as an investigative device, it is important to note that the power now vested there does not have to be. In Florida, for instance, in all noncapital cases the prosecutor may seek subpoenas, grants of immunity, and contempt citations on his own.[175] He does not need to impanel a grand jury to avail himself of these tools. Thus, a better way to focus on the usefulness of the grand jury as an investigative body is to ask whether its retention, at least as an option, offers any advantages over a system which depends entirely on prosecutor- and police-conducted investigations, assuming each system has the same investigative powers.

---

[170] Although Scalia joined the majority in *Cotton,* in other opinions he has argued that even structural error does not require reversal when there is no timely objection. See, e.g., *Neder v. United States,* 527 U.S. 1, 119 S.Ct. 1827 (1999) (Scalia, J., dissenting).

[171] See § 29.05(a).

[172] This type of violation used to require automatic reversal, *Stirone v. United States,* 361 U.S. 212, 80 S.Ct. 270 (1960), but it may now be subject to harmless error analysis (when timely objection is raised) and plain error analysis (when it is not), given the Court's holding in *Cotton.*

[173] 471 U.S. 130, 105 S.Ct. 1811 (1985).

[174] See Fed.R.Crim.P. 7(d) (surplusage in the indictment or information may be stricken).

[175] F.S. 914.001. In many states, the prosecutor has subpoena power, but only in connection with a pending proceeding, such as a grand jury inquest, a preliminary hearing, or trial.

At least three possible advantages of some sort of grand jury system can be advanced. First, the fact that the grand jury is composed of laypeople may have some benefits. As is said about the petit jury,[176] the institution of the grand jury may promote a sense of citizen participation in the criminal process that improves the reputation and credibility of the system as a whole. And the lay nature of the grand jury may make it willing to pursue certain types of investigations—e.g., of political corruption—that the prosecutor would be reluctant to initiate, either because he himself may be involved somehow, or because the targets of the investigation control his future. Most importantly, reliance on a panel of citizens, rather than the prosecutor's office, could be fairer and less partisan, in fact as well as symbolically; the grand jury's mere existence may serve to hold the prosecutor in check from vindictive or ill-advised investigations.

Second, both because of its lay make-up and its history, the investigative scope of the grand jury is likely to be more wide-ranging than the prosecutor's. The prosecutor, for legal or ethical reasons, may feel constrained about using the subpoena process to investigate people who have not yet been formally charged, or who have not at least been targeted by a complaint from a citizen or the police. The grand jury, on the other hand, may engage in virtual fishing expeditions. The most potent evidence of this difference is the fact that, in many states, the grand jury may issue reports on various matters—ranging from conditions in local jails[177] to reports on misconduct of public employees and local government[178]—without rendering any criminal charges. In support of these reports, it is said the grand jury's investigative authority extends to "all that is comprehended in the police power of the state."[179] The modern trend is to limit the use of these reports in a number of ways, most notably by requiring that they not be issued unless the individuals implicated are allowed to testify before the grand jury and append a response to the report.[180] Courts may also order such reports expunged if they draw conclusions beyond the bounds of a legitimate investigation.[181] But, even so limited, they represent a power unlikely to be given to the prosecutor's office, which traditionally has focused on enforcing the criminal law.

A third reason the grand jury might be usefully retained as an investigative option is that a witness may be more likely to talk in front of a grand jury than at the stationhouse or the prosecutor's office, for a number of reasons. Because, in contrast to the person subjected to custodial interrogation, a grand jury witness is not entitled to counsel and may not be entitled to reminders about the right to remain silent,[182] he may feel more compelled to talk. Additionally, the grand jury may provide more secrecy than a prosecutorial investigation, which can encourage disclosures. Finally, if the witness does talk, he is more likely to do so truthfully, since, unlike a stationhouse encounter, he is under oath and can be tried for perjury if he lies.

It can be questioned whether these differences justify maintaining the grand jury as an investigative body. The fact that an unwarned, uncounselled person is less likely

---

[176] See § 27.01.

[177] Ohio Rev.Code § 2939.21; Ala. § 12–16–224.

[178] Ala. § 36–11–3; West's Ann.Cal.Pen.Code § 933.

[179] *In re Report of Grand Jury,* 152 Fla. 154, 11 So.2d 316 (1943).

[180] N.Y.—McKinney's Crim.P.Law §§ 190.85–90(3).

[181] In *Hammond v. Brown,* 323 F.Supp. 326 (N.D.Ohio 1971), aff'd 450 F.2d 480 (6th Cir. 1971), the court expunged a grand jury report finding "beyond doubt" that twenty-five persons it had indicted for the events at Kent State University in May, 1970 had committed the charged offenses.

[182] See § 23.04.

to remain silent is not necessarily a reason for favoring grand juries. And it is questionable whether a grand jury proceeding is more likely than an interview with the prosecutor to remain confidential,[183] or disclose truthful information.[184] Most importantly, the potential benefits of the grand jury's lay nature and its ability to engage in wide-ranging investigations are undercut significantly by the previously discussed realities that the prosecutor dominates the grand jury and the court seldom steps in. Indeed, these facets of the grand jury mean it can easily serve as a shield for prosecutors who would be unwilling to pursue certain illegitimate or questionable investigations on their own.[185] Only if the grand jury is granted more of its traditional independence (through the mechanism of allowing it to hire its own attorney, for instance),[186] and is more closely monitored by the court, is it likely to provide any positive advantages over the prosecutor and the police as an investigative device.

Similar comments can be made about the grand jury's efficacy as a screening mechanism. Here, the alternative is a preliminary hearing, presided over by a judge. As a theoretical matter, it may be useful to have citizens involved in deciding who should be charged with crime or criticized for wrongdoing. But if, in practice, the prosecutor largely controls the evidence which informs these decisions, it is not clear that the grand jury is preferable (especially where, as is true in federal jurisdictions, prosecutorial misconduct is often immune from challenge, in the rare instances when grand jury secrecy allows it to be discovered, and defective indictments no longer require reversal even when timely objection is made).[187] In contrast to the grand jury, the preliminary hearing is conducted in open court, with the defendant and counsel present, and allows consideration of evidence for the defendant, as well as against him.[188] While several jurisdictions require both a preliminary hearing and a grand jury proceeding, the prosecutor has the authority, as discussed in the previous chapter,[189] to avoid the preliminary hearing by first obtaining an indictment. Perhaps the opposite rule would make the most sense: the preliminary hearing should be mandatory, with the grand jury used solely as an investigative body *prior* to the hearing, if it is used at all.[190]

23.08   Conclusion

The grand jury indictment may be issued as an authorization to arrest, or serve as a formalization of the prosecutor's decision to arrest. In either case, the following comments about the grand jury process are applicable.

(1) The federal system and slightly over one-third of the states require that prosecution in felony cases proceed by indictment. In most of the remaining states,

---

[183]   See § 23.03 for a discussion of the many exceptions to the secrecy prohibition.

[184]   In the federal courts, for instance, a witness can be punished for intentionally making false statements to a police officer. 18 U.S.C.A. § 1001. See § 15.02(a)(6).

[185]   See David J. Fine, *Federal Grand Jury Investigations of Political Dissidents*, 7 Harv.Civ.Rts.-Civ.Lib.L.Rev. 432 (1972).

[186]   See, e.g., Hawaii Const. art. 1, § 11.

[187]   See § 23.06(b). Federal grand juries return "no-bills" in less than 1% of the cases, although the rate is higher in some states. At the same time, very few indicted cases are dismissed by a judge for lack of evidence. See Wayne LaFave et al., Criminal Procedure 15.3(b) (2d ed. 1999).

[188]   See generally, Chapter 22.

[189]   See § 22.02(b).

[190]   This was the practice in California, under *Hawkins v. Superior Court,* 22 Cal.3d 584, 150 Cal.Rptr. 435, 586 P.2d 916 (1978), until 1990, when a statewide proposition eliminated the right to a preliminary hearing. West's Ann.Cal. Const. Art. I, § 14.1.

prosecution may proceed by either indictment or information; in the latter case, a preliminary hearing usually serves the charging function.

(2)   The size of the grand jury and the number of votes necessary for an indictment vary considerably among the states. In federal jurisdictions, the grand jury is composed of from 16 to 23 people, with twelve votes needed for an indictment. Neither the pool from which the grand jury is chosen nor the grand jury itself may result from a procedure which purposefully discriminates on the basis of race or gender. Further, the grand jury pool may not result from a procedure which systematically excludes a significant, identifiable segment of society. Finally, the grand jury must be impartial, although ensuring impartiality is difficult, since the defendant is entitled neither to pre- or post-indictment voir dire.

(3)   In order to encourage witnesses to come forward, prevent disclosure of derogatory information, avoid premature disclosure of the investigation to a potential defendant, and protect grand jurors from intimidation or reprisal by the government or targets, neither evidence heard by the grand jury nor the grand jury's deliberations are a matter of public record. However, disclosure of this information may be made under the following circumstances: (a) in most jurisdictions, a witness may disclose his own testimony; after the grand jury's term has ended, he *must* be allowed to do so under the First Amendment; (b) in most jurisdictions, the defendant is entitled to the grand jury testimony of witnesses who testify at trial; (c) the validity of other disclosures requires balancing the need for secrecy (including the impact that disclosure may have on future grand juries) against the specificity and strength of the third party's request, with government agencies more likely to obtain grand jury transcripts than private third parties.

(4)   Under the federal Constitution, a putative defendant or target apparently has no right (a) to appear in front of the grand jury; (b) to counsel, either in the grand jury room or outside for consultation; (c) to be told he is a target, or (d) to a reminder that he has the right to remain silent. However, most jurisdictions, statutorily or by judicial decision, provide all of these rights in one form or another.

(5)   The grand jury has wide-ranging investigative powers, in order to implement its "right to every-man's evidence." Use of subpoenas *ad testificandum* appears to be unrestricted by the Constitution, except that they may not be "too sweeping." Traditionally, a subpoena *duces tecum*, whether issued by a grand jury or another government entity, needed only to meet the following Fourth Amendment requirements: (a) it must state with some particularity what is requested; (b) it must avoid being overly burdensome; and (c) the items it requests must be at least minimally related to the investigation. However, this area of the law is in a state of flux, and a warrant or its equivalent may be required to obtain certain types of information, such as cell-site location data. A subpoena *duces tecum* can also be quashed under the Fifth Amendment if the prosecution cannot state with reasonable particularity the location of the file and its nature, or in the rare event that the act of production it compels is self-incriminating and cannot be immunized. The grand jury's authority to grant immunity allows it to force a witness to testify upon a promise that no future prosecution will be based on that testimony, or on any evidence derived from it. Both the subpoena and immunity powers are enforced by civil and criminal contempt, imposed by the court. In practice, the prosecutor often suggests to the grand jury who to subpoena and immunize, and when the contempt penalty is appropriate.

(6) In the federal courts, a grand jury indictment probably cannot be quashed for insufficient evidence, or on the ground that the evidence considered by the grand jury would be inadmissible at trial. Egregious prosecutorial conduct during the grand jury investigation will only furnish grounds for quashing an indictment if it violates an established rule, and even then a motion for dismissal will usually succeed only if the defendant establishes that the violation substantially influenced the grand jury's decision to indict. An indictment from a grand jury that was selected unconstitutionally will normally be quashed, and any resulting conviction reversed. If timely objection is made, a conviction based on an indictment that does not state the essential elements of the crime or whose primary basis consists of facts not found by the grand jury may also be overturned, but is subject to plain error analysis when raised after trial.

BIBLIOGRAPHY

Bowers, Josh. The Normative Case for Normative Grand Juries. 47 Wake Forest L. Rev. 319 (2012).

Bowman, Frank O. Vox Populi: Robert McCulloch, Ferguson and the Roles of Prosecutors and Grand Juries in High-Profile Cases. 80 Mo. L. Rev. 111 (2015).

Brenner, Susan. The Voice of the Community: A Case for Grand Jury Independence. 3 Va. J. Soc. Pol'y & L. 67 (1995).

Collins, Jennifer M. And the Walls Came Tumbling Down: Sharing Grand Jury Information with the Intelligence Community Under the USA Patriot Act. 39 Am.Crim.L.Rev. 1261 (2002).

Crites, Erin L., Jon B. Gould and Colleen E. Shepard. Evaluating Grand Jury Reform in Two States: The Case for Reform (NACDL, 2011).

Fairfax, Roger A. Grand Jury Discretion and Constitutional Design. 93 Cornell L. Rev. 703 (2008).

____. The Jurisdictional Heritage of the Grand Jury Clause. 91 Minn.L.Rev. 398 (2006).

____ (ed.). Grand Jury 2.0 (2010).

Frankel, Marvin E. The Grand Jury: An Institution on Trial. New York: Hill and Wang, 1977.

Henning, Peter J. Prosecutorial Misconduct in Grand Jury Investigations. 51 S.C.L.Rev. 1 (1999).

Kuckes, Nicki. The Democratic Prosecutor: Explaining the Constitutional Function of the Federal Grand Jury. 94 Geo.L.J. 1265 (2006).

____. The Useful, Dangerous Fiction of Grand Jury Independence. 41 Am.Crim.L. 1 (2004).

Leipold, Andrew. Why Grand Juries Do Not (And Cannot) Protect the Accused. 80 Cornell L.Rev. 260 (1995).

Murphy, Erin. The Politics of Privacy in the Criminal Justice System: Information Disclosure, The Fourth Amendment, and Statutory Law Enforcement Exemptions. 111 Mich. L. Rev. 485 (2013).

Poulin, Anne Bowen. Supervision of the Grand Jury: Who Watches the Guardian? 68 Wash. U.L.Q. 885 (1990).

Richman, Daniel. Grand Jury Secrecy: Plugging the Leaks in an Empty Bucket. 36 Am. Crim. L.Rev. 339 (1999).

Rosenberg, Benjamin E. The Analysis of Defective Indictments after *United States v. Cotton*. 41 Crim.L.Bull. 1 (2005).

Silbert, Earl J. Defense Counsel in the Grand Jury—The Answer to the White Collar Criminal's Prayers. 15 Am.Crim.L.Rev. 293 (1978).

Simmons, Ric. Re-examining the Grand Jury: Is There Room for Democracy in the Criminal Justice System? 82 B.U.L.Rev. 1 (2002).

Slobogin, Christopher. Subpoenas and Privacy. 54 DePaul L. Rev. 805 (2005).

Sullivan, Thomas and Nachman, Robert. If It Ain't Broke, Don't Fix It: Why the Grand Jury's Accusatory Function Should Not Be Changed. 75 J.Crim.L. & Criminol. 1047 (1984).

Washburn, Kevin K. Restoring the Grand Jury. 76 Fordham L.Rev. 533 (2008).

Younger, Richard. The People's Panel. Brown University Press (1963).

Zwerling, Matthew. Federal Grand Juries v. Attorney Independence and the Attorney Client Privilege. 27 Hastings L.J. 1263 (1976).

Chapter 24

DISCOVERY

24.01 Introduction

As in the civil system, broad discovery in criminal cases might accomplish several goals: (1) more rational decisionmaking during pretrial negotiations; (2) better prepared adversaries at trial; (3) conservation of attorney resources that will otherwise be diverted to discovering information; and (4) avoidance of surprise, and the trial disruption and continuances that surprise causes. It was not until the last few decades of the twentieth century, however, that discovery in the criminal justice system began to approach the level necessary to implement these objectives.

Before the middle of the twentieth century, there were few formal provisions permitting discovery in criminal cases. In most jurisdictions, both the defendant and the prosecutor had to rely on the information they could glean from pretrial proceedings. With the adoption, in 1946, of Rule 16 in the Federal Rules of Criminal Procedure, and the proliferation of similar rules at the state level, the scope of discovery began to expand. Rule 16 permits the defendant, upon request, to discover from the prosecution: (1) any written statements or transcriptions of oral statements made by the defendant that are in the prosecution's possession; (2) the defendant's prior criminal record; and (3) documents, photographs, tangible objects, results of physical and mental examinations, and test reports in the prosecution's possession that the prosecution intends to use as evidence or that is deemed "material" to the defense's trial preparation.[1] If the defendant requests any of the items in the latter two categories, Rule 16 grants the prosecutor "reciprocal discovery;" he may request inspection of documents, objects, and test results that the defense intends to introduce at trial.[2] The "work product" (i.e., documents prepared in anticipation of litigation) of both sides is protected, however.[3]

Most state rules are even broader in scope. For example, over half the states not only provide for discovery of the items covered in Rule 16, but also require the prosecution to provide names and addresses of all persons known to have information relevant to the offense charged, as well as any statements about the offense these persons have made.[4] In several of these states, the defense must reciprocate, either by providing a list of all persons whom the defense expects to call as witnesses and any recorded statements they have made,[5] or by simply providing a list of witnesses.[6] In many states, the defense must provide this information even if it has *not* requested

---

[1] Fed.R.Crim.P. 16(a)(1).

[2] Id. 16(b)(1).

[3] Id. 16(a)(2) and 16(b)(2). The one clear exception is that witness statements prepared by the prosecution, which would normally be considered work product, must be provided the defense at least by the completion of the witness' testimony. Fed.R.Crim.P.16(a)(2) (referencing 18 U.S.C.A. § 3500). Furthermore, as of 2002, Rule 16(a)(1)(E) exempts from its protection documents that are "material to preparing the defense," which read literally could include police and other investigative reports normally thought to fall within the work product exemption.

[4] Moore's Federal Practice 216 (1982).

[5] See, e.g., West's Fla.S.A.R.Crim.Pro. 3.220(d)(1)(B)(1).

[6] See, e.g., Hawaii R.Crim.Pro. 16(c)(2)(i).

information from the prosecution.[7] A smaller number of states have adopted "open file" discovery, which additionally requires disclosure to the defense of all tangible objects and all expert reports, even if they will not be introduced at trial, as well as information about any agreements with witnesses whom the prosecution intends to call.[8]

The typical statute also provides for protective orders, and for sanctions if the rules are not followed. For instance, under the federal rules the court has discretion, after making an *in camera* inspection of a requested item, to deny, restrict or defer its disclosure.[9] Upon finding that a party has failed to comply with a discovery rule, a protective order, or other court order regarding discovery, the court may require production of an item, grant a continuance until compliance occurs, "prohibit that party from introducing the undisclosed evidence," or "enter any other order that is just under the circumstances."[10] One type of "order" sometimes relied upon is a charge to the jury telling it that the party has not produced a requested piece of evidence, and that it may draw whatever conclusion it wishes from that fact.

As this brief description indicates, modern discovery rules enable the defense to obtain a substantial amount of information from the prosecution that may otherwise have been difficult to procure prior to trial. At the same time, it should be apparent that discovery under federal and state rules is not a one-way street: the defendant is *required*, under certain circumstances, to disclose information to the prosecution. This chapter will first discuss issues associated with prosecution discovery of the defense's case. It will then address the prosecution's obligations under today's discovery legislation. Finally, it will examine the prosecutor's duty, under the *Constitution*, to disclose exculpatory information and to preserve evidence.

24.02 Discovery by the Prosecution

When disclosure is sought from the defense, there are three possible limitations on discovery: the Fifth Amendment's privilege against self-incrimination, the Sixth Amendment's right to counsel (and the associated work product doctrine), and, in some states, the requirement that the defense ask for information from the prosecution first. These limitations are discussed here, as well as limitations on sanctions that may be imposed on the defense for violating discovery rules.

(a) Fifth Amendment Limitations

As a general proposition, the prosecution cannot compel the defendant to provide inculpatory statements from his own mouth. But the defendant can waive the Fifth Amendment privilege. He can also be granted immunity and forced to talk. Finally, the Fifth Amendment only prohibits compelled *self*-incrimination.[11] These principles have varying application to discovery rules, depending upon the type of discovery at issue.

---

[7] See infra note 30.

[8] These statutes are modeled on American Bar Association Criminal Justice Discovery Standard 11–2.1 (1995).

[9] Fed.R.Crim.P. 16(d)(1).

[10] Fed.R.Crim.P. 16(d)(2).

[11] For a discussion of the scope of the Fifth Amendment, see Chapter 15.

(1) Notice of Alibi and Other Defenses

In *Williams v. Florida*,[12] the Court was faced with a "notice-of-alibi" statute. Such statutes, which exist in every jurisdiction (usually independent of the discovery provisions described earlier), require the defendant to give pretrial notice of an alibi defense (asserting, e.g., that the defendant was a home at the time of the crime) and a list of witnesses who will support it.[13] The majority in *Williams* found that this type of statute does not violate the Fifth Amendment, because it exerts no more compulsion to produce alibi evidence than does the need to avoid conviction at trial itself, and the latter type of pressure has never been found to implicate the Fifth Amendment. The one difference between the command of a notice-of-alibi statute and the "command" that one produce evidence in one's defense at trial is that the former compels the defendant to accelerate the disclosure. In response to this observation, the Court responded: "Nothing in the Fifth Amendment privilege entitles a defendant as a matter of constitutional right to await the end of the State's case before announcing the nature of his defense, any more than it entitles him to await the jury's verdict on the State's case-in-chief before deciding whether or not to take the stand himself." This reasoning would also seem to support statutes that require notification of other defenses, such as insanity or self-defense.[14]

In dissent, Justice Black pointed out that identification of hitherto unknown defense witnesses prior to trial could provide incriminating information or investigative leads. For instance, such a witness could help the prosecution establish that the defendant was in the vicinity of the crime at the time it happened (even though the witness may insist the defendant was not at the precise spot the crime occurred). Or the witness might provide the government with information about other potential witnesses or crimes committed by the defendant. Finally, as occurred in *Williams* itself, pretrial notice might help the prosecution gather evidence that can be used to impeach the alibi witness.

The problem with Black's objection is that, even without alibi notice provisions, the state will eventually find out about the alibi witness at trial, at which time it can ask for a continuance which will give it the same investigative advantages. Unless continuances are barred (which would be unfair to the prosecution), notice-of-alibi statutes and other notice-of-defense statutes are likely to result in no greater infringement of the defendant's interests than would occur without one, at least if the defendant is first given adequate discovery of the prosecution's case so that he can make an intelligent decision about possible defenses. At the same time notice-of-defense statutes are clearly more likely to result in efficient use of judicial resources through minimizing the need for continuances (a point the *Williams* majority emphasized).

In favor of Black's position, however, is the possibility that the defendant may decide to forego the defense after notice is given. In such cases, the notice rule forces the defendant to give the prosecution possibly incriminating information that it otherwise might not have obtained. In this situation, the court could impose a ban on prosecutorial

---

[12]   399 U.S. 78, 90 S.Ct. 1893 (1970).

[13]   See, e.g., Fed.R.Crim.P. 12.1.

[14]   See Fed.R.Crim.P. 12.2(b). However, as discussed in § 24.03(a), a notice-of-defense statute that does not also require the prosecution to provide equivalent information about its rebuttal evidence is unconstitutional.

use of evidence derived from the reneged-upon notice. But determining when such use has occurred can be very difficult. More is said on the "change-of-defense" problem below.

(2) Witness Lists and Statements

As noted in the introduction, many states require the defendant to provide the prosecution with lists of all witnesses (rather than just witnesses who will support a specific affirmative defense), as well as statements from those witnesses. A few jurisdictions even require the defendant to create and document such statements if they do not exist.[15] Clearly, any of this information might prove incriminating or provide investigative leads (for instance, a witness list might lead the prosecution to the sole eyewitness to a crime). But, after *Williams*, these provisions are probably justifiable on the ground that the prosecution will obtain this information at trial in any event. Perhaps the best compromise is to allow the defendant to seek a protective order when he can show that disclosure of certain information will be harmful to him and is not likely to be useful at trial.[16] Thus, the court might decide to protect the identity of a witness who has evidence about other crimes committed by the defendant.

The one piece of information regarding witnesses that the defendant may be able to withhold is whether he himself will testify. In *Brooks v. Tennessee*,[17] the Supreme Court held invalid a state statute requiring that, if the defendant chose to testify, he must do so at the beginning of his case, just after the state has rested. The Court found that the statute violated both the privilege against self-incrimination and the due process right to "the guiding hand of counsel," because it forced the defendant to assess the extent to which his own testimony would be useful or necessary to his defense at the end of the state's case, rather than after he'd had the opportunity to evaluate the impact of his own evidence. Arguably, if a defendant cannot be forced to make a choice about his own testimony after he's seen the state's case, he should not be required to make the choice prior to trial.

However, *Brooks* is not easily reconciled with *Williams,* which upheld a rule forcing the defendant to make an important choice *prior* to viewing the state's evidence at trial. Perhaps the Court considers the right to testify (or remain silent) to be more fundamental than the opportunity to raise an alibi defense or other defenses.[18] Or perhaps the Court is less worried about the element of "surprise" to the prosecution in the *Brooks* context, since the general outline of what a defendant will say at his own trial can usually be anticipated. A final explanation is that *Brooks* merely recognizes the defendant's right to control the presentation of his case, and has no implications for discovery rules. If so, the state *could* force the defendant to reveal prior to trial whether he plans to testify.

The *Williams* "accelerated disclosure" rationale would not seem to justify forcing the defendant to reveal the gist of statements which he does *not* intend to use at trial. Yet, under limited circumstances, the defendant may also be compelled to provide such

---

[15]   See, e.g., R.I. Super.Ct.R.Crim.Pro. 16(a)(8) (if no statement for witness available, defense shall provide "a summary of the testimony such person is expected to give at trial.").

[16]   Cf. *Prudhomme v. Superior Court,* 2 Cal.3d 320, 85 Cal.Rptr. 129, 466 P.2d 673 (1970) (disclosure may be barred depending upon the "incriminating effect" of the item).

[17]   406 U.S. 605, 92 S.Ct. 1891 (1972).

[18]   See Robert Mosteller, *Discovery Against the Defense: Tilting the Adversarial Balance,* 74 Calif.L.Rev. 1567, 1626 (1986). On the right to testify, see § 28.06(a).

statements. In *United States v. Nobles,*[19] the defendant attempted to call as a witness a private investigator retained by the defense; his testimony would have cast doubt on two eyewitnesses for the prosecution. The trial judge ruled that the investigator could not testify until the prosecution received the portion of his investigative report that contained alleged statements from these two witnesses (as determined by the judge *in camera*). Defense counsel refused to submit the report and the investigator was not allowed to testify. On appeal, the defendant argued that the trial court's attempt to compel the disclosure of the investigator's report violated his privilege against self-incrimination.

The Supreme Court did not agree. Emphasizing that the Fifth Amendment is a "personal right,"[20] a unanimous Supreme Court found that it was not implicated here because "[t]he court's order was limited to statements allegedly made by third parties who were available as witnesses to both the prosecution and the defense." Thus, had the court order been implemented, the prosecution would not have received any "personal communications" from the defendant, or any statements from witnesses unknown to the prosecution.

Nobles establishes that the privilege is not violated when the defendant is compelled to provide, at trial, prior recorded statements from witnesses the prosecution knows about and that will further adversarial testing of those witnesses. Since *Nobles* involved an order from the judge at trial, the decision does not make clear whether the defendant can be forced to provide such information prior to trial. However, in light of *Williams'* finding that accelerated disclosure of items that will be disclosed at trial is not violative of the Fifth Amendment, such a practice is probably permissible. Thus, a rule allowing prosecution discovery of statements the defendant takes from prospective witnesses, adopted in several jurisdictions,[21] does not appear to violate the Fifth Amendment even when the statements contain information the defense will not use at trial.

(3) *Identities of Non-Witnesses*

After *Williams*, the defense can be required to disclose the identity of its witnesses prior to trial. Whether the Fifth Amendment prohibits forced disclosure of the identity of a person whom the defense will *not* call as a witness depends upon the source of the information. In *Fisher v. United States,*[22] the Court held that the Fifth Amendment prohibits the state from compelling the defendant to disclose the existence of documentary evidence that could be used against him, and that the attorney-client privilege prohibits compelling the defendant's attorney from surrendering such information (the Fifth Amendment would not prevent the latter disclosure, because, as *Nobles* affirmed, it is concerned only with defendant-directed compulsion). Accordingly, it would appear that the state cannot force the defendant or his attorney to disclose the identity of a non-witness (such as a co-perpetrator) whose existence is known because of the *defendant*. On the other hand, if the defense's knowledge about the existence of incriminating information does not come from the defendant, it is not protected by either the Fifth Amendment or the attorney-client privilege. Thus, if awareness of a non-witness is the result of the *attorney's* efforts (as is the case with most experts, for

---

[19]   422 U.S. 225, 95 S.Ct. 2160 (1975).

[20]   See *Couch v. United States,* 409 U.S. 322, 93 S.Ct. 611 (1973), discussed in § 15.05.

[21]   See, e.g., Minn.R.Crim.P. 9.02–1(3)(b); Wis.R.Crim.P. 971.23(2m)(am).

[22]   425 U.S. 391, 96 S.Ct. 1569 (1976), discussed in § 15.05.

instance), his identity might be discoverable, at least as far as the Fifth Amendment is concerned.[23]

(4) Tangible and Documentary Evidence

After *Williams* and *Nobles*, the Fifth Amendment is unlikely to be infringed by the typical rule allowing the prosecution access to any documents, photographs, and other tangible objects, and the results of physical examinations, psychological evaluations, and scientific tests, that the defendant plans to use at trial. As with other types of information, the more difficult issue is whether the state may discover evidence of this type which the defendant will not use at trial (e.g., a murder weapon, or business records).

Fisher settled that the prosecution cannot force the defendant to admit to the existence of those items that are in the defendant's possession (or are given to his attorney). But *Fisher* also indicated that if the prosecution already knows of their existence, then the Fifth Amendment is not violated by a demand for them, so long as the prosecution is barred from revealing their source. This conclusion derives from the following reasoning: a subpoena for documents or other tangible evidence only compels the act of producing the evidence, not its creation, and this act is incriminating only when the source of the subpoenaed item is a crucial element of the prosecution's case. By barring the prosecution from revealing the source (in effect, "immunizing" the defendant with respect to the fact of production), even this potential for self-incrimination is removed.[24]

Accepting this argument does not mean that all subpoenas for tangible or documentary evidence must be honored by the defense, however. First, as *Fisher* noted, the subpoena cannot, in effect, demand if a document or object exists; rather, it can only compel production of items known to exist. This limitation is bolstered by the Fourth Amendment, which prohibits overbroad or indefinite subpoenas *duces tecum*.[25] Second, even with "immunity" as to the source of the item, subpoenas for certain types of objects, such as contraband or stolen goods, would be invalid, because the factfinder will assume that the source was the defendant regardless of what it is told.[26] Third, some subpoenas may be barred for non-constitutional reasons. Several jurisdictions prohibit use of grand jury subpoenas after an indictment has been returned,[27] apparently on the ground that otherwise they will be abused by evidence-greedy prosecutors.

---

[23] However, as discussed below, see § 24.02(b), there may be Sixth Amendment or work product limitations on the disclosure of such information. See also, *People ex rel. Bowman v. Woodward,* 63 Ill.2d 382, 349 N.E.2d 57 (1976).

[24] See § 15.06(c) for further discussion of this point. Note also that barring information about the source also protects against violation of the attorney-client privilege in those cases where the defense attorney turns over evidence given to him by the defendant in the course of their relationship. See *State ex rel. Sowers v. Olwell,* 64 Wash.2d 828, 394 P.2d 681 (1964).

[25] See § 23.05(a)(1).

[26] Edward A. Tomlinson, *Constitutional Limitations on Prosecutorial Discovery,* 23 San Diego L.Rev. 923 (1986).

[27] See e.g., Colo.Rev.Stat. § 16–5–204(4)(I). Cf. *United States v. Alred,* 144 F.3d 1405 (11th Cir. 1998) (holding that post-indictment subpoenas are still permissible if necessary to determine whether others not indicted were involved in the same crime).

(b) Sixth Amendment Limitations

In addition to his Fifth Amendment argument, the defendant in *Nobles* argued that the court's order deprived him of his right to compulsory process (i.e., the right to call the investigator) and his right to effective confrontation of the prosecution's witnesses. This contention too the Court rejected: "The Sixth Amendment does not confer the right to present testimony free from the legitimate demands of the adversarial system; one cannot invoke the Sixth Amendment as a justification for presenting what might have been a half-truth." In effect, the Court held that once the defense indicated an intent to call the investigator to the stand and ask questions about statements that were contained in his report, it "waived" protection of those portions of the report.

The Court even more explicitly applied waiver analysis to the defendant's claim that the trial court's action denied him effective assistance of counsel and violated the work product doctrine by compromising his ability to investigate and prepare his defense. As to the Sixth Amendment claim that the disclosure contemplated by the trial court would "inhibit other members of the 'defense team' from gathering information essential to the effective preparation of the case," the Court stated: "The short answer is that the disclosure order resulted from respondent's voluntary election to make testimonial use of his investigator's report." Similarly, while the Court stated that the role of the work-product privilege is "even more vital" in the criminal justice system than it is in the civil system and must "protect material prepared by agents for the attorney as well as those prepared by the attorney himself," it concluded that the respondent, "by electing to present the investigator as a witness, waived the privilege with respect to matters covered in his testimony."

The Court's emphasis on waiver *at trial* suggests that the Sixth Amendment and the work product doctrine might protect against *pretrial* discovery of certain types of information, in particular those normally subsumed under the work product doctrine. In fact, most jurisdictions extend protection to "internal memoranda" prepared by either side.[28] But statements *within* those documents may still be discoverable prior to trial under the accelerated disclosure rules discussed above. And *Nobles* suggests that not only favorable statements, but also all other statements that help put those statements in context, would have to be surrendered.

Nobles notwithstanding, a strong argument can be made that discovery rules that require disclosure of statements (or the identities) of persons or the contents of reports the defense does *not* intend to use at trial violate the defendant's right to effective assistance of counsel or the work product doctrine. Some courts have so held.[29] However, the reasoning of these decisions would prevent disclosure only of information the defense developed in preparation for trial; it would not apply to documents or other tangible objects possessed by the defendant prior to being charged. Thus, the Sixth Amendment would not prohibit otherwise valid subpoenas for the latter items.[30]

---

[28] See, e.g., Fed.R.Crim.P. 16(b)(2).

[29] *State v. Williams,* 80 N.J. 472, 404 A.2d 34 (1979) (no discovery of statements not used); *United States v. Alvarez,* 519 F.2d 1036 (3d Cir. 1975) (expert psychiatrists); *State v. Mingo,* 77 N.J. 576, 392 A.2d 590 (1978) (expert reports).

[30] For a discussion of Fifth Amendment restrictions on such subpoenas, see § 24.02(a)(4).

(c) Reciprocity Limitations

At one time, virtually every jurisdiction had adopted the rule that the prosecution could not obtain discovery from the defense unless the defense first requested disclosure from the prosecution. But the clear trend today is to grant the prosecution independent discovery, unconditioned on any requests by the defense (although typically limited to the kinds of information the defense would be authorized to receive had it made a request).[31] The question thus arises whether reciprocity is constitutionally required or whether, instead, it is permissible for the prosecution to obtain information from the defense even when the defense refrains from requesting discovery.

The reciprocity idea apparently is based on a waiver notion; that is, the defense should be able to control its information until it waives that control by requesting information from the prosecution. But if the rationale for discovery is the avoidance of surprise and the thorough preparation of adversaries, then the prosecution should not be barred from obtaining information simply because the defense decides it does not need anything from the prosecution. Or, if the concern is that the defense will otherwise be unable to protect unfavorable information, protective orders are available. In short, independent discovery, as a general matter, would not seem violative of any constitutional provision, provided that, as applied, it does not infringe upon the defendant's Fifth or Sixth Amendment rights.

(d) Sanctions on Defense

The particular sanction to be imposed for violation of a discovery rule is usually left to the trial court's discretion and will not implicate constitutional issues. In *Taylor v. Illinois,*[32] however, the Supreme Court was confronted with the argument that the ultimate sanction of excluding evidence, when imposed on the defense, violates the defendant's right to present evidence on his behalf (under the Compulsory Process Clause of the Sixth Amendment). The trial court in *Taylor* had excluded the testimony of a defense witness who had not been listed prior to trial as required by the rules of discovery, despite counsel's awareness of his existence at least a week prior to trial. The Court found both that exclusion of evidence does not, per se, violate the Compulsory Process Clause, and then found the sanction in this case was appropriate.

The Court first noted that the right to present evidence is not absolute, pointing to its decision in *Nobles,* where exclusion was permitted because of the attorney's failure to cooperate at trial. The defendant in *Taylor* argued that this type of case was different, because the court had available to it a less drastic sanction—such as a continuance or disciplinary action against the attorney—that would still preserve the adversarial process emphasized in *Nobles.* But the Supreme Court noted that less drastic sanctions might also be less effective. Because a primary purpose of the discovery rules is to "minimize the risk that fabricated testimony will be believed," and because it is "reasonable to assume that there is something suspect about a defense witness who is

---

[31] At least 14 states require the defense to disclose names and addresses of all defense witnesses regardless of defense discovery requests, 12 states give the prosecution an independent right to obtain the statements of all defense witnesses, 16 states make documents and tangible objects independently available, and 22 states similarly allow discovery of expert reports. Mosteller, supra note 18, at 1580–82. Ohio, Texas and North Carolina provide even broader discovery, but only North Carolina provides true "open discovery," allowing the defense access to everything in the "files" of the prosecution and police agencies. See N.C. Stat. Ann. § 15A–901 et seq.

[32] 484 U.S. 400, 108 S.Ct. 646 (1988).

not identified until after the eleventh hour has passed," exclusion might be appropriate, particularly where, as here, the failure to list the witness was found to be "willful and blatant" by the trial judge.

The Court did not consider important the fact that allowing the unlisted witness to testify probably would not have prejudiced the prosecution in this case (because the trial judge, prior to ordering exclusion, had conducted a *voir dire* of the witness in the presence of the prosecutor). According to the Court, "[m]ore is at stake than possible prejudice to the prosecution;" also important is "the impact of this conduct on the integrity of the judicial process itself." Nor did the Court accept the argument of the three dissenters that the sins of the lawyer should not be visited on the client, since "it would be highly impracticable to require an investigation into the ... relative responsibility [of the attorney and the client] before applying the sanction of preclusion."

In a similar vein is *Michigan v. Lucas*,[33] where the Court permitted exclusion of a sexual assault victim's past sexual conduct with the defendant because the defendant failed to give notice of intent to use the evidence as required by state rule. Again noting that such a sanction is proportionate when the state seeks to protect against "willful misconduct" designed to obtain "a tactical advantage," the Court held that it did not violate the Sixth Amendment even though sanctions against the attorney and a continuance were available and even though, in contrast to *Taylor*, the evidence was clearly reliable.[34]

24.03   Discovery by the Defense

In the typical case, the defense is more in need of discovery than the prosecution. The government is usually the first on the crime scene, has quality investigative expertise, and possesses formidable financial resources. Operating on its own, the defense team, often court appointed, will normally not have the same access to evidence or the same ability to interpret it as the government. Because it helps equalize the contest between the state and the defendant, extensive discovery by the defense is seen by some as a particularly important aspect of the criminal justice system,[35] and could be said to be required by either the Due Process Clause, the Compulsory Process Clause, or the right to effective assistance of counsel.[36]

Yet a constitutional basis for extensive defense discovery has not developed. Illustrative is the Supreme Court's decision in *Cicenia v. La Gay*,[37] which held that, while it may be "better practice" to give the defense a record of the defendant's confession prior to trial, failing to do so does not violate due process. As discussed in the next section, the courts have recognized a constitutional right to exculpatory information. And, as discussed below, the prosecution is also required by the Due Process Clause to make reciprocal disclosure under some circumstances. But many jurisdictions remain cautious about permitting defense discovery of evidence beyond these minima. This is unfortunate, not only because it impairs defense preparation for plea negotiation and

---

[33]   500 U.S. 145, 111 S.Ct. 1743 (1991).

[34]   For further discussion of these cases, see § 28.06(c)(2).

[35]   Abraham Goldstein, *The State and the Accused: Balance of Advantage in Criminal Procedure*, 69 Yale L.J. 1149 (1960).

[36]   See, e.g., Peter Westen, *The Compulsory Process Clause*, 73 Mich.L.Rev. 71, 121–32 (1974).

[37]   357 U.S. 504, 78 S.Ct. 1297 (1958).

trial, but also because, to the extent the reciprocity doctrine operates, it limits prosecutorial discovery as well.

(a) Mandatory Reciprocal Disclosure by the Prosecution

In *Wardius v. Oregon,*[38] the Supreme Court struck down a notice-of-alibi statute which did not require, in return, that the prosecution notify the defense of any witnesses it intended to offer in rebuttal to the alibi:

> [I]n the absence of a strong showing of state interests to the contrary, discovery must be a two-way street. The State may not insist that trial be run as a "search for truth" so far as defense witnesses are concerned, while maintaining "poker game" secrecy for its own witnesses. It is fundamentally unfair to require a defendant to divulge the details of his own case while at the same time subjecting him to the hazard of surprise concerning refutation of the very pieces of evidence which he disclosed to the State.

This language would seem to extend beyond notice-of-alibi statutes to require prosecutorial disclosure of rebuttal witnesses whenever the state requires the defense to divulge its witnesses supporting a particular defense.

(b) Limitations on Defense Discovery

The result in *Wardius* is compelled under any concept of fairness. But where the defense is asking for information different in kind than it is willing to surrender to the prosecution, certain restrictions can apply. For instance, the Supreme Court has construed Rule 16 of the Federal Rules of Criminal Procedure to prohibit defense discovery beyond the rough reciprocity that *Wardius* establishes. In *United States v. Armstrong,*[39] the Court interpreted that rule's language granting the defendant information "material to the preparation of the defendant's defense" to mean only information relevant to defense efforts to combat the prosecution's case in chief. In the Court's words, when a claim is a "sword" meant to challenge the prosecution's conduct of the case, rather than a "shield" designed to "refute the Government's arguments that the defendant committed the crime charged," it may not form the basis for Rule 16 discovery. Under this definition, the Court concluded, the Rule does not authorize discovery of material relevant to a selective prosecution claim.[40] Other assertions which might be characterized as "sword" claims that do not trigger discovery under Rule 16 include vindictive prosecution allegations,[41] claims regarding the grand jury and jury selection process,[42] and speedy trial claims.[43]

Even access to discovery of information supporting a "shield" claim can be limited, as *Wardius* indicated, when "a strong showing of state interests" can be made. The state interests ranged against granting the defense substantial access to the prosecution's files were summarized in *State v. Eads:*[44]

---

[38]   412 U.S. 470, 93 S.Ct. 2208 (1973).

[39]   517 U.S. 456, 116 S.Ct. 1480 (1996).

[40]   While the Court went on to hold that this type of discovery might be permissible on non-statutory grounds, it required a "rigorous" threshold showing before the request could be granted. See § 21.03(a)(5).

[41]   See § 21.03(b).

[42]   See §§ 23.06(c); 27.03; 27.04.

[43]   See § 25.04(b) (discussing when government-produced delay may support a claim).

[44]   166 N.W.2d 766 (Iowa 1969).

(1) It would afford the defendant increased opportunity to produce perjured testimony and to fabricate evidence to meet the State's case; (2) witnesses would be subject to bribe, threat and intimidation; (3) since the State cannot compel the defendant to disclose ... evidence [protected by the Fifth Amendment], disclosure by the State would afford the defendant an unreasonable advantage at trial; and (4) disclosure is unnecessary in any event because of the other sources of information which defendant has under existing law.

These types of concerns have led some jurisdictions to curtail defense discovery in various ways. For instance, the reciprocity doctrine can be seen as a means of inhibiting scattershot discovery requests by the defense. Additionally, to prevent perjury and witness intimidation, many jurisdictions do not permit witness depositions for discovery purposes, but only to preserve testimony.[45] For the same reasons, the federal courts, pursuant to the so-called Jencks Act, prohibit disclosure of witness identities and statements until the witness has testified at trial,[46] a rule followed by many states.[47]

This last limitation on witness-related information is particularly damaging to the defense. It ensures that this information will be unavailable during plea negotiations. It hampers preparation for trial. And it disrupts the trial process, since the defense may need a continuance to analyze the pretrial statements obtained for the first time at trial. As noted in the introduction to this chapter, many states now have provisions calling for disclosure of such information prior to trial. And some courts have softened the impact of the Jencks Act and similar provisions by permitting pretrial disclosure when the defendant can show hardship would otherwise result.[48]

These efforts at broadening defense discovery are warranted, since the points made in *Eads* do not withstand close analysis. The danger that pretrial discovery will increase perjury is exaggerated: even with no pretrial discovery, the dishonest defendant will be able to change his story to fit the prosecution's facts, because he hears the prosecution's case before he puts on his own evidence. In any event, rather than shackling defense discovery in all cases, the best way to deal with the possibility of perjury is on a case-by-case basis through protective orders and the threat of perjury prosecution. Similarly, intimidation or bribery of witnesses not already known to the defendant is a rare event that can be inhibited through protective orders, letting the defense know the prosecution already has signed statements by the witness, and the threat of criminal and disciplinary action. The defendant's right to remain silent is a fundamental tenet of the accusatorial system which should not work to deny the defendant access to information; moreover, as the preceding section made clear,[49] the Fifth Amendment only prevents prosecution access to *self*-incriminating material possessed by the defense, and does not preclude discovery of most material the defense plans to use at trial. And finally, other sources of

---

[45] See, e.g., Fed.R.Crim.P. 15(a). But see, West's Fla.R.Crim.P. 3.220(d).

[46] 18 U.S.C.A. § 3500. See also, Fed.R.Crim.P. 16(a)(2) and 26.2. The type of "statement" to which the defense is entitled includes only those which are "signed or otherwise adopted or approved" by the witness. *Goldberg v. United States,* 425 U.S. 94, 96 S.Ct. 1338 (1976).

[47] See, e.g., N.Y.—McKinney's Crim.P.Law § 240.45(1)(a). Many of these states also bar *all* prosecution access to statements of defense witnesses, apparently due to the reciprocity notion, but this merely compounds the misery. See § 24.02(c).

[48] For an example of such a decision, and a good description of the injustice and inefficiency caused by the Jencks Act, see *United States v. Algie,* 503 F.Supp. 783 (E.D.Ky. 1980). The Sixth Circuit, construing the Jencks Act strictly, reluctantly reversed the district court. 667 F.2d 569 (6th Cir. 1982).

[49] See § 24.02(a).

"discovery," such as the preliminary hearing, the suppression hearing, or the bill of particulars, are neither dependable nor routine and, in any event, should not be manipulated when fairer, more straightforward discovery devices can be devised.[50]

Some have even argued that the defense's need for information is so great and the prosecution's so minimal that unconditional discovery by the defense is warranted. As explained by the American Bar Association's advisory committee on discovery:

> If disclosure to the accused promotes finality, orderliness, and efficiency in prosecution generally, these gains should not depend upon the possible capricious willingness of the accused to make reciprocal discovery.... Certainly, the usual reasons for denying disclosure to the accused—dangers of "perjury of intimidation of witness"—are not alleviated by forcing the defendant to make discovery, nor are they heightened by his failure to disclose.[51]

Given the fear that the prosecution would be unfairly disadvantaged if reciprocal disclosure were denied, the courts and legislatures have not supported the ABA's position.

24.04   The Constitutional Duty to Disclose Exculpatory Information

The discovery rules discussed previously are concerned primarily with ensuring that each party knows what the other side will present at trial. With a few exceptions, they do not require revelation of material unfavorable to the disclosing side. This pattern follows the paradigm of discovery in civil cases. But, in a departure from that paradigm, the Supreme Court has held that the Constitution requires the prosecution to reveal exculpatory information, a duty that contrasts sharply with the defense's ability, under the Fifth Amendment, to withhold incriminating items.[52] This section discusses the scope of this prosecutorial duty to disclose.

(a) The Duty to Reveal False Testimony

The broad duty to disclose exculpatory information was presaged by a series of decisions requiring the prosecutor to reveal perjured testimony by a prosecution witness. In *Mooney v. Holohan,*[53] the prosecutor allegedly procured perjured testimony to convict the defendant. The Court had no trouble finding that due process was violated when the government "has contrived a conviction through the pretense of a trial which in truth is but used as a means of depriving a defendant of liberty through a deliberate deception of court and jury by the presentation of testimony known to be perjured." And in *Alcorta v. Texas,*[54] the Court made clear that solicitation of perjured testimony was not necessary

---

[50]   Note that many courts specifically reject use of the preliminary hearing as a discovery device, citing the existence of more formal discovery mechanisms. See § 22.04(c).

[51]   ABA Standards Relating to Discovery and Procedure Before Trial, Commentary to § 1.2, at 45 (Approved Draft 1970). The ABA's new standards, however, call for mandatory reciprocal discovery. ABA Standards Relating to Discovery, § 11–2.2 and commentary 38–39 (3d ed. 1996).

[52]   Note that ethical guidelines may impose further obligations on the defense attorney. Compare, e.g., the cases described in § 24.04(a) with ABA Model Rules of Professional Conduct § 3.3(a)(4) (prohibiting lawyer from offering evidence he knows to be false and requiring correction of evidence he later finds to have been false).

[53]   294 U.S. 103, 55 S.Ct. 340 (1935).

[54]   355 U.S. 28, 78 S.Ct. 103 (1957).

in order to find a due process violation; even perjury that is purely the witness' must be corrected if discovered by the prosecutor.

In *Napue v. Illinois,*[55] the Court held that due process is violated not only by perjury concerning the facts of the case (as in *Mooney* and *Alcorta*), but also by fabrication relating to the credibility of the witness. In *Napue,* a witness falsely stated that the prosecutor had not promised him lenient treatment for his testimony. The Court concluded that the prosecutor's failure to correct this statement required reversal of the conviction, since "[t]he jury's estimate of the truthfulness and reliability of a given witness may well be determinative of guilt or innocence, and it is upon such subtle factors as the possible interest of the witness in testifying falsely that a defendant's life or liberty may depend." The facts in *Giglio v. United States*[56] were similar to *Napue* except that the promise of leniency came from another prosecutor, unbeknownst to the examining attorney. Even here, the Court required reversal, since "a promise made by one attorney must be attributed, for these purposes, to the Government." These cases expressed strong support for the notion that any use of false testimony requires reversal, at least when the testimony is important to the case.[57]

(b) The Materiality Test

In *Brady v. Maryland,*[58] the Court announced a rule that, in effect, subsumed the false testimony cases, by making unconstitutional the failure to provide any "exculpatory" information to the defendant. As Justice Douglas stated for the Court: "Society wins not only when the guilty are convicted but when criminal trials are fair; our system of the administration of justice suffers when any accused is treated unfairly." Thus, "the suppression by the prosecution of evidence favorable to an accused upon request violates due process where the evidence is material either to guilt or to punishment, irrespective of the good faith or bad faith of the prosecution."

In *Brady,* this test was applied to require reversal of the defendant's death sentence for murder. Prior to trial, Brady's attorney had requested that the prosecution provide the pretrial statements of Brady's co-defendant. While the prosecution did hand over most of the statements, it did not provide the portion in which the co-defendant had asserted that he committed the murder. This statement would have made no difference at trial, since co-defendants in a murder case were equally guilty under state law, regardless of who pulled the trigger. But, finding that this information could easily have affected the sentencing body, the Supreme Court required a new sentencing proceeding.

Several questions were left unanswered by *Brady,* including how "material" information must be before due process requires its disclosure, and whether the defense has to make a request for the information in order to trigger the prosecution's duty to disclose. In *United States v. Agurs,*[59] the Court clarified both of these points to some extent. In *Agurs,* the defendant had stabbed and killed a male companion with the latter's knife during a brief interlude at a motel. She pleaded self-defense, but was convicted of second degree murder. In arguing for reversal, the defense noted that the

---

[55]   360 U.S. 264, 79 S.Ct. 1173 (1959).

[56]   405 U.S. 150, 92 S.Ct. 763 (1972).

[57]   See also, *Giles v. Maryland,* 386 U.S. 66, 87 S.Ct. 793 (1967).

[58]   373 U.S. 83, 83 S.Ct. 1194 (1963).

[59]   427 U.S. 97, 96 S.Ct. 2392 (1976).

prosecutor had failed to disclose that the victim had a prior criminal record (including guilty pleas to charges of assault and carrying a deadly weapon).

The Supreme Court found that this information did not have to be disclosed under *Brady* because it was not "material" enough, which in turn depended in part on the fact that the defense made no request for it. Justice Stevens, who wrote the Court's opinion, divided the due process duty to disclose into three types. The first was represented by the *Mooney* line of cases. When the prosecutor relies on perjured testimony, he must disclose it if "there is any reasonable likelihood that the false testimony could have affected the judgment of the jury," i.e., most of the time. The second type of duty was represented by *Brady,* where the defense made a specific request for the allegedly exculpatory information. Here again disclosure should be the normal response, because a specific request puts the prosecution on notice that the evidence may be exculpatory. When there is a request, "it is reasonable to require the prosecutor to respond either by furnishing the information or by submitting the problem to the trial judge," and "the failure to make any response is seldom, if ever, excusable." Although Stevens did not explicitly say so, the materiality standard for these first two situations appeared similar to the standard the Court had earlier adopted for determining whether constitutional error is harmless in *Chapman v. California*, which looks at whether evidence would have created a reasonable doubt in the jury.[60]

The third situation occurs when the defense makes either no request (as in *Agurs*) or a general request for "all *Brady* material" or "anything exculpatory," requests that Stevens equated with no request. Here, Stevens stated, a conviction will be overturned for failure to provide information only if it creates a reasonable doubt in the mind of the trial judge as to the defendant's guilt. This standard apparently gives more leeway to the prosecutor than the *Chapman* standard, since it depends upon what the judge thinks about the defendant's guilt, not on how the jury would have voted had it had the evidence in front of it. Stevens seemed to believe this difference was justified because, in a no request situation, the prosecutor will have more difficulty deciding what evidence may be exculpatory.

Assuming there is a realistic difference between the two materiality tests developed in *Agurs,* that decision's emphasis on the existence of a specific request can be questioned, given the fact that the defense often has no idea what kind of information the prosecutor may possess. In the Court's next major decision interpreting *Brady,* *United States v. Bagley,*[61] this distinction was apparently eliminated. At the same time, the Court seemed to reject the *Chapman*/harmless error as the test of "materiality," and instead adopted a narrower definition of that central aspect of *Brady,* regardless of the type of information involved or the existence of a request.

In *Bagley,* there was a specific request for information about "any deals, promises or inducements made to [government] witnesses in exchange for their testimony." Yet the prosecution not only failed to inform the defense that such financial inducements had been made to two witnesses, it also forwarded affidavits from those witnesses that concluded with the statement that they were made without any threats or rewards or promises of reward. Nonetheless, five members of the Court strongly suggested there was no violation of *Brady,* applying a standard of whether "there is a reasonable

---

[60] 386 U.S. 18, 87 S.Ct. 824 (1967), discussed in § 29.05(c).

[61] 473 U.S. 667, 105 S.Ct. 3375 (1985).

probability that, had the evidence been disclosed to the defense, the result of the proceeding would be different."[62] Justice Blackmun, in an opinion joined by Justice O'Connor, explicitly equated this standard with that developed in *Agurs* for no request and general request situations. Three other members of the Court appeared to agree with this equation, and stated further that this standard "is sufficiently flexible to cover all instances of prosecutorial failure to disclose evidence favorable to the accused," including, apparently, the use of perjured testimony. Thus, after *Bagley,* the prosecutor is governed by the "reasonable probability" test in all situations; the "any reasonable likelihood" or harmless error test used in *Agurs* for false testimony and specific requests has been abandoned.

In dissent, Justice Marshall argued that the majority's test created an incentive for prosecutors "to gamble, to play the odds, and to take a chance that evidence will later turn out not to have been potentially dispositive." As Marshall noted, the government's legitimate interest in nondisclosure prior to trial is "minimal;" after trial, its interest in avoiding a retrial because of nondisclosure is greater, but should not be given so much weight that it encourages failure to disclose prior to trial.[63] The proper test, at least when the prosecutor has a sufficient idea of what the defense is seeking, should be the *Chapman*/harmless error standard, because it is more likely to encourage disclosure of information when there is any doubt as to its exculpatory nature and to ensure that the subsequent adjudication will be truly "fair."

The facts of *Bagley* illustrate the point. As the Court noted in *Napue,* "such subtle factors as the possible interest of the witness in testifying falsely" can affect the jury's determination. Thus, the prosecution should not only be required, as in *Napue,* to correct false testimony denying incentives to testify were offered, but also to provide information about such incentives. This is especially so when the defense has made a specific request, both because such a request indicates a belief that the information may be important and because a failure to respond will mislead the defense into believing that investigation (and cross-examination) is unnecessary on this point.[64] Although Blackmun's opinion recognized this latter problem, it contended that the "reasonable probability" test is flexible enough to take such possibilities into account. Although the case was remanded for further deliberations, Blackmun's intimation that due process was not violated in *Bagley* suggests otherwise.[65]

---

[62] In developing this standard, Blackmun relied on the rule for determining when government deportation of witnesses constitutes a denial of the right to present evidence, *United States v. Valenzuela-Bernal,* 458 U.S. 858, 102 S.Ct. 3440 (1982), discussed in § 28.06(b), and the rule for determining when effective assistance of counsel has been denied. *Strickland v. Washington,* 466 U.S. 668, 104 S.Ct. 2052 (1984), discussed in § 32.03(b).

[63] Cf. *United States v. Oxman,* 740 F.2d 1298 (3d Cir. 1984), judgment vac'd 473 U.S. 922, 105 S.Ct. 3550 (1985) (discussing "disturbing" prosecutorial tendency to withhold information because of later opportunity to argue, with the benefit of hindsight, that information was not "material."); See also *Turner v. United States,* ___ U.S. ___, 137 S.Ct. 1885 (2017), where the government conceded it withheld information pointing to other perpetrators (including one who committed similar crimes near the relevant crime scene), as well as impeachment evidence, but was able to convince the Court that the evidence was immaterial.

[64] Cf. *People v. Vilardi,* 76 N.Y.2d 67, 556 N.Y.S.2d 518, 555 N.E.2d 915 (1990) (rejecting *Bagley's* reasonable probability standard and adopting, as a matter of state law, a "reasonable possibility" definition of materiality when there is a specific request).

[65] Automatic disclosure of some types of impeachment evidence might deter witnesses from being completely forthcoming with the prosecutor. But even assuming this is a concern that should trump the defendant's (and the state's) interest in a fair trial, it does not apply in *Bagley,* where the impeachment evidence was a prosecutorial promise, not compromising statements by the witness.

The relatively narrow construction of the materiality rule in *Bagley* may have been subtly modified in *Kyles v. Whitley.*[66] Justice Souter's opinion in that case, joined by four other justices, seemed to construe liberally *Bagley's* requirement that the defendant show a reasonable probability that evidence suppressed by the prosecutor would have changed the trial outcome. Specifically, Souter stated that four aspects of the reasonable probability standard "bear emphasis." First, a "reasonable probability" does not require a preponderance of the evidence showing but rather, as the language suggests, something less. Nor does it require that the defendant show that, with the inclusion of the suppressed evidence, the remaining evidence renders the prosecution's case insufficient. Third, once the defendant has demonstrated a reasonable probability of a different outcome, the appellate court cannot find the failure to disclose harmless, since the reasonable probability test "necessarily entails the conclusion that the suppression must have had 'substantial and injurious effect or influence in determining the jury's verdict.' "[67] Finally, while the prosecution is not necessarily required to disclose each bit of evidence that might prove "helpful" to the defense, it "must be assigned the consequent responsibility to gauge the likely net effect of all such evidence and make disclosure when the point of 'reasonable probability' is reached."

Applying these observations to the facts of the case, the Court reversed Kyles' conviction. Although there were four eyewitnesses who testified that Kyles committed the murder at issue, the prosecutor failed to disclose to the defense: (1) the fact that the initial account of the "strongest" eyewitness described a perpetrator who looked more like the government's informant than Kyles; (2) that another eyewitness' account of the offense at trial was "vastly different" from his original account; (3) that many of the informant's statements about his and Kyles' actions near the time of the offense were contradictory; (4) that the informant was implicated in another murder, as well as other crimes committed in the same area as the murder charged against Kyles; and (5) various other facts conflicting with the prosecution's theory of the case. Justice Scalia's dissent vigorously argued that the government's case remained strong even after taking these various bits of evidence into account. Perhaps the concurring opinion of Justice Stevens, who was joined by Justices Ginsburg and Breyer, best explains why the defendant's position nonetheless attracted a majority. Stevens noted that the jury could not reach a verdict at the defendant's first trial, a fact which he thought "provides strong reason to believe the significant errors that occurred at the second trial were prejudicial." And he also pointed out that "cases in which the record reveals so many instances of the state's failure to disclose exculpatory evidence are extremely rare."

Two other cases illustrate the Court's application of the materiality standard in the capital sentencing context. In *Strickler v. Greene,*[68] the prosecution withheld information indicating that a witness who testified at both the defendant's trial and capital sentencing proceeding had initially experienced significant difficulty in recalling the events in question. The Court found that this suppression of information did not violate *Brady,* because the witness' testimony was largely cumulative and "did not relate to [the defendant's] eligibility for the death sentence," given the prosecution's decision not to rely on it during closing argument. In contrast, in *Banks v. Dretke,*[69] the prosecution's

---

[66]   514 U.S. 419, 115 S.Ct. 1555 (1995).

[67]   Citing *Brecht v. Abrahamson,* 507 U.S. 619, 113 S.Ct. 1710 (1993), a harmless error case discussed in § 33.02(f).

[68]   527 U.S. 263, 119 S.Ct. 1936 (1999).

[69]   540 U.S. 668, 124 S.Ct. 1256 (2004).

failure to disclose was in connection with a witness whose testimony, according to the Court, "was the centerpiece" of the prosecution's penalty phase case. The testimony of the witness, one Farr, was designed primarily to show Banks' dangerousness, an aggravating circumstance under the state's death penalty statute, by linking Banks, who otherwise had no known criminal history, to an alleged plan to commit robberies. Farr's testimony that Banks had offered to help Farr obtain a gun with which to commit robberies, and Farr's assertion that Banks had said he would "take care" of any trouble arising during the robberies, would have been significantly undercut, the Court concluded, had the jury known that Farr had been paid by the police to ask Banks for a gun. The facts that Banks had been convicted for shooting his victim three times to get his car, and had pistol-whipped a brother-in-law during a separate altercation, were not viewed as proof of dangerousness sufficient to make the *Brady* violation immaterial.

The Court has also made clear that, just as good faith on the part of the prosecutor normally does not affect materiality analysis (per its decision in *Giglio*),[70] neither does bad faith conduct. *Brady* itself stated that the rule it announced was aimed at assuring a fair trial, not at correcting prosecutorial misconduct. This point was reemphasized in *Smith v. Phillips*,[71] in which the Court refused to reverse a conviction by a jury that had included a juror who had actively pursued a job with the prosecutor's office throughout the trial. Noting that the trial judge had found no evidence of actual bias on the part of the juror, the Court stated that while it could not condone the failure of the prosecutor to discover and report the juror's activities in a timely fashion, "the touchstone of due process analysis [in *Brady*] cases is the fairness of the trial, not the culpability of the prosecutor."

(c) The Decisionmaker

Three different decisionmakers could make the materiality determination: defense counsel, the trial judge, or the prosecutor. Clearly, the defense attorney is the person best equipped to make the decision as to what is "material" to his case. But such an approach would subvert an important premise of *Brady:* that the prosecution need not turn over its entire file to the defense. The Supreme Court reiterated this premise in *Pennsylvania v. Ritchie*.[72] There, the Pennsylvania Supreme Court had ordered the state child welfare agency to provide defense counsel with files concerning the defendant's daughter, who was allegedly raped by the defendant; under the order, counsel would then make arguments in favor of disclosure at trial.[73] The Supreme Court reversed, holding that the "defendant's right to discover exculpatory evidence does not include the unsupervised authority to search through the Commonwealth's files." As the Court pointed out, "[s]ettled practice is to the contrary," particularly where, as here, confidentiality concerns are significant.

The Court in *Ritchie* did order that the case be remanded, with the suggestion that the trial judge review the files *in camera* and decide what information, if any, was material to the defendant's case. Apparently the Court felt this suggestion appropriate

---

[70]   See § 24.04(a). *Kyles* affirmed that "the individual prosecutor has a duty to learn of any favorable evidence known to the others acting on the government's behalf in the case, including the police."

[71]   455 U.S. 209, 102 S.Ct. 940 (1982).

[72]   480 U.S. 39, 107 S.Ct. 989 (1987).

[73]   The defendant argued that this procedure was required under the Compulsory Process Clause. Stating that the latter provision "provides no greater protections in this area than those afforded by due process," the Supreme Court analyzed the case under *Brady*.

because the file contained statements by the victim, as well as other possibly highly significant information. However, *Ritchie* did not hold, and most courts are reluctant to hold, that such *in camera* review *must* take place upon defense request. The typical holding is that the *Brady* rule "does not make it incumbent upon the trial judge to rummage through the file on behalf of the defendant."[74] In *Ritchie* itself, the Court stated in a footnote that the defendant "may not require the trial court to search through the . . . file without first establishing a basis for his claim that it contains material evidence."

As this language suggests, however, if the defendant is able to make a particularized showing that the prosecution may have exculpatory information, a hearing may be required. In *DeMarco v. United States*,[75] the Supreme Court directed that an evidentiary hearing be held on the defendant's claim that the prosecutor had made an undisclosed promise of leniency to a witness prior to his testimony, based on proof of certain remarks the prosecutor made during the sentencing proceeding. Upon being presented with this type of information, the Court concluded, the trial court should investigate the issue. Presumably, had the same remarks been made prior to trial, the defense could have obtained court intervention as well, if the prosecutor had not cooperated.

When the defense is unable to make such a showing that exculpatory information may exist, the prosecutor generally makes the decision on the materiality issue. This arrangement might not be troubling if, as recommended by the dissent in *Bagley*, the prosecutor resolves doubtful questions in favor of disclosure. But, for reasons discussed above, the majority opinion in *Bagley* is likely to encourage stinginess on the part of the prosecution, a stinginess that the Court's subsequent, more defendant-friendly decisions, all involving capital cases, may not dissipate in the typical case.[76]

(d) Timing of the Disclosure

As noted in the introduction to this chapter, many jurisdictions are moving toward pretrial disclosure of routine discovery items. But most courts hold that a *Brady* disclosure need not be made prior to trial. To some extent, this reluctance is based on the familiar fear that extensive pretrial disclosure might damage the adversary nature of the system.[77] Further, at least one court has contended that the materiality standard "can only be sensibly applied to the suppression of evidence throughout the trial."[78] Consistent with these rulings is the Supreme Court's decision in *United States v. Ruiz*,[79] which held that the prosecutor is not obligated to provide the defendant with impeachment evidence or information supporting an affirmative defense, at least when the defendant has waived the right to such evidence as part of a "fast-track" plea negotiation regime. However, *Ruiz* also intimated that evidence tending to establish "factual innocence" should be disclosed prior to conclusion of plea negotiations.

Most of the courts that have limited *Brady* to disclosure at trial do so not on conceptual grounds but in the belief that, on the facts of the case before them, the defense

---

[74] *United States v. Frazier*, 394 F.2d 258 (4th Cir. 1968), cert. denied 393 U.S. 984, 89 S.Ct. 457 (1968). See also, *United States v. Gonzalez*, 466 F.2d 1286 (5th Cir. 1972).

[75] 415 U.S. 449, 94 S.Ct. 1185 (1974).

[76] See Michael J. Sniffen, *Study Tells of Cases Tainted by Prosecutors: Thousands of Cases Affected by Misconduct, Researchers Say*, S.Fla. Sun Sentinel, June 26, 2003, at A4 (reporting study finding scores of prosecutorial misconduct cases involving withholding information).

[77] See, e.g., *United States v. Evans*, 454 F.2d 813 (8th Cir. 1972).

[78] *United States v. McPartlin*, 595 F.2d 1321 (7th Cir. 1979).

[79] 536 U.S. 622, 122 S.Ct. 2450 (2002), discussed in § 26.02(b)(2).

still had an opportunity to make use of any information revealed. In *United States v. Baxter*,[80] for example, the government's failure to supply the defense with certain evidence prior to trial did not constitute a denial of due process, because the defendants had at least two weeks prior to the conclusion of the trial to examine, evaluate, and introduce any evidence that had come to their attention. Similarly, in *United States v. Harris*,[81] the Third Circuit held that the disclosure of the prosecution's agreement to help one of its witnesses was made in "timely fashion" so long as such disclosure occurred before the conclusion of the witness' trial testimony.

Most of the courts that have not limited *Brady* to disclosure at trial focus on the importance of possibly exculpatory information to defense trial preparation. Illustrative is *Grant v. Alldredge*.[82] There, the government did not disclose until trial that an eyewitness had identified a photograph of someone other than the defendant as the perpetrator of the crime. After speculating that, armed with this information, the defense could have learned more about the identified person, the Second Circuit ordered a new trial, concluding that skilled counsel may have been able to induce a reasonable doubt in the minds of the jurors had it come by the information earlier in the proceedings.[83]

Unless there is fear of witness intimidation, information that is clearly "material" to the defendant's case under *Agurs* and *Bagley* should be disclosed early enough to allow the defense adequate preparation time to make use of it. Disclosure at trial will rarely meet this test. The courts' fear that pretrial disclosure will somehow disadvantage the prosecutor is exaggerated and contrary to the spirit of *Brady*.

An entirely different type of timing issue is whether the *Brady* right can be the basis for obtaining evidence for use in the post-conviction process. In *Dist. Att'y Third Judicial Circuit v. Osborne*,[84] the Court, in an opinion by Chief Justice Roberts, held that "*Brady* is the wrong framework" in this context because the defendant has already been legitimately convicted. Rather, the question is whether the state's procedure for obtaining discovery during post-conviction relief "offends some principle of justice so rooted in the traditions and conscience of our people as to be ranked as fundamental," or "transgresses any recognized principle of fundamental fairness in operation." In *Osborne*, a § 1983 suit, the plaintiff-prisoner wanted access to physical evidence that could be tested for DNA and prove his innocence, using testing procedures that did not exist at the time of his trial. The Alaska courts had denied him access on the grounds (which the state now conceded were erroneous) that the type of DNA testing he sought was available at the time of his trial and that this testing would not conclusively prove his innocence. The Supreme Court nonetheless concluded that because Alaska's judiciary grants convicted offenders the right to raise post-conviction claims based on newly-discovered evidence, including those based on DNA testing, Alaska's post-conviction procedures were not deficient under the procedural due process test described above. The majority also rejected Osborne's argument for a "free-standing" substantive due process right to access DNA evidence, because such a claim would be tantamount to recognizing that state defendants are entitled to federal relief solely on innocence grounds (a type of

---

[80]   492 F.2d 150 (9th Cir. 1973), cert. denied 416 U.S. 940, 94 S.Ct. 1945 (1974).

[81]   498 F.2d 1164 (3d Cir. 1974), cert. denied 419 U.S. 1069, 95 S.Ct. 655 (1974).

[82]   498 F.2d 376 (2d Cir. 1974).

[83]   See also *United States v. Donatelli*, 484 F.2d 505 (1st Cir. 1973).

[84]   557 U.S. 52, 129 S.Ct. 2308 (2009).

claim that Court has yet to recognize[85]), and because recognition of such a right would "short-circuit what looks to be a prompt and considered legislative response" to issues raised by DNA technology, as evidenced by the fact that only a "handful" of states other than Alaska have no statute dealing with them.

Justice Stevens' dissent, joined by three others, pointed out that Osborne's ability to challenge his conviction based on newly discovered evidence was useless unless he could get access to the DNA. Thus Justice Stevens advocated following the test the Ninth Circuit developed in *Osborne*, which provided that the defendant is entitled to evidence from the state "where [such] evidence was used to secure his conviction, the DNA testing is to be conducted using methods that were unavailable at the time of trial and are far more precise than the methods that were then available, such methods are capable of conclusively determining whether Osborne is the source of the genetic material, the testing can be conducted without cost or prejudice to the State, and the evidence is material to available forms of post-conviction relief."

The state in *Osborne* had also argued that procedural due process claims of the type raised in that case could only be heard through a writ of habeas corpus, because such claims challenge the validity of the petitioner's custody. But because the *Osborne* Court proceeded directly to the merits of the state's claim, this jurisdictional issue was left unresolved in that case. In *Skinner v. Switzer*,[86] the state made the same argument, but six members of the Court, in an opinion by Justice Ginsburg, held that when the petitioner is challenging a DNA statute facially, rather than a state court decision applying that statute, he may proceed under § 1983 if the claim is framed in procedural due process terms. In this circumstance, Justice Ginsburg reasoned, granting relief would only trigger a DNA test; it would not *immediately* terminate, accelerate release from, or reduce his custody and thus would not be the type of case that could only be heard on habeas.[87] The Court distinguished Skinner's petition from a 1983 petition challenging a *Brady* decision (the type of claim brought in *Osborne*) because the latter claim depends on a determination of whether withholding information would have affected the outcome of trial,[88] and granting relief thus *does* immediately affect whether the petitioner remains in custody.

Skinner provides a second forum for seeking DNA testing. But *Osborne* suggests that success on the merits will still be difficult, and *Skinner* did not indicate otherwise. Skinner had asserted that Texas' DNA law violated due process by prohibiting testing in cases where trial counsel claims to have intentionally avoiding such testing due to concern it might implicate the defendant. The Court remanded the case to the lower courts rather than resolve this issue.

24.05   The Constitutional Duty to Preserve Evidence

Obviously related to the prosecutorial duty to disclose exculpatory evidence is the duty to preserve such evidence for possible use by the defendant. However, as Justice

---

[85]   See § 34.02(d).

[86]   562 U.S. 521, 131 S.Ct. 1289 (2011).

[87]   Compare *Wilkinson v. Dotson*, 544 U.S. 74, 125 S.Ct. 1242 (2005) (permitting suit challenging administrative process for making parole decision because original conviction not challenged) and *Heck v. Humphrey*, 512 U.S. 477, 114 S.Ct. 2364 (1994) (prohibiting damages suit for illegal arrest and conviction until after conviction has been successfully challenged on federal habeas or in state court).

[88]   For a discussion of *Brady* analysis, see § 24.04(b).

Marshall pointed out for the Court in *California v. Trombetta,*[89] when evidence has been destroyed, not only is its exculpatory value more difficult to evaluate, but a decision in favor of the defendant will bar further prosecution rather than, as in the typical *Brady* situation, merely call for a new trial with the suppressed evidence. Thus, *Trombetta* held, when the defendant makes the claim that exculpatory evidence was destroyed, he has a heavier burden then in the typical *Brady* case. He must not only show that the evidence might have been "expected to play a significant role in the suspect's defense," and that it was of "such a nature that the defendant would be unable to obtain comparable evidence by other reasonably available means," but he must also show that the failure to preserve the evidence resulted from "official animus toward [the defendant] or . . . a conscious effort to suppress exculpatory evidence." This latter requirement obviously departs from the *Brady* standard, which considered prosecutorial intent irrelevant.

In *Trombetta* the state failed to preserve a breath sample taken by police from a suspected drunk driver and tested by them on an instrument that analyzes breath-alcohol levels. The California Court of Appeal ruled that due process required police officers to "establish and follow rigorous and systematic procedures to preserve the captured evidence or its equivalent for the use of the defendant." But a unanimous Supreme Court rejected this rule and found that the defendant here was able to demonstrate neither exculpatory value nor official animus. According to the Court, tests of the breath samples by the defendant would normally merely confirm the results obtained by the state; if inaccuracies in the state's results did occur, they could be shown by other means, such as proof that the machine malfunctioned or that the officer who administered the test erred in operating the machine. Nor was there evidence the police acted in bad faith when they destroyed the breath samples; rather they did so according to routine practice. While the *Trombetta* Court considered the absence of bad faith relevant, it appeared to put the most stress on the failure of the defendant to prove the evidence destroyed had a unique exculpatory value. In *Arizona v. Youngblood,*[90] however, the Court held that "unless a criminal defendant can show bad faith on the part of the police, failure to preserve potentially useful evidence does not constitute due process of law." Chief Justice Rehnquist, writing for the Court, justified this ruling on two grounds. First, he noted, as had the *Trombetta* Court, "the treacherous task of divining the import of materials whose contents are unknown and, very often, disputed." Second, he expressed an "unwillingness to read the 'fundamental fairness' requirement of the Due Process Clause . . . as imposing on the police an undifferentiated and absolute duty to retain and to preserve all material that might be of conceivable evidentiary significance in a particular prosecution." Thus, the behavior of the police now appears to be the key issue in preservation of evidence cases, at least when there is doubt as to the exculpatory significance of the lost or destroyed evidence.[91]

In *Youngblood,* the defendant was convicted of sexual assault of a ten-year-old boy. On appeal the defendant argued that the state's failure to perform tests of semen samples taken from the victim shortly after they were obtained and to refrigerate the boy's clothing (in order to preserve the semen on it), violated due process. Experts at trial

---

[89]   467 U.S. 479, 104 S.Ct. 2528 (1984).

[90]   488 U.S. 51, 109 S.Ct. 333 (1988).

[91]   The Court reiterated this point in *Illinois v. Fisher,* 540 U.S. 544, 124 S.Ct. 1200 (2004), where the Court found no due process violation when cocaine that had been tested was destroyed despite a pending discovery request, because the destruction occurred "in good faith and in accord with . . . normal practice" (and during a ten to eleven-year delay of adjudication caused by the defendant's escape from custody).

had testified that prompt tests might have exonerated the defendant had they been performed. But the Supreme Court found that at most the failure to preserve and test the semen samples was "negligent." In a concurring opinion, Justice Stevens emphasized the latter point, asserting that the interest of the police and the prosecution in preserving the evidence during the investigation phase of a case is "at least as great" as the accused's. He also noted that the defense attorney had emphasized the state's failure to preserve the evidence at trial, and that the court had told the jury that if it found the state "had allowed [the evidence] to be lost or destroyed," it could infer the evidence was exculpatory.

In dissent, Justice Blackmun rejected the Court's focus on police behavior. He asserted that "it makes no sense to ignore the fact that a defendant has been denied a fair trial because the State allowed evidence that was material to the defense to deteriorate beyond the point of usefulness, simply because police were inept rather than malicious." He also questioned the ability of the courts to determine when police have in fact acted in bad faith, as opposed to recklessly or negligently. Instead he proposed the following test: "where no comparable evidence is likely to be available to the defendant, police must preserve physical evidence of a type that they reasonably should know has the potential, if tested, to reveal immutable characteristics of the criminal, and hence to exculpate a defendant charged with crime." On the facts of *Youngblood*, Blackmun argued that this test was met; he also noted that the only evidence implicating the defendant was the testimony of the ten-year old victim.[92]

24.06 Conclusion

Pretrial disclosure of information can facilitate preparation for trial, avoid surprise, and promote efficiency. It may also serve to equalize an investigative process normally weighted in favor of the state. The following observations can be made about statutory and constitutional pretrial disclosure rules.

(1) The typical jurisdiction at a minimum permits defense discovery of the defendant's statements in the prosecutor's possession, as well as documents, tangible objects and test results in the prosecution's possession that it intends to use at trial and are not work product, on condition that the defense reciprocate with like items (other than the defendant's statements) which it intends to introduce at trial. The defense is also typically entitled to any pretrial statements of government witnesses either at the time they testify or at some earlier point.

(2) Although the Fifth Amendment generally protects against compelled disclosure of incriminating information from the defendant, the defendant may be compelled to give notice of witnesses he intends to call in support of an alibi defense, so long as the prosecution is also required to disclose rebuttal witnesses. This accelerated disclosure rationale probably also permits requiring the defendant to reveal most other evidence he plans to use at trial. Moreover, neither the Fifth nor Sixth Amendment permits the defendant to withhold witness statements, other than his own, the existence of which the prosecution is aware and which might assist in challenging trial statements by the witness. However, the Sixth Amendment may prevent pretrial disclosure of the identity of, or statements from, persons the defendant does not plan to use at trial.

---

[92] Fifteen years after the decision Youngblood was exonerated through DNA evidence. Barbara Whitaker, *DNA Frees Inmate Years After Justice Rejected Plea*, N.Y. Times, Aug. 11, 2000, at A12.

(3)   In addition to the state's statutory obligations outlined in (1), the Due Process Clause imposes a limited duty upon the state to provide the defense with any other information "material" to its case. Specifically, the duty is violated if: (a) the prosecutor fails, intentionally or otherwise, to disclose information that is "exculpatory" in the sense that, had the information been disclosed to the defense, there is a reasonable probability that the result of the proceeding would have been different; or (b) the state intentionally and in bad faith destroys evidence possessing an exculpatory value apparent before the evidence was destroyed and of such a nature that the defendant would be unable to obtain comparable evidence by other reasonably available means. In the post-conviction process, a state's procedure for obtaining discovery is unconstitutional only if it offends some fundamental principle of justice; proof that the sought-after evidence is exculpatory, by itself, does not meet this test.

(4)   It is normally up to the prosecutor to decide whether particular information should be disclosed under the standards described in (3) above, although a colorable claim that he possesses exculpatory information should require an *in camera* perusal of the prosecutor's files by the trial court. If it is decided information should be disclosed, the best practice will normally be to do so prior to trial in order to permit the defense adequate time to prepare its case, although many courts have sanctioned disclosure at trial so long as the defendant has some time to evaluate the evidence. In the plea bargaining context, the Due Process clause at most requires the prosecutor to disclose information that tends to show the defendant's "factual innocence."

BIBLIOGRAPHY

Baer, Miriam H. Timing *Brady*. 115 Colum. L. Rev. 1 (2015).

Capra, Daniel J. Access to Exculpatory Evidence: Avoiding the *Agurs* Problems of Prosecutorial Discretion and Retrospective Review. 53 Ford.L.Rev. 391 (1984).

Cassidy, R. Michael. Plea Bargaining, Discovery, and the Intractable Problem of Impeachment Disclosures. 64 Vand. L. Rev. 1429 (2011).

Douglass, John G. Balancing Hearsay and Criminal Discovery. 68 Fordham L.Rev. 2097 (2000).

Feldman, Steven W. The Work Product Rule in Criminal Practice and Procedure. 50 U.Cin.L.Rev. 495 (1981).

Garrett, Brandon. Big Data and Due Process. 99 Cornell L. Rev. 207 (2014).

Garrie, Daniel B. and Gelb, Daniel K. E-Discovery in Criminal Cases: A Need for Specific Rules. 43 Suffolk U. L.Rev. 393 (2010).

Green, Bruce A. Federal Criminal Discovery Reform: A Legislative Approach. 64 Mercer L. Rev. 639 (2013).

Henning, Peter J. Defense Discovery in White Collar Criminal Cases. 15 Ga.St.L.Rev. 601 (1999).

Imwinkelreid, Edward J. The Applicability of the Attorney-Client Privilege to Non-Testifying Experts. 68 Wash.U.L.Q. 19 (1990).

Mosteller, Robert P. Exculpatory Evidence, Ethics, and the Road to the Disbarment of Mike Nifong: The Critical Importance of Full Open-File Discovery. 15 Geo. Mason L. Rev. 257 (2008).

____. Discovery Against the Defense: Tilting the Adversarial Balance. 74 Cal.L.Rev. 1567 (1986).

Podgor, Ellen S. Criminal Discovery of Jencks Witness Statements: Timing Makes a Difference. 15 Ga.St.U.L.Rev. 651 (1999).

Prosser, Mary. Reforming Criminal Discovery: Why Old Objections Must Yield to New Realities. 2006 Wisc.L.Rev. 541.

Serota, Michael. Stare Decisis and the *Brady* Doctrine. 5 Harv. L. & Pol'y Rev. 415 (2011).

Slobogin, Christopher. Discovery by the Prosecution in the United States: A Balancing Approach. 36 Criminal Law Quarterly 423 (1994).

Symposium. New Perspectives on *Brady* and Other Disclosure Obligations: What Really Works. 31 Cardozo L. Rev. 1943 (2010).

Tomlinson, Edward A. Constitutional Limitations on Prosecutorial Discovery. 23 San Diego L.Rev. 923 (1986).

Uphoff, Rodney. The Physical Evidence Dilemma: Does ABA Standard 4–4.6 Offer Appropriate Guidance? 62 Hastings L.J. 1177 (2011).

Westen, Peter. Order of Proof: An Accused's Right to Control the Timing and Sequence of Evidence in His Defense. 66 Cal. L.Rev. 935 (1978).

Chapter 25

THE RIGHT TO SPEEDY TRIAL

25.01   Introduction

The right to speedy trial is explicitly guaranteed by the Sixth Amendment[1] and is applicable to the states through the Fourteenth Amendment.[2] In most jurisdictions, it is also given fairly detailed statutory implementation.[3]

The defendant's interest in securing a speedy trial was first articulated by the Supreme Court in *United States v. Ewell*.[4] There the Court noted that a prompt trial: (1) prevents undue incarceration; (2) minimizes the anxiety accompanying public accusation; and (3) prevents impairment of the defendant's case due to delay. In *Barker v. Wingo*,[5] the Court elaborated on these points. It noted that if the defendant is detained, the time spent in jail disrupts family life and employment, and hinders the defendant's ability to gather evidence, contact witnesses, and otherwise prepare his case. For defendants on pretrial release, the denial of a speedy trial is less oppressive, but, given the possibility of conditional restraints on liberty, can also result in loss of employment or difficulty in finding work. In either case, noted *Barker*, delay in resolving criminal charges increases the drain on resources, the constraints on associating with others, and the exposure to public obloquy. Most importantly, whether the defendant is in or out of jail, delay may lead to loss of exculpatory evidence: witnesses may die or their memories fade, and tangible evidence may disappear.

Society too has an interest in prompt adjudication, an interest that occasionally may run counter to the defendant's interests. In *Barker* the Court articulated a number of reasons why society may desire speedy disposition of criminal cases, only one of which is directly associated with concern over the defendant's welfare. First, the Court noted, ensuring speedy trials reduces the likelihood of crimes being committed by those who are free on pretrial release programs. A second concern is the potential damage to the criminal justice system when delay weakens the prosecution's case and a plea bargain or dismissal results. Thirdly, to the extent that rehabilitative measures are put off by lengthy pretrial delays, the chances for success are diminished. Finally, there is substantial financial cost and administrative burden associated with lengthy pretrial detention. Indeed, it is probable that the impetus behind speedy trial legislation comes as much from fiscal concerns as it does from a desire to protect the defendant's interests.

Whether the state may *force* a speedy trial on a defendant, as is possible with other Sixth Amendment rights such as the right to jury trial,[6] is not clear. But it should not be overlooked that the accused may suffer from a trial that takes place too quickly. The defendant must be given sufficient time to prepare his case. That this need is sometimes

---

[1]   The Sixth Amendment to the United States Constitution reads in relevant part: "In all criminal prosecutions, the accused shall enjoy the right to a speedy and public trial. . . ."

[2]   *Klopfer v. North Carolina,* 386 U.S. 213, 87 S.Ct. 988 (1967).

[3]   See § 25.05.

[4]   383 U.S. 116, 86 S.Ct. 773 (1966).

[5]   407 U.S. 514, 92 S.Ct. 2182 (1972).

[6]   See § 27.02(g)(2).

ignored is borne out by the history of the "mass-production" misdemeanor courts.[7] As the Supreme Court put it in *Ewell*: "The essential ingredient is orderly expedition and not mere speed."

The next three sections of this chapter discuss three aspects of the constitutional right to speedy trial: (1) when it attaches; (2) the appropriate remedy for its violation; and (3) the criteria to be considered in deciding whether the right has been violated. The final section examines statutory attempts to implement the speedy trial ideal, focusing in particular on the Federal Speedy Trial Act.

25.02   When the Right Is Implicated

(a)   The Post-Accusation Rule

In *United States v. Marion,*[8] the defendants moved to dismiss the indictment against them on speedy trial grounds, claiming that the government had known of their identities for three years prior to the indictment. The Supreme Court rejected their claim, holding that the constitutional guarantee of a speedy trial is applicable only after a person has been "accused" of a crime. According to the Court, an accusation for this purpose does not have to be by way of indictment, information or formal charge, but must at least involve "the actual restraints imposed by arrest and holding to answer on a criminal charge." This result followed from the Sixth Amendment's wording (guaranteeing a right to speedy trial in all "criminal *prosecutions*") as well as the fact that the detention, anxiety, and public obloquy that the right is designed to avoid generally do not occur until this point. The Court also noted that, traditionally, statutes of limitations are designed to prevent the prejudice that might flow from pre-accusation delay.

Even after arrest, the defendant must *remain* charged for the right to speedy trial to be implicated. This rule was established in *United States v. MacDonald,*[9] where almost four years of delay occurred between the dismissal of the first charges against the defendant and reindictment on the same charges. Analogizing to the facts of *Marion,* the Court held, 5–4, that "[f]ollowing dismissal of charges, any restraint on liberty, disruption of employment, strain on financial resources, and exposure to public obloquy, stress and anxiety is no greater than it is upon anyone openly subject to a criminal investigation." During the hiatus between the charges, MacDonald had been "free to go about his affairs, to practice his profession, and to continue his life," and thus could not claim Sixth Amendment protection for that period.

In *United States v. Loud Hawk,*[10] the Court held, in another 5–4 decision, that the time period between dismissal of an indictment and its reinstatement should not be considered even if, during that time, the government is pursuing an appeal of the dismissal. Again, because the defendants had been unconditionally released during this period, the Court held that a 46-month period between dismissal and the retrial that followed an appellate court decision in the prosecution's favor was irrelevant to speedy trial analysis. The mere fact that the government's desire to prosecute was a matter of

---

7   See Charles Whitebread, Mass Production Justice and the Constitutional Ideal (1969); Alexandra Natapoff, *Misdemeanors*, 85 S.Cal. L.Rev. 1313 (2012).

8   404 U.S. 307, 92 S.Ct. 455 (1971).

9   456 U.S. 1, 102 S.Ct. 1497 (1982).

10   474 U.S. 302, 106 S.Ct. 648 (1986).

public record did not constitute actual restraint under *Marion*. In dissent, Justice Marshall pointed out that here, unlike in *Marion* and *MacDonald,* the defendants did not have the protection against prolonged pre-accusation delay that is provided by the statute of limitations, since the statute was tolled by the appeal. In further contrast to those cases, the trial court here had the authority, at any time during the appeal, to impose conditions on the defendants' release.

The majority's result is also contrary to the Court's pre-*Marion* decision of *Klopfer v. North Carolina,*[11] in which the Court held that a prosecutorial *nolle prosequi* does not terminate the period of time to be considered for speedy trial purposes. The *nolle prosequi* device is not a dismissal, in that the defendant remains formally accused and can be brought to trial at the whim of the prosecution throughout the time it is in effect. But, functionally, the defendants in *Loud Hawk* were in the same position. In neither type of case is the defendant under any "actual restraint" or subject to anxiety other than that associated with awaiting the outcome of a criminal justice decision (by the prosecutor or the appellate court). At the same time, in both cases, the defendants were the focus not merely of an investigation but of a formal prosecution, a fact which should implicate the Sixth Amendment.

While the Court has been unwilling to apply the Speedy Trial Clause when no charges are pending, it has also held that, when charges are pending, the Clause is triggered even if the defendant does not know about them and is thus not restrained in any way. This was the unusual situation in *Doggett v. United States,*[12] in which the Court upheld, 5–4, the defendant's speedy trial claim. Doggett had left the country just prior to government attempts to arrest him. Apparently unaware that an indictment on drug dealing charges had been issued against him, he returned to the country two and one-half years later, found a job, and was carrying on a law-abiding life when the government discovered his location through a routine computer check and arrested him 8 and one-half years after the indictment.

In holding that this entire period counted for purposes of speedy trial analysis despite the absence of restraint on the defendant, the majority, in an opinion by Justice Souter, distinguished *Marion, MacDonald,* and *Loudhawk* on the ground that those cases "support nothing beyond the principle . . . that the Sixth Amendment right of the accused to a speedy trial has no application beyond the confines of a formal criminal prosecution." This construction of the caselaw clearly undermines the "actual restraint" rule the Court had been developing as the test for when the Speedy Trial Clause applies. But, in defense of its divergent approach, the majority noted that the Clause is meant to protect against not only pretrial detention and the anxiety associated with criminal charges (effects the defendant in *Doggett* obviously could not claim), but also impairment of the defendant's case. This latter form of prejudice, the majority concluded, must be measured from the time the "criminal prosecution" to which the Sixth Amendment refers begins.

Although, after *Doggett,* arrest or accusation alone triggers the Speedy Trial Clause, it is unlikely this rule will affect the outcome of many cases beyond those which would also implicate the Clause under an actual restraint rule. Defendants are rarely unaware they have been indicted for any length of time, and in those situations in which they do

---

[11]   386 U.S. 213, 87 S.Ct. 988 (1967).

[12]   505 U.S. 647, 112 S.Ct. 2686 (1992).

know of the charges but evade restraint by avoiding arrest, the resulting delay will be their fault and thus unlikely to help a speedy trial claim.[13] *Doggett* is likely to have an independent impact only in those rare cases where, like *Doggett* itself, the defendant does not know about the charges for a prolonged period, or in cases where the defendant is aware of the indictment and takes no evasive action, but the government makes no effort to effectuate arrest.

The Court has also held that the speedy trial right is not implicated by delay between conviction and sentencing. In *Betterman v. Montana*,[14] the defendant was jailed for over 14 months while awaiting sentencing, a delay not attributable to the defense. Nonetheless, a unanimous Court held that the speedy trial right "loses force upon conviction," because it is meant to promote the presumption of innocence, avoid lengthy pretrial incarceration, lessen the anxiety associated with public accusation, and limit the effects of delay on the ability to mount a defense. Further, if applied in the post-conviction setting, the remedy for a violation—vacation of the conviction—would be an "unjustified windfall."

(b) Pre-Accusation Delay

As *Marion* noted, statutes of limitations may require the state to bring charges within a certain time after an offense. The statute varies by jurisdiction and charge (with the misdemeanor limitation usually falling between one to five years, while the limit for felonies typically varies between three to ten years). Usually, very serious crimes, such as murder, have no limitation period.[15] Like the speedy trial right, these statutes are designed to ensure that prosecutions are based on reasonably "fresh" evidence.

Marion also recognized, however, that these statutes might not provide sufficient protection against prejudicial pre-accusation delay, in which case due process might be implicated. In the later decision of *United States v. Lovasco*,[16] the Court affirmed that, even if the relevant limitations period has not expired, the Due Process Clause is violated if the delay transgresses "the community's sense of fair play and decency." At the same time, the Court's application of this due process right to the facts of *Lovasco* indicated that it will rarely lead to dismissal of a charge.

In *Lovasco,* two material witnesses died during an eighteen-month delay between the time the government developed sufficient evidence to indict the defendants and the actual indictment. The apparent reason for the delay was a desire to obtain more evidence, even though little new evidence was in fact obtained. The Court held that because thorough investigation can assure against unwarranted prosecutions and relieves the courts of trying insubstantial claims, the government is not obligated to file formal charges as soon as it has probable cause, or even when it has "evidence sufficient to establish guilt." Rather, investigative delay will be unconstitutional only if it is intended "to gain tactical advantage over the accused," or is carried out "in reckless disregard of circumstances . . . suggesting that there existed an appreciable risk that delay would impair the ability to mount an effective defense."

---

[13] See § 25.04(b).

[14] ___ U.S. ___, 136 S.Ct. 1609 (2016).

[15] See West's Fla.S.A.Stat. § 775.15 for an example of typical limitations.

[16] 431 U.S. 783, 97 S.Ct. 2044 (1977).

Lovasco's due process test—requiring both prejudice to the defendant's case *and* prosecutorial bad faith—is not only unduly stringent but incomplete. Analogous to speedy trial analysis of post-accusation delay, an important aspect of pre-accusation delay is the extent to which it subjects the individual to the "public obloquy" to which *Barker* refers. A person under public investigation can suffer as much damage to reputation and financial and occupational interests as an arrested person. It would be preferable to allow the individual under investigation (including persons in MacDonald's position, where charges have been dismissed) to force the prosecution either to arrest or to announce it is foregoing prosecution within a reasonable period of time after an investigation becomes public knowledge.

25.03   The Dismissal Remedy

The sole remedy recognized for violation of the constitutional right to speedy trial is dismissal, a fact that has important consequences for the scope of the right. In *Strunk v. United States,*[17] the defendant was found guilty of interstate transportation of a stolen vehicle after a ten-month delay between indictment and arraignment. On appeal, the Seventh Circuit Court of Appeals held that the defendant had been denied a speedy trial, but went on to hold that the extreme remedy of dismissal was not warranted, since no loss of evidence had been alleged by the defendant. The case was remanded to the district court for reduction of the defendant's sentence by 259 days to compensate for the unnecessary delay between indictment and arraignment. The United States Supreme Court reversed, holding that when a defendant has been denied a speedy trial, dismissal must remain the *only* possible remedy. The Court based its decision on the rationale that failure to afford a defendant a speedy trial, unlike other guarantees of the Sixth Amendment such as public trial, an impartial jury or compulsory service, cannot be cured by granting a new trial. In particular, the Court noted, the prolonged "emotional stress" suffered while awaiting trial and the possible adverse effect on rehabilitation cannot be rectified through a new proceeding.

As the next section makes clear, the severity of the dismissal remedy, and the concern that it will allow dangerous criminals freedom on a technicality, has made courts loathe to find a deprivation of the speedy trial right in all but the most extreme circumstances. One commentator has contended that the dismissal remedy has converted the speedy trial right from the right of any criminal defendant to have a speedy trial into the right of a few defendants—those most egregiously denied a speedy trial— to have the criminal charges against them dismissed.[18] A more flexible approach would make the remedy depend on which of the three interests protected by the speedy trial right is violated: release if prolonged detention is the concern, dismissal without prejudice to the prosecution's ability to reinstate charges if the public obloquy associated with formal charges is the concern, and outright dismissal only if prejudice to the defendant's case has occurred.

25.04   The Constitutional Criteria

The Supreme Court's most comprehensive treatment of the Sixth Amendment's speedy trial guarantee came in *Barker v. Wingo.*[19] In that case, the defendant did not

---

[17]   412 U.S. 434, 93 S.Ct. 2260 (1973).

[18]   Anthony Amsterdam, *Speedy Criminal Trial: Rights and Remedies*, 27 Stanford L.Rev. 525 (1975).

[19]   407 U.S. 514, 92 S.Ct. 2182 (1972).

explicitly raise his speedy trial right until the prosecution had asked for the last of sixteen continuances, which had stretched over five and one-half years from July, 1958 to October, 1963. The delay, all of which was countable under *Marion,* had resulted from the prosecution's repeated attempts to convict Barker's co-defendant (who would otherwise have been able to claim the privilege against self-incrimination when asked to testify against Barker) and, following that conviction in February, 1963, the illness of the chief investigating officer (a key witness). In finding that the defendant's right to speedy trial had not been violated despite the extremely long delay, the Supreme Court articulated a four-factor balancing test to be used in determining whether the right to a speedy trial has been denied:

> (1) the length of the delay; (2) the reason for the delay (e.g. whether the defense or prosecution caused the delay and, if the latter, the degree of good faith effort expended in bringing the case to trial as soon as possible); (3) whether and when the defendant asserted his right; and (4) whether any actual prejudice to the defendant resulted from the delay due to destruction or staleness of evidence, oppressive pretrial incarceration or the creation of excessive anxiety.

None of these factors are to be considered determinative; they are to be balanced against one another in deciding whether the delay is unconstitutional.[20]

(a) Length of Delay

In *Doggett v. United States,*[21] the Supreme Court suggested that a delay of one year might be "presumptively prejudicial" and trigger judicial review. Nonetheless, as *Barker* indicates, the length of the delay can be quite long without violating the Constitution. In *United States v. Loud Hawk,*[22] the delay was two years longer than that in *Barker*— seven and one-half years[23]—and yet the Court still found no violation of the speedy trial right. In *United States v. Eight Thousand Eight Hundred & Fifty Dollars,*[24] a delay of eighteen months prior to a forfeiture proceeding was deemed "quite significant" but again was constitutionally insufficient. In all of these cases, other factors, such as the reason for delay, or the degree of prejudice, counteracted the length of the delay. At most, it appears that the longer the delay, the greater showing the government must make with respect to these other factors.

(b) Reasons for Delay

Barker described three different types of reasons for a delay:

> A deliberate attempt to delay the trial in order to hamper the defense should be weighted heavily against the government. A more neutral reason such as negligence or overcrowded courts should be weighted less heavily but nevertheless should be considered since the ultimate responsibility for such circumstances must rest with government rather than the defendant. [Finally,]

---

[20] The elements set forth in *Barker* are usually applied to each case after trial has been completed, since the fourth element of the *Barker* test—the degree to which the defendant has been prejudiced by the delay—cannot accurately be determined unless there is a trial record available for review. *United States v. MacDonald,* 435 U.S. 850, 98 S.Ct. 1547 (1978), discussed in § 29.03(a).

[21] 505 U.S. 647, 112 S.Ct. 2686 (1992).

[22] 474 U.S. 302, 106 S.Ct. 648 (1986).

[23] At least, this was the Court's computation, although in fact, 46 months of this period did not involve "actual restraint" and should not have been counted. See discussion of *Loud Hawk* in § 25.02(a).

[24] 461 U.S. 555, 103 S.Ct. 2005 (1983).

a valid reason, such as a missing witness . . . should serve to justify appropriate delay.

This language indicates that, analogous to due process analysis of pre-accusation delay, even delay designed to hamper the defense is not an automatic Sixth Amendment violation; at the least some prejudice to the defendant must be shown. At the same time, given the multi-factor nature of the *Barker* test, a so-called "valid reason" for delay does not mean that the delay is constitutionally justifiable; if prejudice is shown, for instance, the speedy trial right may still be infringed. In *Barker,* the Court was confronted with both the first and third type of reason for delay. The Court indicated that the delay caused by the illness of a witness was for a "valid reason," and that some delay in order to convict Barker's co-defendant was also permissible, but that the four years it took to achieve the latter purpose was not justifiable and should count against the government.

In *Loud Hawk,* the Court focused primarily on the second type of reason for delay, since much of the period under consideration resulted from government appeal of decisions by the trial court. In assessing the reasonableness of such appeals, the Court stated that the courts should consider "the strength of the Government's position on the appealed issue, the importance of the issue in the posture of the case, and—in some cases—the seriousness of the crime."[25] Applying these factors in *Loud Hawk,* the Court found no bad faith on the government's part, noting that the strength of the government's positions on appeal had been borne out by the court of appeals' complete reversal of the trial court. The dissenters, quoting the above language from *Barker,* argued that when delay is due to the courts, whether or not it is deliberate, the government, not the defendant, should bear the cost. Here the court of appeals had taken over five years to hear two appeals, which the dissent viewed as "patently unreasonable."

When the delay is the direct result of prosecutorial negligence, on the other hand, a speedy trial claim is more likely to be successful. In *Doggett,* a six year hiatus between the defendant's return to the country and his arrest was due to the government's failure to continue tracking the defendant after it lost him in Panama. These facts alone (there being no proof of particularized prejudice) led five members of the Court to find a violation of the Sixth Amendment. According to the Court:

> Although negligence is obviously to be weighed more lightly than a deliberate intent to harm the accused's defense, it still falls on the wrong side of the divide between acceptable and unacceptable reasons for delaying a criminal prosecution once it has begun. And such is the nature of the prejudice presumed that the weight we assign to official negligence compounds over time as the presumption of evidentiary prejudice grows. Thus, our toleration of such negligence varies inversely with its protractedness, and its consequent threat to the fairness of the accused's trial. Condoning prolonged and unjustifiable delays in prosecution would both penalize many defendants for the state's fault and simply encourage the government to gamble with the interests of criminal suspects assigned a low prosecutorial priority.

Occasionally, the delay will be due to the defendant rather than the government, in which case the persuasiveness of a speedy trial claim will presumably be undermined.

---

[25] With respect to this latter criterion, the Court stated: "[T]he charged offense usually must be sufficiently serious to justify restraints that may be imposed on the defendant pending the outcome of the appeal."

One obvious example of such "culpable" delay is when the defendant escapes from custody.[26] At other times, defense-produced prolongation of the pretrial period will be less deliberate. Some of the delay in *Loud Hawk*, for instance, resulted from defense appeals. The majority concluded that this type of delay usually should not count against the government. According to the Court, where the defendant's claim on appeal is frivolous, as was the case here, he cannot complain about appellate delay; further, even when a claim is "meritorious," the defendant "normally should not be able upon return to the district court to reap the reward of dismissal for failure to receive a speedy trial." The dissent once again disagreed, stating that when the appellate delay is "patently unreasonable" it should not matter that the appeal was initiated by the defense rather than the prosecution.

In *Vermont v. Brillon*[27] the Court emphasized that delay caused by defense counsel is usually charged against the defendant regardless of the defendant's acquiescence to the delay, and held that this is so even when counsel is publicly assigned and the delay is caused in part by contract disputes with the state.[28] Justice Ginsburg's opinion for the Court rejected the Vermont Supreme Court's conclusion that public defenders are state actors for purposes of a speedy trial claim and that their failure to move the case forward should therefore be attributable to the state.[29] "A contrary conclusion," Justice Ginsburg stated, "could encourage appointed counsel to delay proceedings by seeking unreasonable continuances, hoping thereby to obtain a dismissal of the indictment on speedy-trial grounds," and might also lead judges to suspect even legitimate continuance requests. However, she also indicated that delay resulting from a "systemic breakdown in the public defender system" could be charged to the state.

(c) Assertion of the Right

While *Barker* held that failure to assert the right to speedy trial does not constitute a waiver, it emphasized that the "frequency and force of the objections" to delay should be taken into account. The Court noted that "delay is not an uncommon defense tactic," and thus a failure to object could normally be construed as a determination by the defendant that it was not harmful.[30] Indeed, in contrast to its treatment of most other criminal procedure rights, which must be affirmatively waived, the Court stated that "failure to assert the [speedy trial] right will make it difficult for a defendant to prove that he was denied a speedy trial." Accordingly, in *Barker,* the defendant's failure to demand a trial for a substantial period of time (which the Court viewed as a tactical maneuver based on the hope that his co-defendant would be acquitted), weighed heavily against him. Similarly, in *Eight Thousand Eight Hundred & Fifty Dollars,* the defendant's failure to demand an early forfeiture proceeding counted against her.

In *Loud Hawk,* in contrast, the defendants repeatedly moved for dismissal on speedy trial grounds. Nonetheless, concluded the majority, "that finding alone does not

---

[26]   See, e.g., *United States v. Taylor*, 487 U.S. 326, 108 S.Ct. 2413 (1988), discussed in § 25.05(e)(1).

[27]   556 U.S. 81, 129 S.Ct. 1283 (2009).

[28]   As Justice Breyer pointed out in dissent, during the 12-month period that the Vermont Supreme Court clearly attributed to the nonfeasance of Brillon's attorneys, one attorney's contract expired and a second was forced to withdraw "for contractual reasons."

[29]   Cf. *Polk County v. Dodson*, 454 U.S. 312, 102 S.Ct. 445 (1981), discussed in § 32.05 (a public defender does not act under "color of state law" for purposes of § 1983 claims).

[30]   However, the Court was careful to distinguish between a situation in which the defendant knowingly failed to assert the right and "a situation in which his attorney acquiesces in long delay without adequately informing his client," or "a situation in which no counsel is appointed."

establish that [they] had appropriately asserted their rights." The defendants' numerous other repetitive and often frivolous motions at the trial level suggested to the Court that the defendants' speedy trial motions were dilatory rather than motivated by sincere concern over pretrial delay. It appears, then, that to have a good speedy trial claim, the defendant must not only assert the right but must do so in a "sincere" fashion.

(d) Prejudice

As discussed in the introduction, the right to speedy trial exists to prevent oppressive pretrial incarceration, the anxiety and concern accompanying public accusation, and impairment of the defendant's ability to defend himself as evidence disappears or grows stale. If any of these detriments occur due to unnecessary delay, then the right could be said to be violated. But, as with the other factors, the defendant's burden of showing prejudice is, in practice, quite heavy.

In one pre-*Barker* case, *Dickey v. Florida*,[31] the Court found that a seven-year delay, during which two defense witnesses died and a third one became unavailable, merited dismissal. And in *Doggett*, as noted above, the Court was willing to assume prejudice after an eight and one-half year delay, six years of which was attributable to government negligence.

But in *Dickey* the prejudice to the defendant's case was obvious, and *Doggett* involved a relatively minor crime and a sympathetic defendant (who had lived a law-abiding life during the six years). Other Court decisions have been much stricter in evaluating claims of prejudice. For instance, in *Barker,* while admitting that determining whether a loss of memory has occurred is extremely difficult, the Court found no significant prejudice resulted from the 66-month delay; nor was a ten-month period of incarceration considered unconstitutionally oppressive. And in *Loud Hawk,* the Court found that the "possibility" that witnesses had disappeared or suffered memory loss during the seven-and-a-half year hiatus was "not sufficient" to sustain the speedy trial claim. Additionally, the Court stressed that the *government's* case might also be impaired by the passage of time, a curious, if not illogical, attempt at minimizing the possible harm the delay might cause to the defendant's case.

Because prejudice, especially that associated with memory loss, is often difficult to prove, the Court's apparent requirement that substantial, concrete detriment be shown is unrealistic and, together with its prosecution-oriented treatment of the other factors in *Barker's* test, emasculates the right to speedy trial. A better approach would be to presume prejudice if, after a prolonged delay (of over twelve months or so), the defendant asks for a trial, at which point the government must provide a substantial justification for the delay; when there is no assertion of the right, on the other hand, the defendant should prevail only if he can show the delay prejudiced his case. The Court appears to have moved in precisely the opposite direction, however. In *Reed v. Farley*,[32] the Court stated, citing *Barker*, that "[a] showing of prejudice [by the defendant] is required to establish a violation of the Sixth Amendment Speedy Trial Clause."

---

[31] 398 U.S. 30, 90 S.Ct. 1564 (1970).

[32] 512 U.S. 339, 114 S.Ct. 2291 (1994).

25.05   Legislation: The Federal Speedy Trial Act

Barker made no effort to establish explicit time requirements defining the speedy trial right. That task it held constitutionally reserved for the legislatures. Legislatures lost little time in responding to the challenge. Within ten years of *Barker,* over two-thirds of the states had enacted provisions setting time limits on the adjudication process.[33] The model for many of these provisions was the Federal Speedy Trial Act of 1974,[34] which was enacted two years after *Barker.* The rest of this chapter will focus on the Act as the best illustration of attempts to implement legislatively the speedy trial right.

(a) An Overview

The Act requires each federal district court to establish a plan for trying criminal cases within 100 days of arrest or receipt of summons. Failure to abide by the plan can result in dismissal of the indictment; additionally, deliberate dilatory tactics may be sanctioned by fines (in the case of prosecutors), forfeiture of a percentage of compensation (in the case of defense attorneys), suspension (of either attorney, for up to 90 days), or the filing of a report to the appropriate disciplinary body.[35]

Despite these provisions, speedy adjudication is far from assured. The latter sanctions are likely to be infrequently imposed since they require proof of intentional delay, and in any event "are totally ineffective against general institutional delay."[36] Even the dismissal remedy is not a strong incentive against delay, since dismissal may be "without prejudice" (meaning the defendant may be reindicted on the same charge).[37] Moreover, the Act permits several types of delay to be excluded from the time computation and allows both sides to seek continuances under certain circumstances. Thus, while the Act is probably more effective than the Sixth Amendment at pressuring the courts and lawyers to resolve criminal cases promptly,[38] it is no guarantee against prolonged adjudication.

(b) Specific Time Limits

The Act specifies three separate time periods:

(1)   Any information or indictment must be filed within thirty days from the date of arrest or service of summons. If no grand jury is in session within that thirty days, an extension of thirty days will be granted for felony cases.[39] In contrast to the constitutional analysis,[40] several courts have determined that if a person is arrested, but no formal charges are filed, the speedy trial time limits are not activated at the time of

---

[33]   See generally, Robert L. Misner, Speedy Trial: Federal and State Practice 330–735 (1983). From Misner's research, it appears that only about ten states do not have time limits, although they all have constitutional and/or statutory provisions forbidding unnecessary delay.

[34]   18 U.S.C.A. § 3161 et seq.

[35]   18 U.S.C.A. § 3162.

[36]   Misner, supra note 33, at 303.

[37]   See § 25.05(e).

[38]   But see George Bridges, *The Speedy Trial Act of 1974: Effect on Delays in Federal Criminal Litigation,* 73 J.Crim.L. & Criminol. 50, 53 (1982) (finding insignificant increase in speed since Act).

[39]   18 U.S.C.A. § 3161(b).

[40]   See § 25.02(a).

arrest.[41] Moreover, the arrest must be by *federal* officers, not officers of another sovereign, in order to trigger the Act's provisions.[42]

(2)   Trial must take place within seventy days from the filing date of the indictment or information, or from the date the defendant first appears before a judicial officer, whichever is later.[43] In jury cases, trial is deemed to begin when voir dire commences.[44]

(3)   Trial cannot take place less than thirty days from the date on which the defendant first appears through counsel or expressly waives counsel and elects to proceed *pro se,* unless the defendant consents to earlier trial in writing.[45]

(c) Exemptions

Certain periods of delay are excluded from the computation of time limitations.[46] In *United States v. Tinklenberg,*[47] the Supreme Court unanimously held that these periods are excludable even if they do not "actually cause" delay but in fact coincide with delay that would have occurred in any event. These excluded periods include:

(1)   Delays caused by proceedings relating to the defendant, such as hearings on competency to stand trial, hearings on pretrial motions, trials on other charges and interlocutory appeals. The most controversial issue involving this provision is whether the entire postponement resulting from a pretrial motion is always excludable or whether some outer limit must be observed. Until *Henderson v. United States,*[48] several courts had permitted exclusion only of that time found to be "reasonably necessary" to effectuate the purpose of the motion.[49] In *Henderson,* however, the Supreme Court held that neither the statutory language nor the legislative history of the Act called for such a rule. Thus, both the five month delay between the filing of the suppression motion and the hearing on the motion, and the ten month delay between the hearing and the court's final decision (resulting largely from prosecution delay in submitting posthearing material requested by the court) was excludable. However, time granted to the defendant to prepare for pretrial motions is not automatically excludable; rather before any exemption may occur the court must make case-specific findings that the ends of justice outweigh the benefits of a speedy trial to the defendant and to society.[50]

---

[41]   See, e.g., *United States v. Sanchez,* 722 F.2d 1501 (11th Cir. 1984), cert. denied 467 U.S. 1208, 104 S.Ct. 2396 (1984); *United States v. Boles,* 684 F.2d 534 (8th Cir. 1982). A particularly bothersome decision is *United States v. Reme,* 738 F.2d 1156 (11th Cir. 1984), which held that, even if the offense for which the defendant is indicted is only slightly different from that for which he was arrested, time spent in custody between arrest and indictment is excludable.

[42]   *United States v. Manuel,* 706 F.2d 908 (9th Cir. 1983) (initial arrest by tribal authorities did not trigger Act); *United States v. Iaquinta,* 674 F.2d 260 (4th Cir. 1982) (initial arrest by state authorities did not trigger Act even though state officers were assisted by federal officers).

[43]   18 U.S.C.A. § 3161(c)(1).

[44]   *United States v. Richmond,* 735 F.2d 208 (6th Cir. 1984); *United States v. Manfredi,* 722 F.2d 519 (9th Cir. 1983).

[45]   18 U.S.C.A. § 3161(c)(2).

[46]   18 U.S.C.A. § 3161(h)(1)–(9).

[47]   563 U.S. 647, 131 S.Ct. 2007 (2011).

[48]   476 U.S. 321, 106 S.Ct. 1871 (1986).

[49]   See, e.g., *United States v. Novak,* 715 F.2d 810 (3d Cir. 1983); *United States v. Cobb,* 697 F.2d 38 (2d Cir. 1982).

[50]   *Bloate v. United States,* 559 U.S. 196, 130 S.Ct. 1345 (2010).

(2) Delays caused by deferred prosecution upon agreement of defense counsel, prosecutor, and the court. For instance, in *New York v. Hill*,[51] the Court unanimously held that, under the Interstate Agreement on Detainers (an analogue to the Speedy Trial Act in the extradition context), defense counsel may agree with the prosecution to set a new trial date beyond the 180-day time limit.

(3) Delays caused by the absence or unavailability of the defendant or an essential witness.

(4) Delays resulting from the defendant's mental incompetence or physical unfitness to stand trial.

(5) Delays resulting from treatment of the defendant pursuant to the Narcotics Addict Rehabilitation Act.

(6) Analogous to the holding in *United States v. MacDonald*,[52] delays between the dropping of a charge and filing of a new charge for the same or related offense.

(7) Reasonable periods of delay when the defendant is joined for trial with a co-defendant.

(8) Any delay resulting from a continuance granted by the court to serve the ends of justice.

Defendants will occasionally waive the protections of the Act. In *Zedner v. United States*,[53] the Supreme Court held that the time period during which a defendant waives these protections does *not* count as an exemption under the latter provision or any other. In that case Zedner, acting at the behest of the trial court and after two continuances, waived his speedy trial right under the Act "for all time." Six years later he was convicted, after the trial court found that this waiver prevented him from claiming a time bar. A unanimous Supreme Court, in an opinion by Justice Alito, held that under the plain language of the statute the time period affected by Zedner's waiver could not be exempted from the speedy trial calculation. First, the Court pointed out, the Act does not list waiver as one of the exemptions. Second, many of the factors the Act indicates might satisfy the "ends-of-justice" exemption, including the need for a "reasonable time to obtain counsel" and for time for "effective preparation," would otherwise be irrelevant; the defendant could simply waive the time period associated with these factors.

Alito also emphasized that the speedy trial right protects public as well as litigant interests, and thus is not something the defendant "may opt out of . . . entirely." In particular, defendants should not be able to enter into "prospective waivers" of the type involved in *Zedner*. In contrast to a waiver at the time of trial or plea, where the court and prosecutor are ready for a case resolution and thus are likely to want to implement the Act, a prospective waiver occurs at a time when the date of adjudication is not yet foreseeable. In that situation, all parties, court and prosecutor included, might be "all too happy to opt out of the Act, to the detriment of the public interest."

(d) Continuances

As the final exemption provision above makes clear, periods of delay resulting from a continuance are exempted from computation of the time limits if the continuance

---

[51]   528 U.S. 110, 120 S.Ct. 659 (2000).

[52]   456 U.S. 1, 102 S.Ct. 1497 (1982), discussed in § 25.02(a).

[53]   547 U.S. 489, 126 S.Ct. 1976 (2006).

serves the ends of justice. The reasons for any continuance must be set forth in the record or the continuance will not be so exempted. In considering whether to grant a continuance, the federal statute states that the following factors are to be taken into account:[54]

(1)　Whether failure to grant a continuance would be likely to make a continuation of the proceedings impossible or result in a miscarriage of justice. Thus, in *United States v. Martin*[55] the Ninth Circuit permitted a continuance when the validity of a defense raised by the defendant was soon to be considered by the United States Supreme Court, and the Court's decision could conceivably have overruled two Ninth Circuit cases finding contrary to the defendant's position.

(2)　Whether the case is so "unusual or complex" that it is unreasonable to expect adequate preparation within the time limits. *United States v. Perez-Reveles*[56] held that a mere conclusory finding by the trial judge that a case is "complex," when the trial took only two days to complete, involved a single defendant and raised no unusual issues will not constitute an excludable continuance.

(3)　Whether, in a case where arrest precedes indictment, delay in the filing of the indictment occurs because the arrest occurred at a time which made convening a grand jury and obtaining an indictment within the period specified difficult or because the facts upon which the grand jury had to base its determination are unusual or complex.

(4)　Whether the failure to grant a continuance would deny the defendant reasonable time to obtain counsel, would unreasonably deny the defendant or the government continuity of counsel, or would deny counsel for either party reasonable time for effective preparation. For example, the court in *United States v. Nance*[57] exempted three successive continuances totalling three months because they were granted, respectively, when (a) the defendant's lawyer was unavailable due to a death in the family and continuity of representation was considered important; (b) a co-defendant's counsel was unavailable because of his involvement in another trial; and (c) an unrelated trial scheduled by the judge to fill the docket slot left open by the defendant's continued trial took a few days longer than expected. The last continuance was considered justified because it was aimed at taking full advantage of judicial resources and the delay was unforeseeable.

(5)　Whether the continuance was granted for an "inappropriate" reason, such as general congestion of the court's calendar, or lack of diligent preparation or failure to obtain witnesses on the part of the government's attorney. No continuance granted on such grounds will qualify as excludable.

(e)　Dismissal/Reprosecution

Failure to comply with the time limit requirements, after subtracting the allowable exclusions and continuances, results in dismissal of the prosecution. However, discretion is vested in the trial judge to dismiss with or without prejudice. In doing so, the judge is to consider three factors: (1) the seriousness of the offense; (2) the circumstances leading

---

[54]　18 U.S.C.A. § 3161(h)(8)(B)(i–iv).

[55]　742 F.2d 512 (9th Cir. 1984).

[56]　715 F.2d 1348 (9th Cir. 1983).

[57]　666 F.2d 353 (9th Cir. 1982), cert. denied 456 U.S. 918, 102 S.Ct. 1776 (1982).

to dismissal (e.g., who is responsible for the delay); and (3) the effect of reprosecution on the administration of the Act and the administration of justice.[58]

(1) The Courts' Approach

The one Supreme Court decision reaching this issue suggests that the Court believes the harsher dismissal remedy should be used sparingly. In *United States v. Taylor*,[59] the government was prepared to try the defendant one day before expiration of the 70-day deadline established by the statute, but was unable to do so because the defendant had escaped from custody. However, after the defendant was apprehended in another jurisdiction, the government delayed trial for well over a month (at least 15 days of which were nonexcludable), in large part because it was inconvenient for the United States Marshal Service to transfer the defendant to the appropriate jurisdiction at an earlier time. The trial court, applying the three statutory factors noted above, dismissed the charges against the defendant with prejudice. It found that the charges (federal narcotics felonies) were serious. But, with respect to the "circumstances leading to the dismissal" factor, it found that the government's attitude toward reinitiating prosecution had been "lackadaisical." And it concluded that the administration of the Act would be "seriously impaired if the court were not to respond sternly to the instant violation." The Ninth Circuit affirmed.

The Supreme Court held that the dismissal should have been without prejudice. Justice Blackmun, writing for a six-member majority, began by stressing that while the type of dismissal ordered in a particular case is in the discretion of the trial judge, appellate courts should make sure the judge has devoted adequate attention to the three factors set out in the Act, as well as the degree of prejudice to the defendant occasioned by the nonexcludable delay. He included the last consideration based on a reading of the Act's legislative history, which he asserted indicated Congress' desire to have courts consider prejudice in determining a remedy even though it was not specifically included in the statute.

Blackmun then concluded that the trial judge in *Taylor* had failed to explain adequately how she had evaluated these four variables. In particular, the trial court had not sufficiently explained its conclusion, relevant to the second and third statutory factors, that the government was so "lackadaisical" as to deserve the dismissal with prejudice sanction. Blackmun found no evidence in the trial court's opinion that the government had acted in "bad faith", or exhibited "a pattern of neglect" or "antipathy toward a recaptured fugitive." He found the court's determination that there was "no excuse" for the government's conduct insufficient. Additionally, while admitting that the defendant's escape did not restart the clock for purposes of the Act, Blackmun felt the trial court had overlooked the relevance of the escape as a causative factor in the failure of the government to meet the deadline.

Finally, Blackmun stated that the trial court had given insufficient weight to the prejudice issue. He noted that neither the district court nor the circuit court had found that the defendant had been prejudiced by the delay, but that this fact had not seemed to influence either court. Concluded the Supreme Court: "At bottom, the District Court appears to have decided to dismiss with prejudice in this case in order to send a strong message to the Government that unexcused delays will not be tolerated. That factor

---

[58]   18 U.S.C.A. § 3162.

[59]   487 U.S. 326, 108 S.Ct. 2413 (1988).

alone, by definition implicated in almost every Speedy Trial Act case, does not suffice to justify barring reprosecution in light of all the other circumstances present."

The speedy trial claim in *Taylor* was not a particularly strong one. The delay was not very long, and apparently did not prejudice the defendant; moreover, the government probably did not act in "bad faith" and the defendant hardly had "clean hands." However, the Court's willingness to overturn the lower court's decision rather than remand it for further consideration, along with its clearly demonstrated unwillingness to countenance a nonchalant attitude on the part of the government as the sole ground for prohibiting reprosecution, suggests a desire to deter use of the dismissal with prejudice sanction. Additionally, the Court took pains to emphasize that dismissal without prejudice "is not a toothless sanction;" it forces the government to seek a new indictment which, given the time lapse, will be harder to obtain and may be dismissed on statute of limitations grounds.

One can at least conclude that *Taylor* will do nothing to diminish the tendency of most lower courts to rely on the dismissal without prejudice sanction. Although a few courts have held that defendants are entitled to a presumption in favor of dismissal with prejudice,[60] most have decided otherwise.[61] Many have also been willing to interpret the three statutory factors in the prosecution's favor. For instance, many courts are apparently willing to dismiss without prejudice for any type of felony.[62] Similarly, even when it is clear that the delay is the fault of the prosecution, the courts often grant dismissal without prejudice if the violation was not in bad faith,[63] or was justified by a need for further investigation.[64] Even a failure to provide a reason does not necessarily hurt the prosecution.[65] As with the Court's holding in *Taylor,* many of these holdings rely heavily on the finding that the defendant did not appear to be prejudiced by the delay. In contrast, a few isolated decisions have dismissed with prejudice for delays as short as a month, even when the charge is serious and there is no bad faith on the part of the prosecution and no concrete prejudice, in order to send a "message" that compliance with the Act is important.[66]

(2) An Alternative Approach

The ability to dismiss without prejudice substantially detracts from the original purpose of the Act, which was to adopt relatively finite rules governing the duration of adjudication. As one judge stated: "If dismissal without prejudice is permitted, then the defendant has achieved nothing but the privilege of being tried a second time."[67] Indeed, given the authority to dismiss without prejudice, a violation of the statute may result in

---

[60]   See, e.g., *United States v. Angelini,* 553 F.Supp. 367 (D.Mass. 1982), aff'd on other grounds 678 F.2d 380 (1st Cir. 1982).

[61]   See, e.g., *United States v. Williams,* 314 F.3d 552 (11th Cir. 2002) (where the offense is serious, dismissal with prejudice should occur only when there is "a correspondingly severe delay").

[62]   See, e.g., *United States v. Nejdl,* 773 F.Supp. 1288 (D.Neb. 1991) ("in most drug cases, dismissal without prejudice is the rule"); *United States v. Kiszewski,* 877 F.2d 210 (2d Cir. 1989) (perjury to grand jury); *United States v. Bittle,* 699 F.2d 1201 (D.C.Cir. 1983) (possession of stolen mail); *United States v. Hawthorne,* 705 F.2d 258 (7th Cir. 1983) (possession of government checks).

[63]   *United States v. Kiszewski,* 877 F.2d 210 (2d Cir. 1989).

[64]   *United States v. Godoy,* 821 F.2d 1498 (11th Cir. 1987).

[65]   *United States v. May,* 819 F.2d 531 (5th Cir. 1987). But see *United States v. Moss,* 217 F.3d 426 (6th Cir. 2000) (dismissal without prejudice erroneous because it did not adequately address the statutory factors).

[66]   See *United States v. Ramirez,* 973 F.2d 36 (1st Cir. 1992).

[67]   *United States v. Mehrmanesh,* 652 F.2d 766 (9th Cir. 1981) (Fletcher, J. dissenting).

longer delay than would have occurred had the statute never been passed, since the defendant must be reindicted before retrial can take place and the statutory period begins anew.[68]

The preferable approach would be to dismiss with prejudice all cases involving statutory violations that are not clearly the product of defense-caused delay. When non-excludable delay is due to the government or some other entity over which the defense has no control, the government should bear the cost. Given the large number of exemptions to which the prosecution can resort, this approach would not unfairly burden the government; rather, it would encourage the diligence and efficiency necessary to ensure defendants are not detained or made to wait in the community for prolonged periods of time prior to having their case resolved. When, on the other hand, delay is the result of defense tactics or lack of diligence, a dismissal without prejudice might be proper, at least when serious crimes are involved. While the defendant should not be penalized for an attorney's incompetence or miscalculations, neither should the government be forced to dismiss a case which it has attempted to adjudicate promptly.

(f) Burden of Proof

The burden of proving the time limits in the Act have been exceeded is on the defendant, although when the exemption at issue has to do with the absence or unavailability of the defendant or an essential witness, the government bears the burden of coming forward with sufficient evidence to raise the question. Significantly, failure of the defendant to move for dismissal prior to trial or the entry of a plea of guilty or nolo contendere is a waiver of the statutory right.[69]

(g) Sixth Amendment Rights

The Speedy Trial Act does not displace the constitutional right of speedy trial. Section 3173 provides: "No provision of this chapter shall be interpreted as a bar to any claim of denial of speedy trial as required by Amendment VI of the Constitution." If a defendant for some reason cannot make out a violation of his statutory right to speedy trial, he may still argue his constitutional claim, although he is unlikely to be successful.[70]

25.06   Conclusion

The right to speedy disposition of one's charges is embodied both in the Sixth Amendment and legislation in every jurisdiction. The nature of the right varies depending upon its source.

(1) Under the Sixth Amendment, the right does not attach until arrest or indictment (whichever comes first), although the Due Process Clause provides limited protection against excessive and prejudicial pre-accusation delay which is intended to hamper the defense or recklessly causes that result. If the charge or indictment is dismissed and reinstated, the period of dismissal is not relevant to Sixth Amendment analysis unless, during that period, the defendant is subject to restriction on his liberty

---

[68]   Further, the trial judge may extend the period before retrial to 180 days. 18 U.S.C.A. § 3161(d)(2).

[69]   18 U.S.C.A. § 3162(a)(2).

[70]   Cf. Misner, supra note 33, at 325. ("A violation of the Act itself generally will not offend the Sixth Amendment.")

greater than the *possibility* of pretrial detention or bond. The right does not apply post-conviction to the sentencing hearing.

(2) In deciding whether post-accusation delay as defined in (1) violates the Sixth Amendment, four factors should be considered: (a) the length of the delay; (b) the reason for the delay (e.g., whether the defense or prosecution caused the delay and, if the latter, the degree of good faith effort expended in bringing the case to trial as soon as possible); (c) whether and when the defendant asserted his right; and (d) whether any actual prejudice to the defendant resulted from the delay due to destruction or staleness of evidence, oppressive pretrial incarceration or the creation of excessive anxiety. Even when delay is extraordinary, the Supreme Court requires strong proof concerning the other factors before it will find a violation of the Sixth Amendment.

(3) Statutory implementation of the speedy trial concept tends to place more concrete time limits on the period between arrest and adjudication. The federal act, for instance, presumes that if this period exceeds 100 days, the statutory right is violated. However, several types of delays, including the time necessary to hear defense motions, delays resulting from the defendant's incompetence to stand trial, and delays resulting from continuances granted to serve the ends of justice do not count toward the 100-day limit. In contrast, time affected by a defendant's waiver of the speedy trial right *does* count and time the defense spends preparing for pretrial motions may count, depending on the trial court's assessment of the impact on speedy trial interests. The number of exceptions to the time limit requirements of the Act illustrates the difficulty of achieving speedy disposition of cases given the realities of the criminal justice system.

(4) The remedy for violation of the constitutional right is dismissal with prejudice (i.e., prohibition of reprosecution). A violation of the federal act can result in dismissal with or without prejudice, depending upon: (a) the seriousness of the offense; (b) the circumstances leading to dismissal; and (c) the effect of reprosecution on the administration of the Act and of justice.

BIBLIOGRAPHY

Allen, Darren. The Constitutional Floor Doctrine and the Right to a Speedy Trial. 26 Campbell L.Rev. 101 (2004).

Amsterdam, Anthony G. Speedy Criminal Trial: Rights and Remedies. 27 Stan.L.Rev. 525 (1975).

Bridges, George. The Speedy Trial Act of 1974: Effects on Delays in Federal Criminal Litigation, 73 J.Crim.L. & Criminol. 50 (1982).

Cleary, Michael J. Pre-Indictment Delay: Establishing a Fairer Approach Based on *United States v. Marion* and *United States v. Lovasco*. 78 Temple L.Rev. 1049 (2005).

Frase, Richard S. The Speedy Trial Act of 1974. 43 U.Chi.L.Rev. 667 (1976).

Hopwood, Shon. The Not So Speedy Trial Act. 89 Wash. L. Rev. 709 (2014).

Rose, Emily. Speedy Trial as a Viable Challenge to Underfunded Indigent-Defense Systems. 113 Mich. L. Rev. 279 (2014).

Uviller, H. Richard. *Barker v. Wingo*: Speedy Trial Gets a Fast Shuffle. 72 Colum.L.Rev. 1376 (1972).

Part F

ADJUDICATION OF GUILT

Police investigation, the subject of Parts A through D, and the pretrial process, examined in Part E, share a common goal: they both are aimed at identifying those cases that have a good chance of ending in conviction. As a result, most defendants who enter the adjudication phase of the criminal process have committed some crime. But a number of complex mechanisms have been developed in an effort to assure that *only* those defendants who are culpable "beyond a reasonable doubt"[1] are convicted. This Part describes this adjudication process.

Chapter 26 describes the rules associated with guilty pleas and plea bargaining, phenomena little known to the public but responsible for most criminal convictions. If the defendant pleads not guilty, he has the right to be tried by a jury, the subject of Chapter 27. Chapter 28 discusses a number of matters connected with the conduct of trial itself, all stemming from the defendant's constitutionally-based prerogative to confront his accusers. If trial results in conviction, every jurisdiction gives the defendant a statutory right to appeal, the various aspects of which are covered in Chapter 29. As Chapter 30 discusses, if the defendant is acquitted, at either the trial or the appellate stage, he is protected from retrial on the same offense by the Double Jeopardy Clause, which also protects against multiple punishments for the same offense. The right to counsel at the guilty plea, trial and appellate stages is discussed in Part G (in Chapter 31), which deals with the right to counsel generally.

---

[1] Beyond a reasonable doubt is typically defined as "a belief to a moral certainty which does not exclude all possible or imaginary doubt, but which is of such convincing character that a reasonable person would not hesitate to rely and act upon it in the most important of his own affairs." See Smith & Blackmore, Federal Jury Practice and Instructions, § 11.14.

Chapter 26

GUILTY PLEAS AND PLEA BARGAINING

26.01 Introduction

Most convictions in the United States are the result of a guilty plea rather than a bench or jury trial. Some estimates indicate that over ninety percent of all criminal cases are disposed of through guilty pleas.[1] Most of these pleas are the result of "plea bargaining" between the prosecution and the defense, in which the former makes charge or sentencing concessions in exchange for a plea of guilty.

The response to the guilty plea process has been mixed. Most commentators and courts assume that guilty pleas and plea bargaining are essential to the efficient administration of an increasingly overburdened system of criminal justice. As one Manhattan prosecutor stated: "Our office keeps eight courtrooms extremely busy trying 5% of the cases. If even 10% of the cases ended in a trial, the system would break down."[2] As a result, most criticisms of guilty pleas and plea bargains do not call for their elimination, but rather focus on the manner by which they are obtained and the lack of openness surrounding the process.[3]

Some have insisted, however, that juries and judges, not prosecutors and defense attorneys, should be the ultimate arbiters of criminal disputes, and that the degree of discretion plea bargaining gives the prosecution produces inappropriate results.[4] On the latter score, it is often noted that, of two defendants with identical charges, the one who pleads guilty is likely to receive a less severe sentence than the one who goes to trial.[5] Further, the plea bargaining process encourages the prosecutor to overcharge as a negotiating ploy, and may lead to less individualized dispositions, especially in busy urban areas, where bargaining often appears to proceed according to a pre-set "schedule." The end result, it is contended, is inaccuracy.[6] Even the administrative need for plea bargaining has been challenged. The bargaining process, it is asserted, actually contributes to inefficiency, for "defense attorneys commonly devise strategies whose only utility lies in the threat they pose to the court's and prosecutor's time."[7] Furthermore, bargaining is not necessary to obtain guilty pleas, which would still be forthcoming from

---

[1] ABA Project on Standards for Criminal Justice, Standards Relating to Pleas of Guilty, at xi–xii (1998) [hereafter cited as ABA Standards] (93% in federal system and 91% in state systems).

[2] Quoted in Albert Alschuler, *The Prosecutor's Role in Plea Bargaining*, 36 Chi.L.Rev. 50, 54 (1968).

[3] See, e.g., ABA Standards, supra note 1, at xiii–xiv; Kuh, Plea Bargaining: Guidelines for the Manhattan District Attorney's Office, 11 Crim.L.Bull. 48–65 (1975).

[4] See, e.g., Peter Arenella, *Rethinking the Functions of Criminal Procedure: The Warren and Burger Courts' Competing Ideologies*, 72 Geo.L.J. 185, 216–219 (1983); National Advisory Commission on Criminal Justice Standards and Goals, *Courts* Standard 3.1 (1973).

[5] See Michael M. O'Hear, *Remorse, Cooperation, and 'Acceptance of Responsibility': The Structure, Implementation and Reform of Section 3E1.1 of the Federal Sentencing Guidelines*, 91 Nw. U.L.Rev. 1507, 1513–15 (1997) (discussing the acceptance of responsibility discount under federal sentencing guidelines); *United States v. Rodriguez*, 162 F.3d 135 (1st Cir. 1998) (upholding sentences of 17 and 60 months for defendants who pleaded guilty, and sentences of 235 and 270 months for similarly situated co-defendants who did not);. *Frank v. Blackburn*, 646 F.2d 873 (5th Cir. 1980), mod'd 646 F.2d 902 (5th Cir. 1981).

[6] Donald Gifford, *Meaningful Reform of Plea Bargaining: The Control of Prosecutorial Discretion*, 1983 U.Ill.L.Rev. 37.

[7] Alschuler, supra note 2, at 56.

defendants who believe that conviction is likely to occur at trial.[8] A few jurisdictions have forbidden plea bargaining except in unusual circumstances. One study conducted in Alaska after plea bargaining was severely curtailed in that state concluded that "the efficient operation of Alaska's criminal justice system did not depend upon plea bargaining."[9]

There are several points to be made in favor of guilty pleas reached through plea bargaining, however. In response to the disparity concern, it has been argued that a person who pleads guilty is often *deserving* of leniency, since the plea may indicate repentance, a potential for rehabilitation, cooperation with the authorities in bringing to justice other offenders, or a willingness to help the state avoid the delay associated with trial. Indeed, the ABA encourages such leniency in its recommendations concerning plea bargaining, at least when the plea can be viewed as evidence of contriteness, a demonstration of concern for the victim, or a reward for cooperation.[10] With respect to the potential for "inaccurate" dispositions, it is noted that, given the myriad shades of personal culpability, plea bargaining can, at least theoretically, result in more "just" solutions than a trial, which must proceed based on specified charges connected with specific penalties.[11] Finally, the empirical studies indicating that abolition of plea bargaining can "work" also usually show that the discretion once permitted by that practice has merely been shifted to other points in the process, such as charging or sentencing, with not necessarily more just results.[12]

In any event, the courts have come to accept guilty pleas and plea bargaining as a necessary and established part of the criminal justice system. In *Brady v. United States*,[13] the Supreme Court expressed caution about, but still recognized the validity of, the plea bargain system:

> Of course, that the prevalence of guilty pleas is explainable does not necessarily validate those pleas or the system which produces them. But we cannot hold that it is unconstitutional for the State to extend a benefit to a defendant who in turn extends a substantial benefit to the State. . . .

One year later in *Santobello v. New York*,[14] the Court was even more affirmative:

> The disposition of criminal charges by agreement between the prosecutor and the accused, sometimes loosely called "plea bargaining," is an essential component of the administration of justice. Properly administered, it is to be encouraged.

---

[8]   Arenella, supra note 4, at 221–222.

[9]   Michael L. Rubinstein & Teresa J. White, *Alaska's Ban on Plea Bargaining*, 13 Law & Soc'y Rev. 367 (1979). See also, Ronald Wright & Marc Miller, *The Screening/Bargaining Tradeoff*, 55 Stan.L.Rev. 29 (2002) (arguing, based on a study of the New Orleans prosecutor's office, that a system in which the prosecutor's office makes "an early and careful assessment of each case" and charges accordingly can lead to a significant reduction in bargaining); Raymond Parnas & Riley J. Atkins, *Abolishing Plea Bargaining: A Proposal*, 14 Crim.L.Bull. 101, 110–114 (1978).

[10]   ABA Standards, supra note 1, § 1.8(a).

[11]   Thomas Church, Jr., *In Defense of Bargain Justice*, 13 Law & Soc.Rev. 509, 511 (1979).

[12]   Malcom Feeley, *Perspectives on Plea Bargaining*, 13 Law & Soc.Rev. 199, 204 (1979). See also, Robert A. Weninger, *The Abolition of Plea Bargaining: A Case Study of El Paso County, Texas*, 35 U.C.L.A.L.Rev. 265 (1987); Sam W. Callan, *An Experiment in Justice Without Plea Negotiation*, 13 Law & Soc.Rev. 327 (1979).

[13]   397 U.S. 742, 90 S.Ct. 1463 (1970).

[14]   404 U.S. 257, 92 S.Ct. 495 (1971).

This chapter examines: (1) the plea bargaining process; (2) the effect of a bargain once it is made; (3) the rules regarding the "arraignment," or proceeding at which the plea is taken; and (4) the circumstances under which a plea may be challenged.

26.02   The Plea Bargaining Process

(a) Types of Bargains and Pleas

With the few exceptions noted above, every jurisdiction has explicitly provided that the prosecution and the defense may engage in discussions with a view toward reaching a plea agreement.[15] Typically, the prosecution offers one or more of the following concessions: (1) a reduction in charge; (2) dismissal of other pending charges; (3) a promise to recommend or not contest a particular sentence or range of sentences; or (4) a stipulation that a particular sentence is the appropriate disposition. The prosecution may also agree to other conditions, such as maintaining confidentiality about the dismissed charges.

The defendant in return agrees to plead guilty to the proffered charge or charges. In many states, as well as federal court,[16] there are actually two different types of guilty pleas: a straight guilty plea and a plea of nolo contendere.[17] The nolo plea (or plea non vult) means literally: "I do not contest this." In effect, it is identical to the guilty plea, except that it cannot be used against a defendant as an admission of guilt in a subsequent civil case. Thus, it is particularly popular among defendants charged with criminal antitrust violations and the like, since civil litigation often follows the criminal adjudication.[18] In addition to agreeing to plead guilty in one of these ways, the defendant may agree to testify against a co-defendant, forego asserting certain rights, or provide other benefits to the prosecution.

(b) Rights During Bargaining

Plea bargaining is, in effect, the adjudicatory process for defendants who eventually plead guilty. But the rights accorded a defendant during the bargaining process are not as extensive as those enjoyed by the defendant at trial.

(1) The Right to Effective Counsel

The Supreme Court has held that the Sixth Amendment right to counsel attaches whenever, after the initiation of criminal proceedings, "a defendant finds himself faced with the prosecutorial forces of organized society, and immersed in the intricacies of substantive and procedural criminal law."[19] Accordingly, once criminal prosecution begins, the defendant is entitled to counsel during the bargaining process, as well as during arraignment. The prosecutor should not bargain directly with the defendant,

---

[15] See, e.g., Fed.R.Crim.P. 11(e)(1).

[16] See *Hudson v. United States,* 272 U.S. 451, 47 S.Ct. 127 (1926).

[17] In most states, the defendant can plead insanity, which is also a form of guilty plea, in that the defendant admits he committed the crime, but claims that he should not be held responsible for it.

[18] See Charles A. Wright, Federal Practice and Procedure § 177.

[19] *Kirby v. Illinois,* 406 U.S. 682, 92 S.Ct. 1877 (1972).

unless there has been a waiver of counsel.[20] However, there is no right to counsel during bargaining that takes place prior to indictment or formal charge.[21]

The Sixth Amendment also requires that, when the right to counsel attaches, counsel bargain effectively. Counsel should carry out sufficient investigation of the case to permit him to advise his client as to various charging and sentencing options. He should also ensure that his client understands the options available and the consequences of a plea. Thus, as discussed later in this chapter,[22] the Court has held that failure to inform the defendant that a guilty plea could trigger various collateral consequences, such as deportation, is deficient performance.

The Supreme Court has also held, however, that failing to fulfill these tasks is not necessarily ineffective assistance of counsel under the Sixth Amendment. In *Hill v. Lockhart*,[23] it concluded that such a claim will not lie unless the defendant can show "a reasonable probability that, but for counsel's errors, he would not have pleaded guilty and would have insisted on going to trial." In *Hill*, the defendant, who pleaded guilty pursuant to a bargain, claimed that his attorney should have told him that his previous felony conviction meant that he would not be eligible for parole until he had served one-half of his sentence, rather than one-third of his sentence, as was true of first-time offenders. The Court concluded that the defendant failed to allege "any special circumstances that might support the conclusion that he placed particular emphasis on his parole eligibility in deciding whether or not to plead guilty."

When, however, the defendant tells the attorney he would like to appeal a conviction or sentence resulting from a guilty plea and the attorney fails to appeal within the allotted time, the failure not only constitutes deficient performance, it is also automatically prejudicial, even if the plea agreement includes a waiver of the right to appeal. The Court so held in *Garza v. Idaho*,[24] where six members of the Court reasoned that "no appeal waiver serves as an absolute bar to all appellate claims" (including, most obviously, a claim as to whether the plea is voluntary), and thus "a defendant who has signed an appeal waiver does not, in directing counsel to file a notice of appeal, necessarily undertake a quixotic or frivolous quest." To the argument that an attorney's refusal to file such a notice might nonetheless be a justifiable strategy in light of the waiver and the perceived weakness of any claims, the majority noted that a notice of appeal need not indicate the precise basis for appeal, and thus filing is merely a "ministerial" act that does not involve tactical decision-making. As to the prejudice prong, the Court had earlier held that prejudice automatically occurs if an attorney's failure forfeits an appellate proceeding "altogether."[25] To the state's argument that the defendant in such a situation should at least have to indicate what non-waived issue might have been raised on appeal, Justice Kagan pointed out for the majority that, if prejudice were not assumed, a habeas court would have to decide, perhaps years later,

---

[20]   Ethical rules also prohibit such contact. See, e.g., ABA Code of Professional Responsibility, DR 7–104.

[21]   See *United States v. Moody*, 206 F.3d 609 (6th Cir. 2001).

[22]   See *Padilla v. Kentucky*, 559 U.S. 356, 130 S.Ct. 1473 (2010), discussed in § 26.04(a)(2).

[23]   474 U.S. 52, 106 S.Ct. 366 (1985).

[24]   ___ U.S. ___, 139 S.Ct. 738 (2019).

[25]   *Roe v. Flores-Ortega*, 528 U.S. 470, 120 S.Ct. 1029 (2000), discussed further in § 32.04(c)(4).

what the issue might have been, based on assertions made by a defendant who might not be aided by counsel (since there is no right to post-conviction counsel[26]).

When counsel's defective performance during plea bargaining leads the defendant to reject the plea offer and go to trial, a different prejudice standard comes into play. As discussed in Chapter 32,[27] in that situation, a defendant "must show that but for the ineffective advice there is reasonable probability that the plea offer would have been presented to the court (i.e., that the defendant would have accepted the plea and the prosecution would not have withdrawn it in light of intervening circumstance), that the court would have accepted its terms, and that the conviction or sentence, or both, under the offer's terms would have been less severe than under the judgment and sentence that in fact were imposed." If both defective performance and prejudice are found, the usual remedy will probably at most be an entitlement to reconsider the original offer, which, if taken by the defendant, can be accepted or rejected by the court, as with any offer.

(2) The Right to Exculpatory Evidence

By analogy to the trial process,[28] defense counsel should also receive any "exculpatory" information in the prosecution's possession before a final bargain is struck. But, as with ineffective assistance of counsel claims, it is likely that information will be considered exculpatory only if there is a reasonable probability it would have changed the defendant's plea.[29] Further, some courts have distinguished between specific exculpatory evidence, which must be disclosed, and weaknesses in the prosecution's case that would come out at trial (such as a missing witness), which need not be.[30]

Thus, the Supreme Court has held, in *United States v. Ruiz*,[31] that defendants are not entitled either to impeachment evidence or evidence relevant to affirmative defenses prior to entering a plea agreement. Although a failure to provide such evidence might be important in determining whether a defendant has a fair trial, Justice Breyer wrote for a unanimous Court, it does not make a guilty plea involuntary. As other Court decisions have indicated,[32] a plea decision can be voluntary even if based on incomplete information. Further, the pre-plea value of impeachment and affirmative defense information is "often limited," and in the case of impeachment evidence, at least, depends upon the rest of the prosecution's case, which the defendant is *not* entitled to discover, even for trial.[33] At the same time, requiring disclosure of such information at an early stage could disrupt ongoing investigations, expose prospective witnesses and informants to serious harm, and require the government "to devote substantially more resources to trial preparation prior to plea bargaining," thereby making bargaining a much less

---

[26] *Pennsylvania v. Finley*, 481 U.S. 551, 107 S.Ct. 1990 (1987), discussed further in § 31.03(c)(4).

[27] See *Lafler v. Cooper*, 566 U.S. 156, 132 S.Ct. 1376 (2012), discussed in § 32.04(c)(3).

[28] See § 24.04.

[29] See *United States v. Bagley*, 473 U.S. 667, 105 S.Ct. 3375 (1985), discussed in § 24.04(b).

[30] See, e.g., *People v. Jones,* 44 N.Y.2d 76, 404 N.Y.S.2d 85, 375 N.E.2d 41 (1978), cert. denied 439 U.S. 846, 99 S.Ct. 145 (1978). On the other hand, at least one court has held that if counsel is denied full discovery and as a result is unable to evaluate its wisdom, the plea is not valid. *Stano v. Dugger,* 889 F.2d 962 (11th Cir. 1989), rehr'g decided on other grounds 901 F.2d 898 (11th Cir. 1990).

[31] 536 U.S. 622, 122 S.Ct. 2450 (2002).

[32] See *Brady v. Maryland*, 373 U.S. 83, 83 S.Ct. 1194 (1963) (upholding a guilty plea even though the defendant "misapprehended the quality of the State's case"); *McMann v. Richardson*, 397 U.S. 759, 90 S.Ct. 1441 (1970) (upholding a guilty plea even though counsel "misjudged the admissibility" of a confession), discussed in § 26.05(e).

[33] See generally, §§ 24.03(b); 24.04(a)(b).

attractive option. The Court did suggest, however, that any information "establishing the factual innocence" of the defendant should be disclosed prior to entering a plea.

(3) The Right to Be Present

Although the defendant has the right to be present at his trial and other "critical" proceedings,[34] no court has been willing to grant defendants this right during the bargaining process. From a doctrinal perspective, this conclusion can be supported on the ground that bargaining does not involve confrontation of prosecution witnesses, and thus does not implicate the Sixth Amendment right from which the right to be present derives. It could also be based on the practical difficulty of conducting negotiations when the defendant is in jail. On the other hand, the present approach leans heavily on counsel's ability to recall and report accurately all discussions with the prosecution and his ability to divine the defendant's response to variations on the prosecution's offer. Some commentators have suggested that the accused be present during negotiations to improve his understanding of the stakes involved, as well as the attorneys' performance.[35]

(c) Permissible Inducements and Concessions

Brady v. United States[36] is important not only because it was the first Supreme Court opinion that explicitly condoned plea bargaining, but also because it provided the theoretical basis for analyzing the validity of various types of bargains. While indicating that a guilty plea that is "compelled" by the government is invalid under the Fifth Amendment because a defendant is thereby forced to "testify" against himself, it was careful to distinguish between a compelled plea, on the one hand, and a plea that is merely "caused" by a legitimately posed offer. This approach has meant that the Constitution places very few limitations on the types of inducements the state may use to encourage guilty pleas.

(1) Causation v. Compulsion

The defendant in *Brady* was charged with kidnapping under a statute that permitted imposition of the death penalty if a jury so recommended, but provided for a maximum of life at a bench trial. Brady first pleaded not guilty and opted for a jury trial, "apparently because the trial judge was unwilling to try the case without a jury." However, Brady subsequently changed his plea to guilty and was sentenced to 50 years (later reduced to 30 years). Although the trial judge twice questioned him as to the voluntariness of his plea, Brady later argued that it was coerced by the kidnapping statute and, more particularly, by fear of the death penalty.

The Supreme Court, in an opinion by Justice White, rejected this claim. While recognizing that Brady may have been affected by the possibility of a heavier sentence had he gone to trial, White pointed out that this fact would merely prove the statute "caused" the plea, not that it "coerced" the plea. Actual or threatened "physical harm" or "mental coercion overbearing the will of the defendant" would result in a violation of the Fifth Amendment, as would proof that "Brady was so gripped by fear of the death penalty

---

[34] See § 28.03(a).

[35] See, e.g., Norval Morris, The Future of Imprisonment 54 (1974) (proposing a pretrial conference at which the attorneys, the judge, the accused and the victim are present).

[36] 397 U.S. 742, 90 S.Ct. 1463 (1970).

or hope of leniency that he did not or could not, with the help of counsel, rationally weigh the advantages of going to trial against the advantages of pleading guilty." But here White found that at most the specter of capital punishment influenced Brady's decision. He also pointed out that prior to changing his plea from not guilty to guilty, Brady had discovered that his codefendant had agreed to testify against him at trial, suggesting that factors other than the potential death sentence had played a more significant role in encouraging the changed plea. White concluded by quoting a passage from the Fifth Circuit which he suggested stated the voluntariness standard in the guilty plea context:

> [A] plea of guilty entered by one fully aware of the direct consequences, including the actual value of any commitments made to him by the court, prosecutor, or his own counsel, must stand unless induced by threats (or promises to discontinue improper harassment), misrepresentation (including unfulfilled or unfulfillable promises), or perhaps by promises that are by their nature improper as having no proper relationship to the prosecutor's business (e.g. bribes).[37]

Two other decisions handed down the same day as *Brady, McMann v. Richardson*[38] and *Parker v. North Carolina*[39] similarly emphasized the difference between "causation" and "coercion." In each case, the defendant urged that he had been coerced into giving a confession to the police and that his guilty plea was the result of the confession. Justice White, writing for the Court in *McMann,* conceded that if the coercion leading to a confession also tainted the plea, a valid Fifth Amendment claim would exist. But here the defendants were merely alleging a "but for" relationship between the confession and the guilty plea which did not make out a valid involuntariness claim.

(2) *Prosecutorial Inducements*

While *Brady* made clear that a plea is not compelled merely because it results from a difficult choice, it did not address the constitutionality of inducements consciously offered by the state to obtain a plea. In *Bordenkircher v. Hayes,*[40] the Court applied the reasoning of the "*Brady* trilogy" to sanction direct prosecutorial pressure on the defendant during the plea bargaining process, so long as the choices offered by the prosecutor are authorized by law. *Bordenkircher* involved a defendant indicted by a state grand jury for forging a check for $88.30, punishable by 2 to 10 years in prison. The prosecutor offered to recommend a maximum of five years if the petitioner agreed to plead guilty, but also threatened to seek an indictment under the Kentucky Habitual Criminal Act if the petitioner (who had two prior felony convictions) refused to accept his offer. Notwithstanding the mandatory life sentence that would result from a conviction under the recidivist statute, Hayes rejected the offer. He was subsequently indicted and convicted as a habitual criminal. On federal habeas, petitioner did not contest his culpability under the recidivist statute; rather, he argued that his reindictment and conviction for the greater offense was an unconstitutionally

---

[37]　*Shelton v. United States,* 246 F.2d 571 (5th Cir. 1957) (en banc), reversed on other grounds 356 U.S. 26, 78 S.Ct. 563 (1958).

[38]　397 U.S. 759, 90 S.Ct. 1441 (1970).

[39]　397 U.S. 790, 90 S.Ct. 1458 (1970).

[40]　434 U.S. 357, 98 S.Ct. 663 (1978).

"vindictive" punishment, under *North Carolina v. Pearce*,[41] for the exercise of his right to plead not guilty and move to trial.

In a 5–4 decision, the Supreme Court reasserted that an action taken by a defendant in plea negotiations passes constitutional muster if it represents a choice among known alternatives. While reiterating *Pearce's* holding that punishing a defendant "because he has done what the law plainly allows him to do is a due process violation of the most basic sort," the majority, in an opinion by Justice Stewart, concluded that in the " 'give-and-take' of plea bargaining, there is no such element of punishment or retaliation so long as the accused is free to accept or reject the prosecution's offer." The Court emphasized that, while a defendant in Hayes' situation may be discouraged from exercising his right to plead not guilty, "the imposition of these difficult choices [is] an inevitable '—and permissible—' attribute of any legitimate system which tolerates and encourages the negotiation of pleas." By implication, had Hayes pleaded guilty as a result of the prosecutor's threat (rather than proceeded to trial despite the threat), his plea would have been voluntary.

One dissent, written by Justice Blackmun and joined by Justices Brennan and Marshall, alleged the prosecutor had been vindictive in seeking the habitual offender indictment and found his actions unconstitutional under *Pearce*. Blackmun argued that, in the plea bargaining context, the prosecutor should be required to adhere to the charge in his original offer rather than allowed to "up the ante" whenever a defendant refused his offer. Justice Powell, who wrote a second dissent, opted for a voluntariness inquiry. Although prosecutorial discretion should be overridden only in the "most exceptional case," he found that this exception applied here, because the prosecutor "penalize[d] with unique severity [the defendant's] exercise of constitutional rights."

After *Bordenkircher,* it appears that virtually all prosecutorial attempts to "persuade" a defendant to plead guilty through the spectre of higher charges are permissible, so long as: (1) the higher charges are legitimate and (2) they are "openly presented" to the defendant (to use the majority's phrase) so that he knows precisely his choices. Short of abolishing plea bargaining, this may be the only reasonable approach to such threats. As Blackmun recognized, his requirement that prosecutors stick to their original charge might encourage them to choose the higher charge initially, in detriment to defendants seeking pleas. Powell's approach avoids this problem, but requires the courts to engage in proportionality analysis (i.e., was the threat "uniquely severe"?), a very difficult task.[42]

Prosecutors occasionally resort to other types of inducements, some of which may not be permissible. For instance, the majority in *Bordenkircher* cautioned that the case did not "involve the constitutional implications of a prosecutor's offer during plea bargaining of adverse or lenient treatment for some person *other* than the accused, which might pose a greater danger of inducing a false guilty plea by skewing the assessment of the risks a defendant must consider." The Supreme Court has also indicated that use of deception to obtain a guilty plea is unconstitutional,[43] as are threats to manufacture

---

[41]   395 U.S. 711, 89 S.Ct. 2072 (1969), discussed in § 21.03(b).

[42]   Some have suggested, nonetheless, that Powell's approach is not very different from the "unconscionability analysis" used by civil courts in contracts cases. See Franklin Zimring & Richard Frase, The Criminal Justice System 587 (1980).

[43]   *Walker v. Johnston,* 312 U.S. 275, 61 S.Ct. 574 (1941).

evidence or rumors against the defendant if he does not plead guilty.[44] And, of course, as the Court stated in *Brady,* "the State may not produce a plea by actual or threatened physical harm or by mental coercion overbearing the will of the defendant."

On the other hand, as noted earlier, the Court has held that conditioning a plea agreement on waiver of one's right to receive discovery of impeachment information or information supporting an affirmative defense is permissible.[45] Similarly, offering a charge or sentencing concession in return for agreeing not to pursue an appeal or claim some other constitutional right has been found not to violate due process or the Fifth Amendment, on the ground that such waiver, if voluntary, is no different than the waiver of the right to jury trial and other rights that occurs with a guilty plea.[46] The practice of offering leniency in exchange for testimony against another defendant is also well-accepted. One circuit court of appeals panel held that such deals constitute bribery, but that decision was overturned by the full circuit.[47]

(3) Statutory Inducements

At times, the threat of a greater sentence if no plea is forthcoming comes not from the prosecutor but via statute. In *Corbitt v. New Jersey,*[48] the defendant was tried and convicted of first degree murder and sentenced to life imprisonment, as required by a state statute. Had he pleaded guilty, the same statute permitted the judge to sentence him to either life imprisonment or 30 years (the term for second degree murder). The Supreme Court upheld this scheme against a due process claim, concluding that it could not permit bargaining by a prosecutor, as it had in *Bordenkircher,* "and yet hold that the legislature may not openly provide for the possibility of leniency in return for a plea."

Corbitt does not necessarily approve all "legislative bargaining." As the dissent pointed out, this type of bargaining should be distinguished from prosecutorial bargaining, since the former is not based on individualized factors. Justice Stewart, the author of *Bordenkircher,* argued further in a separate opinion that encouraging plea bargaining is not a legislative, but an executive function. Thus, a legislative provision that automatically gives significant benefits to a person who pleads guilty rather than goes to trial should be "clearly unconstitutional." For example, the legislature should not be able to provide "that the penalty for every criminal offense to which a defendant pleads guilty is to be one-half the penalty to be imposed upon a defendant convicted of the same offense after a not guilty plea." The majority in *Corbitt* seemed to agree with this latter conclusion when it reaffirmed the pre-*Bordenkircher* decision of *United States v. Jackson,*[49] which found unconstitutional, on the ground that it "needlessly encourage[d]" guilty pleas, a statute permitting imposition of the death penalty for a

---

[44]　*Waley v. Johnston,* 316 U.S. 101, 62 S.Ct. 964 (1942).

[45]　*United States v. Ruiz,* 536 U.S. 622, 122 S.Ct. 2450 (2002), discussed in § 26.02(b)(2).

[46]　*United States v. Hare,* 269 F.3d 859 (7th Cir. 2001); *People v. Seaberg,* 41 N.E.2d 1022 (N.Y. 1989). But see *United States v. Jeffries,* 265 F.3d 556 (7th Cir. 2001) (defendant is still entitled to appeal if the agreement is involuntary or otherwise unenforceable); *MacDonald v. State,* 778 A.2d 1064 (Del. 2001) (similar holding).

[47]　See *United States v. Singleton,* 144 F.3d 1343 (10th Cir. 1998), rev'd 165 F.3d 1297 (10th Cir. 1999). For discussion see Nancy King, *Why Prosecutors are Permitted to Offer Witness Inducements: A Matter of Constitutional Authority,* 29 Stetson L.Rev. 155 (1999).

[48]　439 U.S. 212, 99 S.Ct. 492 (1978).

[49]　390 U.S. 570, 88 S.Ct. 1209 (1968).

particular offense only after a jury trial.[50] Thus, if, unlike the statute in *Corbitt*, a statute does not permit the greater punishment at the guilty plea as well as trial stage, it may violate due process.

(4) Judicial Inducements

Traditionally, judges have been barred from involvement in the bargaining process, on the grounds that they might be unduly intimidating to the defendant and could have difficulty remaining neutral if they ended up trying him.[51] But in some jurisdictions this practice has gradually given way to limited judicial participation in plea bargaining, as a means of monitoring the process and providing the parties with more information as to potential sentences. Illustrative are the American Bar Association standards, which allow judicial participation at the request of the parties, provided the judge indicates only what charge or sentence concessions would be acceptable, and "never through word or demeanor, either directly or indirectly, communicates to the defendant or defense counsel that a plea agreement should be accepted or that a guilty plea should be entered."[52] Some commentators have gone further, arguing that bargaining should not take place *except* in front of a judge, who, at a transcribed pretrial conference, would hear evidence from both sides, as well as consider a pre-sentence report, and indicate the sentence he would impose if the defendant pleads guilty.[53]

If the judge makes clear at a pretrial conference that a greater sentence will be imposed if the defendant does not plead, is a subsequent plea coerced? Some courts have answered this question affirmatively, on the ground that "[t]he unequal positions of the judge and the accused, one with the power to commit to prison and the other deeply concerned to avoid prison, at once raise a question of fundamental fairness."[54] But, in light of *Bordenkircher* and *Corbitt,* the Supreme Court would presumably answer this question in the negative.[55] Indeed, because defendants know that courts often accept the prosecutor's sentencing recommendations in any event, there is little functional difference, in "inequality" terms, between judicial and prosecutorial threats of this type.[56] Although Federal Rule of Criminal Procedure 11 prohibits judicial involvement in the plea bargaining process, the Supreme Court has held that such involvement can be harmless error. In *United States v. Davila,*[57] the defendant pleaded guilty to a federal conspiracy charge in exchange for the dismissal of 33 other charges, after the judge encouraged him to do so in light of the strength of the government's case. Davila later argued that a guilty plea obtained after this type of judicial involvement in the

---

[50] Although *Jackson* was decided before *Brady*, and struck down the same statute that was involved in that case, Brady's guilty plea occurred well before *Jackson* and its legality was not affected by the decision. As the Court said in *Brady*, a defendant "should not be permitted to disown his solemn admissions in open court . . . because it later develops . . . that the maximum penalty then assumed applicable has been held inapplicable in subsequent judicial decisions."

[51] See, e.g., ABA, Advisory Committee on the Criminal Trial, Standards Relating to Pleas of Guilty 71–74 (1968); Fed.R.Crim.P. 11(e)(1).

[52] ABA Criminal Justice Standard 14–3.3(d) & (c) (3d ed. 1996) (amending the ABA standard cited supra note 52). See also *Ellis v. State*, 744 N.E.2d 425 (Ind. 2001).

[53] See Albert Alschuler, *The Trial Judge's Role in Plea Bargaining, Part I*, 76 Colum.L.Rev. 1059 (1976).

[54] *United States ex rel. Elksnis v. Gilligan,* 256 F.Supp. 244 (S.D.N.Y. 1966).

[55] Note also that, in *Brady*, judicial "unwillingness" to hear Brady's capital charge without a jury was not viewed as unconstitutionally coercive, despite the fact that it meant the defendant could only avoid the possibility of a death sentence if he pleaded guilty.

[56] See, e.g., *Frank v. Blackburn,* 646 F.2d 873 (5th Cir. 1980) (upholding judicial bargaining).

[57] 569 U.S. 597, 133 S.Ct. 2139 (2013).

bargaining process is structural error that requires automatic reversal under Rule 11.[58] A unanimous Court rejected that view, and noted that on remand the lower court should consider the facts that Davila had pleaded guilty three months after the judge's exhortation to plead guilty and did not raise the judicial interference claim at the time of the plea.[59]

If judicial involvement is permissible, the judge should be required, as *Bordenkircher* required of prosecutors, to state with some precision the sentence that will be imposed if a plea of not guilty is entered and conviction follows at trial. Otherwise, there is a grave danger that a judge whose offer is refused will react vindictively and, unconstrained by specific promises, impose a greater sentence than he would have had he not been involved in the negotiations. Alternatively, trial of the defendant who refuses to plead should be assigned to another judge.[60]

(d) Admission of Statements Made in Connection with Bargaining

Under the federal rules, and in most states, "any statement made in the course of plea discussions with an attorney for the government which do not result in a plea of guilty or which result in a plea of guilty later withdrawn" are inadmissible in subsequent proceedings.[61] This rule is obviously designed to encourage bargaining. Note, however, that it is does not cover statements made to the police or other individuals who are not attorneys for the government. The admissibility of these admissions is governed by the law of confessions, even when made under the impression that the non-attorney had bargaining authority.[62] Note further that statements made *after* "plea discussions" and the taking of the plea may be admissible in subsequent proceedings if the plea is later withdrawn.[63]

The Supreme Court has also held that a federal defendant may waive the protection the federal rules afford against using statements made during plea negotiations. In *United States v. Mezzanatto,*[64] the defendant agreed to the prosecution's stipulation that, as a condition of entering into plea negotiations, he waive his right to prevent prosecution use of such statements to impeach him if he later testified at trial. The negotiations failed, the defendant testified at trial and, on the basis of the defendant's prenegotiation waiver, the prosecution was allowed to rebut his testimony with contradictory statements made during the negotiations. The defendant appealed his conviction on three grounds: (1) the right to prevent prosecution use of plea statements is so important to a "fair procedure" that it should be considered unwaivable; (2) allowing such waiver will deter plea bargaining by defendants (who will fear that their negotiation statements might provide the prosecution with rebuttal evidence); and (3) allowing waiver will encourage prosecutorial abuse of the bargaining process. To the first argument Justice Thomas, who wrote the opinion for the Court, responded that, if any rights are non-waivable, only those that are "fundamental to the reliability of the fact-finding process" would fit in this category; since assertion of the right to prevent

---

[58]   See § 29.05(c)(3) for a discussion of structural error.

[59]   See § 26.05(b) for a discussion of harmless error analysis in connection with challenges to violations of Rule 11.

[60]   This is the suggestion of Alschuler, supra note 54.

[61]   Fed.R.Crim.P. 11(f).

[62]   See § 16.03(d)(2) for a discussion of trickery and confessions cases.

[63]   *Hutto v. Ross,* 429 U.S. 28, 97 S.Ct. 202 (1976).

[64]   513 U.S. 196, 115 S.Ct. 797 (1995).

impeachment use of plea statements *detracts* from reliability, it can be waived. Thomas also doubted that routine use of waiver clauses would diminish plea bargaining, both as an empirical matter,[65] and because, as a matter of logic, without the incentive provided by such waiver clauses the prosecution might not be willing to bargain. Finally, Thomas stated that the possibility that some prosecutors might overreach does not require that all such agreements must be invalidated.

Still undecided is whether a waiver clause that allows use of plea statements in the prosecution's case-in-chief is permissible. As the dissenters (Justices Souter and Stevens) pointed out, the Court's reasoning would support such waiver clauses as well. But three Justices in the majority, Ginsburg, O'Connor and Breyer, wrote a concurring opinion suggesting they might be more hesitant to join such a holding, out of fear that these more expansive waiver clauses might "more severely undermine a defendant's incentive to negotiate, and thereby inhibit plea bargaining." Nonetheless, a large number of courts have now held that prosecutors may require defendants wishing to plea bargain to waive *all* protection against use of their plea statements, including statements made during "proffer sessions," when the defense and prosecution meet to discuss the information the defendant might be able to offer on other suspects.[66]

26.03   The Legal Effect of a Bargain

(a) On the Court

As a general rule, the court is not bound by a plea bargain reached by the parties.[67] The one obvious exception is when the court participated in the bargaining process and promised the bargain would be fulfilled.[68] Additionally, when the bargain is a "charge bargain" rather than a "sentence bargain," some courts have held that, because charging is a prosecutorial prerogative, the judge has no authority to reject such a bargain unless the dismissal of charges thereby contemplated is "an abuse of prosecutorial discretion."[69] This distinction between the two types of bargains is somewhat problematic, since most charge reductions are sought precisely because of their effect on sentencing. In any event, when the bargain explicitly seeks a particular sentencing disposition, then the court clearly has authority to reject it.[70]

(b) On the Prosecution

Once the court accepts a bargain, the prosecutor must fulfill any remaining obligations under it (although occasionally disputes arise over what those obligations are

---

[65]   Thomas noted that, while the waiver practice at issue in *Mezzanatto* was in effect in the Ninth Circuit, approximately 92.2% of the convictions obtained were via plea, compared to an 88.8% plea rate in other federal jurisdictions.

[66]   See, e.g., *United States v. Barrow*, 400 F.3d 109 (2d Cir. 2005) (use of proffer statements and omissions to rebut defense attorney's assertions during opening argument and cross); *United States v. Rebbe*, 314 F.3d 402 (9th Cir. 2002) (proffer statement admissible even when defendant does not testify, if defense presents any evidence or arguments inconsistent with statements); *United States v. Burch*, 156 F.3d 1315 (D.C.Cir. 1998) (plea statements admissible in prosecution's case-in-chief).

[67]   See, e.g., Fed.R.Crim.P. 11(c)(3). In the federal courts, the nolo plea is accepted only after considering "the parties' views *and* the interest of the public in the effective administration of justice." Fed.R.Crim.P. 11(a)(3) (emphasis added).

[68]   See § 26.02(c)(4).

[69]   *United States v. Ammidown*, 497 F.2d 615 (D.C.Cir. 1973).

[70]   As to the consequences for the defendant of such a rejection, see § 26.05(b).

and the remedy for breach). Before the court accepts the bargain, on the other hand, the bargain rarely has binding power on the prosecution.

(1) Post-Arraignment

In *Santobello v. New York*,[71] the defendant was indicted on two felony counts. After negotiations the prosecutor agreed to allow the defendant to plead guilty to a lesser-included offense, conviction of which would carry a maximum sentence of one year, and to make no recommendation as to sentence. Accordingly, the defendant withdrew his plea of not guilty and agreed to plead guilty to the lesser charge. The court accepted the plea. At sentencing, a new prosecutor, unaware of the plea negotiations, requested the maximum one-year sentence. The defense counsel objected on the ground that the first prosecutor had promised to make no recommendation as to sentence. The judge, who stated that he was uninfluenced by the recommendation, imposed the maximum sentence.

The Supreme Court held that the plea should be voided as a matter of due process. The Court noted the many benefits associated with disposing of charges after plea discussions, but added that the utilization of this process presupposes fairness in securing agreement between an accused and a prosecutor. The Court concluded that "when a plea rests in any significant degree on a promise or agreement of the prosecutor, so that it can be said to be part of the inducement or consideration, such promise must be fulfilled." Significantly, it was immaterial to the Court that the prosecution claimed its breach of the agreement had been inadvertent.

In deciding whether a due process violation has occurred under *Santobello*, the precise terms of the agreement must be considered. In *United States v. Benchimol*,[72] the plea agreement included a promise by the government that it would recommend probation with restitution. Instead of making this recommendation, the government's presentence report was silent as to recommendation. When defense counsel pointed out this error, the government's attorney agreed that the promise had been made. The court, however, sentenced the defendant to a term of six years under the Youth Corrections Act. The defendant, arguing that the government had not kept its bargain, moved to have his sentence vacated and be resentenced to time served or to be allowed to withdraw his guilty plea. The court of appeals granted relief, finding that the U.S. Attorney should have stated his grounds for making the lenient recommendation and that, by failing to do so, he "left an impression of less-than-enthusiastic support for leniency." The Supreme Court, in a per curiam opinion, reversed, holding that unless the government agrees to support a particular recommendation "enthusiastically," or to give its reasons for a lenient recommendation, it need not do so.

(2) Pre-Arraignment

The prosecutor is given even more leeway with respect to adhering to a bargain *before* the defendant pleads to the court. In *Mabry v. Johnson*,[73] when the defendant's attorney called to accept a dispositional arrangement suggested by the deputy prosecutor, the prosecutor told him that a mistake had been made and withdrew the offer. The prosecutor then proposed a significantly harsher arrangement to which the

---

[71]　404 U.S. 257, 92 S.Ct. 495 (1971).

[72]　471 U.S. 453, 105 S.Ct. 2103 (1985).

[73]　467 U.S. 504, 104 S.Ct. 2543 (1984).

defendant eventually agreed and which the trial judge accepted at arraignment. The Supreme Court unanimously rejected the court of appeals' reasoning that "fairness" precluded the prosecution's withdrawal of the original plea proposal once it was accepted by the defendant. It pointed out that while the defendant in *Santobello* had pleaded guilty on the false assurance by the state that he had bargained for a specific prosecutorial stance toward sentencing, the defendant's ultimate plea in this case was made with full awareness of the consequences and "was thus in no sense the product of governmental deception; it rested on no 'unfulfilled promise' and fully satisfied the test for voluntariness and intelligence." The Court thus declared irrelevant whether the prosecution was negligent in first making and then withdrawing the original offer.

Mabry did not deal with a pre-arraignment defendant who did *not* accept a second offer after the first, accepted offer is withdrawn. But, in a footnote, the Court suggested that this type of defendant would not be entitled to specific performance either, an issue discussed further below, in connection with remedies. Most lower courts have held that the prosecutor should be allowed to withdraw an accepted offer up to the time a plea is entered unless the defendant has "detrimentally relied" on the agreement before it is withdrawn (by, for instance, testifying against a co-defendant pursuant to the agreement).[74] While this rule runs counter to traditional contract doctrine, so does the well-accepted principle that the defendant may refuse to plead guilty at the time of arraignment despite any previous bargains.[75] Thus, the rule has a reciprocal fairness to it.

(3) Remedy for Breach

Of the seven justices who deliberated in *Santobello*, four appeared to agree that if the prosecution fails to abide by an agreement accepted by the court, the defendant is entitled either to specific performance of the agreement (which, in *Santobello*, would have required the prosecutor to make the agreed-upon recommendation to a different judge), or to withdraw the plea. The other three justices appeared to leave the choice of remedy up to the trial court, although they also stated that one or the other remedy might be "required" under some, unspecified circumstances.

If the choice of remedy is the defendant's, it will usually be in favor of specific performance, since a plea withdrawal requires the parties to begin the bargaining process over again, with unclear results. However, in *Mabry,* the Court intimated that the choice may not be the defendant's. In a footnote, the Court stated that "*Santobello* expressly declined to hold that the Constitution compels specific performance of a broken prosecutorial promise . . . ; the Court made it clear that permitting Santobello to replead was within the range of constitutionally appropriate remedies." This somewhat cryptically phrased passage suggests that the defendant can be forced, either pre- *or* post-arraignment, to replead or go to trial rather than be allowed to demand specific performance of an agreed-upon bargain that has been broken.[76]

---

[74] See *People v. Heiler*, 79 Mich.App. 714, 262 N.W.2d 890 (1977). But see, *Cooper v. United States,* 594 F.2d 12 (4th Cir. 1979).

[75] See, e.g., Fed.R.Crim.P. 11(d)(1) (providing that a defendant may withdraw a guilty plea "before the court accepts the plea, for any reason or no reason").

[76] It should also be noted that, if the new charge is greater than the charge involved in the breached bargain, a vindictiveness claim might lie. See § 21.03(b).

While, as discussed above, this approach is usually justifiable for pre-arraignment breaches, it is inappropriate after a plea has been entered, for two reasons. First, after a plea is entered, the defendant is usually not permitted to withdraw it unless the agreement is not fulfilled or an error of constitutional or near constitutional magnitude has occurred.[77] Thus, the "reciprocal fairness" argument in favor of allowing pre-arraignment breaches does not apply here. Second, although in many cases there may be no more "concrete" detrimental reliance on a post-plea bargain than on a pre-plea bargain, allowing the prosecution to breach with impunity an agreement that has been endorsed by the court damages the integrity of the system, not only in the eyes of the defendant but of the public at large as well. Nonetheless most courts hold that the defendant is not entitled to specific performance for post-arraignment breaches.[78]

(c) On the Defendant

As already noted, up until the time of arraignment, the defendant may plead not guilty despite a previous agreement to plead guilty. But if he wants the benefits of the bargain, he may have certain obligations beyond merely pleading guilty at the arraignment. Some courts have reasonably held, for instance, that the prosecution need not abide by an agreement based on inaccurate information provided by the defendant.[79] The agreement itself may also impose obligations on the defendant beyond simply pleading guilty. For instance, one common type of bargain already mentioned is a reduction in charges in exchange for testimony against a codefendant. If the defendant refuses to provide the testimony, the plea might be vacated.

The Supreme Court had occasion to address the latter situation in *Ricketts v. Adamson*.[80] There, the defendant did testify against his two codefendants and helped secure their convictions, in exchange for a reduction in charge from first to second degree murder. However, after he had been sentenced on the latter charge, the codefendants' convictions were overturned on appeal. When the prosecution sought the defendant's testimony at the retrial, the defendant told the prosecution that he believed his obligation to testify had terminated when he had been sentenced and that he would testify again only if the state would release him from custody following the retrial. The prosecution informed the defendant that he was in breach of the agreement and eventually filed an information recharging him with first degree murder. The defendant challenged the validity of the new charge in state court, arguing it violated the Double Jeopardy Clause. The Arizona Supreme Court found that the defendant had breached the agreement and ordered that he be tried on the original first degree murder charge. Despite his indication that he was now willing to testify against the codefendants, the defendant was tried on the charge and sentenced to death.

The Court, in a 5–4 decision authored by Justice White, held that double jeopardy did not bar the first degree murder prosecution because the plea agreement specifically stated that in the event the defendant refused to testify "this entire agreement is null and void and the original charge will be automatically reinstated." The dissent, authored by Justice Brennan, did not contest the notion that the double jeopardy right could be

---

[77]   See § 26.05(b).

[78]   See, e.g., *United States v. Moscahlaidis*, 868 F.2d 1357 (3d Cir. 1989). Occasionally, of course, specific performance is not possible, as when the prosecutor has promised to recommend a sentence that is not legally authorized.

[79]   *Hamlin v. Barrett*, 335 So.2d 898 (Miss. 1976).

[80]   483 U.S. 1, 107 S.Ct. 2680 (1987).

waived through a plea agreement. However, Brennan argued that under the terms of the agreement at issue in *Adamson* the defendant could reasonably have believed he was required to testify only prior to his sentencing (indeed, the express wording of the agreement spoke of the defendant being sentenced "at the conclusion of his testimony");[81] thus, his communication to the state of the terms under which he would testify after sentencing was not *necessarily* a breach of the agreement. The proper procedure, Brennan contended, would have been to submit the disagreement about the interpretation of the plea to the court which accepted the plea; the state should be able to try the defendant on the greater charge only if the court decided the defendant's interpretation was in error and the defendant continued to refuse to testify.

Adamson, like *Mabry*, indicates that the defendant cannot demand specific performance of a broken bargain. Defendants who disagree with the state's interpretation of a plea agreement now do so at the risk of having the entire plea vacated if the prosecution can convince a court its interpretation is correct, regardless of the defendant's subsequent willingness to abide by the agreement as construed by the court.

26.04   Taking the Plea

If a defendant decides to plead guilty, whether pursuant to a bargain or not, the arraignment judge must ensure that the plea meets constitutional and statutory standards. According to the Supreme Court's decision in *Boykin v. Alabama*,[82] it is constitutional error "for the trial judge to accept [a] guilty plea without an affirmative showing that it is intelligent and voluntary." Additionally, local rules often require the judge to inquire into various matters, including most importantly, the nature of any bargains reached.

Very often this procedure will be pro forma, since the parties, through the plea bargaining process, have usually already agreed to and understand the charges involved, the penalties that they would like imposed, and any other relevant quid pro quo. Nonetheless, the Supreme Court has indicated that a direct interview of the defendant by the arraignment judge is important, if not constitutionally required. In *McCarthy v. United States*,[83] it stated:

> By personally interrogating the defendant, not only will the judge be better able to ascertain the plea's voluntariness, but he also will develop a more complete record to support his determination in a subsequent post-conviction attack. . . . Both of these goals are undermined in proportion to the degree the district court judge resorts to "assumptions" not based upon recorded responses to his inquiries.

Summarizing these various requirements, the arraignment judge should address the defendant to ensure: (1) that the plea is "intelligent," i.e., that the defendant understands the elements of the plea and any associated bargain; and (2) that the plea is "voluntary," i.e., that the defendant was not coerced into the plea. Additionally, to ensure that the

---

[81] Contrast the Court's unwillingness to countenance the defendant's literal reading of the plea agreement here with its willingness to allow such a reading when it favors the state. *United States v. Benchimol,* 471 U.S. 453, 105 S.Ct. 2103 (1985), discussed in § 26.03(b)(1).

[82] 395 U.S. 238, 89 S.Ct. 1709 (1969).

[83] 394 U.S. 459, 89 S.Ct. 1166 (1969).

plea is "accurate," the judge should make some effort to ascertain (3) that there is some sort of factual basis for the plea. These aspects of the arraignment are discussed here.

(a) The Intelligent Plea Requirement

Federal Rule 11(b) (formerly 11(c)), which has served as a model for many states, provides that the court may not accept a guilty plea until it has determined that the defendant understands: (1) the nature of the charge or charges to which a plea is offered; (2) the possible sentence and other penalties for each offense to which a plea is offered; and (3) the rights he will be waiving if he pleads guilty, i.e. the rights to: be tried by a jury, the assistance of counsel at trial, confront and cross-examine witnesses against him, and avoid compelled self-incrimination. Rule 11(c)(4) imposes further requirements with respect to ensuring the defendant understands the nature of any plea bargain he has entered into. The discussion here focuses on which, if any, of these requirements are constitutionally necessary, and whether they recognize all crucial aspects of the case which the defendant must understand to ensure a constitutionally adequate plea.

(1) Understanding the Charge

In *Henderson v. Morgan*,[84] the defendant was indicted for first-degree murder, but pleaded guilty to second-degree murder on the advice of counsel and with the agreement of the prosecutor. Five years later he attempted to vacate the conviction on the ground that at the time of his plea he had not known that intent to cause death was an element of second-degree murder. The Supreme Court held that "since respondent did not receive adequate notice of the offense to which he pleaded guilty, his plea was involuntary and the judgment of conviction was entered without due process of law." Because the intent element of a murder charge is a "critical" element of the charge, the fact that neither the judge nor the defense attorney explained this element to Morgan invalidated the plea.

Two things remain unclear after *Henderson*. First is the definition of "critical" elements. In a footnote, the Court stated:

> There is no need in this case to decide whether notice of the true nature, or substance, of a charge always requires a description of the offense; we assume it does not. Nevertheless, intent is such a critical element of the offense of second-degree murder that notice of that element is required.

It would seem that any element, knowledge of which might have the effect of changing the plea of the defendant, should be described. Thus, for instance, the defendant should have notice of every element that has the effect of differentiating the charged offense from a lesser included offense. On the other hand, most courts have held that inquiry into "defenses" would require too much guesswork, especially if dependent upon individualized factors, and that apprising the defendant of their scope is more appropriately the province of the attorney.[85]

The second issue left unclear after *Henderson* is the precise obligation of the judge with respect to notice of those elements that are "critical." Arguably, to ensure an intelligent plea, the judge should inquire into the defendant's understanding of these elements. Yet *Henderson* suggests that even if the judge makes no such inquiry, "a

---

[84] 426 U.S. 637, 96 S.Ct. 2253 (1976).

[85] *United States v. Lumpkins*, 845 F.2d 1444 (7th Cir. 1988) (statute of limitations); *Dismuke v. United States*, 864 F.2d 106 (11th Cir. 1989) (good faith); *United States ex rel. Salisbury v. Blackburn*, 792 F.2d 498 (5th Cir. 1986) (insanity).

representation [on the record] by defense counsel that the nature of the offense has been explained to the accused" will suffice. Indeed, "it may be appropriate to presume that in most cases defense counsel routinely explain the nature of the offense in sufficient detail to give the accused notice of what he is being asked to admit." In the same vein was the Court's statement in *Bradshaw v. Stumpf*[86] that "[w]here a defendant is represented by competent counsel, the court usually may rely on that counsel's assurance that the defendant has been properly informed of the nature and elements of the charge to which he is pleading guilty." Thus, assuming such assurance occurs, the judge need not independently explain the elements of the charge to the defendant.

Henderson also suggests that, even if such a certification by counsel is not made, a plea is valid if the defendant provides a "factual statement or admission necessarily implying that he [met all critical elements]." In such a situation, the judge is again apparently absolved for failing to inquire into the defendant's understanding of the charges. The problem here is that an admission of guilt does not necessarily mean the defendant has thought through whether the prosecution would be able to prove the relevant elements at trial; without information as to the nature of these elements, either from the attorney or the judge, an intelligent decision about whether to plead cannot be made. Nonetheless, lower courts tend to follow this aspect of *Henderson*.[87]

(2) Understanding of Consequences

Prior to 1975, Rule 11 required the court to inform the defendant of the "consequences of the plea." In that year, the Rule was amended to require disclosure concerning the minimum and maximum sentences that might be received, as well as the effect of any special parole term (which can result in confinement beyond the maximum term otherwise provided). In 1989, the Rule was further amended to ensure the defendant is informed of any applicable sentencing guidelines (which had replaced the previous system of flexible sentences and "ordinary" parole five years earlier[88]), as well as any possibility that the court may order the defendant to make restitution to a victim of the offense.[89]

Despite the breadth of the federal rule, still other dispositional information might also be considered important. For instance, the ABA Standards[90] require the judge to inform the defendant of any different or additional punishment that might be authorized by reason of the defendant's previous conviction of an offense. In addition, they require that a defendant be informed of special circumstances relating to release or probation.[91] On the other hand, there is agreement among the lower courts that some "collateral" consequences of a plea, such as loss of the right to vote, need not be described.[92]

---

[86]   545 U.S. 175, 125 S.Ct. 2398 (2005).

[87]   See, e.g., *Commonwealth v. Colantoni,* 396 Mass. 672, 488 N.E.2d 394 (1986).

[88]   See 28 U.S.C.A. § 994(a) (establishing guidelines); 18 U.S.C.A. § 3624(a)(b) (abolishing parole).

[89]   See Fed.R.Crim.P. 11(b)(1).

[90]   See ABA, supra note 1, Standard 14–1.4(a)(iii).

[91]   Cf. *United States v. Littlejohn,* 224 F.3d 960 (9th Cir. 2000) (defendant must be told of loss of federal benefits when it is a mandatory result of conviction).

[92]   See, e.g., *People v. Thomas,* 41 Ill.2d 122, 242 N.E.2d 177 (1968) (loss of right to vote); *Moore v. Hinton,* 513 F.2d 781 (5th Cir. 1975) (loss of driver's license); *Steinsvik v. Vinzant,* 640 F.2d 949 (9th Cir. 1981) (deportation).

As to whether any of this information must be imparted as a *constitutional* matter, a few Supreme Court decisions are relevant. In *Iowa v. Tovar*,[93] the Court unanimously rejected a state court ruling that defendants at guilty plea hearings must be told that waiving an attorney both entails the risk that a viable defense will be overlooked and deprives the defendant of an independent opinion on whether, under the facts and applicable law, it is wise to plead guilty. But the Court also stated that "the constitutional requirement" encompasses telling such a defendant "of the nature of the charges against him, of his right to be counseled regarding his plea, and of the range of allowable punishments attendant upon the entry of a guilty plea." The Court did not elaborate on what might be an "allowable punishment." However, in an earlier case, it held that a pleading defendant need not be told of his parole eligibility under ordinary parole provisions.[94] Although this holding is irrelevant in federal court now that federal parole has been abolished, it obviously is still pertinent in states which have parole provisions.

At the same time, the Supreme Court has held that failure of *defense counsel* to apprise a defendant of certain consequences can amount to ineffective assistance of counsel and invalidation of a guilty plea. In *Padilla v. Kentucky*,[95] counsel erroneously told Padilla that, given the length of time he had lived in the United States (40 years), he did not have to worry about deportation if he pled guilty. Seven members of the Court concluded that, because deportation is a severe penalty (albeit civil in nature), misinformation of this sort constitutes deficient performance for Sixth Amendment purposes, at least when the law regarding deportation is clear.[96] When, as is often the case, the relevant immigration law is unclear, the attorney need only tell noncitizen clients that charges "may carry a risk of adverse immigration consequences." Justice Scalia, in a dissent joined by Justice Thomas, contended that the Sixth Amendment's language guaranteeing effective counsel in "criminal prosecutions" only requires that counsel inform clients of the *criminal* sanctions attendant to a conviction. But given the majority's conclusion in *Padilla*, the Constitution may now require defense attorneys to inform clients of other serious and clearly delineated non-criminal consequences of a guilty plea, including, for instance, sex offender registration and residential restrictions. Whether the judge must inquire into whether counsel has done so is not clear from *Padilla*.

(3) Understanding Rights Waived by a Plea

Prior to 1975, Rule 11 did not require the judge to inform the defendant of the rights waived by a plea, apparently on the highly dubious assumption that simply telling the defendant a guilty plea waives his right to trial is sufficient notice of the other rights he is waiving. The Court's decision in *Boykin* suggested that the federal rule's mandate of explicit notice of the rights waived is constitutionally required. There, the Court stressed that a guilty plea waives the privilege against self-incrimination at trial,[97] the right to

---

[93]   541 U.S. 77, 124 S.Ct. 1379 (2004).

[94]   *Hill v. Lockhart,* 474 U.S. 52, 106 S.Ct. 366 (1985).

[95]   559 U.S. 356, 130 S.Ct. 1473 (2010). *Padilla* was held to be non-retroactive in *Chaidez v. United States*, 568 U.S. 342, 113 S.Ct. 1103 (2013).

[96]   The Court remanded the case to determine whether this deficient performance prejudiced the defendant, an inquiry that involves determining whether the defendant's decision to plead would have been affected by correct information. See § 32.04(c)(3).

[97]   However, a guilty plea does not waive the privilege at sentencing, for otherwise the government "could indict without specifying the quantity of drugs involved, obtain a guilty plea, and then put the defendant

trial by jury and the right to confront one's accusers and concluded: "We cannot presume a waiver of these three important federal rights from a silent record."

This language strongly supports the notion that the judge must determine whether these specific rights are understood, which can usually best be effectuated simply by describing them to the defendant as required by Rule 11. However, the Court later upheld a guilty plea from a defendant who had not been advised of these rights, with no discussion of the point.[98] Furthermore, the Court has suggested that the defendant need not be apprised of statutory, as opposed to constitutional, rights that are waived by a guilty plea.[99] Whatever the constitutional standard is, as noted above, the federal rule and most state rules require that the defendant be apprised of these and other legal rights that might be waived by a plea.[100]

(4) Understanding the Bargain

Before *Brady*, the fact that the parties had bargained was seldom admitted to in open court, given its uncertain legal status. Now that plea bargaining is accepted, most jurisdictions require that the agreement be clearly revealed on the record at the time the guilty plea is taken. The federal rules, for instance, stipulate that the agreement must be disclosed at the time the plea is offered in court (though, on a showing of good cause, the disclosure may be made *in camera*).[101] This type of rule helps ensure that all the parties to the bargain are aware of its terms and agree upon them, and also facilitates later review of the bargain.

The facts of *Blackledge v. Allison,*[102] which involved a plea accepted before *Brady* was decided, are illustrative. There, the only record of the plea was an executed "plea form" from which the judge had read a number of questions, including whether anyone had "made any promises or threats" that influenced the defendant. The defendant later claimed on habeas that his attorney had told him to give a negative answer to this question, but that in fact he had been promised a lesser sentence than he received; in support of this claim, he provided precise information as to the nature of the promise and when it was made. The Supreme Court, taking note of the defendant's proof, and speculating that defense counsel may have advised the defendant to lie at the arraignment given "the ambiguous status of the process of plea bargaining at the time the guilty plea was made," found that the defendant was entitled to a hearing on his claim.

More importantly, the Court went on to note that North Carolina, the state in which the plea took place, had recently reformed its plea practices to require the judge, on the

---

on the stand at sentencing to fill in the drug quantity." *Mitchell v. United States*, 526 U.S. 314, 119 S.Ct. 1307 (1999), discussed in § 15.03(a).

[98] *Brady v. United States*, 397 U.S. 742, 90 S.Ct. 1463 (1970).

[99] *Libretti v. United States*, 516 U.S. 29, 116 S.Ct. 356 (1995)(defendant need not be told of his statutory right to a jury trial on the forfeiture issue, although if defendant can prove he was ignorant of this right at the time of the plea he may have grounds for relief).

[100] In 1999 Rule 11 was amended to require that the trial court ascertain that the defendant understands "the terms of any provision in a plea agreement waiving the right to appeal or to collaterally attack the sentence." See Fed.R.Crim.P. 11(b)(1)(N) (using revised language). This provision was proposed primarily because, with the advent of the federal sentencing guidelines and appeals of sentences received thereunder, an increasing number of plea agreements contain such a waiver provision. See 65 Crim. L.Rep. 142 (1999).

[101] Fed.R.Crim.P. 11(c)(2).

[102] 431 U.S. 63, 97 S.Ct. 1621 (1977).

record, to make "specific inquiry" of both the defendant and the attorneys about whether a plea bargain had been struck and, if so, the nature of the bargain. "Had these commendable procedures been followed in the present case," continued the Court, "Allison's petition would have been cast in a very different light." *Allison* does not constitutionalize disclosure requirements, but provides a strong rationale for them. If procedures like these are followed, it will be difficult for the defendant to later claim that either the prosecutor or his own counsel misled him as to elements of the bargain.

A second requirement relating to the defendant's understanding of the plea bargain has to do with alerting him to the court's possible reaction to the bargain. As discussed later in this chapter,[103] although judicial rejection of agreed-upon terms usually allows the defendant to withdraw his plea, in some jurisdictions a plea of guilty at arraignment may not be withdrawn if the court merely fails to follow, at a subsequent sentencing proceeding, a sentencing recommendation or request made as part of the agreement between the parties. Because this rule is founded on the assumption that the defendant knows the court may arrive at a stiffer sentence, the federal rules require the arraignment judge to inform the defendant who has entered into such a bargain that he may not back out of the plea if, after consideration of the presentence report and other matters, the court decides not to endorse the recommendation or request.[104]

(5) Competence

Occasionally, a person's mental status will be so suspect that he is incapable of understanding the various aspects of a guilty plea and any associated bargain. Typically, such an individual will be found incompetent prior to arraignment and treated to restore his competency. If his competency is restored, he will be given the option, as with any other defendant, of going to trial or pleading guilty. If not restorable, he will normally be hospitalized or released.[105]

Although a competency hearing thus need not be a routine part of the arraignment, a plea can be invalidated if the judge fails to inquire into the effects of obvious mental disability or other disabilities.[106] In most states, no distinction is made between the standard for determining incompetence to plead guilty and the standard for determining incompetence if, instead, the case goes to trial. Some courts have held that this equation is inappropriate.[107] A plea of guilty, these courts state, not only requires an understanding of the legal situation and an ability to communicate with the attorney (which is all that is required before a finding of competence to stand trial),[108] but also requires an understanding of the rights being waived by not going to trial. Additionally, it is argued, a guilty plea requires more "competence" because the defendant, not a jury, is making the dispositive decision.[109]

However, in *Godinez v. Moran*[110] the Supreme Court held that, in federal court, the majority view that the two competencies are synonymous should govern. The majority

---

[103] See § 26.05(b).

[104] Fed.R.Crim.P. 11(e)(3)(B).

[105] This is the procedure applied to those found incompetent to stand trial, described in § 28.03(b)(4).

[106] *Fontaine v. United States,* 411 U.S. 213, 93 S.Ct. 1461 (1973).

[107] See *Sieling v. Eyman,* 478 F.2d 211 (9th Cir. 1973).

[108] See § 28.03(b)(1).

[109] *Sieling,* supra note 108.

[110] 509 U.S. 389, 113 S.Ct. 2680 (1993).

pointed out that, like the person who pleads guilty, a person who proceeds to trial may also have to make decisions about the right to jury, the need to confront accusers, and the right to remain silent (in terms of taking the stand). At the same time, the Court held that, if a defendant does decide to waive any of these rights through a guilty plea or otherwise, the waiver must be a knowing and voluntary, meaning that the defendant must understand the consequences of the waiver (e.g., that a guilty plea means there will be no trial, no ability to confront accusers and no jury) and willingly make it. Others have noted that adopting a higher competency standard for guilty pleas might "create a class of semi-competent defendants who are not protected from prosecution because they have been found competent to stand trial, but who are denied the leniency of the plea bargaining process because they are not competent to plead guilty."[111] Further, it can be assumed that a guilty plea is usually in the best interests of the defendant who has adequate counsel.[112]

(b) The Voluntariness Requirement

Boykin emphasized that a plea may be rendered constitutionally invalid not only by "ignorance" or "incomprehension," but also by "coercion, terror, inducements, [and] subtle or blatant threats." Rule 11(b)(2), similar to most state rules, attempts to protect against the danger of such coercion by requiring the judge to address the defendant personally in court and determine that any offered plea is "voluntary and did not result from force, threats or promises (other than promises in a plea agreement)." As discussed in detail earlier,[113] threats or promises within the context of the bargaining process are unlikely to be deemed coercive.

(c) The Factual Basis Requirement

Rule 11 not only requires the court to ensure that a plea is intelligently and voluntarily given, but also that it make "such inquiry as shall satisfy it that there is a factual basis for the plea."[114] The Advisory Committee notes on this rule state that the factual basis should be developed on the record, "for example, by having the accused describe the conduct that gave rise to the charge."[115] As the Supreme Court stated in *McCarthy v. United States,*[116] "[r]equiring this examination of the relation between the law and the acts the defendant admits having committed is designed to 'protect a defendant who is in the position of pleading voluntarily with an understanding of the nature of the charge but without realizing that his conduct does not actually fall within the charge.' "[117]

McCarthy merely construed Rule 11; it did not explicitly hold that the factual basis inquiry was constitutionally required. However, in *North Carolina v. Alford*[118] the Court appeared to give the *McCarthy* holding constitutional status under at least one specific

---

[111] Note, *Competence to Plead Guilty: A New Standard*, 1974 Duke L.J. 149, 170.

[112] However, *Moran* went on to hold that a person who is competent to stand trial is also competent to waive the right to counsel. For further discussion of this case, see § 28.03(b)(1).

[113] See § 26.02(c).

[114] Fed.R.Crim.P. 11(b)(3).

[115] Quoting *Santobello v. New York,* 404 U.S. 257, 92 S.Ct. 495 (1971).

[116] 394 U.S. 459, 89 S.Ct. 1166 (1969).

[117] In *Mitchell v. United States,* 526 U.S. 314, 119 S.Ct. 1307 (1999), the Court held that statements made in determining a factual basis do not waive the Fifth Amendment privilege at sentencing. See § 15.03(a).

[118] 400 U.S. 25, 91 S.Ct. 160 (1970).

circumstance: when the defendant refuses to admit his guilt. The defendant in *Alford* pleaded guilty to a 30-year term, but insisted on his innocence. The Court first held that "an express admission of guilt . . . is not a constitutional requisite to the imposition of criminal penalty. An individual accused of crime may voluntarily, knowingly, and understandingly consent to the imposition of a prison sentence even if he is unwilling or unable to admit his participation in the acts constituting the crime." The Court then upheld the plea, "[i]n view of the strong factual basis for the plea demonstrated by the State and Alford's clearly expressed desire to enter it despite his professed belief in his innocence." In a footnote, the Court continued:

> Because of the importance of protecting the innocent and of insuring that guilty pleas are a product of free and intelligent choice, various state and federal court decisions properly caution that pleas coupled with claims of innocence should not be accepted unless there is a factual basis for the plea . . . and until the judge taking the plea has inquired into and sought to resolve the conflict between the waiver of trial and the claim of innocence.

Conversely, if such a factual basis is established, a court should not be prevented from accepting an otherwise intelligent and voluntary guilty plea from an individual merely because he refuses to admit his guilt.

A separate question is the scope of the factual basis requirement. Clearly, the judge must determine that there is a factual basis for the charge to which the defendant is pleading guilty. But does the judge have to inquire as well into the factual assumptions underlying any *dispositional* aspects of the plea? In *Libretti v. United States*,[119] the Court appeared to hold that, at least under the terms of Rule 11, the judge need not make this determination. Pointing to the fact that Rule 11(f) refers only to a "plea of guilty," it concluded that the judge must only ascertain the facts underlying the criminal offense, not those related to punishment.

Libretti had entered an agreement to forfeit virtually all of his property to the government in exchange for a recommendation of a reduced sentence. After pleading guilty pursuant to this agreement, he challenged the plea on the ground that the judge had failed to inquire sufficiently into the nexus between the forfeited property and his crimes (involving drug, firearms and money-laundering laws). The Court concluded that the judge had no obligation to do so under Rule 11, because forfeiture is an aspect of punishment, not the charge.

At the same time, in response to Justice Stevens' dissent arguing that the trial court must ensure that any agreement about forfeiting property must be authorized by law,[120] the Court felt it important to discuss in detail the evidence available to the District Court bolstering the propriety of the forfeiture. It further emphasized it was not holding that a district court "must simply accept a defendant's agreement to forfeit property, particularly when that agreement is not accompanied by a stipulation of facts supporting forfeiture, or when the trial judge for other reasons finds the agreement problematic." Also clear is the requirement, under federal sentencing guidelines, that the sentencing judge make certain factual findings before following a prosecutor's sentencing

---

[119]　516 U.S. 29, 116 S.Ct. 356 (1995).

[120]　To use Justice Stevens' example, a wealthy defendant may agree to forfeit all of his property, even that which has no nexus to the crime, in exchange for a more lenient sentence. Such a forfeiture is not authorized by law, and presumably should be rejected by the trial court.

recommendation.[121] Thus, *Libretti* ultimately leaves uncertain the trial court's obligations regarding inquiry into the lawfulness of a plea agreement which deals with forfeiture or other types of dispositions.

26.05 Challenging a Guilty Plea

(a) Substantive and Procedural Options

Although the types of claims that can be raised in an effort to nullify or overturn a guilty plea are numerous, they can be divided into three categories: (1) allegations that the plea is invalid because it was not voluntary or intelligent ("direct" challenges of the plea);[122] (2) allegations that the plea should be nullified because the bargain upon which it was based was breached by the prosecution or was not fully carried out by the court ("breach-of-bargain" challenges);[123] and (3) allegations that the conviction represented by the plea should be overturned because of other defects in the pretrial process, such as an illegal search and seizure or an indictment by an illegally constituted grand jury ("independent" challenges).[124]

The likely success of each type of claim depends in part upon the procedure used to assert them. There are several ways of attacking a guilty plea. The first involves making a "motion to withdraw" a plea. The second is through filing a direct appeal challenging the plea. The third is via a writ of habeas corpus or other collateral relief.

(b) Withdrawal of the Plea

Out of fairness concerns, the general rule is that the defendant may automatically withdraw a plea if the court fails to endorse a bargained-for charge or sentence; every jurisdiction follows the federal practice of permitting withdrawal when the judge rejects a sentence (or a charge) that the parties have agreed is the appropriate disposition.[125] But, under the federal rules and the rules of several states,[126] a withdrawal motion need *not* be granted if the court rejects a sentence that the government merely agreed to "recommend or . . . not to oppose," provided the government carried out its obligation and the judge indicated at arraignment that this action would not be binding on him. This stance is justified on the assumption that the defendant "knew the nonbinding character of the recommendation or request."[127] Other courts reject this position, on the ground that the defendant, in effect, has been falsely induced to plead when the sentence does not coincide with that bargained for.[128]

---

[121] Federal Sentencing Guidelines Manual § 6B2.1(b) (before accepting a sentencing recommendation agreement the judge must determine that the recommended sentence is within the guideline range or departs for "justifiable reasons.").

[122] See § 26.02(c) and § 26.04.

[123] See § 26.03(a) & (b).

[124] A fourth type of challenge to a guilty plea occurs when, subsequent to acceptance of the plea, the legislature reduces the sentence for the relevant charge. In federal cases, the offender is eligible for a sentence reduction in this situation, at least when the plea agreement "expressly uses a Guidelines sentencing range to establish the term of imprisonment." *Freeman v. United States*, 564 U.S. 522, 131 S.Ct. 2685 (2011) (Sotomayor, J., concurring).

[125] See Fed.R.Crim.P. 11(d). *United States v. Hyde*, 520 U.S. 670, 117 S.Ct. 1630 (1997).

[126] Fed.R.Crim.P. 11(c)(3)(B). See, *United States v. Henderson*, 565 F.2d 1119 (9th Cir. 1977); *People v. Lambrechts*, 69 Ill.2d 544, 14 Ill.Dec. 445, 372 N.E.2d 641 (1977).

[127] Advisory Committee Note to Rule 11(c)(3)(B), as amended in 1979 and 2002.

[128] See, e.g., *King v. State*, 553 P.2d 529 (Okl.Crim. 1976).

After a plea is accepted, it may only be withdrawn under limited circumstances. Further, under the federal rules, withdrawal is permitted only prior to the formal imposition of sentence; after the sentencing proceeding the plea may be challenged solely on direct appeal or habeas.[129] Prior to sentencing, the federal standard permits withdrawal if the defendant can show a "fair and just reason" for overturning the plea, which also approximates the test used in most state jurisdictions that limit withdrawals to pre-sentence motions. Under this standard, the defendant must make a plausible showing that one of the three grounds described above are satisfied, i.e. (1) that the plea was coerced, "unintelligent," or in some other way deficient; (2) that the bargain upon which the plea was based has been breached by the prosecution or not endorsed by the court; or, (3) that, for "good reason,"[130] a defense was overlooked prior to the plea that the defendant now seeks to raise.[131]

In some state jurisdictions, a plea may also be withdrawn after the sentencing hearing. Here, however, the prosecution is more likely to be prejudiced by withdrawal and a motion is more likely to reflect second thoughts about a validly entered plea rather than a legitimate challenge. Thus, the defendant is usually required to meet the more stringent "manifest injustice" standard, a term borrowed from the ABA Criminal Justice Standards.[132] For instance, with respect to "independent" challenges to the plea, a "good reason" for not discovering a defense by the time of the plea may be insufficient; rather, the defendant may have to demonstrate that defense counsel error of constitutional magnitude was the cause of the oversight.[133]

(c) Appeal

The defendant may always appeal denial of a withdrawal motion. But once the time for withdrawal has passed (which, as noted above, in many jurisdictions occurs once sentence has been imposed), only "direct" appeal of the plea is possible. Unlike either a withdrawal motion made at the trial level or a habeas petition, an appeal may only raise issues that can be addressed from the trial court transcript (which in the case of a direct appeal of a plea usually consists solely of the arraignment proceedings). Thus, claims that require proof of events beyond the arraignment (e.g., virtually all independent claims and any bargain challenges that require proof of a dispute over the nature of plea discussions) are generally not justiciable on direct appeal.

A few states and the federal government have created a "conditional plea" mechanism, which allows an appeal on specified pretrial motions involving independent challenges (e.g., Fourth Amendment claims).[134] Under these statutes, a defendant is permitted to plead guilty but preserve for appeal, usually on a stipulated factual record, the independent claim; if the appeal prevails, the defendant is allowed to withdraw his plea. The conditional plea procedure is meant to encourage guilty pleas by "factually

---

[129] Fed.R.Crim.P. 11(e).

[130] *United States v. Barker,* 514 F.2d 208 (D.C.Cir. 1975), cert. denied 421 U.S. 1013, 95 S.Ct. 2420 (1975).

[131] Sometimes courts accept the guilty plea but defer acceptance of the underlying plea bargain until a presentence report is prepared. In *United States v. Hyde,* 520 U.S. 670, 117 S.Ct. 1630 (1997), the Court held that withdrawal under these circumstances still requires a fair and just reason.

[132] ABA Criminal Justice Standard 14–2.1(b) (3d ed. 1996).

[133] Cf. § 26.05(e) (discussing independent claims on habeas).

[134] See, e.g., Fed.R.Crim.P. 11(a)(2); *Lefkowitz v. Newsome,* 420 U.S. 283, 95 S.Ct. 886 (1975) (discussing such statutes).

guilty" defendants who otherwise would go to trial (in the process costing the state time and money) merely to sustain a claim that they are not "legally guilty."

Appeals under such statutes aside, the guilty plea challenge most likely to be heard on appeal is of the "direct" variety since, as noted above, appeals must be based on the arraignment transcript. The typical question on these appeals is whether arraignment procedures were followed and, if not, what the remedy should be. In *McCarthy v. United States,*[135] the Supreme Court held that, in the federal system, failure to comply *strictly* with Rule 11's arraignment procedures required reversal on appeal. The Court gave two reasons for this holding: (1) the procedure "is designed to assist the district judge in making the constitutionally required determination that a defendant's guilty plea is truly voluntary;" and (2) "the more meticulously the Rule is adhered to, the more it tends to discourage, or at least to enable more expeditious disposition of, the numerous and often frivolous post-conviction attacks on the constitutional validity of guilty pleas." In *McCarthy,* the arraignment judge's failure to inform the defendant that the crime to which he pleaded guilty required proof of specific intent invalidated the plea, despite the absence of clear proof that the defendant misunderstood this point.

McCarthy's "strict adherence" approach may no longer be good law, however. Rule 11 has since been amended to provide that "[a] variance from the requirements of this rule is harmless error if it does not affect substantial rights."[136] This amendment was adopted because of the current complexity of the rule, and the difficulty of perfect compliance.[137]

Along the same lines is *Peguero v. United States,*[138] in which the Court held that failure to follow the rule[139] requiring that the defendant be informed of his right to appeal a guilty plea is not grounds for reversal when the defendant knew of the right.[140] It is probable that most state appellate courts adopt this "harmless error" approach to such claims as well, especially since the Court has indicated that, under the Constitution, failure to follow even the most important aspects of arraignment procedure does not render a plea invalid if there was other evidence the defendant understood the consequences of the plea.[141]

The Court has also held that, when a defendant lets Rule 11 error pass without objection, on appeal he must show plain error,[142] which requires proof of a reasonable probability that, but for the error, he would not have entered the plea.[143] This is in contrast to the standard of review for the objecting defendant, who is entitled to relief unless the government can show the error was harmless.[144] Thus in *United States v.*

---

[135] 394 U.S. 459, 89 S.Ct. 1166 (1969).

[136] Fed.R.Crim.P. 11(h).

[137] Advisory Committee Note, Rule 11(h).

[138] 526 U.S. 23, 119 S.Ct. 961 (1999).

[139] Formerly F.R.Crim.P. 32(a)(2), now F.R.Crim.P. 32(j)(1)(B).

[140] Although *Peguero* was unanimous, three concurring justices opined that if the defendant who was not told of the right to appeal did not appeal because he remained ignorant of the right, he should not have to show the appeal would have been meritorious in order to obtain relief, because such a showing would impose "a heavy burden" on defendants, who are usually proceeding pro se at that point.

[141] *Henderson v. Morgan,* 426 U.S. 637, 96 S.Ct. 2253 (1976), discussed in § 26.04(a)(1).

[142] *United States v. Vonn,* 535 U.S. 55, 122 S.Ct. 1043 (2002).

[143] *United States v. Benitez,* 542 U.S. 74, 124 S.Ct. 2333 (2004).

[144] See *United States v. Olano,* 507 U.S. 725, 113 S.Ct. 1770 (1993) (distinguishing Federal Rule 52(b)'s plain error rule and Rule 52(a)'s harmless error rule).

Benitez,[145] the judge's failure to warn the defendant that he was barred from withdrawing his plea if the court did not accept the government's recommendation did not require relief, despite the importance of this information, because the defendant did not object to the failure until appeal and was unable to present any evidence that he would have gone to trial had the warning been given (and indeed conceded that his plea agreement had contained the warning).

Similarly, in *Puckett v. United States*,[146] the Court held that prosecutorial breach of a plea bargain is not structural error, and thus is subject to plain error review when timely objection is not made (and presumably does not require automatic reversal even if objection is made).[147] In *Puckett*, despite previously agreeing to a three-level reduction in recognition of the defendant's acceptance of responsibility for his crime, the prosecutor opposed any reduction in charge level at the plea hearing, because the defendant had engaged in criminal activity in the interim. The Court held that the defendant, who did not complain about the breach until appeal, was unable to demonstrate that it affected his sentence as required by the plain error rule, given the trial judge's statement that sentence reductions on acceptance-of-responsibility grounds for a defendant who has engaged in post-agreement criminal activity are so rare as "to be unknown."

(d) Federal Habeas: Direct and Bargain Challenges

While a guilty plea by a state defendant can be challenged collaterally at the state level, this discussion will focus solely on federal habeas review, as representative of the usual approach. To best understand this approach, a distinction should be made between direct and bargain challenges, on the one hand, and independent challenges on the other.

Most relevant to the first two types of challenges is the requirement that a federal defendant's claim on habeas involve "a complete miscarriage of justice" or "an omission inconsistent with the rudimentary demands of fair procedure."[148] Thus, when making a direct or bargain challenge, such a defendant must show significantly more prejudice than he would have to on appeal (or on a pre-sentence withdrawal motion). For example, in *United States v. Timmreck*,[149] the Supreme Court noted that the arraignment judge's failure to inform the defendant of a special parole provision (which ended up adding 5 years to his sentence) would probably have required reversal on appeal under *McCarthy*. But it concluded that, absent a showing that the defendant would have acted differently had he been so informed, relief should not be granted now that the case was in a post-appeal posture.

The extent to which a *state* defendant can challenge a plea in federal habeas court is even more limited, since his claim must generally be based on federal constitutional grounds.[150] Moreover, in *Bousley v. United States*[151] the Court held that failure of either a federal or state petitioner to raise the claim on direct appeal forecloses federal habeas

---

[145]   542 U.S. 74, 124 S.Ct. 2333 (2004).

[146]   556 U.S. 129, 129 S.Ct. 1423 (2009).

[147]   For discussion of the plain error and automatic reversal rules, see § 29.02(e) and § 29.05(c)(2), respectively.

[148]   *Hill v. United States,* 368 U.S. 424, 82 S.Ct. 468 (1962).

[149]   441 U.S. 780, 99 S.Ct. 2085 (1979).

[150]   See generally, § 33.02(d).

[151]   523 U.S. 614, 118 S.Ct. 1604 (1998).

review unless the petitioner can demonstrate "cause" for the failure to appeal or that he is "actually innocent", showings which are very difficult.[152]

(e) Federal Habeas: Independent Challenges

Many independent challenges of guilty pleas cannot be raised on habeas at all. According to the Supreme Court, "a guilty plea represents a break in the chain of events which has preceded it in the criminal process."[153] Thus, while the voluntariness of the plea or its adherence to a previous bargain is subject to attack on habeas, a plea that is valid in these two senses precludes most other claims.

(1) The General Rule

The Supreme Court first addressed the preclusive effect of guilty pleas in a trilogy of cases decided in 1970. In *McMann v. Richardson*,[154] the defendants asserted that their guilty pleas many years earlier had been motivated by coerced confessions. The Court of Appeals held that this type of claim could be heard on habeas, at least when, as was true at the time of the defendants' pleas, state law provided that the voluntariness of a confession was to be decided by the jury, not the judge; it reasoned that the defendants may have been deterred from going to trial by this practice, which had subsequently been found unconstitutional in *Jackson v. Denno*[155] and applied retroactively to defendants who had gone to trial. The Supreme Court reversed, holding that a defendant who pleads guilty "is in a different posture" than one who goes to trial. Had the defendants gone to trial and their confessions erroneously been admitted against them, the Court explained, the basis for conviction might well have been their confessions. In contrast, the sole basis for a defendant's guilty plea is a "counseled admission in open court that he committed the crime charged against him." The confession "is not the basis for the judgment, has never been offered in evidence at a trial, and may never be offered in evidence."[156]

The Court conceded that, had the defendants had the benefit of *Jackson,* their confessions might have been found coerced and kept from the jury (thus obviating the need to plead guilty). But it characterized this possibility as "a highly speculative matter in any particular case and not an issue promising a meaningful and productive evidentiary hearing long after entry of the guilty plea." Further, noted the Court, finding for the defendant would invalidate all pleas motivated by confessions prior to *Jackson.* This "would be an improvident invasion of the State's interest in maintaining the finality of guilty plea convictions which were valid under constitutional standards applicable at the time." The Court might have added, as one commentator has noted, that because its diminishes the need to prepare a case "the entry of the plea itself may . . . impair[ ] the state's ability thereafter to prove the defendant guilty at trial."[157]

---

[152] See generally, § 33.03(d) & (e).

[153] *Tollett v. Henderson,* 411 U.S. 258, 93 S.Ct. 1602 (1973).

[154] 397 U.S. 759, 90 S.Ct. 1441 (1970).

[155] 378 U.S. 368, 84 S.Ct. 1774 (1964), discussed in § 16.06(a).

[156] Note, however, that the distinction between guilty pleas and trial verdicts is no longer as broad as the Court suggests; even defendants who go to trial cannot use habeas to vindicate claims not raised at the time of trial. See § 33.03(c).

[157] Peter Westen, Away From Waiver: A Rationale for the Forfeiture of Constitutional Rights in Criminal Procedure, 75 Mich.L.Rev. 1214, 1236 (1977).

Similarly, in *Brady v. United States,*[158] a companion case to *McMann,* the Court refused to overturn a guilty plea of a defendant charged under a statute which the Court later found unconstitutional because it "needlessly encouraged guilty pleas."[159] To the defendant's argument that his plea was not "intelligent" given this subsequent decision,[160] the Court stated "[t]he rule that a plea must be intelligently made to be valid does not require that a plea be vulnerable to later attack if the defendant did not correctly assess every relevant factor entering into his decision." In the third case of the trilogy, *Parker v. North Carolina,*[161] the Court likewise held that the defendant's coerced confession claim was barred by his guilty plea.

In a later case, *Tollett v. Henderson,*[162] the Court stated its position even more forcefully: "When a criminal defendant has solemnly admitted in open court that he is in fact guilty of the offense with which he is charged, he may not thereafter raise independent claims relating to the deprivation of constitutional rights that occurred prior to the entry of the guilty plea." The Court then held that a defendant who had pleaded guilty could not subsequently challenge on habeas the racial composition of the grand jury which indicted him, a claim that has received very generous treatment from the Court in other contexts.[163] *Tollett* and the cases leading up to it suggested that any claim that does not directly attack the voluntariness or accuracy of the plea would be barred on habeas.

(2) Ineffective Assistance

There are three narrow caveats to *Tollett's* preclusion rule, however. The first was expressed in *McMann:* if the defendant can show that the reason he did not raise the "independent claim" at the time of the plea was that he had received advice from counsel outside "the range of competence demanded of attorneys in criminal cases," then it could be heard on habeas. The Court made clear in *McMann* that mere failure to raise a claim that might have been successful did not mean incompetence under this standard. For instance, it stated, "[t]hat this Court might hold a defendant's confession inadmissible in evidence, possibly by a divided vote, hardly justifies a conclusion that the defendant's attorney was incompetent or ineffective when he thought the admissibility of the confession sufficiently probable to advise a plea of guilty."

The facts of *Parker* concretely illustrate this point. There the defendant, a 15-year-old Afro-American, was questioned for one to two hours late at night, and then questioned again the next morning after receiving a drink of water. Soon thereafter, he confessed to a burglary and rape. Although there was some evidence that the defendant was not given food, was promised "help" if he confessed, and was denied access to an attorney, counsel decided not to challenge the admissibility of the confession after the defendant denied being frightened or receiving any threats or promises. The Court stated that "even if Parker's counsel was wrong in his assessment of Parker's confession, it does not follow his error was sufficient to render the plea unintelligent and entitle Parker to

---

[158] 397 U.S. 742, 90 S.Ct. 1463 (1970).

[159] *United States v. Jackson,* 390 U.S. 570, 88 S.Ct. 1209 (1968), discussed in § 26.02(c)(3).

[160] As to the defendant's argument that his plea was not "voluntary," see § 26.02(c)(1).

[161] 397 U.S. 790, 90 S.Ct. 1458 (1970).

[162] 411 U.S. 258, 93 S.Ct. 1602 (1973).

[163] See § 23.06(c) (discussing challenges of grand jury indictments); § 29.05(c)(2) (discussing harmless error analysis).

disavow his admission in open court that he committed the offense with which he was charged."

The Court's subsequent decision in *Hill v. Lockhart*[164] has further narrowed this aspect of *McMann* and *Parker* to require that the defendant show not just that counsel's performance was "seriously" deficient, but also that there is "a reasonable probability that, but for counsel's errors, [the defendant] would not have pleaded guilty and would have insisted on going to trial." For instance, the Court stated in *Hill,* if the claim is that counsel failed to advise the defendant of an affirmative defense, the defendant must also show that "the affirmative defense would likely have succeeded at trial."

This language implying that prejudice in guilty plea cases is to be gauged by likely success at trial was undermined, however, in *Lee v. United States,*[165] where counsel mistakenly told the defendant that pleading guilty would not lead to deportation. After pleading guilty and finding out that he in fact was subject to deportation, Lee sought collateral relief. The lower court denied the claim on the ground that had Lee gone to trial he very likely would have been deported in any event, especially since he had admitted at the time of arrest that he was in possession of illegal drugs—the conduct that formed the basis for his charges, conviction on which requires deportation under federal immigration law. But the Supreme Court held that, despite the language quoted above, *Hill's* focus is "on a defendant's decisionmaking, which may not turn solely on the likelihood of conviction after trial." Since both Lee and his attorney stated that avoiding deportation was the "determinative issue" in Lee's calculus, a finding of prejudice was required. That ruling was bolstered by the Court's conclusion that insisting on going to trial was not irrational in Lee's case. As Chief Justice Roberts wrote for seven members of the Court:

> But for his attorney's incompetence, Lee would have known that accepting the plea agreement would *certainly* lead to deportation. Going to trial? *Almost* certainly. If deportation were the "determinative issue" for an individual in plea discussions, as it was for Lee; if that individual had strong connections to this country and no other, as did Lee; and if the consequences of taking a chance at trial were not markedly harsher than pleading, as in this case, that "almost" could make all the difference. Balanced against holding on to some chance of avoiding deportation was a year or two more of prison time.[166]

(3) "Incurable" Defects

The second caveat to the *McMann-Tollett* rule was recognized in two subsequent cases. *Blackledge v. Perry*[167] involved a habeas claim that the prosecutor had acted vindictively in violation of due process, by changing the defendant's charge from a misdemeanor to a felony after he had asserted his right to a trial *de novo* upon conviction of the misdemeanor. The Court was willing to consider (and ultimately upheld) this claim, despite the fact that the defendant had pleaded guilty to the felony charge. Unlike the claims involved in *Tollett* and previous cases, the Court explained, this claim "went to the very power of the State to bring the defendant into court to answer the charge

---

[164] 474 U.S. 52, 106 S.Ct. 366 (1985).

[165] ___ U.S. ___, 137 S.Ct. 1958 (2017).

[166] For further discussion of ineffective assistance of counsel claims, see § 32.04(c).

[167] 417 U.S. 21, 94 S.Ct. 2098 (1974), discussed in § 21.03(b).

brought against him." Similarly, in *Menna v. New York*,[168] the Court held that a double jeopardy claim against the prosecution leading to a guilty plea could be heard because this type of claim, if sustained, precludes the state "from hailing a defendant into court on a charge."[169]

Contrary to the Court's assertion, the claim in *Tollett,* concerning the legitimacy of the indicting grand jury, also went to the "power of the state to bring the defendant into court." Thus, it has been argued,[170] the better way of explaining *Blackledge* and *Menna* is that they involved "incurable" constitutional claims which, if sustained, would prevent the state from *ever* trying a defendant on the charge to which he pleaded guilty.[171] On the other hand, a finding for the defendant on the grand jury claim in *Tollett* (and on the assertions in the *McMann-Brady-Parker* trilogy) would not prevent the state from subsequently trying the defendant on the charge (although in *Tollett* the state would have to convene a new grand jury to proceed against the defendant).

Citing *Blackledge* and *Menna*, in *Class v. United States*[172] six members of the Court, in an opinion by Justice Breyer, held that claims that the offense of conviction is unconstitutional may also be heard after an unconditional plea. In *Class*, the defendant pleaded guilty and subsequently appealed on the ground that the relevant statute— prohibiting possession of firearms on U.S. Capitol grounds—was unconstitutional under both the Second Amendment and the due process void-for-vagueness doctrine. Although Class' plea was conditional, it did not reserve this type of claim for appeal. Nonetheless, Breyer concluded that the Class' claims could be heard on appeal because they did not contradict any of the assertions inherent in the plea and "cannot in any way be characterized as part of the trial," but rather "call[ed] into question the Government's power to constitutionally prosecute" him. The dissent, written by Justice Alito, argued that *Class*, *Blackledge* and *Menna* are difficult to distinguish from situations in which the Court has disallowed post-plea appeals, and concluded that this entire line of cases should be reversed, because it "is vacuous, has no sound foundation, and produces nothing but confusion."

(4) Conditional Pleas

The third caveat to *Tollett* was recognized in *Lefkowitz v. Newsome*,[173] where the Supreme Court held that even "curable" post-plea claims can be heard on habeas if they are raised pursuant to a conditional plea statute of the type described earlier.[174] In *Lefkowitz*, the defendant pleaded guilty in state court but preserved a search and seizure claim for appeal under New York's conditional plea statute. The claim was rejected on direct appeal, and the federal habeas court, on authority of *McMann* and *Brady*, refused to hear it. The Supreme Court directed the lower federal court to hold a hearing on the

---

[168]   423 U.S. 61, 96 S.Ct. 241 (1975).

[169]   *In United States v. Broce,* 488 U.S. 563, 109 S.Ct. 757 (1989), the Court limited *Menna* to those cases where the double jeopardy claim can be based on the existing record and does not require an evidentiary hearing.

[170]   Westen, supra note 158, at 1220–21.

[171]   Another claim that fits this category is a claim that the right to speedy trial has been violated. Id. at 1255.

[172]   ___ U.S. ___, 138 S.Ct.798 (2018).

[173]   420 U.S. 283, 95 S.Ct. 886 (1975).

[174]   See § 26.05(c).

claim, concluding that it should be heard so as not to frustrate New York's policy of providing post-guilty plea review of pretrial motions.[175]

(f) The Effect of an Overturned Plea

If the defendant successfully challenges a guilty plea, his remedy depends upon the type of claim asserted. As discussed earlier,[176] if he wins a bargain challenge alleging breach by the prosecution, he should normally obtain specific performance of the bargain (although he may only be entitled to replead). When the defendant wins a direct or independent challenge and the prosecution persists in prosecuting, the defendant may either go to trial or seek to plead again. The primary issue that arises in this situation is whether the prosecutor and judge are bound by the charge and sentence in the original plea bargain or whether, instead, a higher charge or sentence may be imposed.

After a *trial* conviction and a successful appeal, retrial on a higher charge is barred by the Double Jeopardy Clause, on the ground that the trial verdict represents an "implied acquittal" of the greater charge.[177] In the analogous situation in the guilty plea context, however, there has been no such "implied acquittal," but merely a determination by the prosecutor, endorsed by the judge, that an offer on the lesser charge or sentence is more likely to get the defendant to plead guilty. Thus, the Double Jeopardy Clause probably does not bar reprosecution on a greater charge or imposition of a greater sentence than that associated with the challenged guilty plea.[178]

Only slightly more likely to be successful is the claim that, under *Blackledge v. Perry*[179] and *North Carolina v. Pearce,*[180] the higher charge or sentence is a vindictive reaction against the defendant for asserting his right to withdraw or otherwise challenge the plea. In order to avoid chilling the right to appeal after a *trial,* these cases established a "presumption of vindictiveness" when the prosecutor raises the charge or the judge imposes a higher sentence after an appeal is taken. But, in *Alabama v. Smith,*[181] the Court held that the presumption does not apply when the first charge and sentence occur in the guilty plea context, the defendant successfully appeals the plea, and then decides to go to trial, because "the relevant sentencing information available to the judge after the plea will usually be considerably less than that available after trial," and because "the factors that may have indicated leniency as consideration for the guilty plea are no longer present." Accordingly, after a successful challenge of a guilty plea, the prosecutor may charge the original pre-plea-bargain offense and the sentencing judge may impose a higher sentence than originally bargained for.

Smith does not foreclose a finding of vindictiveness in this situation; it merely refuses to apply the *Pearce-Blackledge* presumption. In favor of this rule, it has been argued that if the defendant can always be assured of obtaining the same bargain after seeking to overturn a plea, he will often have nothing to lose and much to gain (including a possible dismissal because of passage of time) by challenging it, at considerable cost to

---

[175] Note that, one year after *Lefkowitz, Stone v. Powell,* 428 U.S. 465, 96 S.Ct. 3037 (1976), held that *no* Fourth Amendment claim (the type of claim at issue in *Lefkowitz*) is reviewable on federal habeas if it received a full and fair hearing in state court. See § 33.02(b).

[176] See § 26.03(b)(3).

[177] *Green v. United States,* 355 U.S. 184, 78 S.Ct. 221 (1957), discussed in § 30.03(a).

[178] For further discussion of this point, see § 30.03(a)(1).

[179] 417 U.S. 21, 94 S.Ct. 2098 (1974).

[180] 395 U.S. 711, 89 S.Ct. 2072 (1969), discussed in § 29.02(d).

[181] 490 U.S. 794, 109 S.Ct. 2201 (1989).

the efficiency of the system.[182] Moreover, a higher post-appeal sentence can be justified on the ground that courts often impose more lenient sentences on those who plead guilty than on those who go to trial. On the other hand, if, after a successful challenge, the prosecutor is typically allowed to bring a higher charge or the judge able to impose a higher sentence than was contemplated in the original bargain, the defendant's right to challenge the plea may be chilled, and prosecutors (if not judges) may be encouraged "to coerce a plea in the knowledge that the defendant may be reluctant to risk a successful appeal."[183] At the least, by analogy to the holding in *Blackledge,* unless some "identifiable conduct" other than the successful plea challenge and the decision to go to trial would justify different treatment, the original bargain should form the basis for further prosecution.

26.06 Conclusion

In terms of case dispositions, guilty pleas—and the plea bargaining process that leads to them—are far more important than trials. Yet, relative to its caselaw on trial adjudication, the Supreme Court has devoted little attention to these topics. As a result, the constitutional limitations on the guilty plea process are still somewhat vague, as the following summary illustrates.

(1) Virtually every jurisdiction permits the defendant and the prosecution to plea bargain, a process that usually involves an agreement by the defendant to plead guilty in exchange for charge concessions or a recommendation regarding sentence by the prosecution. The defendant is entitled to the assistance of an effective attorney during the plea process. However, attorney errors do not require overturning the plea unless without them the defendant would have insisted on going to trial, and the prosecution need not give the attorney impeachment evidence or evidence supporting affirmative defenses prior to the plea. The prosecutor may use the threat of significantly higher charges or sentencing recommendations to induce the defendant to plead guilty, so long as the options presented are legitimate and are openly described to the defendant. The legitimacy of judicial involvement in plea bargaining is not clear, although it is probably constitutional and, properly conducted, perhaps even a preferred method of ensuring the process is monitored and the defendant is given accurate information as to the effect of a plea. Under the federal rules, statements made during negotiations may not be used at trial, unless the defendant agreed to waive his statutory protection in order to engage in plea bargaining. Plea agreements can also include waiver of other rights that are collateral to guilt, such as the right to appeal, although a failure to file notice of an appeal after such a waiver constitutes ineffective of counsel if the defendant specifically asks to the attorney to do so.

(2) Either party may withdraw from the plea bargain prior to the arraignment. Even if they do not, the court need not accept the bargain, unless it has previously agreed to its provisions. If the bargain is rejected by the court, most jurisdictions allow the defendant to withdraw his plea, although in federal court, at least, imposition of a sentence higher than that anticipated by the defendant does not automatically permit withdrawal when the judge has warned the defendant of that possibility unless the sentence was explicitly stipulated by the bargain agreement. After a plea is accepted by

---

[182] *United States ex rel. Williams v. McMann,* 436 F.2d 103 (2d Cir. 1970).

[183] Paul D. Borman, *The Chilled Right to Appeal From a Plea Bargain Conviction: A Due Process Cure,* 69 Nw.U.L.Rev. 663, 713 (1974).

the court, a breach of the agreement by either the prosecution or the defendant should generally lead to specific performance, although it is apparently constitutional, after either type of breach, to force the defendant to replead to a different offer or to go to trial.

(3)   To be valid under the Due Process Clause, a guilty plea must be intelligently and voluntarily made, as affirmatively shown on a record developed by the judge who takes the plea. Ideally, this would require the arraignment judge to develop on the record: (a) that the defendant understands the critical elements of the charges against him, including any elements that differentiate the charge to which he is pleading from lesser included offenses; (b) that he understands the penalties and any important "collateral" consequences associated with the charges, such as deportation; (c) that he understands that by pleading guilty he is waiving his rights to jury trial, confrontation, and trial counsel and his privilege against self-incrimination; (d) that his plea is not the product of coercion other than that associated with having to choose between known alternatives legitimately offered by the prosecutor or by the relevant law; and (e) that there is a factual basis for his plea. All of these requirements are fully incorporated in Rule 11 of the Federal Rules of Criminal Procedure, with the possible exception of (c). The Constitution appears to require that the judge personally determine (d) and (e), and that he at least obtain general representations of counsel as to (a), (b) and (c). An express admission of guilt is not a constitutional requisite to the acceptance of a guilty plea and imposition of a criminal penalty, although the judge should take particular care to obtain a factual basis for the plea when the defendant maintains his innocence.

(4)   In most jurisdictions, prior to formal imposition of sentence, a plea may be withdrawn for any just and fair reason, including proof that (a) the plea was not voluntary or intelligent; (b) the bargain upon which it was based was breached by the prosecutor or not endorsed by the court (as in (2) above); or (c) a previously overlooked defense is now available to the defendant. After the sentencing proceeding, a plea may be withdrawn only if manifest injustice would otherwise result, which probably encompasses grounds similar to those recognized on federal habeas, described below. Direct appeal of a guilty plea is generally limited to claims that can be based on the arraignment transcript (such as whether arraignment procedures or the plea bargain was followed), although some jurisdictions allow conditional pleas, under which the defendant can preserve specified pretrial motions for appeal. Under the federal rules only substantial violations of Rule 11 will result in relief on appeal. A federal habeas corpus hearing on the guilty plea is usually granted only in cases which assert (a) that the plea was not voluntary or intelligent; (b) that there was a significant breach of a plea bargain; (c) that counsel was ineffective; (d) that the state lacks power to bring the charge to which the defendant pleaded (because, for instance, the charge is barred by double jeopardy or is based on an unconstitutional offense); or (e) a claim that was preserved via a conditional plea procedure. For claims (a) and (b) and perhaps (c) and (d), the claim must also have been raised on direct appeal, or the petitioner must provide a good reason why it was not raised on appeal and show also that the error prejudiced his case.

BIBLIOGRAPHY

Alschuler, Albert W. Implementing the Criminal Defendant's Right to Trial: Alternatives to the Plea Bargaining System. 50 U.Chi.L.Rev. 931 (1983).

____. The Defense Attorney's Role in Plea Bargaining. 84 Yale L.J. 1179 (1975).

Batra, Rishi R. Judicial Participation in Plea Bargaining: A Dispute Resolution Perspective. 76 Ohio St. L.J. 565 (2015).

Bibas, Stephanos. Incompetent Plea Bargains and Extrajudicial Reforms. 126 Har. L. Rev. 150 (2012).

____. Harmonizing Substantive-Criminal-Law Values and Criminal Procedure: The Case of *Alford* and Nolo Contendere Pleas. 88 Cornell L.Rev. 1361 (2003).

____. *Apprendi* and the Dynamics of Guilty Pleas. 54 Stanford L.Rev. 311 (2001).

Cassidy, R. Michael. Plea Bargaining, Discovery, and the Intractable Problem of Impeachment Disclosures. 64 Vand. L. Rev. 1429 (2011).

Chin, Gabriel L. Making *Padilla* Practical: Defense Counsel and Collateral Consequences at Guilty Plea. 54 How. L.J. 675 (2011).

Cook, Julian. Plea Bargaining, Sentencing Modifications, and the Real World. 48 Wake Forest L. Rev. 65 (2013).

____. Federal Guilty Pleas Under Rule 11: The Unfulfilled Promise of the Post-*Boykin* Era. 77 Notre Dame L.Rev. 597 (2002).

Dervan, Lucien E. Bargained Justice: Plea-Bargaining's Innocence Problem and the Brady Safety-Valve. 2012 Utah L. Rev. 51.

____. Overcriminalization 2.0: The Symbiotic Relationship Between Plea Bargaining and Overcriminalization. 7 J. L. Econ. & Pol'y 645 (2011).

Easterbrook, Frank H. Plea Bargaining as Compromise. 101 Yale L.J. 1969 (1992).

Fisher, George. Plea Bargaining's Triumph. 109 Yale L.J. 857 (2000).

Gleeson, John. The Sentencing Commission and Prosecutorial Discretion: The Role of the Courts in Policing Sentence Bargains. 36 Hofstra L. Rev. 639 (2008).

Graham, Kyle. Crimes, Widgets, and Plea Bargaining: An Analysis of Charge Content, Pleas, and Trials. 100 Cal. L. Rev. 1573 (2012).

Guidorizzi, Douglas D. Should We Really "Ban" Plea Bargaining?: The Core Concerns of Plea Bargaining Critics. 47 Emory L.J. 753 (1998).

Hessick, Andrew and Reshma Saujani. Plea Bargaining and Convicting the Innocent: the Role of the Prosecutor, the Defense Counsel, and the Judge. 16 BYU J.Publ.L. 189 (2002).

King, Nancy J. When Process Affects Punishment: Differences in Sentences after Guilty Plea, Bench Trial and Jury Trial in Five Guidelines States. 105 Colum.L.Rev. 959 (2005).

Lagoy, Stephen P., Joseph J. Senna, and Larry J. Siegel. An Empirical Study on Information Usage for Prosecutorial Decision Making in Plea Negotiations. 13 Am.Crim.L.Rev. 435 (1976).

Langbein, John H. Torture and Plea Bargaining. 46 U.Chi.L.Rev. 3 (1978).

Leonard, David P. Waiver of Protections Against the Use of Plea Bargains and Plea Bargaining Statements After *Mezzanatto*. 23 Crim. Just 8 (Fall, 2008).

McMunigal, Kevin C. Guilty Pleas, *Brady* Disclosure, and Wrongful Convictions. 57 Case W. Res. L. Rev. 651 (2007).

Nagel, Ilene H. and Steven J. Schulhofer. A Tale of Three Cities: An Empirical Study of Charging and Bargaining Practices Under the Federal Sentencing Guidelines. 66 S.Cal. L. Rev. 501 (1992).

Proctor, Gray and Nancy King. Post-*Padilla*: *Padilla*'s Puzzles for Review in State and Federal Courts. 23 Fed. Sentencing Rep. 239 (2011).

Roberts, Jenny. Effective Plea Bargaining Counsel. 122 Yale L.J. 2650 (2013).

Schulhofer, Stephen. Plea Bargaining as Disaster. 101 Yale L.J. 1979 (1992).

Scott, Robert E. and William J. Stuntz. Plea Bargaining as Contract. 101 Yale L.J. 1909 (1992).

Symposium. Plea Bargaining After *Lafler* and *Frye*. 51 Duq. L. Rev. 533 (2013).

Symposium. Plea Bargaining: The Next Criminal Procedure Frontier, 57 Wm. & Mary L. Rev. 1055 (2016).

Turner, Jenia I. Judicial Participation in Plea Negotiations: A Comparative View. 54 Am. J. Compl. L. 199 (2006).

Weninger, Robert A. The Abolition of Plea Bargaining: A Case Study of El Paso County, Texas. 35 U.C.L.A.L.Rev. 265 (1987).

Westen, Peter and David Westin. A Constitutional Law of Remedies for Broken Plea Bargains. 66 Calif.L.Rev. 471 (1978).

Wright, Ronald and Marc Miller. The Screening/Bargaining Tradeoff. 55 Stan.L.Rev. 29 (2002).

Wright, Ronald F. and Rodney L. Engen. Charge Movement and Theories of Prosecutors. 91 Marq. L. Rev. 9 (2007).

Chapter 27

THE RIGHT TO AN IMPARTIAL
JURY AND JUDGE

27.01   Introduction

Constitutional doctrine governing the identity and role of the decisionmaker at a criminal proceeding has flowed from two premises. Most important has been the belief that the decisionmaker must be neutral (thus helping to assure, it is assumed, accuracy of judgment). To implement this goal, the Sixth Amendment guarantees a trial "by an impartial jury" in all criminal prosecutions, and the Due Process Clause has been found to require an impartial trial judge.[1] Further ensuring that both the jury and the judge have some incentive to be impartial, the Sixth Amendment guarantees a "public" trial, and the First Amendment's protection of freedom of press has been applied to most stages of the criminal process.[2]

The second premise concerning the decisionmaker is that the community should be involved in the decisionmaking process, as a matter of participatory democracy and as a protection against government-dominated justice. The right to jury trial is the most direct attempt at realizing this goal. Additionally, the public trial, attended by the media, assures that interested members of the public will be able to evaluate the decisionmaker and the system in which it operates, and provide feedback.

The impartiality and community participation premises can sometimes conflict. A jury composed of laypeople may not be the most impartial decisionmaker, and the most neutral decisionmaker may not represent the community. Press coverage may improperly influence prospective jurors, disrupt the trial process and distort the deliberations of the judge or the jury. This chapter explores these tensions. The first three sections examine the most significant aspects of the right to jury trial: its scope; the selection of the jury venire; and the selection of the petit jury from the venire. The fourth section looks at the selection of the presiding judge. The final section discusses the role of a free press at a jury or bench trial in re-enforcing or diminishing decisionmaker impartiality.

27.02   The Scope of the Right to Jury Trial

(a)   History and Rationale of the Right

The right to a trial by jury has roots deep in the common law. As early as the Magna Carta, the right was recognized as essential, although in a different form than its modern version: to the barons who drafted that document, a "jury of peers" was a means of ensuring they would be tried by other members of the aristocracy rather than those in the lower classes.[3] Further, the jury in medieval days functioned more like the grand jury of modern times and could be punished if its verdict was contrary to law. By the end

---

[1]   See § 27.05.

[2]   See § 27.06.

[3]   See Frederick Pollock and Frederic Maitland, The History of English Law Before the Time of Edward I, Vol. I, at 173 n. 3 (2d ed. 1899).

of the seventeenth century, however, it had acquired its three essential elements: (1) a group of twelve lay citizens (2) whose unanimous verdict (3) was given exclusive effect.

During the American Revolution the jury was seen as a bulwark against oppression. Colonists considered the jury trial "a valuable safeguard of liberty" and "the palladium of free government."[4] The jury was idealized as a group of citizens acting as a buffer between the criminal accused and the state. Accordingly, the framers of the Constitution were committed to making the jury an integral part of the criminal justice system. Article II, Section 2 provides that "the trial of all crimes, except in cases of impeachment, shall be by jury." And, as noted above, the Sixth Amendment states: "In all criminal prosecutions, the accused shall enjoy the right to a . . . trial, by an impartial jury. . . ."

(1) Application to the States

While the Sixth Amendment guarantee has always been honored in the federal courts, it was not applied to the states until 1968, in *Duncan v. Louisiana*.[5] The tensions which contributed to this delay, and which would later form the basis for diminishing the scope of the jury trial right, are reflected in Justice White's majority opinion in *Duncan* and Justice Harlan's dissent in that case. As it had in earlier cases construing the scope of the right at the federal level,[6] the majority emphasized that the jury not only provides "an inestimable safeguard against the corrupt or overzealous prosecutor and against the compliant, biased, or eccentric judge," but also reflects an "insistence upon community participation in the determination of guilt and innocence." Justice Harlan argued, on the other hand, that the danger of "tyrannous judges" that had so exercised the colonists was largely a relic of the past. And he criticized the lay jury process as cumbersome, costly, and likely to result in defective verdicts, at least in complex legal cases. The majority did not directly respond to Harlan's assertion that the jury is an inefficient decisionmaking institution, but it did state that "we hold no constitutional doubts about the practices, common in both federal and state courts, of accepting waivers of jury trial and prosecuting petty crimes without extending a right to jury trial." As to the claim of erroneous jury verdicts, White noted the results of a "recent and exhaustive study"[7] which had found that, when juries reach a different decision than the judge in a particular case, "it is usually because they are serving some of the very purposes for which they were created and for which they are now employed."

Although the *Duncan* majority strongly endorsed the concept of the jury trial, it did not explicitly decide whether all of the common law attributes of the jury were required as a matter of due process. In defining the scope of the right in later cases, Harlan's arguments in dissent—particularly those having to do with the jury's cumbersome and costly nature—heavily influenced the Court. Additionally, the optimistic view of lay decisionmaking abilities that supported the holding in *Duncan* would later bolster decisions, discussed later in this chapter,[8] allowing experimentation with its size and voting requirements.

---

[4]   Francis Heller, The Sixth Amendment 21–22, 25–26 (1951).

[5]   391 U.S. 145, 88 S.Ct. 1444 (1968).

[6]   *Patton v. United States,* 281 U.S. 276, 50 S.Ct. 253 (1930); *Thompson v. Utah,* 170 U.S. 343, 18 S.Ct. 620 (1898).

[7]   Harry Kalven & Hans Zeisel, The American Jury (1966).

[8]   See § 27.02(d) & (e).

(2) Application to "Sentencing Factors"

In *Jones v. United States*,[9] a majority of the Court for the first time indicated that the Sixth Amendment right to jury trial extends to some aspects of the crime that are not charged in the indictment or information; specifically, the right is violated by sentencing provisions that permit a judge rather than a jury to find facts that lead to a sentence enhancement. In *Jones*, the defendant was sentenced to 25 years for the crime of carjacking. The normal sentence for that crime was 15 years, but the judge had raised the sentence by another ten years under authority of another statute that permitted such an enhancement if the carjacking caused "serious bodily injury". The five-member majority, in an opinion by Justice Souter, held that before such enhancements can occur the government must prove the underlying factual predicate to a jury beyond a reasonable doubt. A contrary holding, Souter reasoned, would "shrink" the jury's role "from the significance usually carried by determinations of guilt to the relative importance of low-level gatekeeping." Pointing to struggles during colonial times over the power of juries to decide facts relevant to punishment, Souter also asserted that such a diminishment of the jury's role would be inconsistent with the Founder's concept of the jury. At the same time, the Court reaffirmed *Almendarez-Torres v. United States*,[10] which had permitted a sentence enhancement based on a judicial finding of prior convictions, because "unlike the factor before us in this case, a prior conviction must itself have been established through procedures satisfying the fair notice, reasonable doubt, and jury trial guarantees."

Within a year, the Court had extended the principle announced in *Jones* to require a jury determination of *all* factors, other than prior convictions, that lead to a sentence longer than the normal maximum sentence. In *Apprendi v. New Jersey*,[11] the defendant was convicted of several weapons offenses against an African-American family, and saw his sentence double after the sentencing judge found that his crimes had been committed "with a purpose to intimidate . . . because of race." In reversing this sentence, Justice Stevens wrote for five members of the Court that, although judges could still find facts that increased a sentence within the legislatively mandated range, "[o]ther than the fact of a prior conviction, any fact that can increase the penalty for a crime beyond the prescribed statutory maximum must be submitted to a jury, and proved beyond a reasonable doubt." To the dissent's contention that a state could avoid this holding simply by increasing its maximum sentences and permitting judges to reduce them based on mitigating findings (e.g., that the offense was not a hate crime or did not involve use of a weapon), Stevens responded that "structural democratic constraints exist to discourage legislatures" from such a major modification but that, if it this type of modification did occur, "we would be required to question whether the revision was constitutional under this Court's prior decisions."

Nonetheless, the Court has extended *Apprendi* to a number of other situations. In *Ring v. Arizona*,[12] the Court applied *Apprendi's* reasoning in finding that a jury must find aggravating circumstances that justify a death sentence. In *Hurst v. Florida*,[13] eight members of the Court voted to extend *Ring* to capital sentencing schemes like Florida's,

---

[9]   526 U.S. 227, 119 S.Ct. 1215 (1999).

[10]   523 U.S. 224, 118 S.Ct. 1219 (1998).

[11]   530 U.S. 466, 120 S.Ct. 2348 (2000).

[12]   536 U.S. 584, 122 S.Ct. 2428 (2002).

[13]   ___ U.S. ___, 136 S.Ct. 616 (2016).

under which the jury's decision is merely advisory and the judge makes the ultimate findings relevant to whether the death sentence is warranted. And in *Southern Union Co. v. United States*,[14] it held that the jury must find the facts relevant to the imposition of fines (e.g., not just that a violation has occurred, but also the number of days a violation occurs).

Even more far-reaching has been the series of decisions that began in *Blakely v. Washington*.[15] That case involved a more complicated but relatively typical sentencing scheme, whereby crimes were divided into a few major categories and assigned certain penalties (e.g., Class B felonies warranted sentences of up to 10 years) but specific crimes were associated with narrower "standard ranges" (e.g., kidnapping, a Class B felony, presumptively carried a range of 49 to 53 months). Blakely, convicted by a jury of kidnapping, received a sentence of 90 months because the judge found that he had acted with "deliberate cruelty," a statutorily enumerated ground for a sentence enhancement. Justice Scalia, writing for the Court, found that this sentence was unconstitutional because "the 'statutory maximum' for *Apprendi* purposes is the maximum sentence a judge may impose solely on the basis of the facts reflected in the jury verdict or admitted by the defendant" (in this case, 53 months). In *United States v. Booker*,[16] decided the next term, a majority of the Court held that the same reasoning applied to the Federal Sentencing Guidelines, which set ranges of sentences with the statutory maxima set by Congress, but frequently permitted sentences beyond that range based on judicial findings of facts not presented to or found by the jury. To avoid the complete dismantlement of that system, Justice Breyer, writing for a different majority, concluded that the provision in the Guidelines that *required* judges to impose a sentence within a given range when they find certain facts should be "excised" from the statute authorizing the Guidelines. By making the Guidelines' ranges "advisory" only, the Court in effect equated the Guidelines maxima with the statutory maxima, meaning that the jury's findings authorize any sentence up to that amount.

In the wake of these decisions, jurisdictions must require that all facts that result in enhancements to statutorily-or guidelines-designated maxima be proven to a jury. To implement that rule, they can recast their sentencing guidelines as non-binding (as the Court did with the Federal Sentencing Guidelines in *Booker*), explicitly increase the guideline range to the statutory maximum, set all sentences at their maximum and permit judges to depart downward, or adhere to an indeterminate sentencing regime. The important point for present purposes is that the *Apprendi* line of cases is a strong reaffirmation of the right to jury trial.

That stance was furthered strengthened by the Court's treatment of sentencing regimes involving mandatory *minimum* sentences. Initially, the Court demonstrated an unwillingness to apply the *Jones-Apprendi* logic to this situation. According to the four member plurality in *Harris v. United States*,[17] (joined by Justice Breyer on the ground that *Apprendi* was wrongly decided), while "any fact extending the defendant's sentence beyond the maximum authorized by the jury's verdict would have been considered an element of an aggravated crime—and thus the domain of the jury—by those who framed the Bill of Rights . . . [t]he same cannot be said of a fact increasing the mandatory

---

[14]   567 U.S. 343, 132 S.Ct. 2344 (2012).

[15]   542 U.S. 296, 124 S.Ct. 2531 (2004).

[16]   543 U.S. 220, 125 S.Ct. 738 (2005).

[17]   536 U.S. 545, 122 S.Ct. 2406 (2002).

minimum (but not extending the sentence beyond the statutory maximum) for the jury's verdict has authorized the judge to impose the minimum with or without the finding." However, in *Alleyne v. United States*,[18] five members of the Court voted to overturn *Harris*. The sentencing provision at issue in that case stated that use of a gun during a crime carried a mandatory five-year minimum, and that brandishing the gun required addition of another two years to the mandatory minimum. The jury found that Alleyne used a gun during the crime, but did not make a specific finding about the brandishing issue. At sentencing, the judge, relying on a presentence report, found that Alleyne had brandished the weapon and added two years to the sentence. Essentially ignoring the historical assertion made in *Harris*, Justice Thomas wrote for four members of the Court that "a fact increasing either end of the range produces a new penalty and constitutes an ingredient of the offense;" thus, he concluded, that fact is an aggravating element that needs to be decided by a jury.[19]

The Court also made clear, however, that in a sentencing regime where the legislature has not specified facts upon which a minimum may be increased, *Apprendi* does not apply and a judge may make the decision about whether to increase the sentence. Reacting to this last point, Chief Justice Roberts' dissent noted, "The majority nowhere explains what it is about the jury right that bars a determination by Congress that brandishing (or any other fact) makes an offense worth two extra years, but not an identical determination by a judge. Simply calling one 'aggravation' and the other 'discretion' does not do the trick." The dissenters argued that a mandatory minimum does not violate the right to jury trial because it does not increase the maximum sentence.

In *United States v. Haymond*,[20] however, a majority affirmed *Alleyne*, and extended it by holding that judges may not impose a mandatory minimum the jury's verdict did not authorize even when the penalty is based on an offense that occurred during supervised release and falls within the range permitted by the original sentence. A jury convicted Haymond of possession of child pornography, which carries a term of zero to ten years. During his 38-month sentence, while Haymond was on supervised release, a judge found that he was again in possession of child pornography. The judge could have sentenced Haymond to up to two more years for this violation, but instead sentenced him to a mandatory minimum of five years under authority of 18 U.S.C. § 3583(k). Justice Gorsuch, writing for four members of the Court (who were joined in the holding by Justice Breyer), in essence found this provision unconstitutional, because the jury had not deliberated on the new pornography charge. To the government's argument that Haymond was always subject to revocation of release if he engaged in misconduct, Justice Gorsuch pointed out that the difference between that situation and this one was *Alleyne*: a *mandatory minimum* must be based on facts found by a jury.

(b) The Right in Noncriminal Proceedings

The Sixth Amendment clearly governs all "criminal prosecutions," and the Seventh Amendment guarantees a right to jury trial in all civil cases in which non-equitable relief

---

[18]   570 U.S. 99, 133 S.Ct. 2151 (2013).

[19]   Justice Breyer adhered to his position that facts like brandishing a weapon are sentencing facts that can be decided by the judge, but he joined the plurality on the ground that *Harris* was inconsistent with *Apprendi*.

[20]   ___ U.S. ___, 139 S.Ct. 2369 (2019).

is sought.[21] But many types of proceedings do not fit cleanly into either category. In *McKeiver v. Pennsylvania,*[22] the Court held that juveniles charged with delinquent acts do not have a right to jury trial. Although the Court had been quite willing to import other adult criminal process rights into this quasi-criminal process,[23] it found that granting the right to those charged with delinquent acts would introduce the "clamor" of the adversary process and thus undermine the "intimacy" that many states consider important in arriving at an appropriate disposition in cases involving children.

Justice Brennan concurred with this conclusion in one of the two cases joined in *McKeiver,* because the state involved (Pennsylvania) permitted public trials, with press coverage, when requested. In the other case, however, Brennan dissented because the proceedings in that jurisdiction (North Carolina) were routinely closed; thus, without a jury, there was no way the "community conscience" could protect against oppression by the courts. The lower courts have generally disregarded Brennan's distinction, extending the holding in *McKeiver* to civil commitment and similar proceedings which are also often closed at the behest of the state.[24]

(c) The Petty Crime Exception

Based on historical precedent, *Duncan* exempted from the jury requirement trials of "petty crimes or offenses." Two years later, in *Baldwin v. New York,*[25] the Court explained that the "disadvantages, onerous though they may be," of punishment for a petty crime are "outweighed by the benefits that result from speedy and inexpensive nonjury adjudication." The "petty offense" exception raises several questions.

(1) The Six-Month Imprisonment Rule

Duncan did not define "petty" offense, other than to suggest that the primary factor in determining crime seriousness should be the nature of the penalty authorized. *Baldwin* reiterated this criterion and concluded that a crime which can bring imprisonment of more than six months implicates the Sixth Amendment. The six-month dividing line was chosen because only one state at the time absolutely prohibited a jury trial for crimes associated with a longer punishment, and because other alternatives— such as the felony-misdemeanor distinction—did not lend themselves to clear definition.

Note that, in contrast to the right to counsel,[26] the right to jury depends upon the punishment that is *possible,* not that which is actually imposed. But when, as in criminal contempt cases, the legislature has not spoken as to the possible punishment, the Court has held that the penalty actually imposed is the correct yardstick.[27] Thus, in *Frank v. United States,*[28] a sentence of three years probation for contempt did not trigger the right, because a probation violation would have, at most, meant six months in prison.

---

[21]   See, e.g., *Beacon Theatres, Inc. v. Westover,* 359 U.S. 500, 79 S.Ct. 948 (1959).

[22]   403 U.S. 528, 91 S.Ct. 1976 (1971).

[23]   See *Application of Gault,* 387 U.S. 1, 87 S.Ct. 1428 (1967) (juveniles have right to adequate notice and counsel, and the privilege against self-incrimination); *Breed v. Jones,* 421 U.S. 519, 95 S.Ct. 1779 (1975) (double jeopardy).

[24]   See, e.g., *Lynch v. Baxley,* 386 F.Supp. 378 (M.D.Ala. 1974).

[25]   399 U.S. 66, 90 S.Ct. 1886 (1970).

[26]   See § 31.02(b).

[27]   See *Bloom v. Illinois,* 391 U.S. 194, 88 S.Ct. 1477 (1968).

[28]   395 U.S. 147, 89 S.Ct. 1503 (1969).

(2) *Relevance of Other Penalties*

Baldwin left open the possibility that, under some circumstances, a prison term of six months or less, in combination with other penalties, might be considered serious for purposes of the right to jury trial. But subsequent decisions have indicated that this possibility is a small one. Most significantly, in *Blanton v. City of North Las Vegas*,[29] the Court held that a defendant is entitled to a jury trial in such a situation "only if he can demonstrate that any additional statutory penalties, viewed in conjunction with the maximum authorized period of incarceration, are so severe that they clearly reflect a legislative determination that the offense in question is a 'serious' one." In *Blanton*, the Court considered a driving while intoxicated statute that authorized a maximum term of six months or, in lieu of a prison sentence, 48 hours of community work while wearing garb identifying the person as a DWI offender. In addition, a person given either penalty suffers an automatic 90-day loss of driver's license, and is required to pay a $200 to $1000 fine and to attend an alcohol abuse education course. A unanimous Court held that the penalties under this statute were not "serious" for purposes of the Sixth Amendment. In a footnote, it concluded that even if the sentence and the license suspension were not concurrent—so that the suspension might occur after six months in jail—"we cannot say that a 90-day suspension is that significant as a Sixth Amendment matter, particularly when a restricted license may be obtained after only 45 days."

Blanton is consistent with previous Court decisions. In *Frank,* the contempt case noted above, the Court suggested that a potential penalty of six months plus a fine would not implicate the Sixth Amendment. And in *Muniz v. Hoffman*,[30] also involving a contempt penalty, the Court held that a fine of $10,000 would not trigger the right to jury trial, at least when, as in *Muniz,* the defendant (a labor union) was an organization. Such a large fine levied on an individual might require a different result, however.

Blanton is also important in establishing that, with the exception of contempt cases (where the penalty is judicially defined) only the legislatively imposed penalty is to be considered in determining whether a crime is serious or petty. According to the Court, "[t]he judiciary should not substitute its judgment as to seriousness for that of a legislature, which is 'far better equipped to perform the task, and . . . likewise more responsive to changes in attitude and more amenable to the recognition and correction of . . . misperceptions in this respect.' " This holding rendered irrelevant, for constitutional purposes, several pre-*Duncan* decisions that had looked at such factors as the morally offensive nature of the offense, in addition to its potential penalty, in deciding the reach of the right to jury trial in federal cases.[31]

(3) *Aggregation of Imprisonment Sanctions*

In *Codispoti v. Pennsylvania*,[32] the two defendants were tried on several different counts of contempt arising from their criminal trial, in a bench proceeding separate from the trial. Although no single sentence imposed during the contempt proceeding amounted to more than six months, the aggregate sentence received by each was well over six months. In this situation, the Court held that the defendants were entitled to a

---

[29] 489 U.S. 538, 109 S.Ct. 1289 (1989).

[30] 422 U.S. 454, 95 S.Ct. 2178 (1975).

[31] See, e.g., *District of Columbia v. Clawans,* 300 U.S. 617, 57 S.Ct. 660 (1937).

[32] 418 U.S. 506, 94 S.Ct. 2687 (1974).

jury trial, reasoning that, despite the petty nature of each offense, "the salient fact remains that the contempts arose from a single trial, were charged by a single judge and were tried in a single proceeding."

Outside of the contempt context, on the other hand, *Codispoti's* aggregation rule does not apply. In *Lewis v. United States,*[33] a five-member majority held that a defendant prosecuted in a single proceeding for multiple petty offenses does not have a right to a jury trial even when the aggregated penalty would clearly exceed six months.[34] The *Codispoti* rule is necessary in contempt proceedings, the *Lewis* majority reasoned, because it is not known before such a trial whether a single contempt penalty will exceed six months, and because a judge may be affected by personal bias where an allegation of contempt is involved; in the non-contempt context, in contrast, the potential sentence can be determined beforehand and a jury is not needed to ensure neutrality. In the latter situation, therefore, the Sixth Amendment requires a jury only when the penalty for any one of the crimes would amount to more than six months.

Even in contempt cases, the *Codispoti* aggregation rule will rarely apply. That is because the Court also indicated in that decision (in dictum) that, if the contempt penalties are imposed "summarily"—that is, for in-court contemptuous conduct as it occurs rather than in a separate proceeding as was the case in *Codispoti*—no jury would be required for individual contempt penalties of six months or less, even if, over the course of the trial, the contempt penalties aggregated to more than six months imprisonment. This position was justified by the "need to maintain order" in the courtroom.[35] Additionally, in *Taylor v. Hayes,*[36] decided the same day as *Codispoti,* the Court held that, even when a separate contempt proceeding is held, as in *Codispoti,* if an appellate court later reduces the aggregate sentence to six months or less the Sixth Amendment is not violated by a bench proceeding.

(d) Jury Size

Traditionally, the jury was twelve strong. In *Williams v. Florida,*[37] the Court held that this number was "a historical accident," and "unnecessary to effect the purposes of the jury system." On the latter point, it declared that reducing the size of the jury would impair neither of the functions of the jury recognized by *Duncan:* such a jury would still interpose "the common-sense judgment of a group of laymen" between the accused and his accuser, and still promote "the community participation and shared responsibility that results from the group's determination of guilt or innocence." To the argument that the smaller group could not as effectively incorporate the community's or the defendant's interests, the Court responded that a six-person jury would provide "a fair possibility for obtaining a representative cross-section of the community," at least "[a]s long as arbitrary exclusions of a particular class from the jury rolls are forbidden." Further, it would not necessarily favor the prosecution, since it reduced the chance of a holdout juror for *both* sides.

---

[33]   518 U.S. 322, 116 S.Ct. 2163 (1996).

[34]   Note also that trying petty offenses separately without juries does not violate the Sixth Amendment.

[35]   Thus, for contemptuous conduct that occurs outside the courtroom (e.g., refusal to obey a discovery order), this rule would not apply.

[36]   418 U.S. 488, 94 S.Ct. 2697 (1974).

[37]   399 U.S. 78, 90 S.Ct. 1893 (1970).

Research subsequent to *Williams* has questioned the assumptions underlying each of these points. Progressively smaller groups are less likely to represent the community; less likely to foster deliberation among members of the group; less likely to listen to a minority (since the minority, if any, will be smaller); more likely to harm the defendant, since the number of hung juries (along with the concomitant retrials) would diminish; and less likely to be reliable.[38] That this research had some persuasive force was borne out by the Court's decision in *Ballew v. Georgia*,[39] which relied heavily on it in concluding that a five-member jury violated the Constitution. Justice Blackmun found it unlikely that five persons could engage "in meaningful deliberation, . . . remember all the facts and arguments, and truly represent[ ] the common sense of the entire community." He conceded, in light of this conclusion, that the distinction between six and five members was arbitrary. But he also noted that, while the reduction from twelve to six members resulted in substantial savings, the reduction from six to five did not.

(e)　Voting Requirements

In two companion cases, *Johnson v. Louisiana*,[40] and *Apodaca v. Oregon*,[41] the Court allowed further experimentation with the jury trial right by approving the use of non-unanimous jury verdicts in criminal trials. In *Johnson*, the Court refused to strike down a Louisiana statute that authorized a 9–3 verdict of guilty in cases where the crime is necessarily punishable by hard labor. In *Apodaca*, the Court sustained three convictions, two of which were based on 11–1 verdicts and one which resulted from a 10–2 decision, the minimum requirement for a conviction under Oregon law.

In *Johnson*, the defendant relied on Fourteenth Amendment claims, since *Duncan's* application of the Sixth Amendment to the states occurred after his trial had commenced and was not applied retroactively. His principal argument was that a non-unanimous verdict failed to meet the standard of proving guilt beyond a reasonable doubt and therefore violated due process. Justice White's majority opinion disagreed:

> In our view, disagreement of three jurors does not alone establish reasonable doubt, particularly when such a heavy majority of the jury, after having considered the dissenters' views, remained convinced of guilt. . . . That want of jury unanimity is not to be equated with the existence of reasonable doubt emerges even more clearly from the fact that when a jury in a federal court, which operates under the unanimity rule and is instructed to acquit a defendant if it has a reasonable doubt . . . cannot agree unanimously upon a verdict, the defendant is not acquitted, but is merely given a new trial.

Of course, this statement overlooks the fact that, under the statutes in question, the result of a hung jury could be conviction, not a new trial.

In *Apodaca* the Court reached the same result even though the defendant's claim was based directly on the Sixth Amendment. Justice White, again speaking for the Court, pointed out that the Sixth Amendment does not speak to the reasonable doubt standard at all. And, with respect to *Duncan's* requirement that the jury interpose the commonsense judgment of a group representative of a cross-section of the community,

---

[38]　See Michael J. Saks, Jury Verdicts 207 (1977); Hans Zeisel, *And Then There Were None: The Diminution of the Federal Jury*, 38 U.Chi.L.Rev. 710 (1971).

[39]　435 U.S. 223, 98 S.Ct. 1029 (1978).

[40]　406 U.S. 356, 92 S.Ct. 1620 (1972).

[41]　406 U.S. 404, 92 S.Ct. 1628 (1972).

he put forward the same generous perception of how juries function that was articulated in *Williams* to justify six-person juries:

> We cannot assume that the majority of the jury will refuse to weigh the evidence and reach a decision upon rational grounds, just as it must do now in order to obtain unanimous verdicts, or that a majority will deprive a man of his liberty on the basis of prejudice when a minority is presenting a reasonable argument in favor of acquittal.

Nor would White accept the "assumption" that the minority, believing it will easily be outvoted, would refrain from making its views known at all.

Justice Douglas vigorously attacked this view of how juries operate in his dissent to both *Johnson* and *Apodaca*. He argued that permitting non-unanimous verdicts diminishes jury reliability because jurors will not debate and deliberate as fully. As soon as the requisite majority is obtained, Douglas contended, further consideration will be precluded. "Indeed, if a necessary majority is immediately obtained, then no deliberation at all is required." In contrast, where unanimity is required, Douglas continued, the majority must win the dissenters over to its side. The ultimate result, even if a guilty verdict, may still reflect the reservations of the uncertain jurors who may force compromise verdicts on lesser-included offenses and lesser sentences. As Douglas put it, "even though a minority may not be forceful enough to carry the day, their doubts may nonetheless cause a majority to exercise caution."

In both *Johnson* and *Apodaca*, the justices were split 4–4 between the views of White and Douglas, leaving Justice Powell as the swing vote. Although Powell agreed that the Sixth Amendment mandates unanimity in a federal jury trial, he concluded that unanimity is not a fundamental aspect of the right to jury trial applicable to the states. Thus, unanimity is only required at the federal level.

Burch v. Louisiana[42] raised the question of how *Williams,* which permitted six person juries, interrelated with *Johnson* and *Apodaca,* which allowed non-unanimous verdicts. There, the Court unanimously found a Louisiana statute that allowed non-unanimous verdicts by six-member juries unconstitutional. It saw little merit to Louisiana's contention that the provision "saved time," especially since only one other state had a similar provision. Thus, *Burch,* like *Ballew,* indicated that the Court was unwilling to carry the administrative convenience rationale to the point where the states are completely free to devise their own jury systems.

Read in conjunction with *Ballew,* the *Burch* decision permits six member juries only if the state additionally requires that decisions by such juries be unanimous. Despite this creation of a "lower limit," the Court's decisions concerning the scope of the jury trial right principally stand for the notion that the unanimous verdict by a twelve-member jury model is an "historical accident" and can be significantly curtailed. Thus, as the law stands today, it is conceivable that a 7–3 verdict by a ten-member jury panel is permissible.[43]

---

[42]   441 U.S. 130, 99 S.Ct. 1623 (1979).

[43]   Cf. Justice Stewart's dissent in *Johnson* (contending that an 8–4 verdict would be constitutional under the majority's reasoning).

(f) Trials *De Novo*

Many states require trial of minor crimes to take place before a judge, but then allow a conviction at this first tier to be "appealed" to a higher trial court, at which a trial *de novo* (i.e., a new proceeding at which evidence from the first trial is inadmissible) takes place in front of a jury. This system allows expedited handling of a large number of less serious offenses. In *Ludwig v. Massachusetts*,[44] the defendant challenged such a system as an impermissible obstacle to exercising the right to jury trial. The Supreme Court rejected the challenge, emphasizing that a Massachusetts defendant who insists on a jury can proceed "immediately" to the jury trial by "admitting sufficient findings of fact" at the first "trial" (resulting in a conviction which would trigger the *de novo* proceeding). In any event, the Court stated, the defendant had "not presented any evidence to show that there is a greater delay in obtaining a jury in Massachusetts than there would be if the Commonwealth abandoned its two-tier system."

The fact remains that the Massachusetts system requires certain defendants who want a jury trial to jump through hoops not normally required, perhaps leading those with fewer resources or less energy to forego their Sixth Amendment right. Further, as the four-member dissent pointed out, if *de novo* appeal is sought, the first trial, whether abbreviated or not (and despite the "inadmissibility" of its outcome in subsequent proceedings), will have an impact on the jury trial, since the judge, as well as any members of the jury familiar with the system, will know a conviction has taken place. The dissenters cogently argued that "[a]ll of the legitimate benefits of the two-tier system could be obtained by giving the defendant the right to waive the first-tier trial completely."[45]

(g) Waiver

A defendant might want to waive the right to jury trial for several reasons. Most obviously, community sentiment against him or the crime he allegedly committed may be so strong that a trial by members of that community could distort the decisionmaking process. Although changes of venue can be sought in such situations, they are rarely granted.[46] Further, some defendants or crimes may be so repulsive that trial by any group of laypeople, no matter where located, poses more of a risk than a proceeding presided over by a less naive judge. Or the case may be a particularly complex one that the defense believes a jury could not easily comprehend.

(1) When Waiver May Occur

In *Patton v. United States*,[47] the defendants made the relatively novel argument that their waiver of the right to a twelve-member jury at the federal level was invalid because they lacked the power to waive the right. But the Supreme Court held that, as is true with other rights, the right to jury trial may be surrendered. The Court concluded that since defendants routinely waive the right to jury trial when they plead guilty, waiver at trial should be permitted as well. Further, as *Patton* itself illustrated, a

---

[44] 427 U.S. 618, 96 S.Ct. 2781 (1976).

[45] Justice Powell, following his reasoning in *Apodaca,* found that the Sixth Amendment prohibited a *de novo* system at the federal level but not at the state level, and thus joined the majority. For the federal rule, see *Callan v. Wilson,* 127 U.S. 540, 8 S.Ct. 1301 (1888).

[46] See § 27.06(b)(2).

[47] 281 U.S. 276, 50 S.Ct. 253 (1930).

defendant can agree to a trial by a jury composed of fewer members than normally required (if, for instance, a juror becomes ill). Although *Patton* was decided before *Duncan* and applied only to federal trials, *Duncan* indicated that *Patton's* holding would apply to the states.

Patton required that the waiver be "express and intelligent." In *United States v. Jackson*,[48] the Court also required that it be voluntary. There the Court found unconstitutional the death penalty provision of the Federal Kidnapping Act, because it permitted imposition of capital punishment only after a jury trial. The Court stated that "the evil in the federal statute is not that it necessarily coerces guilty pleas and jury waivers but simply that it needlessly encourages them." In later cases,[49] however, the Court limited *Jackson* to its facts. Assuming the potential penalties after a jury and non-jury adjudication are the same, choosing the latter is voluntary if it represents a choice between known alternatives.[50]

(2) "Veto" of Waiver

The more controversial issue with respect to waiver of jury trial is whether it may be conditioned on the consent of the court and the prosecution. Most jurisdictions, including the federal courts, allow the judge or the prosecutor to "veto" a defendant's waiver of jury trial.[51] In *Singer v. United States*,[52] the Supreme Court upheld the federal provision, reasoning that "[a] defendant's only constitutional right concerning the method of trial is to an impartial trial by jury." Prosecutorial or judicial refusal to allow waiver simply subjects the defendant to a jury trial, "the very thing that the Constitution guarantees him."

The Court did caution that there might be circumstances, particularly those involving "passion, prejudice [or] public feeling," "where the defendant's reasons for wanting to be tried by a judge alone might be so compelling that the Government's insistence on trial by jury would result in the denial to a defendant of an impartial trial." But it appears that the proof required to meet the Court's "compelling reasons" test is very difficult to produce. One survey of federal cases during an eight-year period after *Singer* found that the prosecutor's decision to block a waiver had never been overruled.[53]

27.03 Selection of Prospective Jurors

(a) The Selection Process and Its Rationale

The selection of the jury is a several stage process. First, a list of names, normally designated the "jury pool", "jury list," or "master jury wheel," is compiled. The pool is usually drawn from voter registration lists (as is typically the case in the federal courts)[54]

---

[48]   390 U.S. 570, 88 S.Ct. 1209 (1968).

[49]   See, e.g., *Parker v. North Carolina,* 397 U.S. 790, 90 S.Ct. 1458 (1970); *Brady v. United States,* 397 U.S. 742, 90 S.Ct. 1463 (1970).

[50]   For further discussion on this point, see § 26.02(c)(2).

[51]   See, e.g., Fed.R.Crim.P. 23(a).

[52]   380 U.S. 24, 85 S.Ct. 783 (1965).

[53]   Note, *Waiving the Right to Jury Trial in the Federal Courts: The Burden of Prejudice"* 7 Suffolk L.Rev. 973 (1973).

[54]   See, 28 U.S.C.A. § 1863(b).

or telephone directories.[55] Some states, however, still operate under a jury commissioner, or "key man," system, in which individuals appointed by a judge are responsible for selecting and maintaining jury lists.[56] Generally, these individuals are directed to pick persons of "known integrity" or who have a "reputation for honesty and intelligence." The result can often be a pool that is not as representative as one chosen by purely random methods.

From the jury pool of eligible jurors, a much smaller "venire" or "panel" is selected, typically through a random process. Again, however, in jurisdictions with a selection procedure that utilizes commissioners, this stage has often been decidedly non-random in nature. As discussed below, such systems have frequently come under constitutional attack.

Once a venire is selected, those qualified for statutory exemption are excused, usually relying on juror qualification forms they have filled out. Typically exempted are (1) aliens; (2) those unable to speak English; (3) those under 18; (4) persons charged with a felony or serving a felony sentence; (5) and those who are suffering from mental or physical incapacity. Additionally, a prospective juror may normally request exemption from duty if he has previously served as a juror, is engaged in a "critical occupation" (often specified by statute and including military, government and professional jobs), or can show that service on a jury would work undue hardship or inconvenience.[57]

The venirepersons not exempted (a group that is still usually called the venire or panel) are further whittled down to jury size through *voir dire*. This process permits the parties to inform themselves about members of the panel so as to be able to exclude, through "challenges," those they find unsuitable.

In describing the ideal jury selection process, the Supreme Court most often speaks of a procedure that seeks a "fair cross-section" of the community and produces, as required by the language of the Sixth Amendment, an "impartial" jury.[58] It should be apparent that these two goals are not necessarily complementary: merely because a jury represents a number of groups in the community does not mean it is impartial, and fashioning an "impartial" jury may often produce one fairly homogenous in composition. Nor are these objectives equally achievable at each stage of the selection process. While the jury pool, and perhaps the venire, are large enough to include members of most significant groups in the community, a twelve or six-member jury cannot be expected to incorporate such diversity, a fact which the Supreme Court has recognized.[59] Conversely, by its very nature, "impartiality," if obtainable at all, can only be approached after *voir dire* has taken place and individual biases of potential jurors are exposed. Thus, the cross-section goal is most effectively implemented early in the jury selection process while impartiality can only be achieved toward the end of that process.

---

[55]　See generally, David Rottman, Carol Flango & R. Shedine Lockley, State Court Organization 255–73 (1995) for a description of state procedures.

[56]　See, e.g., Ala.Code §§ 12–16–31; 12–16–60; Ga. Code Ann. §§ 15–12–20; 15–13–40; Tenn.Code Ann. §§ 22–2–201; 22–2–302, 22–2–304.

[57]　See, e.g., 28 U.S.C.A. §§ 1865(b), 1866(c); ABA Criminal Justice Standard 15–2.1(d) (3d ed. 1996).

[58]　See, e.g., *Strauder v. West Virginia,* 100 U.S. (10 Otto) 303 (1879); *Williams v. Florida,* 399 U.S. 78, 90 S.Ct. 1893 (1970); *Taylor v. Louisiana,* 419 U.S. 522, 95 S.Ct. 692 (1975).

[59]　*Taylor v. Louisiana,* 419 U.S. 522, 95 S.Ct. 692 (1975); *Fay v. New York,* 332 U.S. 261, 67 S.Ct. 1613 (1947).

Ultimately, these realities serve the jury system well. As will become clear in this section, the ideal of a fair cross-section exists as much for the community's and the government's benefit as the defendant's, indeed perhaps more so. Without the cross-section requirement, the community's sense of participation in the criminal justice system would be minimal; concomitantly, the legitimacy of the government could be diminished. On the other hand, a *particular* jury need not reflect an exact cross-section of the community in order to meet public and governmental needs; so long as the jury *pool* includes a cross-section of the locality, over time the diverse segments of that locality will be represented on actual juries. This eventual representation should satisfy any sense of participation the public at large might seek, and any citizen involvement the government desires to achieve.

For his part, the defendant, like the community at large, is not particularly concerned about whether his particular jury reflects a cross-section of the community. Indeed, although he might wish to have members of certain groups on his jury, he will want to *avoid* a jury composed of people whose differences may make it difficult for them to empathize with his story. His primary concern is not whether the jury is representative of the community but whether the group which considers his case is impartial—if not actively partial—toward him. Closely related, but not identical, to this concern is a desire, shared by the barons who signed the Magna Carta,[60] to seek a jury consisting of individuals similar to him, a jury of his "peers." These objectives, ideally, are achieved through *voir dire*.[61]

The remainder of this section considers those stages of the jury selection process concerned primarily with ensuring various segments of the community have a chance at serving on the jury. The next section discusses those aspects of the selection process more clearly aimed at achieving an impartial jury of the defendant's peers, in particular the *voir dire* procedure.

(b) Equal Protection Challenges

Most litigation about the selection of the venire today focuses on application of the Sixth Amendment's "fair cross-section" requirement, discussed in the next subsection. But, prior to the mid-1970's, the only constitutional means of attacking state venire selection procedure was an argument based on the Equal Protection Clause. The theory behind these cases was that intentional exclusion from the venire of members of a "suspect class"—meaning African-Americans and other racial minorities—violated both the right of class members who were tried by a jury selected from that venire and the right of the persons excluded to be in the venire.[62]

Today, as a result of a series of decisions beginning with *Holland v. Illinois*,[63] the Court has made clear that the equal protection challenge is based solely on the second ground; that is, as the Court stated in *Holland*, "a juror's right to equal protection is violated when he is excluded because of his race." The defendant is allowed to make an equal protection challenge not to vindicate any personal right but because the juror has

---

[60] See supra text at note 3.

[61] See generally, Toni Massaro, *Peremptories or Peers? Rethinking Sixth Amendment Doctrine, Images and Procedures*, 64 N.Car.L.Rev. 501 (1986).

[62] *Carter v. Jury Commission of Greene County*, 396 U.S. 320, 90 S.Ct. 518 (1970).

[63] 493 U.S. 474, 110 S.Ct. 803 (1990); see also, *Powers v. Ohio*, 499 U.S. 400, 111 S.Ct. 1364 (1991); *Georgia v. McCollum*, 502 U.S. 1056, 112 S.Ct. 931 (1992), discussed further in § 27.04(d)(2).

"little incentive or resources to set in motion the arduous process needed to vindicate his own rights." The practical consequence of this holding is that, whereas originally an equal protection claim could be raised only by defendants who belonged to the suspect class excluded, now any defendant may raise the claim.

The standing issue aside, the most difficult aspect of an equal protection claim has always been proving an intent to discriminate. The first equal protection attack on selection of the jury, the 1880 decision of *Strauder v. Virginia*,[64] presented no problem in this regard, since it involved a statute that explicitly excluded blacks from jury service. But, after *Strauder,* discrimination took much subtler forms. For the next 85 years, the Court essentially failed to recognize this fact, insisting either on explicit proof of intent to discriminate or on a showing of "virtual exclusion" of all blacks from the venire, in which case the burden shifted to the state to show that the disparity was not intentional.[65]

The obtuse character of the Court's approach was starkly illustrated in *Swain v. Alabama,*[66] decided by the Warren Court. In *Swain,* the Court had neither evidence of virtual exclusion nor direct confirmation of discriminatory intent. The evidence merely showed that, over a several year period, 26% of eligible jurors in the jurisdiction were black, while jury panels averaged 10–15% black. Furthermore, stressed the Court, the jury commissioners "denied that racial considerations entered into their selections of either their contacts in the community or the names of prospective jurors." Under these circumstances, the Court could find no violation of the Equal Protection Clause.[67] It explained away the disparity shown by petitioner's statistics as the result of "an imperfect" but not purposefully discriminatory system which neither excluded nor limited proportionally black representation:

> Neither the jury roll nor the venire need be a perfect mirror of the community or accurately reflect the proportionate strength of every identifiable group. . . .
> We cannot say that purposeful discrimination based on race alone is satisfactorily proved by showing that an identifiable group in a community is underrepresented by as much as 10%.

The naiveté of this language was soon exposed in an article by Professor Finkelstein which showed that the disproportionate and persistent under-representation proven in *Swain* could have resulted by chance only in one out of 100 million trillion venires chosen from the population of Talladega County.[68]

Subsequent decisions showed a Court more sophisticated in its statistical analysis and less willing to give credence to the statements of jury commissioners. Rather than requiring complete or virtual exclusion of African-Americans plus an opportunity to discriminate, the Court was willing to find a prima facie violation of equal protection whenever a "significant" disparity between the proportion of blacks on the jury panels and the proportion in the community existed, and some opportunity to discriminate was

---

[64] 100 U.S. (10 Otto) 303 (1879).

[65] See, e.g., *Cassell v. Texas,* 339 U.S. 282, 70 S.Ct. 629 (1950) (finding proof of actual intent); *Avery v. Georgia,* 345 U.S. 559, 73 S.Ct. 891 (1953) (finding virtual exclusion plus an opportunity to discriminate).

[66] 380 U.S. 202, 85 S.Ct. 824 (1965).

[67] *Swain* also rejected a challenge to the prosecutor's use of peremptories, discussed in § 27.04(d)(1).

[68] Michael O. Finkelstein, *The Application of Statistical Decision Theory to the Jury Discrimination Cases*, 80 Harv.L.Rev. 338, 356–58 (1966).

shown. For example, in *Whitus v. Georgia*,[69] the Court found a prima facie case of purposeful discrimination when, in a county where 42.6% of males over 21 were black, only 3 of 33 prospective grand jurors were black and only seven of 90 persons selected for the petit jury venire were black, and evidence showed that the jury lists had been made up from an earlier list compiled from tax returns that indicated the taxpayer's race. Testimony by the jury commissioners that race was not a factor in compiling the lists did not overcome this presumption; the Court noted that, while unnecessary to the decision, it was "interesting" that, under Finkelstein's analysis, the probability that the venire would randomly contain the number of blacks it did was .000006. Later decisions reached similar results.[70]

In *Castaneda v. Partida*,[71] the Court for the first time applied the equal protection formula to a group other than blacks and may also have further expanded its scope. The respondent's statistics showed that use of the "key man" system in Texas had produced, over an 11-year period, a 40% disparity (79.1% to 39%) between the proportion of those with Spanish surnames in the community and the proportion summoned for grand jury service. After finding that Mexican-Americans are an identifiable class protected by the Equal Protection Clause, five members of the Court, in an opinion by Justice Blackmun, concluded that these statistics made out a prima facie case of discrimination. "Supporting this conclusion" was the fact that the key man selection procedures, although facially constitutional, were highly subjective and susceptible to abuse against Mexican-Americans, since Spanish surnames are easily identifiable. Because the state "inexplicably" produced no evidence from the grand jury commissioners as to their method of selection, the presumption of discrimination was not rebutted. The Court also rejected the state's contention that since Mexican-Americans were the "governing majority" in the county, it must be presumed that governmental discrimination could not have occurred.

The dissent, not unreasonably, argued that relying on gross population statistics rather than "jury-eligible" population statistics as the baseline for judging the disparity was inappropriate, given the fact that neither "tokenism nor absolute exclusion" was involved. But even had the relevant difference in representation been smaller, the majority seemed to indicate that, "in the absence of evidence to the contrary," a finding of discrimination is proper. Unconstitutional disparity exists when it is "sufficiently large [that] it is unlikely [to be] due solely to chance or accident" (a disparity that the Court defined as "more than two or three standard deviations" from the expected representation of the group in question). The Court also stressed that "a selection procedure that is susceptible of abuse or is not racially neutral supports the presumption of discrimination raised by the statistical showing." *Castaneda* thus suggests that when a procedure susceptible of abuse exists, the disparity necessary to show purposeful discrimination may be smaller than would otherwise be required. It also suggests that when the disparity is large, one may presume discrimination regardless of whether the procedure appears to be racially neutral.

---

[69]   385 U.S. 545, 87 S.Ct. 643 (1967).

[70]   See *Turner v. Fouche*, 396 U.S. 346, 90 S.Ct. 532 (1970); *Alexander v. Louisiana*, 405 U.S. 625, 92 S.Ct. 1221 (1972).

[71]   430 U.S. 482, 97 S.Ct. 1272 (1977).

(c) The Fair Cross-Section Requirement

As early as 1942, in *Glasser v. United States*,[72] the Supreme Court interpreted the Sixth Amendment to require a selection process that comports "with the concept of the jury as a cross-section of the community." But that decision applied only to the federal courts. In subsequent years, while relying on the cross-section concept to invalidate federal selection procedures that excluded day laborers[73] and women,[74] the Court refused to consider constitutional challenges against state selection procedures on any grounds other than equal protection.[75]

When *Duncan* applied the Sixth Amendment to the states, however, the stage was set for a new approach. Seven years later, in *Taylor v. Louisiana*,[76] the Court explicitly stated: "We accept the fair cross-section requirement as fundamental to the jury trial guaranteed by the Sixth Amendment." In providing an alternative to equal protection analysis, *Taylor* facilitated challenge of state petit jury selection procedures in three ways. First, it required only a showing of "systematic exclusion;" according to the Court, proving the existence of discriminatory intent is not necessary to show a violation of the fair cross-section requirement. Second, it signaled that the Constitution banned unjustifiable systematic exclusion of *any* significant, distinct group in the community, not just racial minorities. Third, unlike equal protection analysis at the time, *Taylor* permitted a defendant who is not a member of the excluded group to challenge its exclusion. Although, as noted above, this latter difference has since been eliminated,[77] the first two differences remain. Whether they are significant will be examined further below.

The statute in question in *Taylor* automatically exempted women from jury service unless they filed in advance a written notice of their desire to serve as a juror.[78] As a result, women comprised less than 10% of the persons in the jury wheel, despite comprising 53% of the populace. Relying on its earlier decision in *Peters v. Kiff*,[79] the Court first held that Taylor, a male, had standing to challenge this state of affairs. As Justice Marshall's opinion in *Peters* had stated, "[i]llegal and unconstitutional jury selection procedures cast doubt on the integrity of the whole judicial process," and thus should be challengeable by any defendant. The Court then explained why the fair cross-section requirement it had previously applied only to federal cases now applied, post-*Duncan*, to the state jury selection process as well. According to the majority, the jury cannot fulfill its intended purpose of guarding against the exercise of arbitrary power "if the jury pool is made up of only segments of the populace or if large, distinctive groups are excluded from the pool." The Court also emphasized the public's interest in enforcing a cross-section requirement. "Community participation in the criminal law . . . is not only consistent with our democratic heritage but is also critical to public confidence in the fairness of the criminal justice system."

---

[72] 315 U.S. 60, 62 S.Ct. 457 (1942).

[73] *Thiel v. Southern Pacific Co.*, 328 U.S. 217, 66 S.Ct. 984 (1946).

[74] *Ballard v. United States*, 329 U.S. 187, 67 S.Ct. 261 (1946).

[75] See e.g., *Fay v. New York*, 332 U.S. 261, 67 S.Ct. 1613 (1947).

[76] 419 U.S. 522, 95 S.Ct. 692 (1975).

[77] See *Holland v. Illinois*, 493 U.S. 474, 110 S.Ct. 803 (1990), discussed in § 27.03(b).

[78] Prior to *Duncan*, the Supreme Court had upheld an identical state statute against a cross-section claim in *Hoyt v. Florida*, 368 U.S. 57, 82 S.Ct. 159 (1961).

[79] 407 U.S. 493, 92 S.Ct. 2163 (1972).

Applying this reasoning to the facts, the Court held that women compose the type of large, distinctive group that needs to be included in the jury selection process to guard against arbitrariness and foster a sense of community participation. In addition to their obviously significant numbers, women impart "a flavor, a distinct quality" to a jury. In support of this latter statement, the Court pointed to sociological studies reporting that women brought different perspectives and values to jury service than did men. Thus, any "systematic exclusion" of this group, such as occurred under the Louisiana statute, violated the Sixth Amendment.

The Court also rejected the state's argument that making women as eligible for jury service as men would interfere with their "distinctive role in society." The systematic exclusion of all women under a "special hardship or incapacity" category is impermissible since it is "untenable" to suggest that it would be a special hardship for all women to serve. At the same time, the Court sanctioned the granting of individualized exemptions in the cases "of special hardship or incapacity and to those engaged in particular occupations the uninterrupted performance of which is critical to the community's welfare."

Finally, *Taylor* emphasized that while the lists from which jurors are chosen must be representative, the juries chosen from these lists need not mirror the community exactly or reflect every community group. For reasons suggested earlier,[80] this holding is not only practically necessary, but also preferable theoretically. A jury that represents the community may not be impartial. At the same time, the community's interest in participating in and feeling confident about the criminal justice system is adequately taken into account by prohibiting the exclusion of distinctive groups from the panel from which juries are ultimately selected.

The best summary of *Taylor's* holding is found in a later case, *Duren v. Missouri*.[81] There the Court held that a fair cross-section challenge of the jury venire as established in *Taylor* requires the defendant to prove three elements:

> (1) that the group alleged to be excluded is a "distinctive" group in the community; (2) that the representation of this group in venires from which juries are selected is not fair and reasonable in relation to the number of such persons in the community; and (3) that this underrepresentation is due to systematic exclusion of the group in the jury-selection process.

These three elements are discussed in more detail below.

(1) Distinctive Group

There appear to be three requirements a "group" must meet before it comes within the ambit of the Sixth Amendment fair cross-section requirement established in *Taylor* and *Duren*. First, the group must be "large." Second, it must be identifiable. Third, its inclusion in the venire must significantly advance the systemic and community objectives associated with the jury trial right. As summarized by the Court in *Lockhart v. McCree*,[82] these objectives are "(1) 'guard[ing] against the exercise of arbitrary power' and ensuring that the 'commonsense judgment of the community' will act as a 'hedge against the overzealous or mistaken prosecutor;' (2) preserving 'public confidence in the

---

[80] See § 27.03(a).

[81] 439 U.S. 357, 99 S.Ct. 664 (1979).

[82] 476 U.S. 162, 106 S.Ct. 1758 (1986).

fairness of the criminal justice system;' and (3) implementing our belief that 'sharing in the administration of justice is a phase of civic responsibility.' " If the group, in *Taylor's* words, imparts a "flavor, a distinct quality" to the jury deliberation process, then it presumably meets these latter three objectives. On the other hand, the group need not "act or tend to act as a class" in the jury room for it to be "distinctive."

The types of exemptions described in the beginning of this section—having to do with aliens, felons, and so on—systematically exclude from jury service identifiable groups that may be large and perhaps even "distinctive" in the sense just described. But, as *Taylor* emphasized, group exemptions based on a valid state justification will continue to be recognized.[83] Thus, even an exemption that falls predominately on women may not violate the Sixth Amendment if enacted for legitimate reasons. In *Duren,* for instance, the Court suggested that so long as the state exercised "proper caution" in excusing those members of the family responsible for the care of children, a non-gender-based provision to this effect would not violate the Constitution given the important state interest in assuring proper child care.

Valid exemptions aside, there are many groups other than women potentially eligible under *Taylor's* distinctiveness test. In *McCree* the Court indicated, not surprisingly, that the Sixth Amendment requires inclusion of racial groups such as African-Americans and Mexican-Americans in the jury pool (thereby specifically incorporating the equal protection cases into fair cross-section jurisprudence). As Justice Rehnquist wrote for the Court, exclusion of these groups from the venire could produce juries that might be "arbitrarily skewed in such a way as to deny criminal defendants the benefit of the common-sense judgment of the community." Furthermore, such exclusion creates an appearance of unfairness by basing exclusion not on inability to serve but on "some immutable characteristic such as race, gender, or ethnic background," and "improperly deprives members of these often historically disadvantaged groups of their right as citizens to serve on juries in criminal cases."

In applying the *Taylor-McCree* test, lower courts have held that other ethnic groups, including Native Americans[84] and Jews,[85] are "distinct" groups for Sixth Amendment purposes. In contrast, non-ethnic groups, such as blue collar workers[86] and young adults,[87] are generally not included in this category. In short, the courts have not strayed very far beyond traditional equal protection doctrine (which has focused on oppressed minorities and gender) in developing this aspect of the fair cross-section doctrine. One of the cases involving young adults, *Barber v. Ponte,*[88] illustrates the difficulties of extending the doctrine beyond racial, ethnic, and gender lines.

The original decision in *Barber* came from two members of a three-judge panel, which found, in contrast to most precedent, that young adults between the ages of 18 and 34 are a cognizable group (and found further that this group had been systematically

---

[83]   See, e.g., *State v. Brewer,* 247 N.W.2d 205 (Iowa 1976) (state's exemption of those over 65 has a rational basis).

[84]   *United States v. Herbert,* 698 F.2d 981 (9th Cir. 1983); *United States v. Brady,* 579 F.2d 1121 (9th Cir. 1978), cert. denied 439 U.S. 1074, 99 S.Ct. 849 (1979).

[85]   *United States v. Gelb,* 881 F.2d 1155 (2d Cir. 1989).

[86]   *Anaya v. Hansen,* 781 F.2d 1 (1st Cir. 1986).

[87]   *Ford v. Seabold,* 841 F.2d 677 (6th Cir. 1988); *Brown v. Harris,* 666 F.2d 782 (2d Cir. 1981), cert. denied 456 U.S. 948, 102 S.Ct. 2017 (1982); *United States v. Test,* 550 F.2d 577 (10th Cir. 1976).

[88]   772 F.2d 982 (1st Cir. 1985), cert. denied 475 U.S. 1050, 106 S.Ct. 1272 (1986).

underrepresented in the jury pool by a factor of between 19 and 22%). In reaching the conclusion that young adults are distinctive for Sixth Amendment purposes, the judges relied heavily on sociological research, as had the Court in *Taylor*. This research indicated that younger adults have differing opinions from older adults on such matters as "the inference of guilt from silence; the presumption of innocence; the predisposition of the young to break the law; and the performance and prerogatives of the police."[89] The judges concluded that "a gross underrepresentation of young people could be expected to affect a large number of cases, particularly those involving young people."

However, on rehearing en banc, the First Circuit reversed, giving two significant reasons. First, it asserted that the Court in *Taylor* and *Duren* had "wanted to give heightened scrutiny to groups needing special protection, not to all groups generally." The court continued: "[I]f age classification is adopted, surely blue-collar workers, yuppies, Rotarians, Eagle Scouts, and an endless variety of other classifications will be entitled to similar treatment." Second, the majority concluded that the age group identified by the three-judge panel decision was arbitrary.[90] In terms of "specific common characteristics," the court asserted, there are no "clear lines of demarcation" between the 18–34 group and any other group within or overlapping with that range; further, the diversity within that range might be substantial.

Both rationales can be questioned. The first argument seems heavily tinged with equal protection concerns not necessarily relevant to fair cross-section analysis. The Supreme Court's Sixth Amendment cases do not speak of "protecting" groups from discrimination, but of ensuring that groups with a distinctive voice can both contribute to the "common sense" of the jury and experience a sense of participation in the criminal justice process.[91] The majority's concern that this approach will open the door to a wide diversity of claims is understandable. But some of the groups named by the majority may not bring a "distinct flavor" to the jury, and, even assuming they do, they may not be large enough (e.g., Eagle Scouts or Rotarians) or discernible (e.g., "yuppies"), thus failing the other aspects of *Taylor's* distinctive group test.

Lack of discernibility is the *Barber* majority's second rationale for its decision. There is certainly some strength to the point that the group of "young adults" is not "identifiable." But as the dissent (written by one member of the original two-judge majority) noted, "amorphousness is not confined to age groups. In what generation does a Mexican-American or Puerto Rican become simply a Texas [sic] or New Yorker and cease to be part of a cognizable group?" Conundrums such as these make the distinctive group aspect of *Taylor* particularly problematic.

(2) Underrepresentation

In *Taylor*, the Court had no difficulty finding the requisite degree of underrepresentation: while women comprised 53% of the persons eligible for jury service in the relevant jurisdictions, no more than 10% of the persons on the jury wheel were

---

[89] Quoting Donald H. Zeigler, *Young Adults as a Cognizable Group in Jury Selection*, 76 Mich.L.Rev. 1045 (1978).

[90] *Barber v. Ponte,* 772 F.2d 982 (1st Cir. 1985).

[91] Indeed, in *Hamling v. United States,* 418 U.S. 87, 94 S.Ct. 2887 (1974), the Supreme Court assumed, without deciding, that the young do constitute a "cognizable group," but went on to hold that, because "[s]ome play in the joints of the jury selection process is necessary," California's scheme of refilling the jury list every four years (and thus failing to include those who reached 18 in the intervening years) did not violate the Constitution.

women and no women were on the venire from which the petit jury in the defendant's case was drawn. In *Duren*, the defendant presented statistics that only 15% of the persons on venires were women while 54% of the adults in the county were women. Again the Court found the underrepresentation substantial enough to violate the Sixth Amendment.

One might argue that, because *Taylor* was concerned with ensuring a fair cross-section in the jury venire and not with preventing purposeful discrimination, a very small differential should trigger the Sixth Amendment. But among the lower courts, the disparity between a group's representation in the community and in the jury-eligible population must usually be over 10% to be sufficient under the Sixth Amendment.[92] In *Berghuis v. Smith*[93] the Supreme Court declined to reject this approach (which calculates "absolute disparity"), while noting that there are at least two other methods of determining underrepresentation—comparative disparity (computed by dividing absolute disparity by the group's representation in the jury-eligible population and most appropriate where the target group is small) and standard deviation analysis (relied upon in *Casteneda v. Partida*[94]). Whatever method is chosen, it should be remembered that mere proof of a sufficient disparity does not necessarily conclude the case. If the state can give a legitimate reason for the underrepresentation, then the Sixth Amendment is not violated.

(3) Systematic Exclusion

The facts of *Taylor* and *Duren* both illustrate that the Sixth Amendment does not require proof of purposeful exclusion. In *Taylor*, the statute struck down in that case permitted any otherwise qualified woman to serve if she indicated a willingness to do so. No state official prevented women from volunteering for jury service and there was no evidence that the legislature intended to exclude women from such service. In *Duren*, the challenged statutes required women to opt out of service rather than "opt in," arguably a system even less likely to deter female participation in the jury system. Yet the fact that the statutes made opting out especially easy for women (and that local practice was to excuse any woman who failed to appear for jury service), when combined with the statistical showing described above, led the Court to invalidate the Missouri provisions as well.

In short, as the Court said in *Duren*, "[i]n contrast [to the equal protection cases], in Sixth Amendment fair-cross-section cases, systematic disproportion itself demonstrates an infringement of the defendant's interest in a jury chosen from a fair cross section." For instance, if it is shown that a group is significantly underrepresented in the venire because it is underrepresented on the voter registration lists from which the jury pool is randomly selected (which might be true of Mexican-Americans, for example), an equal protection claim would presumably lose (because the exclusion, although systematic, is not intentional). However, a fair cross-section claim might require that some other means of selecting the pool be found that more accurately represents the excluded group.

---

[92] See, e.g., *United States v. Rodriguez*, 776 F.2d 1509 (11th Cir. 1985) ("a prima facie case of underrepresentation has not been made where the absolute disparity . . . does not exceed 10%"); *Porter v. Freeman*, 577 F.2d 329 (5th Cir. 1978) (women underrepresented by 20%).

[93] 559 U.S. 314, 130 S.Ct. 1382 (2010).

[94] 430 U.S. 482, 97 S.Ct. 1272 (1977), discussed § 27.03(b). Note, however, that no court has accepted standard deviation alone as determinative in petit jury cases. *United States v. Rioux*, 97 F.3d 648, 655 (2d. Cir. 1996).

This should not suggest that claims of systematic exclusion are easily won. In *Berghuis v. Smith*,[95] the Court concluded that it is not "unreasonable" to place the burden on the defendant to show that underrepresentation of a distinctive group in a jury pool resulted from systematic exclusion. It further held that exclusion of a group is not necessarily systematic simply because the state had siphoned off many minority jurors to other districts in an effort to improve minority representation in those districts. Nor is systematic exclusion necessarily proven by showing, as Smith alleged, that the jurisdiction: routinely excuses people on a bare allegation of hardship or due to failure to show up for jury service; fails to follow up on non-responses to, or enforce, appearance orders; and uses residential addresses at least 15 months old. The Court stated that *Taylor* had granted states broad discretion to create exemptions to jury service and that *Duren* recognized that "hardship exemptions resembling those Smith assails might well 'survive a fair-cross-section challenge.'"

(d) The Right to the Jury List

In *Test v. United States*,[96] the Supreme Court held that a federal defendant has the right to inspect and copy jury lists in order to prepare challenges to petit and grand jury selection procedures. Relying on the Federal Jury Selection and Service Act, the Court found an unqualified right to inspection in the plain text of the statute and in the statute's overall purpose of assuring that juries are selected at random from a fair cross-section of the community.

Since the decision was based on a federal statute, *Test* has no direct implications for the states. Without unreasonable extension, however, this right of inspection could be seen as part of the constitutional right to have a jury pool and panel selected from a fair cross-section of the community.

27.04 Voir Dire

(a) The Basic Structure

After the jury pool or venire is selected, effort is focused on choosing the members of the jury who will hear the case. At this point, the principal goal is no longer obtaining a cross-section of the community, but rather assuring that the members of the jury are "impartial," as guaranteed by the Sixth Amendment.[97] The principal mechanism for accomplishing this objective is *"voir dire,"* literally, "to see what is said."

Depending upon the jurisdiction, *voir dire* questioning—designed to elicit possible biases among the venirepersons—may be conducted by the judge, the attorneys, or by both.[98] When the judge alone conducts the process, the attorneys typically are allowed to suggest questions to the judge. The advantage of judicial questioning is that attorneys will be prevented from using *voir dire* to "indoctrinate" the jury. The disadvantage is

---

[95]   559 U.S. 314, 130 S.Ct. 1382 (2010). Because *Smith* was a habeas case, the issue was whether the lower court's decision was an "unreasonable" interpretation of the law, and did not directly address the constitutionality of the selection procedure. See § 33.02(c).

[96]   420 U.S. 28, 95 S.Ct. 749 (1975).

[97]   Although normally the impartiality requirement is achieved through regulating the jury selection process, in *Peña-Rodriguez v. Colorado*, ___ U.S. ___, 137 S.Ct. 855 (2017), the Court held that the general rule against not "impeaching" a jury verdict through post-verdict inquiries must give way when a juror gratuitously states after conviction that his or her decision was influenced by racial stereotypes.

[98]   The federal rule leaves the matter up to the judge. Fed.R.Crim.P. 24(a).

that judicial questioning is seldom probing (and may be directed at the entire panel rather than individual jurors). The better practice, probably, is to allow the attorneys to conduct questioning, monitored closely by the judge and other attorney.

In addition to questioning at *voir dire,* attorneys may conduct outside research about prospective jurors. This typically consists of culling demographic information from jury lists.[99] But the attorneys may also pursue more detailed investigation of prospective jurors by interviewing their acquaintances and searching records,[100] or even hiring social scientists to anticipate their attitudes on various issues.[101]

Based on the results of the questioning and other information they have acquired, the defense and the prosecution decide which individuals they would like to exclude from the jury. Each side has an unlimited number of for cause challenges, which permit striking from the jury any venireperson who admits to being or appears to be biased. Each side also has a limited number of peremptories (from 3 to 20 or more, depending upon the jurisdiction, the size of the jury and the type of crime) which it can use to strike any venireperson without explanation.[102]

The following three subsections explore in more depth the questioning process that occurs during *voir dire*, the nature of for cause challenges and the nature of peremptory challenges.

(b) Voir Dire Questioning

Litigation over *voir dire* questioning is most likely to occur when the judge conducts it and refuses to ask questions proffered by the defense. The Supreme Court has held that, under certain circumstances, the judge must ask specific questions about racial prejudice and attitudes toward the death penalty. But otherwise, failure on the part of the judge to ask individualized questions at the defendant's request will not constitute error unless the defendant can show that the failure produced a jury that was prejudiced. This latter burden is very difficult to meet.

(1) Questions About Racial Prejudice

The Supreme Court has held that specific questions about racial prejudice must be asked if racial issues are "inextricably bound with the conduct of the trial." *Ham v. South Carolina*[103] involved a black tried in South Carolina for the possession of marijuana. The defendant was well known in the locale of his trial as a civil rights activist, and his defense was that law enforcement officials had framed him on the narcotics charge to "get him" for those activities. The Court, in an opinion by Justice Rehnquist, unanimously found that Ham's reputation as an activist and the defense he interposed likely intensified any prejudice that individual members of the jury might have harbored against blacks and that, in such circumstances, the defendant was entitled to questioning specifically directed to racial prejudice in order to meet the constitutional requirement that an impartial jury be impaneled. The routine questions asked by the

---

[99] See § 27.03(d).

[100] Extrajudicial communication with veniremen prior to trial is considered unethical. ABA Model Rule of Professional Conduct 3.5(b).

[101] For a critique of this latter practice, see Michael J. Saks, *The Limits of Scientific Jury Selection: Ethical and Empirical*, 17 Jurimetrics J. 3 (1976).

[102] See e.g., Fed.R.Crim.P. 24(b).

[103] 409 U.S. 524, 93 S.Ct. 848 (1973).

trial court (i.e., "Have you formed or expressed any opinion as to the guilt or innocence of the defendant, Gene Ham?; Are you conscious of any bias or prejudice for or against him?; Can you give the State and the defendant a fair and impartial trial?") were insufficient for this purpose.

But the Court strictly limited *Ham* in *Ristaino v. Ross*,[104] in which a black was convicted in state court of violent crimes against a white security guard. The trial judge denied the defendant's motion that a question specifically directed to racial prejudice be asked during *voir dire,* finding the customary questions directed to general bias and prejudice sufficient. The Court upheld the trial judge's decision, construing *Ham* to mean that it is in the trial judge's discretion to determine whether there is a significant likelihood that questioning about racial prejudice would result in a jury less biased on the race issue than a jury not subjected to such questioning. In *Ristaino,* the racial issue was seen as collateral compared to the situation in *Ham;* racial issues did not "permeate" the trial and were not "bound up" with its conduct. Thus questioning about general bias was sufficient. Only in capital cases might more be constitutionally required.[105]

In the federal courts, the rule concerning questioning about racial prejudice is somewhat more generous toward the defendant. The defendant in *Rosales-Lopez v. United States*[106] was convicted of participating in a plan to bring Mexican aliens across the border from Tijuana to California. Prior to *voir dire,* the defendant's counsel had requested the trial judge to ask potential jury members a list of 26 questions, one of which read: "Would you consider the race or Mexican descent of Humber Rosales-Lopez in your evaluation of this case? How would it affect you?" The Supreme Court found no violation, constitutional or otherwise, in the trial judge's refusal to ask this type of question on *voir dire,* given the failure of the petitioner to show that racial issues were a significant aspect of the trial. However, the plurality opinion went on to create, under its supervisory power over the federal courts, a federal rule calling for such questions when there is "a reasonable possibility that racial or ethnic prejudice might have influenced the jury." The plurality also found, after an analysis of the Court's previous decisions, that such a "reasonable possibility" would exist whenever the defendant is "accused of a violent crime [unlike the instant case] and where the defendant and the victim are members of different racial or ethnic groups." But it cautioned that, in most cases, "whether the total circumstances suggest a reasonable possibility that racial or ethnic prejudice will affect the jury remains primarily with the trial court."

(2) Questions About Attitudes Toward the Death Penalty

In order to implement its decisions attempting to maintain jury impartiality in capital sentencing cases, to be discussed below,[107] the Court has required trial judges, at the request of a party, to ask specific questions designed to determine attitudes about the death penalty. The explicit rule announced in *Morgan v. Illinois*[108] was that capital defendants may require potential jurors to disclose whether they would automatically impose the death penalty upon conviction. Six members of the Court, in an opinion by Justice White, concluded that individuals who would do so are unlikely to be discovered

---

[104]   424 U.S. 589, 96 S.Ct. 1017 (1976).

[105]   *Turner v. Murray*, 476 U.S. 28, 106 S.Ct. 1683 (1986) (holding that a *capital sentencing* jury must be asked racial prejudice questions whenever the crime involves racial violence).

[106]   451 U.S. 182, 101 S.Ct. 1629 (1981).

[107]   See § 27.04(c)(2).

[108]   504 U.S. 719, 112 S.Ct. 2222 (1992).

by general questions concerning fairness and impartiality, because they might be unwilling to admit a reluctance to abide by the law, or might, "in good conscience, swear to uphold that law and yet be unaware that maintaining such dogmatic beliefs about the death penalty would prevent [them] from doing so." Although not necessary to its holding, the *Morgan* Court also strongly suggested that the *prosecution* can require the judge to ask specific questions as to whether a potential juror would *refuse* to impose the death penalty under any circumstances. As White stated, "[w]ere *voir dire* not available to lay bare" those who would automatically impose the death penalty, the "right not to be tried by such jurors would be rendered as nugatory and meaningless as the State's right, in the absence of questioning, to strike those who would *never* do so."

(3) Questions About Other Matters

As to *voir dire* questioning on issues other than racial prejudice or the death penalty, it seems clear that constitutional obligations are minimal. For instance, in rejecting Ham's argument that the trial court should also have examined jurors about possible prejudice engendered by his beard, Rehnquist stated "[g]iven the traditionally broad discretion accorded to the trial judge in conducting *voir dire* . . . and our inability to distinguish possible prejudice against beards from a host of other possible similar prejudices, we do not believe the petitioner's constitutional rights were violated when the trial judge refused to put this question." Much the same thing could be said about *voir dire* questioning directed at most other types of possible prejudices.

Post-*Ham* cases do not dispel this notion. In *Hamling v. United States,*[109] the Court held that the trial judge in an obscenity case is not required to inquire into the "whether the jurors' educational, political, and religious beliefs might affect their views on the question of obscenity." And in *Mu'Min v. Virginia,*[110] it concluded that, although there was "a certain common sense appeal" to the argument that the effect of pretrial publicity could not be gauged unless each venireperson was asked specifically what he had heard or read, the judge did not violate the Sixth Amendment by merely asking potential jurors, in groups of four, general questions about whether they had foreknowledge of the case and were able to avoid a fixed opinion about it.

The Court's reasoning in *Mu'Min* is the Court's strongest suggestion that, outside of racial and death penalty issues, the Sixth Amendment imposes few constraints on *voir dire* questioning. Chief Justice Rehnquist characterized as "speculative" the assumption that questioning about the precise content of foreknowledge would cause jurors to consider more carefully whether they were open-minded about the case. He also pointed out that, to prevent other jurors from hearing about the content of the pretrial publicity, the type of *voir dire* proposed by the defendant would necessitate questioning each prospective juror individually, which would be inefficient and might make those questioned feel that they themselves were on trial. Yet Justice Kennedy, one of four dissenters, seemed more realistic when he wrote that, at least when prejudicial pretrial publicity is involved, "findings of impartiality must be based on something more than the mere silence of the individual in response to questions asked *en masse*."

---

[109] 418 U.S. 87, 94 S.Ct. 2887 (1974).
[110] 500 U.S. 415, 111 S.Ct. 1899 (1991).

(c) For Cause Challenges

Typical statutory grounds for challenging jurors include a blood relationship to one of the litigants, a pecuniary interest in the outcome of the case, and previous service on a jury which considered a similar crime or a grand jury which considered the same crime. Additionally, even if not specifically provided for by statute, each party can exclude for cause any juror who "is unable or unwilling to hear the case at issue fairly and impartially."[111]

Challenges on the latter basis are rarely granted, however. First, as noted in the previous subsection, judges are not normally required to ask *voir dire* questions designed to probe into prejudices involving such matters as race or appearance. Second, judges usually accept at face value a potential juror's statement that he will abide by the oath of impartiality. Prejudice is seldom implied, on the reasonable ground that individuals who say they can be impartial should be trusted to abide by their oath. The question of when bias *should* be implied, as a matter of constitutional law, is discussed first, followed by a discussion of the special for cause challenge jurisprudence that has developed in death penalty cases.

(1) Implied Bias

Except for a few decisions involving the impact of pretrial publicity (which, as discussed later in this chapter,[112] have since been significantly limited in scope), there is only one decision in which the Court held that exclusion for cause should have occurred because of implied bias, and that decision involved a very unusual set of facts. In *Leonard v. United States*,[113] the defendant was tried on two similar charges in two separate trials held on the same day. At the end of the first trial, the judge announced that the defendant was guilty, in front of prospective jurors who were in court awaiting the second trial. The Court held that all of the prospective jurors were automatically disqualified, regardless of whether they vowed impartiality.

In other cases, the Court has been hostile to implied bias claims, requiring instead a showing of "actual bias." In *Dennis v. United States*,[114] for instance, the defendant claimed that his conviction on criminal contempt charges for failure to appear before the Committee on Un-American Activities was inherently tainted, because his jury had been composed primarily of employees of the federal government who were subject to a regulation providing for their discharge if they were disloyal to the government. The Court dismissed the claim, observing that "[p]reservation of the opportunity to prove actual bias is a guarantee of a defendant's right to an impartial jury," an opportunity which the defendant had failed to exercise. Similarly, in *Remmer v. United States*,[115] while the Court ruled that an attempt to bribe a juror during the trial in an effort to affect the outcome should be deemed "presumptively prejudicial," it remanded the case to determine "the circumstances, the impact thereof upon the jury, and whether or not [they were] prejudicial."

---

[111] See, e.g., ABA Standards for Criminal Justice Relating to Jury Trial 15–2.5(a) (3d ed. 1996).

[112] See § 27.06(b)(1).

[113] 378 U.S. 544, 84 S.Ct. 1696 (1964).

[114] 339 U.S. 162, 70 S.Ct. 519 (1950).

[115] 347 U.S. 227, 74 S.Ct. 450 (1954).

Thirty years later, the Court adhered to the view that actual bias must generally be shown before the Impartiality Clause is violated. In *Smith v. Phillips*,[116] the Court was unwilling to imply bias from the fact that one of the jurors at the defendant's trial was actively seeking employment with the prosecutor's office before and during the trial. Noting that the trial court had concluded, after a post-trial hearing, that the juror had not been biased, the six-member majority considered irrelevant the federal district court's finding on habeas that "the average man in Smith's position would believe that the verdict of the jury would directly affect the evaluation of his job application." Nor was it impressed with the dissent's argument that post-trial hearings to determine bias were ineffective because they relied primarily, if not entirely, on the suspect juror's testimony. Indeed, five members of the majority appeared to believe that bias can *never* be implied from a juror's circumstances. Of the majority, only Justice O'Connor, in a concurring opinion, insisted that prejudice could still be implied in appropriate circumstances, such as those present in *Leonard*.

(2) Death Penalty Cases

A number of Supreme Court decisions have addressed the extent to which use of for cause challenges affect the impartiality of juries in capital cases. The issue was first addressed in *Witherspoon v. Illinois*,[117] which involved a statute providing for exclusion, in all capital cases, of any venireperson who "expressed scruples" against the death penalty. The Supreme Court held that a death sentence imposed by a jury so selected could not stand, because the for cause exclusions would result in a tribunal "organized to return a verdict of death," or at least "uncommonly willing to condemn a man to die." The Court also concluded that such a jury could not express the conscience of the community, since those who do not harbor doubts about the wisdom of capital punishment are "a distinct and dwindling minority."

Witherspoon noted that the state may continue to exclude jurors in capital cases who indicate that they would *never* consider returning a verdict of death, regardless of the evidence. Several later decisions refined the scope of the for cause challenge in this context. While a juror cannot be excluded merely because he refuses to take an oath affirming that the mandatory penalty of death or life imprisonment would not "affect his deliberations on any issue of fact,"[118] he can be excluded, the Court held in *Wainwright v. Witt*, if his views about the death penalty would "substantially impair[ ] the performance of [his] duties as a juror."[119] Thus, a juror can be excluded if the prospect of the death penalty would "interfere" with his judgment of guilt or innocence,[120] if he indicates that imposing the death penalty is against his "principles,"[121] or if he states that he could only impose the death penalty in "severe" situations and gives as his sole example of such a situation an offender who might otherwise reoffend upon release (in a state where the alternative to execution is life without parole).[122]

---

[116]   455 U.S. 209, 102 S.Ct. 940 (1982).

[117]   391 U.S. 510, 88 S.Ct. 1770 (1968).

[118]   *Adams v. Texas*, 448 U.S. 38, 100 S.Ct. 2521 (1980).

[119]   469 U.S. 412, 105 S.Ct. 844 (1985).

[120]   Id.

[121]   *Darden v. Wainwright*, 477 U.S. 168, 106 S.Ct. 2464 (1986).

[122]   *Uttecht v. Brown*, 551 U.S. 1, 127 S.Ct. 2218 (2007).

These latter decisions come close to allowing exclusion based on a finding of "implied bias" against the state, in interesting contrast to *Smith* and like cases prohibiting exclusion by the defendant on such a basis. Indeed, in *Uttecht v. Brown*, the last mentioned case, Justice Stevens claimed in a dissent joined by three others that the majority had "fundamentally redefined—or maybe just misunderstood—the meaning of 'substantially impaired,' and, in doing so, has gotten it horribly backwards." That standard, Stevens stated, "does not and cannot mean that jurors must be willing to impose a death sentence in every situation in which a defendant is eligible for that sanction. That is exactly the outcome we aimed to protect against in developing the [*Witherspoon-Witt*] standard."[123]

Witherspoon invalidated only the defendant's death sentence, not his conviction. Although the defendant had presented what he called "competent scientific evidence" that "death-qualified juries" are partial to the prosecution not only on the sentencing issue but also with respect to guilt, the Court found the data "too tentative and fragmentary" to require reversal of every conviction returned by such juries. In response to this conclusion, several methodologically improved studies were conducted which indicated that even juries that are selected under the original *Witherspoon* standard (excluding only those who would not impose the death penalty) are more conviction-prone than juries that are not so selected;[124] this research led at least one lower federal court to reverse a conviction by a "death-qualified" jury.[125] However, in *Lockhart v. McCree*,[126] the Supreme Court held that even if research can conclusively prove that death qualified juries are more conviction prone than ordinary juries, no constitutional violation occurs when the prosecution excludes those who cannot impose the death penalty from capital trial juries.

The defendant in *McCree* advanced two separate constitutional grounds for overturning his conviction by a death-qualified jury. The first was that death-qualification results in a jury that violates the Sixth Amendment's fair cross-section requirement because it excludes a "distinctive group," and thus runs afoul of *Taylor v. Louisiana*.[127] In rejecting this argument, Justice Rehnquist's majority opinion first noted that *Taylor* had resisted applying the cross-section requirement to the petit jury, as opposed to the venire. But assuming, without deciding, that *Taylor* covered this situation,[128] the majority concluded that the jurors excluded through the death-qualification process are different from women and the racial groups contemplated by the cross-section requirement, since they are fairly excluded for their inability to be impartial, not because of an "immutable characteristic," and because they can serve in

---

[123] Note that the ruling in *Uttecht* permits exclusion of jurors who do not support the death penalty when the alternative is life without parole. Because a majority of the population rejects the death penalty when life without parole is an option, exclusion of this group from capital cases might result in particularly conviction-and execution-prone juries.

[124] See in particular, Claudia L. Cowan, William C. Thompson & Phoebe C. Ellsworth, *The Effects of Death Qualification on Jurors' Predisposition to Convict and on the Quality of Deliberation*, 8 Law & Hum. Behav. 53 (1984); Bruce Winick, *Prosecutorial Peremptory Challenge Practices in Capital Cases: An Empirical Study and a Constitutional Analysis*, 81 Mich.L.Rev. 1 (1982); George L. Jurow, *New Data on the Effect of a 'Death Qualified' Jury on the Guilty Determination Process*, 84 Harv.L.Rev. 567 (1971).

[125] *Grigsby v. Mabry*, 758 F.2d 226 (8th Cir. 1985).

[126] 476 U.S. 162, 106 S.Ct. 1758 (1986).

[127] 419 U.S. 522, 95 S.Ct. 692 (1975), discussed in § 27.03(c).

[128] As Justice Marshall pointed out in dissent, if the systematic exclusion of a given group takes place at *voir dire*, then, for practical purposes, the infringement of the Sixth Amendment is the same as if it had occurred during selection of the jury pool.

other juries not involving a capital charge, unlike minority groups prevented by exclusion from participating at all in the criminal process.

McCree's second argument was that the death-qualification process made his jury more predisposed to convict than the average jury and thus violated the Impartiality Clause. Rehnquist also rejected this argument. First, he noted that the individual members of McCree's jury were impartial, in the sense they had all promised to abide by their oath. "[E]xactly the same twelve individuals could have ended up on his jury through the 'luck of the draw,' without in any way violating the constitutional guarantee of impartiality." McCree conceded this point, but argued that *Witherspoon* had held that the state may not "slant" a jury by excluding a group of individuals more likely than the population at large to favor the criminal defendant even if, on an individual-by-individual basis, it is "impartial." But Rehnquist distinguished *Witherspoon* on two grounds. First, whereas there had been no legitimate state interest supporting the prosecution's exclusion of scrupled venirepersons from the jury in *Witherspoon*, here the removal of those who could not impose the death penalty served the "entirely proper interest in obtaining a single jury that could impartially decide all the issues in McCree's case." Because the guilt and penalty issues in a capital case are interwoven, duplication of evidence would be required if separate juries were required. Second, in contrast to the trial jury composition issue in *Lockhart*, *Witherspoon* dealt with "the special context of capital sentencing, where the range of jury discretion necessarily gave rise to far greater concern over the possible effects of an 'imbalanced' jury."

In dissent, Justice Marshall, joined by Justices Brennan and Stevens, argued that, in light of the research, the Court's decision gives "the prosecution license to empanel a jury especially likely to return [a guilty] verdict." The state's efficiency and financial interests in a unitary jury, Marshall continued, did not overcome the jury's predisposition toward the prosecution. Capital cases resulting in conviction are a very small proportion of all criminal cases, and in those cases where a new jury is required, alternate jurors can replace any "automatic life imprisonment" jurors on the sentencing jury or evidence can be presented in stipulated summaries rather than re-presented wholesale.

The Court reaffirmed and expanded the reach of *McCree* in *Buchanan v. Kentucky*.[129] There, six justices upheld a death-qualified jury for a joint trial of a capital defendant and a *non*-capital co-defendant (for whom, of course, the state does not need a "death-qualified" jury), in light of the state's interest in avoiding duplicate trials and sentencing proceedings. The Court did not pause to consider Marshall's suggestion in dissent that death-qualified alternates sit during the joint trial and replace any "*Witherspoon*-excludables" at the capital defendant's sentencing proceeding if he is convicted.

If *McCree* and *Buchanan* are wrong, it is because they unreasonably inflate the government's needs rather than unfairly characterize the defendant's interests. Impaneling alternative jurors, as suggested by Marshall, is a minor inconvenience. But Rehnquist's assertion in *McCree* that the conviction-proneness of a jury is not determinative of its ability to weigh the evidence fairly is difficult to dispute. Assuming its members have agreed to abide by the law, such a jury may be just as "accurate" as other juries even if it is more "conviction-prone."

---

[129] 483 U.S. 402, 107 S.Ct. 2906 (1987).

A stronger argument can be made that a death-qualified jury does not represent "community sentiment." But the Court's decision in *Morgan v. Illinois*,[130] undercuts that argument. As noted above,[131] in *Morgan* the Court held that the defendant charged with a capital crime is entitled to specific *voir dire* questions designed to determine whether any potential jurors would automatically impose the death penalty were conviction to result. The obvious predicate to this holding was the Court's conclusion that the defendant has the right to remove such people from the capital sentencing jury; because a person who would automatically vote for the death penalty "will fail in good faith to consider the evidence of aggravating and mitigating circumstances as the instructions require him to do," the Court held that the defendant must be able to excuse him for cause.[132] After *Morgan*, a death-qualified jury is less likely to be imbalanced.[133] Again, however, the burden the state would incur if it were required to seat both types of jurors through trial and replace them at sentencing does not seem particularly significant. Given the *possibility* of bias and lack of community representation that otherwise results, it would seem this burden should be borne.[134]

(d) Peremptory Challenges

In contrast to for cause challenges, peremptory challenges allow removal of a venireperson without explanation; no proof of actual or implied bias is necessary. For example, the defense may use a peremptory challenge to remove a person who glares at the defendant during *voir dire*, while the prosecution may exclude a long-haired college student. Neither of these individuals could typically be excluded from the jury "for cause" (assuming they agree to abide by their oath to consider the evidence impartially) because the reason for exclusion is merely a suspicion based on amorphous assumptions about their attitudes. As the Supreme Court has stated,[135] the peremptory challenge "is often exercised upon the 'sudden impressions and unaccountable prejudices we are apt to conceive upon the bare looks and gestures of another,' upon a juror's 'habits and associations,' or upon the feeling that the 'bare questioning [of a juror's] indifference may sometimes provoke a resentment.'" Peremptory challenges can best be analyzed by looking separately at prosecutorial and defense use.

(1) By the Prosecution

The most controversial issue associated with prosecutorial use of peremptories is whether they may be used to exclude potential jurors because of their race. In *Swain v. Alabama*,[136] the defendant argued that the prosecutor's use of peremptory challenges to strike all prospective black jurors violated the Equal Protection Clause. In rejecting this

---

[130] 504 U.S. 719, 112 S.Ct. 2222 (1992).

[131] See § 27.04(b)(2).

[132] Although this holding resonates with the Impartiality Clause, the majority had to base its decision on the Due Process Clause, because the Sixth Amendment had yet to be applied to capital sentencing proceedings. *Ring v. Arizona*, 536 U.S. 584, 122 S.Ct. 2428 (2002), discussed in § 27.02(a)(2).

[133] It should be noted, however, that there are many more *Witherspoon*-excludables in the community then there are "automatic death penalty" individuals. See studies cited supra note 124.

[134] Of course, even if this approach were adopted, the parties could still use peremptory challenges to remove individuals with the "wrong" attitude about the death penalty. Cf. *Gray v. Mississippi*, 481 U.S. 648, 107 S.Ct. 2045 (1987), where five members of the Court contended the prosecution could do so.

[135] *Swain v. Alabama*, 380 U.S. 202, 85 S.Ct. 824 (1965).

[136] 380 U.S. 202, 85 S.Ct. 824 (1965).

claim, the Court stressed that the function of the peremptory challenge required that its use not be subject to inquiry:

> [The peremptory challenge] is frequently exercised on grounds normally thought irrelevant to legal proceedings or official action, namely, the race, religion, nationality, occupation or affiliations of people summoned for jury duty. For the question a prosecutor or defense counsel must decide is not whether a juror of a particular race or nationality is in fact partial, but whether one from a different group is less likely to be. . . . Hence veniremen are not always judged solely as individuals for the purpose of exercising peremptory challenges. Rather they are challenged in light of the limited knowledge counsel has of them, which may include their group affiliations, in the context of the case to be tried.

The Court acknowledged, however, that a constitutional violation might be established if it could be shown that the prosecutor systematically used the peremptory challenge to exclude blacks from all juries on the basis of race. On this point the Court found the record deficient, despite uncontradicted evidence that no black within memory of anyone living had ever served in any civil or criminal case tried in Talladega County, Alabama, and verified evidence that no black had served there since 1950.

Twenty-one years later, in *Batson v. Kentucky*,[137] the Court reconsidered the *Swain* ruling and partially overruled it by requiring prosecutors to explain their use of peremptories upon a showing by the defendant that they have been used to exclude members of his race. *Batson* focused on *Swain's* conclusion that only proof of repeated striking of blacks over a number of cases would establish an equal protection violation. Terming this "a crippling burden of proof" which in effect made prosecutors' peremptory challenges of blacks "largely immune from constitutional scrutiny," Justice Powell, joined by six other members of the Court (including Justice White, the author of *Swain*), arrived at a new "evidentiary formulation." Borrowing from the Court's equal protection analysis in cases involving selection of jury pools,[138] he concluded that a defendant could make out a prima facie case that use of peremptory challenges has violated the Constitution if he shows (1) that he is a member of a cognizable racial group, (2) that the prosecutor has exercised peremptories to remove members of the defendant's race, and (3) that "these facts and any other relevant circumstances raise an inference that the prosecutor used [peremptories] to exclude the veniremen from the petit jury on account of their race." "Other relevant circumstances" might include a "pattern" of strikes against blacks, and the prosecutor's questions and statements during *voir dire*. Once a prima facie case is established, the prosecution may rebut it by coming forward "with a neutral explanation for challenging black jurors [that] need not rise to the level justifying exercise of a challenge for cause." However, merely stating blacks were excluded on the intuition that they would be partial to a defendant of the same race is insufficient.

Since the prosecutor in *Batson* had not been given the opportunity to explain his peremptory challenges of blacks, the Court had no occasion to apply these guidelines there. The first Court case to do so suggested that the prosecutor's burden under *Batson* will be minimal. In *Hernandez v. New York*,[139] the prosecutor challenged the only three

---

[137]   476 U.S. 79, 106 S.Ct. 1712 (1986).

[138]   See § 27.03(b).

[139]   500 U.S. 352, 111 S.Ct. 1859 (1991).

prospective jurors with Hispanic surnames, as well as an additional Latino. Two of the exclusions were explained on the ground that the individuals had relatives involved in criminal activity; in these cases, the defendant did not press his *Batson* objection. The prosecutor explained the other two exclusions by noting that both of those excluded had looked away from him and been hesitant when stating that they would not consider their own translations of testimony by Spanish-speaking witnesses, but rather would follow the court interpreter's version.

Emphasizing the need to prove intentional discrimination, the Court held, 6–3, that the prosecutor's explanation was race neutral. In response to the defendant's argument that there is a high correlation between Spanish-language ability and race in New York, the Court, in an opinion by Justice Kennedy, noted that the prosecutor relied on the jurors' demeanor as well as their language ability. Moreover, Kennedy asserted, even assuming that most Spanish-speaking individuals would act the same way in such a situation, "[n]othing in the prosecutor's explanation shows that he chose to exclude jurors who hesitated in answering questions about following the interpreter *because* he wanted to prevent bilingual Latinos from serving on the jury."

Kennedy did state that, in a different case, prosecutorial exclusions on grounds of language-ability that had a disproportionate impact on Latinos might not survive a *Batson* claim. But here, stated the Court, the trial court legitimately believed the prosecutor's explanation that he was concerned about the jurors' ability to rely on the interpreter's version of testimony, in light of the prosecutor's sincere demeanor, his willingness to explain his exclusions before the defense made out a prima facie case of discrimination, his statement that he did not know the jurors were Latino (as opposed to people who spoke Spanish), and the fact that many of the victims and prosecution witnesses were Latino (thus suggesting, apparently, that the prosecution would have preferred Latinos on the jury, all else being equal). What was not explained is the rationale for excluding jurors who might consider their own interpretation of a Spanish-speaking person's testimony rather than the interpreter's; if it has any effect on the jury verdict, it is most likely to increase its accuracy.

The Court appeared to relax even further the showing required to avoid a *Batson* challenge in its per curiam opinion in *Purkett v. Elem*.[140] There the prosecutor explained his use of peremptories to strike two blacks on the ground that one had long "unkempt" curly hair, a mustache and a goatee type beard, and the other also had a mustache and a goatee type beard. He concluded by saying "I don't like the way they looked, with the way the hair is cut on both of them. And the mustaches and the beards look suspicious to me."

The Court of Appeals had found that this explanation was not a plausible reason for believing that these persons were unable to perform their duty as jurors. But the Supreme Court upheld the strikes. It reasoned that after the defendant makes a prima facie case that *Batson* has been violated, the second step in *Batson* analysis is simply to determine whether the prosecution can give a race-neutral reason for the strike, no matter how "silly or superstitious," "implausible or fantastic." Then, at the third stage of the analysis, the judge should determine whether the strikes were racially motivated, by looking at the "genuineness" of the reason, not its "reasonableness." Since the reasons given by the prosecutor were race-neutral, and since the state court had found they were

---

[140] 514 U.S. 765, 115 S.Ct. 1769 (1995).

genuine (a credibility assessment that must normally be presumed correct in a habeas proceeding such as *Purkett*[141]), no violation of *Batson* occurred.[142]

While *Hernandez* and *Purkett* seemed to signal a desire to limit the impact of *Batson*, more recent cases have reinvigorated it. In *Johnson v. California*,[143] the Court rejected a ruling by the California Supreme Court holding that, in order to make out a prima facie case of discrimination, the defendant must show racial discrimination is "more likely than not" the explanation for the strikes. Rather, consistent with the above-quoted language in *Batson*, eight members of the Court, in an opinion by Justice Souter, held that the defendant need only demonstrate facts sufficient to establish an "inference" of discrimination. The Court found those facts present in *Johnson*, where the prosecutor excluded all three black members of the jury pool in a case involving a black defendant charged with killing the child of his white girlfriend, and where even the California Supreme Court stated that the removal of all black persons from the pool "certainly looks suspicious." Thus, Justice Souter wrote, the trial judge erred in not requiring the prosecutor to explain the strikes.

In *Miller-El v. Dretke*,[144] handed down the same day as *Johnson*, the Court reversed a conviction and death sentence in a case where the prosecutor used peremptories to strike ten out of 11 eligible African-American venirepersons. Here the issue was not whether the defense made out a prima facie case of discrimination, but whether the prosecution's reasons for the exclusions were race-neutral. Since the case was raised via a writ of habeas corpus, Miller-El had to show that the state court's determination of non-discrimination was unreasonable by clear and convincing evidence.[145] Six members of the Court concluded Miller-El met this standard. Justice Souter's opinion for the Court relied primarily on comparisons of the reasons the prosecutor gave for striking black jury pool members with information known about *non*black pool members who were *not* struck by the prosecution. Thus, the Court discounted the prosecutor's reason for excluding one black—his belief that anyone could be rehabilitated—because at least three nonblack pool members whom the prosecutor had not excluded had made similar statements. Similarly, the Court found specious the prosecutor's explanation that he excluded another black venireperson because of his ambivalence about the death penalty, given that several nonblacks not excluded by the prosecution demonstrated the same ambivalence. The Court also noted that on at least two occasions the prosecution had "shuffled" the jury panel when a predominant number of African-Americans were seated in the front row (a move that meant fewer blacks would be subject to voir dire), and that a higher proportion of blacks than nonblacks had been subjected to graphic depictions of the death penalty designed to test their attitudes toward the death penalty. Finally, Justice Souter pointed out that the Dallas County prosecutor's office that tried Miller-El had at one time followed a policy of systematically excluding African-Americans from the jury.

Justice Thomas, in dissent, contested each of these conclusions. He pointed to several factors besides attitudes about rehabilitation and ambivalence about the death

---

[141] See § 33.05(a).

[142] See also *Rice v. Collins*, 546 U.S. 333, 126 S.Ct. 969 (2006) (youth, lack of ties to the community, and disrespectful demeanor are reasons that satisfy *Batson*).

[143] 545 U.S. 162, 125 S.Ct. 2410 (2005).

[144] 545 U.S. 231, 125 S.Ct. 2317 (2005).

[145] See § 33.02(c).

penalty that distinguished the black and nonblack venirepersons in Miller-El's case, and noted that more blacks than nonblacks had been unsure of their views about capital punishment and thus were more likely to be questioned aggressively about the death penalty. He also pointed out that the racial exclusionary policy in Dallas County had officially ended at least ten years before Miller-El's trial, and that in any event none of the prosecutors in his trial had ever been associated with it.

A similar analysis and result came in *Snyder v. Louisiana*,[146] where the prosecutor used peremptories to remove all five African-Americans on the jury panel. The case focused on the validity under *Batson* of the two reasons the prosecutor gave for excluding one of these five potential jurors: the individual's nervousness, and his expression of concern that jury service would interfere with his teaching job (a concern which, the prosecutor speculated, might lead him to try to truncate jury deliberations). Justice Alito's majority opinion, joined by six others, dismissed the first reason because the record failed to make clear that it was relied upon by the trial judge in granting the prosecutor's challenge. And the majority considered the second reason insufficiently credible, because a juror's desire for a shorter trial could as easily help the prosecution as the defense, the juror's employer had in any event indicated that a trial of a week or less would not interfere with his job, and white jurors who had *not* been excused during the voir dire had disclosed conflicting obligations at least as serious as those described by the excused African-American. Again in dissent, Justice Thomas, after stressing the need to defer to trial judges' assessment of credibility in *Batson* cases, noted that the record was simply silent as to the reason the trial judge granted the prosecutor's challenge, and thus wondered how the majority could justify focusing solely on the job-related reason.

Miller-El and *Snyder* demonstrate the difficulty of implementing *Batson*.[147] Citing that reason, in a concurring opinion in *Miller-El* Justice Breyer suggested reconsideration of *Batson's* test as well as of "the peremptory challenge system as a whole." The following year, in *Rice v. Collins*,[148] he was joined in this sentiment by Justice Souter.

Another reason the Court may feel the need to revisit the *Batson* decision is the number of cases in which its reasoning might apply. Affirming the view that five justices had expressed in the earlier case of *Holland v. Illinois*,[149] *Powers v. Ohio*[150] held, 7–2, that *any* defendant, not just a member of the excluded group, may bring an equal protection claim under *Batson*. The *Powers* Court first found, as it had already held with respect to selection of the jury pool,[151] that preventing exclusion of racial minorities is necessary to ensure fairness in jury selection, promote public confidence in the jury system, and protect "the right not to be excluded from [the jury] on account of race." According to Justice Kennedy, author of the majority opinion, this latter right exists in order to give excluded jurors the opportunity "to participate in the democratic process," prevent "arbitrary use or abuse" of the judicial system, and develop civic mindedness.

---

[146] 552 U.S. 472, 128 S.Ct. 1203 (2008). See also *Foster v. Chatman*, ___ U.S. ___, 136 S.Ct. 1737 (2016); *Flowers v. Mississippi*, ___ U.S. ___, 139 S.Ct. 2228 (2019).

[147] Consider also the possibility that exercising peremptories to obtain a "more racially diverse jury" is a *Batson* violation. See *United States v. Allen-Brown*, 243 F.3d 1293 (11th Cir. 2001).

[148] 546 U.S. 333, 126 S.Ct. 969 (2006).

[149] 493 U.S. 474, 110 S.Ct. 803 (1990).

[150] 499 U.S. 400, 111 S.Ct. 1364 (1991).

[151] See § 27.03(b).

The Court then concluded that the criminal defendant has standing to trigger *Batson* regardless of his race. Applying its well-established three-part test for determining when a party has standing to contest a certain issue,[152] Kennedy concluded that: (1) a criminal defendant suffers "injury-in-fact [from discriminatory exclusion] because an improperly composed trier of fact may affect the fairness of his trial;" (2) the defendant "will be a motivated, effective advocate for the excluded venireperson's rights;" and (3) the excluded juror is unlikely to have any other meaningful means of redress.

In dissent, Justice Scalia, joined by Chief Justice Rehnquist, argued that the *Batson* rule could not reasonably be construed as stemming from the rights of excluded jurors rather than the rights of defendants. He noted, for example, that the excluded juror is not deprived of a benefit, since he can sit on other juries. And limiting peremptories can have a significant adverse impact "[i]n a criminal-law system in which a single biased juror can prevent a deserved conviction or a deserved acquittal." With respect to the majority's standing analysis, Scalia focused on the injury-in-fact issue, arguing that while exclusion of blacks might injure a white defendant, the injury was much more speculative than the Court had required in other cases. In particular, he noted that the Court had consistently refused to recognize third party standing in connection with Fourth and Fifth Amendment rights (i.e., when one's own privacy or autonomy is not violated),[153] despite the fact that, in contrast to the situation in *Powers,* denying standing in such cases very often *ensures* a defendant's conviction. One might also note that, with respect to the second prong of the standing analysis, a white defendant's willingness to protect the equal protection interests of black jurors is unlikely to exist in every case in which exclusion results.

Despite such concerns, the Court extended *Batson* and *Powers* to gender-based use of peremptories in *J.E.B. v. Alabama.*[154] Although admitting that "prejudicial attitudes toward women in this country have not been identical to those held toward racial minorities," Justice Blackmun concluded for six members of the Court that both groups "share a history of total exclusion" from jury service, and that women have suffered a long history of discrimination "which warrants the heightened scrutiny we afford all gender-based classifications today." Applying this heightened scrutiny, the only rationale the majority could find for allowing peremptories to be based on gender alone was the possibility that women might deliberate differently than men.[155] The Court found this "gross generalization" far outweighed by its conclusion, similar to its reasoning in *Powers* with respect to race, that gender-based discrimination in jury selection "causes harm to the litigants, the community, and the individual jurors who are wrongfully excluded." The Court did note, however, that "strikes based on characteristics that are disproportionately associated with one gender could be appropriate." It illustrated the point by stating that even though challenging all persons with military or nursing experience might disproportionately affect men and women, respectively, they would not be impermissible "absent a showing of pretext."

---

[152] See *Singleton v. Wulff,* 428 U.S. 106, 96 S.Ct. 2868 (1976).

[153] See §§ 4.04(c); 16.05(a).

[154] 511 U.S. 127, 114 S.Ct. 1419 (1994).

[155] With its emphasis on overcoming *erroneous* stereotypes based on gender, the Court may have left open a small loophole in its holding in those situations where one can make a clear showing that gender-based differences exist. Cf. Reid Hastie, Stephen Penrod & N. Pennington, Inside the Jury 140 (1983) (concluding there are insignificant differences between male and female verdict preferences, except in rape cases, "where female jurors appear to be somewhat more conviction-prone than male jurors.").

Although *J.E.B.* involved civil litigation (a paternity suit), it undoubtedly applies to prosecutorial use of peremptories, given the decision's multiple references to *Powers*. Furthermore, the holding in *J.E.B.* prohibits gender-based exclusion of men as well as women. Indeed, the action invalidated in *J.E.B.* was Alabama's use of its peremptories to strike nine out of the ten men in the jury pool (apparently the state's theory was that men are likely to be overly sympathetic to the respondent in a paternity action). This aspect of *J.E.B.*, together with other equal protection decisions by the Court,[156] suggests that using strikes to discriminate against whites is also unconstitutional.

The ultimate wisdom of *Batson* and its progeny depends upon the goal of *voir dire*. If its primary goal is to create an impartial jury, then *Batson,* with its attendant difficulties, is arguably unnecessary. Exclusion of racial minorities through peremptories does not automatically create a biased jury, even when the defendant is of the same race (especially if *voir dire* questioning about racial prejudice is allowed).[157] But if, as argued earlier,[158] another goal of *voir dire* is to ensure that defendants have a jury of their "peers," then the holding in *Batson* itself is more easily justified. In effect, *Batson* told prosecutors that they may not construct, through use of peremptories, an all-white jury for the trial of a black defendant. Regardless of how impartial the jury actually is, neither the defendant nor the public is likely to think such a trial is fair, and the integrity of the system is thereby undermined. Of course, this analysis suggests that *Batson* should be limited, as it originally was, to those cases in which the defendant and the excluded jurors are of the same race. Finally, if the goal is to prevent actual and symbolic discrimination against minorities during the *voir dire* process, then *Batson*, as well as *Powers'* expansion of *Batson*, is more supportable. The advisability of this latter goal can be questioned, however, both along the lines suggested by Scalia and because, as discussed below, it leads to a limitation on *defense* use of peremptories as well, a rule that may undermine the protections afforded by the Impartiality Clause.

(2) By the Defense

Despite the usefulness of peremptory challenges as a means of ensuring an impartial jury, the Supreme Court has made clear that they are not guaranteed by the Constitution.[159] Thus, so long as the relevant federal or state law is followed, the defendant's use of peremptories can normally be abridged significantly. For instance, the government may require codefendants to be treated as a single defendant so that each has only a small portion of the number of peremptories he would have if tried separately.[160] Or a defendant may be required by statute to exercise his challenges prior to the state, even though this practice means that some may be wasted on jurors whom the state would have challenged.[161] The state may also require the defendant to use a peremptory to excuse a juror who the judge should have excluded for cause.[162] Similarly, a judge's erroneous but good faith determination that the defendant is not permitted to

---

[156] See, e.g., *University of California Regents v. Bakke,* 438 U.S. 265, 98 S.Ct. 2733 (1978) (strict scrutiny standard applies to discrimination against "innocent" whites as well as blacks).

[157] See § 27.04(b)(1).

[158] See § 27.03(a).

[159] See, e.g., *Gray v. Mississippi,* 481 U.S. 648, 107 S.Ct. 2045 (1987).

[160] *Stilson v. United States,* 250 U.S. 583, 40 S.Ct. 28 (1919).

[161] *Pointer v. United States,* 151 U.S. 396, 14 S.Ct. 410 (1894).

[162] *Ross v. Oklahoma,* 487 U.S. 81, 108 S.Ct. 2273 (1988). However, the defendant may not be forced, as a way of preserving his claim, to use a peremptory to exclude a juror that he alleges should have been excused for cause. *United States v. Martinez-Salazar*, 528 U.S. 304, 120 S.Ct. 774 (2000).

exercise a peremptory challenge against a particular venire member (because, for example, it would discriminate on the basis of race) is not a constitutional violation, even if that determination is a violation of state law.[163] The basis for these decisions appears to be that, so long as the defendant is permitted for cause challenges to remove those obviously biased against him, he will receive the impartial jury to which he is entitled regardless of how his peremptories are restricted.

There is also at least one circumstance where the defendant is prohibited from exercising a peremptory challenge that is *authorized* by law. In *Georgia v. McCollum,*[164] the Court held that the defendant may not use peremptories to exclude potential jurors on the basis of race. The defendants in *McCollum,* who were whites charged with assaulting African-Americans, had indicated an intention to use their peremptories to exclude all the blacks on their panel, and appeared to have sufficient peremptories to do so. In response to a prosecution motion contesting this anticipated action, the trial court entered an order allowing them to use their challenges as they saw fit. On interlocutory appeal, the prosecution argued that this ruling would violate *Powers v. Ohio,* which, as discussed above,[165] held that the Equal Protection Clause prevents prosecution exclusion of racial minorities unless, as established in *Batson v. Kentucky*, a race-neutral explanation is provided. The prosecution contended that the same rule should apply to defendants. The defendants, on the other hand, put forward three principal reasons why the interest of the excluded juror and the community in avoiding discriminatory selection processes should not affect defense use of peremptories: (1) defense use of peremptories does not constitute state action in violation of the Fourteenth Amendment; (2) the prosecution lacks standing to assert an equal protection claim; and (3) a defendant's interest in an impartial trial outweighs the interests of the excluded jurors and the community in avoiding exclusion on the basis of race.

The Supreme Court, in an opinion by Justice Blackmun, rejected all three defense arguments. On the first issue, Blackmun concluded that because peremptories are a creation of state law, and because "a criminal defendant is wielding the power to choose a quintessential governmental body," the defendant's exercise of peremptories is state action.[166] With respect to the prosecution's standing, he noted that "[a]s the representative of all its citizens, the State is the logical and proper party to assert the invasion of the constitutional rights of the excluded jurors in a criminal trial." And while not denying the defendant the right to an impartial trial, Blackmun found "a distinction between exercising a peremptory challenge to discriminate invidiously against jurors on account of race and exercising a peremptory challenge to remove an individual juror who harbors racial prejudice." Thus, analogous to *Batson,* if the prosecution makes out a prima facie case of discriminatory use of peremptories, the defendant must provide a race-neutral reason for exclusion.

In dissent, Justice O'Connor was particularly critical of the majority's state action analysis. As she noted, "[t]he government in no way influences the defense's decision to use a peremptory challenge to strike a particular juror." Perhaps more telling was Justice Thomas' concurrence, in which he reluctantly joined the Court because of

---

[163] *Rivera v. Illinois*, 556 U.S. 148, 129 S.Ct. 1446 (2009).

[164] 502 U.S. 1056, 112 S.Ct. 931 (1992).

[165] See § 27.04(d)(1).

[166] Here Blackmun relied heavily on *Edmonson v. Leesville Concrete Co.,* 500 U.S. 614, 111 S.Ct. 2077 (1991), which the same term as *Powers* had held that *Batson* also applied to private litigants.

precedent. Asserting that the original purpose of applying the Equal Protection Clause to jury selection was to prevent racial bias on the jury, he pointed out that the Court's decision "exalt[s] the right of citizens to sit on juries over the rights of the criminal defendant," and predicted that black defendants in particular "will rue the day this court ventured down this road."

McCollum highlights the tension between the Equal Protection and Impartiality Clauses. As Thomas suggests, while the aspiration to have a discrimination-free society is obviously commendable, making an innocent criminal defendant pay for that aspiration with his liberty or life is not. Admittedly, allowing defendants to use peremptories to remove all African-Americans from the jury may produce a biased decisionmaker, especially in the type of case involved in *McCollum,* where the defendants were white and the victims black. But the opposite may also be true: failing to exclude such persons could lead to a slanted verdict. Furthermore, the defendant is arguably entitled, much more so than the prosecution, to unrestricted peremptories to ensure that he is "comfortable" with the jury that will decide his fate.[167] Finally, *McCollum* will eventually require the Court to decide whether a black defendant can be prevented from excluding whites on the basis of race (for instance, in a case where the victim is white), a case which will raise racial hackles regardless of how it is decided.[168]

Some have argued that abolition of peremptory challenges (for the prosecution as well as the defense) is the only effective way to eliminate their discriminatory abuse against racial and other minorities; at the same time, it would avoid the difficult issues associated with deciding when *Batson* applies.[169] In light of the Court's previous decisions concerning peremptories, this scheme would probably be constitutional. But it would seriously undermine the defendant's ability to maintain impartiality, given the Court's other *voir dire* cases. Specifically, the Court's reluctance to allow individualized questions during *voir dire,*[170] combined with its unwillingness to imply bias from circumstances,[171] means that in many jurisdictions peremptory challenges may be the only way a defendant can remove from the venire individuals strongly suspected of bias. Unless the grounds for challenges for cause and the means of developing those grounds are relaxed considerably, some entitlement to peremptories may be necessary. Again, limiting *Batson's* application to prosecution attempts to remove jurors of the defendant's race may be the best way of reconciling the desire to maintain impartiality with the desire to avoid the appearance of invidious discrimination. An alternative would be to apply *Batson* to both the defense and prosecution, but *only* when racial issues "permeate" the trial.

---

[167] Katherine Goldwasser, *Limiting a Criminal Defendant's Use of Peremptory Challenges: On Symmetry and the Jury in a Criminal Trial,* 102 Harv.L.Rev. 808, 829–831 (1989). Goldwasser also argues that applying *Batson* to defense peremptories may require revelation of confidential communications between attorney and client. Id. at 831–33. In *McCollum,* Blackmun discounted this problem by noting that *Batson* explanations may be made *in camera.*

[168] Similarly, the reasoning in *McCollum* is likely to lead the Court to extend its ruling in *J.E.B. v. Alabama,* 511 U.S. 127, 114 S.Ct. 1419 (1994), discussed in § 27.04(d)(1), which prohibited *gender*-based peremptories by the state, to defense use of peremptories.

[169] See, e.g., Justice Marshall's concurrence in *Batson*; Richard Singer, *Peremptory Holds: A Suggestion (Only Half Specious) of a Solution to the Discriminatory Use of Peremptory Challenges,* 62 U.Det.L.Rev. 275, 286–87 (1985).

[170] See § 27.04(b)(3).

[171] See § 27.04(c)(1).

27.05   The Right to an Impartial Judge

(a) The Constitutional Right

Although the Sixth Amendment speaks only of juries, the Supreme Court has held that the Due Process Clause guarantees the defendant an impartial judge as well, whether he sits with or without a jury. The leading case is *Tumey v. Ohio,*[172] where the judge of a municipal court, who was also the mayor, received the fees and costs he levied against violators. The Court had no trouble finding that a defendant is deprived of due process when the judge "has a direct, personal, substantial pecuniary interest in reaching a conclusion against him in his case." *Tumey* was extended in *Ward v. Monroeville,*[173] where the fees collected by the mayor-judge did not go directly to him, but rather provided a substantial portion of the town's funds. Due process was violated here as well because "the mayor's executive responsibilities for village finances may make him partisan to maintain the high level of contribution from the mayor's court." On the other hand, if the mayor who levies the town's fees is one of only several members of a city commission, as was the case in *Dugan v. Ohio,*[174] then the conflict of interest is not direct enough to trigger a due process violation.

The judicial impartiality issue often arises in contempt cases, where the judge is involved in assessing penalties on a defendant who may have directly insulted him. The Supreme Court has held that, while a judge may normally act summarily in the face of vilification by a party,[175] when a separate contempt proceeding is held at the end of trial, due process may require that another judge preside. This was the holding in both *Mayberry v. Pennsylvania,*[176] where the trial judge gave a defendant who had repeatedly insulted him during the trial a contempt sentence of 11–22 years, and *Johnson v. Mississippi,*[177] where the trial judge had lost to the defendant in a related civil rights suit just prior to the contempt proceeding. Similarly, the Supreme Court held in *Taylor v. Hayes*[178] that a defense attorney was entitled to a new judge at his separate contempt proceeding when the record showed that there had been "marked personal feelings . . . present on both sides." But unless, as *Mayberry* put it, there has been the "sting of slanderous remarks," a new judge is not necessary under the Due Process Clause even when the contempt proceeding is separate. Merely possessing previous knowledge about a case does not disqualify the judge.[179]

At the same time, the defendant need not prove "actual bias" to obtain recusal under the Due Process Clause. In *Rippo v. Baker,*[180] the defendant showed that at the time of his trial the judge was under investigation on bribery charges by the same prosecutor's office that was trying Rippo, and argued that the judge might therefore favor the state in the hopes of obtaining leniency in his own case. Refusing to require proof of actual

---

[172] 273 U.S. 510, 47 S.Ct. 437 (1927).

[173] 409 U.S. 57, 93 S.Ct. 80 (1972).

[174] 277 U.S. 61, 48 S.Ct. 439 (1928).

[175] Note that when the judge acts summarily, he may only impose sentences of six months or less. See § 27.02(c)(3).

[176] 400 U.S. 455, 91 S.Ct. 499 (1971).

[177] 403 U.S. 212, 91 S.Ct. 1778 (1971).

[178] 418 U.S. 488, 94 S.Ct. 2697 (1974).

[179] *Withrow v. Larkin,* 421 U.S. 35, 95 S.Ct. 1456 (1975).

[180] ___ U.S. ___, 137 S.Ct. 905 (2017).

bias, the Court, in a per curiam decision, remanded the case for a determination of whether "the probability of actual bias on the part of the judge or decisionmaker is too high to be constitutionally tolerable,"[181] language suggesting that the mere appearance of bias may be ground for recusal. Similarly, in *Williams v. Pennsylvania*,[182] the Court counseled that the inquiry is "not whether a judge harbors an actual, subjective bias, but instead whether, as an objective matter, the average judge in his position is likely to be neutral, or whether there is an unconstitutional potential for bias." There the Court held due process is violated when a judge presides over a proceeding involving a death sentence that the judge, in his earlier role as a prosecutor, had personally authorized be pursued.

(b) Mechanisms for Assuring Impartiality

There are three mechanisms for assuring an impartial judge. The first two mimic the *voir dire* process in jury selection. In most jurisdictions, a judge can be excused for cause, if it is shown that he is biased for or against a particular party.[183] Additionally, in some jurisdictions, either party can also peremptorily remove a judge, in which case the trial is automatically transferred to another judge (although this second judge can usually only be removed for cause).[184]

Finally, the judicial code of ethics requires a judge to "recuse" or disqualify himself if: (1) "he has a personal bias or prejudice concerning a party, or personal knowledge of disputed evidentiary facts concerning the proceeding;" (2) he or a former partner served as a lawyer or a material witness in the controversy; (3) he or a close relative has a financial or other "substantial interest" in the outcome of the proceeding; or (4) he is related, directly or by marriage, to one of the parties or lawyers.[185]

27.06   Fair Proceedings and Media Access

(a) The Effects of Publicity

The First Amendment guarantees freedom of speech and of the press. In many cases, these provisions do not conflict with the defendant's right to a fair, impartial trial. Indeed, they often protect that right. Out-of-court statements by witnesses and press accounts of criminal proceedings can energize the public against unfair prosecutions. Reports in the media may also lead to the discovery of evidence. Additionally, as discussed further in the next chapter,[186] the right to a public trial, guaranteed to the defendant by the Sixth Amendment as well as to the public by the First, protects against "star chamber" proceedings in which the state metes out justice in private.

However, when extensive or dramatic publicity occurs before or during trial, the fairness of the proceeding may be undermined. Newspaper accounts of a grisly crime, television depictions of a pretrial confession, or descriptions of the defendant's prior offenses can irredeemably infect the minds of both jurors and judges. Additionally, the

---

[181] Citing *Withrow v. Larkin*, 421 U.S. 35, 95 S.Ct. 1456 (1975).

[182] *Williams v. Pennsylvania*, ___ U.S. ___, 136 S.Ct. 1899 (2016).

[183] See, e.g., 28 U.S.C.A. § 144.

[184] See, e.g., Fla.R.Jud.Admin. 2.330(f) (requiring automatic disqualification if motion is accompanied by two affidavits which are judged to state legally sufficient grounds for disqualification, regardless of their credibility).

[185] American Bar Association, Code of Judicial Conduct, Canon 3–C.

[186] See § 28.02.

mere presence of the media in the courtroom may be disruptive or change the behavior of the parties in ways that could lead to unfairness. As a result, various mechanisms have developed for curtailing the impact of publicity or preventing it altogether.

(b) Alleviating the Effects of Publicity

There are several ways a court might be able to diminish the impact of inflammatory press coverage. In rare cases where the effects of the publicity are likely to die out quickly, a continuance might be useful. To counteract more extensive or on-going publicity, the courts typically resort to one of three methods: (1) *voir dire* inquiry; (2) changes of venue; and (3) jury sequestration.

(1) Voir Dire Inquiry

In theory, the voir dire process is the perfect antidote for damaging pretrial publicity. That process could ensure that the jurors who sit on the defendant's case either have not seen or heard the publicity or, if they have, that it has not biased them one way or the other. The Supreme Court, for one, has assumed that this is possible.[187] But empirical research suggests that *voir dire* usually cannot identify all of the potential jurors who have been prejudiced against the defendant by pretrial publicity.[188] Unfortunately, jurors may not recognize their bias or, if they do, may adopt a defensive stance or even lie when the judge or attorneys delve into their attitudes.[189]

Furthermore, whatever chance *voir dire* does have of identifying and excluding prejudiced jurors has been seriously diminished by the Court's own decisions. As discussed earlier in this chapter,[190] the Court has held that the Constitution does not require the trial court to question each juror about the content of publicity he may have heard, even when the publicity has been extensive. Rather, the judge need only ask general questions, to the venire as a whole, inquiring as to whether the venirepersons have a "fixed opinion" about the case. Yet individualized content questioning may be the only way to make a juror realize he is prejudiced. Further, even if, for reasons discussed above, he does not admit to his bias, such questioning can be very useful. The juror's answers about what he has read and heard will allow the defense to exercise more intelligently its for cause and peremptory challenges.

Even in a jurisdiction that allows detailed questioning, however, the usefulness of the information so acquired is significantly limited by other Court decisions addressing the scope of the for cause challenge in high publicity cases. Although Warren Court cases seemed to take the view that extensive publicity allows an assumption of bias on the part of jurors who have been exposed to it (and thus allows excuse for cause), more recent Court opinions have held that, unless an *express* admission of bias is made, a defendant can be forced to use his limited number of peremptory challenges to excuse what may turn out to be a large number of potentially biased jurors.

---

[187] See, e.g., *Nebraska Press Ass'n v. Stuart,* 427 U.S. 539, 96 S.Ct. 2791 (1976), discussed in § 27.06(c)(1); *Press-Enterprise Co. v. Superior Court,* 478 U.S. 1, 106 S.Ct. 2735 (1986), discussed in § 27.06(c)(3).

[188] Norbert L. Kerr, Geoffrey P. Kramer, John S. Carroll & James J. Alfini, *On the Effectiveness of Voir Dire in Criminal Cases with Prejudicial Pretrial Publicity: An Empirical Study,* 40 Amer.U.L.Rev. 665 (1991).

[189] Newton Minow & Fred Cate, *Who is an Impartial Juror in an Age of Mass Media?,* 40 Amer.U.L.Rev. 631, 650–54 (1991).

[190] See *Mu'Min v. Virginia,* 500 U.S. 415, 111 S.Ct. 1899 (1991), discussed in § 27.04(b)(3).

The Warren Court approach is represented by *Marshall v. United States*[191] and *Irvin v. Dowd.*[192] In *Marshall,* the Court held that "persons who have learned from news sources of a defendant's prior record are presumed to be prejudiced," a holding that would seem to flow from the rules of evidence.[193] And in *Irvin,* the Court held that publicity can be so inflammatory that even statements of impartiality can be discounted. In the county in which the *Irvin* trial took place, newspaper, radio and television media reported, just before trial, his conviction for arson 20 years before, his refusal to take a lie detector test and his offer to plead guilty if he received a 99 year sentence. He was described as a confessed slayer of six, a parole violator and a fraudulent check artist by a newspaper that was delivered to 95% of the homes in the county. During a *voir dire* that lasted four weeks, 268 of 430 people examined were excused because they admitted they had made up their minds about the defendant's guilt. Of the 12 jurors selected, eight stated they thought the defendant was guilty, but all said they could render an impartial verdict. The Court conceded that, given the advent of modern communication systems, "[t]o hold that the mere existence of any preconceived notion as to the guilt or innocence of an accused, without more, is sufficient to rebut the presumption of a prospective juror's impartiality would be to establish an impossible standard." Here, however, the expressions of impartiality could "be given little weight" because the *voir dire* transcript reflected a "pattern of deep and bitter prejudice" in the county.

Later decisions of the Court, however, significantly undercut both *Marshall* and *Irvin.* Like these two cases, *Murphy v. Florida,*[194] involved extensive publicity about the defendant's prior crimes, one a murder. But the Court, in an opinion by Justice Marshall, refused to rely on *Marshall's* holding, pointing out that it did not rest on the Due Process Clause, but on the Court's supervisory power over the federal courts. And it distinguished *Irvin* by noting that, whereas the publicity in that case had immediately preceded the trial and created a "circus atmosphere," almost all the news articles in *Murphy* had appeared seven months before the jury was selected and were "largely factual in nature." Marshall also contrasted the fact that whereas 268 of the 430 venirepersons in *Irvin* had been excused for cause, only 20 of the 78 persons examined in *Murphy* were excluded because they indicated an opinion as to his guilt. According to Marshall: "This may indeed be 20 more than would occur in the trial of a totally obscure person, but it by no means suggests a community with sentiment so poisoned against petitioner as to impeach the indifference of jurors who displayed no hostile animus of their own."

In dissent, Justice Brennan disputed Marshall's characterization of the jury as non-hostile. He argued that there had been a "daily buildup of prejudice against Murphy" and that several seated jurors had admitted during *voir dire* that they were predisposed against the defendant (one stated that comments about Murphy by other venirepersons had made him "sick to [his] stomach"). In light of these facts, stated Brennan, "[i]t is of no moment that several jurors ultimately testified that they would try to exclude from their deliberations their knowledge of petitioner's past misdeeds and of his community

---

[191]   360 U.S. 310, 79 S.Ct. 1171 (1959).

[192]   366 U.S. 717, 81 S.Ct. 1639 (1961). See also, *Rideau v. Louisiana,* 373 U.S. 723, 83 S.Ct. 1417 (1963), discussed in § 27.06(b)(2).

[193]   See Fed.R.Evid. 608 (barring introduction of prior crimes except for impeachment purposes or to rebut character evidence).

[194]   421 U.S. 794, 95 S.Ct. 2031 (1975). See also, *Dobbert v. Florida,* 432 U.S. 282, 97 S.Ct. 2290 (1977).

reputation." *Irvin* had settled that "little weight could be attached to such self-serving protestations."

In *Patton v. Yount,*[195] all but 2 of the 162 venirepersons had heard about the case, and 126 of them (a higher percentage than in *Irvin*) were excluded after admitting that they remembered the defendant's first conviction for a gruesome murder and that they "would carry an opinion into the box." Additionally, similar to *Irvin,* of the 14 jurors (including two alternates) who sat on the case, 8 admitted that at some time they had formed an opinion as to the defendant's guilt. One juror and both alternates also stated, in an apparent reluctance to presume innocence, that they would require evidence to overcome their beliefs. The court of appeals held that, even though four years had elapsed between the first conviction (which was reversed on appeal) and the second trial, the passage of time had not served "to erase highly unfavorable publicity from the memory of the community." Additionally, it noted that the publicity just prior to the trial revealed the defendant's prior conviction, his confession and his prior plea of temporary insanity (none of which was admitted at trial).

The Supreme Court reversed by a 6–2 margin (Justice Marshall not participating). The Court held that the fact that the community might remember the first conviction was "essentially irrelevant;" rather, the important question was "whether the jurors at Yount's trial had such fixed opinions that they could not judge impartially the guilt of the defendant." On this point, it first noted that *voir dire* questioning (which was conducted by the attorneys) had revealed that the four-year lapse in time "had a profound effect on the community and, more important, on the jury, in softening or effacing opinion." It also asserted that more recent publicity had not been inflammatory. It concluded that *voir dire* had "resulted in selecting those who had forgotten [that they thought the defendant was guilty] or would need to be persuaded again."

The Court reached a similar conclusion in *Skilling v. United States.*[196] There the defendant, a high level executive of Enron who was charged with fraudulent financial manipulations that destroyed the company, argued that an impartial jury could not be selected in Houston, the site of the defendant's alleged fraud and home to thousands of Enron employees and employees of related companies who lost their jobs, pension funds, or both as a result of the company's demise. Negative publicity about Enron and Skilling had been extensive over the four years between Enron's collapse and the trial; one journalism expert with 30 years' experience stated he could not "recall another instance where a local paper dedicated as many resources to a single topic over such an extended period of time as the Houston Chronicle . . . dedicated to Enron." More than two-thirds of the prospective jurors either knew victims of the Enron debacle or were victims themselves, and two-thirds gave responses during pre-screening or voir dire that suggested anti-Enron bias. Noting that the trial judge's questioning lasted only five hours, Skilling asserted that it failed "adequately to probe the jurors' true feelings." Justice Sotomayor, writing a dissent joined by Justices Breyer and Stevens, agreed that "the court asked very few prospective jurors any questions directed to their knowledge of or feelings about that event." But six members of the Court, in an opinion by Justice Ginsburg, concluded that the voir dire adequately ferreted out biased jurors.

---

[195] 467 U.S. 1025, 104 S.Ct. 2885 (1984).

[196] 561 U.S. 368, 130 S.Ct. 2896 (2010).

Emphasizing that "[n]o hard-and-fast formula dictates the necessary depth or breadth of voir dire," Ginsburg pointed out that the prospective jurors were initially screened via a comprehensive questionnaire drafted "in large part" by Skilling's attorneys. Each venireperson was questioned one-on-one by the judge, thus avoiding the spread of prejudicial information, and the judge repeatedly stated that there were "no right and wrong answers to th[e] questions." Further, Skilling's attorneys were allowed follow-up inquiries, an opportunity they declined in connection with over half the prospective jurors, including eight of the people ultimately selected. And they challenged for cause only one of the jurors eventually seated. Eleven of the seated jurors and alternates reported no connection to Enron, while the other jurors reported at most an insubstantial link, and 14 of the jurors and alternates stated that they had paid scant attention to Enron-related news. Finally, Ginsburg noted that the jury acquitted Skilling on nine counts in the indictment, suggesting impartiality on its part.

The Court's cases indicate that bias due to pretrial publicity cannot be a basis for a constitutional challenge unless a juror candidly admits to bias, or unless recent publicity has been extraordinary in its inflammatory nature and pervasiveness. These requirements probably flow from the fact, recognized in *Irvin,* that very few people in the community will not have heard something about highly publicized cases before trial begins. At the same time, when a large proportion of the venire admits to having strong reactions to a case, as in *Irvin* and *Yount,* and the pretrial publicity includes inadmissible, prejudicial information, as in *Murphy* and *Yount,* the impartiality of those who are seated as jurors cannot be assumed merely because they say they can keep an open mind despite what they have heard. An alternative to the Court's approach, suggested by Judge Stern (a concurring judge on the court of appeals in *Yount*), is to excuse any juror who admits an opinion as to guilt and to refuse to empanel a jury where more than 25% of the veniremen state that they hold an opinion concerning the defendant's guilt (in which case, a change of venue may be appropriate).

(2) Change of Venue

If *voir dire* exposes overwhelming bias against the defendant, or if the trial court is willing to recognize, even without the assistance of *voir dire* questioning, that publicity has been extensive and probably prejudicial, a change of venue can be granted. Illustrative is *Rideau v. Louisiana,*[197] in which the Supreme Court overturned a death sentence because the trial court refused to grant the defendant's motion for a venue change. Two months before trial, Rideau had confessed to a sheriff on film. Within the next two days, the film was broadcast on local television to audiences of 24,000, 53,000 and 29,000 in a 150,000 person parish. Three members of the jury admitted seeing or hearing the interview, but testified they could return an impartial verdict. Calling the defendant's trial "an empty formality" after the television showings, the Supreme Court stated that regardless of the particular responses of the individual jurors during *voir dire*, "due process of law in this case required a trial before a jury drawn from a community of people who had not seen and heard Rideau's interview." In other words, according to the Court, bias should have been presumed with respect to all potential jurors, and Rideau's change of venue motion granted.

Whether *Rideau* would have been decided the same way today, in light of *Murphy* and *Yount,* is unclear. Further complicating the matter, of course, is the fact that pretrial

---

[197] 373 U.S. 723, 83 S.Ct. 1417 (1963).

publicity does not necessarily end at the jurisdiction's borders. With respect to widely known criminal defendants, a careful *voir dire* may be the only option available. On the other hand, when the "media community" is a small one, a change of venue will usually be the best way to ensure a fair trial in cases of extensive publicity, given the inadequacies of *voir dire*.

The Court emphasized this latter consideration in *Skilling*, discussed above. There, the venue was Houston, the country's fourth most populous city. This fact, plus the absence of "blatantly prejudicial information" (like the pretrial admission of guilt in Rideau's case) and the lapse of four years between the collapse of Enron and trial, led the Court to conclude that a change of venue was not constitutionally required. Even the dissenters agreed with this holding, although they accorded the four-year hiatus little weight given the unrelenting nature of the pretrial publicity. Instead, as recounted above, they argued that the trial judge did not do an adequate job of ensuring that the jury's members were impartial.

(3) Sequestration of the Jury

Finding an impartial venue and jury may not be sufficient protection for the defendant, since publicity usually continues, and indeed intensifies, once trial starts. Instructions to members of the jury, warning them that media accounts are not to be taken as evidence, are probably to little avail and may actually stimulate interest in press reports. Thus, the Supreme Court has recognized that sequestration of the jury is a permissible option.[198] If sequestration occurs, however, there is a danger that the jury will resent whichever side it believes is responsible for its confinement (which will usually be the defense). It may be good practice for the judge to tell the jury that its sequestration is by order of the court.

(c) Preventing Pretrial Publicity

Given the problems with alleviating the effects of prejudicial publicity, the courts have attempted various means of inhibiting or preventing media reporting and access to the criminal process, including: (1) "gag orders" on the press; (2) "gag orders" on the participants; and (3) closed proceedings. Of course, these mechanisms do not prevent the press from printing facts that are already a matter of public record. More importantly, the First Amendment, as construed by the Supreme Court, severely limits their usefulness.

(1) Gag Orders on the Media

In *Nebraska Press Ass'n v. Stuart*,[199] the trial judge prohibited media dissemination of certain incriminating information about the defendant (including his confession) that came out in court and from out-of-court statements by the participants. He based the order on a finding that, otherwise, there would be a "clear and present danger that pretrial publicity could impinge on the defendant's right to a fair trial." The Supreme Court firmly repudiated, as an impermissible prior restraint, any bar on media coverage of an open hearing. It further indicated that preventing publication of information from other sources would be permissible only in extreme circumstances, after consideration of: "(a) the nature and extent of pretrial coverage; (b) whether other measures [such as

---

[198] *Sheppard v. Maxwell*, 384 U.S. 333, 86 S.Ct. 1507 (1966).

[199] 427 U.S. 539, 96 S.Ct. 2791 (1976).

changes of venue, continuances, *voir dire*, and admonitions to the jury] would be likely to mitigate the effects of unrestrained pretrial publicity; and (c) how effectively a restraining order would operate to prevent the threatened danger." Here, the impact of the press coverage was "speculative," the alternatives to the gag order had not been carefully considered, and the order might have merely encouraged rumors that "could well be more damaging than reasonably accurate news accounts." The Court also stressed the difficulty of "managing and enforcing pretrial restraining orders," in particular noting the possibility that such an order will inhibit proper coverage of the proceedings.

Subsequent Court decisions in analogous contexts have energetically followed *Nebraska Press*. For instance, in *Smith v. Daily Mail Publishing Co.*,[200] the Court struck down a state statute that criminally penalized publishing, without written order of the juvenile court, the name of any youth charged as a juvenile offender.[201] On the other hand, the Court's opinion in *Nebraska Press* did not rule out the possibility of a restraining order under appropriate circumstances. Particularly in light of the inadequacy of *voir dire* as a corrective device, a narrowly framed order aimed at preventing a "clear and present danger" of prejudicial publicity might be constitutional.[202]

(2) Gag Orders on the Participants

Given the difficulty of stopping the press from reporting information it obtains, courts have sometimes resorted to muffling its source. This practice has been approved, at least tangentially, by the Supreme Court. *Sheppard v. Maxwell*[203] involved such extensive and persistent media coverage that the Court characterized the proceedings as a "Roman holiday." Blaming this state of affairs in part on the participants in the trial, the Court suggested that, under appropriate circumstances, the trial judge has an obligation "to control the release of leads, information, and gossip to the press by police officers, witnesses and the counsel for both sides."

This language could be read to mean that a gag order on trial participants is less likely to run afoul of the First Amendment than a restraining order on the press. Alternatively, *Sheppard* could merely represent a situation where comments by the participants in the trial constituted a "clear and present danger" to the fairness and integrity of the trial. In support of this second interpretation, it could be argued that the concerns the Court later expressed in *Nebraska Press*—i.e., that suppressing dissemination of information by the media might inhibit proper press coverage, and may often be based on mere "speculation" that other alternatives cannot alleviate the effect of publicity—are equally applicable when the gag order is imposed on trial participants. Moreover, such a restraining order prevents the speech of those who are most intimately involved in the trial process and thus most likely to provide useful criticism of it. Many, but not all, lower courts appear to apply some version of the "clear and present danger"

---

[200]   443 U.S. 97, 99 S.Ct. 2667 (1979).

[201]   See also, *Landmark Communications, Inc. v. Virginia*, 435 U.S. 829, 98 S.Ct. 1535 (1978).

[202]   Cf. *Cable News Network, Inc. v. Noriega*, 498 U.S. 976, 111 S.Ct. 451 (1990), where the Court denied certiorari on an Eleventh Circuit opinion upholding a district court restraining order on the media, over a strong dissent by Justices Marshall and O'Connor.

[203]   384 U.S. 333, 86 S.Ct. 1507 (1966).

test before granting a gag order, which might only exist when highly incriminating yet potentially inadmissible evidence (e.g., a confession) could be disclosed.[204]

The professional ethical rules, however, appear to restrict speech (at least by an attorney) to a much greater extent than these lower court decisions contemplate. For instance, the ABA Rules of Professional Responsibility prohibit a lawyer from making any "extrajudicial statement" that "will have a substantial likelihood of materially prejudicing an adjudicative proceeding," a provision which has been broadly interpreted to include statements relating to "the character, credibility, reputation or criminal record of a party, suspect . . . or witness," the identity of a witness, "the expected testimony of a party or witness," the "possibility of a plea of guilty, . . . the performance or results of any examination or test, [and] . . . any opinion as to . . . guilt or innocence."[205]

The rules at one time also specifically permitted an attorney to furnish only a description of the charges and defenses, the arrest and the length of the investigation, the schedule of proceedings, and the identity of the defendant and the arresting officers. In *Gentile v. Nevada State Bar*,[206] the Supreme Court sent mixed messages about this rule, with five members holding that state bars can reprimand attorneys for speech that causes a "substantial likelihood of material prejudice" short of "clear and present danger," and another configuration of five justices concluding that the part of the rule that permits the attorney to describe defenses "without elaboration" was void for vagueness because lawyers "must guess at its contours." As a result, the pretrial statements of Gentile, to the effect that his client was being framed by the police for the actions of one of its officers, could not be the basis for reprimand. Whatever the validity of these ethical restrictions on attorneys after *Gentile*,[207] they clearly do not apply to witnesses or to the defendant himself.

(3) Closure of the Proceedings

A second way of preventing media access to information is to close the relevant proceedings. Here again, however, the First Amendment presents a significant obstacle to the defendant seeking closure in an effort to avoid the effects of negative publicity. The Court's cases indicate that, unless a showing of significant prejudice is made, closure is not appropriate.

The Court's first modern decision on this issue, *Gannett Co., Inc. v. DePasquale*,[208] held that the trial judge may, at the request of the defendant, close a pretrial suppression hearing to avoid a "reasonable probability of prejudice" to the defendant's right to a fair trial. But this holding was based solely on an interpretation of the Sixth Amendment's guarantee of a "public" trial which, the Court rightly noted, is a right of the defendant's and thus may be waived by him. One year later, in *Richmond Newspapers, Inc. v. Virginia*,[209] the Court indicated that, when a First Amendment right is asserted by the

---

[204] See, e.g., *United States v. Regan*, 878 F.2d 67 (2d Cir. 1989); *United States v. Ford*, 830 F.2d 596 (6th Cir. 1987).

[205] ABA Rule 3.6(a)(b) and associated commentary.

[206] 501 U.S. 1030, 111 S.Ct. 2720 (1991).

[207] The ABA rule has now been changed to allow a lawyer to state "the claim, offense, or defense involved," as well as to respond to "recent adverse publicity."

[208] 443 U.S. 368, 99 S.Ct. 2898 (1979).

[209] 448 U.S. 555, 100 S.Ct. 2814 (1980).

press or the public, a defendant will seldom be able to close the proceeding, at least when it is a trial.

The defendant in *Richmond Newspapers* sought closure of his trial because he had been through four previous mistrials, one of which occurred after a prospective juror told jurors who sat on the case about press reports concerning the previous trials. Eight members of the Court found closure under these circumstances inappropriate (with Justice Rehnquist dissenting on the ground that closure agreed to by the parties should be constitutional). Although there were several concurring opinions, the essential rationale of the decision was expressed in an opinion by Chief Justice Burger. Noting that criminal trials "had long been presumptively open," he concluded that "the right to attend criminal trials is implicit in the guarantees of the First Amendment; without the freedom to attend such trials, which people have exercised for centuries, important aspects of freedom of speech and of the press could be eviscerated." A later decision by a full majority of the Court elaborated upon this notion, stating that the public access guaranteed by the First Amendment serves "to ensure that the individual citizen can effectively participate in and contribute to our republican system of self-government," and also "fosters an appearance of fairness, thereby heightening public respect for the judicial process."[210]

As suggested by the reference to trial openness as "presumptive," several members of the Court in *Richmond Newspapers* indicated that a trial could be closed at the defendant's request if "overriding" interests could be shown. But the only specific such interest mentioned in any of the opinions was an allusion to "reasonable restrictions" so as to assure "quiet and orderly" trials and prevent overcrowding in the courtroom. As to the need to avoid the tainting impact of publicity about the trial, the Court pointed out that sequestration of the jury was always possible. Thus, it appears that, for this purpose, closure of trial at the defendant's request will seldom be granted.

Because it dealt with a trial, *Richmond Newspapers* did not explicitly resolve whether *Gannett's* holding concerning a pretrial proceeding would withstand a First Amendment challenge. In *Press-Enterprise Co. v. Superior Court II,*[211] the defendant, with the consent of the state, obtained closure of what turned out to be a 41-day preliminary hearing. Upon challenge by the press, the California Supreme Court upheld the closure, finding a "reasonable likelihood" that the defendant, who was charged with murdering 12 nurses with drug overdoses, would have been prejudiced at trial had the hearing been open to the media. The Supreme Court, in a 7–2 opinion written by Chief Justice Burger, rejected the California court's standard, holding that the defendant must show a "substantial probability" of prejudice from the proceeding. Additionally, it required a showing that other "reasonable" alternatives to closure (such as *voir dire*) will not preserve the accused's right to an unbiased jury.

In justifying this decision, the Court relied on several factors. As it had in *Richmond Newspapers,* the Court stressed that, historically, the preliminary hearing had been open to the public. Further, because many cases end in a guilty plea, "the preliminary hearing is often the final and most important step in the criminal proceeding," especially given its adversarial nature. Finally, Burger noted the absence of public representatives at the preliminary hearing (in contrast, for instance, to the grand jury).

---

[210] *Globe Newspaper Co. v. Superior Court,* 457 U.S. 596, 102 S.Ct. 2613 (1982).

[211] 478 U.S. 1, 106 S.Ct. 2735 (1986).

Given this reasoning, the grand jury process is clearly not covered by *Press-Enterprise II*; unlike the preliminary hearing, it has a tradition of secrecy,[212] and, as Burger pointed out, involves members of the public. Other pretrial hearings (e.g., suppression hearings), vary both in their history and function from the preliminary hearing, but the lower courts tend to allow press access to most such hearings, as well as associated documents, unless the "substantial probability" test is met.[213]

As to the meaning of the "substantial probability" test, *Press-Enterprise II* clearly refused to equate it with the California courts "reasonable likelihood" standard, a standard virtually identical to that used by the trial judge (and approved by the Court) in *Gannett*. At the same time, the Court did not adopt a "clear and present danger" rubric. Thus, closure of pretrial proceedings may be permissible in situations where closure of trial is not. This difference makes some sense, since the alternative to the former (*voir dire*) is not likely to be as successful at alleviating the effects of pretrial prejudicial publicity on potential jurors as the alternative to the latter (sequestration) will be at preventing juror access to publicity about the trial.[214] Furthermore, if a transcript of the closed pretrial proceeding is provided to the press as soon as practicable, a practice approved by the Court in *Gannett,* the infringement of First Amendment interests can be minimized.

(d) The Media in the Courtroom

The mere presence of the public and the media in the courtroom can have an impact on the fairness of a trial, independent of any new reports thereby generated. In *Sheppard,* for instance, the courtroom was packed with members of the public and the media for all nine weeks of the trial, making it "difficult for the witnesses and counsel to be heard," and for Sheppard and his counsel to talk together confidentially. Newsmen also handled and took pictures of exhibits. In reversing Sheppard's conviction on due process grounds, the Court held that this "carnival atmosphere" should have been prevented by limiting the number of reporters in the courtroom and more closely regulating their conduct.

A similar issue arose in *Estes v. Texas,*[215] where pretrial hearings were televised, as well as much of the trial. The Court reversed the defendant's conviction, again on due process grounds, noting that the presence of television cameras could distract the jurors, decrease the quality of testimony, unduly burden the judge and subject him to greater political pressure, and distract the defendant, as well as his attorney. The Court's plurality opinion did not address the First Amendment implications of its decision, although Justice Harlan, who cast the fifth vote, limited his conclusion to the facts of the case and noted that television could be of educational and informational value to the public.

Estes notwithstanding, several states persisted in developing guidelines for permitting television in the courtroom. In *Chandler v. Florida,*[216] the Supreme Court in effect nullified *Estes* and upheld Florida's rule allowing electronic media and still photography coverage of public judicial proceedings, although without specifically

---

[212] See § 23.03.

[213] See, e.g., *In re Search Warrant for Secretarial Area,* 855 F.2d 569 (8th Cir. 1988).

[214] See discussion of *voir dire,* § 27.04(a) & (b).

[215] 381 U.S. 532, 85 S.Ct. 1628 (1965).

[216] 449 U.S. 560, 101 S.Ct. 802 (1981).

addressing First Amendment concerns. The Court instead merely noted that technological advances had diminished many of the distractions originally associated with television coverage (such as bright lighting, numerous technicians and cumbersome equipment), that the Florida rule provided significant procedural safeguards for the defendant, and that there was little empirical data showing that the presence of the broadcast media had an adverse effect on the trial process. Under these circumstances, television coverage is permissible, unless the defendant can show that "the media's coverage of his case—be it printed or broadcast—compromised the ability of the particular jury that heard the case to adjudicate fairly." In the case before it, the Court concluded that the defendants were unable to show that television coverage "impaired the ability of the jurors to decide the case on only the evidence before them or that their trial was affected adversely by the impact on any of the participants of the presence of cameras and the prospect of broadcast."

27.07   Conclusion

The various aspects of the right to trial by an impartial jury and judge can be summarized as follows:

(1)   A defendant has the right to a trial by jury whenever the legislated sentence could result in imprisonment of more than six months for any of the crimes charged or, in contempt cases, whenever the actual punishment imposed at one time (whether summarily or at a separate proceeding) is more than six months. The Sixth Amendment also requires that a jury determine all the facts used to enhance a sentence beyond the statutory or guidelines maximum, or from a life sentence to a death sentence. It also requires that any facts that the legislature requires for a mandatory minimum sentence (even one imposed for acts that occur during supervised release) be found by the jury. The federal model of a twelve-person jury which must vote unanimously for conviction or acquittal is not constitutionally required. Six-person juries which vote unanimously, and twelve-person juries which reach a 9–3 verdict meet constitutional requirements. The right to jury trial may be waived, but can be conditioned on the consent of the prosecution and the court, unless such veto will unduly prejudice the defendant.

(2)   Under the Equal Protection Clause, a jury pool and panel may not be the result of purposeful discrimination against members of a suspect class. Purposeful discrimination is presumed if the disparity between the proportion of the group in the community and the proportion of the group in the jury pool or panel is significant (i.e., over two or three standard deviations) and the jury selection procedures used offer an opportunity to discriminate. Under the Sixth Amendment, a defendant is entitled to a jury pool and panel representing a fair cross-section of the community (although the jury itself need not mirror the community). This requirement is violated whenever (1) a large, identifiable, distinctive group is (2) substantially underrepresented in the pool or panel as a result of (3) systematic exclusion. Distinctiveness is defined primarily not in terms of attitudes possessed by a particular group but by more neutral characteristics, such as race and gender. Although the exclusion of group members apparently need not be intentional to be systematic, proof of underrepresentation similar to that required in equal protection cases will probably be required.

(3)   At *voir dire*, the judge is not constitutionally required to ask any particular questions about prospective juror biases beyond general inquiries about prejudice, except when: (a) racial issues are "inextricably bound up" with issues at trial; or (b) the

defendant is charged with a capital offense, necessitating questions about attitudes toward the death penalty. Challenges for cause are generally allowed only in circumstances specified by statute or if an identifiable bias becomes apparent during *voir dire*. Thus, bias will not normally be implied due to pretrial publicity about the defendant or a prospective juror's employment with the government. Nor may the prosecution use its challenges to fashion a capital sentencing jury devoid of individuals who have merely expressed scruples against the death penalty, since their bias is not clear and such a jury is organized to return a verdict of death. However, the prosecution may exclude from a capital sentencing jury and trial venirepersons who state that under no circumstances would they impose the death penalty or who state that their views about the death penalty would substantially impair the performance of their duties as a juror, just as the defense may exclude those who would automatically impose the death penalty at the sentencing stage. Peremptory challenges may be used to exclude venirepersons as the parties see fit, except that neither the prosecution nor the defense may use them to exclude blacks or other racial minorities solely on the basis of race, nor may prosecutors use them to exclude anyone solely on the basis of gender. If a prima facie case can be made that peremptories have been used in this way, the party using peremptories must convince the court that it genuinely sought exclusion on race-or gender-neutral grounds.

(4) The criminal defendant is entitled, under the Due Process Clause, to an impartial judge, which means the judge may not only not harbor a subjective bias against the defendant, but also must avoid any situation in which there is a potential for bias.

(5) The prejudicial impact of publicity can be alleviated through (a) continuances; (b) exclusion, at *voir dire,* of jurors with a fixed opinion against the defendant; (c) changes of venue, when publicity has been extraordinarily inflammatory and extensive; and (d) jury sequestration. Media dissemination of prejudicial information can be prevented through gag orders on the press or the trial participants, but probably only when there is a clear and present danger that the trial will otherwise be unfair (which is most likely to exist if potentially inadmissible evidence might be disclosed). Additionally, publicity may be prevented by closing pretrial proceedings, if there is a substantial probability of prejudice from the proceeding and there are no other reasonable alternatives to closure (such as *voir dire*). Closure of *trial* to prevent juror exposure to publicity will rarely, if ever, be permissible, given the availability of sequestration. Television is permitted in the courtroom so long as it does not compromise the ability of the jury to adjudicate the case fairly.

BIBLIOGRAPHY

Alschuler, Albert. The Supreme Court and the Jury: *Voir Dire*, Peremptory Challenges and the Review of Jury Verdicts. 56 U.Chi.L.Rev. 153 (1989).

Appleman, Laura I. The Lost Meaning of the Jury Trial Right. 84 Ind. L.J. 397 (2009).

Arenella, Peter. Televising High Profile Trials: Are We Better Off Pulling the Plug? 37 Santa Clara L.Rev. 701 (1997).

Babcock, Barbara. *Voir Dire*: Preserving "Its Wonderful Power." 27 Stan.L.Rev. 545 (1975).

Beale, Sara S. Integrating Statistical Evidence and Legal Theory to Challenge the Selection of Grand and Petit Jurors. 46 Law & Contemp. Probs. 269 (1983).

Bellin, Jeffrey and Junichi P. Semitsu. Widening *Batson's* Net to Ensnare More than the Unapologetically Bigoted or Painfully Unimaginative Attorney. 96 Cornell L. Rev. 1075 (2011).

Collins, Christina. Stuck in the 1960s: Supreme Court Misses an Opportunity in *Skilling v. United States* to Bring Venue Jurisprudence into the Twenty-First Century. 44 Texas Tech L. Rev. 391 (2012).

Crump, Susan W. *Lockhart v. McCree*: The "Biased But Unbiased Juror," What Are the States' Legitimate Interests? 65 Denver L.Rev. 1 (1988).

Ford, Roger A. Modeling the Effects of Peremptory Challenges on Jury Selection and Jury Verdicts. 17 Geo. Mason L. Rev. 377 (2010).

Goldwasser, Katherine. Limiting a Criminal Defendant's Use of Peremptory Challenges: On Symmetry and the Jury in a Criminal Trial. 102 Harv.L.Rev. 808 (1989).

Hannaford, Paula L. Systematic Negligence in Jury Operations: Why the Definition of Systematic Exclusion in Fair Cross Section Claims Must Be Expanded. 59 Drake L. Rev. 761 (2011).

_____. Safeguarding Juror Privacy: A New Framework for Court Policies and Procedures. 85 Judicature 28 (2001).

Isaacson, Robert. Fair Trial and Free Press: An Opportunity for Co-Existence. 29 Stan.L.Rev. 561 (1977).

Kalven, Harry and Harry Zeisel. The American Jury. Boston: Little Brown, 1966.

King, Nancy Jean. The American Criminal Jury. 62 Law & Contemp.Prob. 41 (1999).

Leib, Ethan. Supermajoritarianism and the American Criminal Jury. 33 Hastings Const.L.Q. 141 (2006).

Leipold, Andrew D. Constitutionalizing Jury Selection in Criminal Cases: A Critical Evaluation. 86 Geo. L.J. 945 (1998).

Levenson, Laurie L. Change of Venue and the Role of the Criminal Jury. 66 So. Calif. L.Rev. 1533 (1993).

Marder, Nancy S. *Batson* Revisited. 97 Iowa L. Rev. 1585 (2012).

Massaro, Toni. Peremptories or Peers?—Rethinking Sixth Amendment Doctrine, Images and Procedures. 64 N.Car.L.Rev. 501 (1986).

Minow, Newton and Fred Cate. Who is an Impartial Juror in an Age of Mass Media? 40 Amer.L.Rev. 631 (1991).

Pizzi, William and Morris B. Hoffman. Jury Selection Errors on Appeal. 38 Am.Crim.L.Rev. 1391 (2001).

Prescott, J.J. and Sonja Starr. Improving Criminal Jury Decisionmaking After the *Blakely* Revolution. 2006 Ill.L.Rev. 301.

Rose, Mary R. and Shari Seidman Diamond. Judging Bias: Juror Confidence and Judicial Rulings on Challenges for Cause. 41 L. & Soc'y Rev. 513 (2008).

Sack, Robert D. Principle and *Nebraska Press Association v. Stuart*. 29 Stan.L.Rev. 411 (1977).

Saks, Michael J. Jury Verdicts: The Role of Group Size and Social Decision Rule. Lexington, Massachusetts: Lexington Books, 1977.

Simon, Rita J. The Jury System in America: A Critical Overview. Sage: 1975.

Smith, Abbe. "Nice Work If You Can Get It": "Ethical" Jury Selection in Criminal Defense. 67 Fordham L.Rev. 523 (1998).

Symposium. The Court of Public Opinion: The Practice and Ethics of Trying Cases in the Media. 71 Law & Contemp. Probls. 1 (2008).

Tarkington, Margaret. Lost in the Compromise: Free Speech, Criminal Justice, and Attorney Pretrial Publicity. 66 Fla. L. Rev. 1873 (2014).

Taslitz, Andrew. The Incautious Media, Free Speech and the Unfair Trial: Why Prosecutors Need More Realistic Guidelines in Dealing with the Press. 62 Hastings L.J. 1285 (2011).

Wang, Chenyu. Rearguing Jury Unanimity: An Alternative. 16 Lewis & Clark L. Rev. 38 (2012).

Chapter 28

ADVERSARIAL RIGHTS: OPENNESS, CONFRONTATION, AND COMPULSORY PROCESS

28.01   Introduction

The Sixth Amendment provides in part: "In all criminal prosecutions, the accused shall enjoy the right to . . . public trial[,] to be confronted with the witnesses against him [and] to have compulsory process for obtaining witnesses in his favor." The three rights guaranteed by this language, applied to the states in *In re Oliver*[1] (Public Trial Clause), *Pointer v. Texas*[2] (Confrontation Clause) and *Washington v. Texas*[3] (Compulsory Process Clause), are designed to equalize the contest between the state and the accused and ensure that it is adversarial rather than inquisitional.

The first section of this chapter examines the right to a "public trial," which is meant to promote fair adjudication by bringing the process into the open. The next three sections address the central aspects of an accused's right to confront her accusers: the right to be present, both physically and mentally; the right to force the prosecution to rely on live testimony rather than out-of-court statements; and the right to face and cross-examine those accusers who testify in court. These guarantees help ensure that the defendant is given adequate opportunity to hear and challenge the state's case against her. The final section of the chapter describes the operation of the compulsory process guarantee, which supplements the Confrontation Clause by providing means for the defendant to muster his own evidence against the state's case. Although this chapter focuses primarily on these provisions as they affect the trial process, it also examines their application to other criminal proceedings.

28.02   The Right to Public Adjudication

(a)   Rationale and Scope

As the Supreme Court recognized in *In re Oliver,*[4] "[t]he knowledge that every criminal trial is subject to contemporaneous review in the forum of public opinion is an effective restraint on possible abuse of power. . . . Without publicity, all other checks are insufficient; in comparison of publicity, all other checks are of small account." The Court explained further that "the presence of interested spectators may keep [the accused's] triers keenly alive to a sense of their responsibility and to the importance of their functions."

Although *Oliver* speaks only of trial, its rationale would seem to apply to any formal proceeding where important decisions about the defendant's fate are made. This surmise

---

[1]   333 U.S. 257, 68 S.Ct. 499 (1948).
[2]   380 U.S. 400, 85 S.Ct. 1065 (1965).
[3]   388 U.S. 14, 87 S.Ct. 1920 (1967).
[4]   333 U.S. 257, 68 S.Ct. 499 (1948).

was affirmed in *Waller v. Georgia*,[5] where the Court held that the right to public trial encompassed the right to an open suppression hearing. The right probably applies to most other pretrial proceedings as well, with the exception of the grand jury, which has traditionally operated in secret.[6] Thus, in *Presley v. Georgia*[7] the Court held, per curiam, that the right applies to voir dire proceedings, and may only be overridden under narrow circumstances. In *Presley*, the Court held that the fear that a potential juror would overhear unspecified remarks from the audience was an insufficient reason for excluding the public from the jury selection process.

(b) Closure of Normally Open Proceedings

For the reasons given above, the defendant will usually want an open proceeding. Occasionally, however, she may seek closure, perhaps to mitigate the effects of publicity or to protect privacy interests. Under such circumstances, the Sixth Amendment may be waived.[8] However, the First Amendment's guarantee of a free press permits the public to override this waiver in a number of situations. This issue is discussed elsewhere in this book.[9]

Discussed here are those situations where the defendant (as well as, perhaps, the press) want an open proceeding, but the *state* wishes to close it. In *Waller,* the Court set forth the test for determining when the state may prevail in such circumstances. Closure may occur over a Sixth Amendment objection by the defendant only if: (1) the state proves that an overriding interest requires protection (such as the need to protect juror or witness privacy); (2) the closure is no broader than necessary to protect that interest; (3) reasonable alternatives are considered; and (4) findings adequate to support the closure are made.

In *Waller* itself the Court found that this test was not met. There, the state requested that the suppression hearing be closed because it would be playing a tape that referred to persons not yet indicted. Granting the motion, the judge closed all seven days of the hearing, despite the fact that less than 2½ hours of this period were devoted to playing the tape, and few of the conversations mentioned or involved parties not then before the court. The Supreme Court held that, because the state failed to identify specifically "whose privacy interests might be infringed, how they would be infringed, what portions of the tape might infringe them, and what portion of the evidence consisted of the tapes," and because the closure went far beyond that necessary to protect against inappropriate disclosure, the Sixth Amendment was violated. Accordingly, the defendants were entitled to a new suppression hearing and, if the results of the hearing were significantly different from the first suppression hearing, a new trial.

Globe Newspaper Co. v. Superior Court,[10] a First Amendment case decided before *Waller,* provides another illustration of the Supreme Court's probable approach in this area. There, the Court found unconstitutional a state-requested closure of trial under a statute that automatically denied access to the public in cases involving sex offenses

---

[5]   467 U.S. 39, 104 S.Ct. 2210 (1984).

[6]   See § 23.03.

[7]   558 U.S. 209, 130 S.Ct. 721 (2010).

[8]   *Gannett Co., Inc. v. DePasquale,* 443 U.S. 368, 99 S.Ct. 2898 (1979) (permitting closure of suppression hearing when there is "reasonable possibility" that pretrial publicity will affect fairness of trial).

[9]   See § 27.06(c)(3).

[10]   457 U.S. 596, 102 S.Ct. 2613 (1982).

against minors. The Court did not prohibit closure under all such circumstances, however; rather it held that, upon a motion by the state, the trial court should "determine on a case-by-case basis whether closure is necessary," taking into account "the minor victim's age, psychological maturity and understanding, the nature of the crime, the desires of the victim, and the interests of parents and relatives."[11]

28.03   The Right to Be Present

As the Supreme Court stated in *Illinois v. Allen*,[12] "[o]ne of the most basic of the rights guaranteed by the Confrontation Clause is the accused's right to be present in the courtroom at every stage of his trial." The right of confrontation would be meaningless if the defendant were not present to hear and view the state's evidence. It would also be an empty right if the defendant, though present, could not understand and respond to what he observes in the courtroom. Thus the right to be present actually encompasses two different aspects: physical presence and mental competence. The Supreme Court has also indicated that the right to be present may not be burdened unnecessarily, either through prosecutorial comment about the defendant's failure to take the stand or through manipulating the defendant's appearance. These three concepts are discussed here.

(a) Physical Presence

The defendant's right to be physically present during the proceedings against him is limited in several ways. First, it only applies to "critical" proceedings. Second, it can be voluntarily waived, or forfeited (that is, "involuntarily" sacrificed), by the absence of the defendant. Third, it can be forfeited through misconduct of the defendant at the proceeding.

(1) Proceedings at Which Applicable

Allen speaks of the right to be present "at every stage of [the] trial." In *United States v. Gagnon*,[13] the Court made clear that, because the right to presence has due process as well as confrontation origins, it is not limited to proceedings at which witnesses appear to offer testimony against the defendant but also to all other proceedings at which the defendant's presence " 'has a relation, reasonably substantial, to the fullness of his opportunity to defend against the charge.' " In *Kentucky v. Stincer*,[14] the Court reiterated this principle, finding a right to presence at any stage of the criminal proceeding which is "critical," in the sense that the accused's presence there "would contribute to the fairness of the prosecution."

However, in both *Gagnon* and *Stincer* the Court held that the proceedings at issue did not implicate the right. In *Gagnon,* the judge met in chambers with a juror who had noticed, and apparently become bothered by, the fact that the defendant was sketching the jury; the judge determined that the sketching did not prejudice the juror against the defendant and allowed the juror to continue sitting. The Court held that the absence of the defendants at this "minor occurrence" did not violate due process, since the

---

[11]   See also, *Press-Enterprise Co. v. Superior Court I,* 464 U.S. 501, 104 S.Ct. 819 (1984) (finding unconstitutional, on First Amendment grounds, closure of all but three days of a six-week *voir dire,* without specific findings as to how closure would protect juror privacy).

[12]   397 U.S. 337, 90 S.Ct. 1057 (1970).

[13]   470 U.S. 522, 105 S.Ct. 1482 (1985).

[14]   479 U.S. 1028, 107 S.Ct. 870 (1987).

defendants "could have done nothing had they been present nor would they have gained anything by attending." In *Stincer,* the proceeding involved a pretrial determination of the testimonial competence of children the prosecution planned to offer as witnesses. Here, the questions asked concerned the witnesses' mental competency, not their account of the offense, thus making it less likely the defendant could have pointed to any discrepancies in their testimony. Furthermore, the children were subject to cross-examination at trial (at which the defendant was present), and many of the questions asked at the pretrial proceeding were replicated at trial.

Even when the right to be present is violated, it may be such a *de minimis* violation that reversal is not required. For instance, in *Rushen v. Spain,*[15] the trial judge failed to disclose *ex parte* communications between himself and a juror regarding the juror's reaction to impeachment evidence concerning the murder of an acquaintance of hers. The Supreme Court acknowledged that this *in camera* interview was a violation of the right to be present, as well as the right to counsel at critical stages of trial, but ultimately found it harmless in view of the trial judge's post-trial finding of fact that the jury's deliberations were not biased by the *ex parte* communication. A different holding, stated the Court, would "undermine . . . society's interest in the administration of criminal justice."

(2) Waiver/Forfeiture Through Absence

In contrast to *Rushen,* in both *Gagnon* and *Stincer* defense attorneys had been present during the proceeding which the defendant missed. Thus, an additional argument in favor of the latter decisions might have been that the attorneys waived their clients' right to be present. But this argument is likely to be given short shrift by the Court, since, in *Taylor v. Illinois,*[16] it held that the right cannot be waived by the attorney "without the fully informed and publicly acknowledged consent of the defendant."

On the other hand, the defendant himself can waive the right, or forfeit it through misconduct, in a number of situations. As early as 1912, the Court held that the right to be present may be waived by the defendant. In *Diaz v. United States,*[17] the defendant twice voluntarily absented himself from trial after the trial had begun. The accused also sent a message to the court expressly consenting to the trial continuing in his absence. The Supreme Court held that on these facts waiver of the right to be present was valid. However, it also held that when an accused is charged with a capital offense and is in custody (i.e., has not escaped), the right to be present can never be waived.

The Court has also permitted *implied* waiver of the right to be present. In *Taylor v. United States,*[18] the defendant failed to return to his trial after a noon recess. The jury was admonished that Taylor's absence should not lead to an inference of guilt, but returned a guilty verdict. Taylor was eventually arrested and sentenced, but appealed on the ground that his right to confrontation was violated because he had not "intentionally relinquished a known right." The Court rejected this argument, concluding:

---

[15]   464 U.S. 114, 104 S.Ct. 453 (1983).

[16]   484 U.S. 400, 108 S.Ct. 646 (1988).

[17]   223 U.S. 442, 32 S.Ct. 250 (1912).

[18]   414 U.S. 17, 94 S.Ct. 194 (1973).

It is wholly incredible to suggest that [Taylor] . . . entertained any doubts about his right to be present at every stage of the trial. It seems equally incredible to us, as it did to the Court of Appeals, 'that a defendant who flees from a courtroom in the midst of a trial—where judge, jury, witnesses and lawyers are present and ready to continue—would not know that as a consequence the trial could continue in his absence.'

Taylor suggests that once trial has already commenced with the defendant present, an uncoerced absence will be construed as a forfeiture of the right to be present regardless of whether the defendant has been informed of the consequences of that absence.[19]

Finally, the Court has implied that even when the defendant *never* appears for trial, a waiver may be assumed under appropriate circumstances without violating the Constitution. In *Tacon v. Arizona,*[20] the defendant claimed to be unable to travel from New York to his trial in Arizona because he couldn't afford the trip. The Court granted certiorari to decide whether a state may try a defendant who is *in absentia* for financial reasons. Ultimately, however, it dismissed the writ as improvidently granted, concluding that the only issue raised below was whether the defendant's conduct, which suggested that in fact he could afford the trip, amounted to a "knowing and intelligent" waiver. With this language, the Court strongly indicated that, even in cases not involving escape from custody, one can forfeit one's right to presence without ever appearing at trial.

However, in the federal courts, the Court has held that the express language of Federal Rule 43 prohibits trial of a defendant who absconds prior to trial rather than after its commencement. In *Crosby v. United States,*[21] a unanimous Court held that the Rule's list of situations in which waiver can be implied, which does not include the pre-trial flight scenario, was exclusive. In response to the government's contention that this gap in the list was an oversight, Justice Blackmun's opinion noted some possible justifications for the rule's approach, including the fact that forestalling a trial not yet begun was not as expensive as suspending an ongoing proceeding, and the fact that flight during trial was more probative of a knowing waiver than absconding beforehand.

(3) Forfeiture Through Conduct

A third exception to the right to be present arises when the defendant makes it impossible to conduct an orderly proceeding. In *Illinois v. Allen,*[22] the defendant did not voluntarily leave the courtroom but rather was removed after repeated warnings from the judge that the defendant's abusive and disruptive behavior would result in his removal. The Supreme Court sanctioned this action, holding that the right to be present may be forfeited if the defendant, after being warned, continues to act "in a manner so disorderly, disruptive, and disrespectful of the court that his trial cannot be carried on with him in the courtroom." The Court also noted, however, that this lost right may be reclaimed when an accused is "willing to conduct himself consistently with the decorum and respect inherent in the concept of courts and judicial proceedings."

---

[19] Fed.R.Crim.Proc. 43(c) states that a "defendant who was initially present at trial . . . waives the right to be present . . . when the defendant is voluntarily absent after the trial has begun, regardless of whether the court informed the defendant of an obligation to remain during trial [and] in a noncapital case, when the defendant is voluntarily absent during sentencing."

[20] 410 U.S. 351, 93 S.Ct. 998 (1973) (per curiam).

[21] 506 U.S. 255, 113 S.Ct. 748 (1993).

[22] 397 U.S. 337, 90 S.Ct. 1057 (1970).

The Court recognized alternatives to removal from the courtroom but refused to require their use as a substitute, given the disadvantages associated with them. One alternative—binding and gagging the defendant—would ensure the defendant's presence but might also "have a significant effect on the jury's feelings about the defendant [and act as] something of an affront to the very dignity and decorum of judicial proceedings that the judge is seeking to uphold." Moreover, this approach would severely curtail the defendant's ability to communicate with her attorney, thus denigrating the defendant's right to confront her accusers. The second alternative, a contempt citation, would allow attorney-client communication but would not stop the misconduct of those defendants determined to be disruptive and those charged with serious offenses for whom a contempt sanction might mean little. Thus, held the Court, removal, restraints, and contempt are all permissible solutions to the disruptive defendant, to be used in the judge's discretion.

(b) Competency to Proceed

The Supreme Court has held that conviction of an "incompetent" person violates the Constitution.[23] Two very different reasons support this holding. Most clearly, physical presence without some ability to process events in the courtroom and communicate with one's attorney would be a useless prerogative. A second rationale for the competency requirement is the damage to societal integrity that would occur if the state could convict and sentence individuals who are unaware of what is being done to them.[24] Both rationales support the proposition that the defendant's competence should be assured at *any* proceeding, not just at trial. Thus, this discussion speaks of "competency to proceed" rather than competency to stand trial.

(1) The Standard

The test for determining a defendant's competency to proceed is often said to have been established in the Supreme Court's per curiam decision in *Dusky v. United States.*[25] There the district court judge found the defendant competent because he was "oriented to time and place and [had] some recollection of events." The Solicitor General found this an insufficient basis for a competency determination and suggested to the Court that the test be whether a defendant "has sufficient present ability to consult with his lawyer with a reasonable degree of rational understanding—and whether he has a rational as well as factual understanding of the proceedings against him." The Court adopted the Solicitor General's suggestion and the *Dusky* test has since been treated as setting forth the appropriate criteria for competency to stand trial in the federal courts; most states have followed suit.[26] The Court has since held that a state may place the burden of proving incompetency on the defendant.[27]

---

[23] *Pate v. Robinson,* 383 U.S. 375, 86 S.Ct. 836 (1966); *Bishop v. United States,* 350 U.S. 961, 76 S.Ct. 440 (1956). In reaching this holding, the Court has relied on the Due Process Clause, but its reasoning resonates with right to confrontation concerns.

[24] See Note, *Incompetency to Stand Trial,* 81 Harv.L.Rev. 454, 458 (1967).

[25] 362 U.S. 402, 80 S.Ct. 788 (1960).

[26] See, e.g., West's Fla.S.A.R.Crim.Pro. 3.211(a)(1).

[27] *Medina v. California,* 505 U.S. 437, 112 S.Ct. 2572 (1992). However, the state may, at most, require the defendant to carry this burden by a preponderance of the evidence; imposing a clear-and-convincing evidence standard of proof unfairly burdens the defendant. *Cooper v. Oklahoma,* 517 U.S. 348, 116 S.Ct. 1373 (1996).

It is important to note the distinction between incompetency to proceed and the insanity defense; the two concepts are often confused. The first concerns the defendant's mental condition at the time of the relevant proceeding, while the second involves the defendant's mental state at the time of the offense. Additionally, while the insanity defense contemplates a broad inquiry designed to determine the extent of *any* cognitive *or* volitional impairment at the time of the offense,[28] the competency test focuses on the defendant's mental capacity with respect to two narrowly defined areas: (1) his ability to understand the proceedings against her and (2) his ability to communicate with his lawyer.

With respect to the first prong, it seems clear that the defendant must have some basic understanding of the charges against him, the consequences of conviction on those charges, and the nature of the adversary process. Additionally, as the Supreme Court noted in *Godinez v. Moran*,[29] a person who goes to trial must have the capacity to understand various rights that may be waived during the trial process, including the right to jury trial, the right to remain silent (in connection with deciding whether to take the stand), and the right to counsel.[30] With respect to the second prong, the defendant should be able to recount the pertinent facts surrounding the time of the offense, although several courts have held that amnesia for the time of the offense, by itself, is not an automatic bar to a competency finding.[31] As applied, the competency test is an extremely low standard. Studies indicate that of those who are referred for a competency evaluation (and who thus presumably evidence some degree of mental deficiency), only between ten and thirty percent are found incompetent by the courts.[32]

(2) Raising the Competency Issue

In *Pate v. Robinson*[33] the Court held that a hearing to determine the defendant's competency to stand trial must be held whenever "a sufficient doubt exists as to his present competence." In *Pate*, the trial judge had not held a hearing on the issue despite Robinson's history of mental illness and his assertion of an insanity defense. The Illinois Supreme Court affirmed this denial in light of the mental alertness and understanding displayed in Robinson's "colloquies" with the trial judge. But the Supreme Court required a hearing, stating:

> [The Illinois courts'] reasoning offers no justification for ignoring the uncontradicted testimony of Robinson's history of pronounced irrational behavior. While Robinson's demeanor at trial might be relevant to the ultimate decision as to his [present] sanity, it cannot be relied upon to dispense with a hearing on that very issue.

As Justice Harlan pointed out in dissent, the pattern of Robinson's illness "may best indicate that Robinson did function adequately during most of his life interrupted by periods of severe derangement that would have been quite apparent had they occurred

---

[28]   For a general exposition of these matters, see Wayne LaFave, Criminal Law 402–414 (4th ed. 2003).

[29]   509 U.S. 389, 113 S.Ct. 2680 (1993).

[30]   For further discussion of this case, see § 26.04(a)(5) (concerning *Moran* and the standard for competency to plead guilty) and § 31.04(b) (concerning *Moran* and waiver of counsel).

[31]   See, e.g., *Wilson v. United States*, 391 F.2d 460 (D.C.Cir. 1968).

[32]   Ron Roesch and Stephen Golding, Competency to Stand Trial 48 (1980). The authors note that variations in the rate exist because "many defendants are inappropriately referred, . . . and confusion exists about the proper criteria necessary for a determination of incompetency." Id. at 51.

[33]   383 U.S. 375, 86 S.Ct. 836 (1966).

at trial." Moreover, the trial judge was obviously satisfied as to Robinson's competence and even his attorneys never moved to have his competency examined. Given these facts, the majority decision in *Pate* suggests that a hearing of some sort should be held whenever there is a history of mental aberration, regardless of what other indicia of present mental state may reveal.

This notion is supported by the Court's holding in *Drope v. Missouri,*[34] in which the defendant was charged, along with four others, in the rape and sexual abuse of his wife. During trial, the wife testified that the defendant would sometimes roll down the stairs when he was upset and that the night before trial the defendant had tried to choke her. The second day of trial, the defendant's attorney announced that the defendant had shot himself in the stomach. On these facts, the Court held that the trial judge had an obligation to inquire into the defendant's competency to stand trial despite his apparent lucidity prior to and during the first day of trial.

Pate and *Drope* make clear that the competency issue may be raised at any time prior to or during the proceeding. They further imply, and many states provide, that any party—the defense, the prosecution, or the judge—may raise the issue when a bona fide doubt as to competency exists. If, as suggested above, society too has an interest in trying only competent defendants, this latter rule makes sense. But some commentators believe that only the defense should be able to raise the issue, on the ground that prosecutors and judges may abuse the hospital-based competency evaluation process as an alternative disposition and a means of obtaining discovery.[35]

(3) Self-Incrimination and the Competency Evaluation

As just noted, when the competency issue is raised, most states provide for an evaluation of the defendant's competency by a mental health professional at a state hospital.[36] In *Estelle v. Smith,*[37] the results of such an evaluation were used not only to address the defendant's competency, but also as the basis for testimony at the defendant's sentencing proceeding to the effect that he was dangerous, a finding which permitted the sentencing jury to impose the death penalty on the defendant. The Supreme Court held that because the defense did not initiate the evaluation nor introduce psychiatric testimony of its own at the sentencing proceeding, the admission of the dangerousness testimony violated the Fifth Amendment. Comparing the evaluation in *Smith* to the custodial interrogation setting at issue in *Miranda v. Arizona,*[38] the Court concluded that the only way the state could have introduced such testimony under these circumstances was if the psychiatrist performing the evaluation had informed Smith of his right to remain silent and of the possible uses of any disclosures he might make. Here, there had been no such warnings. On the other hand, the Court noted, had Smith been given the warnings and refused to talk, "the validly ordered competency examination nevertheless could have proceeded upon the condition that the results would be applied solely for that purpose." Later cases also confirmed that if the defendant uses the results of the competency evaluation for another purpose, or raises a mental state issue at trial that might be rebutted through information

---

[34] 420 U.S. 162, 95 S.Ct. 896 (1975).

[35] Stuart Eizenstadt, *Mental Competency to Stand Trial*, 4 Harv.Civ.Rts.Civ.Lib.L.Rev. 379 (1969).

[36] Bruce B. Winick, *Incompetency to Stand Trial* 9–11, in John Monahan & Henry Steadman, Mentally Disordered Offenders: Perspectives from Law and Social Science (1983).

[37] 451 U.S. 454, 101 S.Ct. 1866 (1981).

[38] 384 U.S. 436, 86 S.Ct. 1602 (1966), discussed in pertinent part in § 16.03(a)(3).

obtained at such an evaluation, its results are admissible over a Fifth Amendment objection.[39]

Smith also held that the prosecution's failure to notify the defendant's attorneys about the evaluation violated the Sixth Amendment as construed by *Massiah v. United States*,[40] since the evaluation took place after indictment. But, as with the right to remain silent, the Court concluded that this "right-to-notice" could be waived as well.

After *Smith,* it appears that if a defendant is told about the right to remain silent and the right to notice of counsel, and then agrees to submit to an evaluation on issues other than competency, his disclosures can be used for any purpose designated in the warnings. Given the difficulty of determining when a defendant whose mental capacity is presumably in question has validly waived her Fifth and Sixth Amendment rights, the better approach would be to prohibit use of disclosures made during a court-ordered competency evaluation for any purpose other than the determination of competency itself, unless the defendant uses the results of the evaluation for another purpose or raises another psychiatric issue.[41]

(4) *Disposition of the Incompetent Defendant*

In most jurisdictions, if a defendant is found incompetent to proceed he is usually hospitalized in an effort to restore his competency. Whether it takes place in a hospital or on an outpatient basis, the usual treatment of a person with mental illness who has been found incompetent is psychoactive medication. Courts have also held that the state may forcibly medicate an individual to ensure competency,[42] although the Supreme Court has made clear that such medication may not significantly impair the defendant's ability to communicate with counsel, must be "medically appropriate," and must be both necessary and the less restrictive method of achieving the state's aim of restoring competency.[43]

Despite the efficacy of medication and other treatments in restoring most defendants to competency, an incompetency finding can sometimes lead to indeterminate confinement well beyond the sentence associated with the defendant's charge.[44] In *Jackson v. Indiana*,[45] the Supreme Court held that the Constitution places some limitations on the length of hospitalization of individuals found incompetent. In *Jackson,* the defendant, a 27-year-old deaf mute with a mental level of a pre-school child, was charged with two robberies, one involving property valued at four dollars and the other involving five dollars in cash. The trial court found Jackson incompetent and committed him to a state hospital until the hospital staff considered him "sane." Since there was very little likelihood the defendant's condition would ever improve, this disposition "amounted to a commitment for life," in the words of Justice Blackmun, who wrote the unanimous Court opinion.

---

[39]　See § 15.02(a)(4).

[40]　377 U.S. 201, 84 S.Ct. 1199 (1964), discussed in § 16.02(c).

[41]　Christopher Slobogin, Estelle v. Smith: *The Constitutional Contours of the Forensic Evaluation*, 31 Emory L.J. 71, 87–95 (1982).

[42]　See, e.g., *United States v. Charters*, 863 F.2d 302 (4th Cir. 1988).

[43]　*Sell v. United States*, 539 U.S. 166, 123 S.Ct. 2174 (2003); *Riggins v. Nevada*, 504 U.S. 127, 112 S.Ct. 1810 (1992).

[44]　Winick, supra note 37, at 19–20.

[45]　406 U.S. 715, 92 S.Ct. 1845 (1972).

The Court found Indiana's practice unconstitutional on two grounds. First, it violated the equal protection principle. Because Jackson had not been convicted of crime, the Court held, he should presumptively be able to avoid involuntary hospitalization unless he met the normal criteria for civil commitment of mentally disabled individuals. Yet, under Indiana laws dealing with those found incompetent to stand trial, he was subject to "a more lenient commitment and to a more stringent standard of release" than those subjected to civil commitment. Second, the Due Process Clause "[a]t the least, . . . requires that the nature and duration of commitment bear some reasonable relation to the purpose for which the individual is committed." The duration of the commitment to which Jackson would be subject under Indiana law—a possible lifetime confinement— would not reasonably relate to its purpose.

In effect combining these two lines of reasoning, Blackmun concluded:

> We hold, consequently, that a person charged by a State with a criminal offense who is committed solely on account of his incapacity to proceed to trial cannot be held more than the reasonable period of time necessary to determine whether there is a substantial probability that he will attain that capacity in the foreseeable future. If it is determined that this is not the case, then the State must either institute the customary civil commitment proceeding that would be required to commit indefinitely any other citizen, or release the defendant.

The Court further held that if a defendant is found potentially "restorable" to competency, "his continued commitment must be justified by progress toward that goal."

The Court did not place any outer time limit on the duration of hospitalization authorized by *Jackson,* but did hold that Jackson himself should either be released or civilly committed, given the fact that he had now been confined for three and one-half years "on a record that sufficiently establishes the lack of a substantial probability that he will ever be able to participate fully in a trial." Some jurisdictions have attempted to designate the period after which an unrestorably incompetent defendant must be released or civil committed. For instance, the federal practice is to limit hospitalization on incompetency grounds to between 18 and 24 months.[46] New York limits commitment to 90 days for those charged with misdemeanors and to two-thirds of the maximum sentence for all others.[47] However, one survey of state law found that, forty years after *Jackson*, a majority of jurisdictions ignore or circumvent its requirements,[48] probably because they find it difficult to release or place in relatively insecure civil confinement persons charged with serious crimes.

(c) Prejudicial Aspects of Presence

The defendant's presence in the courtroom could prove prejudicial in two ways. First, if the defendant fails to testify during the proceeding, the jury may draw adverse conclusions. Second, the defendant's physical appearance may have the same effect. To the extent the state takes advantage of, or manipulates, these aspects of presence, the

---

[46] *United States v. Beidler*, 417 F.Supp. 608 (M.D.Fla. 1976).

[47] N.Y.Code Crim.Pro. § 730.50(1), (5).

[48] Nicolas Rosinia, *How "Reasonable" Has Become Unreasonable: A Proposal for Rewriting the Lasting Legacy of* Jackson v. Indiana, 89 Wash. U. L. Rev. 673, 689–90 (2012). See also Grant Morris & J. Reid Meloy, *Out of Mind? Out of Sight: The Uncivil Commitment of Permanently Incompetent Criminal Defendants*, 27 San Diego L.Rev. 1, 77–78 (1993).

Fifth Amendment's prohibition of compelled self-incrimination or analogous due process concerns may be implicated.

(1) Refusal to Testify

Under the Fifth Amendment, the state may not force the defendant to testify.[49] In *Griffin v. California*,[50] the Supreme Court held further that the prosecution may not call attention to the fact that the defendant exercises the right to remain silent, because such statements would make assertion of the Fifth Amendment "costly" and thus constitute "constitutionally impermissible compulsion."[51] While the majority recognized that the jury might assume the non-testifying defendant is guilty in any event, it distinguished that possibility from prosecutorial comment which "solemnizes the silence of the accused into evidence against him." It also pointed out that there are many reasons an *innocent* defendant might not testify, including fear that he will be impeached with prior crimes, "[e]xcessive timidity [or] nervousness when facing others and attempting to explain transactions of a suspicious character," or confusion and embarrassment "to such a degree as to increase rather than remove prejudices against [him]."

In light of these considerations, the Court's later holding in *Carter v. Kentucky*[52]—that the trial court must, at the defendant's request,[53] instruct the jury to draw no adverse inferences from the defendant's failure to take the stand—was not surprising. Further, in *Lakeside v. Oregon*,[54] it held that the defendant cannot *prevent* such an instruction. Finding speculative the defendant's argument that the instruction might call his refusal to testify to the attention of the jury, the Court stated, "[i]t would be strange indeed to conclude that this cautionary instruction violates the very constitutional provision it is intended to protect."

There is also at least one exception to the holding in *Griffin* forbidding prosecutorial comments about failure to take the stand. In *United States v. Robinson*,[55] defense counsel made numerous charges during closing argument that the government had denied the defendant the opportunity to explain his side of the case. Although, according to the defense, these comments had to do with the government's actions during the investigation stage of the proceedings, they may have left the impression that the government had somehow prevented the defendant from taking the stand. The prosecutor, who was permitted to respond to these comments during his closing statement, noted the several occasions prior to trial at which the defendant could have explained himself and ended by saying "[he] could have taken the stand and explained it to you, anything he wanted to. The United States of America has given him, throughout, the opportunity to explain." The Court felt that, in context, this statement was not a violation of *Griffin* but rather a "fair response" to the defense's assertions.

---

[49]　*Malloy v. Hogan,* 378 U.S. 1, 84 S.Ct. 1489 (1964); see also, *Wilson v. United States,* 149 U.S. 60, 13 S.Ct. 765 (1893).

[50]　380 U.S. 609, 85 S.Ct. 1229 (1965).

[51]　For further discussion of *Griffin's* compulsion theory, see § 15.02(c).

[52]　450 U.S. 288, 101 S.Ct. 1112 (1981).

[53]　In *James v. Kentucky,* 466 U.S. 341, 104 S.Ct. 1830 (1984) the Court defined "request" broadly to include a request for an "admonition" as well as a request for an instruction, despite state law distinguishing the two.

[54]　435 U.S. 333, 98 S.Ct. 1091 (1978).

[55]　485 U.S. 25, 108 S.Ct. 864 (1988).

The Court has yet to decide whether *Griffin* applies in capital sentencing proceedings. In *White v. Woodall*,[56] the Court held that a state court's refusal to adhere to *Griffin* in this setting was not "contrary to" Supreme Court precedent. But the post-conviction posture of the case means that the issue has not yet been definitively decided.[57]

(2) Prejudicial Physical Appearance

Related to the *Griffin* line of cases is *Estelle v. Williams*,[58] which held that the state may not compel a defendant to wear jail garb in the courtroom. The fact that the "constant reminder of the accused's condition implicit in such distinctive, identifiable attire may affect a juror's judgment," together with the finding that "compelling an accused to wear jail clothing furthers no essential state policy," led the Court to conclude that such a practice violated the Due Process Clause. However, if, as occurred in *Williams*, the defendant does not object to the clothing, then no constitutional violation occurs, on the assumption that no compulsion has occurred.

In a similar vein, the Court held in *Deck v. Missouri*[59] that the Due Process Clause prohibits the nonconsensual use of visible shackles during trial and during the penalty phase of a capital proceeding, unless the court makes a specific finding that their use is justified by concerns about courtroom security or escape risk. Shackling at trial, Justice Breyer wrote for seven members of the Court, not only was prohibited at common law, but undermines the presumption of innocence, the defendant's ability to consult with counsel, and the dignity of the proceedings. The latter two considerations also argue against use of shackles at the penalty phase of a capital proceeding, the Court concluded. And, although the presumption of innocence no longer applies at that stage, "related concerns" regarding accuracy also support the penalty phase prohibition, because "[t]he appearance of the offender during the penalty phase in shackles . . . almost inevitably implies to a jury, as a matter of common sense, that court authorities consider the offender a danger to the community—often a statutory aggravator and nearly always a relevant factor in jury decisionmaking, even where the State does not specifically argue the point." Justice Thomas in dissent pointed out that the historical ban on restraints had occurred at a time when irons caused significant pain and discomfort. He also argued that shackles are much less prejudicial at sentencing, when the jury knows the person has already been convicted, at the same time they are more necessary, given the increased risk of flight and danger represented by a convicted felon.

(3) Presence During Prosecution's Case

In *Portuondo v. Agard*,[60] the prosecutor stated during her summation that the defendant, who was allowed to testify at the end of his trial, "gets to sit here and listen to the testimony of all the other witnesses before he testifies . . . and think what am I going to say and [h]ow am I going to fit it into the evidence?" The defendant argued that this summation violated his Fifth Amendment right against adverse prosecutorial comment under *Griffin* and prejudiced his Sixth Amendment right to be present during

---

[56]   572 U.S. 415, 134 S.Ct. 1697 (2014).

[57]   See § 33.02(b)(3) for a discussion of federal habeas law.

[58]   425 U.S. 501, 96 S.Ct. 1691 (1976).

[59]   544 U.S. 622, 125 S.Ct. 2007 (2005). But see *Holbrook v. Flynn*, 475 U.S. 560, 106 S.Ct. 1340 (1986) (due process not violated by presence of multiple guards).

[60]   529 U.S. 61, 120 S.Ct. 1119 (2000).

the state's entire case. He also argued that the statements rendered his trial unfair under the Due Process Clause because they used his presence at trial, which was mandatory under state law, to impugn his credibility. This practice, he claimed, was analogous to prosecutorial impeachment using a defendant's silence that occurs after being told of the right to remain silent under *Miranda*, found violative of due process in *Doyle v. Ohio*.[61]

Five members of the Court, per Justice Scalia, rejected all of these arguments.[62] *Griffin* was inapposite, according to the majority, because the prosecutorial comment there urged the jury to do something it was not permitted to do (counting the defendant's silence against him even when it may be due to factors having nothing to do with guilt), while "it is natural and irresistible for a jury, in evaluating the relative credibility of a defendant who testifies last, to have in mind and weigh in the balance the fact that he heard the testimony of all those who preceded him." In response to both the Fifth and Sixth Amendment arguments, the Court cited other decisions that implicitly permitted government actions that had the effect of discouraging exercise of the constitutional rights to be present and to testify.[63] Finally, the majority concluded that the state rule requiring presence at trial was "no worse" in terms of unfairness than requiring the defendant to plead to the charge before, rather than after, all the evidence was in, and that defendants so rarely absent themselves from trial in jurisdictions in which there is no mandatory presence rule that the harm from presence must not be substantial.

Justice Ginsburg in dissent argued that the inference urged by the prosecutor in this case (that a defendant who testifies last and whose testimony is consistent with that of the other witnesses lacks credibility) is no more "natural" or "irresistible" than the inference from silence to guilt involved in *Griffin* or the inference from silence to untrustworthiness involved in *Doyle*. Thus, she suggested, prosecutors should not encourage the inference. Ultimately, however, she did not contest the constitutionality of prosecution arguments that point to specific evidence of testimonial tailoring by the defendant, nor did she find fault with suggestions to that effect if made during cross-examination. Instead she focused solely on the constitutionality of permitting *generic* comments about tailoring during *summation*, as occurred in *Agard*. She concluded that "the interests of truth are not advanced by allowing a prosecutor, at a time when the defendant cannot respond, to invite the jury to convict on the basis of conduct as consistent with innocence as with guilt."[64]

28.04   The Right to Live Testimony: When Hearsay Is Permitted

The Confrontation Clause might be read to require the prosecution to produce all of its witnesses in the courtroom so that the defendant can face and cross-examine them.

---

[61]   426 U.S. 610, 96 S.Ct. 2240 (1976), discussed in § 16.05(b)(2).

[62]   Justices Stevens and Breyer concurred on the ground that the summation did not rise to the level of fundamental unfairness that permits a federal court to set aside a state criminal conviction.

[63]   See, e.g., *Jenkins v. Anderson*, 447 U.S. 231, 100 S.Ct. 2124 (1980) (permitting use of pre-*Miranda* warning silence), discussed in § 16.05(b)(2); *Brooks v. Tennessee*, 406 U.S. 605, 92 S.Ct. 1891 (1972) (implying that the prosecutor may expose testimonial tailoring during cross-examination); *Reagan v. United States*, 157 U.S. 301, 15 S.Ct. 610 (1895) (permitting a judicial instruction to the effect that defendants have strong incentives to give self-serving testimony).

[64]   Ginsburg distinguished *Reagan, supra* note 63, the only Court decision that allows generic comments about defendant credibility after the defense has rested, on the ground that it only addressed whether the instruction at issue violated a statutory, rather than a constitutional, right to testify.

But, as early as 1895 the Supreme Court concluded, in *Mattox v. United States*,[65] that the right of confrontation is "subject to exceptions, recognized long before the adoption of the Constitution." There, it upheld the introduction of testimony given at the defendant's first trial by a witness who died before the defendant's second trial. As the majority elaborated, "[t]o say that a criminal, after having once been convicted by the testimony of a certain witness, should go scot free simply because death has closed the mouth of that witness, would be carrying his constitutional protection to an unwarrantable extent."

The Supreme Court has struggled, however, in determining when other types of "hearsay"—here, meant to describe any testimony that purports to repeat the out-of-court statements of a third person—are admissible under the Confrontation Clause. The rules of evidence in most jurisdictions recognize many exceptions to the general prohibition on hearsay. A central controversy has been the extent to which these exceptions should dictate the scope of the Confrontation Clause. In the 1980s the Court seemed to have adopted one approach to the issue, only to abandon it some twenty-five years later.

In *Ohio v. Roberts*,[66] the Court held that the determination as to whether hearsay is admissible over a Confrontation Clause objection depends on whether it is "reliable." Reliability was to be presumed if the hearsay was admissible under a "firmly rooted exception" to the hearsay rule. If no such exception applied, the hearsay would still be admissible if the government could show the statement possessed "particularized guarantees of trustworthiness." Thus, for instance, in *United States v. Inadi*,[67] the Court held that the co-conspirator exception to the hearsay rule was "firmly rooted." Similarly, in *White v. Illinois*[68] it concluded that the spontaneous declaration and medical treatment exceptions were well accepted, thus rendering admissible over Confrontation Clause objections a child's statements to her babysitter, her mother, and a police officer shortly after the incident and additional statements made to medical personnel at the hospital. In *Idaho v. Wright*,[69] in contrast, the statements of a 2 ½-year-old girl about her mother and her boyfriend in an abuse case were deemed inadmissible, because they did not fall within a recognized exception (they were not made spontaneously or to obtain medical treatment), and were obtained under circumstances lacking sufficient indicia of trustworthiness (given, among other things, the interviewer's suggestive interview technique).

A quarter century after *Roberts*, however, *Crawford v. Washington*[70] jettisoned the analytical framework established in *Roberts*, specifically rejecting reliability as the focus of Confrontation Clause analysis. Instead, in a 7–2 opinion written by Justice Scalia, the Court held that the Clause is meant to prevent the admission of "testimonial" statements by declarants who are not subject to cross-examination either at the time the statements are made or at trial. Although this rule tends to exclude untrustworthy hearsay, it is based on the separate notion that defendants should be able to confront accusers whose statements are the product of government efforts to garner evidence against them.

---

[65]   156 U.S. 237, 15 S.Ct. 337 (1895).

[66]   448 U.S. 56, 100 S.Ct. 2531 (1980).

[67]   475 U.S. 387, 106 S.Ct. 1121 (1986).

[68]   502 U.S. 346, 112 S.Ct. 736 (1992).

[69]   497 U.S. 805, 110 S.Ct. 3139 (1990).

[70]   541 U.S. 36, 124 S.Ct. 1354 (2004).

The Court arrived at this new rationale for the Confrontation Clause primarily through an historical analysis. Scalia asserted that a primary motivation for adding the Clause to the Sixth Amendment was the desire to avoid the "civil-law" (European) practice of private inquisition by judges, as distinguished from the common law practice of "adversarial testing." In particular, he described the outcry over inquisitional practices associated with several political trials of the sixteenth and seventeenth centuries, including that of Sir Walter Raleigh, who was sentenced to death based on statements made by Lord Cobham to the Privy Council after the government refused to produce Cobham for cross-examination. Scalia also noted the strong preference in the colonies for admitting only those statements that had been subjected to cross-examination, and cited several nineteenth century American cases that had even excluded prior testimony by a witness who *had* been subject to cross-examination by the accused at the time of the testimony.

Pointing out that the Confrontation Clause speaks of "witnesses" against the accused, Scalia then concluded, "[t]he constitutional text, like the history underlying the common-law right of confrontation, . . . reflects an especially acute concern with a specific type of out-of-court statement"—"testimonial" statements. Scalia indicated that such statements are most likely to be found in affidavits, custodial examinations, prior testimony that the defendant was unable to cross-examine, or similar formal pretrial statements that declarants are likely to believe will be used in a subsequent prosecution. Conversely, "[a]n off-hand, overheard remark," although it "might be unreliable evidence and thus a good candidate for exclusion under hearsay rules . . . bears little resemblance to the civil-law abuses the Confrontation Clause targeted." This latter statement would suggest that many types of hearsay statements—including excited utterances, dying declarations, co-conspirator statements, statements in business records and the like—do not implicate the Clause, at least when they are made to someone other than a government investigator. However, this part of the Court's opinion was dictum, because the hearsay at issue in *Crawford*—a statement made during police interrogation—was clearly "testimonial."

Crawford left a number of issues unresolved or only partially resolved. When is an out-of-court statement "testimonial"? Are there any circumstances when testimonial statements may be admitted? And does the Confrontation Clause place any constraints on "non-testimonial" evidence?

(a) The Definition of Testimonial Evidence

Crawford stated that the Confrontation Clause "applies at a minimum to prior testimony at a preliminary hearing, before a grand jury, or at a former trial; and to police interrogations." It then went on to recognize, without choosing between them, three more general definitions of testimonial statements. From least to most expansive they were: (1) "extrajudicial statements . . . contained in formalized testimonial materials, such as affidavits, depositions, prior testimony, or confessions"; (2) "ex parte in-court testimony or its functional equivalent—that is, material such as affidavits, custodial examinations, prior testimony that the defendant was unable to cross-examine, or similar pretrial statements that declarants would reasonably expect to be used prosecutorially"; and (3) "statements that were made under circumstances which would lead an objective witness reasonably to believe that the statement would be available for use at a later trial." The Court's later cases have yet to make clear which, if any, of these definitions apply.

In the companion cases of *Davis v. Washington* and *Hammon v. Indiana*,[71] decided three years after *Crawford*, the Court appeared to move away from the first, most restrictive definition but otherwise did little to clear up the ambiguity. In *Davis*, the hearsay was a transcript of a 911 call in which a woman told the operator she was being beaten by Davis and then provided his full name. In *Hammon*, the hearsay also involved an account of a domestic assault, made by the victim to an officer who had responded to her report of a disturbance while the husband was in another room with another officer. The Court, in an opinion by Justice Scalia, held that the first statement was not testimonial while the second one was, with only Justice Thomas dissenting (and only to the latter holding). According to the Court, statements made under police questioning are testimonial when "the circumstances objectively indicate that . . . the primary purpose of the interrogation is to establish or prove past events potentially relevant to later criminal prosecution." In contrast, "statements are nontestimonial when made in the course of police interrogation under circumstances objectively indicating that the primary purpose of the interrogation is to enable police assistance to meet an ongoing emergency." Under that definition, the statement in *Davis* was nontestimonial, because the woman was describing events as they were happening. In contrast, the statement in *Hammon* "took place some time after the events described were over," while the woman was protected by the police; thus, the primary purpose of the questioning was to establish past events and the statement was testimonial. The Court also indicated that even statements made during emergency assistance, as in *Davis*, can "evolve into testimonial statements once that purpose has been achieved," and noted that once Davis drove from the scene the remainder of the 911 call might have been testimonial.

This last-mentioned dictum in *Davis* and the result in *Hammon* indicate that statements need not constitute a "confession," be recorded, or take place at a hearing to be testimonial. At the same time, *Davis* stated "[w]e do not dispute that formality is indeed essential to testimonial utterance." *Hammon* provides some idea of what this "formality" might involve in its explanation of why, despite the fact that a formal interrogation was involved in *Crawford*, the more casual statements made to the officer in *Hammon* were comparable to those made in *Crawford*,

> Both declarants were actively separated from the defendant. . . . Both statements deliberately recounted, in response to police questioning, how potentially criminal past events began and progressed. And both took place some time after the events described were over. Such statements under official interrogation are an obvious substitute for live testimony, because they do precisely what a witness does on direct examination; they are inherently testimonial.

The Court also indicated that "interrogation" is not essential to formality, stating that "[t]he Framers were no more willing to exempt from cross-examination volunteered testimony or answers to open-ended question than they were to exempt answers to detailed interrogation."

If, on the other hand, the statements are made to someone other than a government employee involved in the investigation, they are much less likely to be testimonial. For instance, in explaining why *White v. Illinois* (described above) was "arguably in tension" with its holding, *Crawford* referred solely to *White's* willingness to admit the victim's

---

[71]   547 U.S. 813, 126 S.Ct. 2266 (2006).

statements to the police officer, ignoring the fact that *White* had also found admissible identical statements to the victim's babysitter and mother, and to a nurse and doctor at the hospital; presumably, therefore, these latter types of statements are not testimonial.[72] Even statements made to government employees who are closely related to the police may not trigger the Confrontation Clause; in *Davis*, the Court only *assumed*, without deciding, that the actions of 911 operators are "acts of the police," in order to make it "unnecessary to consider whether and when statements made to someone other than law enforcement personnel are 'testimonial.'" And in *Crawford*, the Court stated that its earlier decision in *Bourjaily v. United States*,[73] upholding statements made to a co-conspirator who turned out to be a government informant, was consistent with the new regime announced in *Crawford*.

The informant in *Bourjaily*, and perhaps at least some of the non-police inquisitors in *White*, if not the 911 operators in *Davis*, were trying to collect information for potential prosecution. So the key variable to the Court might be the lack of "formality" in these situations. For instance, in *Davis* the Court stated that the "solemnity" necessary to make a statement testimonial is reinforced by the fact that making false statements to a government official is usually a crime. That indicia of solemnity is missing in both the non-police questioning in *White* and the conversations with the informant in *Bourjaily*. But not clear is whether this factor should be dispositive, because in some jurisdictions such a crime occurs *only* when the false statements are made to official police officers.[74]

Lower courts have tended to define the scope of testimonial evidence narrowly. Thus, entries found in business, medical and other types of records,[75] and verbal statements made to co-conspirators,[76] doctors and nurses,[77] and other non-law enforcement personnel[78] have not been considered testimonial. However, the Court's insistence that the Confrontation Clause generally prohibits statements obtained in a formal effort to establish useful investigative facts must be kept in mind. Thus, even business records might contain testimonial statements if they are maintained by the police or other investigative agencies and are prepared in anticipation of prosecution.[79] Statements made to individuals who are officially gathering information for the police, even though they are not police themselves, have also been found to be testimonial.[80] As

---

[72]   *Crawford* did cite with approval the old English decision in *King v. Brasier*, 1 Leach 199, 168 Eng. Rep. 202 (1779), where the court reversed a conviction based on a mother's testimony that her child complained of being raped, but this case might well have been based on the incompetency of the child rather than hearsay concerns.

[73]   479 U.S. 881, 107 S.Ct. 268 (1986).

[74]   See Wis.Stat. § 946.41(2)(b) (applying the obstruction of justice statute only to interference with public employees who have authority to "take another into custody").

[75]   See, e.g., *United States v. Garcia*, 452 F.3d 36 (1st Cir. 2006) (warrants of deportation signed by an immigration official who witnessed the deportation are not testimonial); *United States v. Weiland*, 420 F.3d 1062 (9th Cir. 2005) (record of state court convictions certified for defendant's litigation are not testimonial); *United States v. Jamieson*, 427 F.3d 394 (6th Cir. 2005) (business records, including medical records and insurance applications, are not testimonial).

[76]   See, e.g., *United States v. Underwood*, 446 F.3d 1340 (11th Cir. 2006).

[77]   See, e.g., *United Sates v. Peneaux*, 432 F.3d 882 (8th Cir. 2005).

[78]   See, e.g., *United States v. Franklin*, 415 F.3d 537 (6th Cir. 2005)(statement to a friend used against declarant and co-defendant).

[79]   See *State v. Campbell*, 719 N.W.2d 374, 377 n.1 (N.D. 2006) (citing differing judicial views on whether lab reports are testimonial).

[80]   See *United States v. Bordeaux*, 400 F.3d 548 (8th Cir. 2005) (statements given to "forensic interviewer" who is "collecting information for law enforcement" are testimonial). Note also that *Crawford* did

Davis suggests, even "excited utterances" may be testimonial once the police have arrived or the alleged perpetrator is gone.

The Supreme Court confirmed that these latter types of outcomes are usually correct in *Melendez-Diaz v. Massachusetts*,[81] which involved the admissibility of notarized forensic laboratory test results that asserted the substance found in the defendant's possession was cocaine. Justice Scalia, writing for a five-member majority, found that the affidavits were testimonial under *Crawford* because they were "made under circumstances which would lead an objective witness reasonably to believe that the statement would be available for use at a later trial;" in fact "the *sole purpose* of the affidavits was to provide 'prima facie evidence of the composition, quality, and the net weight' of the analyzed substance." The majority rejected a number of objections to this ruling. Because the Confrontation Clause requires that the accused be confronted with the witnesses "against" him, the Court reasoned, prosecution evidence that is created in preparation for trial is testimonial even if it is not "accusatory," is created well after the crime, and provides only a small part of the case against the defendant; nor does the fact it does not involve observations of human actions or can be characterized as neutral or scientific in nature necessarily make it non-testimonial.

The Court also concluded that there is no business or official records exception to the Confrontation Clause's prohibition. While information that is "created for the administration of an entity's affairs and not for the purpose of establishing or proving some fact at trial" is not testimonial, the lab results here clearly were produced for that purpose and thus were testimonial despite the fact they could be described as part of a record kept in the normal course of business. Finally, Justice Scalia dismissed the dissent's concern that the majority's rule would seriously burden government, noting that several states had already adopted the rule and had not suffered serious consequences, in part because so many cases are plea bargained or involve situations in which the defense will not want to contest the drug tests.

Melendez-Diaz was affirmed by the same five-member majority in *Bullcoming v. New Mexico*.[82] Unlike in *Melendez-Diaz*, in *Bullcoming* the state proffered an expert. But because the expert had not conducted the blood test himself, the Court held that the Confrontation Clause was violated. As Justice Ginsburg noted for the Court, the original analyst could have testified about chain of custody issues, the extent to which he adhered to the testing protocol, and why he was unavailable for trial (apparently he had been placed on unpaid leave). Justice Kennedy's dissent pointed out that the original analyst was not likely to remember the particular test in question, and that protocol issues could have been answered by the expert who was present. But Ginsburg reiterated *Crawford's* statement that the text of the Sixth Amendment does not recognize exceptions to the confrontation requirement and thus "does not tolerate dispensing with confrontation simply because the court believes that questioning one witness about another's testimonial statements provides a fair enough opportunity for cross-examination."

In its next case involving expert testimony, however, the Court backtracked from this broad statement, and in the course of doing so created considerable confusion about

---

not question the holding in *Idaho v. Wright* (which excluded statements made to a pediatrician selected by the police).

[81]   557 U.S. 305, 129 S.Ct. 2527 (2009).

[82]   564 U.S. 647, 131 S.Ct. 2705 (2011).

what *Crawford* means. In *Williams v. Illinois*,[83] a forensic specialist for the state lab named Lambatos testified that she had matched a DNA profile of Williams' blood produced by her lab with a profile of semen taken from a rape victim produced by an independent laboratory named Cellmark. No one from Cellmark testified.

Four members of the Court concluded that Lambatos' testimony did not violate the Confrontation Clause, on two different grounds. First, Justice Alito wrote for the plurality, Lambatos' core testimony was that Cellmark's profile and her test of Williams' blood matched; her further statement, in answer to a question from the prosecutor, that the profile was the victim's (a fact corroborated by other proof) was incidental to her testimony and not offered for the truth of the matter asserted. As detailed below,[84] the Court has held that the admission of non-hearsay, even if testimonial, does not violate the Confrontation Clause.

However, both the four dissenters and Justice Thomas, the fifth vote for the result in *Williams*, concluded that Lambatos' testimony would not be relevant to William's guilt without assuming that the Cellmark profile was in fact taken from the victim. Thus Justice Alito's second ground for finding for the state is more important. Even if the testimony about Cellmark's report was hearsay, Justice Alito stated, its introduction did not violate the Confrontation Clause because, in contrast to the test results described by the testimony in *Melendez-Diaz* and *Bullcoming*, it was not "the equivalent of affidavits made for the purpose of proving a particular criminal defendant's guilt." At the time Cellmark's profile was created, the goal was to catch a dangerous rapist who was still at large, not develop a case against Williams, who was not suspected by the police or anyone at Cellmark at the time. Thus, Justice Alito concluded, there was no "prospect of fabrication"; the Cellmark technicians had no incentive to manipulate the testing procedures, especially since they knew that defects in a DNA profile can be detected.

While these latter points support the conclusion that the Cellmark profile was likely to be accurate, that conclusion resonates more with *Roberts* than with *Crawford*. Justice Breyer, who was part of the plurality but wrote a separate concurring opinion, carried this idea further by arguing that DNA profiles like those involved in *Williams* should "lie outside the perimeter of the Clause" unless the defendant can call into question the laboratory's competence, the validity of its accreditation or the existence of a motive to falsify. He also noted that the defense could always call the lab technician as a witness. The dissent, written by Justice Kagan, vigorously contested this approach, iterating the statements in *Melendez-Diaz* and *Bullcoming* that "it's not up to us to decide, ex ante, what evidence is trustworthy and what is not" and that cross-examination of lab technicians the prosecution proffers is the preferable manner of exposing the numerous ways in which test results might be suspect.

The lineup of justices in *Williams* meant that Justice Thomas' opinion—agreeing with the plurality's result but also agreeing with the dissent that the Cellmark testimony was hearsay and that reliability is no longer the Sixth Amendment test—could be deemed controlling. Justice Thomas, alone among the justices, concluded that the Cellmark report was not testimonial because it was not a "solemn declaration or affirmation made for the purpose of establishing or proving some fact" akin to "prior testimony, affidavits, or statements resulting from 'formalized dialogue' such as

---

[83]   567 U.S. 50, 132 S.Ct. 2221 (2012).

[84]   See § 28.04(b)(4).

custodial interrogation." He asserted that, while the reports in *Melendez-Diaz* and *Bullcoming* were formal certifications by the laboratories involved, the report in Cellmark "certified nothing." The dissenters seem more on the mark however, in stating that the distinction between the "certificate" in *Melendez-Diaz* and the "report of laboratory examination" in *Williams* is so slight that it should not be given "constitutional dimension," especially since that approach would provide an incentive for state officials to avoid the certificate label.

The outcome in *Williams* leaves confrontation analysis in disarray. It is not clear the extent to which the definition of testimonial depends on whether the statement is hearsay, reliable, formal or made for the purpose of proving a particular defendant's guilt. However, based on the various opinions in *Williams*, if the latter test is met probably eight justices would agree that the statement is testimonial.

Unfortunately, considerable disagreement also exists about how the purpose test should be applied, as demonstrated by *Michigan v. Bryant*,[85] decided a year before *Williams*, and involving a lay, rather than expert, witness. In *Bryant*, the hearsay statements came from a shooting victim, who claimed Bryant had shot him twenty-five minutes earlier from the back door of Bryant's house six blocks away; the declarant was unavailable for trial because he died from his wounds soon after being taken to the hospital. Applying the test in *Davis*, the Michigan Supreme Court held that the declarant's statements were testimonial because they were made with the "primary purpose" of establishing who shot the declarant rather than of enabling the police "to meet an ongoing emergency." A five-member majority of the Court voted to reverse, on the ground that the statements were made primarily for the latter purpose.[86] Justice Sotomayor wrote for the majority that nothing in the declarant's dialogue with the police indicated either that the threat from the shooter had ended or that it was confined to him. Further, the questions the police asked about who did the shooting and where it took place "were the exact type of questions necessary to 'assess the situation, the threat to their own safety, and possible danger to the potential victim' and to the public."

In dissent, Justice Scalia argued that, since the declarant knew the shooting was "the work of a drug dealer" and was surrounded by five police officers when he made his statements, his purpose in talking to the police was to identify his assailant, not provide information about an imminent threat to himself or others. Justice Scalia equated the declarant's statements and the interview by the police with the testimony of a witness being questioned by a prosecutor at trial. He also took the majority to task for its analogy between *Davis'* emergency exception and evidence law's willingness to consider excited utterances reliable hearsay, as well as for its even broader statement that, in implementing *Davis'* primary purpose rule, "standard rules of hearsay [like the excited utterance rule], designed to identify some statements as reliable, will be relevant." To Scalia, these aspects of the majority opinion were reminiscent of *Ohio v. Roberts* and suggested the majority's intent to overrule *Crawford*. Although the latter step is unlikely, the majority's analysis of the facts of *Bryant* does indicate, at the least, a willingness to interpret *Davis'* emergency exception expansively.

---

[85]   562 U.S. 344, 131 S.Ct. 1143 (2011).

[86]   Justice Thomas concurred on the ground that the declarant's statements "lacked sufficient formality and solemnity" to be considered testimonial and Justice Kagan took no part in the decision.

Further evidence of this willingness came in *Ohio v. Clark*.[87] There the prosecution introduced statements from a three year-old in a child abuse prosecution. The seven-member majority concluded, in an opinion written by Justice Alito, that these statements were not testimonial because they were obtained by teachers, not law enforcement personnel, in the context of an "ongoing emergency . . . aimed at identifying and ending a threat." Further, the declarant's purpose in making the statements was not to provide evidence for prosecution, and in fact a 3 year-old is unlikely ever to be able to form such a purpose. While the majority reiterated that the test for determining whether a statement is testimonial is whether "it was given with the '*primary* purpose of creating an out-of-court substitute for trial testimony,' " Justice Scalia, in concurrence, castigated the majority for implying that purposefulness was not *always* a sufficient condition for making a statement testimonial.

However, all nine justices agreed that the child's hearsay statements were admissible, that the test should be the same whether the statements are made to private actors or state actors, and that the fact that the teachers were required by law to report evidence of abuse to the authorities was irrelevant to the analysis. These conclusions of the full Court raise significant concerns. As the defendant pointed out, the state had prevailed upon the trial court to declare the three year-old incompetent to testify, which meant he could not be cross-examined, but at the same time was able to introduce his testimony via hearsay. Furthermore, like many states, Ohio requires teachers to report suspected abuse to the authorities, so that even if neither the child's nor the teacher's "primary" purpose is to gather evidence, such evidence will virtually always be produced, a fact that teachers and other mandated reporters surely know. Finally, if the Court eventually decides that the sole focus is the *declarant's* purpose, the Court's assertion that young children are unlikely to be thinking of prosecution when they talk suggests that even statements they make to a government-employed interviewer would not trigger the Confrontation Clause. The result is that the Clause may allow introduction of extremely unreliable hearsay. While this result is not inconsistent with *Crawford's* turn away from reliability concerns, it creates significant potential for prosecutorial manipulation of evidence in child molestation cases, which ought to be a concern under the Confrontation Clause.

(b) When Testimonial Evidence Is Admissible

Crawford made clear that out-of-court testimonial statements are presumptively inadmissible. But it recognized four exceptions to this rule—when the maker of statement is unavailable despite the diligent efforts of the prosecution and was subjected to cross-examination at the time the statement was made; where the maker of the statement is unavailable because of misconduct by the defendant; where the maker of the statement is available at trial and the defendant is afforded the opportunity to cross-examine her about the statement; and where the statements are not introduced to prove the truth of the matter they assert. *Crawford* also indicated a fifth possible exception might exist in the case of dying declarations.

(1) Unavailability and Cross-Examination

Crawford summarized previous caselaw as follows: "Testimonial statements of witnesses absent from trial have been admitted only where the declarant is unavailable,

---

[87]   ___ U.S. ___, 135 S.Ct. 2173 (2015).

and only where the defendant has had a prior opportunity to cross-examine." A declarant might be legitimately "unavailable" for courtroom testimony for a number of reasons. One obvious such reason, recognized in *Mattox*, is the death of the declarant prior to trial. The Court has also held that a declarant becomes unavailable for Confrontation Clause purposes when she permanently transfers to a foreign country,[88] cannot be located after a diligent search by the prosecution,[89] validly asserts the Fifth Amendment,[90] or suffers a loss of memory.[91]

According to *Mattox*, the requirement of unavailability as a predicate for admission of out-of-court statements is based on "the necessities of the case, and to prevent a manifest failure of justice." The Court continued:

> [t]he primary object of the [Confrontation Clause] was to prevent depositions or ex parte affidavits, such as were sometimes admitted in civil cases, being used against the prisoner in lieu of a personal examination and cross-examination of the witness in which the accused has an opportunity, not only of testing the recollection and sifting the conscience of the witness, but of compelling him to stand and face the jury in order that they may look at him, and judge by his demeanor upon the stand and the manner in which he gives his testimony whether he is worthy of belief.

Five years later, in *Motes v. United States*,[92] the Court was even more direct, stating that it was inconsistent with the Confrontation Clause "to permit the deposition or statement of an absent witness (taken at an examining trial) to be read at the final trial when it does not appear that the witness was absent by the suggestion, connivance, or procurement of the accused, but does appear that this absence was due to the negligence of the prosecution."

Prosecutorial negligence was apparent in *Motes*, where the witness, who had been in jail, was for some reason released after trial commenced and put in the care of another witness, and did not appear when called even though he had been seen in the courthouse earlier that day. Another case finding such negligence was *Barber v. Page*,[93] where a unanimous Court held that failure to produce a declarant who was in federal prison at the time of the petitioner's trial on state criminal charges violated the Clause. While admitting that the federal authorities had discretion to deny the witness's release for a state trial, the Court noted that the state had not even forwarded a request for his presence. It concluded that "a witness is not 'unavailable' for purposes of the [prior testimony] exception to the confrontation requirement unless the prosecutorial authorities have made a good-faith effort to obtain his presence at trial." In contrast, in *Ohio v. Roberts*,[94] in a part of the opinion unaffected by *Crawford*, the Court held that the declarant's absence was not the prosecution's fault where the prosecution showed

---

[88]   *Mancusi v. Stubbs,* 408 U.S. 204, 92 S.Ct. 2308 (1972).

[89]   *Ohio v. Roberts,* 448 U.S. 56, 100 S.Ct. 2531 (1980). For an example of a witness search that the Court deemed diligent, see *Hardy v. Cross,* 565 U.S. 65, 132 S.Ct. 490 (2011) (state made "constant personal visits" to the last known residence of the witness as well as the home of the witness' father, telephoned family members, and checked hospitals, correctional facilities and the victim's school, among many other places).

[90]   *Lilly v. Virginia,* 527 U.S. 116, 119 S.Ct. 1887 (1999).

[91]   *California v. Green,* 399 U.S. 149, 90 S.Ct. 1930 (1970). See also, *Idaho v. Wright,* 497 U.S. 805, 110 S.Ct. 3139 (1990) (recognizing that incompetency of witness makes her unavailable).

[92]   178 U.S. 458, 20 S.Ct. 993 (1900).

[93]   390 U.S. 719, 88 S.Ct. 1318 (1968).

[94]   448 U.S. 56, 100 S.Ct. 2531 (1980).

that the witness' last contact with her family was by phone several months before trial, during which the witness said she was "travelling" and did not reveal her whereabouts.

Proving the unavailability of the declarant is not enough to overcome a Confrontation Clause objection, however. In *Crawford*, the Court emphasized that "prior opportunity to cross-examine" is a "necessary" condition for admitting such statements. Thus, in *Barber* and a number of other cases,[95] the Court held that even testimony taken at a judicial proceeding is inadmissible if it is not subject to cross-examination (because, for instance, the defendant did not have counsel at the time).

However, as the language in *Crawford* suggests, all that is required is an *opportunity* to cross-examine the declarant, a principle firmly established in earlier cases. *California v. Green*[96] was the first decision to make this point explicit, concluding that preliminary hearing testimony can be admitted even it is not subjected to cross examination, as long as both defense counsel and the declarant are present and counsel is not prevented from cross-examining the witness. In dissent, Justice Brennan argued that, unlike the prior *trial* testimony involved in *Mattox,* the defense might not want or be permitted to cross-examine preliminary hearing testimony aggressively.[97]

Since *Green* involved a declarant who was present at trial but was "unavailable" because of a memory loss, its relaxed standard could have been attributable to the fact that the declarant could be subjected to at least some cross-examination at trial. But in *Roberts* the Court held that pretrial testimony may also be used when a witness is *physically* unavailable at trial so long as there was an opportunity to cross-examine at the pretrial hearing. In *Roberts,* the Court found this latter requirement met even though the *defense* had called the declarant as a witness at the preliminary hearing, because defense counsel had been allowed to ask several leading questions during the hearing.

If the state fails to afford the defendant even the opportunity to cross-examine a testimonial statement made by an unavailable witness, it must be excluded.[98] A pre-*Crawford* case illustrates the import of this rule, although it was decided under *Roberts'* reliability framework. In *Lilly v. Virginia,*[99] the prosecution sought to introduce against Lilly a co-defendant's confession implicating both the co-defendant and Lilly. The trial court permitted, and the Virginia Supreme Court upheld, use of this evidence on the ground that the confession was a declaration against penal interest by the co-defendant. The Virginia Supreme also held that this exception was "firmly rooted," thus, under *Roberts*, establishing a presumption that admission did not violate the Confrontation Clause.

The Supreme Court reversed. Noting that a number of lower court decisions had expressed hesitance in applying the declaration against interest exception to declarations that also inculpate a third party, and that the Court itself had viewed this application of the exception with some suspicion (because of the obvious benefits, in terms of minimizing blame and obtaining deals from the prosecution, that a statement

---

[95]   *Pointer v. Texas*, 380 U.S. 400, 85 S.Ct. 1065 (1965); *Roberts v. Russell*, 392 U.S. 293, 88 S.Ct. 1921 (1968) (per curiam).

[96]   399 U.S. 149, 90 S.Ct. 1930 (1970).

[97]   See § 22.04(c) for a discussion of the scope of cross-examination at the preliminary hearing.

[98]   Unless, as discussed below, forfeiture is involved.

[99]   527 U.S. 116, 119 S.Ct. 1887 (1999).

inculpating others can bring to the maker of the statement),[100] four members of the Supreme Court held that the Virginia court's application of the exception to statements made in custody about third parties was not firmly rooted for purposes of the Confrontation Clause.[101] For present purposes, however, the most important aspect of *Lilly* is Justice Scalia's concurring opinion. Presaging *Crawford*, Justice Scalia joined the result but refused to endorse the majority's reliability analysis. Rather, he concurred on the ground that using the co-defendant's statements against Lilly without making the co-defendant available for cross-examination was "a paradigmatic Confrontation Clause violation."

And so it is, as *Crawford* defined such violations. Under *Crawford's* framework, the co-defendant's confession in *Lilly* was testimonial because it was made to a police officer during interrogation, and was not subject to cross-examination by the defendant either during the interrogation or at trial (where the co-defendant invoked the Fifth Amendment). As *Crawford* later put it, *Lilly* "excluded testimonial statements that the defendant had no opportunity to test by cross-examination."

(2) Forfeiture

When a declarant's unavailability is due to the defendant rather than prosecutorial negligence or one of the other legitimate grounds for unavailability given above, his hearsay statements may be admissible even when not subject to cross-examination. As the Court indicated in *Motes*, a witness' absence due to the "suggestion, connivance, or procurement of the accused" results in a forfeiture of confrontation rights. *Crawford* made clear that it left this part of confrontation analysis unchanged.

Davis and *Hammon*, both of which involved domestic violence, raised this issue more directly. Although *Hammon* found that the statement made to the police officer in that case was testimonial, it cautioned that the statement should be excluded only in the absence of a finding of "forfeiture by wrongdoing," which it noted might be particularly likely to occur in domestic violence cases. The Court also stated that generally the government must show forfeiture by a preponderance of the evidence.[102]

The issue of forfeiture is most likely to arise when the defendant has killed the declarant. A number of courts at one time held that hearsay from the victim is automatically admissible in this situation.[103] In *Giles v. California*,[104] however, the Court, in an opinion by Justice Scalia, rejected this view. Noting that no decision before 1985 had endorsed this definition of forfeiture, the Court instead required the state to show that the murder was motivated by a desire to prevent the victim from testifying against the defendant. In dissent, Justice Breyer, joined by Justices Stevens and

---

[100] See, e.g., *Crawford v. United States*, 212 U.S. 183, 29 S.Ct. 260 (1909); *Douglas v. Alabama*, 380 U.S. 415, 85 S.Ct. 1074 (1965); *Lee v. Illinois*, 476 U.S. 530, 106 S.Ct. 2056 (1986). In *Williamson v. United States*, 512 U.S. 594, 114 S.Ct. 2431 (1994), the Court, without addressing the Confrontation Clause issue, held that the declaration against penal interest provision found in the federal rules of evidence permits use only of self-inculpatory statements, not statements that inculpate a third party, are exculpatory, or are neutral as to interest.

[101] The plurality opinion went on to analyze, as required by *Roberts*, whether the statement was lacking in indicia of reliability, and concluded that it was, for the types of reasons given in the text, as well as the facts that the co-defendant was drunk at the time of the interrogation and was asked leading questions throughout it.

[102] See Fed.R.Ev. 804(b)(6); *United States v. Scott*, 284 F.3d 758, 762 (7th Cir. 2002).

[103] See *Gonzalez v. State*, 195 S.W.3d 114 (Tex.Crim.App. 2006) (collecting cases).

[104] 554 U.S. 353, 128 S.Ct. 2678 (2008).

Kennedy, asserted that the majority had misread pre-1985 precedent. While acknowledging that this precedent did not automatically admit a murdered victim's hearsay, Breyer also asserted that these cases required only that the state demonstrate the defendant was aware, rather than intended, that the killing would prevent the victim's testimony. This rule also made sense, Breyer contended, because of the difficulty of proving a more specific motive and the likelihood that a large number of such cases involve domestic battering situations where the motivation behind the killing is often highly ambiguous. In response to this last point, the majority opinion, echoed by Justice Souter's concurring opinion (which was joined by Justice Ginsburg), emphasized that "[e]arlier abuse, or threats of abuse, intended to dissuade the victim from resorting to outside help would be highly relevant to th[e forfeiture] inquiry, as would evidence of ongoing criminal proceedings at which the victim would have been expected to testify." Note also that many hearsay statements by victims in such cases are not testimonial (because made to civilians or to police in a *Davis*-type situation), and thus are admissible over Confrontation Clause objections in any event.[105]

(3) *Declarant Is Available*

If the declarant is available for cross-examination, the Confrontation Clause does not bar the declarant's out-of-court statements even if they are testimonial. As *Crawford* emphasized, "when the declarant appears for cross-examination at trial, the Confrontation Cause places no constraints at all on the use of his prior testimonial statement."

This language suggests that, to take advantage of this exception, the *prosecution* is required to present the witness who made the out-of-court statement. But suppose the witness is "available" to the defendant via subpoena? The Compulsory Process Clause permits the defendant to subpoena witnesses and have them declared "hostile" so that cross-examination may take place.[106] Some lower courts have held post-*Crawford*,[107] and at least one Supreme Court case suggested pre-*Crawford*,[108] that in some circumstances that right of the defendant is sufficient for Confrontation Clause purposes.

This approach creates several problems, however. First, it allows the prosecution to put the burden, financial and otherwise, on the defendant to produce the witnesses against her. Second, it puts the defense in the difficult tactical situation of deciding whether it wants to cross-examine the declarant before it has heard her direct testimony. Finally, it allows the prosecution to place the defendant in this tactical quandary any time it is not sure the live testimony will be as favorable to the state as the hearsay testimony. As an illustration of the last two points, assume that a child who makes statements to a police officer exhibits confusion about the alleged criminal incident subsequent to her initial hearsay statements. If this child were considered "present for cross-examination" so long as she could be subpoenaed by the defense, the prosecution could decide to present only the latter statements, in the hopes that the defense, unaware

---

[105] Indeed, both Justice Thomas and Justice Alito wrote opinions in *Giles* asserting that the hearsay statement in this case—made by the eventual decedent to a police officer responding to a domestic violence call three weeks before her murder—was nontestimonial.

[106] See § 28.06(b) for further discussion of this aspect of the Compulsory Process Clause.

[107] See, e.g., *State v. Campbell*, 719 N.W.2d 374 (N.D. 2006) (defendant's failure to subpoena forensic lab scientists was a waiver of confrontation right).

[108] *United States v. Inadi*, 475 U.S. 387, 106 S.Ct. 1121 (1986).

of the confusion,[109] will refrain from calling a witness who might merely repeat the content of the statements on the stand.

If the declarant is present for cross-examination however that concept is defined, then, *Crawford* states, any of her prior testimonial statements are admissible. Here *Crawford* was merely reiterating precedent. The first case to contemplate this conclusion was *California v. Green,*[110] which involved not only the admissibility of prior testimony (discussed earlier), but also the admissibility of prior out-of-court statements made to a police officer by the same witness. The witness appeared at trial, but, in the words of the lower court, proved to be "markedly evasive and uncooperative on the stand" and claimed a loss of memory about the event. Although the witness' hearsay statements to the police could not be introduced under the prior testimony rule because they had not been subject to cross-examination, the majority suggested that they might nonetheless be admissible; it noted that neither the lower courts nor the parties had addressed whether the witness' "apparent lapse of memory so affected Green's right to cross-examine [at trial] as to make a critical difference in the application of the Confrontation Clause." And Justice Harlan, in his concurring opinion, stated outright that, if a witness is subject to cross-examination at trial, his out-of-court statement should not be barred merely because he is unable to "recall either the underlying events that are the subject of an extra-judicial statement or previous testimony or recollect the circumstances under which the statement was given."

In *United States v. Owens,*[111] the issue discussed in *Green* was directly confronted. There the victim of an assault, one Foster, could remember very little about the assault, or the conditions under which he made a pretrial statement about it to an FBI agent, because of head injuries suffered during the incident. In holding that Foster's pretrial statement, which implicated the defendant in the assault, was admissible, the Court followed Justice Harlan's reasoning in *Green.* Justice Scalia, writing for a six-member majority, reiterated that the Confrontation Clause guarantees only the opportunity to cross-examine witnesses, not the right to an effective cross-examination. Here, that opportunity was afforded. During defense counsel's examination, Scalia noted, Foster had admitted that he could not remember: (1) seeing his assailant; (2) having visitors at the hospital other than the FBI agent (although he had had several other visitors); (3) hearing anyone suggest to him that the defendant was the assailant; or (4) attributing the assault to someone other than the defendant, as one hospital record suggested he had. Justice Brennan in dissent pointed out that none of this allowed the jury to evaluate the trustworthiness or reliability of the pretrial identification of the defendant as the assailant; neither Foster's perception at the time of the offense nor his memory of the offense at the time of his statement to the agent could be explored because he simply could not remember either event. But, presaging his rejection of *Roberts* in *Crawford,* Scalia discounted the contention that the Confrontation Clause requires hearsay such as this to be examined for "indicia of reliability" or "particularized guarantees of trustworthiness." Echoing the Court's opinion in *Green* with respect to the admissibility of pretrial testimony, Scalia stated: "the traditional protections of the oath, cross-

---

[109] Only if the confusion rises to a recantation that the prosecutor, in her judgment, considers "exculpatory," need it be revealed to the defense. See § 24.04(b).

[110] 399 U.S. 149, 90 S.Ct. 1930 (1970).

[111] 484 U.S. 554, 108 S.Ct. 838 (1988).

examination, and opportunity for the jury to observe the witness's demeanor satisfy the constitutional requirements."

It should be noted, however, that the declarant in *Owens* was "competent" and able to remember making the hearsay statements (although not able to remember their content). These facts might pose important limitations on the admissibility of hearsay by a declarant who is physically "available" to be cross-examined but is experiencing mental impairments of a more serious nature.

(4) *Non-Hearsay Use*

Crawford also reaffirmed *Tennessee v. Street*,[112] where the defendant claimed that his confession was entitled to no weight because it was a coerced imitation of his accomplice's confession. To rebut this claim, the state called the sheriff to read the accomplice's confession to the jury, which was significantly different than the defendant's. The judge allowed the confession to be read, instructing the jury that it was to be considered only to rebut the defendant's imitation claim, not prove the truth of its contents (which implicated the defendant). A unanimous Court upheld this ruling, pointing out that the accomplice's confession was introduced for the nonhearsay purpose of comparing the confessions and proving the defendant's confession was not coerced; accordingly, cross-examination of the alleged accomplice would serve no purpose.

(5) *Dying Declarations*

Mattox recognized in dictum that the "dying declaration" of a witness is admissible over a Confrontation Clause objection. Most such declarations, made at or near the time of death, are non-testimonial. But in a footnote the *Crawford* Court admitted that under the common law such statements were admissible even when made to police officers. Given the historical approach taken in *Crawford*, the Court might thus ultimately feel compelled to permit such statements to be introduced. But, Scalia stated in *Crawford*, "[i]f this exception must be accepted on historical grounds, it is *sui generis*."

(c) When Nontestimonial Evidence Is Admissible

Crawford stated that "where nontestimonial hearsay is at issue, it is wholly consistent with the Framers' design to afford the States flexibility in their development of hearsay law—as does *Roberts*, and as would an approach that exempted such statements from Confrontation Clause scrutiny altogether." Thus, the Court left unclear whether the admissibility of nontestimonial evidence is governed by *Roberts'* reliability analysis or is outside the reach of the Clause. In *Davis*, the Court appeared to elect the latter path. There it stated that "[i]t is the testimonial character of the statement that separates it from other hearsay that, while subject to traditional limitations upon hearsay evidence, is not subject to the Confrontation Clause." Later in the opinion, after repeating the Confrontation Clause's language guaranteeing confrontation of witnesses against the accused, the Court stated: "A limitation so clearly reflected in the text of the constitutional provision must fairly be said to mark out not merely its core, but its perimeter."

In short, *Roberts* and the cases applying its reliability analysis are probably a dead letter. If out-of-court statements are testimonial and introduced to prove the truth of the matter asserted therein, then they are inadmissible unless they were subject to cross-

---

[112]   471 U.S. 409, 105 S.Ct. 2078 (1985).

examination, the declarant is unavailable because of defendant misconduct, or the declarant is available at trial. If they are nontestimonial, their admissibility will likely depend solely on the jurisdiction's rules of evidence and other constitutional doctrines. It is also possible, however, that the Court will eventually decide that nontestimonial evidence is also inadmissible if the declarant is available to testify.[113]

(d) Co-Defendant Confessions

A special type of confrontation case occurs when two or more co-defendants are tried together and the prosecution seeks to convict one of them by introducing his out-of-court stationhouse confession, which also happens to implicate one or more of the co-defendants. If, as is often the case, the maker of the statement refuses to testify (as is his right under the Fifth Amendment),[114] the other defendant or defendants have no "opportunity to cross-examine" him about the confession. *Crawford* affirmed that, in this situation, the confession is inadmissible against the other defendants.

When first confronted with this prosecutorial practice in the 1957 case of *Delli Paoli v. United States,*[115] the Court found no constitutional infirmity, provided that the jury is given a precautionary instruction directing it to consider the confession as evidence only against the defendant who made it. But eleven years later *Delli Paoli* was overruled in *Bruton v. United States.*[116] There, the Court concluded that the jury could not be expected to follow a precautionary instruction of the type mandated in *Delli Paoli,* and that, in any event, the infringement on the defendant's right of confrontation could not be cured by such an instruction.

The *Bruton* majority apparently contemplated that the prosecutor who wishes to use a confession implicating more than one defendant would have to try the defendants separately. Although Justice White argued in dissent that this solution would place a significant burden on witnesses, prosecutors and courts, it is not clear that this is so: if the confessing defendant is tried first and convicted (and thus no longer able to claim the Fifth Amendment), the second defendant, if really guilty, will often see the advantage of pleading to the charge rather than going to a trial at which the first defendant testifies.

Nonetheless, resistance to the severance option persisted. Two other solutions to the "*Bruton* problem," of questionable worth,[117] include bifurcated trials, in which the defendants are tried jointly but a verdict is reached with respect to the non-confessing defendant before the confession is introduced, and multiple trials, in which a separate jury is selected for each defendant and the jury for the non-confessing defendant does not hear the confession. Since *Bruton,* the Court has indicated that there are three other possible solutions to the *Bruton* problem. The first two probably survive *Crawford;* the third—involving "interlocking confessions"—does not.[118]

---

[113] For an argument, based on textual analysis, history and policy, that the Confrontation Clause bars non-testimonial hearsay unless the declarant is unavailable, see Jeffrey Bellin, *The Incredible Shrinking Confrontation Clause*, 92 B.U. L. Rev. 1865 (2012).

[114] See § 28.03(c).

[115] 352 U.S. 232, 77 S.Ct. 294 (1957).

[116] 391 U.S. 123, 88 S.Ct. 1620 (1968). See also, *Douglas v. Alabama,* 380 U.S. 415, 85 S.Ct. 1074 (1965).

[117] See Alex A. Gaynes, *Two Juries/One Trial: Panacea of Judicial Economy or Personification of Murphy's Law?* 5 Am.J.Trial Advoc. 285 (1981).

[118] A fourth situation, involving use of a co-defendant's confession for non-hearsay purposes, was discussed in § 28.04(b)(4).

(1) Redaction

In his *Bruton* dissent, Justice White noted that one alternative to severance was to avoid all references to defendants other than the maker by either deleting them (if the confession is in writing) or prohibiting the relevant testimony (if the statement is described by a witness). He also pointed out that this option would normally be of limited use, since very often the remaining segments of the confession will either make no sense or strongly suggest the participation of another individual, who the factfinder is likely to suspect is a co-defendant in the courtroom.

Nonetheless, in *Richardson v. Marsh,*[119] the Court sanctioned this practice so long as a proper limiting instruction is given and the confession is redacted to eliminate not only the defendant's name but any reference to his existence. Justice Scalia, writing for the Court, admitted that members of the jury hearing such a confession might have difficulty obeying an instruction to disregard its possible inferences about the defendant, but "there does not exist the overwhelming probability of their inability to do so that is the foundation of *Bruton's* exception to the general rule."

The three dissenters disagreed with this conclusion, supporting their position by pointing to the facts of *Marsh,* which involved a prosecution for assault and murder, committed in the course of a robbery. The redacted confession in *Marsh* described a conversation between Marsh's two co-defendants that took place in a car on the way to the scene of the robbery and murder. During the conversation, one of the co-defendants stated that the victims would have to be killed after the robbery. Although the confession did not mention Marsh, other trial evidence made clear she was in the car with the two co-defendants at the time of this conversation. Thus, the jury was sure to infer that Marsh knew about the plans to commit murder unless she could show she did not hear the conversation. Although she so testified (apparently stating that she was in the backseat and that the radio was on), she was prevented from questioning the two co-defendants as to whether they thought she had heard their conversation because they refused to testify.

Marsh did not provide much guidance as to how redaction is to be carried out. In *Gray v. Maryland,*[120] the Court held that editing a co-defendant's confession simply by replacing inculpatory references to the defendant with a blank space or the word "deleted" is not adequate for purposes of the Sixth Amendment. In an opinion by Justice Breyer, five members of the Court concluded that such a confession "so closely resemble[s] *Bruton's* unredacted statements that . . . the law must require the same result [as in *Bruton*]." Jurors are likely to assume that the blank refers to the defendant, Breyer reasoned, because the blank will indicate the existence of a co-defendant and the prosecution will be arguing the defendant helped perpetrate the crime; additionally, instructions that tell the jury not to consider the confession as evidence against the defendant might ironically make clear the blank refers to him. To illustrate a more appropriate redaction, Breyer used the confession transcript at issue in *Gray*: the co-defendant's response to the question about who was in the group that committed the crime, Breyer suggested, should have been changed from "Me, deleted, deleted, and a few other guys" to "Me and a few other guys."

---

[119]   481 U.S. 200, 107 S.Ct. 1702 (1987).

[120]   523 U.S. 185, 118 S.Ct. 1151 (1998).

The four dissenters, in an opinion by Justice Scalia, agreed that the redaction in *Gray* was more likely to incriminate the defendant than a confession that omitted any reference to the defendant's existence, but asserted that *Bruton* only prohibited "powerfully incriminating" confessions and that the redacted confession in *Gray* did not qualify as such. Furthermore, Scalia noted, attempts to omit references to the existence of the defendant would often require changing the meaning of the confession, or even render it nonsensical (as in a conspiracy case, where the confession states that "[Defendant] and I agreed to . . ."). Concluded Scalia, "[t]he risk to the integrity of our system (not to mention the increase in its complexity) posed by the approval of such free-lance editing seems to me infinitely greater than the risk posed by the entirely honest reproduction that the Court disapproves."

(2) Testimony by the Maker of the Confession

Not surprisingly, given the confrontation basis of *Bruton*, the Court has found that *Bruton* is not controlling when the confessing defendant takes the stand and denies the inculpatory admission. The majority in *Nelson v. O'Neil*[121] concluded that the opportunity to cross-examine the declarant at trial, at least when he repudiates the confession, sufficiently protects the non-confessing defendant's right of confrontation. Given the Court's more recent holdings in *Owens* and *Crawford*, it would seem that the crucial issue under current confrontation analysis is whether the declarant is subject to cross-examination; whether she repudiates the out-of-court statements is probably no longer dispositive.

(3) Interlocking Confessions

For a time (before *Crawford*) the Court also recognized a third situation in which *Bruton* was not violated by a joint trial: when the defendant implicated by another's statement has also confessed, and the confessions are very similar in material detail. In *Parker v. Randolph*,[122] which first announced this rule, a plurality of the Court reasoned that, when "interlocking" confessions are involved, a precautionary instruction like that endorsed in *Delli Paoli* was sufficient to protect the defendant's confrontation right. In *Cruz v. New York*,[123] five members of the Court, in an opinion by Justice Scalia, found "illogical" the notion that juries are more likely to obey limiting instructions in interlocking confession cases than in other cases. But the Court still upheld use of interlocking confessions by borrowing from the *Roberts* analysis; Scalia reasoned that the similarity of the confessions is relevant in deciding whether a co-defendant's confession has sufficient "indicia of reliability" to be *directly* admissible against the defendant (in either a joint *or* a severed trial), and noted that an earlier decision, *Lee v. Illinois*,[124] had concluded that the similarity between the two confessions must be significant for this doctrine to be triggered.

Crawford re-interpreted this line of cases, noting that *Lee* had held the accomplice's confession should not have been admitted (albeit because the discrepancies between that confession and the defendant's were "not insignificant") and that *Cruz* and *Parker* had merely addressed whether a limiting instruction could cure prejudice created by

---

[121]   402 U.S. 622, 91 S.Ct. 1723 (1971).

[122]   442 U.S. 62, 99 S.Ct. 2132 (1979).

[123]   481 U.S. 186, 107 S.Ct. 1714 (1987).

[124]   476 U.S. 530, 106 S.Ct. 2056 (1986).

admitting a co-defendant's confession. Be that as it may, it is clear after *Crawford* that a co-defendant's confession that is testimonial (e.g., made to a police officer whose primary purpose is to investigate a crime) may not be introduced against another co-defendant to prove the truth of the matter asserted in the confession unless the confessor is available for cross-examination, even when the defendant has confessed using identical language.

28.05   Challenging Witnesses in the Courtroom

When a prosecution witness does appear in court, two issues arise: when, if ever, the defendant may be denied a face-to-face encounter with that witness, and the extent to which cross-examination of the witness may be limited.

(a)   The Right to a Face-to-Face Encounter

In lay terms, one does not "confront" another unless there is a face-to-face encounter. Nonetheless, under narrow circumstances, the state may prevent the accused from confronting prosecution witnesses who appear in court.

In *Coy v. Iowa*,[125] the Court found unconstitutional a state law that permitted a large screen to be placed between the defendant and two 13-year-old girls who testified that he had sexually assaulted him. Justice Scalia, writing for the Court, emphasized that "the Confrontation Clause guarantees the defendant a face-to-face meeting with witnesses appearing before the trier of fact." But two members of the six-member majority appeared to disagree with this latter statement. Justice O'Connor wrote a concurring opinion, joined by Justice White, which noted that the statute in *Coy* *presumed* that trauma would occur any time a youthful victim testified in such a case. She suggested that had there been an individualized finding that the child witnesses needed special protection, she might support a different result.

In *Maryland v. Craig*,[126] such a finding was made by the trial court pursuant to a Maryland statute which permits a one-way television procedure if the judge determines that face-to-face testimony "will result in the child suffering serious emotional distress such that the child cannot reasonably communicate." Under the statute, once this finding is made, the witness, prosecutor, and defense counsel withdraw to a separate room; the judge, jury, and defendant remain in the courtroom. The defendant can watch direct and cross-examination of the child over the video hookup and remains in electronic communication with his counsel. In a 5–4 decision, the Court upheld this procedure, in an opinion written by O'Connor.

Although recognizing that requiring a face-to-face encounter between defendant and witness forms the "core" of the Confrontation Clause, the majority concluded that the "central concern" of the Clause "is to ensure the reliability of the evidence against a criminal defendant by subjecting it to rigorous testing in the context of an adversary proceeding before the trier of fact." According to O'Connor, this goal can be met even without a face-to-face encounter if other elements of confrontation—physical presence of the accused, oath, cross-examination of the witness, and observation of the witness' demeanor by the trier of fact—are present. Thus actual confrontation, although important, is not an "absolute" requirement.

---

[125]   487 U.S. 1012, 108 S.Ct. 2798 (1988).
[126]   497 U.S. 836, 110 S.Ct. 3157 (1990).

On the other hand, she cautioned, face-to-face confrontation may be dispensed with only if "necessary to further an important public policy and only where the reliability of the testimony is otherwise assured." Since the Maryland procedure provided the defendant with all the above-described components of confrontation except the face-to-face encounter, and consequently "does not impinge upon the truth-seeking or symbolic purposes of the Confrontation Clause," the "critical inquiry" here was the importance of the state's interest in protecting child witnesses. On this point, the Court relied heavily on the fact that a "significant majority" of the states had enacted statutes similar to Maryland's, reflecting the states' traditional interest in protecting the welfare of children and "a growing body of academic literature documenting the psychological trauma suffered by child abuse victims who must testify in court." Accordingly, so long as the trial court determines on a case-by-case basis that such trauma will result if the child is faced with the defendant, the Confrontation Clause is not violated. The Court further held that this individualized decision need not be based on observation of the child in the presence of the defendant. Nor need the trial court explore less restrictive alternatives than the one-way television procedure permitted under Maryland law.

In dissent, Justice Scalia, joined by Justices Brennan, Marshall and Stevens, quoted from his opinion in *Coy:* "[F]ace-to-face presence may, unfortunately, upset the truthful rape victim or abused child; but by the same token it may confound and undo the false accuser, or reveal the child coached by a malevolent adult." He found the state's interest in protecting children more than offset by the defendant's interest in exposing erroneous testimony by children, who are especially manipulable by other adults or likely to confuse fact with fantasy.

(b) The Right to Cross-Examine

As the Supreme Court stated in *Pointer v. Texas,*[127] the decision which applied the Confrontation Clause to the states, "probably no one, certainly no one with experience in the trial of lawsuits, would deny the value of cross-examination in exposing falsehood and bringing out the truth in the trial of a criminal case." Of course, the Court's cases permitting prosecution use of hearsay have seriously undermined the defendant's ability to cross-examine the witnesses against him.[128] But, when the prosecution does present a witness, significant state or court imposed limitations on cross-examination have consistently been rejected by the Court. At the same time, the Court has carefully distinguished between such limitations and other reasons why cross-examination may not be effective.

(1) State-Imposed Limitations

A number of cases demonstrate the Court's consistent willingness to safeguard the defendant's right to cross-examine prosecution witnesses against court rulings or state evidentiary rules that inhibit the right. In *Smith v. Illinois,*[129] for instance, the Court reversed the conviction of a defendant when a prosecution witness who was also a police informant was allowed to conceal his true identity during cross-examination. Although cross-examination was otherwise permitted, this identifying information was viewed as basic material which "opens countless avenues of in-court examination and out-of-court

---

[127] 380 U.S. 400, 85 S.Ct. 1065 (1965).

[128] See in particular § 28.04(b) & (c).

[129] 390 U.S. 129, 88 S.Ct. 748 (1968).

investigation." Moreover, reasoned the Court, such information and the cross-examination it provokes are necessary for jurors to test properly the weight and credibility of a witness' testimony. These factors outweighed any government interest in avoiding revelation of an informant's identity.

Similarly, a state's interest in protecting the anonymity of juvenile criminal offenders does not outweigh a defendant's right to cross-examine witnesses. In *Davis v. Alaska*,[130] the state's chief witness at the defendant's burglary trial was a juvenile who was himself on probation for two burglaries at the time of the crime and at the time of his identification of the accused. Defense counsel sought to bring out this information for the purpose of showing that the witness may have made a hasty and faulty identification of the defendant in order to shift suspicion away from himself or in order to avoid revocation of probation by police who felt he was being uncooperative. But the trial court prohibited him from doing so under authority of a state rule that bars introduction of any juvenile court adjudication except where the trial judge views its use as appropriate. In the Supreme Court, the state argued that this rule protected against further delinquent acts by juvenile offenders and improved their chances for rehabilitation because it prevented potential employers and associates from discovering their youthful transgressions. But the Court, concluding that "[s]erious damage to the strength of the State's case would have been a real possibility had petitioner been allowed to pursue [his] line of inquiry," held by a 7–2 margin that "the right of confrontation is paramount to the State's policy of protecting a juvenile offender."

While cross-examination was merely inhibited in *Smith* and *Davis*, *Chambers v. Mississippi*,[131] involved a state rule that operated to deny any cross-examination. There, the defendant sought to cross-examine one MacDonald, who had confessed on three separate occasions to the murder with which the defendant was charged (although he later repudiated the confessions). Because the state did not put MacDonald on the stand, the defense had to call him. When the defense sought to treat MacDonald as an adverse witness, the trial court judge prohibited cross-examination, on the authority of the state's "voucher" rule, which assumed that the party calling a witness vouches for his credibility. The Supreme Court unanimously reversed the ensuing conviction, reasoning that because MacDonald's confessions tended to exculpate the defendant, his repudiation tended to inculpate the defendant; thus, the trial court's application of the voucher rule abridged the right to cross-examine a clearly adverse witness. As Justice Powell stated for the Court: "The availability of the right to confront and cross-examine those who give damaging testimony against the accused has never been held to depend on whether the witness was initially put on the stand by the accused or by the State."

The due process right to cross-examine witnesses and challenge evidence also applies at capital sentencing proceedings. In *Gardner v. Florida*,[132] the sentencing judge based his death sentence in part on a presentence report that included a confidential portion not disclosed to defense counsel. The Court found that due process was violated when Gardner was sentenced "on the basis of information which he had no opportunity to deny or explain."

---

[130] 415 U.S. 308, 94 S.Ct. 1105 (1974).
[131] 410 U.S. 284, 93 S.Ct. 1038 (1973).
[132] 430 U.S. 349, 97 S.Ct. 1197 (1977).

(2) Discovery for Impeachment Purposes

An argument could be made that the government abridges the right to cross-examine its witnesses when it fails to provide impeachment material. In *United States v. Augenblick*,[133] the defendant contended that his right of confrontation (as well as his prerogative under the Jencks Act[134]) was denied when the government failed to produce tapes containing previous statements of a person who had testified at the defendant's trial. The Court found no constitutional or statutory violation occurred because the government had made a diligent effort to find the tapes. But it added that, "in some situations, denial of production of a Jencks Act type of a statement might be a denial of a Sixth Amendment right."

In *United States v. Bagley,*[135] however, the Court held that the Sixth Amendment does not entitle the defendant to any impeachment evidence beyond what the prosecution must already surrender under the Court's Due Process Clause cases, which limit the prosecutorial duty of discovery disclosure to those items which have "exculpatory" significance.[136] As the Court stated in *Bagley,* "failure [of the prosecutor] to assist the defense by disclosing information that might have been helpful in conducting . . . cross-examination . . . amounts to a constitutional violation . . . only if the evidence is material in the sense that its suppression undermines confidence in the outcome of the trial." The Court went on to suggest that no constitutional violation occurred in *Bagley*, despite proof that the prosecution intentionally withheld from the defense the fact that two of its witnesses signed an agreement giving them money in return for their testimony and "the accomplishment of the objective sought to be obtained by use of such information."

Similarly, in *Pennsylvania v. Ritchie,*[137] the Court held that refusal on the part of a state child welfare agency to provide defense counsel with copies of a report on the defendant's daughter, who was allegedly molested by the defendant, did not violate the Sixth Amendment. Although the rationale for this refusal was similar to that given by the trial court in *Davis* for limiting defense cross-examination of a juvenile witness, the Court distinguished the cases by noting that here the defense's cross-examination at trial was not restricted in any way.[138] Justice Blackmun argued in dissent that the state should not be able to avoid the Confrontation Clause "simply by deciding to hinder the defendant's right to effective cross-examination . . . at the pretrial, rather than at the trial, stage."

The Court has adhered to its ruling in *Ritchie* even in capital cases, where defendants sometimes claim that their ability to cross-examine was compromised because they were given insufficient time to investigate before the sentencing hearing. In *Gray v. Netherland,*[139] involving such a "surprise" claim (as opposed to a "secrecy"

---

[133] 393 U.S. 348, 89 S.Ct. 528 (1969).

[134] 18 U.S.C.A. § 3500 (providing for disclosure to the defense of prior testimony of any government witness testifying at trial). See § 24.01.

[135] 473 U.S. 667, 105 S.Ct. 3375 (1985).

[136] See § 24.04.

[137] 480 U.S. 39, 107 S.Ct. 989 (1987).

[138] However, the majority did remand the case to the trial court for the purpose of determining whether the report contained "material" information that should have been revealed to the defense. For further discussion of this aspect of *Ritchie,* see § 24.04(c).

[139] 518 U.S. 152, 116 S.Ct. 2074 (1996).

claim of the type involved in *Gardner*, discussed above), five members of the Court stressed that "there is no general constitutional right to discovery in a criminal case."[140]

(3) Witness-Created Limitations

When the inability to cross-examine is due to something other than a court ruling or state rule, the Court has been even more unwilling to find the Confrontation Clause implicated. For instance, in *Delaware v. Fensterer*,[141] the defendant was convicted in part on the testimony of the state's expert witness, who could not remember the scientific test he had used to form his opinion. Because this lack of memory was not the fault of the state or the trial court, the Court found no Sixth Amendment violation, despite the deleterious effect it had on defense counsel's ability to discredit the expert's testimony. Borrowing from its hearsay cases,[142] the Court concluded that the Confrontation Clause guarantees only the "opportunity" to cross-examine, not an effective cross-examination.

Similarly, in *United States v. Owens*,[143] discussed earlier in connection with the admission of hearsay, the Court held irrelevant to confrontation analysis the fact that the prosecution witness, who was the victim of the assault for which the defendant was tried, could not remember the assault or any of the surrounding events. So long as the defendant was not denied the opportunity to cross-examine the witness and was thus able to point out to the jury the fact of the memory loss, no Sixth Amendment violation occurred.

28.06   Compulsory Process and the Right to Present Evidence

In *Washington v. Texas*,[144] the decision which applied the Compulsory Process Clause to the states, the Supreme Court stated that this Sixth Amendment provision protects "[t]he right to offer the testimony of witnesses, and to compel their attendance [and] the right to present the defendant's version of the facts as well as the prosecution's to the jury so that it may decide where the truth lies." In short, the Compulsory Process Clause implements the right of the defendant to present a defense. Echoing *Washington*, subsequent cases have found that the Clause, either by itself or in conjunction with other constitutional provisions, guarantees the defendant the right to testify, the right to subpoena witnesses, and the right to examine those witnesses. These three aspects of the Compulsory Process Clause are discussed here.

(a) The Defendant's Right to Testify

Although as recently as the 18th century English courts refused to allow defendants to testify on the ground that such testimony would be self-serving, this rule fell into disrepute by the next century.[145] By the mid-1970's, the Supreme Court had implicitly recognized a right to testify in one's own behalf on several occasions.[146] However, the constitutional status of the right was not explicitly established until 1987, in *Rock v.*

---

[140] See generally, § 24.03 on defense discovery.

[141] 474 U.S. 15, 106 S.Ct. 292 (1985).

[142] See, e.g., *California v. Green,* 399 U.S. 149, 90 S.Ct. 1930 (1970), discussed in § 28.04(c).

[143] 484 U.S. 554, 108 S.Ct. 838 (1988).

[144] 388 U.S. 14, 87 S.Ct. 1920 (1967).

[145] See, e.g., *McVeigh v. United States,* 78 U.S. (11 Wall.) 259 (1870).

[146] *Faretta v. California,* 422 U.S. 806, 95 S.Ct. 2525 (1975); *Brooks v. Tennessee,* 406 U.S. 605, 92 S.Ct. 1891 (1972); *Harris v. New York,* 401 U.S. 222, 91 S.Ct. 643 (1971).

Arkansas.[147] In *Rock,* Justice Blackmun, writing for the Court, found that the right derived from three different constitutional provisions: the Due Process Clause's guarantee of fairness, the Compulsory Process Clause's guarantee that the defendant may call witnesses in her favor, and the Fifth Amendment's protection of silence unless the defendant "chooses to speak in the unfettered exercise of his own will." Underlying all of these provisions, Blackmun concluded, is the notion that the right to testify is necessary to facilitate the truth-seeking function of trial.[148]

Blackmun also stressed that the right to testify is not absolute. It may be restricted to accommodate "legitimate interests in the criminal trial process," so long as the restrictions are not "arbitrary or disproportionate to the purposes they are designed to serve." The question before the Court in *Rock* was whether a state rule barring post-hypnosis testimony was a permissible restriction on the right to testify. Conceding that memories induced through hypnosis can be fabricated or distorted, Blackmun found nonetheless that a *per se* rule such as Arkansas' is unconstitutional because it does not take into account the reasons for undergoing hypnosis, the circumstances under which it took place, or any independent verification of the information it produced. Nor does it recognize that cross-examination, expert testimony and cautionary instructions might counteract the inadequacies of post-hypnotic testimony. A case-by-case approach is mandated, held Blackmun, unless the state can show "that hypnotically enhanced testimony is always so untrustworthy and so immune to the traditional means of evaluating credibility that it should disable a defendant from presenting her version of the events for which she is on trial." In dissent, Chief Justice Rehnquist, joined by three others, argued that "until there is a much more general consensus on the use of hypnosis than there is now, the Constitution does not warrant this Court's mandating its own view of how to deal with the issue."

As *Rock* indicated, the right to testify can be curtailed under narrow circumstances. Both before and after *Rock,* the Court has permitted actions by the judge or the prosecutor that could chill the defendant's decision to testify. For instance, in 1895, in *Reagan v. United States,*[149] the Court upheld an instruction telling the jury that defendants have a powerful interest in being acquitted and might therefore lie. The modern version of that decision came in *Portuondo v. Agard,*[150] where the Court held that, during closing argument, the prosecutor may, without having to offer any specific proof of the allegation, suggest that a defendant who testified last did so in order to make sure his testimony fit with the other evidence. These practices might be justified on the ground that the defendant's credibility is always a legitimate target. But they can also affect an innocent defendant's willingness to testify.[151] More reasonably, in *Brooks v. Tennessee,*[152] the Court implied that prosecutors may, during cross-examination, ask *specific* questions designed to expose a defendant who tailors his testimony to the evidence.

---

[147] 479 U.S. 1079, 107 S.Ct. 1276 (1987).

[148] For similar reasons, once the defendant takes the stand, she may not avoid cross-examination. See § 15.02(a)(4).

[149] 157 U.S. 301, 15 S.Ct. 610 (1895).

[150] 529 U.S. 61, 120 S.Ct. 1119 (2000).

[151] See § 28.03(c)(3).

[152] 406 U.S. 605, 92 S.Ct. 1891 (1972).

(b) The Right to Subpoena Witnesses

The Compulsory Process Clause guarantees the defendant the use of subpoenas to obtain witnesses, documents and objects that are useful to her defense. Each state has statutory rules implementing this right,[153] used primarily to procure evidence the defense will present in its case-in-chief. But subpoenas may also be relied upon to obtain prosecution witnesses whom the prosecution does not have to present in court; indeed, more recent Supreme Court cases allowing the prosecution to introduce hearsay have justified their holdings in part on the defendant's ability to subpoena available witnesses that the prosecution has decided not to present.[154] Although, for reasons discussed earlier in this chapter,[155] placing the burden on the defense to produce prosecution witnesses is both conceptually and practically problematic, the Sixth Amendment subpoena power can be an important means of ensuring that key components of the prosecution's case are not based on extrajudicial statements. Thus the defendant's subpoena power is a significant defense tool.

The Supreme Court has adopted a balancing test in deciding whether the right to subpoena has been infringed, weighing the government's interest in avoiding the cost or inconvenience of helping to produce the witness against the defendant's need for the witness in question. In *Roviaro v. United States,*[156] the government refused to disclose to the defendant, who was charged with transportation of narcotics, the true identity of an informer who had not only received from the defendant a package allegedly containing heroin but had been the only witness to the transaction. The Supreme Court took notice of the government's need to withhold the identity of informants in order to maintain the flow of information from undercover sources, but found it outweighed by the defendant's interest in the testimony of this informant, who "might have disclosed an entrapment . . . thrown doubt upon petitioner's identity or on the identity of the package, [or] testified to petitioner's lack of knowledge of the contents of the package that he 'transported.' "

Roviaro's relatively strong support of the compulsory process right was undercut, however, by the Court's subsequent holding in *United States v. Valenzuela-Bernal.*[157] There the defendant was charged with transporting illegal aliens. Upon the arrest of the defendant and the three individuals in his car, the immigration authorities determined that two of the three passengers were not needed for the prosecution's case and deported them pursuant to immigration bureau policy. The defendant argued that since this deportation made it impossible for him to interview these witnesses prior to trial and to subpoena them for trial he was denied his right to compulsory process.

The Supreme Court, in an opinion authored by Justice Rehnquist, noted that the government had an obligation to deport illegal aliens and that holding cells for illegal aliens were extremely overcrowded. Balanced against these reasons for deporting the individuals seized with the defendant was the defendant's right to witnesses favorable and material to his defense, which Rehnquist found to be weak. Rehnquist rejected the

---

[153] The federal rules, for instance, grant the indigent defendant power to subpoena any witness necessary to an "adequate defense." Fed.R.Crim.P. 17(b).

[154] See, e.g., *United States v. Inadi,* 475 U.S. 387, 106 S.Ct. 1121 (1986); *White v. Illinois,* 502 U.S. 346, 112 S.Ct. 736 (1992).

[155] See § 28.04(b)(1).

[156] 353 U.S. 53, 77 S.Ct. 623 (1957).

[157] 458 U.S. 858, 102 S.Ct. 3440 (1982).

materiality test developed by the court of appeals, which asked whether any "conceivable benefit" might accrue from the deported individuals' presence at trial. Instead, he opted for a standard requiring that defendants provide "some explanation of how [absent witnesses] would have been favorable and material." Here, he found this test not met because the defendant had offered no plausible reason why he would need the two deported individuals in addition to the one who remained. To convict the defendant, the government needed only to show that the defendant knew the third, remaining individual was an alien who had entered the country in the past three years; that individual, Rehnquist pointed out, was fully available for examination. The fact that the other two individuals were eyewitnesses to the incident was not enough.

In dissent, Justice Brennan, joined by Justice Marshall, noted that no inordinate delay in pursuing immigration policies would have been occasioned by postponing the deportation of the first two individuals found in the defendant's car. He also pointed out that in *Roviaro* the Court had not required the defendant to explain how the informant would be useful to him but had merely suggested how he *might* have been helpful. Finally, he noted that the defendant could not be counted upon to give anything more than speculative reasons for requiring the presence of the witnesses when he had not been able to interview them. Indulging in such speculation, Brennan reasoned that the deported individuals could have testified as to the defendant's lack of knowledge with respect to their identity and perhaps concerning whether they had helped entrap the defendant.

Valenzuela-Bernal may have heightened the materiality showing required by the Compulsory Process Clause. It would seem that the government interest in protecting informants (at issue in *Roviaro*) is more important than its interest in reducing the number of aliens incarcerated in this country, especially since, as Brennan points out, deportation can take place after trial. Thus, the proof of materiality necessary to outweigh the government's interest in *Valenzuela-Bernal* should have been correspondingly lower than was necessary in *Roviaro*. But the Court's application of its "some explanation" test in that case appeared to require a *greater* showing of materiality than did the *Roviaro* Court. Put another way, *Valenzuela-Bernal* gives more power to the prosecution to decide what is "material" to the defense's case, a tendency also evident in the Court's confrontation cases.[158]

(c) The Right to Present Evidence

Literally read, the Compulsory Process Clause guarantees only the power to subpoena witnesses, not the right to have those witnesses testify. But the Supreme Court has rejected that interpretation of the Clause; in *Washington v. Texas*,[159] for instance, the Court stated that "[t]he Framers of the Constitution did not intend to commit the futile act of giving to a defendant the right to secure the attendance of witnesses whose testimony he had no right to use."[160] Instead, analogous to its confrontation cases dealing

---

[158] See, e.g., *United States v. Bagley*, 473 U.S. 667, 105 S.Ct. 3375 (1985), discussed in § 28.05(b)(2). Compare also the minimal showing the government must make to obtain a subpoena, discussed in § 23.05(a)(1).

[159] 388 U.S. 14, 87 S.Ct. 1920 (1967).

[160] But see, *Taylor v. Illinois*, 484 U.S. 400, 108 S.Ct. 646 (1988) (affirming *Washington*, but finding the argument that the Clause guarantees only subpoena power "supported by the plain language of the Clause, by the historical evidence . . . by some scholarly comment, and by a brief excerpt from the legislative history of the Clause.").

with cross-examination, the Court has generally disapproved government rules or practices inhibiting or prohibiting direct examination or presentation of other evidence, unless the defense has engaged in misconduct. A separate issue is whether the Clause permits the defendant to immunize witnesses who may have testimony favorable to the defense.

(1) State-Imposed Limitations; Generally

Several cases illustrate the Court's willingness to protect the defendant's opportunity to present evidence on his behalf, regardless of state rules to the contrary. In *Washington*, for instance, the Court struck down a statute which prohibited accomplices from testifying for each other, a rule apparently based on the theory that accomplices are likely to perjure themselves in an effort to gain acquittal for their colleagues in crime. Noting that perjury is more likely to be committed by accomplices who testify for the prosecution *against* one another in an effort to shift blame, the Court concluded that the statute was "absurd." It was also found arbitrary, because it prevented "whole categories of defense witnesses from testifying on the basis of *a priori* categories that presume them worthy of unbelief." Instead, stated the Court, the state must allow the defendant to present a witness "who was physically and mentally capable of testifying to events that he had personally observed, and whose testimony would have been relevant and material to his defense."

The Court's implicit trust of the jury system's ability to gauge credibility was reaffirmed in *Webb v. Texas,*[161] where it reversed, on due process grounds, the conviction of a defendant whose sole witness refused to testify after the trial judge harshly admonished him not to lie on the stand. Holding that the judge's lengthy comments "effectively drove the witness off the stand," the Court concluded that, whatever the judge's belief as to the veracity of the witness, the jury should have been allowed to determine "where the truth lies." For much the same reason, the same term the Court held, in *Cool v. United States,*[162] that a defendant was deprived of his right to compulsory process when the trial court instructed the jury that exculpatory testimony of an accomplice should be disregarded unless the jury decided that such testimony was true beyond a reasonable doubt. The Court also noted that the instruction reduced the government's burden below the reasonable doubt standard.

Other Court cases have also conflated compulsory process and due process concerns in upholding defense attempts to put on material evidence. For instance, in *Chambers v. Mississippi,*[163] discussed earlier in connection with the Confrontation Clause, the defendant sought to prove that another person, MacDonald, had committed the murder with which the defendant was charged. Part of his proof in this regard was to be the testimony of three individuals to whom MacDonald had confessed that he had committed the murder (although all of these confessions were later repudiated). The trial court refused to allow this testimony on the ground that it was hearsay and that Mississippi law did not recognize an exception for declarations against penal interest (although it did recognize an exception for declarations against pecuniary interest). A unanimous Court overturned Chambers' conviction, noting that each of MacDonald's confessions had been made spontaneously to a close acquaintance shortly after the murder, that the

---

[161]   409 U.S. 95, 93 S.Ct. 351 (1972).

[162]   409 U.S. 100, 93 S.Ct. 354 (1972).

[163]   410 U.S. 284, 93 S.Ct. 1038 (1973).

confessions were corroborated (by, e.g., testimony that MacDonald had been seen with a gun shortly after the shooting), that MacDonald stood to gain little and to lose much by confessing, and that in any event he was in the courtroom and could be cross-examined by the state. Holding that "the hearsay rule may not be applied mechanistically to defeat the ends of justice," the Court concluded that "the exclusion of this critical evidence, coupled with the State's refusal to permit Chambers to cross-examine MacDonald,[164] denied him a trial in accord with traditional and fundamental standards of due process." Although framed in due process terms, the compulsory process overtones are apparent.

Similarly, in *Crane v. Kentucky,*[165] the Court held that the state may not exclude "competent, reliable evidence bearing on the credibility of a confession when such evidence is central to the defendant's claim of innocence," because "[w]hether rooted directly in the Due Process Clause . . . or in the Compulsory Process or Confrontation Clauses . . . the Constitution guarantees criminal defendants a 'meaningful opportunity to present a complete defense.' " In *Crane* the defendant wanted to produce extrinsic evidence suggesting his confession was unreliable because it had been obtained when the defendant, a young, uneducated boy, had allegedly been kept against his will in a small, windowless room for a protracted period of time until he confessed to every unsolved crime in the county, including the one he was tried for. The state courts had rejected this testimony on the ground that it was relevant only to the admissibility of the confession, not its credibility once the confession was found voluntary. Noting that there was no physical evidence connecting the defendant to the crime and that the state offered no rational justification for the exclusion of this body of evidence, the Court unanimously reversed the state courts.

In the same vein is *Holmes v. South Carolina,*[166] which struck down a South Carolina rule that prohibited defendants from introducing evidence suggesting a third party committed the crime whenever there is strong forensic evidence of the defendant's guilt. Justice Alito's opinion for a unanimous Court distinguished between evidentiary rules that exclude probative evidence because of its prejudicial impact, which are permissible, from the kind of "arbitrary" rule at issue here, which excluded evidence not because of its own flaws but because of the strength of the prosecution's case. Holmes wanted to show that, similar to the excluded proof in *Chambers,* a man named White had been in the vicinity of the crime the morning it was committed, and that White had subsequently either 'acknowledged Holmes' innocence or admitted his own guilt to four other individuals. The state courts had excluded this evidence because fibers, prints, and blood found at the scene of the crime matched the defendant's. As Justice Alito pointed out, however, "just because the prosecution's evidence, *if credited,* would provide strong support for a guilty verdict, it does not follow that evidence of third-party guilt has only a weak logical connection to the central issues of the case." He also noted defense evidence suggesting that the forensic analysis was flawed and that the police had reason to frame Holmes.

When, in contrast to the type of evidence involved in *Chambers, Crane* and *Holmes,* the evidence the defense seeks to introduce cannot easily be characterized as "competent" and "reliable," the result may be different. In *United States v. Salerno,*[167]

---

[164] See discussion of *Chambers* in § 28.05(b)(1).

[165] 476 U.S. 683, 106 S.Ct. 2142 (1986).

[166] 547 U.S. 319, 126 S.Ct. 1727 (2006).

[167] 505 U.S. 317, 112 S.Ct. 2503 (1992).

the defendant sought to introduce hearsay statements made at his grand jury proceeding by two individuals who refused to repeat the testimony at trial on Fifth Amendment grounds. The prosecution sought to exclude the hearsay on the authority of Federal Rule of Evidence 804(a)(1), which permits introduction of testimony given at another hearing only when the "party against whom the testimony is now offered . . . had an opportunity and similar motive to develop the testimony by direct, cross, or redirect examination." While remanding the case to determine whether the prosecution had had "an opportunity and similar motive" to cross-examine the two individuals during the grand jury hearing,[168] the Court, with only one member dissenting, rejected the defendant's contention that "adversarial fairness" permits the trial court to ignore the similar motive limitation at the defendant's request. The Court based this ruling on its interpretation of the rule rather than on constitutional grounds, but the tone of the opinion suggests that neither the Sixth Amendment nor the Due Process Clause requires admission of hearsay that does not fit within a hearsay exception or at least bears some other indicia of reliability.[169]

Similar in tone is *United States v. Scheffer,*[170] in which the Court upheld a trial court's ruling rejecting use of polygraph evidence by the defendant. The defendant, charged with taking methamphetamines, wanted to introduce the results of a polygraph test to bolster his argument that he had not been lying to investigators when he denied drug use. But Justice Thomas explained that "[t]here is simply no consensus that polygraph evidence is reliable. To this day, the scientific community remains extremely polarized about the reliability of polygraph techniques."

The Court was careful to note several limitations on its holding, however. First, unlike other types of evidence the defendant might present, polygraphs have an "aura of near infallibility" and thus may lead jurors to "give excessive weight to the opinions of the polygrapher, clothed as they are in scientific expertise." Thomas also stressed that "[a] fundamental premise of our criminal system is that the *jury* is the lie detector." Yet, "[u]nlike other expert witnesses who testify about factual matters outside the jurors' knowledge, such as analysis of fingerprints, ballistics, or DNA found at a crime scene, a polygraph expert [supplies] the jury with another opinion, in addition to its own, about whether the witness was telling the truth." Finally, Thomas noted that the trial court's decision did not preclude the defendant from presenting "factual evidence" or "exercis[ing] his choice to convey his version of the facts." Thus, he asserted, the Court's decision was not inconsistent with *Rock,* which had stressed that the accused ought to be allowed "to present his own version of events in his own words."

(2) Sanctions for Defense Misconduct

The Court has veered away from the general rule that the defense should be permitted to present relevant and competent information on its behalf when the state seeks to exclude defense evidence as a sanction. The first case endorsing this view was

---

[168] Justice Stevens, in dissent, argued that the remand was unnecessary, since the prosecution always has the "opportunity and motive" to cross-examine hostile witnesses at a grand jury proceeding, even if that opportunity is not exercised due to a fear of undermining grand jury secrecy or a decision to undermine the witness in other ways.

[169] Compare § 28.04(b)(2).

[170] 523 U.S. 303, 118 S.Ct. 1261 (1998).

Taylor v. Illinois,[171] where the Court approved the trial court's exclusion of a defense witness in an attempted murder case because he had not been listed on the defense's witness list, in violation of state discovery rules. The Court, in an opinion by Justice Stevens, emphasized that the violation had been "willful and blatant," in that the defense attorney had not mentioned the witness until the second day of trial, even though he had visited the witness a week before and had known his name for much longer. Stevens also asserted that trial courts have a "vital interest in protecting the trial process from the pollution of perjured testimony," and noted the trial judge's statement, after conducting a *voir dire* of the witness, doubting his veracity.[172]

As Justice Brennan, joined by two others, pointed out in dissent, the possibility that a witness might lie had never before been thought to prohibit competent witnesses from testifying for the defense. Rather, cases like *Washington* and *Webb* had left that determination up to the jury. A continuance would have been less inimical to the truth-finding process than exclusion, while preventing any prejudice to the prosecution (indeed, in this case even a continuance might not have been necessary, since the prosecution participated in the witness' *voir dire*).[173] As to the need to sanction discovery violations, Brennan noted that the violation here was by the attorney, not the defendant; direct punishment of the attorney would have been much fairer. The majority had anticipated this point by concluding that the defendant should be bound by his lawyer's "tactical" decisions.[174] But here, as Brennan pointed out, the judge was dealing with obvious misconduct, not a tactical error that becomes obvious only in hindsight and thus can more fairly bind the client.[175]

Despite these arguments, three years later the Court reinforced *Taylor's* message that a defendant can be prevented from presenting material evidence as a sanction for his attorney's misconduct. In *Michigan v. Lucas*,[176] the trial judge in a rape trial excluded evidence about the victim's past sexual conduct with the defendant because the defendant had failed to give notice within ten days of arraignment that he planned to present the evidence, as required by statute. Although the Supreme Court remanded the case to determine whether exclusion was appropriate on the facts of *Lucas*, it held that, in principle, such exclusion was permissible. Citing *Taylor*, it stated that the exclusion sanction, despite its severity, might be imposed if, for instance, the court found the defendant's failure was "willful misconduct" designed to obtain "a tactical advantage." According to the Court, this rule was justified because the notice requirement at issue in *Lucas*, which is designed to allow the trial court to conduct a hearing considering the

---

[171] 484 U.S. 400, 108 S.Ct. 646 (1988). Earlier cases had avoided the issue. See, e.g., *Williams v. Florida*, 399 U.S. 78, 90 S.Ct. 1893 (1970); *Wardius v. Oregon*, 412 U.S. 470, 93 S.Ct. 2208 (1973).

[172] Apparently, the basis for the judge's doubt about the witness, aside from the "eleventh hour" nature of his appearance, was that he claimed to have warned the defendant just prior to the shooting that the victim had weapons and was out to get him, but also admitted that he had not formally met the defendant until two years after the incident.

[173] For further discussion of this point in the context of sanctions for discovery violations, see § 24.02(d).

[174] In support of this notion, Stevens also noted the difficulty of determining who is responsible for a violation, since defendants can mislead attorneys about the identity or location of material witnesses. Whatever the validity of this point generally, it did not apply here, since the defendant had told the attorney about the witness sometime before trial.

[175] See § 32.04(c)(4) for further discussion of tactical versus fundamental errors by the attorney.

[176] 500 U.S. 145, 111 S.Ct. 1743 (1991).

admissibility of the evidence, "serves legitimate state interests in protecting against surprise, harassment, and undue delay."[177]

As Justice Blackmun reminded in an opinion concurring with the result, the state also has an interest "in the full and truthful disclosure of critical facts." He continued: "[I]t may be that, in most cases, preclusion will be 'disproportionate to the purposes [the rule is] designed to serve.'" This would seem so in *Lucas,* where the discovery violation could not be attributed to the defendant, the excluded evidence was clearly relevant, and the prosecution could have been granted a continuance if necessary to counter prejudice to its case.

(3) *Immunity for Defense Witnesses*

In *Washington,* the Court cautioned that its decision guaranteeing the defendant the right to present a defense should not be construed "as disapproving testimonial privileges, such as the privilege against self-incrimination." This passage suggests that, in contrast to the power granted the prosecution,[178] the defense cannot seek to immunize witnesses who refuse to provide relevant information on Fifth Amendment grounds. This inequity can be justified on the ground that the prosecution grants immunity to further legitimate societal ends (e.g., as a means of obtaining evidence against more significant offenders), while giving the defense unfettered discretion to grant immunity might have the opposite effect (e.g., immunizing a significant offender to protect a minor offender). On the other hand, when the defendant can show that immunization will likely produce highly relevant information for the defense, and the prosecution cannot show a "strong countervailing interest" in preventing immunization, due process, if not the Compulsory Process Clause, might require that immunity be granted.[179]

28.07 Conclusion

This chapter discussed the various rights, most of them derived from the Sixth Amendment, that are meant to assure that trial and related proceedings arrive at just results. They can be summarized as follows:

(1) Under the Sixth Amendment, the defendant is entitled to insist that his trial, and most pretrial proceedings (other than the grand jury), be conducted in public. However, closure may be allowed (over First Amendment as well as Sixth Amendment objections) if the prosecution can show that: (a) an overriding interest requires protection (such as the need to protect witness privacy); (b) the closure is no broader than necessary to protect that interest; (c) reasonable alternatives are considered; and (d) findings adequate to support the closure are made.

(2) The Confrontation and Due Process Clauses guarantee the defendant the right to be present, while competent, at trial and at all other critical proceedings at which his presence would contribute to the fairness of the prosecution. However, a conviction in absentia is permissible if the defendant intentionally avoids trial or is disruptive in the courtroom. Although the prosecution may remind the jury that a defendant who takes

---

[177] The Court did not assess the constitutionality of the Michigan statute, but noted that "[i]t is not inconceivable" that its 10-day notice rule might be "overly restrictive." It also reminded, however, that it had upheld other notice statutes. See, e.g., *Williams v. Florida,* 399 U.S. 78, 90 S.Ct. 1893 (1970), discussed in § 24.02(a)(1).

[178] See § 15.03(d).

[179] See, e.g., *Government of Virgin Islands v. Smith,* 615 F.2d 964 (3d Cir. 1980).

the stand heard all of the prosecution's case before testifying, it may not comment on the defendant's failure to take the stand at all (under the Fifth Amendment). Nor may the state force the defendant to wear jail garb or force a defendant who has not been found to be a security risk to wear shackles (under the Due Process Clause).

✎ (3) The right of confrontation precludes the use of testimonial evidence (i.e., statements made in formal proceedings, affidavits, and police interrogation or made to law enforcement personnel in other situations where the primary purpose was to establish or prove past events potentially relevant to later criminal prosecution), except when: (a) the declarant can be cross-examined at trial; (b) the declarant is unavailable despite good faith efforts by the prosecution to obtain his presence and the defendant was afforded the opportunity to cross-examine him about those statements prior to trial; (c) the defendant intentionally caused the declarant's unavailability; (d) the statement is not proffered to prove the truth of the matter asserted therein; or (e) (perhaps) the statement is a dying declaration. The admissibility of nontestimonial evidence is apparently not governed by the Confrontation Clause.

(4)　In light of (3), the prosecution must sever the trials of co-defendants when it plans to use a confession from one defendant that implicates both unless: (a) the confessing defendant is subject to cross-examination; (b) the name and references to the non-confessing defendant are deleted from the confession in a way that does not draw attention to the defendant; or (c) the confession is used solely for a non-hearsay purpose.

(5)　The Confrontation Clause guarantees the defendant a face-to-face encounter with accusers whom the prosecution presents unless separation is necessary to further an important public policy, such as protection of child witnesses who have been found in need of protection, and the reliability of the testimony is otherwise assured. The Clause also prevents the state from inhibiting the defendant's opportunity to cross-examine prosecution witnesses. Concealing the identity of a witness, assuring confidentiality of juvenile records and maintaining the viability of a state voucher rule have all been found insufficient reasons for preventing the defendant from developing information through cross-examination. However, the state need not disclose impeachment evidence unless it decides its use would probably affect the outcome of trial.

(6)　Under the Compulsory Process Clause, the Due Process Clause and the Fifth Amendment, the defendant has the right to testify in her own behalf, subject to limitations that are not arbitrary or disproportionate to the purposes they are designed to serve. The Compulsory Process Clause also guarantees the defendant the right to subpoena material and relevant witnesses on her behalf, although the burden is on the defendant to offer a plausible explanation of the witness' relevance when the state asserts an countervailing interest (such as protection of witness identity). Finally, the Compulsory Process Clause and the Due Process Clause protect against state restrictions on defense use of competent and reliable evidence, except when those restrictions are imposed as a sanction for willful and blatant misconduct by the defense.

BIBLIOGRAPHY

Bellin, Jeffrey. Applying *Crawford's* Confrontation Right in a Digital Age. 45 Tex. Tech. L. Rev. 43 (2012).

Cohen, Neil P. Can They Kill Me If I'm Gone: Trial in Absentia in Capital Cases. 36 U.Fla.L.Rev. 273 (1984).

Crawford and Davis: A Symposium. 19 Regent U.L.Rev. 303 (2006–07)).

Davies, Thomas Y. Revisiting the Fictional Originalism in *Crawford*'s "Cross-Examination Rule:" A Reply to Mr. Kry. 72 Brooklyn L.Rev. 557 (2007).

Friedman, Richard D. Confrontation and Forensic Laboratory Reports, Round Four. 45 Texas Tech L. Rev. 51 (2012).

Hewett, Martin A. A More Reliable Right to Present a Defense: The Compulsory Process Right After *Crawford v. Washington*. 96 Geo. L. J. 273 (2007).

Kime, Stacey. Can a Right Be Less Than the Sum of Its Parts?; How the Conflation of the Confrontation Clause and Due Process Diminishes Criminal Defendants' rights. 48 Am. Crim. L. Rev. 1501 (2011).

McGurk, Brett H. The Strategic Implications of *Portuondo v. Agard*. 33 West. L.A. L. Rev. 71 (2001).

Nagareda, Richard A. Reconceiving the Right to Present Witnesses. 97 Mich. L. Rev. 1063 (1999).

Raeder, Myrna S. Thoughts About *Giles* and Forfeiture in Domestic Violence Cases. 75 Brooklyn L. Rev. 1359 (2010).

Ross, Josephine. After *Crawford* Double-speak: "Testimony" Does Not Mean Testimony and "Witness" Does Not Mean Witness. 97 J.Crim.L. & Criminol. 147 (2006).

Simonson, Jocelyn. The Criminal Court Audience in a Post-Trial World. 127 Har. L. Rev. 2173 (2014).

Slobogin, Christopher and Amy Mashburn. The Criminal Defense Attorney's Fiduciary Duty to Clients With Mental Disability. 68 Fordham L.Rev. 1581 (2000).

Westen, Peter. Confrontation and Compulsory Process: A Unified Theory of Evidence for Criminal Cases. 91 Harv.L.Rev. 567 (1978).

____. The Compulsory Process Clause. 73 Mich.L.Rev. 71 (1974).

Winick, Bruce B. Incompetency to Stand Trial: An Assessment of Costs and Benefits, and a Proposal for Reform. 39 Rutgers L. Rev. 243 (1987).

Chapter 29

APPEALS

29.01   Introduction

An "appeal" usually involves an examination of the trial court record by an appellate court in an effort to ascertain whether the relevant substantive and procedural law was properly applied by the lower court. It might also consist of a trial *de novo*, in which the appellate proceeding is actually a new, independent trial in a superior court.[1] In either case, the appeal procedure assures that a convicted offender is afforded the opportunity to obtain one judicial review of his conviction by a tribunal other than the court in which he was tried.

As significant as the opportunity to appeal is, the Supreme Court has never given it constitutional status. In the late 19th century case of *McKane v. Durston*,[2] the Court stated:

> A review by an appellate court of the final judgment in a criminal case, however grave the offense of which the accused is convicted, was not at common law, and is not now, a necessary element of due process of law. It is wholly within the discretion of the state to allow or not to allow such a review.

Although the passage was dictum, it has been continually affirmed by the Court.[3]

The Court's stance on the constitutional status of the right to appeal is unlikely ever to be challenged, because every state, as well as the federal system, provides at least one appeal as of right after conviction, as well as at least one discretionary appeal to a higher level appellate court. In the federal system, for instance, federal convictions may be appealed as of right to the circuit courts of appeal. Further appeal to the Supreme Court is usually dependent upon whether the Court grants a writ of certiorari.[4]

State litigants have somewhat more elaborate appellate opportunities, since they may resort not only to the relevant state courts, but to the United States Supreme Court as well, under certain narrow circumstances. Once the case of a state defendant has been reviewed by the highest available state court, direct appeal to the Supreme Court may be had if the state court ruling invalidated a federal statute or upheld a state statute in the face of a challenge that it was invalid under the federal Constitution.[5] Further, a writ of certiorari from the Court is available where the decision by the highest available state court "draw[s] into question the validity" of a federal or state statute or "where any title, right, privilege or immunity is specially set up or claimed under the Constitution,

---

[1]   See *Blackledge v. Perry,* 417 U.S. 21, 94 S.Ct. 2098 (1974), described in § 29.02(d)(1).

[2]   153 U.S. 684, 14 S.Ct. 913 (1894).

[3]   See *Abney v. United States,* 431 U.S. 651, 97 S.Ct. 2034 (1977); *Ross v. Moffitt,* 417 U.S. 600, 94 S.Ct. 2437 (1974).

[4]   See 28 U.S.C.A. § 1254.

[5]   See 28 U.S.C.A. § 1257(1)(2). While appeal is permitted, the Court may dismiss the claim if no "substantial federal question" is presented. 16 Charles A. Wright, Arthur R. Miller & Edward H. Cooper, Jurisdiction: Civil § 4014.

treaties or statutes of, or commission held or authority exercised under, the United States."[6]

This chapter discusses some of the legal issues that have arisen as a result of the appeals system. Specifically, it addresses (1) constitutional rights designed to ensure a meaningful appeal; (2) the statutory final judgment requirement; (3) limitations on appeals by the prosecution; (4) the harmless error doctrine; and (5) the retroactivity doctrine.

29.02   Assuring a Meaningful Appeal

A number of Supreme Court decisions stand for the proposition that, while a state need not provide an appeals process, if it does so it may not unfairly inhibit use of that process. This notion has been implemented in a number of ways, discussed below.

(a) The Right to Trial Transcripts

The first case to consider constitutional issues in connection with appeals was *Griffin v. Illinois.*[7] There, the Supreme Court held that Illinois appellate procedure violated equal protection because it required defendants to produce transcripts of their trial in order to obtain appellate review, but failed to provide one free of charge to indigent defendants. As the Court put it, the state may not grant the right to appeal "in a way that discriminates against some convicted defendants on account of their poverty."

The Court has vigorously affirmed *Griffin* on several occasions. For example, in *Entsminger v. Iowa,*[8] the Court unanimously held that *Griffin* was violated by a state procedure that allowed defense counsel, rather than the indigent defendant, to decide whether appeal could proceed with less than a complete record. In another case, the Court held that conditioning production of a transcript on the trial judge's assessment of whether "justice will thereby be promoted" violates equal protection.[9]

(b) The Right to Counsel

The Sixth Amendment guarantee of the right to assistance of counsel applies only to "criminal prosecutions," which does not include the appellate process. Thus, the Court has looked to the Equal Protection and Due Process Clauses in defining the scope of the right to counsel on appeal. The watershed case in this regard was *Douglas v. California,*[10] where the Court relied on *Griffin* and equal protection analysis in concluding that the state must provide the indigent defendant with counsel on appeals as of right to provide "meaningful access" to the appellate courts. According to Justice Douglas' majority opinion, "where the merits of the *one and only* appeal an indigent has as of right are decided without benefit of counsel . . . an unconstitutional line has been drawn between rich and poor."

---

[6]   28 U.S.C.A. § 1257(3).

[7]   351 U.S. 12, 76 S.Ct. 585 (1956).

[8]   386 U.S. 748, 87 S.Ct. 1402 (1967).

[9]   *Draper v. Washington,* 372 U.S. 487, 83 S.Ct. 774 (1963); see also *Mayer v. Chicago,* 404 U.S. 189, 92 S.Ct. 410 (1971) (transcript must be provided for appeal of crime punishable only by a fine). Both *Draper* and *Mayer* also suggested, however, that "alternative methods of reporting trial proceedings" would be permissible if they were equivalent to a transcript.

[10]   372 U.S. 353, 83 S.Ct. 814 (1963).

To reach the result in *Douglas,* the Court in effect had to assume that the state cannot prevent *non*-indigent defendants from having appellate counsel. But it was not until *Evitts v. Lucey,*[11] over twenty years later, that the Court firmly guaranteed a right to counsel on appeal for these defendants as well. Justice Brennan's majority opinion based this conclusion both on the "meaningful access" language underlying *Douglas* and on the notion developed in previous due process and Sixth Amendment cases that lawyers are "necessities, not luxuries."[12]

At the same time, the Court has refused to find that either equal protection or due process guarantees a right to counsel on discretionary appeals. In *Ross v. Moffitt,*[13] the majority held that the Equal Protection Clause does not require precisely equal advantages between rich and poor; further, the counselless discretionary review procedure at issue in *Ross* was sufficiently fair because the indigent defendant was able to present both his trial transcript and the appellate briefs (written by a lawyer) submitted at his appeal as of right. *Ross* notwithstanding, most jurisdictions provide counsel to indigents on all appeals.[14]

The underlying right to counsel also determines the extent to which counsel must be "effective" on appeal. In *Evitts,* the Court held that counsel's failure to meet a technical filing deadline for an appeal as of right deprived the defendant of effective assistance, and reinstated the appeal.[15] In contrast, in *Wainwright v. Torna,*[16] counsel's failure to make timely application for *discretionary* review did not require reinstatement of the appeal, since the lawyer's incompetence did not deprive the defendant of any constitutional right to counsel. These and other cases concerning appellate counsel are discussed further in the context of the Court's effective assistance jurisprudence.[17]

The Supreme Court has also unanimously held, in *Martinez v. Court of Appeal,*[18] that there is no right to self-representation at the appellate stage. Although the Sixth Amendment guarantees this right at the adjudication stage,[19] the Court found that neither history nor the Sixth Amendment's structure (which focuses on trial rights) guaranteed a right to proceed *pro se* on appeal. Such a right would have to be grounded in the Due Process Clause and the Court was "entirely unpersuaded that the risk of disloyalty by a court-appointed attorney, or the suspicion of such disloyalty, that underlies the constitutional right of self-representation at trial is a sufficient concern to conclude that such a right is a necessary component of a fair appellate proceeding." The Court has also held, in *Jones v. Barnes,*[20] that if counsel does decide to argue the case on appeal, he, not the defendant, is the arbiter of what will be argued, even if some of the arguments he discards are not frivolous.

---

[11]   469 U.S. 387, 105 S.Ct. 830 (1985).

[12]   Quoting *Gideon v. Wainwright,* 372 U.S. 335, 83 S.Ct. 792 (1963), discussed in § 31.02(b).

[13]   417 U.S. 600, 94 S.Ct. 2437 (1974).

[14]   See commentary to ABA, Criminal Justice Standard 21–1.1.

[15]   See also *Garza v. Idaho,* ___ U.S. ___, 139 S.Ct. 738 (2019), discussed in more detail in § 26.02(b)(1) (holding that the right applies even when the defendant has signed an appeal waiver).

[16]   455 U.S. 586, 102 S.Ct. 1300 (1982).

[17]   For further discussion of the right to counsel on appeal, see § 31.03(c)(1) & (3); for effective assistance issues, see § 32.04(c).

[18]   528 U.S. 152, 120 S.Ct. 684 (2000).

[19]   *Faretta v. California,* 422 U.S. 806, 95 S.Ct. 2525 (1975), discussed in § 31.04(a).

[20]   463 U.S. 745, 103 S.Ct. 3308 (1983), discussed further in § 32.04(c)(2) & (4).

(c) The Right to Pursue "Non-Frivolous" Arguments

Counsel will sometimes perfect an appeal but then decide that there are no substantial appellate claims and withdraw from the case. In *Anders v. California,*[21] the Supreme Court held that withdrawal under these circumstances may take place only after counsel has filed a "brief referring to anything in the record that might arguably support the appeal," the defendant is given a chance to add to this brief, and the appellate court, after reviewing the brief, has determined that the appeal is "wholly frivolous." This procedure was found necessary to assure that appointed counsel thought carefully about deciding to withdraw. Furthermore, violation of this rule can never be harmless error, and cannot be avoided through showing a lack of prejudice, as is the case with most ineffective assistance claims.[22]

However, the Court has also upheld a state rule requiring counsel to submit, in addition to this "*Anders* brief," a statement as to why any issues that might support an appeal *lack* merit. The defendant in *McCoy v. Wisconsin*[23] argued that this rule forced the appellate attorney to make arguments against his client's case; moreover, unlike the wealthy client, the indigent cannot avoid such damaging submissions by hiring another attorney. But the majority held that, rather than rendering counsel ineffective, the statute furthered the aims underlying *Anders* by encouraging diligent research by counsel and assisting the appellate court in assessing frivolousness.

For similar reasons, the Court upheld, in *Smith v. Robbins,*[24] a procedure that obliges counsel who finds the appeal lacking in merit to provide a summary of the case's procedural and factual history, but requires him to remain *silent* on the merits of the case, unless the appellate court directs him to brief a particular issue. Four dissenters argued that this procedure, because it failed to force counsel to describe "arguable" issues and relied on an appellate court to spot those issues, fell well short of the protection contemplated in *Anders*. But the majority found that this procedure ensures that "an indigent's appeal will be resolved in a way that is related to the merit of that appeal," by requiring a "trained legal eye" to search the record and provide at least some assistance to the reviewing court.

(d) The Right to Appeal Without Fear of Retaliation

In *North Carolina v. Pearce,*[25] a defendant who had been reconvicted after a successful appeal received a greater punishment than had been imposed after his original conviction. Although the Supreme Court did not explicitly find that the increase in sentence was in retaliation for the appeal, it concluded that, to prevent the right of appeal from being chilled, due process required that a "defendant be freed of apprehension of such a retaliatory motivation on the part of the sentencing judge." Accordingly, when a sentence is increased after a successful appeal, vindictiveness should be assumed unless the trial judge can provide a reasonable explanation for the increase, consisting of "identifiable conduct occurring after the time of the original sentencing proceeding."

---

[21] 386 U.S. 738, 87 S.Ct. 1396 (1967).

[22] *Penson v. Ohio,* 488 U.S. 75, 109 S.Ct. 346 (1988).

[23] 486 U.S. 429, 108 S.Ct. 1895 (1988).

[24] 528 U.S. 259, 120 S.Ct. 746 (2000).

[25] 395 U.S. 711, 89 S.Ct. 2072 (1969).

(1) When the Presumption of Vindictiveness Applies

In effect, *Pearce* created what has since come to be called a "presumption of vindictiveness"[26] whenever the sentencing judge imposes a heavier sentence after a successful appeal. In *Blackledge v. Perry*,[27] the Court found the presumption also applies to *prosecutorial* decisions that may chill the right to appeal. There the prosecutor raised the charge against the defendant from a misdemeanor to a felony after the defendant had been convicted on the misdemeanor and filed notice of appeal for a trial *de novo* in a higher court. The Supreme Court held that "upping the ante" in this way after a defendant has exercised her right to appeal is presumptively vindictive.

On the other hand, when the sentencing or charging authority lacks the motivation to be vindictive, *Pearce's* presumption of vindictiveness does not apply. For example, in *Colten v. Kentucky*,[28] the Court refused to apply the presumption when the defendant's sentence after a trial *de novo* was higher than the one received at his earlier trial on the same charge. Because *de novo* appeals are fresh determinations of guilt in front of a different judge, the sentencing court is not being asked, as it was in *Pearce*, "to do over what it had thought it had already done correctly," nor even to "overrule" what another court has done. Similarly, the Court found in *Chaffin v. Stynchcombe*[29] that a harsher post-appeal sentence imposed by a jury did not violate due process, because the jury lacked knowledge of the first sentence and because the jury would "have no personal stake in the prior convictions and no motivation to engage in self-vindication."

In *Texas v. McCullough*[30] the second sentencer was the same judge who presided over the first trial. However, the sentence after the first trial was imposed by a jury and the second trial came about because the trial judge herself concluded that certain conduct by the prosecutor required it. Thus, the Court asserted, "unlike the judge who has been reversed, the trial judge here had no motivation to engage in self-vindication." Neither was there "justifiable concern about 'institutional interests that might occasion higher sentences by a judge desirous of discouraging what he regards as meritless appeals.'" The majority rejected as too "speculative" the dissent's argument that the judge may have been vindictive toward the defendant because she was forced to sit through a new trial whose result was a "foregone conclusion."

In possible contrast to these cases is *Thigpen v. Roberts*,[31] where the Court suggested that, in the *Blackledge* context, the presumption of vindictiveness is triggered even when the increase in charge is by a different prosecutor. However, the Court noted that the first prosecutor in this case had assisted the prosecutor at the second adjudication and held that "we need not decide the correct result when independent prosecutors are involved." In light of the Court's subsequent decision in *McCullough,* if the second prosecutor does not know of the first charge, or is from a different office, the Court may find that the institutional pressure to discourage "meritless appeals" does not exist, and thus that the presumption should not apply.

---

[26] See, e.g., *United States v. Goodwin,* 457 U.S. 368, 102 S.Ct. 2485 (1982).

[27] 417 U.S. 21, 94 S.Ct. 2098 (1974).

[28] 407 U.S. 104, 92 S.Ct. 1953 (1972).

[29] 412 U.S. 17, 93 S.Ct. 1977 (1973).

[30] 475 U.S. 134, 106 S.Ct. 976 (1986).

[31] 468 U.S. 27, 104 S.Ct. 2916 (1984).

The Court has also held that, even where the charging or sentencing authority is the same before and after the appeal, the presumption of vindictiveness is not triggered where the first charge and sentence occurred in the plea bargaining/guilty plea context and the second charge and sentence occur in connection with trial. The Court reached this conclusion (in *Alabama v. Smith*[32]) because "relevant sentencing information available to the judge after the plea will usually be considerably less than that available at trial," and because "the facts that may have indicated leniency as consideration for the guilty plea [such as the defendant's willingness to forego trial] are no longer present." Thus, a defendant who successfully overturns a guilty plea may be charged with the original, pre-plea bargain charge and, if convicted on it, subjected to a higher sentence than he received after the plea. The presumption of vindictiveness would apply, however, if the new charge was greater than the charge originally brought by the prosecutor.[33]

(2) Overcoming the Presumption

If the presumption does apply, *Pearce* held that an increased sentence or charge after the exercise of the right to appeal will stand only if the state provides proof of "identifiable conduct occurring after the time of the original sentencing proceeding." Subsequent cases have made clear that this language is not to be interpreted literally. In *Wasman v. United States*,[34] the judge imposed a higher sentence after a successful appeal because of an intervening conviction on another charge. The charge had been pending at the time of the original sentencing, but the judge had stated that he would consider only prior convictions, not pending charges, in imposing sentence. A unanimous Court upheld the new sentence, concluding that although the conviction did not represent new "conduct" by the defendant since the first sentencing, it was a new "event" that could be considered in showing a nonvindictive motive.

Similarly, in *McCullough,* discussed above, the Court concluded that even if, contrary to its holding, vindictiveness were to be presumed, the presumption was overcome in that case. There the judge's sentence after the second trial was thirty years longer than the sentence imposed by the jury after the first trial.[35] The judge justified this differential on the ground that the second trial had presented two new state witnesses who had added to the credibility of the state's case, shed new light on the defendant's personality, and revealed for the first time that he had been released from prison only four months before the murder. She also noted that the defendant had done nothing to rehabilitate himself between trials. According to Chief Justice Burger, this "new objective information . . . amply justified McCullough's increased sentence."

In dissent, Justice Marshall, joined by two others, pointed out that, with the exception of the latter reason, the judge relied on neither "new" conduct nor events to justify her decision. As Marshall noted: "If a court on retrial could justify an increased sentence on the ground that it now had additional knowledge concerning the defendant's participation in the offense, then the *Pearce* limitation could be evaded in almost every

---

[32]   490 U.S. 794, 109 S.Ct. 2201 (1989).

[33]   It would also probably apply when the prosecutor recharges for the original, pre-plea bargaining offense, if the reason the guilty plea was overturned was not involuntariness, but because the prosecution breached the plea bargain agreement. For further discussion of the vindictiveness issue in the guilty plea context, see § 26.02(c)(2).

[34]   468 U.S. 559, 104 S.Ct. 3217 (1984).

[35]   The sentence (50 years) equalled the sentence the same judge had given the defendant's two co-defendants.

case." Put another way, if *McCullough* does stand for the proposition that a higher sentence may be imposed anytime the judge can proffer a "new" explanation for the increase, and defendants know this, the right to appeal may be significantly chilled. Similarly, the likelihood of a higher charge after a successful appeal (or after filing for a trial *de novo,* as in *Blackledge*) is probably lower, but by no means *de minimis,* if prosecutors need merely discover "new information" about the details of the defendant's crime in order to up the ante.

(e) Waiver/Forfeiture of Appeal and Plain Error

The right to appeal can be lost in at least three ways. First, the defendant may voluntarily waive the right to appeal, which usually occurs in connection with the plea negotiation process. Most courts have upheld such waivers, if they are voluntary and the defendant understands their consequences.[36] Second, the defendant may forfeit the right to appeal if he is a "fugitive from justice during the pendency of his appeal."[37]

Third, defendants may forfeit the ability to appeal a particular issue if they did not object and preserve the issue at trial.[38] The Supreme Court has held that even constitutional rights can be forfeited in this way.[39] Moreover, in *Ohler v. United States,*[40] the Court indicated that, in federal court at least, forfeiture can occur *despite* objection, under limited circumstances. Thus, in *Ohler,* the fact that the defendant had made an unsuccessful pretrial motion in limine to exclude his prior convictions was mooted as a means of preserving the issue for appeal when his attorney used those convictions during direct examination at trial, even though the attorney's goal was solely to inoculate the defendant against use of the convictions for impeachment purposes during cross-examination.

The principal exception to the raise-or-waive rule is the plain error doctrine, recognized in federal and virtually all state courts.[41] As defined by the Supreme Court, this doctrine permits courts to reverse convictions when there is "(1) 'error,' (2) that is 'plain,' . . . (3) that 'affect[s] substantial rights' [and that] (4). . . . seriously affects the fairness, integrity, or public reputation of judicial proceedings."[42] No error occurs if the defendant voluntarily waives the right in question. If instead the right is forfeited as opposed to waived, error exists, but it must be obvious ("plain"). Additionally, under the third and fourth prongs, the error must have affected the outcome of the lower court proceedings, although not necessarily in the sense that a factually innocent person is convicted; the court may also consider whether the failure to correct the error is inherently unfair or seriously damages the image of the criminal justice system.[43] The Court has yet to decide whether "structural error" (which, as described later in this

---

[36]   See *United States v. Fisher,* 232 F.3d 301 (2d Cir. 2000) (collecting cases). However, the Supreme Court has held that failing to file a notice of appeal when the defendant asks the attorney to do so constitutes ineffective assistance of counsel even when there has been such a waiver. *Garza v. Idaho,* ___ U.S. ___, 139 S.Ct. 738 (2019).

[37]   *Ortega-Rodriguez v. United States,* 507 U.S. 234, 113 S.Ct. 1199 (1993).

[38]   See, e.g., Fed.R.Crim.P. 51.

[39]   *Yakus v. United States,* 321 U.S. 414, 64 S.Ct. 660 (1944).

[40]   529 U.S. 753, 120 S.Ct. 1851 (2000).

[41]   See, e.g., Fed.R.Crim.P. 52(b).

[42]   *Johnson v. United States,* 520 U.S. 461, 117 S.Ct. 1544 (1997).

[43]   *United States v. Olano,* 507 U.S. 725, 113 S.Ct. 1770 (1993). Consistent with this view is the rule that, even if the unobjected-to trial conduct challenged on appeal is error under law established *subsequent to trial*, the appellate court should consider it. *Henderson v. United States,* 568 U.S. 266, 113 S.Ct. 1121 (2013).

chapter, requires automatic reversal when timely objection is made[44]) always meets the third and fourth prongs of the plain error standard. Justice Scalia, for instance, has asserted that structural errors that are not objected to do not require relief, because "[i]t is a universally acknowledged principle of law that one who sleeps on his rights—even fundamental rights—may lose them."[45]

However, in at least one such situation no prejudice need be shown even when no objection is made. In *Nguyen v. United States*,[46] the Court reversed an appellate court decision upholding a conviction because one of the judges on the appellate panel had not been an Article III judge. Despite the absence of an objection from the defendant, the Court insisted that "*no one* other than a properly constituted panel of Article III judges is empowered to exercise appellate jurisdiction in these cases."

29.03　The Final Judgment Rule

(a)　Defense Appeals

In addition to appeals after conviction and sentence, interlocutory appeals of decisions reached preliminary to adjudication of guilt may occasionally be attempted by the defendant. The procedural viability of these appeals is governed by the final judgment rule, which is observed in some form or other in virtually every jurisdiction.[47] The rule attempts to discourage piecemeal and time-consuming pretrial litigation by providing, as the relevant federal legislation puts it,[48] that only "final decisions" of the trial court are appealable.

A final judgment is not always required to perfect an appeal, however. In *Cohen v. Beneficial Industrial Loan Corp.*,[49] the Supreme Court articulated an exception to the final judgment rule that permits appeal of "a small class [of pretrial judgments] which finally determine claims of right separable from, and collateral to, rights asserted in the action, too important to be denied review and too independent of the cause itself to require that appellate consideration be deferred until the whole case is adjudicated." *Cohen* identified several factors that must be present before a claim may be appealed as a "collateral order." First, a trial court must have made a final determination on the issue, not leaving it open, unfinished or inconclusive. Second, the issue must involve an important right that would "be lost, probably irreparably" if review had to await final judgment. Third, the appealed right must not be an ingredient of the main cause of action. Relatedly, an appeals court must not be required to consider the main cause of action while reviewing the collateral issue. Although *Cohen* was a civil case, it was based on a construction of 28 U.S.C.A. § 1291, which covers both criminal and civil cases, and its reasoning has been applied in a number of Supreme Court cases involving criminal litigation. Many state courts utilize its test in interpreting their own final judgment rules.[50]

---

[44]　See § 29.05(c)(2).

[45]　*Neder v. United States*, 527 U.S. 1, 119 S.Ct. 1827 (1999) (Scalia, J., dissenting).

[46]　539 U.S. 69, 123 S.Ct. 2130 (2003).

[47]　See 15 Wright et al., supra note 5, at § 3918.

[48]　28 U.S.C.A. § 1291.

[49]　337 U.S. 541, 69 S.Ct. 1221 (1949).

[50]　See e.g., *Commonwealth v. Bolden,* 472 Pa. 602, 373 A.2d 90 (1977).

Not surprisingly, given the efficiency concerns underlying the final judgment rule, the Supreme Court has found that only a few types of judicial orders in criminal cases fit within the *Cohen* test. In *Stack v. Boyle*,[51] the Court held, in line with the current federal statute,[52] that the defendant may pursue a pretrial appeal of a judicial decision rejecting an argument that bail was excessive under the Eighth Amendment. It found that the judge's bail determination was sufficiently independent of the main cause of action to be considered a final judgment for appeal purposes, that the issue would be moot if raised after conviction, and that failing to preserve the bail right at the pretrial stage would render the presumption of innocence and the right to an unhampered preparation of one's defense meaningless. Similarly, a pretrial order denying a motion to dismiss an indictment on double jeopardy grounds has been found to fit within the *Cohen* class of cases. As the Court noted in *Abney v. United States*,[53] if a criminal defendant is to avoid exposure to jeopardy a second time and thereby enjoy full protection of the right, his double jeopardy challenge must normally be heard before the second adjudication.[54] The collateral order exception announced in *Cohen* also applies to orders in civil rights cases denying officials qualified immunity.[55] Indeed, the Court has held that, in order to implement the "right" of immune officials to avoid undergoing any unnecessary litigation, the exception permits an immediate appeal on this issue after the summary judgment stage even if an appeal has already been taken after the dismissal stage, given the additional information likely to be available at the summary judgment stage.[56] The Court has also permitted interlocutory appeal of court orders permitting forcible medication of defendants found incompetent to stand trial, in part because by the time of trial the defendant "will have undergone forced medication—the very harm he seeks to avoid," but primarily because of the extremely intrusive nature of such medication.[57]

On the other hand, the Court has indicated that most claims do not come within the collateral order exception. In *Carroll v. United States*,[58] the Court denied the appealability of orders on post-indictment search and seizure motions because, given the fact that seized evidence is usually crucial at trial, such orders are not "independent" of the ongoing case against the defendant.[59] And in *DiBella v. United States*,[60] the Court held that a ruling on a *pre*-indictment order to suppress evidence under the Fourth Amendment normally does not constitute a final judgment either, even though it is less clear that the order is part of the ongoing litigation. The Court, in an opinion by Justice

---

[51]   342 U.S. 1, 72 S.Ct. 1 (1951).

[52]   18 U.S.C.A. § 3147(b).

[53]   431 U.S. 651, 97 S.Ct. 2034 (1977).

[54]   However, in *Illinois v. Vitale*, 447 U.S. 410, 100 S.Ct. 2260 (1980), the Court found that in certain "rare" instances it might be necessary to proceed with the second trial despite the double jeopardy claim in order to determine whether the evidence the prosecution intends to use is sufficiently similar to the evidence it relied upon in the first trial to justify a finding that the "same offense" is involved. See § 30.04(a)(2).

[55]   *Mitchell v. Forsyth*, 472 U.S. 511, 105 S.Ct. 2806 (1985).

[56]   *Behrens v. Pelletier*, 516 U.S. 299, 116 S.Ct. 834 (1996). But see *Will v. Hallock*, 546 U.S. 345, 126 S.Ct. 952 (2006), which limited this right to situations where a substantial public interest would otherwise be imperiled; thus a dismissal of a claim against the *government* on procedural grounds did not require immediate review of a parallel suit against individual agents.

[57]   *Sell v. United States*, 539 U.S. 166, 123 S.Ct. 2174 (2003).

[58]   354 U.S. 394, 77 S.Ct. 1332 (1957).

[59]   The Court found such orders non appealable whether the appeal is brought by the defense *or* the prosecution. But see § 29.04.

[60]   369 U.S. 121, 82 S.Ct. 654 (1962).

Frankfurter, saw little practical difference between pre- and post-indictment rulings of this sort. First, unlike a bail determination, in neither case is the Fourth Amendment ruling "fairly severable" from the rest of the litigation, because it may well determine the conduct of the trial. Second, an appeal could "entail serious disruption" of the litigation process, perhaps becoming "an instrument of harassment, jeopardizing by delay the availability of other essential evidence." Third, "appellate intervention makes for truncated presentation of the issue of admissibility, because the legality of the search too often cannot truly be determined until the evidence at the trial has brought all circumstances to light."

The Court also acknowledged, however, that forcing a litigant to wait until after trial to seek return of property seized by the government may be an insufficient remedy, in that one's right to one's property prior to the post-trial appeal would be "irreparably lost." Thus, the Court held that suppression orders *are* appealable "if the motion is solely for return of property and is in no way tied to a criminal prosecution *in esse* [in being] against the movant." The federal courts have construed this language to permit appeals of denied motions whose "primary purpose" was to seek the return of seized property, if the order occurs in the early phases of the investigatory process.[61] This latter limitation makes sense, since the closer to trial the appeal occurs the more likely it will disrupt the prosecution, result from insincere motives, and not afford relief substantially different from a post-trial appeal.

Also resolved under the *Cohen* criteria was *United States v. MacDonald,*[62] in which the Court held that a defendant may not bring a pretrial appeal of a court's order denying a motion to dismiss an indictment on speedy trial grounds. The Court stressed that the review of such an order normally requires an appeals court to view not just the circumstances leading up to trial, but the quality and amount of evidence at trial itself.[63] Even more important, vacating the defendant's conviction provides an adequate remedy for violation of her Sixth Amendment right; unlike, for instance, the double jeopardy prohibition, the speedy trial right is not a "right not to be tried" but a right to avoid pretrial delay, which in fact could be harmed by allowing pretrial appeal. Finally, if a right to immediate appeal were recognized, "any defendant" could raise such a claim as a dilatory tactic since "nothing about . . . a speedy trial claim . . . inherently limits [its] availability."

Less persuasively, the Court held, in *United States v. Hollywood Motor Car Co.,*[64] that the pretrial appeal of an order denying a motion to dismiss an indictment based on prosecutorial vindictiveness was improper. As in *MacDonald,* the Court found there were adequate post-trial means of protecting the *Pearce-Blackledge* right,[65] specifically, reversal of the conviction and a new trial on charges not tainted by prosecutorial

---

[61]   The courts are split as to whether a pre-indictment post-arrest suppression order of the type at issue in *DiBella* is part of a prosecution *in esse*. Compare *United States v. One Residence and Attached Garage,* 603 F.2d 1231 (7th Cir. 1979) to *Standard Drywall, Inc. v. United States,* 668 F.2d 156 (2d Cir. 1982), cert. denied 456 U.S. 927, 102 S.Ct. 1973 (1982), rehearing denied 457 U.S. 1112, 102 S.Ct. 2917 (1982) (order pending grand jury investigation is nonappealable).

[62]   435 U.S. 850, 98 S.Ct. 1547 (1978).

[63]   See § 25.04(d). Similarly, in *Flanagan v. United States,* 465 U.S. 259, 104 S.Ct. 1051 (1984), the Court held nonappealable an order disqualifying defendants' attorney because the "effect of the disqualification on the defense, and hence whether the asserted right had been violated, cannot be fairly assessed until the substance of the prosecution's and defendant's case is known."

[64]   458 U.S. 263, 102 S.Ct. 3081 (1982).

[65]   See § 29.02(d).

vindictiveness. The Court gave short shrift to the petitioner's argument that, like a double jeopardy violation, *Pearce* and *Blackledge* guaranteed the defendant a right not to be tried on particular charges (here the higher charge motivated by vindictiveness). Rather, it asserted that there is a "crucial distinction between a right not to be tried and a right whose remedy requires the dismissal of charges." Pretrial vindication of the latter type of right usually merely *delays* trial (albeit, in this case, on the lower charge), and thus need not be allowed.[66]

As Justice Blackmun pointed out in dissent, *Hollywood* is not easily reconciled with the Court's past cases. First, the majority's reasoning notwithstanding, a *Pearce-Blackledge* claim—at least one based on vindictiveness in *charging*[67] (the claim at issue in *MacDonald*)—arguably does contemplate a right not to be tried, and thus a post-trial remedy for prosecutorial vindictiveness may be insufficient. The rationale of *Pearce* and *Blackledge* is preservation of the right to appeal by removing inhibitions to its exercise. Allowing the prosecutor to try the defendant on increased charges could create such an inhibition, even if any subsequent conviction could be overturned, since a *third* trial would then be required. Furthermore, unlike determination of a speedy trial claim, whether increased charges are vindictive can be determined from facts already available at the time of the pretrial appeal and collateral to the case against the defendant. Finally, unlike a speedy trial challenge or most other claims, the class of defendants who could plausibly assert a vindictiveness claim is inherently limited and easily ascertained because it is based on an increased charge; thus, the fear of dilatory tactics raised in *MacDonald* is inapposite here.

A more general consideration is that *Hollywood,* like the Court's decisions in this area generally, may have taken insufficient account of the possibility that immediate correction of an erroneous pretrial ruling, particularly if it disposes of the case, will be more efficient than requiring the case to proceed through adjudication before appeal is possible. In civil litigation, for instance, 28 U.S.C.A. § 1292(b) allows district court judges to certify for appeal pretrial rulings that involve "a controlling question of law as to which there is substantial ground for difference of opinion" if immediate appeal would "materially advance the ultimate termination of the litigation." In *Mohawk Industries v. Carpenter*,[68] the Court noted that this option is most likely to be available when the claim involves "a new legal question or is of special consequence." However, at present § 1292(b) applies only in civil cases.

(b) Prosecution Appeals

The final judgment rule may not apply as forcefully to the prosecution as it does to the defense. For instance, as discussed in the next section, some states provide by statute that certain pretrial rulings that the defendant cannot appeal on an interlocutory basis (e.g., suppression hearing rulings) may be appealable pretrial by the prosecution. This stance can be justified on the ground that, analogous to the Court's rationale in *Cohen,* the prosecution might otherwise be "irreparably" barred from any appellate review of

---

[66] See also, *Midland Asphalt Corp. v. United States*, 489 U.S. 794, 109 S.Ct. 1494 (1989) (likelihood that violation of rules governing grand jury process will be found harmless on post-conviction appeal, see § 23.06(b), does not mean interlocutory appeal is permissible, because the only remedy granted by such an appeal would be dismissal of charges, which does not foreclose a new indictment).

[67] Note that if the vindictiveness claim is instead that an increase in sentence is vindictive, then the argument in the text would not follow. See § 29.02(d).

[68] 558 U.S. 100, 130 S.Ct. 599 (2009).

the judgment; if, because of the pretrial ruling, charges are dismissed for lack of evidence or the prosecution fails to obtain a conviction, the Double Jeopardy Clause would bar appeal on the pretrial ruling. Not only might this prevent justice in the individual case; it might also lead to the proliferation of "erroneous" rulings at the trial court level. Furthermore, it might be argued, the prosecution is less likely than the defense to use such appeals as a dilatory tactic.

Of course, even if all of these points are true, pretrial appeals by the prosecution can significantly abridge the defendant's right to a speedy resolution of the charges against him. Nonetheless, most speedy trial statutes exclude any pretrial appeal period from speedy trial calculations.[69] Further, the Supreme Court has suggested it would find no constitutional infirmities in this practice, so long as the prosecution's case is not frivolous.[70]

(c) Third Party Appeals

Third parties may seek to appeal a pretrial ruling in a criminal case in two different contexts. First, the third party may allege that he should not have to follow a given court order, such as a subpoena. In this situation, the Supreme Court held in *Cobbledick v. United States,*[71] the order is not appealable unless the third party refuses to comply and has been held in contempt by the court. However, if a contempt citation is issued, then an appeal is appropriate; a contrary holding "would forever preclude review of the witness' claim, for his alternatives are to abandon the claim or languish in jail."

The second way in which a third party might seek to challenge a criminal trial court ruling is when the ruling is not directed at him, but it nonetheless infringes a legal interest of his. The most obvious example of such a case is when the press protests a closure order or a gag order. In this situation, the third party is usually allowed an interlocutory appeal, on the grounds that its claim is "independent" of the criminal action, even though it may work to delay that action.

29.04   Appeals by the Prosecution

Generally, as Chapter 30 explains,[72] the Double Jeopardy Clause bars government appeal of any acquittal at a jury or bench trial, as well as any other judicial judgment which involves a finding that there is insufficient evidence to convict the defendant. However, other rulings may be appealed by the prosecution, *provided* it has statutory duty to do so. As the Supreme Court stated in *Carroll v. United States:*[73]

> [A]ppeals by the government in criminal cases are something unusual, exceptional, not favored. The history shows resistance of the Court to the opening of an appellate route for the Government until it was plainly provided by the Congress, and after that a close restriction of its uses to those authorized by the statute.

The most common situation covered by such statutes is prosecutorial appeal of a pretrial motion to suppress evidence. For example, on the federal level, 18 U.S.C.A.

---

[69]   See § 25.05(c) for a description of the federal statute on this point.

[70]   See *United States v. Loud Hawk,* 474 U.S. 302, 106 S.Ct. 648 (1986), discussed in § 25.04(b).

[71]   309 U.S. 323, 60 S.Ct. 540 (1940).

[72]   See in particular, § 30.03(a)(2).

[73]   354 U.S. 394, 77 S.Ct. 1332 (1957).

§ 3731 provides for interlocutory prosecutorial appeal of a district court decision to suppress or exclude evidence having a substantial bearing on the case. As noted in the previous section, such provisions are popular because, if the defendant is acquitted at trial (which could easily occur if the suppressed evidence is crucial to the prosecution's case), the Double Jeopardy Clause will bar the prosecution from appealing the adverse pretrial ruling after trial. A pretrial appeal, on the other hand, occurs before jeopardy has attached and thus is not barred.[74]

The Supreme Court has also held that the prosecution may appeal *post*-jeopardy rulings that do not involve a finding that the evidence was insufficient to convict.[75] While this stance can be questioned in some contexts,[76] it seems appropriate when the appealed order is a post-conviction finding by the trial judge "arresting" or "vacating" the jury's guilty verdict on the ground that it is not supported by the evidence. Statutes permitting such appeals do not violate the double jeopardy prohibition because a successful prosecutorial appeal does not subject the defendant to a new trial and additional jeopardy, but merely reinstates the jury verdict.[77]

The prosecution may also appeal a *sentence*, at least in non-capital cases. As discussed in more detail in the next chapter,[78] because capital sentencing procedure resembles a trial, the Supreme Court has held that the Double Jeopardy Clause prohibits an appeal arguing that a life sentence imposed by a judge or a jury should be reconsidered at a new sentencing proceeding and converted into a death sentence.[79] However, because the typical non-capital sentencing proceeding does not resemble a trial either procedurally or in terms of the factors the sentencing tribunal must consider, a prosecution appeal that leads to resentencing in the non-capital context usually does not implicate the Clause, provided, once again, that a statute authorizes the appeal.[80]

29.05   Harmless Error

(a) Various Approaches

When an appellate court finds that error has occurred at the trial level, its simplest option would be reversal of the judgment below, regardless of the type of error involved or the overall strength of the case. For some time during the nineteenth century, "automatic reversal" was, in effect, the rule in England. The so-called Exchequer Rule presumed prejudice from any trial defect, and thus virtually always required a new trial when error was found.[81] But, as might be imagined, this system bred numerous retrials and sometimes multiple retrials in the same case, at considerable damage to judicial economy, the witnesses and the litigants.[82] The lesson of the British experience was not

---

[74]   See § 30.02(b).

[75]   *United States v. Scott,* 437 U.S. 82, 98 S.Ct. 2187 (1978).

[76]   See § 30.03(b).

[77]   Compare *Tibbs v. Florida,* 457 U.S. 31, 102 S.Ct. 2211 (1982), in which the Florida Supreme Court characterized its reversal of the defendant's conviction as a decision that the jury's verdict was against the weight of the evidence. According to the United States Supreme Court, this finding was not an "acquittal" for double jeopardy purposes. Thus, reprosecution was permitted. See § 30.03(a)(2).

[78]   A fuller discussion of this issue is found in § 30.05.

[79]   *Bullington v. Missouri,* 451 U.S. 430, 101 S.Ct. 1852 (1981).

[80]   *United States v. DiFrancesco,* 449 U.S. 117, 101 S.Ct. 426 (1980).

[81]   See Roger J. Traynor, The Riddle of Harmless Error (1970), at 6–10.

[82]   See Steven H. Goldberg, *Harmless Error, Constitutional Sneak Thief,* 71 J.Crim.L. & Criminol. 421, 422 (1980).

lost on American courts. As one American court later put it, treating every error as reversible can be seen as "archaic formalism and . . . watery sentiment that obstructs, delays, and defeats the prosecution of crime."[83]

Accordingly, in addition to requiring timely objection before most claims of error will even be heard,[84] every American jurisdiction has adopted some kind of "harmless error" rule, which allows an appellate court to hold that error is so insignificant that the trial court verdict should stand.[85] While this authority avoids the drawbacks of an automatic reversal rule, it can require very speculative assessments about the impact of error. Further, because harmless error analysis is likely to vary in each case, depending upon the idiosyncrasies of the record, it is difficult to describe in a way that is helpful to courts or litigants. But because the number of harmless error findings today is significant,[86] some understanding of its contours is important.

At least four different definitions of harmless error can be discerned from the cases.[87] The broadest is the so-called "correct ruling" test, which finds an error harmless if the appellate court believes, based on an assessment of all the evidence, that the trial court's verdict is correct. This approach has been criticized because it places the appellate court in the position of second-guessing the trial factfinder, which is not its function and may run afoul of the right to jury trial.[88] The remaining three approaches attempt to correct for this problem. The "overwhelming evidence" test requires looking at all of the "left-over" evidence to determine whether it is so overwhelmingly supportive of the verdict, and the relative significance of the error so small, that the factfinder could not have been affected by the error. Next there is the "cumulative evidence" test, which does not consider all of the untainted evidence, but instead permits a finding of harmlessness only if the factfinder was presented with admissible information that proved the same facts the tainted evidence proved; the theory here is that only in this situation is the factfinder not likely to have placed weight on the error in its deliberations.[89] Finally, there is the "effect of the error" test, which pays no attention to the other evidence, focusing entirely on whether the error could have had any effect on the factfinder.

In practice, there may be very little difference between these tests, since each is subject to manipulation by appellate judges, especially in terms of the degree of certainty required (compare, for example, a test which requires the appellate court to find, "beyond a reasonable doubt," that the trial court reached the correct result and a test which requires the appellate court to find that the error "probably" had no effect on the factfinder).[90] Assuming there is a practical difference between the tests, other problems arise. For instance, because they focus on the effect of the error on the factfinder, the

---

[83]   *United States v. Garsson,* 291 Fed. 646 (S.D.N.Y. 1923).

[84]   See § 29.02(e).

[85]   To be distinguished from the harmless error doctrine is the plain error rule, which determines when an appellate court can hear claims that were not raised at trial. In contrast to harmless error, plain error involves only "defects affecting substantial rights," see, e.g., Fed.R.Crim.P. 52(b), whose recognition is necessary to avoid "a miscarriage of justice." *United States v. Frady,* 456 U.S. 152, 102 S.Ct. 1584 (1982).

[86]   Francis Allen, *A Serendipitous Trek Through the Advance-Sheet Jungle: Criminal Justice in the Courts of Review,* 70 Iowa L.Rev. 311, 329–332 (1985).

[87]   To a large extent, these approaches are adapted from Traynor, supra note 81.

[88]   Id. at 13.

[89]   For the most forceful support of this approach, see Martha Field, *Assessing the Harmlessness of Federal Constitutional Error—A Process in Need of a Rationale,* 125 U.Pa.L.Rev. 15 (1976).

[90]   Stephen Saltzburg, *The Harm of Harmless Error,* 59 Va.L.Rev. 988, 1014 (1973).

last three tests may not be very useful when the error is "non-evidentiary," such as is the case with a violation of the right to counsel. The fourth test can also be criticized on the ground that analyzing the impact of the error in the abstract is a meaningless endeavor. And, as already noted, the first test is thought to be deficient because it places the appellate court in the role of the jury or trial judge.

(b) The Federal Rule for Non-Constitutional Error

In *Kotteakos v. United States,*[91] the Supreme Court deliberated upon the harmless error standard to be applied in the federal courts to non-constitutional error. It specifically rejected a "correct result" test, reasoning that "it is not the appellate court's function to determine guilt or innocence[, n]or is it to speculate upon probable reconviction and decide according to how the speculation comes out." Instead, the Court held error is harmless only when "the error did not influence the jury, or had but very slight effect." Thus, "if one cannot say, with fair assurance, after pondering all that happened without stripping the erroneous action from the whole, that the judgment was not substantially swayed by the error, it is impossible to conclude that substantial rights were not affected." In short, for the purpose of assessing the harmlessness of non-constitutional error in federal court, the Court appeared to adopt a version of the "overwhelming evidence" test, and require a "fair assurance" that it is met.[92]

(c) Constitutional Error

Kotteakos specifically declined to apply its test to departures from "a constitutional norm." Thus, the possibility remained that the Court would adopt a more stringent test, or a rule of automatic reversal, when the error was of constitutional magnitude. The first intimation that the latter approach would not be taken came in *Fahy v. Connecticut,*[93] where the error involved was the introduction of evidence illegally seized under the Fourth Amendment. The Court in *Fahy* held that constitutional error could be harmless where there was no "reasonable possibility" that the error "might have contributed to the verdict," although it eventually concluded that the error in this case was not harmless.[94]

Four years later, in *Chapman v. California,*[95] the Court formally adopted a harmless error test for constitutional error, reframing *Fahy's* language to require the prosecution to prove "beyond a reasonable doubt that the error complained of did not contribute to the verdict obtained." This formulation obviously rejected the "correct result" test, given its emphasis on the effect the error has on the factfinder. Furthermore, it clearly established that the absence of such an effect must be demonstrated by the prosecution, beyond a reasonable doubt, before a harmless error finding will be made, which conforms with the prosecution's burden and standard of proof in criminal cases.[96] But the opinion did not make clear whether the Court meant to adopt an "overwhelming evidence" test, a "cumulative evidence" test, or an "effect of the error" test. Subsequent Court cases seem to have vacillated between the first two standards, and occasionally may even have

---

[91]   328 U.S. 750, 66 S.Ct. 1239 (1946).

[92]   In *Brecht v. Abrahamson,* 507 U.S. 619, 113 S.Ct. 1710 (1993), the Court held that the *Kotteakos* standard also applies on habeas review. See § 33.02(f).

[93]   375 U.S. 85, 84 S.Ct. 229 (1963).

[94]   For further discussion of *Fahy,* see § 29.05(c)(1) below.

[95]   386 U.S. 18, 87 S.Ct. 824 (1967).

[96]   *In re Winship,* 397 U.S. 358, 90 S.Ct. 1068 (1970).

applied the correct result approach. On the other hand, other Court cases have made clear that *certain* types of constitutional error must result in automatic reversal, regardless of its effect on the factfinder. These two lines of cases are discussed below.

(1) The Reasonable Doubt Test

Many of the Court's cases, especially prior to the 1970's, appeared to subscribe to relatively restrictive definitions of harmless error. For instance, in *Fahy*, the Court found that the trial court's admission of illegally obtained evidence (consisting of paint and brushes that the defendant used to paint a swastika on a synagogue) was not harmless, even though there was substantial independent evidence against the defendant, including several admissions and a confession. The majority stressed that the evidence made the arresting officer's testimony "far more damaging than it would otherwise have been," and was used to "forg[e] another link between the accused and the crime charged."

In *Chapman*, the prosecutor's closing argument repeatedly referred to the defendant's failure to take the stand and the judge instructed the jury that it could draw an adverse inference from this failure, clearly violations of the Fifth Amendment rule announced in *Griffin v. California*.[97] The Court found reversal necessary, stating that "though the case in which this occurred presented a reasonably strong 'circumstantial web of evidence' against petitioners, it was also a case in which, absent the constitutionally forbidden comments, honest fair-minded jurors might very well have brought in not-guilty verdicts." The Court found it "completely impossible" to say beyond a reasonable doubt that the error did not contribute to the verdict.

The error in *Harrington v. California*[98] was a violation of *Bruton v. United States*,[99] occurring because the trial court had admitted the confessions of two codefendants who did not take the stand and thus were not subject to confrontation by the defendant, who was implicated by both confessions. In finding this error harmless, Justice Douglas stressed that the confessions were merely "cumulative." Although they placed the defendant at the scene of the crime, so did the defendant's own admissions, the statements of several eyewitnesses, and the statements of a third co-defendant who did take the stand. Thus, concluded Douglas, it was extremely unlikely the illegally introduced confessions contributed to the verdict. He also remarked that the untainted evidence was "so overwhelming" that to reverse the conviction would amount to making a *Bruton* violation an automatic reversal error.

All of these decisions focused primarily on the nature of the tainted evidence and its possible effect on the jury. Arguably, all of them are also consistent with the relatively restrictive "cumulative evidence" test for harmless error. In contrast, many of the Court's cases subsequent to *Harrington* focused almost entirely on the nature and quality of the *legally* admitted evidence and adopted either an "overwhelming evidence" test or a "correct result" approach.

For instance, the error in *Schneble v. Florida*,[100] a capital murder prosecution, again involved a *Bruton* violation, this time the admission of testimony from an officer recounting statements of a codefendant suggesting that Schneble strangled the victim.

[97]   380 U.S. 609, 85 S.Ct. 1229 (1965), discussed in § 28.03(c)(1).

[98]   395 U.S. 250, 89 S.Ct. 1726 (1969).

[99]   391 U.S. 123, 88 S.Ct. 1620 (1968), discussed in § 28.04(d).

[100] 405 U.S. 427, 92 S.Ct. 1056 (1972).

Because "the independent evidence of guilt [was] overwhelming"—in particular Schneble's own "minute and grisly" confession and rope burns on his hands—the Court, in a 6–3 decision authored by Justice Rehnquist, held that the admission of the tainted evidence was harmless beyond a reasonable doubt. In dissent, Justice Marshall, joined by Justice Douglas, the author of *Harrington,* and Justice Brennan, pointed out that the petitioner had originally placed the blame for the murder on his codefendant and had confessed only after "a series of bizarre acts by the police designed to frighten him into making incriminating statements." Although the trial judge had made a threshold finding that Schneble's confession was voluntary, he had instructed the jury that if it doubted the voluntariness of the confession it should disregard it. Marshall argued that there was at least a reasonable possibility that the jury had indeed found Schneble's confession, or at least that part of it stating that he had strangled the victim, involuntary and thus irrelevant, but had convicted him anyway on the strength of the other evidence in the case, including the tainted evidence.

The same term as *Schneble* the Court decided *Milton v. Wainwright,*[101] where the defendant alleged that a confession, obtained by a police officer who posed as a fellow prisoner of the defendant's, should not have been admitted at his trial. Without squarely addressing whether this admission was error, the Court went on to hold that it was harmless in any event, given the fact that three other confessions made by the defendant were *validly* admitted into evidence. Although this result could have been reached under a "cumulative evidence" test, the Court spoke solely of the "overwhelming amount of independent evidence."

Similarly, in *United States v. Hasting,*[102] the Court assumed, without definitively deciding, that the prosecutor had violated *Griffin,*[103] and then declared the error harmless based on an assessment of the remaining evidence, using language that sounded like a correct result test. As Chief Justice Burger stated for the majority, "[t]he question a reviewing court must ask is this: absent the prosecutor's allusion to the failure of the defense to proffer evidence to rebut the testimony of the victims, is it clear beyond a reasonable doubt that the jury would have returned a verdict of guilty?" This formulation subtly rearranges the inquiry from one which focuses on the effect of the error on the jury, as *Chapman* required, to one which looks at whether the remaining evidence supports the jury's guilty verdict.

But the Supreme Court's approach to harmless error is not easily pinned down, perhaps because harmless error analysis is so context-dependent. The same term as *Hasting,* the plurality opinion in *Connecticut v. Johnson*[104] refused to find harmless an erroneous jury instruction, despite overwhelming evidence against the defendant, because of the possible effect of the instruction on the jury. The judge had instructed the jury, in a case where the defendant was charged with a specific intent crime, that every person is "conclusively presumed to intend the natural and necessary consequences of his acts," in clear violation of the Court's ruling in *Sandstrom v. Montana.*[105] The four-

---

[101]   407 U.S. 371, 92 S.Ct. 2174 (1972).

[102]   461 U.S. 499, 103 S.Ct. 1974 (1983).

[103]   As Justice Stevens argued in a concurring opinion, the Court could easily have held no violation occurred, since the prosecutor did not comment on the defendant's failure to take the stand, but only on his failure to present evidence challenging certain aspects of the prosecution's case.

[104]   460 U.S. 73, 103 S.Ct. 969 (1983).

[105]   442 U.S. 510, 99 S.Ct. 2450 (1979) (prohibiting presumptive intent instructions because they violate the proof beyond a reasonable doubt requirement).

member dissent pointed out that the facts of the case definitively established the defendant committed the crime, and argued from this that the jury "could have regarded these facts as dispositive of intent and not relied on the presumption." But the plurality, in an opinion by Justice Blackmun, held that the instruction "permitted the jury to convict respondent without ever examining the evidence concerning an element of the crime charged," and thus could not be considered harmless beyond a reasonable doubt. Justice Stevens joined the result reached by the plurality because he felt the case did not raise a federal question.

For a time it appeared that *Hasting* and *Johnson* could be distinguished from one another on the ground that the latter involved a jury instruction that misconstrued an element of the crime, the impact of which is difficult to gauge regardless of the evidence against the defendant. In *Yates v. Evatt*,[106] for instance, the Court again analyzed the impact of an instruction erroneously telling the jury to presume intent. In a unanimous opinion written by Justice Souter, the Court took to task the South Carolina Supreme Court for finding that the instruction was harmless error, particularly because the test that court applied was whether the other evidence in the case established beyond a reasonable doubt that the jury "would have found it unnecessary to rely" on the unconstitutional presumption. Souter pointed out that this inquiry "will not tell us whether the jury's verdict did rest on that evidence as well as on the presumptions, or whether that evidence was of such compelling force as to show beyond a reasonable doubt that the presumptions must have made no difference in reaching the verdict obtained." It is the latter issue that must be addressed, according to the Court. Although admitting that discerning what the jury actually considered was impossible, the Court emphasized that the reviewing court should conduct harmless error analysis with this ultimate goal in mind.[107]

The same type of reasoning would seem to apply when the judge *fails* to instruct the jury about an element of the crime: in the absence of such an instruction, the jury may well not consider the evidence relevant to that element. But in *Neder v. United States*[108] the Court held that a failure to tell the jury that "materiality" was an element of tax fraud was harmless because the evidence of materiality was "overwhelming" and "uncontested." The dissent focused on whether this type of error was "structural," not on whether harmless error analysis in such cases should focus on the amount of evidence or instead should look at whether the error influenced the jury. Thus, the Court may now have adopted the "correct ruling" or "overwhelming evidence" test for analyzing the harmfulness of *all* non-structural errors.

(2) Errors Requiring Automatic Reversal

In *Chapman*, the Court cautioned that certain constitutional errors may involve "rights so basic to a fair trial that their infraction can never be treated as harmless

---

[106] 500 U.S. 391, 111 S.Ct. 1884 (1991).

[107] The lower courts also generally find that instructions that misstate the prosecution's burden are not harmless, regardless of the evidence presented. See, e.g., *United States v. Jones,* 909 F.2d 533 (D.C.Cir. 1990); *Hall v. Kelso,* 892 F.2d 1541 (11th Cir. 1990); *Reid v. Warden,* 708 F.Supp. 730 (W.D.N.C. 1989); *Groesbeck v. Housewright,* 657 F.Supp. 798 (D.Nev. 1987).

[108] 527 U.S. 1, 119 S.Ct. 1827 (1999).

error." It then cited cases involving a coerced confession,[109] the right to trial counsel,[110] and the right to an impartial judge.[111] In other decisions, the Court has suggested that violation of the right to speedy trial,[112] the Double Jeopardy Clause,[113] and the right to a representative jury[114] and grand jury[115] should never be deemed harmless.

The Court's first attempt to explain in general terms why these types of errors require automatic reversal rather than analysis under the reasonable doubt standard came in *Arizona v. Fulminante,*[116] in the course of "reversing" *Payne v. Arkansas,*[117] the case which *Chapman* cited in support of its statement that admission of a coerced confession is never harmless error. In *Fulminante,* Chief Justice Rehnquist contended for a five-member majority that the "common thread" connecting post-*Chapman* cases permitting a harmless error finding was that they involved "trial error." This type of error, according to Rehnquist, is "error which occurred during the presentation of the case to the jury, and which may therefore be quantitatively assessed in the context of other evidence presented in order to determine whether its admission was harmless beyond a reasonable doubt." Calling admission of an involuntary confession a "classic" trial error, Rehnquist distinguished it from the two other examples *Chapman* gave of automatic reversal situations—"total deprivation of the right to counsel at trial" and a trial judge who was not impartial. These "structural defects" infect the entire trial and thus "defy analysis by 'harmless error' standards."

This conceptualization of harmless error doctrine has some appeal. As noted earlier, the most commonly advocated harmless error standards all focus on the effect of the error on the factfinder, assessment of which is always difficult, but particularly so when the error is "structural." Whether the trial-versus-structural error dichotomy explains all of the Court's cases is not clear, however. For instance, while faulty jury instructions have generally been subject to harmless error analysis in congruence with *Fulminante's* notion that trial errors can be found harmless,[118] the Court has rejected use of that analysis when the judge fails to instruct the jury on the reasonable doubt standard.[119] Further, while *Fulminante* reaffirmed *Chapman's* holding that deprivation of the right to trial counsel should bring automatic reversal, deprivation of that right at pretrial

---

[109]   *Payne v. Arkansas,* 356 U.S. 560, 78 S.Ct. 844 (1958) ("where, as here, a coerced confession constitutes a part of the evidence before the jury and a general verdict is returned, no one can say what credit and weight the jury gave to the confession.").

[110]   *Gideon v. Wainwright,* 372 U.S. 335, 83 S.Ct. 792 (1963), discussed in § 31.02(b).

[111]   *Tumey v. Ohio,* 273 U.S. 510, 47 S.Ct. 437 (1927), discussed in § 27.05(a).

[112]   *Strunk v. United States,* 412 U.S. 434, 93 S.Ct. 2260 (1973).

[113]   *Price v. Georgia,* 398 U.S. 323, 90 S.Ct. 1757 (1970).

[114]   *Taylor v. Louisiana,* 419 U.S. 522, 95 S.Ct. 692 (1975).

[115]   *Vasquez v. Hillery,* 474 U.S. 254, 106 S.Ct. 617 (1986).

[116]   499 U.S. 279, 111 S.Ct. 1246 (1991).

[117]   356 U.S. 560, 78 S.Ct. 844 (1958). The majority in *Fulminante* denied that it was reversing *Payne,* since at the time of the latter decision the harmless error test was whether there was sufficient evidence in the absence of the error to support a conviction. According to the *Fulminante* majority, all *Payne* held was that admission of a coerced confession calls for automatic reversal under this more lenient, pre-*Chapman* test.

[118]   See, e.g., *Yates v. Evatt,* 500 U.S. 391, 111 S.Ct. 1884 (1991) (presumed intent instruction); *Kentucky v. Whorton,* 441 U.S. 786, 99 S.Ct. 2088 (1979) (presumption of innocence instruction).

[119]   *Sullivan v. Louisiana,* 508 U.S. 275, 113 S.Ct. 2078 (1993). Cf. note 106 supra. In *Sullivan,* the Court explained this dichotomy by arguing that failure to instruct on reasonable doubt "vitiates *all* the jury's findings," thus denying the defendant the right to jury trial. Yet a presumption of intent instruction, as in *Yates,* or a failure to instruct the jury on an element of the crime, as in *Neder,* vitiates all the jury's findings about that fact; nonetheless, the Court applied harmless error analysis in these cases.

proceedings can be harmless.[120] Similarly, while a trial court's refusal to allow any summation at the end of trial is structural error,[121] a limitation on the types of arguments that can be made during summation is not.[122] And even when the error affects a structural right, if it is not objected to at trial and instead is raised for the first time during the post-conviction process via an ineffective assistance of counsel claim, reversal is required only when the error resulted in "fundamental unfairness."[123]

Perhaps these decisions can somehow be reconciled with *Fulminante's* categories. As an alternative to *Fulminante's* framework, or as a supplement to it, one might consider Justice Harlan's argument, in his dissents in *Fahy* and *Chapman,* that automatic reversal should be reserved for those errors that significantly detract from the public's image of fairness. This "public intolerance" rationale might better justify the distinction between the reasonable doubt instruction and other instructions and between deprivations of trial and pretrial counsel. It is also echoed in some of the Court's decisions requiring automatic reversal. For instance, in *Vasquez v. Hillery,*[124] where five members of the Court held that racial discrimination in the selection of the grand jury can never be harmless, the primary justification given was that such discrimination "strikes at the fundamental values of our judicial system and our society as a whole." Harlan's public intolerance rationale might also call into question *Fulminante's* explicit holding, at least to the extent it would allow the introduction of a confession that has been beaten out of a suspect.[125]

Finally, some types of error require automatic reversal because they can only occur if the defendant has been prejudiced. For instance, a denial of effective assistance of counsel cannot be found unless the attorney's incompetence is shown to have "deprive[d] the defendant of a fair trial."[126] Similarly, prosecutorial failure to provide material evidence to the defense is not a constitutional violation unless "there is a reasonable probability that, had the evidence been disclosed to the defense, the result of the proceeding would be different."[127] Given the way in which these rights are defined, if a court finds that they have been violated, it cannot rationally decide that the violation is harmless.

29.06 Retroactivity

Two issues that have given the Supreme Court considerable difficulty are whether a new ruling by an appellate or habeas court should be given retroactive application, and if so, to what extent. Prior to the 1965 decision of *Linkletter v. Walker,*[128] the Court applied *each* of its new constitutional holdings to *all* cases that were on appeal or habeas review at the time of the ruling. The principal practical problem with this approach, as the Court recognized in *Linkletter,* was that a new ruling could impose enormous costs

---

[120] See, e.g., *Coleman v. Alabama,* 399 U.S. 1, 90 S.Ct. 1999 (1970) (preliminary hearing counsel); *United States v. Wade,* 388 U.S. 218, 87 S.Ct. 1926 (1967) (counsel at lineups).

[121] *Herring v. New York,* 422 U.S. 853, 95 S.Ct. 2550 (1975).

[122] *Glebe v. Frost,* 574 U.S. 21, 135 S.Ct. 429 (2014).

[123] See *Weaver v. Massachusetts,* ___ U.S. ___, 137 S.Ct. 1899 (2017), discussed in § 32.04(c)(3).

[124] 474 U.S. 254, 106 S.Ct. 617 (1986).

[125] Note that the "coercion" involved in *Fulminante* was not physical, but consisted primarily of veiled threats. See § 16.02(a)(1).

[126] *Strickland v. Washington,* 466 U.S. 668, 104 S.Ct. 2052 (1984), discussed in § 32.03(b).

[127] *United States v. Bagley,* 473 U.S. 667, 105 S.Ct. 3375 (1985), discussed in § 24.04(b).

[128] 381 U.S. 618, 85 S.Ct. 1731 (1965).

on the criminal justice system. Not only would there need to be numerous retrials, but some cases might even have to be dismissed, given the length of time between many convictions and habeas review. Furthermore, commentators noted,[129] this potential cost might in turn deter the creation of new rules.

Since 1965, the Court has embarked on an attempt to narrow the retroactivity doctrine, with several vacillations and false starts. In *Linkletter* and its direct progeny, the Court indicated that whether a constitutional ruling should be given retroactive effect depended upon the nature of the rule at issue; at the same time, all rules that were declared retroactive continued to be given "full" effect (i.e. they were applied to all cases on post-conviction review). Then, beginning in 1982 with *United States v. Johnson*,[130] the Court began to collapse the analysis of when a rule is retroactive into the issue of how retroactive the rule should be by shifting its analysis from the nature of the rule in question to the stage at which one seeks to have it applied. As a result, today every new rule, regardless of its nature, is available to litigants seeking appellate review at the time it was announced. In contrast, litigants seeking collateral review will seldom benefit from retroactivity. These developments are discussed most extensively here, but are also briefly treated in the context of habeas review.[131]

(a) The *Linkletter-Stovall* Rule

The decision considered in *Linkletter* was *Mapp v. Ohio*,[132] which had ruled that the Fourth Amendment exclusionary rule should apply to the states. The defendant's conviction had occurred one year prior to *Mapp,* and the contested search had obviously occurred even earlier. Yet because the defendant was seeking collateral relief at the time *Mapp* was decided, the pre-*Linkletter* approach to retroactivity would have required reversal of his conviction.

The Supreme Court advanced several reasons for not following the traditional approach. First, the exclusionary rule was a judicially created remedy, rather than a direct outgrowth of the Fourth Amendment, and thus more subject to judicial (i.e., the Court's) manipulation in terms of shaping its retroactive application. Second, state officials in the defendant's case had reasonably relied on the Court's decision in *Wolf v. Colorado*,[133] which had explicitly held that although the Fourth Amendment applied to the states, the exclusionary rule did not. Third, and perhaps most importantly, the Court noted that to apply *Mapp* retroactively would flood the courts with retrials and present problems in determining the materiality of lost or deteriorating evidence. Finally, the Court pointed out that, unlike other rights given retroactive application, an illegal search or seizure has no direct bearing on the guilt or innocence of the defendant or on the integrity of the trial.

---

[129] See Francis Allen, *The Judicial Quest for Penal Justice: The Warren Court and the Criminal Cases,* 1975 U.Ill.L.F. 518.

[130] 457 U.S. 537, 102 S.Ct. 2579 (1982).

[131] See § 33.02(c).

[132] 367 U.S. 643, 81 S.Ct. 1684 (1961), discussed in § 2.02.

[133] 338 U.S. 25, 69 S.Ct. 1359 (1949), discussed in § 2.02.

(1) Retroactive Rules: Definition

Although *Linkletter* signaled a new approach to retroactivity analysis, it was not until two years later, in *Stovall v. Denno*,[134] that the Court formalized its new approach. There the Court indicated that retroactivity analysis required assessment of "(a) the purpose to be served by the new standards [meaning the effect the standards had on the accuracy of the truth-finding process], (b) the extent of the reliance by law enforcement authorities on the old standards, and (c) the effect on the administration of justice of a retroactive application of the new standards." In *Stovall*, the Court applied these criteria to find non-retroactive the ruling in *United States v. Wade*[135] that the Sixth Amendment requires counsel at pretrial lineups. While it acknowledged that counsel played some role in assuring the reliability of identifications, the Court noted that *Wade* established a prophylactic rule that applied without regard to the fairness of a particular lineup. Moreover, any suggestivity in an identification procedure could always be challenged on due process grounds. Additionally, law enforcement officials had relied in good faith on accepted doctrine that counsel was not required at lineups. Finally, the Court noted that reopening those cases implicated by the *Wade* ruling would saddle the courts with numerous hearings to determine whether the violation was harmless error and, if not, whether a new trial could proceed using evidence that could easily be stale.

For similar reasons, in *Desist v. United States*,[136] the Court refused to render retroactive the ruling in *Katz v. United States*[137] that non-consensual electronic eavesdropping constitutes a search under the Fourth Amendment; it also held nonretroactive its holdings that jury trials are required for serious contempt charges,[138] that due process prohibits vindictive sentencing after a successful appeal,[139] and that the exclusion of women from jury venires violates the Sixth Amendment.[140] On the other hand, the Court's rulings finding unconstitutional the failure to provide counsel in misdemeanor cases,[141] the use of un-cross-examined preliminary hearing testimony at trial,[142] and the use of non-unanimous six-member juries[143] were given retroactive application, primarily because they were said to affect the truth-finding function. Additionally, in the last two cases, the Court noted that the rulings had been foreshadowed by earlier decisions and thus could have been anticipated by government officials.[144]

---

[134]   388 U.S. 293, 87 S.Ct. 1967 (1967).

[135]   388 U.S. 218, 87 S.Ct. 1926 (1967), discussed in § 17.02(a).

[136]   394 U.S. 244, 89 S.Ct. 1030 (1969).

[137]   389 U.S. 347, 88 S.Ct. 507 (1967), discussed in § 4.03.

[138]   *DeStefano v. Woods,* 392 U.S. 631, 88 S.Ct. 2093 (1968) (finding non-retroactive *Bloom v. Illinois*, discussed in § 27.02(c)(1)).

[139]   *Michigan v. Payne,* 412 U.S. 47, 93 S.Ct. 1966 (1973) (finding non-retroactive *North Carolina v. Pearce,* discussed in § 29.02(d)).

[140]   *Daniel v. Louisiana,* 420 U.S. 31, 95 S.Ct. 704 (1975) (finding non-retroactive *Taylor v. Louisiana*, discussed in § 27.03(c)).

[141]   *Berry v. Cincinnati,* 414 U.S. 29, 94 S.Ct. 193 (1973) (finding retroactive *Argersinger v. Hamlin*, discussed in § 31.02(b)).

[142]   *Berger v. California,* 393 U.S. 314, 89 S.Ct. 540 (1969) (finding retroactive *Barber v. Page,* discussed in § 28.04(a)).

[143]   *Brown v. Louisiana,* 447 U.S. 323, 100 S.Ct. 2214 (1980) (finding retroactive *Burch v. Louisiana,* discussed in § 27.02(e)).

[144]   *Barber,* the confrontation case, had been foreshadowed by *Pointer v. Texas,* discussed in § 28.04(a). *Burch,* the jury voting ruling, had been foreshadowed by *Ballew v. Georgia,* discussed in § 27.02(d).

This latter type of reasoning dovetailed with the idea, first expressed in *Desist,* that the retroactivity issue is moot if the constitutional ruling is not "new." According to *Desist,* a ruling that "simply applie[s] a well-established constitutional principle to govern a case which is closely analogous to those which have been previously considered in the prior caselaw" should apply to all cases subject to judicial review at the time of the rule.[145] If, on the other hand, the decision overrules a previous Supreme Court precedent (as did the *Katz* decision considered in *Desist*), or rejects a practice that the lower courts had generally followed, then a more careful analysis, along the lines suggested in *Linkletter* and *Stovall,* was warranted.

(2) The Effect of Retroactive Rules

While the *Linkletter/Stovall* approach to retroactivity limited the types of cases given retroactive status, it did not change the *effect* of a ruling on retroactivity. *Stovall* affirmed that when a ruling was found retroactive, it generally applied to all cases subject to judicial review at the time of the ruling, even to those being collaterally attacked through a writ of habeas corpus. When a ruling was found nonretroactive, then it applied only to those cases where the right in question was violated after the ruling. Thus, in the latter instance, when the right applied to trial proceedings, the Court's ruling only affected trials commenced after the ruling. If it concerned a police practice, the Court's holding only applied to those cases in which the practice (e.g., a search) occurred after the ruling.

The one major exception to the latter rule was *Johnson v. New Jersey,*[146] which decided the retroactivity of *Miranda v. Arizona.*[147] Although the Court acknowledged the minimal relationship between the *Miranda* requirements and the reliability of a confession, as well as the numerous retrials and releases that retroactive application would require, it gave *Miranda* partial retroactivity, limiting its application to all *trials* which commenced after the date of the decision. This meant that confessions obtained in violation of *Miranda* before that decision was handed down could still be challenged, if the trial using those confessions did not take place until after *Miranda.*

(b) Cases on Appeal

Not all members of the Court agreed with the *Linkletter/Stovall* approach during the seventeen years it held sway. For instance, in *Brown v. Louisiana,*[148] the case which held retroactive the Court's ruling in *Burch v. Louisiana*[149] that unanimity is required for six person juries, two members of the Court joined the majority, but refused to endorse the *Stovall* analysis it used. Rather, Justices Powell and Stevens simply noted that the petitioner should prevail because his case had been on "direct review," or appeal, at the time *Burch* was decided. To find otherwise, they argued, would mean that whenever a right was found nonretroactive, one defendant—the one whose case happened to be chosen by the Court—would fortuitously benefit from the rule announced in his case while others, equally situated on the appellate ladder, would be denied relief.

---

[145] See, e.g., *Lee v. Missouri,* 439 U.S. 461, 99 S.Ct. 710 (1979), holding that *Duren v. Missouri* was merely an "extrapolation" of *Taylor v. Louisiana* (both discussed in § 27.03(c)), and therefore required full retroactive application.

[146] 384 U.S. 719, 86 S.Ct. 1772 (1966).

[147] 384 U.S. 436, 86 S.Ct. 1602 (1966), discussed in § 16.02(d).

[148] 447 U.S. 323, 100 S.Ct. 2214 (1980).

[149] 441 U.S. 130, 99 S.Ct. 1623 (1979).

Thus, their allegiance with the majority was not based on retroactivity analysis *per se,* but on a fairness rationale approaching an equal protection stance. This position had originated with Justice Harlan, in his opinion in *Desist.* Harlan had contended that application of a new rule to cases pending on direct review is *always* necessary, not only to assure equality of treatment, but also to avoid turning the Court into a "super-legislature" that announced rules of prospective impact only.

In part to resolve this disagreement, the Court began to change direction. Two years after *Brown, United States v. Johnson*[150] announced that "retroactivity must be rethought" and in a 5–4 opinion written by Justice Blackmun, established a new framework for examining the question. The opinion began by setting out three "threshold" inquiries designed to determine the applicability of retroactivity analysis. First, as it had in *Desist,* the Court noted that when an opinion "merely has applied settled precedents to new and different factual situations," no retroactivity question arises. Second, departing somewhat from *Desist,* if the new opinion is a "clear break with the past," it should almost always be applied *prospectively* only, because government officials will have reasonably relied upon the earlier rule and because retroactive application will require intolerable disruption of the justice system. Third, however, if the new rule goes to the very authority of the trial court to convict or punish a criminal, then the rule must be applied retroactively even if it is a "clear break". Here the Court was merely affirming the good sense of earlier decisions such as *Robinson v. Neil,*[151] which had applied *Waller v. Florida*[152] retroactively on the ground that after that decision a state court does not have jurisdiction to prosecute a person who had already been prosecuted for the same offense under a municipal ordnance, and thus all cases on review involving this type of violation must grant relief for the petitioner.

The *Johnson* Court focused on distinguishing the second, "clear break" category from the first, "application-of-old-doctrine-to-new-law" category. The clear break cases were seen to fall into three types: (1) those that explicitly overruled a past decision; (2) those that "disapproved a practice this Court arguably has sanctioned in prior cases," and (3) those "which overturn[ed] a longstanding and widespread practice to which this Court ha[d] not spoken but which a near-unanimous body of lower court authority ha[d] expressly approved." As noted above, the Court asserted that if a rule met any of these definitions, then it should generally not be applied retroactively. Yet Blackmun also pointed out, in a footnote, that when a rule's "purpose is to overcome an aspect of the criminal trial that substantially impairs its truth-finding function" it had always been given "complete retroactive effect." Thus, he implied that even a clear break rule, if it affects truth-finding, is to be given retroactive effect.

The rule before the *Johnson* Court was that announced in *Payton v. New York,*[153] requiring an arrest warrant to effect a non-exigent home arrest. The Court concluded that *Payton* neither explicitly overruled a past decision nor disapproved a practice that the Court had sanctioned, and noted that the lower courts had been split on the warrantless house arrest issue. Thus, the rule fit neither the first or second "threshold" categories—it was neither a mere application of past precedent to new facts, nor a clear break with the past. Nor was it a rule that deprived the trial court of jurisdiction, as in

---

[150] 457 U.S. 537, 102 S.Ct. 2579 (1982).

[151] 409 U.S. 505, 93 S.Ct. 876 (1973).

[152] 397 U.S. 387, 90 S.Ct. 1184 (1970), discussed in § 30.06(c).

[153] 445 U.S. 573, 100 S.Ct. 1371 (1980), discussed in § 3.04(b).

Waller. In this situation, the pre-*Johnson* approach would have mandated application of the *Stovall* criteria to ascertain whether retroactive effect should be given; under these criteria and the precedent construing them, such as *Desist,* the rule probably would not have been applied retroactively, since it derived from the Fourth Amendment. But the *Johnson* Court took a different tack. It applied *Payton* to all cases on direct review, agreeing with Harlan that a different holding would increase the risk the Court would "mete out different constitutional protection to defendants simultaneously subjected to identical police conduct."

Thus, *Johnson* suggested that rules that are not clear breaks with the past will always be given retroactive application, at least to cases on appeal. Although *Johnson* was carefully confined to Fourth Amendment cases, nothing in its reasoning logically limited it to those types of claims (which, after all, are the *least* likely to challenge the accuracy of the verdict). Indeed, in *Shea v. Louisiana,*[154] the Court held that *Johnson* applied to Fifth Amendment cases as well. There the Court first held that *Edwards v. Arizona,*[155] which prohibited police from questioning a defendant who has requested counsel, was an "in-between" case like *Payton*—it was neither a straightforward application of *Miranda v. Arizona* nor a clear break from that case.[156] It then concluded that "[t]here is nothing about a Fourth Amendment rule that suggests that in this context it should be given greater retroactive effect than a Fifth Amendment rule." Accordingly, all defendants on direct review at the time *Edwards* was decided were able to benefit from it.

Johnson and *Shea* left retroactivity analysis in a state of confusion. They appeared to endorse Harlan's approach to cases on direct review, except when the ruling was a "clear break with the past" that did not affect the truth-finding function. Why the latter exception should exist was unclear, if the Court agreed with Harlan's sentiment that all cases on direct review should be treated alike.

Thus, in *Griffith v. Kentucky*[157] the Court finally explicitly adopted Harlan's approach for such cases. Justice Blackmun, writing for six members of the Court, reiterated Harlan's two reasons for applying *any* new constitutional ruling to all cases on direct appeal. First, to refrain from doing so would put the Court in the position of acting like a legislature rather than a court, because its rule would have the effect only of prospective legislation rather than backward-looking adjudication. Second, failing to apply all new rulings retroactively would unfairly allow the petitioner whose case was selected by the Court to benefit from the rule while others similarly situated might not, simply because their case was not chosen for review by the Court. After *Griffith,* every rule announced on direct review, even one that is a clear break with the past, applies retroactively to all other cases on direct review.

(c) Cases on Habeas Review

If a rule applies retroactively to cases on habeas review, it applies not only to prisoners who have a habeas petition pending but to any prisoner who might have a claim under the rule. *Johnson* appeared to hold that habeas litigants should not have

---

[154] 470 U.S. 51, 105 S.Ct. 1065 (1985).

[155] 451 U.S. 477, 101 S.Ct. 1880 (1981), discussed in § 16.03(e)(2).

[156] The Court had actually reached this conclusion earlier, in *Solem v. Stumes,* 465 U.S. 638, 104 S.Ct. 1338 (1984), discussed below.

[157] 479 U.S. 314, 107 S.Ct. 708 (1987).

the benefit of a "clear break" rule unless it dealt with the truth-finding function, and should have the benefit of an "in-between" rule, such as *Payton's* holding, only if *Stovall's* three criteria (involving the rule's purpose, the courts' reliance and the effect of retroactive application) were met. This approach seemed to be affirmed two years later in *Solem v. Stumes*.[158] There, the Court refused to apply the *Edwards* rule (later applied to cases on direct review in *Shea*) to cases on habeas, because the *Stovall* criteria were not met. But in *Teague v. Lane,*[159] the Court completely revamped this aspect of retroactivity analysis as well, again relying on an approach suggested by Justice Harlan.

In *Desist* and *Mackey v. United States,*[160] Harlan had argued that retroactivity analysis for decisions reached on collateral review should depend not on the purpose or content of the rule at issue (as the *Stovall* criteria do), but rather on "the purposes for which the writ of habeas corpus is made available." Emphasizing that the writ is a *collateral* remedy, the scope of which can be narrowed in the interest of promoting finality of judgment and comity with state courts, he concluded in *Desist:*

> [T]he threat of habeas serves as a necessary incentive for trial and appellate judges throughout the land to conduct their proceedings in a manner consistent with established constitutional principles. In order to perform this function, the habeas court need only apply the constitutional standards that prevailed at the time the original proceedings took place.

For these reasons, Harlan concluded, a new rule should not be applied retroactively to habeas petitioners. However, given the remedial purposes of the writ, Harlan was willing to recognize two exceptions to this approach, both outlined in *Mackey*. A new rule should be applied to habeas petitioners, he concluded, if it places "certain kinds of primary, private individual conduct beyond the power of the criminal law-making authority to proscribe," or if it involves "procedures that . . . are 'implicit in the concept of ordered liberty.' "

In *Teague,* seven members of the Court agreed to adopt the Harlan approach. Implicitly rejecting *Johnson,* which had not distinguished between cases on direct and collateral review, the majority held that only those new rules meeting one of Harlan's two exceptions should be applied in habeas cases. Four justices, in an opinion by Justice O'Connor, also voted to circumscribe the ability of federal courts to grant relief *even in the case before them* when the claim is raised collaterally rather than on direct review. Relying on the type of reasoning used to justify the holding in *Griffith,* O'Connor stated that "the harm caused by the failure to treat similarly situated defendants alike cannot be exaggerated." Thus, she concluded that "habeas corpus cannot be used as a vehicle to create new constitutional rules of criminal procedure unless those rules would be applied retroactively to *all* defendants on collateral review through one of the two exceptions we have articulated."

The final step taken by the plurality was to circumscribe the authority of federal habeas courts even to *consider* the merits of a habeas claim. If the habeas court decides that the proposed rule, if adopted, would not apply retroactively under *Teague,* then, held the plurality, it should refrain from addressing the merits of the proposed rule. According to O'Connor, this approach avoids the danger of advisory opinions, as well as

---

[158] 465 U.S. 638, 104 S.Ct. 1338 (1984).

[159] 489 U.S. 288, 109 S.Ct. 1060 (1989).

[160] 401 U.S. 667, 91 S.Ct. 1160 (1971) (separate opinion of Harlan, J.).

"the inequity" of treating similarly situated defendants differently. This conclusion was the central focus of Justice Brennan's dissent:

> Out of an exaggerated concern for treating similarly situated habeas petitioners the same, the plurality would for the first time preclude the federal courts from considering on collateral review a vast range of important constitutional challenges; where those challenges have merit, it would bar the vindication of personal constitutional rights and deny society a check against further violations until the same claim is presented on direct review.

But the plurality was more impressed with its perception that the previous approach to retroactivity, which Brennan advocated, "*continually* forces the States to marshal resources to keep in prison defendants whose trials and appeals conformed to then-existing constitutional standards."

As Brennan indicated, the plurality's holding in *Teague* (since affirmed by a majority of the Court[161]) makes challenging the constitutionality of state criminal procedures in federal court much more difficult. State criminal defendants' only avenue of federal relief is the writ of habeas corpus or, as indicated in the introduction to this chapter, a direct appeal or writ of certiorari to the United States Supreme Court. If these defendants are not able to meet *Teague's* requirements for gaining access to a federal habeas court, they are limited to Supreme Court review, which is infrequently granted and is based solely on the state court record (unlike a federal habeas case, for which there is sometimes an additional evidentiary hearing).[162]

Thus, understanding *Teague's* scope is important not only for retroactivity purposes but also in order to delineate its impact on the development of federal constitutional law, in those cases brought by state prisoners in federal court.[163] This objective necessitates looking at two factors: (1) whether the claim at issue merely requires application of clear precedent or instead envisions a "new rule;" and, if the latter, (2) whether it meets one of the two exceptions advanced by Harlan and endorsed in *Teague*. While the discussion here is representative of the Court's cases on these issues, discussion of the federal habeas statute's potential modification of these cases is deferred until Chapter 33, on the writ of habeas corpus.[164]

(1) The Definition of "New Rule"

Consistent with *Desist* and other early retroactivity decisions, nothing in *Teague* prevents a federal habeas court from applying settled law to vindicate a state petitioner's claim. But if the claim contemplates what *Teague* calls a "new rule," then relief may not be granted (or even considered) unless one of the two exceptions are met. In defining the "new rule" concept, *Teague* could have adopted *Johnson's* definition of a "clear break" rule; this notion, it will be remembered, was defined as a holding that overruled a past decision, disapproved a practice the Court had arguably sanctioned, or overturned a

---

[161] See, e.g., *Penry v. Lynaugh,* 492 U.S. 302, 109 S.Ct. 2934 (1989).

[162] See § 33.05(c).

[163] It is important to note that, because a primary goal of *Teague* was to limit federal court second-guessing of state court determinations, *state* courts hearing post-conviction cases need not follow the regime established by *Teague* and related cases, *Danforth v. Minnesota*, 552 U.S. 264, 128 S.Ct. 1029 (2008). Nor, by the same reasoning, should federal courts hearing post-conviction claims brought by federal prisoners have to follow *Teague*.

[164] See § 33.02(c).

longstanding practice which a near-unanimous body of lower court authority had approved. But *Johnson* was not mentioned in the plurality opinion. Rather, O'Connor announced another test, seemingly much broader than the clear break standard: "a case announces a new rule if the result was not *dictated* by precedent existing at the time the defendant's conviction became final."

As Justice Brennan argued in dissent, "[f]ew decisions on appeal or collateral review are '*dictated*' by what came before. Most such cases involve a question of law that is at least debatable, permitting a rational judge to resolve the case in more than one way." This observation was borne out by the Court's post-*Teague* treatment of the rule in *Arizona v. Roberson*,[165] which had held that the holding in *Edwards v. Arizona* (the same ruling at issue in *Shea* and *Stumes*) governed cases where the subsequent police questioning is about a different offense than the one for which the defendant requests counsel. Although the majority in *Roberson* had stated that its rule was within the "logical compass" of and "directly controlled" by *Edwards,* five members of the Court concluded, in *Butler v. McKellar,*[166] that *Roberson's* holding should not be given retroactive effect to habeas litigants. The *McKellar* Court emphasized that since there had been a significant division among lower courts about whether *Edwards* applied to separate offenses, the rule in *Roberson* was "susceptible to debate among reasonable minds," and thus should be seen as "new" for retroactivity purposes.

Other Court decisions have continued to define the new rule concept very broadly. Thus, for instance, in *Gray v. Netherland,*[167] the Court held that a rule that the prosecutor must give a capital defendant notice of specific evidence to be presented at sentencing is not dictated by the holding of *Gardner v. Florida,*[168] finding a violation of due process when a defendant is sentenced to death "on the basis of information which he has had no opportunity to deny or explain." Similarly, in *Beard v. Banks,*[169] the Court held that the ruling in *Mills v. Maryland*[170] holding invalid capital sentencing schemes that require juries to disregard mitigating factors that are not found unanimously was not dictated by the Court's decisions holding that capital sentencing juries must be allowed to consider all mitigating evidence. And in *Stringer v. Black,*[171] the Court stated that *Teague* even bars hearing claims that *are* dictated by precedent, if relief "would effectively create a new rule by extending the precedent to a novel context."[172] This was the rationale in *Chaidez v. United States,*[173] which declared that the Court's holding in *Padilla v. Kentucky*[174] requiring counsel to inform defendants about a guilty plea's effect on deportation was an extension of the Court's decisions requiring counsel to inform defendants of the consequences of a plea.[175]

---

[165]   486 U.S. 675, 108 S.Ct. 2093 (1988), discussed in § 16.03(e)(4).

[166]   494 U.S. 407, 110 S.Ct. 1212 (1990).

[167]   518 U.S. 152, 116 S.Ct. 2074 (1996).

[168]   430 U.S. 349, 97 S.Ct. 1197 (1977), discussed in § 28.05(b)(1).

[169]   542 U.S. 406, 124 S.Ct. 2504 (2004).

[170]   486 U.S. 367, 108 S.Ct. 1860 (1988).

[171]   503 U.S. 222, 112 S.Ct. 1130 (1992).

[172]   See also *Saffle v. Parks*, 494 U.S. 484, 110 S.Ct. 1257 (1990).

[173]   568 U.S. 342, 133 S.Ct. 1103 (2013).

[174]   599 U.S. 356, 130 S.Ct. 1473 (2010), discussed in § 26.04(a)(2).

[175]   See § 26.04(a)(2), and *Hill v. Lockhart*, 474 U.S. 52, 106 S.Ct. 366 (1985) (declining to address application of the Sixth Amendment to failures to inform defendants about the collateral consequences of a plea).

(2) Exceptions to Non-Retroactivity of New Rules

According to *Teague*, a claim that asks a federal habeas court to adopt a new rule may nonetheless be considered, following Justice Harlan's formulation, if it would place "certain kinds of primary, private individual conduct beyond the power of the criminal law-making authority to proscribe," or involves procedures that are "implicit in the concept of ordered liberty." As examples of the first exception, which looks at whether the new rule is substantive rather than procedural, Harlan cited cases involving First and Fifth Amendment claims which, once vindicated, rendered unconstitutional the criminal statute under which the petitioner was prosecuted.[176] In *Penry v. Lynaugh*,[177] the Court also included within this exception claims that place "certain conduct beyond the State's power to punish at all;" it then went on to consider (but ultimately reject) a habeas claim that execution of people with mental retardation is unconstitutional. However, in *Montgomery v. Louisiana*,[178] the Court concluded that its holding in *Miller v. Alabama*[179] that mandatory life without parole sentences for juveniles violate the Eight Amendment was a "watershed rule" because it eliminated the state's power to impose a given punishment. Other claims that might fit this category are those which would eliminate the state's ability to prosecute certain offenses, such as *Pearce-Blackledge* vindictiveness claims,[180] double jeopardy claims of the type recognized by *Johnson* in its third "threshold" inquiry, and claims that a criminal statute does not, as a matter of statutory interpretation, cover the defendant's conduct.[181]

With respect to the second exception, which recognizes that even some new rules about procedure might require retroactive application, the four-member plurality in *Teague* concluded that it should be confined to procedures "without which the likelihood of an accurate conviction is seriously diminished." Harlan had argued in *Mackey* against such a definition, in large part because he found "inherently intractable the purported distinctions between those new rules that are designed to improve the factfinding process and those designed principally to further other values." But O'Connor justified the narrower test, subsequently approved by a majority of the Court,[182] by pointing to more recent cases that made factual innocence the touchstone of analysis in deciding the scope of habeas review.[183] To date, this exception has been construed very narrowly.[184] As the Court stated in *Sawyer v. Smith*,[185] this exception grants retroactive status only to "watershed" rules that "alter our understanding of the bedrock procedural elements

---

[176] *See, e.g., Stanley v. Georgia,* 394 U.S. 557, 89 S.Ct. 1243 (1969) (invalidating obscenity statute).

[177] 492 U.S. 302, 109 S.Ct. 2934 (1989).

[178] ___ U.S. ___, 136 S.Ct. 718 (2016).

[179] 567 U.S. 460, 132 S.Ct. 2455 (2012).

[180] See § 29.02(d).

[181] See, e.g., *Bousley v. United States,* 523 U.S. 614, 118 S.Ct. 1604 (1998) in which the Court held that *Teague's* first exception allows a habeas petitioner to claim that a guilty plea is involuntary when based on erroneous information that the statute under which he pleaded criminalized mere possession of a firearm, when in fact it only penalized active employment of it. For further discussion of *Bousley,* see § 33.03(e).

[182] See, e.g., *Butler v. McKellar,* 494 U.S. 407, 110 S.Ct. 1212 (1990).

[183] See, e.g., *Murray v. Carrier,* 477 U.S. 478, 106 S.Ct. 2639 (1986), discussed in § 33.03(e).

[184] See, e.g., *Butler v. McKellar,* 494 U.S. 407, 110 S.Ct. 1212 (1990); *Gray v. Netherland,* 518 U.S. 152, 116 S.Ct. 2074 (1996) (described supra note 167); *Lambrix v. Singletary,* 520 U.S. 518, 117 S.Ct. 1517 (1997). Even the Court's ground-breaking rule about the Confrontation Clause, announced in *Crawford v. Washington,* 541 U.S. 36 (2004), discussed in § 28.03, is not considered a watershed rule. *Whorton v. Bockting,* 549 U.S. 406 (2007).

[185] 497 U.S. 227, 110 S.Ct. 2822 (1990).

essential to the fairness of a proceeding," and that are an "absolute prerequisite to fundamental fairness."

At the time *Teague* was decided, the Court had already recognized most such rules. Thus, this second exception is rarely applicable. In *Teague* itself, the petitioner argued that *Taylor v. Louisiana's*[186] requirement that jury venires represent a cross-section of the community should also apply to the jury itself. Since *Taylor* had stated that its cross-section requirement should *not* apply to the petit jury, this claim clearly requested a "new rule," which, under *Teague's* new approach, could only be considered by the Supreme Court on habeas review if it met one of the exceptions. The claim clearly does not fit within the first exception, and the Court found that it did not rest on accuracy concerns either, but rather on a desire to foster community participation in the adjudication process. Since the proposed rule would thus not be applied retroactively, it was not considered on its merits.

Two other examples illustrate the near impossibility of meeting *Teague's* second exception. Noting (in 2004) that "we have yet to find a new rule that falls under the second *Teague* exception," the Court in *Beard v. Banks*[187] concluded that assuring that capital sentencing juries consider mitigating circumstances even if they are not found unanimously, as the Court required in *Mills v. Maryland*,[188] is not central to an "accurate determination" of whether a death sentence is appropriate. Although the dissent pointed out that, under the scheme *Mills* invalidated, one juror out of 12 could force a death sentence because he was unwilling to find a mitigator existed, the five-member majority in *Mills* concluded that "the fact that a new rule removes some remote possibility of arbitrary infliction of the death sentence does not suffice to bring it within *Teague's* second exception." Similarly, in *Schriro v. Summerlin*,[189] the same five-member majority held that the rule of *Ring v. Arizona*[190] requiring a jury, rather than a judge, to find all aggravating factors in death penalty proceedings did not meet the second exception. The dissent argued that aggravating factors such as heinousness are best determined according to community sentiment, which is more precisely gauged by a jury than by a judge, but the majority concluded that judicial factfinding does not "seriously" diminish accuracy in this setting.

29.07   Conclusion

The following summarizes those aspects of the appeals process discussed in this chapter.

(1)   The federal Constitution does not guarantee a right to appeal of a criminal conviction. However, if an appeal process is provided, as is the case in every jurisdiction, then: (a) indigent defendants are entitled to complete trial transcripts, free of charge, to perfect the appeal; (b) all defendants are entitled to effective assistance of counsel on appeals as of right (but are not entitled to counsel on discretionary appeals nor to self-representation on appeal); (c) counsel who determines that there is no merit to an appeal must file a brief with the appellate court referring to anything in the record that might arguably support the appeal or in some other way ensure that a "trained legal eye" has

---

[186]   419 U.S. 522, 95 S.Ct. 692 (1975), discussed in § 27.03(c).

[187]   542 U.S. 406, 124 S.Ct. 2504 (2004).

[188]   486 U.S. 367, 108 S.Ct. 1860 (1988).

[189]   542 U.S. 348, 124 S.Ct. 2519 (2004).

[190]   536 U.S. 584, 122 S.Ct. 2428 (2002).

searched the record with the aim of providing at least some assistance to the reviewing court; and (d) the state may not retaliate against defendants who successfully appeal. With respect to the latter issue, a retaliatory motive is presumed when the post-appeal sentence or charge is higher than the pre-appeal sentence or charge, unless the post-appeal decisionmaker lacks the motivation to be vindictive. This presumption can be overcome by showing that the new sentence or charge is plausibly based on an event subsequent to the previous sentence or charge, or on "new" information. The right to appeal can be waived (if done so voluntarily and intelligently) and can also be forfeited through escape from the jurisdiction or a failure to preserve at trial the issue sought to be appealed. In the latter instance, an appellate court can still reverse if the error is plain and affected the outcome of the proceeding and the fairness, integrity and reputation of the criminal justice system.

(2)   In order to avoid piecemeal, disruptive litigation, defense appeals of pretrial rulings are permissible only if the ruling: (a) is final from the trial court's point of view; (b) involves an important right that would be lost, probably irreparably, if review were to await conviction; (c) involves an issue that is independent of the main cause of action, so that elements of the latter will not have be considered by the appellate court before they are considered by the trial court; and (d) concerns an issue which is inherently limited, rather than one which could be raised by any defendant as a dilatory tactic. Under this analysis, rulings regarding bail and double jeopardy are usually appealable prior to trial, whereas rulings regarding the Fourth Amendment, speedy trial, vindictive sentencing, and grand jury matters generally are not. The prosecution is not as firmly bound by the final judgment rule, and may appeal many types of pretrial rulings so long as it has statutory authority to do so and meets the requirements in (3). Third parties may appeal a pretrial ruling holding them in contempt, or involving a legal right (such as First Amendment access to the court) that is independent of the proceedings.

(3)   The Double Jeopardy Clause bars the prosecution from appealing any judgment which determines that there is insufficient evidence to convict the defendant. However, given statutory authorization to do so, the prosecution may appeal any other ruling without violating the Clause, including pretrial rulings that may have a significant impact on its case, post-jeopardy rulings, and sentences.

(4)   Constitutional error that constitutes a structural defect (e.g., a corrupt judge or violation of the right to trial counsel) requires automatic reversal, if timely objection is made. In contrast, constitutional error which can be labelled trial error—error that occurred during the presentation of the case to the jury and may therefore be quantitatively assessed in the context of other evidence presented (e.g., introduction of illegally seized evidence or a coerced confession)—may be found harmless. To be found harmless, the prosecution must show beyond a reasonable doubt that the error did not contribute to the verdict. Non-constitutional error, in federal court at least, is harmless if there is fair assurance that it did not influence the jury.

(5)   A new constitutional ruling is applicable to all cases on direct appeal at the time of the ruling. For a habeas claim brought by a state prisoner which asks a federal court to adopt a "new" rule (i.e., a rule that is not dictated by precedent or is dictated by precedent but represents an extension of that precedent to a novel context), retroactivity analysis is governed by whether the proposed rule (a) places primary, private individual conduct beyond the power of the criminal law-making authority to proscribe (as the Court's decision prohibiting mandatory life without parole sentences for juveniles did)

or (b) is closely associated with accurate factfinding. If the proposed rule fits one of these latter two criteria, then it should be considered on its merits and, if adopted, should be given retroactive application to all other habeas petitioners. If the proposed rule fits neither criterion, then, because it would not be applicable retroactively to other petitioners, the habeas petitioner is not entitled to relief and her claim should not be ruled upon.

BIBLIOGRAPHY

Arkin, Marc. Rethinking the Constitutional Right to a Criminal Appeal. 39 U.C.L.A. L.Rev. 503 (1992).

Bryant, A. Christopher. Retroactive Application of "New Rules" and the Anti-Terrorism and Effective Death Penalty Act. 70 Geo.Wash.L.Rev. 1 (2002).

Carrington, Paul D. Justice on Appeal in Criminal Cases: A Twentieth-Century Perspective. 93 Marq. L. Rev. 459 (2009).

Enzeroth, Lyn S. Reflections on Fifteen Years of the *Teague v. Lane* Retroactivity Doctrine: A Study of the Persistence, the Pervasiveness and the Perversity of the Court's Doctrine. 34 N.M.L.Rev. 161 (2005).

Erlinder, C. Peter and David C. Thomas. Prohibiting Prosecutorial Vindictiveness While Protecting Prosecutorial Discretion. 76 J.Crim.L. & Criminol. 341 (1985).

Fairfax, Roger. Harmless Constitutional Error and the Institutional Significance of the Jury. 76 Fordham L. Rev. 2027 (2008).

Gerson, Gayle. A Return to Practicality: Reforming the Fourth *Cox* Exception to the Final Judgment Rule Governing Supreme Court Certiorari Review of State Judgments. 73 Fordham L. Rev. 789 (2004).

Graham, Michael H. Abuse of Discretion, Reversible Error, Harmless Error, Plain Error, Structural Error: A New Paradigm for Criminal Cases. 43 Crim. L. Bull. 6 (2008).

Junkin, Frederick D. The Right to Counsel in "Frivolous" Criminal Appeals: A Reevaluation of the Guarantees of *Anders v. California.* 67 Tex.L.Rev. 181 (1988).

Kamin, Sam. Harmless Error and the Rights/Remedies Split. 88 Va.L.Rev.1 (2002).

Khanna, Vikramaditya S. Double Jeopardy's Asymmetric Appeal Rights: What Purpose Do They Serve? 82 B.U.L.Rev. 341 (2002).

King, Nancy and Michael E. O'Neill. Appeal Waivers and the Future of Sentencing Policy. 55 Duke L.J. 209 (2005).

Lasch, Christopher N. The Future of Teague Retroactivity, Or "Redressability," after *Danforth v. Minnesota*: Why Lower Courts Should Give Retroactive Effect to New Constitutional Rules of Criminal Procedure in Postconviction Proceedings. 46 Am. Crim. L. Rev. 1 (2009).

Meltzer, Daniel. Harmless Error and Constitutional Remedies. 51 U. Chi. L.Rev. 1 (1994).

Poulin, Anne Bowen. Tests for Harm in Criminal Cases: A Fix for Blurred Lines. 17 U. Pa. J. Const. L. 991 (2015).

____. Government Appeals in Criminal Cases. 77 U. Cinn. L. Rev. 1 (2008).

Rossman, David. "Were There No Appeal": The History of Review in American Criminal Courts. 81 J. Crim. L. & Criminol. 518 (1990).

Sharpless, Rebecca and Andrew Stanton. *Teague* New Rules Must Apply in Initial Collateral Review Proceedings: The Teachings of *Padilla*, *Chaidez* and *Martinez*. 67 U. Miami L. Rev. 697 (2013).

Traynor, Roger J. The Riddle of Harmless Error. Ohio State Univ. Press: 1970.

Chapter 30

DOUBLE JEOPARDY

30.01   Introduction

Both the civil and criminal law have developed doctrines that render legal proceedings conclusive and binding. In civil cases, the doctrine of *res judicata* is based upon the maxim that "no man shall be twice vexed for one and the same cause." Its criminal analogue is the prohibition on double jeopardy.

The common law very early developed two pleas which form the basis for the modern theory of double jeopardy. The plea of *autrefois acquit* forbids retrial of a defendant for the same offense after he has been acquitted. Its counterpart, *autrefois convict* disallows retrial after a prior conviction for the same offense. These rules were adopted by the American colonies, many of which, following the lead of Massachusetts, included double jeopardy provisions in their constitutions.[1]

In *Ex parte Lange*,[2] the Supreme Court held that both the *autrefois acquit* and *autrefois convict* notions were meant to be recognized by that part of the Fifth Amendment which states: "nor shall any person be subject for the same offence to be twice put in jeopardy of life or limb." The Court emphasized that "[t]he 'twice put in jeopardy' language of the Constitution . . . relates to a potential, i.e., the risk that an accused for a second time will be convicted of the 'same offense' for which he was initially tried." Furthermore, stated the Court, the Double Jeopardy Clause not only incorporates the two common law rules but also applies "to all cases where a second punishment is attempted to be inflicted for the same offence by a judicial sentence." Later cases indicated that the Clause also protects the defendant's "valued right to have his trial completed by a particular tribunal," at least to the extent it does not interfere with the "public's interest in fair trials."[3] Thus, the Double Jeopardy Clause, as originally construed by the Court, is meant to protect against: (1) reprosecution after acquittal; (2) reprosecution after conviction; (3) separate punishments for the same offense; and, in some circumstances, (4) reprosecution after an aborted trial.

In *Palko v. Connecticut*,[4] the Supreme Court refused to hold that the protection from double jeopardy is a fundamental right requiring application to the states. But some thirty years later, in *Benton v. Maryland*,[5] the Court reversed itself, finding the Double Jeopardy Clause applicable to the states through the Fourteenth Amendment. Justice Black, in *Green v. United States*,[6] provided the classic description of why the Clause embodies a fundamental principle of justice:

> The underlying idea, one that is deeply ingrained in at least the Anglo-American system of jurisprudence, is that the State with all its resources and

---

[1]   For more on the history of double jeopardy, see Jay A. Sigler, Double Jeopardy: The Development of a Legal and Social Policy 13–37 (1969); Martin L. Friedland, Double Jeopardy 3–17 (1969).

[2]   85 U.S. (18 Wall.) 163 (1873).

[3]   *Wade v. Hunter,* 336 U.S. 684, 69 S.Ct. 834 (1949).

[4]   302 U.S. 319, 58 S.Ct. 149 (1937).

[5]   395 U.S. 784, 89 S.Ct. 2056 (1969).

[6]   355 U.S. 184, 78 S.Ct. 221 (1957).

power should not be allowed to make repeated attempts to convict an individual for an alleged offense, thereby subjecting him to embarrassment, expense and ordeal and compelling him to live in a continuing state of anxiety and insecurity, as well as enhancing the possibility that even though innocent he may be found guilty.

As this chapter illustrates, this avoidance-of-repeated-prosecutions rationale has receded into the background in more recent Supreme Court interpretations of the Clause. In its place, the Court has focused on whether the criminal defendant asserting a double jeopardy claim has been once subjected to a *determination* as to his guilt. Under the Court's new approach, regardless of the number of jeopardizing events to which the individual is exposed (see § 30.02), he is not entitled to the protection afforded by the Clause until he is either convicted, acquitted, or deprived of a chance for acquittal by prosecutorial action (see § 30.03), and then tried again for the "same offense" (see § 30.04) by the same governmental entity or "sovereign" (see § 30.05).

30.02   When Jeopardy Attaches

Two issues arise in determining the threshold issue of when jeopardy attaches for purposes of triggering the double jeopardy prohibition. The first is the type of proceeding that is prohibited after the defendant has once been subjected to jeopardy. If a defendant has been prosecuted in a criminal trial and acquitted or convicted, the Clause clearly prevents a second criminal trial on the same offense. But does it prevent a "civil" proceeding designed, for instance, to confiscate property obtained through the defendant's criminal activities? The second threshold is at what point in the proceeding jeopardy is said to attach. Is a second proceeding barred only once the first proceeding is completed, is it barred once the defendant is charged in the first proceeding, or does jeopardy attach at some point in between these two events?

(a) Type of Proceeding

Although the Fifth Amendment speaks of "jeopardy of life and limb," *Ex parte Lange* established that the Double Jeopardy Clause governs all criminal prosecutions. In support of this holding, the Court noted that when the pleas of *autrefois acquit* and *autrefois convict* were established, they applied to most crimes because virtually all were punishable by death or corporeal punishment. Further, common law courts continued to apply these doctrines even when other punishment was involved.

In establishing whether subjecting a person to a given proceeding or sanction implicates the Clause the Court has used a number of tests. In *Hudson v. United States*,[7] Chief Justice Rehnquist summarized the Court's caselaw as follows. First, a court should determine whether the legislature intended the penalizing mechanism to be criminal or civil; if the latter, only the "clearest proof" will suffice to override legislative intent.[8] In determining whether such proof exists, Rehnquist continued, several factors, taken from the Court's decision in *Kennedy v. Mendoza-Martinez*,[9] should be considered:

(1) "whether the sanction involves an affirmative disability or restraint"; (2) "whether it has historically been regarded as a punishment"; (3) "whether it

---

[7]   522 U.S. 93, 118 S.Ct. 488 (1997).

[8]   See *United States v. Ward*, 448 U.S. 242, 100 S.Ct. 2636 (1980); *Rex Trailer Co. v. United States*, 350 U.S. 148, 76 S.Ct. 219 (1956).

[9]   372 U.S. 144, 83 S.Ct. 554 (1963).

comes into play on a finding of scienter"; (4) "whether its operation will promote the traditional aims of punishment—retribution and deterrence"; (5) "whether the behavior to which it applies is already a crime"; (6) "whether an alternative purpose to which it may rationally be connected is assignable for it"; and (7) "whether it appears excessive in relation to the alternative purpose assigned."

All of these factors, the Court stated, should be determined from the "statute on its face".

Hudson elaborated on the preferred approach by distinguishing and repudiating the approach taken in *United States v. Halper*,[10] decided nine years earlier. In *Halper*, a unanimous Court had annulled a $130,000 civil fine imposed under the federal False Claims Act, after a conviction and sentence for welfare fraud. Noting that this fine equalled roughly eight times the government's costs and was over 200 times greater than the money gained through the fraud, the Court found the fine to be punishment. Although not expressly disputing this outcome, *Hudson* did express concern over *Halper's* failure to even consider legislative intent. *Hudson* also disputed *Halper's* suggestion that sanctions that are not "solely remedial" are serving either retributive or deterrent purposes and are therefore punishment, its readiness to look at the fine imposed rather than the statute on its face, and its focus on the disproportionate nature of the fine to the exclusion of the first six factors noted above.

The majority in *Hudson* also asserted that *Halper's* test "has proved unworkable." Because all civil penalties have some non-remedial deterrent effect, Rehnquist reasoned, they might all implicate the Clause under *Halper's* formulation. Additionally, because application of *Halper's* test requires knowledge of the sanction actually imposed through the civil penalty, when the civil proceeding follows a criminal proceeding a trial might have to take place to determine whether the Clause applies, an event that could permit the second proceeding the Clause is design to prevent. Finally, Rehnquist noted, truly "irrational" sanctions are prohibited by the Eighth Amendment excessive fines prohibition and the Due Process and Equal Protection Clauses.[11]

Four justices expressed misgivings about the majority's endorsement of the idea that only the "clearest proof" that a statute was meant as punishment would overcome a legislature's civil label. Justice Stevens emphasized that the majority's holding still did not make controlling the legislature's denomination. Justice Souter echoed that view and suggested that "clear proof" of legislative mislabeling might increasingly occur in light of "the expanding use of ostensibly civil forfeitures and penalties under the exigencies of the current drug problems, a development doubtless spurred by the increasingly inviting prospect of its profit to the Government." In a similar vein, Justice Breyer, joined by Justice Ginsburg, objected to the majority's statement that analysis should focus on the face of the statute, stating that it is "quite possible that a statute that provides for punishment that normally is civil in nature could nonetheless amount to a criminal punishment as applied in special circumstances."[12]

A survey of Court cases that address the punitiveness of various statutes illustrates that, as applied, the Court's approach is very hard to pin down. Although *Hudson* indicated that its summary of the law applies to all of these cases, it is helpful to divide

---

[10] 490 U.S. 435, 109 S.Ct. 1892 (1989).

[11] See *Alexander v. United States*, 509 U.S. 544, 113 S.Ct. 2766 (1993), discussed in § 5.06(d); *Williamson v. Lee Optical of Okla., Inc.*, 348 U.S. 483, 75 S.Ct. 461 (1955).

[12] Compare the Court's cases construing the definition of "punishment" for purposes of whether the Eighth Amendment's Excessive Fines Clause applies, which look at the fine actually imposed. See § 5.06(d).

them into two categories, those involving fines or some other confiscation of property and those dealing with sanctions involving restrictions on liberty.

(1) Confiscations of Property

Although there are a few exceptions, the bulk of the Court's cases indicate that if the proceeding does not involve a deprivation of liberty it is not punitive for purposes of the Double Jeopardy Clause. *Helvering v. Mitchell*[13] upheld the constitutionality of a tax proceeding, following an acquittal on criminal fraud charges, which resulted in the government recovering the tax deficiency as well as a 50% additional amount specified by statute on account of the fraud. The Court found that, as a matter of statutory interpretation, the additional 50% penalty was meant to be a "remedial sanction" designed to reimburse the government for investigatory and other costs. Similarly, in *United States ex rel. Marcus v. Hess,*[14] the Court upheld a $2,000 per-count civil penalty plus double damages and costs—imposed on individuals who had already been convicted and fined criminally for the same fraud—amounting to almost $50,000 more than the government's actual damages. The Court reasoned that the fine and double damages "do no more than afford the government complete indemnity for the injuries done it," including the costs of detection and investigation.

One Lot Emerald Cut Stones v. United States[15] involved a civil forfeiture seeking return of goods the defendant had allegedly smuggled into the country plus a monetary penalty equal to the value of the goods. The Court found that because the statute "provided a reasonable form of liquidated damages" to the government, it did not put the defendant in jeopardy. The Court reached the same conclusion in considering the forfeiture of weapons at issue in *United States v. One Assortment of 89 Firearms,*[16] based on the type of analysis later summarized in *Hudson*. Specifically, it found that (1) Congress intended the forfeiture to be a remedial civil sanction and (2) confiscation of the guns (possessed without a license) was primarily for remedial purposes and thus was not so clearly punitive in fact that it could not legitimately be viewed as civil in nature.

In contrast to most of the Court's decisions on the punitiveness issue the Court's next two cases, *Halper* and *Montana v. Kurth Ranch,*[17] held that monetary penalties implicated the Double Jeopardy Clause. In *Halper*, as noted above, the Court found a $130,000 fine for conduct associated with welfare fraud to be punitive because it bore no "rational relation" to the government's expenses. In *Kurth Ranch*, a tax levied on marijuana used to convict the defendants on possession charges was found to be punishment despite only somewhat exceeding the government's costs because it was four times the market value of the marijuana seized, conditioned upon commission of a crime, "exacted only after the taxpayer ha[d] been arrested for the precise conduct that g[ave] rise to the tax obligation in the first place [e.g., possession of marijuana]", and imposed after the marijuana had been destroyed.

The holdings in *Halper* and *Kurth Ranch* called into question cases like *Emerald Cut Stones* and *89 Firearms* which, as noted above, found that jeopardy does not attach at civil forfeiture proceedings. Some lower courts concluded that, after *Halper* and *Kurth*

---

[13]   303 U.S. 391, 58 S.Ct. 630 (1938).

[14]   317 U.S. 537, 63 S.Ct. 379 (1943). See also, *Rex Trailer Co. v. U.S.,* 350 U.S. 148, 76 S.Ct. 219 (1956).

[15]   409 U.S. 232, 93 S.Ct. 489 (1972).

[16]   465 U.S. 354, 104 S.Ct. 1099 (1984).

[17]   511 U.S. 767, 114 S.Ct. 1937 (1994).

Ranch, forfeiture of a defendant's property was punishment for double jeopardy purposes because it confiscates property shown to be connected with criminal activity.[18] Many of these courts also relied upon a second Supreme Court decision, *Austin v. United States*,[19] which declared that civil forfeiture *is* punishment for purposes of analyzing the proportionality of government sanctions under the Cruel and Unusual Punishment Clause.

In *United States v. Ursery*,[20] however, eight members of the Court rejected these arguments in a case involving the federal forfeiture statute. Chief Justice Rehnquist's opinion for the Court noted that *Halper* and *Kurth Ranch* had dealt with civil penalties and taxes, not civil forfeiture, and that *Alexander* and *Austin* had only purported to define punishment under the Eighth Amendment. As for the definition of punishment for double jeopardy purposes, the Court adhered to the two-step test used in *89 Firearms* (and subsequently summarized in *Hudson*). First, it found that Congress had clearly intended the statute to be a civil remedy. Second, it held that civil forfeiture proceedings are not in fact so punitive as to render them criminal in nature. To Justice Stevens' argument in dissent that the primary goal of forfeiture statutes is deterrence of criminal activity, the Court responded that forfeiture has other, non-punitive goals as well, such as preventing illegal use of real property, ensuring criminals do not profit from illegal acts, encouraging property owners to monitor use of their property, and compensating the government. The Court also noted that the *in rem* nature of forfeiture proceedings means they are not directed at the criminal defendant, but at the property (and indeed, they are often brought against property owners who are not defendants).[21] Further, in contrast to the typical criminal action, no proof of scienter is required.

Hudson itself held that neither a $100,000 penalty nor a "debarment" from further employment in the banking industry, both imposed for making $900,000 worth of loans that unlawfully allowed Hudson to receive the loans' benefit, were punitive for double jeopardy purposes. The statute authorizing the monetary penalty specifically designated the penalty as civil, and the fact that debarment is imposed by a federal banking agency was "prima facie" evidence the latter penalty was intended to be civil. As to whether there was clear proof the statute was nonetheless punitive, the Court concluded that debarment is "certainly nothing approaching the 'infamous punishment' of imprisonment" and thus was not an "affirmative disability," and that although the defendant's good faith could be taken into account in making both dispositions, neither penalty *required* proof of scienter. Further, as in *Ursery*, the facts that the conduct penalized could also form the basis for a criminal prosecution or that the penalties were meant to and might deter others did not make them punishment.[22]

---

[18]   *United States v. Ursery*, 59 F.3d 568 (6th Cir. 1995); *United States v. $405,089.23 U.S. Currency*, 33 F.3d 1210 (9th Cir. 1994); *United States v. Shorb*, 876 F.Supp. 1183, 1187 n. 46 (D.Or. 1995).

[19]   509 U.S. 602, 113 S.Ct. 2801 (1993), discussed in § 5.06(d).

[20]   518 U.S. 267, 116 S.Ct. 2135 (1996).

[21]   This point was stressed in a concurring opinion by Justice Kennedy, who explained that the *in rem* denomination is a recognition that Congress structured the forfeiture action as a proceeding against the property, not against the defendant.

[22]   Reinforcing this point is *Seling v. Young*, 531 U.S. 250, 121 S.Ct. 727 (2001), where the Court held that once a statute is considered to be non-punitive, an "as applied" challenge will be to no avail.

(2) Deprivations of Liberty

Breed v. Jones[23] exemplifies the second category of cases that have addressed the punitiveness issue. There the Court extended the reach of the Clause to juvenile delinquency proceedings on the ground that "the risk to which the term jeopardy refers is that traditionally associated with actions intended to authorize criminal punishment to vindicate public justice." Under this reasoning, the fact that a juvenile proceeding might be denominated "civil" was not dispositive. Rather, most important was the fact that delinquency proceedings are similar to criminal proceedings in terms of stigma and deprivation of liberty.[24] For much the same reason, a bare majority of the Court held in *United States v. Dixon*[25] that criminal contempt proceedings, at least those that are not summary in nature,[26] result in punishment. Thus, the Double Jeopardy Clause prohibits a delinquency or nonsummary contempt proceeding after a criminal prosecution for the same offense and vice versa.

In contrast to *Jones* and *Dixon* is *Kansas v. Hendricks*,[27] in which the Court found that a "sexual predator" proceeding, which can result in much more serious restrictions on liberty than either juvenile delinquency or contempt proceedings, is nonetheless not punitive for double jeopardy purposes. The statute at issue in *Hendricks* allows additional incarceration of a sex offender who has already served his prison term if the state proves beyond a reasonable doubt that the offender is "likely to engage in predatory acts of sexual violence" as a result of mental abnormality or personality disorder. Writing for five members of the Court, Justice Thomas pointed out that the state's intent was to create a *civil* commitment system for sex offenders and that proof of scienter is not required by the law. He also concluded that the statute is aimed at incapacitation and treatment rather than retribution and deterrence. The statute is not retributive in purpose, he reasoned, because the commitment it authorizes is not in response to (and does not even require proof of) a specific crime; it is not meant to be a deterrent because, according to Thomas, recidivist offenders are usually not deterrable. The Kansas Supreme Court had nonetheless found that the statute violated the double jeopardy prohibition because the Kansas program provided no meaningful treatment to many of the offenders so committed. Thomas responded that the lack of treatment does not make incarceration "punitive"; just as confinement of people with untreatable contagious diseases should not be considered punitive, he reasoned, "it would be of little value to require treatment as a precondition for civil confinement of the dangerously insane when no acceptable treatment existed."[28]

The attachment of jeopardy issue has also arisen in the sentencing context. Traditional sentencing practice and many modern statutory sentencing schemes, including the Federal Sentencing Guidelines,[29] allow enhancement of a sentence in light of other criminal conduct. In a decision handed down ten years before the Double

---

[23]   421 U.S. 519, 95 S.Ct. 1779 (1975).

[24]   See, e.g., *In re Gault*, 387 U.S. 1, 87 S.Ct. 1428 (1967).

[25]   509 U.S. 688, 113 S.Ct. 2849 (1993).

[26]   For a discussion of the distinction between summary and nonsummary contempt proceedings, see § 27.02(c)(3).

[27]   521 U.S. 346, 117 S.Ct. 2072 (1997).

[28]   Relying on similar reasoning, the Court held that the fact the commitment statute had been passed after Hendricks' conviction did not violate the ban on ex post facto criminal laws.

[29]   United States Sentencing Guidelines, § 1B1.3 (allowing consideration of "relevant conduct"); § 4A1.1 (allowing consideration of "criminal history").

Jeopardy Clause was applied to the states in *Benton,* the Court indicated that double jeopardy principles did not bar a federal prosecution or punishment for criminal activity previously used in the sentencing of another crime.[30]

Twenty-six years after *Benton,* the Court reaffirmed this ruling, albeit in somewhat different factual circumstances. In *Witte v. United States,*[31] the defendant's sentence on marijuana charges was significantly lengthened based on the trial court's finding that the defendant had also been involved in cocaine importation. Subsequently, the defendant was tried for the conduct underlying the cocaine importation. The Court nonetheless held that the second prosecution could proceed, concluding that use of criminal conduct to enhance the sentence for another offense does not constitute "punishment" for the conduct so long as the enhanced sentence does not exceed the statutory maximum for the offense; to put the holding in other terms, in these circumstances jeopardy does not attach for conduct used solely at sentencing. This rule applies whether or not the conduct used to enhance a sentence has already led to conviction.

Two factors might soften the impact of this definition of "punishment" for double jeopardy purposes. One is that, at least under the federal sentencing guidelines, sentencing judges are to mitigate sentences for an offense when its underlying conduct has already been taken into account in another sentence,[32] a provision that the *Witte* Court emphasized. Second, the Due Process Clause may impose narrow limits on the extent to which conduct that has not yet been prosecuted or charged may be used to enhance the sentence for another offense, and the Sixth Amendment absolutely bans enhancement above the statutory/guidelines maximum using conduct not proven to a jury beyond a reasonable doubt.[33]

(b) Point in the Proceedings

Assuming a proceeding at which jeopardy can attach, the second issue concerning the threshold of the Double Jeopardy Clause is at what point during that process jeopardy occurs. If the purpose of the Clause is to prevent the embarrassment and harassment from repeated prosecutions, one could argue that jeopardy should attach with the institution of formal charges. If, on the other hand, the primary purpose of the Clause is to prevent the prosecution from honing its case against the defendant, jeopardy might not exist until the prosecution has completed its case against the accused or until the case terminates in a verdict. Under the federal Constitution, the rule falls between these two extremes.

In *Crist v. Bretz,*[34] the Supreme Court held that jeopardy attaches at jury trials when the jury is empaneled and sworn, which had been the federal practice up to that time. To the state's argument that the federal practice was an "arbitrarily chosen rule of convenience" and that, as a constitutional matter, jeopardy should attach when the first witness is sworn, the Court placed emphasis on the defendant's "valued right to have his trial completed before a particular tribunal," and contended that the federal rule has

---

[30]   *Williams v. Oklahoma,* 358 U.S. 576, 79 S.Ct. 421 (1959).

[31]   515 U.S. 389, 115 S.Ct. 2199 (1995).

[32]   USSG § 5G1.3.

[33]   See, e.g., *McMillan v. Pennsylvania,* 477 U.S. 79, 106 S.Ct. 2411 (1986); *Dowling v. United States,* 493 U.S. 342, 110 S.Ct. 668 (1990); § 27.02(a)(2).

[34]   437 U.S. 28, 98 S.Ct. 2156 (1978).

"roots deep in the historic development of trial by jury in the Anglo-American system of criminal justice." According to the Court, "double jeopardy . . . concerns—the finality of judgments, the minimization of harassing exposure to the harrowing experience of a criminal trial, and the valued right to continue with the chosen jury—have combined to produce the federal law that in a jury trial jeopardy attached when the jury is empaneled and sworn." In a concurring opinion, Justice Blackmun added that "the possibility of prosecutorial overreaching in the opening statement" was another reason for rejecting the government's approach.

The latter type of reason has not been persuasive in nonjury cases, however. When trial is in front of a judge alone, jeopardy attaches when the first witness is sworn, despite the fact that opening arguments have been completed at that point.[35] When conviction is by guilty plea, jeopardy attaches when the judge accepts the plea,[36] despite the fact that prior to that event evidence is often presented against the defendant to provide a factual basis for the plea.[37]

If a case is terminated before jeopardy attaches, then reprosecution is possible, even if the termination is on grounds similar to an acquittal. As the Court stated in *Serfass v. United States,*[38] a judicial action labelled an "acquittal" still "has no significance in the [double jeopardy] context unless jeopardy has once attached and an accused has been subjected to the risk of conviction." Furthermore, the Double Jeopardy Clause does not prevent prosecution appeals of pre-jeopardy judicial rulings (although other rules might limit prosecution appeals in this context).[39] Finally, even after jeopardy attaches, if the court is not competent to hear the case on jurisdictional grounds, then reprosecution in an appropriate court is permissible.[40]

30.03   Exceptions to the Double Jeopardy Prohibition

A strict interpretation of the Double Jeopardy Clause would contemplate that once jeopardy has attached, the government would be prohibited from subjecting the defendant to jeopardy again for the same offense. Thus, for instance, not only would a judge or jury verdict bar retrial, but so would any decision by the trial judge to abort the trial before it is complete. Out of concern that the government be assured one fair chance to convict the accused, this interpretation of the Clause has never been favored. The Supreme Court has recognized that the general rule barring retrial on the same charge by the same sovereign after jeopardy has attached may be relaxed in three different situations. The first situation occurs when the defendant has successfully appealed his conviction or otherwise managed to have his conviction overturned. The second arises when the trial judge "dismisses" the case against the defendant prior to verdict. The third occurs when the judge declares a mistrial. In each situation, retrial on the same charge is permitted under certain circumstances.

---

[35]   Id.

[36]   See *Ohio v. Johnson,* 467 U.S. 493, 104 S.Ct. 2536 (1984), discussed further in § 30.04(b)(4).

[37]   See § 26.04(c).

[38]   420 U.S. 377, 95 S.Ct. 1055 (1975). See also, *United States v. Sanford,* 429 U.S. 14, 97 S.Ct. 20 (1976).

[39]   See § 29.04.

[40]   *Kepner v. United States,* 195 U.S. 100, 24 S.Ct. 797 (1904).

(a) Reprosecution After Reversal of Conviction

A defendant who is convicted and does not appeal that conviction or challenges the conviction and loses cannot be retried on the same charge. But when his appeal of the conviction is successful or the defendant is able to overturn his conviction through some other procedural mechanism, it has long been recognized that the government is generally not barred from reprosecution on the original charge.[41] The Supreme Court explained in *Green v. United States*[42] that this result can be justified either on the ground that the defendant has "waived" his plea of former jeopardy by challenging the conviction or, alternatively, that the original jeopardy is "continued" since the first conviction was not final. A better rationale for this rule was provided by Justice Harlan in *United States v. Tateo*.[43] As he noted:

> [I]t would be a high price indeed for society to pay were every accused granted immunity from punishment because of any defect sufficient to constitute reversible error in the proceedings leading to conviction. From the standpoint of a defendant, it is at least doubtful that appellate courts would be as zealous as they now are in protecting against the effects of improprieties at the trial or pretrial stage if they knew that reversal of a conviction would put the accused irrevocably beyond the reach of further prosecution. In reality, therefore, the practice of retrial serves defendants' rights as well as society's interest.

Although reprosecution after a successful appeal is thus generally permissible, there are two limitations on this rule.

(1) The "Implied Acquittal" Doctrine

The first limitation was announced in *Green*, where the defendant was tried for first-degree murder but convicted of second degree murder, a conviction which he successfully appealed. He was then tried on the original first degree murder charge. The Court held that retrial on the greater charge violated the double jeopardy prohibition, because the first jury "was given a full opportunity to return a verdict [on the first degree murder charge] and no extraordinary circumstances appeared which prevented it from doing so." Thus, after the appeal, jeopardy "continued" only for the lesser offense. *Green* stands for the proposition that, when the prosecution presents the factfinder with evidence of a charge and its lesser included offense, conviction on the lesser charge operates as an "implied acquittal" of the greater charge and prosecution on the latter charge is forever barred. The Court has also held that if a prosecution in violation of *Green* takes place, the defendant is entitled to a new trial even if he is convicted only of the lesser offense the second time, since the greater charge against the defendant might have "induced the jury to find him guilty of the less serious offense [rather] than continue to debate his innocence."[44] If, however, the jury foreperson announces the jury has agreed that the defendant is not guilty of the greater offense but is deadlocked on the

---

[41] *Ball v. United States*, 163 U.S. 662, 16 S.Ct. 1192 (1896) (reversal on appeal); *United States v. Tateo*, 377 U.S. 463, 84 S.Ct. 1587 (1964) (reversal by trial judge or habeas court).

[42] 355 U.S. 184, 78 S.Ct. 221 (1957).

[43] 377 U.S. 463, 84 S.Ct. 1587 (1964).

[44] *Price v. Georgia*, 398 U.S. 323, 90 S.Ct. 1757 (1970). But see, *Morris v. Mathews*, 475 U.S. 237, 106 S.Ct. 1032 (1986). Note also that where the appellate court reverses because the defendant was tried under the wrong statute, the defendant may be retried under a different statute because there is no "implied acquittal" for a statutory charge the jury did not consider. *Montana v. Hall*, 481 U.S. 400, 107 S.Ct. 1825 (1987).

lesser offense, and the jury then returns to deliberate further, the announcement does not function as an implied acquittal, because such a statement "lacks the finality necessary to amount to an acquittal."[45]

When the conviction that is appealed was obtained through a guilty plea, then a different analysis applies:

> Unlike the jury in *Green,* the [judge who] is tendered a plea of guilty to the lesser offense does not have the opportunity to convict on the greater offense. Hence, it does not follow from his acceptance of that plea that he has declined the opportunity to convict on the greater charge thus giving rise to an implication of acquittal.[46]

The defendant's only recourse in such a situation is a due process claim arguing that the new charge is a vindictive response to his appeal.[47]

(2) The Evidentiary Insufficiency Exception

There is also one situation in which reprosecution after appeal is barred even on the same charge. As established in *Burks v. United States*[48] this occurs when the appellate court finds that the prosecution has failed as a matter of law to meet its burden of persuasion. In *Burks* the federal appellate court found that the prosecution's evidence had been insufficient to rebut the defendant's prima facie defense of insanity. The Supreme Court saw no reason to distinguish between the defendant who is acquitted pursuant to a directed verdict that the prosecution's evidence is insufficient to warrant submitting the case to the jury (which would clearly bar reprosecution), and the defendant whose conviction is reversed on appeal because the evidence is insufficient to support the jury verdict.

Contrary to the Court's assertion, there is a difference between directed verdicts and appellate reversals: the prosecution might be able to present additional evidence after a motion for directed verdict during trial, whereas it cannot on appeal. But, as the Court stated in *Burks,* appellate reversal on evidentiary sufficiency grounds, like a directed verdict, does "constitute a decision to the effect that the government has failed to prove its case." In contrast, appellate reversals based on procedural errors (e.g., incorrect receipt or rejection of evidence, incorrect instructions or prosecutorial misconduct) "impl[y] nothing with respect to the guilt or innocence of the defendant." Thus, the *Burks* exception is unlikely to protect guilty persons or deter proper appellate decisionmaking, the two reasons given by Harlan in *Tateo* for permitting reprosecution after successful appeals.

Several subsequent decisions have fleshed out the *Burks* holding. In *Hudson v. Louisiana,*[49] the Court emphasized that *Burks* requires only that the evidence against the defendant be *insufficient* to support the conviction, not that there be *no* evidence to support the verdict. In *Hudson,* the defendant moved for a second trial after his

---

[45]   *Blueford v. Arkansas,* 566 U.S. 599, 132 S.Ct. 2044 (2012).

[46]   Note, *Upping the Ante Against the Defendant Who Successfully Attacks His Guilty Plea: Double Jeopardy and Due Process Implications,* 50 Notre Dame Law. 857, 878 (1975). See also, *Ohio v. Johnson,* 467 U.S. 493, 104 S.Ct. 2536 (1984) ("the taking of a guilty plea is not the same as an adjudication on the merits after a full trial.").

[47]   See § 29.02(d).

[48]   437 U.S. 1, 98 S.Ct. 2141 (1978).

[49]   450 U.S. 40, 101 S.Ct. 970 (1981).

conviction, such motion being the only way he could challenge the sufficiency of the evidence under Louisiana law. The trial judge granted the motion, stating: "I heard the same evidence the jury did[;] I'm convinced that there was no evidence, certainly not evidence beyond a reasonable doubt, to sustain the verdict of the homicide committed by this defendant of this particular victim." Justice Powell, writing for a unanimous Court, emphasized that "nothing in *Burks* suggests, as the Louisiana Supreme Court seemed to believe, that double jeopardy protections are violated only when the prosecution has adduced no evidence at all of the crime or an element thereof." Since the trial judge in *Hudson* had ruled that the state had failed to prove its case as a matter of law in the original trial, there were "no significant facts which distinguish [*Hudson*] from *Burks*, and the Double Jeopardy Clause barred the state from prosecuting petitioner a second time."

On the other hand, the Court has also held, in *Tibbs v. Florida*,[50] that a second trial is not barred by the Double Jeopardy Clause when the reversal of the jury's verdict is based on the *weight* of the evidence rather than its sufficiency. Such a reversal could occur pursuant to a state rule authorizing the trial judge to grant a new trial when he finds the jury verdict against the weight of the evidence[51] or, as was true in *Tibbs* itself, after the defendant convinces an appellate court that the jury verdict was against the weight of the evidence. In either case, the *Tibbs* Court held, the second trial does not violate *Burks*.

Justice O'Connor, who wrote the 5–4 opinion, reasoned that *Burks* was based on two policies: (1) that an acquittal, or any action which has the effect of an acquittal, should bar retrial; and (2) that the Double Jeopardy Clause "forbids a second trial for the purpose of affording the prosecution another opportunity to supply evidence which it failed to muster in the first proceeding." She found that a reversal based on a finding by the trial judge (or, as occurred in *Tibbs* itself, an appellate court) that the jury's verdict was not supported by the weight of the evidence does not implicate either of these policies. First, in such cases the judge is merely sitting as a "thirteenth juror" who disagrees with the jury's resolution of the conflicting testimony; "[t]his difference of opinion no more signifies acquittal than does a disagreement among the jurors themselves." Second, in such cases, the state has presented sufficient evidence to persuade a jury to convict; giving the defendant a second chance to seek acquittal under such circumstances does not create " 'an unacceptably high risk that the Government, with its superior resources, [will] wear down [the] defendant and obtain conviction' solely through its persistence."

Yet, as the dissent pointed out with respect to *Tibbs* itself, "[w]ere the state to present this same evidence again, we must assume that once again the state courts would reverse any conviction that was based on it." Since the state was not prevented from producing any of its evidence in the first trial, "the only point of any second trial in this case is to allow the state to present additional evidence to bolster its case." If it does not have such evidence, "reprosecution can serve no purpose other than harassment." As the dissent suggests, *Tibbs* holds that some types of *de facto* acquittals will not bar retrial. On the other hand, a contrary ruling might significantly diminish findings like the one in *Tibbs*, which at least provide the defendant with a new trial.

---

50   457 U.S. 31, 102 S.Ct. 2211 (1982).

51   See e.g., West's Fla.S.A.R.Crim.Pro. 3.600(a)(2).

An implementation question which arises under *Burks* is whether the Double Jeopardy Clause bars retrial when an appellate court decides that certain evidence should not have been admitted by the trial court, and in addition decides that the remaining evidence is insufficient to support the verdict. *Burks* might be read to prohibit retrial in this situation. But in *Lockhart v. Nelson*,[52] the Supreme Court held that a determination of sufficiency for purposes of *Burks* must be based on a review of *all* the evidence, including that found inadmissible by the appellate court. According to Chief Justice Rehnquist, who wrote the 6–3 opinion for the Court,

> The basis for the *Burks* exception . . . is that a reversal for insufficiency of the evidence should be treated no differently than a trial court's granting judgment of acquittal at the close of all the evidence. A trial court in passing on such a motion considers all the evidence it has admitted, and to make the analogy complete it must be this same quantum of evidence which is considered by the reviewing court.

The majority also pointed out that, had the trial court excluded the inadmissible evidence, the prosecution would have had the opportunity to introduce other evidence on the same point, and thus should be allowed to do so via a retrial when the inadmissibility decision is made for the first time by an appellate court. In *Nelson* itself, the Court permitted the state to resentence the defendant as an habitual offender even though his original habitual offender sentence had been overturned after one of the four felonies upon which the sentence had been based was determined to have been nullified by pardon prior to the original sentencing; had this determination been made at the original proceeding, the Court noted, another felony might have been substituted.

(3) The Termination Requirement

Even if the defendant can show that the evidence was insufficient to convict him, the Double Jeopardy Clause affords him no protection against retrial unless the holding favorable to the defendant occurs at the "termination" of the first proceeding against him. In *Justices of Boston Municipal Court v. Lydon*,[53] the defendant chose a bench trial over a jury trial, which under Massachusetts law meant that his first appeal would be a trial *de novo*. After his conviction at the bench trial and pending his trial *de novo*, Lydon motioned for dismissal on the ground that no evidence of criminal intent had been adduced at the bench trial and that retrial was thus barred under *Burks*. The Supreme Court rejected this argument, pointing out that at the time he raised his double jeopardy claim Lydon, in contrast to Burks, had not yet been acquitted but was merely asserting he should have been. Thus, his situation was no different from the defendant appealing a conviction through normal appellate channels; in both cases jeopardy had not yet "terminated." In essence, the *Lydon* Court endorsed the "continuing jeopardy" concept described above and applied it to permit the second trial in the Massachusetts system because it resembled an appeal.

(b) Dismissals Which Are Not "Acquittals"

Burks clearly established that an acquittal by a trial judge or appellate court, even in the face of an adverse jury verdict, bars retrial on the same offense. But what if a judge dismisses the case before the jury returns a verdict? The Court's decisions on this

---

[52]   488 U.S. 33, 109 S.Ct. 285 (1988).
[53]   466 U.S. 294, 104 S.Ct. 1805 (1984).

issue at first endorsed, but then rejected the traditional rationale for the Double Jeopardy Clause—i.e. avoidance of the anxiety and harassment associated with a second trial—and adopted in its place an approach analogous to *Burks*, allowing retrial after every dismissal that is not the equivalent of an acquittal.

In *United States v. Jenkins*,[54] a 1975 decision, the Court held that the Double Jeopardy Clause may bar retrial of a case that has been dismissed even when the dismissal is not "on the merits." In *Jenkins*, the trial court dismissed the indictment on draft evasion charges midway through trial, when it became clear that the defendant's application for conscientious objector status had not been considered by the selective service board before the charges were brought. The prosecution appealed the dismissal. The Supreme Court noted that it was unclear whether the trial court had resolved the factual issues in the case before dismissing the indictment, but held that, regardless, the jeopardy bar applied so long as a successful prosecution appeal would require any further proceedings to resolve the case. In *Jenkins*, the trial court would have had to hear additional evidence, or, at a minimum, make supplemental findings of fact if the government prevailed on appeal, and thus the jeopardy bar prohibited a government appeal of the dismissal.

In a companion case, *United States v. Wilson*,[55] the Court applied the logic behind *Jenkins* in holding that a government appeal was not barred when reversal of the dismissal would *not* necessitate further proceedings. In *Wilson*, the trial court dismissed the indictment after the jury had returned a guilty verdict. Since reversal of the dismissal would result in reinstatement of the jury verdict, rather than retrial, the Double Jeopardy Clause did not apply and prosecution appeal of the dismissal was permissible.

In *Jenkins* and *Wilson*, the Court tried to establish two propositions. First, it differentiated between a mistrial, which it described as a ruling by the trial court that the present trial cannot proceed and that a new one must be held, and a dismissal, which, like an acquittal by verdict, involves a finding favoring the defendant. Second, it refused to distinguish, for purposes of double jeopardy analysis, between dismissals on the merits and those on procedural grounds; according to *Jenkins* and *Wilson*, the Double Jeopardy Clause automatically bars any appeal of a dismissal if its reversal on appeal would require additional proceedings.

Three years later, however, the Court rejected both propositions and overruled *Jenkins*. *United States v. Scott*[56] held that there is *no* functional distinction between a dismissal that is not on the merits and a mistrial. In *Scott*, the defendant moved successfully for dismissal of two counts of his indictment on the ground of prejudicial pretrial delay. The Supreme Court permitted prosecution appeal of this ruling, over a four-member dissent arguing that when the government fails "for any reason to persuade the court not to enter a final judgment favorable to the accused, the constitutional policies underlying the ban against multiple trials become compelling." Instead, Justice Rehnquist's majority opinion found that the appeal sought by the prosecution was a "far cry" from "an all-powerful state relentlessly pursuing a defendant who had either been found guilty or who had at least insisted on having the issue of guilt submitted to the

---

54   420 U.S. 358, 95 S.Ct. 1006 (1975).

55   420 U.S. 332, 95 S.Ct. 1013 (1975).

56   437 U.S. 82, 98 S.Ct. 2187 (1978).

first trier of fact." Rather, here the defendant chose "to seek termination of the proceedings against him on a basis unrelated to factual guilt or innocence of the offense of which he is accused." The Court emphasized that its holding was not based on the finding that the defendant waived jeopardy protection when he made the dismissal motion, but rather on the finding that he had no double jeopardy right to waive.

Thus, just as reprosecution is permitted after the defense obtains reversal of a trial ruling not related to guilt, the prosecution is permitted to appeal any judicial ruling that is not an "acquittal" (and, of course, reprosecute if the appeal is successful). As with the exception established in *Burks* (decided the same term as *Scott*), the central question after *Scott* is the definition of "acquittal." In *Scott*, Rehnquist quoted the year-old language in *United States v. Martin Linen Supply Co.*,[57] to the effect that an acquittal occurs "only upon a jury verdict of not guilty [or when] the ruling of the judge, whatever its label, actually represents a resolution [in the defendant's favor], correct or not, of some or all of the factual elements of the offense charged." According to Rehnquist, for example, judicial dismissal predicated on a finding of insanity (which was the case in *Burks*) or entrapment is an acquittal. "By contrast, the dismissal of an indictment for preindictment delay represents a legal judgment that a defendant, although criminally culpable, may not be punished because of a supposed constitutional violation." Thus, the prosecution may not appeal the former but may appeal the latter. The dissent questioned this distinction between "factual" and "legal" innocence, noting that the applicability of the pretrial delay rule depends as much on an evaluation of the trial evidence as does the validity of an insanity or entrapment defense.[58]

Scott's emphasis on factual matters left open whether a judicial dismissal based purely on a ruling of law would be appealable. Given the fact that barring retrial in such circumstances might prevent retrial of a person for whom the prosecution has produced sufficient evidence to convict, it would not be inconsistent with *Scott* to allow appeal in this type of case, as occurs in some European countries. However, the Court appears to be unwilling to make such a distinction. In *Sanabria v. United States*,[59] decided the same term as *Scott*, the Court held that a dismissal based on an incorrect finding that the dismissed charge was not in the indictment bars reprosecution. In doing so, it stated that, "when a defendant has been acquitted at trial, he may not be retried on the same offense, even if the legal rulings underlying the acquittal were erroneous." Similarly, in *Michigan v. Evans*,[60] the trial judge dismissed an arson charge under the mistaken impression that the charge required proof that the building that had been burned was a dwelling rather than, as allegedly occurred in *Evans*, another type of real property, a clear error of law. Eight members of the Court held that the double jeopardy prohibition barred retrial, because "our cases have defined an acquittal to encompass any ruling that the prosecution's proof is insufficient to establish criminal liability for an offense," even when, as the Court put it in *Fong Foo v. United States*,[61] the acquittal is "based upon an egregiously erroneous foundation.[62]

---

[57]   430 U.S. 564, 97 S.Ct. 1349 (1977).

[58]   See § 25.02(b) for a discussion of the pretrial delay rule.

[59]   437 U.S. 54, 98 S.Ct. 2170 (1978).

[60]   568 U.S. 313, 133 S.Ct. 1069 (2013).

[61]   369 U.S. 141, 82 S.Ct. 671 (1962).

[62]   See also *Arizona v. Rumsey*, 467 U.S. 203, 104 S.Ct. 2305 (1984), discussed in § 30.05(a).

In any event, it is clear that a dismissal that *is* based on an assessment of the sufficiency of the prosecution's factual case against the defendant, whatever its label, is not appealable by the prosecution. In *Smalis v. Pennsylvania*,[63] the Court affirmed that a trial court dismissal on the ground that the prosecution had failed to establish the defendant's guilt beyond a reasonable doubt bars appeal and reprosecution, finding it irrelevant that the state appellate court described the defendant's "demurrer" motion as one that required a legal judgment rather than a factual determination. Similarly, in *Smith v. Massachusetts*,[64] the Court held that a midtrial ruling dismissing a particular charge on insufficient evidence grounds is a judgment of acquittal for double jeopardy purposes, unless the judge reserves the right to reconsider the ruling or state law indicates that such judgments are not final until the end of trial. As Justice Scalia explained in an opinion for five members of the Court, a midtrial ruling might influence defendants' decisions about what evidence to present or whether to present any evidence at all, and the "Double Jeopardy Clause's guarantee cannot be allowed to become a potential snare for those who reasonably rely upon it."[65] In the unusual circumstance where the judge directs a verdict for the defense after the prosecution declares an unwillingness to participate in the trial (in this case, because the court refused to grant a continuance despite the prosecution's inability to locate the defendants), retrial is also barred.[66]

As Rehnquist pointed out in *Scott*, one way of avoiding the situation giving rise to *Scott, Jenkins* and these other cases is to defer the dismissal decision until after the jury has returned a verdict (as in *Wilson*). If the verdict is acquittal, dismissal will of course be unnecessary. If the verdict is a conviction, and the trial judge decides that it cannot stand, the verdict can be reinstated after successful prosecutorial appeal of that decision without violating even *Jenkins'* conception of double jeopardy (because no new proceeding is required by such a practice).

(c) Mistrials

As the Court's discussion in *Jenkins* and *Scott* illustrates, there has been some confusion over the terms "mistrial" and "dismissal." Indeed, in some jurisdictions the terms are nearly interchangeable. But the Court's suggested definition of the two concepts is fairly straightforward. As outlined in *Scott*, the word "dismissal" should be used only to designate judicial decisions that are meant to dispose of the case on the merits either factually or (probably) legally, whereas a mistrial is abortion of trial for any other reason. The most common cause of a mistrial, as that term is traditionally understood, is the inability of the jury to arrive at a unanimous verdict. A mistrial could also be declared when the judge believes a violation of evidentiary or procedural rules or some other circumstance has so influenced the jury that a fair trial, for either the defendant or the government, is impossible.

In *Oregon v. Kennedy*,[67] Justice Stevens helpfully organized the Court's double jeopardy cases involving mistrials into two categories. The first category concerns

---

[63]   476 U.S. 140, 106 S.Ct. 1745 (1986).

[64]   543 U.S. 462, 125 S.Ct. 1129 (2005).

[65]   That rationale suggests, however, that a quick reversal of a midtrial ruling might not trigger the guarantee, and in fact Justice Scalia noted that the Clause has "never been thought to bar immediate repair of a genuine error in the announcement of acquittal."

[66]   *Martinez v. Illinois*, 572 U.S. 833, 134 S.Ct. 2070 (2014).

[67]   456 U.S. 667, 102 S.Ct. 2083 (1982) (Stevens, J., concurring).

mistrials declared over the defendant's objection; here retrial is permitted only when the mistrial was a "manifest necessity." The second category includes mistrials to which the defendant consented, or which result from the defendant's own motion; here retrial is permitted unless the mistrial motion was provoked by prosecutorial "overreaching" designed to secure a second trial. The manifest necessity and prosecutorial overreaching notions are discussed below.

(1)   The Manifest Necessity Doctrine; Prosecution or Judicial Motion

At least since 1824, when it decided *United States v. Perez*,[68] the Supreme Court has recognized that retrial after a mistrial is constitutionally permissible if the mistrial is dictated by "manifest necessity, or the ends of public justice would otherwise be defeated." A more modern formulation of this idea was put forward in *Illinois v. Somerville*,[69] where the Court stated that the double jeopardy ban does not apply when "the defendant's interest in proceeding to verdict is outweighed by the competing and equally legitimate demand for public justice." Further defining the manifest necessity rule is difficult, given the many different reasons for which a mistrial might be granted.

The classic example of "manifest necessity" occurs when the judge declares a mistrial because the jury is unable to reach a unanimous or otherwise legal verdict. As *Perez* indicated, other than dismissing the case permanently, the trial court is left with no other option in such circumstances. Over one and a half centuries later, in *Richardson v. United States*,[70] the Court reaffirmed *Perez* with the following language:

> Without exception, the courts have held that the trial judge may discharge a genuinely deadlocked jury and require the defendant to submit to a second trial. This rule accords recognition to society's interest in giving the prosecution one complete opportunity to convict those who have violated its laws.

The majority rejected Justice Brennan's argument in dissent that the Court's decision in *Burks* barred retrial if a reviewing court felt the jury was deadlocked because of insufficiency in the prosecution's case. Rather, it construed *Burks* as prohibiting retrial only if an appellate court found the prosecution's evidence to be insufficient upon review of a *conviction;* when there is no conviction, but only a hung jury, the prosecution may, in the trial judge's discretion, retry the defendant. Thus, the manifest necessity doctrine permits reprosecution following a hung jury even if the majority of jurors vote to acquit or an appellate court believes the evidence was insufficient to support conviction.

Further, the trial judge has substantial discretion in deciding whether a jury is hung and how much effort to expend in cajoling it to reach a unanimous verdict. Thus, in *Renico v. Lett*,[71] the Court held that it was not unreasonable for a state court to declare a manifest necessity mistrial even though the jury had only deliberated for four hours and the trial judge neither definitively ascertained the jury was deadlocked nor considered options such as polling the jurors, giving an instruction ordering further deliberations, or querying defense counsel about his preferences.[72]

---

[68]   22 U.S. (9 Wheat.) 579 (1824).

[69]   410 U.S. 458, 93 S.Ct. 1066 (1973).

[70]   468 U.S. 317, 104 S.Ct. 3081 (1984).

[71]   559 U.S. 766, 130 S.Ct. 1855 (2010).

[72]   Note that *Lett* was a habeas case and thus its holding does not state a constitutional rule but rather merely prevents a federal habeas court from overturning a state court decision like that in *Lett*. See § 33.02(c).

The Court has also found that manifest necessity justifies retrial after mistrials declared when the trial judge learns that one of the jurors had served on the indicting grand jury,[73] and when war-time exigencies intervene.[74] Sometimes manifest necessity is found in more subtle circumstances. For instance, in *Gori v. United States,*[75] the Court allowed a second trial of the defendant after the judge, apparently prematurely assuming that the prosecutor's questioning of a witness was calculated to inform the jury of the defendant's prior convictions, declared a mistrial without the defendant's consent. In a 5–4 decision, the Court upheld the conviction obtained in a subsequent trial. The Court emphasized that the trial judge declared the mistrial out of "extreme solicitude—an overeager solicitude, it may be—in favor of the accused." The Court may also have been influenced by the fact that the prosecutor probably had not actually committed error at the time the mistrial was declared. It quoted the circuit court opinion in the case to the effect that "the prosecutor did nothing to instigate the declaration of a mistrial and . . . was only performing his assigned duty under trying conditions."

On the other hand, some judicial actions may be so precipitous and so clearly reflect a failure to take into account the alternatives or the defendant's interests that they do not trigger the manifest necessity rule. In *United States v. Jorn,*[76] the trial judge abruptly declared a mistrial after becoming convinced that five government witnesses had not been warned of their constitutional rights, despite the prosecution's assurances that the witnesses had been sufficiently warned. A plurality of the Court held that the trial judge had abused his discretion in not considering the less drastic alternative of a continuance or permitting the defense to object to the mistrial and that, in these circumstances, the Double Jeopardy Clause prohibited reprosecution, the government's claim of undeserved benefit to the defendant notwithstanding. In contrast, when a jury has announced it has agreed the defendant is not guilty of capital murder but remains deadlocked on lesser included offenses, a judge who declares a mistrial on all the charges rather than dismissing the capital murder charge does not prevent application of the manifest necessity doctrine. Stating that "we have never required a trial court, before declaring a mistrial because of a hung jury, to consider any particular means of breaking the impasse," the Court's decision in *Blueford v. Arkansas*[77] held, 6–3, that retrial is permissible on the greater charge as well.

Several cases concern application of the manifest necessity rule in the more "suspicious" situation created when the mistrial motion originates from the prosecution rather than the court. In *Downum v. United States,*[78] for instance, the prosecution requested that the jury be discharged just after it had been empaneled, because one of the government's key witnesses was not available. The defendant motioned to proceed with trial on the five counts for which the witness was irrelevant, but the court denied the motion and declared a mistrial. Here, unlike in *Gori,* the error leading to abortion of the first trial was at least negligent; apparently understaffing in the prosecutor's office had led to the failure to discover the absence of the witness. Moreover, again in contrast to *Gori,* the first jury was discharged out of concern for the prosecution, not the defense. On these facts, the Court, in a 5–4 decision, reversed the conviction. However, in *Illinois*

---

[73]   *Thompson v. United States*, 155 U.S. 271, 15 S.Ct. 73 (1894).

[74]   *Wade v. Hunter*, 336 U.S. 684, 69 S.Ct. 834 (1949).

[75]   367 U.S. 364, 81 S.Ct. 1523 (1961).

[76]   400 U.S. 470, 91 S.Ct. 547 (1971).

[77]   566 U.S. 599, 132 S.Ct. 2044 (2012).

[78]   372 U.S. 734, 83 S.Ct. 1033 (1963).

v. Somerville,[79] the state was permitted to convict the defendant after a mistrial resulting from a defect in the prosecution's indictment. Here the prosecutor's error was grossly negligent, yet the Supreme Court allowed a second trial under a cured indictment.

One possible explanation for the seeming inconsistency between *Downum* and *Somerville* was that in the first case the state could easily have moved for a continuance and avoided the drastic action of a mistrial, while in the latter case, given Illinois' "archaic mode of reading indictments," a mistrial was the only course.[80] In other words, in *Downum* there was a less drastic means of curing the alleged defect, and thus a mistrial was not a "manifest necessity."[81] Second, it has been argued that the type of error in *Downum* is more subject to prosecutorial manipulation:

> If a witness is willing to testify without a subpoena, an unscrupulous prosecutor might indeed fail to subpoena the witness, knowing that he could exploit the witness's unavailability as grounds for a mistrial if the trial proceeded unfavorably. On the other hand, a prosecutor is unlikely to create uncorrectable error in the indictment to preserve the mistrial option because any conviction is automatically reversible.[82]

Downum and *Somerville* might also be distinguished by looking at the extent to which different results in those cases would allow the *defendant* to manipulate the system. Arguably, the defendant is better able to determine prior to trial when an indictment is defective than when the prosecution is missing a key witness; thus, in the former instance, his objection to a mistrial motion after jeopardy has attached is more likely to be a cynical attempt to take advantage of a "technicality" to avoid conviction, rather than a sincere effort to prevent the prosecution from honing its case.

Relatedly, the Court has suggested that one factor to consider in determining whether "manifest necessity" exists is whether the defense is responsible for the mistrial declaration. In *Arizona v. Washington,*[83] the defendant's first conviction was reversed because the prosecutor had failed to disclose exculpatory information to the defense. In his opening statement at the second trial, the defense counsel referred to this lapse on the part of the prosecution. The judge declared a mistrial, on the prosecution's motion, on the ground of possible jury bias. The Supreme Court upheld the defendant's conviction at his third trial despite his argument that the judge had made no express finding that the abortion of the second trial was a manifest necessity. In justifying its decision, the Court noted that the judge allowed both sides to offer arguments pertaining to the mistrial motion, and emphasized that the judge's familiarity with the situation "requires that we accord the highest degree of respect to the judge's evaluation." But the most significant reason for the Court's decision may have been the fact that the mistrial was triggered by defense misconduct.[84] Supporting this interpretation is the Court's

---

[79]　410 U.S. 458, 93 S.Ct. 1066 (1973).

[80]　See Lewis Katz, *Double Jeopardy,* 2 Pub.Def.Rep. 1, 6 (1979).

[81]　Note that *Crist v. Bretz,* 437 U.S. 28, 98 S.Ct. 2156 (1978), discussed in § 30.02(b), also involved a dismissal due to a defective charging instrument, and that there a continuance was possible. However, in that case, the parties stipulated that, if jeopardy were found to have attached when the mistrial was declared, retrial would be barred.

[82]　George Thomas III, *An Elegant Theory of Double Jeopardy,* 1988 U.Ill.L.Rev. 827, 864.

[83]　434 U.S. 497, 98 S.Ct. 824 (1978).

[84]　Katz, supra note 80, at 7.

statement that a mistrial order is not entitled to the same deference when the prosecution is the cause of the order.

Similar in spirit is *United States v. Dinitz,*[85] where the Court concluded that so long as "the defendant retains primary control over the course to be followed in the event of . . . error," the Fifth Amendment will rarely be implicated. There, the defendant's first attorney was expelled from the courtroom for repeated misconduct, and co-counsel was unprepared to proceed with the case. From several alternatives offered by the judge (including a continuance), the defendant asked for a mistrial, to permit him to obtain new counsel. Although conceding that the defendant was confronted with a "Hobson's choice" (i.e., continuing with unprepared counsel or undergoing a new trial), the Court rejected the lower appellate court's conclusion that trial should have been precluded:

> The defendant may reasonably conclude that a continuation of the tainted proceeding would result in a conviction followed by a lengthy appeal and, if a reversal is secured, by a second prosecution. In such circumstances, a defendant's mistrial request has objectives not unlike the interest served by the Double Jeopardy Clause—the avoidance of the anxiety, expense, and delay occasioned by multiple prosecutions.

(2) *Prosecutorial Overreaching; Defense Motion*

When the defense moves for mistrial because of prosecutorial error, a more discerning analysis is necessary. Some hypothetical scenarios suggest why.[86] For instance, a prosecutor might commit repeated prejudicial error merely to subject a defendant he knows he cannot convict to the harassment of multiple trials. Or a prosecutor might try to inject enough unfair prejudice into a trial to ensure a conviction but not so much as to cause a reversal of that conviction. Under such circumstances, the Court's earlier cases suggested, in dictum, that retrial after a mistrial would be barred, to prevent prosecutorial manipulation of the system.[87]

More recent cases suggest a more lenient approach to prosecutorial malfeasance. In *Lee v. United States,*[88] the defendant, just prior to trial, moved to dismiss the information for theft on the grounds that it did not allege the necessary specific intent. The court tentatively denied the motion and defendant's counsel did not object to going forward with the trial. At the close of the evidence, the trial court decided to grant the defendant's motion to dismiss but observed that his guilt had been proved beyond a reasonable doubt. On the facts in *Lee,* the Court held that a retrial was not barred by former jeopardy. The Court viewed the dismissal as functionally indistinguishable from a mistrial, noting that it was not predicated on any determination that the defendant should be acquitted of the crime with which he was charged. It then found: (1) that there was no prosecutorial bad faith, only negligence; (2) that the proceedings continued at the defendant's request and with his consent; and (3) that the trial court's failure to postpone taking evidence was reasonable in light of the last-minute timing of the motion and defense counsel's failure

---

[85] 424 U.S. 600, 96 S.Ct. 1075 (1976).

[86] These examples are taken from Justice Stevens concurring opinion in *Oregon v. Kennedy,* 456 U.S. 667, 102 S.Ct. 2083 (1982).

[87] See, e.g., *Arizona v. Washington,* 434 U.S. 497, 98 S.Ct. 824 (1978) (prohibiting "using the superior resources of the State to harass or to achieve a tactical advantage over the accused"); *United States v. Tateo,* 377 U.S. 463, 84 S.Ct. 1587 (1964) (prohibiting "prosecutorial . . . impropriety . . . result[ing] from a fear that the jury was likely to acquit the accused").

[88] 432 U.S. 23, 97 S.Ct. 2141 (1977).

to request a continuance. *Lee* made clear that whether a trial may take place after a mistrial is declared is not merely dependent upon the culpability of the prosecutor, but on the relative culpability of the prosecution, the defense, and the judge.

In *Oregon v. Kennedy*[89] the Court went a step further by holding that merely negligent prosecutorial action resulting in mistrial will not bar retrial even when the defense does not contribute to the mistrial order. During Kennedy's trial for theft, the state's expert witness, who testified during direct examination concerning the value of the stolen property, admitted on cross-examination that he had once filed a criminal complaint against Kennedy, but that no action had been taken on the complaint. On redirect, the prosecutor tried to rehabilitate her witness by establishing why the witness had filed the complaint, but the defense repeatedly and successfully objected to her questions. Finally, however, having elicited from the witness that he had never done business with the defendant, the prosecutor asked "Is that because he is a crook?" On defendant's motion, the court declared a mistrial and the defendant claimed that his subsequent trial violated the Double Jeopardy Clause.

The Supreme Court rejected the defendant's suggestion that the test for applying the Clause in such situations should be whether the prosecutor "overreached." Rather, after concluding that the dicta in earlier cases offered "no standards for their application," the Court announced that the test should be whether the prosecutor "*intended* to 'goad' the defendant into moving for a mistrial" [emphasis added]. Since the state courts found this intent did not exist in *Kennedy*,[90] the defendant could not invoke the double jeopardy prohibition. Indeed, *Kennedy's* test will seldom ever be met since, as Justice Stevens concurrence pointed out, "[i]t is almost inconceivable that a defendant could prove that the prosecutor's deliberate misconduct was motivated by an intent to provoke a mistrial instead of an intent simply to prejudice the defendant."[91]

30.04 The "Same Offense" Prohibition

If jeopardy has attached on a particular charge and none of the exceptions to the double jeopardy ban described in the previous section apply, then reprosecution is generally barred not only on that charge but also on any other charges that are considered the "same offense." Put another way, those offenses that are the "same" for double jeopardy purposes must usually be joined in the same proceeding if the state wishes to prosecute them. This section discusses the definition of "same offense," the exceptions to the same offense prohibition, and the different definition of "same offense" that is applied when the issue is cumulative punishments rather than multiple prosecutions.

(a) Defining Same Offense

The Fifth Amendment phrase "same offense" has always been defined more broadly than the precise charge involved at the first proceeding; otherwise, the prosecution could repeatedly try the defendant despite the double jeopardy ban, given the wide array of

---

[89] 456 U.S. 667, 102 S.Ct. 2083 (1982).

[90] As Justice Stevens noted in his concurring opinion:

The isolated prosecutorial error occurred early in the trial, too early to determine whether the case was going badly for the prosecution. If anyone was being harassed at that trial, it was the prosecutor, who was frustrated by improper defense objections. . . .

[91] For further development of this point, see Steven Alan Reiss, *Prosecutorial Intent in Constitutional Criminal Procedure*, 135 U.Pa.L.Rev. 1365 (1987).

crimes that any given act might trigger.[92] The courts have devised a number of different standards for determining when related offenses must be joined rather than tried separately. The Supreme Court has vacillated on which standard to use, and has also granted constitutional status to the collateral estoppel principle, which in some instances will bar a second prosecution where the same offense prohibition, at least under some of its guises, would not.

(1) Various Approaches

The test that defines "same offense" most narrowly could be called the "identical evidence" test. The basic thrust of this approach is captured by the original American version, formulated in *Morey v. Commonwealth*:[93] "A conviction or acquittal upon one indictment is no bar to a subsequent conviction and sentence upon another, unless the evidence required to support a conviction upon one of them would have been sufficient to warrant a conviction upon the other." In essence, this test places little limitation on reprosecution beyond prohibiting a trial for any lesser included offense of a crime on which the defendant has already been acquitted or convicted. Under a literal application of *Morey's* standard, for instance, if a person is first convicted of the *lesser* offense, he could still be prosecuted for the greater offense, unless the jury in the first trial was presented evidence relating to the greater offense and could be said to have "impliedly acquitted" the defendant by choosing the lesser charge.[94]

A test that appears to be slightly broader than the identical evidence test could be called the "same element" test. As described by the Supreme Court in *Blockburger v. United States*,[95] this test states that "[w]here the same act or transaction constitutes a violation of two distinct statutory provisions, the test to be applied to determine whether there are two offenses or only one, is whether each provision requires proof of an additional fact which the other does not." Under this type of test, second-degree murder and manslaughter are the "same offense," as are larceny and robbery, and an attempt and the completed offense.[96] The same element test bars consecutive prosecution of an offense and its lesser included offenses regardless of the order of prosecution, and without resort to the implied acquittal idea.

On the other hand, under either the same evidence or same element tests, a single criminal act or transaction may result in a number of "offenses" for double jeopardy purposes. For example, a single criminal act involving three victims can be considered three separate offenses under both tests.[97] A single act might also be in violation of overlapping statutes that require different elements, such as burglary and larceny.[98] Finally, a single transaction may be separable into acts that are chronologically discreet,

---

[92]   For instance, one commentator noted that a single sale of narcotics could, at least in 1958, elicit nine counts under separate federal statutes. Note, *Consecutive Sentences in Single Prosecutions: Judicial Multiplication of Statutory Penalties*, 67 Yale L.J. 916, 928 n. 43 (1958).

[93]   108 Mass. 433 (1871).

[94]   Cf. § 30.03(a)(1).

[95]   284 U.S. 299, 52 S.Ct. 180 (1932).

[96]   See Annotation, *What Constitutes Lesser Offense 'Necessarily Included' in Offense Charged, under Rule 31(c) of Federal Rules of Criminal Procedure*, 11 ALR Fed. 173 (1972).

[97]   See, e.g., *State v. Hoag*, 21 N.J. 496, 122 A.2d 628 (1956), aff'd 356 U.S. 464, 78 S.Ct. 829 (1958). However, if the defendant is acquitted at a trial relating to the first victim, *collateral estoppel* may bar subsequent prosecutions, if the acquittal represents a determination that the defendant was not the perpetrator of the crime. See § 30.04(a)(3).

[98]   See Comment, *Twice in Jeopardy*, 75 Yale L.J. 262, 273 (1965).

and thus are separate offenses under the same evidence approach. For instance, a person who steals a gun, possesses it while breaking and entering a house, and then murders the occupant may, under the same evidence or *Blockburger* approaches, be subjected to three separate trials.[99] In many instances, dissecting a crime into such components is anathema to the values traditionally associated with the protection against double jeopardy.

For this reason, some jurisdictions have developed other approaches to the same offense issue. The broadest category of tests in this regard are the so-called "same transaction" tests, which focus not upon the evidence or elements needed to prove each offense but upon the incident which led to apprehension and prosecution; under a same transaction test, multiple prosecutions based on the number of victims involved in a crime or the number of overlapping statutory offenses it implicates would usually be prohibited. The Court's most vigorous proponent of the transactional approach was Justice Brennan. In his view, as he explained in *Ashe v. Swenson*,[100] "[t]he Double Jeopardy Clause requires the prosecution, except in most limited circumstances, to join at one trial all the charges against a defendant that grow out of a single criminal act, occurrence, episode, or transaction." Jurisdictions that have adopted such an approach[101] have chosen to protect more actively against multiple prosecutions.

However, the transaction approach has problems as well. As one court inquired:

> Assume that one breaks and enters a building to commit larceny of an automobile, does thereafter in fact steal the automobile and drive away, killing the night watchman in the process, and two blocks away runs a red light which brings about his arrest by the municipal police. Could it be said with any logic that a plea of guilty to breaking and entering would bar a subsequent prosecution for murder? If so, presumably a plea of guilty to the traffic offense would likewise, since all arise out of the "same transaction."[102]

Although the effect of the same transaction test in such a scenario can be circumscribed to some extent,[103] the concerns voiced above have led others to propose a "same conduct" test, which falls somewhere in-between the same element and same transaction approaches.[104] This test looks at the conduct that will be shown to prove each offense to determine whether two offenses are the same. Thus, in the above hypothetical, under a same conduct test the breaking and entering and the theft of the automobile would probably be the same offense, because the prosecution would present testimony about the breaking and entering to prove the theft, but the traffic violation and homicide would not be. Under a same element test, on the other hand, none of the crimes would be the same offense; despite their similarity, the breaking and entering and theft charges each include elements the other does not.

---

[99] See *Johnson v. Commonwealth,* 201 Ky. 314, 256 S.W. 388 (1923), where 75 hands of poker were considered to be separate offenses.

[100] 397 U.S. 436, 90 S.Ct. 1189 (1970) (Brennan, J., concurring).

[101] See, e.g., *Boyette v. State,* 172 Ga.App. 683, 324 S.E.2d 540 (1984); *Cowart v. State,* 461 So.2d 21 (Ala.Crim.App. 1984).

[102] *State v. Conrad,* 243 So.2d 174 (Fla.App. 1971).

[103] For instance, as developed in § 30.04(b)(3), if the traffic court lacked jurisdiction to hear the other charges, double jeopardy would not bar a subsequent prosecution on those charges.

[104] See George Thomas III, *Successive Prosecutions for the Same Offense: In Search of a Definition,* 71 Iowa L.Rev. 323, 377–88 (1986).

(2) The Supreme Court's Approach

The Supreme Court's earliest cases appeared to adopt a same element test. Although the *Blockburger* rule quoted above was developed solely as a guide to when multiple punishments may be imposed (an issue discussed below[105]), in *Brown v. Ohio*[106] the Court relied on the rule in deciding when separate prosecutions for related offenses are permitted. In *Brown*, the defendant had taken another person's car and was apprehended nine days later. He pleaded guilty to "joyriding" and was jailed and fined. Upon his release, he was returned to the county where he first gained possession of the automobile and was indicted for auto theft. Although, as the three-member dissent pointed out, this second prosecution was based on a different part of the nine-day period than the original prosecution, the majority characterized the joyriding charge as a single continuing offense.[107] On this assumption, the majority held that the second prosecution was barred because the joyriding charge (which in essence involves operating a car without the owner's consent) did not require proof of any fact that is not also required to prove auto theft.

Although *Brown* resulted in a finding for the defendant, it clearly adopted the relatively narrow *Blockburger* definition of same offense. The same term as *Brown*, however, the Court created an exception to *Blockburger*. In *Harris v. Oklahoma*,[108] the defendant was convicted of felony-murder for his participation in a robbery during which a grocery store clerk was killed. He was later tried and convicted of robbery with firearms. The *Blockburger* test would have permitted the robbery prosecution, since robbery does not require proof of a killing, and felony murder does not require proof of *robbery,* but only some felony. Nonetheless, the Court reversed the robbery conviction, holding that where a conviction for a greater crime, in this case felony murder, cannot be had without conviction for a lesser crime, here the underlying felony, the Double Jeopardy Clause bars prosecution for the lesser crime after conviction of the greater.

Three years later the Court decided *Illinois v. Vitale,*[109] which further called into question the continued vitality of the *Blockburger* rule. There the defendant allegedly caused a fatal car accident. He was issued a ticket charging him with failure to reduce speed, and convicted of that offense. The day after his conviction, the state charged him with two counts of involuntary manslaughter based on his reckless driving. The Supreme Court held that, under the *Blockburger* rule, the second prosecution was not barred. But it also stated in dictum that if, to prove the homicide charges, the prosecution *had* to prove a failure to slow or "conduct necessarily involving such failure," then "his claim of double jeopardy would be substantial."

In *Grady v. Corbin,*[110] the Court held, 5–4, that *Vitale's* dictum should become law. The Court reminded that *Blockburger's* rule had originally been devised purely as a method of determining when multiple punishments for similar offenses are permitted. It then concluded that the definition of same offense for determining when multiple trials may take place must be broader, to prevent reprosecutions that give "the State an

---

[105] See § 30.04(c).

[106] 432 U.S. 161, 97 S.Ct. 2221 (1977).

[107] However, it noted that had Ohio law provided that joyriding was a separate offense for each day in which a motor vehicle is operated without the owner's consent, a different result would have been required.

[108] 433 U.S. 682, 97 S.Ct. 2912 (1977).

[109] 447 U.S. 410, 100 S.Ct. 2260 (1980).

[110] 495 U.S. 508, 110 S.Ct. 2084 (1990).

opportunity to rehearse its presentation of proof, thus increasing the risk of an erroneous conviction for one or more of the offenses charged." Specifically, the Court held, double jeopardy concerns require a "same conduct" definition of "same offense," prohibiting "any . . . prosecution in which the government, to establish an essential element of an offense charged in that prosecution, will prove conduct that constitutes an offense for which the defendant has already been prosecuted."

Within three years, however, the Court had overturned *Grady*. In *United States v. Dixon,*[111] five members of the Court agreed that *Grady* should no longer be the law because it had "no constitutional basis," conflicted with longstanding precedent, and was confusing to apply. Justice Scalia, who wrote the majority opinion, borrowed heavily from his dissent in *Grady* in concluding that the constitutional "same offense" language should not mean two different things depending upon whether separate punishments or separate prosecutions are involved. He then concluded that the *Blockburger* test, which reflected historical tradition, was the appropriate one. He found irrelevant Justice Souter's argument in dissent that this test made it too easy for the government to try a defendant two or more times for essentially the same conduct. But he did note that the "sheer press" of pursuing other prosecutorial business would probably prevent such multiple prosecutions in most cases where they are possible.

As an illustration of how *Grady* conflicted with precedent and had proven "unstable," Scalia pointed to the Court's year-old decision in *United States v. Felix.*[112] That case had in effect disregarded *Grady* in deciding that the government could prosecute a defendant for conspiring to sell drugs two years after he was convicted for attempting to sell the drugs. Chief Justice Rehnquist's opinion in *Felix* implicitly conceded that *Grady's* rule would have prohibited the second prosecution in *Felix,* because the evidence used to prove the overt act required for the conspiracy included conduct proven in the previous attempt trial.[113] But, on authority of *United States v. Bayer,*[114] a forty-six-year-old decision which had relied on the *Blockburger* test, the *Felix* Court held that a conspiracy and the conspired offense are distinct for double jeopardy purposes because the "essence" of a conspiracy offense "is in the agreement or confederation to commit a crime." Because such an agreement is not an element of the substantive offense, and because conspiracy does not require proof of the actus reus for the completed crime or an attempt to commit it, the second prosecution was permissible.

Scalia's final assertion—that *Grady's* test had proven confusing—is supported by its application in *Grady* itself. There, the Court held that the defendant's guilty plea on a ticket charging him with driving while intoxicated and failing to keep to the right of the median prevented his later prosecution for a homicide arising out of the same incident. The *Blockburger* rule would not have barred the second prosecution because the ticket charge did not require proof of death, and manslaughter does not require proof of driving while intoxicated or failing to keep to the right. However, the Court held that, under its new test, the second prosecution was barred because, according to the prosecution's bill of particulars, the state planned to prove manslaughter by proving the

---

[111]   509 U.S. 688, 113 S.Ct. 2849 (1993).

[112]   503 U.S. 378, 112 S.Ct. 1377 (1992).

[113]   In a concurring opinion, however, Justice Stevens argued that even *Grady* would permit the second trial: "the overt acts at issue here did not meaningfully 'establish' an essential element of the conspiracy because there is no overt act requirement in the federal drug conspiracy statute and the overt acts did not establish an agreement between Felix and his coconspirators."

[114]   331 U.S. 532, 67 S.Ct. 1394 (1947).

same conduct that had been at issue in the ticket offense (i.e., operating a vehicle in an intoxicated condition and failing to keep right). At the same time, the Court stated, prosecution on the second set of charges might still be possible if the bill of particulars were amended so as not to rely on conduct for which the defendant had already been convicted (e.g., "if the State relied solely on Corbin's driving too fast in heavy rain to establish recklessness or negligence"). As Justice Scalia noted in his dissent in *Grady,* it was unclear what would happen under the majority's rule if, during a new trial under the amended bill of particulars, a witness testified that the defendant had been weaving across the line: would the trial have to be aborted at this point, because the prosecution had now introduced conduct previously used to convict the defendant on another charge?

Having overturned *Grady* on conceptual and practical grounds, Scalia went on to apply the *Blockburger* test to the two cases at issue in *Dixon.* Both involved prosecution of defendants who had previously been convicted on criminal contempt charges for violating court orders. By distributing cocaine, Dixon had violated a court order forbidding the commission of "any criminal offense" after his release from confinement. Foster had violated a protective order forbidding him to assault "or in any manner threaten" his wife by assaulting her on several occasions. Scalia concluded that, under the *Blockburger* test, Dixon's reprosecution was barred, since the crime of possessing cocaine with the intention of distributing it was in effect a lesser included offense of the "crime" of violating the court order prohibiting commission of any criminal offense (for which he had already been convicted). Similarly, he concluded that Foster could not be prosecuted on a charge of simple assault, since that crime was a lesser included offense of the assault proscribed by the protective order the court had previously found he violated. However, Scalia also concluded that Foster could be tried on both the charge of assault with intent to kill and the charge of threatening to injure or kidnap, as these crimes contained elements in addition to assault and the "crime" of violating the protective order included the element of intentionally violating the court's order, which the two felonies did not.

Justice Scalia obtained only a bare majority on his resolution of Dixon's case (and three of these justices—White, Stevens and Souter—may have joined because they believed Dixon could not be reprosecuted under *Grady,* which they argued should still be the law). A different group of four justices—Rehnquist, Blackmun, O'Connor, and Thomas—dissented with respect to the disposition of the first charge in Foster's case. Although their primary complaint was that criminal contempt convictions should not be considered in double jeopardy analysis,[115] three of these justices also believed that Foster could be tried on the assault charge under the *Blockburger* test.

Although a majority of the Court now subscribes to the *Blockburger* test, that test is not always easily applied, as *Dixon* demonstrates. Furthermore, the possibility remains that a version of the same conduct test will apply in some cases. In particular, *Harris,* the case that bars prosecution for the felony that formed the predicate for a previous conviction of felony murder, is apparently still good law, despite its conflict with *Blockburger.*

(3) Collateral Estoppel

Closely related to the definition of same offense under the Double Jeopardy Clause is the application of the collateral estoppel principle, which was given constitutional

---

[115] See § 30.02(a)(1).

status by the Supreme Court in *Ashe v. Swenson*.[116] Under limited circumstances, this principle can provide as much protection against reprosecution as the same transaction or same conduct tests.

The resolution of *Ashe* illustrates this point. There the state alleged that the defendant had been one of four gunmen to hold up six other men. However, at his trial for robbery of one of the six victims, the defendant was able to cast serious doubt on the reliability of testimony identifying him as a perpetrator and was acquitted. He was then indicted for the robbery of a second member of the group of six victims, and this time he was convicted, the eyewitnesses now being more certain of his identity. This second prosecution would not have been barred under the *Blockburger* rule. But the Supreme Court found it unconstitutional on collateral estoppel grounds. After examining the trial record, it concluded that the original acquittal must have turned upon a finding that the defendant had not been a participant in the robbery and that, under the collateral estoppel principle, "when an issue of ultimate fact has once been determined by a valid and final judgment, that issue cannot again be litigated between the same parties in any future lawsuit." That this result was required under the Fifth Amendment as well as customary practice was also clear to the Court, "[f]or whatever else that constitutional guarantee may embrace, . . . it surely protects a man who has been acquitted from having to 'run the gauntlet' a second time."

The use of collateral estoppel is quite limited, however.[117] First, there must be, as in *Ashe,* clear evidence that the issue sought to be precluded in the second proceeding was resolved in favor of the defendant in the first proceeding. Because an acquittal can usually rely on a number of different factors, ranging from prosecution failure to prove the various elements of the crime to the defendant's success with one or more defenses, determining whether a particular issue was resolved favorably to the defendant can be very difficult.

Use of special verdicts could assuage this problem, but they may not always be useful to the defendant. For instance, in *Turner v. Arkansas*,[118] the defendant was charged, along with his brother, of robbing and murdering a fellow poker player, on a felony murder theory. After being acquitted at this trial, the state courts allowed a second trial of the defendant on the robbery charge, on the assumption that the first jury may have acquitted him of felony murder not because he was "innocent" but because his brother committed the actual killing. Although this assumption was plausible, the Supreme Court held that the second trial should have been prohibited because the judge at the first trial had instructed the jury to find the defendant guilty of felony murder even if he was only involved in the robbery and not the killing. Had there been a special verdict in this case to determine the rationale for the verdict, it may have revealed that the jury *did* disregard the instruction, and acquitted the defendant despite his participation in the robbery (thus presumably eliminating the verdict's collateral estoppel value). Worse for the defendant, a special verdict procedure may have deterred the first jury from acquitting him in the first place, knowing that a nullification of the instruction would eventually be discovered.

---

[116] 397 U.S. 436, 90 S.Ct. 1189 (1970).

[117] Indeed, four members of the Court have signaled that issue preclusion of the type applicable in civil cases should not be imported to criminal cases through the Double Jeopardy Clause. *Currier v. Virginia*, ___ U.S. ___, 138 S.Ct. 2144 (2018).

[118] 407 U.S. 366, 92 S.Ct. 2096 (1972).

Even if the finding upon which the jury based its verdict can be determined through a special verdict procedure or otherwise, it must be precisely identical to the issue sought to be precluded in order for the collateral estoppel doctrine to apply. For example, in *United States v. Smith*,[119] the defendant was acquitted on one count of uttering a forged check. A subsequent trial charging him with forgery of that check was permitted, since the jury in the first trial could have based its acquittal on the identity of the person who uttered the check rather than on the identity of the person who forged it. Similarly, in *Schiro v. Farley*,[120] the Supreme Court found that a jury choice of felony murder from among ten verdict options, including "knowingly" killing, did not preclude the state from arguing in the subsequent death sentence hearing that the homicide was "intentional" and thus aggravated. The Court noted that the jury was not instructed to return more than one verdict and *was* instructed that each variant of murder, including felony murder, required intent. Thus the defendant had "not met his 'burden . . . to demonstrate that the issue whose relitigation he seeks to foreclose was actually decided' in his favor." In contrast, in *Yeager v. United States*,[121] the Court held that where a jury acquits on a count that requires a certain finding (here that the defendant did not act on insider trading information) a retrial on any hung count that would require a contrary finding to convict is barred, even if the jury's failure to reach a unanimous decision on the hung count is inconsistent with the acquittal. According to the Court, for double jeopardy purposes, "[a] hung count is not a relevant part of the record of the prior proceeding." However, if a conviction that is irreconcilably inconsistent with an acquittal by the same jury is later vacated on appeal on grounds unrelated to the inconsistency, retrial on the reversed conviction is not barred.[122] In such cases, the Court has held in its inconsistent verdict cases,[123] it is "unknowable" which of the verdicts—conviction or acquittal—the jury meant. The one exception to this rule, of course, is when the appellate court reverses the conviction on *Burks* grounds of insufficient evidence.

Third, a finding in a previous proceeding will not be given preclusive effect unless it involved, in *Ashe's* language, an "ultimate" issue. Thus, while a finding that the defendant was not the perpetrator of a multi-victim crime, such as was involved in *Ashe,* will bar subsequent prosecution for the same transaction, a finding by the jury that the prosecution's key witness was not "credible" would probably not be given preclusive effect.[124] Another example of the ultimate fact limitation comes from *Bobby v. Bies*,[125] where the Supreme Court held that a finding that a capital defendant is intellectually disabled for purposes of determining mitigation does not preclude the state from subsequently litigating the defendant's intellectual disability under *Atkins v. Virginia*.[126] The latter case, decided after Bies was sentenced to death, prohibited execution of people with intellectual disability; in support of his claim that *Atkins* now barred his execution, Bies argued that the trial court's finding that intellectual disability was a mitigating factor in his case estopped the state from arguing that he was not intellectually disabled for purposes of *Atkins*. In rejecting that contention, a unanimous

---

[119] 470 F.2d 1299 (5th Cir. 1973).

[120] 510 U.S. 222, 114 S.Ct. 783 (1994).

[121] 557 U.S. 110, 129 S.Ct. 2360 (2009).

[122] *United States v. Powell*, 469 U.S. 57, 105 S.Ct. 471 (1984).

[123] *Bravo-Fernandez v. U.S.*, ___ U.S. ___, 137 S.Ct. 352 (2016).

[124] See *Schleiss v. State,* 71 Wis.2d 733, 239 N.W.2d 68 (1976).

[125] 556 U.S. 825, 129 S.Ct. 2145 (2009).

[126] 536 U.S. 304, 122 S.Ct. 2242 (2002).

Court noted that: (1) the state court's original determination of intellectual disability was not necessary to the ultimate disposition in his case because the disposition was a death sentence, not an "acquittal" and (2) the state's interest in litigating the intellectual disability issue at Bies' trial, pre-*Atkins*, was significantly less than it is post-*Atkins*, given that, prior to *Atkins*, intellectual disability was not a bar to execution and prosecutors knew that capital sentencing juries often treated that condition as an aggravating factor rather than as a mitigator.

Note, however, that if the issue resolved at the first proceeding is "ultimate," it can have an estoppel effect even if the final verdict was not an acquittal. For instance, one court found that a defendant may not be prosecuted for an assault that occurred during a robbery if he has already been convicted of receiving the property stolen during the robbery.[127]

Finally, collateral estoppel may be used only against a party that lost on the issue sought to be estopped, by at least the standard of proof required in the second proceeding. Given the identity of parties requirement, collateral estoppel cannot be used in a proceeding brought by a different sovereign.[128] And given the identity of proof requirement, a finding in a criminal trial that there is a reasonable doubt on a particular issue usually cannot be used to estop a civil proceeding where stronger proof is required. For instance, in *United States v. One Assortment of 89 Firearms*,[129] the Supreme Court held that an acquittal on criminal charges did not bar, in a subsequent forfeiture proceeding, a finding by a preponderance of the evidence that the defendant engaged in the same criminal activity. And in *One Lot Emerald Cut Stones and One Ring v. United States*,[130] the Court disallowed the defendant's use of his acquittal on smuggling charges in a forfeiture proceeding where the government did not have to show criminal intent.[131]

Based on similar reasoning, the Court has held that the collateral estoppel doctrine does not always bar use of conduct for which the defendant was acquitted even in subsequent *criminal* proceedings, so long as the evidence has some credibility and the proceeding is for a different offense (thus avoiding the double jeopardy prohibition). For example, in *Dowling v. United States*,[132] the state used eyewitness testimony at the defendant's robbery trial that linked the defendant to a separate robbery for which he had been acquitted, in an attempt to show, *inter alia,* that the defendant used the same modus operandi in both. The Court pointed out that, according to prior caselaw,[133] such prior act evidence is admissible under Federal Rule of Evidence 404(b) (dealing with prior bad acts) if the jury can reasonably conclude that the act occurred and that the defendant was the actor. Thus, merely because the defendant had managed to raise a reasonable doubt as to whether he was guilty of the first robbery did not bar evidence of that robbery at a trial for another robbery.

---

[127] *Hinton v. State,* 36 Md.App. 52, 373 A.2d 39 (1977).

[128] See § 30.06 for further discussion of the different sovereign doctrine.

[129] 465 U.S. 354, 104 S.Ct. 1099 (1984).

[130] 409 U.S. 232, 93 S.Ct. 489 (1972).

[131] Note that if the proceedings are reversed—that is, the civil proceeding precedes the criminal action—collateral estoppel could apply (because a finding by a preponderance of the evidence would certainly suggest a reasonable doubt). However, application of the estoppel doctrine is not *constitutionally* required in this situation, since jeopardy has not attached at the civil proceeding. See § 30.02(a).

[132] 493 U.S. 342, 110 S.Ct. 668 (1990).

[133] *Huddleston v. United States,* 485 U.S. 681, 108 S.Ct. 1496 (1988).

The question might arise whether the *state* can estop the defendant from asserting a defense, proven unsuccessful in a previous trial. For instance, if the prosecution in *Ashe* had convicted the defendant in the first trial, could it claim that this verdict showed beyond a reasonable doubt that the defendant was also involved in the robbery of the other five victims? Although the technical requirements of collateral estoppel might be met in this situation, it probably runs afoul of the right to jury trial for each offense.[134]

(b) Exceptions to the Same Offense Prohibition

There are at least four exceptions to the general rule that a prosecution will be barred if the defendant can show that he has already been "acquitted" of or convicted for the "same offense." They occur when the second prosecution: (1) is based on conduct or events that have occurred after the first prosecution; (2) results from the defendant's own motion; (3) is based on a charge over which the court for the original prosecution did not have jurisdiction; or (4) is based on a charge which was originally filed by the prosecution, but which was dismissed by the arraignment judge over the prosecution's objection in the course of taking a guilty plea.

(1) New Conduct or Event

The first exception to the same offense prohibition occurs when an essential element of an offense does not develop until after prosecution of a lesser offense. In *Diaz v. United States*,[135] the defendant was convicted of assault and battery, but the victim later died. In rejecting the defendant's attempt to interpose a double jeopardy bar on the subsequent homicide prosecution, the Court stated:

> The death of the injured person was the principal element of the homicide, but was no part of the assault and battery. At the time of the trial for the latter the death had not ensued, and not until it did ensue was the homicide committed. Then, and not before, was it possible to put the accused in jeopardy for the offense.

In *Garrett v. United States*,[136] the Court reaffirmed the *Diaz* rule, at the same time expanding its scope. There, the defendant pleaded guilty to one count of importing marijuana. Two months later, the government indicted the defendant under the "continuing criminal enterprise" (CCE) provision of the Comprehensive Drug Abuse Prevention and Control Act of 1970. The defendant's prior importation conviction was introduced at his trial on the CCE charge as proof of one of the three predicate offenses that must be proven to authorize the enhanced penalties of the Act. Five members of the Court concluded that the prosecution on the CCE charge was not barred because that charge was based on new conduct after the first prosecution. To the dissent's argument that the government had enough evidence at the time of the first prosecution to bring a CCE charge (albeit one of shorter duration), a plurality of four justices responded that "one who at the time the first indictment is returned is continuing to engage in other conduct found criminal" cannot object to multiple prosecutions; the fact that a CCE charge could have been brought at the time of the first prosecution was irrelevant to double jeopardy analysis. Justice O'Connor saw "merit" to the dissent's position, but joined the plurality given her belief that the government should be allowed to decide

---

[134] See *Simpson v. Florida*, 403 U.S. 384, 91 S.Ct. 1801 (1971).

[135] 223 U.S. 442, 32 S.Ct. 250 (1912).

[136] 471 U.S. 773, 105 S.Ct. 2407 (1985).

when to prosecute criminal activity that continues after prosecution for a predicate offense, so long as there is no evidence of "governmental oppression of the sort against which the Double Jeopardy Clause was intended to protect."

Diaz permitted a second prosecution for the "same offense" when the offense involved was impossible to charge at the time of the first prosecution. *Garrett* obviously extends the *Diaz* rationale to permit such prosecutions even when the second charge could have been joined at the first trial, so long as the relevant conduct continues after the first indictment. This ruling might have particularly significant consequences in cases involving crimes defined as a continuing course of conduct (such as CCE charges, "racketeering" or "RICO" charges, and conspiracies).[137] But now that *United States v. Felix*[138] has decided that a conspiracy and the associated substantive offense are not the "same" for double jeopardy purposes (and thus may be tried in separate trials in any event), *Garrett*'s broadening of the *Diaz* exception is likely to add little to the prosecution's arsenal.

(2) Severance by the Defendant

In *Jeffers v. United States*,[139] a plurality of the Court announced another exception to the same offense prohibition. In *Jeffers*, a grand jury returned two separate indictments against the defendant, one charging him, along with nine others, of conspiring to distribute narcotics, and the other charging him individually with a CCE violation. Prior to the trial on the conspiracy charge, the government made a motion to join the CCE charge, to which the defendant and his co-conspirators successfully objected. He and six of the co-conspirators were found guilty of the conspiracy offense, and the defendant alone was then tried and convicted on the severed CCE charge.

The Court assumed that the conspiracy and the CCE charge were the same offense for double jeopardy purposes (an assumption that may be inaccurate after *Felix*[140]). But it went on to uphold the second conviction on grounds analogous to its mistrial jurisprudence.[141] According to the plurality opinion, because the defendant "was solely responsible for the successive prosecutions," he could not prevent the second one.

While plausible on its face, this reasoning can be questioned, at least on the facts of *Jeffers*. As the dissent pointed out, the defendant could not "be held responsible for the fact that two separate indictments were returned, or for the fact that other defendants were named in the earlier indictment, or for the fact that the Government elected to proceed to trial first on the lesser charge." The plurality's only response to this argument was to suggest that had there been "proof" that joinder would have so severely prejudiced the defendant that his "Sixth Amendment right to a fair trial" would be abridged, a different result might have been necessary. Assuming this degree of prejudice is not shown, when joinder and double jeopardy principles clash, *Jeffers* requires the defendant, not the government, to make the hard choice.

---

[137] George Thomas III, *An Elegant Theory of Double Jeopardy*, 1988 U.Ill.L.Rev. 827, 878.

[138] 503 U.S. 378, 112 S.Ct. 1377 (1992), discussed in § 30.04(a)(2).

[139] 432 U.S. 137, 97 S.Ct. 2207 (1977).

[140] But see *Rutledge v. United States*, 517 U.S. 292, 116 S.Ct. 1241 (1996), discussed in § 30.04(c).

[141] See *United States v. Dinitz*, 424 U.S. 600, 96 S.Ct. 1075 (1976), discussed in § 30.03(c)(2).

(3) Jurisdictional Bar

The third exception to the same offense prohibition occurs when the lesser charge is tried to an inferior court with no jurisdiction over the greater charge. In such a case, jeopardy does not attach for the greater offense. In *Waller v. Florida*,[142] the Supreme Court intimated otherwise when it held that a municipal proceeding upon the lesser offense would bar a state action on the greater. But that decision was premised on a finding that municipalities and the state in which they are located are not separate sovereigns for purposes of the Double Jeopardy Clause.[143] The jurisdictional issue was not explicitly addressed. In *Fugate v. New Mexico*,[144] on the other hand, an evenly divided Court (Justice Powell not participating) let stand a New Mexico Supreme Court decision holding that a defendant's conviction in municipal court on charges of driving while intoxicated and careless driving did not bar his subsequent prosecution, in higher court, for vehicular homicide based on the same incident, because the lower court had no jurisdiction to hear the greater charge.[145]

Assuming the prosecution has, or should have had, possession of all the relevant evidence at the time of the first prosecution (in other words, assuming the *Diaz* exception does not apply), it is not clear why multiple prosecutions should be allowed merely because the prosecution made the mistake of trying the less serious crime first, in a court of limited jurisdiction. Apparently *Fugate* is based on the idea, similar to that voiced in *Garrett, Jeffers* and the Court's mistrial cases, that the prosecution should not be penalized by the same offense prohibition when it has not *intentionally* sought to subject the defendant to multiple trials. Again, the defendant is made to suffer multiple prosecutions due to the prosecution's oversight or inefficiency. If a jurisdictional bar exception is necessary, a more sensible version, suggested by Justice Brennan, would permit multiple prosecutions only if no single court had jurisdiction over both offenses.[146]

(4) Guilty Pleas over Prosecution Objection

A final exception to the same offense prohibition occurs in the relatively rare situation represented in *Ohio v. Johnson*.[147] There the defendant, over the prosecution's objection, convinced the trial judge to dismiss murder and aggravated robbery charges after pleading guilty to the lesser included offenses, respectively, of manslaughter and grand theft. The Supreme Court reversed the Ohio Supreme Court's ruling that the Double Jeopardy Clause barred trial on the murder and aggravated robbery charges, pointing out that the defendant "had not been exposed to conviction on the charges to which he pleaded not guilty, nor has the state had the opportunity to marshal its evidence and resources more than once or to hone its presentation of its case through a trial." The situation in *Johnson* "has none of the implications of an 'implied acquittal' which results from a verdict convicting a defendant on lesser included offenses rendered by a jury charged to consider both greater and lesser included offenses." Further, the Court stressed that the defendant "should not be entitled to use the Double Jeopardy

---

[142] 397 U.S. 387, 90 S.Ct. 1184 (1970).

[143] See § 30.06(c).

[144] 471 U.S. 1112, 105 S.Ct. 2349 (1985).

[145] Note that in *Grady*, involving similar facts, the court in which the first prosecution took place had jurisdiction over both charges.

[146] See *Ashe v. Swenson,* 397 U.S. 436, 90 S.Ct. 1189 (1970) (Brennan, J., concurring).

[147] 467 U.S. 493, 104 S.Ct. 2536 (1984).

Clause as a sword to prevent the State from completing its prosecution on the remaining charges."

This exception too is questionable. It is true, as noted earlier,[148] that when a judge accepts a plea to which the prosecution agrees, the resulting conviction cannot be seen as an "implied acquittal" of any greater charge, because the judge never considered the greater charge. But the judge in *Johnson* clearly did consider, and decided to dismiss, the greater charges. Arguably, the fact that the prosecution disagreed with this dismissal has no more relevance for double jeopardy purposes than its disagreement with a jury verdict or a midtrial dismissal on the merits; in all of these cases jeopardy has attached and a final disposition of the "same offense" reached. Perhaps the distinction is that the prosecution in *Johnson* was never given the chance to marshal its evidence on the greater charges. It might also be said that judges do not have "jurisdiction" to dismiss charges over prosecutorial objection, in which case it could be claimed that jeopardy never attached.[149]

(c) Cumulative Punishments

Whether two offenses constituting the "same offense" are tried successively, as permitted by the above exceptions to the same offense prohibition, or together, as is more normally the case, a central question is whether the punishment for each may be imposed cumulatively or whether the government is limited to seeking the stiffest penalty from among those available. If the definition of same offense used to determine the validity of multiple prosecutions were also used to determine the validity of multiple punishments, the latter approach would be constitutionally required in at least some types of cases (for instance, where the defendant is convicted of felony murder and the underlying felony). But the Supreme Court has held that whether cumulative punishment for two offenses is barred by the Double Jeopardy Clause depends in the first instance on what the legislature intended when it enacted the two offenses, not on whether the offenses are the "same offense" as that term is used in determining whether multiple prosecutions are permissible.

While alluding to this position in *Albernaz v. United States,*[150] the Court's first explicit statement to this effect came in *Missouri v. Hunter.*[151] In *Hunter,* the defendant was convicted at one trial under two separate Missouri statutes, one proscribing robbery in the first degree, the second prohibiting "armed criminal action" (i.e., "use a gun, go to jail"). He received consecutive terms of ten years for the robbery and fifteen years for the armed criminal action even though the former offense is a lesser included offense of the latter. The Court's majority opinion, written by Chief Justice Burger, conceded that the Court was bound by the Missouri Supreme Court's ruling that the two statutes at issue defined the same crime under *Blockburger.* But the Chief Justice went on to conclude that *Blockburger* was irrelevant in this case because the Missouri legislature had made "crystal clear" that it intended the penalty imposed for violation of the armed criminal action statute to be in addition to any other penalty imposed for crimes committed simultaneously with it. In such a situation, "a court's task of statutory construction is at an end and the prosecutor may seek and the trial court or jury may impose cumulative

---

[148] See § 30.03(a)(1).

[149] Cf. *Kepner v. United States,* 195 U.S. 100, 24 S.Ct. 797 (1904), noted in § 30.02(b).

[150] 450 U.S. 333, 101 S.Ct. 1137 (1981).

[151] 459 U.S. 359, 103 S.Ct. 673 (1983).

punishment under such statutes in a single trial." As it had suggested in *Albernaz,* the Court held that *Blockburger* merely provided a rule of statutory construction which becomes unnecessary when the legislature's actions are unambiguous.

On the other hand, when the there is no legislative history, *Blockburger's* rule becomes important. That was the situation in *Rutledge v. United States*,[152] where the Court held that an offender may not be punished for both conspiracy to distribute cocaine and engaging in a continuing criminal enterprise (CCE) involving distribution of that cocaine. The government had argued that conviction on the CCE charge did not require an "agreement," as does conspiracy, but rather only that the parties were acting "in concert." Applying *Blockburger*, a unanimous Court found no difference between the two concepts and thus ordered that one of the offender's two sentences be vacated.

Hunter's holding was limited to multiple punishments imposed at a single trial. It is not implausible to suggest that, on those occasions when two different crimes constituting the same offense are tried separately (as in the four situations discussed above), punishment should have to be imposed concurrently. As the Court has recognized in a different double jeopardy context, "it might be argued that the defendant perceives the length of his sentence as finally determined when he begins to serve it, and that the trial judge should be prohibited from thereafter increasing the sentence."[153] But in *Garrett,* where the defendant received five years and a $15,000 fine after his first trial on the marijuana importation charge, the Court cited *Hunter* in upholding an additional 40 years imprisonment and $100,000 in fines on the CCE charge, based on its assessment of the CCE statute's legislative history.[154] Thus, it appears that the cumulative punishment rule announced in *Hunter* is the same whether charges are tried together or separately. The sole limitation on legislative discretion with respect to cumulation of sentences is the Eighth Amendment's ban on disproportionate, cruel and unusual punishment.[155]

30.05　Resentencing

To be distinguished from cumulation of separate sentences for more than one statutory offense (which triggers an inquiry into whether the punishments are for the "same offense" for double jeopardy purposes) is the practice of increasing a single sentence imposed after an appeal or discovery of a defect in the sentencing procedure. One could argue that the Double Jeopardy Clause prohibits this practice, by analogy to the implied acquittal doctrine, which provides that a conviction on one charge bars subsequent prosecution on a greater charge when the factfinder had the opportunity to consider evidence on the latter charge.[156] But the Supreme Court has indicated that there are a number of situations where a sentence for a particular charge may be increased after it has been imposed. The law of resentencing is best considered by dividing it into the three contexts in which it can occur.

---

[152]　517 U.S. 292, 116 S.Ct. 1241 (1996).

[153]　*United States v. DiFrancesco,* 449 U.S. 117, 101 S.Ct. 426 (1980) (rejecting this argument, however, when the defendant is on notice that his sentence can be appealed by the prosecution).

[154]　The *Garrett* Court also characterized as "reasonabl[e]" the conclusion in *Jeffers* that Congress had *not* meant to cumulate the *conspiracy* and CCE penalties involved there, since in contrast to the offenses involved in *Garrett,* "the dangers posed by a conspiracy and a CCE were similar and thus there would be little purpose in cumulating the penalties."

[155]　And this limitation is virtually non-existent. See *Solem v. Helm,* 463 U.S. 277, 103 S.Ct. 3001 (1983).

[156]　See § 30.03(a)(1).

(a) After Reversal of Conviction

In *North Carolina v. Pearce,*[157] the defendant successfully appealed his conviction, was retried on the same charge, and received a harsher sentence than the one he received after his first conviction. While the Court held that due process might be implicated if the harsher sentence were vindictively imposed as a penalty for appealing the conviction,[158] it concluded that the *Double Jeopardy Clause* does not bar the stiffer penalty, so long as it is legally authorized, and so long as the defendant is given credit for time served. The Court reasoned that the original conviction had, "at the defendant's behest, been wholly nullified and the slate wiped clean."

This latter statement contradicts the sense of the Court's earlier holding in *Green v. United States,*[159] to the effect that a defendant who has successfully appealed cannot be reprosecuted on the original charge if the jury rejected it at the first trial. In a later decision affirming *Pearce,* the Court provided a better (although not necessarily persuasive) reason for rejecting the idea that "the imposition of a particular sentence is an 'implied acquittal' of any greater sentence." In *United States v. DiFrancesco,*[160] discussed further below in connection with prosecution appeals of sentences, the Court pointed out that many of the traditional reasons for barring reprosecution—i.e., saving the defendant the expense and anxiety of another trial, and preventing the prosecution from securing an unwarranted conviction by wearing the defendant down with a well-practiced case—are not implicated by normal resentencing, because no formal proceeding is involved.

However, in *Bullington v. Missouri,*[161] the Court held that when the sentencing process *is* more formalized, the *Pearce-DiFrancesco* reasoning does not apply. In *Bullington,* the defendant, after being convicted of capital murder and sentenced in a separate sentencing proceeding to life imprisonment, moved for a judgment of acquittal or, in the alternative, a new trial. The latter motion was granted because his trial and sentencing jury had been unconstitutionally selected. The prosecution then informed the defendant that, at the second trial, it planned to once again seek the death penalty.

In holding that the prosecution was limited to obtaining life imprisonment, the Court emphasized the similarity between the capital sentencing procedures under Missouri law and a trial on the issue of the defendant's guilt or innocence. Justice Blackmun, writing for a majority of five justices, pointed out that, after *Burks v. United States,*[162] a defendant may not be retried if he obtains a reversal of his conviction on the ground that the prosecution lacked sufficient evidence to prove its case. He then noted that, while, in "the usual sentencing proceeding . . . it is impossible to conclude that a sentence less than the statutory maximum 'constitute[s] a decision to the effect that the government has failed to prove its case,'" the procedure established by Missouri's capital sentencing statute *"explicitly requires* the jury to determine whether the prosecution has 'proved its case.'" In particular, Blackmun pointed to the fact that, under Missouri law, the capital "presentence hearing resembled and, indeed, in all relevant respects was like

[157] 395 U.S. 711, 89 S.Ct. 2072 (1969).
[158] See § 29.02(d).
[159] 355 U.S. 184, 78 S.Ct. 221 (1957), discussed in § 30.03(a).
[160] 449 U.S. 117, 101 S.Ct. 426 (1980).
[161] 451 U.S. 430, 101 S.Ct. 1852 (1981).
[162] 437 U.S. 1, 98 S.Ct. 2141 (1978), discussed in § 30.03(a)(2).

the immediately preceding trial on the issue of guilt or innocence," including the requirement that the prosecution prove its case in support of the death penalty beyond a reasonable doubt. Since Bullington had received a life sentence rather than the death penalty during the first trial, the latter penalty was off the table during the second trial.

Bullington was applied in *Arizona v. Rumsey*,[163] which involved a capital sentencing proceeding similar to the Missouri procedure at issue in *Bullington* except that the judge, rather than the jury, had sentencing authority. In *Rumsey,* the judge sentenced the defendant to life imprisonment. The defendant appealed to the Arizona Supreme Court and the prosecution cross-appealed. While it rejected the defendant's claim, the Arizona court agreed with the state that the judge had misconstrued an aggravating circumstance permitting imposition of the death penalty and remanded the case for a new penalty hearing. Upon receiving a death sentence at the new hearing, the defendant again appealed, this time on double jeopardy grounds. The Supreme Court found that the trial judge's first ruling was an implied acquittal of the death penalty even though erroneous. "Reliance on an error of law . . . does not change the double jeopardy effects of a judgment that amounts to an acquittal on the merits."

On the other hand, where the sentencing judge *imposes* the death penalty and a reviewing court finds the sentence erroneous because an aggravating circumstance identified by the judge does not exist, the sentencing court may reimpose capital punishment even if it has previously rejected the remaining aggravating circumstances. In *Poland v. Arizona*,[164] the sentencing judge imposed the death penalty on the ground the defendant's crime had been particularly "heinous" but specifically held that it had not been committed for pecuniary gain, another aggravating circumstance. The Arizona Supreme Court held that the crime had not been heinous but that the sentencing judge had misinterpreted the pecuniary gain provision, and remanded for resentencing. Despite *Poland's* similarity to *Rumsey*, the U.S. Supreme Court refused to find that the defendant had been "acquitted" by the sentencing judge of the pecuniary gain circumstance, on the ground that *Bullington* prohibits resentencing only when a court has found the death penalty "inappropriate" and that here no court had done so; since the sentencing court had imposed the death penalty and the reviewing court had indicated it did not consider the matter closed, the state was allowed a "clean slate" hearing on the pecuniary gain circumstance.

Similarly, analogous to the trial context, a capital sentencing proceeding that ends because of a deadlocked jury does not bar resentencing. Pennsylvania capital sentencing law requires the judge to impose a life sentence when the jury fails to reach a unanimous verdict on sentence. In *Sattazahn v. Pennsylvania*,[165] Sattazahn received a life sentence under this provision when his jury deadlocked 9 to 3 (in favor of life). He then successfully appealed his conviction, and was reconvicted and resentenced, this time to death. His claim that this second sentence violated the Double Jeopardy Clause was rejected by five members of the Court. Justice Scalia, writing for the majority, concluded that because the initial jury had never unanimously found an absence of aggravating circumstances, Sattazhan was never "acquitted" with respect to capital punishment and thus could be subject to resentencing and the death penalty without violating the Double Jeopardy Clause. The dissent, by Justice Ginsburg, expressed concern about the

---

[163]   467 U.S. 203, 104 S.Ct. 2305 (1984).

[164]   476 U.S. 147, 106 S.Ct. 1749 (1986).

[165]   537 U.S. 101, 123 S.Ct. 732 (2003).

holding's chilling effect on defendants' decision to appeal convictions in capital cases and its approval of a process that subjects successful appellants to two capital sentencing proceedings. But Scalia correctly pointed out that the Court's current double jeopardy jurisprudence does not bar a second proceeding unless the initial proceeding results in an acquittal or an uncontested conviction and sentence.[166]

Bullington left unclear whether its exception to *Pearce* and *DiFrancesco* is applicable to non-capital sentencing proceedings that resemble a trial. In *Monge v. California*,[167] the Court held that it is not. Justice O'Connor's opinion for five members of the Court stated that *Bullington* should be limited to capital cases because the death penalty process is uniquely concerned with assuring reliability; the heightened procedures in place there are constitutionally required rather than a "matter of legislative grace" as is the case with noncapital sentencing. Thus, the state may reinstitute or enhance a noncapital crime after it is overturned on grounds of evidentiary insufficiency, even when the first proceeding is trial-like. In *Monge* itself, that meant that the fact that an appeals court had reversed Monge's sentence on the ground that the prior conviction used to enhance it had not been proven beyond a reasonable doubt would not prevent the same penalty from being imposed at a new sentencing hearing.

(b) After Prosecution Appeal of Sentence

As discussed earlier in this chapter,[168] the prosecution usually may not appeal an acquittal, or appeal a dismissal that is the equivalent of an acquittal. But in those situations just discussed where a particular sentence does not represent an "acquittal" on any greater sentence, the prosecution may appeal a sentence, so long as there is statutory authorization to do so. This was the holding in *United States v. DiFrancesco*,[169] where the Court upheld a federal provision authorizing prosecution appeal of sentences imposed under a "dangerous special offender" statute. In addition to noting that a successful prosecutorial appeal under this provision did not subject the defendant to the ordeal of a new trial-like proceeding, the Court emphasized that because the defendant was aware that his special offender sentence was subject to appellate review, his legitimate expectations would not be defeated should his sentence be increased. Adhering to the rationale of *Missouri v. Hunter*,[170] the Court also held that an increased sentence as a result of the appeal would not violate the ban on cumulative punishments, because the new sentence would still be within specified legislative limits, of which the defendant was, or should have been, aware.

DiFrancesco's emphasis on the fact that the defendant was on notice that his sentence could be changed suggests that a defendant's expectations with respect to his sentence may be important for double jeopardy purposes. The same theme was sounded in *Pennsylvania v. Goldhammer*,[171] where the defendant appealed a multicount conviction. The state appellate court, after reversing the one count against the defendant which carried a term of imprisonment and affirming the other counts (which carried a suspended sentence), refused on double jeopardy grounds the state's request to remand

---

[166]   See § 30.03(a).

[167]   524 U.S. 721, 118 S.Ct. 2246 (1998).

[168]   See § 30.03(a) & (b).

[169]   449 U.S. 117, 101 S.Ct. 426 (1980).

[170]   459 U.S. 359, 103 S.Ct. 673 (1983), discussed in § 30.04(c).

[171]   474 U.S. 28, 106 S.Ct. 353 (1985).

for (enhanced) resentencing on the affirmed counts. Disagreeing with the state court's reasoning, the Supreme Court remanded the case for reconsideration in light of *DiFrancesco,* and directed the state court to consider "whether the Pennsylvania laws in effect at the time allowed the State to obtain review of the sentences on the counts for which the sentence had been suspended." If there were such a procedure, resentencing would be permitted. But if, to the contrary, there were no review procedure, *Goldhammer* implies that the defendant's expectation of finality in his sentence could not be upset by reimposing part or all of the suspended sentence.

(c) After Discovery of a Defect in the Sentence

A final resentencing situation involves neither resentencing after a reversal of a conviction or a prosecutorial attempt to appeal the sentence. Rather, it occurs when the sentencing judge seeks to redress a legal error in the original sentence. For instance, in *Ex parte Lange,*[172] the trial court imposed the maximum one-year term of imprisonment and the maximum $200 fine, under a statute that authorized only imprisonment *or* a fine. After paying the fine, the defendant petitioned for release, but the trial court instead ordered the refund of the defendant's money and reimposed the imprisonment term of one year. The Supreme Court held that this solution violated the Double Jeopardy Clause's ban on multiple punishments, because the $200 was now beyond the reach of the judiciary (since it was in the state treasury), and the new one-year term was added to the five days the defendant had already served. *In re Bradley*[173] involved a very similar fact pattern, except the judge, after returning the fine, was careful to avoid imposing more than the maximum prison term. Nonetheless, the Court once again found that the new sentence was barred, because the defendant had fully satisfied one of the two sentencing alternatives.

The Court has not considered the Double Jeopardy Clause a shield against correction of all judicial errors, however. For instance, in *Bozza v. United States,*[174] the Court upheld an increase in sentence designed to meet the mandatory minimum required by statute. The Court noted that the correction was made within hours of announcing the original sentence, and that it merely provided what was required by law, before the defendant had satisfied the sentence. This holding conforms to the usual mandate that the trial judge may correct an illegal sentence at any time before it is satisfied (in contrast to *Lange* and *Bradley*, where the illegal sentence has already occurred).[175]

A different scenario confronted the Court in *Jones v. Thomas.*[176] There, the defendant was convicted of felony murder and the underlying felony of attempted robbery and sentenced to consecutive terms of life imprisonment and 15 years respectively. Some years later, after the defendant had already served sufficient time to satisfy the latter sentence, a state appellate court held, consistent with *Harris v. Oklahoma,*[177] that the felony murder statute did not authorize separate punishments for the murder and the underlying felony. While the defendant argued that, under *Bradley,*

---

[172] 85 U.S. (18 Wall.) 163 (1873).

[173] 318 U.S. 50, 63 S.Ct. 470 (1943).

[174] 330 U.S. 160, 67 S.Ct. 645 (1947).

[175] See, e.g., Fed.R.Crim.P. 35(a).

[176] 491 U.S. 376, 109 S.Ct. 2522 (1989).

[177] 433 U.S. 682, 97 S.Ct. 2912 (1977), discussed in § 30.04(a)(2).

he should thus be freed, the Supreme Court upheld the trial court's conclusion that it only needed to credit the time served against his life sentence for felony murder. The Court distinguished *Bradley* on two grounds. First, in *Bradley* the legislature had obviously conceived of the penalties involved as alternative punishments for the crime, whereas the penalty for robbery could not be seen as an alternative for the felony murder sentence, and thus was not a legitimate substitute. Second, while crediting was possible in *Jones,* because both penalties involved imprisonment, it had not been possible to credit the fine against the imprisonment penalty in *Bradley.*

Echoing the expectation theme from *DiFrancesco* and *Goldhammer,* the Court also noted that Jones could not have expected to serve only an attempted robbery sentence, given his original sentence. At the same time, it implied that, under normal circumstances, a defendant has a "legitimate expectation of finality" in the sentence he receives, at least once he has served it, and perhaps even once he has started serving it. Consistent with this observation is the federal practice that, except in those situations described in this section, a sentence cannot be enhanced once imposed. *Goldhammer,* while noting this fact, ventured "no comment on this limitation."

30.06   The Dual Sovereignty Doctrine

Even when the defendant is acquitted at trial, or is convicted and does not appeal, there is one situation in which he can be reprosecuted for the identical offense. That is when the entity that brings the second prosecution is a separate sovereign from the first prosecuting entity. The basis for this rule is that separate sovereigns have the right to enforce their own laws, irrespective of the impact that prerogative may have on the individual defendant. While this reasoning has some appeal when dealing with international crime, it makes less sense within the United States, even acknowledging the federal nature of our system. Nonetheless, in 2019 the Supreme Court affirmed the dual sovereignty doctrine by a vote of 7–2,[178] relying on its reading of eighteenth century history, its precedent, and the conclusion that "offense" is a term "defined by law, and each law is defined by a sovereign." In dissent, Justice Gorsuch reasoned that "if double jeopardy prevents *one* government from prosecuting a defendant multiple times for the same offense under the banner of separate statutory labels [as it does under *Blockburger v. United States*[179]], on what account can it make a difference when *many* governments collectively seek to do the same thing?"

(a)   Federal-State/Tribe Prosecutions

The first exposition of the dual sovereignty doctrine arose in the context of federal and state prosecutions for the same crime.[180] As articulated in *United States v. Lanza,*[181] the doctrine states that "an act denounced as a crime by both national and state sovereignties is an offense against the peace and dignity of both and may be punished by each." This rule was reaffirmed in two 1959 decisions, *Bartkus v. Illinois*[182] and *Abbate v. United States.*[183] In *Bartkus,* the defendant was tried first in federal court for robbery of a federally insured savings and loan bank. After a federal acquittal, he was

---

[178]   *Gamble v. United States,* ___ U.S. ___, 139 S.Ct. 1960 (2019).

[179]   284 U.S. 299, 52 S.Ct. 180 (1932), discussed in § 30.04(a)(2).

[180]   See *Moore v. Illinois,* 55 U.S. (14 How.) 13 (1852).

[181]   260 U.S. 377, 43 S.Ct. 141 (1922).

[182]   359 U.S. 121, 79 S.Ct. 676 (1959).

[183]   359 U.S. 187, 79 S.Ct. 666 (1959).

tried and convicted in state court for the same act. The reverse situation occurred in *Abbate* (i.e., a state trial was followed by federal trial for the same act) but both prosecutions ended in conviction. Both instances of multiple trials were upheld, given the possibility that the defendant's acts "may impinge more seriously on a federal [state] interest than a state [federal] interest." Illustrating this point in *Bartkus*, the Court noted that a contrary ruling could allow a defendant who has been convicted of a federal civil rights offense, carrying no more than a few years sentence, to prevent state prosecution on homicide charges (although this holding assumes, in possible conflict with the Court's current jurisprudence,[184] that these crimes are the "same offense" for double jeopardy purposes). Similarly, in *Abbate*, the Court pointed out that the defendants were arguing that their state convictions, "resulting in three months' prison sentences[,] should bar this federal prosecution which could result in a sentence of up to five years."

Two decades later, the Court affirmed the reasoning of these cases in *United States v. Wheeler*.[185] There, the defendant asserted that Navaho Tribal court proceedings that resulted in his conviction for contributing to the delinquency of a minor were a bar to federal prosecution for the same offense. The Court rejected his claim, holding that the Tribe, like a state, constitutes a sovereign independent of the United States because "the ultimate source of the power under which the respective prosecutions were undertaken" is different. The Tribe's authority to prosecute, the Court found, stemmed from its " 'primeval sovereignty' rather than a delegation of federal authority."[186]

As several commentators have pointed out, the dual sovereignty notion established in these cases is contrary to the historical development of the Double Jeopardy Clause, the apparent intent of the framers of the Constitution, and the policy, endorsed in virtually all of the Court's other double jeopardy decisions, against subjecting defendants to multiple prosecutions for the same offense.[187] At the least, these factors should not be outweighed by any "interest" a separate sovereign may have in reprosecuting for the same offense unless the interest is extremely significant.[188] The federal government has, in effect, recognized this "independent interest" limitation by barring federal trial "when there has already been a state prosecution for substantially the same act or acts" unless an Assistant Attorney General directs otherwise. The Supreme Court noted this policy in *Petite v. United States,*[189] (with the consequence that it has since come to be called the "*Petite* policy"), and went so far as to hold, in *Rinaldi v. United States,*[190] that a federal district court abused its discretion by refusing to vacate a conviction upon a motion made by the government pursuant to this policy.

---

[184] See § 30.04(b).

[185] 435 U.S. 313, 98 S.Ct. 1079 (1978).

[186] See also *United States v. Lara*, 541 U.S. 193, 124 S.Ct. 1628 (2004) (tribal trial of non-tribal member did not bar federal prosecution for same offense because tribal power to try members of a different tribe stems from "inherent *tribal* sovereignty" not "delegated *federal* authority"). However, because of its historical dependence upon the federal government, Puerto Rico is not considered a separate sovereign double jeopardy purposes. *Puerto Rico v. Sanchez Valle*, ___ U.S. ___, 136 S.Ct. 1863 (2016).

[187] See Ronald Allen, Bard Ferrall & John Ratnaswamy, *The Double Jeopardy Clause, Constitutional Interpretation and the Limits of Formal Logic*, 26 Valparaiso U.L.Rev. 281, 300–306 (1991).

[188] See, e.g., Walker T. Fisher, *Double Jeopardy, Two Sovereignties, and the Intruding Constitution*, 28 U.Chi.L.Rev. 591 (1961).

[189] 361 U.S. 529, 80 S.Ct. 450 (1960).

[190] 434 U.S. 22, 98 S.Ct. 81 (1977).

(b) State-State Prosecutions

Despite the Court's apparent willingness to contemplate adding some form of a "separate interests" requirement to the dual sovereignty doctrine (at least when one of the sovereigns is willing to endorse it), it has flatly refused to adopt the requirement as a matter of constitutional law. In *Heath v. Alabama*[191] the Court upheld the Alabama conviction of the defendant for the hired murder of his wife after he had pleaded guilty to the same crime in Georgia. The Court, in an opinion by Justice O'Connor, first found that:

> The States are no less sovereign with respect to each other than they are with respect to the Federal Government. Their powers to undertake criminal prosecutions derive from separate and independent sources of power and authority originally belonging to them before admission to the Union and preserved by the Tenth Amendment.

The Court then explicitly rejected the contention that a defendant subject to dual prosecutions should be able to avoid the second unless doing so would frustrate the interests of the second sovereign. Ignoring the rationale underlying *Bartkus* and *Abbate*, it found the states' interest in prosecuting "irrelevant" in assessing whether two states may prosecute the same crime.

In dissent, Justice Marshall, joined by Justice Brennan, argued that allowing two states to prosecute for the same offense differed from federal-state dual prosecution. "[I]n contrast to the federal-state context, barring the second prosecution [in the two state context] would still permit one government to act upon the broad range of sovereign concerns that have been reserved to the States by the Constitution." He also pointed out that in this case Georgia officials, after obtaining a guilty plea from the defendant, had not only cooperated with Alabama officials in securing the defendant's second conviction but played "leading roles as prosecution witnesses in the Alabama trial." He argued that either double jeopardy or due process was violated by this "relentless prosecution."

(c) State-Municipal Prosecutions

In *Waller v. Florida,*[192] the Supreme Court held that contrary to federal, state and tribal governments, municipalities are not sovereign entities, but rather "subordinate governmental instrumentalities created by the State to assist in the carrying out of state governmental functions." Thus, multiple prosecutions for the "same offense" by a city and the state are barred by the Double Jeopardy Clause. However, if the municipal prosecution was not for the same offense,[193] or, as discussed earlier in this chapter,[194] the municipal court lacked jurisdiction over a more serious version of the same offense, then reprosecution in state court is permitted.

30.07   Conclusion

The Double Jeopardy Clause in the Fifth Amendment has spawned a very complex set of rules governing when the government may subject a defendant to separate

---

[191]   474 U.S. 82, 106 S.Ct. 433 (1985).

[192]   397 U.S. 387, 90 S.Ct. 1184 (1970).

[193]   As the lower court in *Waller* found on remand.

[194]   See § 30.04(b)(3).

prosecutions, separate punishments, and increased punishment for the same offense. These rules are summarized below:

(1) Fifth Amendment protection against reprosecution is not triggered unless jeopardy attaches. Jeopardy attaches only in those proceedings the legislature intends to be criminal or that result in clearly punitive sanctions (because, inter alia, scienter is required, a deprivation of liberty is involved, and the sanctions are aimed at retribution and deterrence), and only after the jury is impaneled (in jury trials), the first witness is sworn (in bench trials), or a guilty plea is accepted (when conviction is by plea).

(2) Once jeopardy on a particular charge has attached, reprosecution for the same charge is prohibited unless: (a) the defendant is convicted and obtains a reversal on grounds other than evidentiary insufficiency; (b) the charge is dismissed by the judge on grounds not amounting to a factual determination that the defendant is innocent; or (c) a mistrial is declared for reasons of manifest necessity (when declared over the defendant's objection) or on grounds not involving prosecutorial error designed to provoke a mistrial motion from the defendant (when declared on the defendant's motion).

(3) Also barred is prosecution for any other offense, not joined in the first prosecution, that is the "same offense" under the *Blockburger* test (which looks at whether each crime requires proof of an element the other does not), except when: (a) the second prosecution is based in part on new conduct committed or events occurring after the first prosecution; (b) the defendant is responsible for preventing joinder of the second offense with the first offense on grounds that do not amount to unconstitutional prejudice; (c) the court that heard the first prosecution lacked jurisdiction to try the second offense; or (d) the first offense was resolved through a guilty plea that was objected to by the prosecution. Also barred is a prosecution based on an ultimate fact that a previous tribunal has clearly determined against the same sovereign. The state is permitted to cumulate punishments when the relevant statutes or legislative history allow such cumulation or, in the absence of guidance from these sources, when the offenses are different under the *Blockburger* test.

(4) A sentence for a particular charge, once imposed, may not be increased when: (a) the original sentence was imposed at a capital sentencing proceeding by a unanimous jury; (b) the increase results from an appeal or motion by the prosecution that is not specifically authorized by statute; or (c) the defendant has fully satisfied the original sentence (or has begun serving an unappealed sentence?), and has a legitimate expectation in its finality.

(5) The foregoing rules barring reprosecution and cumulative sentences are not applicable to prosecutions brought by separate sovereigns. The federal government, each state government, and each Indian tribe is considered a separate sovereign. Municipalities are not sovereign entities for double jeopardy purposes.

BIBLIOGRAPHY

Allen, Ronald and John Ratnaswany. *Heath v. Alabama*: A Case Study of Doctrine and Rationality in the Supreme Court. 76 J.Crim.L. & Criminol. 801 (1985).

Amar, Akhil. Double Jeopardy Law Made Simple. 106 Yale L.J. 1807 (1997).

Cantrell, Charles L. Double Jeopardy and Multiple Punishment: An Historical Analysis. 24 S.Tex.L.J. 735 (1983).

Curtis, Justin. The Meaning of Life (or Limb): An Originalist Proposal for Double Jeopardy Reform. 41 U.Rich.L.Rev. 991 (2007).

Fellmeth, Aaron Xavier. Civil and Criminal Sanctions in the Constitution and Courts. 94 Geo.L.J. 1 (2005).

Findlater, Janet E. Retrial After a Hung Jury: The Double Jeopardy Problem. 129 U.Pa.L.Rev. 701 (1981).

Guerra, Sandra. The Myth of Dual Sovereignty: Multijurisdictional Law Enforcement and Double Jeopardy. 73 N.C. L.Rev. 1160 (1995).

Jahncke, Elizabeth S. *United States v. Halper*, Punitive Civil Fines, and the Double Jeopardy and Excessive Fines Clauses. 66 N.Y.U. L.Rev. 112 (1991).

Klein, Susan. Double Jeopardy's Demise. 88 Cal.L.Rev. 1001 (2000).

Ponsoldt, James F. When Guilt Should Be Irrelevant: Government Overreaching as a Bar to Reprosecution Under the Double Jeopardy Clause After *Oregon v. Kennedy*. 69 Cornell L.Rev. 76 (1983).

Poulin, Anne Bowen. Double Jeopardy and Multiple Punishment: Cutting the Gordian Knot. 77 Colo.L.Rev. 595 (2006).

____. Double Jeopardy Protection from Successive Prosecution: A Proposed Approach. 92 Geo. L.J. 1183 (2004).

____. The Limits of Double Jeopardy: A Course in the Dark? 39 Vill. L.Rev. 627 (1994).

Rosenthal, Kenneth. Prosecutor Misconduct, Convictions, and Double Jeopardy: Case Studies in an Emerging Jurisprudence. 71 Temp. L.Rev. 887 (1998).

Rudstein, David. Prosecution Appeals of Court-Ordered Midtrial Mistrials: Permissible Under the Double Jeopardy Clause? 62 Cath. U. L. Rev. 91 (2012).

____. A Brief History of the Fifth Amendment Guarantee Against Double Jeopardy. 14 Wm. & Mary Bill Rts.J. 193 (2005).

____. Civil Penalties and Multiple Punishment Under the Double Jeopardy Clause: Some Unanswered Questions. 46 Okla. L.Rev. 587 (1993).

Schulhofer, Stephen J. Jeopardy and Mistrials. 125 U.Pa.L.Rev. 449 (1977).

Steinglass, Joshua. The Justice System in Jeopardy: The Prohibition on Government Appeals of Acquittals. 31 Ind. L.Rev. 353 (1998).

Stinneford, John. Dividing Crime, Multiplying Punishments. 48 U.C.Davis L. Rev. 1955 (2015).

Symposium. The Rodney King Trials: Civil Rights, Prosecutions, and Double Jeopardy. 41 U.C.L.A. L.Rev. 5009 (1994).

Thomas, George III. Double Jeopardy: The History, the Law (1998).

Westen, Peter and Richard Drubel. Toward a General Theory of Double Jeopardy. 1978 Sup.Ct.Rev. 81 (1978).

White, Thomas. Limitations Imposed on the Dual Sovereignty Doctrine by Federal and State Governments. 38 N. Ky. L. Rev. 173 (2011).

Part G

THE ROLE OF THE DEFENSE LAWYER

The Sixth Amendment to the United States Constitution provides "in all criminal prosecutions, the accused shall enjoy the right . . . to have the Assistance of Counsel for his defense." This language, applied to the states in *Gideon v. Wainwright,*[1] has raised two central questions. First, what aspects of the criminal process comprise the "criminal prosecution"—that is, when is a criminal defendant entitled to have counsel present, at state expense if necessary? Second, what is "assistance"—that is, what, beyond mere physical presence, does the Constitution require of the attorney representing a criminal defendant?

Chapter 31 discusses the first issue, which has been an important aspect of the Supreme Court's concern over the fairness of the criminal process since the 1930's. It examines not only the Court's treatment of the Sixth Amendment, but also its use of the Fifth and Fourteenth Amendments in determining when the right to counsel attaches.

The second question—which raises what has come to be called the effective assistance of counsel issue—is addressed in Chapter 32. The chapter examines the various factors that the courts have looked at in determining whether the acts or omissions of a lawyer rise to the level of a constitutional violation.

---

[1]   372 U.S. 335, 83 S.Ct. 792 (1963).

Chapter 31

THE RIGHT TO COUNSEL

31.01 Introduction

As fundamental as the right to counsel may seem today, it developed much later than many of the other rights discussed in this book. In England, for instance, the right to jury trial was mentioned in the thirteenth century Magna Carta, and the antecedents to the double jeopardy prohibition developed at about the same time, but a right to counsel was not recognized until the late seventeenth century. Even then, in the Treason Act of 1695, criminal defendants were allowed counsel only if they could afford one, and only when charged with misdemeanors or treason.[1] Accordingly, self-representation was the norm under English common law.[2] In part the resistance to counsel was due to the Crown's fear that presence of an attorney would unduly strengthen the cause of its political enemies in courts of law.[3] But in part it may also have been due to a distaste for lawyers. The West New Jersey Charter of 1676 explicitly guaranteed criminal defendants the right to *avoid* hiring lawyers.[4]

These attitudes changed in this country as counsel came to be seen as an important bulwark against tyranny; a contributory development was the rise of the public prosecutor, who confronted the defendant with a powerful, well-informed adversary familiar with court procedures and personnel.[5] Thus, the Declaration of Independence specifically complained of the denial of counsel, twelve of the original thirteen states guaranteed a right to counsel for felony cases in their constitutions and, of course, the right was included in the Sixth Amendment.[6]

Even with these developments, the right to counsel existed only for those who could afford one. It was not until 1932 that the Supreme Court recognized an entitlement to defense counsel, and even then the entitlement existed only on a case-by-case basis.[7] It took another three decades for the Court to hold, in *Gideon v. Wainwright*, that *every* criminal defendant is guaranteed counsel at trial. The first section of this chapter examines the development of the right to trial counsel, while the second section looks at the right to counsel at other stages of the criminal process. The following sections discuss related matters, specifically: waiver of counsel and the right to self-representation; the right to counsel of one's choice; the right to expert assistance other than counsel; and the state's right to require reimbursement for attorney services rendered to a defendant when he was indigent.

---

[1]   Francis Heller, The Sixth Amendment to the Constitution of the United States 10 (1951). Moreover, up to the end of the seventeenth century, counsel was permitted to argue only questions of law, not fact. Note, *An Historical Argument for the Right to Counsel during Police Interrogation*, 73 Yale L.J. 100, 1028 (1964).

[2]   *Faretta v. California*, 422 U.S. 806, 95 S.Ct. 2525 (1975) (citing 1 F. Pollock & F. Maitland, The History of the English Law 211 (2d ed. 1909)).

[3]   Heller, supra note 1, at 10 (citing 5 W. Woldsworth, A History of English Law 196 (1927)).

[4]   Id. at 17.

[5]   Id. at 21.

[6]   See *Powell v. Alabama*, 287 U.S. 45, 53 S.Ct. 55 (1932).

[7]   See § 31.02(a).

31.02 The Right to Counsel at Trial

The right to counsel at trial developed over four decades. For some time, beginning in 1932, the Court relied on the Due Process Clause and analyzed the right on a case-by-case basis. Even after the Sixth Amendment was applied to the states in 1963, it took several decisions to define precisely the types of cases which trigger the right. Today the Sixth Amendment guarantees counsel at any criminal trial that results in deprivation of liberty. The Due Process Clause remains relevant to analysis of those trials that are not seen to be part of the "criminal prosecution."

(a) Due Process Origins

The constitutional right of an indigent defendant to the assistance of court-appointed counsel was first recognized in *Powell v. Alabama*.[8] In that case nine black defendants were charged with the rapes of two white women. No inquiry was made into whether the defendants had, or were able to employ, counsel. The trial court appointed the entire membership of the local bar to represent the defendants at arraignment. However, no specific lawyer was designated to represent the defendants until the morning of the trial. Eight of the defendants were subsequently convicted and sentenced to death. The Supreme Court reversed the convictions on two separate grounds: (1) the defendants possessed a right to retain their own counsel, which was violated when the trial court denied them an opportunity to seek legal representation; and (2) the defendants had a right to appointed counsel if they could not retain counsel, which was violated by the trial judge's careless manner of appointing their attorneys.

The Court did not base these holdings on the Sixth Amendment, but relied instead on the Due Process Clause. The Court found that the long history of permitting an accused to rely on his own attorney, dating back to colonial times,[9] made the right to retained counsel a fundamental guarantee protected by due process. More significantly, the majority held that, even when counsel cannot be retained, defendants like those in *Powell* were entitled to effective legal representation paid for by the state, not only during trial but "during perhaps the most critical period of the proceedings," from arraignment to the beginning of trial. Although there was little historical support for this second right, the Court found it to be a natural corollary to the due process right to a fair hearing. In the words of Justice Sutherland:

> The right to be heard would be, in many cases, of little avail if it did not comprehend the right to be heard by counsel. Even the intelligent and educated layman has small and sometimes no skill in the science of law. If charged with crimes, he is incapable, generally, of determining for himself whether the indictment is good or bad. He is unfamiliar with the rules of evidence. Left without the aid of counsel he may be put on trial without a proper charge, and convicted upon incompetent evidence, or evidence irrelevant to the issue or otherwise inadmissible. He lacks both the skill and knowledge adequately to prepare his defense, even though he have a perfect one. He requires the guiding hand of counsel at every step in the proceedings against him. Without it, though he be not guilty, he faces the danger of conviction because he does not know how to establish his innocence. . . .

---

[8]   287 U.S. 45, 53 S.Ct. 55 (1932).

[9]   See § 31.01.

The right to appointed counsel established in *Powell* was limited to "capital case[s], where the defendant is unable to employ counsel, and is incapable adequately of making his own defense because of ignorance, feeble-mindedness, illiteracy or the like." But the Court's emphasis on the need for the legal expertise and knowledge of a lawyer argued for a more general rule. Indeed, six years later, in *Johnson v. Zerbst*,[10] the Court recognized, at the federal level, a Sixth Amendment right to appointed trial counsel in *all* criminal prosecutions which sought to deprive the defendant of life or liberty. Justice Black, echoing *Powell,* stated that the Sixth Amendment "embodies a realistic recognition of the obvious truth that the average defendant does not have the professional legal skill to protect himself."

However, *Johnson* refused to extend its ruling to the states. This holding was reaffirmed four years later in *Betts v. Brady*,[11] which held that "[t]he Due Process Clause of the Fourteenth Amendment does not incorporate, as such, the specific guarantees found in the Sixth Amendment." The majority in *Betts* opted for continuing the due process case-by-case approach in state cases, requiring examination of whether the particular circumstances indicated that the absence of counsel would result in a lack of fundamental fairness. In doing so, the Court seemed particularly concerned that the *Johnson* rule would impose too heavy a burden on the states and perhaps even open the door to requiring counsel in some types of civil cases.[12]

Betts' due process analysis, to which the Court adhered for the next twenty-one years, rarely resulted in upholding a denial of counsel,[13] whether the denial occurred at trial or at equivalent adjudicatory proceedings, such as guilty plea hearings.[14] Nonetheless, it was criticized from its inception; for instance, Justice Black argued in his *Betts* dissent that the due process approach was both unworkable, given the impossibility of assessing how the trial would have come out had counsel been available, and unrealistic, given its refusal to recognize *Powell's* implicit message that a denial of counsel deprives the defendant of a basic tool to his defense.

(b)　The Sixth Amendment Actual Imprisonment Threshold

These concerns finally persuaded a majority of the Court to overrule *Betts* in *Gideon v. Wainwright*,[15] which held that the Sixth Amendment's guarantee of counsel for indigent criminal defendants was fully incorporated by the Fourteenth Amendment. The Court, in an opinion by Justice Black, relied heavily on *Powell* in deciding the right was of a fundamental nature. Black reemphasized the need for legal knowledge and expertise at a criminal trial, concluding that "lawyers in criminal courts are necessities, not luxuries." The strongest indications of this "obvious truth," in his view, were the facts "[t]hat government . . . hires lawyers to prosecute and defendants who have money hire lawyers to defend."

---

[10]　304 U.S. 458, 58 S.Ct. 1019 (1938).

[11]　316 U.S. 455, 62 S.Ct. 1252 (1942).

[12]　At one point, the Court noted that "as the Fourteenth Amendment extends the protection of due process to property as well as to life and liberty, if we hold with the petitioner, logic would require the furnishing of counsel in civil cases involving property."

[13]　See Jerold Israel, Gideon v. Wainwright: *The 'Art' of Overruling*, 1963 Sup.Ct.Rev. 211, 249–251.

[14]　See, e.g., *Moore v. Michigan*, 355 U.S. 155, 78 S.Ct. 191 (1957).

[15]　372 U.S. 335, 83 S.Ct. 792 (1963).

Gideon involved a felony prosecution and later cases referred to that decision as establishing the right to counsel only in felony cases.[16] In *Argersinger v. Hamlin,*[17] however, a unanimous Court held the right to counsel applicable to misdemeanors as well, at least where the defendant receives a jail term. The Court squarely rejected the contention that the right to counsel should, like the right to jury trial,[18] apply only to offenses punishable by imprisonment for six months or more. Unlike the jury right, the right to counsel had historically been accorded those charged with minor crimes. Furthermore:

> The requirement of counsel may well be necessary for a fair trial even in petty-offense prosecution. We are by no means convinced that legal and constitutional questions involved in a case that actually leads to imprisonment even for a brief period are any less complex than when a person can be sent off for six months or more.

Indeed, the opinion noted, the greater likelihood of mass production justice at the petty-offense level might create a special need for counsel in that context.

Conversely, the Court has refused to find a right to counsel at trial where the loss of liberty is merely a *possibility* and does not, in fact, occur. In *Scott v. Illinois,*[19] a five member majority concluded that "the central premise of *Argersinger*—that actual imprisonment is a penalty different in kind from fines or the mere threat of imprisonment—is eminently sound." A finding otherwise would only "create confusion and impose unpredictable, but necessarily substantial, costs on 50 quite diverse states." Thus, where there is no confinement, the right to counsel does not attach. Presumably, however, if the state does not provide an indigent accused counsel in the belief he would only receive a fine, and the accused is later given a jail sentence, the conviction would have to be overturned.

The efficiency argument that is the principal foundation for *Scott* is open to question. As Justice Brennan pointed out in dissent, the defendant in *Scott*—who was charged with a theft offense that carried a maximum penalty of $500 and a year imprisonment, but who received only a $50 fine (and thus was not entitled to counsel under the majority's rule)—would have received counsel in 33 states. Brennan also noted that the majority's actual imprisonment test would mandate time-consuming decisions before trial about the likely disposition of the case, occasionally leading to inaccurate predictions that might require retrials, and could also lead to "unequal treatment" because indigents charged with the same offense would not necessarily always be accorded the same "right" to counsel. Thus he advocated an "authorized imprisonment" threshold for the Sixth Amendment.

Even the dissent's authorized imprisonment test does not recognize the Sixth Amendment's application to "all criminal prosecutions," which would include trials involving charges that could bring only a fine. Nor does it take into account the fact that non-incarcerative penalties can carry consequences as harsh as imprisonment. But it may be advisable given the fact that many states still criminalize very minor offenses, such as traffic violations.

---

[16]   See, e.g., *Mempa v. Rhay,* 389 U.S. 128, 88 S.Ct. 254 (1967).

[17]   407 U.S. 25, 92 S.Ct. 2006 (1972).

[18]   See § 27.02(c)(1).

[19]   440 U.S. 367, 99 S.Ct. 1158 (1979).

Scott's thrust was undercut somewhat in *Baldasar v. Illinois,*[20] which held that an uncounselled misdemeanor conviction, although valid under *Scott,* may not be used to enhance a later sentence beyond a term of imprisonment of six months or more. But *Baldasar,* a per curiam decision with three separate opinions, was overturned 14 years later in *Nichols v. United States.*[21] In that decision, Chief Justice Rehnquist wrote for five members of the Court that uncounselled convictions may be used for *any* enhancement, regardless of length, because doing so does not change the penalty received for the uncounselled offense. Further, he reasoned, since it is well settled that a judge determining the length of sentence may consider any antisocial conduct of the defendant that is proven by a preponderance of the evidence,[22] "[s]urely . . . it must be constitutionally permissible to consider a prior uncounselled misdemeanor conviction based on the same conduct where that conduct must be proven beyond a reasonable doubt." Rehnquist also rejected the defendant's due process argument that, if uncounselled convictions can be used to enhance sentence, defendants are entitled to notice of that fact. He concluded that it would be difficult to memorialize such notice (since many misdemeanor courts are not of record) and even more difficult to convey accurately enhancement law in the fifty states. In any event, he asserted, defendants are likely to know that their misdemeanor conviction can lead to harsher punishment after a subsequent conviction.

Justice Blackmun, joined by Justices Stevens and Ginsburg, adhered to the position he took in *Baldasar* that uncounselled convictions cannot be used for enhancement purposes. While he agreed with the majority that its ruling did not change the sentence received for the uncounselled conviction, he pointed out that, when used to enhance, such convictions still lead directly to further imprisonment (in Nichols' case, the enhancement attributable to his uncounselled DUI conviction was over two years). The dissenters also rejected Rehnquist's comparison to the sentencing process. While admitting that the sentencing judge can consider unconvicted conduct proven at the preponderance level, they emphasized that evidence of such conduct is subjected to cross-examination by counsel in front of the judge, something that obviously is not true of evidence in an uncounselled misdemeanor case. In any event, they noted, convictions tend to receive more weight in the sentencing process than other conduct. As he had in *Baldasar,* Blackmun concluded that, if the dissent's position pressured the states into providing counsel in misdemeanor cases, that would be preferable to allowing possibly unreliable evidence to bolster sentence enhancement.

In *Alabama v. Shelton*[23] the Court addressed the implications of *Argersinger* and *Nichols* for defendants who receive a suspended sentence at trial. The state argued that counsel should not be required at this type of proceeding because punishment is not immediately imposed, and might never be; as a result, the counsel issue should be

---

[20]   446 U.S. 222, 100 S.Ct. 1585 (1980).

[21]   511 U.S. 738, 114 S.Ct. 1921 (1994). *See also United States v. Bryant,* ___ U.S. ___, 136 S.Ct. 1954 (2016) (holding unanimously that an uncounseled conviction in tribal court that results in imprisonment permitted by the Indian Civil Rights Act may be used to enhance sentence).

[22]   The case upon which Rehnquist relied for this proposition, *McMillan v. Pennsylvania,* 477 U.S. 79, 106 S.Ct. 2411 (1986), has since been overruled in *Alleyne v. United States,* 570 U.S. 99, 133 S.Ct. 2151 (2013), based on the theory that sentencing enhancement factors must be found by a jury beyond a reasonable doubt. See § 27.02(a)(2), But since there is no right to jury in the misdemeanor cases at issue here, this aspect of his reasoning is probably still intact.

[23]   535 U.S. 654, 122 S.Ct. 1764 (2002).

addressed only if and when the state seeks to revoke probation.[24] But the Court, in an opinion by Justice Ginsburg, reasoned that imprisonment after a probation revocation proceeding is based on the original, underlying offense, not the conduct leading to revocation of probation. Thus, unless counsel is provided for the underlying offense at the time of conviction, imposition of a suspended sentence violates *Argersinger*.

The state also argued its position was supported by *Nichols*, which allowed enhanced imprisonment to be based on an uncounselled conviction. But the Court distinguished *Nichols* by noting that the uncounselled conviction there was used to increase a sentence for a conviction on which the defendant *was* represented. The uncounselled conviction in that case was treated merely as evidence of prior criminal activity, which *Nichols* had held could consist of *any* credible evidence when used to enhance a sentence.

Shelton's impact on the processing of misdemeanors could be significant. At the time of that decision, as many as half the states did not provide counsel at misdemeanor proceedings in cases involving suspended sentences.[25] The Court refused to decide whether the impact of its decision could be avoided by imposing a suspended sentence that, by law, could never be enforced, instead leaving it to the courts of Alabama to decide whether such a sentence would be valid as a matter of state law. It did note that states could still impose pretrial probation, which withholds adjudication of guilt and imposition of sentence for the underlying offense unless and until the defendant breaches the pretrial conditions. But the option of allowing uncounselled misdemeanant offenders to relitigate their guilt, with counsel, if and when the state seeks to revoke probation is apparently foreclosed by *Shelton*. The four dissenters, in an opinion written by Justice Scalia, were particularly critical of this aspect of the opinion, stating that "the Court's decision imposes a large, new burden on a majority of the States, including some of the poorest."

(c) Non-Criminal Trials

Because the Sixth Amendment applies only to "criminal prosecutions," the Due Process Clause still retains some vitality in determining whether litigants in other types of proceedings are entitled to counsel. In *In re Gault*,[26] the Supreme Court held that juveniles subjected to delinquency proceedings that "may result in commitment to an institution in which the juvenile's freedom is curtailed" are guaranteed counsel as a matter of due process. It is not clear whether, after *Argersinger,* this due process right has been modified by the "actual imprisonment" threshold applied in Sixth Amendment cases. But, aside from this possible limitation, *Gault* established that the right to counsel in delinquency proceedings is not subject to the case-by-case determination approach endorsed in *Betts*.

On the other hand, in *Vitek v. Jones*,[27] the Court held that prisoners subjected to transfers from prisons to mental health facilities are entitled only to "a qualified and independent advisor . . . who may be . . . a licensed psychiatrist or other mental health professional." And in *Parham v. J.R.*,[28] it concluded that children subjected to

---

[24] Note that counsel is not constitutionally required at all revocation proceedings. See § 31.03(c)(2).

[25] This, at least, was the assertion of Justice Scalia in dissent.

[26] 387 U.S. 1, 87 S.Ct. 1428 (1967).

[27] 445 U.S. 480, 100 S.Ct. 1254 (1980).

[28] 442 U.S. 584, 99 S.Ct. 2493 (1979).

commitment by their parents are not entitled to any advocate, although commitment must be based on a decision by a "neutral" decisionmaker. Both decisions stemmed in part from the fear that the presence of counsel would make proceedings designed to determine what is "best" for the individual too adversarial and formalistic.

For different reasons, in *Middendorf v. Henry*,[29] the Court found that due process does not require counsel at military summary courts-martial. The Court first concluded that, even though a loss of liberty can result from such proceedings, they are not criminal prosecutions under the Sixth Amendment because they are inquisitorial rather than adversarial and are meant to enforce disciplinary rules. It then held that counsel was not required under the Due Process Clause because: (1) Congress had determined that counsel should not be provided; (2) the hearings were brief and informal; and (3) the "defendant" had the option of selecting a "special" courts-martial proceeding, where counsel would be provided (but which also usually resulted in more serious penalties).[30]

Civil contempt proceedings can also result in incarceration, often for six months or longer. But in this situation as well the Court held, in *Turner v. Rogers*,[31] that there is no "automatic" right to counsel. In particular, where the opposing side in the underlying proceeding is not represented by counsel and the state provides "substitute procedural safeguards" for the contempt proceeding the Due Process Clause does not require an attorney. However, in *Turner* itself, involving an attempt to obtain child support from Turner by his ex-wife, a bare majority of the Court remanded the case even though the ex-wife was not represented, because Turner had not received substitute safeguards such as "clear notice" that his ability to pay would constitute the critical question in his contempt proceeding or a form designed to elicit information about his financial circumstances. The four dissenters, in an opinion by Justice Thomas, argued that this result stretched the Due Process Clause beyond its parameters and failed to take adequate account of the interests of the ex-wife and children in need of support.

31.03   Counsel at Other Stages of the Criminal Process

Until *Gideon,* the Court's focus in right to counsel cases was primarily on trial and other adjudicatory proceedings. But after that decision, the Court increasingly turned its attention to determining the extent to which the state must provide counsel at earlier and later stages of the process. The Sixth Amendment was the principal referent for these cases, but given the Court's definition of when a "criminal prosecution" begins and ends, due process, equal protection, and the privilege against self-incrimination have also played a role in these opinions.

(a) Under the Sixth Amendment

The Court's Sixth Amendment treatment of the right to counsel at stages other than trial can be divided into two distinct periods. During the first period, which lasted only six years, the Court employed what it called "critical stage" analysis. The second period, beginning in 1973, continues to use the critical stage rubric, but actually focuses more closely on whether the stage in question is a "trial-like confrontation." Also during this

---

[29]   425 U.S. 25, 96 S.Ct. 1281 (1976).

[30]   Two members of the five-member majority agreed with this analysis but emphasized as well that the military is a "specialized society" meriting different treatment.

[31]   564 U.S. 431, 131 S.Ct. 2507 (2011).

second period, the Court made clear how it would define "criminal prosecution" for purposes of Sixth Amendment analysis. These three issues are discussed below.

(1) Critical Stage Analysis

The most articulate exposition of the critical stage framework came in *United States v. Wade*,[32] decided four years after *Gideon*. There the Court established a two part test to determine when counsel is required under the Sixth Amendment: (1) "whether potential substantial prejudice to the defendant's rights inheres in the particular confrontation;" and (2) whether counsel can "help avoid that prejudice." The Court then applied this two-step analysis in finding a right to counsel at post-indictment lineup procedures. Justice Brennan's majority opinion first noted that lineups are susceptible to rigging and other "innumerable dangers and variable factors which might seriously, even crucially, derogate from a fair trial." At the same time, Brennan stressed, given the impact of eyewitness testimony, "[t]he trial which might determine the accused's fate may well not be that in the courtroom but that at the pretrial confrontation, with the State aligned against the accused, the witness the sole jury, and the accused unprotected against the overreaching, intentional or unintentional, [of the state]." Unless the state, by statute or regulation, establishes procedures "which eliminate the abuse and unintentional suggestion at lineup proceedings and the impediments to meaningful confrontation at trial," counsel must be provided the indigent accused subjected to a post-indictment lineup, to deter use of suggestive procedures and to enable counsel to expose any residual suggestiveness at a subsequent suppression hearing or at trial.

The *Wade* Court claimed that the critical stage analysis it described explained all of the Court's earlier due process decisions. It noted, for example, that in *Powell* the Court had characterized the period from arraignment to trial as "perhaps the most critical period of the proceedings." Also said to be consistent with critical stage analysis were the Court's earlier due process decisions finding a right to counsel at a preliminary hearing whenever state law provides that defenses not raised at that point are abandoned,[33] and whenever a plea of guilty made at the hearing, though non-binding, could be used as evidence at a later proceeding.[34] Finally, the *Wade* Court viewed its holding to be consonant with its two recent decisions involving police questioning, *Massiah v. United States*[35] (requiring counsel during any post-indictment questioning) and *Miranda v. Arizona*[36] (requiring counsel during custodial interrogation, regardless of when it takes place). This was so because both cases viewed the presence of counsel as an important means not just of ensuring intelligent decisionmaking, but also of deterring police abuse and exposing improprieties at later proceedings.

However in a companion case to *Wade*, *Gilbert v. California*,[37] the Court made clear that not every stage of the criminal process is "critical." *Gilbert* involved the taking of handwriting exemplars in the absence of counsel. In finding that the Sixth Amendment is not implicated by this investigative procedure, the Court stressed that once the sample is taken it can be analyzed at any time, by the defense as well as by the prosecution.

---

[32] 388 U.S. 218, 87 S.Ct. 1926 (1967).

[33] *Hamilton v. Alabama*, 368 U.S. 52, 82 S.Ct. 157 (1961).

[34] *White v. Maryland*, 373 U.S. 59, 83 S.Ct. 1050 (1963).

[35] 377 U.S. 201, 84 S.Ct. 1199 (1964), discussed in § 16.02(c).

[36] 384 U.S. 436, 86 S.Ct. 1602 (1966), discussed in § 16.02(d).

[37] 388 U.S. 263, 87 S.Ct. 1951 (1967), also discussed in § 17.02(a).

Moreover, additional samples can be obtained at any time. Thus, the absence of counsel does not seriously impede efforts at challenging the prosecution's evidence: "Knowledge of the techniques of science and technology is sufficiently available, and the variables in techniques few enough, that the accused has the opportunity for a meaningful confrontation of the Government's case at trial through the ordinary processes of cross-examination of the Government's expert witnesses and the presentation of the evidence of his own experts."[38]

The Court continued to employ critical stage analysis for several years after *Wade*. In *Mempa v. Rhay*,[39] decided the same term as *Wade*, the Court found sentencing proceedings to be a critical stage. And in *Coleman v. Alabama*[40] the Court went beyond its earlier due process decisions in holding that *any* preliminary hearing designed to determine whether the prosecution has a prima facie case implicates *Wade's* test, because at the hearing counsel can expose weaknesses in the state's case and thereby protect the accused against an erroneous or improper prosecution.

(2)　Trial-Like Confrontation Analysis

Because it believed that critical stage analysis swept too broadly, the post-Warren Court developed a second mode of analyzing the Sixth Amendment right to counsel, first articulated in *United States v. Ash*.[41] The defendant in that case argued that his Sixth Amendment right was violated when his attorney was barred from observing prosecution witnesses study photo displays for purposes of identification prior to trial. This argument was quite plausible under critical stage theory, given the similarity between the lineup in *Wade* and the photo array at issue in *Ash*. But the Court held otherwise, in the process establishing what could be called the "trial-like confrontation" test for the right to counsel. As Justice Blackmun, the author of the majority opinion, described the new test, the key inquiry in determining when the right to counsel attaches is whether—as at trial—the proceeding at issue confronts the accused with the "intricacies of the law and the advocacy of the public prosecutor."

The Court's principal objection to the critical stage test appeared to be its open-endedness. As Justice Blackmun stated, that test, "if applied outside the [trial-like] confrontation context, [would] result in drastic expansion of the right to counsel," including, for instance, a right to counsel at prosecutorial interviews of the victim and other witnesses. This latter example is worth looking at in more detail, given the Court's reference to it. On the one hand, any improper "suggestions" made during such an interview will be less subtle than those that might occur during a photo array, and thus are more likely to come out later even if counsel is not present; in short, it is not clear that critical stage theory would require counsel at such interviews. But if it does (in which case it might also require counsel at analogous events such as *police* interviews of witnesses), *Wade's* approach is admittedly in tension with the adversarial premise of the criminal justice system, which puts limits on the extent to which the defense may discover the prosecution's case prior to trial.[42] *Ash* attempted to avoid that tension by

---

[38]　See also, *Schmerber v. California,* 384 U.S. 757, 86 S.Ct. 1826 (1966), in which the Court rejected defendant's claim that, in compelling him to submit to a blood test after he objected to it on advice of counsel, police violated his Sixth Amendment right to counsel.

[39]　389 U.S. 128, 88 S.Ct. 254 (1967).

[40]　399 U.S. 1, 90 S.Ct. 1999 (1970), discussed in § 22.04(a).

[41]　413 U.S. 300, 93 S.Ct. 2568 (1973).

[42]　See § 24.03 on discovery by the defense.

limiting the pretrial right to counsel to those situations where the defendant is faced by government agents and needs aid in coping with legal problems.

Applying this test to the photo display at issue in *Ash,* Blackmun concluded that the Sixth Amendment was not implicated, since the defendant is usually not present during such displays and confrontation with the prosecution thus does not occur. Theoretically, that should have concluded the Court's reasoning. But the majority, perhaps demonstrating some ambivalence about the new test, went on to address the types of concerns that underlie critical stage analysis as well. Anticipating the dissent's argument that a photo display could easily be rigged in the prosecution's favor and that, as assumed in *Wade,* the presence of the defense attorney would deter such a practice, Blackmun made two points. First, he noted that the defense has equal access to the photos and the identifying witnesses after the identification takes place, as well as the opportunity to cross examine the witnesses at trial. Second, he argued that the prosecution could be depended upon to prevent any residual possibility of abuse. "The primary safeguard against abuses of this kind is the ethical responsibility of the prosecutor, who, as so often has been said, may 'strike hard blows' but not 'foul ones.' " As the dissent pointed out, however, the basis of *Wade* was the need to observe police-witness interaction *during* the photo identification process, a process in which the prosecutor is seldom involved. Indeed, the reasoning of *Ash* would not support even *Wade's* holding, since the prosecutor is often not involved in lineups and defense counsel can gain access to the lineup witnesses.

The "trial-like confrontation" threshold for the right to counsel developed in *Ash* was next applied in *Gerstein v. Pugh.*[43] After holding that a person whose arrest is not authorized by a warrant or indictment is entitled to a post-arrest judicial determination that the arrest is founded on probable cause, the Court addressed whether the hearing it had mandated "must be accompanied by the full panoply of adversarial safeguards— counsel, confrontation, cross-examination and compulsory process for witnesses." In finding that the *Gerstein* hearing is not a "critical stage," Justice Powell compared the preliminary hearing at issue in *Coleman v. Alabama* (noted above) to the *Gerstein* hearing:

> First, under Alabama law the function of the preliminary hearing was to determine whether the evidence justified charging the suspect with an offense. A finding of no probable cause could mean that he would not be tried at all. The Fourth Amendment probable cause determination is addressed only to pretrial custody. To be sure, pretrial custody may affect to some extent the defendant's ability to assist in preparation of his defense, but this does not present the high probability of substantial harm identified as controlling in *Wade* and *Coleman.* Second, Alabama allowed the suspect to confront and cross-examine prosecution witnesses at the preliminary hearing. The Court noted that the suspect's defense on the merits could be compromised if he had no legal assistance for exploring or preserving the witnesses' testimony. This consideration does not apply when the prosecution is not required to produce witnesses for cross-examination.

This language, like the opinion in *Ash,* does not entirely ignore the types of concerns that inspired critical stage analysis. But *Gerstein,* like *Ash,* signals a retreat from the

---

[43]   420 U.S. 103, 95 S.Ct. 854 (1975), discussed in § 20.02.

latter approach to the Sixth Amendment. Assuming, as Justice Powell asserted, that lack of counsel at the initial appearance will not seriously detract from a defendant's ability to mount a successful defense at trial,[44] it could still result in "the continuing incarceration of a presumptively innocent person" (in the words of four concurring justices, who felt that the Court did not need to reach the right to counsel issue in *Gerstein* but suggested they might find contrary to the majority). Indeed, *Gerstein's* reasoning could conceivably support the position that there is no right to counsel at the bail hearing, a proceeding that also affects "only" pretrial custody and does not directly compromise "the suspect's defense on the merits."[45] However, given the fact that the bail hearing involves both the prosecutor and the defendant, as well as cross-examination of prosecution witnesses, it is likely to be considered a "critical stage" even under trial-like confrontation analysis.[46]

One other decision illustrates the Court's continuing adherence to the trial-like confrontation approach. In *Estelle v. Smith*,[47] the Court held that the Sixth Amendment requires notice to the defense attorney of a state-requested psychiatric evaluation, but refused to hold that there is a right to counsel *during* such an evaluation. This result can be justified on trial-like confrontation grounds (since the prosecutor is not present during psychiatric evaluations). But it is difficult to reconcile with traditional critical stage analysis, given the impact of psychiatric testimony in criminal cases and the difficulty of reconstructing its basis merely from the defendant's report.[48]

(3) The Definition of "Criminal Prosecution"

One year before *Ash*, the Court had significantly limited the scope of *Wade* in another way, by holding, in *Kirby v. Illinois*,[49] that criminal prosecution does not begin until indictment, formal charge or the "initiation of adversary proceedings." This holding conforms to the commonsense meaning of the Sixth Amendment's language. But, as Justice Brennan pointed out in dissent, the issue of when criminal prosecution begins is peripheral to the nature of the inquiry under *Wade's* critical stage analysis—whether the defendant's case at trial has been prejudiced by the absence of counsel.[50] Indirectly, then, *Kirby* helped set the stage for *Ash's* later ruling that only confrontation with the prosecutor (which will normally occur only after charges have been brought) implicates the right to counsel.

The Court reiterated this point in *Rothgery v. Gillespie Cty., Texas*.[51] There, eight members of the Court first made clear what had been suggested in *Kirby* and reiterated

---

[44] But see, *Hamilton v. Alabama,* 368 U.S. 52, 82 S.Ct. 157 (1961), discussed supra note 33; *Moore v. Illinois,* 434 U.S. 220, 98 S.Ct. 458 (1977) (holding that when a showup is conducted during the initial appearance with the prosecutor present, counsel is required).

[45] Note, however, that *Gerstein* was also based on the finding that since it is "reasonable" under the Fourth Amendment to detain a person based on an arrest warrant, issued *ex parte,* it is also reasonable to deny counsel at the initial appearance, reasoning that would not apply to the bail hearing.

[46] See § 20.03(d).

[47] 451 U.S. 454, 101 S.Ct. 1866 (1981).

[48] Christopher Slobogin, Estelle v. Smith: *The Constitutional Contours of the Forensic Evaluation Process*, 31 Emory L.J. 71, 114–135 (1982).

[49] 406 U.S. 682, 92 S.Ct. 1877 (1972).

[50] *In United States v. Gouveia,* 467 U.S. 180, 104 S.Ct. 2292 (1984), the Court did indicate that, if a delay in bringing charges (and the consequent delay in obtaining counsel) was a "deliberate device to gain an advantage over [the defendant] and . . . caused him actual prejudice in presenting his defense," a due process claim would lie. See *United States v. Lovasco,* 431 U.S. 783, 97 S.Ct. 2044 (1977), discussed in § 25.02(b).

[51] 554 U.S. 191, 128 S.Ct. 2578 (2008).

in dictum in Supreme Court decisions like *Brewer v. Williams*[52] and *Michigan v. Jackson*[53]: the initiation of adversary proceedings can occur as early as the initial appearance in front of a judicial officer,[54] even if formal charges, in the form of an indictment or information, have not yet been filed. However, Souter also stated—and four of the justices emphasized in separate opinions—that this holding only determines when the Sixth Amendment attaches, not when defendants are entitled to counsel. That issue is resolved through the critical stage/trial-like confrontation analysis discussed above. Thus, for instance, *Rothgery* does not reverse *Gerstein's* holding that the state need not provide counsel *during* the initial appearance, nor does it necessarily require counsel at bail hearings that occur after that proceeding.[55]

At the other end of the process, the Court has indicated, the "criminal prosecution" concludes with sentencing (at which, as noted earlier, *Mempa v. Rhay* found a Sixth Amendment right to counsel). In *Gagnon v. Scarpelli,*[56] for instance, the Court held that a post-sentence probation revocation hearing is not part of the criminal prosecution because the only issue presented is whether to revoke probation, which is a determination based on conduct subsequent to commission of the original offense. And in *Ross v. Moffitt,*[57] the Court excluded appeals from Sixth Amendment coverage because "it is ordinarily the defendant, rather than the state, who initiates the appellate process, seeking not to fend off the efforts of the State's prosecutor but rather to overturn a finding of guilt." Thus, the defendant on appeal is using counsel as a "sword" to upset the verdict, not "as a shield" to protect him against a prosecution. In apparent conflict with this reasoning, however, the Court has intimated that the right to counsel does apply during a post-verdict proceeding on a motion for a new trial, despite the fact that counsel's goal in such a proceeding is to challenge the jury's verdict.[58]

(b) Under the Fifth Amendment

Although pre-charge confrontations with the state do not implicate the Sixth Amendment, *Miranda v. Arizona*[59] held that the Fifth Amendment's privilege against self-incrimination entitles indigent defendants to counsel during *any* custodial interrogation, pre- or post-charge, to counteract the "inherent coerciveness" of such encounters. Because the Fifth Amendment bars compelled self-incrimination "in any criminal case," *Miranda* avoids *Kirby's* criminal prosecution threshold. Further discussion on the Fifth Amendment right to counsel is found elsewhere in this book.[60]

(c) Under the Equal Protection and Due Process Clauses

Just as the Fifth Amendment has mitigated to some extent the Sixth Amendment's post-charge threshold for determining when the right to counsel first attaches in the criminal process, equal protection and due process analysis has, under limited

---

[52] 430 U.S. 387, 97 S.Ct. 1232 (1977), discussed in § 16.04.

[53] 475 U.S. 625, 106 S.Ct. 1404 (1986), discussed in § 16.04(c).

[54] See § 20.02 for a discussion of the initial appearance.

[55] See § 20.03(d).

[56] 411 U.S. 778, 93 S.Ct. 1756 (1973).

[57] 417 U.S. 600, 94 S.Ct. 2437 (1974).

[58] *Marshall v. Rodgers*, 569 U.S. 58, 133 S.Ct. 1446 (2013) (per curiam) (assuming, without holding, that a motion for a new trial is a critical stage for Sixth Amendment purposes), discussed further in § 34.01(d).

[59] 384 U.S. 436, 86 S.Ct. 1602 (1966).

[60] See, in particular, §§ 16.02(d)(1) & 16.03(e)(2).

circumstances, provided a basis for a right to counsel at post-sentencing stages where the Sixth Amendment does not apply. In particular, the Court has looked at the right to counsel at appeals as of right, probation and parole revocation proceedings, discretionary appeals and habeas proceedings.

(1) Appeals as of Right

The first case to rely on the Equal Protection Clause as a basis for the right to counsel was *Douglas v. California*,[61] which held, the same term as *Gideon*, that indigents are entitled to counsel on appeals as of right. *Douglas* built on *Griffin v. Illinois*,[62] which had concluded that the Equal Protection Clause requires the state to provide indigent appellants with a trial transcript when state law requires submission of such a transcript in order to obtain an appeal; otherwise, held the Court, the state would be granting the right to appeal in a way "that discriminates against some convicted defendants on account of their poverty." Similarly, in *Douglas*, the Court held that "where the merits on the *one and only* appeal an indigent has as of right are decided without benefit of counsel, . . . an unconstitutional line has been drawn between rich and poor." The Court added that without counsel "[t]he indigent, where the record is unclear or the errors are hidden, has only the right to a meaningless ritual, while the rich man has a meaningful appeal."

In dissent, Justice Harlan argued that due process should have been the focus of the Court's analysis. Harlan pointed out that, as a practical matter, the criminal process can never fully equalize justice between the rich and the poor. Further, he argued, the focus of equal protection—the provision of equal treatment—is not necessarily relevant to whether an attorney is needed to assure a fair hearing, and thus diverges from the premise of *Powell*. Even under due process analysis, however, Harlan found no right to counsel on the facts of *Douglas*, given the state appellate court's explicit obligation under the California rules to appoint counsel when it found an attorney would be of value.

When it revisited the right to appellate counsel issue over two decades later, the Court adopted Harlan's conceptual approach, but arrived at a different result. *Douglas* had held that indigents were entitled to appellate counsel whenever non-indigent defendants were, but the decision could not, given its equal protection grounding, guarantee counsel to *all* defendants (non-indigent as well as indigent) in the first instance. In *Evitts v. Lucey*[63] the Court held, 7–2, that as a matter of due process *every* defendant is entitled to counsel on appeals of right. In arriving at this result, Justice Brennan's opinion relied both on *Douglas'* depiction of a counselless appeal as a "meaningless ritual," and *Gideon's* observation that in an "adversarial system of justice . . . lawyers are 'necessities,' not luxuries."

(2) Probation and Parole Revocations

The Court conformed even more closely to Harlan's analysis in the earlier case of *Gagnon v. Scarpelli*,[64] which held that, as a matter of due process, indigents subject to probation or parole revocation proceedings are entitled to counsel only on a case-by-case basis, depending upon the complexity of the issues and the indigent's capacities. The

---

[61]   372 U.S. 353, 83 S.Ct. 814 (1963).

[62]   351 U.S. 12, 76 S.Ct. 585 (1956), discussed in § 29.02(a).

[63]   469 U.S. 387, 105 S.Ct. 830 (1985), discussed in more detail in § 32.04(c)(4).

[64]   411 U.S. 778, 93 S.Ct. 1756 (1973).

majority also left the impression that, under this case-by-case analysis, counsel would usually not be provided in such proceedings; it stressed that revocation decisions are typically based on acts that have already been proven in a separate proceeding or are admitted, and that mitigating circumstances, if advanced, often are "not susceptible of proof or [are] so simple as not to require either investigation or exposition by counsel."

Furthermore, as it had in cases limiting or rejecting the right to counsel in non-criminal cases,[65] the Court asserted that the quasi-judicial role thrust upon the fact-finding body by the presence of lawyers might make the probation or parole decisionmakers "less tolerant of marginally deviant behavior and feel more pressure to reincarcerate than to continue non-punitive rehabilitation." Indeed, in light of these considerations, the Court reserved the question of whether the state could prohibit reliance on *retained* counsel in such proceedings.[66]

(3) Discretionary Appeals

A year after *Scarpelli*, in *Ross v. Moffitt*,[67] the Court evaluated whether indigents are entitled to counsel in preparing a petition for a *discretionary* appeal (as opposed to the appeal as of right at issue in *Douglas* and *Evitts*). Justice Rehnquist began by noting that since appellate counsel is used as a sword rather than a shield, and since there is no constitutional right to appeal,[68] the state "does not automatically . . . act . . . unfairly by refusing to provide counsel to indigent defendants at every stage of the [appellate process]." Although this language suggested a due process analysis, Rehnquist proceeded to conclude that the issue of whether the state has in fact acted unfairly toward indigent defendants "is more profitably considered under an equal protection analysis." He noted that, under North Carolina's system, the appellate court deciding whether to review a defendant's case automatically receives the trial transcript, the brief filed in the lower appellate court and, if one is issued, the lower appellate decision. These documents, together with any *pro se* offering the defendant might wish to make, provide the poverty-stricken with access to North Carolina's appellate process not appreciably different from that provided nonindigent defendants.[69]

It is not clear why Rehnquist felt the need to resuscitate equal protection doctrine, which Justice Harlan had so roundly criticized in his *Douglas* dissent. In any event, the central question would seem to be whether the absence of counsel led to an unfair hearing, a due process question. On the fairness issue, Justice Douglas' dissent, joined by Justices Brennan and Marshall, pointed out the technical aspects of certiorari and review proceedings and argued that only a lawyer can make an effective and comprehensive presentation of the defendant's case in such situations. Douglas agreed with Judge Haynsworth (who wrote the opinion for a unanimous Fourth Circuit panel in the case) that there is "no logical basis for differentiation between appeals of right and permissive review procedures in the context of the Constitution and the right to counsel."

---

[65]   See § 31.02(c).

[66]   Note that in some states, revocation of probation comes before the imposition of sentence, and thus is akin to the situation addressed in *Mempa v. Rhay*. See *Ex parte Shivers,* 501 S.W.2d 898 (Tex.Crim.App. 1973). At the federal level, Congress has provided counsel in parole proceedings. 18 U.S.C.A. §§ 3006A(g), 4214.

[67]   417 U.S. 600, 94 S.Ct. 2437 (1974).

[68]   See § 29.01.

[69]   The Court did not address the issue of whether counsel would be required if an indigent defendant's petition for appellate review were accepted. Most states provide counsel at this point.

This type of reasoning influenced the Court in *Halbert v. Michigan*,[70] which considered the constitutionality of a Michigan rule denying state-paid counsel to indigent defendants who seek leave to appeal their guilty plea (while automatically providing appellate counsel when the indigent defendant appeals after conviction at trial). Relying on *Douglas* and due process notions of fairness rather than equal protection analysis,[71] the Court held that counsel must be provided to those who seek leave to appeal a guilty plea. Under Michigan law an appeal after a guilty plea is "discretionary," as was the appeal at issue in *Ross*, and of course counsel is provided during the guilty plea process, analogous to the representation at trial of those who appeal a conviction. But appeal of the plea is also likely to be the defendant's only chance to obtain review of the conviction, as was the case with the appeal of right involved in *Douglas*. Further, the appeal under Michigan's process is focused solely on correcting error rather than, as is often the case with the upper level type of appeal in *Ross*, designed to address issues of significant public moment that are less likely to require the focused attention on counsel. Finally, unlike the defendant seeking the discretionary appeal in *Ross*, defendants who plead guilty in Michigan's system have no brief from a previous counsel-assisted appeal, nor do they have an appellate opinion on which to base arguments. For these reasons, Justice Ginsburg, in an opinion for seven members of the Court, concluded that Halbert was entitled to counsel to help prepare his request to obtain leave to appeal his guilty plea. The Court further intimated that, given the fundamental nature of this right, prosecutors would not be able to obtain a waiver of it.

(4) Habeas Proceedings

In *Pennsylvania v. Finley*,[72] the Court relied on the combined due process/equal protection analysis used in *Ross* in holding that there is no constitutional right to counsel at state postconviction proceedings.[73] Chief Justice Rehnquist, writing for the Court, found that a right to habeas counsel is not required by the Due Process Clause because state "[post]conviction relief is even further removed from the criminal trial than is discretionary direct review" (the procedure at issue in *Ross*) and likewise is not a required avenue of relief. Nor, analogous to the reasoning of *Ross*, does the Equal Protection Clause support such a right, so long as the defendant has access to the trial record and the appellate briefs and opinions. The Court did suggest that the Due Process Clause places some obligation on the state to consider a petitioner's habeas claim; in *Finley* itself, the Court held that the habeas court's independent review of the record after counsel's withdrawal notification was sufficient for this purpose.

In *Murray v. Giarratano*,[74] the petitioner, on death row in Virginia, argued that *Finley's* rejection of a right to counsel in state postconviction proceedings should be limited to noncapital cases. Chief Justice Rehnquist, writing for a plurality of four, conceded that, because of the penalty involved, the Court's decisions had provided

---

[70]   545 U.S. 605, 125 S.Ct. 2582 (2005).

[71]   Justice Thomas, in dissent, argued that Michigan's distinction between defendants who plead guilty and defendants who go to trial was "sensible," given the briefer record and minimal number of issues that can be raised by the former group. As noted above, however, the majority did not base its reasoning on a discrimination-type rationale.

[72]   481 U.S. 551, 107 S.Ct. 1990 (1987).

[73]   The precise issue addressed by the Court was whether a habeas litigant is entitled to an *Anders* brief, see § 29.02(c), which the Court held was dependent upon whether such a litigant is entitled to counsel in the first instance.

[74]   492 U.S. 1, 109 S.Ct. 2765 (1989).

greater procedural protections in capital cases. But he pointed out that all of these decisions involved *trial* procedures. Because he found these safeguards "sufficient to assure the reliability of the process by which the death penalty is imposed," he concluded that any further distinction between capital and noncapital cases is unnecessary, especially in postconviction proceedings, which are "an adjunct to state criminal proceedings and serve a different and more limited purpose than either trial or appeal."

Justice Kennedy, in a concurring opinion joined by Justice O'Connor (also a member of the plurality), seemed less willing to force state habeas petitioners to proceed without counsel. He noted that a substantial proportion of such petitioners succeed in vacating their death sentences; moreover, he pointed out that the complexity of the law in this area "makes it unlikely that capital defendants will be able to file successful petitions for collateral relief without the assistance of persons learned in the law." However, he joined the Court's judgment because he felt that mechanisms other than counsel might provide "meaningful access" to the courts.[75] He concluded by saying:

> While Virginia has not adopted procedures for securing representation that are as far reaching and effective as those available in other States, no prisoner on death row in Virginia has been unable to obtain counsel to represent him in postconviction proceedings, and Virginia's prison system is staffed with institutional lawyers to assist in preparing petitions for postconviction relief. I am not prepared to say that this scheme violates the Constitution.

Given Kennedy's opinion, state habeas petitioners may be entitled to counsel if they can show the state is not providing an adequate substitute.

Although there is no right to counsel at state postconviction proceedings, the Constitution does entitle prisoners to some aid in raising claims on habeas. In *Johnson v. Avery,*[76] the Court ruled that a state may not prohibit inmates from helping each other in preparing habeas corpus petitions unless it provides some reasonable alternative to assist illiterate or poorly educated inmates. And in *Bounds v. Smith,*[77] the Court held that the right of access to the courts requires that prison authorities assist inmates in preparation and filing of meaningful legal papers by providing prisoners with adequate law libraries, adequate assistance from persons trained in the law, or other means of assuring adequate access to the courts. This right was significantly limited, however, in *Lewis v. Casey,*[78] which held that, before special programs or other large-scale relief will be granted under *Bounds*, litigants must show that inadequacies in prison legal research facilities caused actual inability to gain access to the courts on a systemwide basis.

31.04 Waiver of the Right to Counsel

The right to counsel can be waived. Waiver of the right during the interrogation process is discussed in Chapter 16. Here the focus is on the right to waive counsel and represent oneself at trial and related proceedings.

---

[75] Here he referred to *Bounds v. Smith,* infra note 77, which held that prisoners are guaranteed such access under the Due Process Clause and which has since been significantly limited (see below).

[76] 393 U.S. 483, 89 S.Ct. 747 (1969).

[77] 430 U.S. 817, 97 S.Ct. 1491 (1977).

[78] 518 U.S. 343, 116 S.Ct. 2174 (1996).

(a) The Right to Self-Representation

Although it has long been established that the right to counsel may be waived, it was not until relatively recently, in the case of *Faretta v. California*,[79] that the Supreme Court recognized that a criminal defendant has a constitutional right to represent himself at trial once waiver has taken place. Faretta was charged with grand theft. At arraignment a public defender was appointed to represent him, but well before trial he requested permission to act as his own lawyer. The trial court at first accepted his waiver of counsel but later revoked it, at least in part because Faretta's answers to questions about the hearsay rule and *voir dire* challenges did not satisfy the judge. Faretta's subsequent request for leave to act as counsel was denied as were his attempted motions on his own behalf. Throughout the subsequent trial, the judge required that Faretta's defense be conducted only through his appointed attorney. At the conclusion of the trial, the jury found the defendant guilty. The California court of appeal affirmed the trial court's ruling that Faretta had no federal or state constitutional right to represent himself.

The United States Supreme Court vacated judgment in a 6–3 opinion authored by Justice Stewart. In establishing the right to self-representation, Stewart found support in English and early American history, and the fact that some state constitutions recognized the right. But he also concluded that the privilege of self-representation could be derived from the Sixth Amendment itself, which guarantees the accused "assistance" of counsel:

> The language and spirit of the Sixth Amendment contemplate that counsel, like the other defense tools guaranteed by the Amendment, shall be an aid to a willing defendant—not an organ of the State interposed between an unwilling defendant and his right to defend himself personally. . . . An unwanted counsel "represents" the defendant only through a tenuous and unacceptable legal fiction. Unless the accused has acquiesced in such representation, the defense presented is not the defense guaranteed him by the Constitution, for in a very real sense, it is not his defense.

The Court acknowledged the validity of the dissent's point that recognizing a right to self-representation "seems to cut against the grain" of the basic premise in *Powell*, *Gideon*, and *Argersinger* that the lawyer is essential to a fair trial. But the majority asserted that the framers placed the "inestimable worth of free choice" above the right to counsel, and noted that, in some cases, *pro se* representation may be more effective. Moreover, while it:

> is undeniable that in most criminal prosecutions defendants could better defend with counsel's guidance than by their own unskilled efforts . . . where the defendant will not voluntarily accept representation by counsel, the potential advantage of a lawyer's training and experience can be realized, if at all, only imperfectly. To force a lawyer on a defendant can only lead him to believe that the law contrives against him.

The majority also rejected the dissent's argument that the state's strong societal interest in providing a fair trial permitted it to insist upon representation by counsel: "Although

---

[79]   422 U.S. 806, 95 S.Ct. 2525 (1975).

[the defendant] may conduct his own defense ultimately to his own detriment, his choice must be honored out of 'that respect for the individual which is the lifeblood of the law.' "

Assuming a right to self-representation, several implementation issues arise. The first is whether a pro se defendant is entitled to "standby counsel" to assist in preparing and presenting his case. Concerned about difficulties of implementation and the unusual role in which it casts counsel, virtually all courts have held that there is no constitutional right to such hybrid representation.[80] A second issue is the extent to which the state must provide law library access to such defendants. Lower courts have split on this issue.[81] In *Kane v. Espitia*,[82] the Supreme Court used this split to bolster its conclusion that the California courts were reasonable in deciding that denial of such access was not a violation of the Sixth Amendment, and thus that relief on such a claim was not available through federal habeas.

(b) The Definition of Waiver

Faretta notwithstanding, not every defendant who might want to proceed without counsel is allowed to do so. As early as 1938, in *Johnson v. Zerbst*,[83] the Supreme Court held that an individual may waive his right to counsel only so long as his waiver is "competent and intelligent" and cautioned that courts should "indulge every reasonable presumption against waiver." In *Carnley v. Cochran*,[84] the Court added that presuming waiver of counsel from a silent record is impermissible. To sustain a claim that counsel was waived, "the record must show, or there must be an allegation and evidence must show, that an accused was offered counsel but intelligently and understandingly rejected the offer. Anything less is not waiver." In *Von Moltke v. Gillies*,[85] a four justice plurality opinion went even further, stressing that the judge deciding whether to allow waiver of counsel at trial "must investigate as long and as thoroughly as the circumstances of the case before him demand." Justice Black's opinion continued:

> To be valid such waiver must be made with an apprehension of the nature of the charges, the statutory offenses included within them, the range of allowable punishments thereunder, possible defenses to the charges and circumstances in mitigation thereof, and all other facts essential to a broad understanding of the whole matter. A judge can make certain that an accused's professed waiver of counsel is understandingly and wisely made only from a penetrating and comprehensive examination of all the circumstances.

The lower appellate courts did not always followed *Von Moltke's* formulation precisely, but they at least considered the critical issue to be "what the defendant understood—not what the [trial] court said."[86]

---

[80]   See e.g., *United States v. Treff*, 924 F.2d 975 (10th Cir. 1991); *People v. Dennany*, 445 Mich. 412, 519 N.W.2d 128 (1994)(collecting cases). But see *Hill v. Commonwealth*, 125 S.W.3d 221 (Ky. 2004). The extent to which standby counsel may be *forced* on a pro se defendant is discussed in § 31.04(c).

[81]   Compare *Milton v. Morris*, 767 F.2d 1443, 1446 (9th Cir. 1985) with *United States v. Smith*, 907 F.2d 42, 45 (6th Cir. 1990) (holding that waiver of counsel encompasses waiver of law library access).

[82]   546 U.S. 9, 126 S.Ct. 407 (2005).

[83]   304 U.S. 458, 58 S.Ct. 1019 (1938).

[84]   369 U.S. 506, 82 S.Ct. 884 (1962).

[85]   332 U.S. 708, 68 S.Ct. 316 (1948).

[86]   *United States v. Harris*, 683 F.2d 322 (9th Cir. 1982).

Although these decisions suggested that courts should not readily accede to waivers of counsel, they left the precise waiver standard somewhat ambiguous. In an effort to clarify that standard, courts have often analyzed the issue in terms of whether a person who is competent to stand trial (which, as discussed elsewhere in this book,[87] requires a finding that the defendant understands the criminal process and can communicate with his attorney) is also competent to waive the right to counsel. A number of courts refused to equate the two competencies, on the ground that the latter decision is more significant and involves more difficult issues.[88] Early Supreme Court cases lent credence to that view. In *Massey v. Moore,*[89] for instance, the Court stated that "[o]ne might not be insane in the sense of being incapable of standing trial and yet lack the capacity to stand trial without benefit of counsel." And in *Westbrook v. Arizona,*[90] the Supreme Court also suggested that courts may not rely on a competency to stand trial finding in determining whether a person is competent to waive the right to counsel and conduct her own defense.

At the same time, *Faretta* made clear that the typical defendant should be able to waive trial counsel. It indicated, for instance, that a valid waiver can occur even if the defendant is not well versed in legal technicalities. Although it remanded the case to the lower courts, the Court strongly implied it would find Faretta competent to waive counsel. Stewart noted that Faretta had unequivocally, and in a timely fashion, asked to represent himself, that he appeared to be "literate, competent and understanding," and that he acted freely in making his request. The Court concluded that assessing how well Faretta understood the hearsay rule and *voir dire,* as the trial judge had done, was inappropriate, "[f]or his technical legal knowledge, as such, was not relevant to an assessment of his knowing exercise of the right to defend himself."

In *Godinez v. Moran,*[91] the Court appeared to relax even further the competency required to waive counsel, explicitly holding that a person who is competent to stand trial is also competent to waive counsel, and thus able to go to trial or plead guilty without counsel's assistance. In an opinion by Justice Thomas, the Court rejected the circuit court's holding that a person is competent to waive counsel only if she is both competent to stand trial *and* able to make a "reasoned choice" about the alternatives involved. Thomas pointed out that a defendant who is competent to stand trial is permitted to waive the right to jury trial and the right to silence, and then asserted that "there is no reason to believe that the decision to waive counsel requires an appreciably higher level of mental functioning than the decision to waive [these] other constitutional rights." Although conceding that a client who is competent to stand trial is not necessarily capable of doing a good job of self-representation, the Court stated that "a criminal defendant's ability to represent himself has no bearing upon his competence to *choose* self-representation."

In dissent, Justice Blackmun stated the majority's "attempt to extricate the competence to waive counsel from the competence to represent oneself is unavailing, because the former decision necessarily entails the latter." He noted that, while Moran had been able to understand his charges and their consequences, he was severely

---

[87]   See § 28.03(b)(1).

[88]   See, e.g., *Sieling v. Eyman,* 478 F.2d 211 (9th Cir. 1973) (standard for pleading guilty higher); *United States v. McDowell,* 814 F.2d 245 (6th Cir. 1987) (standard for waiving counsel higher).

[89]   348 U.S. 105, 75 S.Ct. 145 (1954).

[90]   384 U.S. 150, 86 S.Ct. 1320 (1966).

[91]   509 U.S. 389, 113 S.Ct. 2680 (1993).

depressed and on several different medications at the time he fired his attorneys, pleaded guilty to capital charges, and refrained from presenting evidence at sentencing. Thus, Blackmun argued, further inquiry should have occurred. The majority's only concession to Blackmun's point was to require that the defendant not only be competent to waive counsel, but that the judge additionally find the waiver to be "knowing and voluntary." However, Thomas also made clear that "[t]he purpose of the 'knowing and voluntary' inquiry . . . is [merely] to determine whether the defendant actually does understand the significance and consequences of a particular decision and whether the decision is coerced." That requirement does not involve any investigation into the individual's ability to represent himself.

In *Indiana v. Edwards*,[92] however, the Court backed away from this language, holding that a state may force counsel on a defendant who is competent to stand trial and wants to go to trial if the trial judge finds that the defendant is not "mentally competent" to proceed *pro se*. The Court claimed it was not reversing this aspect of *Moran*, because that case only dealt with whether a state could *permit* a defendant to represent himself, not with whether it could *deny* her the right to self-representation. Be that as it may, Justice Breyer's opinion for the Court reasoned that, given the variable nature of mental disability, denying the *Faretta* right to a mentally ill but competent defendant is permissible if necessary to assure the dignity and fairness of trial. In dissent, Justice Scalia, joined by Justice Thomas, the author of *Moran*, stated that, outside of situations where a defendant is disruptive,[93] the right to self-representation, asserted by a defendant who is competent to exercise it, should be absolute. Scalia noted that undermining the *Faretta* right by imposing counsel on a defendant who understood its consequences might insult, rather than reinforce, the defendant's dignity, and detract from the trial's fairness as well, at least in the defendant's eyes.

Edwards did not resolve how a trial judge is to determine whether a defendant who is competent to stand trial with counsel can nonetheless be foreclosed from standing trial without one, other than to say that the inquiry involves assessing the individual's ability to carry out "basic trial tasks." Presumably, this ability includes the capacity not only to communicate with the attorney but also the ability to communicate to the judge and the witnesses in a minimally coherent fashion. But arguably that ability is also required for competency to stand trial *with* counsel, given the possibility the defendant will testify. Ultimately, *Edwards* may significantly undermine *Faretta*.

In any event, the combined effect of *Moran* and *Edwards* is to allow a defendant with mental difficulties who is nonetheless competent to stand trial to plead guilty on his own with little further inquiry,[94] while preventing that same defendant from representing himself at trial, even with standby counsel.[95] That result that may be

---

[92]   554 U.S. 164, 128 S.Ct. 2379 (2008).

[93]   See § 28.03(a)(3).

[94]   The impact of *Moran* is exacerbated by the holding in *Iowa v. Tovar*, 541 U.S. 77, 124 S.Ct. 1379 (2004), discussed in § 26.04(a)(2), where the Court held that the trial court need not inform defendants at guilty plea hearings that waiving an attorney both entails the risk that a viable defense will be overlooked and deprives the defendant of an independent opinion on whether, under the facts and applicable law, it is wise to plead guilty.

[95]   See § 31.04(c).

efficient. But it will not always achieve the fairness and dignity goals the court claims it is trying to advance.[96]

(c) Standby Counsel

The potentially harmful consequences of self-representation can be mitigated to some extent by appointing "standby counsel" for defendants who have been found capable of proceeding *pro se*. Indeed, the Supreme Court has permitted the trial judge to force such counsel of pro se litigants. In *McKaskle v. Wiggins*,[97] it unanimously held that, even when it occurs over the *pro se* defendant's objection, a court may appoint standby counsel "to relieve the judge of the need to explain and enforce basic rules of courtroom protocol or to assist the defendant in overcoming routine obstacles that stand in the way of the defendant's achievement of his own clearly indicated goals."

This conclusion helped redress a problem created by *Faretta,* where the Court had stated, in a footnote, that "[t]he right of self representation is not a license . . . not to comply with relevant rules of procedural and substantive law." From this the majority concluded that "whatever else may or may not be open to him on appeal, a defendant who elects to represent himself cannot thereafter complain that the quality of his own defense amounted to a denial of 'effective assistance of counsel.'" The lower courts have adhered to this view.[98] But in his *Faretta* dissent, Chief Justice Burger pointed out that such a position was "totally unrealistic," at least when the defendant had represented himself so poorly that he may have been erroneously convicted. Through recognizing the institution of standby counsel, *Wiggins'* holding helps strike an accommodation between the right to self-representation and the spectacle of *pro se* defendants attacking their own conduct as a means of obtaining retrial.

While the entire Court agreed that standby counsel may be appointed to fulfill the minimum role described above, it could not reach a consensus as to the propriety of further actions by standby counsel. Six members of the Court concluded that actions of standby counsel do not violate *Faretta* so long as: (1) the defendant retains actual control over the case presented to the jury; and (2) the jury retains the perception that he represents himself. The three dissenting members, on the other hand, found this test unworkable, as well as violative of *Faretta:* the actual control standard placed "the burden . . . on the *pro se* defendant to comprehend counsel's submissions" and assert they were contrary to his objectives, and the jury perception prong was inconsistent with *Faretta's* emphasis on the "defendant's own perception of the criminal justice system." The dissent preferred the test adopted by the lower court, allowing the trial judge to suggest that the defendant consult with counsel on procedural and evidentiary matters, but requiring that standby counsel be "seen and not heard" until the defendant expressly asks for his assistance.

The difference between these tests is illustrated by the way their proponents applied them to the facts in *Wiggins*. The defendant there agreed to the participation of two standby counsel provided by the court, but then frequently changed his mind as to the extent of their participation, sometimes asking the attorneys to make objections directly

---

[96]   See Christopher Slobogin, *Mental Illness and Self-Representation:* Faretta, Godinez *and* Edwards, 7 Ohio St. J. Crim. L. 391 (2009).

[97]   465 U.S. 168, 104 S.Ct. 944 (1984).

[98]   See, e.g., *Green v. State,* 759 P.2d 219 (Okl.Crim. 1988); *Commonwealth v. Celijewski,* 324 Pa.Super. 185, 471 A.2d 525 (1984); *State v. Brown,* 33 Wash.App. 843, 658 P.2d 44 (1983).

to the court without consulting him, sometimes conferring with them during his cross-examination of witnesses, and sometimes requesting that they not be present even for consultation. On several occasions, one of the attorneys engaged in "acrimonious" exchanges with the defendant and made objections or motions without consulting the defendant. The majority concluded that "[o]nce a *pro se* defendant invites or agrees to any substantial participation by counsel, subsequent appearances by counsel must be presumed to be with the defendant's acquiescence, at least until the defendant expressly and unambiguously renews his request that standby counsel be silenced." The Court found no such request; applying the two-part test described above, it concluded that since most of the incidents of which the defendant complained occurred when the jury was not in the courtroom, and that since all conflicts between the defendant and counsel that did occur in front of the jury were resolved in the defendant's favor, no violation of *Faretta* occurred. The dissenters, on the other hand, concluded that their test would prohibit the actions taken by the standby attorneys in this case, since they had "distracted Wiggins and usurped his prerogatives, altered the tenor of the defense, disrupted the trial, undermined Wiggins' perception that he controlled his own fate[,] . . . induced a belief—most assuredly unfounded, but sincerely held nevertheless—that 'the law contrived against him' [citing *Faretta*,] and undoubtedly reduced Wiggins' credibility and prejudiced him in the eyes of the jury."

The majority in *Wiggins* also stated, in dictum, that "*Faretta* does not require a trial judge to permit 'hybrid' representation of the type Wiggins was actually allowed." This language suggests that, once a defendant has decided to proceed *pro se,* he may not depend on standby counsel taking over the role of representing him; that is, while he may ask standby counsel for advice about law and tactics, he is not *entitled* to have the attorney perform actual courtroom functions. Although this notion may require some fine distinctions between what standby counsel is allowed to do and what he is required to do, several courts have adopted it. For instance, one court upheld a trial court's denial of a *pro se* defendant's request to have standby counsel argue a motion in *limine,* on the ground that such conduct would amount to "hybrid" representation not guaranteed under *Faretta*—either the defendant must accept counsel as the tactical decisionmaker for the entire case or pursue the case himself.[99]

(d) Reasserting the Right to Counsel

Possibly relevant to whether defendants are entitled to hybrid representation is caselaw addressing whether a defendant who validly waives his right to counsel may reassert it at a later proceeding. In *Marshall v. Rodgers,*[100] the defendant waived his right to counsel on three separate occasions prior to trial, and eventually represented himself at the trial. After conviction, he asked for counsel to assist him in filing a motion for a new trial, but the trial judge refused and the California Supreme Court upheld the refusal, primarily because the defendant had given no reason for the request. The defendant then sought federal habeas relief. While the district court affirmed, the Ninth Circuit, based on its own precedent and precedent from other circuits, held that the trial court's refusal to appoint counsel violated the Sixth Amendment. The U.S. Supreme Court reversed, holding that the California Supreme Court's holding was not an

---

[99] *State v. Cooley,* 468 N.W.2d 833 (Iowa App. 1991); see also, *State v. Gethers,* 497 A.2d 408 (Conn. 1985).

[100] 569 U.S. 58, 133 S.Ct. 1446 (2013).

"unreasonable application" of clearly established Supreme Court caselaw,[101] because it (the U.S. Supreme Court) had yet to address the issue. However, the Court also noted that its opinion was not meant to "suggest or imply that the underlying issue, if presented on direct review, would be insubstantial." Thus, a refusal to appoint counsel for an indigent defendant who has previously waived counsel but now is willing to be represented by counsel may violate the Sixth Amendment.

31.05   The Right to Counsel of One's Choice

The indigent defendant has a right to counsel, but not to counsel of his choice. The non-indigent defendant obviously has greater control over the identity of counsel, but even his choice may be restricted under certain circumstances.

(a) The Indigent's Right

The right to counsel does not guarantee the indigent accused a right to a particular attorney. Ideally, perhaps, the state should provide the indigent with enough money to hire the counsel of his choice. But in *Wheat v. United States,*[102] the Supreme Court stated that "a defendant may not insist on representation by an attorney he cannot afford." Some lower courts have also held, primarily for economic and administrative reasons, that the indigent defendant is not even entitled to his choice from among those on the court appointed list or in the public defender's office.[103]

Once an indigent has appointed counsel, he can obtain a replacement if he shows "good cause, such as a conflict of interest, a complete breakdown of communication, or an irreconcilable conflict" for believing that an "unjust verdict" would otherwise result.[104] As might be imagined, however, such cause is difficult to show. In particular, the Court has held that the lack of a "meaningful relationship" with the attorney is not cause.[105]

(b) The Non-Indigent's Right

When the defendant has sufficient financial resources, the government may not, generally speaking, prevent him from retaining the attorney of his choice. After several cases containing dictum to this effect, a closely divided Court firmly established the rule in *United States v. Gonzalez-Lopez,*[106] in an opinion written by Justice Scalia. While conceding that the trial court had erroneously rejected Gonzalez-Lopez' counsel of choice under the applicable state law, the government argued that the *Sixth Amendment* is not violated by such a rejection unless substitute counsel is ineffective, as defined by the Supreme Court's cases.[107] Scalia responded that the right to effective assistance is meant to ensure a fair trial, while the right to counsel of one's choice is meant to guarantee a separate interest of the defendant's. "To argue otherwise," Scalia stated, "is to confuse the right to counsel—which is the right to a particular lawyer regardless of comparative effectiveness—with the right to effective counsel—which imposes a baseline requirement of competence on whatever lawyer is chosen or appointed." The Court also held that

---

[101] See § 33.02(c) for a description of this standard.

[102] 486 U.S. 153, 108 S.Ct. 1692 (1988).

[103] See Peter Tague, *An Indigent's Right to the Attorney of His Choice,* 27 Stan.L.Rev. 73, 79 (1974).

[104] *McKee v. Harris,* 649 F.2d 927 (2d Cir. 1981), cert. denied 456 U.S. 917, 102 S.Ct. 1773 (1982).

[105] See *Morris v. Slappy,* 461 U.S. 1, 103 S.Ct. 1610 (1983), discussed in § 32.04(c)(1).

[106] 548 U.S. 140, 126 S.Ct. 2557 (2006).

[107] See *Strickland v. Washington,* 466 U.S. 668, 104 S.Ct. 2052 (1984), discussed in § 32.02.

violation of the right to one's counsel of choice is "structural error" that is not subject to harmless error analysis,[108] primarily because of the difficulty of determining how rejected counsel would have carried out the representation.

In dissent, Justice Alito, joined by three others, argued that the Sixth Amendment only guarantees the assistance of whatever counsel the defendant has. He also pointed out that both the Court, in decisions involving conflicts and forfeitures (to be described below), and the states, through implementation of their practice rules (also noted below), have on occasion prevented defendants from obtaining their counsel of choice. The majority emphasized, however, that its ruling in *Gonzalez-Lopez* affected only those cases where the judge clearly violates a legitimately established rule, and thus did not apply in the situations noted by Alito.

There are at least four exceptions to the counsel-of-choice right, all noted by the majority or dissent in *Gonzalez-Lopez*. The conflicts exception, discussed in more detail in the next chapter,[109] was announced in *Wheat,* where the Court held that a trial court may override the defendant's choice whenever it believes that, in light of that attorney's other clients, a serious potential for conflict of interest may develop. A second exception arises when the defendant's attorney is not qualified to practice law under state or federal rules governing attorney credentials.[110] In some states, a third situation in which a defendant is not entitled to his counsel of choice exists when a defendant wants to discharge an attorney and acquire another more to his liking.[111] A fourth exception, one which is likely to have a much more significant impact on defendants' ability to select counsel than these other situations, occurs when, pursuant to the provisions of a "forfeiture statute," the defendant is unable to pay for the attorney of his choice because his assets are frozen and made subject to later forfeiture.

In *Caplin & Drysdale v. United States,*[112] the Supreme Court rejected a Sixth Amendment challenge to such a statute. The Comprehensive Forfeiture Act of 1984[113] authorizes the trial court, in cases involving certain federal offenses, to issue a restraining order prohibiting transfer of any of the defendant's assets it believes to be derived from drug-law violations, and further authorizes forfeiture of those assets upon conviction of the defendant. The petitioner in *Caplin & Drysdale* was a law firm representing a defendant who had been tried under the federal continuing criminal enterprise (CCE) statute and whose assets had been forfeited under the Forfeiture Act. The firm's primary contention was that the Act impermissibly burdens a criminal defendant's Sixth Amendment right to counsel because it deprives him of funds with which to pay for private legal representation.[114] In a 5–4 opinion, the court rejected this claim. Justice White, who wrote the majority opinion, concluded that "[a] defendant has no Sixth Amendment right to spend another person's money for services rendered by an

---

[108] See § 29.06.

[109] See § 32.04(b)(4), which deals with conflicts of interest.

[110] Cf. *Leis v. Flynt,* 439 U.S. 438, 99 S.Ct. 698 (1979).

[111] *Ungar v. Sarafite,* 376 U.S. 575, 84 S.Ct. 841 (1964).

[112] 491 U.S. 617, 109 S.Ct. 2646 (1989).

[113] 21 U.S.C.A. § 853.

[114] In a case decided the same day as *Caplin & Drysdale,* the Court held that nothing in the language or legislative history of the Act suggested that Congress meant to exempt from its scope sufficient proceeds to pay for legal representation. *United States v. Monsanto,* 491 U.S. 600, 109 S.Ct. 2657 (1989).

attorney, even if those funds are the only way that that defendant will be able to retain the attorney of his choice."

The petitioner had argued that his assets were not "another's" in the same way stolen property is and that, in any event, allowing payment of drug-related proceeds to an attorney would not transgress the objective of the Forfeiture Act because the defendant would still be dispossessed of the assets. But White pointed to three reasons why the government has an interest in gaining control over *all* the defendant's assets: (1) the money raised under the Act provides financial support for law enforcement efforts; (2) the Act ensures that property belonging to others will be preserved for later reclamation; and (3) the Act, at least as applied in CCE cases, "lessen[s] the economic power of organized crime and drug enterprises." These interests, concluded the Court, override any Sixth Amendment interest in permitting defendants to use forfeitable assets in their defense.

In dissent, Justice Blackmun characterized as "weak" the government interests identified by the majority, especially since at the time a restraining order is issued the government has only made a probable cause showing that the defendant has violated the law.[115] He also contended that the effect of the Court's decision would be to deny the defendant the right to retain counsel "he has chosen and trusts." Blackmun pointed out that a defendant whose assets are frozen could be forced to accept a public defender or court-appointed attorney who may lack the experience necessary for CCE litigation, which is often lengthy and complex. Even if the defendant is able to retain a private attorney, the quality of his representation may be sullied by concern over finances. The attorney may be reticent about investigating the case thoroughly because of the Act's provision that only bona fide purchasers of forfeitable property (i.e., people with no reason to believe that the property is subject to forfeiture) may keep it. Moreover, the "attorney who fears for his fee will be tempted to make the Government's waiver of fee-forfeiture the *sine qua non* for any plea agreement, a position which conflicts with his client's best interests."

Blackmun also conjectured on the long-term effects of the Court's holding:

> The long-term effects of the fee-forfeiture practice will be to decimate the private criminal-defense bar. As the use of the forfeiture mechanism expands to new categories of federal crimes and spreads to the States, only one class of defendants will be free routinely to retain private counsel: the affluent defendant accused of a crime that generates no economic gain. As the number of private clients diminishes, only the most idealistic and the least skilled of young lawyers will be attracted to the field, while the remainder seek greener pastures elsewhere.

Echoing Blackmun, some commentators have argued that forfeiture statutes such as those involved in *Caplin & Drysdale,* together with other aggressive prosecutorial maneuvers (e.g., law office searches and subpoenas of attorney records) will have a detrimental impact on the quality and morale of the defense bar.[116] Nonetheless the

---

[115] In *Monsanto,* supra note 114, the majority responded to this point by stating that if the government may restrain persons prior to trial based on a probable cause showing, as it may do under *United States v. Salerno,* 479 U.S. 1026, 107 S.Ct. 867 (1987) (discussed in § 20.03(c)(2)), then it may restrain the transfer of property on such a showing as well. However, the Court reserved the question as to whether a hearing must be held before a restraining order under the Forfeiture Act may be issued.

[116] William Genego, *The New Adversary,* 54 Brooklyn L.Rev. 781 (1988).

Court has subsequently reaffirmed the government's authority to confiscate property that might be used to compensate an attorney, so long as there is a probable cause finding that the defendant has committed a crime and that the confiscated property will ultimately be forfeitable because of its nexus to the crime.[117] However, in *Luis v. United States*,[118] the Court held that the government may not confiscate or freeze "untainted" assets if doing so would hinder the ability to hire counsel. A bare majority of the Court held that the Sixth Amendment right to counsel outweighs the government's interest in securing assets that might be used to pay criminal fines or provide restitution to the victim when those assets have no nexus to the crime.

31.06 The Right to Expert Assistance

Many issues that might be raised during a criminal trial—e.g., the interpretation of forensic tests, the defendant's sanity at the time of the offense, proper accounting practices (in fraud and tax cases)—are often beyond the competence of the lawyer as well as the competence of the defendant. Defense counsel may also find it difficult to track down exculpatory evidence without the aid of a trained investigator. Most jurisdictions authorize support for the indigent defendant and his counsel in obtaining such expert assistance.[119] For example, 18 U.S.C.A. § 3007A(e)(1) requires the trial court to provide for "investigative, expert, or other services" upon a showing that the service is "necessary for an adequate defense."

In *Ake v. Oklahoma*,[120] the Supreme Court held that when the service requested is psychiatric assessment of either the defendant's sanity at the time of the offense or his future dangerousness when that issue is relevant under a state's capital sentencing statute, government support is constitutionally mandated by the Due Process Clause, at least when the defendant can make a preliminary showing that these issues are likely to be a "significant factor" at trial or sentencing. In arriving at these conclusions, Justice Marshall, writing for the Court, looked at three factors—the "private interest" in obtaining the safeguard sought, the state interests that will be affected if the safeguard is provided, and the probable value of the safeguard sought. He found the criminal defendant's interest in an accurate resolution of the criminal responsibility and dangerousness issues compelling. Conversely, the only state interest he could identify in the case of psychiatric assistance was financial in nature, and this interest, concluded Marshall, was minimal given the fact that many states, as well as the federal government, provide such assistance. Finally, Marshall noted the "pivotal role" played by psychiatry in criminal proceedings. In insanity cases, the expertise of psychiatrists in identifying the " 'elusive and deceptive' symptoms of insanity," when combined with the complex and foreign nature of the issue, made psychiatrists " 'a virtual necessity if an insanity plea is to have any chance at success.' " Similarly, in capital cases a psychiatrist could be useful at exposing the shortcomings of the dangerousness predictions made by the state's experts.

Ake has potentially far-reaching consequences for the defense of criminal cases. It could be read to hold that if the defendant can show an issue will be a "significant factor" in his case and that expert assistance could play a "pivotal role" in the resolution of this

---

[117] *Kaley v. United States*, 571 U.S. 320, 134 S.Ct. 1090 (2014).

[118] ___ U.S. ___, 136 S.Ct. 1083 (2016).

[119] See Norman Lefstein, Criminal Defense Services for the Poor, App. B. (1982).

[120] 470 U.S. 68, 105 S.Ct. 1087 (1985).

issue, the state will not be able to deny such assistance on the ground of financial burden. Some of Justice Marshall's language is quite sweeping: "We recognized long ago that mere access to the courthouse doors does not by itself assure a proper functioning of the adversary process, and that a criminal trial is fundamentally unfair if the State proceeds against an indigent defendant without making certain that he has access to the raw materials integral to the building of an effective defense." Consistent with this language, the Court emphasized in *McWilliams v. Dunn*[121] that "*Ake* requires more than just an examination. It requires that the State provide the defense with 'access to a competent psychiatrist who will conduct an appropriate [1] examination and assist in [2] evaluation, [3] preparation, and [4] presentation of the defense.'" Thus, even though McWilliams, convicted of capital murder, was able to procure state-paid neuropsychological testing before his sentencing, *Ake* was violated because the trial court rejected a request for a second expert to interpret the test, assist with preparing a defense strategy, and testify at trial.

On the other hand, the Court specifically limited its holding to the provision of *one* psychiatrist for the defendant; it also stated, consistent with its right to counsel holdings, that it did not mean "that the indigent defendant has a constitutional right to choose a psychiatrist of his personal liking or to receive funds to hire his own." Thus, assuming the appropriate showing by the defendant, the state may be able to satisfy *Ake* by providing the defendant with one *state-employed* expert, so long as that expert is not so closely tied to the prosecution that his "neutrality" is questionable. Furthermore, it is unlikely that a defendant will be entitled to an expert in non-psychiatric fields, state-employed or otherwise, merely upon a showing that the expert's area of competence will be a "significant factor" in his case.[122] Rather, like the federal statute described above, the courts will probably impose a requirement that the defendant show a "particularized need" for the expertise in question. For instance, merely because ballistics testimony will be pivotal in a case does not necessarily mean that the defendant is entitled to a ballistics expert. A court may well find that the state's experts can be trusted to arrive at generally accurate conclusions, and that cross-examination will adequately expose any possible inadequacies in their testimony.[123]

Perhaps relevant to the constitutional issue is the Court's interpretation of the federal statute that provides indigent defendants with funds for experts and investigators. Analogous to the general provision in 18 U.S.C. § 3007(e)(1), noted earlier, that authorizes funds for services "necessary to an adequate defense," 18 U.S.C. § 3599(a) authorizes federal courts to provide funding to a party who is facing a death sentence and is "financially unable to obtain adequate representation or investigative, expert, or other reasonably necessary services." In *Ayestas v. Davis*,[124] the Court had occasion to interpret this language in a case in which the Fifth Circuit had held that, at least in habeas cases, the defendant must show both a "substantial need" for services and "a viable constitutional claim that is not procedurally barred." The Court held that this standard was too demanding because "substantial need" suggests a greater burden

---

[121]   ___ U.S. ___, 137 S.Ct. 1790 (2017).

[122]   Indeed, a number of courts have held that even obtaining a psychiatrist requires a greater showing, perhaps fearful that experts would contribute to speculative defenses. See, e.g., *Clark v. Dugger*, 834 F.2d 1561 (11th Cir. 1987); *Sabiar v. State*, 526 So.2d 661 (Ala.Crim.App. 1988).

[123]   See, e.g., *Moore v. Kemp*, 809 F.2d 702 (11th Cir. 1987) (en banc) (defendant not entitled to expert to review tests performed by state crime lab).

[124]   ___ U.S. ___, 138 S.Ct. 1080 (2018).

that "reasonably necessary," and because it suggested that the defendant must prove that he will win if the services are provided. However, the Court left open the possibility that funding could never be reasonably necessary for a procedurally defaulted claim.

31.07   Reimbursement of Defense Fees

Many states require convicted indigent defendants to reimburse the state for the costs of their legal defense if they become financially able to make such reimbursement. While the Court has held that such programs may not discriminate arbitrarily against particular offenders or groups of offenders, it has refused to invalidate them altogether.

Rinaldi v. Yeager[125] involved a New Jersey statute that required unsuccessful criminal appellants who were incarcerated to reimburse the state, to the extent possible, for expenses incurred in providing trial transcripts. The statute was attacked as a violation of *Griffin v. Illinois*,[126] because forcing the indigent to pay for the cost of a transcript chilled his right to appeal while the rich defendant would not be so discouraged. The Supreme Court struck down the statute, but not on this ground; rather it held that applying the statute only to incarcerated defendants but not to those on probation or suspended sentence constituted invidious discrimination in violation of equal protection principles.

James v. Strange[127] involved a Kansas statute permitting the state to recover attorney's fees and other legal defense costs expended for the benefit of indigent defendants. Any debt incurred under the statute became a lien on the real estate of the defendant and could be executed by garnishment or any other statutory method. The indigent defendant was not, however, accorded the same limitations on wage garnishment and other exemptions afforded other civil judgment debtors. The district court invalidated the statute on the grounds that it "needlessly encourages indigents to do without counsel and consequently infringes on the right to counsel as explicated in *Gideon v. Wainwright*." The Supreme Court again affirmed on different grounds, holding that, by depriving indigent defendants of the protective exemptions enjoyed by other civil judgment debtors, the state had violated the Equal Protection Clause.

In *Fuller v. Oregon,*[128] the Court finally squarely addressed the constitutionality of a recoupment statute that requires reimbursement of legal expenses by indigent defendants who are found guilty and are later able to repay. In *Fuller,* appointed counsel represented the defendant on his guilty plea and at other court proceedings. The defendant was sentenced to five years probation, conditioned upon compliance with the requirements of a work-release program and upon reimbursement to the county for the fees of the attorney and an investigator. The Court held the Oregon scheme did not violate equal protection principles because the convicted defendant from whom reimbursement was sought was accorded all the exemptions enjoyed by other judgment debtors and because remission was allowed in the case of manifest hardship. The Court refused to invalidate the statute because of its distinction between those defendants ultimately convicted and those acquitted. This distinction, stated the Court, "reflects no more than an effort to achieve elemental fairness and is a far cry from . . . invidious discrimination. . . ." The opinion stressed the serious imposition by society upon a

---

[125]   384 U.S. 305, 86 S.Ct. 1497 (1966).

[126]   351 U.S. 12, 76 S.Ct. 585 (1956), discussed in § 29.02(a).

[127]   407 U.S. 128, 92 S.Ct. 2027 (1972).

[128]   417 U.S. 40, 94 S.Ct. 2116 (1974).

defendant who is forced to submit to a prosecution that results in acquittal. The effort to make up for the imposition by releasing acquitted defendants from reimbursement liability met the constitutional standard of objective rationality.

Fuller also rejected the argument that the recoupment scheme infringed on the defendant's right to counsel. As in *Strange,* the appellant had argued that knowledge that he might be required to repay the expenses of his defense might encourage him to decline the services of an appointed attorney and thus chill his exercise of his constitutional right to counsel. In rejecting that contention, the Court reasoned that the Oregon statute was carefully tailored to impose an obligation only upon those who actually become capable of repaying the government without hardship. The Court further observed that a defendant who is just above the indigency line must often make substantial financial sacrifices to retain a lawyer: "We cannot say that the Constitution requires that those only slightly poorer must remain forever immune from any obligation to shoulder the expenses of their legal defense, even when they are able to pay without hardship."

31.08   Conclusion

The several aspects of the right to counsel discussed in this chapter can be summarized as follows:

(1)   Under the Sixth Amendment, a criminal defendant has the right to counsel at any criminal trial that actually results in the loss of liberty or that results in a suspended sentence of imprisonment that can be imposed at some later point in time.

(2)   The right to counsel at other stages of the criminal process is governed by several different constitutional provisions. Those stages considered part of the criminal prosecution (i.e., from formal charging through sentencing) are governed by the Sixth Amendment, which today appears to require counsel only at those stages: (a) that involve a trial-like confrontation involving the prosecutor and the intricacies of the law; and (b) that can cause substantial prejudice to defendant's rights which counsel can help avoid. Until 1973 only the latter showing was required. Applying one or both of these standards, the Court has found that there is a right to counsel at post-charging lineups, preliminary hearings to determine probable cause, guilty plea arraignments, and sentencing, but not at handwriting samplings, photo array identifications, preliminary hearings to determine probable cause to detain, and psychiatric evaluations.

For stages not considered part of the criminal prosecution, the Court has employed either Fifth Amendment, due process, or equal protection analysis. Under the Fifth Amendment, there is a right to counsel at all custodial interrogations. Under the Due Process and Equal Protection Clauses, there is a right to counsel at appeals as of right. Under the Due Process Clause, there is a right to counsel at discretionary appeals that are functionally equivalent to appeals as of right (such as appeals of guilty pleas), and a limited right to counsel (depending upon the complexity of the issues and the defendant's capacities) at parole and probation revocation proceedings. Except perhaps in extraordinary circumstances (such as a capital case), there is no right to counsel at discretionary appeals that occur after direct review or on petitions for collateral review.

(3)   The defendant has a Sixth Amendment right to represent himself if (a) he validly waives the right to counsel and (b) in those cases where he goes to trial rather than pleads guilty, he can carry out basic trial tasks. A waiver of the right to counsel is

valid if the defendant meets the criteria for competency to stand trial and makes a knowing and voluntary decision to relinquish counsel by demonstrating actual awareness that he will be representing himself and what that entails. To meet the basic trial tasks standard, a defendant probably needs to be able to communicate coherently in the courtroom but need not demonstrate technical knowledge of trial rules and procedures. At the same time, the trial court may appoint standby counsel to assist the defendant; such counsel may participate in the case, even over the defendant's objection, so long as the defendant retains actual control over the case presented to the jury and the jury retains the perception that he represents himself.

(4)   An indigent defendant is not entitled to any particular attorney. A non-indigent defendant's choice of attorney may constitutionally be limited by: (a) conflict of interest considerations; (b) attorney qualification rules; or (c) forfeiture statutes that operate to deprive him of resources to pay for the attorney of his choice (although confiscation of untainted funds that works to deprive the defendant of the ability to pay for any attorney is not permitted).

(5)   An indigent defendant has the right, under the Due Process Clause, to psychiatric consultation whenever he can show that his sanity or dangerousness is likely to be a significant factor at trial. However, the defendant is entitled to only one psychiatrist for such evaluations, and he is not necessarily entitled to the psychiatrist of his choice. Whether other types of expert assistance need be provided by the state may depend upon a number of factors, including (a) whether experts normally play a pivotal role in the resolution of the issue on which the defendant seeks expert assistance and (b) whether the alternatives to providing the defendant with expert assistance—e.g., cross-examination of the state's experts—provide adequate expertise to the defendant.

(6)   The state may require indigent defendants to reimburse the state for the costs of their legal defense once they become financially able to do so, so long as the reimbursement statute does not discriminate arbitrarily against particular defendants or groups of defendants. Requiring defendants who are convicted to reimburse the state while relieving those who are acquitted from this obligation does not constitute such arbitrary discrimination.

BIBLIOGRAPHY

Anderson, Helen A. Penalizing Poverty: Making Defendants Pay Their Court Appointed Counsel Through Recoupment and Contribution. 41 Mich. J. L. Ref. 323 (2009).

Anderson, James M. and Paul Heaton. How Much Difference Does the Lawyer Make? The Effect of Defense Counsel on Murder Case Outcomes. 122 Yale L.J. 154 (2012).

Backus, Mary Sue. The Right to Counsel in Criminal Cases: A National Crisis. 57 Hastings L.J. 1031 (2006).

Bailey, Carlton. *Ake v. Oklahoma* and an Indigent Defendant's "Right" to an Expert Witness: A Promise Denied or Imagined? 10 Wm. & Mary Bill Rts. J. 401 (2002).

Baxter, Heather. *Gideon*'s Ghost: Providing the Sixth Amendment Right to Counsel in Times of Budgetary Crisis. 2010 Mich. St. L. Rev. 341.

Berger, Vivian O. The Supreme Court and Defense Counsel: Old Roads, New Paths—A Dead End? 86 Colum.L.Rev. 9 (1986).

Bibas, Stephanos. Shrinking *Gideon* and Expanding Alternatives to Lawyers. 70 Wash. & Lee L. Rev. 1287 (2013).

Chin, Gabriel J. and Scott C. Wells. Can A Reasonable Doubt Have an Unreasonable Price? Limitations on Attorneys' Fees in Criminal Cases. 41 B.C.L.Rev. 1 (1999).

Chused, Richard H. *Faretta* and the Personal Defense. The Role of a Represented Defendant in Trial Tactics. 65 Cal.L.Rev. 636 (1977).

Cleary, John J. Federal Defender Services: Serving the System or the Client? 58 Law & Contemp. Probs. 65 (1995).

Colbert, Douglas. Prosecution Without Representation. 59 Buff. L. Rev. 333 (2011).

Colquitt, Joseph A. Hybrid Representation: Standing the Two-Sided Coin on Its Edge. 38 Wake Forest L.Rev. 55 (2003).

Costello, Margaret A. Fulfilling the Unfulfilled Promise of *Gideon*: Litigation as a Viable Strategic Tool. 99 Iowa L. Rev. 1951 (2014).

Drinan, Cara H. Getting Real about *Gideon*: The Next Fifty Years of Enforcing the Right to Counsel. 70 Wash. & Lee L. Rev. 1309 (2013).

_____. The Revitalization of *Ake*: A Capital Defendant's Right to Effective Assistance. 60 Okla. L. Rev. 283 (2009).

Duke, Steven B. The Right to Appointed Counsel: *Argersinger* and Beyond. 12 Am.Crim.L.Rev. 601 (1975).

Etienne, Margareth. The Declining Utility of the Right to Counsel in Federal Criminal Courts: An Empirical Study of the Diminished Role of Defense Attorney Advocacy under the Sentencing Guidelines. 92 Cal. L. Rev. 425 (2004).

Freedman, Eric. M. *Giarratano* is a Scarecrow: The Right to Counsel in State Capital Post-Conviction Proceedings. 91 Cornell L.Rev. 1079 (2006).

Genego, William. The New Adversary. 54 Brooklyn L.Rev. 781 (1988).

Gianelli, Paul. *Ake v. Oklahoma*: The Right to Expert Assistance in a Post-Daubert, Post-DNA World. 89 Cornell L.Rev. 1305 (2004).

Green, Bruce A. "Through a Glass, Darkly": How the Court Sees Motions to Disqualify Criminal Defense Lawyers. 89 Colum. L.Rev. 1201 (1989).

Herman, Lawrence and Charles A. Thompson. *Scott v. Illinois* and the Right to Counsel: A Decision in Search of a Doctrine? 17 Am.Crim.L.Rev. 71 (1979).

Lewis, Anthony. Gideon's Trumpet (1964).

Marcus, Paul. Why the United States Supreme Court Got Some (But Not a Lot) of the Sixth Amendment Right to Counsel Analysis Right. 21 St. Thomas L. Rev. 142 (2009).

Mayeux, Sara. What *Gideon* Did. 116 Colum. L. Rev. 15 (2016).

Metzger, Pamela. Beyond the Bright Line: A Contemporary Right-to-Counsel Doctrine. 97 Nw.U.L.Rev. 1635 (2003).

Moskovitz. Myron. Advising the Pro Se Defendant: The Trial Court's Duties Under *Faretta*. 42 Brandeis L.Rev. 329 (2003/04).

Poulin, Anne Bowen. The Role of Standby Counsel in Criminal Cases: In the Twilight Zone of the Criminal Justice System. 75 N.Y.U.L.Rev. 676 (2000).

Primus, Eve Brensike. A Structural Vision of Habeas Corpus. 98 Cal. L. Rev. 1 (2010).

Ribstein, Sarah. A Question of Costs: Considering Pressure on White Collar Criminal Defendants. 58 Duke L.J. 857 (2009).

Schulhofer, Stephen J. and David D. Friedman. Rethinking Indigent Defense: Promoting Effective Representation Through Consumer Sovereignty and Freedom of Choice for All Criminal Defendants. 31 Am. Crim. L. Rev. 73 (1993).

Slobogin, Christopher. Mental Illness and Self-Representation: *Faretta*, *Godinez* and *Edwards*. 7 Ohio St. J. Crim. L. 391 (2009).

Tague, Peter. Ensuring Able Representation for Publicly-Funded Criminal Defendants: Lessons from England. 69 U.Cin.L.Rev. 273 (2000).

Winick, Bruce. Forfeiture of Attorney's Fees Under RICO and CCE and the Right to Counsel of Choice. 43 U.Miami L.Rev. 763 (1989).

Chapter 32

EFFECTIVE ASSISTANCE OF COUNSEL

32.01   Introduction

The right to counsel is empty unless counsel adequately represent their clients. An attorney who does not investigate the factual basis of his client's charges, assert the relevant defenses, or attempt to cross-examine witnesses at trial can hardly be said to provide "counsel" at all. Following this reasoning, courts have interpreted the Sixth Amendment to prohibit "ineffective" counsel, that is, attorney conduct that fails to provide "assistance" to the accused as required by the Right to Counsel Clause. Ineffective assistance claims are not malpractice actions; they cannot result in money damages payable by the attorney. Rather, the remedy for failing to abide by the demands of the Sixth Amendment is reversal of the conviction resulting from ineffective assistance.

At least three phenomena have led to a vast increase in ineffective assistance claims since the early 1960's. First, the Supreme Court's announcement in *Gideon v. Wainwright*[1] that the Sixth Amendment right to counsel is applicable to all state felony prosecutions predictably resulted in a proliferation of such claims. Compounding this increase was the simultaneous rise of the public defender movement, which relied primarily upon young and inexperienced practitioners.[2] A final factor that has stimulated ineffective assistance claims has been the Supreme Court's efforts to limit habeas corpus actions. As detailed elsewhere in this book, the Court has significantly curbed the ability of federal habeas courts to declare "new rules,"[3] to rule on *any* Fourth Amendment claim,[4] and to grant post-conviction relief on constitutional claims that were not raised at trial.[5] When a habeas petition is denied on any of these grounds, the only alternative remaining to the aggrieved prisoner is to claim that his counsel did not effectively deal with the alleged constitutional violation before or during trial.

Thus, despite attempts to narrow its scope, the right to effective assistance of counsel has become an issue of substantial concern. This chapter discusses when the right applies, past and present standards defining the right, and ways of improving representation by defense counsel.

32.02   When the Right Applies

(a)   Linkage to Right to Counsel

The right to effective assistance of counsel is linked to the right to counsel. Only when the right to counsel attaches is there a constitutionally-based right to effective assistance. Thus, in *Wainwright v. Torna*,[6] the Supreme Court held that failure to make a timely application for a discretionary appeal could not constitute ineffective assistance

---

[1]   372 U.S. 335, 83 S.Ct. 792 (1963).

[2]   See generally, Joel Jay Finer *Ineffective Assistance of Counsel*, 58 Cornell L.Rev. 1077 (1973).

[3]   See *Teague v. Lane,* 489 U.S. 288, 109 S.Ct. 1060 (1989), discussed in § 33.03(c).

[4]   See *Stone v. Powell,* 428 U.S. 465, 96 S.Ct. 3037 (1976), discussed in § 33.02(b)(1).

[5]   *Wainwright v. Sykes,* 433 U.S. 72, 97 S.Ct. 2497 (1977), discussed in § 33.03(c).

[6]   455 U.S. 586, 102 S.Ct. 1300 (1982).

of counsel, since there is no right to counsel at discretionary appeals.[7] Similarly, in *Pennsylvania v. Finley,*[8] the Court first concluded that there is no right to counsel at state post-conviction proceedings and then held that, given this finding, no claim of ineffective assistance of counsel can be made in connection with such proceedings.

In contrast, there clearly is a right to effective assistance of counsel at trial, sentencing, appeals as of right and other settings in which the right to counsel attaches.[9] Furthermore, the Court has held that when a claim, such as claim of ineffective trial counsel, cannot be raised until the post-conviction process, either by law or as a practical matter, then a failure by counsel to raise it at that proceeding may constitute ineffective assistance for purposes of demonstrating cause in habeas proceedings. This complicated notion is discussed further in the chapter on habeas.[10]

(b) Retained Counsel

If there is a right to counsel at the proceeding in question, then the right to effective assistance does not vary depending upon whether counsel is retained or appointed. For some time, most courts held otherwise, on one of two theories. According to some courts, if defense counsel was privately retained the defendant was held to be estopped from asserting a claim of ineffective assistance because he was bound, on an agency rationale, by the conduct of the attorney whom he employed. The prevailing theory was explained by the Supreme Court of California in *People v. Stevens.*[11] Rejecting a claim that a mistrial should have been declared because of the alleged gross incompetence of the defendant's retained attorney, the court observed: "If there was any error in this regard, it was merely an error of judgment on the part of the defendant in the selection of counsel to represent him." Courts also rejected claims of ineffective assistance of retained counsel on the ground that there was no "state action" depriving the defendant of life or liberty without due process of law. In the words of the First Circuit in *Farrell v. Lanagan:*[12]

> The petitioner's claim that his counsel was so inadequate as to constitute . . . [a] violation of his constitutional rights is . . . not borne out. Counsel was selected and paid for by the petitioner's family, and accepted by him. [E]ven if incompetency of counsel so selected be assumed, it would not follow from that that the state deprived petitioner of any constitutional right in his trial and conviction.

In *Cuyler v. Sullivan,*[13] however, the Supreme Court firmly held that the performance of the retained attorney is to be judged by the same standards as the conduct of the appointed attorney. In doing so, it quickly dispensed with the absence of state action argument:

> The vital guarantee of the Sixth Amendment would stand for little if the often uninformed decision to retain a particular lawyer could reduce or forfeit the defendant's entitlement to constitutional protection. Since the State's conduct of a criminal trial itself implicates the State in the defendant's conviction, we

---

[7]   See *Ross v. Moffitt,* 417 U.S. 600, 94 S.Ct. 2437 (1974), discussed in § 31.03(c)(3).

[8]   481 U.S. 551, 107 S.Ct. 1990 (1987), discussed in § 31.03(c)(4).

[9]   See § 31.03.

[10]   See § 33.03(d)(3).

[11]   5 Cal.2d 92, 53 P.2d 133 (1935).

[12]   166 F.2d 845 (1st Cir. 1948). See also *Dusseldorf v. Teets,* 209 F.2d 754 (9th Cir. 1954).

[13]   446 U.S. 335, 100 S.Ct. 1708 (1980).

see no basis for drawing a distinction between retained and appointed counsel that would deny equal justice to defendants who must choose their own lawyers.

Although *Cuyler* did not directly debunk the agency argument, its holding has led the lower courts to reject that rationale as well and find that, for purposes of ineffective assistance claims, there is no distinction between retained and appointed counsel.[14] The fallacy of the agency analogy is easily exposed. Agency theory presupposes a principal capable of supervising the agent. Yet the assumption underlying the Court's right to counsel decisions is that the person accused of a crime engages counsel to conduct his defense because he is not able to defend himself. Presumably, such a person is *not* in a position to guide and control the conduct of his lawyer. Moreover, agency theory developed primarily as a means of compensating innocent third parties for the actions of a principal's agent. In the counsel context, there is no innocent third party who will benefit from making the defendant liable for his attorney's incompetence.[15]

32.03   The Substantive Standard

(a) Differing Approaches in the Lower Courts

Until the 1960s, most courts rejected an ineffective assistance of counsel claim unless counsel's efforts were so incompetent as to render the trial "a farce or mockery of justice."[16] On its face, this standard put an unduly heavy burden on the defendant. Moreover, the "farce and mockery" standard was extremely vague, and seemed unfair in light of the more exacting requirements demanded of other professions.

Beginning in the early 1960's, most courts attempted to articulate a more rigorous standard. For instance, the United States Court of Appeals for the District of Columbia held that the appropriate test for ineffective assistance of counsel is whether gross incompetence "blotted out the essence of a substantial defense."[17] Other courts adopted a malpractice-type standard. The Third Circuit, in *Moore v. United States*,[18] declared: "The standard of the adequacy of legal services as in other professions is the exercise of the customary skill and knowledge which normally prevails at the time and place." Still other courts, finding *Moore's* test too demanding (on the ground that performance that falls below the norm is not necessarily negligent or incompetent), adopted variations on the notion of "reasonable" competence.[19] Under each of these tests, the defendant also had to show that any incompetence was detrimental to his case.

Although these attempts at clarifying the definition of ineffective assistance improved upon the old farce and mockery test, they too were ambiguous and, in the

---

[14]   See e.g., *Scott v. Wainwright,* 698 F.2d 427 (11th Cir. 1983); *Perez v. Wainwright,* 640 F.2d 596 (5th Cir. 1981).

[15]   Jon R. Waltz, *Inadequacy of Trial Defense Representation as a Ground for Post-Conviction Relief in Criminal Cases,* 59 Nw.U.L.Rev. 289, 297 (1964).

[16]   See, e.g., *Edwards v. United States,* 103 U.S.App.D.C. 152, 256 F.2d 707 (1958), cert. denied 358 U.S. 847, 79 S.Ct. 74 (1958).

[17]   *Scott v. United States,* 427 F.2d 609 (D.C.Cir. 1970).

[18]   432 F.2d 730, 736 (3d Cir. 1970).

[19]   See, e.g., *Cooper v. Fitzharris,* 586 F.2d 1325 (9th Cir. 1978) ("reasonably competent attorney acting as a diligent conscientious advocate"); *United States v. Easter,* 539 F.2d 663 (8th Cir. 1976) ("customary skills and diligence that a reasonably competent attorney would perform under similar circumstances"); *Beasley v. United States,* 491 F.2d 687 (6th Cir. 1974) ("counsel reasonably likely to render and rendering reasonably effective assistance").

words of one judge, provided the courts with little more than a "semantic merry-go-round."[20] Recognizing this problem, Judge Bazelon, in his opinion for the D.C. Circuit Court of Appeals in *United States v. Decoster (Decoster I)*,[21] borrowed from the American Bar Association's Standards for the Defense Function in an attempt to define more succinctly some of the duties counsel owes his client. Based on the Standards, Bazelon concluded, for instance, that "[c]ounsel should confer with his client without delay and as often as necessary to elicit matters of defense, or to ascertain that potential defenses are unavailable." In addition, "[c]ounsel should promptly advise his client of his rights and take all actions necessary to preserve them." Failure to perform functions such as these did not automatically lead to a finding of ineffective assistance. Rather the defendant first had to show that any violation of these standards was "substantial," which required showing that the violation was egregious or repeated. Secondly, the prosecution was given an opportunity to establish that the defendant was not prejudiced by the violation. But, taken as a whole, the definition of ineffective assistance in *Decoster I* was not only more refined, but more stringent, than earlier definitions. As Judge Bazelon later stated,[22] the approach taken in *Decoster I* "gave content to what previously had been empty verbal formulations."

Greater clarity for attorneys and judges was not the only purpose behind the *Decoster I* standard. According to Bazelon's subsequent characterization of it, this standard was meant to focus on the "quality of counsel's performance rather than looking to the effect of counsel's actions on the outcome of the case," a perspective that had two advantages. First, it would go further toward eliminating "second-class justice for the poor," because it would "proscribe second-class performances by counsel, whatever the consequences in a particular case." Second, it would "reduce[ ] the likelihood that any particular defendant will be prejudiced by counsel's shortcomings," and thus reduce the need to engage in "the inherently difficult task of speculating about the precise effect of each error or omission by an attorney." Although the prejudice inquiry would still be made when error was found, the prosecution bore the burden of showing a lack of prejudice. Furthermore, this inquiry would be "distinct from the determination of whether the defendant has received effective assistance," and "considered only in order to spare defendants, prosecutors and the courts alike a truly futile repetition of the pretrial and trial process."

Ultimately, however, Judge Bazelon's approach did not find favor in the lower courts, or even in his own court. *Decoster I* was overruled three years after it was decided. In *United States v. Decoster (Decoster III)*,[23] the majority intentionally avoided setting forth *any* definitive standards beyond requiring a finding of "serious incompetency," on the ground that it is impossible to define "effectiveness" without reference to the facts of the specific case. As Judge Leventhal wrote:

> [The court] must be wary lest its inquiry and standards undercut the sensitive relationship between attorney and client and tear the fabric of the adversary system. A defense counsel's representation of a client encompasses an almost

---

[20]   *Cooper v. Fitzharris,* 551 F.2d 1162 (9th Cir. 1977) (Duniway, J., concurring), vacated 586 F.2d 1325 (9th Cir. 1978) (en banc).

[21]   487 F.2d 1197 (D.C.Cir. 1973).

[22]   *United States v. Decoster (Decoster III)*, 624 F.2d 196 (D.C.Cir. 1976) (Bazelon, J., dissenting).

[23]   624 F.2d 196 (D.C.Cir. 1976).

infinite variety of situations that call for the exercise of professional judgment. . . .

Leventhal offered several reasons in favor of rejecting what he called the "categorical" approach in favor of a flexible "judgmental" approach. The latter approach "preserves the freedom of counsel to make quick judgments," at the same time it deters intentional inadequacy as a means of obtaining reversal in a weak case. The judgmental approach also "avoids the possibility that there will be frequent and wide-ranging inquiries into the information and reasoning that prompted counsel to pursue a given course." Such inquiries are problematic not only because they might inhibit counsel's behavior, but because they are time-consuming and may require revelation of attorney-client discussions. Furthermore, in an effort to avoid the post-trial reviews the categorical approach would require, the court and perhaps even the prosecution might feel the need to monitor defense attorneys' behavior, not only during trial but during the pre-trial process. In short, "[e]fforts to improve the performance of defense counsel should not imperil [the] protection [of the adversary system]." The *Decoster III* court also required, contrary to *Decoster I* but in line with the majority stance, that the *defendant* show that any alleged ineffective assistance prejudiced his defense.

(b) The Supreme Court's Approach

Until 1984 the United States Supreme Court provided the lower courts with very little guidance on the ineffective assistance of counsel issue. The one decision in which it made any type of generalized pronouncement prior to that time was in the narrow context of representation during the pleading process. In *McMann v. Richardson*,[24] a 1970 decision, the Court stated that an attorney's performance at the guilty plea stage was effective so long as the advice he rendered was "within the range of competence demanded of attorneys in criminal cases." Arguably, this standard is an exacting one, since the measuring stick it establishes is not attorney performance generally, but the performance of attorneys in *criminal cases.* But for fourteen years the Court did little to elucidate this language,[25] with the result that the lower courts continued to debate the appropriate ineffective assistance standard.

When the Court finally did make its first direct statement on the scope of the ineffective assistance doctrine, it opted for a "judgmental" approach similar to that taken in *Decoster III*, by a margin of 8–1. At several points in *Strickland v. Washington*,[26] the Court echoed Judge Leventhal's rejection of "mechanical rules" as a means of defining the Sixth Amendment. It also held, as had *Decoster III*, that, except in a few types of cases where prejudice is presumed, the defendant bears the burden on this issue. Thus, Justice O'Connor, in her majority opinion, set forth a test with two components:

> First, the defendant must show that counsel's performance was deficient. This requires showing that counsel made errors so serious that counsel was not functioning as the "counsel" guaranteed the defendant by the Sixth Amendment. Second, the defendant must show that the deficient performance prejudiced the defense. This requires showing that counsel's errors were so

---

[24]   397 U.S. 759, 90 S.Ct. 1441 (1970).

[25]   The one significant exception was *Tollett v. Henderson,* 411 U.S. 258, 93 S.Ct. 1602 (1973), discussed in § 32.04(b)(2).

[26]   466 U.S. 668, 104 S.Ct. 2052 (1984).

serious as to deprive the defendant of a fair trial, a trial whose result is unreliable.

A year later, in *Hill v. Lockhart,*[27] the Court held that *Strickland's* two-prong test also applied to guilty plea cases, although the prejudice prong was defined somewhat differently to require the defendant to show that "there is a reasonable probability that, but for counsel's errors, he would not have pleaded guilty and would have insisted on going to trial."[28] And one year after *Hill,* it applied *Strickland* to appeals as of right.[29]

(1) The Performance Prong

In elaborating on the first prong announced in *Strickland,* Justice O'Connor repeated *McMann's* language and stated that "[t]he proper measure of attorney performance remains simply reasonableness under prevailing professional norms." O'Connor posited three such norms: (1) a duty to avoid conflicts of interest; (2) a duty "to advocate the defendant's cause," which includes the duties "to consult with the defendant on important decisions and to keep the defendant informed of important developments"; and (3) a duty "to bring to bear such skill and knowledge as will render the trial a reliable adversarial testing process." Elsewhere in the opinion she stated that "counsel has a duty to make reasonable investigations or to make a reasonable decision that makes particular investigations unnecessary." This was the extent of the Court's effort to develop guidelines. And in analyzing whether an attorney met these standards, Justice O'Connor wrote, "[j]udicial scrutiny of counsel's performance must be highly deferential." Moreover, "counsel is strongly presumed to have rendered adequate assistance and made all significant decisions in the exercise of reasonable professional judgment."

The Court reasons for this relatively undemanding definition of attorney error were similar to those advanced in *Decoster III.* According to the Court, "[i]ntrusive post-trial inquiry into attorney performance or . . . detailed guidelines for its evaluation would encourage the proliferation of ineffectiveness challenges." Further:

> Criminal trials resolved unfavorably to the defendant would increasingly come to be followed by a second trial, this one of counsel's unsuccessful defense. Counsel's performance and even willingness to serve could be adversely affected. Intensive scrutiny of counsel and rigid requirements for acceptable assistance could dampen the ardor and impair the independence of defense counsel, discourage the acceptance of assigned cases, and undermine the trust between attorney and client.

Although the Court has thus refused to develop rigid guidelines for attorneys, it has suggested that conduct that is ethical under the professional codes of responsibility cannot be error for purposes of the Sixth Amendment. In *Nix v. Whiteside,*[30] the five-member majority stated that since the attorney's conduct in that case (i.e., threatening to withdraw if the defendant committed perjury) did not breach "any recognized professional duty, it follows that there can be no deprivation of the right to assistance of counsel under the *Strickland* standard." At the same time, the *Nix* majority was quick to state that it was not adopting a categorical approach; a mere breach of an ethical

---

[27] 474 U.S. 52, 106 S.Ct. 366 (1985).

[28] The definition of prejudice caused by error during the plea bargaining process has been further refined since *Hill.* See § 32.04(c)(3).

[29] *Smith v. Murray,* 477 U.S. 527, 106 S.Ct. 2661 (1986).

[30] 475 U.S. 157, 106 S.Ct. 988 (1986), discussed in more detail in § 32.03(b)(3).

canon would not mean the performance prong has been violated. According to the Court, "a court must be careful not to narrow the wide range of conduct acceptable under the Sixth Amendment so restrictively as to constitutionalize particular standards of professional conduct and thereby intrude into the State's proper authority to define and apply the standards of professional conduct applicable to those it admits to practice in its courts."[31]

(2) The Prejudice Prong

With respect to the prejudice prong, the majority in *Strickland* first noted that certain situations are so likely to be prejudicial to the defendant that prejudice is presumed. Here it referred to decisions, discussed in more detail below,[32] which found ineffective assistance in cases involving government rules or rulings that inhibit the functioning of counsel, and conflicts of interest occasioned by dual representation. But in all other situations, the defendant must affirmatively prove that "there is a reasonable probability that, but for counsel's unprofessional errors, the result of the proceeding would have been different." Similar to its generous view of attorney conduct under the performance prong, the Court cautioned that in analyzing the degree of prejudice to the defendant, the court "should presume, absent challenge to the judgment on grounds of evidentiary insufficiency, that the judge or jury acted according to law." In short, the Court's definition of prejudice in those cases where prejudice is not presumed requires the defendant to make a strong showing of "innocence" on either factual or technical "legal" grounds.[33]

In justifying its decision to place the burden on the defendant to prove prejudice rather than on the prosecution to show its absence, the majority reasoned that "[t]he government is not responsible for, and hence not able to prevent, attorney errors that will result in reversal of conviction or sentence." Although this statement is true in the individual case, it is the government which, in the case of indigents, appoints and pays for the attorney; thus, the government's inadequate funding of its legal defense system could be "responsible" for attorney error in an indirect sense. Further, of course, the defendant often has no more control over the attorney than does the government. At the same time, it might be pointed out that the defense is usually in the best position to prove the facts relevant to the prejudice inquiry, and thus should bear the burden on this issue.

With respect to its definition of prejudice, the Court explained that it chose to focus on the error's effect on the outcome of the case because the purpose of the Sixth Amendment's guarantee is "to ensure that a defendant has the assistance necessary to justify reliance on the outcome of the proceeding." Responding to the defendant's proposal to base the prejudice inquiry on whether the error "impaired presentation of the defense," Justice O'Connor stated: "Since any error, if it is indeed an error, 'impairs' the presentation of the defense, the proposed standard is inadequate because it provides no way of deciding what impairments are sufficiently serious to warrant setting aside

---

[31]   The remaining four members of the Court concurred only in the judgment, criticizing in particular the majority's linkage between the rules of professional conduct and proper conduct under the Sixth Amendment.

[32]   See § 32.04(a) & (b).

[33]   Note that in *Kimmelman v. Morrison*, 477 U.S. 365, 106 S.Ct. 2574 (1986), Justice Powell wrote a concurring opinion suggesting that *Strickland's* prejudice prong should be limited solely to cases of factual innocence, an argument which has yet to be squarely addressed by the Court.

the outcome of the proceeding." As this latter statement suggests, under the Court's "judgmental" approach the prejudice inquiry may well determine when a particular act or omission fails to meet the performance prong (e.g., failure to raise a certain defense may be "error" when it results in an unjust conviction, but not "error" when the defense was weak.) This is in distinct contrast to the categorical approach, which attempts to pre-define the type of conduct that is deficient and engages in the prejudice inquiry only after error has been found.

32.04   Application of the Standard

As noted above, *Strickland* outlined three general categories of ineffective assistance claims. The first involved state interference with counsel's ability to represent his client, the second concerned conflicts of interest, and the third included most attorney-produced errors. This section adopts *Strickland's* general organization of the cases.

(a) State Interference Cases

In *Strickland,* the Court stated that "[a]ctual or constructive denial of the assistance of counsel" and "various kinds of state interference with counsel's assistance" are "legally presumed to result in prejudice." The reason for this presumption in state interference cases, according to the majority, is that "prejudice in these circumstances is so likely that case-by-case inquiry into prejudice is not worth the cost." Furthermore, "such circumstances involve impairments of the Sixth Amendment right that are easy to identify and, for that reason and because the prosecution is directly responsible, easy for the government to prevent." It should also be noted that, in contrast to the "categorical" approach criticized by Judge Leventhal in *Decoster III,*[34] a rule that treats government interference as presumptively violative of the Sixth Amendment is not likely to inhibit defense tactics, occasion judicial or prosecutorial monitoring of counsel, or "reward" inept conduct designed to ensure a reversal.

The Court's cases involving state interference can be divided into three categories: (1) denial or late appointment of counsel; (2) obstruction of counsel's performance; and (3) intrusion into the attorney-client relationship. Although prejudice is often presumed in these situations, in each the Court has identified some situations where official intermeddling with the right to counsel does not eliminate the need to inquire into its effect on the defendant's case.

(1) Denial or Late Appointment of Counsel

The clearest example of state action that results in ineffective assistance of counsel is when the government fails to provide or denies counsel at a stage of the proceeding at which the right to counsel attaches.[35] Here, as *Strickland* makes clear, prejudice must be presumed. However, the denial of counsel must be "complete," so that "counsel [is] either totally absent, or prevented from assisting the accused during a critical stage of the proceeding."[36] In *Wright v. Van Patten,*[37] the Court held that permitting counsel to appear by speakerphone at a plea hearing was not so clear a violation of the Sixth

---

[34]   See § 32.03(a).

[35]   See §§ 31.02 and 31.03 for a discussion of when the right attaches.

[36]   *United States v. Cronic*, 466 U.S. 648, 104 S.Ct. 2039 (1984).

[37]   552 U.S. 120, 128 S.Ct. 743 (2008).

Amendment that habeas relief was required, despite the fact that the speakerphone arrangement prevented counsel from observing the demeanor of the client (and thus whether he was confused or resistant to the plea), and allowed everyone in the courtroom to hear conversation between the attorney and the defendant.

A related situation—what *Strickland* labelled "constructive denial" of counsel— occurs when an attorney is appointed at such a belated point in the process that the defendant is, in effect, denied counsel. An example is *Powell v. Alabama,*[38] where the court appointed the entire local bar to assist a lone attorney, appearing for the first time on the day of trial in representing nine defendants. Without bothering to assess counsel's performance at trial, the Court concluded that "such designation of counsel as was attempted was either so indefinite or so close upon the trial as to amount to a denial of effective and substantial aid in that regard."

However, tardy appointment of counsel is not always a violation of the Sixth Amendment. In *Avery v. Alabama,*[39] eight years after *Powell,* the Court upheld a conviction in a capital case when counsel was appointed only three days before trial, on the ground that, despite counsel's statement to the contrary, three days was not unreasonably short under the circumstances. And in *Chambers v. Maroney,*[40] the Court explicitly refused to adopt "a per se rule requiring reversal of every conviction following tardy appointment of counsel," in a case where the late appointment at most prevented counsel from making pretrial suppression motions that would have failed in any event.

Following these decisions, but before *Strickland,* some lower courts had held that a late appointment should establish a presumption of prejudice which the prosecution must overcome.[41] But in *United States v. Cronic,*[42] a companion case to *Strickland,* the Court indicated that the usual late appointment case should be treated no differently than cases in which no state negligence was involved; in other words, the burden of showing prejudice should still be on the defendant. In *Cronic,* the Court refused to find ineffective assistance of counsel when the attorney was allowed only twenty-five days to investigate a case which took the government four-and-one-half years to prepare; the majority concluded that "the period of 25 days . . . is not so short that it even arguably justifies a presumption that no lawyer could provide the respondent with the effective assistance of counsel required by the Constitution." It went on to note that while the government's prolonged investigation was necessary because the check kiting scheme with which the defendant was charged involved banks in several jurisdictions and thousands of documents, the defendant's only defense was the absence of an intent to defraud; viewed in this light, the preparation time allowed did not prejudice the defendant.

A lower court decision that probably summarizes the law on this issue is the pre-*Strickland* case of *Moore v. United States,*[43] where the court stated that "[t]he question necessarily involves a comparison of the time of the appointment with all the attendant circumstances, such as the gravity of the charge, the experience of appointed counsel, the extent of his knowledge and participation in similar cases, his opportunity for

---

[38]　287 U.S. 45, 53 S.Ct. 55 (1932), discussed in § 31.02(a).

[39]　308 U.S. 444, 60 S.Ct. 321 (1940).

[40]　399 U.S. 42, 90 S.Ct. 1975 (1970).

[41]　See, e.g., *Coles v. Peyton,* 389 F.2d 224 (4th Cir. 1968).

[42]　466 U.S. 648, 104 S.Ct. 2039 (1984).

[43]　432 F.2d 730 (3d Cir. 1970).

preparation and even what he may have been told by the defendant which may reduce the area of necessary preparation." *Moore* specifically disapproved an earlier case suggesting that lateness of appointment creates a burden-shifting presumption of inadequate representation,[44] but it also held that untimely appointment of counsel raises a "strong inference of prejudice."

(2) Obstruction of Counsel's Performance

Assuming counsel has been retained or appointed with sufficient time to prepare, there are any number of ways the state can obstruct his effectiveness. The Supreme Court's cases appear to hold that if the obstruction of counsel prevents him from carrying out a well-established prerogative, then prejudice is presumed. On the other hand, other limitations on counsel are subjected to the same analysis as other ineffectiveness claims.

In *Cronic,* the Court listed several decisions that it depicted as cases where prejudice was presumed because of state interference with retained or appointed counsel. *Ferguson v. Georgia,*[45] decided before *Gideon,* held that due process was violated by a state statute barring the defendant from having his testimony elicited by counsel through direct examination. Post-*Gideon* cases cited in *Cronic* were *Brooks v. Tennessee,*[46] which held unconstitutional a statute that restricted counsel's choice of when to put the defendant on the stand; *Herring v. New York,*[47] which struck down a statute giving the judge in a non-jury trial the power to deny defense counsel closing summation; *Davis v. Alaska,*[48] which found the Confrontation Clause violated by a prohibition on defense counsel's attempt to use a juvenile record to impeach a witness; and *Geders v. United States,*[49] which held unconstitutional a judge's order directing a defendant not to consult with his attorney during an overnight recess that fell between direct and cross-examination. In each of these cases, the state action, in *Herring's* words, interfered with "the traditions of the adversary factfinding process," and thus required reversal even when actual prejudice was not shown by the defendant.

Two later cases indicate that the Court is willing to place significant limitations on this analysis, however. In *United States v. Bagley,*[50] the Court refined *Davis* by indicating that where the infringement on counsel's cross-examination results not from a prohibition on using evidence already obtained but from a state refusal to *provide* impeachment evidence, and that refusal is justifiable under the Court's due process analysis in discovery cases,[51] no automatic Sixth Amendment violation occurs. And in *Perry v. Leeke,*[52] which upheld a judge's prohibition on communication between the defendant and his attorney during a 15-minute recess in his testimony, the Court distinguished *Geders* by noting that the overnight gag order there could have prevented discussion of "matters that the defendant [has] a constitutional right to discuss with his lawyer," such as overall strategy. In *Leeke,* on the other hand, there was "a virtual

---

[44] See *United States ex rel. Mathis v. Rundle,* 394 F.2d 748 (3d Cir. 1968).

[45] 365 U.S. 570, 81 S.Ct. 756 (1961).

[46] 406 U.S. 605, 92 S.Ct. 1891 (1972), discussed in § 24.02(a)(2).

[47] 422 U.S. 853, 95 S.Ct. 2550 (1975).

[48] 415 U.S. 308, 94 S.Ct. 1105 (1974).

[49] 425 U.S. 80, 96 S.Ct. 1330 (1976).

[50] 473 U.S. 667, 105 S.Ct. 3375 (1985), discussed in § 28.05(b)(1).

[51] As *Bagley* also held, the prosecution need disclose only "exculpatory" information, i.e., information that will have a "reasonable probability" of changing the "result of the proceeding." See § 24.04(b).

[52] 488 U.S. 272, 109 S.Ct. 594 (1989).

certainty that any conversation between the witness and the lawyer would relate to ongoing testimony;" thus, the order in that case treated the defendant like any other witness (in light of the traditional rule that witnesses are not permitted to talk to others during testimony), and should not lead to a presumption of prejudice.

(3) Intrusion into the Attorney-Client Relationship

Several cases involve government eavesdropping on attorney-client conversations through the use of undercover agents or other devices. It appears to be established, as *Strickland* suggested, that the government may not use information gained in such exchanges against the defendant.[53] But if the government avoids using such information, then the invasion, by itself, probably does not violate the Sixth Amendment unless some other type of prejudice is shown. In effect, barring such prejudice, the state has not actually "interfered" with the defense's case.

In *Weatherford v. Bursey*,[54] an undercover police officer had been arrested with the defendant for vandalizing a selective service office. Trying to maintain his undercover stature, the officer met with the defendant and his attorney at two strategy sessions, at the defendant's request. He also told the defendant that he would not testify at the defendant's trial, apparently in the honest belief that he would continue to be undercover. At the time of trial, however, his value as an agent had diminished and he was called by the prosecution to testify as to his undercover activities and the events on the day of the vandalizing. Emphasizing that the agent had not testified about the attorney-client conversations and that none of the state's evidence or strategy was based on those conversations, the Court held that no per se violation of the Sixth Amendment right to counsel occurred. The defendant's desire for private conversations with his attorney, by itself, did not outweigh the state's need to protect the identity of its agents who might need to be present at attorney-client meetings to maintain their cover.

In *United States v. Morrison*[55] the Court suggested that it would reach the same result, at least functionally, even when a state intrusion does not result from the need to prevent the "unmasking" of an agent. In *Morrison,* the agent gratuitously met with the defendant and disparaged defense counsel. The Court assumed, without deciding, that this action was a violation of the Sixth Amendment. But it went on to hold that the lower court's dismissal of the charge against the defendant, with prejudice, was not warranted, given the absence of any showing that the agent's contact with the defendant prejudiced representation of her case.[56]

(b) Conflict of Interests Cases

The second category of ineffective assistance claims identified in *Strickland* involves conflicts between the attorney's and the client's interests. Such conflicts can stem from an attorney's attempt to represent more than one co-defendant in the same trial, the attorney's prior representation of a prosecution witness in the current trial, the fact that

---

[53]   See, e.g., *O'Brien v. United States,* 386 U.S. 345, 87 S.Ct. 1158 (1967).

[54]   429 U.S. 545, 97 S.Ct. 837 (1977).

[55]   449 U.S. 361, 101 S.Ct. 665 (1981).

[56]   The lower courts are divided on the issue, with some still finding a per se violation when the prosecution "improperly" obtains information relating to a confidential defense strategy, see, e.g., *United States v. Costanzo,* 740 F.2d 251 (3d Cir. 1984); others requiring the prosecution to show no prejudice, see, e.g., *United States v. Mastroianni,* 749 F.2d 900 (1st Cir. 1984); and others requiring the defense to show prejudice, see, e.g., *United States v. Irwin,* 612 F.2d 1182 (9th Cir. 1980).

the attorney's fee is coming from a third party, an attorney's contract with a publishing company for the defendant's story, and a host of other situations, most of which are dealt with by the professional codes of conduct.[57]

The Court has held that, as with state interference cases, cases where such conflict is shown often do not require a showing of prejudice in order to implicate the Sixth Amendment. Again, *Strickland* provides the Court's best summary of its reasons for this rule. First, "the duty of loyalty [is] perhaps the most basic of counsel's duties." Second, "it is difficult to measure the precise effect on the defense of representation corrupted by conflicting interests." Third, and perhaps most importantly, the courts have the "ability . . . to make early inquiry in certain situations likely to give rise to conflicts" and thus avoid them. When the court fails to avert obvious conflicts, in a sense the state is once again "interfering" with the defendant's right to counsel.

Even so, as with cases involving direct state interference with counsel, an irrebuttable presumption of prejudice is not ironclad in conflicts cases. For the presumption to operate, it must be shown that the trial court should have detected the potential for conflict prior to trial. If the latter showing is not made, then an ineffective assistance claim will succeed only if there is proof that an "actual" conflict "adversely affected" the lawyer's performance, a standard that appears to come close to requiring a showing of prejudice. Further, the presumption does not operate unless the conflict is between "legitimate" interests. These principles are discussed here. Also examined is the somewhat countervailing notion of whether a defendant can waive his right to conflict-free counsel.

(1) The Judicial Notice Requirement

In *Glasser v. United States*,[58] the trial court had insisted that the same attorney represent co-defendants in a conspiracy prosecution. In evaluating the case, the Court did not require a specific showing of prejudice, but only proof that the accused's defense was rendered less effective by the joint appointment than it would have been had the defendants had separate attorneys. This threshold was met by a showing that arguably inadmissible evidence was admitted without objection against one defendant, and that the attorney failed to cross-examine witnesses who might have helped one defendant but would have hurt the other.

In *Holloway v. Arkansas*,[59] the majority read *Glasser* as holding that requiring joint representation over timely objection demands automatic reversal, unless the court first satisfies itself that no conflict exists. When no such judicial inquiry is made, prejudice is presumed, because a rule requiring proof of prejudice after trial would not be susceptible to "intelligent, even-handed application." *Holloway* also suggested that even an unsupported request for separate counsel should usually be granted since, as Chief Justice Burger pointed out for the majority, "compelled disclosure" of the reasons for such a request might risk revelation of confidential information and "creates significant risks of unfair prejudice, especially when the disclosure is to a judge who may be called upon later to impose sentences on the attorney's clients." Not surprisingly in light of this language, *Holloway* had the effect of imposing a duty on trial courts to appoint separate

---

[57] See, e.g., American Bar Association, Model Code of Professional Responsibility, Canon 5; ABA Model Rules of Professional Conduct, Rules 1.7–1.9.

[58] 315 U.S. 60, 62 S.Ct. 457 (1942).

[59] 435 U.S. 475, 98 S.Ct. 1173 (1978).

counsel any time defense counsel makes a conflict of interest claim, at least in multiple representation cases.[60]

More difficult are those cases where a pretrial request for separate counsel is not made. In *Cuyler v. Sullivan,*[61] the Court held that, under such circumstances, the trial court has a duty to inquire into possible conflicts only in the presence of "special circumstances" involving "actual conflict." These circumstances were found not to exist in *Sullivan*: despite the fact that the same attorneys represented three defendants, the conflicts issue was not only not raised prior to trial, the defendants were tried at separate trials, and counsel for Sullivan presented a defense that was compatible with the view that none of the three defendants were connected with the crime.

As the dissent pointed out, a rule putting the burden on the trial court to inquire into possible conflicts in all joint representation cases would not be unduly burdensome; indeed, the federal rules soon thereafter adopted this practice.[62] Although the *Sullivan* majority refused to constitutionalize such a rule, in *Wood v. Georgia*[63] the Court did emphasize that "*Sullivan mandated* a reversal when the trial court has failed to make an inquiry even though 'it knows or reasonably should know that a particular conflict exists.'" Thus, *Wood* suggested that an inquiry into conflict must be made not only when the defense raises the issue prior to trial but also when the record otherwise suggests a "potential" for conflict. Because the potential conflict in *Wood* concerned payment of the defendants' attorneys fees by their employer (who had an interest in shifting liability to the employees), it also seemed to extend that rule beyond the joint representation context involved in *Holloway* and *Sullivan.*

However, in *Mickens v. Taylor*[64] the Court undermined both aspects of *Wood*. In *Mickens*, the attorney for the defendant, charged with capital murder "following the commission of an attempted forcible sodomy," had represented the victim of the murder at the time of his death. The trial judge likely knew of this potential conflict,[65] because she appointed the lawyer as Mickens' counsel the day after she dismissed the charge against the victim (on the ground that he was dead), using a docket sheet that listed the attorney as the victim's lawyer. Yet the judge made no inquiry into Mickens' representation, and the attorney apparently saw no reason to raise the conflict with either the judge or the client.

Five members of the Court, in an opinion by Justice Scalia, held that these failures did not require reversal. Scalia reasoned that the *Holloway* and *Sullivan* presumption of prejudice rules existed to ensure reliable verdicts, and that the judge's knowledge or ignorance of a conflict would not affect that variable. Nor would the failure to make an inquiry at trial necessarily make it harder for reviewing courts to analyze the conflict, "particularly since those courts may rely on evidence and testimony whose importance only becomes established at the trial." Thus, inquiry by the trial court is not mandated

---

[60] See, e.g., *Smith v. Anderson,* 689 F.2d 59 (6th Cir. 1982); *Bishop v. Parratt,* 509 F.Supp. 1140 (D.Neb. 1981); *Brooks v. Hopper,* 597 F.2d 57 (5th Cir. 1979).

[61] 446 U.S. 335, 100 S.Ct. 1708 (1980).

[62] See Fed.R.Crim.P. 44(c).

[63] 450 U.S. 261, 101 S.Ct. 1097 (1981).

[64] 535 U.S. 162, 122 S.Ct. 1237 (2002).

[65] Cf. ABA Model Rule of Professional Conduct 1.7 ("A lawyer shall not represent a client if the representation of that client may be materially limited by the lawyer's responsibilities to another client . . . unless (1) the lawyer reasonably believes the representation will not be adversely affected; and (2) the client consents after consultation . . .").

when there is no defense objection, even when the defense attorney, as in this type of case, might not want to object. Scalia stated that *Wood* did not decide to the contrary, noting that the Court in that case had remanded rather than reversing the conviction.

The majority in *Mickens* also suggested that, when the conflict consists of successive representation as in *Mickens*, rather than joint representation as in *Holloway*, even a conflict brought to the attention of the judge will not require reversal for a failure to inquire, unless it is "actual" in the sense contemplated by *Sullivan*. Whether the actual conflict requirement should be extended to such cases remains, the Court said, an "open question." If it is, then other types of conflicts, such as the conflict involved in *Wood*, would presumably also require proof of actual conflict regardless of whether objection or judicial inquiry is made. The three dissenters disagreed with this approach, at least on the facts of *Mickens*. Justice Stevens believed that the conflict in the case was "intolerable," and that *Wood* required reversal of Mickens' conviction because the judge knew or should have known of it. Justice Souter worried that, without a reversal remedy in such situations, there will be little incentive for judges who suspect conflict to inquire in cases where no objection is made. And Justice Breyer, joined by Justice Ginsburg, argued that the trial judge's "active role in bringing about the incompatible representation" meant that the state had created a "structural defect" that mandated reversal. According to Breyer, "[t]his kind of breakdown in the criminal justice system creates, at a minimum, the appearance that the proceeding will not 'reliably serve its function as a vehicle for determination of guilt or innocence,' " and the resulting criminal punishment will not "be regarded as fundamentally fair."

(2) The Actual Conflict Requirement

As noted above, a second holding in *Sullivan* was that in those situations in which reversal isn't required because of a failure to inquire, a postconviction ineffective assistance claim will not be successful based merely on a "potential" conflict, but only when the defendant can show an "actual conflict of interest adversely affected his lawyer's performance." Although the Court did not have occasion to apply this test in *Sullivan* (the case was remanded on the issue), it did interpret the actual conflict standard in *Burger v. Kemp*.[66] There two lawyers from the same firm represented Burger and his co-defendant Stevens, both of whom were charged with capital murder. Assuming, without holding, that two attorneys can be considered as one for purposes of the Sixth Amendment, the Court found no constitutional violation in *Burger*. It was admitted that the two lawyers consulted together frequently on both cases and that Burger's lawyer wrote the appellate brief for Stevens as well. Burger argued that this relationship created an actual conflict of interest, as shown by his attorney's failure to make a "lesser culpability" argument at the plea negotiation and appellate stages, despite Burger's relative youth and evidence from Burger and another witness suggesting that Burger originally resisted Stevens' plan to commit murder. The Court called this evidence weak, especially since it was Burger who eventually committed the murder. It also concluded that even if there had been an actual conflict of interest, the joint representation did not "adversely" affect Burger's case. In particular, leaning heavily on counsel's explanations of his actions, it noted that Burger's counsel attempted to portray Stevens as the principal architect of the crime throughout Burger's trial.

---

[66]   483 U.S. 776, 107 S.Ct. 3114 (1987).

As the dissent reiterated, however, the lesser culpability argument was *not* pressed at plea bargaining or on appeal, despite the relevance of such information under the state's death penalty statute. It was during these two phases of the process that Burger was most likely to be harmed by a fear on the part of his lawyer that the lesser culpability argument would damage Stevens' case, since the plea negotiations for the two defendants went on simultaneously and their appeals were combined, whereas their trials were severed. While the majority's insinuation that the outcome of Burger's case was not affected by any conflict that existed may be correct, that factor is supposedly irrelevant in conflict of interest cases.

Burger illustrates the fine line between *Sullivan's* "actual conflict" test and the prejudice inquiry. Similar in tone to *Burger* are most lower court decisions dealing with post-conviction conflicts claims. For instance, in *Riley v. State*,[67] the court found that joint representation (not objected to prior to trial) had no adverse effect on counsel's performance despite evidence that he failed to develop the defendant's "social history" and instead chose to emphasize the co-defendant's greater culpability.[68] Addressing the type of conflict involved in *Mickens*, *State v. Stephani*[69] held that prior representation of a victim by a public defender's office will generally not support a post-conviction claim of ineffective assistance.[70] One other example of how the adverse effect test might be applied comes from the concurring opinion in *Mickens*. Although they joined the majority opinion in that case focusing solely on the judicial notice issue, Justices Kennedy and O'Connor also expressed the opinion that the attorney's representation in that case was not adversely affected by his previous representation of the victim because the defense at trial had been that the defendant was not at the scene of the rape-murder ("hardly consistent with the theory that there was a consensual encounter" with the victim) and attacking the victim's character at sentencing would have backfired.

(3) The Legitimate Interest Requirement

There may be circumstances where even an actual conflict of interest does not lead to a Sixth Amendment violation. In *Nix v. Whiteside*,[71] the defendant, charged with murder, insisted on testifying that he had seen "something metallic" in the victim's hand, although none of the eyewitnesses to the event had seen a gun and no gun was found. Counsel told the defendant that if he testified falsely counsel would feel obligated to advise the court that he felt the defendant was committing perjury; moreover, counsel would seek to withdraw from representing the defendant and might be allowed to impeach any false testimony given. As a result, the defendant made no mention of a gun in his testimony; he was convicted of second degree murder. He subsequently sought federal habeas relief, alleging denial of effective assistance.

The circuit court of appeals upheld the claim, in part on the ground that *Sullivan* required prejudice be presumed when there is an actual conflict of interest. The Supreme

---

[67]   585 A.2d 719 (Del. 1990).

[68]   But see, *Armstrong v. State,* 573 So.2d 1329 (Miss. 1990) (lack of mitigating evidence in 14 year-old's sentencing proceeding compared to evidence presented by same attorney for co-defendant demonstrated an actual conflict of interest adversely affecting representation).

[69]   369 N.W.2d 540 (Minn.App. 1985). See also, *People v. Wilkins,* 28 N.Y.2d 53, 320 N.Y.S.2d 8, 268 N.E.2d 756 (1971).

[70]   However, some courts presume prejudice in cases where the defense counsel has represented a victim or complaining witness. See, e.g., *People v. Pinkins,* 272 Cal.Rptr. 100 (Cal.App. 1990); *People v. Stoval,* 40 Ill.2d 109, 239 N.E.2d 441 (1968).

[71]   475 U.S. 157, 106 S.Ct. 988 (1986).

Court unanimously rejected this reasoning. As Chief Justice Burger stated for the Court, "[i]f a 'conflict' between a client's proposal and counsel's ethical obligation gives rise to a presumption that counsel's assistance was prejudicially ineffective, every guilty criminal's conviction would be suspect if the defendant had sought to obtain an acquittal by illegal means." Elsewhere in the opinion, Burger elaborated on the interests involved:

> [The lawyer's] admonitions to his client can in no sense be said to have forced respondent into an *impermissible* choice between his right to counsel and his right to testify as he proposed for there was no *permissible* choice to testify falsely. For a defense counsel to take steps to persuade a criminal defendant to testify truthfully, or to withdraw, deprives the defendant of neither his right to counsel nor the right to testify truthfully. . . . A defendant who informed his counsel that he was arranging to bribe or threaten witnesses or members of the jury would have no "right" to insist on counsel's assistance or silence. Counsel would not be limited to advising against that conduct.

In a similar vein, the four concurring justices noted that whereas the Court's other conflicts cases had involved a conflict between a legitimate interest of the client and other interests, here, on the assumption that the attorney's assessment of the defendant's story was correct, the defendant had no legitimate interest to protect.[72] When such is the case, the presumption of prejudice normally associated with conflicts cases does not apply.

(4) Waiver

Occasionally, a defendant will be aware of a possible adverse interest on the part of his attorney but nonetheless want to "waive" his right to conflict-free counsel, perhaps because he believes the attorney is his best advocate and that the conflict will not affect that advocacy. In *Wheat v. United States*,[73] the Supreme Court held that such waivers were possible. But it also held that the trial judge may, in his discretion, override the defendant's choice of counsel whenever it finds an "actual" conflict or a "serious potential" for conflict. Perhaps more importantly, the Court held that, in light of the fact that allowing waiver of the right to conflict-free counsel might subject trial courts to assertions of error "no matter which way they rule," the judge's decision as to when a "serious" potential for conflict has developed should be given "substantial latitude" by the appellate courts.

Wheat requested the trial judge to substitute for his counsel an attorney named Iredale, who also represented his two codefendants. Although all three defendants indicated they were willing to waive their right to conflict-free counsel, the trial judge rejected the request. The Supreme Court upheld the judge's decision. The entire Court agreed that the presumption in favor of defendant's counsel of choice could be overcome by either an actual conflict or a serious potential for conflict, because the integrity of the trial process and the "ethical standards of the profession" might otherwise be compromised. However, the Court split 5–4 over whether the trial judge should be allowed "substantial latitude" in deciding whether serious potential conflict existed; it also split by a like margin over whether such potential existed in this particular case.

---

[72] However, the concurring members were unwilling to join the majority in finding that the Sixth Amendment could never be violated in such circumstances. Rather they merely concluded that, on the facts of the case, the defendant was not prejudiced by being prevented from testifying falsely.

[73] 486 U.S. 153, 108 S.Ct. 1692 (1988).

The facts in *Wheat* illustrate the difficulty of gauging the "potential for conflict." One of Wheat's two codefendants had completed plea negotiations at the time Wheat's request for Iredale occurred, although the court had not yet accepted the plea. The second codefendant was to testify at Wheat's trial. The majority asserted that if the first codefendant's plea had not been accepted and Wheat had testified at the resulting trial of the codefendant, or if the second codefendant had needed to be vigorously cross-examined during Wheat's trial, then Iredale would have been faced with difficult and perhaps impossible-to-reconcile ethical conflicts. Thus the judge's finding that the potential for conflict was serious was proper. The dissent asserted, on the other hand, that at the time of the request for Iredale, it was clear that the first codefendant's plea would be accepted (in fact it was). It was also clear that, while the second codefendant would testify at Wheat's trial, he would not mention Wheat because he had never met him and could not identify him (which turned out to be the case; indeed, because of the general nature of the testimony there was no cross-examination). Moreover, had cross-examination been necessary, Wheat's initial counsel, who indicated a willingness to stay with Wheat's case, could have conducted it, thereby avoiding the conflict.

It should be emphasized that *Wheat's* willingness to give broad discretion to the trial judge insulates not only decisions to appoint separate counsel, but also decisions to allow waiver. The Court noted that, although it was sustaining the trial court's judgment in the case, another court might have allowed waiver, "with equal justification," and neither would necessarily be right. Any waiver of conflict which is proffered must of course be intelligent and voluntary and requires careful analysis by the court.[74] It also should be noted that *Wheat's* analysis could apply to other types of conflicts claims that the defendant wants to waive (e.g., counsel's prior representation of the victim, counsel's obligation to testify as a witness at trial).

(c) Attorney Errors: Relevant Considerations

When state interference with counsel or conflicts of interests are not involved, *Strickland* required that the defendant making an ineffective assistance claim "affirmatively prove" a reasonable probability that attorney error affected the outcome of the case. The prejudice inquiry is necessary in such cases, the Court explained, because "[a]ttorney errors come in an infinite variety and are as likely to be utterly harmless in a particular case as they are to be prejudicial. They cannot be classified according to likelihood of causing prejudice."

The Court is correct that attorney errors are not easily susceptible to classification. But the Court's decisions do reveal some common threads of analysis. In cases that do not involve interference with counsel or conflicts of interest, the Court has identified four factors that are relevant to determining whether an attorney's conduct constitutes defective assistance of counsel that should lead to reversal of a conviction: (1) the specificity of the ineffective assistance claim; (2) whether a "reasonable" explanation for the attorney's conduct exists (which encompasses the performance prong); (3) the extent to which the conduct affected the outcome of the case (which operationalizes the prejudice prong); and (4) the extent to which the defendant should have control of the action taken by the attorney or instead is a tactical decision that is within the attorney's prerogative.

---

[74]　See, e.g., *United States v. Petz,* 764 F.2d 1390 (11th Cir. 1985).

(1) Specification of the Error

In *United States v. Cronic*,[75] the companion case to *Strickland*, the Court strongly suggested that ineffective assistance claims based on the "overall performance" or character of the defense attorney will rarely succeed. In *Cronic*, the Tenth Circuit Court of Appeals had overturned a conviction for a "check" kiting scheme after "inferring" that the defendant's counsel was ineffective. This inference was based on a number of factors, including the youth and inexperience of the attorney (whose expertise was real estate and who had never tried a jury case), and the short period of time (25 days) he had to prepare for what appeared to be a serious, complex charge involving thousands of documents. A unanimous Court reversed the Tenth Circuit's judgment, finding that while these factors "may affect what a reasonably competent attorney could be expected to have done under the circumstances, . . . none identifies circumstances that in themselves make it unlikely that respondent received the effective assistance of counsel." On remand, the Court noted, the defendant would be able to make out a claim of ineffective assistance "only by pointing to specific errors made by trial counsel."

The Court's insistence that ineffectiveness claims not rest on inferences but rather be based on findings of specific attorney error is consistent with most lower court decisions. For instance, well before *Cronic* courts usually concluded that a showing of defense counsel's general inexperience or youth, without more, is not sufficient under the Sixth Amendment.[76] Similarly, lack of experience in the trial of criminal cases has been deemed immaterial without a showing of specific prejudice.[77] A number of older cases take an identical attitude toward claims that defense counsel's effectiveness was impeded by mental illness,[78] advanced age,[79] deafness,[80] or intoxication.[81] And, as already noted, most courts are in line with *Cronic* in being unwilling to assume that late appointment, by itself, leads to a violation of the Sixth Amendment.[82]

A defendant might take a slightly different tack by arguing that he could not work with counsel given personal antagonisms or disagreements (falling short of a potential conflict of interest of the type described earlier).[83] For instance, in *Morris v. Slappy*,[84] the Ninth Circuit Court of Appeals held that the right to effective assistance would "be without substance if it did not include the right to a meaningful attorney-client relationship." But the Supreme Court's reaction to this holding, although only dictum, made clear that it would not constitutionalize such a rule: "No court could possibly guarantee that a defendant will develop the kind of rapport with his attorney—privately retained or provided by the public—that the Court of Appeals thought part of the Sixth Amendment guarantee to counsel." A poor attorney-client relationship, without proof of specific instances of deficient conduct, is unlikely to lead to reversal.

---

[75] 466 U.S. 648, 104 S.Ct. 2039 (1984).

[76] See, e.g., *Spaulding v. United States*, 279 F.2d 65 (9th Cir. 1960).

[77] *State v. Crowe*, 190 Kan. 658, 378 P.2d 89 (1963).

[78] *Hagan v. United States*, 9 F.2d 562 (8th Cir. 1925).

[79] *United States v. Estep*, 151 F.Supp. 668 (N.D.Tex. 1957), aff'd 251 F.2d 579 (5th Cir. 1958).

[80] *People v. Butterfield*, 37 Cal.App.2d 140, 99 P.2d 310 (1940).

[81] *State v. Keller*, 57 N.D. 645, 223 N.W. 698 (1929).

[82] See § 32.04(a)(1).

[83] See § 32.04(b).

[84] 461 U.S. 1, 103 S.Ct. 1610 (1983).

(2) Existence of a Reasonable Explanation

Assuming a specific "error" is identified, it will still not violate the performance prong of *Strickland* if there is a "reasonable" explanation for the action. Occasionally, there will be no such explanation. For instance, on remand in *Cronic*, the Tenth Circuit found that the Sixth Amendment was violated because counsel's failure to argue lack of intent, the one obvious defense to the check-kiting charge, could not be explained under any rational strategy.[85] Similarly, in *Kimmelman v. Morrison*[86] the Supreme Court found the incompetence prong of *Strickland* violated by counsel's "total failure" to conduct pretrial discovery. This failure prevented him from finding out about a warrantless search of his client's apartment until trial, at which time it was too late, under New Jersey rules, to make a motion for suppression. Because counsel could offer only "implausible," non-strategic explanations for the lack of preparation (e.g., counsel said he thought the state was obligated to provide the defense with all inculpatory information), the Court found it "unreasonable."[87] The Court has also held that failure to inform a noncitizen client about deportation consequences of a guilty plea when those consequences are clear is not excusable.[88]

The Court has been particularly attentive to the "reasonable explanation" issue in death penalty cases. In *Wiggins v. Smith*[89] seven members of the Court agreed that counsel's failure, in a capital case, to seek a social history report, discover evidence of child abuse and other aspects of the client's history, and inquire further into or present mitigating evidence about his significant mental deficiencies could not be explained as a "tactical" decision, especially in light of the absence of significant aggravating factors. According to the Court, "*Strickland* does not establish that a cursory investigation automatically justifies a tactical decision with respect to sentencing strategy. Rather, a reviewing court must consider the reasonableness of the investigation said to support that strategy."

Similarly, in *Rompilla v. Beard*,[90] another capital case, the Court found no reasonable explanation for defense counsels' failure to look at the case file of a prior crime—a crime which the prosecution had indicated would be a central part of its case in aggravation, and which, given its similarity to the current charge, would likely seriously undermine the defense's main mitigation argument that residual doubt remained about whether Rompilla committed the murder. The four-member dissent pointed out that Rompilla's two defense counsel had worked hard representing Rompilla, interviewing five family members and retaining three mental health experts. But Justice Souter concluded for the majority that this investigative effort was not enough, stating: "We . . . cannot think of any situation in which defense counsel should not make some effort to learn the information in the possession of the prosecution and law enforcement authorities." *Rompilla* may not, as the dissent suggested, create a "rigid" rule that defense counsel must examine the case files of all convictions on which the prosecution

---

[85]   *United States v. Cronic*, 839 F.2d 1401 (10th Cir. 1988).

[86]   477 U.S. 365, 106 S.Ct. 2574 (1986).

[87]   Along similar lines, in *Hinton v. Alabama*, 571 U.S. 263, 134 S.Ct. 1081 (2014), the Court held that defense counsel's ignorance about statutory funding for expert witnesses—an ignorance that led him to employ an expert "*he himself* deemed inadequate" (emphasis in original)—was defective performance.

[88]   *Padilla v. Kentucky*, 559 U.S. 356, 130 S.Ct. 1473 (2010), discussed in § 26.04(a)(2).

[89]   539 U.S. 510, 123 S.Ct. 2527 (2003).

[90]   545 U.S. 374, 125 S.Ct. 2456 (2005).

relies, but the latter statement from Souter does seem inconsistent with the case-by-case approach endorsed in *Strickland*.[91]

Indeed, in most cases claiming ineffective assistance the Court has been able either to find a reasonable explanation for the alleged error or to hypothesize one. In *Strickland,* for instance, the Court came up with its own explanation for why, despite significant evidence of mental dysfunction in the defendant, counsel failed to obtain a psychiatric examination and develop and present character evidence at the defendant's capital sentencing proceeding. The Court speculated that, given the strength of the case against the defendant, trial counsel "could reasonably surmise" that such evidence would have been "of little help." Further, defendant's testimony at the earlier plea colloquy had revealed the substance of what there was to know about his emotional problems; restricting character testimony to this information ensured that contrary psychological evidence and the defendant's criminal history (which counsel had successfully moved to exclude) would not be introduced by the state. Similarly, in *Burger v. Kemp,*[92] the failure to discover and introduce evidence of the defendant's personality and unhappy childhood at a capital sentencing proceeding was not ineffective assistance when based on a conclusion that such evidence may have harmed the defendant as much as it may have helped him.[93]

As a third example, counsel's failure in *Bell v. Cone*[94] to present any mitigating evidence or make a closing argument at a capital sentencing proceeding was not ineffective assistance because, according to the majority, the mitigating medical evidence had just been presented at trial, the defendant's mother and other character witnesses would not have been effective or might have revealed harmful information, and a closing argument would have allowed rebuttal by the lead prosecutor, "who all agreed was very persuasive." Justice Stevens, the lone dissenter, argued that counsel's nonfeasance was a "total failure to subject the prosecution's case to adversarial testing," a situation that *Cronic* had recognized should result in a presumption of prejudice. But the Court concluded that, at most, counsel's alleged failures occurred only at "specific points," and that, in any event, there were plausible explanations for them.[95]

The reasonableness of the attorney's conduct has also been construed in connection with appellate counsel. In *Smith v. Murray,*[96] the Court found that counsel's failure to advance a particular claim on appeal (later upheld by the Supreme Court in another case) was not ineffective assistance. The fact that an amicus brief submitted at the time of appeal had focused on that claim and that other courts had recognized similar claims

---

[91] Especially since *Rompilla* (and *Wiggins* as well) were habeas cases, and thus the Court had to find not only that *Strickland* was violated, but that the lower courts' decisions to the contrary were an "unreasonable" interpretation of that case. See § 33.02(b)(3) for a discussion of the standard of review in habeas cases. See also *Porter v. McCollum*, 558 U.S. 30, 130 S.Ct. 447 (2009).

[92] 483 U.S. 776, 107 S.Ct. 3114 (1987).

[93] See also, *Darden v. Wainwright,* 477 U.S. 168, 106 S.Ct. 2464 (1986) (reliance solely on a plea of mercy at sentencing explicable by a desire to prevent prosecution use of prior criminal record, an unfavorable psychiatric report, and information about defendant's mistress).

[94] 535 U.S. 685, 122 S.Ct. 1843 (2002).

[95] See also *Knowles v. Mirzayance*, 556 U.S. 111,129 S.Ct. 1411 (2009) (no ineffective assistance where counsel decided not to raise an insanity defense at the second stage of trial even though it was the only defense available to the defendant, because the jury had already rejected a virtually identical claim at the first, guilt stage of trial, where the state, rather than the defendant, had the burden of proof, and the defendant's parents had refused to testify in support of the defense).

[96] 477 U.S. 527, 106 S.Ct. 2661 (1986).

was not dispositive. Quoting from *Strickland*, the Court emphasized that "[a] fair assessment of attorney performance requires that every effort be made to eliminate the distorting effects of hindsight, to reconstruct the circumstances of counsel's challenged conduct, and to evaluate the conduct from counsel's perspective at the time." Here counsel had researched a number of issues and decided that the claim in question was not supportable under prevailing law, and had vigorously argued several other issues on the appeal. *Smith* illustrates *Strickland's* conclusion that, when counsel conducts a reasonable investigation and decides to advance only one of several arguments, his choice is "virtually unchallengeable."

The Court has also been willing to find explanations for what appear to be significant lapses in legal knowledge. The pre-*Strickland* case of *Tollett v. Henderson*,[97] involved counsel's failure to challenge the racial composition of the grand jury that indicted the defendant, who pleaded guilty on counsel's advice. Although, as the dissent pointed out, there was strong evidence suggesting that counsel was not even aware that such a claim could have been made, the Court found that the attorney's omission may have been dictated by tactical considerations:

> Often the interests of the accused are not advanced by challenges that would only delay the inevitable date of prosecution, or by contesting all guilt. A prospect of plea bargaining, the expectation or hope of a lesser sentence, or the convincing nature of the evidence against the accused are considerations that might well suggest the advisability of a guilty plea without elaborate consideration of whether pleas in abatement, such as unconstitutional grand jury selection procedures, might be factually supported.

This language suggests that the Court is willing to go to some length in providing reasons supporting counsel's allegedly deficient conduct.[98]

In contrast, a number of lower court cases are, like the Court's decision in *Kimmelman*, bottomed on a finding that counsel's ignorance of the law was inexcusable. For instance, attorney error has been found when counsel did not challenge the legality of a search that produced heroin because he was unaware of the rule that allowed him to do so;[99] counsel failed to object to illegally seized evidence because he misread the leading case on the issue;[100] counsel advised a plea of guilty to the charge of forgery, unaware that under the controlling law the defendant could be prosecuted only under a statute proscribing misuse of credit cards, which carried a lighter penalty;[101] and "counsel induced the defendant to plead guilty on the *patently erroneous* advice that if he does not do so he may be subject to a sentence six times more severe than that which the law would really allow."[102]

A final consideration in analyzing the reasonableness of an explanation for attorney conduct is whether the defendant's own malfeasance contributed to it. This type of

---

[97] 411 U.S. 258, 93 S.Ct. 1602 (1973).

[98] The Court may have also been influenced by the rather dubious assumption that some attorneys would be willing to be labelled "ineffective" if failing to raise a grand jury challenge would allow retrial after conviction. See § 33.03(c).

[99] *People v. Ibarra*, 60 Cal.2d 460, 34 Cal.Rptr. 863, 386 P.2d 487 (1963).

[100] *People v. Coffman*, 2 Cal.App.3d 681, 82 Cal.Rptr. 782 (1969).

[101] *In re Williams*, 1 Cal.3d 168, 81 Cal.Rptr. 784, 460 P.2d 984 (1969).

[102] *Cooks v. United States*, 461 F.2d 530 (5th Cir. 1972).

explanation surfaced in *Hill v. Lockhart*,[103] involving counsel's advice to plead guilty. There the majority suggested that the defendant was not prejudiced by his attorney's failure to discover, prior to the plea, a previous felony conviction, and his concomitant failure to inform the defendant that under state law the conviction acted to postpone defendant's parole eligibility. Two members of the Court joined in the decision on the ground that the attorney's failure was not defective performance, since the defendant had signed a "plea statement" indicating he had no prior felonies and the attorney was entitled to rely on this information. This type of reasoning is buttressed by *Strickland,* which stated that counsel need not pursue a particular line of investigation when the "defendant has given counsel reason to believe that [such action] would be fruitless or even harmful."[104]

Similar reasoning justified the Court's decision in *Burt v. Titlow*[105] refusing to find ineffective assistance. There, defense counsel failed to retrieve the defendant's file from his former counsel before recommending that the defendant demand an even lower sentence than had been negotiated by the former attorney; when the defendant followed the new attorney's recommendation, the prosecution withdrew the plea offer (which had been based on a manslaughter charge) and the defendant was convicted of second degree murder at trial. The Court pointed to evidence that the defendant had insisted on his innocence to the new attorney and that the defendant had been told by his former counsel that the state had sufficient evidence to convict him of first degree murder. Under these circumstances, the Court held, unanimously, that counsel was justified in not making any further effort to learn the strength of the state's case before recommending withdrawal of the plea. Again, the defendant's own actions were said to undercut his ineffective assistance claim.

This rationale was carried even further in *Schriro v. Landrigan*,[106] where the Court held that an attorney's failure to fully investigate mitigating evidence in a capital case is not ineffective assistance when the defendant refuses to permit any mitigating evidence to be presented, even if the defendant's demand may not be good strategy. Although the four-member dissent pointed out that the discovery of new mitigating evidence might have changed the defendant's negative attitude, the majority stated that a defendant's decision to forego the introduction of mitigating evidence need not be "informed and knowing." Thus, in *Landrigan*, the defendant's statement that he did not want to introduce any mitigating evidence, after interrupting his attorney's attempt to introduce testimony from his mother and ex-wife, was treated as a waiver of *all* mitigating evidence. That evidence, post-sentence investigation revealed, included proof of a brain disorder, significant medical consequences of his mother's drinking and drug use, and an abusive upbringing within his adoptive family, none of which the defense attorney investigated or attempted to introduce. The Court went on to find that this mitigating evidence would not have changed the outcome of the capital sentencing proceeding in any event, since much of it would have been alluded to by the mother and ex-wife had they testified and the sentencing judge had heard this testimony by way of

---

[103]   474 U.S. 52, 106 S.Ct. 366 (1985).

[104]   See also *Parker v. North Carolina*, 397 U.S. 790, 90 S.Ct. 1458 (1970) (failure to challenge admissibility of confession despite evidence of improper promises made during interrogation not ineffective assistance when defendant told lawyer that he had not been threatened or promised help and that he had not been frightened during the interrogation).

[105]   571 U.S. 12, 134 S.Ct. 10 (2013).

[106]   550 U.S. 465, 127 S.Ct. 1933 (2007).

the attorney's proffer. But this prejudice inquiry, as the dissent noted, was more of an "afterthought;" the principal holding in the case was that a defendant's unwillingness to present mitigating evidence can absolve attorneys of any duty to find it.

(3)　The Prejudice Inquiry

After *Strickland*, even if attorney error is found there must also be a "reasonable probability" that it affected the outcome of the case. This is so even when the attorney's failure leads to "structural error" that under traditional harmless error analysis requires automatic reversal.[107] In *Weaver v. Massachusetts*,[108] the claim was that the defendant's trial counsel failed to object to a closure of the jury selection process that resulted in his mother and minister, among others, being excluded from voir dire. The Court acknowledged that, had counsel objected, on appeal the error could not have been found harmless because the right affected was structural. But when raised through an ineffective assistance of counsel claim during the post-conviction process, *Strickland's* outcome test applies, supplemented by an inquiry into whether any other type of fundamental unfairness occurred. The majority found no such prejudice here, because the error was unlikely to have affected the outcome of the trial, there was no evidence of the type of judicial or prosecutorial misconduct that the public trial right is meant to deter, the unselected jurors were in the courtroom and thus at least some outsiders observed the selection process, and the rest of the trial was conducted in public.

Nonetheless, the Court has found prejudice in a number of cases, including in the *Wiggins v. Smith* and *Rompilla v. Beard* decisions noted in the previous section. In *Wiggins*, after holding that counsel's failure to investigate and present evidence of the defendant's social history at the capital sentencing proceeding was unreasonable, the Court concluded that there was a reasonable probability that at least one juror would have resisted a death sentence had the evidence been presented. As the Court noted, counsel did not tell the jury about the defendant's diminished mental capacities, his abuse as a young child by his alcoholic mother, his repeated physical and sexual abuse during his subsequent years in foster care, or his homelessness after foster care. And in *Rompilla* the Court found prejudice in defense counsels' failure to review the prosecution's file on a prior conviction it planned to use as an aggravator in a capital case. Even though the file revealed nothing that would undermine the validity of the prior conviction, it did contain leads that would have given counsel information they did not obtain from other sources, including records that suggested their client suffered from mental illness, mental retardation, and fetal alcohol syndrome, and had been seriously abused as a child by his alcoholic parents. As Justice Souter put it, this "evidence adds up to a mitigation case that bears no relation to the few naked pleas for mercy actually put before the jury," and could well have influenced the jury to give Rompilla a life sentence.

As noted earlier, when the defendant pleads guilty and then wants to overturn the conviction based on an assertion of ineffective assistance, prejudice is measured by looking at whether there is a reasonable probability that, but for counsel's errors, the defendant would not have pleaded guilty and would have instead insisted on going to trial.[109] The Court has emphasized that the key issue here is not whether the defendant

---

[107]　See § 29.05(c)(2) defining structural error and the rule of automatic reversal.

[108]　___ U.S. ___, 137 S.Ct. 1899 (2017).

[109]　*Hill v. Lockhart*, 474 U.S. 52, 106 S.Ct. 366 (1985).

would have succeeded at trial nor whether most defendants would have nonetheless taken the plea, but instead whether, but for the error, the defendant in question would have decided differently.[110]

Prejudice is defined somewhat differently when the error leads the defendant to *reject* a plea offer and go to trial. In *Lafler v. Cooper*,[111] the defendant turned down a plea offer for a recommended 51-to-85 month sentence on a murder charge because his attorney incorrectly told him that state law prevented a murder conviction when the victim is shot below the waist. Lafler went to trial, was convicted and received a mandatory minimum sentence of 185–360 months. In *Missouri v. Frye*[112] the attorney never communicated the plea offer, which contemplated a 90-day sentence recommendation for a fourth offense of driving with a revoked license. Frye went to trial, was convicted and received a sentence of three years. In both cases, the Court assumed the deficiency prong was met.[113] With respect to the prejudice prong, it held that where the alleged prejudice is having to stand trial, a defendant "must show that but for the ineffective advice there is reasonable probability that the plea offer would have been presented to the court (i.e., that the defendant would have accepted the plea and the prosecution would not have withdrawn it in light of intervening circumstance), that the court would have accepted its terms, and that the conviction or sentence, or both, under the offer's terms would have been less severe than under the judgment and sentence that in fact were imposed."

The state contended that *Strickland's* prejudice prong is not met if, as occurred in both *Lafler* and *Frye*, the defendant is convicted after a fair trial. Similarly, Justice Scalia, who wrote the dissent in both cases, distinguished cases like *Padilla v. Kentucky*,[114] where the defendant pleaded guilty after receiving ineffective advice from counsel, from *Lafler* and *Frye*, where the defendant went to trial as a result of bad advice. In the latter cases, he argued, counsel's inadequacy does not call into question "the basic justice of a defendant's conviction or sentence." Further, Scalia stated, since there is no right to a plea bargain, ineffectiveness of counsel in the course of the bargaining process does not deprive a defendant of any constitutionally protected interest.

But Justice Kennedy, who wrote for the five-member majority in both cases, stated that the Sixth Amendment reaches to all critical stages of the criminal proceeding,[115] and that, far from curing the error in these cases, trial can "cause" it by resulting in a longer sentence. Perhaps more importantly, Justice Kennedy stated that the notion that a fair trial "wipes clean any deficient performance by defense counsel during plea bargaining . . . ignores the reality that criminal justice today is for the most part a system of pleas, not a system of trials." Thus *Lafley* and *Frye* signal that the Court is willing to pay more attention to the central adjudicative mechanism in today's criminal process.

However, the Court's remedy for *Strickland* violations in the plea bargaining context gives the trial court and prosecution considerable discretion. In *Lafley*, the court held that the correct remedy was for the state to reoffer the original plea agreement but

---

[110]   *Lee v. United States*, ___ U.S. ___, 137 S.Ct. 1958 (2017), discussed in § 26.05(3)(2).

[111]   566 U.S. 156, 132 S.Ct. 1376 (2012).

[112]   566 U.S. 134, 132 S.Ct. 1399 (2012).

[113]   In *Frye*, the Court explicitly held that defense counsel has the duty to communicate formal offers from the prosecution that may be favorable to the accused.

[114]   See § 26.04(a)(2).

[115]   See § 31.03.

that, if it is accepted, the trial court could still decide to reject the bargain (authority it has with any agreement[116]) and let the trial conviction and sentence stand or even impose some other disposition. In *Frye*, the Court noted that the prosecutor had the authority, under Missouri law, to cancel the plea offer in light of a subsequent driving offense committed by Frye, and thus a reoffer of the plea might not be necessary.

Wiggins, *Smith*, *Lafler* and *Frye* notwithstanding, the Court has usually been unwilling to find prejudice results from attorney error. In most of the cases discussed in the previous section in which the Court found that no error occurred, it went on to find, additionally, that had error occurred, no prejudice resulted. Similarly, while finding that there was no excuse for the attorney's ignorance of state discovery rules in *Kimmelman*, the Court remanded the case for an inquiry into whether the unargued Fourth Amendment claim was meritorious and, if so, whether exclusion of the evidence would have affected the outcome of the trial. This resolution made clear that a lack of prejudice will defeat an ineffective assistance of counsel claim even if there is no reasonable explanation for the attorney's act or omission.

Lockhart v. Fretwell[117] carried this idea even further by linking prejudice to the time at which the ineffective assistance claim is made. There, the Court assumed that counsel had incompetently failed to raise a constitutional claim. But it also noted that the claim was based on a decision that had since been overruled. As a result, seven members of the Court found that counsel's inadequacy caused no prejudice to the petitioner, concluding that a contrary finding would allow him to receive "a windfall to which the law does not entitle him."

Furthermore, the *Strickland* majority emphasized that a reviewing court need not always determine whether an attorney's performance was defective before evaluating prejudice: "If it is easier to dispose of an ineffectiveness claim on the ground of lack of sufficient prejudice, which we expect will often be so, that course should be followed." For example, in *Hill v. Lockhart*, discussed in the previous section, the majority saw no need to address whether the attorney's failure to discover the defendant's prior conviction was error, since it found there was no "reasonable probability" that the defendant's "ignorance" about the conviction and its effect on his parole eligibility would have changed the decision to plead guilty.

Note that, under the Court's cases, the converse of *Strickland's* proposition is not true: a clear showing of prejudice does not eliminate the requirement that it be caused by attorney conduct that is "deficient." This fact is illustrated by *Smith v. Murray,* where, it will be remembered, the attorney failed to raise a claim on appeal that probably would have resulted in reversal. Despite the impact of the attorney's omission on the outcome of the case, the Court found, as noted above, that it did not constitute unreasonable behavior under the performance prong of *Strickland,* and thus did not violate the Sixth Amendment. Similarly, in *Roe v. Flores-Ortega*,[118] the Court held that, while a failure to file notice of appeal when there are non-frivolous appellate issues may well constitute prejudice, the failure must result from deficient performance—such as ignoring a client's

---

[116]　See § 26.03(a).

[117]　506 U.S. 364, 113 S.Ct. 838 (1993).

[118]　528 U.S. 470, 120 S.Ct. 1029 (2000), discussed further in § 32.04(c)(4).

instructions about appeal or failing to consult with the client about appeal—for there to be ineffective assistance of counsel.[119]

(4) The Defendant's Control over the Decision

A final inquiry in ineffective assistance of counsel cases is the extent to which an attorney's failure to follow the client's wishes, or ascertain what those wishes are, is defective performance and, if so, automatically prejudicial. In *Faretta v. California*,[120] the Supreme Court held that defendants have the right to represent themselves. This holding suggested that, even when represented, defendants should have some control of their case. Indeed, construed broadly, the *Faretta* principle would mean that an attorney commits "error" anytime he acts against his client's wishes or fails to consult him on a particular decision. But in *Jones v. Barnes*,[121] the Court rejected this interpretation of *Faretta*. At the same time, it indicated that an attorney's failure to follow his client's wishes on certain "fundamental" issues might violate the Sixth Amendment, and that in such cases prejudice might be presumed.

The specific holding in *Jones* was that a defendant cannot compel his attorney to argue particular claims on appeal, even claims that are concededly "nonfrivolous," when the attorney has decided, in the exercise of his professional judgment, not to present them to the court. A contrary finding, ruled the majority, would undermine counsel's ability to choose the most effective arguments. Justice Brennan's dissent contended that *Faretta* allowed only those "restrictions on individual autonomy and dignity . . . necessary to vindicate the State's interest in a speedy, effective prosecution;" thus, the appellate attorney's role should be limited to giving advice on appropriate arguments, which the defendant is free to accept or reject. But the majority rejected this conclusion, reasoning that counsel's decision to override the defendant's wishes, "far from being evidence of incompetence, is the hallmark of effective appellate advocacy."

Jones appears to hold that most tactical aspects of the defense are the attorney's domain. In particular, decisions about what claims to investigate and pursue and what witnesses to present—the focus of virtually all of the "attorney error" cases discussed to this point—are ultimately the attorney's, and thus cannot form the basis for an ineffective assistance claim unless they are unreasonable and affected the outcome of the case. Although he did not go as far as the majority even Brennan, in his *Jones* dissent, conceded that defense counsel must be given "decisive authority" in making "the hundreds of decisions that must be made quickly in the course of a trial." Other Court decisions have held that the defendant is bound by the acts of his lawyer-agent with respect to evidentiary objections,[122] agreements to scheduling delays that result in waiver of speedy trial rights,[123] and a decision to permit a magistrate rather than a district court judge to preside over jury selection.[124]

---

[119] See also, *Glover v. United States*, 531 U.S. 198, 121 S.Ct. 696 (2001) (holding that any increase in sentence caused by counsel's ineffectiveness is prejudice, but pointing out that ineffectiveness still needs to be proven).

[120] 422 U.S. 806, 95 S.Ct. 2525 (1975), discussed in § 31.04(a).

[121] 463 U.S. 745, 103 S.Ct. 3308 (1983).

[122] *Henry v. Mississippi*, 379 U.S. 443, 85 S.Ct. 564 (1965).

[123] *New York v. Hill*, 528 U.S. 110, 120 S.Ct. 659 (2000).

[124] *Gonzalez v. United States*, 553 U.S. 242, 128 S.Ct. 1765 (2008).

However, in a footnote, the majority in *Jones* also quoted approvingly from the ABA Model Rules of Professional Conduct to the effect that the client should hold the ultimate authority to make certain "fundamental" decisions, such as whether to plead guilty, waive the right to jury trial, testify on his own behalf, or forego an appeal.[125] It is not entirely clear why these decisions might be considered "fundamental," and other decisions, such as whether to raise a certain defense, call a particular witness, or request the exclusion of the public from trial, are not. The best explanation may be that the former decisions are thought to go beyond pure "strategy" and involve issues that are so closely tied to a person's sense of autonomy that the defendant should be allowed to make them regardless of their tactical impact.[126] In any event, *Jones'* dictum raised the possibility that attorney failure either to discover or to follow a defendant's wishes with respect to such a "fundamental" decision might be automatic error, at least when the defendant is competent.[127]

Some early post-*Jones* subsequent decisions seem to confirm that view. In *Evitts v. Lucey,*[128] for instance, counsel failed to file a "statement of appeal" along with his motion for an appeal, an omission that resulted in the dismissal and was presumably not in accordance with the defendant's wishes. The Court found, 7–2, that this failure constituted ineffective assistance, without assessing the validity of the foreclosed claims (although the Court explicitly avoided deciding whether a failure to appeal is presumptively prejudicial, given the state's concession in that case that the attorney's failure had a "drastic" impact on the defendant). And in *Penson v. Ohio,*[129] the Court held that a violation of the holding in *Anders v. California*[130] (requiring that appellate counsel who wish to withdraw from an appeal file a brief noting possible arguments) requires reversal "[b]ecause the fundamental importance of the assistance of counsel does not cease as the prosecutorial process moves from the trial to the appellate stage, the presumption of prejudice must extend as well to the denial of counsel on appeal."

In *Roe v. Flores-Ortega,*[131] however, the Court took a more nuanced view. There counsel did not file a notice of appeal after the defendant pleaded guilty to second degree murder, and it was conceded that counsel had not obtained the defendant's consent to forego the appeal. The Supreme Court held that whether these omissions amounted to ineffective assistance of counsel required *both* a showing of defective performance and of prejudice. While performance is clearly defective if the lawyer disregards a defendant's instructions to file an appeal, failure to file when there has been no communication regarding appeal is not automatically ineffective assistance, six members of the Court concluded. Justice O'Connor wrote for the majority that a constitutional duty to consult about appeal exists only when "a rational defendant would want to appeal . . . or this particular defendant reasonably demonstrated to counsel that he was interested in appealing." While the majority speculated that, under this standard, the courts would find a duty to consult in the "vast majority" of cases, it also explained that the duty might be somewhat lessened when the defendant has pleaded guilty, as occurred here. A plea

---

[125] Rule 2.1(a).

[126] See Monroe H. Freedman, *Personal Responsibility in a Professional System*, 27 Cath.U.L.Rev. 191 (1978).

[127] For the Court's definition of competence in this context, see § 28.03(b)(1).

[128] 469 U.S. 387, 105 S.Ct. 830 (1985).

[129] 488 U.S. 75, 109 S.Ct. 346 (1988).

[130] 386 U.S. 738, 87 S.Ct. 1396 (1967), discussed in § 29.02(c).

[131] 528 U.S. 470, 120 S.Ct. 1029 (2000).

both reduces the scope of appealable issues and may indicate that the defendant seeks an end to judicial proceedings.[132]

As to the prejudice analysis, the Court unanimously held, following the logic of *Strickland* and *Hill*, that the defendant must demonstrate that "but for counsel's deficient failure to consult about an appeal, he would have timely appealed." Here evidence that there were nonfrivolous grounds for appeal or that the defendant promptly expressed a desire to appeal will be "highly relevant."[133] The Court also recognized that both the defective performance and prejudice inquiries might be met by showing nonfrivolous grounds for appeal, but iterated that, even with such a showing, the ultimate inquiry under the prejudice prong is whether the defendant would have appealed but for the lack of consultation.

After *Flores-Ortega*, then, failure to obtain the client's consent with respect to a decision that is regarded as fundamental is probably, but not automatically, ineffective assistance of counsel. What if the attorney does consult with the defendant about a fundamental issue but the defendant fails to register a choice? In *Florida v. Nixon*,[134] a capital murder case, defense counsel Corin explained to Nixon that, given the overwhelming evidence against him, the best strategy was to concede guilt at trial; that move would, in Corin's estimation, preserve the defense's credibility for sentencing, where it could present extensive evidence of mental illness in mitigation. Although Corin had represented Nixon on two previous criminal charges and believed he had a good relationship with him, Nixon would neither approve nor reject this strategy, and provided little if any direction during preparation for the case. Nonetheless, at trial Corin stated during opening argument that "there won't be any question, none whatsoever" that Nixon committed the charged murder, cross-examined the state's witnesses only for the purpose of clarification, and did not present a defense case, although he did contest several jury instructions. At the penalty phase, in contrast, he presented eight mitigation witnesses.

The Florida Supreme Court held that Corin's failure to obtain Nixon's affirmative and explicit consent to this strategy was presumptively ineffective assistance of counsel, under *Cronic's* rule that "if counsel entirely fails to subject the prosecution's case to meaningful adversarial testing, then there has been a denial of Sixth Amendment rights that makes the adversary process itself presumptively unreliable." But a unanimous Supreme Court (Chief Justice Rehnquist not participating) held that this was a misreading of *Cronic*. In capital cases, Justice Ginsburg stated for the Court, defense attorneys "face daunting challenges in developing trial strategies, not least because the defendant's guilt is often clear." As Corin had suggested to Nixon, contesting the prosecution's case during the adjudication phase in such cases can be a "counterproductive course." At the same time, conceding guilt at trial is not, contrary to the Florida Supreme Court's suggestion, like pleading guilty, because the latter tactic forfeits all trial rights and increases the likelihood the state will present "aggressive

---

[132] Note also that, in the habeas context, attorney failure to meet a filing deadline, even if grossly negligent, does not violate the Sixth Amendment because there is no constitutional right to counsel in that context, see § 33.03(d)(3), although such failure can be judicially mitigated through equitable tolling, at least in capital cases. *Holland v. Florida*, 560 U.S. 631, 130 S.Ct. 2549 (2010), discussed in § 33.04(d).

[133] In *Garza v. Idaho*, ___ U.S. ___, 139 S.Ct. 738 (2019), discussed further in § 26.02(b)(1), the Court made clear that the defendant's desire to appeal is not only highly relevant, it is dispositive on both the performance and prejudice prongs, even when there has been an appeal waiver.

[134] 543 U.S. 175, 125 S.Ct. 551 (2004).

evidence of guilt" during sentencing. Thus, when counsel decides to go to trial and concede guilt, as Corin did, his "strategic choice is not impeded by any blanket rule demanding the defendant's explicit consent."

However, if, unlike in *Nixon*, the client specifically forbids counsel to concede guilt, counsel's conduct is not only deficient but automatically results in reversible error, with no showing of prejudice required. In *McCoy v. Louisiana*,[135] defense counsel told the jury his client had killed three people, over McCoy's explicit objection. The Court held, 6–3, that such an error is structural and thus not subject to harmless error review.

In other situations not involving decisions that are clearly the defendant's, however, counsel's refusal to follow a client's explicit direction will usually not constitute automatic error. In at least one situation, the Court has so held: in *Nix v. Whiteside*,[136] discussed earlier, the Court held that refusing to permit a defendant who wants to testify to get on the stand is not reversible error if the defendant plans to testify falsely. Recall also the *Landrigan* decision, in which the Court refused to find a failure to pursue mitigating evidence inadequate because the defendant had indicated he did not want such evidence presented. While this holding could be read to suggest that the decision about whether to present mitigating evidence is the defendant's, the Court did not explicitly so decide. In other words, it is not clear that the Court would have found the attorney's performance inadequate had he presented such evidence *against* the defendant's wishes, since, as in *Nixon*, the defendant's "strategy" could be seen as "counterproductive."[137]

32.05   Methods of Improving Representation

In rejecting a "categorical" approach to ineffective assistance claims, the Supreme Court's opinion in *Strickland* emphasized that "the purpose of the effective assistance guarantee is not to improve the quality of legal representation." At the same time, it added that this goal is "of considerable importance to the legal system." Of particular concern is the quality of representation provided the indigent, who are often saddled with court appointed attorneys with little knowledge of the criminal system, or public defenders with little experience of any kind.

Various proposals have been made to rectify this situation. For instance, several commentators have argued that inadequate representation could be greatly reduced by creating a separate criminal bar. One proposal advocates the following measures: (1) a special examination dealing with criminal procedure, evidence, and trial tactics; (2) previous misdemeanor experience as a prerequisite to representing a defendant in a felony case; (3) providing counsel with a checklist of functions that he must perform preparatory to a trial or guilty plea; (4) increased compensation for appointed attorneys; and (5) limitations on the number of cases public defender offices may deal with each year.[138]

Several other proposals might supplement, or provide alternatives to, the creation of a separate bar. For instance, in his dissent in *United States v. Decoster III*,[139] Judge

---

[135] ___ U.S. ___, 138 S.Ct. 1500 (2018).

[136] 475 U.S. 157, 106 S.Ct. 988 (1986).

[137] But see *Rodriguez v. United States*, 395 U.S. 327, 89 S.Ct. 1715 (1969) (defendant entitled to resentencing and appeal when counsel failed to bring a requested appeal).

[138] Joel Jay Finer, *Ineffective Assistance of Counsel*, 58 Cornell L.Rev. 1077 (1973).

[139] 624 F.2d 196 (D.C.Cir. 1976).

Bazelon suggested that "[b]efore trial—or before a guilty plea is accepted—defense counsel could submit an investigative checklist certifying that he has conducted a complete investigation and reviewing the steps he has taken in pretrial preparation, including what records were obtained, which witnesses were interviewed, when the defendant was consulted, and what motions were filed." Bazelon believed that this "worksheet" would "heighten defense counsel's sensitivity to the need for adequate investigation," which, together with judicial oversight of the attorney's conduct at trial, would prevent deprivation of constitutional rights. To the majority's argument that this intrusive inquiry might "tear the fabric of the adversary system," Bazelon responded "for so very many indigent defendants, the adversary system is already in shreds." Another proposal is to impose immediate sanctions on attorneys whose assistance has been found ineffective, and to encourage defendants who are unable to obtain appellate or habeas relief due to a failure to meet the prejudice prong under *Strickland* to sue attorneys under a "malpractice" standard, which does not require a prejudice showing.[140]

Of course, the latter type of suit could not be brought under § 1983, since that avenue of relief is only available for a *constitutional* (i.e., Sixth Amendment) violation,[141] which would require a showing of prejudice. Even if prejudice could be shown, however, the courts have restricted § 1983 actions against defense attorneys. The Fourth Circuit has held that court-appointed attorneys, in the performance of their duties, enjoy absolute immunity from such suits.[142] And the Supreme Court has held that public defenders also enjoy absolute immunity from suit under § 1983,[143] except when the attorney has intentionally conspired with state officials to deprive the defendant of federal constitutional rights.[144]

On the other hand, a few courts have recognized the viability of injunctive relief under § 1983 designed to improve representation. One of the earliest to do so was *Luckey v. Harris*,[145] which involved a suit asking for various changes in Georgia's system for appointing counsel, based on allegations that "inadequate resources, delays in the appointment of counsel, pressure on attorneys to hurry their clients' case to trial or to enter a guilty plea, and inadequate supervision" denied indigent criminal defendants their Sixth Amendment, Eighth Amendment and due process rights. The district court dismissed the suit for failure to state a claim upon which relief could be granted, in part because the plaintiffs did not allege and prove the "future inevitability of ineffective assistance" under the state system. But the Eleventh Circuit reversed and remanded, concluding that even though the alleged deficiencies might not inevitably affect the outcome of the plaintiffs' trials (and therefore would not result in prejudice to them), they might still routinely lead to poor attorney performance and thus cause "ineffectiveness" cognizable under the Sixth Amendment. It further noted that *Strickland's* deferential scrutiny of ineffective assistance claims derived in large part from concerns that a more exacting standard would reduce finality, create post-trial burdens that would discourage counsel from accepting cases, and diminish the

---

[140] Harvey E. Bines, *Remedying Ineffective Representation in Criminal Cases: Departures from Habeas Corpus*, 59 Va.L.Rev. 927 (1973).

[141] See § 2.05(a)(3).

[142] *Minns v. Paul*, 542 F.2d 899 (4th Cir. 1976).

[143] *Polk County v. Dodson*, 454 U.S. 312, 102 S.Ct. 445 (1981).

[144] *Tower v. Glover*, 467 U.S. 914, 104 S.Ct. 2820 (1984).

[145] 860 F.2d 1012 (11th Cir. 1988).

independence of counsel, considerations that do not apply when only prospective relief is being sought.[146]

32.06 Conclusion

The Sixth Amendment right to effective assistance of counsel can be summarized as follows:

(1) The right attaches only at proceedings at which the right to counsel attaches. Thus, for instance, there is no right to effective assistance of counsel at discretionary appeals or post-conviction proceedings. At those proceedings at which the right attaches, both retained and appointed counsel must be effective.

(2) Ineffective assistance occurs when attorney error prejudiced the defendant's case. Counsel is presumed to be competent and the defendant bears the burden on the prejudice issue. Thus, the defendant must normally show: (a) that counsel's performance was so deficient that he violated his duties to avoid conflicts of interest, consult with the defendant on important decisions, keep the defendant informed of important developments, and bring to bear such skill and knowledge as will render the trial a reliable adversarial testing process; and (b) that, except where prejudice is presumed as described in (3), there is a reasonable probability that, but for counsel's unprofessional errors, the result of the proceeding would have been different. In those cases where the attorney errs in providing advice to a defendant during plea negotiations and the defendant goes to trial, the defendant must show that but for the ineffective advice there is reasonable probability that the plea offer would have been presented to the court, that the court would have accepted its terms, and that the conviction or sentence received under the offer's terms would have been less severe than under the judgment and sentence that in fact were imposed. If instead the defendant pleads guilty based on counsel's deficient advice, the sole issue is whether this particular defendant would have decided differently had he received adequate advice.

(3) Prejudice is presumed when: (a) the government denies or constructively denies counsel to the defendant; (b) the government interferes with counsel's traditionally recognized roles, such as conducting cross-examination, conferring with his client, or making closing arguments; (c) the trial court fails to inquire into a conflict of interest involving joint representation that is brought to its attention by the defense; (d) the defendant can show the existence of an actual conflict between his legitimate interests and his attorney's interests that adversely affected his attorney's performance; or (e) the attorney overrides the defendant respecting fundamental issues such as whether to plead guilty, waive the jury, testify truthfully, concede guilt at trial, or appeal (including appeal of a conviction based on a plea bargain that includes a plea waiver). In all other cases, the defendant must show prejudice as defined in (2), caused by a specific act or omission on the part of the attorney for which there is no reasonable explanation. A failure to investigate or to challenge the prosecution's evidence or allegations may be unreasonable, but a wide range of tactical considerations, hypothesized as well as proven, in addition to any malfeasance by the defendant in communicating with the attorney, is taken into account in evaluating the reasonableness of an explanation for attorney conduct.

---

[146] See also *Miranda v. Clark County*, 319 F.3d 465 (9th Cir. 2003).

(4) Methods of improving representation beyond that afforded by the Sixth Amendment include creation of a separate criminal defense bar, performance checklists, more vigorous judicial oversight, sanctions and civil suits against attorneys who commit non-prejudicial error, and injunctive actions designed to correct systemic deficiencies.

BIBLIOGRAPHY

Anderson, Heidi Reamer. Qualitative Assessments of Effective Assistance of Counsel. 51 Washburn 571 (2012).

Appel, Brent R. The Limited Impact of *Nix v. Whiteside* on Attorney-Client Relations. 136 U. Pa. L. Rev. 1413 (1988).

Bibas, Stephanos. Regulating the Plea-Bargaining Market: From Caveat Emptor to Consumer Protection. 99 Cal. L. Rev. 1117 (2011).

Blume, John H. and Stacey D. Neuman. It's Like Déjà vu All Over Again: *Williams v. Taylor*, *Wiggins v. Smith*, *Rompilla v. Beard*, and a (Partial) Return to the Guidelines Approach to the Effective Assistance of Counsel. 34 Am. J. Crim. L. 127 (2007).

Gable, Elizabeth and Tyler Green. *Wiggins v. Smith*: The Ineffective Assistance of Counsel Standard Applied Twenty Years After *Strickland*. 17 Geo.J.Leg.Ethics 755 (2004).

Green, Bruce A. Lethal Fiction: The Meaning of "Counsel" in the Sixth Amendment. 78 Iowa L.Rev. 433 (1993).

Herbert, Wm. C. Turner. Off the Beaten Path: An Analysis of the Supreme Court's Surprising Decision in *Mickens v. Taylor*. 81 N.C.L.Rev. 1268 (2003).

King, Nancy. Enforcing Effective Assistance after *Martinez*. 122 Yale L.J. 2428 (2013).

____. Plea Bargains that Waive Claims of Ineffective Assistance: Waiving *Padilla* and *Frye*. 51 Duq. L. Rev. 647 (2013).

Klein, Richard. The Emperor *Gideon* Has No Clothes: The Empty Promise of the Constitutional Right to Effective Assistance of Counsel. 13 Hastings Const.L.Q. 625 (1987).

Lefstein, Norman. Client Perjury in Criminal Cases: Still in Search of an Answer. 1 Geo. J. Legal Ethics. 521 (1988).

Lowenthal, Gary T. Joint Representation in Criminal Cases: A Critical Appraisal. 64 Va.L.Rev. 939 (1978).

Myers, Richard E. The Future of Effective Assistance of Counsel: Rereading *Cronic* and *Strickland* in Light of *Padilla*, *Frye*, and *Lafler*. 45 Tex. Tech. L. Rev. 229 (2012).

Place, Thomas M. Deferring Ineffectiveness Claims to Collateral Review: Ensuring Equal Access and a Right to Appointed Counsel. 98 Ky. L. Rev. 301 (2010).

Primus, Eve Brensike. Structural Reform in Criminal Defense: Relocating Ineffective Assistance of Counsel Claims. 92 Cornell L.Rev. 679 (2007).

Roberts, Jenny. Effective Plea Bargaining Counsel. 122 Yale L.J. 2650 (2013).

Slobogin, Christopher and Amy Mashburn. The Criminal Defense Lawyer's Fiduciary Duty to Clients with Mental Disability. 68 Fordham L.Rev. 1581 (2000).

Thomas, George C., III. History's Lesson for the Right to Counsel. 2004 Ill.L.Rev. 543.

Uphoff, Rodney. Who Should Control the Decision to Call a Witness?: Respecting a Criminal Defendant's Tactical Choices. 68 U.Cin.L.Rev. 763 (2000).

Uviller, Richard. Calling the Shots: The Allocation of Choice Between the Accused and the Counsel in the Defense of a Criminal Case. 52 Rutgers L.Rev. 719 (2000).

Part H

THE RELATIONSHIP BETWEEN THE FEDERAL AND STATE COURTS

As the contents of this book attest, since the 1950's the Supreme Court has increasingly focused its attention on the substantive constitutional rights of the criminally accused. But a substantive right is of no value unless its possessor has a forum in which to vindicate it. As the Warren Court expanded the scope of the Bill of Rights, it became clear that the state courts, which did not always agree with the new federal standards and were often opposed to federal intervention in the area of criminal procedure, could effectively nullify the Court's work by failing to provide a fair assessment of the newly created rights. Thus the ability of the state criminal defendant to obtain review in federal court became a pressing concern. Chapter 33 is devoted primarily to the issue of when federal relief should be granted to such defendants (although it also discusses federal habeas relief for federal prisoners).

While many state courts in the 1960's were reluctant to enforce the standards announced by the Warren Court, more recently a countertrend has emerged. As the post-Warren Court slowed the extension of federal constitutional rights, some state courts have rejected its pronouncements by interpreting their state constitutions to require more defendant-oriented procedures than the federally-announced constitutional minimum. Chapter 34 analyzes this modern state court reaction to the retrenchment of the post-Warren Court.

Chapter 33

FEDERAL HABEAS CORPUS:
THE CLOSING DOOR

33.01 Introduction

Generally, a state criminal defendant can gain access to the federal courts only when an error of federal constitutional dimension is alleged. Assuming the defendant has exhausted state court remedies, such access can be achieved in one of two ways. Either the defendant can petition the Supreme Court for direct review of the alleged constitutional errors,[1] or he can petition a United States district court to issue a "writ of habeas corpus," a "collateral" remedy challenging the legitimacy of the detention.[2] The tremendous number of criminal cases generated each year prevents direct review by the Supreme Court from being an effective remedy for state prisoners. The Court's entire criminal docket consists of from fifteen to thirty cases in each term, and some of these are appeals or habeas claims from *federal* prisoners.[3] Thus, the only realistic access to further federal review of state court decisions is through the vehicle of habeas corpus petitions to the lower federal courts.

The writ of habeas corpus has a long history. It appears to have originated in thirteenth century England as a means of ensuring that a party would appear before the court; literally, "habeas corpus" means "you have the body."[4] During the fifteenth and sixteenth centuries, in the midst of the common law courts' struggle to assert power, the writ developed into a device for challenging another court's jurisdiction to detain a person.[5] But it was not until the seventeenth century that the "Great Writ," as Blackstone called it,[6] became a vehicle for challenging arbitrary confinements by the Crown. Under the Habeas Corpus Act of 1679, Parliament attempted to undercut the king's persistent detention of persons in the absence of probable cause by giving the courts statutory authority to recognize the writ. Although the Act specifically dealt only with arrested persons (rather than those who had been convicted), it appears that the courts used the writ to release convicted individuals as well, at least when the detaining court lacked jurisdiction.[7]

In the United States most colonies recognized the writ, and the United States Constitution specifically provides that the "privilege of the Writ of Habeas Corpus shall not be suspended."[8] However, the Habeas Clause was probably meant to refer only to the suspension of habeas in *state* courts for *federal* prisoners (virtually all of whom, at

---

[1]   See § 29.01.

[2]   As used here, the "writ of habeas corpus" refers to the writ of habeas corpus *as subjiciendum*, which challenges the legality of detention. See *Fay v. Noia*, 372 U.S. 391, 83 S.Ct. 822 (1963) (describing other writs).

[3]   In the 2005 Term, for example, of the 83 cases disposed of with a full opinion, the Court decided 12 state criminal cases on certiorari or appeal and 10 habeas corpus cases involving state or federal prisoners. *The Supreme Court, 2005 Term*, 91 Harv.L.Rev. 372, 382 (Table III).

[4]   *Developments in the Law—Federal Habeas Corpus*, 83 Harvard L.Rev. 1038, 1042 (1970).

[5]   Id. at 1042–43.

[6]   3 Blackstone Commentaries at 129.

[7]   *Bushell's Case,* 124 Eng.Rep. 1006 (C.P. 1670).

[8]   U.S. Const., Art. I, § 9, cl. 2.

that time, were kept in state prisons).[9] Thus, the more important early development in American habeas law was the federal Judiciary Act of 1789,[10] which provided that *federal* courts could issue the writ, but still only for federal prisoners. Nearly eight decades later, Congress enacted the Habeas Corpus Act of 1867,[11] which authorized federal courts to issue a writ of habeas corpus in "all cases where any person may be restrained of his or her liberty in violation of the constitution, or of any treaty or law of the United States." This language extended the federal writ to state prisoners as well.

The modern successor of the Act of 1867, found in 28 U.S.C.A. §§ 2241–2255, continues to grant the federal writ to "any prisoner" who is "in custody in violation of the Constitution or laws or treaties of the United States."[12] But, until 1996, congressional enactments were otherwise silent as to the substantive scope of the writ, and only slightly more detailed in dealing with habeas procedures.[13] Thus, the extent to which habeas review was available to state and federal prisoners was left largely up to the courts. In 1996, with the passage of the Antiterrorism and Effective Death Penalty Act (AEDPA),[14] Congress purported to radically reform habeas review.[15] Yet many of the Act's provisions either codify previous caselaw or rely on its reasoning.[16] Thus, Supreme Court decisions construing the pre-1996 habeas statutes remain important.

In construing these provisions, the Supreme Court has fluctuated in its approach. The history of the writ up to the 1970's reflects a constant expansion of its scope, to the point where it became available to virtually any prisoner asserting a constitutional claim that had not been deliberately waived at trial or on direct review. Since that time, however, the Court has significantly reduced the availability of the writ, both substantively and procedurally. In the course of doing so, it has sought to reinvigorate state systems of review as the final arbiter of most federal constitutional claims, a development that has been dubbed the "New Federalism."[17]

The member of the Court who most vigorously pushed for a broad, easily pursued writ of habeas corpus was Justice Brennan. In *Sanders v. United States,*[18] for instance, he stated:

> Conventional notions of finality of litigation have no place where life or liberty is at stake and infringement of constitutional rights is alleged. If "government

---

[9]   William F. Duker, A Constitutional History of Habeas Corpus 129 (1980).

[10]   1 Stat. 81–82 (1789).

[11]   14 Stat. 385 (1867).

[12]   28 U.S.C.A. § 2241(c)(3) (1948).

[13]   The statutes merely prohibited "abuse of the writ", id. at § 2244, required exhaustion of state remedies, id. § 2254(b)(c) and required that state court findings of fact be presumed correct. Id. at 2254(d).

[14]   Amending 28 U.S.C.A. §§ 2244, 2253, 2254, and 2255, and Rule 22 of the Federal Rules of Appellate Procedure, and adding §§ 2261 through 2266 on habeas corpus procedures in capital cases.

[15]   The Explanatory Statement of the Senate-House conference committee stated that the Act was meant to "to curb the abuse of the statutory writ of habeas corpus, and to address the acute problems of unnecessary delay and abuse in capital cases." 104th Cong. 2d Sess. No. 104–518. However, congressional enactments that restrict the scope of the writ beyond that established by the courts could violate the Suspension Clause of the U.S. Constitution. See *Felker v. Turpin*, 518 U.S. 651, 116 S.Ct. 2333 (1996), discussed in § 33.04(b).

[16]   See §§ 32.02 and 33.03.

[17]   See, e.g., Richard A. Michael, *The 'New Federalism' and the Burger Court's Deference to the States in Federal Habeas Proceedings*, 64 Iowa L.Rev. 233 (1979).

[18]   373 U.S. 1, 83 S.Ct. 1068 (1963).

[is] always [to] be accountable to the judiciary for a man's imprisonment," access to the courts on habeas must not be thus impeded.

Along the same lines, in *Kaufman v. United States*,[19] he argued that federal habeas review of both federal and state court convictions is necessary to provide "adequate protection of constitutional rights."

When a state (as opposed to a federal) conviction was involved, the Warren Court cited additional reasons for expanding federal review. In *Kaufman,* for instance, the Court stated that "federal courts [should] have the 'last say' with respect to questions of federal law." Further, Brennan later asserted, "[s]tate judges popularly elected may have difficulty resisting popular pressures not experienced by federal judges given lifetime tenure designed to immunize them from such influences."[20] Others have pointed to differences in the means of selection, salary, workload, and attitudes of federal and state judges as reasons for entrusting the ultimate decision about constitutional issues to federal judges.[21] Undoubtedly underlying these arguments was the fear that, without federal review of state decisions, the impact of the "revolution" in criminal procedure that occurred during the 1960's would be blunted in many states.

The post-Warren Court's restriction of access to the federal courts has been fueled by several countering concerns. Perhaps foremost among these is a desire for "finality." As Justice O'Connor stated, convictions that are reversed on habeas can exact significant costs on society, since "[p]assage of time, erosion of memory, and dispersion of witnesses may render retrial difficult, even impossible."[22] Further, according to Justice Powell, open-ended collateral review tends to distract prisoners from seeking rehabilitation, and undermines society's "psychological" desire to have a final conclusion to criminal matters.[23] A related limiting rationale cited by the post-Warren Court is efficiency. Habeas review places a heavy burden on the federal courts; in 1970, when the scope of habeas review was at its broadest, there were over 9,000 federal habeas petitions filed.[24] Consideration of these claims, Justice Powell noted, detracts from the federal courts' ability to decide other issues, yet rarely results in reversal of an earlier decision.[25]

With respect to the claim that federal review of state cases is an important means of ensuring quality justice, the post-Warren Court has had two responses. First, it manifests greater faith in the capabilities of state court judges. As the Court stated in *Stone v. Powell,*[26] "[d]espite differences in institutional environment and the unsympathetic attitude to federal constitutional claims of some state judges in years past, we are unwilling to assume that there now exists a general lack of appropriate sensitivity to constitutional rights in the trial and appellate courts of the several States." Similarly, Justice O'Connor, a former state appellate judge, has noted (in an article written before she became a justice) that many state judges are not elected, thus

---

[19]   394 U.S. 217, 89 S.Ct. 1068 (1969).

[20]   *Stone v. Powell,* 428 U.S. 465, 96 S.Ct. 3037 (1976) (Brennan, J., dissenting).

[21]   See, e.g., Burt Neuborne, *The Myth of Parity*, 90 Harv.L.Rev. 1105 (1977).

[22]   *Engle v. Isaac,* 456 U.S. 107, 102 S.Ct. 1558 (1982).

[23]   *Stone v. Powell,* 428 U.S. 465, 96 S.Ct. 3037 (1976).

[24]   *Federal Habeas Corpus and Its Reform: An Empirical Analysis*, 13 Rutgers L.J. 675, 677 n. 2 (1982). Note that, by 1980, after the post-Warren Court had significantly reduced the scope of the writ, the number of petitions was still slightly over 7,000 and much of this reduction could have been due to the increased availability of § 1983 claims. Id.

[25]   *Schneckloth v. Bustamonte,* 412 U.S. 218, 93 S.Ct. 2041 (1973) (Powell, J., concurring).

[26]   428 U.S. 465, 96 S.Ct. 3037 (1976).

reducing their sensitivity to "majoritarian pressures." She also asserted that many lawyers see "no great difference in the quality of judges or justice between the state and federal courts."[27] The second response to the argument that federal courts must be the ultimate arbiter of federal rights has been an emphasis on the concept of "comity," or respect for the judgment of state courts. According to Justice O'Connor, this concern is not just symbolic. She has argued that federal review (by a single-judge district court) of state appellate decisions undermines "morale" at the state level; this in turn leaves state judges less willing to enforce constitutional rights, to the detriment of the majority of state litigants, who never seek federal habeas review.[28]

This chapter discusses how these various perspectives on the writ of habeas corpus have influenced its substantive and procedural scope. Specifically, it will address judicial pronouncements and legislative provisions concerning: (1) the types of claims that may be heard pursuant to the writ; (2) the extent to which claims can be foreclosed pursuant to state rules; (3) the exhaustion requirement; (4) limitations on successive petitions; (5) the custody requirement; (6) the ability of federal habeas courts to engage in independent fact-finding; and (7) special provisions for indigent habeas petitioners.

33.02   The Substantive Scope of the Writ

(a)   From *Watkins* to *Brown*: Expansion of the Writ

As noted in the introduction, the common law writ of habeas corpus focused on whether the detaining court had "jurisdiction" over the defendant. This concept was given a narrow definition by Chief Justice Marshall in *Ex parte Watkins*,[29] decided in 1830. Federal habeas review was denied in that case, despite a claim that the indictment failed to state a crime, because the state trial court had "general jurisdiction of the subject;" the fact that the state court's decision may have been erroneous was irrelevant.

Gradually, however, the jurisdiction concept expanded to encompass claims that were not purely "jurisdictional." In the 1879 decision of *Ex parte Siebold*,[30] for instance, the Court permitted habeas review of a conviction based on a statute alleged to be unconstitutional, despite the state court's technical jurisdiction over the matter, on the ground that a conviction based on such a law would be "not merely erroneous, but . . . illegal and void." Some 35 years later, in *Frank v. Mangum*,[31] the Court indicated that a conviction rendered by a mob-dominated tribunal was a violation of due process and subject to federal habeas review, unless the state provided an adequate post-conviction "corrective process."[32] And in *Johnson v. Zerbst*,[33] the Court held that a federal trial

---

[27]   Sandra D. O'Connor, *Trends in the Relationship Between the Federal and State Courts from the Perspective of a State Court Judge*, 22 Wm. & Mary L.Rev. 801 (1981). The latter assertion was based on a study which showed that significantly more lawyers preferred to file their claims in state rather than federal court. However, the survey also showed that although 125 lawyers saw no difference between the quality of state and federal judges, 95 felt that federal judges were more qualified, while only 25 felt the opposite. Id. at 817.

[28]   Id. at 801.

[29]   28 U.S. (3 Pet.) 193 (1830).

[30]   100 U.S. (10 Otto) 371 (1880).

[31]   237 U.S. 309, 35 S.Ct. 582 (1915).

[32]   In *Frank*, the Court found that such process was present and denied relief. However, in *Moore v. Dempsey*, 261 U.S. 86, 43 S.Ct. 265 (1923), it granted relief, apparently on the ground that post-conviction state procedure had been inadequate.

[33]   304 U.S. 458, 58 S.Ct. 1019 (1938).

court's failure to provide counsel in violation of the Sixth Amendment resulted in a loss of "jurisdiction," thus allowing habeas review as a remedial measure.

Finally, in the 1942 decision of *Waley v. Johnston*,[34] the Court explicitly dispensed with jurisdictional analysis, concluding that the writ extended "to those exceptional cases where the conviction has been in disregard of the constitutional rights of the accused." However, like *Frank*, *Waley* limited use of the writ to those situations where it was "the only effective means of preserving [the defendant's] rights." This formulation appeared to give a federal habeas court discretion to hear any federal constitutional claim, but only if, to use *Frank's* phrase, the "corrective process" provided below was inadequate.

Then, in 1953, the Court decided *Brown v. Allen*,[35] which apparently eliminated the latter half of this formulation. There, the Court held that a federal habeas court could consider a jury discrimination claim and a coerced confession claim even though both had been fully litigated and rejected by the state courts. While stating that the federal court should generally accord conclusive weight to state court findings of fact (unless there was a "vital flaw" in its procedure), the Court stressed that the federal habeas court should reach its own conclusion on the law. For roughly twenty years after it was decided, *Brown* held the federal courtroom door wide open to prisoners, both state and federal,[36] who sought review of constitutional claims that had previously been raised at the trial level.[37]

(b) The Full and Fair Hearing Exception

The first inroad into the broad reach of habeas established in *Brown* came in *Stone v. Powell*.[38] There the Court held that "where the State has provided an opportunity for full and fair litigation of a Fourth Amendment claim," a federal court should not grant review of the claim. According to the Court, affording habeas review of Fourth Amendment claims would provide little benefit, at great cost. Justice Powell, writing for a six-member majority, noted first that the deterrent effect of excluding illegally seized evidence at trial is unlikely to be "enhanced" by permitting exclusion after conviction and appeal, "years after incarceration of the defendant." Nor did the Court believe that habeas review was necessary to keep state courts in line; it rejected "a basic mistrust of state courts as fair and competent forums for adjudication of constitutional rights." At the same time, habeas review undermines the government's interest in conserving judicial resources, and in promoting finality and comity. Furthermore, even a successful Fourth Amendment claim exacts a cost, because it "deflects the truthfinding process and often frees the guilty."

Stone established, then, that adequate state process could bar certain types of claims from habeas review. Although the full and fair hearing exception has never been given its full potential scope (and in fact has been limited to Fourth Amendment claims), its history is instructive on the Court's efforts to limit federal habeas review. Below is

---

[34] 316 U.S. 101, 62 S.Ct. 964 (1942).

[35] 344 U.S. 443, 73 S.Ct. 397 (1953).

[36] In *Kaufman v. United States*, 394 U.S. 217, 89 S.Ct. 1068 (1969), the Court made clear that *Brown* extended to federal prisoners as well.

[37] When the petitioner did not raise the claim at the guilt adjudication stage, a different analysis—based on the scope of procedural default—applied. See § 33.03.

[38] 428 U.S. 465, 96 S.Ct. 3037 (1976).

described the Court's struggle over the types of claims to which the exception applies, the definition of "full and fair hearing," and Congress' attempts to deal with both matters in the AEDPA.

(1) The Scope of the Exception

Despite its focus on the nature of the state's process, *Stone* was not a reversion to the pre-*Brown* rule that provision of adequate "corrective processes" by the state would bar federal habeas review of *any* constitutional claim. For instance, three years after *Stone,* in *Jackson v. Virginia,*[39] the Court explicitly refused to apply the full and fair hearing exception to a claim alleging that a conviction was not based on proof beyond a reasonable doubt. The Court concluded that, given its prior holding in *In re Winship*[40] requiring state prosecutions to meet the reasonable doubt burden for each essential element of the offense, a state prisoner is entitled to have a federal court determine not only "whether the jury was properly instructed but [also] whether the record evidence could reasonably support a finding of guilt beyond a reasonable doubt." Justice Stewart's majority opinion specifically rejected application of *Stone* to this type of claim, asserting that federal courts would not be unduly burdened by such review and that "[t]he constitutional issue presented in this case is far different from the kind of issue" present in *Stone.*

This language in *Jackson* suggested that the post-Warren Court would continue to apply the full and fair hearing limitation to review of claims unrelated to the guilt of the petitioner. But the same term as *Jackson* the Court decided *Rose v. Mitchell,*[41] which refused to apply *Stone* to bar consideration of discrimination in the grand jury selection process, a claim unrelated to guilt. Justice Blackmun's majority opinion distinguished equal protection petitions from Fourth Amendment claims on several grounds. First, while the latter claim focuses on police behavior, a claim concerning the operation of the grand jury system involves allegations that the *judiciary* has violated the Constitution; in this situation, the Court doubted that state courts would give the claim a full and fair hearing. As Blackmun put it, "[t]here is a need in such cases to ensure that an independent means of obtaining review by a federal court is available on a broader basis than review only by this Court will permit." Second, collateral review of equal protection claims is less likely to cause "friction" with state courts because it is of less recent vintage and more firmly grounded in the Constitution than the judicially created exclusionary rule. Third, whereas applying the exclusionary rule at the habeas stage is unlikely to have much of a deterrent effect, the "educative" effect of quashing indictments on racial discrimination grounds "is likely to be great," and yet cost society little, because reindictment is usually possible. Finally, the Court noted that a racial discrimination claim seeks to vindicate interests that "are substantially more compelling than those at issue in *Stone.*"

Rose left the Court's approach to the substantive scope of the writ of habeas corpus unclear. Blackmun's first rationale for the holding in that case—that, for institutional reasons, state courts may not fairly adjudicate claims against the grand jury selection process—is probably the strongest. The other three reasons all rest, at bottom, on the somewhat dubious assertion that discrimination claims are inherently more important

---

[39]   443 U.S. 307, 99 S.Ct. 2781 (1979).

[40]   397 U.S. 358, 90 S.Ct. 1068 (1970).

[41]   443 U.S. 545, 99 S.Ct. 2993 (1979).

than the privacy rights protected by the Fourth Amendment. Further, the first reason is consistent with the focus in *Stone* and earlier Court cases on the quality of the state's corrective processes (although, as an empirical matter, it is not clear that state courts lack objectivity in evaluating discrimination claims lodged against the grand jury selection process). A number of other constitutional claims alleging even more direct misconduct by state court judges would presumably be reviewable on habeas under this theory.[42]

The Court's next case dealing with the substantive scope of habeas, *Kimmelman v. Morrison*,[43] did little to clear up confusion as to whether the substantive scope of the writ would focus on the guilt-relatedness of the claim, the adequacy of state corrective processes, or a mixture of the two. There defense counsel failed to seek exclusion of evidence that may have been illegally seized from the defendant's apartment. The claim on habeas was not based directly on the Fourth Amendment,[44] but rather focused on the ineffectiveness of counsel. Justice Brennan's opinion for the Court distinguished this case from *Stone* by stressing that the exclusionary rule is a judicially created right "designed to safeguard Fourth Amendment rights generally," while the Sixth Amendment right to effective assistance is a trial-related, "personal" right. Thus, he concluded, the latter right is deserving of the added protection of federal review whenever it is raised. Furthermore, Brennan pointed out, prohibiting federal habeas review of such claims would often foreclose their review altogether, because defendants may not discover counsel's incompetence before state review is exhausted (although in *Morrison* itself, the petitioner did raise the ineffectiveness claim at both the appeal and habeas stages in state court).

Justice Brennan also rejected the state's argument that the Court's holding would emasculate *Stone* by allowing petitioners to raise Fourth Amendment claims in the guise of Sixth Amendment arguments. Brennan emphasized that the two-prong incompetence and prejudice standard for ineffective assistance, as outlined in *Strickland v. Washington*,[45] was a "rigorous" one, requiring a strong presumption of attorney competence and a strong presumption that, even if counsel's inadequacy is established, the attorney's conduct did not affect the outcome of the proceeding. Thus, for instance, a strategic decision not to assert a Fourth Amendment claim, or a concededly incompetent failure to assert such a claim that does not affect the outcome of the trial, would not amount to ineffective assistance and would not lead to reversal by a federal habeas court. In *Morrison* itself, the Court found that the attorney's failure to make the suppression motion, which apparently resulted from his ignorance of state discovery and motion rules, was incompetent. But it remanded the case for a determination as to whether the Fourth Amendment claim was meritorious and, if so, whether excluding the evidence would have affected the outcome of the trial.

Brennan's disclaimers notwithstanding, the Court's disposition of *Morrison* makes clear that, when framed as part of a Sixth Amendment violation, the validity of a Fourth Amendment claim will now have to be considered by the federal habeas court. Perhaps

---

[42] See, e.g., *North Carolina v. Pearce,* 395 U.S. 711, 89 S.Ct. 2072 (1969) (vindictive sentencing by judge), discussed in § 29.02(d); *Chambers v. Mississippi,* 405 U.S. 1205, 92 S.Ct. 754 (1972) (judicial infringement of confrontation and compulsory process rights), discussed in §§ 28.05(b)(1), 28.06(b).

[43] 477 U.S. 365, 106 S.Ct. 2574 (1986).

[44] Given the Court's procedural default decisions, see § 33.03(c) & (d), such a claim probably would have been barred procedurally as well as substantively.

[45] 466 U.S. 668, 104 S.Ct. 2052 (1984), discussed in § 32.03(b).

concerned about this undermining of *Stone* Justice Powell, the author of that decision, wrote a concurring opinion (joined by Chief Justice Burger and Justice Rehnquist) which argued that failure to raise a Fourth Amendment claim should *never* constitute prejudice under *Strickland*. Powell contended that only if the claim underlying a Sixth Amendment petition relates to the accuracy of the factual guilt adjudication should a federal habeas court hear the claim.

If Powell's position had been adopted, then the post-Warren Court would have made a strong move toward a guilt-related definition of the writ's substantive scope. But since six members of the Court did not join Powell's opinion in *Morrison,* this is not yet the Court's stance. Moreover, to the extent Brennan is right that ineffective assistance claims tend to evade discovery until after much or all of the state process is complete, *Morrison* resonates with the lack of corrective process approach. Finally, one might argue that, as the Court subsequently recognized in another context,[46] ineffective assistance is "imputed" to inadequate monitoring by the state courts and is thus less likely to be fairly considered by them.

A claim based on *Miranda v. Arizona,*[47] on the other hand, would seem a good candidate for the full and fair hearing exception to habeas review, because it usually does not lead one to question the guilt of the petitioner, as did the claim in *Jackson,* nor does it implicate the state's judiciary, as did the claims in *Rose* and *Morrison* or usually evade review on appeal at the state level, as might occur with an ineffective assistance claim. But in *Withrow v. Williams,*[48] the Court held, 5–4, that *Stone* does not apply to such claims. Justice Souter reasoned for the Court that *Miranda,* although "prophylactic," safeguards the Fifth Amendment, "a fundamental *trial* right" founded on historical principles, and thus is distinguishable from *Mapp's* exclusionary rule, the claim involved in *Stone*. Further, the right protected by *Miranda* is not "necessarily divorced" from the correct ascertainment of guilt. "Most importantly," Souter stated, eliminating habeas review of *Miranda* claims will not reduce the federal courts' docket, because most of these claims can be reframed as due process involuntariness issues.

In dissent, Justice O'Connor, joined by Chief Justice Rehnquist, questioned all of these reasons. Her principal contention was that, while the Fifth Amendment's prohibition on compelled statements is a "fundamental right," *Miranda* permits exclusion even of uncompelled statements and thus is *not* based on "fundamental" principles. For the same reason, *Miranda* claims have little to do with preventing unreliable verdicts, and are not easily transformable into voluntariness claims. Thus, O'Connor concluded, *Miranda* claims should be subject to the full and fair hearing exception. In a separate dissent, Justice Scalia, joined by Justice Thomas, went even further, arguing for a broad full and fair hearing exception for all claims that do not go "to the fairness of the trial process or to the accuracy of the ultimate result."

(2) Criteria for a Full and Fair Hearing

Under *Stone,* a Fourth Amendment claim must be accorded federal habeas review only when the state fails to provide a "full and fair opportunity to litigate the claim." Whether this language is meant to be a modern version of *Frank's* relatively narrowly

---

[46] See *Murray v. Carrier,* 477 U.S. 478, 106 S.Ct. 2639 (1986), discussed in § 33.03(d).

[47] 384 U.S. 436, 86 S.Ct. 1602 (1966), discussed in § 16.02(d).

[48] 507 U.S. 680, 113 S.Ct. 1745 (1993).

conceived *lack*-of-corrective-process standard is not clear.[49] Most lower courts seem to construe the phrase more broadly than *Frank's* mob-domination fact pattern might suggest. For instance, in *Lee v. Winston*,[50] the Fourth Circuit permitted federal review of a surgical attempt to obtain a bullet because the state court had given defense counsel only three days to prepare for the pre-surgery hearing and had repeatedly refused to grant counsel's requests for a continuance to obtain expert medical assistance, despite his "obviously diligent effort to obtain" such assistance.[51]

However, assuming adequate process, the mere fact that the state court erroneously applied the Fourth Amendment will generally not suffice to meet the full and fair hearing requirement. Otherwise, *Stone* would be emasculated. In *Stone* itself the Court denied relief even though it noted that, in one of the two cases at issue there, the state court had incorrectly applied the law.[52] Most lower courts have reached similar conclusions.[53]

(3) 1996 Habeas Reform

The AEDPA on its face appears to eliminate the full and fair hearing exception. The section of the AEDPA that deals with the substantive scope of habeas jurisdiction permits review of a state court determination *whenever* the determination "resulted in a decision that was contrary to, or involved an unreasonable application of, clearly established Federal law, as determined by the Supreme Court of the United States."[54] As discussed below,[55] this provision is interpreted very narrowly. Nonetheless, it indicates that even if there *is* a reasonable determination of the facts at the state level, a claim should be heard whenever the state decision runs counter to well-established federal law. Thus, read literally this language requires, contrary to *Stone*, that a federal habeas court hear a claim challenging a clearly erroneous application of Fourth Amendment law even when there has been a full and fair hearing. Lower courts, however, have refused to find that this provision overrules *Stone*, given the absence of any explicit reference in the statute to the *Stone* exception.[56]

(c) The New Rule Exception

As described in more detail elsewhere in this book,[57] independently of its attempts to define the "jurisdiction" of federal habeas courts, the Supreme Court has also developed an approach to retroactivity doctrine which, in its most recent guise, effectively bars federal habeas review of most claims seeking a "new" constitutional

---

[49] The *Stone* Court made reference to *Townsend v. Sain*, 372 U.S. 293, 83 S.Ct. 745 (1963), which developed the somewhat looser standard determining when federal habeas courts may hold an evidentiary hearing. See § 33.05(c). However, this reference was preceded by a "Cf." signature, which makes *Townsend's* relevance to the issue ambiguous.

[50] 717 F.2d 888 (4th Cir. 1983).

[51] The Supreme Court subsequently accepted the case, noting that the state did not challenge the lack-of-fair-hearing finding. *Winston v. Lee,* 470 U.S. 753, 105 S.Ct. 1611 (1985).

[52] The Nebraska Supreme Court had referred to information not available to the magistrate, a practice which the U.S. Supreme Court noted it had found inappropriate "several times."

[53] Philip Halpern, *Federal Habeas Corpus and the Mapp Exclusionary Rule After* Stone v. Powell, 82 Colum.L.Rev. 1, 17–18 (1982).

[54] 28 U.S.C.A. § 2254(d).

[55] See § 33.02(c).

[56] See, e.g., *Lee v. Johnson*, 1999 WL 409456 (E.D.N.Y. 1999); *Weeks v. Angelone*, 4 F.Supp.2d 497 (E.D.Va. 1998); *Tokar v. Bowersox*, 1 F.Supp.2d 986 (E.D.Mo. 1998).

[57] See § 29.06(c).

ruling. This exception to federal habeas jurisdiction has had a much more significant impact on the scope of habeas review than the full and fair hearing exception. Furthermore, the new rule exception has had a major impact on the development of federal constitutional law, since many of the Supreme Court's groundbreaking pronouncements, both for the defense and for the government, have come on habeas review.[58]

For many years, the extent to which a constitutional rule was applied to other pending cases depended upon a complicated analysis examining the extent to which government officials could have anticipated the rule, the purpose of the rule, and the effect its retroactive application would have on the administration of justice.[59] But in two decisions handed down in the late 1980's, the Court held that retroactivity doctrine would no longer depend upon these types of factors, but rather on whether the rule was announced on direct review or on habeas. The first decision was *Griffith v. Kentucky*,[60] which involved the retroactivity of a rule announced on direct review by the Court. There, the Court stressed the frequent inequity caused by the claim-oriented approach to retroactivity, which granted relief to the petitioner whose case happened to be selected by the Court but often denied it to others similarly situated, simply because their case was not chosen for review. Accordingly, the Court held that any rule it announced on direct review of state or federal cases, regardless of its "purpose" or the effect on the administration of justice, should apply to all other cases pending on direct review.

Two years later, in *Teague v. Lane*,[61] the Court reached quite a different result with respect to habeas review. The Court first asserted that the principal purpose of federal habeas review is to deter state courts from misapplying federal law prevailing at the time of trial and appeal. From this, it concluded that there was no purpose in giving retroactive effect to "new" rules announced by a federal habeas court; such an approach would have no deterrent effect on the state courts. Thus, only those rules that are "dictated by precedent" at the time of conviction should affect other cases on collateral review. More importantly for present purposes, the Court then relied on *Griffith's* "equity" idea in deciding that, because the "harm caused by the failure to treat similarly situated defendants alike cannot be exaggerated," the habeas court confronted with a "new" claim should not even consider its merits in the case before it; to permit such consideration would unjustly be favoring the petitioner.

In short, *Teague* held that unless a claim is "dictated by precedent," it cannot be heard by a federal habeas court.[62] *Teague* did announce two narrow exceptions to this rule, however. The first is when the "new" claim goes to the ability of the court to hear the case (e.g., a claim that the statute upon which conviction is based is unconstitutional, or a claim that the prosecution was barred by double jeopardy). This exception is similar to the view of habeas "jurisdiction" recognized by the Court in cases like *Siebold*, and will only rarely be applicable. The second exception is when the claim implicates procedures "central to an accurate determination of innocence or guilt," thus resurrecting *Stone's* emphasis on the guilt-relatedness of the claim. It is extremely

---

[58] See Justice Brennan's dissent in *Teague v. Lane,* 489 U.S. 288, 109 S.Ct. 1060 (1989) (listing cases that would not have been decided had the new rule exception been in effect).

[59] See, e.g., *Brown v. Louisiana,* 447 U.S. 323, 100 S.Ct. 2214 (1980), discussed in § 29.06(a)(1).

[60] 479 U.S. 314, 107 S.Ct. 708 (1987).

[61] 489 U.S. 288, 109 S.Ct. 1060 (1989).

[62] Note, however, that *Teague* does not constrain the authority of *state* courts to give broader effect to new rules than is required by that opinion. *Danforth v. Minnesota,* 552 U.S. 264, 128 S.Ct. 1029 (2008).

unlikely that the Court will create a new rule in this latter category because, as *Teague* itself indicates, at this point in the history of criminal procedure jurisprudence there are probably very few unresolved "watershed" issues affecting fundamental aspects of justice.[63] Given the narrowness of these exceptions,[64] the extent to which *Teague* affects habeas review will depend largely on how the Court determines whether a rule is "dictated by precedent." As discussed in Chapter 29,[65] to date, its interpretation of this phrase has been relatively restrictive, with the consequence that the scope of federal habeas review is significantly reduced from pre-*Teague* days.

In 1996, Congress reduced the scope of federal habeas review even further. As noted in the previous section, the AEDPA permits federal habeas relief regarding a state court determination of law made at a fair hearing only if the determination is "contrary to, or involved an unreasonable application of, clearly established Federal law, as determined by the Supreme Court of the United States."[66] In *Williams v. Taylor*,[67] five members of the Court, in an opinion by Justice O'Connor, reached three conclusions about this language. First, the limitation to cases involving "clearly established" Supreme Court law, while similar-sounding to *Teague's* restriction of habeas to cases involving rules governed by existing precedent, in fact "bears only a slight connection to our *Teague* jurisprudence;" under the AEDPA, only state court decisions applying *holdings* (as opposed to dicta) from the *Supreme Court* may be heard.[68] Second, a state court decision is "contrary to" such precedent only if it "arrives at a conclusion opposite to that reached by this Court on a question of law" or "decides a case differently than this Court has on a set of materially indistinguishable facts."[69] Finally, a state court decision involves an "unreasonable application" of clearly established federal law only if it was "objectively unreasonable;" an incorrect ruling is not necessarily an unreasonable one, according to the Court. In *Harrington v. Richter*,[70] the Court stressed that, because the test is objective, a state court's determination can be reasonable even if that court provides no reasons for its opinion, so long as "fair-minded jurists" could reach the same result.[71]

Occasionally, even this narrow definition of "unreasonable" is met. For instance, in *Williams* the Court held that the Virginia Supreme Court had unreasonably construed the prejudice prong *of Strickland v. Washington*,[72] by requiring something more than a reasonable probability that ineffective assistance would have changed the outcome of the case.

---

[63] See, e.g., *Sawyer v. Smith*, 497 U.S. 227, 110 S.Ct. 2822 (1990) (holding that to qualify under the second exception, a rule "must not only improve accuracy, but also 'alter our understanding of the *bedrock procedural elements*' essential to the fairness of a proceeding").

[64] See § 29.06(c)(2) for further explication of these exceptions.

[65] See § 29.06(c)(1).

[66] 28 U.S.C.A. § 2254(d)(1).

[67] 529 U.S. 362, 120 S.Ct. 1495 (2000).

[68] See, e.g., *Carey v. Musladin*, 549 U.S. 70, 127 S.Ct. 649 (2006) (AEDPA exception does not apply because previous Court decisions dealing with prejudicial impact of courtroom procedures [see § 28.03(c)(2)] dealt only with state-initiated practices, not with private-actor conduct such as, in this case, family members wearing buttons with victim's picture on it).

[69] The law relevant to this determination is the law at the time of state-court adjudication on the merits. *Greene v. Fisher*, 565 U.S. 34, 132 S.Ct. 38 (2011).

[70] 562 U.S. 86, 131 S.Ct. 770 (2011).

[71] However, when the habeas court can "look through" the state appellate court decision to a lower court opinion that does provide a rationale, it must do so. *Wilson v. Sellers*, ___ U.S. ___, 138 S.Ct. 1188 (2018).

[72] 466 U.S. 668, 104 S.Ct. 2052 (1984), discussed in § 32.03(b).

Usually, however, the Court reaches the opposite result. In *Ramdass v. Angelone*,[73] for instance, five members of the Court held that the Virginia Supreme Court's interpretation of *Simmons v. South Carolina*,[74] which requires the judge to inform capital sentencing juries when a defendant is parole ineligible, was not unreasonable. There the Virginia Supreme Court had held that, even though Ramdass had already been convicted for three independent felonies—a fact that would normally render him parole ineligible under Virginia law—the final judgment on the third felony had not been entered until 19 days after his capital sentencing hearing, and thus the trial court's failure to give a *Simmons* instruction did not violate the Constitution. In a similar vein was *Bell v. Cone*,[75] where the claim was that counsel's failure to offer any mitigating evidence or make a closing argument at Cone's capital sentencing proceeding constituted ineffective assistance of counsel. The defense counsel's explanations for his inaction were not very persuasive,[76] and the Sixth Circuit Court of Appeals found that counsel's failure to plead for mercy after the prosecution's closing argument amounted to a failure to subject the prosecution's case to adversarial testing. But the Supreme Court held that it was reasonable for the state court to find that *Strickland* was not violated on these facts. Whether the decision would have been different had the case come to the Court on direct appeal is not clear, but the Court stressed again, as it had in *Williams*, that "an unreasonable application is different from an incorrect one."[77]

AEDPA's unreasonable application rule only applies if the state court adjudicated the federal claim on its merits.[78] Thus, federal habeas petitioners have argued that when a state court does not directly address a federal claim (and the claim was not procedurally defaulted), the claim may be raised in federal court. But the Supreme Court has construed the phrase "adjudicated on the merits" broadly. In *Harrington v. Richter*,[79] it held that when a state court summarily rejects all claims without discussion, it has adjudicated all of them, state and federal, on the merits. And in *Johnson v. Williams*,[80] it held that the same rule presumptively applies when the state court addresses some of the claims raised by a defendant but not a claim that is later raised again in a federal habeas proceeding. According to the Court, only if the petitioner can show that the federal claim was "inadvertently overlooked" by the state court, based on a showing, for instance, that "the state standard is less protective [than the federal standard] or that the federal precedent was mentioned in passing," might the presumption be rebutted, "either by a habeas petitioner (to show that the federal court should consider the claim

---

[73]   530 U.S. 156, 120 S.Ct. 2113 (2000).

[74]   512 U.S. 154, 114 S.Ct. 2187 (1994).

[75]   535 U.S. 685, 122 S.Ct. 1843 (2002).

[76]   For instance, as Justice Stevens noted in dissent, the attorney explained the failure to present character witnesses on the ground that their cross-examination would allow the state to bring out Cone's crimes after his service in Vietnam, despite the facts that these offenses were already in the record and that his entire defense at trial had been that Cone had changed because of the war.

[77]   See also, *Price v. Vincent*, 538 U.S. 634, 123 S.Ct. 1848 (2003)(state supreme court did not render an "unreasonable" interpretation of the Double Jeopardy Clause in deciding that an acquittal of first degree murder did not occur when the trial judge stated, in response to a defense motion for a directed verdict, that "what we have at the very best is Second Degree Murder . . . I think that Second Degree Murder is an appropriate charge as to the defendants.").

[78]   28 U.S.C.A. § 2254(d). Furthermore, in determining whether a state court decision is reasonable the federal habeas court is limited to the record that was before the state court that adjudicated the claim on the merits. *Cullen v. Pinholster*, 563 U.S. 170, 131 S.Ct. 1388 (2011).

[79]   562 U.S. 86, 131 S.Ct. 770 (2011).

[80]   568 U.S. 289, 133 S.Ct. 1088 (2013).

de novo) or by the State (to show that the federal claim should be regarded as procedurally defaulted)."

The AEDPA may restrict habeas review to a greater extent than *Teague* did in still another way. The only other situation besides the clearly-established-law scenario in which the AEDPA permits a federal court to grant relief is when the state court decision is "based on an unreasonable determination of the facts."[81] This provision may well encompass *Teague's* second exception to its prohibition against new rules (i.e., the exception that allows new rule claims that implicate "procedures central to an accurate determination of innocence or guilt"). But neither this language nor the clearly-established-law provision seems to recognize *Teague's* other, "lack of jurisdiction," exception. It remains to be seen whether the Supreme Court will agree that habeas relief can be denied to a person whose act is beyond criminal proscription (e.g., a conviction under an unconstitutional statute).[82]

(d) The Federal Question Requirement

Even *Brown,* which represented federal habeas jurisdiction at its most expansive, limited federal habeas claims by state prisoners to those based on the federal constitution. This limitation is generally not controversial, but it was tested in dramatic fashion in *Herrera v. Collins,*[83] where the Court held noncognizable a habeas petitioner's claim that he was entitled to vacation of his death sentence because of newly discovered evidence showing his innocence of the underlying crime. The petitioner argued that his execution under these circumstances would violate the Eighth Amendment's cruel and unusual punishment clause. But at least two members of the Court concluded that such a claim is not based on the Constitution, and four others concluded that the claim in this particular case was not cognizable.

Supporting the first point of view, Chief Justice Rehnquist's majority opinion began by asserting that a claim of newly discovered evidence, by itself, is factual, not constitutional, in nature. Many lower court opinions had reached the same conclusion,[84] based on an unelaborated statement in *Townsend v. Sain,*[85] decided ten years after *Brown,* that "the existence merely of newly discovered evidence relevant to the guilt of a state prisoner is not a ground for relief on federal habeas corpus." Rehnquist's opinion in *Herrera* explained that, "[i]n light of the historical availability of new trials . . . and the contemporary practice in the States, we cannot say that Texas' refusal to entertain petitioner's newly discovered evidence eight years after his conviction transgresses a principle of fundamental fairness 'rooted in the traditions and conscience of our people.' " He also pointed out that the state of Texas provided for clemency hearings, which "is the historic remedy for preventing miscarriages of justice where judicial process has been

---

[81]   28 U.S.C.A. § 2254(d)(2).

[82]   Cf. *Felker v. Turpin,* 518 U.S. 651, 116 S.Ct. 2333 (1996)(recognizing that congressional restriction of the writ may violate the Suspension Clause of the Constitution).

[83]   506 U.S. 390, 113 S.Ct. 853 (1993).

[84]   See e.g., *Boyd v. Puckett,* 905 F.2d 895 (5th Cir. 1990); *Stockton v. Virginia,* 852 F.2d 740 (4th Cir. 1988).

[85]   372 U.S. 293, 83 S.Ct. 745 (1963).

exhausted." Thus, a state prisoner's claim of actual innocence should not be cognizable in federal court.[86]

Despite this analysis, Rehnquist ended the opinion by looking at the petitioner's claim of new evidence. He stated that, even if one assumed a "truly persuasive case" of "actual innocence" raised a constitutional issue, the evidence presented by Herrera was not that case. Justice Scalia, joined by Justice Thomas, refused to join this final part of the opinion, agreeing with Rehnquist' initial analysis and arguing that federal judicial resources should not be expended on assessing whether such claims are "truly persuasive." That view probably represented the Chief Justice's view as well, but the last part of his opinion was necessary to obtain a majority. Justices O'Connor, Kennedy and White rejected the proposition that the Constitution does not prevent execution of the innocent, and joined the majority's result solely on the ground that Herrera's affidavits fell short of showing actual innocence. Justice Blackmun, joined by Justices Stevens and Souter, agreed with the petitioner that the Eighth Amendment would be violated by execution of an innocent person and concluded that, to obtain relief under this provision, a prisoner would have to show that he was "probably innocent" (a standard they believed was met in *Herrera*).[87]

It is important to distinguish the type of claim in *Herrera* from a claim which asserts that the state presented insufficient evidence to allow the jury to convict beyond a reasonable doubt, which the Court has held may be the subject of habeas review.[88] As Rehnquist pointed out in *Herrera*, in reviewing the latter type of claim the federal court inquires into whether the jury made a rational decision based *on the evidence before it*, in light of proof-beyond-a-reasonable-doubt requirement. In its comprehensive revision of federal habeas law in 1996, Congress adhered to this distinction by permitting review of state court decisions based on an unreasonable determination of facts "in light of the evidence presented in the State court proceeding,"[89] while prohibiting claims based solely on newly discovered evidence.[90]

(e) The Fundamental Defect Exception

While, with the exceptions noted above, federal *constitutional* claims are justiciable on habeas, other federal claims, whether brought by a federal or state prisoner, may only be raised in a federal habeas court if they involve a fundamental defect. The rule in federal cases was established in *Hill v. United States*,[91] where the Supreme Court held

---

[86] Rehnquist contrasted this holding with the cases holding that a claim of actual innocence, *coupled* with a federal constitutional claim, permits a habeas petitioner to avoid the Court's rules barring habeas review for procedural reasons. See generally, § 33.03(e).

[87] A subsequent case characterized the test as whether the petitioner demonstrated "a case of conclusive exoneration." *House v. Bell*, 547 U.S. 518, 126 S.Ct. 2064 (2006).

[88] *Jackson v. Virginia*, 443 U.S. 307, 99 S.Ct. 2781 (1979), discussed in § 33.02(b)(1). See also, *Fiore v. White*, 531 U.S. 225, 121 S.Ct. 712 (2001)(holding that failure to prove a basic element of the crime, as construed by the state supreme court, was a due process violation cognizable on federal habeas).

[89] 28 U.S.C.A. § 2254(d)(2).

[90] Another provision in the AEDPA, dealing solely with capital cases, states that a federal court may consider a claim not raised at the state level if it is "based on a factual predicate that could not have been discovered through the exercise of due diligence in time to present the claim for State or Federal post-conviction review." § 2264(a)(3). However, this provision also requires, in § 2264(b), that the petitioner meet all of the requirements of § 2254(d), which requires as well an erroneous interpretation of federal law in those situations in which a claim is not based on "evidence presented in the State court proceeding." See § 33.02(b)(3). Thus, the new legislation does not appear to change the result in *Herrera*.

[91] 368 U.S. 424, 82 S.Ct. 468 (1962).

that a federal prisoner can obtain relief for a non-constitutional violation only if "a complete miscarriage of justice" or "an omission inconsistent with the rudimentary demands of fair procedure" would otherwise result. The Court went on to deny collateral relief to the claimant, who had shown that the sentencing court violated Federal Rule of Criminal Procedure 32(a) by failing to permit him to make a statement and present information in mitigation of sentence, but who had not objected to the failure at the time. This "fundamental defect" limitation on habeas review was reaffirmed in *United States v. Timmreck*,[92] where the Court held that a federal sentencing court's violation of Rule 11, which requires the court accepting a plea to inform the defendant of special parole provisions, is not a basis for habeas relief, absent a showing that the defendant would have acted differently had he been so informed.

The *Hill-Timmreck* line of cases, involving federal prisoners seeking relief under § 2255, did not address whether the fundamental defect rule should apply when *state* prisoners seek federal habeas review, under § 2254. Arguably, the two situations should be treated differently for a number of reasons: (1) the federal prisoner has already had a federal forum (at trial and on appeal), whereas the state prisoner has not; (2) the need to promote uniform application of federal law among the states militates in favor of giving broader federal habeas relief to state prisoners; and (3) outside of the Constitution, few federal laws are implicated in state trials, meaning that the fundamental defect limitation is not needed as screening device. However, in *Reed v. Farley*,[93] the Supreme Court held that, when the federal law in question is statutory rather than constitutional, *Hill's* fundamental defect rule should apply to state prisoners as well. Justice Ginsburg's opinion for five members of the Court did not directly address any of the above concerns. Instead it merely stressed that Reed's claim—that the state court which tried him had violated the federal Interstate Agreement on Detainers when it commenced his trial after the statute's deadline for trying transported prisoners—was not deserving of relief, primarily because Reed had not specifically raised the issue at the trial level.

(f) Harmless Error

As described elsewhere in this book,[94] the Supreme Court has developed two tests for determining when error committed at the trial level is harmless and thus does not require reversal. The test used when the error is constitutional in dimension, usually associated with *Chapman v. California*,[95] is whether the error is "harmless beyond a reasonable doubt." When the error is not of constitutional dimension, on the other hand, the test, devised in *Kotteakos v. United States*,[96] is whether the error had "substantial and injurious effect or influence in determining the jury's verdict." In *Brecht v. Abrahamson*,[97] the Court held, 5–4, that the latter test should apply on habeas review. Chief Justice Rehnquist's opinion emphasized the differences between collateral and direct review—in particular, the fact that collateral review often involves federal review of state court decisions, usually at a much later time when retrial is often difficult—in deciding that the *Chapman* standard intrudes too significantly on state's interests and

---

[92]   441 U.S. 780, 99 S.Ct. 2085 (1979).

[93]   512 U.S. 339, 114 S.Ct. 2291 (1994).

[94]   See § 29.05.

[95]   386 U.S. 18, 87 S.Ct. 824 (1967).

[96]   328 U.S. 750, 66 S.Ct. 1239 (1946).

[97]   507 U.S. 619, 113 S.Ct. 1710 (1993).

"is at odds with the historic meaning of habeas corpus—to afford relief to those whom society has 'grievously wronged.' "[98]

Justice Stevens, who provided the fifth vote for the majority, stated that he joined the Court's opinion because "the way we phrase the governing standard is far less important than the quality of the judgment with which it is applied," and found the *Kotteakos* standard "appropriately demanding." The dissenters, all of whom wrote separate opinions, subscribed to the general notion that the harmless error standard should not vary according to the posture of review, but rather depend upon the type of error. The dissenters' position seems more persuasive. While the collateral nature of habeas review may support limitations on its scope, it should not affect the care with which the federal courts analyze those claims they do confront. Consistent with this view, the Court subsequently concluded that reversal is required in those rare instances when a habeas court decides that the evidence is "evenly balanced" on the issue of whether the *Kotteakos/Brecht* test is met; in such circumstances, which Justice Breyer's majority opinion equated with a "grave doubt" as to whether the error is harmless, finding against the defendant simply because the defendant has the burden of proof on the harmlessness issue is inappropriate.[99]

In *Davis v. Ayala,*[100] however, five members of the Court put a gloss on this position that appears to weaken the harmless error rule. The majority, in an opinion by Justice Alito, concluded that a state court's determination that constitutional error is harmless is to be interpreted through the prism of the AEDPA. Thus, a federal court cannot grant habeas relief unless the harmless error analysis itself "was contrary to or involved an unreasonable application of clearly established federal law as established by the Supreme Court, or was based on an unreasonable determination of facts."

(g) Application of the Writ in Wartime and Outside the United States

The Constitution specifically permits suspension of the writ of habeas corpus "in cases of Rebellion or Invasion" when "the public Safety may require it."[101] Although the Constitution does not specify which branch of government may suspend the writ, traditionally the authority to do so has been thought to be vested in Congress. Beginning in the 2004 Term, the Supreme Court has decided a number of cases in which the *executive* branch argued that it could significantly abridge the scope of the writ in order to pursue the "war on terrorism."

In *Hamdi v. Rumsfeld,*[102] the Defense Department argued that Hamdi, an American citizen found in the warzone in Afghanistan and subsequently transferred to a brig in South Carolina, could be detained indefinitely, based solely on a declaration by a Defense Department official (one Michael Mobbs) that Hamdi was an "enemy combatant." Among other facts, the "Mobbs Declaration" asserted that Hamdi had been affiliated with a Taliban unit during the United States' engagement with the Taliban and that, once

---

[98]　The Court followed this same reasoning in holding that *Brecht*, not *Chapman*, applies in habeas cases regardless of whether the state appellate court applied *Chapman. Fry v. Pliler*, 551 U.S. 112, 127 S.Ct. 2321 (2007).

[99]　*O'Neal v. McAninch,* 513 U.S. 432, 115 S.Ct. 992 (1995).

[100]　___ U.S. ___, 135 S.Ct. 2187 (2015).

[101]　U.S. Const., Art. I, § 9, cl. 2.

[102]　542 U.S. 507, 124 S.Ct. 2633 (2004).

detained, he had surrendered an assault rifle. Hamdi argued that both his detention and the procedure used to justify it were unconstitutional.

A divided Court authorized long-term detention of enemy combatants, but only when they have been so designated by a process considerably more elaborate than that represented by the Mobbs Declaration. A four-member plurality, in an opinion by Justice O'Connor, first found that the government has authority to detain enemy combatants in the Afghanistan conflict. Hamdi had argued that his detention violated 18 U.S.C. § 4001(a), which provides that "[n]o citizen shall be imprisoned or otherwise detained by the United States except pursuant to an Act of Congress." But the plurality concluded that Congress passed such an act with its post-9/11 Authorization of Military Force resolution authorizing the President to "use all necessary and appropriate force" against "nations, organizations or persons" that he determines "planned authorized, committed or aided" the al Qaeda terrorist attacks. The plurality further found that the detention authorized by the resolution was constitutional, relying principally on the Court's World War II decision in *Ex parte Quirin*,[103] which permitted military detention of enemy combatants, including those who are American citizens.

But the plurality also concluded that, in making the determination whether a particular person is an enemy combatant and thus subject to *Quirin*, the Due Process Clause guaranteed Hamdi more process than the Defense Department's "Mobbs' Declaration" provided. Stating that "[i]t is during our most challenging and uncertain moments that our Nation's commitment to due process is most severely tested," Justice O'Connor wrote that citizens seeking to challenge their classification as enemy combatants are entitled to notice describing the factual basis for that classification, a "fair opportunity to rebut the Government's factual assertions before a neutral decisionmaker," and the right to counsel. At the same time, the plurality suggested, the exigencies of wartime might permit the hearing to take place in front of a military tribunal, hearsay might be admissible, and the government might be entitled to a rebuttable presumption in favor of its evidence.

The plurality picked up a fifth vote on the issue of whether the government has authority to detain citizens as enemy combatants from Justice Thomas, who argued that government decision-making during wartime should be given great deference. As a result of that position, however, Thomas disagreed with the plurality's resolution of the due process issue. On the latter score the plurality obtained two additional votes from Justices Souter and Justice Ginsburg. Although these two justices contended that the congressional resolution only authorized military action, not detention of enemy combatants, they were willing to join the plurality's conclusion that, assuming such detention could occur, Hamdi was entitled to a judicial determination of his classification. More specifically, they agreed with the plurality's requirements regarding notice, the ability to challenge the government's evidence, and the rights to a neutral decisionmaker and counsel. Justice Souter's opinion for the two justices also made clear, however, that they were not necessarily willing to go along with the plurality's suggestions regarding burden-shifting and adjudication in a military tribunal.[104]

---

[103]　317 U.S. 1, 63 S.Ct. 2 (1942).

[104]　In a dissenting opinion, Justice Scalia, joined by Justice Stevens, argued that a citizen who is alleged to be in league with an enemy may only be detained indefinitely if Congress suspends the writ of habeas corpus; otherwise, he must be tried for treason or released. Thus, these two justices disagreed with the plurality's first holding, and would have required a full-blown trial in situations where the writ has not been suspended.

Because Hamdi was an American citizen detained in the United States, the Court did not question his ability to bring his claim in a federal habeas court. In the companion cases of *Rasul v. United States* and *Al Odah v. United States*,[105] the Court considered whether *foreign nationals* detained during hostilities have access to the federal courts via the writ. Specifically, the Court looked at whether Australian and Kuwaiti citizens captured during fighting between the U.S. and the Taliban in Afghanistan could use habeas to challenge their detention in the military facility at Guantanamo Bay, Cuba. Justice Stevens, for five members of the Court, concluded that they could.

The majority avoided deciding whether the *Constitution* requires that such individuals are entitled to the writ. Rather it interpreted § 2241, the federal habeas statute, to permit such claims, relying heavily on the 1973 Supreme Court holding in *Braden v. 30th Judicial Circuit Court of Ky.*[106] that the statute gives federal district courts jurisdiction to hear not only claims by petitioners within their territory but also claims against custodians of petitioners who can be reached by service of process. The government contended that such process could not reach the custodians of persons in Guantanamo Bay because of the "long-standing" rule that federal statutes should not be given extraterritorial application unless Congress has clearly manifested such intent,[107] which was lacking in § 2241. But Justice Stevens responded that, by the terms of the United States' agreement with Cuba, the United States exercises "complete jurisdiction and control" over Guantanamo Bay, and thus no extraterritorial application of jurisdiction was required to hear the petitioners' claims.

Because *Rasul* and *Al Odah* interpreted only the habeas statute and avoided any constitutional analysis, Congress was left with the authority to amend it. In 2005, it passed the Detainee Treatment Act (DTA), which directed that the Defense Department's Combatant Status Review Panel (CSRP) was to be the only entity that could make the factual determinations raised by a habeas petition, and further provided that only the D.C. Circuit Court of Appeals had jurisdiction to review the Panel's decisions. In *Hamdan v. Rumsfeld*,[108] the Court held that the DTA was inapplicable to petitioners held in Guantanamo prior to its passage. Consistent with *Rasul*, it also held that foreign nationals could use the writ to challenge the legitimacy of the process mandated by the DTA and that this process was not permissible under either the Uniform Code of Military Justice or the Geneva Convention.

In an apparent attempt to nullify *Hamdan*, Congress passed the Military Commissions Act of 2006, which provided that no alien found to be an enemy combatant by a CSRP could use habeas to challenge his detention or the procedures used to determine his status. The Court's response to that Act came two years later, in *Boumediene v. Bush*.[109] There it finally held that the *Constitution* guarantees foreign nationals held at Guantanamo access to federal district court via a writ of habeas corpus, unless Congress formally suspends the Writ pursuant to Article I, § 9 of the Constitution which, as noted above, allows such suspension "when in cases of Rebellion or Invasion public Safety may require it." The 5–4 decision, authored by Justice Kennedy, stated that, because no such finding had been made by Congress, the Military Commissions Act

---

[105] 542 U.S. 466, 124 S.Ct. 2686 (2004).

[106] 410 U.S. 484, 93 S.Ct. 1123 (1973).

[107] See *EEOC v. Arabian American Oil Co.*, 499 U.S. 244, 111 S.Ct. 1227 (1991).

[108] 548 U.S. 557, 126 S.Ct. 2749 (2006).

[109] 553 U.S. 723, 128 S.Ct. 2229 (2008).

was unconstitutional. Although conceding that the historical record and precedent were unclear as to whether the Writ extended to a detention center on foreign soil like Guantanamo, the majority concluded that earlier decisions on the application of constitutional rights to territories outside the U.S. focused on whether the U.S. had uncontested control of the area in question and whether the military mission would be compromised by granting habeas rights.[110] Given the United States' solid authority over Guantanamo, both of these considerations favored extending the historic role of the Writ in maintaining "the delicate balance of governance" to Guantanamo detainees.

Although the Court noted that the DTA process did not provide counsel and involved prolific use of hearsay, it did not specify the procedures that such habeas review should require, other than to state that the proceeding should provide some mechanism for assessing "the sufficiency of the government's evidence" and for receiving exculpatory evidence not introduced in previous proceedings. Nor did the Court indicate how quickly a habeas hearing must be granted, although it did note with disapproval that many of the detainees at Guantanamo had been held there up to six years. Finally, the Court did not attempt to delineate the issue to be addressed in such proceedings: does the government merely have to show the petitioner is an "enemy combatant," or must it also show the individual is dangerous? But *Boumediene* at least clearly established that federal courts have jurisdiction over habeas claims brought by Guantanamo detainees, whether citizens or aliens.[111]

Given the fact that, for obvious reasons, no particular court had been designated as having authority over Guantanamo Bay, this holding meant that any district court could hear the petitioners' claims. Normally, however, only the district court in the jurisdiction with custody has jurisdiction, as the Court made clear in *Rumsfeld v. Padilla*.[112] There it dismissed a habeas claim brought in New York on the ground it should have been filed in South Carolina district court against the director of the brig in that state, where Padilla was housed.

For petitioners who are in custody somewhere other than the United States and territories over which it has complete jurisdiction and control, the reach of the writ is less clear. In *Johnson v. Eisentrager*,[113] decided in 1950, the Court held that aliens detained outside the sovereign territory of the United States may not invoke the writ. That case involved 21 German citizens captured in China during World War II who were tried and convicted of war crimes by an American military commission in Nanking and incarcerated in Germany. When, however, the captured combatant held outside the United States is an American citizen, a foreign national who has received no judicial process, or a citizen of a country not at war with the United States, the Court's more recent decisions in *Hamdi*, *Rasul* and *Al Odah* at least leave open the possibility that the writ is available to contest detention by American authorities.

---

[110] See *Reid v. Covert*, 354 U.S. 1, 77 S.Ct. 1222 (1957); *Johnson v. Eisentrager*, 339 U.S. 763, 70 S.Ct. 936 (1950); *Dorr v. United States*, 195 U.S. 138, 24 S.Ct. 808 (1904).

[111] On the same day, however, it also held that federal habeas courts may not enjoin the United States government from transferring to Iraqi custody individuals alleged to have committed crimes in Iraq and detained there; the possibility that such transfer would result in torture, the Court stated, should be resolved politically, not judicially. *Munaf v. Geren*, 553 U.S. 674, 128 S.Ct. 2207 (2008).

[112] 542 U.S. 426, 124 S.Ct. 2711 (2004).

[113] 339 U.S. 763, 70 S.Ct. 936 (1950).

33.03   The Effect of Default Under State Procedural Rules

Virtually every state prohibits defendants from raising a claim on appeal or other post-conviction proceedings if it was not raised when the error occurred or within a certain time after trial. The subject addressed here is the extent to which such "procedural default" rules act to bar habeas review. The Supreme Court has taken at least four different approaches to the issue. At first, a failure to abide by the state rule was an absolute bar to habeas review unless the state rule was not an "adequate and independent" basis for the dismissal. The Warren Court soon rejected this approach, substituting a much more defendant-oriented "deliberate bypass" rule that focused on whether the defendant's default was an intentional waiver of the claim. The post-Warren Court, finding the deliberate bypass rule too generous to habeas petitioners, largely replaced it with a requirement that the defendant show "cause" as to why he failed to raise the claim, and show further that failure to vindicate the claim would "prejudice" his case. Most recently, the Court has created an "actual innocence" exception to the cause and prejudice requirement that allows review of defaulted claims which are guilt-related.

(a)   The Adequate and Independent Requirement

In *Daniels v. Allen*,[114] a companion case to *Brown v. Allen*,[115] the Supreme Court held that when a defendant has defaulted at the state level federal habeas review is barred as well, so long as the state rule is adequate and independent. The effect of this rule was made apparent in *Daniels*, where the defendant raised the same types of arguments as Brown (i.e., coerced confession and jury selection claims), but was denied federal relief because his attorney failed to perfect his state appeal. As Justice Black stated in dissent, this result, combined with *Brown's* holding that any properly raised constitutional claim could be raised on habeas, meant that the Court would "grant a second review where the state has granted one but . . . deny any review at all where the state has granted none."

The only hope for a defendant under *Daniels* was to show that the state default rule was either "inadequate" or that it was not the basis for the dismissal of his claim, which would suggest there was no "independent" state ground for the dismissal. Neither showing was easily made. The adequacy inquiry appeared to boil down to whether the rule served any legitimate purpose. Only a procedural rule that was an "arid ritual of meaningless form," often ignored by the state courts, was likely to be found inadequate.[116] With respect to the second issue, only if the state court clearly decided the case on substantive grounds could one argue that the rule was not the basis for the dismissal.[117]

Because the Court's current habeas jurisprudence still views state procedural default rules as a limitation on habeas review, these considerations remain relevant today. On the "adequacy" issue, as recently as 1989 at least four members of the Court seemed willing to hold that a procedural rule that is not "consistently or regularly

---

[114]   344 U.S. 443, 73 S.Ct. 397 (1953).

[115]   344 U.S. 443, 73 S.Ct. 397 (1953), discussed in § 33.02(a).

[116]   *Staub v. City of Baxley,* 355 U.S. 313, 78 S.Ct. 277 (1958).

[117]   See *Irvin v. Dowd,* 359 U.S. 394, 79 S.Ct. 825 (1959).

applied" would not be a legitimate ground for barring habeas review.[118] This position seems defensible, at least when the state uses its rule as means of punishing particular defendants or thwarting federal review by simply refusing to hear a claim.[119] The Court has also held, in *Lee v. Kemna*,[120] that there are "exceptional cases in which exorbitant application of a generally sound rule renders the state ground inadequate to stop consideration of a federal question." Thus, for example, in *Osborne v. Ohio*,[121] the Court held that, even though the trial attorney had failed to object contemporaneously to the judge's instruction regarding the elements of the crime, a habeas challenge to those instructions could be heard because the lawyer had made his position clear prior to the charge and the trial judge had rejected it "in no uncertain terms." Similarly, in *Kemna* itself the Court held that trial counsel's failure to put in writing the reasons for his motion for a continuance, as required by state rule, did not bar habeas relief, because his oral continuance motion and other information in the record meant the rule's "essential requirements . . . were substantially met" and that "[n]othing would have been gained by requiring [counsel] to recapitulate in rank order the showings the [state rule] requires."[122] In contrast, a regularly applied state rule providing that procedural default occurs when a defendant raises a claim on state collateral review that could have been, but was not, raised on direct appeal is a bar to federal habeas review.[123]

Other relatively recent cases deal with the second, "independence" prong, having to do with determining whether the state's default rule was really the basis for the state court decision. A number of decisions have endorsed the idea that a state court's consideration of a defaulted claim excuses the litigant's failure to abide by the rule. In *Ulster County Court v. Allen*,[124] for instance, the Court stated that if state courts themselves bypass a procedural default, a federal court "implies no disrespect" to state interests if it does the same. After *Harris v. Reed*,[125] it appeared that, as a means of easing the determination of this issue, the state court wanting to avoid federal review would have to make a "plain statement" that its default rule was an independent ground for its ruling, a phrase borrowed from Court's cases describing the circumstances under which the Court can review state court decisions against the prosecution.[126]

However, in *Coleman v. Thompson*,[127] the Court held that federal habeas review is presumptively barred simply if it "fairly appears" on the record that the state court's dismissal was based "primarily" on the state procedural rule. The Court rejected a plain statement requirement because such a requirement would evidence a "loss of respect" for state court decisions and "put too great a burden on the state courts." Thus, in

---

[118] *Dugger v. Adams*, 489 U.S. 401, 109 S.Ct. 1211 (1989) (Blackmun, J., dissenting).

[119] Cf. *NAACP v. Alabama ex rel. Flowers*, 377 U.S. 288, 84 S.Ct. 1302 (1964). However, the mere fact that a state procedural rule is discretionary does not make it inadequate, given the need to give states flexibility in their approach to default. *Beard v. Kindler*, 558 U.S. 53, 130 S.Ct. 612 (2009).

[120] 534 U.S. 362, 122 S.Ct. 877 (2002).

[121] 495 U.S. 103, 110 S.Ct. 1691 (1990).

[122] The Court also noted that the continuance motion was made under exigent circumstances (alibi witnesses had suddenly disappeared), that neither the trial court or the prosecutor had pointed out the failure to put the motion in writing at the time of trial, and that no published Missouri opinion had ever required perfect compliance with the continuance rule.

[123] *Johnson v. Lee*, ___ U.S. ___, 136 S.Ct. 1802 (2016).

[124] 442 U.S. 140, 99 S.Ct. 2213 (1979).

[125] 489 U.S. 255, 109 S.Ct. 1038 (1989).

[126] See *Michigan v. Long*, 463 U.S. 1032, 103 S.Ct. 3469 (1983), discussed in § 34.04.

[127] 501 U.S. 722, 111 S.Ct. 2546 (1991).

Coleman, the Court refused to allow federal review of a claim that was dismissed on procedural grounds, even though the state court did so only after deciding its action would not abridge one of the petitioner's federal constitutional rights, and without plainly stating the dismissal was on procedural grounds. In *Ylst v. Nunnemaker*,[128] the Court moved even further from a plain statement rule by holding that when an upper level state court does not indicate the ground for dismissal, federal courts should "presume" that the basis for dismissal is the same ground that lower state courts explicitly relied upon (which may often be procedural default).

However, *Ylst* also noted that a state court decision not to hear a claim because it has already been heard in another state proceeding is not based on a procedural default rule. Thus, as the Court later stated in *Bell v. Cone*[129] "when a state court declines to review the merits of a petitioner's claim on the ground that it has done so already, it creates no bar to federal habeas review."

(b) The Deliberate Bypass Rule

Daniels' holding that federal habeas review was barred by a default under a state rule that is adequate and independent retained vitality until 1963. In that year, the Court decided *Fay v. Noia*,[130] which held that the need to prevent unconstitutional detentions outweighed the state's interest in an "airtight system" of procedural rules, and that habeas review should therefore usually be available to those state defendants who violate them. Justice Harlan wrote in dissent that, with this reasoning, the Court "turned its back on history and struck a heavy blow at the foundations of our federal system." But the majority opinion, authored by Justice Brennan, contended that sufficient deference to state rules was evidenced by the denial of direct review to the noncomplying defendant, who then had the burden of seeking habeas relief. According to Brennan, "the only concrete impact the assumption of federal habeas jurisdiction in the face of a procedural default has on the state interest [in orderly criminal procedure] is that it prevents the State from closing off the convicted defendant's last opportunity to vindicate his constitutional rights, thereby punishing him for his default and deterring others who might commit similar defaults in the future."

The majority did admit, however, that its holding could lead to occasional abuse by state defendants who might withhold claims until habeas as a means of obtaining a retrial after conviction. Thus, it held that "the federal judge may in his discretion deny relief to any applicant who has deliberately bypassed the orderly procedure of the state courts and in so doing has forfeited his state court remedies." At the same time, the majority made clear that it expected this discretion to be rarely exercised. In defining the deliberate bypass concept, it placed emphasis on *Johnson v. Zerbst*,[131] which had described waiver as "an intentional relinquishment or abandonment of a known right or privilege." Furthermore, the Court held that the relinquishment of state remedies must be "the considered choice of the petitioner;" thus, "a choice made by counsel not participated in by the petitioner does not automatically bar relief." Finally, its disposition of the case before it indicated that even some intentional defaults by the petitioner would not constitute a "deliberate bypass;" the Court granted review of Noia's

---

[128]   501 U.S. 797, 111 S.Ct. 2590 (1991).

[129]   556 U.S. 449, 129 S.Ct. 1769 (2009). See also, *Wellons v. Hall*, 558 U.S. 220, 130 S.Ct. 727 (2010).

[130]   372 U.S. 391, 83 S.Ct. 822 (1963).

[131]   304 U.S. 458, 58 S.Ct. 1019 (1938).

coerced confession claim even though he had affirmatively decided not to appeal, because his decision was based on financial considerations and fear that he might receive the death penalty on a retrial.

The Court later modified somewhat its stance that the defendant be personally involved in every waiver, In *Henry v. Mississippi,*[132] it held that, for certain types of constitutional claims involving tactical decisions, intentional bypass by counsel alone would be sufficient.[133] Moreover, a few lower courts were quite willing to presume waiver from a silent record, or give great weight to an attorney's explanations as to why he did not pursue a particular claim.[134] Nonetheless, *Fay* was a major step, at least as significant as *Brown,* toward creating federal oversight of the state court system. It provided ready access to the federal courts for state prisoners whose counsel was unaware of, or insensitive to, constitutional issues.

(c) Development of the Cause and Prejudice Standard

Ten years after *Fay,* the Court began the process of dismantling the deliberate bypass rule and replacing it with the so-called "cause and prejudice" standard. Today, unless a claim goes to the "actual innocence" of the petitioner,[135] or is barred at the state level on grounds that are not "adequate or independent" (as defined earlier), the latter analysis determines whether a defaulted claim in a noncapital case will be heard on habeas review.[136]

The first case to endorse the cause and prejudice standard was *Davis v. United States,*[137] which involved an allegation by a federal prisoner that the grand jury that indicted him had been selected in a racially discriminatory manner. Although the claim had not been raised either prior to trial or on appeal, the petitioner argued that it should be heard on habeas because there had been no deliberate bypass. The Court held, in essence, that even if the latter assertion were true, relief should not be granted. While the Court conceded that *Fay* had been applied to federal prisoners,[138] it ignored that decision and chose to decide whether § 2255, the federal prisoner analogue to § 2254, allowed collateral review in the circumstances presented in *Davis.*

The majority first noted that, had Davis brought his claim on direct review, it would have been barred by Federal Rule 12(b)(2), which provides that an appeal does not lie for a federal defendant unless he can show "cause" why an objection was not made prior to trial. The Court then concluded that it was "inconceivable that Congress, having in the criminal proceeding foreclosed the raising of a claim such as this after the commencement of trial in the absence of a showing of 'cause' for relief from waiver, nonetheless intended to perversely negate the Rule's purpose by permitting an entirely different but much more liberal requirement of waiver in federal habeas proceedings." Thus, as a matter of statutory interpretation, the Rule 12(b) standard should apply under § 2255 as well. Furthermore, the Court held, in addition to showing cause the

---

[132] 379 U.S. 443, 85 S.Ct. 564 (1965).

[133] See also, *Murch v. Mottram,* 409 U.S. 41, 93 S.Ct. 71 (1972).

[134] See Note, *Federal Habeas Corpus and the Doctrine of Waiver Through the Deliberate Bypass of State Procedures,* 31 La.L.Rev. 601, 606–08 (1971).

[135] See § 33.03(e).

[136] For the special rules in capital cases under the AEDPA, see § 33.03(f).

[137] 411 U.S. 233, 93 S.Ct. 1577 (1973).

[138] *Kaufman v. United States,* 394 U.S. 217, 89 S.Ct. 1068 (1969).

defendant must show "actual prejudice" to his case should the court fail to grant relief, a stipulation that went beyond the terms of Rule 12(b) but that had been developed in earlier cases construing the rule.[139] Since Davis had neither explained his failure to make a pretrial motion nor shown any "actual" prejudice to his case resulting from the improper selection process,[140] he was denied relief. This disposition of the case strongly suggested that mere proof that there had been no "deliberate bypass" would seldom satisfy the "cause" prong.

Three years later, without mentioning the deliberate bypass standard, the Court applied the cause and prejudice rule to a habeas petition by a *state* prisoner. In *Francis v. Henderson*,[141] the petitioner alleged the same type of claim—racial discrimination in the selection of his grand jury—at issue in *Davis*. Citing "considerations of comity and concern for the orderly administration of criminal justice," the Court held that the rule developed in *Davis* should apply here as well, and denied relief.

Although *Davis* and *Francis* established the cause and prejudice standard as an alternative to the deliberate bypass rule, their impact could have been quite limited, given the fact that both involved claims against the indictment process. As Justice Stewart wrote for the Court in *Francis*, applying the state's procedural default rule to such claims would be useful because "[i]f its time limits are followed, inquiry into an alleged defect may be concluded and, if necessary, cured before the court, the witnesses and the parties have gone to the burden and expense of a trial." On the other hand, if the rule is denigrated by allowing habeas review even when it is violated, "there would be little incentive to comply with its terms when a successful attack might simply result in a new indictment prior to trial." These points do not apply to defaults at trial or on appeal, nor do they apply to pretrial defaults on claims that might prevent trial entirely.

However, in *Wainwright v. Sykes*,[142] the Court indicated that the cause and prejudice standard would govern analysis of virtually all defaulted claims. There, the Court held that habeas review was barred because the defense had failed to make a "contemporaneous objection" during trial to the admission of a confession allegedly obtained in violation of *Miranda*. In denying habeas review of this claim, the Court made clear that, while it was not overturning *Fay's* result on the facts of that case, in the more typical case a failure to raise a claim within the period allowed by state law would foreclose habeas review unless the cause and prejudice standard was met.

Justice Rehnquist's opinion for the Court justified this rejuvenation of the procedural default principle on several grounds. First, he emphasized the valid state interests protected by default rules, including the desire to develop the factual record when recollections "are freshest," and the goal of encouraging finality by forcing the parties to put their best case forward at the time the motion should be made. Second, he asserted that the cause and prejudice standard would make less likely the "sandbagging" alluded to in *Francis,* whereby lawyers intentionally defer raising a constitutional claim at the state level in the hope that a federal court will later decide the question favorably and require a retrial. Relatedly, the cause and prejudice standard better served the adversarial process, because the narrowly-defined deliberate bypass standard had the

---

[139] See, e.g., *Shotwell Mfg. Co. v. United States,* 371 U.S. 341, 83 S.Ct. 448 (1963).

[140] The Court noted that, while prejudice is presumed when racial discrimination of the grand jury is shown upon timely objection, it must be proven when such objection is not made.

[141] 425 U.S. 536, 96 S.Ct. 1708 (1976).

[142] 433 U.S. 72, 97 S.Ct. 2497 (1977).

tendency, Rehnquist asserted, of making federal habeas the "determinative" proceeding, thus minimizing the importance of trial as a "decisive and portentous event."

The rationales underlying *Sykes* are open to serious question, even accepting the Court's objectives of promoting comity, efficiency and finality. Because the deliberate bypass standard presumably deters any intentional failure to raise a claim at the state level, the only additional purpose served by the cause and prejudice standard is to penalize inadvertent attorney error. Accordingly, *Sykes* does not increase the chance an objection will be made at or prior to trial, and makes "the choice between *Fay* and *Sykes* . . . neutral with respect to the goals of promoting determinations based on fresh evidence and deciding all issues in one proceeding."[143] Furthermore, as Justice Brennan put it in his dissent, the assertion that a "meaningful number of lawyers" would risk the sandbagging feared by the majority "offends common sense," and in any event is deterred by the deliberate bypass standard as well. Perhaps more importantly, as subsequent discussion makes clear, the refusal to recognize attorney error as automatic "cause" has not stymied habeas petitioners, as the *Sykes* majority apparently hoped, but merely transformed the procedural default issue into an ineffective assistance of counsel issue, which continues to require federal habeas review and second-guessing of state court determinations in many situations.

Nonetheless, the Court has maintained its adherence to the cause and prejudice standard, and extended its scope to apply to all defaults at the state level. In *Murray v. Carrier*,[144] the petitioner argued that habeas review of a claim presented at trial and not defaulted until appeal should not be governed by the *Sykes* rule—or at least should be subject to a "lesser" cause requirement—because its effect on the state's interests is relatively minimal. Unlike habeas review of a claim defaulted prior to or during trial, he argued, review of a defaulted appellate claim does not detract from the significance of trial, nor does it deter development of a full trial record or affect the trial court's ability to correct the error during trial. Moreover, while the fast pace of trial may make it necessary to bind a defendant to his counsel's acts or omissions, the more reflective process on appeal does not require such a rule.

But the Court, in an opinion by Justice O'Connor, found that appellate default rules still promoted significant state objectives, including "the opportunity to resolve the issue shortly after trial, while evidence is still available both to assess the defendant's claim and to retry the defendant effectively if he prevails in his appeal." Perhaps revealing the real rationale behind the *Sykes* rule, she also stated that the difference between a failure to detect a colorable claim and a deliberate decision not to raise it "is much too tenuous a distinction to justify a regime of evidentiary hearings into counsel's state of mind in failing to raise a claim on appeal." For much the same reasons, the Court has also held that the cause and prejudice standard governs defaults on appeal of state post-conviction determinations.[145]

The one type of default left untouched by *Carrier* and previous decisions was that involved in *Fay*: a failure to bring any appeal at all (as opposed to a failure to raise a particular claim on appeal). In *Sykes*, the majority opinion had been careful to state that it was only "the sweeping language of *Fay*, going far beyond the facts of the case eliciting

---

[143] *The Supreme Court, 1976 Term*, 91 Har.L.Rev. 70, 214–221 (1977).

[144] 477 U.S. 478, 106 S.Ct. 2639 (1986).

[145] *Coleman v. Thompson*, 501 U.S. 722, 111 S.Ct. 2546 (1991).

it, which we today reject." As Chief Justice Burger's concurring opinion explained, *Fay* "applied the 'deliberate bypass' standard to a case where the critical procedural decision—whether to take a criminal appeal—was entrusted to a convicted defendant." The case for holding that only the deliberate bypass standard need be met in this situation was strengthened by the Court's recognition, in another context,[146] that the decision to forego an appeal (along with the decisions to plead guilty, waive jury trial, and testify) is a "fundamental" one that belongs to the defendant. One could thus argue that when this decision is made by counsel alone, or over the objection of the defendant, and claims are thereby defaulted, habeas review of those claims should automatically be allowed.

But in *Coleman v. Thompson*[147] the Court held that "there is no reason that the [cause and prejudice] standard should not apply to a failure to appeal at all." According to the Court, "[a]ll of the State's interests—in channeling the resolution of claims to the most appropriate forum, in finality, and in having an opportunity to correct is own errors—are implicated whether a prisoner defaults one claim or all of them." Justice O'Connor, who wrote the majority opinion, also noted that by applying the cause and prejudice standard to all default situations, "we . . . eliminate inconsistency between the respect federal courts show for state procedural rules and the respect they show for their own." Thus, *Fay's* deliberate bypass rule has apparently been eliminated altogether as a means of evaluating the impact of default on habeas review.[148]

(d) The Definition of Cause and Prejudice

The adoption of the cause and prejudice standard in *Sykes* and later cases has occasioned considerable litigation as to the definition of cause. In *Carrier*, the Court summarized a number of decisions on this issue by stating that "cause for procedural default must ordinarily turn on whether the prisoner can show that some objective factor external to the defense impeded counsel's efforts to comply with the State's procedural rule." It then gave three illustrations of such "external impediments:" (1) when the factual or legal basis of the claim was not reasonably available at the time the claim should have been made; (2) when state officials interfere with counsel's ability to avoid default; and (3) when default is the result of attorney error rising to the level of ineffective assistance of counsel. (The Court was able to characterize the latter type of cause as an "external impediment" by "imputing" to the state the responsibility for a trial conducted without adequate defense counsel.) These three types of cause, as well as the possible definitions of prejudice in this context, are discussed below.

(1) Cause: Novel Claims

Cause deriving from the novel legal basis of the claim is illustrated by two pre-*Carrier* decisions. In *Engle v. Isaac*,[149] the defendants were tried and convicted of

---

[146] See *Jones v. Barnes,* 463 U.S. 745, 103 S.Ct. 3308 (1983), discussed in § 32.04(c)(4).

[147] 501 U.S. 722, 111 S.Ct. 2546 (1991).

[148] The one possible exception to this statement may involve "jurisdictional" claims. In the guilty plea context, for instance, the Court has indicated that such claims (e.g., double jeopardy claims, or claims of vindictive prosecution) may be raised on habeas even after a voluntary and intelligent plea by a competently represented defendant, because they go to the "very power of the State to bring the defendant into court to answer the charge brought against him." *Blackledge v. Perry,* 417 U.S. 21, 94 S.Ct. 2098 (1974), discussed in § 26.05(e)(3). Note also that attorney failure to raise an appeal may constitute ineffective assistance, thus meeting the cause and prejudice test. See § 33.03(d)(3).

[149] 456 U.S. 107, 102 S.Ct. 1558 (1982).

homicide under an Ohio instruction placing the burden of proving self-defense on the defense. On habeas, the defendants challenged this instruction for the first time, claiming that there was "cause" for not objecting earlier because at the time of their trial both Ohio law and the federal law in their circuit clearly placed the burden of proving self-defense on the defense. But the Court, in an opinion by Justice O'Connor, rejected this argument by concluding that "the futility of presenting an objection to the state courts cannot alone constitute cause for a failure to object at trial. . . . Even a state court that has previously rejected a constitutional argument may decide, upon reflection, that the contention is valid." The Court also pointed out that, well before the defendant's trial, the Court's decision in *In re Winship*[150] had required the prosecution to prove beyond a reasonable doubt every essential element of the crime charged, and dozens of courts outside the defendants' circuit had found *Winship* required the prosecution to bear the burden on affirmative defenses. The Court concluded that "[w]here the basis of a constitutional claim is available, and other defense counsel have perceived and litigated that claim, the demands of comity and finality counsel against labelling alleged unawareness of the objection" sufficient cause for purposes of earning federal review.

In contrast, in *Reed v. Ross,*[151] which involved the same type of instruction at issue in *Engle* but concerned a trial that took place *before Winship*, the Court found cause present. Justice Brennan's majority opinion concluded that the Court's own previous sanctioning of the prevailing practice,[152] the pervasive support for the instruction in most jurisdictions, and the minimal number of lower court cases supporting its unconstitutionality (a total of two), justified this result. The four dissenters, in an opinion by Justice Rehnquist, disagreed, finding that "it has long been assumed that proof of a criminal charge beyond a reasonable doubt is constitutionally required."

Even if a claim is shown to be "novel," this aspect of cause is likely to be of minimal use to habeas petitioners, given the Court's more recent decision in *Teague v. Lane.*[153] As discussed earlier in this chapter,[154] *Teague* held that a federal habeas court may not consider a "new" rule unless (1) it goes to the trial court's jurisdiction to hear the claim or (2) it involves an allegation relating to factual innocence. Thus, a petitioner who meets the cause prong by showing his claim is "novel" will automatically be barred from habeas review under *Teague,* unless he meets one of that case's two exceptions. Most claims will not meet either exception; indeed, although the question of what the prosecution must show to prove guilt, at issue in *Engle* and *Reed,* would seem to come under *Teague's* second exception, language in *Engle* suggests it would not reach that conclusion.[155]

To be distinguished from novel legal claims are constitutional claims based on newly discovered facts. *Teague* would not affect such claims, because it is based on the retroactive effect of new legal *rules,* applied to facts found by the state courts. However, to meet this aspect of cause, the Court will probably require strong proof that the fact could not have been discovered prior to trial, thus merging this type of cause with either the state interference aspect of cause (when the information was withheld by the state)

---

[150] 397 U.S. 358, 90 S.Ct. 1068 (1970).

[151] 468 U.S. 1, 104 S.Ct. 2901 (1984).

[152] In *Leland v. Oregon,* 343 U.S. 790, 72 S.Ct. 1002 (1952), the Court upheld a statute requiring the defendant to bear the burden of proving insanity.

[153] 489 U.S. 288, 109 S.Ct. 1060 (1989).

[154] See § 33.02(c).

[155] See § 33.03(e).

or the ineffective assistance aspect of cause (when the information could have been discovered by the defense).[156]

(2) Cause: State Interference

The second type of cause identified in *Carrier* requires proof that the state has somehow caused the default. This could occur in at least three different ways. First, state officials might inhibit or actually prevent filing of the objection. In *Carrier*, the Court illustrated this scenario by reference to a case in which a prison official had suppressed the petitioner's appeal papers.[157]

Second, state officials might make early objection impossible because they prevent discovery of crucial information. In *Amadeo v. Zant*,[158] for instance, the Court found cause for not raising a jury selection claim, after it was shown that the district attorney's office concealed a memorandum to line staff that seemed to encourage underrepresentation of blacks and women on the master list from which all grand and petit juries were drawn. Similarly, in *Strickler v. Greene*,[159] it found cause when the prosecution, which supposedly followed an "open file" discovery policy and told the defense attorney that all relevant information had been disclosed, failed to provide the attorney with documents that would have been useful for impeachment purposes.

A third way in which state action could result in "cause" is when the state's judiciary applies its default rules so inconsistently that the default is more a matter of state arbitrariness than defense inadvertence. This type of state interference involves the same types of actions that are relevant in determining whether a state procedural rule provides an "adequate" basis for dismissal of the claim.[160] Numerous other examples of all three types of state interference can be culled from the cases.[161]

(3) Cause: Ineffective Assistance

Unless a claim is so novel that even competent attorneys would not be aware of it, or unless the state interferes with a competent attorney's ability to develop or raise a claim,[162] *Carrier* suggests that cause will exist only upon a showing of ineffective assistance of counsel. Moreover, according to that decision, "the question of cause for a procedural default does not turn on whether counsel erred or on the kind of error counsel

---

[156] In any event, as discussed in § 33.05(c), under the AEDPA federal courts are not permitted to hold evidentiary hearings to adduce new evidence unless the facts "were not previously discoverable through the exercise of due diligence" and there is "clear and convincing evidence that but for the constitutional error, no reasonable factfinder would have found the applicant guilty of the underlying offense," a standard that significantly limits those situations in which newly discovered evidence may be heard by a federal habeas court.

[157] *Dowd v. United States ex rel. Cook,* 340 U.S. 206, 71 S.Ct. 262 (1951).

[158] 486 U.S. 214, 108 S.Ct. 1771 (1988).

[159] 527 U.S. 263, 119 S.Ct. 1936 (1999).

[160] See § 33.03(a).

[161] See Anthony Amsterdam, *Search, Seizure, and Section 2255: A Comment,* 112 U.Pa.L.Rev. 378, at 385 n. 34 (1964).

[162] See *Banks v. Dretke,* 540 U.S. 668, 124 S.Ct. 1256 (2004) (finding cause where the prosecution did not disclose, either at trial or at post-conviction proceedings, that one of the key witnesses against the defendant had been paid to set up the defendant's arrest and that another key witness lied when he stated at trial that he had not been coached by the government).

may have made," but on whether counsel is ineffective as defined in *Strickland v. Washington*[163] (the Court's leading case on the issue).

Strickland's two-prong "deficient performance-and-prejudice" standard for determining when counsel has been ineffective is discussed in detail elsewhere in this book,[164] and will not be elaborated upon here. However, three points are worth emphasizing in this context. First, given the narrow definition of "deficient performance" found in *Strickland* and its progeny, only egregious error for which there is no reasonable explanation will constitute cause. Thus, while an attorney's abandonment of his client without notice (resulting in a failure to file a notice of appeal in a timely fashion) will constitute cause,[165] an attorney's failure to argue a claim even though it was raised in an amicus brief and later sustained by the Court in a subsequent case was found to be insufficient cause, because the attorney was "reasonable" both in his assessment that the claim was weak, given the law at that time, and in his desire to focus on other appellate claims.[166] *Carrier* provides another illustration of the Court's approach. There, counsel in a rape and abduction trial failed to argue on appeal the trial court's rejection of two pretrial discovery motions requesting the victim's statements. According to the Court, while this failure was "more easily described as an oversight" rather than a "misjudgment," it did not justify delving into counsel's state of mind and did not establish cause.

The second point with respect to the ineffective assistance aspect of cause follows from the first. Consistent with *Sykes'* rejection of the deliberate bypass rule, error that does not amount to ineffective assistance fails to establish cause even if it is not attributable to the defendant in any way. As the Court stated in *Carrier,* "[s]o long as the defendant is represented by counsel whose performance is not constitutionally ineffective, we discern no inequity in requiring him to bear the risk of attorney error that results in a procedural default." The one exception to this rule may occur when counsel decides not to take a direct appeal. Although *Coleman* made clear that the cause and prejudice standard applies in this situation, an attorney's failure to consult with his client on the "fundamental" decision to forego an appeal may automatically constitute ineffective assistance of counsel,[167] and therefore also constitute cause.

However, in *Edwards v. Carpenter*,[168] the Court unanimously held that the latter claim must itself be raised at the state level in accordance with the relevant state rule, or cause shown why it was not raised. To hold otherwise, the Court reasoned, "would render *Carrier's* exhaustion requirement illusory," because offenders with ineffective assistance claims could simply wait until state remedies were no longer available and then proceed to federal court. Since Carpenter did not raise his ineffective appellate counsel claim in state court within 90 days of the end of the appeals process, as required by state rule, he had to show either cause for his failure, or that the state's 90-day rule was "inadequate,"[169] before he could obtain access to federal relief.

---

[163] 466 U.S. 668, 104 S.Ct. 2052 (1984).

[164] See § 32.03(b).

[165] *Maples v. Thomas*, 565 U.S. 266, 132 S.Ct. 912 (2012).

[166] *Smith v. Murray*, 477 U.S. 527, 106 S.Ct. 2661 (1986).

[167] See § 32.04(c)(4).

[168] 529 U.S. 446, 120 S.Ct. 1587 (2000).

[169] See § 33.03(a).

Finally, the Court has held that attorney error at proceedings at which the right to counsel does not attach can never amount to cause, because the right to effective assistance is not implicated. This was another conclusion reached in *Coleman,* where the petitioner argued that his attorney incompetently defaulted a claim on an appeal of a state habeas decision. The Court first noted that, while there is a right to counsel on direct appeal of a conviction,[170] it had also held that there is no constitutional right to an attorney in state postconviction proceedings.[171] From this, it concluded that the right to counsel could not attach at *appeal* of such proceedings either. Accordingly, the error claimed by the petitioner "cannot be constitutionally ineffective." As the Court put it, for purposes of establishing cause, "it is not the gravity of the attorney's error that matters, but that it constitutes a violation of petitioner's right to counsel, so that the error must be seen as an external factor, i.e. 'imputed to the State.' " When such is not the case, the Court reiterated its stand in *Carrier* that "the petitioner bears the risk in federal habeas for all attorney errors made in the course of the representation."

An important exception to the rule that an ineffective assistance claim only lies when the underlying right to counsel exists arises when the ineffective assistance at the state post-conviction proceeding results in the failure to raise a claim of ineffective assistance of *trial* counsel and, under the relevant state law, that collateral proceeding is the only stage at which such claims may be raised. In this situation, seven members of the Court concluded in *Martinez v. Ryan,*[172] the prisoner is denied fair process unless he can raise the claim on federal habeas. Although the exception purports to apply solely when the state has expressly chosen to permit an ineffective trial counsel claim only on collateral review (and not on appeal) and only when the claim is "substantial," Justice Scalia asserted in dissent that no functional difference existed between that situation and those claims—including many other ineffective assistance claims and new evidence claims—that only come to light after the appellate process is complete. Given the ubiquity of ineffective assistance of trial counsel claims made on collateral review, Scalia averred that *Ryan's* holding in essence established a right to (effective) counsel at initial collateral review proceedings. Instead, he argued, the Court should adhere to its holdings in *Carrier* and *Coleman* that only when factors "external" to the prisoner's defense (e.g., state interference with counsel) cause an inability to raise a claim should cause be recognized.

Despite Justice Scalia's concerns, one year later the Court expanded *Martinez* to those situations in which the state technically does permit an ineffective trial counsel claim to be brought on direct appeal but in fact has made it "nearly impossible" to raise such a claim. *Trevino v. Thaler*[173] involved the post-conviction procedure in Texas, where the two primary mechanisms for bring an ineffective assistance of counsel claim were to assert the claim on direct appeal or through a motion for a new trial to develop a record. The first option, the Court held, was inadequate because the trial record, which is all that is available on appeal, rarely provides sufficient information for a claim about counsel's misconduct. And the motion for a new trial to develop the record "is usually inadequate because of Texas rules regarding time limits on the filing, and the disposal, of such motions and the availability of trial transcripts." A number of states have

---

[170] See *Evitts v. Lucey,* 469 U.S. 387, 105 S.Ct. 830 (1985) and discussion in § 32.04(c)(4).

[171] See, e.g., *Pennsylvania v. Finley,* 481 U.S. 551, 107 S.Ct. 1990 (1987), discussed in § 31.03(c).

[172] 566 U.S. 1, 132 S.Ct. 1309 (2012).

[173] 569 U.S. 413, 133 S.Ct. 1911 (2013).

procedural regimes like the one in Texas, so *Trevino* is evidence that, as Justice Scalia predicted in *Martinez*, the Court is effectively establishing a right to counsel at the initial state collateral review proceeding, at least for claims that require more than a trial transcript to develop.

Four years later, however, the Court made clear that *Martinez* and *Trevino* establish only a limited exception to *Coleman*, by expressly holding that the ineffectiveness of state post-conviction counsel does not provide sufficient cause for procedural default on a claim that appellate counsel was ineffective. In *Davila v. Davis*,[174] trial counsel's objection to a proposed jury instruction was overruled by the trial court. On appeal, counsel did not challenge the instruction, a fact that state collateral review counsel failed to raise. The petitioner argued in federal habeas court that, even though normally there is no right to (effective) counsel at post-conviction proceedings, this failure provided the cause necessary to permit challenge of the instruction in federal habeas court, citing *Martinez* and *Trevino*. But Justice Thomas reasoned for the Court that, unlike in those cases, here the state had not established a procedural structure that prevented or made "nearly impossible" raising the claim at the next stage of the process; rather, the state's process was reasonable because ineffective appellate claims can only be raised at post-conviction proceedings and the failure to raise such a claim on collateral review is entirely the defense's fault. To the four dissenters' argument that, given the fact that there is no right to counsel on collateral review, the majority's holding makes challenging appellate counsel's ineffectiveness much more difficult than challenging trial counsel's ineffectiveness, Thomas stated that "[t]he criminal trial enjoys pride of place in our criminal justice system in a way that an appeal from that trial does not." He also noted that in the typical case of this sort, at least one court—the trial court—would have ruled on the objection (unlike in a case like *Martinez*, where by definition no trial objection would have been made).

As noted above, one reason for the cause requirement when a state prisoner brings a claim in federal habeas court is federal-state comity. That rationale disappears when the claimant is a federal prisoner. But for judicial economy reasons the Court has also required federal prisoners to show cause and prejudice when the claim was not raised below.[175] However, in *Massaro v. United States*,[176] the Court unanimously decided that federal prisoners may bring an ineffective assistance of counsel claim on habeas even if it was not raised on direct appeal. As it would subsequently reason in *Martinez* and *Trevino*, the Court stated that, because evaluation of such claims often requires facts that are not found in the trial transcript, it is usually best carried out in a habeas court, which—unlike an appellate court—has the capacity to conduct hearings. A contrary holding would "creat[e] the risk that defendants would feel compelled to raise the issue before there has been an opportunity fully to develop the factual predicate for the claim." Further, it would put appellate counsel in an "awkward position vis-a-vis trial counsel" because in developing the trial record for appeal the former attorney relies on the latter, who may not be very forthcoming if one of the appellate claims is ineffective assistance. The Court also rejected as too difficult to administer a procedure that precludes habeas review of ineffective counsel claims that can be assessed based on the trial record or do not suffer from conflict between trial and appellate counsel. A growing number of states

---

[174]   ___ U.S. ___, 137 S.Ct. 2058 (2017).

[175]   *United States v. Frady*, 456 U.S. 152, 102 S.Ct. 1584 (1982) (construing 28 U.S.C.A. § 2255).

[176]   538 U.S. 500, 123 S.Ct. 1690 (2003).

adopt the *Massaro* approach in assessing ineffective assistance claims raised at state collateral proceedings.[177]

(4) Prejudice

Until *United States v. Frady*,[178] a companion case to *Engle*, none of the Court's cases had directly addressed the "prejudice" prong of the cause and prejudice standard. *Frady* did not produce a clear definition of the term either, but it did reject at least one possible interpretation of it. The petitioner's contention in *Frady* was that prejudice should be equated with the "plain error" rule applicable in cases on direct appeal, which under the federal rules allows the appellate court to decide a claim "affecting substantial rights" even when it has not been brought to the attention of the court.[179] But the Court, in another opinion by Justice O'Connor, held that a habeas petitioner must clear a "significantly higher hurdle" than the litigant on direct review in order to obtain relief.

The Court was ambiguous as to what that hurdle might be. But it did find that the error raised by Frady—an erroneous instruction on "malice" at his homicide trial—would not be heard on habeas review because it did not inflict "actual and substantial disadvantage, infecting his entire trial with error of constitutional dimension," and thus was not prejudicial under the cause and prejudice standard. In reaching this conclusion, the Court stressed that the trial judge and nine appellate judges, over the course of several different proceedings, had found that the evidence of intent in Frady's case clearly supported his conviction. This treatment suggested that the Court might conduct the prejudice inquiry in line with an "overwhelming evidence" version of the harmless error test;[180] under this approach, the prejudice prong would only be met if the untainted evidence against the defendant failed to substantiate his guilt.

It is more likely that the Court meant to adopt the slightly narrower (i.e. more prosecution-oriented) formulation of the prejudice inquiry found in discovery and ineffective assistance cases. That conclusion is based on a reading of the Court's decision in *Strickler v. Greene*,[181] where the Court stated that the prejudice inquiry in procedural default analysis is "parallel" to the materiality inquiry mandated by *Brady v. Maryland*[182] in determining whether evidence is exculpatory. The latter test looks at whether there is a "reasonable probability" that the error affected the "outcome of the proceedings" (rather than, as in constitutional harmless error analysis, whether there is a *possibility* that the error affected the outcome).[183] The same test applies in determining whether ineffective assistance of counsel has prejudiced the defendant. Examples of how this test is applied by the Court are found in the chapters on discovery and ineffective assistance.[184]

It may be that the difference between these standards is so subtle that the choice between one or the other makes little practical difference. But, at least in theory, *Greene's* conflation of the various prejudice standards facilitates analysis under the

---

[177] See *Commonwealth v. Grant*, 572 Pa. 48, 813 A.2d 726, 735–738 & n. 13 (2002) (discussing cases).

[178] 456 U.S. 152, 102 S.Ct. 1584 (1982).

[179] Fed.R.Crim.P. 52(b).

[180] See § 29.05(a).

[181] 527 U.S. 263, 119 S.Ct. 1936 (1999). See also, *Banks v. Dretke*, 540 U.S. 668, 124 S.Ct. 1256 (2004).

[182] 373 U.S. 83, 83 S.Ct. 1194 (1963).

[183] See § 29.05(c).

[184] See § 24.04(b) (*Brady* claims); § 32.04(c)(3) (ineffective assistance claims).

cause and prejudice standard whenever (as will often be the case) the asserted cause is either a failure to produce exculpatory evidence or ineffective assistance. In *Brady* cases, as the Court pointed out in *Strickler,* if the defendant shows both that the prosecution suppressed evidence and that the suppression affected the outcome of trial, then cause and prejudice for purposes of habeas review is automatically established. Similarly, if in ineffective assistance cases both the deficient performance and prejudice prongs are met, the *Sykes* test is presumably met.

(e)   The Actual Innocence Exception

In *Engle,* the Court stated that "[w]hile the nature of a constitutional claim may affect the calculation of cause and actual prejudice, it does not alter the need to make that threshold showing." Nonetheless, perhaps spurred by the dissent's argument that requiring proof of cause in every case would result in "miscarriages of justice," the *Engle* Court also stated that "[i]n appropriate cases," the principles of comity and finality that underlie the cause and prejudice standard "must yield to the imperative of correcting a fundamentally unjust incarceration." In *Murray v. Carrier,* the Court made this point more explicit, by admitting that there might be "extraordinary" cases where a fundamental miscarriage of justice would result if the cause prong had to be met before habeas review were granted. It went on to hold that "where a constitutional violation has probably resulted in the conviction of one who is actually innocent," the level of "prejudice" is sufficient by itself to entitle the petitioner to federal review. In the companion case of *Kuhlmann v. Wilson,*[185] the Court elaborated on the actual innocence standard as follows: "the prisoner must show a fair probability that, in light of all the evidence, including that alleged to have been illegally admitted (but with due regard to any unreliability of it) and evidence tenably claimed to have been wrongly excluded or to have become available only after the trial, the trier of the facts would have entertained a reasonable doubt of his guilt."[186]

The scope of this exception is very narrow. The language in *Kuhlmann* suggests that it focuses entirely on claims that adduce *facts* proving innocence; unlike a harmless error test,[187] for instance, the impact of instructions on the accuracy of a verdict may well be irrelevant.[188] Further suggesting the narrow scope of the exception is the Court's statement in *Sawyer v. Whitley*[189] that a "prototypical" example of actual innocence is "where the State has convicted the wrong person of the crime."

A separate issue is the standard of proof necessary to show innocence. As noted above, *Kuhlmann* stated that innocence can be shown by a "fair *probability*." Similarly, in *Carrier* the Court asserted that the petitioner need only show the error "has *probably* resulted in the conviction of one who is actually innocent." In *Schlup v. Delo,*[190] the Court formally adopted the preponderance standard, framing the actual innocence inquiry in terms of whether "it is more likely than not that no reasonable juror would have

---

[185]   477 U.S. 436, 106 S.Ct. 2616 (1986).

[186]   Quoting Henry Friendly, *Is Innocence Irrelevant? Collateral Attack on Criminal Judgments,* 38 U.Chi.L.Rev. 142, 160 (1970).

[187]   See § 29.05(c)(1).

[188]   Although both pre-*Carrier* cases, it is noteworthy that relief was denied in both *Engle,* involving an erroneous burden of proof instruction, and *Frady,* involving an erroneous malice instruction. See also, *Dugger v. Adams,* discussed below.

[189]   505 U.S. 333, 112 S.Ct. 2514 (1992).

[190]   513 U.S. 298, 115 S.Ct. 851 (1995).

convicted [the petitioner]." *Schlup* explicitly rejected a requirement that actual innocence be shown by clear and convincing evidence, a standard that, as discussed below, it had previously adopted in the capital sentencing context. Its primary justification for this distinction centered on efficient use of judicial resources: while the range of mitigating factors that "probably" would preclude a death sentence are legion, the Court concluded that actual innocence claims connected with conviction were likely to be "extremely rare," or at least "rarely successful," and thus a more-likely-than-not standard could be countenanced in that context.

House v. Bell[191] provides a good example of how *Schlup's* preponderance standard plays out. In that case, the Court noted that (1) DNA testing had established that semen found on the victim came from her husband (not the petitioner); (2) the victim's blood may have ended up on the petitioner's pants because both items had been packed in the same box; and (3) credible evidence was presented to the effect that the husband had the motive and opportunity to commit the crime. Calling the issue "close," Justice Kennedy concluded for five members of the Court (Justice Alito not participating) that House's procedurally defaulted claims should be heard. In doing so, the Court specifically rejected the government's argument that passage of the AEDPA since *Schlup* adopted the preponderance test had raised the actual innocence standard in first-time habeas actions to the "clear and convincing evidence" level. Kennedy noted that this language appears only in the AEDPA's provisions dealing with successive petitions and with requests for evidentiary hearings.[192]

The Court also emphasized that, in applying *Schlup*, the court should consider all relevant evidence, including evidence that was wrongly excluded or was unavailable at trial. It also stated that even witness credibility may need to be assessed. Further, the "court's function is not to make an independent factual determination about what likely occurred, but rather to assess the likely impact of the evidence on reasonable jurors."

In *Bousley v. United States*,[193] the Court applied *Schlup's* preponderance standard to errors associated with adjudication by plea as well, despite the fact that claims raised in connection with guilty pleas (which resolve most cases) are less likely to be "rare." Bousley argued that his guilty plea was involuntary because at the time of his plea he had been informed by the lawyers and the judge that the statute penalizing "using" a firearm, under which he was charged, covered *possession* of a firearm, an interpretation that was later declared incorrect in the Supreme Court's decision in *Bailey v. United States*.[194] Applying the *Schlup* standard, the Court held that the defendant, who claimed he had merely possessed a gun at the time of the offense, should prevail on his habeas claim if he could show that he probably was not guilty of the using-a-firearm offense as defined in *Bailey* or of any other more serious offenses that were "forgone" by the prosecution because of the guilty plea.

In dissent, Justice Scalia, joined by Justice Thomas, argued that the *Schlup* standard was inappropriate for guilty plea cases because the judicial efficiency rationale of that case does not apply; given their much greater number and the fact that any

---

[191] 547 U.S. 518, 126 S.Ct. 2064 (2006).

[192] See §§ 33.04(b)(2) & 33.05(c).

[193] 523 U.S. 614, 118 S.Ct. 1604 (1998).

[194] 516 U.S. 137, 116 S.Ct. 501 (1995). The Court first held that the retroactivity prohibition on applying new rules in federal habeas cases did not apply in a case such as this, where the petitioner claimed that the statute under which he was convicted did not apply to him. See § 33.02(c).

Supreme Court decision construing the elements of a crime might trigger an involuntariness claim like Bousley's, such cases will generate many more actual innocence claims than will trials. Scalia also noted that, in contrast to the relative ease with which the relevant facts can be ascertained when trials have occurred, evidence about the facts necessary to show guilt or innocence is scanty in cases resolved through pleas; in the case of "forgone" charges, such evidence may even be non-existent, since the charges might never have been formally filed and in any event no factual basis on them will be developed at arraignment.

While the Court has adhered to the *Schlup* standard in assessing innocence claims associated with any aspect of the conviction process, it has rejected that standard at capital sentencing. The standard in the latter context was set out in *Sawyer v. Whitley*.[195] The majority opinion, written by Chief Justice Rehnquist, rejected the state's contention that a capital defendant is only "innocent" of a death penalty if he should not have been convicted for intentional murder. At the same time, it found overbroad petitioner's contention that review should always be granted if the claimed constitutional error caused "a fair probability that the admission of false evidence, or the preclusion of true mitigating evidence . . . resulted in a sentence of death." The Court noted that, given the breadth of mitigating factors that are relevant at capital sentencing proceedings, this test would have a damaging effect on "finality" in capital cases. Instead, the Court held that "[s]ensible meaning is given to the term 'innocent of the death penalty' by allowing a showing in addition to innocence of the capital crime itself a showing that there was no aggravating circumstance or that some other condition of eligibility had not been met." Thus, the petitioner must "show by clear and convincing evidence that . . . no reasonable juror would have found [him] eligible for the death penalty."

The Court made clear that, under this standard, merely showing that mitigating evidence was not presented due to ineffective assistance of counsel or some other reason would be insufficient, because mitigating evidence, no matter how powerful, does not focus on the petitioner's "eligibility" for the death sentence. Furthermore, it strongly suggested that unless the petitioner's claims undermine *all* of the aggravating circumstances found by the sentencing jury, the actual innocence exception is not met. In *Sawyer* itself, the petitioner had been convicted and sentenced to death for torturing a woman and then setting her on fire, in concert with one Charles Lane. The petitioner claimed that the prosecution withheld evidence that would have impeached its principal witness (Sawyer's girlfriend), as well as a hearsay statement by the girlfriend's four-year-old son that suggested Sawyer had "tried to help the lady" at the time the fire was lit but was pushed backed in a chair by Lane. The Court found that, in light of other facts adduced at trial, as well as the relevant state law, this evidence, even if credited, did not show Sawyer was "innocent" of the jury's findings in aggravation that the crime was heinous and committed during an aggravated arson; undisputed evidence showed that Sawyer had helped his co-defendant beat and kick the victim, submerge her in a bathtub and pour scalding water on her prior to the burning, and Louisiana law held liable principals who "aid and abet in [the crime's] commission, or directly or indirectly counsel or procure another to commit the crime."[196]

---

[195]   505 U.S. 333, 112 S.Ct. 2514 (1992).

[196]   The three dissenters agreed with this result, but argued that the Court should define actual innocence in the capital sentencing context to require the defendant to show that "the alleged error more likely than not created a manifest miscarriage of justice."

Earlier Court cases dealing with capital sentencing claims are consonant with *Sawyer*. In *Smith v. Murray*,[197] for instance, the claim involved the admissibility of psychiatric testimony to the effect that the defendant was "dangerous." Although the Court conceded that this testimony was obtained in violation of the Fifth Amendment,[198] it found that, because the testimony had not been false or misleading and because the evaluation on which it was based "neither precluded the development of true facts nor resulted in the admission of false ones," admission of the testimony did not lead to the imposition of capital punishment on one who was actually "nondangerous." Similarly, in *Dugger v. Adams*,[199] the Court held that an erroneous instruction to the jury that the judge had the ultimate "responsibility" for imposing the death penalty was not reviewable under the actual innocence exception, given the fact that the trial judge found an equal number of aggravating and mitigating circumstances in affirming the jury's death sentence. According to the Court, "[d]emonstrating that an error is by its nature the kind of error that might have affected the accuracy of a death sentence is far from demonstrating that an individual defendant probably is 'actually innocent' of the sentence he or she received."

The Court has yet to address whether the actual innocence exception applies to non-capital sentencing determinations. In *Dretke v. Haley*,[200] the petitioner contended, and the state conceded, that his enhanced (three-strikes) sentence was invalid, because conviction for one of the predicate offenses had not been final at the time of sentencing. Although he had failed to raise this claim on appeal, he argued that this default should be excused because he was actually "innocent" of the enhanced sentence, given the absence of a crucial predicate for it. The Court recognized the potential viability of the claim, but dismissed it because the lower courts had not considered all related nondefaulted claims and other grounds to excuse the default (such as counsel's failure to notice that the petitioner was ineligible for an enhanced sentence). Unless the petitioner loses on all of these claims, the Court held, the actual innocence issue should not be addressed. The Court further made clear that it was declining to answer the question of whether the actual innocence doctrine applies to non-capital cases.

(f) Procedural Default in Capital Cases

For capital cases only, the 1996 Antiterrorism and Effective Death Penalty Act radically departed from the foregoing procedural default framework. Under the Act, failure to raise a claim in a death penalty case bars habeas review unless the failure is:

(1)   "the result of State action in violation of the Constitution or laws of the United States";

(2)   "the result of the Supreme Court's recognition of a new Federal right that is made retroactively applicable"; or

(3)   "based on a factual predicate that could not have been discovered through the exercise of due diligence in time to present the claim for State or Federal post-conviction review."[201]

---

[197] 477 U.S. 527, 106 S.Ct. 2661 (1986).

[198] See *Estelle v. Smith,* 451 U.S. 454, 101 S.Ct. 1866 (1981), discussed in § 28.03(b)(3).

[199] 489 U.S. 401, 109 S.Ct. 1211 (1989).

[200] 541 U.S. 386, 124 S.Ct. 1847 (2004).

[201] 28 U.S.C.A. § 2264(a).

While it may expand habeas jurisdiction in some respects, this language also eliminates ineffective assistance of counsel as a basis for cause, and substantially reduces the scope of the actual innocence exception just discussed.

The first exception probably incorporates the situations described earlier as "state interference" bases for cause, including when the default occurs due to state processes that cannot be called adequate and independent.[202] The second exception is meant to allow defaulted claims when *Teague's* two categories of justiciable new rules apply; as discussed earlier, very few claims qualify under *Teague's* categories in any event.[203] The third exception, which looks at whether there has been a failure to discover facts rather than to raise legal claims, has no direct analogue in the Court's cause and prejudice jurisprudence but, as noted earlier,[204] allowing such claims to be heard would not be inconsistent with the Court's case law if the failure were due to the state or to incompetent counsel. However, the precise language of the third provision appears to reject attorney incompetence as a reason for failing to discover facts, since it only allows such facts to be heard if they could *not* have been discovered through "due diligence," meaning that facts that were undiscovered because of attorney incompetence may not be heard. Even more surprisingly, none of these provisions recognizes an actual innocence exception (unless it is based on new evidence that could not have been discovered with due diligence).[205]

Note again that these provisions only apply in capital cases.[206] The AEDPA does not contain any provisions governing procedural default in noncapital cases, which means, however ironically, that the "more protective" cause-and-prejudice rules developed by the Court apply in the latter context.

33.04 Other Procedural Hurdles

(a) The Exhaustion Requirement

Generally, state prisoners must seek vindication of their federal constitutional rights in state court before proceeding to federal court. According to the Supreme Court, this "exhaustion" requirement is based on the comity principle. It "serves to minimize friction between our federal and state systems of justice" by preventing disruption of state proceedings and giving state courts an opportunity to correct federal violations before a federal court does.[207] Justice O'Connor has further asserted that ensuring state court review will improve competence among state courts, because it makes them "increasingly familiar with and hospitable toward federal constitutional issues."[208]

---

[202] See § 33.03(d)(2).

[203] See § 33.02(c).

[204] See § 33.02(d)(2) & (3).

[205] However, in *House v. Bell*, 547 U.S. 518, 126 S.Ct. 2064 (2006), the Court appeared to hold that the actual innocence exception still applies in capital cases.

[206] Cf. *Lindh v. Murphy*, 521 U.S. 320, 117 S.Ct. 2059 (1997)(concluding that these provisions of the AEDPA do not apply to noncapital cases). The AEDPA also provides that, even if timely objection is made, ineffective post-conviction counsel claims may not be heard in capital cases in those states which provide for the "appointment, compensation and payment of reasonable litigation expenses of competent counsel in state post-conviction proceedings." 28 U.S.C.A. § 2261(e).

[207] *Duckworth v. Serrano,* 454 U.S. 1, 102 S.Ct. 18 (1981).

[208] *Rose v. Lundy,* 455 U.S. 509, 102 S.Ct. 1198 (1982).

Some commentators, however, believe the exhaustion requirement "is at best a nuisance and a wasted effort, and at worst offends comity interests rather than advancing them."[209] By the time most non-exhausted claims are presented in federal court, they are defaulted in any event; returning the claim to a state court to have it confirm that fact is inefficient. In the few cases where the state court does reach the merits of a non-exhausted claim, the federal court will still often reconsider the case from scratch, resulting in further inefficiency; furthermore, as Justice Blackmun has pointed out, "[r]emitting a habeas petitioner to state court to exhaust a patently frivolous claim . . . hardly demonstrates respect for state courts."[210] As to Justice O'Connor's hope that the requirement increases state court competence, one commentator has argued that "state courts have been addressing federal constitutional issues for a long time, . . . and it is condescending at best to suggest that with more practice they might improve their ability to recognize and respect federal rights."[211]

For some time the Supreme Court seemed willing merely to express a preference against habeas review when review by state courts remained available,[212] but by 1944 the Court considered it well settled that "ordinarily an application for habeas corpus by one detained under a state court judgment of conviction will be entertained . . . only after all state remedies available, including all appellate remedies in the state courts and in this Court by appeal or writ of certiorari have been exhausted."[213] The current federal habeas statute, § 2254(b), summarizes current law with respect to exhaustion. It states that the writ is not available to the applicant "unless it appears that the applicant has exhausted the remedies available in the courts of the State, or that there is either an absence of available State corrective process or the existence of circumstances rendering such process ineffective to protect the rights of the prisoner." The Supreme Court has adhered to this formulation in virtually all cases, although it continues to affirm the idea that the exhaustion requirement is not "jurisdictional" and thus can occasionally be waived by a federal court when "the interest of comity and federalism will be better served by addressing the merits forthwith."[214]

Discussed here are four issues that arise with some frequency in connection with the exhaustion requirement: (1) the meaning of § 2254's phrase "remedies available in the courts of the state;" (2) the meaning of that section's "ineffective" state "corrective process;" (3) the extent to which the precise claim raised on federal habeas must have been presented in state court; and (4) the correct procedure when a habeas petition contains both exhausted and non-exhausted claims.

(1) Available State Remedies

In *Brown v. Allen*[215] the Court held that a state prisoner who has fully pursued direct review at the state and Supreme Court level need not seek state collateral

---

[209] Barry Friedman, *A Tale of Two Habeas*, 73 Minn.L.Rev. 247, 310 (1988). See also, Paul M. Bator, *Finality in Criminal Law and Federal Habeas Corpus for State Prisoners*, 76 Harv.L.Rev. 441, 483 (1963).

[210] *Rose v. Lundy,* 455 U.S. 509, 102 S.Ct. 1198 (1982) (Blackmun, J., concurring).

[211] Friedman, supra note 210, at 312–13.

[212] See e.g., *Ex parte Royall,* 117 U.S. 241, 6 S.Ct. 734 (1886).

[213] *Ex parte Hawk,* 321 U.S. 114, 64 S.Ct. 448 (1944).

[214] *Granberry v. Greer*, 481 U.S. 129, 107 S.Ct. 1671 (1987). See also § 2254(b)(2) (allowing a federal court to deny a habeas petition on merit grounds notwithstanding a lack of exhaustion).

[215] 344 U.S. 443, 73 S.Ct. 397 (1953).

remedies in order to meet the exhaustion requirement. And in *Fay v. Noia*,[216] the Court eliminated the need to pursue a direct appeal to the Supreme Court before exhaustion occurs. Thus only state appellate remedies need be sought to meet the exhaustion requirement. However, review must normally be sought up through the highest court level, which usually means the state supreme court.

Fay also stressed that only *available* state remedies need be pursued to satisfy the exhaustion requirement. It went on to hold that exhaustion rules did not bar Noia's claim, despite the fact that he had not appealed his claim in state court, because the time to appeal had expired. However, in *O'Sullivan v. Boerckel*[217] the Court held that failure to seek *discretionary* review with the state's highest court within the time allotted for such review results is a violation of the exhaustion principle unless the petitioner can show cause for the failure and prejudice from it. In other words, the Court applied its reasoning in the procedural default cases to the exhaustion context.[218] The four dissenters argued that discretionary review should not be considered necessary for exhaustion because in most, if not all, states the supreme court, worried about judicial resources, *discourages* prisoners from seeking such review. The majority conceded that its holding would possibly increase filings to the state supreme courts and thus "disserve . . . comity," but maintained that the exhaustion requirement is unmet whenever, using the language of § 2254(c), the petitioner "has the right under the law of the State to raise, *by any available procedure*, the question presented." Justice Souter, who provided the fifth vote for the result, emphasized the majority opinion's suggestion that, if a state supreme court plainly stated a desire to avoid discretionary review petitions, the exhaustion requirement would not bar a subsequent federal habeas petition. If state courts follow this suggestion, *Boerckel* may be of limited impact. In *Ylst v. Nunnemaker*,[219] the Court noted that a state court refusal to revisit a claim on the ground it has already done so is not a procedural bar. This dictum was converted to a holding in *Cone v. Bell*.[220] The latter case made clear that in this situation the claim is ripe for federal review because exhaustion has occurred.

(2) Ineffective Corrective Processes

The last clause of § 2254(b) makes clear that even exhaustion of available remedies is not required when circumstances render the state process "ineffective to protect the rights of the prisoner." In *Duckworth v. Serrano*,[221] the Court construed this language to mean that this exception to the exhaustion requirement exists only if there is "no opportunity to obtain redress in state court or if the corrective process is so clearly deficient as to render futile any effort to obtain relief." Under this definition of ineffective process, few situations will merit suspension of the exhaustion requirement. Inadequate process may be found, however, when there has been an inordinate delay at the state level,[222] or where procedural snarls or obstacles preclude an effective state remedy.[223]

---

[216] 372 U.S. 391, 83 S.Ct. 822 (1963).

[217] 526 U.S. 838, 119 S.Ct. 1728 (1999).

[218] See § 33.03(d). It is not clear whether the Court will apply the same reasoning to direct appeals and thus overturn *Fay*. See § 33.03(d)(3).

[219] 501 U.S. 797, 111 S.Ct. 2590 (1991).

[220] 556 U.S. 449, 129 S.Ct. 1769 (2009).

[221] 454 U.S. 1, 102 S.Ct. 18 (1981).

[222] See e.g., *Lowe v. Duckworth,* 663 F.2d 42 (7th Cir. 1981).

[223] *Bartone v. United States,* 375 U.S. 52, 84 S.Ct. 21 (1963).

(3) The Fair Presentation Requirement

If adequate process was available in the state appellate courts, the habeas petitioner must not only have presented his case to them but also have given them a "fair opportunity" to consider the same issues presented in the habeas petition.[224] Otherwise considerations of comity require dismissal of the petition. The post-Warren Court has strictly construed this requirement.

For example, in *Anderson v. Harless*[225] the petitioner was convicted of murder by a jury that may have been improperly instructed about the burden of proof as required by the Court's decision in *Sandstrom v. Montana*.[226] In his state appeals, the petitioner argued simply that the instruction was erroneous, citing to a state case but not *Sandstrom*. The Supreme Court, in a 6–3 opinion, held that the petition could not be heard on habeas because the *Sandstrom* claim had not been presented in state court. According to the Court:

> [I]t is not enough that all the facts necessary to support the federal claim were before the state courts . . . or that a somewhat similar state-law claim was made. . . . [T]he habeas petitioner must have "fairly presented" to the state courts the "substance" of his federal habeas corpus claim.

Similarly, a petitioner cannot assume that state courts will peruse lower court opinions to ascertain the federal nature of his claim; if the petitioner does not state in his petition that his claim is federal and fails to append the relevant lower court opinions, he has not fairly presented the claim to the state courts. Holding otherwise, the Court concluded in *Baldwin v. Reese*,[227] "would impose a serious burden upon judges of state appellate courts, particularly those with discretionary review powers," because it would require them to read through lower court opinions and briefs in every instance. Moreover, the Court noted, to ensure the fair presentation requirement is met in such a case all the petitioner need do is indicate in his petition that the claim is a federal one.[228]

In contrast to the situation in *Reese*, where the petitioner does not add a new claim at the federal level but merely supplements the *evidence* the fair presentation requirement is not necessarily violated. In *Vasquez v. Hillery*,[229] the petitioner, at the federal district court's request, presented statistical evidence showing discrimination in the selection of his grand jury that had not been available in state court. Although the state argued that introduction of this evidence rendered the petitioner's claim a "wholly different animal," the Supreme Court pointed out that the new information did not change the nature of the discrimination claim but merely provided more sophisticated data that improved the reliability of the district court's decision. Whether the same holding would be required in a case in which the federal court did not make a request for the supplemental evidence is not clear. As the Court stated, "the circumstances present no occasion for the Court to consider a case in which the prisoner has attempted

---

[224] *Picard v. Connor,* 404 U.S. 270, 92 S.Ct. 509 (1971).

[225] 459 U.S. 4, 103 S.Ct. 276 (1982).

[226] 442 U.S. 510, 99 S.Ct. 2450 (1979).

[227] 541 U.S. 27, 124 S.Ct. 1347 (2004).

[228] The petitioner also argued that the exhaustion requirement was met because, even though he did not label his ineffective assistance claim federal, federal and state law on the issue were identical. Over Justice Stevens' dissent, the Court deemed this argument waived, since it had not been raised in the courts below.

[229] 474 U.S. 254, 106 S.Ct. 617 (1986).

to expedite federal review by deliberately withholding essential facts from the state courts."

In addition to considering whether the precise claims raised on federal habeas were presented fairly at the state level, the federal habeas court must consider the *type* of state proceeding at which the claims were presented. In *Pitchess v. Davis*,[230] for instance, the Supreme Court found that motions to the California Court of Appeal and the California Supreme Court for a pretrial writ of prohibition were not sufficient, by themselves, to exhaust state remedies, because such writs are granted only when "extraordinary relief" is required, and thus did not accurately represent the typical state review process. Similarly, in *Castille v. Peoples*,[231] a unanimous Court found that the fair presentation requirement was not met when the only state court consideration of the claims in the petitioner's federal habeas petition was on a petition for "allocatur review," which under Pennsylvania law is not a matter of right but is granted "only when there are special and important reasons therefor."

(4) Mixed Petitions

Frequently, a habeas petition will include both exhausted and non-exhausted claims, the latter involving issues not litigated at the state level because the state court focused on other claims or because the defendant later appended them to the petition as it worked its way up the appellate ladder. Until the Court's decision in *Rose v. Lundy*,[232] the majority of circuits had held that a federal district court confronted with a "mixed" petition must pass upon the fully exhausted claims immediately (if they can be separated from the non-exhausted claims), on the ground that the federal interest in safeguarding the rights of prisoners and swiftly adjudicating disputes outweighed any federal-state comity concerns that might force delayed consideration of a properly presented issue.[233] In *Lundy*, however, the Supreme Court decided that district courts must *dismiss* habeas petitions containing both unexhausted and exhausted claims, in order to "encourage state prisoners to seek full relief first from the state courts, thus giving those courts the first opportunity to review all claims of constitutional error." This holding applies even when the exhausted claims are based on allegations or facts entirely separate from those forming the basis for the non-exhausted claims. A majority of the Court also held, however, that the defendant who has mixed claims can amend his petition to delete the non-exhausted claims and proceed with federal review of his exhausted claims.[234]

Alternatively, the petitioner may withdraw the petition or obtain an abeyance from the federal court, seek state relief on the non-exhausted claims, and return to federal court with the same petition.[235] However, in *Rhines v. Weber*,[236] the Court unanimously held that the stay-and-abeyance order may only be granted for a "reasonable time" and only when (1) "there was good cause for the petitioner's failure to exhaust his claims first

---

[230] 421 U.S. 482, 95 S.Ct. 1748 (1975) (per curiam).

[231] 489 U.S. 346, 109 S.Ct. 1056 (1989).

[232] 455 U.S. 509, 102 S.Ct. 1198 (1982).

[233] See, e.g., *Miller v. Hall,* 536 F.2d 967 (1st Cir. 1976); *Tyler v. Swenson,* 483 F.2d 611 (8th Cir. 1973); *Hewett v. State of North Carolina,* 415 F.2d 1316 (4th Cir. 1969).

[234] The drawback to this approach, discussed in § 33.04(b)(2), is that a subsequent petition raising the deleted (and now exhausted) claims is likely to be considered an "abuse of the writ" and thus denied without considering the merits.

[235] *Slack v. McDaniel*, 529 U.S. 473, 120 S.Ct. 1595 (2000).

[236] 544 U.S. 269, 125 S.Ct. 1528 (2005).

in state court;" (2) the unexhausted claims are not "plainly meritless;" and (3) "there is no indication that the petitioner engaged in intentionally dilatory litigation tactics." Furthermore, a petitioner is not entitled to an explanation of this option, or to a warning that if he decides to go back to state court and exhaust his unexhausted claims the filing deadline may have expired by the time he returns to federal court.

(b) Successive Petitions

Prisoners will often file more than one habeas petition in the course of their imprisonment. These successive petitions raise two different issues: (1) what is the preclusive effect of having raised the same claim in a previous petition?; and (2) what is the preclusive effect of not having raised a claim in a previous petition?[237] Today, it appears that the same claim may not be raised twice and that a new claim may seldom be raised in a second petition; the combined effect of these rules is that most habeas petitioners are limited to one petition relating to the criminal proceeding that resulted in their detention.[238]

(1) Raising the Same Claim

The common law position with respect to successive petitions was that res judicata does not apply to habeas petitions; thus, the petitioner who failed on one habeas petition could go to another habeas court. In the 1924 decision of *Salinger v. Loisel,*[239] the Supreme Court suggested that this rule rested on the fact that appeal of a decision by a habeas (federal district) court had not been available at common law. Now that such appeal was available, the Court concluded, the previous presentation of a habeas claim should be "considered, and even given controlling weight." However, the Court continued to adhere to the rule that a previous petition on the same claim should not automatically preclude renewed consideration.

In *Sanders v. United States,*[240] the Warren Court reaffirmed *Salinger,* but stressed the part of that decision that refused to apply res judicata principles to habeas. Echoing its other habeas decisions, it held that "[t]he inapplicability of res judicata to habeas . . . is inherent in the very role and function of the writ," because "[c]onventional notions of finality have no place where life or liberty is at stake and infringement of constitutional rights is alleged." Thus, only if "the ends of justice would not be served by reaching the merits of the subsequent application" should a successive petition be denied. Although the petitioner bore the burden of proving that "justice" required review of his second petition, this burden could be met by showing, for example, that the earlier hearing was not "full or fair," or that there had been "an intervening change in law or some other justification for having failed to raise a crucial point or argument in the prior application."

The "ends of justice" language in *Sanders* came from the provision on successive petitions in the 1948 version of § 2244. In 1966, three years after *Sanders,* Congress

---

[237] Note that *Teague v. Lane,* discussed in § 33.02(c), has limited the cases in which these issues are relevant to those involving claims dictated by precedent or those meeting one of *Teague's* two exceptions.

[238] However, if a previous petition was considered something other than a habeas petition by the petitioner and the district court subsequently recharacterizes it as a habeas petition, the consequences of the recharacterization must be explained to the petitioner or the successive petition bar does not apply. *Castro v. United States,* 540 U.S. 375, 124 S.Ct. 786 (2003).

[239] 265 U.S. 224, 44 S.Ct. 519 (1924).

[240] 373 U.S. 1, 83 S.Ct. 1068 (1963).

deleted reference to the "ends of justice" in § 2244, and added subsection (b), which provided that a successive application "need not be entertained [unless it contains a] factual or other ground not adjudicated in the hearing on the earlier application." In *Kuhlmann v. Wilson*,[241] the Court held that this amendment did not eliminate *Sander's* "ends of justice" rule. But a plurality of the Court went on to reconstrue the meaning of that rule. The plurality emphasized that, at the time of the 1966 amendment, Congress had been concerned with the "heavy burden" created by successive petitions, and had wanted to introduce "a greater degree of finality of judgments in habeas corpus proceedings." To "accommodate Congress' intent . . . with the historic function of habeas corpus to provide relief from unjust incarceration," the plurality held that the "ends of justice" test is met only when the petitioner "supplements his constitutional claim with a colorable showing of factual innocence." This ruling clearly limited the ability to obtain a second habeas review of the same claim.

In 1996, Congress went even further, passing a provision that appears to render moot the *Sanders* line of cases. The Antiterrorism and Effective Death Penalty Act simply declares that "[a] claim presented in a second or successive habeas corpus application under section 2254 that was presented in a prior application shall be dismissed."[242] In *Felker v. Turpin*[243] the petitioner argued that this modification of habeas law amounted to a "suspension" of the writ and thus was prohibited under Art I, § 9, cl. 2 of the Constitution. However, the Supreme Court held that the new restrictions on successive petitions were "well within the compass" of the Court's previous decisions defining abuse of the writ, and were therefore constitutional.

Not all second petitions raising the same claim are "successive," however. In *Gonzalez v. Crosby*,[244] the Court held that a motion for relief from judgment that a previous petition was time-barred, made under Federal Rule of Civil Procedure 60(b), is not a successive petition because it does not address the "merits" of the petition, only its justiciability (although such a motion should only be granted under "extraordinary circumstances"[245]). Similarly, in *Stewart v. Martinez-Villareal*,[246] the Court held that if the earlier petition was dismissed on a "technical" ground (such as failure to exhaust state remedies or, as in *Martinez-Villareal* itself, a finding that petitioner's claim that he was incompetent to be executed was premature), the subsequent petition is to be considered the same petition for federal habeas purposes. And in *Slack v. McDaniel*,[247] the Court held that a petition containing claims that were previously presented in a mixed petition dismissed under *Rose v. Lundy*,[248] before the district court adjudicated any of the claims in the petition, is not a second or successive petition but rather should be treated like any other first petition.

---

[241] 477 U.S. 436, 106 S.Ct. 2616 (1986).

[242] 28 U.S.C.A. § 2244(b)(1).

[243] 518 U.S. 651, 116 S.Ct. 2333 (1996).

[244] 545 U.S. 524, 125 S.Ct. 2641 (2005). See also *Calderon v. Thompson*, 523 U.S. 538, 118 S.Ct. 1489 (1998).

[245] See *Ackermann v. United States*, 340 U.S. 193, 71 S.Ct. 209 (1950). In *Gonzalez*, the Court held that such circumstances did not exist—even though, after the petitioner's previous petition was dismissed, the Court had held that petitions such as his were not time-barred—given the reasonableness of the lower courts' contrary holdings about that issue at the time they were handed down.

[246] 523 U.S. 637, 118 S.Ct. 1618 (1998).

[247] 529 U.S. 473, 120 S.Ct. 1595 (2000).

[248] 455 U.S. 509, 102 S.Ct. 1198 (1982), discussed in § 33.04(a)(4).

Furthermore, in *Magwood v. Patterson*[249] five members of the Court, in an opinion authored by Justice Thomas, held that the successive petition prohibition only applies to successive applications challenging the *same* state-court judgment. In *Magwood*, the petitioner's first federal habeas petition resulted in reversal of his death sentence and an order to resentence. Upon receiving a second death sentence, the petitioner filed another habeas writ, which contained for the first time a claim that could have been included in the first petition. Nonetheless, the Court held the claim must be heard because it was contained in the first petition to challenge the *second* state court sentence.

(2) Raising a Different Claim

Sanders also addressed the converse of the issue just discussed: the appropriate disposition of a petition that includes a claim *not* raised in a previous petition. *Sanders* held that the proper response in such a situation depends upon whether there has been "abuse of the writ." Purporting to summarize a number of cases on the issue, it concluded that such abuse normally occurs only when the government can show that there has been a deliberate decision to avoid asserting the claim in the previous petition or hearing.[250] Obviously borrowing from its reasoning in *Fay v. Noia*,[251] the Court reasoned that any other standard would be "unfair," particularly since such writs are often brought by a petitioner "typically unlearned in the law and unable to procure legal assistance in drafting his application."

Not surprisingly, given the repudiation of *Fay* in its later procedural default cases,[252] the Court subsequently rejected this approach. In *McCleskey v. Zant*,[253] the Court broadened the definition of writ abuse to include any situation where the petitioner making a new claim in a successive petition is unable to meet the narrowly defined cause and prejudice standard developed in those cases. Under this standard, even inadvertent failure to raise the claim in the first petition will usually prevent it being considered in a subsequent petition. And even if the petitioner can overcome this hurdle, unless he can also show that the claimed error affected the outcome of his trial (i.e. "prejudice"), the claim will usually not be heard.[254] Justice Kennedy, who wrote the majority opinion, first found that the federal habeas statute, which at that time provided that a new ground in a successive petition shall be dismissed if "the applicant has . . . on the earlier application deliberately withheld the newly asserted ground *or* otherwise abused the writ,"[255] was ambiguous as to the rule to be followed. He then rejected the deliberate bypass rule in favor of the cause and prejudice standard, given the need to promote finality and efficiency in the collateral review process.

Zant's analogy between successive petition and procedural default cases seems inapt. As Justice Marshall argued in dissent, one of the major reasons earlier decisions

---

[249] 561 U.S. 320, 130 S.Ct. 2788 (2010).

[250] Here the Court referred to *Wong Doo v. United States,* 265 U.S. 239, 44 S.Ct. 524 (1924), where the Court upheld dismissal of a due process claim that was raised in a previous petition, but not argued at the hearing on the petition.

[251] 372 U.S. 391, 83 S.Ct. 822 (1963), discussed in § 33.03(b).

[252] See, e.g., *Wainwright v. Sykes,* 433 U.S. 72, 97 S.Ct. 2497 (1977), discussed in § 33.03(c).

[253] 499 U.S. 467, 111 S.Ct. 1454 (1991).

[254] However, consistent with its other habeas cases, see e.g., § 33.03(e), the Court held that the petitioner can always obtain review if he can make a plausible case that the error he is claiming permitted the conviction of an innocent person.

[255] 28 U.S.C.A. § 2254(b) (1948) (emphasis added).

had adopted the narrow cause and prejudice standard in procedural default cases was to protect against federal encroachment of *state* procedural rules, a concern that is not implicated when the relevant previous petition was in federal court. Furthermore, as *Sanders* noted, usually the habeas petitioner is unassisted by counsel, unlike the litigants in the Court's procedural default cases, who all had counsel, albeit possibly incompetent ones, at the stage they defaulted.[256] Justice Marshall also contended that the Court's new rule will decrease efficiency, because petitioners will now assert all conceivable claims in their first petition, however weak, rather than hold back an as-yet unrecognized claim in the hopes that future case law will give it more credibility. Finally, the majority's apparent assumption that the deliberate bypass standard does not provide an effective barrier to abuses of the writ seems unfounded.[257]

Whatever the merits of these arguments, they are now moot. In the Antiterrorism and Effective Death Penalty Act, Congress restricted new claims presented in a second petition to the following: (1) a claim that "relies on a new rule of constitutional law, made retroactive to cases on collateral review by the Supreme Court, that was previously unavailable;" or (2) a claim "the factual predicate [for which] could not have been discovered previously through the exercise of due diligence" and which "would be sufficient to establish by clear and convincing evidence that, but for constitutional error no reasonable factfinder would have found the applicant guilty of the underlying offense."[258] This language permits a successive petition only when one of *Teague's* very narrowly defined exceptions are met,[259] or when new facts are discovered that clearly establish the constitutional error led to conviction of an innocent person.

In *Tyler v. Cain*,[260] the Court interpreted the AEDPA's "made retroactive to cases on collateral review by the Supreme Court" language for the first time, and once again emphasized how narrow *Teague's* exceptions are. The petitioner in *Tyler* had filed five federal habeas petitions prior to the Supreme Court's decision in *Cage v. Louisiana*,[261] which held unconstitutional jury instructions that lead the jury to believe it need not find proof beyond a reasonable doubt to convict. In his sixth petition, Tyler argued that the instructions in his case violated *Cage*. Under AEDPA, this type of successive petition could be heard only if *Cage*, which clearly announced a new rule, has been "made retroactive" by the Supreme Court. Construing "made" to mean the same thing as "held," the Court, in a 5–4 opinion authored by Justice Thomas, concluded that the Court had yet to do so. Although *Cage* itself had held that the instruction violated the Due Process Clause, and a later case, *Sullivan v. Louisiana*,[262] had held that this violation was "structural" and deprived a defendant of a "basic protection . . . without which a criminal

---

[256] See § 33.06 on the right to counsel during habeas review.

[257] See, e.g., *Woodard v. Hutchins,* 464 U.S. 377, 104 S.Ct. 752 (1984) (applying deliberate bypass rule in refusing to hear new claims raised immediately after Supreme Court denied writ of certiorari on old claims); *Antone v. Dugger,* 465 U.S. 200, 104 S.Ct. 962 (1984) (applying bypass rule in refusing to hear new claims previously raised in state courts).

[258] 28 U.S.C.A. § 2244(b)(2).

[259] Note that even a claim that is "dictated by precedent" cannot be made in a second petition. For a description of *Teague* and its exceptions, see § 33.02(c). One of the many oddities of the Act (for others, see § 33.03(f)) is that it eliminates at least one, and possibly both, of *Teague's* exceptions in the provisions dealing with the substantive scope of the writ (see § 33.02(c)), but does not do so in the provisions dealing with evidentiary hearings (see § 33.05(c)), the definition of cause (except in capital cases) (see § 33.03(f)) and successive petitions (see above).

[260] 533 U.S. 656, 121 S.Ct. 2478 (2001).

[261] 498 U.S. 39, 111 S.Ct. 328 (1990).

[262] 508 U.S. 275, 113 S.Ct. 2078 (1993).

trial cannot reliably serve its function," the Court noted there still had been no express holding making *Cage* retroactive pursuant to *Teague*. It also indicated that such a holding was not a foregone conclusion, because structural error rules, although always reversible error,[263] are not necessarily true "watershed rules" that "alter our understanding of the bedrock procedural elements essential to the fairness of a proceeding." Only the latter type of rule triggers *Teague's* second exception allowing retroactive application of new rules.[264]

There is at least one circumstance, however, where a successive petition is permitted on a new claim even when neither *Teague* nor the new-facts innocence exception applies. This occurs when an offender who has been sentenced to death argues that he is incompetent to be executed in his second petition. In *Panetti v. Quarterman*,[265] the Court held that requiring offenders who file a habeas petition attacking the legality of their conviction or sentence to include incompetency claims years before their execution date is set and when they may not even evidence symptoms of mental disorder would not promote the judicial conservation and streamlining aims of AEDPA.

(c) The Custody Requirement

Historically, the writ of habeas corpus directed the prisoner's jailer to "bring forth the body" of the prisoner to the court. Accordingly, the federal habeas statutes have all provided that the writ extends only to those "in custody." But the legislation has never defined this phrase. While "custody" clearly encompasses those petitioners who are actually imprisoned on criminal charges,[266] it has been defined more broadly by the Supreme Court in decisions construing the habeas statutes.

Jones v. Cunningham,[267] a Warren Court decision, marked the first major decision expanding the custody concept. Noting that the writ had been made available to aliens seeking entry into the United States despite their ability to go anywhere else in the world, Justice Black's majority opinion stated:

> Of course, [the] writ always could and still can reach behind prison walls and iron bars. But it can do more. It is not now and never has been a static, narrow, formalistic remedy; its scope has grown to achieve its grand purpose—the protection of individuals against erosion of their rights to be free from wrongful restraints upon their liberty.[268]

This language suggested that many types of non-prison restrictions other than parole could satisfy the custody requirement. Indeed, in *Hensley v. Municipal Court*,[269] the Court appeared to do away with the custody requirement almost entirely by hearing collaterally the claim of a petitioner who was released on his own recognizance pending execution of his sentence for a misdemeanor conviction. As one justification for this

---

[263] See § 29.05(c)(2) for further discussion of this aspect of harmless error analysis.

[264] See § 29.06(c)(2) for discussion of this exception to *Teague*.

[265] 551 U.S. 930, 127 S.Ct. 2842 (2007).

[266] This may include prisoners who are detained past the 120-day deadline set by the Interstate Agreement on Detainers for setting a trial date once a prisoner is transferred from one state to another, *if* timely objection is made. See *Reed v. Farley*, 512 U.S. 339, 114 S.Ct. 2291 (1994).

[267] 371 U.S. 236, 83 S.Ct. 373 (1963).

[268] Black also noted that the lower courts had permitted habeas relief in cases involving induction into the military and child custody disputes.

[269] 411 U.S. 345, 93 S.Ct. 1571 (1973).

action, the Court pointed out, quoting *Jones,* that the petitioner was subject to "restraints not shared by the public generally." However, the Court also noted that here petitioner's imprisonment was not remote but certain and immediate if habeas relief were denied; due to a number of stays he had been able to complete the appeals process at the state level. Thus, ultimately *Hensley* may stand only for the proposition that when a petitioner who has been released on his own recognizance has exhausted his state remedies, and imprisonment is accordingly impending, he is entitled to habeas relief.

The Court affirmed this interpretation of *Hensley* in *Justices of Boston Municipal Court v. Lydon.*[270] In *Lydon,* the petitioner was convicted of a misdemeanor and released on his own recognizance pending a trial *de novo* which, under Massachusetts law, functions as an appeal of misdemeanor cases. He then sought dismissal of the second prosecution, on the ground that the evidence at his first trial had been insufficient and that double jeopardy therefore barred the second trial. Upon rejection of this argument by the *de novo* court, he was permitted interlocutory appeal of his double jeopardy claim through the state appellate system and was denied relief. The Supreme Court permitted his subsequent habeas petition because he had exhausted his state remedies, although on an interlocutory basis rather than, as in *Hensley,* after final judgment on direct appeal. The Court made clear that the rationale for finding Lydon was in custody was not his release terms alone but the fact that "there are no more state procedures of which Lydon may avail himself to avoid an allegedly unconstitutional second trial."

As a general rule, of course, once a person completes a particular sentence, he is no longer in "custody." Furthermore, in *Lackawanna Cty. Dist. Atty. v. Coss,*[271] the Court rejected the claim that a state petitioner is still in "custody" for a completed sentence when the underlying conviction for that sentence is used to enhance a current sentence.[272] According to the Court, if the prior conviction is not set aside by the time of the second sentence, it is presumptively valid and may be used to enhance the new sentence, unless it was obtained in violation of the right to counsel.[273] Similarly, a person challenging the constitutionality of a parole revocation is not in custody if the underlying sentence has been served by the time the petition is heard, given that use of the revocation in subsequent parole revocation, sentencing, and trial proceedings is neither certain or probable, but only a possibility.[274]

On the other hand, in *Garlotte v. Fordice*[275] the Court held that a petitioner is still in custody for purposes of challenging a sentence he has already served if he is serving another sentence that was ordered to run consecutively with the one under attack and that was enhanced as a result of it. It has also held that a petitioner may challenge a sentence he has not yet begun to serve if he is currently serving a sentence that is part of a consecutive sentence order.[276] Finally, a person who has served his sentence is in

---

[270] 466 U.S. 294, 104 S.Ct. 1805 (1984).

[271] 532 U.S. 394, 121 S.Ct. 1567 (2001).

[272] See also *Daniels v. United States*, 532 U.S. 374, 121 S.Ct. 1578 (2001) (same holding for federal petitioners). Cf., *Maleng v. Cook*, 490 U.S. 488, 109 S.Ct. 1923 (1989) (holding that a petitioner *is* in custody if he is subject to a state detainer designed to ensure he will be available to serve an enhanced sentence based in part on the expired term).

[273] See also, *Custis v. United States*, 511 U.S. 485, 114 S.Ct. 1732 (1994).

[274] *Spencer v. Kemna*, 523 U.S. 1, 118 S.Ct. 978 (1998). See also, *Lane v. Williams*, 455 U.S. 624, 102 S.Ct. 1322 (1982).

[275] 515 U.S. 39, 115 S.Ct. 1948 (1995).

[276] *Peyton v. Rowe*, 391 U.S. 54, 88 S.Ct. 1549 (1968).

custody for habeas purposes if he remains subject to significant "civil disabilities" such as prohibitions on holding certain offices, voting in state elections, and serving as a juror.[277]

(d) Filing Deadlines

The only time limit the common law imposed on the filing of a habeas petition derived from the doctrine of laches, which required the state to show it was prejudiced by the delay. The AEDPA, however, requires that most petitions be filed within one year from the date on which the judgment being challenged becomes final on direct review, excluding any period during which a properly filed collateral attack was pending before state courts.[278] If the petitioner does not seek collateral review, the limitations period for habeas under AEDPA begins when the time for seeking such review in the state's highest court expires.[279]

For state prisoners, a petition is "properly filed" if the application is filed in the appropriate court under proper procedures,[280] even if some of the claims in the petition are procedurally barred under state law.[281] A petition is "pending" not only when a state court is actively considering the petition, but also during the time between a lower state court's decision and the filing of a notice to appeal to a higher state court, so long as that delay does not violate state procedural rules.[282] For federal prisoners, the claim must be filed within a year of the Supreme Court's decision to affirm conviction on direct review or to deny a petition for a writ of certiorari, or when the time for filing a certiorari petition expires.[283]

Statutory exceptions to these deadlines include situations where the state does not have a competent post-conviction bar, the state otherwise impedes timely filing, the claim was initially recognized by the Supreme Court after the deadline and is considered retroactive by the Court,[284] or the claim is based on newly discovered evidence that could not have been discovered with due diligence.[285] In *Johnson v. United States*,[286] the Court

---

[277] *Carafas v. LaVallee*, 391 U.S. 234, 88 S.Ct. 1556 (1968).

[278] A motion to reduce sentence is considered "collateral review." *Wall v. Kholi*, 562 U.S. 545, 131 S.Ct. 1278 (2011). Additionally, a state court grant of an out-of-time direct appeal during collateral review can toll the statue under some circumstances. *Jimenez v. Quarterman*, 555 U.S. 113, 129 S.Ct. 681 (2009).

[279] *Gonzalez v. Thaler*, 565 U.S. 134, 132 S.Ct. 641 (2012).

[280] 28 U.S.C.A. §§ 2244(d)(1)(A) & 2263. In capital cases in states which have a competent post-conviction bar, the filing deadline is *six months* from the "final state court affirmance of the conviction and sentence on direct review or the expiration of the time for seeking review," tolled by certiorari petitions filed with the Supreme Court and initial state collateral challenges. Id.

[281] *Artuz v. Bennett*, 531 U.S. 4, 121 S.Ct. 361 (2000). However, if the petition is barred by a state *statute of limitations* (i.e., filing deadline) as opposed to a procedural default rule, then it is not properly filed. *Pace v. DiGuglielmo*, 544 U.S. 408, 125 S.Ct. 1807 (2005).

[282] *Carey v. Saffold*, 536 U.S. 214, 122 S.Ct. 2134 (2002). For state prisoners, federal writs do not toll the deadline; only pending state claims do. *Duncan v. Walker*, 533 U.S. 167, 121 S.Ct. 2120 (2001). Nor does a cert petition to the Supreme Court toll the statute. *Lawrence v. Florida*, 549 U.S. 327, 127 S.Ct. 1079 (2007).

[283] *Clay v. United States*, 537 U.S. 522, 123 S.Ct. 1072 (2003).

[284] If this exception applies, the one-year period begins at the time the new right is recognized, not when it is made retroactive. *Dodd v. United States*, 545 U.S. 353, 125 S.Ct. 2478 (2005).

[285] See 28 U.S.C.A. § 2264. Another exception exists when the claim "relates back" to facts set forth in the original pleading. *Mayle v. Felix*, 545 U.S. 644, 125 S.Ct. 2562 (2005) (recognizing this rule, but finding it inapplicable to a post-deadline claim that a pretrial interrogation violated the Fifth Amendment, because the claim differed in "time and type" from the petitioner's pre-deadline claim challenging admission of videotaped testimony from a prosecution witness).

[286] 544 U.S. 295, 125 S.Ct. 1571 (2005).

held that a state court decision vacating a conviction that is a predicate for an enhanced sentence could be a "newly discovered" fact meeting the latter exception. However, the petitioner must show "due diligence" in seeking the vacatur of the conviction; in *Johnson*, the Court held that a delay of more than three years between the conviction leading to the enhanced sentence and the motion for vacatur was too long, rejecting Johnson's excuse that the delay was due to the lack of counsel and sophistication about the process.[287]

Other exceptions to the deadlines have been established by the courts. In *McQuiggin v. Perkins*,[288] the Supreme Court created an exception for petitioners who can present evidence of actual innocence. As indicated elsewhere,[289] this is a hard standard to meet, because the petitioner must show that "it is more likely than not that no reasonable juror would have convicted him in the light of the new evidence." Thus, *Perkins* reasoned, additional time may be necessary. The Court also indicated that the reason for the delay can be taken into account in evaluating the validity of the actual innocence claim.

Courts have also recognized equitable tolling of the one-year period. In *Holland v. Florida*,[290] the Supreme Court affirmed the holdings of eleven circuit courts of appeal to this effect. Justice Breyer concluded for the Court that permitting tolling under AEDPA was warranted because the one-year rule is not jurisdictional, habeas has traditionally been governed by equitable principles, and such an exception was not inconsistent with AEDPA's language. In *Holland*, the petitioner's petition was foreclosed by the filing period because his court-appointed attorney (1) failed to file it on time, despite several letters from Holland reminding him to do so, (2) failed to research the law relating to the time limit, despite the fact that Holland provided him with the relevant legal rules, and (3) failed to inform Holland of the state court decision that began the time period, despite Holland's repeated requests for that information. Holland also repeatedly asked the Florida courts for a new attorney, to no avail. The Eleventh Circuit was willing to assume the attorney's behavior constituted gross negligence, but since there was no proof of "bad faith, dishonesty, divided loyalty, mental impairment or so forth," refused to toll the limitation period. In reversing, the Supreme Court admitted that it had decided, in *Coleman v. Thompson*,[291] that habeas petitioners "must bear the risk of attorney error." But it concluded that this language had no bearing in *Holland* because *Coleman* had involved attorney failure to abide by a *state* rule, not AEDPA. It then called the Eleventh Circuit's approach "overly rigid" and remanded the case to the district court, instructing it to look at whether the case involved "extraordinary circumstances" sufficient to toll the period, and noting that Holland's efforts to rectify his attorney's omissions were entitled to considerable weight.

33.05   Independent Factfinding

In *Brown,* it will be remembered, the Court contemplated that the federal habeas court hearing a state case would arrive at an independent conclusion of law, but would

---

[287] Furthermore, the Court reiterated, once vacatur is obtained, the one-year filing deadline for federal habeas relief begins anew.

[288] 569 U.S. 383, 133 S.Ct. 1924 (2013).

[289] See § 33.03(e).

[290] 560 U.S. 631, 130 S.Ct. 2549 (2010).

[291] 501 U.S. 722, 111 S.Ct. 2546 (1991), discussed in this respect in § 33.03(d)(3).

normally rely on the state court's findings of fact unless its proceedings suffered a "vital flaw." As Justice Frankfurter explained in one of the two majority opinions in *Brown,* this distinction between the credence given a state court's findings of fact, as opposed to its findings of law, rested on the premise that the former "may have been made after hearing witnesses no longer available or whose recollection later may have been affected by the passage of time." Yet *Brown* clearly contemplated that the federal habeas court had the authority to convene an evidentiary hearing when there were "unusual circumstances." Both caselaw and statutory amendments have subsequently provided more direction as to when federal courts may second-guess state court determinations of facts and hold hearings to redetermine the facts.

(a) The Presumption of Correctness

In 1966 Congress, perhaps concerned about the scope of federal review, added subsection (d) to § 2254. That section provided that factual findings by a state court "shall be presumed to be correct" by the federal habeas court unless the state proceeding was deficient in one of eight ways, such as failing to provide a full and fair hearing, failing to resolve the factual dispute, or resolving it in a way that was not fairly supported by the record. Six of these factors were taken from the Supreme Court's opinion in *Townsend v. Sain,*[292] which, as described in more detail below,[293] laid down rules for determining the closely related question of when a federal habeas court may conduct an evidentiary hearing. Adding to *Townsend's* list, § 2254(d) labelled as "deficient" and therefore not entitled to the presumption findings by a court that lacked jurisdiction over the subject matter or that failed to appoint counsel for an indigent.

In 1996, the AEDPA eliminated the eight factors listed in § 2254(d). In their place, the Act merely states that "a determination of a factual issue by a State court shall be presumed to be correct" and that the petitioner bears the burden of proving otherwise. Despite the deletion of these factors, they may still be useful in guiding the determination as to whether the state process is so deficient that the presumption is overcome. However, the Act also states that the petitioner must be denied relief unless the state court's decision was based on an "unreasonable determination of the facts" in light of the evidence in state court,[294] which suggests the showing of inadequacy must be significant.

Even before the AEDPA's changes, the presumption was difficult to rebut. In *LaVallee v. Delle Rose,*[295] the lower federal courts held that the state court failed "to resolve" a factual dispute over the voluntariness of a confession, because it did not indicate the extent to which it relied on the petitioner's own description of how the confession was obtained; accordingly, the state court's findings with respect to the facts surrounding the confession could not be "presumed correct." The Supreme Court reversed in a 5–4 judgment. Finding that the petitioner's testimony could be reconstructed from the state record, it concluded that the district court should have

---

[292] 372 U.S. 293, 83 S.Ct. 745 (1963).

[293] See § 33.05(c).

[294] 28 U.S.C.A. § 2254(d)(2). Most courts have combined these provisions to require that the petitioner show clear and convincing evidence that the state court factual determination was unreasonable, apparently on the assumption that even a defective state process may not result in an unreasonable determination. See, e.g., *Lenz v. Washington,* 444 F.3d 295, 300 (4th Cir. 2006). To date the Supreme Court has not addressed this issue. See *Wood v. Allen,* 558 U.S. 290, 130 S.Ct. 841 (2010).

[295] 410 U.S. 690, 93 S.Ct. 1203 (1973).

presumed that the trial judge took into account and legitimately rejected that testimony. Further, given this presumption, the defendant could overturn the state court's finding of involuntariness only by "convincing evidence" independent of the petitioner's account, effectively precluding the confessions claim.

Other Court decisions reached similar results. In *Maggio v. Fulford*,[296] the Court refused to sustain a federal habeas court's overruling of a state court's finding that the petitioner was competent to stand trial, because the federal court, in reaching its conclusion, had relied heavily on expert testimony that had been explicitly discounted by the state court. And in *Marshall v. Lonberger*[297] the Court again chastised a federal court's reassessment of witness credibility, this time in refusing to sustain a reversal of a guilty plea conviction that rested on the petitioner's state court testimony that he had not understood the consequences of his plea. The majority reasoned that since the state court was familiar with the circumstances surrounding the defendant's guilty plea, including the fact that he was represented, was intelligent, and had been informed of his charges, his testimony that he had thought he was pleading guilty only to battery (and not to attempted murder as well) must have been rejected by the state court; therefore, it should not have been considered by the federal court.

In both of these cases, the Court's application of the presumption of correctness rule had the effect of resolving the case against the petitioner. In contrast, in *Miller-El v. Dretke*,[298] a post-AEDPA decision, the Court found the evidence "too powerful to conclude anything but discrimination" in violation of *Batson v. Kentucky* occurred, and thus held that the state court's conclusion rejecting the *Batson* claim was "wrong to a clear and convincing degree [and] unreasonable as well as erroneous."

(b) Mixed Questions of Fact and Law

While today the issue has been mooted by the AEDPA, probably the most important inquiry with respect to the presumption of correctness prior to 1996 was the difference between a "fact" and a legal conclusion. In *Sumner v. Mata*,[299] the Court held that the constitutionality of a lineup procedure is solely a factual determination, suggesting that judgment calls (in this case, how suggestive an identification procedure is) would often be entitled to a presumption of correctness. However, this position was undermined in *Miller v. Fenton*.[300] There, in an opinion written by Justice O'Connor, the Court held that the voluntariness of a confession is not subject to the presumption of correctness.

Miller appeared to rest on three separate grounds. The first was the long tradition of treating the voluntariness issue as a legal, as opposed to factual, question in appeals and habeas cases. The second was the recognition that voluntariness involves a "hybrid" assessment, but one which is ultimately probably more properly characterized as "legal": it contemplates deciding whether the techniques involved in obtaining a confession (a factual issue) "are compatible with a system that presumes innocence and assures that a conviction will not be secured by inquisitorial means" (a legal issue). Finally, on a more practical level was the question of whether "one judicial actor is better positioned than another to decide the issue." Questions of credibility of witnesses or jurors and

---

[296] 462 U.S. 111, 103 S.Ct. 2261 (1983).

[297] 459 U.S. 422, 103 S.Ct. 843 (1983).

[298] 545 U.S. 231, 125 S.Ct. 2317 (2005), discussed in § 7.04(d)(1).

[299] *Sumner v. Mata*, 455 U.S. 591, 102 S.Ct. 1303 (1982).

[300] 474 U.S. 104, 106 S.Ct. 445 (1985).

evaluations of state of mind are better left to the trial court, while appellate review is appropriate when the trier of fact may have been biased or "the relevant legal principle can be given meaning only through its application to the particular circumstances of a case." In assessing voluntariness, the "subsidiary" findings on things like the length and circumstances of the interrogation, the defendant's prior experience with the legal process and his familiarity with the *Miranda* warnings are entitled to a presumption of correctness on habeas review. But in making the determination of whether, in the totality of the circumstances, the confession was obtained in a constitutional manner, "the state-court judge is not in an appreciably better position than the federal habeas court." Moreover, while credibility assessments are made in open court, confessions are obtained "in a secret and invariably more coercive environment" which, "together with the inevitable and understandable reluctance to exclude an otherwise reliable admission of guilt . . . elevate[s] the risk that erroneous resolution of the voluntariness question might inadvertently frustrate the protection of the federal right."

Miller and subsequent decisions[301] indicated that issues involving a mixture of law and fact could be considered on federal habeas. However, in 1996, the AEDPA required federal habeas court deference to all determinations of law made by state courts, unless they are "contrary to, or involve[ ] an unreasonable application of, clearly established federal law."[302] The legislative history of this provision indicates that it is meant to adopt the minority position in *Wright v. West*,[303] a 1992 case in which three justices had argued that *Miller* was wrong. Thus, the presumption of correctness now appears to apply to "mixed" claims as well as to purely factual claims.[304]

(c) Evidentiary Hearings

An issue closely related to when state findings must be presumed correct is when, if ever, the federal court may conduct its own hearing to determine facts. As noted above, in *Townsend v. Sain* the Court undertook to define more carefully the circumstances under which such a hearing should take place. According to Chief Justice Warren's opinion in that case, a hearing is required whenever:

> (1) the merits of the factual dispute were not resolved in the state hearing; (2) the state factual determination is not fairly supported by the record as a whole; (3) the fact-finding procedure employed by the state court was not adequate to afford a full and fair hearing; (4) there is a substantial allegation of newly discovered evidence; (5) material facts were not adequately developed at the state court hearing; or (6) for any reason it appears that the state trier of fact did not afford the habeas applicant a full and fair hearing.

As the Supreme Court later stated, *Townsend* "substantially increased the availability of evidentiary hearings in habeas corpus proceedings and made mandatory much of what had previously been within the broad discretion of the District Court."[305]

---

[301] See *Thompson v. Keohane*, 516 U.S. 99, 116 S.Ct. 457 (1995) (*Miranda* "custody" is a mixed question).

[302] § 2254(e)(1).

[303] 505 U.S. 277, 112 S.Ct. 2482 (1992).

[304] Although congressional enactments may be declared unconstitutional under the Suspension Clause if they unduly restrict the scope of the writ, *Felker v. Turpin*, 518 U.S. 651, 116 S.Ct. 2333 (1996), this particular change will probably withstand such a challenge, given the strong support for it in *Wright* and the resolution of *Felker* itself, upholding a similar restriction in the Act on successive petitions. See § 33.04(b).

[305] *Smith v. Yeager*, 393 U.S. 122, 89 S.Ct. 277 (1968).

However, in *Keeney v. Tamayo-Reyes*,[306] the Court significantly reduced the availability of such hearings. *Townsend* had held that the one circumstance in which a defendant who met one of its six criteria would *not* obtain a federal hearing was when he "deliberately bypassed" an opportunity to develop the facts at the state level. The deliberate bypass language was taken from *Fay v. Noia*,[307] decided the same term. As described earlier in this chapter,[308] *Fay's* deliberate bypass rule was subsequently replaced with the "cause and prejudice" rule, which requires a defendant who fails to raise a claim at the state level to show, in effect, that the reason for the failure was either ineffective assistance of counsel or state interference with the defendant's ability to raise the claim ("i.e., cause"), and that the claim would have affected the outcome of the case (i.e., "prejudice"). In *Tamayo-Reyes,* the Court, by a 5–4 margin, applied the cause and prejudice rule to failures to raise factual issues as well. As Justice White stated for the majority, "it is . . . irrational to distinguish between failing to properly assert a federal claim in state court and failing in state court to properly develop such a claim, and to apply to the latter a remnant of a decision that is no longer upheld with regard to the former."

The AEDPA, as construed by the Supreme Court, in large part incorporates the holding of *Tamayo-Reyes.* Under § 2254(e)(2) of the Act, when there has been a "failure to develop a factual basis" at the state proceeding, an evidentiary hearing at the federal level may be obtained only when the petitioner can show: (1) that "the claim is based on a new rule of constitutional law, made retroactive to cases on collateral review by the Supreme Court, that was previously unavailable," or (2) that the claim is based on "a factual predicate that could not have been previously discovered through the exercise of due diligence," *and* (3) that there is "clear and convincing evidence that but for constitutional error, no reasonable factfinder would have found the applicant guilty of the underlying offense."[309] Although this provision's requirement that the actual innocence standard always be met appears to restrict the availability of evidentiary hearings even more than *Tamayo-Reyes*, in *Williams v. Taylor*[310] the Court held that it is triggered only when the failure to develop a factual basis is the defendant's fault. If, on the other hand, the failure is due to obstruction by the state or is no one's fault, then a petitioner who can meet the *Tamayo-Reyes* cause and prejudice standard will receive an evidentiary hearing. Since a petitioner who can show he was not at fault for purposes of § 2254(e)(2) will also generally be able to prove cause, the petitioner who can avoid that section in effect need only prove prejudice.

If, however, the failure to develop a factual basis *is* the defendant's fault, then the AEDPA requires (using the numbering in the previous paragraph) that either provisions (1) or (2), as well as provision (3), be met. As discussed earlier,[311] very few rules will be granted retroactive status, thus rendering (1) of limited value to petitioners seeking relief. Similarly, meeting (2) will be difficult, because most facts *"could have been previously discovered with due diligence;"* only the discovery of truly new evidence will satisfy this clause. Finally, the additional requirement that the petitioner produce *clear*

---

[306] 504 U.S. 1, 112 S.Ct. 1715 (1992).

[307] 372 U.S. 391, 83 S.Ct. 822 (1963).

[308] See § 33.03(b) & (c).

[309] 8 U.S.C.A. § 2254(e)(2)(A) & (B).

[310] 529 U.S. 420, 120 S.Ct. 1479 (2000).

[311] See § 33.02(c).

and convincing evidence of innocence due to a *constitutional* error[312] reduces the possibility of an evidentiary hearing to virtually zero in cases where the failure to develop a factual basis is the defendant's fault.

Another significant limitation on evidentiary hearings in federal habeas court was announced in *Cullen v. Pinholster*,[313] which held that determinations of whether a state court holding is an unreasonable interpretation of federal law under § 2254(d)(1) must, in fairness to the state court, be based on the record before the state court. That holding means that evidentiary hearings are not permitted if the petitioner's claim rests solely, as it often will, on the assertion that the state court's ruling was unreasonable. Now evidentiary hearings may occur only if the requirements of § 2254(e)(2) are met and the contested claim was not adjudicated on the merits in state court, was based on a state ground later found inadequate, or fits a few other very narrow circumstances.[314]

33.06   The Right to Assistance on Collateral Review

As discussed in Chapter 31, the Supreme Court has concluded that criminal prosecution ends at sentencing,[315] the Sixth Amendment's guarantee of the "assistance of counsel in all criminal prosecutions" does not apply to habeas proceedings. Nor does due process or equal protection analysis support a right to counsel on habeas, because the petitioner has access to the briefs and other documents from the direct appeal. Thus, in *Pennsylvania v. Finley*,[316] the Court denied a right to counsel at state post-conviction proceedings, and in *Murray v. Giarratano*[317] it refused to make an exception to *Finley* for capital cases.

Because *Finley* is based on the assumption that the petitioner has had at least one counseled post-conviction review on the relevant claim, one could argue that, with respect to claims that could not have been brought on direct appeal, a right to counsel should exist at collateral proceedings. As noted earlier in this chapter,[318] the Court ultimately accepted this rationale in *Trevino v. Thaler*,[319] which in effect recognizes a right to counsel at the initial state post-conviction proceeding for claims that trial counsel was ineffective and other claims (like the failure to provide exculpatory evidence) that could not be raised on appeal, because if no counsel is provided, petitioners automatically have cause for federal habeas purposes. However, for other types of claims, there remains no right to counsel at state post-conviction proceedings. While the Court would likely hold that federal prisoners are likewise not constitutionally entitled to counsel, the point is moot because federal law provides free counsel to indigent petitioners.[320]

---

[312] See § 33.02(d), discussing why discovery of new evidence, standing alone, may not be justiciable on habeas.

[313] 563 U.S. 170, 131 S.Ct. 1388 (2011).

[314] See Justice Breyer's concurring opinion in *Pinholster*.

[315] See § 31.03(a)(3).

[316] 481 U.S. 551, 107 S.Ct. 1990 (1987).

[317] 492 U.S. 1, 109 S.Ct. 2765 (1989). However, six justices indicated that habeas counsel might be required in capital cases where there was no adequate substitute. See § 31.03(c)(4).

[318] See § 33.03(d)(3).

[319] 569 U.S. 413, 133 S.Ct. 1911 (2013).

[320] 18 U.S.C.A. § 3599.

Counterbalancing its refusal to recognize a right to state habeas counsel, the Court has held, in *Bounds v. Smith*,[321] that state and federal prisoners have a "constitutional right of access to the courts," although it has also stated that this right of access does not require states to create special programs for prisoners except upon proof of systemwide inability to gain access.[322] In an earlier case, *Johnson v. Avery*,[323] the Court ruled that a state may not prohibit inmates from assisting each other in preparing habeas corpus petitions, at least without providing some reasonable alternative to assist illiterate or poorly educated individuals. Finally, building on its holding in *Griffin v. Illinois*,[324] the Court has held that the indigent habeas petitioner is entitled, under the Equal Protection Clause, to a free transcript of his trial proceeding, at least when a lower court certifies that his claim is not "wholly frivolous."[325]

Federal law also provides that petitioners are entitled to funding for experts and investigative services that are "reasonably necessary."[326] However, this funding appears to be limited to petitioners in capital cases. It may also be unavailable to petitioners whose claims have been procedurally defaulted.[327]

An issue closely related to whether counsel must be provided at habeas proceedings is whether the habeas court must grant a stay if the petitioner is not competent at the time of the proceeding, and thus cannot assist counsel. In the joined cases of *Ryan v. Gonzalez* and *Tibbals v. Carter*,[328] a unanimous Court held that a stay might be appropriate if the habeas claim "could substantially benefit from the petitioner's assistance" and the petitioner is likely to regain competence "in the foreseeable future." However, it continued, "[w]here there is no reasonable hope of competence, a stay is inappropriate and merely frustrates the State's attempts to defend its presumptively valid judgment." The Court noted that many habeas claims are record-based, and thus do not require the participation of the petitioner. But even if a claim does require such participation, a petitioner who is unlikely to be restored to competency must either pursue it through counsel or forfeit it. The Court refused to find that a right to competency in such situations stems either from the right to counsel (when, as in federal cases, it is recognized statutorily) or from the requirement that defendants be competent when tried,[329] a right the Court concluded does not apply to habeas proceedings.

33.07   Conclusion

The availability of the writ of habeas corpus as a device for seeking federal court post-conviction review of constitutional claims was at one time quite limited, then expanded during the Warren Court years to permit virtually any constitutional claim that was not intentionally defaulted, and since has been severely constricted by both the Supreme Court and Congress. The following paragraphs first describe the judicial approach to the writ up to 1996, and then summarize the ways in which the 1996

---

[321] 430 U.S. 817, 97 S.Ct. 1491 (1977).

[322] *Lewis v. Casey*, 518 U.S. 343, 116 S.Ct. 2174 (1996).

[323] 393 U.S. 483, 89 S.Ct. 747 (1969).

[324] 351 U.S. 12, 76 S.Ct. 585 (1956), discussed in § 29.02(a).

[325] *United States v. MacCollom*, 426 U.S. 317, 96 S.Ct. 2086 (1976); see also, *Smith v. Bennett*, 365 U.S. 708, 81 S.Ct. 895 (1961).

[326] 18 U.S.C.A. § 3599(a).

[327] *Ayestas v. Davis*, ___ U.S. ___, 138 S.Ct. 1080 (2018).

[328] 568 U.S. 57, 133 S.Ct. 696 (2013).

[329] See § 28.03(b).

Antiterrorism and Effective Death Penalty Act (AEDPA) purportedly changed the scope of the writ.

(1)   According to Supreme Court caselaw, the following claims are not cognizable on habeas: (a) Fourth Amendment claims for which there has been a full and fair hearing in state court; (b) any other federal constitutional claims that advance a "new rule" (i.e., a rule that is not "dictated by precedent"), unless they are subject to retroactive application because they go the jurisdiction of the trial court or are "watershed rules" central to the accurate determination of innocence or guilt; (c) claims that consist solely of allegations that the petitioner is factually innocent; and (d) federal statutory claims that do not constitute a fundamental defect in the proceedings below. The AEDPA changed (b) by providing that even a claim that is dictated by precedent is not justiciable on habeas unless it is dictated by a "clearly established" *Supreme Court* rule and is an "objectively unreasonable" (as opposed to incorrect) application of the precedent; the same rule apparently applies to a state court's harmless error analysis. AEDPA may also have changed the Court's rules in two other respects. First, it may require federal courts to hear Fourth Amendment claims even after a full and fair hearing at the state level, if the claim involves an unreasonable state court application of clearly established Supreme Court precedent. It also may eliminate review of new rule claims that challenge the jurisdiction of the trial court.

(2)   A claim, even though cognizable, will not be heard on federal habeas if a procedural default rule that is "adequate" (i.e., consistently and not exorbitantly applied) barred it from being heard at the trial, appellate or post-conviction levels. However, this procedural bar does not apply if the petitioner is able to show "cause" as to why the claim was not raised and "prejudice" to his case if the claim is not vindicated. Cause exists only if: (a) the legal or factual basis of the claim was novel at the time of the default; (b) the government interfered with counsel's ability to raise the claim; or (c) the default resulted from ineffective assistance of counsel (in the latter instance the ineffective assistance claim must also have been raised either at the state appellate proceeding or the initial state post-conviction proceeding). Prejudice probably exists only if there is a reasonable probability that vindicating the claim would affect the outcome of the state proceeding. The cause and prejudice standard does not apply, however, when: (a) the default rule is inconsistently applied (in state cases); (b) the rule is not the true basis for the dismissal (in state cases); or (c) the claim alleges a violation which has probably resulted in the conviction of one who is actually innocent or in the imposition of a death sentence for which there is clear and convincing evidence that no aggravating circumstance or other condition of eligibility exists (in state and federal cases). The AEDPA does not appear to change this law except in capital cases; in such cases, ineffective assistance of counsel is generally no longer a basis for cause, and a claim of actual innocence, by itself, is not grounds for review. Rather, the capital petitioner must show the error was the result of government interference, violated a rule that would be applied retroactively under 1(b), or is based on facts that could not have been discovered prior to state or federal post-conviction review through the exercise of due diligence.

(3)   According to Supreme Court caselaw prior to 1996, even a non-defaulted cognizable claim will not heard if: (a) the petitioner has not fairly presented the claim to all available state appellate courts (i.e., met the exhaustion requirement); (b) the claim was included in a previous habeas petition and is not related to factual innocence; (c) the claim was *not* included in a previous habeas petition and cause and prejudice, as defined in (2), cannot be shown; or (d) the petitioner is not in custody, with custody meaning that

there is some restraint on his freedom, either presently or impending, beyond a release on his own recognizance. The AEDPA does not purport to change substantially the law regarding exhaustion of state remedies. However, it eliminates the factual innocence exception to the general rule that a claim may be raised only once, and permits a new claim in a second petition only if the Supreme Court has explicitly held the claim to be retroactive for reasons stated in 1(b) above, or is based on newly discovered evidence that supports a claim of factual innocence. Finally, AEDPA generally requires that habeas petitions be filed within one year from the time the judgment being challenged becomes final on direct review, excluding any period during which a properly filed collateral attack was pending before state courts. The one-year limitation can be tolled by a federal court under appropriate circumstances and in cases involving viable actual innocence claims.

(4)   Prior to 1996, Supreme Court caselaw required that state findings of fact, but not findings of mixed fact and law, be presumed correct unless the petitioner can show that the state process was deficient, and permitted an evidentiary hearing in federal court only when the petitioner could show cause why the facts were not developed at the state level and that the failure to do so was prejudicial, analogous to the law summarized in (2). Under the AEDPA, findings of mixed fact and law, as well as pure findings of fact, are presumed correct. When a failure to develop facts at the state level is the defendant's fault, an evidentiary hearing may be held only if the claim would be applied retroactively under 1(b) or its factual predicate could not have been previously discovered through the exercise of due diligence, and there is clear and convincing evidence that the petitioner is innocent. Otherwise, an evidentiary hearing is held when the defendant can show cause and prejudice as defined in (2).

(5)   There is no right to counsel at state or federal habeas proceedings, although there is, in effect, a right to counsel at the initial state collateral proceeding for claims like ineffective trial counsel that as a practical matter can only be raised at that proceeding. State and federal prisons are under an obligation to provide legal assistance to prisoners to ensure adequate access to habeas review, and the courts must provide free transcripts to indigent petitioners, at least for non-frivolous petitions.

BIBLIOGRAPHY

Bator, Paul M. Finality in Criminal Law and Federal Habeas Corpus for State Prisoners. 76 Harv. L .Rev. 441 (1963).

Bellamy, Lisa. Playing for Time: The Need for Equitable Tolling of the Habeas Corpus Statute of Limitations. 32 Am. J. Crim. L. 1 (2004).

Blume, John H. AEDPA: The "Hype" and the "Bite." 91 Cornell L. Rev. 259 (2006).

Burns, Amy Knight. Insurmountable Obstacles, Structural Errors, Procedural Default, and Ineffective Assistance. 64 Stanford L. Rev. 727 (2012).

Fallon, Richard H., Jr. Habeas Corpus Jurisdiction, Substantive Rights, and the War on Terror. 120 Harv.L.Rev. 2029 (2007).

Friendly, Henry. Is Innocence Irrelevant? Collateral Attack on Criminal Judgments. 38 U.Chi.L.Rev. 142 (1970).

Halliday, Paul D. and G. Edward White. The Suspension Clause: English Text, Imperial Contexts, and American Implications. 94 Va. L. Rev. 575 (2008).

Harnett, Edward A. The Constitutional Puzzle of Habeas Corpus. 46 B.C. L.Rev. 251 (2005).

Hoffstadt, Brian M. How Congress Might Redesign a Leaner, Cleaner Writ of Habeas Corpus. 49 Duke L.J. 947 (2000).

Jeffries, John and William Stuntz. Ineffective Assistance and Procedural Default in Federal Habeas Corpus. 57 U.Chi.L.Rev. 681 (1990).

King, Nancy. Enforcing Effective Assistance after *Martinez*. 122 Yale L.J. 2428 (2013).

King, Nancy and Joseph Hoffmann. Habeas for the Twenty-First Century: Uses, Abuses, and the Future of the Great Writ (2011).

Kovarsky, Lee. Prisoners and Habeas Privileges Under the Fourteenth Amendment. 67 Vand. L. Rev. 609 (2014).

Lasch, Christopher. The Future of *Teague* Retroactivity or "Redressibility," after *Danforth v. Minnesota*: Why Lower Courts Should Give Retroactive Effect to New Constitutional Rules of Criminal Procedure in Postconviction Proceedings. 46 Am. Crim. L. Rev. 1 (2009).

Marceau, Justin F. Is Guilt Dispositive? Federal Habeas After *Martinez*. 55 Wm. & Mary L. Rev. 2071 (2014).

____. Challenging the Habeas Process Rather Than the Result. 69 Wash. & Lee L. Rev. 85 (2012).

Neuman, Gerald L. The Habeas Corpus Suspension Clause After *Boumediene v. Bush*. 110 Colum. L. Rev. 537 (2010).

Primus, Eve Brensike. A Crisis in Federal Habeas Law. 110 Mich. L. Rev. 887 (2012).

Rosenberg, Yale L. Jettisoning *Fay v. Noia*: Procedural Defaults by Reasonably Incompetent Counsel. 62 Minn.L.Rev. 341 (1978).

Semeraro, Steven. Enforcing Fourth Amendment Rights Through Federal Habeas Corpus. 58 Rutgers L.Rev. 983 (2006).

Solimine, Michael E. and James L. Walker. Constitutional Litigation In Federal and State Courts: An Empirical Analysis of Judicial Parity. 10 Hast.L.J. 213 (1984).

Steinman, Adam N. Reconceptualizing Federal Habeas Corpus for State Prisoners: How Should AEDPA's Standard of Review Operate after *Williams v. Taylor*? 2001 Wisc.L.Rev. 1493.

Stevenson, Bryan A. The Politics of Fear and Death: Successive Problems in Capital Federal Habeas Corpus Cases. 77 N.Y.U. L. Rev. 699 (2002).

Tague, Peter W. Federal Habeas Corpus and Ineffective Representation of Counsel: The Supreme Court Has Work to Do. 31 Stan. L. Rev. 2 (1979).

Turner, Kendall. A New Approach to the *Teague* Doctrine. 66 Stan. L. Rev. 1159 (2014).

Uhrig, Emily Garcia. A Case for a Constitutional Right to Counsel in Habeas Corpus. 60 Hastings L.J. 541 (2009).

Vladeck, Stephen. Using the Supreme Court's Original Habeas Corpus Jurisdiction to "Ma[k]e" New Rules Retroactive. 28 Fed. Sent. Rptr. 225 (2016).

Wiseman, Samuel R. Habeas After *Pinholster*. 53 B.C. L. Rev. 953 (2012).

Yackle, Larry. State Convicts and Federal Courts: Reopening the Habeas Corpus Debate. 91 Cornell L. Rev. 541 (2006).

Chapter 34

STATE CONSTITUTIONS AS AN INDEPENDENT SOURCE OF RIGHTS

34.01 Introduction

This book has concentrated on developments in federal constitutional law, primarily at the Supreme Court level, and on federal and state statutes that regulate criminal procedure. Until now, little attention has been given to state court efforts to put their own stamp on the criminal process. As the preceding chapters amply demonstrate, since the early 1970's the Supreme Court has narrowed the thrust of Bill of Rights protections established by the Warren Court. Some state courts have accepted this retrenchment with little or no visible reaction, adhering to the Supreme Court's rulings. But many state courts have rejected post-Warren Court holdings, relying on state constitutions as an independent source of rights. These latter decisions represent a new field of criminal procedure deserving of examination.

The rationale for these state-law decisions is inherent in the language of the Tenth Amendment, which states that "[t]he powers not delegated to the United States by the Constitution, nor prohibited by it to the States, are reserved to the States respectively, or to the people." Although not relying on this provision, the Supreme Court itself has, on several occasions, explicitly endorsed the idea that state law restrictions on state action may exceed those under federal law. For instance, in *Cooper v. California,*[1] the Court reminded: "Our holding, of course, does not affect the State's power to impose higher standards on searches and seizures than required by the Federal Constitution if it chooses to do so."[2]

The first section of this chapter examines state constitutional lawmaking from an historical perspective. The second section then analyzes the various approaches depicted in the historical account. The third section describes the Supreme Court's reaction to state court rejection of its holdings.

34.02 The Four Phases of State-Federal Judicial Interplay

State court views on the relative importance of state and federal law can be divided into four historical phases, the last three of which overlap considerably.[3] The first phase, from the founding of the republic until approximately the middle of the twentieth century, has been called the "dual federalism" period, since the Bill of Rights had no binding effect on state courts. The second phase, which peaked during the early 1970's, might be called the "co-option" period, because the advent of the incorporation doctrine, combined with the activism of the United States Supreme Court, created the impression that federal law stated the exclusive standard on constitutional issues. The third phase,

---

[1] 386 U.S. 58, 87 S.Ct. 788 (1967). See also, *City of Mesquite v. Aladdin's Castle, Inc.,* 455 U.S. 283, 102 S.Ct. 1070 (1982).

[2] By the same token, state courts can develop rules based on state law that are not as protective as federal law, although these rules will not go into effect unless the federal courts modify their interpretation of the relevant constitutional provision so as to allow the state rule.

[3] The first three phases described below duplicate phases described by Ronald Collins, *Reliance on State Constitutions: Some Random Thoughts,* 54 Miss.L.J. 371, 378–79 (1984).

from the early 1970's to the present, has been called the "New Federalism" period because, as noted in the introduction, state courts have been much more willing to diverge from the federal standard. The final phase, still nascent, could be called the "forced-linkage" era. This term is meant to describe the impact of electoral decisions requiring state courts to equate state constitutional law with federal constitutional law.

(a) Dual Federalism

During the first 150 years under the federal Constitution, the criminal process guarantees found in the Fourth, Fifth, Sixth, and Eighth amendments applied only to federal cases. Since its ratification in 1868, the Fourteenth Amendment has provided a vehicle for guaranteeing these rights to state criminal defendants through the "incorporation" principle. But as described elsewhere in this book, it was not until well into the twentieth century that the Supreme Court indicated any willingness to find the various criminal process rights so fundamental that the states could not abridge them.[4] Only after the Warren Court invigorated the incorporation idea, beginning with *Mapp v. Ohio*,[5] in 1961, could the state criminal defendant depend upon Fourth Amendment protections, the privilege against self-incrimination, the Double Jeopardy Clause, Sixth Amendment trial rights, and protection against cruel and unusual punishment.

Before the 1960's, then, state courts were almost entirely free to develop their own rules of criminal procedure, despite the fact that state constitutional provisions were usually similar or identical to the analogous federal provisions. State courts interpreted their provisions in one of three ways. They either explicitly followed federal court interpretations of federal provisions;[6] viewed federal case law as a helpful guidepost, but not dispositive;[7] or ignored it altogether.[8] Often, the latter two approaches resulted in state standards that were more prosecution-oriented than those applied at the federal level. For example, numerous state courts refused to follow *Weeks v. United States*,[9] which required that illegally seized evidence be excluded from federal prosecutions.[10] But occasionally state courts were more energetic than the federal courts in protecting the rights of criminal defendants. For instance, at least one state court found a right to counsel at criminal trials well before *Johnson v. Zerbst*[11] guaranteed that right at the federal level.[12] In any event, during this phase, the independence of state and federal law was an accepted fact.

---

[4] See § 1.01. The first Supreme Court case that relied on the federal Constitution to overturn a state criminal conviction was *Powell v. Alabama*, 287 U.S. 45, 53 S.Ct. 55 (1932), discussed in § 31.02(a).

[5] 367 U.S. 643, 81 S.Ct. 1684 (1961).

[6] See, e.g., *Griggs v. Hanson*, 86 Kan. 632, 121 P. 1094 (1912).

[7] See, e.g., *State v. Miles*, 29 Wash.2d 921, 190 P.2d 740 (1948) (relying in part on *United States v. Di Re*, 332 U.S. 581, 68 S.Ct. 222 (1948)); *People v. Exum*, 382 Ill. 204, 47 N.E.2d 56, 59 (1943) (relying in part on *Haywood v. United States*, 268 Fed. 795 (7th Cir. 1920)).

[8] See Shirley S. Abrahamson, *Criminal Law and State Constitutions: The Emergence of State Constitutional Law*, 63 Tex.L.Rev. 1141, 1144–46 (1985).

[9] 232 U.S. 383, 34 S.Ct. 341 (1914).

[10] See, e.g., *Elkins v. United States*, 364 U.S. 206, 80 S.Ct. 1437 (1960) (appendix listing state decisions following and rejecting *Weeks*).

[11] 304 U.S. 458, 58 S.Ct. 1019 (1938).

[12] See *Carpenter v. County of Dane*, 9 Wis. 274 (1859).

(b) Co-Option

In the 1960's, the Supreme Court's activism significantly altered the pattern of state constitutional interpretation. The Warren Court not only applied most federal criminal rights guarantees to the states, but also interpreted those guarantees in a way that radically restructured the criminal process. Within a decade of its decision in *Mapp* requiring the states to exclude evidence obtained in violation of the Fourth Amendment, the Court had expanded tremendously the types of searches requiring exclusion.[13] Within seven years of its finding in *Gideon v. Wainwright*[14] that the Sixth Amendment's counsel guarantee applied to the states, the Court extended the right beyond trial proceedings to police questioning, lineups, preliminary hearings, and sentencing.[15] And two years after the Court found the privilege against self-incrimination to be a fundamental right,[16] it decided *Miranda v. Arizona,*[17] causing an upheaval in the law of confessions.

This revolution in criminal procedure made state constitutional interpretation seem irrelevant. State litigants and courts were inclined to view the federal standards as the sole source of criminal procedure law.[18] State courts either interpreted similar federal and state standards similarly, or more commonly, simply neglected to consider the independent significance of state constitutional law. For instance, in Florida between 1961 and 1983, over two-thirds of the state courts' search and seizure decisions made no mention of the state constitutional provision,[19] even though, due to an amendment in 1968, during the last fifteen years of this period the language of the provision differed significantly from the Fourth Amendment.[20] On those rare occasions when Florida courts did refer to the state provision, they almost always interpreted it to coincide with federal standards. Indeed, in 1980, the Florida Supreme Court adopted as its own a lower court opinion concluding that "the search and seizure provision of the Florida Constitution imposes no higher standard than that of the Fourth Amendment to the United States Constitution."[21]

(c) New Federalism

Developments at the Supreme Court level also prompted the third phase in state constitutional interpretation. The post-Warren Court's retrenchment on the Warren Court's groundbreaking decisions has made clear that federal standards do not necessarily represent the most "progressive" approach to criminal procedure. As the Court has constricted the scope of the Bill of Rights, state courts have disinterred state law and increasingly adopted standards more rigorous than those announced by the

---

[13]   See, e.g., §§ 6.04(a); 14.02(d).

[14]   372 U.S. 335, 83 S.Ct. 792 (1963).

[15]   See § 31.03(a)(1).

[16]   *Malloy v. Hogan,* 378 U.S. 1, 84 S.Ct. 1489 (1964).

[17]   384 U.S. 436, 86 S.Ct. 1602 (1966).

[18]   See A.E. Dick Howard, *State Courts and Constitutional Rights in the Day of the Burger Court*, 62 Va.L.Rev. 873–86 (1976).

[19]   See Christopher Slobogin, *State Adoption of Federal Law: Exploring the Limits of Florida's 'Forced Linkage' Amendment*, 39 Fla.L.Rev. 653, 668 (1987).

[20]   The 1968 version of Florida's search and seizure provision specifically protected "communications" as well as persons, papers, houses and effects, and explicitly stated that illegally seized evidence should be excluded.

[21]   *State v. Hetland,* 366 So.2d 831 (Fla.App. 1979), aff'd 387 So.2d 963 (Fla. 1980).

Supreme Court. For instance, between 1970 and 1986 over 300 state decisions went beyond Supreme Court pronouncements, and more than half of those decisions involved criminal procedure.[22]

State court reaction against the Supreme Court has been particularly energetic with respect to search and seizure, perhaps because the post-1970 Supreme Court has been especially antagonistic to the Fourth Amendment. Indeed, the first Supreme Court criminal procedure decision to encounter significant state court resistance involved a search and seizure issue. In *United States v. Robinson*,[23] the Supreme Court held that a full search is permissible after a lawful custodial arrest, regardless of the crime giving rise to the arrest. Within four years of *Robinson*, four different state courts had held, based on state constitutional language, that the nature of the offense is relevant to whether a full search is justified.[24] Similarly, the courts of at least four states refused to follow *United States v. White*[25] on state law grounds, finding untenable the Court's opinion that monitoring a private conversation with a body bug is not a search.[26] At least three states' courts,[27] again relying on their constitutions, have declined to adopt the Supreme Court's totality of the circumstances approach to the probable cause inquiry established in *Illinois v. Gates*.[28] Other Supreme Court Fourth Amendment decisions that at least one state court has found unpersuasive include *Smith v. Maryland*,[29] holding that a person does not have a reasonable expectation of privacy in the identity of phone numbers called;[30] *United States v. Leon*,[31] establishing that a search pursuant to an invalid warrant is lawful if the searching officer believed in objective good faith that the warrant was valid;[32] and *Atwater v. Lago Vista*,[33] permitting custodial arrest for a minor crime.[34] State courts have also relied on their own constitutions in refusing to follow the implications of Supreme Court decisions such as *Ohio v. Robinette* (allowing officers to ask for consent to search a car after a traffic stop is completed)[35] and *Jacobsen v. United States* (allowing police to replicate a private search).[36] These examples far from

---

[22] Ronald Collins & Peter Galie, *The Methodology*, Nat'l L.J., Sept. 29, 1986, at S-8 (collecting over 300 such cases decided since 1970).

[23] 414 U.S. 218, 94 S.Ct. 467 (1973).

[24] See *Zehrung v. State*, 569 P.2d 189 (Alaska 1977); *People v. Brisendine*, 13 Cal.3d 528, 119 Cal.Rptr. 315, 531 P.2d 1099 (1975); *People v. Clyne*, 189 Colo. 412, 541 P.2d 71 (1975); *State v. Kaluna*, 55 Hawaii 361, 520 P.2d 51 (1974); *State v. Caraher*, 293 Or. 741, 653 P.2d 942 (1982).

[25] 401 U.S. 745, 91 S.Ct. 1122 (1971).

[26] *State v. Glass*, 583 P.2d 872 (Alaska 1978); *State v. Sarmiento*, 397 So.2d 643 (Fla. 1981); *People v. Beavers*, 393 Mich. 554, 227 N.W.2d 511 (1975); *State v. Brackman*, 178 Mont. 105, 582 P.2d 1216 (1978).

[27] *State v. Kimbro*, 197 Conn. 219, 496 A.2d 498 (1985); *Commonwealth v. Upton II*, 394 Mass. 363, 476 N.E.2d 548 (1985); *People v. Johnson*, 66 N.Y.2d 398, 497 N.Y.S.2d 618, 488 N.E.2d 439 (1985).

[28] 462 U.S. 213, 103 S.Ct. 2317 (1983).

[29] 442 U.S. 735, 99 S.Ct. 2577 (1979).

[30] See *People v. Blair*, 25 Cal.3d 640, 159 Cal.Rptr. 818, 602 P.2d 738 (1979); *People v. Sporleder*, 666 P.2d 135 (Colo. 1983); *State v. Hunt*, 91 N.J. 338, 450 A.2d 952 (1982).

[31] 468 U.S. 897, 104 S.Ct. 3405 (1984).

[32] *State v. Cline*, 617 N.W.2d 277 (Iowa 2000) (citing similar holdings in Connecticut, New Mexico, Michigan and Pennsylvania); *State v. Novembrino*, 105 N.J. 95, 519 A.2d 820 (1987); *People v. Bigelow*, 66 N.Y.2d 417, 497 N.Y.S.2d 630, 488 N.E.2d 451 (1985).

[33] 532 U.S. 318, 121 S.Ct. 1536 (2001).

[34] *State v. Brown*, 99 Ohio St.3d 323, 792 N.E.2d 175 (2003); *State v. Bauer*, 307 Mont. 105, 36 P.3d 892 (2001).

[35] *State v. Smith*, 184 P.3d 890 (Kan. 2008) (also repudiating implications of *Muehler v. Mena*, discussed in § 3.02(d)). *Robinette* is discussed in § 11.03(b)(2).

[36] *State v. Eisfeldt*, 185 P.3d 580 (Wash. 2008). *Jacobsen* is discussed in § 4.02(c).

exhaust the list of issues on which state courts have come to independent conclusions on search and seizure issues.[37]

Nor is the New Federalism limited to rejecting the Supreme Court's Fourth Amendment decisions. For instance, several state courts have refused to follow the Court's decision in *Harris v. New York*[38] permitting use of statements obtained in violation of *Miranda* for impeachment purposes.[39] Decisions holding inapplicable other Supreme Court rulings concerning the interrogation process are numerous.[40] Court holdings on issues as disparate as double jeopardy[41] and the right to jury trial[42] have also been repudiated. Measuring the extent of the New Federalism with a different gauge, even as early as the mid-1980's, at least thirty-five courts had flexed state constitutional muscle on at least one issue of criminal procedure.[43]

The New Federalism phase is neither insignificant nor isolated, and is likely to continue in the criminal procedure area. Factors that will fuel further state constitutional developments include the Supreme Court's likely persistence in its prosecution-oriented tendencies and state courts' unwillingness to relinquish the power they have discovered and come to enjoy since the 1970's.

A factor that could severely curtail the New Federalism, however, is the hostile reaction of state citizens to their courts' activism. Chief Justice Burger, for one, sought to encourage this reaction while he was on the Court. In a concurring opinion to a dismissal of a writ of certiorari, he stated that "when state courts interpret state law to require more than the Federal Constitution requires, the citizens of the state must be aware that they have the power to amend state law to ensure rational law enforcement."[44] As discussed below, in at least two states the electorate has exercised this power.

(d) Forced Linkage

Linkage of federal and state standards can occur in two ways. Linkage most frequently occurs when state courts interpret their constitutional provisions to conform

---

[37]   See list of cases in Collins & Galie, supra note 22, at S-9, S-12.

[38]   401 U.S. 222, 91 S.Ct. 643 (1971).

[39]   *People v. Disbrow,* 16 Cal.3d 101, 127 Cal.Rptr. 360, 545 P.2d 272 (1976); *Commonwealth v. Triplett,* 462 Pa. 244, 341 A.2d 62 (1975); *State v. Santiago,* 53 Hawaii 254, 492 P.2d 657 (1971). See also, *State v. Davis,* 38 Wash.App. 600, 686 P.2d 1143 (1984) (rejecting *Fletcher v. Weir,* discussed in § 16.05(b)(2)).

[40]   See, e.g., *People v. Harris,* 77 N.Y.2d 434, 568 N.Y.S.2d 702, 570 N.E.2d 1051 (1991) (rejecting *New York v. Harris,* discussed in § 2.03(d)); *People v. Houston,* 42 Cal.3d 595, 230 Cal.Rptr. 141, 724 P.2d 1166 (1986) (rejecting *Moran v. Burbine,* discussed in § 16.04(a)); *People v. Pettingill,* 21 Cal.3d 231, 145 Cal.Rptr. 861, 578 P.2d 108 (1978) (rejecting *Michigan v. Mosley,* discussed in § 16.03(e)(1)).

[41]   See, e.g., *State v. Kennedy,* 295 Or. 260, 666 P.2d 1316 (1983) (rejecting *Oregon v. Kennedy,* discussed in § 30.03(c)(2)); *People v. Paulsen,* 198 Colo. 458, 601 P.2d 634 (1979) (rejecting *United States v. Scott,* discussed in § 30.03(b)); *State v. Hogg,* 118 N.H. 262, 385 A.2d 844 (1978) (rejecting *Bartkus v. Illinois,* discussed in § 30.06(a)).

[42]   See, e.g., *Baker v. City of Fairbanks,* 471 P.2d 386 (Alaska 1970) (rejecting *Baldwin v. New York,* discussed in § 27.02(c)(1)); *State v. Becker,* 130 Vt. 153, 287 A.2d 580 (1972) (same); *Holland v. State,* 91 Wis.2d 134, 280 N.W.2d 288 (1979) (rejecting *Apodaca v. Oregon,* discussed in § 27.02(e)); *Gilbreath v. Wallace,* 292 Ala. 267, 292 So.2d 651 (1974) (rejecting *Williams v. Florida,* discussed in § 27.02(d)).

[43]   See Collins & Galie, supra note 22, at S-9, S-12. The supreme courts of Washington, Alaska, California and New Jersey have been particularly active. Some state legislatures have also repudiated Supreme Court holdings. See Stephen Arons and Ethan Katsh, *Reclaiming the Fourth Amendment in Massachusetts,* 2 Civ.Liberties Rev. 82 (Winter 1975) (legislation overturning *Robinson*).

[44]   *Florida v. Casal,* 462 U.S. 637, 103 S.Ct. 3100 (1983) (Burger, C.J., concurring).

with the federal courts' interpretation of similar federal provisions.[45] This approach does not force linkage on the courts, because state judges control conformity with federal interpretation and can selectively apply it as they see fit. This form of linkage is merely a judicially adopted aid to judicial decisionmaking.

The second type of linkage is that which the electorate imposes on the courts.[46] Many state constitutions provide for amendment through initiative or referendum.[47] The citizens of two states, California and Florida, have used the amendment process to require their courts to follow certain aspects of federal law. The California provision accomplishes this objective indirectly by stating that all "relevant evidence" is admissible in criminal proceedings.[48] Under this provision, California courts remain free to develop the substantive law as they see fit, but the exclusionary remedy is available only in those situations dictated by federal law.[49] The Florida provision differs in two ways. First, it focuses solely on search and seizure law, rather than impinging on every substantive area where exclusion may be the sought-after remedy. Second, it provides that the state search and seizure provision "shall be construed in conformity with the 4th Amendment to the United States Constitution as interpreted by the United States Supreme Court."[50] Thus, in contrast to the California provision, the Florida amendment eliminates the power of the Florida courts to develop their own substantive law in the search and seizure area.

The impetus for these two provisions was the same. In California, law enforcement groups were primarily responsible for the drafting of a number of constitutional measures, ultimately proposed in 1982, which came to be called the Victims' Bill of Rights.[51] The pre-vote literature devoted considerable attention to the exclusionary rule provision, describing it as a means of counteracting the California courts' tendency to be "too concerned with rights of defendants."[52] Thus, approval of the provision was probably in large part a reaction to perceived state court activism in search and seizure law.

Law enforcement groups also initiated Florida's amendment, which was even more clearly the result of dissatisfaction with a specific state court ruling. Although, as noted earlier,[53] Florida courts had tended to mimic federal law, the one significant Florida Supreme Court decision that did not track Supreme Court precedent (*State v. Sarmiento*,[54] rejecting the Supreme Court's ruling that use of a bugged undercover agent

---

[45] See, e.g., *State v. Jackson*, 672 P.2d 255 (Mont. 1983); *Brown v. State*, 657 S.W.2d 797 (Tex.Crim.App. 1983) (en banc).

[46] The discussion here focuses on direct action by the electorate. The legislature may also impose linkage on the courts. See, e.g., Fla.Stat. § 933.19(1) (1985) (providing that the opinion in *Carroll v. United States*, 267 U.S. 132, 45 S.Ct. 280 (1925), is "adopted as the statute law of the state applicable to searches and seizures under § 12, Art. 1 of the State Constitution").

[47] See, e.g., Alaska Const. art. XIII, § 1; Fla. Const. art. XI, §§ 1, 3, 5; N.Y. Const. art. XIX, § 1. "Initiative" refers to a proposal initiated by the populace. "Referendum" refers to a proposal initiated by the legislature and submitted to the electorate.

[48] Cal. Const. art. I, § 28(d).

[49] In *California v. Greenwood*, 486 U.S. 35, 108 S.Ct. 1625 (1988), the Supreme Court rejected the argument that this provision violated the Due Process Clause because it permits introduction of evidence seized in violation of state law.

[50] Fla. Const., art. I, § 12.

[51] Donale E. Wilkes, *First Things Last: Amendomania and State Bills of Rights*, 54 Miss.L.J. 223, 253–54 (1984).

[52] Id. at 254, n. 168.

[53] See § 34.02(b).

[54] 397 So.2d 643 (Fla. 1981).

was not a search) immediately led law enforcement groups to propose the amendment. Within two years, after receiving vigorous backing from the Governor, it was passed.[55]

34.03   An Assessment of the Different Approaches to State Constitutional Interpretation

Of the various approaches that state courts could take to federal constitutional law, a cautious version of the New Federalism probably best balances the tradition of federalism with principles of judicial decisionmaking. Co-option is clearly an inappropriate response to the need for a policy governing state court consideration of federal law. Linkage, while attractive in some respects, is ultimately repugnant to our notion of parallel systems of government. Forced linkage of the type California and Florida have adopted is especially so. On the other hand, wide-open state activism runs counter to judicial decisionmaking goals of clarity, efficiency, and principled reasoning. In short, under a balanced approach to judicial regulation of criminal procedure, state courts would have the authority to develop standards more protective than those the federal courts have produced, but they would be circumspect in doing so.

(a) Differences in Local Law

The justification for state court independence is most clear when the organic state law is different from federal law. Most commentators and jurists agree that interpretive variance is permissible when based on something uniquely local.[56] Thus, a significant difference in the state constitutional provision's language or its legislative history may be a proper justification for departure from the federal interpretation of the analogous federal provision. For instance, New York's constitution speaks of a right to counsel "in any trial in any court whatever,"[57] language which on its face appears to be broader than the Supreme Court's holding that the Sixth Amendment guarantees counsel only at proceedings which result in imprisonment.[58] Similarly, judicial history indicating state court adoption of a standard more expansive than a subsequently established federal standard is clearly a proper basis for ignoring the federal standard.[59]

Finally, a distinct "local morality" is generally a valid reason for diverging from federal standards. A good example of this latter idea is *Ravin v. State*,[60] in which the Alaska Supreme Court established a state constitutional right to private, in-home possession and use of marijuana by adults (and thus prohibited searches for marijuana in such circumstances). The court relied in part on the observation that Alaska "has traditionally been the home of people who prize their individuality and who have chosen to settle or to continue living here in order to achieve a measure of control over their own life style which is now unattainable in many of our sister states."

---

[55] Slobogin, supra note 19, at 671–73.

[56] See, e.g., Eugene L. Shapiro, *State Constitutional Doctrine and the Criminal Process*, 16 Seton Hall L.Rev. 630, 650–54 (1986); Developments in the Law, *The Interpretation of State Constitutional Rights*, 95 Harv.L.Rev. 1324, 1361 (1982).

[57] N.Y. Const. art. I, § 6.

[58] *Argersinger v. Hamlin*, 407 U.S. 25, 92 S.Ct. 2006 (1972), discussed in § 31.02(b).

[59] See, e.g., *People v. Paulsen*, 198 Colo. 458, 601 P.2d 634 (1979) (rejecting *United States v. Scott*, 437 U.S. 82, 98 S.Ct. 2187 (1978), on the basis of state precedent).

[60] 537 P.2d 494 (Alaska 1975).

(b) When Local Factors Are Absent: The Cases For and Against Linkage

Beyond these relatively rare "local factor" situations, the value of the New Federalism is much in dispute. Three arguments have been advanced to support the proposition that, despite their technical independence from federal law, state constitutional provisions should not be interpreted any differently from analogous federal provisions when local textual, historical or cultural differences are absent. First is a desire to avoid the uncertainty and confusion among state officials that might result from having two interpretations of the same text. Second is the notion that having two sets of courts address the same issue is unnecessary unless the state courts offer unique insight on the issue based on local factors. Third is the complaint that state activism that is not based on local factors is a result-oriented reaction to federal precedent and therefore unprincipled.

(1) Uncertainty

Jurists frequently make the uncertainty argument. For instance, Chief Justice Erickson of the Colorado Supreme Court has contended that police should be able to rely on United States Supreme Court decisions as the final word.[61] In the Fourth Amendment context, the Arizona Supreme Court has expressed a similar sentiment, stating "one of the few things worse than a single exclusionary rule is two different exclusionary rules."[62]

The uncertainty argument may be a reason for leaning toward linkage. But it does not persuasively support the conclusion that linkage should be required, as is the case in Florida and California. Uncertainty is a fact of constitutional adjudication, particularly in the criminal procedure area. Even if state courts were bound to the federal standard, disputes would arise over the meaning of most decisions. State officers would still be confronted with a complex array of rules in these cases. Further, even when clear standards are attainable, the claim that uncertainty results when two different court systems address the same issue is easily exaggerated. Unless a state court announces a more protective standard, the federal minimum applies. In those rare instances when the state court arrives at a different standard, that standard will control. In short, only one standard will apply to state officials at any given time.[63]

(2) Duplication of Review

The second argument against state court activism, that the dual review contemplated under the New Federalism unnecessarily shackles state legislatures and officials, is most forcefully presented by Professor Maltz.[64] The dual layer of review is unnecessary, he argues, because state courts are no better situated than federal courts to interpret constitutional language, except when textual differences, legislative history, or local morality create special considerations under state law. In all other circumstances, contends Maltz, neither the competence nor the institutional traits of the state courts distinguish them from the federal courts enough to merit allowing them

---

[61] *People v. Sporleder,* 666 P.2d 135 (Colo. 1983) (Erickson, C.J., dissenting).

[62] *State v. Bolt,* 142 Ariz. 260, 689 P.2d 519 (1984).

[63] An exception to this conclusion occurs when state officers work with federal officers in investigating interstate crime or some other offense which involves dual jurisdiction.

[64] Earl M. Maltz, *The Dark Side of State Court Activism,* 63 Tex.L.Rev. 995, 1005–06 (1985).

independent review of constitutional issues and burdening state legislation with another judicial hurdle.

Like the uncertainty argument, the "duplication-of-review" argument might predispose one toward linkage, but it is not a persuasive reason for requiring it. There are three related reasons for permitting, if not encouraging, state courts to diverge from federal precedent even when the reason for doing so is not among those Maltz identifies.

First, federal courts, and especially the Supreme Court, may be constrained in interpreting particular constitutional language because their rulings govern more than one state. For example, the Supreme Court might construe the Fourth Amendment quite differently if freed from the specter of requiring exclusion in all fifty states every time it announces a new search and seizure principle. Professor Sager has persuasively argued that the underenforcement that may result from this type of institutional pressure on the Supreme Court justifies more expansive state court interpretations.[65] Non-judicial considerations that are irrelevant to the state should not drive state constitutional law.

Second, linkage denies federal and state courts the benefit of the state court's reasoning on the proper interpretation of particular language. Such reasoning has played a valuable role in the past. At times, state court reasoning has proven influential even at the United State Supreme Court level.[66]

Finally, linkage prevents the experimentation of which Justice Brandeis spoke so fondly in *New State Ice Co. v. Liebmann.*[67] According to Brandeis:

Denial of the right to experiment may be fraught with serious consequences to the Nation. It is one of the happy incidents of the federal system that a single courageous State may, if its citizens choose, serve as a laboratory; and try novel social and economic experiments without risk to the rest of the country.

This refrain, which has appeared in many Supreme Court opinions,[68] is particularly germane when speaking of the rights of the criminally accused. As Judge Abrahamson of the Wisconsin Supreme Court has pointed out, state constitutional provisions concerning criminal procedure are "less encrusted with layers of court decisions" than their federal counterparts and thus allow state courts "to rethink the fundamental issues."[69]

(3) Result-Oriented Decisionmaking

For these reasons, duplicative review can fulfill an important role, even when local interpretation factors are absent. But it still might be viewed as improper because it encourages unprincipled decisionmaking. The third argument against state court activism, that it is often result-oriented, is the most prevalent. Many commentators view the current renaissance in state constitutional litigation as an ideological reaction to the

---

[65] See Lawrence G. Sager, *Fair Measure: The Legal Status of Underenforced Constitutional Norms*, 91 Harv.L.Rev. 1212, 1242–63 (1978).

[66] See Robert F. Utter, *Swimming in the Jaws of the Crocodile: State Court Comment on Federal Constitutional Issues When Disposing of Cases on State Constitutional Grounds*, 63 Tex.L.Rev. 1025, 1040 (1985).

[67] 285 U.S. 262, 52 S.Ct. 371 (1932).

[68] See, e.g., *Chandler v. Florida,* 449 U.S. 560, 101 S.Ct. 802 (1981); *Reeves, Inc. v. Stake,* 447 U.S. 429, 100 S.Ct. 2271 (1980).

[69] Abrahamson, supra note 8, at 1181.

retrenchment of the United States Supreme Court, rather than as an objective effort to develop state constitutional doctrine.[70]

The claim that state court activism is result-oriented overlooks the possibility that a judicial decision can be principled simply because it is analytically persuasive. A state court decision need not rely on state constitutional language, history, or precedent to meet this requirement. Admittedly, a state court that strikes out on its own path without giving due deliberation to relevant federal precedent is also likely to be forsaking judicial neutrality. This type of decisionmaking is much more likely to create uncertainty and suggest the type of institutional deficiency that prompts criticism of duplicative review.[71] But if the state court deals with federal precedent and persuasively demonstrates that federal court reasoning is unacceptable, its result can no more be called unprincipled than can the original federal holding. As the Oregon Supreme Court stated, "a state's constitutional guarantees were meant to be . . . truly independent of the rising and falling tides of federal case law both in method and specifics."[72] In short, while linkage with federal law should probably be "presumed," that presumption should be one that can be overcome if the state court gives careful attention to federal doctrine before rejecting it.

(c) A Case Study

The Mississippi Supreme Court's original opinion in *Stringer v. State (Stringer I)*[73] illustrates the type of reasoning that might legitimize state repudiation of a federal standard. The opinion, written by Justice Robertson, declined as a matter of state law to adopt the United States Supreme Court's holding in *United States v. Leon*,[74] which interpreted the Fourth Amendment to allow the introduction of evidence seized pursuant to an invalid warrant if, at the time of its seizure, the seizing officer reasonably believed that the warrant was valid. Justice Robertson's opinion offered at least three different bases for rejecting *Leon's* holding.

The first ground *Stringer I* advanced for repudiating *Leon* focused on explicit differences between federal and state law. Justice Robertson noted that the exclusionary rule has been a recognized facet of Mississippi law since 1922,[75] and that state cases since then had continuously affirmed, even after *Mapp,* the availability of the exclusionary sanction under state law. These facts alone, Robertson asserted, justified a decision to reject *Leon's* good faith exception to the exclusionary rule. Mississippi's pre-*Mapp* judicial history established the state's independent interest in excluding illegally seized evidence, regardless of how federal courts chose to sanction illegal searches.

---

[70]   See, e.g., George Deukmejian & Clifford K. Thompson, Jr., *All Sail and No Anchor-Judicial Review Under the California Constitution*, 6 Hastings Const. L.Q. 975 (1979); Martineau, *Review Essay, The Status of State Government Law in Legal Education*, 53 U.Cin.L.Rev. 511, 516 (1984).

[71]   For a somewhat contrary position, arguing for a "self-reliant" approach to state constitutional interpretation, see Ronald Collins, *Reliance on State Constitutions—Away From a Reactionary Approach*, 9 Hastings Const. L.Q. 1 (1981).

[72]   *State v. Kennedy*, 295 Or. 260, 666 P.2d 1316, 1323 (1983).

[73]   No. 54,805 (477 So.2d 1335). On petition for rehearing, the Mississippi Supreme Court withdrew its original opinion in *Stringer* and substituted a second opinion upholding the result, but on a different ground. 491 So.2d 837 (Miss. 1986). The original opinion, written by Justice Robertson, became the concurring opinion in the second *Stringer* decision.

[74]   468 U.S. 897, 104 S.Ct. 3405 (1984), discussed in § 2.03(c)(1).

[75]   *Tucker v. State,* 128 Miss. 211, 90 So. 845 (1922).

The *Stringer I* court also based its position on a perception that local systemic tendencies differed from those influencing the United States Supreme Court. Justice Robertson found that the good faith exception in *Leon* "more reflects a shift in judicial/political ideology than a judicial response to demonstrable and felt societal needs." In Mississippi, at least, no such societal needs were demonstrable. Justice Robertson noted that only once in thirteen years had the Mississippi Supreme Court used the exclusionary rule to keep out evidence police had seized under a groundless warrant, suggesting that a good faith exception would not result in much of a change to exclusion practices in the state. At the same time, he pointed out that the effect of *Leon* could potentially be particularly insidious in Mississippi "where most judges issuing warrants have had no formal legal training."

Finally, *Stringer I* attacked *Leon's* logic. The majority in *Leon* justified its holding with a cost-benefit analysis. On the one hand, it reasoned, the loss of convictions due to a blanket exclusionary rule is significant. On the other hand, exclusion would not deter officers acting in good faith reliance on a warrant and would be unnecessary to deter the magistrate issuing the warrant, assuming the necessary detachment from the law enforcement process. This analysis did not persuade Justice Robertson. He pointed to the Supreme Court's own statistics for the proposition that exclusion of evidence actually aborts few prosecutions.[76] He also noted that the benefit of exclusion is substantial because it motivates the magistrate to be careful in calculating probable cause. Conversely, if the good faith rule of *Leon* were adopted, the magistrate would have little incentive to act properly. A warrant is obtained in an *ex parte* proceeding from which there is no appeal. Moreover, because of judicial immunity, the magistrate does not experience even the slim deterrent effect that fear of civil liability produces.

Ultimately, however, the *Stringer I* court grounded its decision not on cost-benefit concerns but on what it considered the "fundamental logic of the exclusionary rule." Justice Robertson asserted that the exclusionary rule is meant to leave the state no better or worse off than if the illegal search and seizure had not occurred, citing *Nix v. Williams*,[77] a recent United States Supreme Court decision that had relied on this proposition in addressing the scope of the exclusionary rule in the derivative evidence context. He then reasoned that because the good faith exception violates this precept by allowing the state to benefit from an illegal search, it cannot be countenanced. The *Stringer I* court also restated its adherence to the rationale for the exclusionary rule advanced in *Weeks v. United States*,[78] and endorsed by the Mississippi Supreme Court when it established the state exclusionary rule in 1922: admitting illegally obtained evidence "would be to affirm by judicial decision a manifest neglect if not an open defiance of the prohibitions of the Constitution."

Stringer I exemplifies a state court's use of state precedent, local morality, and logical refutation to justify a position different from the United States Supreme Court's. The logical component of its attack on *Leon* is of particular interest. Justice Robertson's opinion evaluated the good faith exception in terms already recognized by the federal courts. He engaged in cost-benefit analysis, as had *Leon,* and relied on the reasoning not only of *Weeks,* but of the Court's recent decision in *Nix v. Williams*. The opinion thus

---

[76] The Leon Court had noted that the exclusionary rule "results in the nonprosecution of between 0.6% and 2.35% of individuals arrested for felonies."

[77] 467 U.S. 431, 104 S.Ct. 2501 (1984), discussed in § 2.04(d).

[78] 232 U.S. 383, 34 S.Ct. 341 (1914).

reaches its contrary decision within the parameters previous federal law had sketched out. Although concern about creating uncertainty and engaging in unnecessary duplication of review might make a state court cautious about rejecting federal precedent, it should not prevent principled state court analysis of the type *Stringer I* illustrates.

34.04   The Supreme Court's Reaction to the New Federalism

Because the Supreme Court will not review a decision resting on adequate state grounds,[79] a state court that bases its ruling on the state constitution effectively precludes Supreme Court oversight, so long as the ruling meets the minimum federal constitutional standard. This policy insulates those state court decisions that construe the state bill of rights to provide greater protection than the federal Bill of Rights. The result is that law enforcement officials who feel burdened by the broader state constitutional requirements are unable to seek remedies in a federal forum.

Apparently frustrated by this fact, the post-Warren Court has indicated that the state ruling must *clearly* rest on a state constitutional ground before that ground will be considered adequate and independent. In *Michigan v. Long*,[80] for instance, despite the fact that the Michigan Supreme Court held a vehicle search invalid because it was "proscribed by the Fourth Amendment to the United States Constitution *and* art. 1, § 11 of the Michigan Constitution," the Court remained "unconvinced that the lower court's decision rests upon an independent state ground." Justice O'Connor, writing for the majority, noted that although the Michigan Constitution had been cited twice by the Michigan Supreme Court, the lower court had relied exclusively on federal cases. Justice Stevens, in a vigorous dissent to this part of the opinion, argued that historically the presumption has always been against asserting jurisdiction over cases where there may be an independent state ground. He cautioned against the issuance of advisory opinions: "We do not sit to expound our understanding of the Constitution to interested listeners in the legal community; we sit to resolve disputes. If it is not apparent that our views would affect the outcome of a particular case, we cannot presume to interfere."

But the Court appears to have put the burden on the state court to show its decision rests on independent grounds. As Justice O'Connor wrote for the majority, "[i]f a state court chooses merely to rely on federal precedents as it would on the precedents of all other jurisdictions, then it need only make clear by a plain statement in its judgment or opinion that the federal cases are being used only for the purpose of guidance, and do not themselves compel the result that the court has reached." If the state court fails to make such a "plain statement," the Supreme Court is not precluded from reviewing the decision.

The Court reaffirmed this stance in *Arizona v. Evans*,[81] over a dissent by Justice Ginsburg arguing that *Long* should be overruled. Ginsburg asserted that "[a]lthough it is easy enough for a state court to say the requisite magic words, the court may not recognize that its opinion triggers *Long's* plain statement requirement." As an example, she pointed to the Arizona Supreme Court's decision in *Evans,* a case raising the issue

---

[79]   *Herb v. Pitcairn,* 324 U.S. 117, 65 S.Ct. 459 (1945). See generally, Charles A. Wright, Federal Courts, § 39 (1983).

[80]   463 U.S. 1032, 103 S.Ct. 3469 (1983). See also *Montana v. Jackson,* 460 U.S. 1030, 103 S.Ct. 1418 (1983) (per curiam).

[81]   514 U.S. 1, 115 S.Ct. 1185 (1995).

of whether good faith reliance on inaccurate computer records should trigger the exclusionary rule.[82] The Arizona court had stated that it found the U.S. Supreme Court's most relevant decision, *United States v. Leon* (on good faith reliance on warrants),[83] "not helpful," thus indicating, according to Ginsburg, that it did not consider federal law apposite. That *Long* nonetheless allowed the U.S. Supreme Court to accept the case undermined federalism principles, Ginsburg argued; to Stevens' point (in his *Long* dissent) that *Long* undermines the federal court tradition of avoiding constitutional questions when alternative grounds exist, Ginsburg added that the decision leads to premature interference with state court endeavors to deal with new problems. Thus, she concluded, the presumption in *Long* should be reversed: a state court decision should be assumed to be based on *state law* unless the state court indicates otherwise. The majority in *Evans* ignored these points, however, insisting that under *Long* state courts are still "absolutely free" to interpret state constitutional provisions.[84]

34.05 Conclusion

State court reliance on state constitutions as an independent source of rights is widespread. This chapter's assessment of this development can be summarized as follows:

(1) State courts have always had the authority to interpret state law differently from federal precedent. With the advent of incorporation, many states simply followed federal law. But, as the U.S. Supreme Court has retrenched on Warren Court precedent, many state courts have repudiated federal law in favor of more protective rules based on state constitutions. In response to this development, the electorates in a few states have adopted constitutional amendments requiring linkage between state constitutional law and Supreme Court precedent in certain areas of criminal procedure.

(2) Forced linkage between analogous federal and state constitutional provisions undercuts state court analytical independence, thus compromising the ability of state courts to reflect local legal and moral preferences, stimulate thought among other courts, and experiment with important concepts. Unlimited state activism promotes uncertainty, questionable duplication of review, and result-oriented jurisprudence. Presumptive linkage is probably the preferable approach to state court treatment of federal law. Under this approach, state courts would not lightly repudiate a federal ruling, but they would be free to do so when state precedent, local morality, or careful analysis suggests that the federal standard should not be adopted as the state standard.

(3) State court decisions that do not include a plain statement that federal cases in the opinion are being used only for the purpose of guidance and do not themselves compel the result that the court has reached are not based on an adequate and independent state ground and may be reviewed and overturned by the federal courts.

BIBLIOGRAPHY

Abrahamson, Shirley S. Criminal Law and State Constitutions: The Emergence of State Constitutional Law. 63 Tex.L.Rev. 1141 (1985).

---

[82] See § 2.03(c)(3).

[83] 468 U.S. 897, 104 S.Ct. 3405 (1984), discussed in § 2.03(c)(1).

[84] See also *Florida v. Powell*, 559 U.S. 50, 130 S.Ct. 1195 (2010), where the Court held that *Long's* plain statement rule was not met despite the state court's consistent reference to state law as an independent basis for its decision.

Bonventre, Vincent Martin. Changing Roles: The Supreme Court and the State Courts in Safeguarding Rights. 74 Albany L. Rev. 841 (2007).

Brennan, William J. State Constitutions and the Protection of Individual Rights. 90 Harv.L.Rev. 489 (1977).

Cauthen, James N.G. Expanding Rights Under State Constitutions: A Quantitative Appraisal. 63 Alb.L.Rev. 1189 (2000).

Collins, Ronald and Peter J. Galie. Models of Post-Incorporation Judicial Review: 1985 Survey of State Constitutional Individual Rights Decisions. 55 U.Cin.L.Rev. 317 (1986).

Gardner, James A. Interpreting State Constitutions: A Jurisprudence of Function in a Federal System (2005).

Hershkoff, Helen. Positive Rights and State Constitutions: The Limits of Federal Rationality Review. 112 Harv. L.Rev. 1131 (1999).

Howard, A.E. Dick. State Courts and Constitutional Rights in the Day of the Burger Court. 62 Va.L.Rev. 873 (1976).

Howard, Robert M., Scott E. Graves and Julianne Flowers. State Courts, the U.S. Supreme Court and the Protection of Civil Liberties. 40 Law & Society 845 (2006).

Maltz, Earl M. The Dark Side of State Court Activism. 63 Tex.L.Rev. 995 (1985).

McCarthy, Francis B. Counterfeit Interpretations of State Constitutions in Criminal Procedure. 58 Syracuse Law Review 79 (2007).

Saylor, Thomas G. Fourth Amendment Departures and Sustainability in State Constitutionalism. 22 Widener L. J. 1 (2012).

Slobogin, Christopher. State Adoption of Federal Law: Exploring the Limits of Florida's "Forced Linkage" Amendment. 39 U.Fla.L.Rev. 653 (1987).

Sykes, Diane. The "New Federalism":" Confessions of a Former State Supreme Court Justice. 38 Oklahoma City University Law Review 367 (2013).

Wilkes, Donald E. First Things Last: Amendomania and State Bills of Rights. 54 Miss.L.J. 223 (1984).

Table of Cases

Index

References are to Pages